OXFORD MEDIEVAL TEXTS

General Editors

THE LETTER COLLECTION OF PETER ABELARD AND HELOISE

The Paraclete. Engraved by J. Storer and published by Longman, Hurst, Rees, & Orme, Paternoster Row (London), 1 Sept. 1809 (Troyes, Médiathèque, estampe 104/16)

THE LETTER COLLECTION OF PETER ABELARD AND HELOISE

EDITED WITH A REVISED TRANSLATION BY

DAVID LUSCOMBE

after the translation by
Betty Radice

CLARENDON PRESS · OXFORD

OXFORD
UNIVERSITY PRESS

Great Clarendon Street, Oxford OX2 6DP,
United Kingdom

Oxford University Press is a department of the University of Oxford.
It furthers the University's objective of excellence in research, scholarship,
and education by publishing worldwide. Oxford is a registered trade mark of
Oxford University Press in the UK and in certain other countries

First edition published in 2013
Impression: 1

The Letters of Abelard and Heloise translated by Betty Radice.
First published by Penguin Books Ltd. 1974

British Library Cataloguing in Publication Data
Data available

ISBN 978-0-19-822248-4

Typeset by Anne Joshua, Oxford
Printed in Great Britain by
CPI Group (UK) Ltd, Croydon, CR0 4YY

For all the grandchildren,
Thomas, Holly, Eloise, Megan,
Joseph, and Bethan

PREFACE AND ACKNOWLEDGEMENTS

CRITICAL editions of the Latin text of the letters in the letter collection of Heloise and Abelard were published by J. T. Muckle and T. P. McLaughlin between 1950 and 1956 in separate issues of the journal *Mediaeval Studies*. In 1959 Jacques Monfrin also published a justly acclaimed edition of the autobiographical letter which opens the collection, the *Historia calamitatum*. Monfrin had reservations about the work of Muckle, and Giovanni Orlandi had well-founded reservations about the editions of both Muckle and Monfrin. A much-liked translation into English of a large part of the collection was published by Betty Radice in 1974 and revised by Michael T. Clanchy in 2003. The present edition of the Latin text results from a fresh collation of the manuscripts, including some which have not been edited before, and from a review of studies of the text and of its transmission made in the last sixty years and earlier. Bringing the English translation of 1974, now revised by myself, on to pages facing the Latin text will surely help readers to understand both text and translation better. In the notes I have tried to take account of and to take forward numerous contributions that have been made to both scholarly understanding and public controversy, especially in recent decades. No doubt shortcomings will be found but there would be more were it not for all the support I have received during the preparation of this work. Those who have helped include the students whom I have taught over many years and from whom I have always gained encouragement. Countless librarians and keepers of manuscripts have unfailingly responded to my requests. The givers of grants include the University of Sheffield, the British Academy, and, especially, the Leverhulme Trust. To Julia Barrow, James Binns, Bonnie Blackburn, Christopher Brooke, Janet Burton, Morn Capper, Paul Cole, William Courtenay, David d'Avray, Peter Dronke, Louk Engels, Pat Holland, Stephen Jaeger, Michael Jones, Anne Joshua, Matthew Kempshall, Julie Kerr, Edmund King, Rosalind Love, Giovanni Orlandi(†), William Radice, Julia Smith, Claire Thomson, Fr Chrysogonus Waddell, OCRO, Charles West, Ed Wilson, and to many others, I owe many significant and several very considerable debts, and I am most grateful to them all. My wife has been exceedingly patient with me when working both at home and away.

D.L.

CONTENTS

LIST OF ILLUSTRATIONS

ABBREVIATED REFERENCES

For abbreviations of the titles of the writings of Abelard and Heloise see Appendix B: Writings of Peter Abelard and Heloise. For other short titles not listed below see the Bibliography: Primary Sources and Secondary Works.

AHDLMA	*Archives d'histoire doctrinale et littéraire du moyen âge* (Paris, 1926/1927–)
BGPTMA	Beiträge zur Geschichte der Philosophie (27, 1928/30–) und Theologie des Mittelalters (Münster, 1– , 1891–)
BnF	Bibliothèque nationale de France
Briquet	C. M. Briquet, *Les Filigranes* (4 vols., 2nd edn.; Leipzig, 1923)
CCCM	Corpus Christianorum. Continuatio Mediaeualis (Turnhout, 1966–)
CCSL	Corpus Christianorum. Series Latina (Turnhout, 1953–)
Checklist	J. Barrow, C. Burnett, D. Luscombe, 'A checklist of the manuscripts containing the writings of Peter Abelard and Heloise and other works closely associated with Abelard and his school', *Revue d'histoire des textes*, xiv–xv (1984–5), 183–302
Comm. Rom.	Peter Abelard, *Commentaria in epistolam Pauli ad Romanos*, ed. E. M. Buytaert (Petri Abaelardi Opera Theologica, i; *CCCM* xi; 1969), pp. 39–340
Cousin	*Petri Abaelardi Opera*, ed. V. Cousin (2 vols.; Paris, 1849, 1859)
CSEL	Corpus scriptorum ecclesiasticorum Latinorum (Vienna, 1866–)
Duchesne–d'Amboise **Du**:	*PETRI ABAELARDI SANCTI GILDASII IN BRITANNIA ABBATIS, ET HELOISAE CONIVGIS EIUS . . . OPERA, nunc primum ex MMS. codd. eruta, & in lucem edita, studio ac diligentia ANDREAE QUERCETANI, Turonensis . . . PARISIIS . . . M.DCXVI*

Amb:	*PETRI ABAELARDI FILOSOFI ET THEOLOGI, ABBATIS RVYENSIS, ET HELOISAE CONIVGIS EIVS . . . OPERA, NVNC PRIMVM EDITA EX MMS. CODD. V. ILLVST. FRANCISCI AMBOESII . . . PARISIIS . . . M.DCXVI . . .*
Hicks	*La Vie et les Epistres Pierres Abaelart et Heloys sa fame. Traduction du XIIIe siècle attribuée à Jean de Meun. Avec une nouvelle édition des textes latins d'après le ms. Troyes Bibl. mun. 802*, ed. E. Hicks, i: *Introduction, textes* (Nouvelle bibliothèque du moyen âge, xvi; Paris, 1991)
IRHT	Institut de Recherche et d'Histoire des Textes, Paris
JL	*Regesta Pontificum Romanorum ab condita Ecclesia ad annum post Christum natum MCXCVIII*, ed. P. Jaffé (2nd edn., rev. W. Wattenbach, 2 vols.; Leipzig, 1885–8). Contributors: P. Ewald, F. Kaltenbrunner, and S. Loewenfeld
Levitan	*Abelard and Heloise: The Letters and Other Writings*, trans. with introduction and notes by W. Levitan (Indianapolis, IN, 2007)
McLaughlin with Wheeler	*The Letters of Heloise and Abelard: A Translation of their Collected Correspondence and Related Writings*, trans. and ed. M. M. McLaughlin with B. Wheeler (The New Middle Ages; New York, 2009)
MGH	Monumenta Germaniae Historica
Monfrin	*Abélard, Historia Calamitatum. Texte critique avec une introduction*, ed. J. Monfrin (Bibliothèque des textes philosophiques; Paris, 1959; 4ème tirage,1978)
OMT	Oxford Medieval Texts
Pagani	*Epistolario di Abelardo ed Eloisa*, ed. Ileana Pagani, con considerazioni sulla trasmissione del testo di Giovanni Orlandi (Classici Latini; Turin, 2004)
PG	*Patrologiae cursus completus, Series Graeca*, ed. J. P. Migne (167 vols.; Paris, 1857–66)
PL	*Patrologiae cursus completus, Series Latina*, ed. J. P. Migne (221 vols.; Paris, 1844–64)
PL Supplementum	*Patrologiae Latinae Supplementum*, ed. A. Hamman and L. Guillaumin (5 vols.; Paris, 1958–74)
PL clxxviii	*Petri Abaelardi abbatis Rugensis Opera omnia juxta editionem Parisiensem anni 1626* [sic; recte 1616],

	suppletis quae in ea desiderabantur opusculis accedunt Hilarii et Berengarii Abaelardi discipulorum Opuscula et Epistolae (Paris, 1855; repr. Turnhout, 1979)
Radice	*The Letters of Abelard and Heloise*, trans. with an Introduction and Notes by Betty Radice, rev. M. T. Clanchy (Penguin Classics; London, 2003)
S. Bernardi Opera	*Sancti Bernardi Opera*, ed. J. Leclercq with C. H. Talbot and H. M. Rochais (8 vols.; Rome, 1957–77)
SChr	Sources chrétiennes (Paris, 1941–)
Smits	*Peter Abelard. Letters IX–XIV*, ed. E. R. Smits (Groningen, 1983)
SN	Peter Abelard, *Sic et Non: A Critical Edition*, ed. B. B. Boyer and R. McKeon (Chicago, 1976–7)
TChr	Peter Abelard, *Theologia Christiana*, ed. E. M. Buytaert (Petri Abaelardi Opera Theologica, ii; *CCCM* xii; 1969), pp. 69–372
TSum	Peter Abelard, *Theologia 'Summi boni'*, *Theologia 'Scholarium'*, ed. E. M. Buytaert and C. J. Mews (Petri Abaelardi Opera Theologica, iii; *CCCM* xiii; 1987), pp. 83–201
Vulg.	*Biblia Sacra iuxta Vulgatam Versionem*, adiuvantibus B. Fischer, I. Gribomont, H. F. D. Sparks, W. Thiele recensuit et brevi apparatu instruxit R. Weber (2 vols.; Stuttgart, 1969)
Vulg. (Clementine)	*Biblia Sacra iuxta Vulgatam Clementinam nova editio*, ed. A. Colunga and L. Turrado (6th edn.; Biblioteca de autores cristianos; Madrid, 1982)
Ziolkowski	*Letters of Peter Abelard: Beyond the Personal*, trans. J. M. Ziolkowski (Washington, DC, 2008)

Other Abbreviations

add.	*addition/ added*
al.	*alternatively; elsewhere*
c.	chapter
conj.	*conjecture/conjectured*
corr.	*corrector/correction/corrected*
del.	*deletion/deleted*
dioc.	diocese
ditto.	*dittography*
eras.	*erased/erasure*

exp.	*expunction/ expunged*
introd.	introduction
l./ll.	*line/lines*
marg.	*margin*
om.	*omitted*
Ps.-	Pseudo-
rubr.	*rubric*
s.	*saeculum*/century
st.	stanza/stanzas
subscr.	*subscript/subscribed*
superscr.	*superscript/superscribed*
tr.	*transposition/transposed*
v/vv.	verse/verses

INTRODUCTION

HISTORY AND LEGEND

The distinguished historian David Knowles wrote once that Abelard, 'the protagonist in one of the most celebrated dramas of passion in the Western world . . . thanks to Petrarch, to Pope, to Rousseau, to Walter Pater, to George Moore, to Miss Waddell, and to many others, has long since broken out of the historical framework into the land of myth and romance'.[1] This puts the matter well although an important qualification needs to be made because even in their lifetime and before Petrarch sympathetic and romantic testimonies to Abelard and Heloise also abound.[2] These were later elaborated considerably. Charlotte Charrier, in her book *Héloïse dans l'histoire et dans la légende*, published in 1933, surveyed and listed much of the literature and of the legends that were spawned from their correspondence. Notably, in 1675 there appeared *Les Amours d'Abailard et d'Héloïse*, a fanciful reworking of *Letter* 1 passed off as an *Histoire* by a writer who has been identified as Alluis, a lawyer of Grenoble.[3] Some years later a dilettante rewriting of *Letters* 2–4 in French made a greater impression.[4] The writer, Rabutin, seems to have been influenced by the *Lettres portugaises* which appeared in France in 1669.[5] His work was sent to Madame de S(évigné) with a letter in which Rabutin wrote of the *Letters* of Abelard and Heloise: 'Je me suis amusé à en traduire quelques-unes qui m'ont donné beaucoup de plaisir. Je n'ai jamais vû un plus beau Latin, sur tout celui de la

[1] Knowles, *Evolution of Medieval Thought*, p. 116; 2nd edn., p. 106. Details of works cited, especially those cited more than once, are usually given in a shortened form with full details being provided in the Bibliography at the end of the volume and in the list of Abbreviations above. The writings of Abelard and Heloise, unlike works by other writers, are usually cited in a brief form without the name of their author e.g. *Letter* 1, *Sermon* 2, etc.; full details of their editions are given in Appendix B: Writings of Peter Abelard and Heloise.

[2] See especially Dronke, *Abelard and Heloise in Medieval Testimonies* (repr. in Dronke, *Intellectuals and Poets*, pp. 247–94); Luscombe, *The School of Peter Abelard*, pp. 1–13; also the notes on the history of the texts of the *Letters* on pp. xxxviii–cii below.

[3] Charrier, *Héloïse*, pp. 407–11.

[4] *Les Lettres de Messire Roger de Rabutin* (1687), Seconde partie, pp. 116–51. I have used the Nouvelle édition, Seconde partie (1720), pp. 107–39. For an assessment ('a very personal translation') see Brook, 'Bussy-Rabutin and the Abelard–Heloise correspondence'.

[5] Charrier, *Héloïse*, pp. 411–17.

Religieuse . . .'.[6] Madame de S(évigné) replied: 'vous avez tout au moins donné de l'esprit à Heloïsse, tant elle en a. Notre ami C**** qui connoît l'Original, dit que non, mais que vôtre François a des délicatesses & des tours que le Latin n'a pas.'[7] Translations and other productions took off, as may be seen from the long lists compiled by Charrier up to 1933, or shortly before, of *traductions fidèles*, *traductions fantaisistes, traductions françaises, allemandes, anglaises* (including Alexander Pope's *Eloisa to Abelard*, published in 1717), *espagnoles, italiennes*, and *portugaises*, of biographies, essays, novels, plays, poems, parodies, and works of art of many kinds.[8] Charrier's enquiries need to be extended beyond 1933—the year in which Helen Waddell published her richly sweet novel *Peter Abelard*, which has since been reprinted nearly forty times, most recently by the publisher Constable in 1987. Michael Clanchy expressed the view in 1997 that Abelard's (and Heloise's) reputation had now declined in popular esteem.[9] Had renewal of controversy since 1972 over the genuineness of the correspondence of Abelard and Heloise, and of further correspondence that has been associated with them, made it more difficult for creative writers and artists to find inspiration there? This seems improbable, for translations continue to be made or reprinted and the lists compiled by Raffaella Asni of plays, operas, musicals, films, television productions, musical recordings, and recitals given, for the most part, in the last thirty years of the twentieth century show a continuing vitality.[10] Over the same period scholarly enquiries into the lives and writings of Abelard and Heloise and also on the subject of medieval religious women have been very lively to the point where a new edition of the letter collection clearly seems a worthwhile endeavour.[11]

THE LETTER COLLECTION

Letter collections were regularly made in the twelfth century and surviving collections include the correspondence of leading figures

[6] *Les Lettres*, letter XLV, pp. 107–8: Chaseu, 12 Apr. 1687.

[7] Ibid., letter XLVI, p. 139: Paris, 18 Apr. 1687.

[8] Charrier, *Héloïse*, pp. 601–55.

[9] Clanchy, *Abelard*, p. 328.

[10] Asni, 'Abélard et Héloïse sur l'écran et la scène'.

[11] A good edition and English translation of the uncollected letters have been published, respectively, by Smits in 1983 and Ziolkowski in 2008. An edition published by Könsgen in 1974 of other love letters—*Epistolae duorum amantium*—sparked debate over their authorship (see below, pp. xxxii–xxxiv).

and writers such as Bernard of Clairvaux, John of Salisbury, and Peter the Venerable.[12] John knew Abelard; Bernard and Peter knew and corresponded with both Abelard (d. 1142) and Heloise (d. 1164). Their collection is both small and unusual: it contains only eight of their own letters arranged in sequence. There are twelve surviving medieval copies of this collection and one copy of a thirteenth-century translation in old French. Although some copies are less complete than others in what they contain, the unity of the collection is unmistakable in all of them and, with the exception of a single MS,[13] the order in which the letters are presented is always the same, whatever omissions there are.

A key question for readers of these letters has been their truthfulness, especially as regards the claims, some of them contested by Heloise herself, that Abelard made about their relationship in *Letter* 1. Yet Peter Dronke has shown, with a wealth of testimonies to this relationship, that 'all the attitudes revealed in the letters can be paralleled in early testimonies outside the letters' and that 'the majority of contemporaries of whom we have evidence, and the generations immediately following, up to the time of Jean de Meun, were convinced of the uniqueness and stature of Abelard's and Heloise's love, and regarded their tragedy with wonderment and compassion'.[14]

The aggression, sensuality, tension, alarm, and grief which are displayed so openly in the first five letters and in the beginning of the sixth should not disguise the search for a well-thought-out framework in which Heloise and Abelard could live their lives, a search which begins already (although acrimoniously and with no little disagreement) in *Letter 1* and which continues in the next letter, where Heloise begins to formulate requests for guidance from Abelard for her sisters at the Paraclete even before expressing her own need for solace and support. The collection seems to trace the turning away of two people not from love but from quarrelling and to the practice of prayer and of a religious life supported by study of the Scriptures with the aid of the writings of the Church Fathers. Heloise's letters

[12] The best introduction to medieval letter writing and collecting is Constable, *Letters and Letter-Collections*; the introduction to Constable's edition of the *Letters* of Peter the Venerable is also of great value (i. 1–44).

[13] The MS is Paris, BnF lat. 13057 (MS F) and the exception is of no consequence. See below, p. lxi.

[14] Dronke, *Abelard and Heloise in Medieval Testimonies*, pp. 30–1; repr. in Dronke, *Intellectuals and Poets*, p. 278.

are in part influenced by the letters from legendary women to absent husbands or lovers that are found in Ovid's *Heroides*. But from the sixth letter forward the focus is always upon the kind of life that religious women should lead. The *Rule* which Abelard composed owes much to the questions put to him by Heloise and also owes much to the erudite, spiritual guidance that St Jerome had given to pious, educated ladies with whom he had corresponded many centuries earlier. The collection as a whole has something of the character of a documentary record and narrative of the foundation of the abbey of the Paraclete, keenly showing first the earlier lives and troubles of the founder and the first abbess and then exploring, with the aid of a panoramic presentation of examples of religious men and women throughout history, the principles upon which daily life in the abbey should be based.

OTHER LETTERS

The couple mention in their letter collection that they corresponded on other occasions also.[15] And there are other letters extant, not part of the collection, which were ostensibly written by and to each other as well as several letters sent by them to other persons or sent to them by others. Some of these are found in manuscripts in the company of related texts, including the collection itself; others were printed by Duchesne–d'Amboise from different sources and unknown manuscripts. Most, but not all of these, are recorded in *PL* clxxviii and given a number from 9 upward, even when they were printed not there but in other volumes of the *Patrologia Latina*.

Of these uncollected letters some are isolated pieces on diverse subjects, unaccompanied by earlier or later correspondence:

Letter 11, from Abelard to the abbot and monks of St-Denis, concerns the identity of the patron saint of the abbey. It is part of the dispute which Abelard recalls in *Letter* 1, 33 and it is generally found in MSS which contain materials for the lives of Denis and other

[15] *Letter* 1, 16: 'even when separated we could enjoy each other's presence by exchange of written messages in which we could write many things more audaciously than we could say them' ('nosque etiam absentes internuntiis inuicem liceret presentare et pleraque audacius scribere quam colloqui'); *Letter* 1, 21: 'the girl found that she was pregnant and immediately wrote me a letter full of rejoicing' ('puella se concepisse comperit et cum summa exultatione mihi super hoc ilico scripsit'); *Letter* 2, 16: 'when in the past you sought me out for sinful pleasures your letters came to me thick and fast' ('cum me ad turpes olim uoluptates expeteres, crebris me epistolis uisitabas').

saints.[16] *Letter* 12, from Abelard to a regular canon, defends the view that the monastic life is superior to the clerical.[17] *Letter* 13 defends, against a critic, the use of logic in enquiry into Christian faith.[18] *Letter* 14, from Abelard to bishop 'G.' of Paris—probably Bishop Gilbert or Gerbert (1116–25 January 1124) rather than Bishop Galo (1104–16)—and to his clergy, asks for a meeting at which the theological teachings of Roscelin of Compiègne would receive correction; in Paris, BnF lat. 2923 this letter is the final item in a valuable collection which consists of *Letters* 1–8, the *Apologia* of Berengar (written in defence of Abelard), two other letters of Berengar, Abelard's *Soliloquy*, and his *Confessio fidei 'Vniuersis'*.[19] *Letter* 15 is a tirade, in parts an unseemly one, from Roscelin to Abelard following a letter, now lost, sent by Abelard to the canons of St-Martin's at Tours around the years 1119/20.[20] *Letter* 16 is from Fulk, prior of Deuil, offering Abelard mock consolation following his castration.[21] This found its way into collections of material chiefly relating to Abelard and his fights; for example, Paris, BnF lat. 2545 contains *Letters* 1–8, then the letter from Fulk, which is followed by letters of Bernard, abbot of Clairvaux, directed against Abelard's erroneous teaching, a collection of nineteen specified errors imputed to him, a letter from Pope Innocent II formally condemning him following the council held at Sens, and finally Abelard's *Confessio fidei 'Vniuersis'*. A similar

[16] Ed. Smits, pp. 249–55; *PL* clxxviii. 341–4; trans. Ziolkowski, pp. 138–46. Cf. also Smits, pp. 77–100, 137–53; Ziolkowski, pp. 133–8; *Checklist* no. 280.

[17] Ed. Smits, pp. 257–69; *PL* clxxviii. 343–52; trans. Ziolkowski, pp. 158–74. Cf also Smits, pp. 100–1, 153–72; Ziolkowski, pp. 147–58; *Checklist* no. 281. There are links between this *Letter* and *Sermon* 33 and *Adtendite*. It is uncertain whether the *Letter* was directed against a particular Premonstratensian canon such as Norbert of Xanten or Philip of Harvengt. For other polemical writings of this time concerning 'the respective superiority of the monastic and clerical ways of life' see Constable, *The Reformation of the Twelfth Century*, pp. 134–5.

[18] Ed. Smits, pp. 271–7; *PL* clxxviii. 351–6; trans. Ziolkowski, pp. 179–87. Cf. also Smits, pp. 100, 172–88; Ziolkowski, pp. 175–8; *Checklist* no. 282.

[19] Ed. Smits, pp. 279–80; *PL* clxxviii. 355–8; trans. Ziolkowski, pp. 194–6. Cf. also Smits, pp. 101–7, 189–202; Ziolkowski, pp. 188–94; *Checklist* nos. 135 and 283. For Berengar's works see the editions by R. M. Thomson and J. Leclercq; also *PL* clxxviii. 1857–76. See too Luscombe, *The School of Peter Abelard*, pp. 29–49 and Niggli, 'Berengar von Poitiers'.

[20] Ed. Reiners, pp. 63–80; *PL* clxxviii. 357–72. *Checklist* nos. 82, 315, and 394; Dalarun and others, *Les Deux Vies de Robert d'Arbrissel*, pp. 624–30.

[21] *PL* clxxviii. 371–6; a fragment, injurious to papal Rome and omitted from *PL* clxxviii. 375A, but present in the editions of Duchesne–d'Amboise, p. 222 and of Cousin, i. 706–7, was also published by Van den Eynde, 'Détails biographiques sur Pierre Abélard', p. 219. *Checklist* nos. 132, 142, 157, 386. For an English trans. see the Bibliography: Primary Sources.

and slightly fuller collection of such materials, including Fulk's letter, is found in Paris, BnF n. acq. lat. 1873.

The *Confessio fidei 'Vniuersis'*, just mentioned, is an open letter, submissive in manner, addressed to the church at large and briefly but formally refuting the charges of heresy that were presented against Abelard at the council of Sens in 1140 or 1141.[22] The best copy of this much travelled *Confessio* is found in a MS which also contains a *Letter* which Walter of Mortagne wrote to Abelard in 1136 or 1137 to try to bring into the open growing concerns about Abelard's views concerning the Trinity after his return to teaching in Paris.[23] *Letter* 17 is a personal *Confession of faith* addressed by Abelard to Heloise ('my sister Heloise, once dear to me in the world, now dearest to me in Christ') in which he declares to her that, although logic has made people hate him, his faith is founded on the rock on which Christ built his church. This *Confession* has survived through being part-copied by Berengar in the *Apologia* he wrote in defence of Abelard after the council of Sens;[24] it was also translated into old French.[25] An unnumbered *Letter* (*Epistola contra Bernardum*) which Abelard sent to rally his supporters and bitterly blaming Bernard of Clairvaux was first published in full in 1953 from a MS in Heidelberg where it follows a shortened copy of Bernard's *Letter* 189 which is also part of the tussles surrounding the council of Sens.[26] At this time also Abelard addressed an *Apologia* to Bernard in an attempt to deliver a full answer to each of the accusations made against him. Only a fragment of this *Apologia* has survived; it was first published from a Munich MS in 1930.[27]

[22] *PL* clxxviii. 105–8; new edn. by Burnett in 'Peter Abelard, *Confessio fidei "Universis"*', pp. 132–8. Old French trans. in Paris, BnF fr. 920, ed. Hicks, pp. 151–5. See also Zerbi, 'San Bernardo di Chiaravalle', pp. 49–73.

[23] Burnett in 'Peter Abelard, *Confessio fidei "Universis"*', pp. 117–19; *Checklist* no. 273. Walter of Mortagne, *Epistola ad Abaelardum*, ed. Ostlender, pp. 34–40. See on this letter Ott, *Untersuchungen zur theologischen Briefliteratur*, pp. 234–66.

[24] Ed. Thomson, pp. 117–18; *PL* clxxviii. 1862 and 375–8. *Checklist* no. 377.

[25] Ed. Burnett in '*Confessio fidei ad Heloisam*', pp. 152–5 (Latin and French versions); *PL* clxxviii. 375–8. Old French trans. ed. Hicks, pp. 149–50. English trans. by Radice, pp. 211–12. *Checklist* no. 272.

[26] Ed. Leclercq in 'Études sur S. Bernard et le texte de ses écrits', pp. 104–5 and Klibansky in 'Peter Abailard and Bernard of Clairvaux', pp. 6–7; trans. Ziolkowski, pp. 108–10. See also Leclercq, 'Autour de la correspondance de S. Bernard', pp. 185–92; Ziolkowski, pp. 99–108, and, on Bernard's role in procuring the condemnation of Abelard, Zerbi, 'San Bernardo di Chiaravalle'. *Checklist* nos. 50 and 284.

[27] Abelard, *Apologia contra Bernardum*, ed. Ruf and Grabmann; also ed. Buytaert (*CCCM*, xi; 1969), pp. 341–68; trans. Ziolkowski, pp. 116–29. See also Ziolkowski, pp. 111–15.

Nos. 18 to 27 are not printed in *PL* clxxviii. but references are given there to the other volumes of the *Patrologia Latina* in which they are found. They consist of *Letters* sent by Bernard of Clairvaux and by Pope Innocent II in the process of securing Abelard's condemnation for heresy in 1140 or 1141[28] and of a *Letter* sent by Peter the Venerable, abbot of Cluny, to the pope following this condemnation to ask that Abelard, who had now made peace with Bernard of Clairvaux, might live out his remaining days in the abbey of Cluny.[29] Nos. 28 to 30, also not printed in *PL* clxxviii, refer to the very moving *Letters* that were exchanged between Peter the Venerable and Heloise following Abelard's death on 21 April 1142.[30]

Peter of Celle, from *c.* 1145 to 1162 abbot of Montier-la-Celle near Troyes in Champagne, may have written a *Letter* to Heloise in which a prior of Saint-Ayoul in Provins is mentioned, but there is no certainty.[31] Two further letters to Heloise, abbess of the Paraclete, were written by Hugh Métel (*c.*1080–*c.*1150), an Augustinian canon of St-Leo at Toul, praising her qualities as a writer.[32] In addition,

[28] Bernard, *Letters* 187–90, 191 (written in the name of the archbishop of Reims), 192–3, 194 (from Pope Innocent), in *S. Bernardi Opera*, ed. Leclercq and Rochais, viii. 9–48; Innocent, *Letter* 448 (*PL* clxxix. 517BC).

[29] *The Letters of Peter the Venerable*, ed. Constable, i, no. 98, pp. 258–9. Cf. Constable's notes in *Letters*, ii. 164–5; also Zerbi, 'In Cluniaco vestra sibi perpetuam mansionem elegit', pp. 373–95. Peter the Venerable wrote two letters 'ad Petrum quendam scholasticum' to persuade one Peter to turn away from the schools and philosophy and to embrace the spiritual life, nos. 9–10, ed. Constable, *Letters*, i. 14–17. Constable notes (*Letters*, ii. 101–2) that the identification of Abelard as the recipient is uncertain but more likely than an identification with Peter of Poitiers; Robl, 'Petrus Venerabilis', argues that the letters were an attempt by Peter the Venerable in 1140 or early in 1141 to save Abelard from further criticism of his teaching.

[30] Ed. Constable as letters 115 (Peter), 167 (Heloise), and 168 (Peter) in *Letters*, i. 303–8 and 400–2. The first of these was translated into old French, ed. Hicks, pp. 156–61. Cf. Constable's notes in *Letters*, ii. 177–8, 209–10; also *Checklist* no. 412. The Absolution that Heloïse requested from Peter is printed twice in *PL* clxxviii. 68B and 91C. Schmid, 'Bemerkungen zur Personen- und Memorialforschung', pp. 110–17, draws attention to the association in prayer ('Gebetsverbrüderung') of Cluny and the Paraclete.

[31] *Letter* 25 in *The Letters of Peter of Celle*, ed. Haseldine, pp. 80–3 (no. 35 in *PL* ccii, where the recipient is named as Matilda of Fontevrault). Evidence of the recipient is given in the rubric in Oxford, St John's College 126: 'Abbatisse de paraclito que pro fugitiuo rogabat' and the salutation: 'Domine sue seruus suus . . .'. Haseldine, *Letters of Peter of Celle*, p. 80n, observes that in this MS 'rubrics and salutations are generally confused' but the reference to Saint-Ayoul, 'which was in Provins and thus very close to Le Paraclet, does support the identification of Heloise as the more likely recipient'.

[32] Hugh Métel, *Letters* 16 and 17, ed. and trans. Mews, 'Hugh Métel', pp. 89–91; ed. Hugo, ii. 348–9. See further de Fortia d'Urban, *Histoire et ouvrages de Hugues Métel*, pp. 29–51; *Histoire littéraire de la France*, xii. pp. 493–511; Ott, *Untersuchungen zur theologischen Briefliteratur*, pp. 47–56, and Mews, 'Hugh Métel', pp. 76–86.

Hugh Métel joined the hue and cry against Abelard by writing a hostile *Letter* to him generally denouncing his heresies and by writing a *Letter* to Pope Innocent II on the same subject and after the manner of Bernard's *Letter* 190 to Innocent.[33]

OTHER LETTERS RELATING TO THE ORATORY OF THE PARACLETE

Letter 9 is addressed by Abelard to the nuns of the Paraclete to urge them to study the Bible.[34] As so often, Abelard commends the example of St Jerome, who had urged celibate Christian ladies in Rome during the fourth century to study Scripture and to become proficient, like Heloise, in the three languages in which the Bible was found, Hebrew, Greek, and Latin.[35] Like some of the other surviving letters written by Abelard (e.g. nos. 12 and 13), no. 9 lacks a salutation and a valediction, and the suggestion has been made that it is the last part, accidentally detached, of the *Rule*. For the *Rule* ends, now addressing the nuns directly, with mention of Jerome and of the women he supervised, and this is the topic developed in no. 9. But no. 9 is not found in any manuscript which contains the letter collection and, although some of its contents pick up and develop themes found in the letter collection, it may have been an address prepared separately for the nuns.[36]

[33] Hugh Métel, *Letters* 4 and 5, ed. Hugo, ii. 331–4. See further de Fortia d'Urban, *Histoire et ouvrages de Hugues Métel*, pp. 29–51; *Histoire littéraire de la France*, xii. 493–511; Ott, *Untersuchungen zur theologischen Briefliteratur*, pp. 47–56; and Mews, 'Hugh Métel', esp. pp. 67–8.

[34] *Letter* 9 (ed. Smits, pp. 219–37; *PL* clxxviii. 325–36; trans. Ziolkowski, pp. 10–33). See further Smits, pp. 49–69, 113–20; Ziolkowski, pp. 3–10, and *Checklist* nos. 146 and 278. In Paris, BnF lat. 14511 *Letter* 9 is accompanied by Abelard's *Confessio fidei 'Vniuersis'*, *Sermon* 14, *Expositio Symboli Apostolorum, Expositio Symboli Athanasii*, and *Problemata Heloissae*.

[35] Abelard wrote that Heloise knew all three languages (ed. Smits, p. 231 *ll.* 299, 308–9, p. 233 *ll.* 360–4; trans. Ziolkowski, pp. 25–6, 28). In a letter to Heloise warmly praising her learning Peter the Venerable hints at her knowledge of Hebrew: 'the name Deborah, as your erudition knows, means "bee" in Hebrew' (*hoc nomen Debora, ut tua nouit eruditio, lingua Hebraica apem designat*), *Letter* 115, ed. Constable, *Letters*, i. 303–8, at p. 305. Cf. Jerome, *Liber interpretationis Hebraicorum nominum, De Genesi, D*: 'Debbora apis siue eloquentia' (ed. de Lagarde, *CCSL* lxxii. 64; *PL* xxiii. 777). On the level of knowledge gained by Heloise of Greek and Hebrew see Smits, pp. 115–18 and p. 203, n. 3.

[36] *Letter* 9 begins by repeating some of what is written towards the end of the *Rule*. The importance of the study of the three languages for understanding the Bible is not one of the matters raised by Heloise in *Letter* 6, where she presented her requirements to Abelard and several times invoked the writings of Jerome. It is prominent in Abelard's Pentecost *Sermon* (*Sermon* 18, *PL* clxxviii. 505–12, at 511–12) which was addressed to the sisters of the Paraclete (507B). Van den Eynde, 'Chronologie des écrits d'Abélard à Héloïse', pp. 342–3, calls *Letter* 9 'une espèce de mémoire, que les éditions appellent *Epistola*, mais qui, en

Letter 10 is from Abelard to Bernard, abbot of Clairvaux, following a visit made by Bernard to the Paraclete between about 1131 and 1135 and following a complaint Bernard had made that the nuns had unconventionally replaced in the Lord's Prayer the words 'daily bread' (Luke 11: 3) by 'supersubstantial bread' (Matthew 6: 11), the latter being Abelard's considered preference.[37] Abelard responded with a wide-ranging counter-attack on unconventional usages practised in the Cistercian order. In Paris, BnF lat. 13057 *Letter* 10 accompanies *Letters* 16, 2–7, 1 and the *Confessio fidei 'Vniuersis'*.[38]

Finally, but most interestingly, there is a number of letters which were written by Abelard and by Heloise and which are found as prefaces to other writings. Each of these is like a satellite of the collected correspondence. Twice in the collected correspondence Abelard invited the nuns to bring him their questions about Scripture.[39] They did so. A letter from Heloise, in which she asked him to provide solutions to forty-two questions or *Problemata* about biblical texts, recalls Abelard's exhortations to the community to seek to understand Scripture—and she quotes St Jerome in support as Abelard was wont to do.[40] Her letter heads the one surviving MS copy of these questions and answers.[41] In a letter in

réalité, est une exhortation adressée directement aux soeurs'. I incline to agree. Monfrin, incidentally (p. 60; also Monfrin, 'Le Problème de l'authenticité', pp. 416–17), concluded from his study of the MSS that no part of the letter collection, not even *Letter* 1, is known to have circulated independently of the collection. *Letter* 9 did circulate independently and was not included in the collection.

[37] See Abelard, *Sermon* 14 (*PL* clxxviii. 491AC, 493D–4D) and Smits, p. 206, n. 33.

[38] Ed. Smits, pp. 239–47; *PL* clxxviii. 335–40; trans. Ziolkowski, pp. 85–98. Cf also Waddell, 'Peter Abelard's *Letter 10* and Cistercian liturgical reform'; Smits, pp. 70–6, 120–36; Ziolkowski, pp. 75–84. *Checklist* nos. 142 and 279.

[39] 'Sin . . . in iis etiam que ad Deum pertinent magisterio nostro atque scriptis indiges, super his que uelis scribe mihi, ut ad ipsam rescribam prout Dominus mihi annuerit', *Letter* 3, 1; 'imitamini saltem et amore et studio sanctarum litterarum beatas illas sancti Ieronimi discipulas Paulam et Eustochium quarum precipue rogatu tot uoluminibus ecclesiam predictus doctor illustrauit'; *Rule* 8, 117.

[40] 'saepius intantum Scripturae sacrae doctrinam commendasti . . . Addebas insuper ad exhortationem nostram ipsam Scripturae lectionem non intellectam esse quasi speculum oculis non videntis appositum', *PL* clxxviii. 678B. One of the quotations from Jerome used in Heloise's letter—'Ama scientiam Scripturarum et carnis uitia non amabis' (Jerome, *Letter* 125 to Rusticus (ed. Hilberg, *CSEL* lvi. 130; *PL* xxii. 1079)—appears towards the end of the *Rule* 123 and at the beginning of *Letter* 9 in which Abelard exhorts the nuns to study the Bible (ed. Smits, p. 219; *PL* clxxviii. 325B; trans. Ziolkowski, p. 11).

[41] *PL* clxxviii. 677–8 (letter), 678–730 (*Problemata* and solutions). The letter is courteous: 'dilecte multis sed dilectissime nobis'. Trans. McNamer, *The Education of Heloise*, pp. 111–83; trans. Levitan, pp. 257–9 (letter only). *Checklist* no. 298. See also Smith, 'The *Problemata* of Heloise'.

which Abelard fondly addressed sister Heloise, once dear in the world, now most dear in Christ, he writes that Heloise and her spiritual daughters have asked insistently how Abelard was to carry out his plan to compose for them an exposition of the three places in the Old Testament which were the most difficult to understand—the opening of the book of Genesis, the Song of Songs, and the first and last of the visions in the prophecy of Ezekiel. Whether Abelard did meet their request for an exposition of the Song of Songs and of Ezekiel is not known, although the suggestion has been made that one was written on the Song of Songs.[42] But he wrote that he would start at the beginning with Genesis, and his exposition of the account of creation given in Genesis 1–2: 25, the *Expositio in Hexameron*, survives together with the preface addressed to Heloise.[43] In the work Abelard wove together moral and allegorical exegesis but placed both upon a literal and historical foundation: the six days of creation are explored in the light of natural philosophy but they are a mirror also of the ages of the world and of the path of the human soul. Abelard met a further request from Heloise to write *Sermons* for her and her spiritual daughters gathered together, as he writes in his letter-preface, 'in our oratory' (*in oratorio nostro*). He tells her that he has followed the order of the feasts in writing or arranging these sermons and that they follow upon his completion, also at her request, of a little book

[42] See De Santis, 'Abelardo interprete del Canto dei Cantici per il Paracleto?', who suggested that Abelard may have composed some homilies on verses in the Song of Songs: in *Sermon* 29, addressed to the nuns of the Paraclete—brides of Christ—Abelard remarked that for their edification they have heard a description of the bride in the Canticle (3: 1–2) seeking her beloved ('ad exhortationem vestram diligenter descriptam'). Abelard certainly liked to turn to the Song of Songs when reflecting on contemplation but Pagani, 'Il Cantico nella produzione paraclitense di Abelardo', p. 428, is right to doubt whether the verb *describere* (unlike a verb such as *exponere*) provides sufficient evidence that an *expositio* had been written on the Song of Songs.

[43] 'Supplicando itaque postulas et postulando supplicas, soror Heloysa, in seculo quondam cara, nunc in Christo carissima, quatinus in expositionem horum tanto studiosius intendam quanto difficiliorem eorum esse constat intelligentiam, et specialiter hoc tibi et filiabus tuis spiritualibus persoluam. Vnde et rogantes uos rogo, ut que me rogando ad hoc compellitis, orando deum michi efficaciam impetretis. Et quoniam, ut dici solet, a capite inchoandum est, tanto me amplius in exordio Genesis uestre orationes adiuuent, quanto eius difficultatem ceteris constat esse maiorem, sicut expositionum raritas ipsa protestatur . . . Quam nunc quidem expositionem ita me uestrarum instantia precum aggredi cognoscatis . . .', Letter-preface to the *Expositio in Hexameron* (ed. Romig and Luscombe, *CCCM* xv. 3–5, at pp. 4–5; *PL* clxxviii. 731–2, at 731C–732C; trans. Ziolkowski, pp. 60–3 (and see Ziolkowski, pp. 52–60)). For the text of this *Expositio* see *CCCM* xv. 5–111; *PL* clxxviii. 731–84. *Checklist* no. 286.

of hymns and sequences.[44] In fact, Abelard had composed and sent to the Paraclete three books of hymns (133 hymns in total), each book prefaced with an explanatory, and affectionate, letter.[45] Heloise

[44] 'Libello quodam hymnorum vel sequentiarum a me nuper precibus tuis consummato, veneranda in Christo et amanda soror, Heloissa . . .' ('Having completed recently a small book of hymns and sequences at your entreaty, Heloise, sister to be revered in Christ and loved . . .'); 'In his autem scribendis seu disponendis ordinem festivitatum tenens, ab ipso nostrae redemptionis exordio sum exorsus' ('Moreover, in maintaining the sequence of the feast days when writing or rather arranging these, I have begun at the very beginning of our redemption') (*I sermoni di Abelardo per le monache del Paracleto*, ed. De Santis, p. 86 (it is not clear why De Santis omits from her edition the words from 'veneranda' to 'Heloissa'); *PL* clxxviii. 379–80; trans. Ziolkowski, pp. 70 and 72). The letter concludes as it begins with affection: 'Farewell in the Lord, you who are his handmaiden, once dear to me in the world, now dearest to me in Christ; then wife in flesh, now sister in spirit and consort in the profession of a sacred way of life' ('Vale in Domino eius ancilla, mihi quondam in seculo chara, nunc in Christo charissima, in carne tunc uxor, nunc in spiritu soror atque in professione sacri propositi consors') (*I sermoni di Abelardo per le monache del Paracleto*, ed. De Santis, p. 86; *PL* clxxviii. 379–80; trans. Ziolkowski, p. 72 (and see Ziolkowski, pp. 64–70)). Which of the thirty-four sermons printed in *PL* clxxviii. 379–610 were included in Abelard's gift to the Paraclete is not fully clear but see Van den Eynde, 'Le Recueil des sermons de Pierre Abélard' and also *I sermoni di Abelardo per le monache del Paracleto*, ed. De Santis, who edits six sermons addressed to the nuns of the Paraclete. No medieval manuscript copy of the sermons or of the introductory letter survives. However, twenty-two sermons in the collection printed in *PL* clxxviii follow the sequence of major feasts from the Annunciation to Pentecost. The remainder include sermons on saints. Among these, *Sermon* 33 on St John the Baptist (*PL* clxxviii. 582–607) outlines Abelard's ideas on monastic life. *Sermon* 30 (*PL* clxxviii. 564–9) is an appeal for gifts for the Paraclete convent. Another *Sermon* (inc. '*Adtendite*'), not in the printed collection but probably by Abelard, was found and ed. by Engels; see also Waddell, '*Adtendite a falsis prophetis*', who called it 'more a diatribe than a sermon' which 'shows him at his worst' (pp. 372, 397).

[45] The three letter-prefaces found in the *Hymnarius Paraclitensis* are in *Hymn Collections from the Paraclete*, ed. Waddell, ii. 5–9 (addressed to Heloise and the sisters: 'soror michi Heloysa, in seculo quondam cara, nunc in Christo karissima'; 'sponse Christi uel ancille'), 47–9 ('dilectissime Christi filie'), 89–90 ('sorores karissime Christoque dicate'); *Peter Abelard's Hymnarius Paraclitensis*, ed. Szövérffy, ii. 9–13, 79–81, 169–70; *Petri Abaelardi . . . Hymnarius Paraclitensis*, ed. Dreves, pp. 25–7, 93–4, 193–4; *PL* clxxviii. 1771–2, 1787–8, 1801–4; *The Hymns of Abelard in English Verse*, trans. Sister Jane Patricia, pp. 31–4, 57–8, 95–6; trans. Ziolkowski, pp. 40–51. On these prefaces see further *Hymn Collections from the Paraclete*, ed. Waddell, i, pp. ccxii–ccxiii, ccxxii, ccxxv; *Peter Abelard's Hymnarius Paraclitensis*, ed. Szövérffy, ii. 30–5; Ziolkowski, pp. 34–40; *Checklist* nos. 23 and 291. 'Superlatives of endearment', as Dronke once wrote (*Medieval Latin and the Rise of the European Love-Lyric*, i. 198–9), belong to the tradition of monastic letters and it is not easy to distinguish traditional courtesies and passion. Abelard shows affection for Heloise and the sisters but uses similar salutations at the beginning of *Letter* 10 to Bernard of Clairvaux ('dilectissimo fratri Bernardo') before roundly denouncing Cistercian usages (ed. Smits, p. 239; *PL* clxxviii. 335; trans. Ziolkowski, p. 85), and in *Letter* 11 to Abbot Adam and the monks of Saint-Denis ('Ade dilectissimo patri suo abbati . . . unaque fratribus et commonachis suis carissimis Petrus . . . Valete in Domino dilectissimi', ed. Smits, pp. 249, 255; *PL* clxxviii. 341A, 344D; trans. Ziolkowski, pp. 138, 146) whom he excoriated in *Letter* 1, 33, 46–51. As regards the *libellus* Waddell ('Peter Abelard as creator of liturgical texts', pp. 283–4) has suggested that the original little book may have included Mass

requested hymns more than once ('sepius' according to Abelard) but also once in a letter which was not dissimilar to *Letter* 6 in that she outlined in some detail what she expected from Abelard for the Paraclete. Her letter asking for hymns does not survive independently but Abelard quoted, or at least paraphrased, parts of it in his letter-preface to the first book.[46] The structure of the hymn books offers parallels with the *Exposition* of the *Hexameron*: the night hymns are about the work of the six days of creation while the day hymns offer allegorical and moral interpretations of this. All four works—*Problemata*, *Expositio*, *Hymnarius*, *Sermones*—are partners of the letter collection, a fact which has a bearing upon interpretations of the collection and which also reinforces arguments in favour of its authenticity.

AUTHORSHIP AND AUTHENTICITY OF THE LETTER COLLECTION

In 1972 the two-centuries-old debates over the genesis and the genuineness of the letter collection were spectacularly reignited by John F. Benton.[47] The ensuing controversies were prolonged: some held that the collection was a forgery of the thirteenth century, others that Abelard wrote all the letters, and others that Heloise rewrote them. Notable contributors to the debates, beside Benton himself, have included Christopher Brooke, Peter Dronke, Hubert Silvestre, Peter von Moos, and Fr Chrysogonus Waddell.

My own judgement is that the collection is genuine, that is, that the letters were written by Abelard and Heloise. We may never know how they were redacted and whether they were all written for dispatch,

sequences as well as hymns—sequences are mentioned in Abelard's preface to his *Sermons*; see the previous note—and that the many sequence incipits found in the *Ordinary of the Paraclete* may include sequences composed by Abelard; on this see below, p. xxxviii. Ziolkowski, pp. 67–70 has suggested that the six *Planctus* (*Laments*) which Abelard composed on six Old Testament themes may be numbered among the sequences.

[46] 'Cum autem a diuersis diuersa michi responderentur, tu inter cetera talem memini subiecisti rationem: "Scimus", inquiens, ". . . Discretio uestra diiudicet". His uel consimilibus uestrarum persuasionibus rationum ad scribendos . . . hymnos animum nostrum uestre reuerentia sanctitatis compulit.' For the passages reproduced by Abelard see *Hymn Collections from the Paraclete*, ed. Waddell, ii. 5, *ll.* 13 – 9, *l.* 10.

[47] Benton, 'Fraud, fiction, and borrowing in the correspondence of Abelard and Heloise'. A penetrating account of earlier debates and disagreements is given by Moos, *Mittelalterforschung und Ideologiekritik: Der Gelehrtenstreit um Heloise*, who encountered criticism, however, over his appreciation of the work of Gilson, from Kolb writing in *Euphorion*, lxviii (1974), 286–95.

separately and successively, prompting replies in the form we have, or whether, perhaps, the collection arose from a compact between Heloise and Abelard jointly to share their thoughts and experiences in a literary work of the greatest artistry cast in the form of an epistolary dialogue prefaced by the *Historia calamitatum*, or whether one or both of the pair chose to review and revise or extend an earlier, less elaborate correspondence (of which there is no trace) that had been exchanged between them. But what is clear is that the collected letters of Heloise and Abelard cannot be considered apart from the other surviving letters exchanged between them—that is, the letters accompanying and prefacing the books of hymns and sequences, the biblical problems, the *Hexameron* commentary, and the sermons as well as the letter addressed to the nuns of the Paraclete on study. This correspondence and the collected letters constitute a single achievement, that of providing the abbey of the Paraclete with some of the materials it needed to establish its identity and to shape its future in the light of the exceptional circumstances of its foundation and in the light also of a comprehensive historical account of the lives, aims, and achievements of religious women since time began. The careful attempts that were made not only to write but to arrange and introduce the books of hymns, the biblical problems, the commentary, the sermons, *and* the collection of eight letters beginning with the *Historia calamitatum* and ending with the treatise on religious women and then the *Rule*, as well as the contrast that these carefully mounted arrangements offer to the unstable and fluid texts of several of Abelard's other writings for other readers in other contexts—his heavily revised *Theologiae*, the varying texts of the *Sententie* emerging from his school, the differing versions of his *Sic et non*[48]—all combine to suggest that the collected correspondence was brought together under the very eyes of those who proposed and composed, arranged and preserved the books of hymns and sermons and expositions.[49] The making and keeping of the collected correspondence should not

[48] See Luscombe, *The School of Peter Abelard*, 95–6; Häring, 'Abelard yesterday and today', and *Petrus Abaelardus. Glossae super Peri hermeneias*, ed. Jacobi and Strub, Introduction, pp. liii–lxi.

[49] The *Hexameron* commentary is not an exception: one of the four MSS in which it survives contains an 'abbreviation' of the work, and another contains interventions and corrections made by scribes or editors, but these differences are small in comparison with the changes brought into the *Theologiae*, *Sententie*, and the *Sic et non*. Moreover, the introductory letter to Heloise clearly states that the *Hexameron* commentary was both requested by her and specially written for her and her spiritual daughters (see n. 43 above).

be considered apart from this wider activity of Heloise and Abelard on behalf of and in association with the Paraclete community.

STYLE AND STRUCTURE

There was an art of writing letters and this, the *dictamen*, was developed in Italy in the late eleventh century and then in France during the twelfth.[50] Teachers of *dictamen* usually divided a letter into five parts: an opening *salutatio*, an introductory *captatio benevolentiae*, *narratio*, *petitio*, and *conclusio*. All these elements are found in the collection edited here and with much ornamentation. Each letter has a rhetorical structure with its own series of movements among which are found salutation and valediction, consolation, lament, self-analysis, reproach, antithesis, emphatic repetition, exclamations, clusters of citations from authorities, and much else.[51] The collection is, moreover, arranged in the form of a dialogue with each succeeding letter being a reply to an earlier one. There is, furthermore, a vast network of connections between the *Letters* of Abelard and Heloise and their other writings, including their other letters, connections that take the form of repeated use by both writers of similar words, phrases, ideas, and arguments as well as of citations from, and allusions to, biblical, patristic, and classical sources. They include but also go far beyond the commonplace.[52] Engels ('Abélard écrivain') drew attention to this

[50] For guides see Camargo, *Ars dictaminis, ars dictandi*; Murphy, *Rhetoric in the Middle Ages* and *Medieval Rhetoric: A Select Bibliography*.

[51] See the analyses in Dronke, 'Heloise's *Problemata* and letters', pp. 57–60 (repr. Dronke, *Intellectuals and Poets*, pp. 302–8) and id., *Women Writers of the Middle Ages*, pp. 112–28. Howlett ('Some criteria for editing Abelard') has studied the numerological patterning of some of the rhythms and the structure found in *Letter* 1. Spatial patterns were not uncommon in ancient, medieval, and later literature. Howlett identifies chiastic, symmetrical, parallel, and diagonal word patterns: 'elements from each section of the narrative are woven into other sections' (p. 202). Cf. Howlett, 'Arithmetic rhythms in Latin letters', pp. 202–17 for a similar study of Peter the Venerable's letter to Heloise (no. 115; see n. 30 above). Levitan, p. xix, notes that the name of Heloise is mentioned with symmetry twice in *Letter* 1: 2,031 words from the beginning and then 2,231 words from the end.

[52] Silvestre (who considered the *Letters* to be a forgery) rightly entered a *caveat* (review of Jaeger, 'The Prologue to the "*Historia Calamitatum*"'): many expressions found in the letter collection and in other writings by Abelard and Heloise were the common property of other writers of the time and earlier. Jaeger also warns agains reliance upon commonplace expressions to support views about authorship ('The Prologue to the *Historia calamitatum*', p. 12 and n. 40): 'The only kind of stylistic features useful for determining the authenticity of an individual passage in a work suspected of being a literary imitation are phrasings and syntactic formulations which are unique and inconspicuous, combine two or more unimportant and unrelated phrases and occur infrequently, preferably only once, in genuine works . . . Hence common words and phrases in Abelard, like *tanto-quanto*, *detrimentum*

in compelling fashion; the notes to the re-presentation by Pagani of the editions made by Muckle and McLaughlin are full of such indications, as is the present edition.

Engels also highlighted in 'Abélard écrivain' the clearly didactic character of most of Abelard's writing, including his letters to Heloise: at the centre of Abelard's preoccupations was his wish to teach, to provide *doctrina*, *eruditio*, *expositio*, and *intelligentia*, especially of Christian faith.[53] Engels further noted that, although Abelard frequently cites classical authors, his style reflects Augustine's *De doctrina christiana*. Most importantly also, Peter Dronke drew attention to the tradition of monastic and classical exchanges of letters and verses between men and between men and women: the correspondence of Abelard and Heloise, he wrote, 'however much it mirrors an emotional life incomparably deeper and more manifold than is mirrored in any of the letters just cited,[54] is grounded, as can be seen from almost every page, in Cicero and in the letters of Seneca and Jerome. It is precisely Christian monastic *amicitia* which provides the pretext (the only possible one) for the entire correspondence'.[55]

In parts of the collected correspondence, as well as in the letter from Heloise with which the *Problemata* begin and in her letter to Peter the Venerable, different types of rhythmic cadences or *cursus* are deployed by both writers. There have been a number of studies made of this in the light of Tore Janson's book on *Prose Rhythm in Medieval Latin* published in 1975. The methods used include a test, familiar to statisticians as the χ^2 test, which enables the deliberate use of particular types of cadence to be distinguished from occurrences that may be fortuitous by first squaring the number of observed frequencies (o) minus the number of expected frequencies (e) and then dividing the result by the number of expected frequencies: $(o-e)^2/e$. The results help in finding differences of style between the letters of Abelard and Heloise and other medieval Latin texts. Heloise liked to use *cursus velox*, where the emphasis is placed on the 7th and 2nd last syllables of a clause,[56] and *cursus tardus*, where the emphasis is

famae, *vehementer*, *res ipsa clamat*, *fragilior sexus* . . . are quite useless, even as clues, where there is suspicion of literary imitation.'

[53] Abelard's style was also often allusive, as East ('Abelard's allusive style') has noted.

[54] These include letters from the circle of St Boniface (716–20), from Alcuin (*c*.740–804) and St Anselm of Bec and Canterbury (*c*.1033–1109). Dronke, *Medieval Latin and the Rise of the European Love-Lyric* (2nd edn.), i. 196–200.

[55] Dronke, *Medieval Latin and the Rise of the European Love-Lyric* (2nd edn.), i. 200.

[56] e.g. in *Letter* 4, **12**: débeam de commíssis, pótius de amíssis, témperant improuísis.

placed on the 6th and 3rd last syllables,[57] and also, although less often, *cursus planus* (5th and 2nd last).[58] Sometimes particular types of *cursus* are bunched together in continuous series and sometimes different varieties are used together, and with great artistry, to create particular effects, with the expected word order being adjusted if need be. Abelard also showed a liking for *cursus uelox*[59] and for *cursus tardus*.[60] With these he sometimes also mingled *cursus planus*.[61] But both Abelard and Heloise are apparently unusual in their time in preferring 'slow' to 'swift' cadences and Heloise herself shows a striking preference, greater than Abelard's, for the deliberate use of 'slow' endings in conjunction also, within sentences, with rhythmic parallelism and rhymes.[62]

EPISTOLAE DVORVM AMANTIVM

In 1974 Ewald Könsgen published an edition of a collection of 113 love-letters between a man and a woman that were copied, sometimes in abbreviated form but more often fully, at the abbey of Clairvaux by one Johannes de Vepria in 1471.[63] They are found in

[57] e.g. in *Letter* 4, **8** and **9**: péne reddíderas, caúsa progénitam, feminárum perníciem.

[58] e.g. in *Letter* 6, **9**: uíris iniúngat, quánta et fórti, íta distínxit.

[59] e.g. in *Letter* 3, **4** and **5**: iústi reperiúntur, únicam interfécit, aúdeat instruáris, féminam supplicántem.

[60] e.g. in *Letter* 3, **5** and **6**: fréquens orátio, iústi assídua, matúre attúlerit, látet prudéntiam, and in *Letter* 5, **14**: frúi preséntia, móri non uídeo, túa desíderas.

[61] e.g. in *Letter* 5, **13**: ípsis atténdunt, consórtem habére, toleráre non pótest.

[62] See Dronke, 'Heloise's *Problemata* and letters' (published in 1980), *Women Writers of the Middle Ages* (1984), pp. 110–12, and 'Heloise, Abelard, and some recent discussions' (1992); also Dronke and Orlandi, 'New works by Peter Abelard and Heloise?' (2005). Dronke suggested that, in their practice of *cursus*, Abelard and Heloise were both influenced by a minority current of prose rhythm traceable in France and also advanced by the Italian Adalbertus Samaritanus in his *Praecepta dictaminum*, which began to circulate in 1115. Janson, 'Schools of cursus in the twelfth century and the letters of Heloise and Abelard' (1988), was sceptical about the influence of Adalbertus and relied largely on observed rather than expected frequencies of the use of different cadences to reach the conclusion (p. 195) that '*cursus* usage makes it very probable, though not completely certain, that we have to do with one author, or at least with one editor'. Cupiccia, after further calculations of the use of the *cursus* in the correspondence ('Progressi nello studio del cursus', published in 1998), concluded that Abelard and Heloise wrote their own letters, with Heloise showing a preference for *velox* and Abelard for *tardus*. Orlandi, 'Metrica e statistica linguistica' (2000), p. 29, suggested that Cupiccia's calculations needed to be reviewed. A further scan of the rhythms found was given by Dronke and Orlandi in 'New works by Peter Abelard and Heloise?' (2005) and leads to the view that another letter collection which is about to be discussed here, *Epistolae duorum amantium*, is not the work of Abelard and Heloise. For an introduction to formal elements and techniques practised in the composition of medieval Latin prose, including the *cursus* and rimes, see Bourgain with Hubert, *Le Latin médiéval*, pp. 393–528.

[63] *Epistolae duorum amantium: Briefe Abaelards und Heloises?*, ed. Könsgen.

one MS in Troyes, Médiathèque 1452. The pieces are sometimes in verse and rhyming prose and the man's writing style is different from that of the woman. As there was some reason to think that the originals were of twelfth-century date and from the region of Troyes, and as the letters show that the man taught the woman, whom he regarded as exceptionally talented and who regarded him as a great philosopher and poet who was, nonetheless, hounded by envious rivals, especially among the *Francigenae*, Könsgen raised the question whether these *Epistolae duorum amantium* were relics of early love-messages between Abelard and Heloise. Peter Dronke cautioned that 'these letters take their place within a specific tradition, one that we can follow at Regensburg in Bavaria and Le Ronceray on the Loire in the late eleventh century, and again in Bavaria, at Tegernsee in the early twelfth'; from these places groups of amatory letters from young women and their teachers, written in verse or in rhyming prose, also survive. Dronke further suggested that the Troyes collection is stylistically close to the Tegernsee letters but different from the letter collection of Abelard and Heloise.[64] But Constant Mews answered Könsgen's question affirmatively, basing his arguments (in part at least) on a small selection of phrases, words, and ideas found in the *Epistolae*, and he reproduced Könsgen's edition of the fragments in 1999 with an English translation made by himself and N. Chiavaroli.[65] Mews found support for his view about the authorship of these letters. Jaeger, for example, concluded from his study of correspondences between the *Epistolae* and other evidence concerning Abelard and Heloise that their ascription to Abelard and Heloise had reached 'the point of virtual certainty'.[66] Mews continued to promote his

[64] Dronke, *Abelard and Heloise in Medieval Testimonies*, pp. 24–6 (repr. Dronke, *Intellectuals and Poets*, pp. 270–2); further observations in Dronke, *Women Writers of the Middle Ages*, pp. 92–7. The Regensburg and Tegernsee love-verses and letters have been ed. and trans. by Dronke, *Medieval Latin and the Rise of the European Love-Lyric*, ii. 422–47, 472–82; for some of the Le Ronceray letters see Bulst, 'Liebesbriefgedichte Marbods'. Von Moos was also sceptical ('Die Bekehrung Heloises', p. 120, n. 44; repr. in von Moos, *Abaelard und Heloise: Gesammelte Studien*, p. 39, n. 44). For poetic influences observable in the *Epistolae duorum amantium* see Stella, '*Epistolae*'.

[65] Mews, *The Lost Love Letters of Heloise and Abelard*, with a translation by Chiavaroli and Mews.

[66] Jaeger, '*Epistolae duorum amantium* and the ascription to Heloise and Abelard', p. 149. See too Ward and Chiavaroli, 'The young Heloise and Latin rhetoric'; Clanchy, 'The letters of Abelard and Heloise in today's scholarship', pp. lxxv–lxxxi; Piron, *Lettres des deux amants* (Piron reproduces Könsgen's Latin text and adds a French trans.).

case,[67] although other scholars were or remained sceptical.[68] The case for the attribution of the *Epistolae duorum amantium* to Abelard and Heloise weakened appreciably when Ziolkowski ('Lost and not yet found') found significant differences of vocabulary, prose rhythm, prosody, and allusion between the *Epistolae* and the letters and poetry of Abelard and, even more, when Dronke and Orlandi ('New works by Abelard and Heloise?') scanned the *Epistolae* and *Letters* 2–6 and applied the statistical χ^2 test (on which see above). Their conclusion was that the case for the attribution is extremely feeble ('estremamente debole', p. 164).[69] Furthermore, when Marenbon looked into the supposed web of philosophical links between the *Epistolae* and Abelard's thought, he found not only that it was 'based on misrepresentation and misunderstanding of Abelard', but that it is 'evidence *against* the identification of the Man and Woman with Abelard and Heloise'.[70]

THE DEVELOPMENT OF THE ORATORY OF THE PARACLETE

In the Troyes MS 802, as well as in **Amb**, the letter collection, which ends with the *Rule* or *Institutio*, is followed by some brief *Institutes* or *Statutes* which begin with the words *Institutiones nostre*. These present a short series of instructions which implicitly supplement and adapt some provisions of the *Rule* of St Benedict and, it would seem, of the

[67] Mews, 'Thèmes philosophiques dans les *Epistolae duorum amantium*: Les premières lettres d'Héloïse et Abélard'; 'Philosophical themes in the *Epistolae duorum amantium*: The first letters of Heloise and Abelard'; 'Les Lettres d'amour perdues d'Héloïse et la théologie d'Abélard'; 'On some recent publications relating to Peter Abelard', p. 123; *Abelard and Heloise*, pp. 62–79; 'Cicero and the boundaries of friendship in the twelfth century'; 'Heloise'.

[68] See Constable, 'Sur l'attribution des *Epistolae duorum amantium*' and 'The authorship of the *Epistolae duorum amantium*'; Dronke in a review of Wheeler, ed., *Listening to Heloise* (*International Journal of the Classical Tradition*, viii (2001–2), 134–9); von Moos, 'Die *Epistolae duorum amantium* und die säkulare Religion der Liebe', together with an *excursus* added in *Abaelard und Heloise: Gesammelte Studien*, pp. 282–92.

[69] Dronke and Orlandi (pp. 154–62) recognized that there is a degree of arbitrariness involved in attempts at scanning because there may be differences between a grammatically correct reading and what was actually written by writers in accordance with their own phonetic practices: where an accent should be placed within sentences and within words reflects in part the way in which Latin was actually spoken. But in the case of Abelard, they wrote, help is also available from study of his poetry, especially his hymns and his *Planctus*, where metres and rhymes are more easily identified, and, in general, they show his observance of rules laid down by the ancient grammarians.

[70] Marenbon, 'Lost love letters? A controversy in retrospect', 273, 279.

Rule also provided by Abelard, and which are to be uniformly practised in the mother and daughter houses that now made up an unnamed order of nuns which we may presume to be that of the Paraclete.[71] The *Institutes* appear to have come into being during the lifetime of Heloise (d. 1164), when the Paraclete had become head of a small order which included six other houses, with extensive properties, that were spread over an area stretching nearly 130 km from the abbey of La Pommeraye in the south (north of Sens) to the priory of Saint-Martin-aux-Nonnettes in the north (near Senlis), with the priories of Trainel, Saint-Flavit, Laval, and Noëfort lying in between (see Map 1).[72] Fr Chrysogonus Waddell has shown that the *Institutes* adapt material found in statutes of the Cistercian order of monks dating from before 1147 and also that they are in harmony with some of the prescriptions found in Abelard's *Rule* and concerning, for example, clothing, beds, bedding, and wine, but not in harmony with those concerning bread, meat, eggs, cheese, milk, and fish nor with his provision for a male superior and a deaconess.[73] There are also differences between the *Institutes* and Abelard's *Rule* regarding the detailed arrangement of daily and seasonal tasks to be undertaken in

[71] 'Domino super nos prospiciente, et aliqua loca nobis largiente, misimus quasdam ex nostris ad religionem tenendam numero sufficiente. Annotamus autem boni propositi nostri consuetudines, ut quod tenuit mater incommutabiliter, teneant et filie uniformiter', ed. from the Troyes MS in *The Paraclete Statutes*, ed. Waddell, pp. 9–15, at 9; *Amb* is reproduced in *PL* clxxviii. 313C–317B, at 313D; see above at pp. xiii–xv. The likelihood that these *Institutes* emanate from the abbey of the Paraclete, founded in honour of the Holy Spirit, is supported by the singing on the most solemn days, and the saying on all other days, of *Veni sancte Spiritus* (*The Paraclete Statutes*, ed. Waddell, p. 12; *PL* clxxviii. 515C), a brief antiphon, not the longer sequence which is now better known, according to Van den Eynde, 'En marge des écrits d'Abélard', pp. 72–3.

[72] *The Paraclete Statutes*, ed. Waddell, p. 79 (map) and pp. 113–14. Cottineau lists these houses apart from Saint-Flavit and Saint-Martin-aux-Nonnettes in his *Répertoire*. Charrier, *Héloïse*, pp. 274–7, documents their foundation and indicates their location. See too Niggli, 'Heloisa', pp. 36–9 and Porter, 'The convent of the Paraclete'.

[73] See the commentary by Waddell in *The Paraclete Statutes*, pp. 28–65 (the nature and sources of *Institutiones nostre*), 87 (clothing), 92–3 (bedding), 94–8 (bread, eggs, cheese, milk, fish, wine, meat), 99–102 (abbess and prioress), 199–203 (summary). Many convents of the time adopted Cistercian usages. Bernard, abbot of Clairvaux, visited the Paraclete in the early 1130s and his visit may have helped the Paraclete to do so as well. Abelard acknowledged in *Letter* 10 (ed. Smits, p. 239, trans. Ziolkowski, p. 85, and see the comments made above, p. xxv) that Bernard had been received by the sisters like an angel and the occasion had been one of supreme joy and encouragement for them. Within a decade of his strongly fought and successful campaign to have Abelard condemned as a heretic in 1140 or 1141, Bernard wrote to Pope Eugenius III on behalf of Heloise. His letter (no. 278, *S. Bernardi Opera*, ed. Leclercq and Rochais, viii. 190) is given the date of 1150 by its editors. In 1147 Eugenius had confirmed to Heloise, abbess, and the sisters of the monastery of the Holy Spirit the possesssions of their house (JL 9155; *Checklist* no. 420).

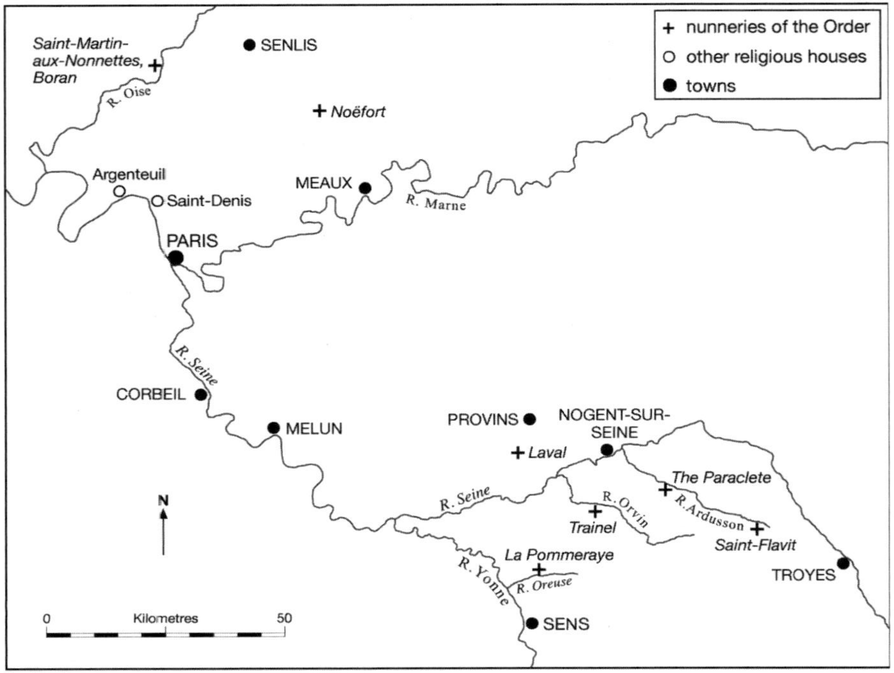

MAP 1. Nunneries of the Order of the Paraclete

the oratory, the cloister, the refectory, and the dormitory.[74] The *Institutes* are followed in the Troyes MS 802 by a collection of other texts taken from various sources, one of them dating from 1231, and all concerning convents of women.[75]

In addition, other documents that once belonged to the Paraclete shed light on its observances. Notable among these are the *Ordinary of the Paraclete* written in the late thirteenth century in Old French, the Paraclete Necrology or 'Book of Burials', which gives obits and indicates burial sites and which is followed in a manuscript copy of the thirteenth century (Paris, BnF fr. 14410) by a directory or order of processions, and the Paraclete *Breviary* (or Diurnal) with a Calendar written in the late fifteenth or early sixteenth century.[76] Waddell, in his editions and studies of these texts, has shown how they can be used to reconstruct the physical layout of the oratory and of the burial sites, how influential Cistercian practices became in the order of the Paraclete, but also the extent to which some of Abelard's written contributions for the community seemingly remained in use in the celebration of the divine offices. The identification of these contributions is not always certain but Abelard did apparently select and arrange antiphons, responsories, and hymns for Holy Week and for the feast of the Transfiguration.[77] In some collects an unusual formula is found which also appears in *Letter* 3, 11 where Abelard asks the nuns to pray for him.[78] Some of his sermons remained

[74] *The Paraclete Statutes*, ed. Waddell, pp. 127–98. For a summary see Waddell, 'Heloise and the abbey of the Paraclete'.

[75] These other texts are printed in *PL* clxxviii. 317B–326A (from 'Ex concilio Triburiensi, capitulo x' onwards). See Van den Eynde, 'En marge des écrits d'Abélard'; Benton, 'The Paraclete and the Council of Rouen of 1231'; *The Paraclete Statutes*, ed. Waddell, pp. 19–21.

[76] See *The Old French Paraclete Ordinary*, ed. Waddell, i (introduction and commentary; for the Calendar see the comments on pp. 319–36), *The Old French Paraclete Ordinary*, ii (edition of the Ordinary and—on pp. 112–24—of the order of processions), *The Paraclete Breviary*, iiiA–C (edition of the Breviary). For the Book of Burials and the *Obituary of the Paraclete* see *The Old French Paraclete Ordinary*, ed. Waddell, i, pp. xiv, 313–18; partly ed. in *Obituaires de la Province de Sens*, iv: *Diocèses de Meaux et de Troyes*, ed. Molinier, pp. 388–403 and 404–30; also in *Collection des principaux obituaires et confraternités du diocèse de Troyes*, ed. Lalore, pp. 12, 446–60. See also *Répertoire des documents nécrologiques français*, ed. Lemaître, pp. 519–20, nos. 1094–7, and, not least, Waddell's essay on 'Cistercian influence'.

[77] *The Old French Paraclete Ordinary*, ed. Waddell, i. 354–6, 361–3.

[78] *The Paraclete Statutes*, ed. Waddell, pp. 137–9, and *The Old French Paraclete Ordinary*, ed. Waddell, i. 377–9, 369–70 and 353–4. The collects are in *The Paraclete Breviary*, ed. Waddell, iiiC, pp. 401–2 and *The Paraclete Breviary*, iiiB, p. 258, *ll.* 4–6. Waddell (in *The Old French Paraclete Ordinary*, i. 209–10 and 378) compares the close of Abelard's *Sermon*

required reading in the refectory.[79] His cycle of Sunday and weekday hymns did not survive in use but many of his hymns do appear in the *Ordinary* along with hymns from Cistercian and Gallican sources.[80] Suggestions that Abelard composed some of the sequences mentioned in the *Ordinary*, including an Easter sequence (*Epithalamica*), an All Souls' Day sequence (*De profundis*), a sequence for the feast of St Lucy (*Virgines castae*), and one for St John the Evangelist (*Eia, karissimi*), have not all won general acceptance.[81]

HISTORY OF THE TEXT

The Surviving Manuscripts

There are good descriptions of some of the manuscripts of the collected letters of Abelard and Heloise (*Letters* 1–8 and the *Rule*), especially those made by Monfrin, pp. 9–61. I focus here on contents and features of the manuscripts that are especially relevant to Abelard and Heloise and illuminate in different ways the history of the

31 on St Stephen and 'other deacons who serve saintly widows' (*PL* clxxviii. 573AB) and the close of *Sermon* 32, also on St Stephen (*I sermoni di Abelardo per le monache del Paraclito*, ed. De Santis, p. 233; *PL* clxxviii. 582A), with the collect on the feast of St Philip, in *The Paraclete Breviary*, iiiB, pp. 258, *ll.* 4–6.

[79] 'Les sermons au mestre' and 'les sermons maistre pierre' are mentioned in the Ordinary, *The Old French Paraclete Ordinary*, ed. Waddell, ii. 24′, *ll.* 12–13, 57′, *l.* 20, 40′, *l.* 13.

[80] *Hymn Collections from the Paraclete*, ed. Waddell, i. 54–86; also *The Old French Paraclete Ordinary*, ed. Waddell, i. 356–9; *The Paraclete Statutes*, ed. Waddell, p. 141.

[81] The first two of these sequences accompany Abelard's *Planctus VI: David super Saul et Jonathan* in Paris, BnF n. acq. lat. 3126, on which see Huglo, 'Un Nouveau Prosaire nivernais', esp. p. 18. Other studies of the contents of this MS from Nevers include Iversen, 'Continuité et renouvellement à Nevers' and 'Pierre Abélard et la poésie liturgique'. All four sequences are mentioned in the *Ordinary of the Paraclete* (*The Old French Paraclete Ordinary*, ed. Waddell, ii. 31′, *l.* 12, p. 100′, *l.* 9, p. 47′, *l.* 20, p. 48′, *l.* 27) and have been printed in *Analecta Hymnica Medii Aevi*, viii (1890), pp. 45–7; x (1891), pp. 54–5; liv (1915), pp. 133–5, and xliv (1904), pp. 163–4. See *The Old French Paraclete Ordinary*, ed. Waddell, i. 125–6, 183–4, 298–9, 347–50, and 183–4. *Epithalamica* has also been ed. by Dronke, 'Amour sacré et amour profane', pp. 394–5; by Waddell with melody and trans., '"Epithalamica"', pp. 248–52; by Iversen, 'Pierre Abélard et la poésie liturgique', pp. 259–60; and with trans. by Bell in *Abelard after Marriage*, pp. 21–3. *Virgines castae* has been ed. by Iversen, 'Pierre Abélard et la poésie liturgique', pp. 254–5 and with trans. by Bell in *Peter Abelard after Marriage*, pp. 16–20. Dronke and Orlandi, 'New works by Abelard and Heloise?', pp. 123–35, give reasons for doubting that *De profundis* was written as late as the 1130s or by Abelard, that *Virgines castae* was written later than the 11th c. or in France, and that *Eia, carissimi* was composed by Abelard; however, *Epithalamica* (on which see also Dronke, 'Amour sacré et amour profane') may well be by a poet or poetess at the Paraclete who knew Abelard's hymns well. For further illustration of the early development of the Paraclete oratory see Luscombe, 'Pierre Abélard et l'abbaye du Paraclet'.

collection—its transmission and its losses, its arrangement and presentation, its readers and posssessors. The descriptions of surviving manuscripts follow a common pattern—location, date,[82] and provenance, contents that are relevant to the collection, date, physical features, spelling and punctuation, former possessors, and lastly a summary of other available descriptions with some further references. These descriptions do not pretend to be complete but to provide such information as sheds most light in each case on the copying of the text, its qualities, and its reception. Where a siglum is given, the MS has been used in the edition (or in the case of **V**, a lost MS, in the stemma only).

Short titles of works and brief mentions of authors by name are filled out towards the end of the descriptions under the heading *Descriptions and further references* or in the *Bibliography* or the list of *Abbreviations*.

Brugge, Stadsbibliotheek 398 (Ter Doest, s. xiv²)

Contents: Fos. 17–21ᵛ, excerpts from Berengar's *Apologia* prefaced by summaries of Berengar's invectives against Bernard of Clairvaux (*In apologia berengarii pictauensis quam fecit pro defensione magistri petri abaelardi quedam inuectiones continentur contra beati bernardi doctrinam et eius eloquenciam ex qua notare aliqua decreui*); excerpts also from Berengar's *Letter to the Bishop of Mende* ending: *si quid in personam hominis dei dixi, ioco legatur non serio*. Ed. Thomson, pp. 111–30, 134–6; Cousin, ii. 771–88; *PL* clxxviii. 1857–73B.

Thomson prints the summaries[83] and follows De Poorter, *Catalogue*, in using a short title also found in the MS: *Invectiones Berengarii*.

Fo. 21ᵛ, two excerpts from *Letter* 1, **2–3** (inc. *Petrus abaelardus opido quodam oriundus* . . . expl. . . . *succensa est inuidia*) and **26** (inc. *Quod nunc apud nos* . . . expl. . . . *religionem referebant*). In the first excerpt the autobiographical format is converted to a biographical one (e.g. *Petrus abaelardus* in place of *Ego*; *terre sue* in place of *terre mee*; *est* in place of *sum*, etc.). These excerpts are followed on fos. 21ᵛ–22 by two other passages of unknown origin presented in the same manner as those from *Letter* 1 (same handwriting, new paragraphs, no

[82] When a precise date cannot be given to a MS, dates are shown in the following manner: s. xivⁱⁿ (early 14th c.), s. xiv² (second half of the 14th c.), s. xiv$^{\text{med/ex}}$ (mid/late 14th c.).

[83] A minor correction: for *tamen ob id* (Thomson, p. 128, n. 262) read *ob hoc*.

headings), one about *religio*, the other about *eloquentia*, with references to Augustine, Rabanus, and Quintilian.

In general, these excerpts reflect an interest in eloquence and an interest also in Bernard, abbot of Clairvaux, on the part of late 14th-c. Cistercian monks at the abbey of Ter Doest (at Lissewege, about 8 km north of Brugge) who had studied in Paris at the Collège Saint-Bernard, which had been founded by 1248 for students who were Cistercians. De Poorter in his *Catalogue* describes the contents of fos. 22–25^{v}, 64–84^{v}, 85–94, and 95–105 as school exercises (*exercices scolaires*) in which essays are written, extracts copied from school textbooks, and references made to authorities including the Bible, Porphyry, Aristotle, Augustine, Seneca, etc. The collection reflects university teaching and learning in Paris in the second half of the 14th c. Similar dissertations and hands are found in MSS 189, 222, and 530; see A. de Poorter and M. Alliaume, 'Catalogue des Manuscrits mathématiques et astronomiques de la Bibliothèque de Bruges', *Annales de la Société d'Émulation de Bruges* 65 (1915–22), pp. 13–50 at 14. The handwriting on fos. 17–25 is very similar to that in MS 530, fo. 9 onwards. The copyist was probably a monk of Ter Doest; a key figure in the making of these copies seems to be William Smidt, doctor of theology and abbot of Ter Doest, *c.*1357–86.

Physical features. Parchment. 105 fos. 210 × 154 mm. 1 col.; not ruled. Leather binding on oak boards now lacking a clasp and apparently original except for the spine which has been restored. A parchment slip affixed to the outside of the rear binding contains a summary of contents written apparently in a 14th-c. hand with red initials *C* and *I*: *Compendium uite beati iob co(mpos)itu(m) a petro blesensi Inuectiones berengarii in beati bernardi doctrinam de*(?) *eloquenciam cum aliis multis.* (The *Compendium in Job* by Peter of Blois is printed in *PL* ccvii. 795–826; J. Gildea, 'Extant Manuscripts of *Compendium in Job* by Peter of Blois', *Scriptorium*, xxx (1976), 285–7 lists about 130 copies). A similar summary of contents is found on fos. 1 (18th c.) and 2^{v} (17th c. or earlier). Similar slips written by 14th–15th-c. hands are found on MSS 222 and 530. Between fos. 17 and 25, *c.*43 lines per leaf. Fos. 17–25 form one quire of ten leaves (first missing); the strings and also the stub before fo. 17 are visible. A new hand appears on fo. 26. The three quires that form fos. 26–47 contain a single work for which De Poorter in the *Catalogue* made up a title: 'Instructions sur les devoirs d'un abbe' (inc. *Inter ceteras sollicitudines* *que abbati incumbent . . .*). Similar rubricated capitals, both large and small, and similar rubricated paragraph marks are found on fos. 17–47. The writing area on fos. 17–47 is enclosed within a rectangular border consisting of two lines. The small, regular, upright, well-spaced hand, with both looped and loopless ascenders and descenders, found on fos. 17–25, and a similar hand found on fos. 26–47, are not found elsewhere in this codex, but the first is not dissimilar to some of the other hands that appear.

The readings found in the two short excerpts from *Letter* 1 have not been noted in the present *apparatus criticus*. Thomson (pp. 106–9) lists four MSS which contain or once contained works of Berengar and some at least of the correspondence of Heloise and Abelard. These are **A**, **Y**, **V**, and the Brugge MS (respectively in Thomson these are **B**, **C**, the lost St-Victor MS, and **E**). The Brugge excerpts from *Letter* 1 show a slight but not conclusive lean to a group of MSS (on which see below, pp. cxvi–cxviii) which includes **Y**, whereas Thomson finds that the Berengarian passages in the Brugge MS bring it closer to a group which includes **A** (Thomson: **B**) than they do to another group which includes **Y** (Thomson: **C**). Examples from *Letter* 1 include the following: 1, **2**^{l}, *tantum* **Y**; 1, **26**^{w}, *helie uel helisei*, **CSR**.

Former possessors. Cistercian abbey of Ter Doest, diocese of Tournai (inside rear binding: *Liber cappelle Thosan*). Ter Doest was incorporated into the mother house of Dunes, diocese of Thérouanne, in 1624; the MS appears in the catalogue which A. Sanderus reproduced from the 1638 catalogue he received from Ch. de Visch (De Poorter, *Catalogue*, p. 14): *Bibliotheca Belgica Manuscripta*, i. 187: *Petrus Blesensis. Compendium uitae S. Iob, cum aliquot aliis paruis Tractatibus.*

Descriptions and further references. A. De Poorter, *Catalogue des manuscrits de la Bibliothèque publique de la ville de Bruges* (Catalogue général des manuscrits des bibliothèques de Belgique; Gembloux and Paris, 1934), ii. 446–9. Thomson, 'The satirical works of Berengar', p. 107. *Checklist* nos. 21 and 377. A. Pelzer, 'Livres de philosophie et de théologie de l'abbaye de Ter Doest à l'usage du maître cistercien Jean Sindewint de 1311 à 1319', *Annales de la Société d'Émulation de Bruges*, lxiii (1913), 5–36. For two examples of monks of Dunes who studied at the Collège Saint-Bernard see T. Sullivan, *Parisian Licentiates in Theology*, i. 160–1, 285–6.

D Douai, Bibliothèque municipale 797 (s. xv)

Contents. Vol. iv, fos. 321–328^{v}, *Letter* 1 and part of *Letter* 2, incomplete through loss of folios.

Physical features. MS 797 consists of four volumes containing the *Speculum historiale* of Vincent of Beauvais copied in the late 13th c. by Roger of St-Amand, monk of Marchiennes (fo. 320rb). Fos. 321–8 in vol. iv are an added quire of unknown provenance and different parchment. The strings that hold the leaves together go through the rear board of the binding as well as through quires containing the *Speculum*. Perhaps the MS is one of those rebound under abbot Jacques Coene in the first half of the 16th c. (Dehaisnes, *Catalogue*, p. v). 1 column. Writing area 300 × 177 mm. 51/57 long lines ruled in pencil. Gothic cursive bookhand of a formal kind, with well-rounded, open letters, providing also the long heading to *Letter* 1. Pale brown ink. Unfilled spaces for initial capitals which occur in *Letter* 1 at the same breaks as are found in **T** except for two breaks that occur in **58** *(Q)uorum* (not *Hoc*), and in **60** *(E)rat* (not *Cum*). No subheadings or illuminations. No annotations.

Spelling. *-ci-*, not *-ti-*, *u* rather than *v*, sometimes *y* rather than *i* (*laycarum* but *immo*), double consonants (*tollerabilius*) but some single (*facilime*). *Punctuation* is almost non-existent.

Former possessors. The earliest possessor of the added quire (fos. 321–8) is unknown; the earliest possessor of the *Speculum* is the Benedictine abbey of Marchiennes, east of Douai, diocese of Arras (*ex libris* in vol. i, fo. 240^{v}, vol. iii, fo. 204^{v}, perhaps from the first half or mid-16th c.). Quintinus Algambe, Marchiennes, 1569 (vol. iv, fo. 320va). Vol. ii of MS 797 is listed by A. Sanderus in *Bibliotheca Belgica Manuscripta* i. 60: *Speculum Historiale, a Libro 9. vsque ad 17.* (reproduced by Dehaisnes, *Catalogue*, Appendix III, p. 771, no. 123). Guilmot in his 1806 inventory gives four class marks: 38, 421, 424, 439 (*Inventaire des livres de la Bibliothèque publique de la ville de Douai* (Douai, 1820), p. 650). No. 756 (4 vols.) in H.-R. Duthilloeul, *Catalogue descriptif et raisonné des manuscrits de la Bibliothèque de Douai* (Douai, 1846), pp. 269–70.

Descriptions and further references. Monfrin, pp. 22–3. C. Dehaisnes, *Catalogue général des manuscrits des Bibliothèques publiques des Départements, ancienne série* 6: *Douai* (Paris 1878), pp. 493–4. Handwritten notice in IRHT by M. M. Lebreton. T. Falmagne, 'La Tradition manuscrite du sermonnaire attribué à Jean de Villers (mort en 1336)', *Scriptorium*, xlvi (1992), 28–49, at 45. *Checklist* no. 37.

Notre Dame, Indiana, University Memorial Library 30 (between 1463 and 1484)

Contents. Fos. 162^{v}–163^{v}, *Ex Epistolis Abaelardi parisiensis rapulata Et heloyssa sua* (title on fo. 162^{v}): excerpts from all the *Letters* except *Letter* 3 and the *Rule*, and from works of Berengar. Ed. Luscombe, 'Excerpts from the Letter Collection'. These excerpts have been chosen on account of their value as aphorisms and proverbs; sometimes a heading has been added in Latin or German to indicate a topic, e.g. 'Minerva', 'prosperity', 'St Joseph', 'beautiful-ugly'. The MS also includes excerpts from letters and other writings by Aeneas Sylvius Piccolomini, Cyprian, Pope Gregory I, St Bernard of Clairvaux, and Leonardo Bruni Aretino.

Physical features. Paper. 203 × 305 mm. 1 col. 46–52 lines. Attractive, small, well-spaced, regular Gothic cursive bookhand sloping to the right with straight descenders and with both looped and loopless ascenders. The readings found in these short fragments are generally good but variants have not been noted in the *apparatus criticus* to the present edition. Sometimes the text aligns more closely with **BRDY** (ed. Luscombe, excerpt 21 *l.* 1: *Amico* as in **RY**; *l.* 2: *vestram dilectissime* as in **BRDY**). But more often they part company (excerpt 10, *l.* 12: *difficulter* but *difficiliter* **BRDY**; excerpt 21 *l.* 5: *quadam*, *om.* **BRDY**; excerpt 24, *l.* 1: *animus meus* but *animus* only in **RY**; *l.* 3: *nusquam* but *numquam* **BRY**; excerpt 28 *l.* 2: *piscatus fuerit* as in **ACEF**, *piscaverit* in other mss; *l.* 4: *extraverit* but *extraverunt* **BR**; excerpt 30, *l.* 3: *interdictis* but *intermissis* **BRY**).

Spelling. *-ci-*, not *-ti-*; *-h-* sometimes included (*pythagorei*, *achademiam*).

Former possessors. Johannes Andree of Neisse by 1484, and, after his death in or before 1484, Joseph Czelfkendorf (?) in Cracow; Martin Leheure, 1484; the church of Reichenbach (perhaps the Reichenbach south of Leipzig and close to the modern Czech border), 1493.

Descriptions and further references. Luscombe, 'Excerpts from the letter collection' (edn., pp. 539–44). J. A. Corbett, *Catalogue of the Medieval and Renaissance Manuscripts of the University of Notre Dame* (Notre Dame, Ind., 1978), pp. 135–57. *Checklist* nos. 91, 377.

Y Oxford, Bodleian Library Add. C 271 (s. xiv^{ex}/possibly xv^{in})

Contents. Fos. 76ra–81va, Berengar, *Apologia*; fos. 81va–83ra, id., *Letter to the Bishop of Mende*; fo. 83$^{ra–vb}$, id., *Letter against the Carthusians* (incomplete at end as in **A**). Ed. Thomson, 'The satirical works of Berengar of Poitiers', pp. 111–38; Cousin, ii. 771–91; *PL* clxxviii. 1857–76.

Fos. 83vb–84va, Abelard, *Soliloquy*, ed. Burnett, 'Peter Abelard "Soliloquium"'; Cousin, ii. 727–9; *PL* clxxviii. 1876–80.

Fos. 84va–85v^{a}, Abelard, *Confession of faith 'Vniuersis'*, ed. Burnett, 'Peter Abelard, *Confessio fidei "Universis"*'; Cousin, ii. 719–23; *PL* clxxviii. 105–8.

Fos. 85vb–106va, *Letters* 1–4 and part of 5. The scribe breaks off in the middle of fo. 106va, leaving the rest of the folio blank.

The earlier fos. 2–75 include apologetical writings by Rufinus (*Apologia in sanctum Hieronimum*, *PL* xxi. 541–624) and Jerome (*Apologia adversus libros Rufini*, *Epistola Ieronimi ad Thesiphontem urbicum*, *Dialogus adversus Pelagianos*, respectively in *PL* xxiii. 397–492, *PL* xxii. 1147–61, and *PL* xxiii. 495–590). Together with fos. 76–106 they form a collection which consists from fo. 14 onwards almost entirely of quarrelsome works. Another 'Berengar MS'—Paris, BnF lat. 1896—is rather similar in this respect; see Burnett, 'Peter Abelard "Soliloquium"', p. 864; Thomson, 'The satirical works of Berengar of Poitiers', p. 106; *Bibliothèque nationale. Catalogue général des manuscrits latins* (Paris, 1940), ii. 228–9. It may be significant that this copy of the *Letters* of Abelard and Heloise stops near the middle of *Letter* 5 (and not by virtue of any damage in the MS): the subsequent *Letters* are not quarrelsome. On the other hand, the patristic works found before fo. 76 are also not always complete.

Physical features. Parchment. Binding, stamped blue calf with gold ornament, *c*.1800. 109 fos. (1 and 107 ff. are flyleaves). 310 × 225 mm; writing area 185 × 135 mm. 2 cols. of 40 lines. Ruled. Large and medium-sized initials coloured red and blue are fancily decorated with ornamental strokes and swinging lines running into and up and down the margin; small initials are coloured red and blue alternately. Fos. 2–106 were originally parts of a larger MS: the folio numbers 81–154, 157–87 that are found in a 14th/15th-c. hand in the upper right-hand corner of the recto sides (2 leaves have been cut out between 154 and 157) correspond to fos. 2–75, 76–106. From fo. 76^{r} onwards another but imperfect series of folio numbers is found, also in a 14th/15th-c. hand, in the lower right-hand corner of some recto folios: 1–6 (fos. 76r–81r), 1–2 (fos. 88r–89r), vj (fo. 101r). They enumerate folios within their quire, and correctly so, but they do not suggest that fos. 2–75 and 76–106 have separate provenances, for the present volume is written by a number of similar hands and the layout and decoration are similar throughout.

Quires. (1 flyleaf), 1–2 (8 leaves each), 3 (12), 4 (8), 5–6 (12; 2 fos. missing after quire 6), 7 (12 followed by the 2 fos. missing after quire 6), 8 (12), 9 (8), 10 (13 but missing 2). The strings are visible in the middle of all 10 quires. The missing fos. after quire 6 lay between fos. 61–2 (formerly 140–1); the added fos. after fo. 73 are fos. 74–5 (formerly 153–4) and belong to quire 6. The 2 fos. cut away in quire 10 without loss of text lay between fos. 95/96 and 106/107. Catchwords giving the first words of the following quire are found in the lower margin on fos. 87vb and 95vb (quires 8/9, 9/10).

One copyist whose Gothic bookhand is clear, but who was nevertheless imperceptive, has filled fos. 76–106. There are some differences, not of importance, between the ways in which the Berengar/Soliloquy material and the Abelard/Heloise material have been edited (for the *Soliloquy* see Burnett, 'Peter Abelard "Soliloquium"', pp. 863–4). On fos. 85–106 the scribe omits words from time to time and makes false starts and false stops; he leaves blank spaces when he cannot read his exemplar. He made corrections himself and it is perhaps he who both marked words for correction which were, nonetheless, left untouched and supplied some corrections in the margin in pencil so as to enable erasure and substitution to take place on the line. An intelligent 15th-c. corrector (Y^1), working according to sense rather than from another MS, confronted mistakes by writing a correction or supplying a missing word, usually above the line or in an unfilled space but sometimes in the margin. His nib is fine, his writing small but clear, and his appearances, which are quite frequent, start before the Berengar/Abelard/Heloise material commences, e.g. on fo. 64ra. A slap-dash hand of the 15th c. (Y^2) provides titles on fos. 85va, 97vb, 100ra, 102ra, 104va at the opening of each *Letter*. A few annotators show occasional interest but add nothing of significance.

Spelling. *-ci-* rather than *-ti-*; *h* is both dropped (*eloyssam*) and added (*hostio*); *p* is sometimes preferred to *b* (*optinuit*), *q* to *c* (*sequture*) and *y* to *i* (*layca*). Sometimes consonants are doubled (*intollerabiles*). An unusual feature is *-xc-* (*excecrabilem*, *excercuimus*). *Punctuation* is by stop, medial pause, and question mark.

Former possessors. Origin unknown; 'not Italian . . . almost certainly French and could date from the early 15th c. rather than the late 14th. It has good pen-flourished initials in characteristic French style' (letter from the late A. de la Mare to C. Burnett, dated 17 Nov. 1982). According to a note on fo. 1^{v}—a flyleaf which does not have the quality of the folios with text—the MS was bought for 1 silver mark by P. de Rota, canon and treasurer of Cambrai, on 1 February 1471 from Jo. Lambert, also canon of Cambrai, and given to Anthony de Rota: *Hunc librum emit P. de Rota canonicus et thezaurarius Cameracensis de executione domini Jo. Lamberti canonici Cameracensis pro marcha argenti quem dedit et donavit Anthonio de Rota juniori, sicuti alios omnes libros suos donavit atque donat in elemosinam. Datum prima Februarii A.D. M^{o} CCCC^{o} LXXI°. P. de Rota scripsit*. Bought by the Bodleian Library from the bookseller H. Grevel on 21 Feb. 1885 for £7 (flyleaf, fo. 1^{v}). According to Monfrin, p. 24n., the Rotas appear several times in a repertory published by the Archives départementales du Nord, *Répertoire numérique de la série H*, ii: *Ordres religieux divers*, ed. P. and A.-M. Piétresson de Saint-Aubin (Avesnes-sur-Helpe, 1943).

Descriptions and further references. F. Madan, *Summary Catalogue of Western MSS in the Bodleian Library* (Oxford, 1895–1953), v (1905), p. 644, no. 29565. Monfrin, pp. 23–5. Thomson, 'The satirical works of Berengar', p. 107. Burnett , 'Peter Abelard "Soliloquium"', pp. 863–4. *Checklist* nos. 99, 377. Burnett, 'Peter Abelard *Confessio fidei "Universis"*', pp. 122–3, finds, in respect of the Abelard/Heloise material, that **Y** and **A** share similar features (for **A** see p. lviii below) and that **J** and the lost MS Paris, Abbey of St-Victor GGG 17, also belong to this 'Berengar tradition'. For modification of this last point see pp. xcvii–xcviii below, Paris, Abbey of St-Victor GGG 17.

J Paris, BnF fr. 920 (Gontier Col, s. xiv^{ex}/before *c*.1418)

Contents. Pp. 1–214, *Letters* 1–7, translated into old French. Ed. Beggiato in *Le lettere di Abelardo ed Eloisa*, i. 7–235; ed. Hicks, pp. 2–147. *Letter* 1, ed. Charrier in *Jean de Meun*. Colophon on p. 214: *Ci fenist le livre de Maistre Pierre Abaielart et de ses espitres et les espitres que Heloys lui renvouoit, et la response que Maistre Pierre lui faisoit encontre*. Jean de Meun counted the *Epistres Pierres Abaelart et Heloys sa fame* among the works he translated from Latin into French near the end of the 13th c. but whether *his* translation is the one found in this MS has been questioned; see Hicks, pp. xxvi–xxxiii. The translation includes interpolations, glosses, and mistakes, some of them being taken from the Latin version that was used; see *Le lettere di Abelardo ed Eloisa*, ed. Beggiato, ii. 19–30; Hicks, pp. xxxvi–xlii.

Pp. 215–16 are blank and conclude a quire.

Pp. 217–18, Abelard, *Confession of faith to Heloise (La Confession d'Abaelart a Heloys jadis sa femme)*, old French translation. Ed. Beggiato in *Le lettere di Abelardo ed Eloisa*, i. 237–9; ed. Burnett, '*Confessio fidei ad Heloisam*', pp. 154–5; ed. Hicks, pp. 149–50.

Pp. 218–22, Abelard, *Confession of faith 'Vniuersis' (. . . La confession d'Abaelart general et especial contre aucuns articlez contre lui imposéz)*, old French translation. Ed. Beggiato in *Le lettere di Abelardo ed Eloisa*, i. 241–6; ed. Hicks, pp. 151–5.

Pp. 223–32, Peter the Venerable, abbot of Cluny, *First Letter to Heloise (. . . l'espitre de Pierre, abbé de Clugny, envoyee a Helois lors abesse du Paraclit, translatee de latin en françoys . . .)*, old French translation. Ed. Zink, 'Traduction française attribuée à Jean de Meun de la lettre de Pierre le Vénérable à Héloïse'; ed. Beggiato in *Le lettere di Abelardo ed Eloisa*, i. 247–59; ed. Hicks, pp. 156–61.

The last three items, dating apparently from the late 14th c., are not the work of the translator of *Letters* 1–7.

Pp. 233–41 and 243 are blank. Pen trials on pp. 232 and 242.

Physical features. Paper. 242 pp. following three flyleaves and followed by six more. 280 × 210 mm; writing area 198/203 × 134/135 mm. Nine quires of twelve leaves and one of 14 (+ 2 missing). 1 column. 22 to 31 lines. Watermarks: paschal lamb (on a flyleaf), two different royal crowns, three fleurs-de-lis, and an anchor; Bozzolo (p. 200) finds analogues, dated between 1393 and 1400, in Briquet no. 12 (paschal lamb) and in V. A. Mošin and S. M. Traljic, *Filigranes des XIIIe et XIVe ss.* (2 vols.; Zagreb 1957), i, nos. 146 (anchor), 708 (fleur-de-lis), and 3240 (crown). Pp. 1–232 are written in a very elegant cursive hand by a single scribe, Gontier Col (*c.*1350–*c.*1418), secretary to King Charles VI. Coloured filigree initials. Col perhaps trusted his exemplar too much, writing e.g. *paradiz* instead of *paracliz*; Bozzolo, 'L'Humaniste Gontier Col', p. 207; Hicks, p. xxxvi.

It is usually possible to find in the Latin versions of *Letters* 1–7 readings which the French translator had before his eyes, and some of these readings, taken from Hicks's edition of the translation, have been included in the apparatus of the present edition in order to show this and thus to extend understanding of the transmission of the *Letters*. But the translator also had a mind of his own and, as Monfrin showed (pp. 30–1), in many respects—in word order, for example, or in tenses—it is unwise to rely on the French version to make a choice between variants in the Latin.

Of one of the last three items in this MS, the *Confession of faith 'Vniuersis'*, Burnett, in 'Peter Abelard, *Confessio fidei "Universis"*', 122–3, finds that the text of **J** shares similar features with **AY**. **AY** and the lost MS **V** (Paris, Abbey of St-Victor, GGG 17; see pp. xcv–xcviii below), contain—or in the case of **A** (where some folios have been lost) may be presumed to have once contained—both the *Confession of faith 'Vniuersis'* and the *Confession of faith to Heloise* (which was copied by Berengar in his *Apologia*).

Former possessors. Gontier Col. Purchased in 1642 by Julien Brodeau (d. 1653), *jurisconsulte* (see the second flyleaf), and listed in his library in February 1657: *Libri manuscripti in-fol.: Epistres de Abailar et Heloise et autres, en francois*, Archives nationales, minutier central, étude 122, liasse 466, fo. 87^{v}. Later numbered 7273^{2} in the Bibliothèque nationale. On Brodeau's library see Delisle, *Cabinet*, i. pp. 300–3.

Descriptions and further references. Bozzolo, 'L'Humaniste Gontier Col'. Monfrin, pp. 29–31. Jean de Meun, *Traduction*, ed. Charrier, pp. 1–8. Beggiato in *Le lettere di Abelardo ed Eloisa*, ii. 7–30. Hicks, pp. xxxiv–xxxvi. On the relationship of the French translation of the *Confession of faith 'Vniuersis'* to the Latin MS tradition, see Burnett, 'Peter Abelard, *Confessio fidei "Universis"*', pp. 123, 130; likewise for the *Confession of faith to Heloise*, Burnett, '*Confessio fidei ad Heloisam*', p. 148. *Checklist*, no. 121. I have not seen E. Schultz, '"La Vie et les Epistres Pierres Abaelart et Heloys sa fame": A Translation by Jean de Meun and an Old French Translation of Three Related Texts: A Critical Edition of MS 920 (Bibliothèque Nationale)' (Ph.D. thesis, University of Washington, 1969). According to the summary of this unpublished dissertation provided in *Dissertation Abstracts International*, 31, no. 2 (Humanities and Social Sciences), August 1970, p. 767-A, Dr Schultz justifies the attribution of the translation of *Letters* 1–7, but not of the three additional items, to Jean de Meun.

H Paris, BnF n. acq. fr. 20001 (Paris, 1 December 1361)

Contents. Fos. 11–12va, *Letter* 7 (*inc.* at **43**: *celibi se uite dicarent . . .*), *Letter* 8 (rubr. *Epistola magistri petri abaielardi concludendo pariter de supradictis*). Colophon: *Expliciunt epistole petri abaielardi et heloyse primitus eius amice postmodum uxoris. Scripte parisius per me mathiam rivalli in domo episcopi ambianensis. Anno domini millesimo. ccc^{o}. lx^{o}. primo mense decembri*. The rest of fo. 12^{v} is blank.

Physical features. Parchment. Two columns. 52 lines. Ruled. A high-grade Gothic bookhand, regular, clear, evenly spaced and square. Rubrics with folio numbers in the upper margins as follows: fo. 11r: *abaiel. .ii^{c}.xxviii*; fo. 11^{v}: *Epistola*; fo. 12^{r}: *abaiel. .ii^{c}.xxix*. One decorated initial with filigrees.

Fos. 5–15 once formed part of Dijon, Bibliothèque municipale 525 (298) which presented a collection of works in Old French including the *Roman de la Rose* and a translation of Boethius' *Consolation*. These folios were some of those stolen from the Dijon MS in the mid-17th c.; they entered the Bibliothèque nationale in Paris at the beginning of the 20th c. The stolen folios are not entirely continuous and, apart from the extract from the *Letters*, contain works written in the vernacular. The Dijon MS has a table of contents which indicates that the MS once contained the *Letters* 1–8 but not the *Rule* (below, p. lxxxii). The table gives detailed headings of the *Letters* with folio numbers that commence at fo. ij^{c}iiij . These headings were published by H. Omont and are reproduced in the apparatus to the present edition. Only the end of *Letter* 7 and *Letter* 8 are found on two of the folios which came to Paris, their original numbers being ij^{c}xxviij and ij^{c}xxix. Authorities cited in the text attract underlining in red. Copied by Mathias Rivalli (or Rival or Rivau) at the Parisian residence of Jean de Cherchemont, royal chancellor (1321–2, 1323–8), bishop of Amiens (1325–73), formerly bishop of Troyes (1324–5).

Spelling. Some examples are *-cio*, *-cia*, not *-tio*, *-tia*; *suspictione*; *transfferendis*; *longinco*; *lingas*. *Punctuation* normally consists of a stop.

Former possessors. Jean de Cherchemont; see also the Dijon MS below, pp. lxxxii–lxxxiii.

Descriptions and further references. H. Omont, 'Bibliothèque nationale. Nouvelles acquisitions du département des manuscrits de la Bibliothèque nationale pendant les années 1900–1902', *Bibliothèque de l'École des Chartes*, lxiv (1903) at pp. 243–4; id., 'Notice sur quelques feuillets retrouvés d'un manuscrit français de la Bibliothèque de Dijon', *Romania*, xxxiv (1905), 364–74, with details on pp. 373–4 of headings added later in a table of contents written in Old French. E. Langlois, *Les Manuscrits du Roman de la Rose: Description et classement* (Travaux et Mémoires de l'Université de Lille, NS, Droit-Lettres, vii; Paris, 1910), pp. 122–5. Monfrin, p. 50. Huot, *Romance of the Rose*, pp. 75–84. The colophon is listed in *Colophons de manuscrits occidentaux des origines au XVIe siècle* by the Bénédictins de Bouveret, vol. iv (Spicilegium Friburgensis Subsidia, v; Fribourg, 1976), p. 185. *Checklist*, no. 154.

B Paris, BnF lat. 2544 (s. xiii^{ex}/xiv)

Contents. Fos. 3–41, *Letters* 1–8 followed on fo. 41rb by rubr. obits of Abelard and Heloise written by the copyist of the *Letters*: *Anno domini MCLXIIII Heloysa obiit Paracliti Abbatissa. Anno domini MCXLII obiit Petrus Abahelardi perypateticus.* The rest of the column is blank.

Physical features. Parchment, much creased. 40 fos. + 2 parchment leaves added at the front +1 at the back, continuously numbered now 1–43. Fo. 1^{r+v} gives Easter tables for the years 1200–1349 with historical notes from 1252 to 1276, written by a hand not found elsewhere in the codex and published in *Recueil des historiens des Gaules et de la France*, xxiii (Paris, 1894), p. 142. Fo. 2 is blank; fos. 41^{v}–43^{v} contain sparse notes of no relevance to the other contents. The medieval numbering *i–xxxix* is found on fos. 3–41, which are formed by five quires of eight leaves (1 missing at the end of quire 8). Catchwords are found at the end of quires 1–4. 245 × 165 mm.; writing area 190 × 65 mm. 2 columns. Usually 42 lines. Not ruled. Bound in red morocco with the emblem of King Louis-Philippe (1830–48); the tight binding hides some text in the second column of the verso side. Text not very tidily copied by one Gothic bookhand, sloping backwards, abbreviating heavily. The letters are quite round. Letters *b* and *l* have clubbed heads or a flat line *in lieu*. Larger initials are decorated with marginal filigrees and are coloured red and blue alternately; they occur at the beginning of each *Letter* and in the earlier parts of *Letter* 1. Small initials are overpainted red. Rubrics are found within *Letter* 1 and at the beginning of *Letters* 2 and 3. The title before *Letter* 1 was added later and spaces are left unfilled for rubrics within *Letter* 1, before **35** and **48** and in **60** before *Erat*. Some marginal notes; many *nota* signs, typically indicating quotations in the text and found particularly in *Letters* 6–7.

The scribe had difficulty reading his exemplar and its abbreviations. Some similar words separated by *uel* (e.g. *cruciare vel curare* in *Letter* 2, **5**) may reflect uncertain readings in the exemplar or its parent; and there are unfilled spaces, some of which the scribe later filled. In *Letter* 1, **12**, a space is filled conjecturally by a later hand writing *machinabantur* where *accendebatur* should appear. Most corrections are made by the scribe and by expunction with the correction sometimes added in the margin. There appears to be another corrector writing with a thin nib and a third corrector who writes in the margin, but neither of these appears often. **B**'s exemplar is similar to that used by **R**: see *Letter* 1, **31–2**, where **BR** both leave a space unfilled. In *Letter* 7, **35–9** there is a long lacuna in both **B** and **R**.

Spelling. *-ci-* is preferred to *-ti-*; double consonants (*coggamur*, *appollo*) sometimes, but sometimes not (*acusaret*, *asiste*); added *d* and *g* before consonants (*adgerem*, *cognabar*); *-h-* appears and disappears (*talamis*, *adholescentiam*); *t* often in place of *d* (*aput*) and *y* in place of *i* (*ymaginis*). The insular *enim* (*·n·*) is sometimes used, as it is in **R**. *Punctuation* is by full and medial stops.

Former possessors. Master Jacobus de Gantis (mid-14th c.; fo. 42^{v}). One magister Jacobus de Gandavo intervened in an affair concerning the Faculty of Medicine in Paris in 1331; see *Chartularium Universitatis Parisiensis*, ed. H. Denifle and A. Chatelain (Paris, 1891), ii. 368, note to no. 928. Probably Jacques Le Batelier of Aviron near Évreux, a late-16th-c. *jurisconsulte* in Évreux. Paul Petau (1568–1614; fo. 3^{r}) obtained it from Le Batelier of Aviron. Not mentioned in K. A. De Meyier, *Paul en Alexandre Petau en de Geschiednis van hun Handschriften* (Leiden, 1947). Colbert 4284 (fo. 1^{r}). Bibliothèque du roi 4353 (fo. 1r). B. de Montfaucon, in *Bibliotheca Bibliothecarum Manuscriptorum nova* (Paris, 1739), ii. 1365D, recorded at Évreux cathedral a MS which contained *Vita Petri Abaelardi Britonis*. In the upper margin of fo. 3, where *Letter* 1 begins, a later hand has written: *Vita magistri Petri Abahelardi* (the rest is lost through trimming).

Descriptions and further references. Muckle, 'Abelard's letter of consolation', pp. 165–6. Monfrin, pp. 20–1, 42. *Checklist*, no. 131.

E Paris, BnF lat. 2545 (s. xv^{ex}/xvi)[84]

Contents. Fos. 1–53^{v}, *Letters* 1–8 with a shortened version of the *Rule*. There are no titles, although another hand has added in the margin (before trimming) at the beginning of *Letter* 2: *(prim)a heloysse ad. p. A.*

The colophon on fo. 53^{v} notes that the venerable Peter Abelard was a contemporary of the blessed Bernard and gives the dates when Bernard became a monk and died. The opening of this colophon is also given in **C** (fo. 207^{v}; see p. lxiv below).

Fos. 54–55^{v}, Fulk of Deuil, *Letter to Abelard* (*Epistola fulconis prioris de dyagillo* (another hand adds: *Ad petrum Abaillardi*). (*P*)*etro Deo gracias cucullato frater fulco uite consolacionem presentis et future* . . .). Ed. Cousin i. 703–7; *PL* clxxviii. 371–6. A passage in which the papal court is criticized (*O miserum ualde . . . dementie est*), omitted by Duchesne–d'Amboise and therefore missing in *PL* clxxviii. 375AB, is printed by Cousin, i. 706, *l.* 5 up–p. 707, *l.* 14 and, from this MS and Paris, BnF lat. 13057, by Van den Eynde, 'Détails biographiques', p. 219.

Fo. 55^{v}, Bernard, abbot of Clairvaux, *Letter* 188 (*Epistola b(ernardi) ad cardinales contra petrum abaelardi*). The text breaks off at . . . *credere dedignatur*. In *S. Bernardi Opera*, ed. Leclercq and Rochais, viii. 10–11, *l.* 10; *PL* clxxxii. 352A–353B *l.* 5.

Fos. 55^{v}–56, Bernard, abbot of Clairvaux, *Letter* 191 (*Item ipse b(ernardus) pape innocentio ex persona Remensis archiepiscopi*). The text breaks off at . . . *in eo iniquitas*. In *S. Bernardi Opera*, ed. Leclercq and Rochais, viii. 41–2, *l.* 2; *PL* clxxxii. 357B–C7.

Fo. 56, Bernard of Clairvaux, short extract from *Letter* 191 (*Episcopi capitula librorum eius a sanctis patribus condempnata ne morbus serperet medicinali necessitate abiudicauerunt*) followed by *Capitula haeresum XIX* (this title is not in the MS), in *S. Bernardi Opera*, ed. Leclercq and Rochais, viii. 42, *ll.* 10–13, p. 39, *l.* 2–p. 40; *PL* clxxxii. 358A *ll.* 1–6; Mews, 'The lists of heresies', pp. 108–10.

Fo. 56^{r+v}, Pope Innocent II, *Letter* 447 (*Innocencius papa secundus contra petrum abaelardum*). Extracts from the Bull *Testante apostolo* (*Marcianus . . . esse censemus*). *PL* clxxix. 516B, *l.* 10–C, *l.* 8, 517A, *l.* 5–B, *l.* 1; JL, no. 8148. Also among Bernard's *Letters* at 194, in

[84] Very late 15th or 16th c. according to Monfrin, p. 27. But for a comparable example, dated 1418, of steeply sloping *cursiva currens* see pl. 97 (Tours, Bibliothèque municipale 157) in A. Derolez, *The Palaeography of Gothic Manuscript Books from the Twelfth to the Early Sixteenth Century* (Cambridge, 2003).

S. Bernardi Opera, ed. Leclercq and Rochais, viii. 47, *ll.* 10–19, 48, *ll.* 5–12; *PL* clxxxii. 360C, *l.* 8–D, *l.* 7, 361A, *l.* 12–B, *l.* 8.

Fos. 56^{v}–57^{v}, Abelard, *Confession of faith 'Vniuersis'* (*Epistola petri abaelardi contra calu(m)pnias objectorum capitulorum responsio*), ed. Burnett, 'Peter Abelard, *Confessio fidei "Universis"*', pp. 132–8; Cousin, ii. 719–23; *PL* clxxviii. 105–8.

The rest of fo. 57^{v} is blank.

All these materials are also found in the same arrangement but with some additions in **C** (below, pp. lxiv–lxv) and they resemble those in the lost MS Paris, Abbey of St-Victor GGG 17 (below, pp. xcv–xcvii).[85]

Physical features. Paper. 58 fos. 280 × 200 mm (after trimming); writing area 200 × 135 mm. One column. 41–6 lines. Bound in red morocco with the emblem of King Louis-Philippe (1830–48). Five quires of 10 leaves, one of 8 (enumerated in the lower margin of the recto sides as follows: *a.i, a.ii, a.iii* . . .; another hand has added folio numbers from 1 to 57 in the top right-hand corner of the recto sides). A small, clear, everyday, speedy, cursive script with typical 'secretary' features such as loops, ascenders, and descenders, but also with lots of mistakes and crossings out. Dark brown ink. Heavy, large letters are used to indicate the opening of each *Letter* and sometimes sections within them; some initial letters have not been entered into the spaces left for them. No rubrics. Some marginal notes in a different hand (not the notes found in Duchesne–d'Amboise) draw attention to contents; some passages are underlined. Watermarks: fo. 3, an animal, perhaps a dog (cf. Briquet, no. 3607, etc.); last fo., three fleurs-de-lis (cf. Briquet, no. 1813, etc.; found in early 16th-c. examples in northern France and the Low Countries).

Muckle, 'Abelard's letter of consolation', p. 167, described this copy of *Letter* 1 as 'fairly good', which is a rather generous view. The scribe, who makes many slips, expunges mistakes and enters corrections as he proceeds. He also leaves blank spaces for words to be added later, so his exemplar was poor. A thin nib (**E***corr.*), in the hand

[85] Burnett, in 'Peter Abelard, *Confessio fidei "Universis"*', pp. 123–4, 130, noted that in CE, and also in MSS bearing the *sigla* WOL, the *Confessio fidei 'Vniuersis'* bears the title *Epistola petri abaelardi contra calumpnias obiectorum capitulorum responsio*. A similar title is found in a now lost MS included in the sale in 1799 of MSS that formerly belonged to Claude-Robert Jardel (1712–88). See Bondéelle-Souchier, 'Claude-Robert Jardel', pp. 618–19 and n. 22, 624 and esp. p. 636, no. 49: '*Petri Abaelardi contra calumnias objectas responsio, epistolae 2 Alexandri papae ad archiepiscopum et canonicos Remenses, Carmina in laudem Susannae*. Ms in-4° du XIIIe s. Aucune de ces pièces n'a été imprimée.' (In fact the *Confessio* had been printed twice in **Amb**).

perhaps of the same scribe, fills some of these spaces, supplies corrections above the line, and sometimes clarifies the abbreviations used. The text is also marked with vertical lines and underlines where corrections need to be made which have not always been entered. An example of the difficulties encountered and not always overcome is found in *Letter* 6, **22**, where the text should read *uictitent*: *uictaretur* **C** *euitassent* **E***corr*.

E is copied from an exemplar similar to, if not the same as, that used by **C**. For example, in *Letter* 1, **52** **CE** both have *mo* followed by a blank space instead of *mobilitate*, and in *Letter* 1, **63** **CE** both present alternative readings (*autem siue namque*). Monfrin, p. 28, like Muckle, 'Abelard's letter of consolation', p. 167, finds **E** to be the more careful of the two, but he thought that the revisions and corrections found in **E** include conjectures, as the example just given of *euitassent* seems to show. In *Letter* 7 and the *Rule*, **CE** share omissions in common. Burnett, 'Peter Abelard, *Confessio fidei "Universis"*', pp. 123–4, noted that **CEF** form a group that provides a poor text of the *Confession of faith 'Vniuersis'*. On the other hand some readings (listed below, p. cxx) provided by **CEF** are good.

Spelling is inconsistent. The copyist sometimes joins words (*ingentibus*), sometimes divides them (*in firmo*), often writes double consonants (*sponssi*, *Heloyssa*) but sometimes not (*asistatis*, *falor*) and sometimes writes *b* where a double consonant might be expected (*obmittam, subgestione)*; sometimes adds *h* (*lachrimas*, *helizabet*), sometimes not (*ebreorum*, *elizabet*). *d* is sometimes preferred to *t* (*capud*, *uelud*), *q* to *c* (*loqutus*, but *longinco*) and *-ti-* to *-ci-* (*consolationem*). *y* and *i* are used interchangeably. Both Arabic and Roman numerals are found. *Punctuation* with a stop occurs rarely.

Former possessors. **E** is more likely than **C** to be the MS obtained in Brittany by F. d'Amboise (*Nanneticus*, below p. xci and Monfrin, pp. 39–40; also below, p. lxvii). Étienne Baluze (1630–1718), cod. 346 (fo. 1); entered the Bibliothèque du roi in 1719, cod. 5492[3] (fo. 1). On Baluze see Delisle, *Cabinet*, i. 364–7.

Descriptions and further references. Muckle, 'Abelard's letter of consolation', p. 167. Monfrin, pp. 27–8, 39–40. Burnett, 'Peter Abelard, *Confessio fidei "Universis"*', pp. 123–4. *Bibliotheca Baluziana seu Catalogus librorum bibliothecae Steph. Baluzii* . . . (3 parts in 2 vols. published by Gabriel Martin; Paris, 1719), iii. 57. *Catalogus codicum manuscriptorum Bibliothecae Regiae*, Pars III, iii (Paris, 1744), p. 295

(MS 2545). L. Delisle, 'État sommaire', *Bibliothèque de l'École des Chartes*, xxxv (1874), 267–76. P.-M. Bondois, 'Concordance des numéros des MSS du fonds Baluze', *Bibliothèque de l'École des Chartes*, ciii (1942), 339–47, esp. p. 343. *Checklist* nos. 132, 382, 386.

Paris, BnF lat. 2816 (perhaps shortly after 1616)

Contents. A notebook in 8° containing excerpts from various writers. On pp. 218–27 the title *Petrus Abaelardus* introduces extracts with short glosses from the writings of Abelard and Heloise:

Pp. 218–20, *Epistolae Petri Abaelardi et Heloissae*: excerpts from *Letters* 1–8 and the *Rule*.

P. 220, *Epistolae aliae*, including the *Letter* of Fulk of Deuil and Abelard, *Letters* 12, 13, 10, and 9.

P. 221, excerpts from the three extant works of Berengar.

P. 221, excerpts from an *Exposition of the Lord's Prayer* (*Expositio in orationem dominicam*, sometimes attributed to Abelard; *PL* clxxviii. 611–18 and cf. *Checklist* no. 348), and from Abelard, *Exposition of the Apostles' Creed* (*Expositio in symbolum apostolorum*, *PL* clxxviii. 617–30).

P. 221, excerpts from the *Problems of Heloise* (*Problemata Heloissae*), from *Against Heresies* (*Adversus Haereses*; *PL* clxxviii. 1823–46) with a brief mention of Abelard, and from Abelard's *Exposition of the Epistle to the Romans* (*Expositio in epistolam Pauli ad Romanos*).

Pp. 221–4, excerpts from Abelard, *Sermons*.

Pp. 225–7, excerpts from Abelard, *Theologia 'Scholarium'* under the title *Introductio ad Theologiam.*

Marginal notes sometimes indicate a topic, e.g. *amor sensu(alis)*, *monachi*, *monachae*, *foemina*, *amor sanctus*, *matrimonium*, etc. (cf. Notre Dame MS 30, above p. xliii).

All the material on pp. 218–27 seems to consist of transcripts from Duchesne–d'Amboise. They follow the sequence in which this is presented in the edition of Duchesne–d'Amboise (of which the contents are summarized by Monfrin, pp. 44–6). The excerpts from *Letters* 1–8 are also numbered as in Duchesne–d'Amboise. The copyist rarely departs from the text found there and gives no indication of following any of the known MSS.

Physical features. Paper. One column. Clear and neat cursive script with well-spaced, rounded letters.

Former possessors. Not known.

Descriptions and further references. Bibliothèque nationale, Catalogue général des manuscrits latins (Paris, 1952), iii. 107 (here the MS is dated to the late 16th c.—before the publication in 1616 of the edition of Duchesne–d'Amboise). Van den Eynde, 'Le Recueil des sermons de Pierre Abélard', p. 18. *Checklist* no. 133.

A **Paris, BnF lat. 2923** (s. xiii$^{med/ex}$)

Contents. Fos. 1–42^{v}, *Letters* 1–8. Two folios are missing between fos. 37 and 38, leaving a lacuna in *Letter* 7, **23–33** from *domina mea* to *Ipse tuum cognosce Dominum.*

Fos. 43–5, Berengar, *Apologia* (incomplete through loss of folios between fos. 44 and 45 and lacking Abelard's *Confession of faith to Heloise*), ed. Thomson, 'The satirical works of Berengar', pp. 111–30; *PL* clxxviii. 1857–70.

Fos. 45–7, Berengar, *Letter to the Bishop of Mende*, ed. Thomson, 'The satirical works of Berengar', pp. 134–8; *PL* clxxviii. 1871–4.

Fo. 47^{r+v}, Berengar, *Letter against the Carthusians* (incomplete at the end as in **Y**), ed. Thomson, 'The satirical works of Berengar', pp. 131–3; ed. Leclercq, 'Autour de la correspondance de S. Bernard', pp. 192–8; *PL* clxxviii. 1875–80.

Fos. 47^{v}–48^{v}, Abelard, *Soliloquy*, ed. Burnett, 'Peter Abelard, "Soliloquium"', pp. 885–91; Cousin, ii. 727–9; *PL* clxxviii. 1876–80.

Fos. 48^{v}–49^{v}, Abelard, *Confession of faith 'Vniuersis'*, ed. Burnett, 'Peter Abelard, *Confessio fidei "Universis"*', pp. 132–8; Cousin, ii. 719–23; *PL* clxxviii. 105–8.

Fo. 50^{r} Abelard, *Letter* 14 *to the bishop and clergy of Paris*, ed. Smits, pp. 279–80; Cousin, ii. 150–1; *PL* clxxviii. 355–8; trans. Ziolkowski, pp. 194–6.

The codex includes thereafter Cassiodorus, *Letters*; two *Artes dictandi*; Stephen of Tournai, *Letters*;[86] a formulary of letters; notes by Petrarch of significant dates. It thus offers a varied selection of finely written letters.

Physical features. Parchment. 220 × 150 mm. 2 columns of 42/43 lines; writing area 170/150 × 50/45 mm in each column. Tightly rebound in 1975; the script in the inner folds is difficult to see and the strings are not visible after fo. 38. Quires 1–5 (8 leaves each but quire 5 lacks two leaves between fos. 37 and 38) are numbered *i–v* on the last folio of the quire; quires 1–2 have catchwords in the lower margin

86 Étienne de Tournai, *Lettres. Nouvelle édition*, ed. J. Desilve (Valenciennes, 1893).

of the last folio. Hereafter (from fo. 38) the quiring is not currently detectable; the *Catalogue général* reports that the next quire (quire 6) has eight leaves. On the other hand, Monfrin, p. 18, seemingly found that quire 5 has twelve leaves (two missing) and quires 6 and 7 have four leaves each. Brown ink. A Gothic bookhand, upright with well-rounded, well-spaced but stubby letters. A 'rotunda' script which may suggest a southern European scribe.

Apart from the scribe, at least two other hands have worked on the texts relating to Abelard, including Petrarch who annotated them (see Nolhac, *Pétrarque* below). Where Abelard in *Letter* 1, **72**, writes of his fall from his horse Petrarch writes *et me nocte*—perhaps a reference to his own fall from a horse on leaving Parma on 23 February 1345. Signs (such as pointing fingers and groups of dots) and keywords are added in the margins by a number of hands. The text scribe corrected his work by rectifying omissions or by expunction followed by an immediate correction on the same line or above the mistake or, sometimes encircled, in the margin. At least one other hand carefully revised the copy in a similar manner, using a thin nib, cancelling mistakes and squeezing corrections in between the lines. Some emendations are found without cancellation of the text as copied, e.g. *colloquia* above *loquela*, *uictitare* above *mocitare*, *in al(io) sceviores* above *saniores* (*Letter* 1, **39**, **52**, **60**), *rem vel estimem* following *estima* (*Letter* 2, **3**). The third of these examples, which relates to the unruly monks of the abbey of St-Gildas, clearly suggests that this corrector had access to a second exemplar. Petrarch apparently made one correction: *ei* to *egi*, *Letter* 1, **17**.

Apart from the second *ars dictaminis* (a later addition), the codex was produced as a single entity. The illuminated initials on a gold background, some historiated, highlight this unity at the beginning of each section. On fo. 1, two cowled figures clothed in black tunics face one another, each holding a bound volume closed with a thong; the face of one of these is scratched out—perhaps that of Heloise or perhaps the *amicus* to whom *Letter* 1 was addressed. This illumination has been reproduced on several occasions e.g. *Abélard et Héloïse, Correspondance*, ed. Gréard, p. 3; C. Charrier, *Héloïse*, planche 22; Luscombe, *The School of Peter Abelard*, frontispiece.

On fo. 43, at the opening of the *Apologia* of Berengar, a hooded figure is painted, wearing a pink tunic and cowl. On fo. 51, at the opening of the *Letters* of Cassiodorus, a crowned Theodoric with a short beard appears seated with crossed legs, wearing a blue cloak over a red tunic and black hose and shoes. On fo. 94 a seated figure (presumably Stephen, bishop of Tournai), clothed in a black cloak and hood over a white tunic, displays a book with outstretched hands. All these figures are painted on a gold background and seated. The illuminations, the rubricated titles, the colouring in red and blue of the small initials, and the decorated capital letters with marginal filigrees, the paragraph markers also, display the unified character and purpose of this codex. According to Jeudy, 'La Correspondance d'Abélard et Héloïse', p. 880, the paintings are Parisian.

Spelling is inconsistent but the scribe habitually prefers *-ci-/-cci-* to *-ti-/-cti-* (*eciam*, *accione*), *f* to *ph* (*profanus*), *i* to *j* (*peiores*, *iam*), *is* to *hiis*, *-n-* to *-m-* (*inmoderata*, *conpulsi*, *nunquam*), *-t* to *-d* (*set*, *aput*), and *y* to *i* (*tyrannus*, *ymaginem*). He adds *c* in *nichil* and *michi*. He does not write *h* between consonants (*sepulcrum*, *lacrimas*) but oscillates with *h* elsewhere (*habundaret*, *rithmo*, *monasticham*; *ebriantur*, *adibenda*; *thimotheum* but also *timotheo*, and *hieremie* but also *ieronimus*). Doubled consonants (*subbortum*, *euuangelium*, *horrissoni*) and their absence (*facilime*, *apeti*) are both found. Other inconsistencies include *contempnere/contemtores*, *admirare/ammonet*, *nunquam/nuncquam*. Sometimes *in* is separated from the rest of a word (*in iurie*, *in uitaui*). *Punctuation* is similar to **T** and includes stops, medial pauses, and question marks.

Muckle, 'Abelard's letter of consolation', p. 165, judged that **A**'s copy of *Letter* 1 'gives a fairly good text but not so good as *Ms* Troyes 802, as the variants listed in this edition show. There are several corruptions and bad readings.' Burnett, 'Peter Abelard, *Confessio fidei "Universis"*', pp. 122–3, finds that the copies of the *Confession of faith 'Vniuersis'* in **AY** are similar; they share divergent readings and a common title; they copy in the margins the *capitula* repudiated in the *Confession*, and place the *Confession* after the *Soliloquy*, which itself follows the three letters of Berengar. **B**, Paris, BnF lat. 1896 (which lacks the *Letters* of Abelard and Heloise but has the three letters of Berengar, the *Soliloquy*, and the *Confession*; see Burnett, 'Peter Abelard "Soliloquium"', p. 864) and the 'lost' part of MS, Paris, Abbey of St-Victor GGG 17, also belong to this 'Berengar tradition'. Within this tradition, according to Burnett, **A** gives the best readings, but the group is not reliable and may stem from one poor witness of the late 13th c. For a modification of the point made about the St-Victor MS see below, pp. xcvii–xcviii, Paris, Abbey of St-Victor GGG 17.

Former possessors. Some references made in the first *ars dictaminis* led Leclercq, 'L'Amitié dans les lettres au Moyen Âge', to suggest that the copy was made in southern France. Jeudy, on the other hand ('La Correspondance d'Abélard et Héloïse', p. 880), found the decoration to be Parisian. Petrarch (after *c*.1337). Dronke, *Abelard and Heloise in Medieval Testimonies*, pp. 58–60 (repr. in *Intellectuals and Poets*, pp. 291–4), gives reasons for thinking that the poet Giovanni Boccaccio read Petrarch's MS copy and drew upon its contents for the portrayal of his heroine in *Fiammetta*. Visconti-Sforza, dukes of Milan, at Pavia, inventory of 1426, no. 70; see E. Pellegrin, *La Bibliothèque des Visconti et des Sforza, ducs de Milan au XVe siècle* (Paris, 1955), p. 87. The library of the dukes of Milan was acquired by King Louis XII in 1499/1500. The MS appears in the inventory made in 1518 of the library of the counts of Blois, table 7 XIII, and later passed into the royal library (Rigault 1561, Dupuy 1702, Regius 4353); Delisle, *Cabinet*, i: *Livres des ducs de Milan et de Pétrarque*, pp. 125–40, at p. 139.

Descriptions and further references. *Bibliothèque nationale. Catalogue général des manuscrits latins*, iii (Paris, 1952), pp. 282–4. P. de Nolhac, *Pétrarque et l'humanisme* (2nd edn., 2 vols.; Paris, 1907, repr. 1965), i. 103 (the Pavia inventory of 1426); ii. 217–25. Nolhac writes (ii. 219): 'Abélard a trouvé en lui (*sc*. Pétrarque) un lecteur attentif et même passioné'; Petrarch had the habit of addressing Peter and Heloise as if he were talking to them, e.g. *Letter* 2, **9**: *ualde perdulciter ac blande. per totum. agis heloysa*; *Letter* 5, **12**: *Non ineleganter ais Petre*. In vol. ii on pp. 220–4 Nolhac discusses and printes many of Petrarch's annotations; a few supplements are given by Burnett, 'Peter Abelard "Soliloquium"', p. 861. Leclercq, 'L'Amitié dans les lettres au Moyen Âge', pp. 391–9. Muckle, 'Abelard's letter of consolation', pp. 164–5. Monfrin, pp. 18–19, 23–4. Thomson, 'The satirical works of Berengar of Poitiers', pp. 106–7. Smits, pp. 101–3. Burnett, 'Peter Abelard "Soliloquium"', pp. 859–62. *Checklist* nos. 135, 377.

Editions made from this MS include Cousin (see Cousin, i. 2); *Abélard et Héloïse, Correspondance*, trans. Gréard; Muckle, 'Abelard's letter of consolation', 'The personal letters', 'The letter of Heloise on the religious life'; McLaughlin, 'Abelard's Rule'; Monfrin.

F **Paris, BnF lat. 13057** (after 1592)

Contents. Pp. 1–10, Fulk of Deuil, *Letter to Abelard* (*Epistola Fulconis prioris de Diogillo ad Petrum Abaelardum* (another hand adds: *Dei gratia cucullatum*). Cousin, i. 703–7; *PL* clxxviii. 371–6. Van den Eynde, 'Détails biographiques sur Pierre Abélard', p. 219 (see above, p. lii, *Paris, BnF lat. 2545*).

Pp. 10–119, *Letters* 2–7. Most of p. 119 is blank.

P. 120, blank apart from the word *Epistolae*.

Pp. 121–80, *Letter* 1. P. 180 blank after the end of *Letter* 1 apart from the word *Vniuersis*.

Pp. 181–6, Abelard, *Confession of faith 'Vniuersis'*. In another hand: *Epistola tertia*, and in a further hand: *edita est 20*. Ed. Burnett, 'Peter Abelard, *Confessio fidei "Universis"*', pp. 132–8; Cousin, ii. 719–23; *PL* clxxviii. 105–8.

Pp. 187 and 188 blank apart from the mention, in another hand, of the next work, *In sequentem Apologiam Argutus Petrus Abailardus a S. Bernardo, quod in oratione Dominica . . .*

Pp. 189–97, Abelard, *Letter* 10 to Bernard of Clairvaux on the Lord's Prayer: *Apologia quedam sui*. Another hand adds *edita est V in 2º ordine*. Ed. Smits, pp. 239–47; Cousin, ii. 618–24; *PL* clxxviii. 335–40; trans. Ziolkowski, pp. 85–98. Smits, pp. 70–6, at 71, suggested that the source of this sole extant MS copy of *Letter* 10 was a (now lost) Clairvaux MS. The catalogue of Clairvaux MSS made by Mathurin de Cangey *c.*1521 includes *Apologia Abaelardi ad Bernardum de Oratione dominica*. See A. Vernet, *La Bibliothèque de l'abbaye de Clairvaux du XIIe au XVIIIe siècle*, i: *Catalogues et répertoires* (Paris, 1979), p. 544, no. 1425. Smits also suggested, with evidence, that Duchesne may have obtained the Clairvaux copy with the help of Nicolas Camuzat, canon of Troyes (see below, p. xciii, *Nicolas Camuzat*).

Pp. 198–207 blank.

Physical features. Paper. 275 × 190 mm; writing area 230 × 130 mm. One column. 26–32 lines per folio. Not ruled. Soft leather binding contemporary with the MS; on the spine: *Epistolae mutuae P. Abelardi et Heloyse post eorum conversionem*. The codex may have been assembled from separate fascicles by someone who provided, as well as some titles and marginal notes, page numbers (A+207) in the upper corner of the written area, and also letters and numbers (in the lower margin of pages with odd numbers) that indicate the quires (e.g. M, M. 2, M. 3). A second set of page numbers has been added on the upper corner of pp. 1–119 and also on pp. 189–97, where the numbers are 1–9. The first words of the next page have been written by the scribe in the lower margin of pages with even numbers. Fifteen quires of six leaves, then one of 4, one of 6, one of 4. Brown ink. No illumination or colouring. Watermark: a shield which contains a cross supported by a bird. Similar examples from 1525/1540 are given in Briquet, i: no. 1255. Two hands, an annotator/corrector and a copyist who writes a careful, regular, cursive script of which the striking features are the long, left-sloping ascenders of the letter d in an otherwise upright script with squat letters and pronounced vertical ascenders and descenders. Salutations are detached from the opening of the *Letters* of Abelard and Heloise and written by the scribe in larger letters like titles. Titles are provided for two pieces which are not part of this correspondence. On p. A a 17th-c. reader has written: *Epistolae omnes huius Codicis* (add.: *ab Abaillardo et ad Abailardum scriptae*) *euulgatae fuerunt ab Andrea Duchesne*. The numbers given to works published in Duchesne–d'Amboise are found here, e.g. for *Letter* 2: *edita ordine* 2^{a}, for *Letter* 3: *edita ordine* 3^{a}, for the *Confession of faith*: *edita est 20*. Since *Letter* 2 is Heloise's response to her reading of *Letter* 1, the misplacement of *Letter* 1 in this codex after *Letter* 7 has no implication for the structure of the collection as a whole and seems to be the consequence of a misarrangement of the quires: *Letters* 2–7 occupy quires 1–10, *Letter* 1 quires 11–15.

Quotations from the Vulgate appear to have been 'modernized' in the light of the revised edition issued by Pope Clement VIII in 1592 and this gives us a *terminus a quo* for dating the MS; see *Letters* 4, **9** and 7, **17**. Many additions have been made in the margins, usually by a blotchy hand, sometimes by the copyist. They become very infrequent after *Letter* 5 but they include (a) variant readings and conjectures prefaced by *alias*, *al.*(= *alias*, *aliter*, or *alibi*) or *uel*; (b) identifications of, and adjustments to, biblical and other quotations, sometimes in the light of printed editions, e.g. in *Letter* 1, **24**: *Hieronymi in primo libro contra Iouinianum: To(mo) 2. epistolarum. pag. 71*; (c) comments which serve as glosses (*uidelicet* . . .) or markers or subheadings, e.g. at *Letter* 1, **21**: *Heloysa se sentit grauidam*; (d) additional information, e.g. in *Letter* 1, **3** (about William of Champeaux): *Hic fuit initiator monasterii Sancti Victoris parisiensis. Vide librum secundum Antiq. Par. pa. 404*;[87] **9** (about Anselm of Laon): *Hic scripsit breues enarrationes in Cantica Canticorum et Apocalypsim, anno*

[87] Possibly from one of the impressions of Bonfons, *Les Fastes: Antiquitez et choses plus remarquables de Paris*, livre 2, ch. 5.

1550 per Poncetum le Preux Luteciae impressae;[88] **5** (*Corbolii*): *Corbeil*; **47** (about Dionysius Areopagita): *Immo vero e duobus unicum facit Dionysium, si exemplari Basiliae impressa fides est.*[89] There are also some notes by another hand. They could possibly signify work in progress towards annotating a planned, printed edition. Burnett, in 'Peter Abelard, *Confessio fidei "Universis"*', p. 124, suggested, since the text of the *Confessio* is similar to that found in Duchesne–d'Amboise, that the copy may have been prepared for the use of Duchesne or d'Amboise. It does not seem to be a transcript from Duchesne–d'Amboise. It lacks the *Argumentum* which prefaces each of the *Letters* in the printed edition; more significantly, the many omissions in **F** that are common to **CE** are not found in **Amb** and there are differences between the annotations in **F** and **Amb**. For example, in Duchesne–d'Amboise the mention of William of Champeaux in *Letter* 1, **3**, is supported by a reference to Otto of Freising; that of Anselm of Laon (**9**) is supported by a reference to the *Historia Restaurationis Ecclesiae Laudunensis*, and that of Dionysius Areopagita (**47**) is supported by a reference to Pope Innocent III.

On the other hand, some similarities between the texts as copied in **F** and as printed in **Amb** (see below, pp. cxxiv, cxxvi) suggest that **F** was intended to prepare the way for a printed edition and both **Amb** and **Amb**^{I} had it to hand when collating MSS and reviewing the results. A striking feature of **F** is the way the copyist seems to have consulted editions of sources cited in the *Letters* and, in the light of what he found, has adjusted the citations in ways that are not found in other witnesses. This is especially so in *Letter* 7, where there are many citations; see pp. cxx–cxxi below and also the *apparatus criticus*. However, these emendations are rarely found in Duchesne–d'Amboise, perhaps because they saw them as alterations of the contents of the MSS they used earlier.

Spelling is to some extent classicized. Dipthongs are written and grave accents are frequent (*uerae*, *uerè*). Double consonants (*Heloyssam*) are rare; *b* is found in place of *p* (*obtineres*); *-ci-* and *-ti-* are both found; *h*

[88] Not found. The notice of Anselm of Laon in the *Histoire littéraire de la France*, x. 170 (repr. in *PL* clxii. 1173–86, at 1183B) mentions an earlier and similar edition: 'Simon Fontaine . . . publia à Paris, en 1549, les Commentaires sur le Cantique des cantiques et sur l'Apocalypse, sous le nom d'Anselme de Laon: Enarrationes Anselmi Laudunensis in Cantica canticorum et in Apocalypsim.'

[89] In *Veterum quorundam breuium theologorum . . . elenchus* (Basel, 1550, *Praefatio*, p. 2), Denis, bishop of Athens, is conflated with Denis, the martyr in the reign of Domitian in AD 96.

appears and disappears (*charissima*, *Iesum*); *-mn-* is preferred to *-mpn-* (*condemnabit*) and *-n-* to *-m-* (*tanquam*, *circuncisione*); *qu* is sometimes preferred to *c* (*quotidie*); *-th-* is preferred to *-ct-* (*authoritas*); *y* is often but not always preferred to *i* (*hysopi*, *idola*). Arabic numerals are used. Some words are written in Greek (in transliteration). Lines of verse are written separately, indented, and sometimes underlined. *Punctuation* is clear and includes commas.

F and **CE** form a group which includes the *Letters*, Fulk's *Letter*, and Abelard's *Confession of faith 'Vniuersis'*. The copies are late, none earlier than the late 15th c., and poor since they make mistakes in common.

Former possessors. Perhaps Duchesne or d'Amboise. Benedictine abbey of St-Germain-des-Prés, diocese of Paris; *ex libris* on p. A with shelf mark: N. 834, *olim* 690.[90] The MS was at St-Germain by 1677 or earlier for it appears in the catalogue of 1677 (Paris, BnF fr. 5792) printed by Montfaucon in *Bibliotheca Bibliothecarum Manuscriptorum nova* (1739), ii. 1136A: *690 Petri Abailardi Epistolae*. This catalogue reproduced earlier MS numbers dating from at least 1653. New class marks were given *c.*1740. The MS entered the Bibliothèque nationale in 1795/6.

Descriptions and further references. Muckle, 'Abelard's letter of consolation', p. 167. Monfrin, pp. 28 and 41, n. 80. L. Delisle, *Inventaire des MSS latins conservés à la Bibliothèque Impériale sous les nos. 8823–18613 et faisant suite à la série dont le catalogue a été publié en 1744* (Paris, 1863–71), p. 87. Smits, pp. 70–5. Burnett, 'Peter Abelard, *Confessio fidei "Universis"*', pp. 123–4. *Checklist* no. 142.

Paris, BnF lat. 13826 (s. xvii)

Contents. Pp. 1–66, *Letter* 8 and the *Rule*.

Physical features. Paper. In the upper margin of p. 1: *Petri Abaelardi epistola octaua* (another hand adds: *edita*): *Quae est eiusdem Petri ad heloissam Institutio, seu Regula Sanctimonialium*. A good transcript of the edition of Duchesne–d'Amboise with the *Argumentum* which was added at the head of the *Letter* and with the same page layout as in the edition (pp. 131–97). The copyist sometimes incorporates into the text readings which were presented as variants in the margins of the

[90] The MS catalogue of printed books in the library of St-Germain-des-Prés made by Luc d'Achéry in 1643 lists a copy of the Duchesne–d'Amboise edition among *Patres latini*, G. 5 (Paris, BnF lat. 13082, p. 120).

edition (**Amb**[1]); he concludes his work on p. 66 with the words *Deo gratias*. The library of the abbey of St-Germain-des-Prés, where this transcript may well have been made, acquired a copy of Duchesne–d'Amboise by 1643 (see above p. lxiii, n. 90). Whether intentionally or otherwise, this copy of *Letter* 8 and the *Rule* complements **F**, another MS of St-Germain, which contains *Letters* 1–7 only.

Former possessors. Benedictine abbey of St-Germain-des-Prés, diocese of Paris; *ex libris* on p. 1 with the shelf mark N.1301_2. The flyleaf contains the numbers 749 and 1301. Listed in the 1677 catalogue (Paris, BnF fr. 5792) printed by Montfaucon in *Bibliotheca Bibliothecarum Manuscriptorum nova*, ii. 1137E: *749 Petri Abailardi Epistola octava ad Heloissam*. Before expunction the catalogue entry continued: *(in codice 749 epistola haec non reperitur)*. In the margin of the catalogue: *ordo novus* 1301_2. New class marks were given *c.*1740. The MS entered the Bibliothèque nationale in 1795/6.

Descriptions and further references. L. Delisle, *Inventaire des MSS latins conservés à la Bibliothèque Nationale sous les numéros 8823–18613 et faisant suite à la série dont le catalogue a été publié en 1744* (Paris, 1863–71); id., *Inventaire des MSS de S. Germain-des-Prés* (Paris, 1868), p. 118: *Règle des religieuses, par Abélard. XVIIs*. McLaughlin, 'Abelard's Rule', p. 241. *Checklist* no. 144.

C Paris, BnF n. acq. lat. 1873 (north-east Italy, s. xv^{ex})

Contents. The codex consists of two parts brought together at a later date. The contents of part 2 (fos. 136–217) concern Abelard and Heloise:

Fos. 136–207^v, *Letters* 1–8 with a shortened version of the *Rule*. On fo. 207^v the opening only is presented of a colophon also found in **E** (fo. 53^v; see p. lii above).

Fos. 207^v–210, Fulk of Deuil, *Letter to Abelard* (*Epistola Fulconis prioris de Dygillo ad Petrum Abaelardum*). Cousin, i. 703–7; *PL* clxxviii. 371–76; Van den Eynde, 'Détails biographiques sur Pierre Abélard', p. 219 (see above, p. lii, *Paris, BnF lat. 2545*).

Fo. 210^{r+v}, Bernard, abbot of Clairvaux, *Letter* 188 (*Epistola Bernardi ad cardinales contra Petrum Abaelardum*), incomplete, in *S. Bernardi Opera*, ed. Leclercq and Rochais, viii. 10–11, *l.* 10; *PL* clxxxii. 351–353B *l.* 5 (. . . *credere dedignatur*).

Fo. 210^v–211, id., *Letter* 191 (*Item ipse pape Innocentio ex persona Remensis archiepiscopi*), incomplete, in *S. Bernardi Opera*, ed. Leclercq and Rochais, viii. 41–2, *l.* 2; *PL* clxxxii. 357B–C *l.* 7 (. . . *est in eo iniquitas*).

Fos. 210^{v}–211, Bernard, short extract from *Letter* 191 (*Episcopi capitula librorum ejus a sanctis patribus condempnata ne morbus serperet medicinali necessitate adjudicaverunt*) followed by *Capitula haeresum XIX* (this title is not in the MS), in *S. Bernardi Opera*, ed. Leclercq and Rochais, viii. 42, *ll.* 10–13, pp. 39–40; *PL* clxxxii. 358A *ll.* 1–6; Mews, 'The lists of heresies', pp. 108–10.

Fo. 211, *Litterae domini Innocentii* (*Innocentius papa secundus contra Petrum Abaelardum*), extracts from the Bull *Testante apostolo* (*Marcianus . . . esse censemus*): Innocent II, *Letter* 447, *PL* clxxix. 516B *l.* 10–C *l.* 8, 517A *l.* 5–B *l.* 1. JL, no. 8148. Also among Bernard's *Letters*, *Letter* 194, in *S. Bernardi Opera*, ed. Leclercq and Rochais, viii. 47, *ll.* 10–19, p. 48, *ll.* 5–12; *PL* clxxxii. 360C *l.* 8–D *l.* 7, 361A *l.* 12–B *l.* 8.

Bernard, *Letter* 192, incomplete, in *S. Bernardi Opera*, ed. Leclercq and Rochais, viii.. 43–4; *PL* clxxxii. 358B–359A.

Fos. 211–212^{v}, Bernard, excerpt from *Letter* 189 (*Bernardus ad papam Innocentium contra idem* [sic] *Abaelardum*), in *S. Bernardi Opera*, ed. Leclercq and Rochais, viii. p. 13, *l.* 21–p. 15, *l.* 13; *PL* clxxxii. 355A *l.* 8–356B *l.* 10.

Fos. 212^{v}–215, Bernard, extracts from *Letter* 190, in *S. Bernardi Opera*, ed. Leclercq and Rochais, viii. 17, *ll.* 7–20, p. 20, *l.* 14–p. 21, *l.* 8, p. 24, *l.* 22–p. 26, *l.* 6, p. 26, *l.* 15–p. 27, *l.* 6, p. 27, *ll.* 10–18, p. 228, *ll.* 18–20; *PL* clxxxii. 1053D *l.* 4–1056A *l.* 2, 1057C *l.* 7–1058B *l.* 5, 1061B *l.* 6–1062C *l.* 3, 1062D *l.* 7–1063B *l.* 14, 1063C *l.* 6–1063D *l.* 5, 1064C *ll.* 7–10 (. . . *preceptum unius pomi et pro certo difficulter multum arguit videris fratrem si vis*).

Fo. 215, Bernard, *Letter 193*, incomplete, in *S. Bernardi Opera*, ed. Leclercq and Rochais, viii. 44–5; *PL* clxxxii. 359.

Fos. 215^{v}–217, Abelard, *Confession of faith 'Vniuersis'* (*Epistola Petri Abaelardi contra calumpnias objectorum capitulorum responsio*), ed. Burnett, 'Peter Abelard, *Confessio fidei "Universis"*', pp. 132–8; Cousin, ii. 719–23; *PL* clxxviii. 105–8.

This material relating to Abelard and Heloise is the same as that found in **E** and was copied from a similar or the same exemplar (above, pp. lii–liii) but **C** also has passages taken from *Letters* 192, 189, 190, and 193 of Bernard. It is also similar to that once found in the lost MS, Paris, Abbey of St-Victor GGG 17 (below, p. xcv).

Fo. 217^{v} is blank.

Physical features. Paper. Part 1 of the codex (fos. 1–115) contains a Hebrew–Latin dictionary copied at Padua in 1494 (fo. 115: *Finis in scribendo mihi obtigit: Die viiii*^{o} *Januarii M*^{o} *CCCC*^{o} *LXXXXIIII*^{o}*, hora nona, in episcopio Patavino. Laus Deo. Jo. Bar.*). Part 2 (fos. 116–217) contains the work of two hands of the late 15th c. The first hand has worked on two quires with 10 leaves; it supplies (fos. 116–130^{v}) book 2 of the *Differentiae* of Isidore of Seville (*PL* lxxxiii. 69–98) and (fos. 130^{v}–132^{v}) Pseudo-Seneca, *Libellus de moribus* (*PL* lxxii. 29–32C); fos. 133–135^{v} are blank. The second hand (fos. 136–217) has worked on seven quires of 12 leaves of which the last lacks two. Here we have the material relating to Abelard and Heloise. At the end of fo. 147^{v} the first word of the next quire (the 2nd) and at the end of fo. 159^{v} the first two words of the next quire (the 3rd) are given. The watermark on fos. 116–217 is a crown surmounted by a fleur-de-lis; a near likeness is found in Briquet, ii, no. 4838 (Treviso, 1530) and many comparable examples are also Italian. The codex is bound in soft parchment.

Fos. 136–217 measure 295 × 205 mm. One column. Not ruled. The writing space varies: 235/220 × 145/135 mm; so does the number of lines: 36/41. Some folios have been misplaced as a result of rebinding: from fo. 172^{v} pass to 184^{r}–188^{v}, 191^{r}–195^{v}, 183, 189, 173–182^{v}, then to 190, and then 196^{r}–207^{v}. One small, everyday cursive hand with lots of loops; good spacing in general between words and lines; long ascenders and descenders. The ink varies from being pale, faded, and faint in places to dark brown. A smaller script and a new nib start at fo. 175^{r} and there is a further change of nib at fo. 203^{v}. On occasions the scribe divides the text of *Letter* 1 and of the *Rule* into sections separated by a space of one or two lines. The copy is slapdash in spite of appearances. No illumination and almost no rubrication, although unfilled spaces are left for the initial capital letters of all eight *Letters* and of the *Rule*, and here the scribe sometimes writes the initial in minuscule in the margin. Some marginal annotations but none of significance. Quotations in the text are often incomplete or abbreviated and conclude with *etc* or *etc usque*. There are also omissions, some in spaces left unfilled. The scribe expunges his mistakes and adds the correction on the same line. Gaps in his exemplar caused problems (e.g. *Letter* 1, 5) nor did he always successfully decipher what he found, and he apparently overlooked some passages.

Spelling, *punctuation* and division into sentences are careless, increasingly so towards the end of the collection. The scribe likes double consonants (*heloyssam*, *pittagorius*, *aspiccere*). He sometimes adds consonants (*inscructabile, pascienter*) and sometimes omits them (*adiscimus*). He likes to use *h (helias*, *ephiphania*, *marchi*) but is occasionally flexible (*auriet*, *exibuerint*, *pulcre*). He sometimes adds *b* before a consonant (*obmittam*, *subcumbere*) and uses *n* in preference to *m* (*inpendisse*) and *qu* instead of *c* (*quoctas*). He oscillates over the use of *y* and *i* (*dyaconissas*, *cothidyano* but *presbiteros*, *egiptiaca*). *Punctuation* is often absent when most necessary; the scribe also relies on initial capitals to indicate the end of one sentence and the start of another. The modern question mark ? is used; numerals are in Arabic.

Former possessors. The watermark suggests that this copy of the Abelard material may have a north Italian provenance. The Paduan origin of part 1 of the codex—Padua and Treviso are some 50 kilometres apart—gives support to the possibility that both parts originated in the north-east of Italy. **C** could be *Nanneticus*, the Nantes MS obtained by d'Amboise, but **E** is a more likely candidate for the reasons given by Monfrin, pp. 39–40 (see *Nanneticus* below, p. xci). Frederick North, 5th Earl of Guildford (1760–1827); purchased by Sir Thomas Phillipps in 1830 during the sale of Lord Guildford's MSS and sold by Phillipps in 1903 as MS 6217 to the Bibliothèque nationale, Paris.

Descriptions and further references. Muckle, 'Abelard's letter of consolation', p. 167. Monfrin, pp. 25–7. H. Omont, *Catalogue des MSS de la Bibliothèque de Sir Thomas Phillipps récemment acquis pour la Bibliothèque nationale* (Paris, 1905), pp. 29–30 (also in *Bibliothèque de l'École des Chartes*, lxiv (1903), 513–14). A. N. L. Munby, *The Formation of the Phillipps Library up to the Year 1840* (Phillipps Studies, no. 3; Cambridge, 1954), pp. 56, 159. Brief mention by Burnett, 'Peter Abelard, *Confessio fidei "Universis"*', p. 120. *Checklist* no. 157.

R Reims, Bibliothèque municipale 872 (s. xiii^{ex}/xiv^{in})

Contents. Fos. 112–54, *Letters* 1–8. Other contents are the supposed letters of Seneca to St Paul (fos. 1–2c), Seneca's letters to Lucilius, 1–88 (fos. 2c–87d), Seneca's *Natural Questions* (not complete, fos. 88–109), followed by the *Natural Questions* of Adelard of Bath (not complete, fos. 109–111). Fos. 158–161vb contain 14th-c. notes on writings by Seneca and Cicero.

Physical features. Parchment. The codex is a single entity, as is shown by the copying and decoration throughout and by the catchwords at the end of quires. The folios were numbered by Gilles d'Aspremont (Aegidius de Asperomonte), canon of Reims between 1384 and 1414, on 29 October 1412 (fo. 161^{v}); Gilles did likewise for other MSS then at Reims. An Augustinian hermit and of Italian origin, Sartelli being his Italian name, Gilles held canonries and other offices both in Reims and elsewhere. Between 1374 and 1413 his name appears in documents of the University of Paris, where he became a regent master in arts and theology and where he was rector in 1382. From 1377 he helped to build up the library of the Collège de Dormans-Beauvais in Paris (see below, p. lxxxvii). See Alexandre and others, *Bibliothèque municipale de Reims* (listed below), pp. 16–20; *Fasti Ecclesiae Gallicanae*, iii: *Diocèse de Reims* by P. Desportes (Turnhout, 1998), p. 117; H. Denifle and Ae. Chatelain, *Chartularium universitatis Parisiensis* (Paris, 1894–7), iii, nos. 1433, 1477, 1541, 1679 (pp. 255, 314, 451, 606; also p. 260, n. 43); iv, nos. 1745, 1786, 1793, 2001, 2003 (pp. 27, 61, 76, 272, 274); T. Kouamé, *Le Collège de Dormans-Beauvais*, pp. 449, 450; T. Sullivan, *Parisian Licentiates in Theology*, ii. 63–6. The codex was rebound in the 15th c. in leather on beech boards now lacking a clasp. The folios measure 195 × 275 mm. 2 columns enclosed within a ruled frame. 37 lines. Ruled. Writing area 60 × 90 mm per column. Quires of 12 leaves with catchwords on fos. 123^{v}, 135^{v}, and 147^{v}—the following quire lacks the last two leaves. Gothic bookhand with an oval aspect but the spacing of characters is irregular and abbreviations are sometimes too compressed. Minims can be confused and confusing e.g. *uineam* for *unicam*. Initials and other large capitals are decorated and coloured red and blue alternately with marginal filigrees; the initial letter of each *Letter* is more sumptuous than other initials. New sentences do not always begin with a capital letter but just run on. The copyist of **R** reviewed his work, making corrections above the line and in the margins where he also added occasional brief notes. Quotations are sometimes reduced to the initial letters of words. The exemplar copied in **R** is similar to one copied in **B** and, like the scribe of **B**, that of **R** had difficulty in reading it and left spaces unfilled, e.g. on fo. 117ra (*Letter* 1, 31). Another hand has frequently added *nota* in the margins with a vertical line in the text to indicate the beginning and the end of the passage being noted (often a quotation from the Bible or one of the Church Fathers) and a line in the margin to indicate its extent. He did likewise in other parts of the codex. Another medieval hand has occasionally tried to edit the text, e.g. in *Letter* 1 he unnecessarily corrected *hec florere* (3), and changed some spellings of nouns—*archydiaconus*, *catalaunensi*, *porphyrius* (**6**).

Spelling. *-ci-*, not *-ti*, *-i-*, not *-j-*, *u* and not *v* (including capital *U*). Frequently single consonants are found where doubles might be expected (*agressus*, *amiratus*, *acusans*, *asiste* but *leccionem*, *hiis*, *legittime*). The scribe liked to write *y*, not *i*, in some words such as *dyalectica*, *dyocesim*, *archidyaconus*, *hystoria*, *inhyant*, *ysayam*, but he was inconsistent (*istoriam*, *simbolum*, *martirium*). He was also inconsistent in his use and non-use of *h* in such words as *ester*, *talamis*, *scolis*, *omicidia/chorinthios*, *iherosolime*, *luchas*, *perhenniter*, *rethibus*; also *habundantia*, *hebrietas*, *honera*, and *habraham*. The insular *enim* (·*n*·) is sometimes used, as it is in **B**. *Punctuation*, usually just a dot, sometimes none at all, is careless.

Former possessors. The cathedral chapter of Reims from at least 1412. Clearly listed (although without mention of its Abelardian content) in the inventories of the chapter library made in 1456 (Reims, Bibliothèque municipale 1992, fo. 23^{v}, no. 439) and in 1684 (Reims, Bibliothèque municipale 1994, fo. 95).

Descriptions and further references. Monfrin, pp. 21–2. *Catalogue général des manuscrits des bibliothèques publiques de France. Départements* 39: *Reims*, ii (1) (by H. Loriquet (Paris, 1904), pp. 187–90. Detailed description of the binding by J.-L. Alexandre, G. Grand, G. Lanoë, *Bibliothèque de Reims* (Reliures médiévales des bibliothèques de France (IRHT), iv; Turnhout 2009), p. 402. *Checklist* no. 164.

S The Schøyen collection (Oslo and London) 2085 (*c*.1330–60)

Contents. Fos. 1–74^{v}, *Letter* 1 (**23–6**, **38–75**), *Letters* 2–7 (**1–17**).

Physical features. Parchment of reasonably good quality but stained in places, especially in the inner margins. 74 unnumbered folios with two modern vellum flyleaves. Modern binding covered with off-white leather bearing on the front an inscription in small capital letters: ABELARD HELOISE.

The first and the last folios are worn, which suggests that the MS lay unbound for a long time. 230 × 150 mm. 1 column. 25 lines. Ruled in pencil; pricked in the margins. Writing area 145/150 × 95/

100 mm. Ten regular quires survive with catchwords on the verso side of fos. 4, 12, 20, 28, 36, 44, 52, 60, 68. A first quire of eight leaves (which presumably contained the earlier part of *Letter* 1) is missing; the second (now the first) has lost four leaves (between fos. 2 and 3, also part of *Letter* 1); eight quires of 8 follow; the last quire (now the 10th) lacks the final two leaves, which were cut out. The codex originally had further quires which have since been removed; it is not possible therefore to know whether these included the rest of *Letter* 7 and *Letter* 8 with or without the long or the short version of the *Rule*. Brown ink. Gothic bookhand of high calligraphic quality, very regular and legible. The script and the decoration suggest a date in the first half or the middle of the fourteenth century. But the scribe was not a careful copyist and there are many howlers. Scribal corrections are made by means of inserting subscript dots or simple crossing out and, when adding rubrics, the scribe made some further corrections of the text in red. Rubricated titles divide the text of *Letter* 1 and introduce *Letters* 2–7. These divisions open with initial capitals decorated with 'frog spawn', usually blue with red filigrees, some red with brown or mauve. Small initials in the text have red highlights. No clear evidence of origin or provenance, although the decoration suggests northern France or the environs of Paris rather than Paris itself (Jeudy) or central/east France (Sotheby's; Specialist in charge: Dr Christopher de Hamel). A corrector, using a thin nib, appears infrequently. Some brief marginal annotations in a lighter ink and in a cursive hand of the early 15th c., with indications of sources of quotations found in the text and with some comments and readers' marks. The annotator found much to admire in the *Letters*. For example, at the close of *Letter* 1, during Abelard's exhortation to his friend to follow the will of God, he offers support, and he does so again during *Letter* 3 in which Abelard tries to justify his silence and recommends that Heloise take to prayer, and again in *Letter* 6, **25** when St Paul is cited on the subject of piety. However, the copy appears to have found few readers.

Jeudy has shown that the texts in **S** resemble **T** and **BRDY** in their additions, omissions and shared readings, but that they do not derive directly from the group **BRDY**.

Spelling. The scribe sometimes writes a single consonant where a double might be expected (*ocultum*) and vice versa (*transfferretur*), consistently prefers *-ci-* to *-ti-*, sometimes intrudes *-h-* (*methaphoram*, *monachos*) but sometimes does not (*incoando*, *monacum*), and sometimes prefers *k* to *c* (*karissima*); *-i- and -y-* are interchangeable (*hystoria*, *historie*); *fariseus* is also found. His abbreviations are clear. Jeudy noticed some omissions of *enim* and some occasions when the Tironian ꝫ (*enim*; cf. **BR**) seems mistakenly to have become *.pp*. *Punctuation*, in the form of stops, colons, and medial stops, is spasmodic; many sentences run on.

Former possessors. Robert de Billy (1869–1953), a French diplomat, ambassador, and bibliophile, the editor also of *Marcel Proust, lettres et conversations* (3rd edn.; Paris 1930), purchased this MS of the *Letters* from Henri Leclerc in 1910 (cat. 30 (1910), no. 8621). I have not been able to locate a copy of this catalogue. Jeudy reproduced pencilled notes made by a French bookseller inside the front cover when this was *cartonnage gris*. The more recent vellum binding with pastedowns inside has covered these notes and they are no longer visible but Jeudy recorded that they give a guide price of 350F, class marks, and the date of the MS. It was later the private property of Robert de Billy's grandson, Daniel Appia, and was sold through Sotheby's to Bernard Quaritch Ltd on 5 December 1995 (lot 33). The guide price given by Sotheby's was £30–40,000. The MS is now MS 2085 in the Schøyen collection (Oslo and London) and is currently in Norway.

The MS is not the missing part of Dijon, Bibliothèque municipale 525, fos. 204–27 (below, p. lxxxii), from which only the final lines of *Letter* 7 and *Letter* 8—missing in **S**—survive now in **H** (Paris, BnF n. acq. fr. 20001, fos. 11–12^{v}; above, pp. xlix–l and below, p. cxviii). The copies are contemporaneous but quite different in many other ways.

Descriptions and further references. Jeudy, 'La Correspondance d'Abélard et Héloïse' (with a photograph of one folio on p. 135); 'Un Nouveau Manuscrit de la *Correspondance* d'Abélard et Héloïse', with a photograph of fos. 19^{v} and 38^{v} between pp. 876 and 877. *Sotheby's. Western Manuscripts and Miniatures. Sale LN5691 London, Tuesday 5th December 1995, no. 33* (with four photographs). Listed, with a photograph of one folio, as MS 2085 on the website of the Schøyen collection ⟨http://www.schoyencollection.com⟩.

T Troyes, Médiathèque 802 (perhaps shortly before 1236/8)

Contents. The codex has three parts, the first of which contains the Abelard/Heloise material and other texts concerning religious women on fos. 1–103.

Fos. 1–88vb, *Letters* 1–8 with the *Rule*. The *Rule* ends near the bottom of fo. 88vb where the last line and a half are blank.

Fos. 89–102va, a collection (inc. *Institutiones nostre*), not found in any other extant MS, of documents concerning women religious. Published under the title *Excerpta ex regulis Paracletensis monasterii* by Duchesne–d'Amboise, pp. 198–213, from a MS belonging to the Paraclete (*in Paracletensi . . . sequentia reperimus, et videntur esse Heloissae*); Cousin, i. 213–24; *PL* clxxviii. 313–26. See Van den Eynde, 'En marge des écrits d'Abélard', pp. 70–84, esp. pp. 76–84; Waddell, *The Paraclete Statutes*. The documents are:

fos. 89–90va, *PL* clxxviii. 313C–317B: *Institutiones nostre*. A formulation of uniform observances of the mother and daughter houses of an unnamed order of nuns—presumably the order of the Paraclete. *The Paraclete Statutes*, ed. Waddell, pp. 9–15 with facsimile of T on pp. 5–8.

fos. 90va–93ra, *PL* clxxviii. 317B–322C *l.* 1: Canons 187–215 in *Panormia* (commonly attributed to Ivo of Chartres, d. 1115), III, *De virginibus, viduis et abbatissis*, *PL* clxi. 1175A–1182A . Identified by Van den Eynde, 'En marge des écrits d'Abélard', p. 75.

fo. 93^{ra+b}, *PL* clxxviii. 322C *l.* 2–323A *l.* 8: Canons headed *De monialibus* and *De sanctimonialibus*, the latter consisting of canons 2 and 4 of the Council of Rouen, 1231 (canon 2—for men—is adapted here for the use of women). Identified by Benton, 'The Paraclete and the Council of Rouen of 1231'.

fos. 93rb–94rb, *PL* clxxviii. 323A *l.* 9–326A: Eleven statutes of the Praemonstratensian General Chapter concerning nuns of the order issued between 1174 and 1236/8. Identified and ed. by Van den Eynde, 'En marge des écrits d'Abélard', pp. 76–83. Van den Eynde believed that T contains a slightly earlier version of the text issued in 1236/8. The copy ends near the bottom of fo. 94rb, where two lines are blank.

fos. 94va–102va: Chapters 7–28 of the *Institutio sanctimonialium Aquisgranensis* (*Explicit regula sanctimonialium*, fo. 102va), ed. from other MSS by A. Werminghoff in *MGH*, Leges, Sectio 3, Concilia 2, Concilia aevi karolini, i (1); Hannover, 1906), pp. 422–56, at 442–56. A codification of regulations for nuns drawn up at the synod of Aachen in 816 (along with a similar work for canons, ed. Werminghoff, pp. 307–421). Monfrin, pp. 12–13.

Fo. 102vb in a hand of the 15th/16th c.:

Epitaphium magistri Petri Abaelardi fondatoris monasterii Paracliti 'Petrus in hac petra latitat . . .'. Ed. from a lost Paraclete Latin necrology by Camuzat, fo. 348 (see below, p. xciii); Duchesne–d'Amboise, sig. e.iiii^{v} and p. 342 from the same necrology; Cousin, i. 717; *PL* clxxviii. 103D; Mews, 'La Bibliothèque du Paraclet', *Appendice* (with Burnett), pp. 65–6. *Checklist* nos. 249a, 449.

Epitaphium Eloyse abbatisse Paracliti 'Hoc tumulo abbatissa jacet Heloysa . . .'. First ed. Camuzat, fo. 348^{v} (see below, p. xciii) from a lost Paraclete Latin necrology; Duchesne–d'Amboise, sig. e iiii^{v} from the same necrology; Cousin, i. 719; *PL* clxxviii. 104; Mews, 'La Bibliothèque du Paraclet', *Appendice* (with Burnett), pp. 62–3; Dronke, *Abelard and Heloise in Medieval Testimonies*, p. 50 (repr. in *Intellectuals and Poets*, p. 285), from Bern, Bürgerbibliothek 211; Dronke dates the composition to the 12th c. *Checklist* nos. 249a, 454.

'*Ego Petrus cluniacensis abbas . . .*', Peter the Venerable, 'open' absolution of Abelard. First printed from a lost Paraclete Latin necrology by Camuzat, fo. 348 (see below, p. xciii), then by M. Marrier and A. Duchesne, *Bibliotheca Cluniacensis* (Paris, 1614), *notae*, col. 155, on which see *The Letters of Peter the Venerable*, ed. Constable, ii. 210 and 47; Duchesne–d'Amboise, sig. e iiii^{v} and p. 345, from the necrology used by Camuzat; Cousin, i. 717; *PL* clxxviii. 68B, 91C. First printed from **T** by U. Wawrzyniak, *Philologische Untersuchungen zum 'Rithmus in Laude Saluatoris' des Petrus Venerabilis: Edition und Kommentar* (Lateinische Sprache und Literatur des Mittelalters, xxii; Frankfurt a. M., 1985), pp. 46–7. Also Mews, 'La Bibliothèque du Paraclet', *Appendice* (with Burnett), p. 62. *Checklist* no. 249a.

These three texts (two epitaphs and absolution) are also found together at the end of the *Breviary of the Paraclete* in the late 15th-c. Chaumont MS, Bibliothèque municipale 31, where they fill the empty verso side of the final folio 245^{v} (just as they do in **T**) and where the absolution appears between the two epitaphs as in the MS seen by Camuzat. Ed. from the Chaumont MS by F. Carnandet in *Notice sur le Bréviaire d'Abailard*, p. 2 and by Waddell in *The Paraclete Breviary*, iiiC, p. 439. See also Waddell, *The Old French Paraclete Ordinary*, i. 388: 'Excursus VIII: Epitaphs and Letter of Absolution', where Waddell suggests that 'the combination of these three texts . . . may date back to the first translation of the remains of Abelard and Heloise from the *petit moustier* to the abbey church, under the authority of Catherine de Courcelles, 2 May 1497'. On this translation see Charrier, *Héloïse*, pp. 305–8 and Mews, 'La Bibliothèque du Paraclet', pp. 42–6.

Fo. 103 is blank.

Physical features. Parchment. The three parts of the present codex were first brought together in the early 18th c. and the folios are now continuously numbered. Fos. 1–103 present the Abelard/Heloise material and other texts concerning religious women. Fos. 104–55 (part 2) contain a *Libellus Quinti Iulii Hilarionis* (fo. 104, in a hand of the 9th/10th c.) and a *Chronicon Hieronymi* (fo. 111^{v}), both being parts of the compilation better known as the *Chronicle* of 'Fredegar' (ed. B. Krusch in *MGH*, Scriptores rerum Merovingicarum, ii). Fos. 156–241 (part 3), written by various hands, contain a 10th-c. copy from St Sulpice of Bourges of the writings of Denis the pseudo-Areopagite in the Latin translation of John the Scot, although an 18th-c. hand attributes the translation to John the Saracen (*fl.* 12th c.).

Fos. 1–103 measure 255 × 190 mm. Ten quires of 8 leaves (quire 7 lacks the last leaf but no text is missing; a second scribe started work on the seventh leaf), one quire of 10 (*Institutiones nostre* begin on the last leaf), one of 8, and one of 6 (not six leaves stitched together, as has been thought; the parchment of the first and last leaves is a single piece). Some quire numbers have survived trimming during binding: *iiii* (fo. 32^{v}), *v* (fo. 40^{v}). Ruled. 2 columns. 31 lines per column. Writing area 205 × 150 mm (205 × 70 mm per column). Large initials alternately red and blue throughout. Larger initials and marginal filigrees at the beginning of each *Letter* and, within *Letter* 1, at the beginning of each section that is introduced with a rubricated subheading; also from fo. 90^{v}. Rubrics normally written by the text hands. In addition the 15th/early 16th-c. hand which has written epitaphs on fo. 102vb has added some rubrics in the margins of the early folios containing *Letter* 1 (1^{va+b}, 2^{r}, 2^{va+b}, 3^{r}, and 7^{v}). Two chief scribes (**T**, **T**^{2}) writing a very clear and similar Gothic bookhand, with generous spacing, the first using a paler brown-black ink, the second a darker, shinier black ink. **T**^{2}, with a slightly more vertical emphasis, takes over on fo. 55vb in mid-column in the course of *Letter* 7 at the end of **40** and continues to fo. 102va. Low ascenders throughout. Most of the many rubricated subheadings are reproduced in the margins in Duchesne–d'Amboise, but they are rare after *Letter* 1 and the spaces left vacant for them are largely unfilled. The copy is corrected with greater care up to fo. 55 than after, usually by **T** but writing more open and more angular letters, sometimes over an erasure or in a blank space. After fo. 55^{v} corrections tend to be added in black ink above the line and without expunction.

Several hands have shown interest in making alterations to the copy. Typically, the main scribe, T, places dots under words copied wrongly and proceeds immediately along the line to write the correction. Corrections made by T are also often made over an erasure of what was originally copied, with an erasure often also in the margin nearby. In these cases corrected material has been put in the margin by a reviser for T to see when he came to review what he had copied. T then erased his own incorrect copy, wrote the correction over this erasure and finally erased what had been put in the margin. Since the marginal matter has been erased it is not possible to identify the hand of this diligent corrector but it is unlikely to be T. One reviser, T^1, makes additions in the margin in pencil up to fo. 89ra where *Institutiones nostre* begin. He[91] is not one of the scribes nor a rubricator but a corrector and perhaps also an annotator. His additions are very brief and sometimes consist of no more than the initial letter of a word. His letters are larger, less regular, and less neat than those of the scribes and he often puts a mark—for example, a sloping single or double line or an underline—by text that is to be corrected. The marginal corrigenda written by T^1 are faint, so faint at times and especially so after fo. 55vb when T^2 took over from T, that the scribe may not have noticed all of them; even with ultra-violet light many obscurities remain.[92] But the scribe's eye has also occasionally jumped over perfectly legible additions made by T^1. Sometimes T^1 puts a cross in the margin by text which is left unchanged. The additions (the epitaphs and the absolution) on fo. 102vb seem to have been written over notes in pencil that are possibly due to T^1.

So far we have distinguished three or four hands but there are more. Some of the corrections made over erasures in the text close to erasures in the margin are not made by T but by a less calligraphic, less angular and more rounded hand, T^3. T^4 uses a very thin nib, marking corrections and transpositions that should be made with thin lines or dots and entering corrections with superscript letters. T^3 and T^4 appear less frequently than T^1. T^5, a flowing and later hand using a pale ink, makes just two corrections. Faint pencil notes and trials follow on fo. 103^{r+v}.

[91] Here and elsewhere I write 'he' only for the sake of convenience: the scribes in T could have been nuns. On nuns and canonesses as scribes see e.g. H. Schmidt-Glintzer, ed., *Die gelehrte Bräute Christi: Geistesleben und Bücher der Nonnen im Mittelalter* (Wolfenbütteler Hefte, xxii; Wiesbaden, 2008), and A. Beach, *Women as Scribes: Book Production and Monastic Reform in Twelfth-Century Bavaria* (Cambridge, 2004).

[92] In the *apparatus criticus* illegible additions by T^1 are not usually mentioned.

Spelling. Joining and separation of words both occur (*quicum*, *in tolerabili*); *-i-*, *-u-*, *-V-* in preference to *-j-*, *-v-*, *-U-*; *-t-* generally in preference to *-c-*, *d* in preference to *t* (*capud*) and *y* rather than *i* (*ethyopissa*), but not always, nor is the difference between *c* and *t* always clear. Double consonants appear (*ammiramur*). *Punctuation* is regular and mainly consists of stops, medial pauses, and question marks.

Former possessors. There is no indication in the codex of the origin of Part 1. It was perhaps copied shortly before 1236/8 (the approximate date of the final version of Praemonstratensian statutes copied on fos. 93rb–94rb) with additions of the 15th/early 16th c. on fo. 102vb. See Dalarun, 'Nouveaux Aperçus', pp. 23–5. Before the mid-14th c. it was in the Chapter of the Cathedral of Notre Dame, Paris. The lists of books in the Chapter reproduced by Delisle, *Cabinet*, iii. 1–5 and by B. Guérard in the *Collection des cartulaires de France*, iv: *Cartulaire de l'Eglise Notre Dame de Paris*, i (Paris, 1850), p. 462 and ii (Paris 1850), pp. 349–52, offer no relevant information. Purchased with four other books from the Chapter on 21 March 1347 (fo. 103^{v}; for the date see Monfrin, p. 13) by *Robertus de Bardis, cancellarius Parisiensis* (Roberto de' Bardi, a former pupil of Marsilius of Padua; doctor of theology by January 1334; collector of the works of St Augustine; canon of Notre Dame from 6 September 1335; Chancellor of the University of Paris 1336–49; friend of Petrarch, whom he offered to crown in Paris; d. 1349[93]).

François Pithou (1543–1621) inherited the library of his father Pierre Pithou 'I' (1496–1554) from Pierre's eldest son Jean, who died in 1602, and he also inherited the library of his brother Pierre Pithou 'II' (1539–96). All of them were avid collectors of books and mansucripts which they freely exchanged between themselves[94] and Pierre the father was a remarkable scholar.[95] It is difficult to know which books François had acquired himself and which he had inherited.[96] François stipulated in his will (1617) that his library be

[93] For a summary of Roberto's career see Courtenay, *Parisian Scholars in the Early Fourteenth Century*, pp. 207–8; G. Pozzi, 'Il Vat. Lat. 479 ed altri codici annotati da Roberto de' Bardi', *Miscellanea del Centro di Studi Medievali*, serie II. Pubblicazioni dell'Università Cattolica del Sacro Cuore, NS lxii (Milan, 1958), pp. 125–65 (on his collection of the *Sermons* of St Augustine); id., 'Roberto de' Bardi e sant'Agostino', *Italia medioevale e umanistica*, i (1958), pp. 139–53.

[94] See Bibolet, 'Les Pithou et l'amour des livres', p. 302.

[95] His findings and publications have been listed by Fragonard in Fragonard and Leroy, eds., *Les Pithou*, pp. 469–72.

[96] Bibolet, '*Bibliotheca Pithoena*', p. 505.

given to the college he proposed to found in his own large house in Troyes and which the Oratorians established in 1630.[97] The codex with its three parts bound together is listed (among *Auteurs Ecclésiastiques* and with the *Cotte: Ji 12*) in the *Catalogue des manuscrits de la bibliothèque de François Pithou* made by P.-J. Grosley in his *Vie de Pierre Pithou avec quelques mémoires sur son Père et ses Frères* (2 vols.; Paris, 1756), ii. 269 ff., at p. 278 (*Opera et Epistolae Abelardi. Ejusdem Constitutiones regulares secundum Canones. Q. Julii Hilarionis liber. S. Dionysii opera ex Interpret. Sarraceni*). Also (among *Auteurs servans à l'histoire*) at p. 284: *S. Hieronymi Cronicon*—(under *MSS. Init.*) *Oper. Abelardi*—*Ji.12 / Idacii Lemov. Episc. Chronicon*—*ibidem*—*idem*. (The two chronicles are parts of the *Chronicle* of 'Fredegar'.) Grosley, on pp. 272–3, complained that MSS at the Collège de Troyes had been rebound according to their size and without regard to content, with *cahos* (*sic*) being the result. Grosley regularly prints the figures and letters (the *Cotte*) found on the spines of the books and the title of the first work found within (p. 273: *l'unique fil qui puisse conduire dans ce labyrinthe*). On a parchment pastedown, now inside the present, more recent, covers of T and probably taken from the spine of a former binding, is a barely legible fragment of what appears to be the title, written in a 17th/18th-c. hand, of the first work: (*a*)*belar(di* (space of seven letters) *constitut)iones (regul)ares secundum canones*. According to the *Catalogue général*, corrections in the hand of Pierre Pithou are found in the copy of Quintus Julius Hilarion; this hand is not found anywhere in Part 1. In the lower margin of fo. 1^r a 17th/18th-c. hand provides a title and an *ex libris*: *Epistolae et alia opera Abaelardi / Eiusdem Constitutiones Regulares secundum Canones / Ex Libris Oratorii Collegii Trecensis*. The same hand provides titles and *ex libris* of the Oratory in the other two parts of the codex on fos. 104^r and 156^{r+v}. Listed in the 18th-c. catalogue of the Oratory in Troyes, Médiathèque 700, fo. 136. Martène and Durand, *Voyage littéraire de deux religieux bénédictins*, i. 94, were shown *lettres de Pierre Abaillard* on their visit to Troyes. At the Revolution the MS entered the Bibliothèque municipale (now the Médiathèque).

Which MS was seen by d'Amboise at the Paraclete after 1593 (the year when Marie III de la Rochefoucauld assumed her duties as abbess) is a question that has received more than one answer. The text of the

[97] The will is printed in Fragonard and Leroy, eds., *Les Pithou*, pp. 457–8. On the foundation of the College see Murard, 'Les Pithou et l'école', and Enright, 'Peace and the politics of education'.

Letters, the *Rule*, and the pieces that follow as they were printed by Duchesne–d'Amboise is very similar indeed to that found in **T** (see pp. cxxiii–cxxiv below) but not sufficiently similar to eliminate all doubt that d'Amboise made use of **T** itself, for there are occasions when what had been corrected in **T** appears uncorrected in **Amb**,[98] and occasions too when differences between the two may reflect differences between MSS but may, on the other hand, reflect editorial adjustments made in **Amb**.[99] Monfrin, pp. 14–18, 41, suggested that the MS seen by d'Amboise at the Paraclete is now lost but that it was one of a number of similar copies, including **T**, made within the order of the Paraclete for each of the different convents: *une hypothèse simple* (p. 17). It was unlikely, according to Monfrin, that the Marie III de la Rochefoucauld (abbess 1593–1639), who in 1621 arranged for the tombs of Heloise and Abelard to be placed side by side under the high altar, would have allowed such a significant MS to be removed from the abbey by d'Amboise or that d'Amboise (d. 1619), if he did borrow it, would have given it to François Pithou or that Pithou (d. 21 Jan. 1621) would have had time to acquire it from the heirs of d'Amboise. Mews ('La Bibliothèque du Paraclet', pp. 39–46) advanced a different and in some ways a less simple hypothesis: **T** began life at the Paraclete in the late 13th c. but soon went to Paris. It was returned to the Paraclete after the rebuilding of the abbey in 1366. The transfer by Abbess Marie III de la Rochefoucauld of the tombs of Abelard and Heloise removed them from sight; seen in this light, she could well have allowed d'Amboise to take **T** away with him with the result that later visitors to the abbey left no record of having seen it.[100] In the *Voyage littéraire de deux religieux bénédictins*, i. 94, Martène and Durand reported that *les lettres de Pierre Abaillard* was one of the principal items they saw in the Oratory library in Troyes, and this is certainly **T**, but the detailed

[98] Examples include: *Letter* 6, **21**: humilitatem **T** *before exp. of* h *and* m utilitatem **ACEFBRS** humilitatem **Amb** vilitatem, *& in al(io) Cod(ice)* vtilitatem **Amb**^{I} proufit **J**; **25**: ad modum **TAmb** ad modicum **T**^{I}**ACEFBRS***Vulg*. *Rule* **27**: inquam **TAmb** ita(que) **T**^{I} *in marg. which has been trimmed* itaque **CE**; **29**: deuote (*exp.*) diligenter suscipiat **T** diligenter suscipiat **CE** deuote et diligenter suscipiat **Amb**; **111**: carnales (*exp.*) curiales **T** curiales **CE** carnales **Amb**. On this see also pp. cxxiii–cxxiv below.

[99] For example, the collection of *consuetudines* which follows the *Rule* in both **T** and **Amb** (inc. *Insitutiones nostre*) generally uses the first person plural (*sequimur*, *conseruamus*, *uiuimus*) but sometimes **T** uses the third person plural (*reuertuntur*, *ueniunt*, *legunt et cantant*). On such occasions **Amb** uses the first person plural (*reuertimur*, *uenimus*, *legimus et cantamus*).

[100] D'Amboise wrote that the abbess Marie was a relative of his ('cognatae meae', *Praefatio apologetica*, *PL* clxxviii. 75D).

account they give (on pp. 84–6) of their visit, at Pentecost in 1709, to the abbey of the Paraclete (*si fameuse par la retraite d'Abaillard & d'Eloise*) and its archives makes no mention of a copy of the *Letters*. What happpened to the Paraclete MS used by d'Amboise is not known, but reasons are given below (pp. cxxiii–cxxvi) to support the view that **T** is not the Paraclete MS used by d'Amboise although it is very similar to it.

Recently, Dalarun ('Nouveaux Aperçus') has suggested that William of Auvergne, bishop of Paris from 1228 to 1249, would have been interested enough in the contents of a MS such as **T** to wish to acquire a copy for the library of the cathedral chapter in Paris and to add to it other legislative material. William is known to have visited the abbey of Prémontré in 1237 when statutory reform was taking place within the Praemonstratensian order and he had given the pallium to archbishop Maurice of Rouen in the cathedral of Rouen in 1231, the year when Maurice promulgated new canons; on both occasions, therefore, William had the opportunity to take an interest in the recent legislation issued for nuns at Prémontré and Rouen and found in **T** on fos. 93^{r}–94^{r}. Dalarun ('Nouveaux Aperçus', pp. 23–4) presents good palaeographical reasons for bringing back the date when **T** has generally been thought to have been copied. His hypothesis regarding William of Auvergne, however, rests on circumstantial arguments. There is no direct evidence that Ermengarde, abbess of the Paraclete from 1209 to 1248, sent to William the abbey's manuscript copy of the correspondence, or had another copy made for him, or that the presence of **T** in Paris was originally due to William or that he was responsible for the appearance of recent legislation in **T**.

A further hypothesis concerning the origins of **T** has been advanced more recently by McLaughlin with Wheeler, apparently without knowledge of Dalarun's work but building, as Dalarun also does, upon Benton's identification in **T** of two canons arising from the council of Rouen held in 1231. As Benton pointed out in his study of 'The Paraclete and the Council of Rouen of 1231', a possible explanation of the presence of these canons in **T** may lie in the fact that the abbess of the Paraclete from 1249, Marie Rigaud, was the brother of Eudes Rigaud, who was consecrated archbishop of Rouen in March 1248, and who visited the Paraclete in the following year on three occasions.[101] McLaughlin with Wheeler suggested that the

[101] 10–12 June, 28 Sept., and 7–8 Nov. 1249, with a further visit on 15–16 Jan. 1253, Eudes Rigaud, *Regestrum visitationum*, ed. Bonnin, pp. 39, 52, 53, 177; trans. Brown, pp. 42, 58, and 59 only (lacks the 1253 visit).

occasion for bringing together in a MS such as **T** a collection of documents on the regulation of religious houses of women may have been concerns about relationships between the houses of the order that had led to the establishment in 1247 of an enquiry by Pope Innocent IV. This is a possibility but, as they admitted, it is 'far from conclusive'.[102] As for **T** being in Paris in 1347, McLaughlin with Wheeler draw attention to the activities of a family from Sens who were book producers and traders in Paris from 1270 to *c.*1342. If one of the family had access to MSS at the Paraclete (as he is known to have had at a nearby monastery), the appearance of a copy of the correspondence from the Paraclete on the doorstep of the home of Jean de Meun or in the rue Saint-Jacques becomes imaginable.[103]

[102] McLaughlin with Wheeeler, Appendix 2, pp. 317–25, at 321. There are some mistakes in references given there to the *Cartulary of the Paraclete*. The relevant documents in chronological order are these:

no. 53. By 1147 (pp. 71–3). Letter from Hugh, archbishop of Sens, about the abbey of La Pommeraye. The first abbess, Gertrude, a nun of the Paraclete, was canonically elected at the Paraclete. Subsequent elections, following the custom of other churches, should be made at and from within the commuity of La Pommeraye whenever possible; otherwise from the Paraclete. The abbess of La Pommeraye should visit the Paraclete once a year and sit in chapter with the abbess of the Paraclete; the latter should also visit the former once a year and sit in chapter with her.

no. 26. 30 May 1247 (pp. 42–3). Pope Innocent IV appoints the cardinal bishop of Albano to investigate an appeal made by nuns in a priory of the Paraclete that they had the right to participate with the nuns of the Paraclete in the election of the abbess but admittance to the election had been refused.

no. 246. 11 June 1249 (pp. 222–4). Odo (or Eudes), archbishop of Rouen, following a visit to the Paraclete, reports the results of an audit made of the goods of the abbey by his sister M(arie) and others.

no. 251. 25 Mar. 1251 (p. 228). A letter from the prioress and convent of La Pommeraye, brought by five of the nuns to the abbess and convent of the Paraclete, to request that Agnes *de Pratis*, having been canonically elected as abbess of La Pommeraye, should take up her office.

no. 28. 25 Apr. 1254 (pp. 44–5). Pope Innocent IV to abbess Marie of the Paraclete agreeing to her request and that of her brother, the archbishop of Rouen, that, should she ever cease to be abbess, she could resume the place she had formerly as a nun and in which she had been succeeded by Agnes, later abbess of La Pommeraye.

no. 258. 24 Dec. 1255 (pp. 233–4). A letter sent by three officials of the church of Sens in which they adjudicate upon the division of opinion between the abbess and convent of the Paraclete on one hand and the prioresses and convents on the other over the claim made by the latter that they should participate in the election of an abbess with the nuns of the Paraclete on an equal basis. They declare that, whenever a vacancy occurs, each priory should send at its own expense seven nuns with their prioress to take part in the election of an abbess along with seven nuns of the Paraclete. The nuns sent by the priories shall be considered to be nuns of the Paraclete and should be admitted as such and with fraternal charity into the dormitory, refectory, chapter, choir, and elsewhere.

[103] McLaughlin with Wheeler, Appendix 2 at pp. 324–5. For this family from Sens, and the location of one of them in the rue Saint-Jacques, see Rouse and Rouse, 'The Book Trade

Whatever its actual provenance, **T** is unique among the surviving MSS of the letter collection and best among them reflects the history and aims of the founders and the foundation of the Paraclete, for **T** alone presents the entire collection with the full text of the *Rule*. The purposes for which other texts, both old and new, concerning the religious life of women were copied in **T** by the scribes who copied the letter collection remain unclear but they enhance the value of the codex as a collection of sources for the history of female monasticism.

Descriptions and further references. Monfrin, pp. 9–18, 57. *Catalogue général des manuscrits des Bibliothèques publiques des Départements*, in 4° (Paris, 1855), ii. 332–4. *The Paraclete Statutes*, ed. Waddell. Bibolet, '*Bibliotheca Pithoena*'. Dalarun, 'Nouveaux Aperçus'. McLaughlin with Wheeler, Appendix 2, pp. 317–25. *Checklist* no. 181.

Lost or Uncertainly Identified Manuscripts and Other Testimonies to the Letter Collection Prior to the First Printed Edition

These are listed according to the source of information or their possessor.

Buonaccorso

See below, *Jean de Montreuil.*

Chalon-sur-Saône, Benedictine priory of St Marcel, diocese of Chalon-sur-Saône (long before 1749)

Letters of Abelard and Heloise

Descriptions and further references. According to F. H. S. Delaulnaye, *Lettres d'Héloïse et d'Abailard* (Paris, 1796), i. 111, 'Les religieux de cette abbaye ont possédé longtemps une épaisse liasse de ses lettres et de celles d'Héloïse dont, à ce qu'il parait, ils ne fesaient pas un très-grand cas. Ils les avaient encore en 1749. A cette époque, un maître des comptes de Dole emprunta cette liasse aux religieux avec promesse de la rendre à leur première réquisition. Oncques depuis on n'en a entendu parler.' Abelard had left the abbey of Cluny to spend his last days as a sick man in this Cluniac priory, where he died.

at the University of Paris, ca. 1250–ca. 1350', in *Authentic Witnesses: Approaches to Medieval Texts and Manuscripts*, esp. pp. 282–93, and Rouse and Rouse, *Illiterati et uxorati: Manuscripts and their Makers*, i. 81–98.

Could this 'thick bundle' have been his personal file of his letters and of those of Heloise? *Checklist* no. 220.

Christine de Pisan

Christine de Pisan (1365–*c*.1429) seems to show knowledge of the Latin text of *Letter* 2, **10** when she accuses Pierre Col of being like Heloise, who would rather be Abelard's *meretrix* or whore than a queen: 'Tu ressanbles Helouye du Paraclet qui dist que mieux ameroit estre *meretrix* appellee de maistre Pierre Abalart que estre royne couronne'; *A Maistre Pierre Col* (2 Oct. 1402), ed. Hicks in *Le Débat sur le Roman de la Rose*, p. 146. Her *Livre de la Cité des Dames* (1405) shows similarities with *Letter* 6. But L. C. Brook is doubtful that she drew her knowledge of holy women directly from the *Letters*, 'Christine de Pisan, Heloise, and Abelard's holy women'.

Claude Fauchet

See below, *Vatican, Biblioteca apostolica Vaticana, Ottob. lat. 2537*.

Dijon, Bibliothèque municipale 525 (298) (Paris, c.1355/1362)

Letters 1–8.

A table of contents at the beginning of this Dijon MS lists *les Epistres Pierre Abaielart et de Heloyse, qui fu s'amie et puis sa feme, et sont en latin ii^{c}iiij*. This entry in the table is followed by summaries in French of each of the *Letters*, *Letter* 1 being in addition divided into twelve chapters. This table was reproduced by Omont in his 'Notice' (mentioned below), pp. 373–4 and its contents are included in the apparatus to the text of the *Letters* in the present edition. The codex once contained 258 fos. but this was before the loss in the 17th c. of thirty-seven fos. These fos. included the *Letters* on fos. 204–27 (fo. ii^{c}iiii onward in the medieval numbering) up to almost the end of *Letter* 7. The remainder of *Letter* 7 (the final lines only) and *Letter* 8, which were once in this MS as fos. ii^{c}xxviii and ii^{c}xxix, are now in *Paris, BnF n. acq. fr. 20001*, fos. 11–12^{v} (see above, pp. xlix–l). The other fos. remain lost.

The contents of the codex are mostly poems in old French beginning with the *Roman de la Rose*; the final item is an old French version of Boethius' *Consolation of Philosophy*. These contents have been described as 'an anthology built on the *Rose*' and 'not simply built up piecemeal' but for study as a whole with cross-references added by the scribe (Huot, *Romance of the Rose*, pp. 75,

79). The scribe was Mathias Rivalli, who wrote three colophons in this MS dated 1355, 1361, and 1362 and who also described himelf as a cleric from the diocese of Poitiers. Huot (*Romance of the Rose*, p. 79, Plate 6 on p. 80, and p. 83) has shown how, in the margins of his copy of the *Rose* where the story of Abelard and Heloise is told (*v.* 8729 onward), and also in his copy of other vernacular texts, Mathias gives references to specific passages in his copy of the *Letters*. It would seem that Mathias did not have access to the old French version of the *Letters* (for which see above, *Paris, BnF fr. 920*, at pp. xlvi–xlviii).

Former possessors. Jean de Cherchemont, bishop of Amiens (1325–73); see above p. xlix, Paris, BnF n. acq. fr. 20001. In the 16th c. Jehan Regnault at Dijon (inside the front binding: *Ce livre appartient a Jehan Regnault, demeurant a Dijon*; his signature follows. See *Catalogue des manuscrits portant des indications de date*, vi. 199). Not Robert de Billy (above p. lxxi).

Physical features. Copied by Mathias Rivalli (or Rival or Rivau) at the Parisian residence of Jean de Cherchemont.

Descriptions and further references. Above, pp. xlix–l. G. Paris, 'Notice du manuscrit de la bibliothèque de Dijon no. 298[2]', *Bulletin de la Société des anciens textes français*, i (1875), 44–9. H. Omont, 'Notice sur quelques feuillets retrouvés d'un manuscrit français de la bibliothèque de Dijon', *Romania*, xxxiv (1905), 364–74. C. Samaran and R. Marichal, *Catalogue des manuscrits en écriture latine portant des indications de date, de lieu ou de copiste*, vi (Paris, 1968), p. 199; Plates LVIII, LX. Bénédictins de Bouveret, *Colophons des manuscrits occidentaux des origines au XVIe siècle* (Spicilegium Friburgensis Subsidia, ii–vii; 6 vols.; Fribourg, 1965–82), iv. 185, no. 13551. Huot, *Romance of the Rose*, pp. 75–84. *Checklist* no. 224.

Étienne Gourmelon

Epistolae of Abelard and Heloise.

Former possessors. Philippe Desportes (1546–1606), the celebrated poet, abbot of the Benedictine abbey of Tiron, diocese of Chartres, obtained from Étienne Gourmelon a manuscript of the *Epistolae* that was used by d'Amboise and Duchesne in their 1616 edition. Étienne Gourmelon, a surgeon and professor at the Collège de France, was born in Finistère and died at Melun in 1593.

Descriptions and further references. Monfrin, p. 41, who excludes the possibility that this MS is **F** on the ground that **F** arrived at St-Germain-des-Prés over half a century before any of the MSS of Desportes. *Checklist* no. 223. Also see below, Duchesne–d'Amboise, p. cix.

Étienne Pasquier

Étienne Pasquier (1529–1615), lawyer, historian, and friend of both Claude Fauchet and Pierre Pithou (cf. p. lxxxii and lxxvi above), summarized *Letters* 1 and 2 and transcribed some passages in these letters from a MS of which he wrote: 'Il est tombé entre mes mains un livre de ses Epitres manuscrit' (col. 587A in the edition mentioned below). He published them in 1560, along with two lines taken from an *Epitaph* for Abelard (inc.: 'Petrus in hac petra . . .'; cf. pp. lxxii–lxxiii above), in *Les Recherches de la France revues et augmentées d'un livre et de plusieurs chapitres par le mesme autheur.* This work, which appears to be the first printed work to reproduce any of the writings of Abelard or Heloise, was widely read over several centuries. In it Pasquier communicated his fascination with the lives of Abelard ('un esprit fort universel') and Heloise ('extremement sage'). In writing *Les Recherches* Pasquier profited from the advice and work of Pierre Pithou;[104] it is possible that he gained his knowledge of Abelard and Heloise from the manuscript which belonged to the latter, particularly since it contains the *Epitaph* just mentioned. *Les Recherches*, the work of a lifetime written between 1557 and 1615, the first book being published in 1560, received its first complete edition in 1621. I have consulted the Amsterdam edition of 1723 (Étienne Pasquier, *Oeuvres complètes*, i); see especially book III, ch. 6, col. 181BD (*Letter* 1, **47–8**); book VI, ch. 17, cols. 587A–592C (*Sommaire de la vie de Pierre Abelard, & des amours de luy, & d'Heloïse*; with extracts from *Letters* 1 and 2); book IX, cols. 894D–895A, 895D, 896D, and 897A. At col. 895A Pasquier writes of Fulbert, Heloise's uncle according to *Letter* 1, **17**: *quelques-uns le disent père.*

Although Pithou's MS may have been consulted by Pasquier, Dorothy Thickett, in *Etienne Pasquier (1529–1615): The Versatile Barrister of Sixteenth-Century France* (London, 1979), p. 171, writes that Pasquier used MSS belonging to the abbey of St-Victor as well as to friends, and in a letter to me dated 14 October 1980, she wrote:

[104] Cf. Roudaut, 'Note sur Étienne Pasquier et Pierre Pithou'.

'Pasquier *could* have purchased a MS. as he & Fauchet often did & shared it. St Victor was the richest & most accessible library for scholars, despite what old Rabelais says . . . It was there that Pasquier, at the end of the 16th c(entury) studied the MS of the Rehabilitation Trial of Joan of Arc & he was allowed to have it at home nearby on le Quai de la Tournelle.' So Pasquier may have known the now lost St-Victor MS GGG 17 (pp. xcv–xcviii below), although it does not appear to have contained the *Epitaph* mentioned above. On the other hand, **A** or **B** may have been accessible to him in or near Paris. In citing *Letter* 1, **47** Pasquier writes 'perlustrauerat'; **A** has 'perlustrauerit' while other MSS have 'perlustrauit'. But in citing *Letter* 1, **59** he follows the reading found in **BRSDY**: 'facilius me ad sectam suam inclinari'. When he comes to Abelard's account of the foundation of the oratory of the Paraclete (col. 591A; *Letter* 1, **54**) Pasquier observes that *Paracletum* (consoler) is the opposite of *Paraclytum* (flatterer) and he refers to a recent case of a canon of Chartres, Maistre Jean Sabelat, who was suspended from saying Mass for following *l'ignorance du commun peuple* and *le commun usage* in using the word *Paraclit* instead of *Paraclet*. All the known medieval MSS of *Letter* 1 have *Paraclitum*; Pasquier, **FAmb** and the *Vulgate* have *Paracletum*. Finally, Pasquier quotes a humorous remark made about Abelard—*Remarque qui m'a semblé ne devoir estre oubliée*—by the 13th-c. civil lawyer Accursius, when commenting on the law *Quinque. Finium regund. C.*: 'Petrus Abellardus qui se jactavit quod ex qualibet, quantumcunque difficili littera traheret aliquem intellectum, hic dixit, Nescio.'

Pasquier was also a friend of André Duchesne, who, together with François d'Amboise, produced the first edition of the works of Abelard and Heloise in 1616 (below, pp. civ–cxi). Duchesne published in 1610 *La Jeunesse*, a collection of Pasquier's prose and verse which includes *Colloques d'amour* and twenty-four *Lettres amoureuses*, and in 1619 he helped to publish a posthumous edition of Pasquier's letters.[105] D'Amboise, in the *Praefatio apologetica* which he added to the 1616 edition of the works of Abelard and Heloise, also expressed his esteem for Pasquier, who had been his *praeceptor* and who had just died. He had, according to d'Amboise, written wonderfully about the couple—their loves, their moral qualities, and their admirable teaching.[106] According to D. R. Kelly, *Foundations of*

[105] *La Ieunesse d'Etienne Pasquier et sa suite* (Paris, 1610), with a preface by André du Chesne; *Les Lettres d'Etienne Pasquier* (2 vols., Paris, 1619).

[106] *PL* clxxviii. 97C–98A.

Modern Historical Scholarship: Language, Law and History in the French Renaissance (New York, 1970), ch. 10, Pasquier revised the conventional Italianate view of the revival of learning: good letters had made their appearance in France at least by the 12th c. in the persons of Abelard, Bernard of Clairvaux, Peter Comestor, and others, and Paris university was to be the model for others.

See also P. Boutellier, 'Un Historien du XVIe siècle, Etienne Pasquier', *Bibliothèque d'Humanisme et Renaissance*, vi (1945), 357–92. Monfrin, p. 50. *Checklist* no. 259.

Humfrey, Duke of Gloucester

epistolas Petri Abailardi secundo folio <u>*dicens uos*</u>

Date. Before 25 February 1444.

Former possessor. Humfrey, duke of Gloucester (1390–1447), youngest son of King Henry IV and youngest brother of King Henry V,who presented the MS to the University of Oxford. He gave at least 281 books to the University between 1439 and 1444. About sixteen of these are known to survive and have been identified so far, but 274 are listed in surviving indentures and this MS was part of the third donation made on 25 February 1444.

Descriptions and further references. The MS, which is not Oxford, Bodleian Library, Add. C 271 (on which see pp. xliv–xlvi above), is listed in an indenture between the Duke of Gloucester and the University of Oxford, ed. A. Sammut in *Unfredo, Duca di Gloucester e gli umanisti italiani* (Medioevo e umanesimo, xli; Padua, 1980), pp. 60–84, at 80; also in *Epistolae Academicae Oxonienses*, ed. H. Anstey (Oxford History Society Publications, xxxv–xxxvi; Oxford, 1898), i. 232–7, at 235: *'Epistolas' Petri Abaralardi secundo folio dicens*. *Checklist* no. 232. On the Duke and his books see R. M. Thomson, 'The Reception of the Italian Renaissance in Fifteenth-Century Oxford: The Evidence of Books and Book-Lists', *Italia medioevale e umanistica*, xlviii (2007), 59–75. *Duke Humfrey and English Humanism in the Fifteenth Century: Catalogue of an Exhibition held in the Bodleian Library Oxford* (Oxford, 1970).

Hyde abbey (Benedictine), Hampshire

Petrus Abellardus in epistolar. ad Helu(isam)

Former possessor. Hyde abbey. The MS is listed in the early sixteenth-century catalogue of the abbey.

Descriptions and further references. English Benedictine Libraries: The Shorter Catalogues, ed. R. Sharpe and others (Corpus of British Medieval Library Catalogues, iv; The British Library in association with the British Academy, 1996), B52.6 (at p. 259).

Jean de Dormans

Epistole P. Abailardi, in gallico, XL s. Seemingly, a French translation of some *Letters* of Abelard.

Former possessor. Jean de Dormans, bishop of Lisieux from 1359, bishop of Beauvais from 1360, cardinal from 1368; chancellor of France from 1358, 1361, and 1373; founder of the Collège de Dormans-Beauvais in Paris in 1370; d. 1373.

Descriptions and further references. L. Douët d'Arcq, *Inventaire de la bibliothèque du roi Charles VI* (Paris, 1867), p. 225. *Checklist* no. 225. On Jean de Dormans and his library see Kouamé, *Le Collège de Dormans-Beauvais*, pp. 496–9, and E. Pellegrin, 'La Bibliothèque de l'ancien collège de Dormans-Beauvais à Paris', *Bulletin philologique et historique (jusqu'à 1715) du Comité des travaux historiques et scientifiques*, Années 1944–1945 (1947), 99–164.

Jean Gerson

Jean Gerson (1363–1429), the celebrated Parisian master of theology, preacher, and chancellor, replying in 1402–3 to Pierre Col during the *querelle* over the *Roman de la Rose*, declared that he had tasted the *Letters* of Heloise and Abelard as a young man along with the writings of other dubious authors used in the *Roman*: 'Boecium, Ovidium, Therencium, Juvenalem, Alanum, et de Sancto Amore, Abaelardum cum sua Heloyde, Marcianum Capellam et si qui sunt alii', *Responsio ad Scripta cuiusdam*, ed. Hicks in *Le Débat sur le Roman de la Rose*, p. 172. In his *Traité contre le Roman de la Rose* (1402) Gerson described the *Letters* as no less dangerous than Ovid's *Art of Love* but the *Roman* was worse than these: 'Et que tele oeuvre soit pieur que celle d'Ovide, certes je le maintieng . . . sont translatés, assemblés et tirés come a violence et sans propos autres livres plusseurs, tant d'Ovide come des autres, qui ne sont point moins deshonnestes et perilleux (ainsy que sont les dis de Heloys et de Pierre Abelart et de Juvenal et des fables faintes—toute a ceste fin maudite—de Mars et Venus et de Vulcanus et de Pigmalion et de Adonis et autres)', ibid., pp. 76–7. See also Mews, 'Interpreting Abelard and Heloise in the fourteenth and early fifteenth centuries'.

Jean de Hesdin

Epistolae; *Apologia* of Berengar.

Former possessors. Unknown.

Descriptions and further references. Jean de Hesdin, a Hospitaller who was a regent master of theology in the University of Paris and who flourished in the 1360s and 1370s, read a copy of the *Letters* and of the *Apologia* of Berengar. In a lecture on Titus he wrote: . . . *aliqui sanam doctrinam predicanti aut docenti contradicunt per ignorantiam, invidiam, malitiam, arrogantiam. Primo per ignorantiam, sicut narrat Berengarius in apologia pro magistro Petro Abelardi* [sic] *quod in consilio senonensi prelati plures qui erant ibi dictis magistri Petri contradicebant magis ex ignorantia quam alia causa*. Also: . . . *ita fuit de Alebardo Petro* [sic] *quia, ut ipse dicit in principio epistolarum suarum, Anselmus decanus laudunensis contradicebat sibi ex invidia, quia plures scholares sequebantur eum et doctrinam suam*. See Smalley, 'Jean de Hesdin', pp. 292–4; repr. in Smalley, *Studies in Medieval Thought*, pp. 354–6.[107] I have slightly adjusted Smalley's edn. of these excerpts in the light of the Oxford MS, Balliol College 181. Smalley observed (pp. 318–19; repr. pp. 380–1) that Jean 'stood for medieval classical culture as opposed to early humanism . . . He remembered Abelard and Gilbert de la Porrée as fighters for freedom of debate in the schools.' Like the excerptors in Brugge, Stadsbibliotheek 398, and in Notre Dame, Indiana, University Memorial Library 30, like the copyists also of **AY** and the lost MSS of Paris, St-Victor GGG 17, and of Pico della Mirandola, and like the translator of **J**, Jean perhaps knew a MS of the 'Berengar type' which contained both the *Letters* and the writings of Berengar. *Checklist* no. 231.

Jean de Meun and Le Roman de la Rose

The second version of the *Le Roman de la Rose*, composed by Jean de Meun *c.*1275–80, reinforces a diatribe against marriage with the tale of Heloise's objections to marrying Abelard (ed. Lecoy, ii. *vv*. 8729–8802; ed. Langlois, iii, *vv*. 8759–8832). Jean studied in Paris *c.*1255

[107] Courtenay, *Parisian Scholars in the Early Fourteenth Century*, p. 77 suggests that he may be identical with Jean de Hadin, a member of the order of Hospitallers, who would have been a student in the faculty of theology in 1329.

and continued to live there until 1305. He knew the *Letters* and translated them into French. Here in the *Rose* he shows his knowledge of *Letters* 1 and 2. Heloise's arguments against marriage, as described by Abelard in *Letter* 1, **24–6**, are reproduced:

. . . argumenz a lui chastier
qu'il se gardast de marier,
e li provoit par escritures
e par resons que trop sont dures
condicions de mariage . . ..
(Lecoy, *vv.* 8737–41; Langlois, *vv.* 8767–71).

Especially close to the text of *Letter* 2, **10**, is the protestation by Heloise that she would rather be Abelard's mistress than his wife:

'Se li empereres de Rome,
souz cui doivent estre tuit home,
me daignet volair prendre a fame
e fere moi du monde dame,
si vodroie je mieuz, fet ele,
et Dieu a tesmoign en apele,
estre ta putain apelee
que empereriz coronee.'
(Lecoy, *vv.* 8787–94; Langlois, *vv.* 8817–24).

No French text was more widely read and cited during the late Middle Ages than the *Rose*, which gave rise to widespread debate and diverse interpretations concerning love and marriage. In a reworking of the poem *c.*1290, a Picard cleric, Gui de Mori, proposed the deletion of the story of Abelard and Heloise, but it survived in the known copies (see Huot, *Romance of the Rose*, p. 105). In the 14th c. in the *Livre de Leesce* Jehan le Fèvre countered the misogamy shown in the *Lamentations* of Matheolus (late 13th c.) by turning to the story in the *Rose* and by commending Abelard as 'sages et bien araisonnés' for giving Heloise the chance to live 'chastement' at the Paraclete (ed. Van Hamel, ii. 88, *vv.* 2785–94, and see p. 250).The poet Geoffrey Chaucer (1340/45–1400) translated part of the *Rose* into English and Heloise appears in his *Canterbury Tales*. In the prologue to the *The Wife of Bath's Tale* the wife of Bath tells how she had exchanged blows with Jankin, her fifth husband ('som-tyme . . . a clerk of Oxenford', *l.* 527), and burnt the 'book of wikked wyves' which so amused him and in which Jerome's *Against Jovinian* was found along with other books and many stories, including the story of 'Helowys,

That was abbesse nat fer fro Parys' (*ll.* 677–8). See Mann, *Feminizing Chaucer*, pp. 41–5; Wilson and Makowski, *Wykked Wyves*, pp. 151–60.

Jean de Meun's translation of the *Letters* into French

Around the year 1302, in the letter he wrote dedicating to King Philip the Fair his translation of Boethius's *Consolation of Philosophy*, Jean counted *la Vie et les Epistres Pierres Abaelart et Heloys sa fame* among the works he had translated from Latin into French.[108] Doubts have been expressed, however, about Jean being the translator of the old French version found in Paris, BnF fr. 920 (above, pp. xlvi–xlviii).

Jean de Montreuil

Epistolae Petri Abaialardi

Former possessors. On 2 July 1395 Coluccio Salutati (1331–1406), chancellor of Florence from 1375 to 1406, asked Jean de Montreuil (1354–1418), secretary to King Charles VI of France, if he could provide a correct and old copy of the *Letters* for they are exceptionally charming: 'Interim te rogatum velim quod epistolas Petri Abaialardi, si non habes, inquiri facias et ex tuis vel repertis studeas meo nomine quanto correctius poterit exemplari, sed si de antiqua littera haberi possent, libentius acciperem; nulle quidem littere sunt meis oculis gratiores.' This request was met and in the following year on 14 July 1396 Salutati wrote again to Jean de Montreuil to ask him to send a copy of the *Letters* to Buonaccorso Pitti (1354–*c*.1430), the Florentine merchant and author of the *Cronica* (1412–30). Salutati expressed his joy that Abelard's name was becoming well known again in France and in Italy too: 'Epistolas optatas Abaialardi Bonaccurso tradas; gaudeoque nomen eius, quod nesciebatur in Gallia, tibi forte et multis aliis renovasse, quod Italis etiam tradam'; *Epistolario di Coluccio Salutati*, ed. F. Novati (Fonti per la Storia d'Italia; 4 vols.; Rome, 1891–1911), iii, letters 8 and 20 at pp. 76 and 146. Like his friend Gontier Col (above, pp. xlvi–xlviii), Jean de Montreuil campaigned in favour of the *Roman de la Rose*.

Descriptions and further references. Monfrin, p. 50. *Checklist* no. 244. E. Hicks and E. Ornato, 'Jean de Montreuil et le débat sur le *Roman de la Rose*', *Romania*, cxcviii (1977), 34–64, 186–219. I have not seen

[108] Ed. in V. L. Dédeck-Héry, 'Boethius' *De Consolatione* par Jean de Meun', *Mediaeval Studies* 14 (1952), pp. 165–275, at 168.

L. Mirot, *Bonacurso Pitti, aventurier, joueur, diplomate et mémorialiste* (Paris, 1932).

Nanneticus

In the *Praefatio apologetica* which François d'Amboise (1550–1619) provided in the **Amb** version of Duchesne–d'Amboise (on which see below, pp. civ–cxi), he wrote that he had collected MSS of the writings of Abelard and Heloise in various provinces, one of which was a copy of the *Letters* which he obtained from Nantes in Brittany. Possibly he did so when , in his early thirties, he was a Conseiller to the Parlement de Bretagne (1583–5), which then met in Rennes twice a year.[109] Duchesne–d'Amboise used it for their edition of the *Letters* and the *Rule*, at the end of which they noted its extent: *Huc usque Nanneticum exemplar . . .* (*PL* clxxviii. 313). Monfrin, pp. 39–40, thought that *Nanneticus* is **E**—Paris, BnF lat. 2545. He based his view on the fact that Cousin, i. 2, saw the name of François d'Amboise in **E**: although Cousin in fact wrote 2544, this must be a slip because MS lat. 2544 (unlike *Nanneticus*) does not contain the *Rule*. The name is not found in MS lat. 2545 today but it could well have been there before the MS acquired its present binding and perhaps before it suffered the loss of its former cover or flyleaves and *ex libris*. For further reasons for identifying *Nanneticus* with **E** see below, p. cxxiv.

Nicolas de Baye

(1) 'Les epistres Pierre Abalart, en papier, commençans ou iie fueillet *ulterius*, prisiées ii s'. (*ulterius*: *Letter* 1, 8).

(2) 'Les Epistres de Pierre Abalard et viii cayers de luy mesmes, tenans ensemble, le premier commençant *tripartite*, prisié xiii s'. Perhaps *Letters* 1–8 with a quire of 8 leaves containing the *Rule* which begins *Tripartitum*.

Other manuscripts in the possession of Nicolas de Baye included:

(3) 'La Exortacion Pierre Abalard, avec aultres traictiez, commençans ou iie fueillet *cum utreque*, prisié x s'. Unspecified works together with (probably) *Exhortatio ad fratres et commonachos*, which is mentioned in Abelard's *Soliloquy* (ed. Burnett in 'Peter Abelard "*Soliloquium*"', pp. 888–9; *PL* clxxviii. 1877D–1878A) but which is now lost.

[109] 'quotquot exemplaria nancisci potui in variis provinciis . . . Itaque unum exemplar epistolarum nactus sum in Armorica, in qua juvenis prima auspicia coepi laticlavii et meae senatoriae dignitatis' (*PL* clxxviii. 75D).

(4) 'xx cayers en parchemin, contenans les sermons Pierre Abalart, prisiez xxiiii s.' *Sermons.*

(5)'les Sermons Pierre Abalard, sans ays, commençans ou iie fueillet *non esset*, prisié ii s'. *Sermons* (*non esset*: *Sermon* 1, *PL* clxxviii. 382B).

Nicolas de Baye (*c.*1364–9 May 1419), first called Colecon le Crantinat, greffier (clerk) of the Parlement de Paris from 1400, canon of the cathedral of Notre Dame, Paris, from 1414. A contemporary of Gontier Col. An inventory of his extensive collection of books is printed by A. Tuetey, *Journal de Nicolas de Baye, greffier du parlement de Paris 1400–1417* (2 vols.; Société de l'histoire de France; Paris, 1888), ii, pp. lxxvii–xcvii: (1) no. 136, p. xci, (2) no. 181, p. xcv, (3) no. 179, p. xcv, (4) no. 121, p. xc, (5) no. 184, p. xcv. (1) was *laissé à Longchamp*; the name of *M. Dreue, doyen* appears in the inventory at (2), (3), (4), and (5). *Checklist* no. 212.

No surviving MS fits the details given in the *Journal* for either copy of the *Letters.*

Nicolas Camuzat

In his *Promptuarium sacrarum antiquitatum Tricassinae dioecesis* (Troyes, 1610) Nicolas Camuzat (1575–1665), canon of Troyes, offered some notes and printed some pieces relating to the abbey of the Paraclete:

fo. 345^{v}: *Historica narratio de prima institutione coenobij Sanctimonialium Paracleti ord. S. Benedicti in Tricassina dioecesi.*

(1) fo. 345^{v}, a brief extract from *Letter* 1, **52**, describing Abelard's removal to a place of solitude in the countryside near Troyes, followed by his students. Some readings are:

> *calamis* (*reeds*) as in **E**, **F** where it is added as a variant in the margin, **Y**, and **Amb**. Not *callis* (*skins*) as in **TCBRD**; *cannis* **A** on the third attempt; deleted in **F**.
>
> *primo* as in **ACEFRDY**. Not *primum* as in **TBAmb**.
>
> *pulmo*, not *culmo*; *vero*, not *vere*; om. *sibi*. These variants are not attested in the MSS or **Amb**.

Too short an extract to show conclusively which MS source was used, but the first variant suggests that Camuzat may have seen a MS similar to **E** or **F**.

(2) fo. 346^{r+v}, a note on the the celebration in Camuzat's time of

the divine office in the Paraclete on the feast of Pentecost, *Graecanico idiomate* (sic);

(3) fos. 346^{v}–347, the bull of Pope Innocent II confirming at Auxerre on 28 November 1131 the foundation of the abbey of the Paraclete. *Checklist* no. 416.

(4) fos. 347^{v}–348, charter of Hugh of Toucy, archbishop of Sens (1142–68), noting, for the purpose of the election of an abbess, that the abbey of La Pommeraye is within the order of the Paraclete. Duchesne–d'Amboise, pp. 355–6 (no. 11); *PL* clxxviii. 1847–8; *Cartulary of the Paraclete*, ed. Lalore, pp. 71–3. See *The Paraclete Statutes*, ed. Waddell, pp. 38–9. *Checklist* no. 434.

fo. 348: *Excerpta ex M.S. Codice obituum coenobij Paracletici*

(5) fo. 348, *Epitaphium Abailardi*, '*Petrus in hac petra latitat . . .*'. See **T** above, pp. lxxii–lxxiii.

(6) fo. 348^{r+v}, Absolution by Peter the Venerable of Abelard, '*Ego Petrus Cluniacensis . . .*'. See **T** above, p. lxxiii.

(7) fo. 348^{v}, *Epitaphium Heloissae*, '*Hoc tumulo abatissa iacet prudens Heloysa . . .*'. See **T** above, p. lxxiii.

(8) fo. 348^{v}, excerpts from the same book (*Ex eodem libro ad. 21. Aprilis*) on the removal of the remains of Abelard and of Heloise in May 1497 (*Ex eod. Lib. ad diem 16. Maij.*)

On the necrologies of the Paraclete and their use by Camuzat and by Duchesne–d'Amboise see Mews, 'La Bibliothèque du Paraclet', pp. 52–4.

(9) fo. 349, a list of five daughter houses of the abbey of the Paraclete.

Camuzat made a list of MSS of the abbey of Clairvaux between 1617 and 1640. He is likely have communicated to Duchesne a copy of *Letter* 10 from a Clairvaux MS (see above, p. lx, *Paris, BnF lat. 13057*). Camuzat also seems to have communicated to Duchesne a Clairvaux MS containing a part of a *Disputatio* against the teachings of Abelard (now known to have been written by Thomas of Morigny) in which are found extracts from Abelard's *Apologia contra Bernardum*. (This *Apologia* is not *Letter* 10.) The evidence is a note by Duchesne in this MS, now Budapest, Országos Széchényi könyvtár, Széchényi 16 (1053 Q. Lat.), fo. 71^{v} (copied by Häring, 'Thomas of Morigny, *Disputatio*', p. 306): *ce liure m'a esté envoyé en don par Mr. Camuzat Chanoine de Troyes 1609, au treys(?) du Januier*. A note in Duchesne–d'Amboise on p. 1194 confirms this: *habeo nunc ipsissimum exemplar dono viri docti et humani Nicolai Camusatij Canonici Ecclesiae Trecensis* . . . See for this and other examples of close collaboration between Camuzat and Duchesne, Häring, 'The writings against Gilbert of Poitiers by Geoffrey of Auxerre', pp. 22–8, and *Petri Abaelardi Opera Theologica*, ed. Buytaert, i. 345–50 (on the Budapest MS) and 359–68 (edn. of the *Apologia* with the extracts found in the *Disputatio*). *Disputatio* ed. from the Budapest MS most recently by Häring, 'Thomas of Morigny, *Disputatio*'; on the Budapest MS see here pp. 302–10. *Checklist* nos. 24, 268, 396.

Papire Masson

Letters of Abelard and Heloise

Former possessor. Papire (or Jean-Papire) Masson (1544–1611), the author of the *Annalium libri quatuor* (Paris, 1577). Duchesne (below, p. cx) mentioned Masson as the provider of a manuscript of the *Letters* which he used in the edition of 1616. The MS has not been identified and the account that Masson gave of Abelard's life in the *Annales* was based on other sources. These sources include Otto of Freising, Petrarch, *Letters* of Bernard of Clairvaux and Pope Innocent II, the correspondence of Peter the Venerable with Pope Innocent II and Heloise, the preface to Abelard's collection of *Sermons*,[110] an epitaph, and the *Chronicle* of the abbey of Morigny. This is a relatively long survey of Abelard's life: it amounts to nearly half of Masson's account of the reign of King Louis VII. D'Amboise summarizes it in his *Praefatio apologetica* in the edition of 1616 (reproduced in *PL* clxxviii. 95D–96A) but with no mention of any manuscript of the *Letters* either here or in his list of those who supplied him with MSS (*PL* clxxviii. 75–6).[111]

[110] For this Masson (*Annalium*, book 3, pp. 259–60) used a MS from the Sorbonne which may or may not be the one seen by Duchesne and which may or may not also be one of the manuscripts bequeathed to the Sorbonne in 1500 by Jean l'Huillier (*c.*1420–1500) who was a professor at the Sorbonne before becoming bishop of Meaux in 1483. His will, dated 19 July 1500, was printed by L. Thuasne, 'Jean l'Huillier, évêque de Meaux et la bibliothèque du collège de Sorbonne', *Revue des bibliothèques*, vii (1897), 126–39 at 131–9. The relevant entry in the will (p. 136) is this: 'Item aliud volumen Petri Abaelardi in quo continentur sermones ad virgines Paraclitenses et alia quaedam.' See *I sermoni di Abelardo per le monache del Paracleto*, ed. De Santis, pp. 35–6, 85–6.

[111] One of the histories included by d'Amboise in his survey in the *Praefatio apologetica* of printed sources for the life of Abelard is *L'Histoire de France* by Bernard de Girard, Seigneur d'Haillan, Historiographe de France (*PL* clxxviii. 84AB), whom d'Amboise calls a great friend, now dead but formerly abbot *in commendam* of the monastery of St-Gildas de Rhuys in Brittany, where Abelard himself had been abbot. The first edition appeared in

Descriptions and further references. Papirii Massoni Annalium Libri Quatuor (Paris, 1577), book 3, pp. 255–61 (the account of the reign of King Louis VII is found on pp. 253–67). Duchesne–d'Amboise, *Praefatio ad lectorem* (*Du*, last page; reproduced by Monfrin, p. 41, n. 82). Duchesne–d'Amboise, *Praefatio apologetica* (*Amb*, reproduced in *PL* clxxviii. 95D–96A). P. Ronzy, *Un Humaniste italianisant: Papire Masson 1544–1611* and *Bibliographie critique des oeuvres imprimées et manuscrites de Papire Masson 1544–1611* (Bibliothèque de l'Institut français de Naples, Series i, vols. i–ii; Paris, 1924). Monfrin, p. 42. *Checklist* no. 239.

Paraclete, convent of the

Letters 1–8, *Rule*, and *Institutiones nostre*.

Former possessor. The abbey of the Paraclete.

Descriptions and further references. Seen by d'Amboise on a visit to the Paraclete in or after 1593 and used by Duchesne–d'Amboise for their edition (1616). Monfrin, pp. 15–18 suggested that the Paraclete and the other convents belonging to this order of nuns possessed copies of the letter collection and of regulations for the nuns of the order. Unlike Monfrin, Mews, 'La Bibliothèque du Paraclet', pp. 39–46, favours the identification of the Paraclete copy with **T**. See above, pp. lxxvii–lxxxi and below, pp. cix–cx, cxxiii–cxxiv. *Checklist* no. 248.

V Paris, Abbey of St-Victor GGG 17

Letters 1–8 with the *Rule* (short version).

The contents and folio numbers are given in the early 16th-c. catalogue of Claude de Grandrue: *Epistole Petri Abaelardi. Prima 2. secunda 15. tercia 19. quarta in qua ejus regula pro monialibus de Paraclito 28. Item epistule Eloysse abbatisse de Paraclito ad Petrum Abaelardi prima 13. secunda 17. tercia 23. Item epistola cujusdam ad Petrum Abaelardi 49. Item quedam sancti Bernardi et quorumdam aliorum contra dicta magistri Petri Abaelardi 51. Epistula Petri Abaelardi contra calumnias quorundam capitulorum sibi objectorum 54 . . .*

Paris in 1576. D'Amboise noted that this history gives a full account of the relationship between Abelard and Heloise. Girard makes no direct reference to their correspondence but he clearly draws upon the narrative found in *Letter* 1 (*L'Histoire*, pp. 426–7). He also gives an account of Abelard's condemnation for erroneous teachings at the council of Sens in 1140 or 1141 which reports errors not found in any of the other sources known to me.

Apologia Berengarii contra beatum Bernardum Clarevallensem et alios qui condemnaverunt Petrum Abaelardum 319.

What Grandrue calls Abelard's fourth *Letter* seems to occupy twenty-two folios. Comparison with the space occupied by the other *Letters* suggsts that it comprises *Letters* 7, 8, and the *Rule*. There follows the *Letter* of (presumably) Fulk of Deuil, various *Letters* of Bernard of Clairvaux and others against Abelard, Abelard's *Confession of faith 'Vniuersis'*, and then (separated by over 250 folios) the *Apologia* of Berengar.

Other authors listed by Grandrue and represented in this codex include St Augustine, Gerson, and Petrarch.

Former possessor. Simon de Plumetot (1371–1443), a lawyer and the possessor of an extensive library who had studied at the abbey of St-Victor and became chancellor of the chapter of Bayeux, perhaps had a copy of the *Letters* which went to the library of the abbey of St-Victor. On this possibility see Ouy, 'Simon de Plumetot', p. 381 and also p. 358*inf.* Plumetot is known to have copied, and to have given to the abbey of St-Victor, Abelard's *Theologia 'Scholarium'* (now Paris, BnF lat. 14793) and to have possessed a copy of the *Problemata Heloissae* and of *Letter* 9 (now Paris, BnF lat. 14511), which he also gave to St-Victor *c.*1440. See *Checklist* nos. 149 and 146 and Ouy, 'Simon de Plumetot', p. 377 and plate 54a.

Duchesne (Duchesne–d'Amboise, below, p. cx) wrote that he used a Victorine MS for the 1616 edition and he indicated that this MS contained all the *Letters* and the *Rule*. A 17th-c. note added to the catalogue of the library of St-Victor made in 1514 by Claude de Grandrue (d. 1520) states that fos. 1–57 were taken away from MS GGG 17 before Jean Picard examined the MS in 1604 (Monfrin, p. 43; fos. 2–55 according to Ouy and Gerz von Büren, *Le Catalogue de la bibliothèque de l'abbaye de Saint-Victor*, p. 346). Monfrin, p. 43, wondered whether the note was mistaken because it was written more than twelve years before the 1616 edition appeared. On the other hand, Léopold Delisle thought that the management of the abbey library was very lax[112] and d'Amboise seems to have been in the habit

[112] 'Les chanoines de Saint-Victor avaient ouvert leur bibliothèque à différents savants . . . Le plus souvent on enlevait des manuscrits tout entiers; mais quelquefois des amateurs délicats se bornaient à arracher dans un volume les cahiers qui renfermaient les meilleurs morceaux'; Delisle, *Le Cabinet des manuscrits*, ii. 231. See more fully on such losses Ouy, *Les Manuscrits de l'abbaye de Saint-Victor*, pp. 30–4; also for Pasquier, p. lxxxv above.

of taking MSS away from their owners.[113] Moreover, as Monfrin imdicated more than once (pp. 35, 39 nn. 73–4, 41 nn. 79, 82), d'Amboise had planned his edition many years earlier (*jampridem*)[114] and wrote that the *Letters* were printed from his MSS.[115]

Apart from the inclusion of Berengar's *Apologia* (much later, on fo. 319) the items relating to Abelard and Heloise resemble those in **CE**, especially **E**. As the folios said to have been removed from **V** before 1604 were fos. 1–57 (fos. 2–55 according to Ouy and Gerz von Büren, *Le Catalogue de la bibliothèque de l'abbaye de Saint-Victor*, p. 346), and as the Abelard/Heloise material in **E**—the only material in this 15th-c. MS—fills fos. 1–57^{v}; the question arises whether **E** is the missing part of **V**. In both MSS *Letter* 2 is entitled the first *Letter* of Heloise and in both MSS the genitive case is used for Abelard's name (*petrus abaelardi*). **E** is a paper, not a parchment, MS; most of **V** was also paper (Ouy and Gerz von Büren, *Le Catalogue de la bibliothèque de l'abbaye de Saint-Victor*, pp. xxxvii–xxxviii). **E** could also have been written in the early 15th c., before the death of Simon de Plumetot in 1443. However, there are differences between the foliation of **E** and **V** which suggest that, while similar, they may not be identical. In **E** and in **V** *Letter* 1 begins on fos. 1 and 2 respectively, 2 on 14 and 13, 3 on 17 and 15, 4 on 19 and 17, 5 on 22 and 19, 6 on 27 and 23, 7 on 32 and 28, 8 and the *Rule* on 40 and on an unspecified folio in **V**, the *Letter* from Fulk (presumably in both MSS) on 54 and 49, *Letters* from Bernard and others on 55v and 51, and the *Confession of faith* on 56v and 54. Since the letter from Fulk starts in **E** twenty-two folios after the start of *Letter* 7 and (it would appear) in **V** twenty-one folios after the start of *Letter* 7, it would seem that **V** like **E** had the shortened version of the *Rule*.

Burnett in 'Peter Abelard, *Confessio fidei "Universis"*', pp. 122–3, notes that this lost MS, like **AYJ**, would have contained, as well as the *Confession of faith 'Vniuersis'*, the *Confession of faith to Heloise* which is known from the copy provided by Berengar in his *Apologia*. Other

[113] D'Amboise seems to have gathered in, sought out, obtained, or received some of the other MSS he needed to use (*collegerim*, *conquisierim*, *nancisci*, *nactus sum*, *michi communicavit*, *ex Filippo Porteo*, *ex monasterio Paracletensi*, etc.), and some have also thought that he did not return the Paraclete MS (see **T** above, pp. lxxviii–lxxix).

[114] D'Amboise recalled in his *Praefatio apologetica* (reproduced in *PL* clxxviii. 75D) his acquisition in his youth of a copy of the correspondence in Brittany; see above, p. xci. He obtained another copy from Philippe Desportes, who had died in 1606 (*PL* clxxviii. 75D).

[115] See the title page of **Amb**, below p. cv.

features that Burnett finds in the 'Berengar tradition' (see **A** above, p. lviii) are not found in this collection.

Descriptions and further references. Catalogue of Claude de Grandrue, 1514 (Paris, BnF lat. 14767, fo. 209^{r-v}), ed. Ouy and Gerz von Büren, *Le Catalogue de la bibliothèque de l'abbaye de Saint-Victor*, pp. 345–6. On Simon's collection of MSS: Ouy, *Les Manuscrits de l'abbaye de Saint-Victor*, pp. 15–19. Monfrin, pp. 42–3. Thomson, 'The satirical works of Berengar of Poitiers', p. 108. *Checklist* no. 256.

Philippe Desportes, abbot of Tiron

See Étienne Gourmelon.

Pico della Mirandola(?)

P(apirus) Berengarii Apologia is listed in a 16th-c. inventory of the library of Giovanni Pico della Mirandola (1463–94). It may be the same MS which is listed in the 1498 inventory of Pico's library made by Antonio Pizzamano, apostolic protonotary, for Cardinal Domenico Grimani (d. 1523), who bought the library in the same year. The 1498 inventory survives in a MS in Modena where the first part of the description is unreadable but it ends: . . . *Abelardi ms in pap(iro)*. If so, this would suggest that Pico possessed a paper copy of the *Letters* which (like **AY** and the lost MS Paris, St-Victor GGG 17 (above, pp. xcvi–xcviii)), included the *Apologia* of Berengar. On the fate of Grimani's library see Kibre, pp. 20–1.

P. Kibre, *The Library of Pico della Mirandola* (New York 1936), p. 149, item 207 in the 16th-c. inventory contained in Vatican Library lat. 3436. F. Calori Cesis, *Giovanni Pico della Mirandola* (Mirandola, 1897), p. 36, from the 1498 inventory in the partially illegible Modena MS.

Poems in the Orleans MS, Bibliothèque municipale 284 (238), p. 183

Affinities and correspondences have been found between expressions used, and events alluded to, in the *Letters* and in two poems copied in the late 12th/early 13th c. in the Orleans MS, Bibliothèque municipale 284 (238), p. 183, and written before, probably much before, the death of Heloise in 1163. The poet perhaps knew Abelard and Heloise personally and shared their thoughts, or he had read some of their *Letters*. He knew of Heloise's unwillingness to take the veil and of Abelard's castration. The two poems open with the words 'Parisius Petrus est velata matre profectus' and 'Ornavere due te quondam, Gallia, gemme'.

Dronke, *Abelard and Heloise in Medieval Testimonies*, pp. 19–21; edn., pp. 45–8; repr. *Intellectuals and Poets*, pp. 262–5; edn. pp. 280–4; Benton in *Abaelardiana*, i, pp. 273–6; Dronke, ed. in *Abaelardiana*, ii, pp. 278–9.

Richard de Bazoques

Abaelardus, Ad Heloyssam

Former possessors. Unknown.

Descriptions and further references. Between 1392/3 and 1408 or later Richard de Bazoques (b. 1360) made a list of the books he possessed or had read (*Memoria librorum quos . . . studui*). It is encyclopedic. One title listed (no. 109) is *Abaelardus, Ad Heloyssam*. Another is the very popular *Roman de la Rose* (no. 128). Richard had become head of a school in Conches in Normandy before studying in the faculty of theology in the University of Paris. His *reportationes* of lectures given to him there by master Pierre Plaoul in 1392/3 survive in Paris, BnF lat. 3074. He also became a schoolmaster in Évreux in Normandy (*fl.* 1406–13). In addition to his *Memoria* he wrote a short treatise on counterpoint (*Tractatus de concordanciis cantus*) and copied texts which survive in Paris, BnF lat. 2994; they include a work by Isidore of Seville and another by St Augustine. He became a priest in 1413 at the age of 52.

J. Bignami-Odier and A.Vernet, 'Les Livres de Richard de Bazoques', *Bibliothèque de l'École des Chartes*, cx (1952), 124–53, at p. 148, no. 109; reprinted in Vernet, 'Études médiévales', p. 524. E.-A. Van Moë, 'Richard de Bazoques, maître d'école à Évreux au début du xve siècle', *Bibliothèque de l'École des Chartes*, xcix (1938), 423–4. P. Glorieux, 'L'Année universitaire 1392–1393 à la Sorbonne à travers les notes d'un étudiant', *Revue des sciences religieuses*, xix (1939), 429–82. *Checklist* no. 213. K. Busby, *Codex and Context: Reading Old French Verse Narrative in Manuscript* (2 vols.; Faux titre, ccxxii; Amsterdam, 2002), ii. 740.

Rogier Benoîton

Epistole Petri Abahelardi

Former possessors. Maître Rogier Benoîton (d. before 24 June 1481), canon of Bourges, Chartres, and Clermont. From at least 1436 until

1444, secretary to Martin Gouge de Charpaigne, bishop of Clermont (1415–44); Martin Gouge was well connected to the circle of Parisian humanists in the early years of the 15th c. Then secretary to Jacques de Comborn, bishop of Clermont (1444–75), Benoîton was also a royal notary-secretary from at least 1441.

Descriptions and further references. The account book of Roger Benoîton includes a catalogue of his very well-stocked and varied library drawn up in November 1470 (Archives départementales du Puy-de-Dôme, Registres, première sér.; Étiquettes jaunes, liasses 30, c. 1, fos. 96–9). See A. Bossuat, 'Jacques de Comborn, évêque de Clermont, et son secrétaire: Notes sur l'humanisme en Auvergne au xve siècle', in *Recueil de travaux offerts à M. Clovis Brunel* (Mémoires et documents publiés par la Société de l'École des Chartes; 2 vols.; Paris, 1955), i. 152–73, at 155–6. The catalogue of 261 manuscripts and incunabula has been printed by A.-M. Chagny-Sève and G. Hasenohr, 'En Auvergne au xve siècle: Le chanoine Roger Benoîton et ses livres', in Nebbiai-Dalla Guarda and Genest, eds., *Du copiste au collectionneur. Mélanges . . . André Vernet*, pp. 412–66, esp. pp. 442–50. The letters of Abelard appear in a section of the catalogue dedicated to works of rhetoric and poetry. Other collections of letters and also a *dictamen* are grouped together within this section, chosen no doubt as examples of fine writing; Abelard's letters (no. 72, p. 444) follow the letters of Peter of Blois (1130/5–1211/12) and are followed by the letters of Nicolas de Clamanges (d. 1437), one of the early French humanists and an admirer of Petrarch. *Checklist* no. 216.

Simon de Plumetot

See above, p. xcvi, *Paris, Abbey of St-Victor GGG 17*.

Vatican, Biblioteca Apostolica Vaticana, Ottob. lat. 2537, fos. 139–44

Vie de Pierre Abellard extraicte de ses espitres: a detailed résumé made by the historian Claude Fauchet (1530–?1602) in French from an unnamed manuscript of *Letter* 1 with notes on *Letters* 2–6. Fauchet does not rely on the old French translation (above, pp. xlvi–xlvii, Paris, BnF fr. 920). He gives in Latin the salutation at the head of *Letter* 2 but the MS he used is not known. Ed. J. G. Espiner-Scott in *Documents concernant la vie et les oeuvres de Claude Fauchet* (Paris, 1938), pp. 180–8. Monfrin, p. 51. *Checklist* no. 227.

Rejected Manuscripts

British Library, Royal 8. F. XV

Contents. Fos. 1–2^{v}, *Capitula haeresum XIV*; fos. 2^{v}–7^{v}, Bernard of Clairvaux, *Letter* 190; fos. 40^{v}–43^{v}, Bernard of Clairvaux, *Letters*, among which are *Letters* 188, 338, 337, 189, 194.

Former possessors. Byland abbey (O.Cist.), diocese of York; Henry Savile (A. G. Watson, *The Manuscripts of Henry Savile of Banke* (London 1969), p. 18); John Theyer (fo. 1; *c.*1597–1673), then Charles Theyer his grandson (*b.* 1651); Robert Scott, bookseller, who sold the Theyer collection of around 800 MSS. 312 of the MSS were bought by King Charles II (1660–85). A catalogue of the royal purchases was made by Scott and by William Beveridge, later bishop of St Asaph, and William Jane in 1678 (*British Library, Royal MSS, appendix 70*).

Descriptions and further references. E. Bernard, *Catalogi Librorum Manuscriptorum Angliae et Hiberniae* (Oxford, 1697), ii. 199, no. 6434.64. Bernard stated that this MS contains the *Capitula* and *Letters* of Abelard: *Capitula Petri Abaelardi et Epistolae eius.* This misled Casimir Oudin, *Commentarius de scriptoribus ecclesiae antiquis illorumque scriptis tam impressis quam manuscriptis . . . ad annum 1460* (Frankfurt and Leipzig, 1722), ii, col. 1171. G. F. Warner and J. R. Gilson, *Catalogue of Western Manuscripts in the Old Royal and King's Collections* (London, 1921), i. 272; Häring, 'Die vierzehn *capitula heresum*', pp. 37–8; H. Rochais and E. Manning, *Bibliographie générale de l'ordre cistercien: Saint Bernard* (La documentation cistercienne, xxi; Rochefort, 1979–82), no. 4019. *Checklist* no. 67. See also *Rawlinson's edition, 1718* (pp. cxi–cxii below).

British Library, Royal 16. F. II, fos. 137–187^{v}

Heloise, Art d'amour.

Despite the explicit on fo. 187^{v} (*Cy finent les epistres de l'abesse Heloys du Paraclit, laquelle abaye maistre Pierre Abaielart fonda ainçois qu'il mourust*), this 15th- or 14th-c. treatise on love is an anonymous forgery written in French and based on Andreas Capellanus, *De amore*, book 1, but showing some familiarity with the correspondence of Abelard and Heloise. Heloise is referred to sixty-two times. Probably copied in England *c.*1480 and richly illuminated; at Richmond Palace in 1535. Ed. L. C. Brook in *Two Late Medieval*

Love Treatises (Medium Aevum Monographs, NS xvi; 1993), pp. 35–71.

G. F. Warner and J. P. Gilson, *Catalogue of Western MSS in the Old Royal and King's Collections* (1921), ii. 203–4. Dronke, *Abelard and Heloise in Medieval Testimonies*, pp. 29–30, 41 n. 69, 52–4; repr. in *Intellectuals and Poets*, pp. 276–8, 287–8. F. Guichard-Tesson and M. Felberg-Levitt, '*Heloys du Paraclit*: Le défi d'éditer une traduction du xve siècle', in G. Di Stefano and R. M. Bidler, eds., *Autour de Jacques Monfrin: Néologie et création verbale. Actes du colloque international. Université McGill, Montréal, 7–8–9 octobre 1996* (Le Moyen français, xxxix–xli; Montreal, 1996), pp. 269–95. J. Backhouse, 'Founders of the Royal Library: Edward IV and Henry VII as Collectors of Illuminated Manuscripts', in D. Williams, ed., *England in the Fifteenth Century: Proceedings of the 1986 Harlaxton Symposium* (Woodbridge, Suffolk, 1987), pp. 23–41, at 37. *Checklist* no. 69.

Summary Table of Surviving or Lost or Uncertainly Identified Manuscripts in Approximate Chronological Order, and of their Provenance or Earliest Known Possessors

lost	before 1163	the writer of poems in Orleans, Bibl. mun. 284 (238)
lost	before 1236/8	the abbey of the Paraclete
Troyes, Médiathèque 802	before 1236/8	Paris cathedral chapter
Paris, BnF lat. 2923	mid/late 13th c.	France; Petrarch after *c.*1337
lost	by *c.*1275–80	Jean de Meun
Reims, Bibl. mun. 872	late 13th/early 14th c.	Reims cathedral
Paris, BnF lat. 2544	late 13th/14th c.	Master Jacobus de Gantis
Schøyen collection (Oslo and London) 2085	*c.*1330–60	Paris region
lost	by the 1360s/1370s	Jean de Hesdin
Paris, BnF n. acq. fr. 20001	1 Dec. 1361	Jean de Cherchemont
lost	before 1373	Jean de Dormans
lost	*c.*1380	Jean Gerson
lost	by 1395/6	Jean de Montreuil
Brugge, Stadsbibl. 398	late 14th c.	abbey of Ter Doest
Oxford, Bodl. Library Add. C 271	late 14th/possibly early 15th c.	France; Jo. Lambert of Cambrai

Paris, BnF fr. 920	late 14th c. or before *c.*1418	Gontier Col
lost	before 1409	Richard de Bazoques
lost	before 9 May 1419	Nicolas de Baye (1)
lost	before 9 May 1419	Nicolas de Baye (2)
lost	before 25 Feb. 1444	Humfrey, duke of Gloucester
Douai, Bibl. mun. 797	15th c.	abbey of Marchiennes
Paris, BnF lat. 2545	15th c.	Nantes
Notre Dame, Indiana, University Memorial Library 30	1463–84	Johannes Andree of Neisse
lost	in or before late 1470	Rogier Benoîton
lost	by 1494	Pico della Mirandola (?)
Paris, BnF n. acq. lat. 1873	late 15th c.	north-east Italy
lost	before early 16th c., perhaps before 1443	Paris, abbey of St-Victor
lost	before early 16th c.	Hyde abbey, Hampshire
lost	before 1593	Étienne Gourmelon
Paris, BnF lat. 13057	after 1592	André Duchesne or François d'Amboise
lost	before 1602 (?)	Claude Fauchet
lost	by 1610	Nicolas Camuzat
lost	by 1611	Papire Masson
lost	by early 17th c.	convent of the Paraclete
Paris, BnF lat. 2816	from 1616	unknown
Paris, BnF lat. 13826	17th c.	abbey of St-Germain-des-Prés, Paris
lost	long before 1749	priory of St-Marcel, Chalon-sur-Saône

The table shows a total of thirty-seven manuscripts of which sixteen survive, and of these thirteen are copies or excerpts made before the sixteenth century. If we include the copies that do not survive, those that can be given an approximate date are distributed through the centuries roughly in the following way: one from the twelfth century, six from the thirteenth, ten from the fourteenth, ten from the fifteenth, and eight or nine from the sixteenth or early seventeenth century. These are small totals and not too much should be read into them,[116] but they suggest a modest growth in the circulation (or at

[116] Comparisons are fickle but the number of surviving medieval (pre-16th c.) MSS of this collection—thirteen—does not look unusual when set against the figures I find in

least of the survival) of the text towards the end of the Middle Ages, following a reclusive period of about a hundred years when the collection slumbered, as it were, perhaps in some convents of the order of the Paraclete or in a Parisian library, where Jean de Meun may have been one of the earliest to appreciate and to bring to light its literary and intellectual significance. Manuscripts of French origin clearly predominate, although the collection did travel further afield, especially from the late fourteenth century, and found its way into abbeys in England and the Low Countries, into the hands of educated clerics in north-eastern Europe, and into the private libraries of patrons and scholars such as Humfrey, duke of Gloucester (d. 1447), and, apparently, Pico della Mirandola (d. 1494). The attraction of the collection as an example of fine letter-writing to humanist scholars within and without France is particularly striking and is likely to be due first of all to the work of Jean de Meun.

Printed Editions of the Letter Collection before 1800

Duchesne–d'Amboise, 1616

The project to collect MSS and to print for the first time the letter collection of Abelard and Heloise seems to have been conceived and started by François d'Amboise (1550–1620), a poet and lawyer who, among his other high-ranking offices, was a Conseiller to the Parlement of Brittany from 1583 to 1585 and a Conseiller d'État from 1604.[117] André Duchesne of Tours (1584–1640) appears to have broadened the project to include other writings of Abelard and Heloise, all printed in 1616. Duchesne was a formidable scholar whose other achievements around this time include the *Bibliotheca Cluniacensis* (with M. Marrier, 1614), *Histoire d'Angleterre, d'Écosse et d'Irlande* (1614), editions of the writings of Alcuin (1617), of Alain Chartier (1617), of the *Historiae Normannorum Scriptores Antiqui*

studies of some other notable 12th-c. letter collections. Most of these figures are approximate but they seem fairly close to being accurate: nineteen for Arnulf, bishop of Lisieux (d. 1182), eight for John of Salisbury (not counting letters found in other writers' letter collections; d. 1180), twenty for Peter, abbot of Celle and bishop of Chartres (d. 1183), thirty-five for Peter the Venerable, abbot of Cluny (d. 1156), and twenty-four for Thomas Becket (d. 1170). The much higher figures for some writers of letters—some 200 for Peter of Blois (d. 1211/1212) and some 400 for St Bernard, abbot of Clairvaux (d. 1153)—are quite exceptional.

[117] See Ughetti, *François d'Amboise*, and the introduction to vol. i of his edition of the *Oeuvres complètes* of François d'Amboise, pp. v–xxvii.

(1619), of the *Letters* of Étienne Pasquier (1619), and as well an *Histoire des Papes jusqu'à Paul V* (1619).[118]

There are two versions, with two different title pages, of the *editio princeps* published in 1616:

Du:

PETRI ABAELARDI SANCTI GILDASII IN BRITANNIA ABBATIS, ET HELOISAE CONIVGIS EIVS, QUAE POSTMODUM PRIMA COENOBII PARACLITENSIS ABBATISSA FUIT, OPERA, nunc primum ex MMS. Codd. eruta, & in lucem edita, studio ac diligentia ANDREAE QVERCETANI, Turonensis . . . PARISIIS . . . M.DCXVI, CUM PRIVILEGIO REGIS.

Amb:

PETRI ABAELARDI, FILOSOFI ET THEOLOGI, ABBATIS RVYENSIS, ET HELOISAE CONIVGIS EIVS, PRIMAE PARACLETENSIS ABBATISSAE, OPERA, NVNC PRIMVM EDITA EX MMS. CODD. V. ILLVST. FRANCISCI AMBOESII, Equitis, Regis in sanctioro (sic) *Consistorio Consiliarij, Baronis Chartrae, &c. Cum eiusdem Praefatione Apologetica, & Censura Doctorum Parisiensium. PARISIIS . . . M.DCXVI, CUM PRIVILEGIO REGIS.*

The letter collection is printed in both versions on pp. 3–197 and is reprinted from **Amb** in *PL* clxxviii. 113–314. Both versions were published by Nicolas Buon of Paris, a publisher chiefly of religious books and of the poetic works of Ronsard.[119] They present the same corpus of texts, with copious and scholarly notes to *Letter* 1 written by André Duchesne and with the same *index rerum et verborum*. But in other respects the two versions are significantly different.[120] **Du** was put on sale first, **Amb** shortly afterwards, but with the same date on the title page.

The *Praefatio ad lectorem* which Duchesne wrote and published in **Du** shows that it was Duchesne who did most of the editorial work. Duchesne writes that, although d'Amboise planned an edition of the

[118] See R. Barroux, revised by E. Bury, 'Duchesne (André)', in *Dictionnaire des lettres françaises*, ed. G. Grente, *Le XVIIe siècle* (rev. edn.; Paris, 1996), pp. 408–9.

[119] See H.-J. Martin, *Livre, pouvoirs et société à Paris au XVIIe siècle (1598–1701)* (2 vols.; Histoire et civilisation du livre, iii; Paris,1969), i. 49, 337–8.

[120] On these differences see esp. Monfrin, pp. 31–9; Engels and Kingma, '*Hos ego versiculos*', and *Histoire littéraire de la France*, xii (1763), 'Pierre Abélard', pp. 86–152, at 149–50 (reproduced in *PL* clxxviii. 9–54, at 51–2). Also, R. Barroux, 'Amboise (François d')' in *Dictionnaire des lettres françaises*, ed. G. Grente, *Le seizième siècle* (Paris, 1951), pp. 40–1.

letter collection, he collated the MSS supplied by d'Amboise and extended the project to bring into use other MSS and to include other writings by Abelard and Heloise. Duchesne contributed, besides the *Praefatio ad lectorem*, twenty-seven *Testimonia veterum de Petro Abaelardo et Heloisa*, many of which showed how bitter and acrimonious their lives had been, and extensive notes to the text of *Letter* 1 on pp. 1139–97. **Du** is dedicated to Benjamin de Brichanteau, bishop of Laon (1612–19) and abbot of Ste-Geneviève, both being places with which Abelard had been associated (sigs. a ij and a iij). The dedication is made over the name of Duchesne and the title page also bears his name.

We do not know what may have been discussed between d'Amboise and Duchesne about the reissue, the clear purpose of which was to demonstrate firmly and authoritatively that Abelard had been a good and faithful Catholic. But he had been condemned for erroneous teachings and his name appeared in the *Index* of prohibited books.[121] In publishing his writings Duchesne had taken a risk—as was proved by the swift issue of a *Censure* of errors found in Abelard's newly printed and newly available writings by theologians in Paris. To this d'Amboise responded with arguments designed to show that, although Abelard had sometimes made mistakes, he was not alone in this and did not deserve to be listed on the *Index*.[122] The volume was revised so as to show that the responsibility for its publication lay with the high-ranking François d'Amboise.

To this end in **Amb**

(i) the name of Duchesne disppeared from the title page and a statement was made that the edited works came from MSS in the possession of d'Amboise (*opera nunc primum edita ex mms. codd. v. illust. Francisci Amboesii*);

(ii) the *Praefatio ad lectorem* found in **Du** was omitted;

[121] Abelard had been named in the *Indices librorum prohibitorum* issued by Pope Paul V, 1559 ('libri et scripta omnia prohibentur'); Pius IV, 1564 (the 'Trent' *Index* in which Abelard is listed among the *Auctores primae classis*); Sixtus V, 1590; and Clement VIII, 1596; ed. F. H. Reusch, *Die Indices Librorum Prohibitorum des sechzehnten Jahrhunderts* (Tübingen, 1886; repr. 1961), pp. 200, 275, 509, 537.

[122] Abelard remained on the *Index*. See F. M. Capiferreus, *Elenchus librorum omnium Tum in Tridentino Clementinoque Indice, tum in aliis omnibus sacrae Indicis Congregationis particularibus Decretis usque ad annum 1640 prohibitorum* (Rome, 1640), p. 307: *Petrus Abailardus in indice appendicis primae classis*. In an earlier edition of this work (Rome, 1632), p. 500, Abelard was included *in Indice primae Classis*. There were six classes, the top two being the first and its appendix.

(iii) Duchesne's name was removed from the summary given of the royal privilege of 1615;

(iv) the *Testimonia veterum* found in **Du** were re-used in a newly written *Praefatio apologetica* addressed (*PL* clxxviii. 71–2), not to the bishop of Laon but to Nicolas Brulart de Sillery, Chancellor of France and Navarre, with the request that he give support to Abelard just as Augustus Caesar had given support to Virgil. Abelard had been condemned at Sens for theological teachings which he had rightly disowned or concerning which he had been misinterpreted. He had later been released from his excommunication by Pope Innocent II.[123] This *Praefatio apologetica* was written by d'Amboise;

(v) an *Admonitio ad lectorem* was added which is followed by a copy of Abelard's *Confessio fidei 'Vniuersis'* and of his *Confessio fidei* to Heloise in which he had repudiated the accusations of error made against him and professed his faith in the teachings of the Church. Both *Confessions* were already printed in the volume (on pp. 308–9 and 330–3) but were included here to emphasize the purity and sincerity of Abelard's Catholic faith: *Etsi, Lector, Apologetica Epistola*

[123] **Amb** prints from an unnamed manuscript containing *Letters* of Bernard of Clairvaux a previously unprinted list of errors which, it is claimed, had been wrongly imputed to Abelard: 'etsi in epistolis sub nomine Bernardi editis non reperiuntur, tamen quia in quodam ms. reperi (ne quid dissimulem) bona fide transcribenda curavi: non quod putem tam perversae mentis fuisse Abaelardum, aut quanquam alium, ut tam absurdis et impiis sententiis voluerit debacchari, sed ut quo magis absona et impia sunt illa dogmata, eo magis judicentur aliena, et multis parasangis distantia a mente et intellectu tam pii et bene morati monachi, qui libros, ex quibus excerpta est major ac periculosior articulorum pars, numquam agnovit. Quod si ex veris ejus dictatis quaedam arguantur, oportuit ad verum ejus sensum recurrere, et non contra eum verba decurtata retorquere'; *Praefatio apologetica* (*PL* clxxviii. 78D–79A; **Amb**, sig. b ij^{v}). A list of seventeen errors follows at 79B–80A (**Amb**, sigs. b ij^{v}–b iij). This is a variant version of the list of up to nineteen errors which was brought to light for the first time by Leclercq in 1953 ('Études sur S. Bernard', pp. 101–3) and which were found as an addition to the end of Bernard's *Letter* 190 but only in some thirty of the 117 MSS of the *Letter* that are now known (*S. Bernardi Opera*, ed. Leclercq and Rochais, viii. 39–40, and see *Introduction*, pp. xi–xii). Leclercq had not noticed the list printed in **Amb**, but the variant readings it offers are also found in various MSS of *Letter* 190: as in d'Amboise, no. 17 follows no. 7 in eleven MSS, and, as in d'Amboise, no. 14 is missing from one MS. See also Leclercq, 'Les Formes successives', pp. 101–5. D'Amboise believed that Abelard should not have been listed in the *Index librorum prohibitorum*: 'Quod si aliquid ejus operum in manus venisset eorum, qui indicem librorum suspectae fidei sarcinarunt, certe aut in eo nomen Abaelardi delevissent, de quo nihil mali viderant, nihil comperti habuerant, aut permisissent ejus opera per doctores expurgata in lucem prodire; sicut nunc ea damus reip(ublicae) Christianae et catholicae, tersa sane et laevigata pumice theologorum Parisiensium, qui ut sunt acris judicii senatores, nulla ex iis expungenda, sed si quae duriuscula videbantur, aut molliori interpretatione temperanda judicarunt, aut sapienter cavenda monuerunt'; *Praefatio apologetica* (*PL* clxxviii. 102D–103A; **Amb**, sig. 'c iv').

quam Abaelardus ipse pro defensione sua scripsit, iam inter alias eius Epistolas semel inserta fuerit; tamen, quia fidei Catholicae puram ac sinceram professionem continet . . . (sig.*);

(vi) on sig. * * ij onwards (*PL* clxxviii, 109–12) the recent *Censura Doctorum Parisiensium* was printed. This lists over forty comments on passages found chiefly in the writings of Heloise and Abelard as printed in **Du** (with page references given; these are converted into column numbers in *PL* clxxviii) and prepared by theologians in Paris following the publication of **Du**. Abelard's works, the reader is told in a short introduction to the *Censura* which is likely to have been written by d'Amboise since its intent is similar to that of his *Praefatio apologetica*, are very pious and learned (*pia admodum et erudita*) but, as is commonly the case in ancient writings, blemishes or moles (*naevi*) have been found in them. Abelard's *Apologia* (that is, his *Confessio fidei 'Vniuersis'*) shows that he agreed with the Church in everything (*Ecclesiae in omnibus assentientem*). If any reader with keener sight subsequently spots more of the same, all Catholics will be truly grateful;[124]

(vii) there was also added a title page before the *Letters* begin on p. 3. This highlights the contribution made by d'Amboise through the provision of his MSS:

MAGISTRI PETRI ABAELARDI NANNETENSIS THEOLOGI ACVTISSIMI, ET HELOISSAE EIVS CONIVGIS, PRIMAE PARACLETI ABBATISSAE, EPISTOLAE. Recens editae ex MSS. Codd. illustrissimi viri FRANCISCI AMBOSII (sic), *Regis in sanctiore Consistorio Consiliarij, Equitis, Baronis Chartrae supra Ledum* . . . Cum argumentis Fr S.H.Guil.;

(viii) a list of *errata* that had been found in the copies as printed so far and a *series cartarum* to guide the printer on the arrangement of the contents were also added.

To judge from surviving copies, more impressions were made of **Amb** than of **Du**.[125] I have not attempted detailed collation of any

[124] See also the end of the passage cited from the *Praefatio apologetica* in the previous note. Five of the strictures in the *Censura* relate to the correspondence of Heloise and Abelard: 1. and 2. Abelard (*Letter* 1, **58**) and Heloise (*Letter* 2, **2**) are unjustifiably hostile to Saint Bernard and Saint Norbert. 3. Heloise writes imprudently (*Letter* 2, **5**) of her wrongful love. 4. It is wrong to write (*Letter* 7, **50**) that the Church teaches that a deceased catechumen cannot be saved. 5. It is wrong to assert that conjugal acts cannot be completely free of sin (*Rule* **80**).

[125] Sixteen copies of the 1616 edition are listed in the *Catalogue collectif de France*, of which nine are **Amb**. All fourteen copies listed in the *National Union Catalogue* of libraries

copies, but Engels and Kingma showed that **Du** underwent some changes in the course of printing, notably the removal of the *Capitula haeresum* from p. 275. Pierre Bayle complained in his *Dictionnaire* that, although the edited volume was very good, *mille fautes* had been missed by its correctors, including differences in the date of publication given on the title page (1606, 1616, 1626).[126] I have seen differences in the arrangement of the preliminary and final contents in copies of **Amb**.[127]

Sources:

According to d'Amboise three MSS had been seen that contain the *Letters* (*Praefatio apologetica*, sig. a iiijv; *PL* clxxviii. 75D–76A):

i. *unum exemplar Epistolarum nactus sum in Armorica . . .*

This is *Nanneticus*; see above, p. xci.

ii. *Alterum ex Filippo Portaeo Abbate Tyronio Poeta excellentissimo & mihi amicissimo, qui affirmabat se accepisse ab haeredibus Stefani Gormeleni Curiosolitae . . .*

Not found; see above, p. xcviii, Philippe Desportes.

iii. *Tertium ex Monasterio Paracletensi, ad quod profectus sum.*

Monfrin suggested that d'Amboise, who was shown MSS in the

in the United States of America are **Amb**. There are at least thirteen copies of **Amb** listed in the *Copac Academic and National Library Catalogue* in the United Kingdom. There is only one copy of **Du** in the British Library (223.k.12), which has two handwritten indications of ownership on the title page: 'dono domini le gris' and in another hand 'Jacobi tavelli senon(. . .) Dono domini quercetani 1618'.

126 See Bayle, *Dictionnaire historique et critique* (1702), i. 'Amboise (François d')', pp. 185–6. Bayle also thought (p. 186, n. B) that the *Praefatio apologetica* provided by d'Amboise backfired. For Bayle's entries on 'Abélard (Pierre)' and 'Bérenger (Pierre)' see i. 17–23 and 559–63.

127 See also Engels and Kingma, '*Hos ego versiculos*'. The correct sequence is: *a–f*, *, **, with + placed at the end of the volume, the sequence of contents thus being: (i) *Praefatio apologetica*, (ii) *Elenchus operum hoc volumine contentorum*, (iii) *Summa privilegii*, (iv) *Admonitio ad lectorem*, (v) *Apologia* (or *Confessio fidei 'Universis'*), (vi) *Confessio fidei ad Heloissam*, (vii) *Censura Doctorum Parisiensium*, (viii) *Errata quaedam*, (ix) *Series cartarum*). However, in Cambridge University Library in Acton b. 51.1, the arrangement of the preliminary pieces following the *Praefatio apologetica* is faulty because *f* and + are placed after * and ** as follows: (iv) *Admonitio ad lectorem* (*), (v) *Apologia* (*)), (vi) *Confessio fidei ad Heloissam* (**), (vii) *Censura Doctorum Parisiensium* (**ij), (ii) *Elenchus operum hoc volumine contentorum* (*f*), (iii) *Summa privilegii* (*f*2 verso) followed immediately by (viii) *Errata quaedam* and (ix) *Series cartarum* (+). In British Library 1125 i. 1, where *f* is misplaced between * and **, a disordered sequence of preliminary pieces follows the *Praefatio apologetica:* (iv), (v), (ii), (iii), (vi), (vii). In British Library G. 12722 (viii) and (ix) follow (vii) immediately and are not placed at the end of the volume.

Paraclete by the abbess Marie III de la Rochfoucauld (who assumed her responsibilities as abbess in 1593), used a MS similar to **T** but not **T**; Mews, 'La Bibliothèque du Paraclet', suggested that it was **T**. See **T** above, pp. lxxvii–lxxix.

Apart from the MSS supplied to him by d'Amboise (*manuscriptorum Codicum copiam*), Duchesne (**Du**, *Praefatio ad lectorem*, last page) reports other MSS containing the letter collection which he used (*lectionibus optima fide ac studio supplevimus*) and names their owners:

iv. *bonae scilicet memoriae Pauli Petavij Senatoris in Parisiensi Curia dignissimi* . . . Probably **B**: Paris, BnF lat. 2544, above p. li; Monfrin, p. 42.

v. *Papyrij Massoni Foresij in eadem Curia Advocati* . . . Unidentified. Monfrin, p. 42. See Papire Masson above, pp. xciv–xcv.

vi. *Canonicorum Regularium S. Victoris, Ordinis S. Augustini*. Probably the lost MS, Paris, abbey of St-Victor GGG 17, discussed above, pp. xcv–xcviii.

On p. 198 (= *PL* clxxviii. 313–14), where the edition of the *Letters* and the *Rule* ends and that of the *Institutiones* [here: *Instructiones*] *nostrae* . . . begins, we read in both **Du** and **Amb**:

HVC VSQUE NANNETICVM exemplar, itemque Uictorianum. Sed in Paracletensi, (quod & auctius ubique passim) sequentia reperimus. Et uidentur esse Heloissae.

These three MSS are: *Nanneticus* (of Nantes in Brittany)—i above; *Uictorianus*—vi above; *Paracletensis*—iii above. According to **Du** and **Amb**, the first two of these lack the text which follows the *Rule*, *Institutiones nostrae* . . ., and are shorter than the third. *Nanneticus* could, therefore, be **C** or **E**, which contain less text than was printed, but it is likely to be **E** for reasons given by Monfrin, p. 40 and summarized above, *Nanneticus*, p. xci; see also below, p. cxxiv. The only surviving MS with all these texts is **T**, which is, indeed, ampler than **E**, and also **CF**, which suppress passages found in **T**.

Physical features. At the head of each letter is a summary (*Argumentum*) written by an unknown third party (*Fr. S. H. Guil.*). Pages are numbered and at the bottom of the recto side are found what appear to be quire numbers (3 leaves per quire), e.g. F, Fij, Fiij. Of special interest are the marginalia, which highlight the contents of the *Letters* and give references—not always accurate or precise—to the sources cited; they also give variant readings found in the MSS or suggested by their editor. Generally the text as printed is similar to **T**. Both the text and the marginal variants in Duchesne–d'Amboise also find support in **F** against the other MSS, which makes one wonder whether **F** was associated in some way with the preparation of the 1616 edition, but no other evidence has come to light and Monfrin, p. 28 was uncertain about the circumstances in which **F** was produced.

Spelling. Duchesne–d'Amboise may have adapted this to suit their preferences. Inconsistencies abound (*-ae*/*-e*; *-cia*/*-tia*; *Hierosolymam*/*Hierusalem*); *h* is sometimes added (*Arimathia*/*Arimatia*, *Hester*/*Ester*; *Anthonius* and *authoritas* are usual) as are *b* and *d* before other consonants (*substinet*, *adsistere*); *v* is preferred to *u*; *y* is sometimes used in preference to *i* (*mystice* but *historia*); double consonants are also found but not too frequently (*millia* but *quatuor*). Initial capitals are frequent (*Monachos*, *Philosophia*) as are grave accents over vowels (*cùm*, *à*).

Descriptions and further references. Monfrin, pp. 31–46. Leclercq, 'Notes abélardiennes', pp. 59–62. Smits, pp. 12–14; Engels and Kingma, '*Hos ego versiculos*'; De Santis in *I Sermoni di Abelardo per le Monache del Paracleto*, pp. 38–47.

Rawlinson's edition, 1718

Petri Abaelardi Abbatis Ruyensis et Heloissae Abbatissae Paracletensis epistolae A prioris Editionis Erroribus purgatae, & cum Cod. MS. collatae Curâ Ricardi Rawlinson . . . (London 1718; reprinted with a new title page at Oxford in 1728).

Monfrin, pp. 46–50, provides a thorough description of the contents of this volume. He thought that Richard Rawlinson (1690–1755), a collector and antiquary who here reproduced and revised the *Letters* and other pieces taken from the 1616 edition of Duchesne–d'Amboise, claimed falsely to have also used a MS which belonged to a Gloucestershire friend whose name was kept secret out of his false modesty. On page ii of his *Praefatio* Rawlinson wrote: 'Amico Claudiocestriensi hic gratias publicas solvimus qui pro singulari humanitate nobis MS. tum Codicem mutuo dedit, nomen vero Viri de me bene meriti malus pudor celat.' Monfrin showed that variant readings in the text supposedly taken from this MS were in all likelihood invented by Rawlinson, who, in reproducing the summaries of the *Letters* found in the 1616 edition, also changed them to please himself. Rawlinson could have cited, had he chosen to do so, a MS listed by E. Bernard in his *Catalogi Librorum Manuscriptorum Angliae et Hiberniae* (2 vols., Oxford, 1697), ii. 199, no. 6434.64. This MS, now British Library, Royal 8. F. XV, belonged to Charles Theyer of Gloucestershire, and Bernard stated that it contained letters of Abelard; see Rejected Manuscripts above at p. ci. There is one weakness in Monfrin's otherwise sound argument: he wrote (p. 48) that the entire library which Charles Theyer (b. 1651) inherited from his father John Theyer (d. 1673) had entered the royal library in the late seventeenth century. In fact, the Theyer collection that had been kept at Cooper's Hill, Brockworth, Gloucestershire, totalled some 800 MSS. Charles II (king, 1660–85) bought 312 of these MSS for the royal collection and it is only these which are listed in Bernard's *Catalogi*, so it is possible that a copy of the *Letters* was among the MSS not bought by the king. But I have not listed this possibility among the Lost MSS since no known MS of the *Letters* gives any support to the variant readings offered by Rawlinson.

See Muckle, 'Abelard's letter of consolation', pp. 169–70. *Checklist* no. 67. M. Clapinson, 'Rawlinson, Richard (1690–1755)' and T. Harmsen, 'Rawlinson, Thomas (1681–1725)', *Oxford Dictionary of National Biography* (Oxford, 2004). C. Fell-Smith, rev. R. J. Haines, 'John Theyer d. 1673', *Oxford Dictionary of National Biography* (Oxford, 2004).

Printed Editions from 1800 of the Letter Collection which Use One or More Manuscripts, both Latin and French

1806 M.-J.-J. Briall, *Recueil des historiens des Gaules et de la France* (Paris), xiv. 278–94. Most of *Letter* 1 from Duchesne–d'Amboise and **A**.

1849 *Petrus Abaelardus. Opera*, ed. V. Cousin with the assistance of C. Jourdain and E. Despois (2 vols.; Paris; repr. Hildesheim, 1970), i. 1–37, 72–213. On pp. 38–71 Cousin reproduces Duchesne's notes on *Letter* 1 with emendations and additions inserted between square brackets. From Duchesne–d'Amboise, **TABE**, and **J**.

1850 F. Génin, 'Première Lettre d'Abailard, traduction inédite de Jean de Meun', in *Bulletin du Comité historique des monuments écrits de l'histoire de France, Histoire-Sciences-Lettres*, ii (Paris),

175–91, 265–92. The old French translation of *Letter* 1. From **J**.

1934 C. Charrier, *Jean de Meun. Traduction de la première épître de Pierre Abélard (Historia Calamitatum)* (Paris). Includes **T** as well as **J**.

1950 J. T. Muckle, 'Abelard's letter of consolation to a friend', *Mediaeval Studies*, xii. 163–213 (*Letter* 1). From Duchesne–d'Amboise and **ABCDEFRTY**.

1953 J. T. Muckle, 'The personal letters between Abelard and Heloise', *Mediaeval Studies*, xv. 47–94 (*Letters* 2–5 and part of 6). From Duchesne–d'Amboise and **ABCDEFRTY**.

1955 J. T. Muckle, 'The letter of Heloise on the religious life and Abelard's first reply', *Mediaeval Studies*, xvii. 240–81 (*Letters* 6–7). From Duchesne–d'Amboise and **ABCEFRT**.

1956 T. P. McLaughlin, 'Abelard's rule for religious women', *Mediaeval Studies*, xviii. 241–92 (*Letter* 8 and the *Rule*). From Duchesne–d'Amboise and **ABCEHRT**.

1959 *Abélard, Historia calamitatum*, ed. J. Monfrin (Paris; reprinted several times) (*Letters* 1, 2, 4, and part of 5). Duchesne–d'Amboise and **ABCDEFRTYJ**.

1969 E. Schultz, '"La Vie et les Epistres Pierres Abaelart et Heloys sa fame": A Translation by Jean de Meun and an Old French Translation of Three Related Texts: A Critical Edition of MS 920 (Bibliothèque Nationale)' (Ph.D. diss., University of Washington). **J**.

1977 *Le lettere di Abaelardo ed Eloisa nella traduzione di Jean de Meun*, ed. F. Beggiato, i: *Testo*; ii: *Introduzione – Apparato – Note – Indice selettivo delle forme – Indice dei nomi propri* (2 vols.; Modena). **J**. In the apparatus Beggiato gives readings from MSS containing the Latin text, but seems to rely for these on the editions of Muckle and Monfrin.

1991 *La Vie et les epistres Pierres Abaelart et Heloys sa fame. Traduction du XIIIe siècle attribuée a Jean de Meun. Avec une nouvelle édition des textes latins d'après le ms. Troyes Bibl. mun. 802*, ed. E. Hicks (Nouvelle bibliothèque du moyen âge, xvi; Paris), i. 1–147. An edition with the Latin and medieval French texts of the *Letters* printed *en face*. **J** and **T**. Like Beggiato (1977) Hicks presents readings from MSS containing the Latin text, but explains (p. lii) that he has used the editions of Muckle and Monfrin as his base (*comme base*).

2004 *Epistolario di Abelardo ed Eloisa*, ed. I. Pagani *con Considerazioni sulla trasmissione del testo di* G. Orlandi (Classici italiani; Turin). Largely based on the editions of Muckle and McLaughlin with an Italian translation printed *en face*.

Further information on modern editions is given by Muckle 'Abelard's letter of consolation', 168–71 and Monfrin, pp. 51–3.

THE PRESENT EDITION

Relationships between the Manuscripts

The MSS differ in their contents as follows:

T contains *Letters* 1–8 with the *Rule*;

CE contain *Letters* 1–8 with a shortened version of the *Rule*;

ABRH contain *Letters* 1–8 without the *Rule*.

All other MSS—**FSDY** and **J**—contain fewer than eight *Letters*. In general, the MS tradition is cohesive, which is not to say that the tradition is uniformly of good quality, for it is not. The MSS are found within two broad constellations, **TACEF** and **BRSHDY**. Within the first constellation **CEF** are close to each other and **A** is closer to **CEF** than is **T**. The source of **J** lies within this first constellation. In the second constellation **BR** have a common ancestor as do **DY**. In preparing the first printed edition **Amb** and **Amb**^{1} drew upon the first constellation alone. Whatever were the exemplars from which extant copies have been made, they were somewhat corrupt or hard to read. Copyists in both constellations betray both confusion and misunderstanding or transmit earlier errors at particular places in the text as the following examples show.[128]

Letter 1, 8^{h}—Aiacis: alacis **T** ailacis **T**^{4} Aiacis **F** (**F** *is a careful reviser*) a laicis **B** alaicis **R** ayacis **D** dya **Y** *followed by a space* Aiaus **J**; **42**^{a}—ubi uidelicet uim: ubi uidelicet inde **TCE** uidelicet inde ubi (ubi *superscr.*) **A** ubi uidelicet uim (uidelicet *exp.*, uim *superscr.*) inde **F** ubi uidelicet ui **BRDY** ubi uidelicet unde **S** ubi uidelicet iudicium **Amb** ou . . . leur force **J**; **52**^{z}—et arx mentis: et arx (et ars **T**^{4} *in marg.*) mentis **TF** arx (*?; superscr. by another hand*) mentis **A** et ars (*?*)

[128] In the lists which follow the first reading shown is usually the one preferred in the present edition.

militibus **C** appri (*?*) militibus **E** et ars mentis **BRSDY**; **68**[j]—ascriberent (*cf. Orlandi, 'Minima Abaelardiana', p. 134*): conscriberent **TACEFDY** al. adscriberent *add.* **F** *in marg.* conscriberant *?***B**, **RS**; **70**[f]—ut (*cf. Orlandi, 'Minima Abaelardiana', p. 134*): et **TACEFBRSDY**

Letter 2, **10**[d]—meas uoluptates: meas uoluptates aut uoluntates **TBRSYAmb** (perhaps an imported gloss rather than a variant); **10**[n]—et infaustis thalamis: et (et *add.* **T**[1] *in marg.*) in faustis thalamis **TACEFAmb** infaustisque thalamis (talamis **B**) **BR** infaustis talamis **S** infaustisque his talentis **Y**

Rule **114**[d]—si: si uel se *all codd.*

The MS tradition is, nonetheless, cohesive overall; the copyists tackled with unequal success exemplars that rested, ultimately, upon a stable, if uneven, foundation. And the overall cohesiveness of the MS tradition is reinforced by cross-contamination between and within the two main constellations. This cross-contamination suggests that the letter collection had been copied frequently enough before the relatively late and contaminated copies that we have began to appear.[129] It is certainly too extensive to be explained entirely by accidental coincidences, although such coincidences may well account for some of the examples shown here:[130]

Letter 1, **25**[o]—Quis: Que **TACEFBRS**; **42**[b]—ullatenus: nullatenus **CEBRSDY**; **52**[f]—primum: primo **ACEFRDY**; **53**[m]—ut *om.* **CEFDY**; **54**[a]—nomine **TBRSDYAmb** honore **ACEFAmb**[1] en l'onnour **J**; **57**[x]—confirmatione: consummatione **TRY**; **61**[y]—sustentaret: sustentarent **ACEFDY**; **67**[o]—eis: ei **TAS** eis **CEFBRDY**;

[129] That allusions to the lives of Heloise and Abelard were made widely and early is clear from Dronke's *Medieval Testimonies*; early diffusion of their correspondence may have favoured this. In addition to the epitaphs for Heloise and Abelard copied in a late 12th-c. *florilegium* from Schaffhausen (Zurich, Zentralbibliothek C 58) and discussed and edited in *Medieval Testimonies* (pp. 21, 49–50; repr. in *Intellectuals and Poets*, pp. 265, 284–5), J.-Y. Tilliette has found a small (anti-Abelard) dossier which includes epitaphs and epigrams apparently concerning Heloise's uncle Fulbert and also (although mistakenly) William of Champeaux. Tilliette reasonably asks whether this suggests 'l'influence diffuse de l'*Historia calamitatum*' ('Le Sens et la composition du florilège de Zurich', p. 161, n. 25).

[130] The excerpts printed by Pasquier in his *Recherches* (see pp. lxxxiv–lxxxv above) confirm the impression given by the surviving MSS of a cohesive collection with many variations of detail. Pasquier's variant readings seem to confirm cross-contamination between the lines of transmission but some may be the result of hasty transcription. Examples: *Letter* 1 at **47** perlustrauit: perlustrauerat *Pasquier* perlustrauerit **A**; at **52** culmum: culmen *Pasquier* and **S**; at **54** memoria: memoriam *Pasquier* and **F**; at **59** posse *om. Pasquier* and **BRSDY**.

71[v]—machinamenta: ex machina uitam *A before self-corr.* machina uitam **Y** *before corr. by* **Y**^{1}

Letter 2, **15**[h]—precedere: procedere **CEBY**

Letter 4, **9**[d]—uerbis: uerba **CEFY**

Letter 5, **26**[k]—in idipsum: ipsum **AR**

Letter 6, **11**[g]—que *om.* **T** *(but add.* **T**^{1}*)***BRS**; **12**[l]—Iacob **T**^{1}**ACE-FAmb**^{1}: Iob **TBRSAmb**; **16**[j]—statuunt: statuerunt **T** *(but marked for corr. by* **T**^{1}*)***BRS**; **18**[s]—dulcem et barbaram: dulce et herbarum **TBRS**; **20**[e]—fieret: fiet **T** (fieret **T**^{1})**BRS**; **23**[k]—ita que: itaque que **TBRS**; **28**[a]—Nec: Ne **ABRS**; **29**[g]—concessa est: concessa **ACFB-SAmb**; **32**[i]—a temptatione: attempcione **ES**

Letter 7, **13**[a]—Demum: Deinde **CFBRSAmb**^{1}; **16**[c]—excubabant: excubant **TABRS** (**E** *was uncertain and wrote only* excu).

The titles given to the letters vary. Subtitles have been added to *Letter* 1 in **TABS**, but not consistently, and to the *Rule* identically in **TAmb**; there is, however, no copy of the *Rule* in **ABS**. Rubrics, more common in **T**, **A**, **B**, and **S** than in other MSS, seem to have been adopted selectively:

Letter 1, **24**, **30**, **43**, **65**.

Letters 2, 1; 3, 1; 4, 1; 5, 1; and 6, 1.

BRSHDY

Throughout the correspondence this group, which lacks the *Rule*, is the weaker of the two main groups:

Letter 1, **2**[c]—quod *om.* **BRDY**; **11**[f]—sententiarum: scienciarum **BRDY**; **11**[b]—prophetia: prophetica **BRD**; **17**[h]—quibusdam: quibus **BRD** quibusque **Y**; **28**[b]—et: ut **BRD** et **Y** *over eras.*; **28**[i]—mihi: sibi **BRDY**; **30**[o]—tonsis: tensis **BR** censis **DY**; **30**[p]—offeretis: offerens **B** offeres **RY** offerentes **D**; **30**[t]—atritis: ac tritis **BRY**; **40**[d]—opprimitur: primitur **BRDY**; **43**[g]—meis *om.* **BRSDY**; **47**[f-f]—qua in: quam **BR** quam in **S** qua **D**; **52**[k]—intrauerint: intrauerit **BRSD**; **57**[j]—Qui adheret . . . Item *om.* **BRDY**; **57**[y]—traditur: tradimur **BRSDY**; **57**[k]—quoque: que **BR** qui **DY**; **61**[b]—etiam: in **B** *om.* **RDY**; **61**[b]—asportabant: apportabant **BY** aportabant **RD**; **61**[e]—aut omnino: an omnino **BS** an animo **R** aut animo **D**; **63**[c]—per *om.* **BRSDY** *add.* **Y**^{1}; **64**[o]—gratior: grauior **BRD**; **71**[f]—Dei *om.* **BRSDY**; **71**[b]—mortuus occumberet: occumbit *BRDY* occumberet **S**; **72**[e]—aliquo: aliqua **BRDY** aliquam **S**

Letter 2, **1**[k]—quidam: quidem **BRS**, ?**D**, **Y**; **5**[c]—sed *om.* **RDY**; **5**[m]—gessisti: fecisti **BRD**, **Y** *before corr. by* **Y**

Letter 3, 1[l]: prioratum: primatum **BRY**

Letter 5, 1[g]: preposuit: preposui **BRSY**

Letter 7, 13[h]—commemorat *om.* **BRS**; 13[i]—terre *om.* **BR**; 15[s]—ad Aaron: Aaron **BRS**.

Sometimes copyists in this second group are confused and disagree, with **BR/BRS** and **DY** tending to occupy different camps:

Letter 1, 5[l]—quamtotius: quanto **BR** quamcito **DY**; 61[w]—se et concubinas suas: se et concubinas suas et **BRS** ut se concubinas suas et **D** ut se et concubinas suas et **Y**; 62[c]—et quantum: et **RD** et quam **S** et **Y** *before exp.* cum **Y**[1]; 62[u]—Illud autem plurimum me cruciabat: Illud autem plurimum me erudiebat (cruciebat **S**) **BRS** Iuxta illud incidit in cillam cupiens uitare carybdim. Illud autem plurimum me cruciabat *add.* **D** Illud autem plurimum me erudiebat. Iuxta illud incidit in scillam cupiens uitare caribdim *add.* **Y** (This short addition in **DY** is perhaps a reader's note); 71[g]—circumferar: circumferat **ABRS** circumferor **DY**

Letter 8, 2[e]—nitentes: intendentes **B** intentes **R** utentes **H**

Muckle in 'Abelard's letter of consolation', pp. 171–2, Monfrin, and Orlandi, '*Minima Abaelardiana*', looked at the relationships between **BRDY**, a group that is now enlarged by the addition of **S** and **H**. Monfrin, pp. 53–5 found that attempts at correction by **DY** of errors in **BR** seem to show that the exemplar followed by **DY** was later than that available to **BR**. An example he gave is this:

Letter 1, 34[t–t]—concitaui: concitari **BR** contigit concitari **DY**

Like Monfrin, Orlandi also separated **BR** and **DY**—they are clearly two different groups—but he found, like Muckle before him, that sometimes **B** itself separates from **RDY**. (One small correction should be made to Orlandi, p. 64, where he refers to Muckle, p. 184, nn. 45–6 (= *Letter* 1, 20[f]): here we have an example of the division between **B** (which reads 'a') and **RDY**[1] ('ante'), not between **BR** and **DY**). Further examples of the split **B/RDY** (where **RDY** combine in error) include:

Letter 1, 6[r]—patentissimis: paucissimis **RDY**; 6[f]—rem: esse **RDY**; 30[f–f]—quod secundum . . . apud Deum *om.* **RDY**; 31[j]—uelum ab altari tulit: uelum altari tulit **RDY**; 32[b]—adhuc conualueram: conualueram **RDY**

Letter 2, 4[l]—uno modo potes: potes **R** *after vacant space*, modo potes **DY**; 5[c]—sed de tuis: de tuis **RDY**

S seems to have used a less corrupt copy than the ones available to **BRDY** and therefore escapes some of their agreements:

Letter 1, **57**[j–j]—nostrum uocauerimus oratorium uni ipsius persone nos dedicasse fateamur, sed propter eam quam supra reddidimus causam in memoria scilicet nostre consolationis **S** uel in memoria scilicet nostre consolationis nostrum uocauerimus (uacauerimus **D**) oratorium uni ipsius persone nos dedicasse fateamur (fatemur **Y**) sed propter eam (eam *om.* **D**) quam supra reddidimus causam **BRDY**

H has a part of *Letter* 7 as well as *Letter* 8, which are not found in **SDY**. It allies sometimes with **BR** but not always and it does not depend on their exemplar. Examples of agreement between **BRH** are:

Letter 7, **43**[n]—propenticon: propenticum **BRH**; **46**[b]—necdum: nec **BRH**; **49**[i]—commemorans: commemoratus **BRH**; **50**[g]—incitata: incitati **BRH**; **50**[t]—salutem: salute **BRH**; **50**[g]—ad castimoniam: castimonie **BRH**

As Orlandi, '*Minima Abaelardiana*', pointed out in respect of **BRDY**, this group, in spite of its shortcomings, sometimes presents a preferable reading missing elsewhere. But this occurs very infrequently. A much noted example is this:

Letter 1, **47**[r]—auctoritatem . . . grauiorem **BRSDY** auctoritatem . . . gratiorem **TACEF**

TACEF

The first main group is not always more reliable than the second:

Letter 1, **8**[v]—lectionem Prisciani in qua: lectiones Prisciani in qua **T** lectionem precipuum (prisciani *add. in marg.* **E**; praecipuam **F**) in qua **EF**; **8**[w]—amisit: admisit **TCE**; **8**[z–z]—multum tempus: tempus **ACEF**; **42**[a]—ubi uidelicet uim: ubi uidelicet inde **TCE** uidelicet inde (uim *superscr. add.*) **A** ubi uidelicet (uidelicet *exp.*) uim (uim *superscr. add.*) inde **F**; **47**[r]—grauiorem: gratiorem **TACEF**; **48**[z]—obseruari: obseruare **TCEF**; **60**[u]—excubans *om.* **TACEF**

Letter 2, **8**[i]—conuersacionis: conuersionis **TCEF**

Letter 6, **23**[o]—sicut non est impar meritum patientie in Petro . . . et in Iohanne . . . sic non est impar meritum continentie in Iohanne . . . et in Abraham: **T**[1] marks the words from *patientie* to *meritum* for corr. and they are om. by **ACEF**, thus removing the comparison necessary to complete the sentence. It survives only in **BRS**

Rule **14**[a]—Paulinum: Paulum **TCE**; **14**[e]—nostra: nostram **TCE**; **14**[g]—Macharios: Macharium **TCE**; **14**[h]—auctoritatem: materiam **TCE**; **24**[e]—unus: unius **TCE**

T contains corrections (see above, p. lxxv), some of which were highlighted by **T**[1], who may have simply checked the copy made by the main scribe **T** against the exemplar which was in use. However, in **A** a reader has consulted a second MS: *Letter* 1, **60**[j]—saniores: in al⟨io⟩ sceuiores *superscr. add. by another hand.* A close link between **T** and **A** is found in *Letter* 7 at **14**[k]: whereas **CEFBRS** all write 'stagnum mariam', both **T** and **A** write 'stagnum marian' but **T** does so after first writing 'stagnum mariam'.

T and **CEF** agree in error once: *Letter* 1, **48**[z]—obseruari: obseruare **TCEF**. But **A** and **CEF** agree in error quite often and Orlandi, 'Considerazioni sulla trasmissione', pp. 58–60, rightly considered **ACEF** to form a distinct group:

Letter 1, **8**[z–z]—post multum tempus **T** post tempus **ACEF** post multum temporis **BRDY**; **24**[p]—ubi et ipse illas . . . rationes . . . concludens . . . inquit: ubi et illas . . . rationes . . . concludens . . . inquit **AEF** ubi et ei illas rationes . . . concludens . . . inquit **C**; **37**[d]—diffamauerunt: diffamauerant **ACE** difamuirant **F**; **47**[h]—conscripsit: scripsit **ACEF**; **54**[a]—in honore sancte Trinitatis **ACEF** *followed by* **Amb**[1] in nomine sancte Trinitatis **TBRSDY** *followed by* **Amb** en l'onnour de la Sainte Trinité **J**; **65**[k]—carpebam: querebam **A** habebam ?**C**, **EF**; **70**[m]—respirarem: respirare **ACEF**

Letter 3, **12**[c]—absens: absentibus **ACEF**

Letter 4, **1**[c]—diaconissam abbati: diaconissam abbati abbatissam **ACEF**

Letter 5, **1**[o]—adiecisti: deiecisti **ACEFY**; **19**[g]—piscauerit: piscatus fuerit **ACEF**; **27**[h]—crucis *om.* **ACEF**; **31**[m]—tue infirmitati nature diuina indulgetur miseratione: tue infirmitatis nature diuina indulgetur miseratione **ACEF**; **35**[v]—Vale in Christo . . . Amen *om.* **ACEF**

Letter 6, **4**[l]—numquam hospitium uiris prebeat: umquam hospitium uiris prebeat **ACEF**; **12**[a]—Perpende itaque: Perpende **ACEF**; **12**[g]—Quibus . . . equiparare possemus *om.* **ACEF**; **18**[h]—indignans quod . . . superent: indignans quod . . . superant **ACEF**; **23**[q]—patientie . . . meritum *om.* **ACEF**; **23**[s]—et *om.* **ACEF**

CEF

CEF share many errors and **CE** worked from a common exemplar, as Monfrin, pp. 55–6 showed. This exemplar was a poor one as was the exemplar available to **F**:

Letter 1, **26**[v]—secundum: super **CEF**; **26**[n]—uis aliqua: uis aliqua seu uis aliquod **CEF**

Letter 7, **2**[m]—quam imitarentur: postquam imitaretur C potius quam imitaretur **EF**; **14**[d]—commemorat: commemorat *inserted into* **E**; narrat *inserted into* **F**; **43**[h]—magni: *vacant space in* **C**; *om.* **EF**

Rule, **78**[c]—nos: uos uel nos *CE*

CEF are notable for their shared omissions, especially but not only in *Letter* 7 and in the *Rule* (lacking in **F**), where they plainly suppress even quite long passages. In *Letter* 7, on rejoining the text following a lacuna, and in the *Rule* (notably at **67**), **CE** sometimes make suitable adjustments of phrase, thereby indicating that these omissions from their common exemplar had been deliberate.[131]

However, as Orlandi, '*Minima Abaelardiana*', has also pointed out, **CEF** sometimes (although not often) offer acceptable or improved readings not found elsewhere:

Letter 1, **26**[a]—insignes olim philosophorum **CEF** insignes olim philosophos **TABRDY**; **49**[r]—quorum prior antea mihi familiaris extiterat et ualde dilexerat: **CEF** *write* . . . et ualde me dilexerat; **50**[v]—particeps esse sustineret: particeps esse uellet **CEF**

Letter 7, **2**[d]—cultui assiduam: cultui semper assiduam **CEF**

Rule **116**[g] (lacking in **F**)—alii **TAmb** aliis **CE**

F—a copy made *c.*1600 from one or more poor exemplars—clearly strove to make improvements, often (it would appear—cf. Monfrin, p. 28; Orlandi, '*Minima Abaelardiana*', pp. 60–1) by consulting editions of texts cited in the *Letters*. There are many examples of this, the following being taken from *Letter* 7, which contains many quotations from earlier sources:[132]

Letter 7, **12**[h]—omnibus uobis: uobis **F** *and Vulg*; **12**[i]—coram: coram omni **F** *and Vulg*; **12**[n]—Nicholaum: Nicholaum aduenam **F** *and Vulg*; **12**[f]—substantiam: necessaria **F** *and Augustine*; **12**[g]—non putat: putat non potuisse **F** *and Augustine*; **12**[j]—audiant **TACEBRS**: audiat **F** *and Augustine*; **12**[k]—cognoscant **TACEBRS**: cognoscat **F** *and Augustine*; **12**[l]—euangelizans: praedicans et euangelizans **F** *and Augustine*; **12**[n]—immundis: malignis **F** *and Vulg*; **14**[u]—tante doctrine et uite continentie: tanta doctrina et uitae continentia **F** *and Jerome*; **14**[a]—sic: sic et **FAmb** *and Jerome*; **14**[f]—imitantur **TACEBRS**: nituntur **F** *and Jerome*; **19**[a]—Maximo: Maximiano **F** *and Gregory*;

[131] Levitan, p. 230, nn. 197, 198, p. 249, n. 261, seems to hold that what is missing from these MSS but is present in another may herald a later interpolation into the text.

[132] I have compared current standard printed editions of works cited in the letter collection. These editions, which are listed in the *Bibliography: Primary Sources*, do not necessarily present the cited texts as they may have been found by **F** in other printed editions. Nonetheless, there does seem to be sufficient evidence overall that **F** emended the letter collection from available editions in this way.

19[b]—abbatissas: abbatissas fieri **F** *and Gregory*; 19[w]—hoc ipsum: idipsum **F** *and Jerome*; 19[a]—precipit: praecipiat **F** *and Jerome*; 19[e]—patrem: patrem quidem **F** *and Jerome*; 21[i]—est: **F** *adds in the marg.* viros? virgo? *Jerome writes* virgo; 24[f]—Nolo: nolo te **F** *and Jerome*; 31[h]—Noli me: Noli **F** *and Jerome*; 43[c]—sibillam: Sibillas **F** *and Jerome*; 43[b]—pondus tenuit tot cauernis patentibus? Itane Deus omnipotens terreno: pondus super cribum tenuit? Quia tot cavernis patentibus nihil inde in terram cadere permisit? Itane Deus omnipotens qui ipsa creavit elementa **F** *and Augustine*; 48[b]—non queo: nequeo **F** *and Jerome*; 48[d]—deuinctus: devictus **F** *and Jerome*; 48[i]—anime: animae hominis **F** *and Augustine*; 48[n]—non: ipse non **F** *and Augustine*; 48[q]—Respondit: Rescripsit **FAmb[1]** *and Augustine*; 49[w]—infancia: adolescentia **F** *and Jerome*; 49[t]—noscerem: nossem **F** *and Jerome*.

F also gives readings not found in **CE**, sometimes by way of giving alternatives in the margin (usually after writing *al.*). Examples include:

Letter 1, 37[l]—correctionem **TDY** correptionem **ACEF** *al.* correctionem **F**; 40[i]—confessus **TACEBRSD** confusus **FY** *al.* confessus **F** 42[a]—inde **TACE** ui **BRDY** unde **S** uim **F**—*and compare* **J**: force

Letter 6, 18[n]—sicera **TABRS**: sincera **CEF** *but* **F** *adds in the marg.* F(orte) sicera

This may reflect access by **F** to a second exemplar and Orlandi, 'Considerazioni sulla trasmissione', p. 62, gives in support examples where **F** would not have needed to but did alter what is found in **CE** or their source, or might not be expected to correct errors carried by **CE** or their source without the help of another exemplar. They include:

Letter 1, 21[s]—peperit **C** *and* **E** *before corr.*: pareret **F** *and other MSS*; 31[l]—obligauit **CEDY** alligauit **F** *and other MSS*.

Other examples, given by Orlandi, 'Considerazioni sulla trasmissione', pp. 62–3, that appear to suggest that **F** used an exemplar unknown to **CE** would convince if the readings of Muckle that he follows were present in the MSS. But several are not:

Letter 1, 8[q]—Orlandi, p. 62 (referring to Muckle, 'Abelard's letter of consolation', p. 179, n. 82): deserat **CE** dimiserat **F** *and other MSS*. In fact, only **E** shows 'deserat'.

Letter 1,74[e]—Orlandi, p. 62 (referring to Muckle, 'Abelard's letter of consolation', p. 210, n. 77): magis **CE** iugiter **F** *and other MSS*. In fact, only **C** shows 'magis'.

Letter 2, **7**[w]—Orlandi, p. 62 (referring to Muckle 'The Personal Letters', p. 70, n. 62): tue unice **CE** tuae **F** *and other MSS* (the reference is to a vineyard). In fact, **F** shows 'tuae uineae'.

Letter 2, **11**[r]—Orlandi, p. 62 (referring to Muckle, 'The Personal Letters', p. 71, n. 95): in terra **CE** in terris **F** *and other MSS; also in Cicero*. In fact, **F** shows 'in terra'.

Letter 3, **4**[t]—Orlandi, p. 63 (referring to Muckle, 'The Personal Letters', p. 74, n. 35): eorum **CE** rebus **F** *and other MSS*. In fact, **F** shows 'eorum'.

Letter 3, **5**[s]—Orlandi, p. 63 (referring to Muckle, 'The Personal Letters', p. 75, n. 46): ualeat **CE** ualet **F** *and other MSS*. In fact, **F** shows 'ualeat'.

So, there is evidence in support of the possibility that **F** from time to time drew upon an exemplar unlike **CE**, but it is less than Orlandi thought, and **CEF** have a strong group identity.

F also occasionally attempted a Greek word where other MSS used or tried to use a transliteration:

Letter 7, **13**[k]—semneion: *ςεμνύον*; **13**[l]—monasterium: *μοναςύριον*

A reader also helped to improve **F**:

Letter 1, **36**[q]—Conano: caneno **CEF** Conone *add. by an annotator in marg.* **F**; **52**[e]—callis: calamis **EY** callis *exp.* **F** *corr.* al. calamis **F**

J

J, which lacks *Letter* 8 and the *Rule*, seems to have had access to a MS in the constellation where **TACEF** are also found:

Letter 1, **4**[c]—etatis: etatis mee **CEF** mon aage **J**; **47**[r]—gratiorem **TACEF***Amb* grauiorem **BRSDY** plus aggreable **J**; **52**[r]—recordatione (recordationem **TCE**) . . . cogat animam (anima **T**) compati contreigne l'ame a piteusement souffrir la remembrance **J**

Unlike Monfrin, p. 58 I do not find **J** to be particularly close to **T**; at times it is, but at other times not:

Letter 1, **42**[t]—nitebatur **TAmb** utebatur **ACEFBRSDYAmb**[1] il s'apuioit **J**; **54**[a]—honore **ACEFAmb**[1] nomine **TBRSDYAmb** en l'onnour **J**

J offers a good reading not found in MSS other than **F**:

Letter 1, **42**[a]—ubi uidelicet (uidelicet *exp.*) uim (*superscr.*) **F** ou . . . leur force **J**

There is a unique link with **Y** in the form of an additional phrase, perhaps added by a reader in the margin of an earlier copy and later imported awkwardly into the text. It is taken from a Psalm at *Letter* 1,

11[h]. There is also a suspicion of a link between **Y** and **J** in a problematic phrase in *Letter* 1, **12**[t]: que nemini umquam ulterius acciderat **TBD**; que nemini nuncquam acciderat **A**; que (qui **E**) nemini umquam acciderat **CEF** que nemini nunquam ulterius acciderat **R**; que nemini unquam alterius acciderat **Y** *which marks* -us *for exp. so as to read* alteri   qui n'estoit onques avenue a autres **J**

Amb

It is not certain that **Amb** (or **Amb**^{1}) used **T**. If he did not, he used a MS which was very similar to it and, indeed, for the subtitles of the *Rule*, identical. Examples of many similarities between **Amb** and **T** include:

Letter 1, **18**[f]—recessus: regressus **TAmb**; **29**[e]—conuersationi: conuersioni **TAmb**; **42**[t]—nitebatur **TAmb**: utebatur **ACEFBRS-DYAmb**^{1}

Letter 2, 8[i]—conuersacionis: conuersionis **TCEFAmb**; **9**[c]—ut: et **TAmb**

Letter 3, **6**[c]—mature: nature **TAmb**; 7k memorauimus: commemorauimus **T** (*after corr. of* memorauimus), **Amb**

Letter 4, **11**[c]—effectu: affectu **TAmb**

Letter 5, **8**[p]—humilitatis: utilitatis **T**; vilitatis **Amb**; **15**[g]—nec: ne **TAmb**; **27**[k]—tam: tunc **TAmb**; **33**[c]—quippe est: est quippe **TAmb**

Letter 6, *salutation*—Suo: Domino **TAmb**; **9**[b]—moderatrix sit: mediatrix sit **TAmb**

Letter 7, **43**[pq]—monachas que uiros: uniuiras *superscr. add.* **T**, *add.* **Amb**; **43**[r]—monachos: uniuirgines *superscr. add.* **T**, *add.* **Amb**

Rule **36**[j], **39**[c], **88**[a], **97**[o], **108**[c]—*headings add. in marg.* **TAmb**; **82**[q]—expergiscimini: expergimiscimini **TAmb**; **116**[g]—aliis: alii **TAmb**; **120**[f]—Athanasius: Anastasius **TAmb**; **120**[h]—ut: quod **TAmb**.

There is also some similarity between **Amb** and **T**^{1} but this is not sufficient evidence that **Amb** used **T**:

Rule **6**[c]—silentium: silentio **T**^{1}**Amb**.

The possibility that **Amb** used **T** is weakened, if not excluded, by his oversight of, or failure to appreciate, corrections made in **T**:

Letter 1, **29**[d]—uestes quoque (quoque *exp.* **T**) **TAmb**; **29**[e]—conuersationi: conuersioni **T** *before corr. by* **T**^{1}, **Amb**

Letter 6, **21**[i]—utilitatem: humilitatem **T** *before exp. of* h *and* m humilitatem **Amb**; **25**[m]—ad modicum **T**^{1}**ACEFBRS** *and Vulg.* ad modum **TAmb**

Rule **16**[f]—insuper: insuper e *add.* **T** *before exp.* insuper et **Amb**; **27**[b]—itaque: inquam **TAmb** ita(que) **T**[1] *in marg. which has been trimmed*; **29**[q]—deuote (*exp.*) diligenter suscipiat **T** deuote et diligenter suscipiat **Amb**; **111**[a]—carnales (*exp.*) curiales **T** carnales **Amb**; **121**[e]—cognoscuntur (*exp.*) opponuntur **T** cognoscuntur opponuntur **Amb**

Amb seems, therefore, to have used a MS similar to **T** but lacking the corrections made in **T**.

Amb also presents readings and mistakes found in the **CEF** subgroup which are not found in *T*:

CEF

Letter 1, **6**[w]—ad cetera dialectice: ad (a **E**) dialectice (Dialecticae **Amb**) lectionem ?**C**, **EFAmb**; **46**[l]—haberet: haberent **CEFAmb**; **46**[n]—sustineret: sustinerent **CEFAmb**

Letter 3, **12**[g]—uestre: nostre **CEFAmb**

Letter 6, **15**[h]—superaddimus: superaddidimus **CEFSAmb**.

CE

Letter 7, **6**[q]—deuotionis: delationis **CEAmb**

Rule **4**[d]—est **CEAmb**; **19**[g]—non *om.* **CEAmb**; **120**[g]—uie (uiae **Amb**) **CEAmb**

CF

Letter 1, **7**[j]—in me quid: in me quod **CFAmb**

E

Letter 1, **6**[t]—rationibus: disputationibus **EAmb**; **11**[w]—concurrere: accedere **EAmb**

F

Letter 1, **5**[t]—remotus: remotus quasi **FAmb**; **20**[m]—castricianum (castricanum **E**) **TACEBRDY** Sabinianum **FAmb**; **54**[f] *et seq.*—Paraclitum: Paracletum **FAmb**; **57**[h]—conicimus: cogitamus **FAmb**; **63**[t]—Illuc itaque: Illuc namque **FAmb**

Letter 6, **12**[u]—debent **TACEBRS**: debet **FAmb**; **17**[g]—dum quando **TACEBRS**: cum **FAmb**

Letter 7, **14**[b]—et *om.* **FAmb**; **14**[a]—sic: sic et **FAmb**

The reading common to **Amb** and **CF** is not sufficient to prove that **Amb** knew **C**. It is more likely that **Amb** knew and used **E** and **F** (see above, pp. xci and lxii). For reasons also given above (pp. xcvi–xcvii) it is likely that **Amb** knew the now lost **V**.

Amb may have made original contributions, e.g. at *Letter* 1, **42**[a]—

uim: iudicium **Amb**; **73**[g]—suspitiens: aspiciens **Amb**. **Amb** also seems to have tried to improve the accuracy of some of the citations from authorities:

Rule **68**[l]—aut quam: aut melior sit quam **Amb** *and Jerome*; **68**[o, q, r, v, y]—aut: aut melior quam **Amb** *and Jerome.*

Amb[I]

Amb[I] seems to have reread MSS and has added variant readings in the outer margin of **Amb**, usually introducing them with *al.* Faced, for example, in *Letter* 1, **47**[a], with the name 'Huldonium' he adds in the margin: '*al.* Hilduinum *et recte*' ('*or/elsewhere* Hilduin *and rightly so*'). This form of the name is found among the surviving MSS only in **F**, which was an active seeker after emendations. It is tempting, and not implausible, to think that **Amb**[I] is André Duchesne at work in revising the original transcriptions of François d'Amboise. Certainly **Amb**[I] compared MSS. For example, in *Letter* 6, **21**[i], where the correct reading (found in **ACEFBRS**) seems to be 'utilitatem', **Amb** prints 'humilitatem', which is found, before correction, only in **T**, where, after expunction of 'h' and 'm', it is reduced to 'uilitatem'. In the margin **Amb**[I] gives 'vilitatem, *& in al(io) Cod(ice)* vtilitatem'. Similarly on other occasions **Amb**[I] notes two different readings, one found only in **F**, the other found in other extant MSS:

Letter 1, **11**[u]—concurrere **TACBRDY**: accedere **EAmb** contendere **F** contendere vel concurrere **Amb**[I]

Letter 6, **3**[e]—conuersionis **TACEBRS** professionis **F** conuersationis **Amb** conuerssionis, & professionis **Amb**[I] conversion **J**

On one occasion **Amb**[I], having noted or thought of a good variant reading (which is otherwise only found in **F**), provides a second reading which, he wrote, he found in the MS of the Paraclete (and which agrees with **TABR**):

Letter 7, **6**[q]—deuotionis: delationis **Amb** dilectionis. Par(acletensi) Cod(ice) deuotionis **Amb**[I]

Two variants might seem to suggest that **Amb**[I] read **T**:

Letter 1, **29**[e]—**T** writes 'conuersioni', **Amb**[I], like **T**[I], gives 'conuersationi', but so do **ACEFBRDY**.

Rule **120**[g]—uite **TAmb**[I] uie **CE** uiae **Amb**, but 'uite' is fairly obviously a correct reading.

On two other occasions **Amb**[I] shows no knowledge of corrections made in **T**:

Letter 1, 8[u–u]—*tr. by* **T**[1] *of* discipulos habebat qualescumque; 8[b]—conuersus: compulsus **T** *before corr.*, **Amb**[1]

On the other hand, **Amb**[1] avoids at least one of the mistakes of **T**:

Letter 5, 8[p]—humilitatis: utilitatis **T**.

And on one occasion **Amb**[1] provides a third reading from a MS which is not among those extant:

Rule 13[d]—rerum **TAmb** uirorum **CE** virorum *&* *in aliq.* vitiorum **Amb**[1]

These examples, taken together, seem to show that **Amb**[1], like **Amb**, is more likely to have used a MS similar to **T** than **T** itself.

On occasions **Amb**[1] allies with two or more of the **CEF** subgroup:

Letter 1, 30[c]—demonstrandus: denotandus ?**C**, **E** *before corr.*, **FAmb**[1]; 42[t]—nitebatur: utebatur **ACEFBRSDYAmb**[1]; 53[l]—meliouerunt: incolauerunt **CEAmb**[1] incoluerunt **F**; 61[d]—compellerer: compellerent **EFAmb**[1]; 63[g]—Argenteoli: argentolii **CEFAmb**[1]

Letter 3, 11[v]—Oratio: Oremus **CEFAmb**[1]

Letter 6, 14[h]—exequare: adequare **EFAmb**[1]

Letter 7, 15[j]—Honorianensi **TAEBRSAmb**: honoriacensi **C** Honoriacensi **FAmb**[1]

Possibly some of his readings represent misreadings of a MS in this group:

Letter 8, 3[n]—compositione **TAmb** computatione **C** compunctione ?**E** compactione **Amb**[1]

Rule 26[b]—cantricem **TAmb** cantatricem **CE** cartaticem *sed male* **Amb**[1]

Amb[1] also allies with **E**, **F**, **FY**, and **Y** but never with **C** alone: with **E**:

Letter 1, 14[d–d]—superesse philosophum estimarem: superiorem philosophum existimarem **EAmb**[1]

with **F**:

Letter 1, 5[o]—importunitas: opportunitas **FAmb**[1]; 11[q]—magisterio: magistro **FAmb**[1]; 11[p–p]—sacre lectionis expertem: sacre lectionis inexpertum **FAmb**[1]; 13[m]—gratiam: gloriam **FAmb**[1]; 51[m]—conuenire: congruere **FAmb**[1]; 56[c]—factum: festum **FAmb**[1]; 58[f]—retinente: resonante **FAmb**[1]; 64[h]—commodis: praediis **FAmb**[1]; 64[m]—commouet affectus: permouet et (et *om.* **Amb**[1]) affectus **FAmb**[1]; 67[j]—immundis: malignis **FAmb**[1]

Letter 5, 15[c]—imprudentes: impudentes **FAmb**[1]; 26[f]—castigat: flagellat **FAmb**[1]

Letter 6, 33[f]—aliquid: aliud **FAmb**[1]

Letter 7, **19**[t]—quo scriptum: qui scriptus **FAmb**^{I}; **24**[c]—consortia: consortium **FAmb**^{I} 48[q]—Respondit: Rescripsit **FAmb**^{I}

with **FY**:

Letter 1, **40**[i]—uel confessus: uel (et **F**) confusus **FYAmb**^{I}

with **Y**:

Letter 1, **53**[n]—Quia: qui (**Y** *after exp. of* a) **YAmb**^{I}

For some readings in **Amb** which are not found in extant MSS **Amb**^{I} provides variants which are found in such MSS:

Letter 1, **6**[r]—correxisset **Amb** correxerit **Amb**^{I}; **6**[s]—dimisisset **Amb** dimiserit **Amb**^{I}; **7**[o]—in locum **Amb** ad officium **Amb**^{I}; **8**[g]—discipulos **Amb** discretos **Amb**^{I}; **11**[u]—conclamantes: inclamantes **Amb**^{I}

Occasionally **Amb**^{I} either follows a MS of which we have no knowledge or offers an emendation of his own or simply makes a mistake:

Letter 1, **16**[l]—facillime: facere **Amb**^{I}; **39**[c]—intemptantis: intentandum **Amb**^{I}; **53**[h]—poterant: potuerant **Amb**^{I}; **55**[m]—diuersa: diuisa **Amb**^{I}

Letter 2, **3**[o]—naufragiis: naufragus **Amb**^{I}; **5**[d]—intenderes: studeres **Amb**^{I}

Rule **22**[h]—magisterio: ministerio **Amb**^{I}

But **Amb**^{I} does indicate use of one or more inextant MSS:

Rule **13**[d]—rerum **TAmb** uirorum **CE** virorum *& in aliq.* vitiorum **Amb**^{I}

Stemma

Surveys of the relationships between the MSS and their transmission have been made by Muckle, 'Abelard's letter of consolation', pp. 171–2 (with stemma on p. 172), Monfrin, pp. 53–9 (with stemma on p. 58), and Orlandi, '*Minima Abaelardiana*' and 'Considerazioni sulla trasmissione' (with stemma in 'Considerazioni', p. 56). Muckle regarded **T** and **A** as the best MSS. Monfrin, pp. 56–9 thought (at least for *Letter* 1) that **T**, **A**, and **J**, together with the common ancestors of **CEF** and **BRDY**, independently spring from a shared source. He found also that **T**, **A**, and **J** share no errors in common and never combine in opposition to **CEFBRDY**. Unlike Muckle, he did not attach the **CEF** group to **A**, and he separated **BR** and **DY**. Orlandi thought that **A** derived from a sub-archetype which was not accessible to **CE** or **F** which occupied lower places in the line of transmission, and that **F** did not stem from the immediate source of **CE**. All agreed that **CEF** are often corrupt, although **F** made corrections.

Cross-contamination between the groups **TACEF** and **BRSHDY** makes the presentation of a stemma difficult, and a legible result can only be an oversimplification of the reality. **Y**, in particular, sides occasionally with the first group against the second and, on one occasion, with **J**. Offered here is a stemma largely similar to that provided by Orlandi, 'Considerazioni sulla trasmissione', p. 56, adjusted in the light of the observations made above, but failing to show justly the extent of cross-contamination. The stemma also records **S**, **H**, and **V** (**V** being the lost MS of Paris, abbey of St-Victor GGG 17; see above, pp. xcv–xcviii).

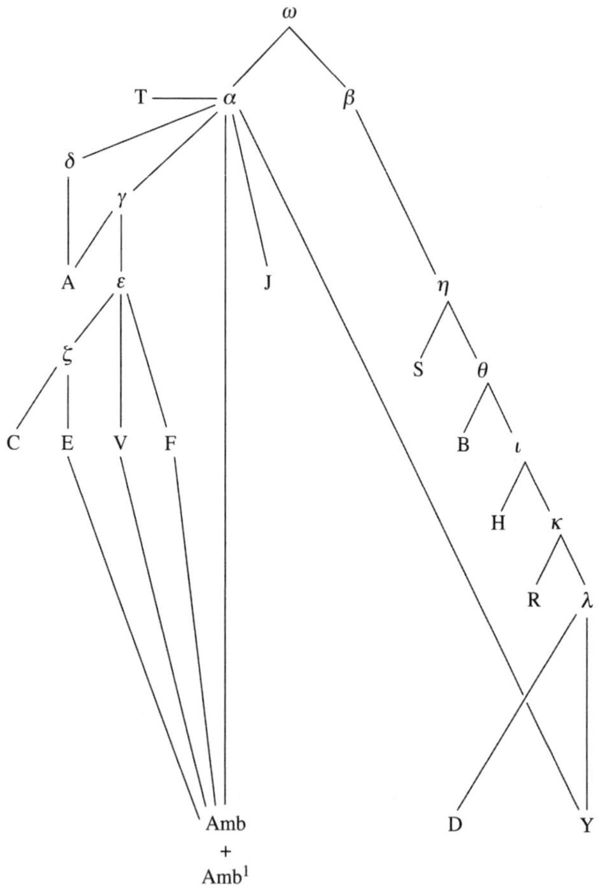

The Edition

The present edition of the letter collection of Heloise and Abelard results from a fresh study and collation of the Latin MSS and is based on those MSS (apart from the lost MS **V** included in the stemma) to which sigla have been given in the descriptions given above—**TACEFBRSHDY**—as well as on the *editio princeps*, **Amb**, together with the revisions of **Amb**[1]. **S** and **H** have not been used in previous editions. **J** is cited occasionally to illustrate differences between the Latin copies; I have relied on the edition by Hicks for this.

Editions of the letter collection and translations of it into several languages are widely available and have proved generally acceptable for gaining and promoting knowledge of what their authors wrote to and about each other. Yet there is a clear need for a new edition. The best critical editions since that of Duchesne–d'Amboise in 1616 are those of Muckle and McLaughlin, which were published between 1950 and 1956 in separate issues of the journal *Mediaeval Studies*, and that of Monfrin, published in 1959, which is limited to *Letters* 1, 2, 4, and part of 5. All these editions are very good. But Monfrin had serious reservations about some of Muckle's work and Orlandi has published serious reservations about some of the work of both Muckle and Monfrin. In 1972 the renewal of controversy over the authorship of the collection led to a flurry, even a blizzard, of publications arising from close reading of the edited texts. It is, therefore, desirable to re-edit the collection, taking much recent scholarship into account.

A few examples may help to illustrate why this seems advisable and what some of the consequences are. They are not chosen to undermine any of the excellent work of previous editors or other scholars but to show how review of the MSS and use of other scholarship does bring benefits.

Letter 1, 8[q]. Here William of Champeaux returns to the Mont Sainte-Geneviève and sends away the master who had replaced him. There is an alternative reading to the effect that William abandoned this master. Orlandi, 'Considerazioni sulla trasmissione', p. 62, referring to Muckle, 'Abelard's letter of consolation', p. 179, n. 82, thought that **Amb** tried to correct this alternative found in **CE**: deserat **CE** deseruerat **Amb**. In fact, 'deserat' is found only in **E**, which helps to support the view presented above (p. xci) that **Amb** had access to **E**, not **C**, and that **E**, not **C**, is *Nanneticus*, the codex named in **Amb**. **Amb**^{I} presents the correct reading found in other MSS: 'dimiserat'. Monfrin, p. 67 does not record any variant here.

Letter 1, **40**^{i}. During the enquiry at Soissons in 1121 into Abelard's teaching on the divine Trinity, bishop Geoffrey of Chartres spoke up for Abelard to be given, in accordance with canonical procedure, a chance to reply to his accusers so that if he is proved wrong or confesses his error he can be totally silenced. All MSS have 'conuictus uel confessus' save **FY**, followed by **Amb**^{I}, which write 'conuictus et confusus'—'if he is proved wrong and becomes confused'—although **F** then adds in the margin the reading found in other MSS: 'uel confessus'. Orlandi, '*Minima Abaelardiana*', p. 132 and n. 10, in the course of a brilliant quest for emendations that might be made to Monfrin's text of the letter, and looking closely for good readings carried by **BRD** and **Y**, preferred 'confusus' to 'confessus', which he thought to be a little unlikely and a scribal corruption of 'confusus'. But it would seem less likely for Geoffrey to be expecting the air to be cleared through confusion than through confession. In the *Decretum* of Geoffrey's predecessor as bishop of Chartres—the celebrated theologian-canonist Ivo—as well as in the *Panormia* commonly attributed to Ivo the words 'conuictus' and 'confessus' are habitually coupled in references to any cleric called to account for some irrregularity.[133] Abelard knew the *Decretum* very well and a large number of entries in his *Sic et non* come from there.[134] Monfrin, incidentally, recorded 'confusus' in **Y** only.

In *Letter* 1, **47**, Abelard answers a question, put to him by a fellow monk of St-Denis, whether the Venerable Bede or Hilduin, a former abbot of St-Denis, had been right about the identity of the abbey's founder. He does this by saying that Bede, 'to whose writings all the Latin churches have recourse', seemed to him to be 'the more weighty authority'—*auctoritatem . . . grauiorem*. Previous editions have given *auctoritatem . . . gratiorem* or 'the more agreeable authority', which

[133] See Ivo of Chartres, *Decretum* VI, *cap*. 232: 'De clericis convictis et confessis' (*PL* clxi. 495C; also Burchard of Worms, *Decretum* II, *cap*. 187: 'De clericis convictis et confessis', *PL* cxl. 656D, who cites the same canon from an African council). Also Ivo, *Decretum* VI, *cap*. 122: 'si ipse confessus non fuerit . . . si . . . non fuerit . . . convictus' (*PL* clxi. 475A), and *Panormia* III, *cap*. 143: 'clericus adulterasse convictus vel confessus'; *cap* . 150: 'non . . . confessus . . . sed . . . convictus'; IV, *cap*. 111: 'convictus vel confessus'; *cap*. 135: 'convictus aut sponte confessus' (*PL* clxi. 1162D, 1166A, 1205D, 1210D). References to Ivo's *Decretum* have been checked against the electronic edition in progress (release of 02/2009: ⟨http://project.knowledgeforge.net/ivo⟩)

[134] See the long lists of parallel passages made by Boyer and McKeon in their edition of *SN*, pp. 635–45.

weakens the reply and, more significantly, is inconsistent both with what is found in Abelard's letter on this subject (*Letter* 11 to the abbot of St-Denis), where Abelard writes *grauioribus . . . auctoritatibus*, and with what is found in the prologue to his *Sic et non*, where, writing about ways of evaluating authorities where they disagree, and quoting St Isidore, Abelard states that preference should be given to the more powerful authority (*potior . . . auctoritas*, ed. Boyer and McKeon, p. 97, *l.* 194) . The correct reading in *Letter* 1 is carried within the weaker of the two main groups of MSS, **BRSDY**, none of which MSS was seen by Duchesne and d'Amboise. Both Muckle and Monfrin, as E. Jeauneau suspected ('Pierre Abélard à Saint-Denis', p. 164n), had adopted an incorrect reading. Monfrin recorded the correct reading as a variant in his *apparatus criticus*; Muckle had not noticed it.

A final example concerns the use in the correspondence of two closely related words: *conuersio* and *conuersatio*. In the course of a fascinating discussion bearing upon the authorship of the collection, E. Gilson in his *Heloise and Abelard* at p. 153, showed that for *conversio* 'the usual meaning of the term' is 'entrance into religion'; '*Conversatio* on the contrary stands, in the language of Abélard and Héloïse, for the monastic state of life'. I have respected this distinction in both text and translation; the MSS were more flexible. *Conuersio* is the better reading in *Letter* 5, 1[q] (nostre conuersationis ad Deum **TEAmb**[1] nostre conuersionis (*tr.* **F**) ad Deum **ACFBRSYAmb**), while *conuersatio* is the better reading in *Letter* 1, **29**[e] (uestes . . . religionis que conuersioni monastice conuenirent **T** *before corr. by* **T**[1], **Amb** uestes . . . religionis que conuersationi monastice conuenirent **ACEFBRDYAmb**[1]) and in *Letter* 6, **3**[e] (conuersionis statum habitumque **TACEBRS** *and Muckle* professionis statum habitumque **F** conuersationis statum habitumque **Amb**) and **16**[g] (ad monasticam conuersionem currentes **TACEFBRSAmb**[1] *and Muckle* ad monasticam conuersationem currentes **Amb**).

In this edition the *Letters* have been divided into consecutively numbered sections. A concordance of the column numbers in Migne, the line numbers in Monfrin, the page numbers in Muckle and McLaughlin, and the section numbers in the edition by Pagani is placed at the end of the volume; for all these editions see Appendix B: Writings of Abelard and Heloise.

I have tried not to give too ready a preference to any one MS such as **T** or to any one group of MSS: **TACEF** are generally more reliable than **BRSHDY** but they too stumble from time to time. On the other hand, I have not always adopted emendations made by **F** around the year 1600, preferring in regard to some of these to accept earlier readings common to the medieval copies. It would, for example, be reasonable to accept a correction made by **F** and **Amb**[1] in *Letter* 5 at **26**[f] in the verse taken from Hebrews 12: 6 ('flagellat autem omnem filium quem recipit'), but all the earlier MSS present 'castigat', not 'flagellat', which is found in the printed Vulgate (Clementine). So 'flagellat' has gone into the *apparatus criticus*. Likewise, to offer another example, it would be correct to write, as **F** does following Pope Gregory himself, Maximianus, not Maximus, in *Letter* 7 at **19**[a], but that is not the name of the bishop of Syracuse that the earlier copyists found. Similarly, I have not substituted the name of Pelagius for that of Jerome in the text of *Letter* 7, **18**. Correction in such cases as these of Maximus and Jerome is made in the notes. But when, as in *Letter* 1, **14**, most of the medieval copies (**TACEBR**) offer a reading (*necdum/not yet*) which makes poor sense and which **F** (*nedum*/let alone; not to speak of) is right to correct, I have accepted the emendation made by **F**: the philosophers of pagan antiquity were not, as the medieval copies wrongly suggest, later to become the divines of the early Christian church.

For the most part the *apparatus criticus* is negative: the MS readings which are indicated in the apparatus are variants from the text as edited and presented here. MSS which give a chosen reading are, however, sometimes indicated when the choice seems especially significant. Even so, this apparatus is fuller than might be expected because so many differences of opinion have arisen over details in the texts and their interpretation that I have chosen to be generous in showing the evidence of the MSS. The variants shown have not always or usually been chosen for the purpose of displaying error or suggesting a plausible alternative, although there are many errors and many plausible alternatives, and some examples of both have been given earlier in this Introduction. The variants shown help to demonstrate the stemma, with the important qualification (previously mentioned) that contamination of the MSS often infringes and defies the usual groupings to which the MSS adhere, but this too (namely, to show contamination) is a valid criterion for their frequent inclusion in the apparatus. On the other hand, agreements or differences between the present text and those established by Duchesne–d'Amboise, Muckle, McLaughlin, and Monfrin have been indicated only occasionally. Where I do depart, usually although not always without comment, from the findings of these and of other scholars, I have endeavoured to do so only after careful checking of the evidence.

Generous notes on spelling and punctuation have accompanied the descriptions of the MSS given above. Their copyists exhibit no underlying consistency in this regard and the spelling of the texts has not been normalized in this edition. It largely reflects that of **T**, which seems to be the earliest witness. While this does not represent the orthography of Abelard or Heloise writing perhaps a hundred years earlier, it fairly represents something close to what their readers encountered, especially in the thirteenth and fourteenth centuries.[135] I have in general indicated in full the variant spellings of personal names and of place names. The punctuation is my own but this, and the numbering of the sections, has been guided by the breaks found in the MSS. In accordance with the editorial guidelines for volumes in the Oxford Medieval Texts series, *v* is printed as *u*, and *j* as *i*.

A second apparatus shows sources of quotations and allusions when they have been found. It also records similar passages in other writings of Heloise and Abelard, the titles of which—unlike those of other writers—are usually given without the name of their author. Thus, *Letter* 2 means Heloise, *Letter* 2, and *Sermon* 32 means Abelard, *Sermon* 32. Notes on some of the contents of the texts that are cited will be found as well as references to further relevant literature. As in this Introduction, so too in this apparatus, references to works cited are usually given in a shortened form: full details will be found in Appendix B or C or the Bibliography at the end of the volume or in the list of Abbreviations at the front.

The Translation

The translation by B. Radice, *The Letters of Abelard and Heloise* (Penguin Classics; London, 1974) has been used. A full translation of *Letter* 7, which was summarized in this volume and numbered *Letter* 6, has been made by the late B. Radice for the present edition. Where I have thought it good to do so, I have 'silently' made some alterations.

[135] On medieval orthography—'la réalité, c'est la diversité' (p. 77)—and the editing of texts, Tombeur's essay '*De polygraphia*' is valuable.

Summary of Manuscript Witnesses to Each of the *Letters* and of their Extents

Abelard, *Letter* 1 (*Historia calamitatum*) **TACEFBR, S** (23–6, 38–75), **DY**, and **J**

Heloise, *Letter* 2 **TACEFBRS, D** (breaks off at the word *alienis*, 7^v^) **Y**, and **J**

Abelard, *Letter* 3 **TACEFBRSY** and **J**

Heloise, *Letter* 4 **TACEFBRSY** and **J**

Abelard, *Letter* 5 **TACEFBRS, Y** (breaks off at *Hoc saltem uno*, 16^r^), and **J**

Heloise, *Letter* 6 **TACEFBRS** and **J**

Abelard, *Letter* 7 **T, A** (1–23, 33–51), **C** (1–8, 11–37, 40–1, 43–51), **E** (1–8, 11–37, 40–1, 43–51), **F** (1–8, 11–37, 40–1, 43–51), **B** (1–35, 40–51), **R** (1–35, 40–51), **S** (breaks off at 17), **H** (lacks text before *celibi se uite dicarent* . . . 43i), and **J**

Abelard, *Letter* 8 **TACEBRH**

Abelard, *Institutio* or *Rule* **T, C** (1–22, 24–38, 40, 51, 67–74, 77–102, 105–28), **E** (1–22, 24–38, 40, 51, 67–74, 77–102, 105–28)

SIGLA

Amb	*Petri Abaelardi . . . Opera*, ed. A. Duchesne and F. d'Amboise (Paris, 1616), pp. 3–197
Amb^{1}	The reviser of **Amb**
A	Paris, BnF lat. 2923, fos. 1–42^{v}
B	Paris, BnF lat. 2544, fos. 3–40^{v}
C	Paris, BnF n. acq. lat. 1873, fos. 136–207^{v}
D	Douai, Bibliothèque municipale 797, vol. iv, fos. 321–328^{v}
E	Paris, BnF lat. 2545, fos. 1–53^{v}
F	Paris, BnF lat. 13057, pp. 10–180
H	Paris, BnF n. acq. fr. 20001, fos. 11–12va
J	Paris, BnF fr. 920, pp. 1–214 (ed. Hicks)
R	Reims, Bibliothèque municipale 872, fos. 112–54
S	The Schøyen collection (Oslo and London) 2085, fos. 1–74^{v}
T	Troyes, Médiathèque 802, fos. 1–88^{v}
Y	Oxford, Bodleian Library Add. C 271, fos. 85^{v}–106^{v}

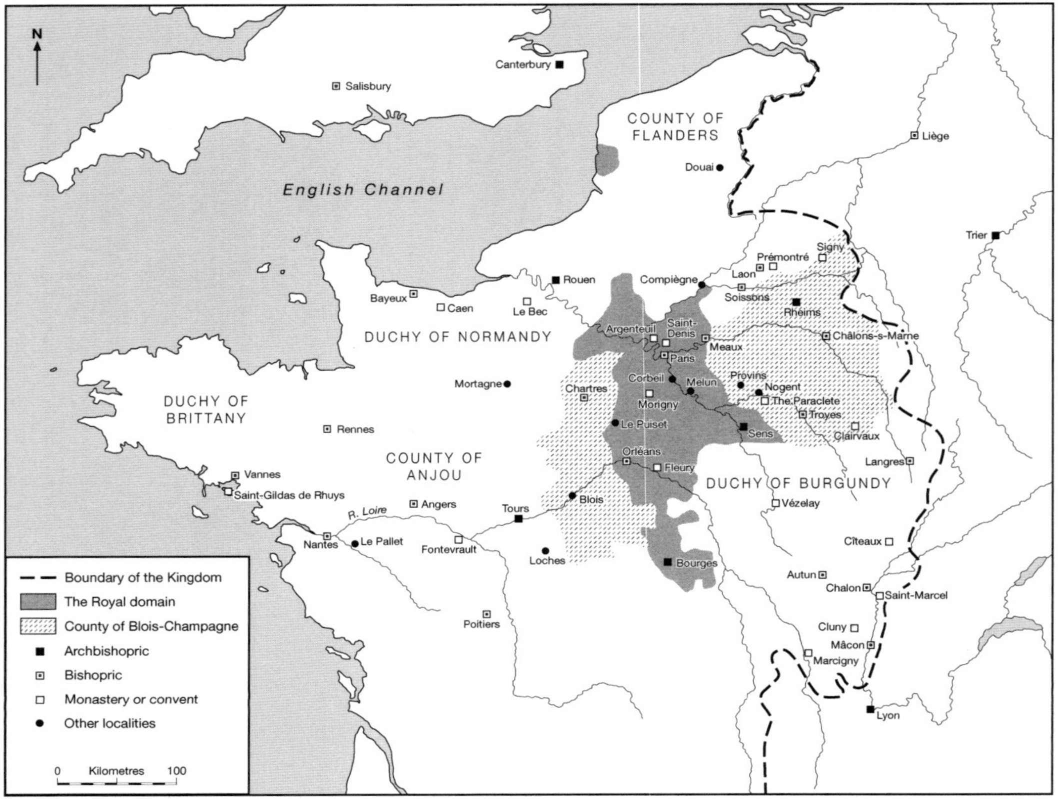

Map 2. The Kingdom of France in the time of Abelard and Heloise

THE LETTERS

⟨EPISTOLA I⟩

ABAELARDI AD AMICVM SVVM CONSOLATORIA

1. Sepe humanos affectus aut prouocant aut mitigant amplius exempla quam uerba.[1] Vnde post nonnullam[a] sermonis ad presentem habiti consolationem,[b] de ipsis calamitatum mearum experimentis consolatoriam[c] ad[d] absentem[2] scribere decreui, ut in comparatione mearum tuas aut nullas aut modicas temptationes recognoscas et[e] tolerabilius feras.[3]

2. [a]DE LOCO NATIVITATIS EIVS[a]

Ego igitur[b] oppido quodam oriundus quod[c] in ingressu minoris Britannie[d] constructum,[e] ab urbe Nannetica uersus orientem octo, credo,[f] miliariis[g] remotum, proprio uocabulo Palatium appellatur, sicut[h] natura terre mee uel generis animo leuis,[4] ita et ingenio extiti[i] ad litteratoriam disciplinam facilis.[5] Patrem autem habebam litteris

Letter 1 *T* fos. 1ra–18ra; *A* fos. 1ra–14ra; *C* fos. 136^{r}–154^{r}; *E* fos. 1^{r}–14^{v}; *F* pp. 121–180; *B* fos. 3ra–13vb; *R* fos. 112ra–125vb; *S* fos. 1^{r}–19^{v}; *D* fos. 321^{r}–328^{r}; *Y* fos. 85vb–97vb; *Amb* pp. 3–41; *Amb*^{1} *variants in the margins of Amb*; *J* pp. 1–58. *Headings are found in the following witnesses*: *Rubr TA* (*cf. Heloise in Letter* 2, 1: 'missam ad amicum pro consolatione epistolam'); Epistolae uenerabilis magistri Petri Abaelardi *F;* Vita magistri Petri Abahelardi . . . (*the rest is lost through trimming*) *add. in B by another hand;* Epistola magistri p. abaielardi ad amicam suam de temptacionibus et calamitatibus in suis euentibus habitis et qualiter suam heloysam sibi copulauit primitus in amorem et postmodum in uxorem *D;* Sequitur prologus de statu et uita magistri abealardi [*sic*] *add. Y*^{2} *in vacant space;* Les Epistres Pierre Abaielart et de Heloyse, qui fut s'amie et puis sa feme, et sont en latin IJ^{C}IIIJ. Premierement il devise ou prologue ou il fu né *table in H of the* (*missing*) *contents of Dijon MS 525;* EPISTOLA I. Quae est HISTORIA CALAMITATUM ABAELARDI Ad Amicum scripta *Amb*

1 [a] nullam *A before corr. by another hand; B before corr.;* non nullam *Y* [b] meam *add. Y* [c] consolotoriam *A* [d] *om. C* [e] aut *D*

2 [a–a] *rubr. TAB* [b] in *add. DY* [c] *om. BRDY* [d] est *add. CEF* [e] constrictum *A before corr. by another hand;* constructo quod *DY* [f] circiter *F* [g] miliaria *F* [h] sed *CEF* [i] et *add. TACEBRDY;* also *Muckle, Monfrin, and F. Châtillon, 'Notes abélardiennes, I', pp. 277–311;* et *F;* extiti *Amb, and Orlandi, 'Minima Abaelardiana', p. 133*

---

[1] For other instances where Abelard juxtaposes 'words' (which instruct) and 'examples' (which provoke or empower) see *Letter* 9: 'Beatus Hieronymus . . . non tam verbis hortatur quam exemplis invitat' (*PL* clxxviii. 325AB and cf. 336A: 'tam scriptis quam exemplis . . . incitat'); *Hymn* 120 (Szövérffy 119), *De sancto Gilda, abbate*, I, *v.* 3: 'uerbis nos instruunt, exemplis prouocant'; *Sermon* 17 (*PL* clxxviii. 504C): 'ut Ecclesiam sibi commissam non solum erudirent uerbis, uerum etiam confirmarent exemplis'. Cf. *Proverbia* (Walther), no. 8420: 'Exemplo melius quam uerbo quisque docetur.' For the expression 'affectus

LETTER 1

A LETTER OF CONSOLATION FROM ABELARD TO A FRIEND

1. There are times when examples are better than words for stirring or soothing human feelings;[1] and so I have chosen to follow up the words of consolation I gave you in person with the experiences of my own misfortunes, hoping thereby to give you comfort in absence.[2] In comparison with my trials you will see that your own are nothing, or only slight, and will find them easier to bear.[3]

2. HIS BIRTHPLACE

I was born on the borders of lower Brittany, about eight miles, I think, east of Nantes, in a town called Le Pallet. I owe my volatile temperament[4] to my native soil and ancestry and also my natural ability for learning letters.[5] My father had acquired some knowledge

prouocant' cf. below **64**: 'humanos commouet affectus'; also *Letter* 3, **9**: 'ut exemplo . . . prouocarentur'. Other examples are given by Jaeger, 'The Prologue to the *Historia calamitatum*', pp. 2–4, of counterparts in Antiquity as well as in other works by Abelard.

[2] 'ad presentem . . . ad absentem': cf. *Carmen ad Astralabium*, ed. Rubingh-Bosscher, *v.* 961: 'scripto te faciet presentem quilibet absens'; also *Letter* 2, **4**. Other mentions of the recipient of *Letter* 1 occur below at **8** and **74** and in *Letter* 2 at **1**, **2**, and **5**. This long-standing and much-suffering friend and companion may have been with Abelard in the schools of Paris and have made a religious profession.

[3] 'ut in comparatione . . . feras': cf. below **74**; also *Sermon* 12 (*PL* clxxviii. 483A): the sufferings of martyrs were nothing or little ('nulla . . . uel parua') in comparison with the Lord's passion. For the theme that consolation comes from comparison of greater with lesser examples, and for other examples of the use by Abelard of similar phrasings, see Jaeger, 'The Prologue to the *Historia calamitatum*', pp. 5–9, who cites *Confessio fidei 'Vniuersis'* (ed. Burnett, p. 132; *PL* clxxviii. 105–6), *Sermon* 26 (*PL* clxxviii. 543B), *Sermon* 29 (*PL* clxxviii. 555D). For such expressions used since Antiquity cf. Silvestre, review of Jaeger, 'The Prologue'.

[4] 'animo levis': for some contemporary parallels see Wollin, 'Ein Liebeslied des Petrus Abaelardus', pp. 132 (4) and 136–7.

[5] Abelard may have been born in 1079. The county of Nantes in lower Brittany was Frankish and lay between the Armorican peninsula and the mainland; being on the river Loire, Nantes was also well connected to France. On its rather independent position within the duchy of Brittany see Everard, *Brittany and the Angevins*, pp. 27–33, esp. pp. 28–9; also Tonnerre, 'Le Comté Nantais à la fin du XIe siècle'. The chronicler Richard of Poitiers wrote (in the 1140s) that Abelard ('Baalardus') was born in Nantes of a Poitevin father and a Breton mother ('Nannetis oritur, patre Pictavus et Brito matre', *Chronicon*, ed. Waitz, p. 81, *l.* 26) The historian Otto of Freising, who was born by 1115 and who studied in Paris, gives an account of Abelard's life in his *Gesta Friderici*, i. 49 (ed. Waitz and von Simson, pp. 68–9). This largely confirms the account given here up to the synod of Soissons. Otto, who thought Abelard arrogant and rash, mentions his birth in Brittany and his early

aliquantulum imbutum antequam militari cingulo insigniretur; unde postmodum tanto litteras amore complexus est, ut quoscumque filios haberet litteris antequam armis instrui disponeret.[6] Sicque profecto actum est. Me[j] itaque primogenitum suum quanto cariorem habebat tanto diligentius erudiri curauit. Ego uero quanto amplius et facilius in studio litterarum profeci tanto ardentius[k] eis inhesi, et in tanto[l] earum amore illectus[m] sum ut militaris glorie pompam cum hereditate et prerogatiua primogenitorum[n] meorum fratribus derelinquens, Martis[o] curie[7] penitus abdicarem ut[p] Minerue gremio[8] educarer; et quoniam dialecticarum rationum armaturam omnibus philosophie documentis pretuli, his armis alia commutaui et tropheis bellorum[q] conflictus pretuli disputationum.[9] Proinde diuersas disputando perambulans prouincias,[10] ubicunque[r] huius [s]artis uigere studium audieram,[s] peripateticorum emulator[t] factus sum.[11]

3. [a]DE PERSECVTIONE MAGISTRI SVI GVILLELMI IN EVM[a]

Perueni tandem Parisius,[b] ubi iam maxime disciplina hec florere consueuerat,[12] ad Guillelmum[c] scilicet[d] Campellensem[e] preceptorem[f] meum in hoc[g] tunc magisterio [h]re et[h] fama precipuum; cum quo aliquantulum moratus, primo ei aceptus, postmodum grauissimus

[j] Sic *Amb* [k] in *add. EF* [l] tantum *Y* [m] illesus *T;* illexus *BR* [n] postgenitorum *D* [o] mris *Y before corr. to* martis me *above the line* [p] de *D* [q] bellator *D* [r] ubique *CER* [s] artis uigere sciui studium *Y with* sciui *add. by* Y[1] [t] ambulator *Amb*[1]

3 [a–a] *rubr. TAB;* Le ij[e] chapitre, comme il ala a Paris aus escoles *table in H of the (missing) contents of Dijon MS 525* [b] Parisios *?E, FAmb* [c] Guillhelmum *T;* guillermum *E* [d] simul *Y* [e] campellesem *A* [f] preceptore *T before exp.* [g] hac *C* [h–h] reque *C;* re quoque et *F*

---

dedication to the study of letters. In a very short biography of Abelard (found in the Munich MS, Clm 14160, fo. 1[r]) which reports a joke about Peter's nickname—*Baiolardus* from *baiare* (to lick) and *lardum* (lard)—and Peter's retort that he called himself *Habelardum* (have-lard) on account of his mastery of the arts—he is said to be English by birth; see Hödl, *Die Geschichte der scholastischen Literatur*, p. 78; Mews, 'In search of a name', pp. 172–3. (The version published in *PL* clxxviii. 57B–58B and by Poole, *Illustrations*, pp. 314–15 lacks a final sentence).

[6] For one of his brothers, Dagobert, Abelard wrote his *Dialectica* (ed. de Rijk, pp. 142 *l.* 15, 146 *l.* 23, 535 *l.* 7), having kept in mind his brother's requests and also his wish that his nephews be educated (p. 146, *ll.* 21–9). Porcarius, who became a canon of the cathedral of Nantes, may also be a brother of Abelard (see n. 235 below). Another brother (*germanus*), Radulphus, is mentioned in the *Obituary of the Paraclete* for 4 Sept. (*Obituaires de la Province de Sens*, iv, ed. Molinier, p. 422A, where mention is also made of a sister, Denise or Dionysia ('Dionisia, magistri nostri Petri germana', 4 Dec., ibid., p. 428E; *Collection des principaux obituaires*, ed. Lalore, no. 393, p. 472) and of two nieces of Abelard, Agnes, prioress ('Agnes, priorissa, neptis magistri nostri Petri', 28 Feb., p. 390n., from the Troyes

of letters before he was a knight, and later on his passion for learning was such that he intended all his sons to have instruction in letters before they were trained to arms.[6] His purpose was fulfilled. I was his firstborn, and being specially dear to him had the greatest care taken over my education. For my part, the more rapid and easy my progress in my studies, the more eagerly I applied myself, until I was so carried away by my love of letters that I renounced the glory of a soldier's life, made over my inheritance and rights of the eldest son to my brothers, and withdrew altogether from the court of Mars[7] in order to be brought up in the bosom of Minerva.[8] I preferred the weapons of dialectical reasonings to all the teachings of philosophy, and armed with these I chose the conflicts of disputes instead of the trophies of war.[9] I began to travel about in various provinces debating,[10] like a true peripatetic philosopher, wherever I had heard there was a keen interest in this art.[11]

3. HIS PERSECUTION BY MASTER WILLIAM

At last I came to Paris, where dialectic had long been particularly flourishing,[12] and to my teacher, William of Champeaux, who at the time was the supreme master of the subject, both in reputation and in fact. I stayed with him for a time, but though he welcomed me at first he soon took a violent dislike to me because I set out to refute some of

MS, Médiathèque 2450, an 18th-c. copy of the Latin necrology), and Agatha, a nun ('Agatha, Deo sacrata, neptis magistri nostri Petri', 25 May, p. 395n; 'Agace, Niece maistre pierre' according to the late 13th-c. French version often called the 'Book of Burials' or 'Livre des sépultures' (Paris, BnF fr. 14410, fo. 14^{v}), p. 395A; previously *Collection des principaux obituaires*, ed. Lalore, no. 92, p. 452); also in Duchesne–d'Amboise, pp. 1187–8. See *Checklist* nos. 122, 401, 411.

[7] 'Martis curie': cf. Juvenal, *Satires*, ix. 101.

[8] 'Minerue gremio': cf. Suetonius, *De uita caesarum*, *Caligula*, *cap*. xxv, 5.

[9] On dialectic as the science of disputing well cf. Ps.-Augustine, *Principia dialecticae* 1 (*PL* xxxii. 1409): 'Dialectica est bene disputandi scientia.' Cited by John of Salisbury, one of Abelard's pupils in the late 1130s, in his *Metalogicon*, ii. 4 (ed. Hall, p. 60, *ll*. 2–3).

[10] Cf. the *Vita* of Robert of Arbrissel (written by Baudri of Bourgueil, d. 1130), who had left Brittany in the 1080s to study in France and Paris: 'Perambulat regiones et provincias irrequietus et in litterarum studiis non poterat non esse sollicitus . . . Franciam adiit et urbem quae Parisius dicitur intravit'; ed. Dalarun and others, *Les Deux vies*, p. 144; *PL* clxii. 1047A. Also Mews, 'Robert of Arbrissel, Roscelin and Abélard', p. 34, n. 7.

[11] On Abelard's early education in dialectic see Appendix A, 1.

[12] 'Perveni tandem Parisius': cf. the similar passage found in Baudri's *Vita* of Robert of Arbrissel cited in n. 10. The date of Abelard's arrival in Paris is uncertain but seems to be *c*.1100. On the city of Paris and its dilapidated mediocrity around the year 1100, largely confined as it was to the Ile de la Cité, on the city's houses, streets, and bridges, on its small population of about 3,000 persons, on the royal palace and the cathedral and other religious establishments, and on its political and military insecurity and instability, see especially Bautier, 'Paris au temps d'Abélard', and Halphen, *Paris sous les premiers Capétiens*, pp. 5–15, 23–5.

extiti, cum nonnullas scilicet eius sententias refellere[i] conarer[j] et ratiocinari[k] contra eum sepius aggrederer et nonnumquam superior in [l]disputando[m] uiderer.[n] [13] Quod quidem[o] et ipsi[l] qui inter conscolares[p] nostros precipui habebantur tanto maiori sustinebant indignatione quanto posterior habebar[q] etatis et studii tempore. Hinc calamitatum mearum, que nunc usque perseuerant, ceperunt exordia; et quo [r]amplius fama extendebatur[r] nostra, aliena in me succensa est inuidia.[s]

4. Factum[a] [b]tandem est[b] ut, supra uires etatis[c] de ingenio meo presumens, ad scolarum[d] regimen[e] adolescentulus[14] aspirarem, et locum in quo id agerem prouiderem,[f] insigne uidelicet tunc temporis Meliduni[g] castrum et sedem regiam.[15] Presensit hoc [h]predictus magister meus,[h] et quo longius posset scolas nostras a se remouere conatus, quibus potuit modis latenter machinatus est ut priusquam a suis recederem [i][j]scolis, nostrarum[j] preparationem scolarum[i] prepediret et prouisum mihi[k] locum auferret. Sed quoniam de potentibus terre nonnullos [l]ibidem habebat emulos,[l] [m]fretus eorum[m] auxilio uoti mei compos[n] extiti, et plurimorum mihi assensum ipsius inuidia manifesta conquisiuit.[16]

5. Ab[a] hoc autem[b] [c]scolarum nostrarum[c] tirocinio[d] ita in arte dialetica nomen meum dilatari cepit, ut non solum [e]condiscipulorum meorum,[e] uerum etiam ipsius magistri fama contracta paulatim [f]extingueretur. Hinc[g] factum est ut de[f] me amplius ipse[h] presumens ad castrum Corbolii,[i] [j]quod Parisiace urbi[j] uicinius[k] est, quamtotius[l] scolas nostras transferrem, ut inde uidelicet [m]crebriores disputationis[m]

[i] refellerer *C before corr.* [j] canerer *C* [k] rationari *A* [l–l] *add. T*³ *over eras.* [m] disputanto *T*³ [n] uidere *C after eras. of final* r [o] que *CEF* [p] scolares *RDY* [q] haberer *D* [r–r] extendebatur fama *Y with* fama *add. by Y*¹ [s] De inicio magisterii sui *rub. add. A*

4 [a] *the initial letter lacks in T* [b–b] est tandem *A* [c] mee *add. CEF;* mon *J* [d] scolarem *C;* scholarem *F* [e] regiminis *C before exp. of* is [f] *om. CEF* [g] meldunum *CE;* Meledunense *F;* meleduni *BRY;* Meldunum *Amb;* Meliduni *Amb*¹; *in the upper margin of T, on fo. 1*$^{va+b}$*, a 15th-/early 16th-c. hand has added a rubr. partly lost through trimming:* . . . apud melidunum Deinde apud Corbolium; Comme il ala tenir les escoles a Meleun, puis a Corbeil *table in H of the (missing) contents of Dijon MS 525* [h–h] magister meus predictus *D* [i–i] scolis nostrarum preparationem *A;* scolis nostrarum preparationum scolarum *Y* [j–j] scolas (scolis *partly exp. F*) nostras *CEF* [k] nobis *F* [l–l] *om. D* [m–m] *possibly* que eorum *F* [n] *om. R*

5 [a] ob *R* [b] *om. D* [c–c] nostrarum scolarum *CE* [d] creatus *?C;* exordio *EAmb;* tyrocinio *Amb*¹ [e–e] causa discipulorum meorum *A;* condiscipulorum suorum *D; in E the letters before and after* discipulorum *are unclear* [f–f] *T*³ *over eras.* [g] Hinc *D signals a new paragraph* [h] ipsum *CE* [i] corbilii *A before corr. by another hand;* carbolii *CY;* corobolii *E* [j–j] *C writes* etc Parisiace urbi nam in isto spacio *then leaves a space and repeats* Hinc (*with a large initial*) . . . Parisiace [k] uicinus *R;*

his opinions and frequently reasoned against him. On several occasions I appeared to be his superior in debate.[13] Those who were considered the leaders among my fellow-students were also annoyed, and the more so as they looked on me as the youngest and most recent pupil. This was the beginning of the misfortunes which have dogged me to this day and, as my reputation grew, so other men's jealousy was aroused.

4. It ended by my setting my heart on running a school of my own, young as I was,[14] and estimating my capacities too highly for my years; and I had my eye on a site suited to my purpose—Melun, an important stronghold at that time and a royal residence.[15] My master suspected my intentions, and, in an attempt to remove my school as far as possible from his own, before I could leave him he secretly used every means he could to thwart my plans and keep me from the place I had chosen. But among the powers in the land he had several enemies, and these men helped me to obtain my desire. I also won considerable support simply through his unconcealed jealousy.[16]

5. Thus my school was launched and my reputation for dialectic began to spread, with the result that the fame of my old fellow-students and even that of the master himself declined and gradually came to an end. Consequently, being more sure of myself, I made haste to transfer my school to Corbeil, a stronghold nearer Paris, where I could embarrass

uicinum *Y* [l] quanto *BR;* quamcito *DY* [m–m] crebriores disputations *A before corr.;* crebrioris disputationis *F*

[13] Otto of Freising, *Gesta Friderici*, i. 49 (ed. Waitz and von Simson, p. 69), writes that Abelard found William's teaching vacuous and that he did not put up with it for long. On William of Champeaux see Appendix A, 2.i.

[14] 'adolescentulus': according to Isidore of Seville, 'adolescentia' lasted from year 15 to 28 (*Etymologiae*, xi. 2. 3–4).

[15] Melun is 55 km south-east of Paris on the river Seine; King Philip I (1060–1108) died at Melun and King Louis VI (1108–37) used it as a centre for royal government. On the political aspects of this and of Abelard's subsequent relocations see Bautier, 'Paris au temps d'Abélard', esp. pp. 53–77.

[16] Bautier, 'Paris au temps d'Abélard', pp. 54, 60–2, identified as the most important figure who enabled Abelard to set up his school in Melun Stephen de Garlande, a member of one of the principal castellan families in the French royal domain, from 1105 royal chancellor, and also from 1104 an archdeacon of the cathedral of Notre Dame in Paris with houses near the north gate of the cathedral close (Bautier, 'Paris au temps d'Abélard', p. 29, n. 7). In 1101, when King Philip I was seeking the election of Stephen as bishop of Beauvais, Ivo, bishop of Chartres, described him as an uneducated playboy and womanizer (Ivo, *Letter* 87, *PL* clxii. 167–8). Stephen quarrelled with the king in 1105 and this may be the time when Abelard first left Melun and went to Corbeil.

assultus nostra[n] daret importunitas.[o] [17] Non multo autem interiecto tempore, ex[p] immoderata studii afflictione correptus[q] infirmitate[r] coactus sum repatriare, et per annos aliquot[s] a Francia remotus,[t] querebar ardentius ab his quos dialetica sollicitabat doctrina.[18]

6. Elapsis autem paucis annis, cum ex infirmitate iam dudum conualuissem, preceptor meus ille Guillelmus[a] Parisiacensis[b] archidiaconus, habitu pristino commutato,[c] ad [d]regularium clericorum[d] ordinem se conuertit; ea ut referebant[e] intentione ut quo religiosior crederetur[f] ad maioris prelationis gradum[g] promoueretur, sicut in proximo contigit, eo Catalaunensi[h] episcopo facto. Nec tamen hic sue conuersionis[i] habitus aut ab urbe Parisius[j] aut a[k] consueto philosophie studio eum[l] reuocauit, sed in ipso quoque monasterio ad quod se causa religionis contulerat statim more solito publicas exercuit scolas.[19] Tum[m] ego[n] ad eum reuersus ut ab ipso rethoricam[o] audirem, [p]inter cetera[p] disputationum nostrarum conamina antiquam eius de uniuersalibus sententiam[q] patentissimis[r] argumentorum[s] rationibus[t] ipsum commutare, immo[u] destruere compuli.[v] [20] Erat autem [w]in ea sententia[w] de communitate uniuersalium, ut eamdem essentialiter rem totam[x] simul singulis suis inesse astrueret indiuiduis,[y] quorum quidem nulla esset[z] in essentia[a] diuersitas sed sola multitudine accidentium[b] uarietas. Sic autem[c] istam tunc[d] suam correxit sententiam,[e] ut deinceps rem[f] eamdem[g] non[h] essentialiter sed indifferenter[i] diceret. Et[j] quoniam de uniuersalibus [k]in hoc ipso precipua semper est apud dialeticos questio, ac tanta[l] ut eam Porphirius[m] quoque in *Ysagogis*[n] suis cum de uniuersalibus[k][o] scriberet definire non presumeret,[p] dicens:

[n] nostras *BRD and Y before corr. by another hand* [o] opportunitas *FAmb*[1] [p] *om. E* [q] corporis *EF;* correctus *R* [r] infirmitate *C followed by repetition of* non multo . . . infirmitate [s] aliquos *DY* [t] quasi *add. FAmb*

6 [a] Guillhelmus *T* [b] Parisiensis *BR;* Par. *DY* [c] commutata *C after corr.* [d–d] scolarium regularium *D* [e] afferebat *F;* al. referebant *add. F in marg.* [f] ordinaretur *C* [g] gradus *C* [h] cataulanensi *TA;* cathelanensi *C;* catholanensi *E;* Catalaunensi *F;* catalanensi *B;* catala⟨u *add. by corr.*⟩nensi *R;* Cathalanensi *D, Y after eras. of final* s [i] conuersationis *C;* conversacion *J* [j] par̄ *CY;* parisiaca *E;* Parisiensi *F* [k] *om. RDY* [l] *om. TACEBRD;* eum *FY*[1]. *Cf. Orlandi, 'Minima Abaelardiana', p. 133* [m] cum *C;* tunc *BRDY* [n] exemplo *E;* extemplo ego *F* [o] rectoriam *Y before corr. in marg. by another hand* [p–p] interest *B;* inter eum *R;* inter cause *D;* inter *Y followed by eras.* [q] scienciam *BRY* [r] paucissimis *RDY* [s] authorum *F* [t] disputationibus *EAmb* [u] seu *Y* [v] *In the upper margin of fo. 2*[r] *in T a 15th-/early 16th-c. hand has added a rubr.:* De impugnatione magistri sui et conuersione ipsius apud parisium [w–w] in eadem sententia *CEF;* prius in ea sciencia *BR;* prius in hac sciencia *DY* [x] tantam *C after corr. of* totam [y] et diuiduis *C* [z] est *D* [a] esse *CF* [b] actionum *F* [c] ante *BRD* [d] *om. CE;* rem RD, *exp. Y* [e] scienciam *B* [f] esse *RDY* [g] eadem *B* [h] *om. C* [i] in indifferenter *A;*

him through more frequent confrontations in debate.[17] However, I was not there long before I fell ill through overwork and was obliged to return to my own country. For some years, being far from France, I was more keenly missed by those eager for instruction in dialectic.[18]

6. A few years later, when I had long since recovered my health, my teacher William, archdeacon of Paris, changed his former way of life and entered the order of regular canons with the intention, it was said, of gaining promotion to a higher prelacy through a reputation for increased piety. He was soon successful, becoming bishop of Châlons. But this religious life of his did not remove him from either the city of Paris or his habitual study of philosophy, and he soon resumed his public teaching in his usual manner in the very monastery to which he had retired to follow the religious life.[19] I returned to him to hear his lectures on rhetoric, and, in the course of our engagements in debates, with very clear reasoned arguments I made him amend, or rather abandon, his previous opinion about universals.[20] For his opinion about the community of universals was that he could prove that the same thing is essentially, wholly, and simultaneously present in its individuals, and that these individuals, which do not differ in essence, differ only in the quantity of their accidents. But he corrected this view of his so as to say that the thing is not the same in essence but in non-difference. The chief question facing dialecticians about universals has always centred on this, so much so that even Porphyry did not venture to settle it when he dealt with universals in his *Isagoge*, but only mentioned it

indiuidualiter *Amb;* indifferenter *Amb*[1] [j] Caeterum *F* [k–k] *om. D* [l] *om. Y* [m] porfirius *A;* phorphirius *C;* phorpfirius *E;* potius *F* [n] ysogogis *TA* [o] uerbalibus *F* [p] presunent *D*

---

[17] 'castrum Corbolii': Bautier, 'Paris au temps d'Abélard', p. 62, links Abelard's move to Corbeil with the presence there of count Eudes, who had also fallen out with King Philip in 1104/5.

[18] Bautier, 'Paris au temps d'Abélard', p. 62, links Abelard's return to his native Brittany, on grounds of ill-health, with the fighting that broke out between the Garlandes, in alliance with Milo of Troyes and the Rocheforts, who had taken the young prince Louis into their keeping. Only when the cloud of disgrace was lifted from the Garlandes, probably in 1108, did Abelard return to Francia. Anseau de Garlande then became the royal seneschal and Stephen once more the royal chancellor. A later dating is suggested by Mews, 'William of Champeaux: The foundation of Saint-Victor', pp. 98, 103. On the Garlande family and the struggles for offices in the royal entourage at the time see Bournazel, *Le Gouvernement capétien*, pp. 34–40, 111–15.

[19] See Appendix A, 2.ii.

[20] See Appendix A, 2.iii.

'Altissimum [q]enim est[q] huiusmodi negotium',[21] cum hanc ille correxerit[r] immo coactus dimiserit[s] sententiam,[t] in tantam [u]lectio eius[u] deuoluta[v] est negligentiam, ut iam [w]ad cetera dialectice[w] uix admitteretur quasi in hac scilicet de uniuersalibus[x] sententia[y] tota huius artis[z] consisteret summa.[22]

7. Hinc[a] tantum roboris[b] et auctoritatis nostra suscepit disciplina, ut hii qui antea uehementius magistro [c]illi nostro[c] adherebant et maxime nostram infestabant doctrinam, ad nostras conuolarent[d] scolas, et ipse qui in scolis Parisiace sedis magistro successerat nostro locum mihi suum offerret, ut ibidem cum ceteris nostro se traderet magisterio ubi antea suus[e] ille et noster magister floruerat.[23] Paucis itaque diebus ibi me dialectice studium regente, quanta inuidia tabescere, quanto dolore estuare ceperit[f] magister noster non est facile exprimere; nec concepte miserie estum diu sustinens, callide aggressus[g] est me [h]tunc etiam[h] remouere.[i] [24] Et quia [j]in me quid[j] aperte ageret[k] non habebat,[l] ei scolas auferre molitus est, pessimis[m] obiectis[n] criminibus, qui mihi suum concesserat magisterium, alio quodam emulo meo [o]ad officium eius[o] substituto.[25]

[q–q] est enim *DY* [r] correxisset *Amb;* correxerit *Amb*[1] [s] dimisit *?A, D;* dimisisset *Amb;* dimiserit *Amb*[1] [t] scienciam *BRD, Y before corr.* [u–u] lectio huius *BR;* lectio huiusmodi *D;* huiusmodi lectio *Y* [v] devolata *T* [w–w] ad (a *E*) dialectice lectionem *?C, EF;* ad Dialecticae lectionem *Amb;* ad caetera Dialecticae *Amb*[1] [x] uerbalibus *F* [y] sciencia *BRDY* [z] *om. A*

7 [a] *om. C* [b] *add. in A by A*[3] [c–c] nostro illi *CF* [d] conualerent *B, R before corr.;* doctrinas *add. Y before exp.* [e] summus *Y* [f] cepit *T* [g] eggressus *D* [h–h] etiam tunc *CEF* [i] Comme .j. sien maistre et aucuns clers eurent envie sur lui, et la fu le commencement de ses doleurs *add. H in the table of the* (*missing*) *contents of Dijon MS 525* [j–j] in me quod *CFAmb;* in me quam *E;* quid in me *BR;* in me *D;* quod in me *Y* [k] aget *R* [l] michi *add. Y*[1] [m] turpissimis *CEF* [n] abjectis *CE* [o–o] ad eius officium *CEF;* in locum eius *Amb;* ad officium eius *Amb*[1]

[21] Porphyry, *Isagoge*, i. 10, trans. Boethius (ed. Minio-Paluello with the aid of Dod, *Aristoteles Latinus*, i. 6–7, p. 5, *ll.* 14–15).

[22] On the problem of universals see Appendix A, 2.iv.

[23] There appears to have been a number of schools for boys in the close on the north side of the cathedral of Notre Dame (the 'Tresantia') and also elsewhere on the Ile de la Cité. Bautier ('Paris au temps d'Abélard', p. 63) suggested but without proof that William's successor in his school was Gilbert or Gerbert, who became chancellor of the cathedral chapter and was bishop of Paris from 1116 to 1123. According to Mews, 'William of Champeaux, Abelard and Hugh of Saint-Victor', p. 142–3; 'William of Champeaux, the foundation of Saint-Victor', pp. 98–101, he was Goscelin or Jocelyn of Vierzy, later (1126–52) bishop of Soissons. But, according to the writer of the *Vita Gosvini*, i. 2 (see n. 25 below), Jocelyn, called *magister*, was an outspoken critic of Abelard, describing him as no

as the 'ultimate difficulty'.[21] Consequently, when William had corrected or rather had been forced to give up his position, his lecturing fell into such disregard that he was scarcely accepted on any other points of dialectic, as if in this view about universals lay the whole of this art.[22]

7. My own teaching gained so much strength and authority from this that the most vigorous supporters of my master who had hitherto been the most hostile among my critics now flocked to join my school. Even William's successor as head of the Paris school offered me his chair so that he could join the others as my pupil, in the place where his master and mine had won fame.[23] Within a few days of my taking over the teaching of dialectic, William was eaten up with jealousy and consumed with anger to an extent it is difficult to convey and, being unable to control the violence of his resentment for long, he made another artful attempt to banish me.[24] I had done nothing to justify his acting openly against me, so he launched an infamous attack on the man who had put me in his chair, in order to remove the school from him and put it in the hands of some other rival of mine.[25]

teacher or disputant but a quibbling scoffer and jester who was stubbornly wrong ('Magistrum Petrum . . . disputatorem non esse, sed cavillatorem; et plus vices agere joculatoris quam doctoris, et quod instar Herculis clavam non leviter abjiceret apprehensam, videlicet quod pertinax esset in errore, et quod si secundum se non esset, nunquam acquicsceret veritati', ed. Gibbons, reproduced in Grondeux, 'Guillaume de Champeaux', p. 16; excerpts in *Recueil des historiens*, xiv, ed. Delisle, pp. 442–3). If this is true, Jocelyn would hardly have been willing to give up his post to let Abelard back into the schools of Paris.

[24] The attempts to prevent Abelard teaching in Paris may underlie a humorous tale told by James of Vitry (*c.*1165–1240) in one of his *exempla*. James wrote that he had heard (*audivi*) that master Peter Abelard, who taught crowds of students in Paris, overcame an order from the king of France to stop him teaching on his lands by climbing a tree and, when forbidden to teach in the air, by taking to a boat (no. 51, ed. Frenken in *Die Exempla des Jacob von Vitry*, p. 123).

[25] This second substitute for William may be Goswin; see Mews, 'William of Champeaux, Abelard, and Hugh of Saint-Victor', pp. 143–5; 'William of Champeaux, the foundation of Saint-Victor', pp. 101–2; Grondeux, 'Sainteté et grammaire', 'Guillaume de Champeaux', and n. 28 below. In the *Vita prima* devoted to him, Goswin appears as a teacher of Priscian at Douai who came to Paris, challenged Abelard, and soon after (1114/15) became a monk; see nn. 28 and 142 below. In the *Vita*, on the occasion when, against the advice of Jocelyn, Goswin challenged Abelard when lecturing, Goswin's inexperience and youth are highlighted, not any responsibility he may have had for teaching in Paris ('adolescens', 'uix juuenescentem', 'pubescere incipientem', 'tantillo juueni', 'juuenculum'), *Vita Gosvini*, ed. Gibbons, i. 7 and reproduced in Grondeux, 'Guillaume de Champeaux'; excerpts in *Recueil des historiens*, xiv, ed. Delisle, pp. 442–8. Abelard also described himself as a precocious *adolescentulus* when he first began to run a school (4 above).

8. Tunc ego Melidunum[a] reuersus scolas ibi[b] nostras sicut antea constitui; et quanto manifestius eius me persequebatur inuidia tanto mihi [c]auctoritatis amplius[c] conferebat iuxta illud poeticum:

Summa petit liuor: perflant[d] altissima uenti.[26]

[e]Non multo autem post,[e] cum ille intelligeret [f]omnes fere[f] discretos[g] de religione eius plurimum hesitare et de conuersione[h] ipsius uehementer susurrare, quod[i] uidelicet [j]a ciuitate minime[j] recessisset, transtulit se et conuenticulum fratrum cum scolis suis ad uillam quandam ab urbe remotam.[27] Statimque ego Meliduno[k] Parisius redii, pacem ab illo ulterius[l] sperans. Sed quia, ut diximus, locum nostrum[m] ab emulo nostro fecerat occupari,[n] extra ciuitatem in monte Sancte Genouefe[o] scolarum nostrarum castra posui, quasi eum obsessurus qui locum occupauerat nostrum.[28] Quo audito magister noster, statim ad[p] urbem impudenter rediens, scolas quas tunc habere poterat et conuenticulum fratrum ad pristinum reduxit monasterium, quasi militem suum quem dimiserat[q] ab obsidione nostra liberaturus.[r] Verum cum illi[s] [t]prodesse intenderet[t] maxime nocuit. Ille quippe antea aliquos [u]habebat qualescunque discipulos,[u] maxime propter [v]lectionem Prisciani in qua[v] plurimum ualere credebatur.[29] Postquam

8 [a] e melduno *E;* Meldunum *F;* meledunum *DY;* Meledunum *Amb;* Melidunum *Amb*¹. *In the margin of fo. 2*^rb *in T a 15th-/early 16th-c. hand has added a rubr.:* de recessu a parisiense ciuitate ad mildunum [b] ibidem *CE;* itidem *F* [c–c] amplius auctoritatis *D* [d] perfluant *T before corr.;* perfluat *C* [e–e] non merito aliq̄ post tempus *E* [f–f] fere omnes *CEF* [g] discipulos *Amb;* discretos *Amb*¹ [h] conversacion *J* [i] eo quod *DY* [j–j] minime a ciuitate *T;* ac (de *B*¹) ciuitate minime *BR* [k] e melduno *E;* Meleduno *FAmb;* meleduno *DY* [l] interius *Y* [m] magnum *?C* [n] occupati *A before corr. by another hand* [o] genoufe *A before corr. by another hand. In the margin of fo. 2*^va *in T a 15th-/early 16th-c. hand has added a rubr.:* De eius regressu ad montem sancte genouefe extra ciuitatem et conflictu contra magistrum suum [p] ab *C* [q] dimiserat *TACFBRDYAmb*¹*;* deserat *E;* deseruerat *Amb* [r] deliberaturus *D* [s] ille *D* [t–t] intenderet prodesse *A after corr. by another hand from* intendere prodesse [u–u] discipulos habebat qualescumque *T but T*¹ *marks* qualescumque *and writes* ⟨di⟩scipulos *in the* (*now trimmed*) *marg.;* avoit il avant aucuns desciples tiex quiex *J* [v–v] lectiones prisciani in qua *T;* lectionem prisciani (priscinani *D;* presciani *Y*) in qua *ACBRDY;* lectionem precipuum (prisciani *add. in marg.*) in qua *E;* lectionem praecipuam in qua *F;* lectionem in qua *Amb;* lectiones Prisciani in quibus *Amb*¹*;* la leccon de Prescien que *J*

---

[26] Ovid, *Remedia amoris*, 369; also cited by Abelard in *Epistola contra Bernardum* (ed. Klibansky in 'Peter Abailard and Bernard of Clairvaux', p. 7, *l.* 21; trans. Ziolkowski, p. 109), and in *Carmen ad Astralabium*, ed. Rubingh-Bosscher, *v.* 327.

[27] On William's moves see Appendix A, 2.v.

[28] The Mont Sainte-Geneviève was the property of the abbey of Sainte-Geneviève, an abbey of secular canons whose dean was (perhaps from 1110) now Stephen de Garlande. The Mont, with its abbey dating from Merovingian times (the burial place of Clovis and his queen Clotilde), was still a rural area with fields and vines, one vineyard being owned by the

8. I then returned to Melun and set up my school there as before; and the more openly his jealousy pursued me, the more widely my reputation spread, for, as the poet says:

> Envy seeks the heights, winds sweep the summits.[26]

But not long after, when he heard that there was considerable doubt about his piety amongst almost all thoughtful men and a good deal of gossip about his conversion, as it had not led to his departure from Paris, he removed himself and his little community, along with his school, to a vill far away from the city.[27] I promptly returned to Paris from Melun, hoping for peace henceforth from him, but since he had filled my place there, as I said, by one of my rivals, I took my school outside the city to the Mont Sainte-Geneviève, and set up camp there in order to lay siege to my usurper.[28] The news brought William back to Paris in unseemly haste to take what he could of his school and of his small group back to his former monastery, as if to deliver from my siege the knight he had abandoned. But his good intentions did the man very serious harm. He had previously had a few pupils of a sort, largely because of his teaching of Priscian, for which he had some reputation.[29] But as soon as his master arrived he lost them all and

wealthy Garlande family until 1134 when a small *bourg* with scattered houses slowly began to develop. It was not until 1209 that a wall was built around most of the Mont that brought it within the city of Paris. Cf. Halphen, *Paris sous les premiers Capétiens*, pp. 23–7; Boussard, *Nouvelle Histoire de Paris*, pp. 186–94; Bautier, 'Paris au temps d'Abélard', pp. 25 and 63; and, for the architecture of the abbey, Vieillard-Troïekouroff, 'L'Église Sainte Geneviève'. One of Abelard's auditors on the Mont, Goswin (*c.*1086–1166), was highly critical of him. His *Life* records that Abelard attracted many students but made enemies. Goswin describes him as learned and eloquent but also as an inventor of unheard-of novelties ('probatae quidem scientiae, sublimis eloquentiae, sed inauditarum erat inventor et assertor novitatum'). Goswin sought to interrupt one of Abelard's public lectures on dialectic given on the Mont, facing him like David before Goliath. Master Jocelyn (later bishop of Soissons, 1126–52; see n. 23 above) had attempted to dissuade him from doing so, but Goswin claims to have had the better of the confrontation, about which, however, he gives no details. Goswin later (*c.*1120) became prior of St-Médard in Soissons (see n. 142 below) and in 1131 abbot of Anchin. See *Vita prima Gosvini*, i. 2, ed. Gibbons in *Vita Gosvini*; reproduced in Grondeux, 'Guillaume de Champeaux'; *Recueil des historiens*, xiv (excerpts from the *Vita prima* (written *c.*1173) and *Vita secunda* (after 1174), ed. Delisle, pp. 442–8); also Robl, 'Goswin von Anchin', pp. 271–2, 284–5.

[29] On William's place in the teaching of Priscian's *Institutiones grammaticae* (written in the early 6th c.; ed. Hertz in Keil, *Grammatici latini*, ii–iii) see Fredborg, 'Speculative grammar', and Rosier-Catach, 'Grammar', pp. 196–200. Books i–xvi ('Priscian maior') were on the parts of speech; books xvii–xviii ('Priscian minor') dealt with syntax. As R. W. Hunt once wrote ('Studies on Priscian', pt. i, p. 194), 'no study of the logical doctrines of the early twelfth century would be adequate which did not take account of Priscian and of the glossators of his works'.

autem magister aduenit, omnes penitus amisit;[w] et [x]sic a[x] regimine scolarum cessare[y] compulsus est. Nec post [z]multum tempus,[z] quasi iam ulterius de mundana desperans gloria, ipse[a] quoque ad monasticam conuersus[b] [c]est uitam.[c] Post reditum uero magistri nostri ad urbem, quos conflictus disputationum scolares nostri tam cum ipso quam cum discipulis eius habuerint,[d] et quos fortuna euentus in his bellis dederit nostris, immo mihi[e] ipsi[f] [g]in eis,[g] te quoque res ipsa dudum edocuit. Illud uero Aiacis,[h] ut[i] temperantius loquar, audacter proferam:

Si queritis huius
Fortunam pugne, non sum superatus ab illo.[30]

[j]Quod si ego taceam,[k] res ipsa clamat et ipsius rei finis indicat.[j] [31]

9. Dum[a] uero hec agerentur, karissima mihi mater mea Lucia[b] [c]repatriare me[c] compulit;[d] que[e] uidelicet post conuersionem Berengarii[f] patris mei ad professionem monasticam idem facere disponebat.[32] Quo completo[g] reuersus sum in Franciam, maxime ut de diuinitate addiscerem,[h] quando[i] iam sepefatus[j] magister noster[k] Guillelmus[l] in episcopatu Catalaunensi[m] pollebat.[33] In hac autem lectione magister eius[n] Anselmus Laudunensis maximam ex antiquitate auctoritatem tunc tenebat.[34]

10. [a] QVANDO LAVDVNVM VENIT AD MAGISTRVM ANSELMVM[a]
Accessi[b] igitur[c] ad hunc senem,[35] cui [d]magis longeuus[d] usus quam ingenium uel memoria[e] [f]nomen comparauerat.[f] Ad quem[g] si quis de aliqua questione pulsandum[h] accederet incertus,[i] redibat[j] incertior.

[w] admisit *TCE, Y before exp. of* d [x–x] se de *E;* sic de *F* [y] *om. BRD, superscr. by another hand in Y* [z–z] tempus *ACEF;* multum temporis *BRDY* [a] ipsum *D* [b] compulsus *T before corr., Amb*¹ [c–c] uitam *C unfilled space in E* [d] habuerit *B* [e] misi *E* [f] *om. CEF* [g–g] *marked for corr. in Y* [h] ailacis *T*⁴ *seeking to correct* alacis *T;* a laicis *B;* alaicis *R;* ayacis *D;* dya *Y followed by space;* Aiaus *J* [i] et *T;* mes que je parolles *J* [j–j] *om. Y* [k] taceram *E;* tacerem *Amb*

9 [a] Dudum *D* [b] Liucia *F* [c–c] me repatriare *Y* [d] *In the top margin of fo. 2vb in T a 15th-/early 16th-c. hand has added a rubr.:* De repatriatione eius [e] Quod *A* [f] Berangarii *D* [g] complecto *D* [h] addicerem *T* [i] quam *E before corr. by another hand;* quoniam *Amb*¹ [j] sepe prefatus *E;* sepe fatus *R* [k] *om. C* [l] Guillhelmus *T* [m] cataulanensi *A;* cathalanensi *CEY;* Cathalan *abbrev. D* [n] *om. CF*

10 [a–a] *rubr. T; space for rubr. AR;* Quando uenit laudunum ad magistrum anselmum *rubr. B;* Le iij^e chapitre, comment il ala ouir de divinité et comment il en leut après, dont les estudiens orent envie sur lui *table in H of the (missing) contents of Dijon MS 525* [b] *large initial capital in TBR and unfilled space in D* [c] ergo *F* [d–d] longeuus magis *BRD;* longenus magis *Y* [e] memoriam *R* [f–f] usum comparauerant *F* [g] quam *D* [h] pulsanda *Y* [i] indeus *C* [j] redibit *F before corr.*

had to retire from running a school. Soon afterwards he appeared to lose hope of future worldly fame, and he too was converted to the monastic life. The bouts of argument which followed William's return to the city between members of my school and him and his followers, and the successes in these skirmishes which fortune gave my own followers, and indeed me too, you have long known from the affair itself. But I shall not go too far if I boldly say with Ajax that

> If you ask the issue of this fight,
> I was not vanquished by him.[30]

Should I keep silence, the facts cry out and tell the outcome.[31]

9. Meanwhile my dearest mother Lucy insisted that I return to Brittany, for after my father Berengar's entry into monastic life she was preparing to do the same.[32] When she had done so I returned to France, with the special purpose of studying divinity, to find my master William (whom I have often mentioned) already established as bishop of Châlons.[33] However, in this field his own master, Anselm of Laon, was then the leading authority because of his great age.[34]

10. WHEN HE WENT TO MASTER ANSELM AT LAON

I therefore approached this old man,[35] who owed his reputation more to long practice than to intelligence or memory. Anyone who knocked at his door to seek an answer to some question went away more

[30] Ovid, *Metamorphoses*, xiii. 89–90. Cf. Taylor, 'A second Ajax'.

[31] 'Quod si ego taceam . . .': cf. *Letter* 2, 5; also Roscelin's *Letter* to Abelard, with disparaging comments on Abelard's affair with Heloise: 'quamuis eam lingua taceat, tamen eam res ipsa clamat' (ed. Reiners p. 78, *ll.* 6–7; *PL* clxxviii. 369B (*Letter* 15)). Cf. also Luke 19: 40; Terence, *Eunuch* 705, Cicero, 1 *In Catilinam*, viii. 21 ('cum tacent, clamant'), and Châtillon, 'Notes abélardiennes (suite). IV'.

[32] Lucy's becoming a nun is mentioned in a 12th-c. poem which begins: 'Peter set out for Paris when his mother had taken the veil' / 'Parisius Petrus est velata matre profectus' (ed. Dronke in *Abelard and Heloise in Medieval Testimonies*, p. 45, trans. p. 19; repr. in *Intellectuals and Poets*, p. 280, trans. p. 263; also in *Abaelardiana*, ii. 278–9. Her name appears in the *Obituary of the Paraclete* on 19 Oct.: 'Lucia, mater magistri Petri' (*Obituaires de la province de Sens*, ed. Molinier, iv. 424G; cf. also there, but inaccurately, n. 6).

[33] The return to France took place after May/Aug. 1113 when William had become bishop of Châlons. The short biography mentioned above in n. 5 records Abelard's progression to the study of divinity from the study of grammar and dialectic; see Hödl, *Die Geschichte der scholastischen Literatur*, p. 78; Mews, 'In search of a name', pp. 172–3.

[34] For Anselm of Laon see Appendix A, 3.i.

[35] According to Isidore of Seville, 'senex' is aged between 50 and 70 years (*Etymologiae*, xi. 2. 6).

Mirabilis quidem [k]in oculis erat[k] auscultantium,[l] sed nullus[m] in conspectu questionantium. Verborum usum habebat mirabilem, sed sensu[n] contemtibilem et ratione uacuum. Cum ignem accenderet, domum suam fumo implebat, non luce illustrabat.[36] Arbor eius tota in foliis aspicientibus a longe conspicua uidebatur, sed propinquantibus et diligentius intuentibus infructuosa reperiebatur.[37] Ad hanc[o] itaque cum accessissem ut fructum inde colligerem, deprehendi illam[p] esse ficulneam cui maledixit Dominus,[38] seu illam ueterem quercum[q] cui Pompeium[r] Lucanus comparat dicens:

Stat magni nominis umbra,
Qualis frugifero quercus[s] sublimis in agro, etc.[t] [39]

11. Hoc igitur comperto non multis diebus in umbra eius ociosus iacui; paulatim[a] [b]uero me iam[b] rarius [c]et rarius[c] ad lectiones eius accedente, quidam tunc inter discipulos eius eminentes grauiter id ferebant, quasi tanti magistri contemptor fierem.[40] Proinde[d] illum quoque aduersum me latenter commouentes, prauis suggestionibus ei me inuidiosum fecerunt. Accidit autem quadam die ut, post aliquas[e] sententiarum[f] collationes,[41] nos scolares inuicem iocaremur. Vbi [g]cum me[g] quidam animo[h] intemptantis[i] [42] interrogasset[j] quid[k] mihi de diuinorum lectione librorum uideretur, qui nondum[l] nisi[m] in philosophicis[n] studueram, respondi: saluberrimum quidem huius lectionis esse studium ubi salus anime cognoscitur, [o] sed me

[k–k] erat in oculis *CFDY* [l] consultancium *D;* ascultancium *Y* [m] *E after corr.; om. D* [n] sensu *TBRAmb;* sensum *ACEFY;* censum *D;* il avoit sens despitable et vuit de reson *J* [o] hunc *Y* [p] eam *F* [q] quartum *C* [r] pompeteium *D* [s] quartus *C* [t] *om. F*

11 [a] paulatim *exp. Y* [b–b] me iam (iam *exp. by another hand*) vero *Y* [c–c] *add. in marg. R; om. DYAmb* [d] Ideo *F* [e] aliquarum *B* [f] scienciarum *BRDY* [g–g] me cum *A* [h] non *C* [i] intentantes *F* [j] interrogassent *F* [k] que *E* [l] iunondum *R before corr.;* iumdum *?D*; numdum *Y* [m] *om. Y* [n] phisicis *C;* psicis *E;* philosophis *D;* Physicis *Amb* [o] recognoscitur *D*

[36] Cf. *Sermon* 17 (*PL* clxxviii. 501D): 'Lex . . . tam fumo potius quam luce referta'; also Isa. 6: 4: 'domus repleta est fumo', and Horace, *Ars poetica* 143–4.

[37] For similar remarks, though not directed against Anselm, see *Carmen ad Astralabium*, ed. Rubingh-Bosscher, *vv.* 11–16:

Fructu, non foliis pomorum quisque cibatur
et sensus uerbis anteferendus erit.
ornatis animos captet persuasio uerbis;
doctrine magis est debita planicies.
copia uerborum est ubi non est copia sensus,
constat et errantem multiplicare uias.

uncertain than he came. Anselm could win the admiration of an audience but he was useless when put to the question. He had a remarkable command of words but their meaning was worthless and lacked reason. The fire he kindled filled his house with smoke but did not light it up.[36] He was a tree in full leaf which could be seen from afar, but on closer and more careful inspection proved to be barren.[37] I had come to this tree to gather fruit, but I found it was the fig tree which the Lord cursed,[38] or the ancient oak to which Lucan compares Pompey:

> There stands the shadow of a noble name,
> Like a tall oak in a field of corn, etc.[39]

11. Once I discovered this I did not lie idle in his shade for long. My attendance at his lectures gradually became more and more infrequent, to the annoyance of some of his leading pupils, who took it as a sign of contempt for so great a master.[40] They began secretly to turn him against me, until their base insinuations succeeded in rousing his jealousy. One day it happened that, after some discussions of sentences,[41] we students were joking amongst ourselves, when someone rounded on me[42] and asked what I thought of reading sacred Scripture when I had hitherto studied only philosophy. I replied that concentration on such reading was most beneficial for the salvation of the soul, but that I found it most surprising that for educated men

Orderic Vitalis in book 11 of his *Ecclesiastical History* (written perhaps *c.*1136/7) records King Henry I of England telling his brother Duke Robert of Normandy before the battle of Tinchebray (1106) that Robert occupied the land like a barren tree, being duke in name only: 'Tu enim terram ut arbor infructuosa occupas . . . Dux quidem nomine tenus uocaris' (ed. and trans. Chibnall, vi. 866–7).

[38] Cf. Mark 11: 13–14, 20–1; partly cited in *Sermon* 11 (*PL* clxxviii. 460B). Cf. Matt. 21: 19; Luke 13: 6–9.

[39] Lucan, *De bello ciuili*, i. 135–6. Echoes of Lucan, i. 129–45 suffuse this portrait of Anselm: Pompey was 'the Great' but his younger rival, Julius Caesar, would win victory over him; the oak towers over the field but is hollow and leafless; it offers little shade, its roots are weak, and the first strong wind would bring it crashing down. Cf. von Moos, 'Lucan und Abaelard', pp. 425–7 (repr. in *Abaelard und Heloise*, pp. 109–11) and Worstbrock, 'Ein Lucanzitat'. For detailed commentary on Lucan's verses see *Lucan*, ed. Roche, pp. 185–90.

[40] For criticism of Anselm, see Appendix A, 3.ii.

[41] 'sententiarum collationes', a reflection of Anselm's way of teaching by taking a question, reviewing apparent differences (e.g. 'God does not will evil'; 'God wills everything that happens'), and reconciling them in a conclusion or sentence, is found in a letter he wrote late in 1116 to an abbot of St Lawrence near Liège (ed. Lottin, *Psychologie et morale*, v. 175–8; *PL* clxii. 1587–92). See too Giraud, 'L'École de Laon entre arts du langage et théologie'.

[42] 'animo intemptantis': cf. 39 below.

uehementer mirari quod his qui litterati sunt ad expositiones sanctorum intelligendas ipsa eorum scripta uel glose non sufficiunt,[p] ut alio scilicet non egeant magisterio.[q] Irridentes[r] plurimi qui aderant an hoc ego possem et aggredi presumerem[s] requisierunt. Respondi [t]me id[t] si uellent experiri paratum esse. Tunc inclamantes[u] et amplius irridentes, 'certe', inquiunt, 'et nos assentimus. Queratur itaque[v] et tradatur uobis[w] expositor alicuius inusitate[x] scripture, et probemus quod uos[y] promittitis.' Et consenserunt omnes[z] in obscurissima Hiezechielis[a] prophetia.[b] [43]Assumpto itaque expositore statim in crastino eos ad lectionem inuitaui.[c] [44] Qui inuito mihi consilium dantes, dicebant ad rem tantam non esse properandum,[d] sed diutius in expositione rimanda[e] et firmanda[f] mihi hanc[g] inexperto uigilandum.[h] Indignatus[i] autem respondi non esse mee consuetudinis per usum proficere sed per ingenium;[45] atque adieci[j] uel me[k] penitus desiturum[l] esse uel eos[m] pro arbitrio meo ad lectionem accedere non differre. Et prime quidem lectioni nostre [n]pauci tunc[n] interfuere, quod[o] ridiculum omnibus uideretur me adhuc quasi penitus [p]sacre lectionis expertem[p] id tam propere[q] aggredi. Omnibus tamen qui affuerunt in tantum lectio illa grata extitit ut eam singulari preconio extollerent, [r]et me[s] secundum hunc nostre lectionis tenorem ad glosandum compellerent.[r] [t]Quo quidem[t] audito, hii qui non interfuerant ceperunt ad secundam et terciam lectionem certatim concurrere[u] [v]et omnes pariter[v] de transcribendis[w] glosis quas prima die inceperam in ipso earum[x] initio plurimum solliciti esse.[46]

[p] sufficiant *Amb* [q] magistro *FAmb*[1] [r] prudentes *CEF* [s] presumere *AE* [t–t] id me *CEF* [u] inclinantes *Y;* conclamantes *Amb;* inclamantes *Amb*[1] [v] inquam *add. F;* inquam *Amb;* itaque *Amb*[1] [w] nobis *FBRDAmb;* vobis *Amb*[1] [x] et usitate *C;* in visitate *D;* in sitate *Y before corr.* [y] nos *BR* [z] *om. E* [a] iezechielis *A;* azechielis *C;* ezechielis *EFY;* hezechielis *R;* bezechielis *D* [b] prophetica *BRD* [c] inuita *Y before corr. by Y*[1] [d] procedendum *D* [e] timenda *marked for corr. in Y* [f] firmandi *Y* [g] *om. CEF;* mesmement a moy qui ne l'avoye onques esprouvee *J;* hactenus *conj. Muckle;* adhuc *conj. E. Franceschini in Aevum 35 (1961), p. 396* [h] sed ego immemor huius uerbi psalmiste. domine non est exaltatum cor meum neque elati sunt oculi mei *add. Y;* Et je, malement remenbrables de celui Psialme qui dist: Sire Dieux, mes cuers n'est pas essauciez, ne mes yex ne sont pas eslevez *J* (Ps. 130:1) [i] *In the margin of T on fo. 3*[rb] *a 15th-/early 16th-c. hand has added a rubr.*: Quod sacros cepit legere libros scolastice et nouas cudere glosas. [j] adhereri *B before corr. by another hand;* adiri *R;* audiri *D;* addidi *Y* [k] *om. D* [l] desisturum *BR* [m] eas *CE* [n–n] *om. E* [o] eo quod *DY* [p–p] sacre lectionis in expertem *C;* facere lectiones Inexpertem *E;* sacre lectionis inexpertum *FAmb*[1]*;* sacre lectionis experturus *?B after corr. of* experte*;* sacre lectionis experturus *R;* sacre lectionis studium in expertum *D;* qui ne savoie aussi comme neant *J* [q] proprie *BR* [r–r] *om. C* [s] ut *D* [t–t] quo qui *E;* quo *F* [u] accedere *EAmb;* contendere *F;* contendere *vel* concurrere *Amb*[1] [v–v] *om. E* [w] conscribendis *A* [x] eorum *TACEF*

glosses or the writings of the saints themselves were not sufficient for understanding their expositions without the need for further instruction. There was general laughter, and I was asked by many of those present if I could or would venture to tackle this myself. I said I was ready to try if they wished. Still laughing, they shouted: 'Right, that's settled! We'll find for you a commentator on a little-known text and test what you say.' And they all agreed on the extremely obscure prophecy of Ezekiel.[43] I took the commentator and promptly invited them all to hear my lecture the very next day.[44] They then pressed unwanted advice on me, telling me not to hurry over something so important but to remember my inexperience and give longer thought to working out and confirming my exposition. I replied indignantly that it was not my custom to benefit by practice, but to rely on my own natural ability,[45] and either they must come to my lecture at the time of my choosing or I would abandon it altogether. At my first lecture there were certainly not many people present, for everyone thought it absurd that, having up to now completely lacked knowledge of the Scriptures, I should attempt this so soon. But all who came liked it so much that they commended the lecture particularly widely, and urged me to provide glosses on the text on the same lines as my lecture. The news brought people who had missed my first lecture flocking to the second and third ones, all alike most eager also to make copies of the glosses which I had begun on the first day.[46]

[43] Cf. *Expositio in Hexameron, praefatio* (ed. Romig and Luscombe, pp. 3–4; *PL* clxxviii. 731–2), where Abelard supports the view that the beginning of Genesis, the Song of Songs, and the book of Ezekiel are the most difficult books of the Old Testament to understand, the latter on account especially of Ezekiel's first vision of animals and wheels and his last vision of the building on the mountain. He cites in support Origen's commentary on the Song of Songs and the prologue to Jerome's *Expositio* of Ezekiel.

[44] On expositors and expositions of Scripture (commentators and commentaries) cf. *TChr*, i. 117 and *TSch*, i. 180; also the *Rule* **64**, where the reference to *expositiones* is to commentaries that are suitable for reading out loud in the refectory or in chapter. The expositor of Ezekiel chosen to be the guide to Abelard's reading could have been Jerome or Gregory the Great or Rabanus Maurus (d. 856), who used both Jerome and Gregory, or Origen or (as J. Châtillon thought, 'Abélard et les écoles', p. 153), a collection of glosses available in the school at Laon. On such glosses, which went out of use with the development during the early-to-mid-century of the *Gloss*, see Smalley, 'Les Commentaires bibliques de l'époque romane'. The *Gloss* on Ezekiel, which was not yet available, includes excerpts from Rabanus and, largely through Rabanus, from Jerome (the greatest number), Gregory, and Origen. Abelard was to turn to Jerome's commentary of Ezekiel in his *Sic et Non* (ed. Boyer and McKeon, p. 658, etc.) and more so than to Gregory's *Homilies* on Ezekiel (ibid., p. 657, etc.).

[45] 'ingenium': cf. **2** and **10** above and *TSch*, ii. 2 (p. 313 *l.* 7)

[46] Cf. the description by Anselm of Bec, in a letter written *c.*1077 to archbishop Lanfranc of Canterbury, of the enthusiasm shown for making copies of his *Monologion*: 'De quo

12. [a] DE PERSECVTIONE EIVS QVOQVE IN EVM[a]

Hinc[b] itaque predictus senex uehementi[c] commotus inuidia et[d] quorumdam persuasionibus iam aduersum me, ut supra memini, et tunc stimulatus, non[e] minus in sacra lectione me[f] persequi cepit quam antea Guillelmus[g] noster in philosophia.[47] Erant autem [h]tunc in scolis huius[h] senis duo qui ceteris preminere uidebantur, Albericus[i] scilicet Remensis et Lotulfus[j] Lumbardus;[k] qui quanto de se maiora presumebant, amplius aduersum me accendebantur.[l] [48] Horum itaque maxime suggestionibus, sicut[m] postmodum deprehensum est, senex ille perturbatus impudenter[n] mihi interdixit inceptum glosandi opus in loco magisterii sui amplius exercere, hanc uidelicet causam pretendens, ne si forte in illo opere aliquid per errorem[o] scriberem,[p] utpote rudis adhuc in hoc studio, ei deputaretur.[q] [49] Quod cum ad aures scolarium peruenisset, maxima commoti sunt indignatione super tam[r] manifesta liuoris calumpnia, que[s] nemini umquam[t] acciderat. Que quanto[u] manifestior tanto mihi honorabilior extitit et persequendo[v] gloriosiorem effecit.[50]

13. [a]QVANDO NOVISSIME PARISIVS FLORVIT[a]

Post[b] paucos itaque dies, Parisius reuersus, scolas[c] [d]mihi iamdudum[d] destinatas atque oblatas[e] unde primo fueram[f] expulsus, annis[g] aliquibus quiete possedi; atque ibi in ipso statim scolarum initio glosas illas Ezechielis[h] quas Lauduni[i] inceperam[j] consummare studui.[k] [51] Que

12 [a] *rubr. TAB* [b] *large decorated initial in TBR; unfilled space for this in D* [c] uehementis *D* [d] *om. BRDY* [e] *add. Y*[1] [f] *om. Y* [g] Guillhelmus *T* [h–h] in scolis huius tunc *DY* [i] albertus *D* [j] lotulphus *CE;* loculfus *FRD;* Loculphus *Amb;* Lotulphus: *sed Othoni Frisinghensi* Leutaldus Nouariensis *Amb*[1] [k] lombardus *FBRD;* Lombardus *Amb* [l] machinabantur *inserted by a reader into vacant space in B* [m] *written in E by another hand* [n] impendentur *D* [o] ibi *add. T where marks for exp. were add. and then eras., add. BRD;* escripsisse par aventure aucune chose par erreur en ceste oeuvre *J* [p] scribere *C* [q] imputaretur *Y after corr. by another hand of* deputaretur [r] causa *C* [s] qui *E* [t] ulterius *add. TBD;* nuncquam *A;* nunquam ulterius *R;* unquam alterius *add. Y but* -us *is marked for exp., so as to read* unquam alteri*;* qui n'estoit onques avenue a autres *J* [u] quanta *T* [v] persecutum *Amb*[1]

13 [a–a] *rubr. T* (uenit *T;* floruit *T*[1]) *in marg. AB;* Puis revint à Paris et en leu, et se commenca a orgeuillir et incliner aus vices *table in H of the (missing) contents of Dijon MS 525* [b] *large initial in A; decorated initial in BR* [c] que *add. CEF* [d–d] iam michi dudum *D;* iamdudum mihi *F* [e] ablatas *CE* [f] fueram *Ecorr.* [g] armis *D* [h] hiezechielis *TBR;* iezechielis *A;* azechielis *C;* Ezechielis *EFY;* bezechielis *D* [i] dudini *A before unclear corr.;* laudinij *E;* meleduni *DY* [j] *om. D* [k] studiui *T*

---

opusculo hoc praeter spem euenit, ut non solum illi quibus instantibus editum est, sed et plures alii illud uelint non solum legere sed etiam transcribere' ('against expectation it has happened that not only those at whose urging this little work was published but many others too wanted not only to read it but also to copy it'); Anselm, *Opera*, ed. Schmitt, i. 6. A similar comment is found in the prologue to this work (ibid., pp. 7–8).

12. ANSELM'S PERSECUTION OF HIM

The old man was now wildly jealous and, being already set against me by the suggestions of some of his pupils, as I said before, he began to attack me for lecturing on the Scriptures no less than my master William had done earlier in philosophy.[47] There were at this time two prominent students in the old man's school, Alberic of Reims and Lotulf of Lombardy, whose hostility to me was intensified by the good opinion they had of themselves.[48] It was largely through their insinuations, as was afterwards proved, that Anselm lost his head and curtly forbade me to continue the work I had begun on glossing in his place of teaching, on the pretext that any error which I might put in writing through lack of training in the subject would be attributed to him.[49] When this reached the ears of the students, their indignation knew no bounds. This was an act of sheer spite and calumny, such as had never been directed at anyone. But the more open it was, the more it brought me renown, and through persecution my fame increased.[50]

13. WHEN HE AGAIN FLOURISHED IN PARIS

A few days after this I returned to Paris, to the school which had long ago been intended for and offered to me, and from which I had been expelled at the start. I remained in possession of it there in peace for several years, and as soon as I began my course of teaching I set myself to complete the glosses on Ezekiel which I had started at Laon.[51] These

[47] Jaeger, *The Envy of Angels*, pp. 217–18, draws attention to a similar occurrence in the mid-10th c. as told by Otloh of St Emmeram in his *Vita Wolfkangi* cc. 4–5, ed. Waitz, p. 528): Master Stephen of Novara's exposition of Martianus Capella failed to satisfy his students in Würzburg. So they asked a fellow student, Wolfgang of Regensburg, to provide a commentary and this was a success. An angered Stephen sought in vain to prevent Wolfgang's future progress.

[48] On Alberic and Lotulf see **36**, **37**, **39**, **42**, and **58** below; also *Letter* 2, **2**.

[49] John of Salisbury commented in his *Metalogicon* (finished in 1159), i. 5 (ed. Hall, p. 21 *ll.* 34–5) that no one harassed Anselm and his brother Ralph with impunity ('nemo lacerauit impune'); the only people they displeased were heretics and the shameful ('solis displicuerunt hereticis, aut flagitiorum turpitudine obuolutis').

[50] Another instance of acute tension arising between a dominant master and others present in his school occurred *c.*1117–20 when Walter of Mortagne, the tutor of a young man (Hugh, later abbot of Marchiennes), attacked some teachings of master Alberic at Reims. This was followed by Walter (who was to be bishop of Laon from 1155 till his death in 1174) being forced to leave the city to teach elsewhere (see *Vita Hugonis*, ed. Martène and Durand, cols. 1711–13).

[51] Abelard's glosses on Ezekiel have not been found. He seems in later years to have wanted to produce commentaries on the Song of Songs and on Ezekiel to accompany the commentary on the *Hexameron* that he sent to Heloise and the sisters at the Paraclete (see above, *Introduction*, p. xxvi).

quidem[l] adeo legentibus acceptabiles fuerunt, ut me non minorem gratiam[m] in sacra lectione adeptum[n] iam crederent quam in philosophica[o] uiderant.[p] Vnde utriusque lectionis studio scole nostre uehementer multiplicate, quanta mihi de pecunia lucra,[q] quantam gloriam[r] compararent[s] [t]ex fama[t] te quoque latere non potuit.[52]

14. Sed quoniam prosperitas [a]stultos semper[a] inflat,[53] et[b] mundana tranquillitas uigorem eneruat animi[c] et per carnales illecebras facile resoluit, cum iam me solum in mundo [d]superesse philosophum estimarem,[d][54] nec ullam[e] ulterius inquietationem formidarem, frena libidini[f] cepi laxare, qui antea[g] uixeram[h] continentissime. Et quo amplius in philosophia uel sacra lectione profeceram,[i] amplius[j] a philosophis et diuinis immunditia uite recedebam. Constat[k] quippe philosophos nedum[l] diuinos, id est sacre[m] lectionis[55] exhortationibus intentos, continentie decore[n] maxime[o] polluisse. Cum[p] igitur totus[q] in superbia atque[r] luxuria laborarem,[s] utriusque morbi remedium diuina mihi gratia licet nolenti contulit. Ac primo luxurie, deinde superbie; luxurie quidem his me priuando quibus hanc[t] exercebam, superbie uero que[u] mihi[v] ex litterarum maxime scientia nascebatur, iuxta illud Apostoli: 'scientia inflat',[56] illius libri quo maxime gloriabar combustione me humiliando.[w] Cuius nunc[x] rei utramque[y] historiam uerius ex ipsa re quam [z]ex auditu cognoscere te uolo, ordine[a] quidem[b] quo processerunt.

[l] *om. F* [m] gloriam *FAmb*¹ [n] adeptam *DY* [o] philosophia *D* [p] uiderent *D;* uideretur *marked for corr. in Y* [q] lucrum *Y* [r] *om. Y* [s] comparent *B;* compararant *D* [t–t] et famam *Y*

14 [a–a] semper stultos *Y after exp. of* stultos *before* semper [b] ac *C* [c] animum *R* [d–d] superesse superiorem philosophum estimarem *add. C;* superiorem philosophum existimarem *EAmb*¹ [e] ulla *C* [f] bibidini *T before corr.;* libidinis *CBRDY;* libidini *Rcorr.;* a luxure *J* [g] aliter *?E after corr.;* alias *CF* [h] uixerem *D* [i] proficerem *Y* [j] eo amplius *F* [k] gustat *B, R before corr.* [l] necdum *TACEBR;* nedum *F;* mundum *D;* nundum *Y* [m] sacra *BR* [n] decare *C before corr. by a modern hand* [o] *om. F* [p] Dedum *C* [q] tota *D* [r] et *E* [s] laborem *D* [t] *om. Amb* [u] qui *D* [v] *om. CEF* [w] habundando *C* [x] nec *E* [y] utrumque *C* [z–z] *om. C* [a] ordinem *F* [b] quoque *EF*

[52] Otto of Freising, *Gesta Friderici*, i. 49 (ed. Waitz and von Simson, p. 69), writes that Abelard now taught in Paris, proving to be both a subtle and a humorous philosopher. The short biography of Abelard found in a 12th-c. MS containing a copy of Abelard's *Ethics* (see n. 5 above), after crediting him with 'an unbelievable intelligence, an unsurpasssed memory and superhuman capacity', records that Abelard began to teach both dialectic and theology (divinity) publicly in Paris, and that in a short time he easily surpassed all other masters in France: 'Mox ergo socios habere, et parisiis palam dialetice atque diuinitatis lectiones dare cepit. Et facile omnes francie magistros in breui superuenit'; ed. Hödl, *Die Geschichte der scholastischen Literatur*, p. 78; Mews, 'In search of a name', pp. 172–3.

proved so popular with their readers that they judged my reputation to stand as high for my reading of the Scriptures as it had previously done for philosophy. The numbers in the school increased enormously as the students gathered there eager for instruction in both subjects, and the wealth and fame this brought me must be well known to you.[52]

14. But success always puffs up fools with pride,[53] and worldly calm weakens the spirit's resolution and easily destroys it through carnal temptations. I began to think myself the only philosopher in the world,[54] with nothing to fear from anyone, and so I yielded to the lusts of the flesh. Hitherto I had been entirely continent. But now the further I advanced in philosophy and theology, the further I fell behind the philosophers and the divines in the impurity of my life. It is well known that the philosophers, let alone the divines, by which is meant those who have devoted themselves to the teachings of Holy Scripture,[55] were especially glorified by their chastity. Since therefore I was wholly enslaved to pride and lust, God's grace provided a remedy for both these evils, though not one of my choosing: first for lust, then for pride. For lust by depriving me of those organs with which I practised it, and for pride which had grown in me through my learning—for in the words of the Apostle, 'Knowledge puffs up'[56]—when I was humiliated by the burning of the book of which I was so proud. The true story of both these episodes I now want you to know from the facts, in their proper order, instead of from hearsay.

[53] Cf. Prov. 1: 32; 1 Cor. 8: 1.

[54] In *Collationes* 4 (written perhaps while he was at St-Gildas, between 1127 and about 1132), Abelard allows one of the participants in his dialogue, a Philosopher, to pour 'the oil of flattery' on his head: 'Your wonderful book, the *Theologia*, proves the sharpness of your intellect, and illustrates how abundant a treasury your memory is of the views both of philosophers and Christian writers'; 'without doubt, in both fields—philosophy and sacred doctrine ('philosophicis et diuinis sententiis')—you have excelled all other masters, even your own, and even the acknowledged writers in each of the disciplines' (ed. Marenbon and Orlandi, pp. 4–5; *Dialogus*, ed. Thomas, *ll.* 40–52; *PL* clxxviii. 1613CD). In his *Metalogicon*, i. 5 (ed. Hall, p. 20 *ll.* 13–15), John of Salisbury wrote with approval that 'the Peripatetic from Le Pallet ("Peripateticus Palatinus"), who excelled all his contemporaries in his distinction as a logician, was the only one who was thought to really understand Aristotle'.

[55] 'sacra lectione', 'sacre lectionis': neither 'theology' nor 'Holy Scripture' (Radice) quite catches the meaning of 'sacra lectio'. Smalley in *The Study of the Bible in the Middle Ages*, pp. 26–36, at p. 27, wrote of *lectio divina* or *lectio sacra*: 'Bible study includes the study of Catholic tradition which St Augustine does not distinguish from Scripture. It is part of theology . . . Scripture is the starting point.'

[56] 1 Cor. 8: 1; also cited in *TSum*, ii. 9; *TChr*, iii. 8-a (*CT*), 15; *TSch*, i. 104, ii. 31.

15. Quia igitur scortorum[z] immunditiam semper abhorrebam et ab accessu[a] et frequentatione nobilium feminarum studii scolaris assiduitate reuocabar[b] nec laicarum conuersationem multum noueram,[c] praua [d]mihi, ut dicitur,[d] [57] fortuna blandiens commodiorem [e]nacta est occasionem,[e] qua[f] me facilius de sublimitatis huius fastigio prosterneret,[g] imo superbissimum nec accepte gratie memorem[h] diuina pietas humiliatum sibi uendicaret.[58]

16. [a]QVOMODO IN AMOREM HELOYSE LAPSVS VVLNVS INDE TAM MENTIS QVAM CORPORIS TRAXIT[a]

Erat[b] quippe in ipsa ciuitate Parisius[c] adolescentula[59] quedam nomine Heloysa,[d] neptis canonici cuiusdam qui Fulbertus uocabatur, qui[e] eam quanto amplius diligebat tanto diligentius in omnem qua[f] poterat scientiam litterarum promoueri studuerat.[60] Que cum per faciem non esset infima, per habundantiam litterarum erat suprema. Nam quo bonum hoc,[g] litteratorie scilicet scientie, in mulieribus[h] est rarius, eo amplius puellam commendabat et in toto regno nominatissimam fecerat.[61] [i]Hanc igitur,[i] omnibus circunspectis que[j] amantes allicere

15 [a] assensu *D;* excessu *Amb* [b] inuocabar *E* [c] nouem' *Y* [d–d] ut dicitur mihi *D* [e–e] occasionem dedit (dedit Y^1) *Y* [f] quam *T* [g] prosternerent *R* [h] memore *D*

16 [a–a] *rubr. TB; ARD begin a new paragraph;* Le iiij^e chapitre, comme il fist s'amie de Heloyse, et comment ils usoient de leurs amors *table in H of the (missing) contents of Dijon MS 525* [b] *large decorated initial TR; large initial A; space in D* [c] Parisiensi *F* [d] Heloyssa *YF* [e] quanto *D* [f] in quam *BRDY;* quam *CEF* [g] huiusmodi *CE;* huius *F* [h] mulier *D* [i–i] Hunc igitur *Y;* Hanc *F* [j] qui *Y*

---

[57] For some similar sayings to the effect that fortune, when it entices and flatters, also ensnares and deceives, see Walther, *Proverbia*: 'Fortuna cum blanditur, captatum venit' (no. 9847), 'Fortuna blanda hamata' (37025g1), 'Fortuna cum blanditur, fallit' (37027), 'Fortuna fallacior quo blandior' (37027g1).

[58] Fulk, prior of Deuil (a Benedictine priory and dependency of St-Florent of Saumur, situated at Deuil-la-Barre, a suburb now in the north of Paris near Montmorency), in a strongly worded letter written to Abelard after his castration, wrote that there were rumours that Abelard consorted with prostitutes and spent his surplus earnings on a life of fornication: 'illud quod sic te, ut aiunt, praecipitem dedit, singularum scilicet feminarum amorem, et laqueos libidinis earum, quibus suos capiunt scortatores, melius mihi videor praeterire'; 'Quidquid vere scientiae tuae venditione perorando praeter quotidianum victum et usum necessarium, sicut relatione didici, acquirere poteras in voraginem fornicariae consumptionis domergere non cessabas. Avara meretricum rapacitas cuncta tibi rapuerat. Nulla audierunt saecula meretricem velle alteri misereri . . .'; *Epistola ad Abaelardum*, *PL* clxxviii. 372B, 372D–373A. F. Châtillon, 'Notes abélardiennes. III', pp. 318–34, accepted Fulk's opinion. Heloise in *Letter* 2, 12 wrote that women were attracted to Abelard.

[59] 'adolescentula': see n. 14 above.

[60] There have been many attempts to trace the family history of Heloise. Bautier, 'Paris au temps d'Abélard', pp. 75–7, gives reasons for thinking that her family was a noble one in

15. I had always held myself aloof from unclean association with prostitutes. Constant application to my studies had prevented me from approaching and keeping company with noble ladies, and I did not know much about the way of life led by lay women. Perverse Fortune flattered me, as the saying goes,[57] and found an easy way to bring me toppling down from my pedestal, or rather, despite my overbearing pride and heedlessness of the grace granted me, God's compassion claimed me humbled for Himself.[58]

16. HOW HAVING FALLEN IN LOVE WITH HELOISE HE WAS WOUNDED IN MIND AND BODY

There was in the city of Paris at the time a young woman[59] named Heloise, the niece of Fulbert, one of the canons, and so much loved by him that he had done everything in his power to advance her education in letters.[60] In looks she did not rank least, while in the abundance of her learning she was supreme. A gift for letters is so rare in women that it added greatly to her charm and had made her very famous throughout the realm.[61] I considered all the usual attractions

the Paris area and that it is not unlikely that Heloise belonged on her father's side to a branch of the Beaumont family or of the closely related family of Montmorency-Bantelu; further, that she had Chartrain connections on her mother's side. The Montmorencys were dominant in the Val d'Oise; the advowson of the convent of Argenteuil, where Heloise had earlier been educated (see **29** below), was in the hands of one of their number. Her mother's name, Hersindis, appears in the *Obituary of the Paraclete* ('Hersindis, mater domine Heloise, abbatisse nostre', *Obituaires de la province de Sens*, ed. Molinier, iv, 1 Dec., p. 428D; *Collection des principaux obituaires*, ed. Lalore, no. 391, p. 472) as does her uncle's name, which is given as Hubert—either incorrectly for Fulbert or she had another uncle called Hubert who was also a canon ('Hubertus canonicus, domne Heloise auunculus', 26 Dec., ed. Molinier, p. 429D; ed. Lalore, no. 405, p. 473). Robl, '*Hersindis Mater*', suggested that Heloise's mother was Hersindis of Champagne, whose grandmother was Eremburg of Montmorency and whose great-grandmother was Heloise, daughter of Odo, count of Blois, Tours, Chartres, and Troyes, but that Heloise's father is unknown and that she was not the child of Hersindis' husband, Herin of Montsoreau (which is in the Loire valley near Saumur). From 1104 Hersindis was the first prioress of the abbey of Fontevraud, which is 15 km south-east of Saumur. The unfolding of Abelard's affair with Heloise in canon Fulbert's house, and Abelard's ensuing castration, are narrated, with hostility, by Roscelin, once Abelard's teacher in Loches. Roscelin considered the castration to be divine punishment (*Letter* to Abelard, ed. Reiners, p. 78, *ll.* 18–21; *PL* clxxviii. 369C (*Letter* 15)). Silvestre, who thought that *Letter* 1 was a forgery, rightly drew attention, in 'Pourquoi Roscelin n'est-il pas mentionné dans l'*Historia calamitatum*?', to similarities between the accounts given by Roscelin in 1119–20 and by Abelard over ten years later.

[61] For similar praise of the 'girl . . . whose face had set her above many, whose philosophy had set her above all other girls, she through whom alone Gaul has worth' ('Quam facies multis, quam philosophia puellis / Pretulerat cunctis, qua sola Gallia pollet'), see the poem which begins 'Peter set out for Paris when his mother had taken the veil' / 'Parisius Petrus est uelata matre profectus', ed. Dronke in *Abelard and Heloise in Medieval Testimonies*, p. 45, trans. p. 19; repr. in *Intellectuals and Poets*, pp. 280–1, trans. p. 263; also

solent, commodiorem[k] censui in amorem mihi copulare, et me id facillime[l] credidi posse. Tanti quippe tunc[m] nominis eram et iuuentutis et forme gratia[n] preminebam, ut quamcunque feminarum nostro dignarer amore nullam[o] uererer repulsam. Tanto autem[p] facilius hanc mihi puellam consensuram[q] credidi quanto amplius eam[r] litterarum scientiam et[s] habere et diligere noueram, nosque etiam[t] absentes scriptis internuntiis inuicem licere[u] presentare, et pleraque[v] audacius scribere quam colloqui,[62] et sic semper iocundis interesse colloquiis.

17. In huius itaque adolescentule amorem totus inflamatus, occasionem[a] quesiui qua [b]eam mihi[b] [c]domestica et cotidiana conuersatione[c] familiarem[d] efficerem et facilius ad consensum traherem. Quod[e] quidem ut fieret, egi cum[f] predicto[g] puelle auunculo, quibusdam[h] ipsius amicis interuenientibus, quatinus me in domum suam, que scolis nostris proxima erat, sub quocumque procurationis precio susciperet,[i] hanc uidelicet[j] occasionem[k] pretendens, quod studium nostrum domestica nostre familie cura plurimum prepediret, et impensa[l] nimia[m] nimium me[n] grauaret.[63] Erat autem cupidus ille ualde atque erga neptim[o] suam, ut amplius semper in doctrinam proficeret[p] litteratoriam, plurimum studiosus. Quibus quidem[q] duobus facile eius[r] assensum[s] assecutus sum et quod optabam obtinui, cum ille uidelicet et[t] ad pecuniam totus inhiaret et neptim[u] suam ex doctrina nostra aliquid percepturam crederet. Super quo uehementer[v] me deprecatus, supra quam sperare[w] presumerem uotis meis accessit, et amori[x] consuluit, eam uidelicet totam nostro magisterio committens, ut quotiens mihi[y] a scolis reuerso uaccaret, tam in die quam in nocte ei [z]docende operam[z] darem, et eam si neglegentem[a] sentirem uehementer constringerem. In qua re quidem quanta eius simplicitas esset uehementer ammiratus, non minus apud me obstupui quam si[b]

[k] est *add. R before corr.* [l] facere *Amb*[1] [m] *om. D* [n] gratiam *A before corr. by another hand* [o] ullam *C* [p] *om. BRDY* [q] concensuram *T before corr. by another hand in marg.*; consensum' *Y* [r] eam *ditto. T* [s] *om. F* [t] *exp. B* [u] liceret *codd., Amb;* licere *conj. Orlandi, 'Minima Abaelardiana', p. 133* [v] plerique *B;* plerumque *Y*

17 [a] actionem *C* [b–b] michi eam *D* [c–c] domestica conuersatione *RD;* per (*add. Y*[1]) domesticam conuersationem *Y* [d] ei *add. C;* et *add. EF* [e] Quo *C* [f] cum *invisible in B through tight binding* [g] predicte *E* [h] quibus *BRD;* quibusque *Y* [i] reciperet *CEF* [j] *om. Y* [k] actionem *C* [l] expensa *D* [m] *om. Muckle* [n] *om. CEF* [o] neptem *CF;* neptiem *Ecorr.* [p] proficet *D* [q] *om. ACEF* [r] *add. T*[1] *in marg.* [s] essensum *A before corr. by another hand* [t] *om. Y* [u] neptem *CEF* [v] frequencius *C* [w] sapere *Y* [x] amore *C* [y] me *EF* [z–z] dicende uel docende *C;* docende uel docere operam *E* [a] negantem *Y* [b] *om. DY*

for a lover and decided she was the one to bring to my bed, confident that I should have an easy success, for at the time I had youth and exceptional good looks as well as my great reputation to recommend me, and feared no rebuff from any woman by whom I might be honoured in sharing love. Knowing her knowledge and love of letters I thought she would be all the more ready to consent, and that even when separated we could enjoy each other's presence by exchange of written messages in which we could write many things more boldly than we could say them,[62] and so need never lack the pleasures of conversation.

17. All on fire with love for this young woman I sought an opportunity of getting to know her through private daily meetings and so more easily winning her over. With this end in view I came to an arrangement with her uncle, with the help of some of his friends, whereby he should take me into his house, which was very near my school, for whatever sum he liked to ask. As a pretext I said that my household cares were hindering my studies and their expense was far, far too much for me to bear.[63] Fulbert dearly loved money, and was moreover always ambitious to further his niece's education in letters, two weaknesses which made it easy for me to seek his assent and obtain my desire. He was all eagerness for my money and confident that his niece would profit from my teaching. This led him to make an urgent request which furthered my love and fell in with my wishes more than I had dared to hope: he gave me complete charge over the girl, so that I could devote all the leisure time left me by my school to teaching her by day as well as night, and if I found her idle I was to punish her severely. I was amazed by his simplicity; if he had entrusted a tender lamb to a ravening wolf it would not have

in *Abaelardiana*, ii. 278–9 (for *Abaelardiana* see the *Bibliography*: *Secondary Works*). Cf. also (as Silvestre pointed out in his review of *Abaelardiana*, ii, p. 805; the italics are his) Peter the Venerable, *Letter* 115 to Heloise: '. . . *nomen* non quidem adhuc religionis tuae, sed honestorum tamen et laudabilium studiorum tuorum, michi fama innotuit. Audiebam tunc temporis, *mulierem* . . . *litteratoriae scientiae*, quod *perrarum* est, et studio licet saecularis sapientiae, summam operam dare', ed. Constable, i. 303.

[62] Cf. *Carmen ad Astralabium*, ed. Rubingh-Bosscher, *vv.* 961 and 964: 'scripto se faciet presentem quilibet absens'; 'queque loqui pudeat scribere multa licet'. Also Ovid, *Heroides*, iv. 10: 'dicere quae puduit, scribere iussit amor'. For some further examples of this topos cf. Schaller, 'Probleme der Überlieferung', p. 26, n. 7.

[63] The cathedral close contained the properties and most of the canons' houses (there were about fifteen) that belonged to the chapter of Notre Dame on the Ile de la Cité, but Robl, '*Hersindis Mater*', pp. 63–4, suggested that Fulbert's house was situated just outside the close between the west front of the cathedral and the Petit Pont, and closer to Abelard's place of teaching.

agnam teneram famelico lupo committeret.[64] Qui cum eam mihi non solum docendam, uerum etiam uehementer constringendam[c] traderet, quid aliud[d] agebat quam ut[e] uotis meis [f]licentiam penitus daret,[f] et occasionem, etiam si[g] nollemus, offerret,[h] [i]ut quam uidelicet[i] blanditiis non possem, minis[j] et uerberibus facilius flecterem?[65] Sed duo erant que eum maxime a turpi[k] suspicione reuocabant, amor uidelicet neptis et continentie mee fama[l] preterita.[m]

18. Quid[a] plura? Primum domo una coniungimur, postmodum animo.[66] Sub occasione[b] itaque discipline,[c] amori penitus uaccabamus,[d] et secretos[e] recessus,[f] quos [g]amor optabat,[g] studium lectionis offerebat.[h] Apertis itaque libris, plura de amore quam de lectione uerba se ingerebant, plura erant oscula[i] quam sententie; sepius ad sinus quam ad libros reducebantur manus, crebrius oculos amor in se reflectebat[j] quam [k]lectio in scripturam[k] dirigebat. Quoque[l] minus suspicionis haberemus, uerbera[m] quandoque dabat amor, non furor, gratia, non ira, que omnium ungentorum suauitatem transcenderent.[n] Quid denique? Nullus[o] a cupidis intermissus est gradus amoris,[67] et si quid insolitum amor excogitare potuit, est additum; et quo minus ista fueramus experti gaudia, ardentius illis insistebamus, et minus in fastidium uertebantur.

19. Et[a] quo me amplius hec uoluptas[b] occupauerat, minus philosophie uaccare poteram et scolis[c] operam dare. Tediosum mihi uehementer erat ad scolas procedere uel in eis morari; pariter et laboriosum, cum nocturnas amori uigilias et diurnas studio conseruarem. Quem etiam ita negligentem et tepidum lectio tunc habebat, ut iam nichil ex ingenio sed ex usu cuncta proferrem, nec iam nisi recitator pristinorum essem inuentorum, et si qua[d] inuenire liceret, carmina[e] essent amatoria, non philosophie secreta; quorum etiam carminum pleraque [f]adhuc in multis,[f] sicut[g] et ipse nosti, frequentantur et decantantur

[c] astrigendam *C* [d] habebat *add. A before exp.* [e] *om. A* [f–f] penitus daret licentiam *CEF* [g] etsi *B;* et si *RY* [h] breviter offerret *?C, ?E, F* [i–i] uidelicet *exp. but reinstated in marg. by corr. R;* uidelicet ut quam *DY* [j] *illegible in C;* saltam minis *D;* saltem minis *Y* [k] turbi *T before corr. to ?*turpi *by T*[1] *in marg.* [l] *om. D* [m] preterite *CE* praeteritae *F*

18 [a] Quis *D* [b] actione *C* [c] *add. Ycorr. in unfilled space* [d] uocabamus *A before corr. by another hand* [e] ac *add. D* [f] regressus *TAmb;* recessus *Amb*[1]; les secrez departemens et les repostailles *J* [g–g] optabat amor *BRDY* [h] afferebat *C* [i] obscula *Y before corr. by exp.* [j] flectebat *Y* [k–k] leccioni scripturam *D;* lectioni scripturam *Y* [l] Quodque *R before corr. by a 15th-c. hand, D* [m] uerba *CBRD* [n] transcenderetur *C;* transcenderet *BRY* [o] nullis *B*

surprised me more.[64] In handing her over to me to punish as well as to teach, what else was he doing but giving me complete freedom to realize my desires, and providing an opportunity, even if I did not make use of it, for me to bend her to my will by threats and blows if persuasion failed?[65] But there were two special reasons for his freedom from base suspicion: his love for his niece and my previous reputation for continence.

18. Need I say more? We were united, first under one roof, then in heart;[66] and so with our lessons providing the opportunity we abandoned ourselves entirely to love. Her studies allowed us the private seclusion that love desired and then, with our books open before us, more words of love than of our reading passed between us, and more kissing than ideas. My hands strayed oftener to her bosom than to her books; love drew our eyes to look on each other more than reading kept them on our texts. To avert suspicion I sometimes struck her, but these blows were prompted by love and tender feeling rather than anger and irritation, and were sweeter than any balm could be. In short, our desires left no stage of lovemaking untried,[67] and if love could devise something new, we welcomed it. We entered on each joy the more eagerly for our previous inexperience, and were the less easily sated.

19. Now the more I was taken up with these pleasures, the less time I could give to philosophy and the less attention I paid to my school. It was utterly wearisome for me to have to go to the school or to be there, and as hard too to spend my days on study when my nights were sleepless with lovemaking. As my interest and concentration flagged, my lectures lacked all inspiration and were merely conventional; I could do no more than repeat what had been said long ago, and when inspiration did come to me, it was for writing love songs, not the secrets of philosophy. A lot of these songs, as you know, are still popular and sung in many places, particularly by those who enjoy

19 [a] ex *RY* [b] voluntas *Y* [c] scolas *C* [d] quidem *DY* [e] cachimna *A*[2] *after corr. of* cacimna [f-f] in multis adhuc *CEF* [g] sed *E*

[64] 'si agnam . . .': cf. Terence, *Eunuch* 832: 'ouem lupo commisisti'.

[65] Cf. Ovid, *Ars amatoria*, i. 440, 673: 'blanditias ferat illa tuas'; 'uim licet apelles: grata est uis ista puellis'.

[66] 'Primum . . . animo': cf. Ovid, *Metamorphoses*, xiv, 78: 'animoque domoque'; Ovid, *Heroides*, vi. 55.

[67] 'gradus amoris': cf. Ovid, *Ars amatoria*, i. 482.

regionibus, ab his maxime quos uita [h]similis oblectat.[h] [68] Quantam autem[i] mestitiam,[j] quos gemitus, que lamenta nostri super hoc scolares assumerent, ubi uidelicet hanc animi mei occupationem immo perturbationem presenserunt,[k] non est facile dicere[l] uel cogitare.[69]

20. Paucos[a] enim iam res tam manifesta decipere poterat, ac[b] neminem, credo, preter[c] eum ad cuius ignominiam maxime id spectabat,[d] ipsum uidelicet puelle auunculum. Cui quidem[e] hoc cum a[f] nonnullis nonnumquam[g] suggestum fuisset credere non poterat, tum, ut supra memini, propter[h] immoderatam sue neptis amicitiam, tum etiam propter ante acte uite mee continentiam cognitam. Non enim[i] facile de his quos plurimum diligimus turpitudinem suspicamur,[j] nec in uehementi dilectione turpis suspitionis labes potest inesse.[k] Vnde et illud est beati Ieronimi[l] in epistola ad Sabinianum:[m] 'Solemus mala domus nostre scire nouissimi [n]ac liberorum ac[n] coniugum uitia, uicinis canentibus, ignorare.'[70] Sed quod nouissime[o] scitur, utique sciri quandoque contingit, et quod omnes deprehendunt, non est facile unum latere.

21. Sic itaque pluribus euolutis mensibus et de nobis accidit. O quantus in hoc cognoscendo dolor auunculi! Quantus in separatione amantium dolor ipsorum! Quanta sum erubescentia confusus![a] Quanta contritione super afflictione puelle sum afflictus! Quantos[b] meroris ipsa de uerecundia mea sustinuit estus! Neuter quod sibi, sed quod alteri contigerat[c] querebatur; neuter sua, sed alterius plangebat incommoda.[d] Separatio autem hec corporum maxima erat copulatio animorum, et negata sui copia amplius amorem [e]accendebat,[f] et

[h–h] simul oblectat *T;* similis oblectabat *Y;* simul oblectabat *Amb;* similis oblectat *Amb*[1]*;* qui se delitent en tele vie mener *J* [i] animi *E* [j] mesticam *T* [k] persenserunt *BRDY;* ilz sentirent *J* [l] *om. TABR;* n'est pas legeire chose neis a penser *J*

20 [a] Paucas *E* [b] aut *A corr. over eras.* [c] pretus *D* [d] spectat *A* [e] *om. CEF* [f] ante *RDY*[1] [g] nonnuncquam *A;* non umquam *D* [h] per ?*E* [i] Comme il furent pris ou present meffait. *Non enim*; a tel seing *no*[a] *table in H of the (missing) contents of Dijon MS 525* [j] suspicamus *BRD* [k] deesse *C* [l] Iheronimi *T;* Hieronymi *F* [m] castricianum *TACBRDY;* castricanum *E;* Sabinianum *FAmb* [n–n] et . . . et *Y* [o] nouissimum *F*

21 [a] effusus *R before corr.* [b] quantas *C* [c] contingerat *CE* [d] commoda *D* [e–e] (ascen)debat . . . in nobis est *T compresses the writing here, perhaps in order to keep to a set column length* [f] ascendebat *T;* accendebant *E;* embrasoit *J*

---

[68] Cf. *Letter* 2, 13. No such 'carmina amatoria' have been identified with certainty, although suggestions have been made, especially with regard to some songs in the *Carmina Burana* collection. For two of these, *Hebet sidus* and *Parce continuis*, see the *Bibliography:*

the kind of life I led.[68] But the grief and sorrow and laments of my students when they realized my preoccupation, or rather confusion of mind, are hard to admit or call to mind.[69]

20. Few could have failed to notice something so obvious, in fact no one, I fancy, except the man whose honour was most involved—Heloise's uncle. Several people tried on more than one occasion to draw his attention to it, but he would not believe them because, as I have said, of his boundless love for his niece and my well-known reputation for chastity in my earlier life. We do not easily think ill of those whom we love most, and the taint of suspicion cannot exist along with warm affection. Hence the remark of St Jerome in his letter to Sabinian: 'We are usually the last to learn of evil in our own home, and the faults of our wife and children may be the talk of the town but do not reach our ears.'[70] But what is learned last is learned eventually, and what everyone has found out cannot easily be hidden from anyone.

21. Several months passed and then this happened to us. Imagine the uncle's grief at the discovery, and the lovers' grief too at being separated! How I blushed with shame and contrition for the girl's plight, and what sorrow she suffered at the thought of my disgrace! All our laments were for one another's troubles, and our distress was for each other, not for ourselves. Separation drew our hearts still closer while frustration inflamed our passion even more; then we

Primary Sources; also *Checklist* nos. 353, 361, and 313. Likewise for *Omnia sol temperat* and *Huc usque, me miseram*, see the *Bibliography: Primary Sources*. Wollin, 'Ein Liebeslied des Petrus Abaelardus', considers that Abelard is the author of an anonymous, personal-love poem, *Primo quasdam eligo*, contained in a 12th-c. collection now in Florence; for these verses also see the *Bibliography: Primary Sources*.

[69] An indication of Abelard's distraction may be found in his *Dialectica*, ii. 1; iii. 1 (ed. de Rijk, pp. 151 *l*. 15, 152 *l*. 21, 319 *ll*. 1–2, 6), where he illustrates types of sentence construction with examples which include 'osculetur me amica', 'festinet amica', 'Petrum diligit sua puella uel eius amica', and 'Petrus diligit suam puellam'. Cf. also iii. 1, where Abelard illustrates the difference between wobbly inference and strong belief (ed. de Rijk, p. 277 *ll*. 33–7): 'Etsi enim cognoscam non necessarium esse ad amorem puelle quod sepe deprehensa est in nocte cum iuuene loquens secreto, tamen facile per hoc colloquium amorem suspicor et concedo, ex eo scilicet quod huiusmodi colloquia numquam uideamus contingere nisi inter amantes' ('although I know that when a girl is often found talking secretly at night with a young man they are not necessarily in love, yet such talk easily gives rise to suspicion and to this thought because we only find such conversations taking place between lovers').

[70] Jerome, *Epistola* CXLVII *ad Sabinianum*, 10 (ed. Hilberg, lvi. 327; *PL* xxii. 1203); also cited in the *Rule* 34. Castricianus is also assumed to be the recipient of the same letter to Sabinian in *Sic et Non c*. 31, 22. Cf. *Carmen ad Astralabium*, ed. Rubingh-Bosscher, *vv*. 183–4: 'oprobriis aurem propriis dat nemo libenter; / nec te nec quemquam talia scire uolet'. Also Juvenal, *Satires*, x. 342.

uerecundie[g] transacta[h] [i]iam passio inuerecundiores[j] reddebat; [k]tantoque uerecundie[ki] minor extiterat passio quanto conuenientior uidebatur actio.[l] Actum itaque in nobis est[e] quod in Marte et Venere deprehensis poetica[m] narrat fabula.[71] Non multo[n] autem post, puella[o] se concepisse comperit,[p] et cum summa exultatione mihi super hoc ilico scripsit, consulens quid de hoc ipse faciendum deliberarem. Quadam itaque nocte, auunculo eius absente, sicut nos condixeramus,[q] eam de domo auunculi furtim sustuli et in patriam meam[r] sine mora transmisi; ubi apud sororem meam tam diu conuersata est donec pareret[s] masculum quem Astralabium[t] nominauit.[72]

22. Auunculus autem eius post ipsius recessum quasi in insaniam conuersus, [a]quanto estuaret dolore,[a] quanto afficeretur[b] pudore, [c]nemo nisi[c] experiendo[d] cognosceret.[e] Quid autem in me ageret, quas [f]mihi tenderet[f] insidias, ignorabat. Si me interficeret seu in aliquo corpus meum debilitaret, id potissimum[g] metuebat ne[h] dilectissima neptis[i] [j]hoc in[j] patria mea plecteretur. Capere me et[k] inuitum alicubi coercere nullatenus ualebat, maxime cum ego mihi super hoc plurimum prouiderem,[l] quod eum, si ualeret uel auderet,[m] citius agredi[n] non dubitarem.

23. Tandem [a]ego eius[a] immoderate anxietati admodum compatiens, et de dolo quem[b] fecerat amor tanquam de summa proditione me [c]ipsum uehementer[c] [d]accusans, conueni[d] hominem supplicando et promittendo[e] quamcunque[f] super hoc emendationem ipse constitueret, nec ulli [g]mirabile id[g] uideri[h] asserens quicumque [i]uim amoris[i] expertus fuisset,

[g] uerecundia *BR;* uerecondie *D* [h] et *add. C;* translata *B before corr.* [i–i] *om. E* [j] inuerecundiorum *C;* in uerecundiores nos *D;* inuerecundiores nos *Y* [k–k] Tantaque uerecondie *D;* Tantaque uerecundie *Y* [l] actu *T;* le fais nous sembloit *J* [m] portica *A* [n] Comme elleli escript que elle estoit ensainte. *Non multo*; a tel seing 6 *table in H of the* (*missing*) *contents of Dijon MS 525; the sign* 6 *is rolled over to the right* [o] *om. E* [p] conceperit *B;* comperit *Y*[1] *over eras.* [q] consideramus *B* [r] *om. BR* [s] peperit *C, E before corr. to ?*perit [t] stralabium *C*

22 [a–a] *om. A* [b] efficeretur *D;* conficeretur *Y* [c–c] nisi nemo *T with inversion signs;* nemo (nemo *after corr.*) nisi *E* [d] experimento *CEF* [e] *superscr. by Acorr.* [f–f] intenderet *Y* [g] potissime *BRDY* [h] me *B;* me *R after eras. of* ne [i] sua *add. Y* [j] in hoc *T and perhaps also marked for corr.* [k] *om. Y* [l] prouiderem Et *D;* prouiderem. Et *Y* [m] audiret *C* [n] ingredi *T before corr.*

23 [a–a] eius ego *E* [b] quasi *E before corr.* [c–c] uehementer ipsum *CEF* [d–d] accusans quem *E;* accusans Quem *D;* accusans cautionem quem *Y* [e] promittando *T* [f] quandoque *BR* [g–g] id mirabile *CEF* [h] assumens *add. T before exp. of* assumens [i–i] ueri amoris *CE;* ueri amoris flammae *F;* la force d'amours *J*

---

[71] Cf. Ovid, *Ars amatoria*, ii. 561–600: 'fabula narratur . . .'; Ovid, *Metamorphoses*, iv. 171. As Dronke and Orlandi have observed ('New works by Abelard and Heloise?', p. 143),

became more abandoned as we lost all sense of shame and, indeed, shame diminished as we found more opportunities for lovemaking. And so we were caught in the act as the poet says happened to Mars and Venus.[71] Soon afterwards the girl found that she was pregnant, and immediately wrote me a letter full of rejoicing to ask what I thought she should do. One night then, when her uncle was away from home, I removed her secretly from his house, as we had planned, and sent her straight to my own country. There she stayed with my sister until she gave birth to a boy, whom she called Astralabe.[72]

22. On his return her uncle went almost out of his mind—one could appreciate only by experience his transports of grief and mortification. What action could he take against me? What traps could he set? He did not know. If he killed me or did me personal injury, there was the danger that his beloved niece might suffer for it in my country. It was useless to try to seize me or confine me anywhere against my will, especially as I was very much on guard against this very thing, knowing that he would not hesitate to assault me if he had the courage or the means.

23. In the end I took pity on his boundless misery and went to him, accusing myself of the deceit that love had made me commit as if it were the basest treachery. I begged his forgiveness and promised to make any amends he might think fit. I protested that I had done nothing unusual in the eyes of anyone who had known the power of

the joy felt by Heloise on finding that she was pregnant and her furtive removal to Brittany are the reverse of the situations found in *Carmina Burana*, no. 126, where a pregnant girl laments her pregnancy and the flight of her 'amicus' to Francia 'a finibus ultimis' to escape her father's rage; the poem is unlikely to have been written by Heloise, as was suggested by Ruys, 'Hearing medieval voices', pp. 91–9.

[72] The sister is likely to be Denise or Dionysia, on whom see n. 6 above. 'Petrus Astralabius, magistri nostri Petri filius' ('Peter Astralabe, son of our master Peter') was commemorated in the *Obituary of the Paraclete*, 30 Oct. (*Obituaires de la province de Sens*, ed. Molinier, iv. 425D; *Collection des principaux obituaires*, ed. Lalore, no. 376, p. 471). The unusual name chosen for him by Heloise, which is that of an astronomical instrument, then still rare in Christendom, used to study the movements of stars, may, according to East, 'Abelard's anagram' and Cook, 'The shadow on the sun', be part of an anagram: the letters 'Astralabius puer dei' can be arranged to read 'Petrus Abaelardus II'. However, the arrangement of these words in this way is not supported by known texts. In verses of advice for Astralabe Abelard calls him the joy of his life ('uite dulcedo paterne', *Carmen ad Astralabium*, ed. Rubingh-Bosscher, *v.* 1). Cf. also on Astralabius and the *Carmen* Brinkmann, 'Astrolabius'. After Abelard's death, Heloise asked Peter the Venerable, abbot of Cluny, to seek a prebend for Astralabe in Paris or elsewhere; Peter replied that he would try to do so but bishops, he had often found, could be difficult (*Letters of Peter the Venerable*, ed. Constable, i. 400–2, nos. 167–8); on this see below, 71 and n. 235.

et qui quanta ruina[j] summos quoque uiros ab ipso statim humani generis exordio mulieres deiecerint[k] memoria retineret.[l] [73] Atque ut amplius eum mittigarem, supra quam sperare poterat obtuli me ei satisfacere, eam scilicet quam corruperam[m] mihi matrimonio copulando, dummodo[n] id[o] secreto fieret, ne fame detrimentum incurrerem. Assensit[p] ille, [q]et tam sua[q] quam suorum fide et osculis eam quam requisiui concordiam mecum iniit,[r] quo me facilius proderet.

24. [a]DEHORTATIO SVPRADICTE PVELLE A NVPTIIS[a]

Ilico[b] ego[c] ad patriam meam reuersus amicam reduxi ut[d] uxorem facerem, illa tamen [e]hoc minime[e] approbante, immo penitus duabus de causis dissuadente, tam scilicet pro periculo quam pro dedecore meo. Iurabat illum [f]nulla unquam[f] satisfactione super hoc placari posse, sicut postmodum cognitum est. Querebat[g] etiam quam[h] de me gloriam[i] habitura[j] esset, cum me ingloriosum efficeret, et se et me pariter humiliaret; quantas ab ea mundus penas exigere deberet, si tantam ei lucernam auferret;[k] [74] quante maledictiones,[l] quanta dampna[m] ecclesie, quante philosophorum lacrime hoc matrimonium essent sequuture; quam indecens, quam lamentabile esset, ut quem omnibus [n]natura[o] creauerat,[n] uni me femine dicarem et[p] [q]turpitudini tante[q] subicerem.[75] Detestabatur uehementer[r] hoc matrimonium,[s] quod mihi per omnia probrosum esset [t]atque honerosum.[t] Pretendebat infamiam mei pariter et difficultates matrimonii,[u] ad quas quidem uitandas[v] nos exortans Apostolus ait: 'Solutus es ab uxore? Noli querere uxorem. Si autem acceperis uxorem, non peccasti; et si nupserit uirgo, non peccabit.[w] Tribulationem tamen[x] carnis habebunt huiusmodi. Ego autem [y]uobis parco',[y] [76] etc.[z] Item:[a] 'Volo [b]autem uos[b]

[j] *add. E in vacant space* [k] *illegible in C;* deiecerunt *EFBRDY* [l] retinet *CF* detinet *E* [m] corrumperam *E;* corruperem *D* [n] dum modo *TD;* de modo *B* [o] *S begins* [p] Assensum *CE* [q–q] et causa *C;* tam sua *E* [r] uel iniit *D*

24 [a–a] *rubr.* (de hortatione *S*) *TABS;* Le v[e] chapitre, comme il la vouloit espouser, mais elle ne vouloit, et li monstroit par raisons qu'il ne le feist mie *table in H of the* (*missing*) *contents of Dijon MS 525* [b] *initial lacking in TD; large initial in ABRS;* Illico *after corr. from* Illici *Y* [c] enim *T before corr. by* T^1*; om. DY* [d] et *D* [e–e] minime hoc *F* [f–f] nulla nunquam *T, perhaps over eras.* [g] Querebam *Y before corr. by exp.* [h] qua *B* [i] gloria *BR* [j] habita *S* [k] aufertur *D* [l] maledictionis *R before corr.* [m] *T over eras.* [n–n] creauerat natura *S* [o] *om. R;* deus *DY* [p] ut *Y* [q–q] turpidudini *R;* tante me *add. CEF* [r] uehenter *A before corr. by another hand* [s] et *add. DY* [t–t] *TACB;* atque onerosum *E after exp. of* h, *SAmb; om. RDY;* atque in honerosum *F before del. of* honerosum *and add. in marg. of* al. onerosum*;* (atque) inhonorosum Amb^1 [u] matrimonio *C* [v] uacandas *C* [w] peccauit *F* [x] tantum *?D* [y–y] parco uobis *T* [z] Et *add. T before corr.* [a] *om. A* [b–b] *om. CE;* uos *F*

love, and recalled how since the beginning of the human race women had brought the noblest men to ruin.[73] Moreover, to conciliate him further, I offered him satisfaction in a form he could never have hoped for: I would marry the girl I had wronged. All I stipulated was that the marriage should be kept secret so as not to damage my reputation. He agreed, pledged his word and that of those close to him, and sealed the reconciliation I desired with kisses. But his intention was to make it easier to betray me.

24. THE GIRL'S EXHORTATION AGAINST MARRIAGE

I set off at once for Brittany and brought back my friend to make her my wife. But she was strongly opposed to the proposal, and argued hotly against it for two reasons: the risk involved and the disgrace to myself. She swore that no satisfaction could ever appease her uncle, as we subsequently found out. What honour could she win, she protested, from a marriage which would dishonour me and humiliate us both? The world would justly exact punishment from her if she removed such a light from its midst.[74] Think of the curses, the harm to the Church, and the grief of philosophers which would greet such a marriage! Nature had created me for all mankind—it would be a sorry scandal if I should bind myself to a single woman and submit to such base servitude.[75] She most strongly rejected this marriage; it would be nothing but a disgrace and a burden to me. Along with the loss to my reputation she put before me the difficulties of marriage, which the apostle Paul exhorts us to avoid when he says: 'Has your marriage been dissolved? Do not seek a wife. If, however, you do marry, there is nothing wrong in it; and if a virgin marries, she has done no wrong. But those who marry will have pain and grief in this bodily life, and my aim is to spare you',[76] etc. And again: 'I want you to be free from

[73] Cf. Gen. 3; Judg. 16; 1 Tim 2: 14. On the ruin of great men by women cf. also *Letters* 4, **9–10** and 5, **24**; *TChr*, ii. 89; *Carmen ad Astralabium*, ed. Rubingh-Bosscher, *vv.* 547–56, and *Planctus IV: Israel super Samson*, *vv.* 38–9: 'O semper fortium / ruinam maximam, / et in exitium / creatam feminam!' (ed. Meyer, *Gesammelte Abhandlungen*, i. 370; ed. Dronke in *Poetic Individuality in the Middle Ages*, ii, 2a, p. 122; *PL* clxxviii. 1821).

[74] 'penas exigere': cf. Lucan, *De bello ciuili*, viii. 103; 'lucernam': cf. Matt. 5: 14; John 5: 35.

[75] Cf. 1 Cor. 7: 3–4 ('the husband cannot claim his body as his own; it is his wife's', etc.). Cf. also *TChr*, ii. 97 ('Seruum . . . se efficit qui se uinculis nuptiarum adstringit'), *Sermon* 33 (*PL* clxxviii. 582D), and *Problemata* 14 (*PL* clxxviii. 701D) on marriage as subjection and as a tie beyond comparison ('seruitus', 'uinculum').

[76] 1 Cor. 7: 27–8.

sine sollicitudine esse',[77] etc. Quod si nec[c] Apostoli consilium nec sanctorum exhortationes de tanto[d] matrimonii[e] iugo[f] susciperem, saltem, inquit, philosophos consulerem,[g] et que[h] super hoc ab eis uel de eis scripta sunt attenderem; quod plerumque [i]etiam sancti[i] ad increpationem nostram diligenter faciunt.[78] Quale illud[j] est beati Iheronimi,[k] in primo[l] *Contra Iouinianum*, ubi scilicet commemorat Theophrastum,[m] intolerabilibus nuptiarum molestiis assiduisque inquietudinibus ex magna parte diligenter[n] expositis, uxorem sapienti non esse ducendam euidentissimis rationibus astruxisse,[o] [79] ubi et ipse[p] illas exhortationis[q] philosophice[r] rationes tali fine concludens: 'Hoc',[s] inquit, 'et huiusmodi[t] Theophrastus[u] disserens,[v] quem non suffundat[w] Christianorum?',[x] etc.[80] Idem in eodem : 'Cicero', inquit, 'rogatus ab Hyrtio[y] ut post repudium Therentie[z] sororem eius duceret,[a] omnino[b] facere supersedit, dicens non posse se[c] et uxori et philosophie [d]operam pariter[d] [e]dare.'[81] Non[e] ait: 'operam dare' sed adiunxit 'pariter', nolens quicquam agere quod studio equaretur philosophie.

25. Vt autem[a] hoc[b] philosophici[c] studii nunc omittam impedimentum, ipsum consule honeste conuersationis statum. Que enim conuentio scolarium[d] ad pedissequas, scriptoriorum[e] ad cunabula,[f] librorum siue tabularum[g] ad colos, stilorum siue calamorum ad fusos? Quis[h] denique sacris uel philosophicis[i] meditationibus intentus, pueriles[j] uagitus, nutricum[k] que hos mittigant nenias,[l] tumultuosam[m] familie

[c] *add. F in unfilled space* [d] uidelicet *add. CEF* [e] matrimonium *T* [f] *om. CE;* periculo *F* [g] consularem *C* [h] qui *E* [i–i] sancti etiam *D* [j] id *E;* istud *BRDY* [k] Ieronimi *BRDY;* Hieronymi *F* [l] libro *add. CEF* [m] theofrastum *Y* [n] *om. D* [o] abstruxisse *T and Monfrin;* astruxisse *ACEFBRSDY and Muckle;* adstrinxisse *Amb;* afferme *J. Orlandi, 'Minima Abaelardiana', p. 133, notes that* astruo *or* adstruo *are found in other writings of Abelard. Cf. TChr* ii. 97: 'uxorem sapienti non esse ducendam plurimis adstruit rationibus'. [p] ipsas *T before corr.; om. AEF;* ei *C* [q] exhortationibus *CEF;* exortationes *S;* exhortationes *D* [r] philosophie *AEFY* [s] Haec *Jerome* [t] huius *B; om. E* [u] Theopharastrus *E;* thophrastus *S;* theofrastus *Y* [v] deserens *E* [w] suffunderat *E;* suffundit *R* [x] christianum *E;* est *add. S* [y] hircio *ACFBR;* irtio *S;* hurio *Y* [z] Terentie *F* [a] duxeret *DY* [b] omnia *E* [c] *om. BRDY* [d–d] pariter operam *EFY. Cf. Jerome* [e–e] (? dare sed) adiunxit pariter nolens quicquam agere. Non *ditto. B*

25 [a] de *D* [b] hec *Y* [c] philosophie *Ycorr. over eras.* [d] scolarum *CEBRSDY;* escolles *J* [e] scriptorum *A by exp.* [f] cumula *S* [g] tabulorum *D* [h] Quid *D* [i] philosophis et *B;* philosophis *RS* [j] puerorles *E* [k] nutricumque *DY* [l] uenias *T before corr. by T¹ in marg., CESR; om. D* [m] tumultuosa *C;* tumultuosam que *D, Ycorr.*

[77] 1 Cor. 7: 32. [78] Cf. *TChr*, ii. 87, 94–101.
[79] Cf. *TChr*, ii. 97: 'Has profecto molestias atque turpitudines assiduasque inquietudines

anxious care',[77] etc. But if I would accept neither the advice of the Apostle nor the exhortations of the Fathers on the heavy yoke of marriage, at least, she argued, I could listen to the philosophers, and pay regard to what had been written by them or concerning them on this subject—as for the most part the Fathers too have carefully done when they wish to rebuke us.[78] For example, St Jerome in the first book of his *Against Jovinian* recalls how Theophrastus sets out in considerable detail the unbearable annoyances of marriage and its endless anxieties, in order to prove by the clearest possible arguments that a wise man should not take a wife;[79] and he brings his reasoning from the exhortations of the philosophers to this conclusion: 'Can any Christian hear Theophrastus argue in this way without a blush?',[80] etc. In the same book Jerome goes on to say that 'after Cicero had divorced Terentia and was asked by Hirtius to marry his sister he firmly refused to do so, on the grounds that he could not devote his attention to a wife and philosophy alike.'[81] He does not simply say 'devote attention', but adds 'alike', not wishing to do anything which would be a rival to his study of philosophy.

25. But apart from the hindrances to such philosophic study, consider, she said, the true conditions for a dignified way of life. What harmony can there be between pupils and serving women, desks and cradles, books or tablets and distaffs, pens or quills and spindles? Who can concentrate on thoughts of Scripture or philosophy and be able to endure babies crying, nurses soothing them with lullabies, and all the noisy crowd of men and women about the house?

coniugiis inesse Theophrastus nouerat, qui pene omnibus diligenter expositis, uxorem sapienti non esse ducendam plurimis adstruit rationibus.'

[80] Jerome (*c*.345–420), *Aduersus Iouinianum*, i. 48 (*PL* xxiii. 278BC); cited more fully in *TChr*, ii. 101. Jerome's *Against Jovinian* contains a vituperative refutation of Jovinian's view, condemned as heretical in 393, that Christian marriage is of itself as meritorious before God as celibate asceticism. On the Jovinianist controversy see Hunter, *Marriage, Celibacy, and Heresy in Ancient Christianity*. Jerome's work inspired anti-feminist writing over many centuries; see Wilson and Makowski, *Wykked Wyves*; Mann, *Feminizing Chaucer*, pp. 39–69, and, for the 12th c., Delhaye, 'Le Dossier anti-matrimonial'. The highly entertaining *Dissuasio Valerii ad Ruffinum philosophum ne uxorem ducat* (*The Dissuasion of Valerius to Rufinus the philosopher that he should not take a wife*), written by Walter Map (d. 1209/10) probably early in the 1180s, was one such misogynist work inspired by *Aduersus Iouinianum*; it survives in over fifty manuscripts. On the unusualness in medieval literature of anti-feminist satire being uttered by a woman, see Mann, *Feminizing Chaucer*, pp. 41–2; in *Letter* 2, **10** Heloise accepts Abelard's account of her protestations but points out that it was incomplete. Theophrastus: *c*.370–288/5 BC, a peripatetic and associate of Aristotle.

[81] Jerome, *Aduersus Iouinianum*, i. 48 (*PL* xxiii. 278C); also cited in *TChr*, ii. 101. Cf. Walter Map's *Dissuasion*, dist. iv, ch. 3 (ed. James, rev. Brooke and Mynors, p. 301).

tam in uiris quam in[n] feminis turbam sustinere poterit? Quis[o] etiam [p]inhonestas[q] illas[p] paruulorum sordes assiduas tolerare ualebit?[82] Id, inquies, diuites[r] possunt,[s] quorum palatia uel domus ample [t]diuersoria habent,[t] quorum opulentia[u] non sentit expensas[v] nec cotidianis sollicitudinibus cruciatur.[w] Sed non est, inquam, hec conditio[x] philosophorum que diuitum, nec qui opibus[y] student uel secularibus[z] implicantur curis diuinis seu philosophicis uacabunt[a] officiis.

26. Vnde et insignes olim philosophorum,[a] mundum maxime contempnentes,[b] [83] nec tam relinquentes seculum quam fugientes, omnes sibi uoluptates[c] interdixerunt ut in unius philosophie requiescerent amplexibus. Quorum unus et maximus Seneca,[d] [84] Lucilium[e] instruens, ait: '[f]Non cum[f] uaccaueris[g] philosophandum est. Omnia[h] negligenda[i] sunt ut huic assideamus, cui[j] nullum tempus satis magnum est. Non multum refert [k]utrum omittas philosophiam an intermittas;[k] non enim ubi interrupta est manet.[l] Resistendum[m] est occupationibus, nec explicande [n]sunt sed submouende.'[n] [85] Quod nunc igitur [o]apud nos amore Dei[o] sustinent qui uere[p] monachi dicuntur, hoc desiderio philosophie qui nobiles in gentibus extiterunt philosophi.[86] In omni [q]namque populo,[q] tam gentili scilicet[r] quam iudaico siue christiano, aliqui semper extiterunt fide seu morum honestate ceteris preminentes, et se a[s] populo aliqua continentie uel abstinentie singularitate[t] segregantes.[u] Apud Iudeos quidem antiquitus Nazarei, qui se Domino secundum[v] legem consecrabant,[87] siue filii prophetarum [w]Helye uel Helysei[w] sectatores[x] quos,[y] beato attestante Iheronimo,[z] [88] monachos legimus in ueteri Testamento;

[n] *om. F*   [o] Que *TACEFBRS;* Quis *DYAmb*   [p–p] inhonestas ipsas *BRSD;* ipsas inhonestas *Y*   [q] honestas *CEF*   [r] dicens *C, ?E, ?F*   [s] post' *Y*   [t–t] diuersoria haberent *A;* habent diuersoria *F*   [u] opulancia *D*   [v] experientiam *E*   [w] cruciantur *CEF*   [x] condictio *E*   [y–y] nec (*om. D*) qui operibus *BRDY*   [z] scolaribus *ACEF*   [a] uacabant *ABRD;* uacant *Y after corr. of* uacabant; entendront *J*

26 [a] philosophos *TABRSDY;* philosophorum *CEF;* Philosophi *Amb, also Muckle and Monfrin;* li . . . philosophe *J. Orlandi, 'Minima Abaelardiana', p. 132, draws attention to the use of the partitive* 'multi philosophorum' *below in* **52**.   [b] condempnantes *D*   [c] uoluntates *D*   [d] ad *add. E*   [e] lucillium *CEF;* Bucilium *D;* Valerius *J*   [f–f] Non com *T;* Non nisi (*add.* Y^1) cum *Y*   [g] *illegible before and after corr. B;* uacauerit *D*   [h] alia *add. F*   [i] negligentia *T before corr. by* T^1 *in marg.*   [j] cum *D;* sibi *E*   [k–k] obmittas philosophiam an intermittas *CE;* intromittas philosophiam an inter mittas *BR;* intermittas philosophiam an dimittas *D;* interdimittas philosophiam an dimittas *Y*   [l] mane *D*   [m] restendum *Y before corr. by* Y^1 [n–n] sed submouende sunt *F*   [o–o] amore dei apud nos *E*   [p] *om. S*   [q–q] populo namque *A*   [r] *om. D*   [s] *om. C*   [t] singulari te *R;* singulari se *S*   [u] segreg° *E*   [v] super *CEF*   [w–w] helie uel helisei *CSR;* helie uel heliseiis *E;* Helye uel Helisei *F;* helielis elisei *D*   [x] seccatores *D*   [y] *om. Y*   [z] Ieronomio *CD;* Ieronimo *BRY;* Hieronymo *F*

Who will put up with the constant muddle and squalor which small children bring into the home?[82] The wealthy can do so, you will say, for their mansions and large houses can provide privacy and, being rich, they do not have to count the cost nor be tormented by daily cares. But philosophers, I say, lead a very different life from rich men, and those who are concerned with wealth or are involved in mundane matters will not have time for the claims of Scripture or philosophy.

26. Consequently, the great philosophers of the past have despised the world,[83] not renouncing it so much as escaping from it, and have denied themselves every pleasure so as to find peace in the arms of philosophy alone. The greatest of them, Seneca,[84] gives this advice to Lucilius: 'Philosophy is not a subject for idle moments. We must neglect everything else to concentrate on this, for no time is long enough for it. Put it aside for a moment, and you might as well give it up, for once interrupted it will not remain. We must resist all other occupations, not merely finish them off but reject them.'[85] This is the practice today through love of God of those among us who truly deserve the name of monks, as it was of distinguished philosophers amongst the pagans in their pursuit of philosophy.[86] For in every people, pagan, Jew, or Christian, some men have always stood out for their faith or upright way of life, and have cut themselves off from their fellows because of their singular chastity or austerity. Amongst the Jews in times past there were the Nazirites, who dedicated themselves to the Lord according to the Law,[87] and the sons of the prophets, followers of Elijah or Elisha, whom the Old Testament calls monks, as St Jerome bears witness;[88] and in more recent times the

[82] 'Quis denique . . . tolerare ualebit': cf. Jerome, *De perpetua uirginitate Beatae Mariae aduersus Heluidium*, 20 (*PL* xxiii. 204) and Abelard, *Sermon* 33 (*PL* clxxviii. 582D).

[83] 'philosophorum mundum maxime contempnentes': cf. *TChr*, ii. 68; *Sermons* 6 and 33 (*PL* clxxviii. 425C, 591C); *Collationes* 81 (ed. Marenbon and Orlandi, pp. 100–1; *Dialogus*, ed. Thomas, *ll.* 1532–3; *PL* clxxviii. 1642A); *Soliloquium* (ed. Burnett, p. 888; *PL* clxxviii. 1877D).

[84] Cf. *Rule* **96**; also *Letter* 12: 'Seneca maximus ille morum philosophorum' (ed. Smits, p. 265; *PL* clxxviii. 350B. 'Seneca, that greatest moral philosopher', trans. Ziolkowski, p. 170).

[85] Seneca, *Epistola ad Lucilium*, lxxii. 3.

[86] Cf. *TChr*, ii. 60.

[87] Cf. Num. 6: 18–21; Judg. 13: 5–7, 16: 17; Lam. 4: 7; Amos 2: 11–12. Also *Letter* 7, **15–17** and *Rule* **82**. The Nazirites were Israelites who consecrated themselves to God, took vows to abstain from the produce of the vine, to grow their hair long, and to avoid contact with a dead body.

[88] Jerome, *Epistola* CXXV *ad Rusticum monachum*, 7 (ed. Hilberg, lvi. 125; *PL* xxii. 1076); 4 Kgs. (2 Kgs.) 6: 1–4. Cf. below **52**, *Letter* 7, **2** and **13**, and *Rule* **12**; *Sermons* 16, 23, and 33 (*PL* clxxviii. 499D, 525C, 585BC), and *Letter* 12 (ed. Smits, p. 262; *PL* clxxviii. 347D–348A; trans. Ziolkowski, pp. 164–5).

nouissime autem tres ille philosophie[a] secte, quas Iosephus [b]in libro[b] *Antiquitatum*[c] distinguens, alios Phariseos, alios Saduceos,[d] alios nominat Esseos.[e][89] Apud nos uero monachi, qui uidelicet[f] aut communem apostolorum uitam aut priorem illam et[g] solitariam[h] Iohannis[i] imittantur.[90] Apud gentiles autem,[j] ut dictum est, philosophi; non enim [k]sapientie uel philosophie nomen[k] tam ad scientie perceptionem[l] quam ad uite religionem referebant, sicut ab ipso etiam huius nominis ortu[m] didicimus, ipsorum quoque[n] testimonio sanctorum.[o] Vnde et illud est beati Augustini, octauo *de ciuitate Dei* libro, genera quidem[p] philosophorum distinguentis:[q] 'Italicum [r]genus auctorem habuit[r] Phitagoram[s] Samium,[t] a quo et fertur[u] ipsum philosophie nomen[v] exortum; nam[w] cum antea sapientes appellarentur qui modo quodam laudabilis uite aliis prestare uidebantur,[x] iste interrogatus quid[y] profiteretur,[z] philosophum se esse respondit, [a]id est[a] studiosum uel[b] amatorem sapientie,[c] quoniam[d] sapientem profiteri arrogantissimum[e] uidebatur.'[91] [f]Hoc itaque loco cum dicitur: 'qui modo quodam laudabilis uite aliis prestare uidebantur',[f] etc., aperte monstratur sapientes gentium, id est philosophos, ex laude uite potius quam scientie[92] sic esse nominatos. Quam sobrie autem atque continenter ipsi uixerint,[g] non est nostrum modo ex[h] exemplis[i] colligere, ne[j] Mineruam ipsam[k] uidear docere.[l][93] Si[m] autem sic[n] laici gentilesque uixerint,[o] nulla scilicet [p]professione religionis[p] astricti, quid te clericum atque canonicum facere oportet, ne diuinis officiis turpes preferas[q] uoluptates, ne te precipitem[r] hec Caribdis[s] absorbeat,[t] ne obscenitatibus[u] istis te[v] impudenter atque irreuocabiliter immergas?[94]

[a] philosophorum *Y;* philosophice *conj. Orlandi, 'Minima Abaelardiana', p. 133. Cf. TChr. ii. 67*: 'tria genera philosophorum et eorum sectas'. [b–b] *add.* T^1 *in marg., add.* T^3 *in a vacant space on the line;* in historiis *S* [c] in antiquitatum *TBR;* Antiquitatum decimo octavo *add. F* [d] seduceos *S* [e] ebuseos *E after corr.* [f] uero *D* [g] *om. C* [h] sollicitariam *CD;* solutariam *S* [i] Ioannis *E after corr., F* [j] aliqui *E* [k–k] philosophie uel sapientie nullum *E* [l] preceptionem *SY* [m] ortum *D* [n] *om. F* [o] sanctorum testimonio *E* [p] quedam *F* [q] distinguens *F* [r–r] genus actorem habuit *T;* autem (*before del.*) genus auctorem habuit *E;* ergo auctorem habuit *FY;* genus ergo auctorem habuit *B;* genus habuit *R;* ergo habuit auctorem *S;* genus autem auctorem habuit *D* [s] Phitagoram *TR;* phitagorem *AD;* pithagorem *C;* pytagorum *E;* Pytagoram *F;* pitagoram *BY;* pictagoram *S* [t] Samiam *F* [u] reffertur *C;* refertur *E;* etiam ferunt *F* [v] n^m *C;* nullum *E* [w] *om. B* [x] etc. aperte *add. and exp. Y* [y] quem *E after corr.* [z] proficeretur *ACD* [a–a] *om. C* [b] et *BRDY;* ou *J* [c] sciencie *S* [d] quem *R* [e] arrogatissimum *S* [f–f] *om. D* [g] vixerunt *Y* [h] *om. SY* [i] *S breaks off here due to the loss of 4 fos.* [j] nec *T before corr. by* T^1 [k] *om. BRDY, J* [l] dicere *C* [m] Sic *R before corr.* [n] hic *T before corr. by* T^1 [o] uixerunt *AF* [p–p] religionis professione *Y* [q] proferas *RD* [r] precipite *BR* [s] caripdis *C* charybdis *F* [t] absorberat *D* [u] obcenitatibus *T* [v] de *A before corr. by* A^1

three sects of philosophy described by Josephus in a book of his *Antiquities*, the Pharisees, Sadducees, and Essenes.[89] Today we have monks who imitate either the communal life of the apostles or the earlier, solitary life of John.[90] Among the pagans, as I said, are the philosophers: for the name of wisdom or philosophy used to be applied not so much to acquisition of learning as to a religious way of life, as we learn from the first use of the word itself and from the testimony of the saints themselves. And so St Augustine, in the eighth book of his *City of God*, distinguishes between types of philosopher: 'The Italian school was founded by Pythagoras of Samos, who is said to have been the first to use the term philosophy; before him men were called "sages" if they seemed outstanding for some praiseworthy manner of life. But when Pythagoras was asked his profession, he replied that he was a philosopher, meaning a student or lover of wisdom, for he thought it too presumptuous to call himself a sage.'[91] So the phrase 'if they seemed outstanding for some praiseworthy manner of life', etc., clearly proves that the sages of the pagans, that is, the philosophers, were so called as a tribute to their way of life, not to their learning.[92] There is no need for me to give examples of their chaste and sober lives—I should seem to be teaching Minerva herself.[93] But if laymen and pagans could live in this way, that is, bound by no religious profession, is there not a greater obligation on you, as clerk and canon, not to put base pleasures before your sacred duties, and to guard against being sucked down headlong into this Charybdis, there to lose all sense of shame and be plunged forever into a whirlpool of impurity?[94] If

[89] Josephus, *Antiquitates Iudaicae*, xviii. 2. 2–5 (ed. Dindorfius, i. 694–5; trans. Whiston, p. 477; trans. Feldman, *Josephus in Nine Volumes*, ix. 9–21) and Jerome, *Aduersus Iouinianum*, ii. 14 (*PL* xxiii. 303B). This is the only reference to *Antiquitates Iudaicae*, xviii (11–22) listed in Schreckenberg, *Die Flavius-Josephus-Tradition*. Cf. *TChr*, ii. 67.

[90] Cf. *Letter* 7, **13** and **27**; *Rule* **12** and **112**.

[91] Augustine, *De ciuitate Dei*, viii. 2 (ed. Dombart and Kalb, xlvii. 217; ed. Hoffmann, i. 355; *PL* xli. 225); also cited in *TChr*, ii. 38.

[92] 'ex laude uitae potius quam scientie': same words in *TChr*, ii. 39.

[93] Examples are abundantly given in *TChr*, ii. 43–115. In his *Soliloquium* (ed. Burnett, p. 888; *PL* clxxviii. 1877D–1878A) Abelard states that he has written for his fellow monks an *Exhortatio* on the faith, the way of life, and the moral discipline practised by the philosophers. This work is lost; cf. *Checklist* nos. 212, 316.

[94] Repeated attempts were made to enforce clerical celibacy. Although clerics could be in very minor grades (cf. *Letter* 7, **42**), as a teacher Abelard may also have been a canon in Paris (or Sens; cf. Cousin, i. 46). Clerical marriage had been forbidden by Pope Gregory VII, for example at the Lenten synod of 1075. The first Lateran Council of 1123 (can. 21) also forbade clerical concubinage and clerical marriage; the second Lateran Council of 1139 (can. 7) invalidated the marriages of clergy who, although already married, would not accept

Qui si clerici prerogatiuam non curas, [w]philosophi saltem[w] defende dignitatem; si reuerentia Dei contempnitur, amor saltem honestatis impudentiam temperet. Memento Socratem uxoratum fuisse, et quam fedo casu hanc philosophie labem ipse primo[x] luerit, ut deinceps ceteri exemplo eius cautiores efficerentur. Quod nec ipse preterit Iheronimus,[y] ita in primo *Contra Iouinianum*[z] de ipso scribens Socrate: 'Quodam autem tempore, cum infinita conuitia ex superiori loco ingerenti[a] Xanthippe[b] restitisset,[c] aqua[d] profusus[e] immunda, [f]nichil respondit amplius[f] quam, capite deterso:[g] "Sciebam",[h] inquit, "futurum ut ista tonitrua ymber sequeretur."'[95] [i]Addebat denique[j] ipsa et quam periculosum[k] mihi esset eam reducere et quam[l] sibi carius existeret mihique honestius amicam dici quam uxorem,[96] ut me ei sola gratia conseruaret,[m] non [n]uis aliqua uinculi nuptialis[n] constringeret,[o] tantoque[p] nos ipsos ad tempus separatos gratiora[q] de conuentu nostro [r]percipere gaudia,[r] quanto[s] rariora.[i]

27. Hec et similia persuadens seu dissuadens, cum meam [a]deflectere non posset stultitiam[a] nec me sustineret offendere, suspirans[b] uehementer[c] et[d] lacrimans perorationem[e] suam[f] tali fine terminauit: 'Vnum,' inquid, 'ad ultimum restat ut in perditione duorum minor non succedat[g] dolor quam precessit amor.' Nec in hoc ei, sicut uniuersus agnouit[h] mundus, prophecie defuit spiritus.[97]

28. Nato itaque[a] paruulo nostro, sorori mee commendato, Parisius occulte reuertimur; et[b] post paucos dies, nocte secretis[c] orationum

[w–w] philosophiam saltem *E;* saltem philosophi *F* [x] prius *DY;* premierement *J* [y] Ieronimus *ACBDRY;* Hieronymus *FAmb* [z] *add. in E in vacant space by another hand* [a] ingerende *C;* ingerendi *?E* [b] xantippe (uxori sue *superscr. add. Y*[1]) *CY;* xantipe *add. in E in vacant space by another hand;* Xantippe *F;* xanchippe *R;* xanthipe *D* [c] recepisset *DY* [d] aquam *CE* [e] perfusus *F and Jerome;* lui versa *J* [f–f] nil amplius respondit *F* [g] demisso *EAmb*[1] [h] sciebat *BR* [i–i] *this passage is missing from J; Jean de Meun knew it* (*Roman de la Rose; ed. Lecoy, vv.* 8747–58*; ed. Langlois, vv.* 8777–88) [j] deinceps *Y* [k] tecum *add. and exp. B* [l] quomodo *CEF* [m] *om. E* [n–n] uis aliqua uinculi nuptiali *T;* uis aliqua seu uis aliquod uinculi nuptialis *CEF;* uis aliqua nuptialis *RDY* [o] astringeret *D* [p] tantaque *E* [q] *om. D* [r–r] perrecepere (*crossed out*) precepere (*before corr.*) percepere (*after corr.*) gaudia *T;* concipere gaudia *B;* percepere gaudia graciora *D. Cf. Orlandi, 'Minima Abaelardiana', pp. 133–4* [s] quam *CE*

27 [a–a] non posset stultitiam refrenare (refrenare *add. Y*[1]) *Y* [b] superans *B before corr.* [c] offendere *add. and exp. T* [d] in *C* [e] per orationem *TR;* orationem *C, inserted into a vacant space in E, FY* [f] nostram *CEF* [g] succedet *E* [h] ignouit *C*

28 [a] Comme il l'espousa. *Nato itaque*; a tel seing—*the sign being three triangles; table in H of the (missing) contents of Dijon MS 525* [b] ut *BRD;* et *Y over eras.* [c] secretarum *A, ?E after corr.;* secretiarum *C;* secretiorum *F*

you take no thought for the privilege of a clerk, you can at least uphold the dignity of a philosopher, and let a love of propriety curb your shamelessness if the reverence due to God means nothing to you. Remember Socrates' marriage and the sordid episode whereby he did at least remove the slur it cast on philosophy by providing an example to be a warning to his successors. This too was noted by Jerome, when he tells this tale of Socrates in the first book of his *Against Jovinian*: 'One day, after he had withstood an endless stream of invective which Xanthippe poured out from a window above his head, he felt himself soaked with dirty water. All he did was to wipe his head and say: "I knew that those claps of thunder would lead to rain."'[95] Finally Heloise went on to the risks I should run in bringing her back, and argued that the name of friend instead of wife would be dearer to her and more honourable for me[96]—only love freely given should keep me for her, not the constriction of a marriage tie, and if we had to be parted for a time, we should find the joy of being together all the sweeter the rarer our meetings were.

27. But at last she saw that her attempts to persuade or dissuade me were making no impression on my foolish obstinacy, and she could not bear to offend me. So amidst deep sighs and tears she ended with these words: 'We shall both be destroyed. All that is left us is suffering as great as our love has been.' In this, as the whole world knows, she showed herself a true prophet.[97]

28. And so, when our little one was born, we entrusted him to my sister's care and returned secretly to Paris. A few days later, after a

the obligation of continence (Mansi, *Concilia* 21, cols. 286BC, 527–8). The effectiveness of such measures varied widely. See esp. Brooke, *The Medieval Idea of Marriage*, pp. 61–92; also Brooke, 'Gregorian reform in action'. Abelard makes no mention of any canonical objection to his marriage being raised by Fulbert or by the priest who blessed the marriage (**28** below) or by himself.

[95] Jerome, *Aduersus Iouinianum*, i. 48 (*PL* xxiii. 279A); cited more fully in *TChr*, ii. 96.

[96] Cf. *Letter* 2, **10**, where Heloise complains that Abelard here overlooks her plea that, rather than be his wife, she would prefer to be his beloved friend or 'amica' (which he did not overlook) or even his concubine or 'concubina uel scortum' (which he does not mention); cf. Ovid, *Heroides*, vii. 169: 'Si pudet uxoris, non nupta, sed hospita dicar' / 'If some scruple prevents you calling me wife, then let me be merely your hostess' (trans. Isbell, p. 64). Brooke, *The Medieval Idea of Marriage*, explores the problems created in the 11th and 12th cc. by pressure on clergy not to marry and examines examples of clerical concubines and of the clerical dynasties that were sometimes created: 'the arguments of Heloise . . . echo a world in which there was a real choice between being a wife and being a concubine' (p. 91).

[97] In *SN* c. 122–35 Abelard presents *auctoritates* which illustrate a wide range of views on chastity, fornication, concubinage, and marriage, both clerical and lay.

uigiliis in quadam ecclesia[d] celebratis, ibidem summo mane, auunculo eius atque quibusdam nostris uel[e] ipsius amicis assistentibus, nuptiali[f] benedictione confederamur; moxque occulte diuisim abscessimus[g] nec nos ulterius nisi raro latenterque uidimus, dissimulantes plurimum quod egeramus. Auunculus autem ipsius atque domestici eius, ignominie sue solatium querentes, nostrum[h] matrimonium diuulgare et fidem mihi[i] super hoc[j] datam uiolare ceperunt, [k]illa autem e contra[k] [l]anathematizare et iurare[l] quia falsissimum esset.[98] Vnde uehementer ille commotus[m] crebris eam contumeliis afficiebat.

29. Quod cum ego cognouissem, transmisi [a]eam ad abbatiam[a] quandam sanctimonialium prope Parisius que Argenteolum[b] appellatur, ubi ipsa[c] olim puellula educata fuerat atque erudita, [d]uestesque ei[d] religionis que conuersationi[e] monastice conuenirent, excepto uelo, aptari feci[f] et his eam indui.[99] Quo audito, auunculus et consanguinei seu affines eius [g]opinati sunt me nunc [h]sibi plurimum[h] illusisse,[i] et ab ea moniali facta me sic facile uelle[j] expedire. Vnde uehementer indignati et aduersum me coniurati, nocte quadam[k] quiescentem[l] me[m] atque dormientem in secreta hospicii mei camera, quodam mihi seruiente per pecuniam corrupto,[gn] crudelissima et pudentissima[o] ultione punierunt, et quam[p] summa ammiratione mundus excepit, eis uidelicet corporis mei[q] partibus amputatis quibus id quod plangebant commiseram. Quibus[r] mox in fugam conuersis,[s] duo qui comprehendi potuerunt oculis et genitalibus priuati sunt, quorum [t]alter ille fuit[t] supradictus seruiens qui, cum in obsequio meo[u] mecum maneret, cupiditate ad proditionem[v] ductus est.[100]

30. [a]DE PLAGA ILLA CORPORIS[a]

Mane[b] autem facto, tota ad me ciuitas[c] congregata, quanta stuperet ammiratione, quanta se affligeret lamentatione, quanto me clamore

[d] ecclesia *corrupt in R* [e] et *FBRD;* m *Y before corr. in marg.;* et *J* [f] *Ecorr. adds* ti *above the line* [g] obscessimus *C;* accessimus *D;* recessimus *Y* [h] initum *TAC;* unitum *BRD* [i] sibi *BRDY* [j] *om. CEF* [k–k] illa contra autem *BR;* illam autem *D;* illa autem *Y;* elle encontre *J* [l–l] iurare (*add. on the line by a corr. in E*) et anathematizare et iurare *CE;* iurare et anathematizare *F* [m] canonicus *D*

29 [a–a] ad ablaciam *D* [b] argentalium *C;* argentolium *EFD* [c] ita *BR;* itaque *D;* utique *Y* [d–d] uestes quoque ei *T before corr. by exp., Amb;* uestesque ei (ei *add. by a corr.*) *R* [e] conuersioni *T before corr. by T*[1], *Amb;* conuersationi *ACEFBRDYAmb*[1]*;* conversacion *J. Cf. Gilson, Heloise and Abelard, p. 152* [f] *om. A* [g–g] *T over eras.; eras. also in marg.* [h–h] plurimum sibi *CE;* plurimum eis *F* [i] illuxisse *TAmb;* illusisse *Amb*[1] [j] *om. Amb* [k] Comme l'en li copa les couilles; a tel seing S. *Nocte quadam table in H of the (missing) contents of Dijon MS 525* [l] qui ascentem *D* [m] *om. B* [n] corrupte *D* [o] prudentissima *C* [p] in *add. D* [q] meis *R*

private vigil of prayer at night in a certain church, at dawn we were joined together with a nuptial blessing in the presence of Fulbert and of some of our friends and his. Afterwards we parted secretly and went our ways unobserved. Subsequently our meetings were few and furtive, in order to conceal as far as possible what we had done. But Fulbert and the members of his household, seeking satisfaction for the dishonour done to him, began to spread the news of our marriage and break the promise of secrecy they had given me. Heloise cursed them and swore that there was no truth in this.[98] In exasperation Fulbert heaped abuse on her on several occasions.

29. As soon as I discovered this, I removed her to an abbey of nuns near Paris called Argenteuil, where she had been brought up and educated as a small girl, and I also had made for her a religious habit suited to the religious life, with the exception of the veil, and dressed her in this.[99] At this news her uncle and his relatives and connections imagined that I had tricked them and had found an easy way of ridding myself of Heloise by making her a nun. Wild with indignation they bound themselves by oath against me, and one night, as I rested and slept peacefully in an inner room in my lodgings, they bribed one of my servants to admit them, and there they punished me with a most cruel and shameful vengeance of such appalling barbarity as to shock the whole world: they cut off the parts of my body whereby I had committed the wrong of which they complained. Then they fled, but two who could be caught were blinded and castrated, one of them being the servant I have mentioned who had been led by greed while in my service to betray me.[100]

30. THE WOUND ON HIS BODY

Come the morning the whole city gathered before my house, and the scene of horror and amazement, mingled with lamentations, cries,

[r] de plaga illa corporis *rubr. add. here in marg. of T by ?T³; ?*quomodo scilicet castratus fuit *follows in a 15th-/early 16th-c. hand* [s] conuersus *D* [t–t] alter fuit ille fuit *CE;* fuit alter ille *F* [u] me *B* [v] prodicioni *B*

30 [a–a] *rubr. add. B; in vacant space in text; vacant space in R;* Le vj^e chapitre, le dul qui en ot, et la plainte de ses escoliers *table in H of the (missing) contents of Dijon MS 525* [b] *decorated initial in R; space left for initial in D* [c] *in T the letter* s *is add. by T⁴*

[98] Cf. Mark 14: 71.

[99] Argenteuil, on the north bank of the river Seine, is some 16 km west of Paris.

[100] On Abelard's castration see Appendix A, 4.

uexarent,[d] quanto planctu perturbarent,[e] difficile, immo impossibile, est exprimi.[101] Maxime uero clerici ac precipue scolares nostri intolerabilibus me lamentis et eiulatibus[f] cruciabant, ut[g] multo[h] amplius ex eorum compassione quam ex uulneris lederer passione et plus erubescentiam quam plagam sentirem et pudore magis quam dolore affligerer.[102] Occurrebat animo quanta[i] modo[j] gloria[k] pollebam, quam facili et turpi casu[l] hec[m] humiliata, immo penitus esset[n] extincta, quam iusto Dei iudicio [o]in illa[o] [p]corporis mei portione[p] plecterer[q] in qua deliqueram, quam iusta[r] proditione is quem antea prodideram[s] uicem mihi retulisset, quanta laude mei emuli tam manifestam equitatem[t] efferrent, quantam perpetui doloris contritionem[u] plaga[v] hec parentibus meis[w] et amicis esset collatura, quanta dilatatione[x] hec singularis infamia uniuersum mundum esset occupatura. Qua[y] mihi [z]ulterius uia[z] pateret![a] Qua fronte in publicum prodirem,[b] omnium digitis demonstrandus,[c] omnium linguis corrodendus,[d] omnibus monstruosum spectaculum futurus![e] Nec me etiam parum confundebat [f]quod, secundum occidentem[g] legis litteram, tanta sit apud Deum[f] eunuchorum abhominatio ut homines, amputatis uel attritis[h] testiculis eunuchizati, intrare ecclesiam tanquam olentes et immundi prohibeantur;[i] et in sacrificio quoque talia penitus animalia[j] respuantur libro Numeri,[k] capitulo[l] septuagesimo quarto:[m] 'Omne animal quod est[n] contritis, uel tonsis,[o] uel sectis ablatisque testiculis, non offeretis[p] Domino.'[103] [q]Item in Deuteronomii[q] capitulo[r] uicesimo primo:[s] 'Non intrabit eunuchus, atritis[t] uel amputatis testiculis et absciso[u] ueretro, ecclesiam[v] Domini.'[w] [104]

[d] uerarent *A;* uexaret *F;* uexarant *D* [e] pertubaret *F* [f] eiulationibus *E* [g] et *A* [h] merito *E* [i] quam *D* [j] nuper *add. DY* [k] gloriam *C* [l] causa *D* [m] hic *E* [n] est *E* [o–o] nulla *B* [p–p] mei corporis portione *BRY;* mei corporis *D* [q] placerer *C;* nisi *add. by another hand in B* [r] iusta *Y after corr.* [s] prodiderem *D* [t] etatem *C;* equitatem *Ecorr.;* crudelitatem *F* [u] *Y after corr.* [v] *E after corr.* [w] *om. CEF* [x] dilacione *A* dilatione *Y* [y] Que *CEF* [z–z] uia ulterius *tr.CEF* [a] paterer *A* [b] cum *add. DY* [c] Denotandus *?C, E before corr., FAmb*[1] [d] corrodendum *T;* corrodandus *D* [e] essem *add. Y*[1] [f–f] *om. RDY* [g] accidentem *C* [h] attrictis *Y before corr.* [i] prohibentur *C* [j] aliam *E;* alia *?B* [k] Leuitici *F and Vulg.* (*Clementine*) [l] capite *F;* capituli *B before corr.* [m] 22 *F and Vulg.* (*Clementine*) [n] uel *Vulg.* (*Clementine*)—a better reading [o] tunsis *F;* tensis *BR;* censis *DY* [p] offerens *B;* offeres *RY;* offerentes *D* [q–q] deuteronom̄ *TA;* deutero *E;* Deuteronom. *F;* in deuteronomio *BR;* Item in Deuteronomio *DY. The second of these two biblical quotations is introduced awkwardly in most MSS, but the addition of* Item *in DY brings the text into conformity with one of the characteristic means* (*others being* Et, Et alibi, *and* Et iterum) *by which Abelard presents supplementary authorities. For examples of chains of quotations often introduced by* Item *see TChr* ii, *TSch* iii *and Letter* 6, 14–23. [r] capite *F;* capituli *B before corr.* [s] 23 *F and Vulg.* (*Clementine*) [t] ac tritis *BRY* [u] aborso *C* [v] in ecclesiam *Y* [w] dei *T*

and groans which exasperated and distressed me, is difficult, no, impossible, to describe.[101] In particular, clerics and, especially, members of my school tormented me with their unbearable weeping and wailing until I suffered much more from their sympathy than from the pain of my wound, and felt the misery of my mutilation less than my shame and humiliation.[102] All sorts of thoughts filled my mind: how brightly my reputation had shone, and now how easily in an evil moment it had been dimmed, or rather completely blotted out; how just a judgement of God had struck me in the parts of the body with which I had sinned, and how just a reprisal had been taken by the very man I had myself betrayed. I thought how my rivals would exult over my unmistakable punishment, how this bitter blow would bring lasting grief and misery to my relatives and friends, and how fast the news of this unheard-of disgrace would spread over the whole world. What road could I take now? How could I show my face in public, to be pointed at by every finger, derided by every tongue, a monstrous spectacle to all I met? I was also appalled to remember that, according to the cruel letter of the Law, a eunuch is such an abomination to the Lord that men made eunuchs by the amputation or mutilation of their members are forbidden to enter a church as if they stank and were unclean; even animals in that state are rejected for sacrifice in the book of Numbers, chapter 74: 'You shall not present to the Lord any animal whose testicles have been bruised or crushed or cut and taken away.'[103] And in Deuteronomy, chapter 21: 'A eunuch whose testicles have been crushed or cut away and whose organ has been severed shall not enter the church of the Lord.'[104]

[101] Jaeger, 'The Prologue to the *Historia calamitatum*', pp. 9–10, draws attention to the use of a similar syntactic frame to describe another moment of anguish as relatives watch Susanna being led off to trial: 'quanto pudore confusi, quantis lacrymis perfusi'; *Sermon* 29 (*PL* clxxviii. 559A).

[102] Fulk of Deuil in his *Letter* to Abelard also writes of the widespread shock and grief felt in the city ('pene tota civitas') by the bishop, by a multitude of canons and clergy and others, both men and women, *PL* clxxviii. 374CD.

[103] Not Numbers but Leviticus; Lev. 22: 24 in modern numbering. Some Bibles of the 11th or 12th c., e.g. Cambridge, Pembroke College, MSS 49 and 50, also number this chapter 22, others (like Abelard) 74, e.g. British Library, Add. MSS 14788 (1148, from l'Abbaye du Parc, near Leuven in Belgium), 17737 (*c.*1155, from Floreffe, near Namur in Belgium), 28106 (1094–7, from Stavelot, near Liège in Belgium), and Harley 2798 (1172, from Arnstein, Bavaria). Practices varied considerably: the chapter is numbered 45 in the Bible copied for Frowin, abbot of Engelberg, 1143–78 (Engelberg, Stiftsbibliothek , MS 3, fo. 52; ⟨http://www.e-codices.unifr.ch⟩); in *Comm. Rom.*, iv (ix. 12, ed. Buytaert, p. 234, *l.* 102) Lev. 25 is numbered 84.

[104] Deut. 23: 1 in modern numbering. Some Bibles of the 11th or 12th c., e. g. British Library, Add. MS 17737 and Cambridge, Pembroke College, MS 53, also number this

31. In tam misera[a] me[b] contritione[c] positum, confusio, fateor, pudoris potius quam[d] deuotio conuersionis[e] ad monastichorum latibula claustrorum[f] compulit,[105] illa tamen prius ad imperium nostrum sponte uelata et monasterium[g] ingressa.[h] [106] [i]Ambo[j] itaque[k] simul sacrum habitum suscepimus, [l]ego quidem in[l] abbatia sancti Dyonisii,[m] illa in[n] monasterio Argenteoli[o] supradicto.[107] [p]Que quidem, memini,[p] cum eius adolescentiam a[q] iugo monastice [r]regule tanquam intolerabili[r] pena[s] plurimi frustra deterrerent ei [t]compacientes, in illam[t] Cornelie[u] querimoniam inter lacrimas et singultus[v] [w]prout poterat[w] prorumpens[108] ait:

'O maxime coniux![x]
O thalamis[y] [z]indigne meis,[z] hoc[a] iuris habebat
In tantum fortuna capud?[b] Cur[c] [d]impia nupsi,[d]

31 [a] miseria *B* [b] mei *R before corr.* [c] contri(c *exp.*)tione *Y* [d] postquam *C;* potius(*Ecorr.*)quam *E* [e] conuersationis *C; om. J* [f] claustrarum *C* [g] in ministerium *B* [h] ingressa *R before del. of* -a [i] *beginning of vacant space in BR, ending in* **32** *at* abbate [j] Comme il fist Heloyse nonain et lui moine. *Ambo; 8 table in H of the (missing) contents of Dijon MS 525. The added reference to Amb should be to p. 18.* [k] *A in another hand;* ita *D* [l–l] eius quidem in *C;* ego (*superscr. Ecorr. after exp.*) quidem in *E;* Ego uero in *add. B in vacant space by another hand;* in *R;* Ego uidelicet in *DY* [m] dionisii *A;* Dionysii *F* [n] *add. in Y by Y*[1] [o] argentolii *CEF* [p–p] Que (qui *add. and exp.*) ut (ut *superscr. corr.*) memini *F;* Que (*vacant space*) memini *B;* quidem memini *R;* Sepe quidem memini *D;* Sepe quidem memini quod (quod *Y*[1]) *Y;* Et remembray que *J* [q] tam *D, Y before exp. by another hand* [r–r] *vacant space in B;* regularitatem quam intolerabili *R;* regularitatis quam intolerabili *D;* re (*exp. Y*) regularitatis quasi (quam *before exp.*) intolerabili *Y* [s] pene *CEFY* [t–t] *vacant space in B* [u] uxorem pompei *add. D;* uxoris pompeii *add. Y* [v] singulatus *D* [w–w] *om. B* (*which leaves vacant space*), *RDY* [x] coniunx *TA* [y] thalamus *R* [z–z] *om. BR* [a] hic *E* [b] *E after corr.;* caput *F;* apud *D* [c] *E after corr.* [d–d] *om. B, which leaves a vacant space;* inpias (*vacant space*) si *R*

---

chapter 23, others not. It is 24 in British Library Add. MS 14788, 91 in Engelberg, Stiftsbibliothek 3, 98 in British Library Harley 2803 (1148, from Worms, Middle Rhineland), and 107 in British Library Add. MS 28106 and Harley 2798. Sometimes a higher range of numbers appears along with a lower range in the text and in the margins. In 'Fraud, fiction and borrowing', pp. 495–6, Benton (and cf. Orlandi, '*Minima Abaelardiana*', pp. 132–3) correctly observed that this chapter in Deuteronomy would have been numbered 107 in (at least some) pre-13th-c. Bibles, but he was mistaken to think that a lower range of numbers first occurs as a result of renumbering in the early 13th c. The chapter divisions used today were certainly championed by Peter the Chanter (d. 1197) and employed by his pupil Stephen Langton (d. 1228) in his *Distinctiones*—see Quinto, *Doctor Nominatissimus: Stefano Langton*, pp. 62–71; D'Esneval, 'La Division de la Vulgate latine en chapitres', pp. 560–1, and Light, 'Versions et révisions du texte biblique'—but they were not wholly new. Benton did later withdraw his view about there being here evidence of 13th-c. interpolation into the text of the *Letter*, having found 'great inconsistency in the chapter numbers of pre-Langton Bibles' ('The correspondence of Abelard and Heloise', p. 99, n. 9), and he noted variations in the numberings given to chapters in Deuteronomy in other works

31. I admit that it was shame and confusion in my remorse and misery rather than any dedication to enter the religious life which drove me to seek shelter in monastic cloisters.[105] Heloise had already agreed to take the veil at my request and entered the monastery.[106] So we both together put on the religious habit, I in the abbey of St-Denis, and she in the monastery of Argenteuil which I spoke of before.[107] There were many people, I remember, who in pity for her youth tried to dissuade her from submitting to the yoke of monastic rule as a penance too hard to bear, but all in vain. She broke out as best she could through her tears and sobs into Cornelia's famous lament:[108]

O most renowned of husbands,
So undeserved a victim of my marriage, was it my fate
To bend that lofty head? What prompted me

of Abelard: the modern chapter numbers 4 and 7 appear as 15 and 23 in *TChr*, ii. 18 (ed. Buytaert, p. 140), 30: 11–13 and 30: 14 appear as 57 and 58 in *Comm. Rom.*, iv (x. 9, ed. Buytaert, p. 251), but 16 as 81 in *Sic et Non* c. 138, 56. See on this also Luscombe, 'From Paris to the Paraclete', pp. 254–5.

[105] In *Sermon* 8, for Palm Sunday, Abelard, reflecting on Ecclus. 4: 25 ('there is a shame that bringeth sin, and there is a shame that bringeth glory and peace'), distinguished between confusion which is good and which leads to proper repentance and confusion which leads the other way (*PL* clxxviii. 442CD).

[106] A 12th-c. poem (cited above at n. 32) contrasts the willingness of Abelard's mother to take the veil with the unwillingness of Heloise to do so: 'the mother spontaneously takes the veil, the beloved friend ('amica') unwillingly . . . She obeyed, nor could she have left unfulfilled for her husband whatever love can fulfill' ('Sponte parens, invita quidem velatur amica . . . Paruit illa, / Nec quid amor pos(s)it non implevisse mari(to)'), ed. Dronke in *Abelard and Heloise in Medieval Testimonies*, p. 45, trans. p. 19; Dronke, 'Orleans, Bib. Mun. 284', p. 278 and *Intellectuals and Poets*, p. 280, trans. p. 263. In an extract from a (lost) Calendar of the abbey of the Paraclete printed by Duchesne–d'Amboise, p. 1187, Heloise is named as a nun at Argenteuil: 'primo Petri Abaelardi coniux, deinde Monialis & Priorissa Argentolij'. Cf. *Letter* 2, **9** and **15**, and *Letter* 4, **14**.

[107] François Villon (1431–63) recalled these events in his *Ballade des dames du temps jadis*: 'Ou est la tres saige Esloÿs, / Pour qui chastré fut et puis moyne / Pierre Esbaillart a Saint Denis? / Pour son amour eust ceste essoyne', *Le Testament Villon*, *ll.* 337–40, ed. Rychner and Henry, i. 44; the editors note in their Commentary (ii. 54) that the epithet 'saige' appears often in the old French translation of the *Letters* (often attributed to Jean de Meun). Cf. also Otto of Freising, who wrote in his *Gesta Friderici*, i. 49 (ed. Waitz and von Simson, p. 69) that at a well-enough known moment Abelard became a monk at St-Denis; Otto also states that Abelard now read and thought by day and night and became ever more learned and clever. In an addition to the *Chronicle* of William of Nangis (*fl.* late 13th c.; ed. Géraud, i. 33) Abelard is said to have been married before he entered St-Denis and later became an abbot in Brittany, his birthplace: 'Petrus Abaelardus, magister in dialectica insignis et celeberrimus, primo uxoratus, deinde S. Dionysii in Francia monachus, post in Britannia, unde natus fuerat, abbas constitutus.' Ferroul, 'Bienheureuse castration', explores reasons why Abelard separated from Heloise.

[108] Cf. Lucan, *De bello ciuili*, viii. 87: 'gemitu rumpente querellas' / 'her wailing broke out into complaints' (trans. Duff).

Si miserum factura[e] fui? Nunc accipe penas
Sed quas sponte luam.'[f] [109]

Atque[g] in his uerbis ad altare mox properat, et confestim ab episcopo [h]benedictum uelum[h] ab[i] altari tulit,[j] et se [k]professioni monastice[k] coram [l]omnibus alligauit.[l]

32. Vix autem de uulnere adhuc[a] conualueram,[b] cum ad me confluentes[c] clerici,[d] tam ab abbate[e] nostro [f]quam a me[f] ipso continuis supplicationibus, efflagitabant[g] quatinus[h] [i]quod hucusque[i] pecunie uel laudis cupiditate[j] egeram nunc[k] amore Dei operam studio darem, attendens[l] quod mihi fuerat a Domino talentum commissum, ab ipso esse cum usuris[m] exigendum,[110] et qui[n] diuitibus maxime hucusque[o] intenderam, pauperibus erudiendis amodo studerem;[111] et[p] ob[q] hoc maxime dominica manu me nunc[r] tactum esse cognoscerem, quo liberius[s] a carnalibus illecebris et tumultuosa uita seculi abstractus[t] studio litterarum uaccarem,[u] nec tam[v] mundi quam Dei uere philosophus fierem.

33. [a]Erat autem abbatia[a] illa nostra ad quam me contuleram secularis[b] admodum[c] uite atque turpissime,[d] cuius abbas ipse quo ceteris[e] prelatione maior tanto uita [f]deterior atque[f] infamia notior erat.[112] Quorum quidem intolerabiles spurcitias ego frequenter atque uehementer modo priuatim[g] modo publice redarguens, omnibus me supra modum onerosum[h] atque odiosum effeci. Qui ad cotidianam discipulorum nostrorum instantiam maxime gauisi occasionem [i]nacti sunt[i] qua[j] me [k]a se[k] remouerent.[113]

[e] factum *D* [f] *om. BRD* [g] que *B; om. RD;* Et *Y* [h–h] *om. B;* benedictum illum *R* [i] *om. RDY* [j] tuli *B* [k–k] monastice professioni *T;* professioni *Y* [l–l] omnibus (*om. Y*) obligauit *CEDY; om. B;* omnibus *R*

32 [a] *om. RDY;* encore *J* [b] conualuerem *R* [c] conflueentes *A before corr.;* confuluentes *C; om. B;* confluerent *RDY;* venant *J* [d] qui *add. DY* [e] *end of vacant space in BR beginning in* 31 [f–f] *om. D* [g] afflagitabant *CEF;* flagitabant *BRDY* [h] quatenus *Y*¹ *after corr. from* quanta [i–i] quodhuc usque *C;* quod adhucusque *BRY;* adhuc usque *D* [j] cupiditati *B* [k] non *Y* [l] accedens *C* [m] usura *E* [n] quod *A* [o] huc usque *T* [p] ut *C* [q] ab *C* [r] tunc *D* [s] libera liberius *R before corr.* [t] astractus *B before corr.* [u] uocarem *D* [v] *om. C*

33 [a–a] Erant (*B corr. from* Erat) autem monachi in abbatia *B in another hand in vacant space* [b] scolarium *E* [c] ad modum *R* [d] continentes se *add. B in another hand in vacant space* [e] *om. C;* quanto ceteris *F* [f–f] *om. CE;* et *F;* deterior eius atque *B in another hand in vacant space;* pires en vie *J* [g] priuatum *D* [h] reddidi *add. F* [i–i] excogitati sunt *B in another hand in vacant space;* nocti sunt *D* [j] que *C* [k–k] *om. A;* ad se *BR*

To marry you and bring about your fall?
Now claim your due, and see me gladly pay.[109]

So saying she hurried to the altar, quickly took up the veil blessed by the bishop, and publicly bound herself to the monastic life.

32. I had still scarcely recovered from my wound when clerics came thronging round to pester the abbot and myself with repeated demands that I should now, for love of God, continue the studies which hitherto I had pursued only in desire for wealth and fame. They urged me to consider that the talent entrusted to me by God would be required of me with interest;[110] that instead of addressing myself to the rich as before I should devote myself to educating the poor,[111] and recognize that the hand of the Lord had touched me for the express purpose of freeing me from the temptations of the flesh and the distractions of the world so that I could devote myself to learning and thereby prove myself a true philosopher not of the world but of God.

33. But the abbey to which I had withdrawn was completely worldly and depraved, with an abbot whose pre-eminent position was matched by his evil living and notorious reputation.[112] On several occasions I spoke out boldly in criticism of their intolerably foul practices, both in private and in public, and made myself such a burden and nuisance to them all that they gladly seized on the daily importunities of my pupils as a pretext for having me removed from their midst.[113]

[109] Lucan, *De bello ciuili*, viii. 94–8. Cf. von Moos, 'Cornelia und Heloise' and 'Lucan und Abaelard', pp. 438–40 (repr. in *Abaelard und Heloise*, pp. 121–3).

[110] 'mihi fuerat . . . exigendum': cf. Matt. 25: 14–30. Cf. *TSch*, *prefacio* 3: '(scolares nostri) unanimiter postulant ne talentum michi a domino commissum multiplicare differam; quod cum usuris utique districtus ille et horrendus iudex quando exigat ignoratur.'

[111] Cf. *TSch*, *prefacio* 4: 'Addunt etiam . . . ut sicut mores et habitum ita commutem et studium et humanis diuina preferam uolumina . . . et qui olim studium ad lucrandam pecuniam institueram, nunc ad lucrandas animas hoc conuertam . . .'.

[112] The disrepute of the abbey before Suger succeeded Adam as abbot in 1122 was deplored by Bernard, abbot of Clairvaux, in a letter sent *c.*1127 to Suger (*Letter* 88, 4, ed. Leclercq and Rochais in *S. Bernardi Opera*, vii. 201–10, here p. 203, *ll.* 18–23) and has been compounded by claims that Adam forged documents in favour of his house; cf. Van de Kieft, 'Deux diplômes faux de Charlemagne'; Du Pouget, 'La Légende carolingienne à Saint-Denis'. Also Grant, *Abbot Suger*, pp. 182–5. For generalized criticism of ostentatious abbots and self-indulgent monks cf. *TChr*, ii. 57, 71.

[113] See Jeauneau, 'Pierre Abélard à Saint-Denis'.

34. Diu itaque illis instantibus atque importune pulsantibus, abbate quoque nostro et fratribus interuenientibus, ad cellam quandam recessi, scolis more solito uaccaturus.[114] Ad quas quidem tanta scolarium multitudo[115] confluxit, ut nec[a] locus ospitiis nec terra sufficeret alimentis. Vbi, quod[b] professioni mee conuenientius erat, sacre plurimum lectioni studium intendens, [c]secularium artium[c] disciplinam quibus amplius assuetus fueram et quas a[d] me plurimum[e] requirebant non penitus abieci; sed de his quasi[f] hamum quendam[g] fabricaui [h]quo illos[h] philosophico sapore[i] inescatos ad uere philosophie lectionem attraherem, sicut et summum Christianorum philosophorum[j] Origenem[k] [116] consueuisse *Hystoria* meminit *ecclesiastica.*[117] Cum autem[l] in diuina scriptura non minorem mihi[m] gratiam quam in seculari Dominus contulisse[n] uideretur,[o] ceperunt admodum ex utraque lectione [p]scole nostre[p] multiplicari et cetere [q]omnes uehementer[q] attenuari.[r] [s]Vnde maxime magistrorum inuidiam atque odium aduersum me [t]concitaui,[st] qui in omnibus que poterant mihi derogantes, duo precipue absenti mihi[u] semper obiciebant[v] quod scilicet proposito monachi ualde sit contrarium secularium[w] librorum studio detineri, et quod[x] sine magistro ad magisterium diuine lectionis accedere presumpsissem, ut sic[y] uidelicet omne[z] mihi doctrine scolaris[a] exercitium interdiceretur; ad quod incessanter [b]episcopos, archiepiscopos, abbates,[b] et quascunque[c] poterant [d]religiosi nominis[d] personas incitabant.[e] [118]

34 [a] ne *C* [b] *T here adds a rubr. in the outer marg.*: de libro theologie sue et persecutione (persecutionem *before corr.*) quam inde sustinuit a condiscipulis. *In the inner marg. a sign indicates where this rubr. should rightly be.* [c–c] scolarium artium *CEDY;* secularium *B followed by vacant space* [d] ad *E* [e] plurimi *Y* [f] *om. Y* [g] quandam *BD* [h–h] quos illos *C;* quos illo *D* [i] sapose *D* [j] philosophum *F* [k] arigenem *C;* originem *BR* [l] *om. D* [m] *om. R* [n] concessisse *DY* [o] uidetur *BR* [p–p] nostre scole *E* [q–q] uehementer omnes *CEF* [r] accencari *D* [s–s] *om. C* [t–t] concitaui *E;* me concitari *BR;* me contigit concitari *DY* [u] *om. DY* [v] abiciebant *CE* [w] secularum *A;* scolarium *CE* [x] quo *BR* [y] sit *BR* [z] etiam *Y* [a] scolares *A* [b–b] archiepiscopos, episcopos et abbates *BRDY;* les evesques et les arcevesques, les abbés *J* [c] quoscunque *F* [d–d] religiosas nominis *E;* religionis *B* [e] inuitabant *F*

[114] The cell to which the abbot released Abelard was presumably a dependency of the abbey of St-Denis. In a letter to Abelard (ed. Reiners, pp. 78–80; *PL* clxxviii. 369D–370D (*Letter* 15)) Roscelin, who calls Abelard a quasi-monk, wrote that he moved out of St-Denis into an obedience (a dependency) and then into another church of the abbey through the abbot's kindness. But by teaching he attracted a large number of barbarians ('congregata barbarorum multitudine') and breached the duty of a monk not to teach. And at a late hour ('sero') he took his earnings to a prostitute ('meretricem'). If this is meant to refer to Heloise who was at Argenteuil, a location near Paris would seem likely. However, according to Benton, ('Fraud, fiction and borrowing', p. 487; repr. in Benton, *Culture, Power and*

34. As pressure continued for some time and these demands became insistent, my abbot and the monks intervened, and I retired to a cell where I could devote myself to teaching as before.[114] And there my pupils gathered in crowds[115] until there were too many for the place to hold or the land to feed. I applied myself mainly to study of the Scriptures as being more suitable to my present calling, but I did not wholly abandon instruction in the profane arts in which I was better practised and which was most expected of me. In fact I used them as a hook, baited with the taste of philosophy, to draw my listeners towards the study of the true philosophy—as was the practice of the greatest of the Christian philosophers, Origen,[116] as recorded in the *Ecclesiastical History*.[117] When it became apparent that God had granted me no less a gift for expounding Scripture than secular literature, the numbers in my school began to increase for both, while elsewhere they diminished rapidly. This roused the envy and hatred of other masters against me; they set out to disparage me in every way they could, and two of them especially were always attacking me behind my back for occupying myself with secular literature in a manner totally unsuitable to my monastic calling, and for presuming to set myself up as a teacher of sacred learning when I had had no teacher myself. Their aim was for every form of teaching in a school to be forbidden me, and to this end they were always trying to win over bishops, archbishops, abbots, in fact anyone of account in religion whom they could approach.[118]

Personality, p. 434), other possibilities include possessions of St-Denis, near Nogent-sur-Seine in Champagne, which were no more than 5 km away from where Abelard was later to found his oratory of the Paraclete; Benton mentions the priory of Marnay, the church of Fontaine-Macon, and the grange of Aulne. The cell is less likely to have been the priory of St-Ayoul, in Provins, which belonged to St-Pierre in Troyes, even though at **49** below Abelard recalls having stayed there earlier. Maisoncelle in Champagne has also been suggested but it too did not belong to St-Denis. When Abelard later fled to Champagne he was more specific about his location (**49** and **52** below), adding that he had known the places earlier. Otto of Freising, in *Gesta Friderici*, i. 49 (ed. Waitz and von Simson, p. 69), wrote that some time after his entry into St-Denis ('post aliquod tempus') Abelard returned to public teaching, having gained release from obedience to his abbot ('ab obedientia abbatis sui solutus'). This last point is inconsistent with Abelard's account in **50–1** and **60** below.

[115] Cf. Roscelin's reference to 'barbarorum multitudine' cited in the previous note.

[116] 'summum Christianorum philosophorum Origenem': similar praise of Origen (*c.*185/6–after 251) is found in **65** below, *Letter* 5: **22** , *Letter* 7: **47**, *Rule* **126**, and *Sermon* 31 (*PL* clxxviii. 571BC).

[117] Eusebius, *Historia ecclesiastica*, vi. 19 (ed. Mommsen, pp. 557–65; *PG* xx. 567C–570B).

[118] One of these two critics many have been Roscelin, who objected, in his *Letter* to Abelard (ed. Reiners, p. 80; *PL* clxxviii. 370D–372A (*Letter* 15)), that teaching was not

35. [a]DE LIBRO THEOLOGIE SVE ET PERSECVTIONE QVAM INDE SVSTINVIT A CONDISCIPVLIS[a]

Accidit[b] autem mihi ut ad ipsum fidei nostre fundamentum humane rationis similitudinibus disserendum primo me applicarem, et quendam theologie[c] tractatum[d] de unitate et trinitate diuina scolaribus nostris componerem,[e] [119] qui humanas et philosophicas rationes requirebant,[f] et [g]plus que[g] intelligi quam que dici[h] possent efflagitabant,[i] dicentes quidem uerborum superfluam esse prolationem quam intelligentia non sequeretur, nec credi posse [j]aliquid nisi primitus intellectum,[j] et ridiculosum[k] esse aliquem[l] aliis predicare quod nec[m] ipse nec illi quos[n] doceret intellectu [o]capere possent,[o] Domino ipso arguente quod ceci essent duces cecorum.[120]

36. Quem quidem tractatum cum uidissent et legissent plurimi, cepit [a]in commune[a] omnibus plurimum placere quod[b] in eo pariter

35 [a–a] *as has been noted above, a sign in the inner marg. of T indicates that this rubr. should be placed here; CBR leave vacant space;* Le vij[e] chapitre, comme pour .I. tracté de theologie qu'il fist, il fu accusé et souffri plusieurs ennuis *table in H of the (missing) contents of Dijon MS 525* [b] *large initial in CEBRY, decorated in BR; unfilled space left for initial in D* [c] *om. Y* [d] tractum *D* [e] *ditto. E;* exponerem *Y* [f] inquirebatur *C;* inquirebant *EF* [g–g] plus quam *E;* que plus *BRDY* [h] didisci *B;* didici *R* [i] afflagitabant *CE* [j–j] nisi primitus ad intellectum *C;* nisi primitus aliquid intellectum *EF* [k] ridiculosum *TCEFAmb and cf. TSch* ii. 58, *l.* 907*;* rediculosum *A;* ridiculum *BRDY;* oultraiges *J* [l] aliquid *F* [m] ne *T* [n] quod *CEF* [o–o] cape possent *A;* possent capere *E;* capere posset *DY*

36 [a–a] *add. in vacant space by Ecorr.* [b] et *F;* eo quod *DY*

---

compatible with the monastic life; hence Abelard was not living the life of a monk. But he was also not a cleric or a layman, nor should he be called *Petrus*, a masculine noun, nor even a man, since he had lost that part of his body that made him male. And since he was an incomplete man Roscelin chose to leave his letter incomplete. In his *Dialectica*, ii. 1 (ed. de Rijk, p. 145 *ll.* 16–22) Abelard complained that his rivals and detractors were motivated by envy to put difficulties in the way of his life, his writings, his teaching, and his studies: 'Etsi enim invidia nostre tempore vite scriptis nostris doctrine viam obstruat studiique exercitium apud nos non permittat . .'. This may well include his monastic life although Marenbon, *The Philosophy of Peter Abelard*, pp. 40–2, thinks not, as Abelard also wrote later in the same work (*Dialectica*, iv. 1, ed. de Rijk, p. 469 *ll.* 1–9) that his rivals further protested that no Christian should treat of or teach matters that did not relate to Christian faith. Disputes about what monks could or could not do beyond their penitential task of mourning for the sins of the world in contemplative solitude were not unknown: at about this time (between 1119 and 1122) Rupert of Deutz, monk and abbot, wrote an *Altercatio monachi et clerici quod liceat monacho praedicare* (*PL* clxx. 537–42) in defence of monastic teaching and preaching; he was countered in the 1150s by a regular canon, Philip of Harvengt, abbot of Bonne Espérance, in his *De institutione clericorum* (*PL* cciii. 665–1206). At 6 above Abelard was uncomplimentary about William of Champeaux combining entry into religious life as a regular canon with continuing teaching. The charge that Abelard was not qualified to teach divinity (*diuina lectio*) because he had not studied under a master does

35. HIS BOOK OF THEOLOGY AND THE PERSECUTION IT RECEIVED FROM FELLOW PUPILS

Now it happened that I first applied myself to expounding the basis of our faith using analogies based on human reason, and I composed a treatise on the theology of the Divine Unity and Trinity[119] for the use of my students who were asking for human and philosophical reasons and who were demanding something intelligible rather than mere words. In fact, they said that words were superfluous if understanding could not follow them, that nothing could be believed unless it was first understood, and that it was absurd for anyone to preach to others what neither he nor those he taught could grasp in the intellect: the Lord himself criticized the blind who are leaders of the blind.[120]

36. After the treatise had been seen and read by many it began to please everyone generally very much, as it seemed uniformly to satisfy

not mean that he needed to have a formal qualification such as the *licentia*, which was still to be developed; see Delhaye, 'L'Organisation scolaire'.

[119] 'theologie tractatus': *Theologia 'Summi boni'* (= *TSum*). For a fuller statement of the need for understanding before preaching cf. *TSch*, ii. 49–60. Between 1118 and 1121, Abelard wrote to G., bishop of Paris (Gilbert or Gerbert, d. 1123, not his predecessor Galo, who was bishop 1104–1115/16), and to his clergy to complain, on the strength of a report from a student, that his old enemy (Roscelin, although he is not named) had vomited accusations over a work of his on the holy Trinity ('opusculo quodam nostro de fide sancte trinitatis'—'a certain little work of ours on faith in the holy Trinity'—surely *TSum*). Abelard states that he had written this work chiefly to show that his adversary taught tritheism and he requested the bishop of Paris to call a meeting at which either he himself or Roscelin (whom Abelard calls a pseudo-dialectician and a pseudo-Christian) would receive correction (*Letter* 14, ed. Smits, pp. 279–80; *PL* clxxviii. 355–8; trans. Ziolkowski, pp. 194–5; and see Smits, pp. 189–202). At the close of *TSum*, 101 (ed. Buytaert and Mews, p. 201) Abelard attacked unnamed and boastful critics who sought a fight but not the truth. Roscelin (on whom see also Appendix A, 1 and nn. 114 and 118 above) was one of these.

[120] Cf. Matt. 15: 14. 'Nothing could be believed unless it was first understood': the pupils seem, in effect, to reject what Anselm of Bec and Canterbury (d. 1109) wrote: 'I do not seek to understand so that I may believe, but I believe so that I may understand' (*Proslogion* 1 in *Opera omnia*, i, ed. Schmitt, p. 100; English trans., ed. Davies and Evans, p. 87). Some twenty years later Bernard of Clairvaux accused Abelard of disregarding the words of the Prophet Isaiah: 'unless you will have believed you will not understand' (7: 9, Septuagint version; *Letter* 338 to Cardinal Haimeric, ed. Leclercq and Rochais in *S. Bernardi Opera*, viii. 278). Yet Abelard, as David Knowles wrote (*Evolution of Medieval Thought*, p. 123; 2nd edn., pp. 112–13), 'though he does not mention (Anselm's) motto, *credo ut intelligam*, would certainly have echoed it, though perhaps on a slightly more superficial level and with more emphasis on the last word'. Likewise, Grabmann, *Geschichte*, ii. 174–5; Thomas, 'Anselms *fides quaerens intellectum*'; Luscombe, 'St Anselm and Abelard'. As St Augustine of Hippo wrote, faith, while it opens the way to understanding, itself requires some prior understanding; *Enarrationes in Psalmum cxviii* (*Sermo* 18, *PL* xxxvii. 1552–3); *Sermo* 43. vii. 9 (*PL* xxxviii. 257–8).

omnibus satisfieri super hoc questionibus uidebatur.[121] Et quoniam questiones iste pre omnibus difficiles uidebantur,[c] quanto earum[d] maior [e]extiterat grauitas, tanto solutionis earum censebatur maior[e] subtilitas. Vnde emuli mei uehementer accensi concilium[f] contra me congregauerunt, maxime duo illi antiqui insidiatores,[g] Albericus scilicet et Lotulfus,[h] qui iam defunctis magistris eorum et nostris, Guillelmo[i] scilicet atque Anselmo, post [j]eos quasi[j] regnare se[k] solos[l] appetebant, atque etiam[m] ipsis tanquam heredes succedere.[n] [122] Cum autem [o]utrique Remis[o] scolas regerent, crebris suggestionibus [p]archiepiscopum suum Radulfum aduersum[p] me commouerunt ut, ascito Conano[q] Prenestino episcopo qui tunc legatione fungebatur in Gallia,[r] conuenticulum quoddam[s] sub nomine concilii[t] in Suesionensi[u] ciuitate celebrarent,[v] meque [w]inuitarent[x] quatenus illud opusculum[y] quod[z] de Trinitate composueram mecum[wa] afferrem; et factum est ita.[123]

[c] et *add.* T^4 [d] eorum *CE* [e–e] *om. D* [f] consilium *AC* [g] insidiatorum *E* [h] loculphus *CEF* [i] Guillhelmo *T* [j–j] q. *R;* quos *Y* [k] *om. CEF* [l] soli *F* [m] *om. ACEF;* aussi *J* [n] sucodere *R before corr.* [o–o] remeñ *Ecorr. in vacant space;* Remenses *F* [p–p] archiepiscopum suum Radulphum aduersum *EFY;* suum archiepiscopum aduersum *D* [q] Cardinali *DY* (li *over eras. in Y*)*;* caneno *CEF* (Conone *add. by an annotator in marg. F*) [r] galla *D* [s] quemdam *T before corr. by* T^1 *in marg., Amb;* quonddam *before corr. by exp. Y* [t] consilii *DCE* [u] successioni *C;* suessionensi *FR* [v] celebraret *Y where the final* e *is written over an eras.* [w–w] *om. B* [x] inuitaret *Y where* -et *is written over an eras.* [y] opus clarum *Amb* [z] *om. D* [a] mequam *?E before corr.*

---

[121] In his *Collationes* 4 (ed. Marenbon and Orlandi, pp. 4–5; ed. Thomas, *ll.* 50–2; *PL* clxxviii. 1613D), Abelard allows the Philosopher to flatter his 'wonderful book, the Theologia': 'the more (envy) has persecuted it, the more it has covered it with glory'. The reference is either to *TSum* or to its successor, *TChr*, which was written after *TSum* had been condemned.

[122] Anselm of Laon and William of Champeaux died in 1117 and 1121 respectively. Alberic and Lotulf, who, according to Abelard, had created difficulties for him when at Laon (cf. **12** above) and were to do so again in the future (cf. **58** below), now taught in Reims, where Alberic, later to be archbishop of Bourges (1136–41), was archdeacon; cf. Williams, 'The cathedral school of Reims'. Lotulf came from Novara in Lombardy; cf. Van den Eynde, 'Du nouveau sur deux maîtres lombards', pp. 7–8. Alberic was warmly commended for his teaching of Scripture by Adalbert of Sarrebrück, his student during the 1130s and archbishop of Mainz from 1137 to 1141 (Anselm of Havelberg, *Vita Adalberti II Moguntini*, ed. Jaffé, p. 586, *vv.* 599–606), and by the poet Hugh Primas (*fl.* 1130s/1140s) for making Reims an outstanding centre for the study of theology and the Bible (*Poem* 18, ed. McDonough, pp. 61–5; trans. Adcock, pp. 45–9). Lotulf seems to have contributed to the compilation of sentences of theology that emanated from the school at Laon; Giraud ('Le Recueil de Sentences de l'école de Laon: *Principium et causa*', pp. 257–8) draws attention to sentence collections attributed to him in two MSS in the Bayerische Staatsbibliothek in Munich, Clm 14730 (fos. 73–82, 'Sententie a magistro Uutolfo collecte. Principium et causa . . .') and Clm 19112 ('Sententie a Loitolfo collecte in quo due ceterniones de diuinitate', fo. 177[v]). Both Alberic and Lotulf are also described as excellent

on all the questions.[121] And, the questions seeming to all to be difficult, the importance of the problems was matched by the subtlety of my solution of them. My rivals were therefore much annoyed and convened a Council against me, especially those two old opponents, Alberic and Lotulf, who, now that our former masters, William and Anselm, were dead, were trying to reign alone in their place and succeed them as their heirs.[122] Both of them were heads of the school in Reims, and there, by repeated insinuations, they were able to influence their archbishop, Ralph, to take action against me and, along with Conan, bishop of Praeneste, who held the office of papal legate in Gaul at the time, to hold an assembly, which they called a Council, in the city of Soissons, where I was to be invited to come provided that I brought my little treatise on the Trinity. And so I did.[123]

masters by Otto of Freising—'egregii uiri et nominati magistri'—in his account of this council held in 1121 (*Gesta Friderici*, i. 49, ed. Waitz and von Simson, p. 69); Otto studied in France from about 1125. Alberic did receive criticism from Walter of Mortagne (n. 50 above), and Lotulf ('magister . . . Franciae') was to come under attack from Gerhoh of Reichersberg during the pontificate of Honorius II (1124–30) for holding an adoptionist view of Christ's sonship of God; see Gerhoh of Reichersberg, *Letter* 21, written to cardinals in Rome in 1163–4 (*PL* cxciii. 575–85, esp. 576CD); also Classen, *Gerhoch von Reichersberg*, pp. 90, 392–3, and Van den Eynde, 'Du nouveau sur deux maîtres lombards', pp. 7–8. Without naming Alberic, Abelard was later to criticize teachings which appear to be Alberic's own on the salvation of those who died before the incarnation of Christ, and on the continuing virginity of Mary, the mother of Jesus, and also to renew the criticism he made at the council of Soissons (**39** below) that Alberic, in effect, maintained that God begat himself (*TSch*, ii. 64; *TChr*, iv. 78, *ll.* 1134–46. Relevant sources are assembled in *Sic et Non*, c. 84, 62, and 15).

[123] Ralph: archbishop 1106–24. Conan of Praeneste: legate in France of Pope Paschal II in 1114–15 and of Popes Gelasius II and Callixtus II in 1117–21; see Schieffer, *Die päpstlichen Legaten in Frankreich*, pp. 198–212 (pp. 210–11 for the synod of Soissons); Dereine, 'Conon de Preneste'. Conan was in Soissons in 1121 before he returned to Rome where, on 17 Apr. and together with thirty other cardinals, he witnessed a privilege granted by Callixtus II (JL 6901; *Italia pontificia*, i. 125, n. 5; text printed in the *Bullaire du pape Calixte II, 1119–1124: Essai de restitution*, ed. V. Robert (2 vols., Paris, 1891), i. 334–6) . He appears in this year in a confirmation of the possessions of the monastery of St-Jean-des-Vignes, Soissons (*Papsturkunden in Frankreich*, NF iv: *Picardie*, ed. Ramackers, no. 13, pp. 81–2) and was present at the settlement in Soissons of a dispute over the possessions of St-Aubin, Bapaume (*Papsturkunden in Frankreich*, NF vii: *Nördliche Ile de France und Vermandois*, ed. Lohrmann, no. 24b, pp. 263–4). This settlement was decided by Bishop Geoffrey of Chartres, Abbot Godfrey of St-Médard, Soissons, Abbot William of St-Thierry, Reims, and Abbot Fulbert of St-Sépulcre, Cambrai. Bishop Geoffrey and the abbot of St-Médard both appear in Abelard's account of the council. In his account of the hearing at the 'prouincialis synodus' held in Soissons (*Gesta Friderici*, i. 49, ed. Waitz and von Simson, p. 69) Otto mentions the presence of the papal legate but gives him no name. Abelard's is the only 'eyewitness' account; no official proceedings survive of the hearing of the case or of any other business brought before the council, on which, and on other proceedings concerning suspected errors in theological teaching in the 11th and 12th cc., see Miethke, 'Theologenprozesse'.

37. Antequam autem[a] illuc[b] peruenirem, duo[c] illi predicti emuli nostri ita me in clero et populo diffamauerunt,[d] ut pene me populus paucosque qui aduenerant ex[e] discipulis nostris prima[f] die nostri aduentus lapidarent, dicentes [g]me tres[g] deos predicare et scripsisse, sicut ipsis persuasum fuerat.[124] Accessi autem, mox ut ad ciuitatem ueni, ad legatum, eique libellum nostrum inspiciendum[h] et diiudicandum tradidi;[i] [j]et me,[j] si aliquid scripsissem[k] aut dixissem quod a catholica fide dissentiret, paratum esse ad correptionem[l] uel[m] satisfactionem obtuli. Ille autem statim [n]mihi precepit[n] libellum ipsum[o] archiepiscopo illisque emulis meis defferre, quatinus ipsi inde[p] iudicarent[q] qui me super hoc accusabant, [r]ut illud [s]in me etiam[s] compleretur:[t] 'Et inimici nostri sunt iudices.'[r] [125]

38. Sepius autem illi inspicientes atque reuoluentes libellum, nec quid in audientia proferre[a] aduersum me auderent inuenientes, distulerunt usque in finem concilii[b] libri ad quam[c] anhelabant[d] dampnationem. Ego autem singulis diebus, antequam sederet[e] concilium,[f] in publico omnibus secundum [g]quam scripseram[g] fidem catholicam disserebam, et[h] cum magna ammiratione omnes qui audiebant tam uerborum apertionem[i] quam sensum[j] nostrum commendabant. Quod cum populus et clerus inspiceret, ceperunt ad inuicem dicere: '"Ecce" nunc "palam loquitur", et nemo [k]in eum aliquid dicit;[k] et concilium[l]

37 [a] nunc *D* [b] illud *C* [c] duoli *D* [d] diffamauerant *ACE;* difamauirant *F* [e] ad *A before corr. by exp. by another hand* [f] primo *F* [g–g] me tres *in E an illegible add. is made here in a vacant space* [h] incipiendum *E before superscr. corr.* [i] *add. Ecorr. in vacant space* [j–j] *om. F* [k] scripssem *A* [l] correctionem *TDYAmb;* correptionem *ACEF* (*al.* correctionem *add. F in marg.*), *Amb*[1]; corretionem *B after exp. of* p; correpcionem *R* [m] et *F* [n–n] precepit mihi *DY* [o] illum *Y* [p] me *Amb* [q] iudicaretur *C* [r–r] *om. E* [s–s] etiam in me *F* [t] compelleretur *D;* complerentur *Y before exp. and corr.*

38 [a] *om. CEF* [b] consilii *CED* [c] quem *CY* [d] hanelabant *D* [e] . . . deret *F before corr. by another hand; al.* sederet *add. F in marg.;* cederet *Amb*[1] [f] consilium *CEDY* [g–g] qua scripseram *A;* scripturam *C;* quam scripturam *E;* quod scripseram *FBRDY;* si comme je l'avoye escript *J* [h] *S resumes here* [i] operationem *?C, D* [j] censum *D* [k–k] dicit in eum aliquid *CEF* [l] consilium *CED*

[124] Mob violence had led to the burning of two peasants suspected of being heretics in Soissons in 1114; see Guibert of Nogent, *De vita sua*, iii. 16–17, ed. Labande, pp. 428–35; Eng. trans. by Swinton Bland, revised by Benton, pp. 212–14; see also Russell, *Dissent and Reform in the Early Middle Ages*, pp. 78–81. Earlier, perhaps in 1092, after an investigation at a council in Soissons into Roscelin's views on the divine Trinity, Ivo, bishop of Chartres, wrote to him that the citizens of Soissons, if they knew about his obduracy, would suffocate him under a pile of stones in their customary way ('more suo subito ad lapides convolarent et lapidum aggere obrutum praefocarent'; *Letter* 7, ed. Leclercq, p. 24; *PL* clxii. 17C). In his

37. But before I could make my appearance, my two rivals spread such defamatory rumours about me amongst the clerks and people that I and the few pupils who had accompanied me narrowly escaped being stoned by the people on the first day we arrived, for preaching and having written (so they had been told) that there are three Gods.[124] I called on the legate as soon as I entered the city, handed him the little book for him to inspect and form an opinion, and declared myself ready to be censured and to make amends if I had written or said anything at odds with the Catholic faith. But he told me at once to take the book to the archbishop and my opponents, so that my accusers could form their own judgement, and the words 'Our enemies are the judges' be fulfilled in me.[125]

38. However, though they read and reread the book again and again they could find nothing they dared charge me with at an open hearing, so they adjourned the condemnation they were panting for until the final meeting of the Council. For my part, every day before the Council sat, I spoke in public on the Catholic faith in accordance with what I had written, and all who heard me were full of praise both for my presentation and for my interpretation. When the people and the clergy saw this they began to say '"Here he is, speaking openly", and

Epistola de incarnatione uerbi, c. 1, Anselm wrote that Roscelin would not have accepted the accusations brought against him at the council convened by Archbishop Rainald of Reims had he not feared being killed by the people ('nisi quia a populo interfici timebat'; *Opera*, ii, ed. Schmitt, pp. 4–5). In *TSum*, with an unnamed Roscelin in view, Abelard refutes tritheism, and in *Letter* 14 to the bishop and clergy of Paris Abelard wrote that Roscelin had earlier been condemned at Soissons for preaching tritheism ('tres deos', ed. Smits, p. 279; *PL* clxxviii. 356D; trans. Ziolkowski, p. 194). In a long and strongly worded letter to Abelard written *c.*1120 Roscelin responded to a (lost) letter sent by Abelard to the canons of St-Martin of Tours which contained criticisms of himself. *Inter alia*, but chiefly, Roscelin in this letter amassed patristic evidence in support of his view that the divine substance was in a certain sense divisible, although he denied that he was a Sabellian heretic (ed. Reiners, p. 78 *ll.* 23–8; *PL* clxxviii. 366A (*Letter* 15)). Sabellianism is the antithesis of tritheism. For the controversy see Mews, 'St Anselm and Roscelin, 2'; also Mews, introduction to *TSum*, pp. 41–6. Otto of Freising in *Gesta Friderici*, i. 49 (ed. Waitz and von Simson, p. 69) reported that Alberic of Reims and Letald (Letaldus) of Novara judged Abelard to be Sabellian and that he was condemned on this account: 'Sabellianus hereticus iudicatus.' Otto explained that Abelard applied his philosophical teaching about words and names to the theology of the Trinity with the result that the three divine persons became simply names: 'Sententiam ergo vocum seu nominum in naturali tenens facultate non caute theologiae admiscuit. Quare de sancta trinitate docens et scribens tres personas—quas sancta aecclesia non vacua nomina tantum sed res distinctas suisque proprietatibus discretas hactenus et pie credidit et fideliter docuit—nimis adtenuans . . .'. See Folz, 'Otton de Freising' and Vergani, '*Sententiam vocum seu nominum*'; also Zerbi, 'La Condanna di Soissons (1121)'.

[125] Deut. 32: 31.

ad finem festinat, maxime in eum, ut audiuimus, congregatum.[m] Numquid[n] iudices cognouerunt quia[o] ipsi potius quam ille[p] errant?'[126] Ex quo emuli nostri [q]cotidie magis ac magis[q] inflamabantur.

39. Quadam autem die, Albericus[a] [b]ad me animo[b] intemptantis[c] [127] cum quibusdam discipulis suis accedens, post quedam blanda colloquia,[d] dixit se mirari [e]quoddam quod[e] in libro illo notauerat, quod scilicet, cum[f] Deus Deum genuerit[g] nec nisi unus Deus sit, negarem tamen [h]Deum se ipsum[h] genuisse. Cui[i] statim respondi:[j] '[k]Super hoc,[k] si [l]uultis, rationem[l] proferam.' 'Non[m] curamus', inquit ille, 'rationem humanam aut sensum uestrum[n] in talibus, sed auctoritatis uerba solummodo.'[o] [p]Cui ego:[p] 'uertite, inquam,[q] folium libri, et inuenietis[r] auctoritatem'. Et erat[s] presto liber[t] quem [u]secum ipse detulerat.[u] Reuolui ad locum quem noueram, quem ipse minime compererat[v] [w]ut qui non nisi mihi nocitura[w] querebat; et uoluntas Dei fuit, ut [x]cito mihi occurreret[x] quod uolebam. Erat autem sentencia intitulata[y] 'Augustinus, *De Trinitate*[z] libro primo: "Qui putat [a]eius potentie Deum[a] ut se ipsum ipse[b] genuerit, eo plus errat,[c] [d]quod non solum[d] Deus[e] ita non est, sed nec [f]spiritualis creatura nec corporalis.[f] Nulla enim omnino res est que se ipsam gignat."'[g] [128] Quod cum discipuli eius qui aderant[h] audissent, obstupefacti erubescebant. Ipse autem, ut se quoquomodo[i] protegeret, 'bene', inquit, 'est intelligendum'. Ego autem subieci[j] hoc non esse nouellam[k] sed ad presens

[m] congregati *Y* [n] Nunquam *CE;* Nonquid *BRS;* Non quid *D* [o] quod *F* [p] ipse *D* [q–q] magis ac (et *Y*) magis cotidie *BRSDY*

39 [a] abbericus *E* [b–b] animo ad me *F* [c] Interptantis *S;* intentatis *Amb;* intentandum *Amb*[1] [d] loquela *A before superscr. corr. by another hand* [e–e] quoddam (*exp. E*) quoddam *E;* quidem quod *F;* quedam quod *D;* quedam que *Y* [f] eum *BR* [g] genuit *CEF* [h–h] se ipsum deum *BRSDY* [i] Cum *A before corr.* [j] respondit *T before exp.; om. E* [k–k] super *C; om. E* [l–l] uultis super rationem ?fundi *add. E* [m] nam *C* [n] nostrum *EF* [o] tantummodo *CEF* [p–p] *exp. E, restored by Ecorr.* [q] *om. CEF* [r] iuuentutis *E* [s] *om. D* [t] *E after corr.* [u–u] ipse secum tulerat *CEF;* secum attulerat *BRDY;* secum ipse abtulerat *S* [v] comparerat *E;* comperaret *S* [w–w] aut qui non nisi nocitura mihi *TA;* aut non nisi mihi nocitura *CF;* aliqui non nisi mihi nocitura *E;* aut qui nisi nocitura (noscitura *Y*) mihi *BRSDY;* aut qui non nisi mihi nocitura *Amb;* utpote qui (*or* ut qui *or* prout qui) non nisi nocitura mihi *conj. Orlandi, 'Minima Abaelardiana', p. 134, who also draws attention to* utpote qui at **48** and **49** *below* [x–x] cito occurreret mihi *T;* mihi cito occurreret *BRSDY* [y] ventilata *Y* [z] Le tracté qu'il fist se commence: *Augustinus de Trinitate—there follows a sign consisting of three oblongs in the table in H of the (missing) contents of Dijon MS 525* [a–a] potentie eius deum *A;* eius posse deum *E* eius esse potentie Deum *F;* eius potencie domini *S* [b] *superscr. F; om. DY* [c] erat *D;* eruat *Y* [d–d] quia non solus *Y* [e] deum *T before corr.* [f–f] spiritualis nec corporalis creatura *F* [g] gignat ut sit *F;* gignit *B;* gingnat *D* [h] auderant *D* [i] quo[o] *C*

no one utters a word against him. The Council which we were told was expressly convened against him is quickly coming to an end. Can the judges have found that the error is theirs, not his?'[126] This went on every day and added fuel to my enemies' fury.

39. And so one day Alberic sought me out with some of his followers, intent on attacking me.[127] After a few polite words he remarked that something he had noticed in the book puzzled him very much; namely, that although God begat God, and there is only one God, I deny that God had begotten Himself. I said at once that if they wished I would offer an explanation on this point. 'We take no account of human reason,' he answered, 'nor of your interpretation in such matters; we recognize only the words of authority.' 'Turn the page,' I said, 'and you will find the authority.' There was a copy of the book at hand, which he had brought with him, so I looked up the passage which I knew but which he had failed to see, as if he had looked only for what would damage me. By God's will I found what I wanted at once: a sentence headed 'Augustine, *On the Trinity*, Book 1': 'Whoever supposes that God has the power to beget Himself is in error, and the more so because it is not only God who lacks this power, but also any spiritual or corporeal creature. There is nothing whatsoever which begets itself.'[128] When his followers standing by heard this they blushed in embarrassment, but he tried to cover up his mistake as best he could by saying that this should be understood in the right way. To that I remarked that this was nothing new, but it

[j] subiecsi *C;* subiunxi *Amb*[1] [k] nouellum *FAmb;* non illam *D; vacant space in Y*

[126] Cf. John 7: 26. The reference is to Christ teaching in the Temple; a further comparison with Christ is made later at **40**, one with Daniel at **43**, and one with St Athanasius being hounded by heretics at **59**. For a comparison made later (in his *Letter against Bernard*, *Epistola contra Bernardum*) of himself with the martyr St Vincent of Saragossa, see n. 180 below. Cf. Frank, 'Abelard as imitator of Christ'; Jaeger, 'Peter Abelard's silence'.

[127] 'animo intemptantis': cf. above at **11**.

[128] Augustine, *De trinitate*, i. 1 (*PL* xlii. 820); cited in *TSum*, ii. 62; also in *TChr*, iii. 109; *TSch*, ii. 64 and 146, and *SN* c. 15, 1. The problem whether one can say that the one God begets God but does not beget himself was explored in *TSum*, iii. 51–67. Abelard almost certainly alludes to his confrontation on this point at Soissons with Alberic of Reims ('in Francia qui se quasi singularem diuinae Paginae magistrum omnibus praefert' / 'who presents himself in France to all as if he were unique as a master of the divine page') in *TChr*, iv. 78; cf. *TSch*, ii. 63–4. The quotation from Augustine also appears in Roscelin's *Letter* to Abelard in which he upbraids Abelard for not having mastered sacred Scripture: 'te in sacrae scripturae eruditione manifestum sit nullatenus laborasse' (ed. Reiners, pp. 68 and 69; *PL* clxxviii. 363B and 362D (*Letter* 15)).

nichil attinere,[l] cum [m]ipse uerba tantum,[m] non sensum, requisisset; si autem sensum et rationem attendere uellet, paratum me dixi ei[n] ostendere secundum eius sententiam[o] quod in eam lapsus[p] esset[q] heresim [r]secundum quam[r] is qui pater est[s] sui ipsius filius[t] sit. Quo ille audito, statim quasi furibundus effectus ad minas conuersus est, asserens nec rationes meas nec auctoritates mihi in hac causa[u] suffragaturas[v] esse. Atque ita recessit.

40. Extrema uero die concilii,[a] priusquam[b] residerent,[c] diu legatus ille atque archiepiscopus cum emulis meis et quibusdam[d] personis deliberare ceperunt quid de me ipso et[e] libro nostro statueretur, pro quo[f] maxime conuocati fuerant.[g] Et quoniam ex uerbis meis aut scripto quod erat in presenti [h]non habebant[h] quid in me pretenderent, omnibus aliquantulum conticentibus[i] aut iam mihi minus aperte[j] detrahentibus, Gaufridus,[k] Carnotensis episcopus, qui ceteris episcopis et religionis nomine et sedis dignitate precellebat,[129] ita exorsus est: 'Nostis, Domini omnes qui adestis, hominis huius doctrinam, [l]qualiscunque sit, eiusque[l] ingenium in quibuscunque studuerit multos assentatores[m] et sequaces habuisse, et magistrorum tam suorum quam nostrorum famam maxime compressisse, et quasi eius[n] uineam [o]a mari[o] usque ad mare palmites suos[p] extendisse.[130] Si hunc preiuditio, quod non[q] arbitror, grauaueritis, etiamsi recte,[r] multos uos offensuros sciatis et non deesse plurimos qui eum defendere uelint, presertim cum in presenti scripto nulla uideamus que [s]aliquid obtineant aperte calumpnie.[s] Et quia iuxta illud Iheronimi:[t] "Semper in propatulo[u] [v]fortitudo[w] emulos habet,[v]

Feriuntque[x] summos
Fulgura[y] montes",[131]

[l] actinere *D;* pertinere *Y* [m–m] ipse tantum uerba *BRSY;* tantam uerba *D* [n] *om. BRSDY* [o] scienciam *D* [p] *om. Y* [q] *om. D* [r–r] secundum (*after corr. by T*¹ *in marg.*) quam *TAEFAmb;* quod *CBRSD;* quam *Y;* selon laquelle *J* [s] *om. D* [t] *ditto. B before corr.* [u] perte *C;* parte *EF* [v] suffragatas *F*

40 [a] consilii *CDY* [b] postquam *CEF* [c] desiderent *CE;* desederant *F;* recederent *DY* [d] quibus *A* [e] de *add. E* [f] et *add. Y* [g] fuerunt *D* [h–h] nihil habebatur *Y* [i] contiscentibus *CE* [j] *om. D* [k] Gauffridus *F* [l–l] qualisque sit eiusque *C;* qualiscunque sit eiusque sit *E;* qualis est eiusque *BRSDY* [m] assectatores *Amb;* assentatores *Amb*¹ [n] *om. B* [o–o] *om. D* [p] suas *C;* non *add. D* [q] *om. T;* ce que je ne croy pas *J* [r] recto *A* [s–s] aliquid erroris (erroris *add. Y*¹) obtineant aperte *Y* [t] Ieronimi *CBRDY;* Hieronimi *E;* Hieronymi *F* [u] propatibulo *BRD* [v–v] emulos habet fortitudo *S* [w] fortitudo *A after corr.* [x] feriunt quoque *C;* fererunt quoque *E;* feriuntque suos *B before corr. by exp.;* fuerunt que *D* [y] Fulmina *Jerome*

was irrelevant at the moment as he was looking only for words, not interpretation. But if he was willing to hear an interpretation and a reasoned argument I was ready to prove to him that by his own understanding he had fallen into the heresy of supposing the Father to be His own Son. On hearing this he lost his temper and turned to threats, asserting that neither my explanations nor my authorities would help me in this case. He then went off.

40. On the last day of the Council, before the session was resumed, the legate and the archbishop began to discuss at length with my opponents and other persons what decision to take about me and my book, as this was the chief reason for their being convened. Since they could find nothing to bring against me either in my words or in the treatise which was before them, and everyone stood silent for a while or now criticized me less openly, Geoffrey, bishop of Chartres, who was pre-eminent among the other bishops on account of his reputation for holiness and the importance of his see,[129] spoke as follows: 'All of you who are present, my lords, know that this man's teaching, whatever it is, and his intelligence have won him many supporters and followers in everything he has studied. He has greatly lessened the reputation both of his own teachers and of ours, and his vine has spread its branches from sea to sea.[130] If you injure him through prejudice, though I do not think you will, you must know that even if your judgement is deserved you will offend many people, and large numbers will rally to his defence, especially since in this treatise before us we can see nothing which is obvious calumny. Jerome has said that "Courage which is unconcealed always attracts envy, and

lightning strikes
the mountain peaks."[131]

[129] Geoffrey II of Lèves, bishop of Chartres, 1116–49. See Grant, 'Geoffrey of Lèves' and 'Arnulf's mentor'; Grauwen, 'Gaufried, bisschop van Chartres'.

[130] Cf. Ps. 79 (80): 9–12 (8–11), 71 (72): 8; also, Bernard of Clairvaux, *Letter* 191 to Pope Innocent II in 1140 on Abelard's heresies (sent in the name of the archbishop of Reims and others, ed. Leclercq and Rochais in *S. Bernardi Opera*, viii. 42, *l.* 4).

[131] Jerome, *Hebraicae quaestiones in libro Geneseos, prologus* (ed. de Lagarde, p. 1; *PL* xxiii. 983B), citing Horace, *Carmina*, ii. 10, 11–12: 'feriuntque summos fulgura montes'; cf. Jerome, *Epistola* LX, 16 and CVIII, 18 (ed. Hilberg, liv. 570 *l.* 1 and lv. 329 *l.* 5; *PL* xxii. 600 and 893). The same verse from Horace is also cited in *Epistola contra Bernardum* (ed. Klibansky, 'Peter Abailard and Bernard of Clairvaux', p. 7; trans. Ziolkowski, p. 109) where 'fulgura', Klibansky notes (p. 7, n. 22), would be more rightly written than 'fulmina'; also found in the *Carmen ad Astralabium*, ed. Rubingh-Bosscher, *v.* 328: 'montes fulgura

uidete ne plus ei nominis conferatis[z] uiolenter agendo, et plus nobis[a] criminis[b] ex inuidia quam ei ex iusticia conquiramus.[c] "Falsus" enim "rumor", ut predictus doctor meminit, "cito opprimitur[d] et uita posterior iudicat de priori."[e][132] Si autem canonice [f]agere in eum[f] disponitis, dogma eius uel scriptum[g] in medium proferatur, et interrogato libere respondere[h] liceat ut, conuictus [i]uel confessus,[i] penitus obmutescat, iuxta illam saltem[j] beati Nichodemi[k] sententiam qua[l] Dominum ipsum[m] liberare cupiens aiebat: "Numquid[n] lex nostra[o] iudicat hominem, nisi[p] audierit ab ipso prius, et cognouerit[q] quid faciat?"'[133] Quo audito, statim emuli mei obstrepentes[r] exclamauerunt: 'O sapientis[s] consilium,[t] ut contra eius uerbositatem contendamus cuius[u] argumentis uel[v] sophismatibus[w] [x]uniuersus obsistere mundus[x] non posset!' Sed, certe, multo[y] difficilius erat cum [z]ipso contendere Christo,[z] ad quem[a] tamen audiendum[b] Nichodemus[c] iuxta legis[d] sanctionem[e] inuitabat.[134]

41. Cum autem episcopus[a] ad id quod proposuerat [b]eorum animos[b] inducere[c] non posset, alia uia eorum[d] inuidiam[e] refrenare attemptat,[f] dicens ad discussionem[g] tante rei paucos qui aderant non[h] posse sufficere, maiorisque examinis[i] causam hanc indigere; in hocque[j] ulterius tantum [k]suum esse[k] consilium ut ad[l] abbatiam meam, hoc est monasterium sancti Dyonisii,[m] abbas meus, qui aderat, me reduceret ibique, pluribus ac doctioribus[n] personis conuocatis,

[z] auferatis *E superscr. corr. of* conferatis [a] uobis *DY* [b] crimina *CE;* criminum *F* [c] conqueramus *S before corr., D;* conquiratis *Y after corr. of* conquiramus [d] primitur *BRDY* [e] priore *codd.;* priori *Jerome. Cf. Bergh, 'Studia critica', p. 21* [f–f] in eum agere *CEFY* [g] scripta *E* [h] ostendere *F* [i–i] uel (et *F*) confusus *FYAmb*[1]; *al.* uel confessus *add. F in marg.;* ou regiehissans *J;* uel confusus *preferred by Orlandi, 'Minima Abaelardiana', p. 132 and n. 10 but cf. Ivo of Chartres, Decretum VI, cap. 232:* 'De clericis convictis et confessis' (*PL clxi.* 495C)*; also the Introduction above at p. cxxx* [j] *om. D* [k] nycodemi *E;* nichomedi *Y* [l] quam *BRSD* [m] christum *Y* [n] Nuncquid *A;* Nonquid *RS;* Non quid *D* [o] uestra *A* [p] ubi non (non *add. Y*[1]) *Y* [q] recognouerit *D* [r] obstrepantes *E;* obstupentes *Y* [s] sapiens *Amb;* sapientis *Amb*[1] [t] concilium *B* [u] eius *Y* [v] et *BRSDY* [w] sophismantibus *T;* sophismatibus non *CE;* sophismatibus nunc *F* [x–x] uniuersus mundus *C;* mundus uniuersus obtinere *D;* uniuersis uniuersus o(bsistere) m(undus) *add. Y* [y] merito *E* [z] ipso contendere *C;* christo contendere *EF* [a] quam *D, ?E* [b] eos *add. ?D over eras., add. Y* [c] nychodemus *E* [d] legum *E* [e] sanctorum *D*

41 [a] christo *C* [b–b] animos eorum *DY* [c] in inducere *R* [d] illorum *BRSY* [e] inuidia *CD; add. Y*[1] [f] acceptat *C* [g] decisionem *Y* [h] *om. E* [i] examimnis *A before corr. by A*[1]; examinacionis *S;* libra *add.* D; examines libra (*after exp. of* circa) *Y* [j] hoc quod *E;* hoc quoque *F* [k–k] esse suum *S* [l] *add. in Y by Y*[1] [m] dionisii *AS* Dionysii *F* [n] doctoribus *D*

Beware lest violent action on your part brings him even more renown, and we are more damaged ourselves by our envy than he is by the justice of the charge. Jerome also reminds us that "A false rumour is soon stifled, and a man's later life passes judgement on his past".[132] But if you are determined to act against him canonically, let his teaching or his writing be put before us, let him be questioned and allowed to give free reply, so that if he is proved wrong or confesses his error he can be totally silenced. This will at least be in accordance with the words of holy Nicodemus, when he wished to set free the Lord himself: "Does our law permit us to pass judgement on a man unless we have first given him a hearing and learned the facts?"'[133] At once my rivals broke in with an outcry: 'Wise advice that is, to bid us compete with the ready tongue of a man whose arguments and sophistries could triumph over the whole world!' But it was surely far harder to compete with Christ, and yet Nicodemus asked for him to be given a hearing, as sanctioned by the law.[134]

41. However, when the bishop could not persuade them to agree to his proposal, he tried to curb their hostility by other means, saying that the few people present were insufficient for discussing a matter of such importance, and this case needed more consideration. His further advice was that my abbot, who was present, should take me back to my abbey, the monastery of St-Denis, and there a larger number of more

percuciunt'—MSS *PMO* and *L* but 'fulmina' in MS *B*. Ziolkowski, p. 107, draws attention to a story about Abelard told by Gerald of Wales in 1191 (Gerald had first visited Paris as a young man in 1165 or shortly before) in which the same verse from Horace appears: 'In his own day, and with Philip I, King of the French, listening to him, Peter Abelard is said to have made a memorable reply to a certain Jew, who was urging the same sort of objection to the Christian religion (*viz., that God does not stop lightning from damaging churches*). "It cannot be denied", said he, "that as it rushes down from on high, lightning often strikes the loftier things on earth and those sublime in nature like itself. It is contrived in all malice by the devils in hell . . . It sometimes strikes human beings, and it can do great harm to the faithful and the objects of their cult. No one ever saw lightning hit a public lavatory, or even heard of such a thing: by the same token it never falls on any of your Jewish synagogues"'; *Itinerarium Kambriae*, i. 12 (ed. Dimock, p. 95; *The Journey through Wales*, trans. Thorpe, p. 153).

[132] Jerome, *Epistola* LIV *ad Furiam de uiduitate seruanda*, 13 (ed. Hilberg, *CSEL* liv. 480; *PL* xxii. 556).

[133] John 7: 51. Documentation of the procedure to be followed when an accusation is levelled against a cleric is brought together by Ivo, Geoffrey's predecessor as bishop of Chartres, in *Decretum*, vi, c. 312–48 (working edn. by M. Brett online: ⟨http://project.knowledgeforge.net/ivo/index.html⟩ (accessed 3 June 2011); *PL* clxi. 509A–517A): the accused and the accusers, the witnesses, and the judges should be present; there should be thorough inquiry and questioning; the case should be heard within the ecclesiastical province and within a church (Soissons was within the province of Reims).

[134] Cf. John 3: 1–10 and n. 126 above.

diligentiori examine quid[o] super hoc faciendum esset[p] statueretur. Assensit[q] [r]legatus huic[r] [s]nouissimo consilio,[s] et ceteri omnes. Inde mox legatus assurrexit, ut missam celebraret antequam concilium[t] intraret, et mihi per episcopum illum [u]licentiam constitutam[u] mandauit,[v] reuertendi scilicet ad monasterium nostrum, ibi[w] expectaturo quod [x]condictum fuerat.[x]

42. Tunc emuli mei, nichil se egisse cogitantes si extra diocesim suam hoc negotium ageretur, [a]ubi uidelicet uim[a] minime[b] exercere ualerent,[c] qui scilicet[d] de iusticia minus confidebant, archiepiscopo persuaserunt hoc sibi ualde ignominiosum esse si ad aliam audientiam causa hec transferretur, et periculosum[e] fieri si[f] sic euaderem. Et statim ad legatum concurrentes, eius[g] immutauerunt sententiam, et ad hoc inuitum pertraxerunt, ut librum[h] sine ulla inquisitione dampnaret atque in conspectu omnium statim combureret, et me in alieno[i] monasterio perhenni clausura cohiberet. Dicebant enim ad dampnationem[j] libelli satis hoc esse debere quod nec romani pontificis[k] nec ecclesie auctoritate eum commendatum legere[l] publice presumpseram,[m] atque ad transcribendum[n] iam pluribus eum ipse prestitissem; et hoc perutile futurum fidei christiane si exemplo mei multorum similis[o] presumptio preueniretur.[p] [135] Quia[q] autem legatus ille minus quam necesse[r] esset[s] litteratus fuerat, plurimum archiepiscopi consilio nitebatur,[t] sicut et[u] archiepiscopus illorum. Quod cum Carnotensis [v]presensisset episcopus,[v] statim machinamenta hec[w] ad me retulit, et me uehementer hortatus[x] est ut hoc[y] tanto leuius tolerarem quanto uiolentius [z]eos[z] agere omnibus patebat; atque hanc tam manifeste inuidie uiolentiam eis plurimum obfuturam,[a] et mihi profuturam non dubitarem; nec de clausura monasterii ullatenus[b] perturbarer, sciens profecto legatum ipsum,[c] qui coactus hoc[d] faciebat, post paucos dies cum hinc recesserit me penitus liberaturum.[e] Et sic me, ut potuit, flentem flens et ipse consolatus est.

[o] quid ?E   [p] *add. Ecorr. in vacant space*   [q] Assensus D   [r–r] huic legatus E   [s–s] consilio nouissimo BRSDY   [t] consilium CEFDY   [u–u] licentia constituta Y   [v] mandiuit A; mandaret ?E, F   [w] sibi Y *before exp. of* s   [x–x] predictum fuerat C; cum dictum fuerat S; dictum fuerit D; condictum fuerit Y

42 [a–a] ubi uidelicet inde TCE; ubi (ubi *add. above* inde *by another hand*) uidelicet inde A; ubi (uidelicet *exp.*) uim (uim *superscr.*) inde F; ubi uidelicet ui BRDY; ubi uidelicet unde S; ubi uidelicet iudicium *Amb;* ou . . . leur force *J*   [b] maxime minime T *before corr.;* minime *corr. in E to clarify abbrev.*   [c] *om.* Y; possent Y^1 [d] solum RDY   [e] periculosam E; periculum S   [f] ut Y   [g] *om.* Y   [h] liber D   [i] alio BRSDY (*add.* Y *in vacant space*)   [j] condempnationem Y   [k] pontifices Y *before corr. by* Y^1 [l] *add.* T *over eras.*   [m] presumpserem D   [n] A *after superscr. corr. by another hand*   [o] similis T *over eras.; eras.*

learned men should be assembled to go into the case thoroughly and decide what was to be done. The legate agreed with this last suggestion, and so did everyone else. Soon after, the legate rose to celebrate Mass before going into the Council. Through Bishop Geoffrey he sent me the permission agreed on: I was to return to my monastery and await a decision.

42. Then my rivals, thinking that they had achieved nothing if this matter were taken outside their diocese, where they would have no influence—it was plain that they had little confidence in the justice of their cause—convinced the archbishop that it would be shameful for him if the case were transferred and heard elsewhere, and it would be dangerous if I were allowed to escape as a result. They hurried to the legate, made him reverse his decision and pressed him unwillingly to condemn the book without any inquiry, burn it immediately in the sight of all and condemn me to perpetual confinement in a different monastery. They said that the fact that I had dared to read the treatise in public and must have allowed many people to make copies without the approval of the authority of the Pope or the Church should be quite enough to condemn it, and that the Christian faith would greatly benefit if an example were made of me and if similar presumption in many others were forestalled.[135] As the legate was less learned than he should have been, he relied mostly on the advice of the archbishop, who in turn relied on theirs. When the bishop of Chartres saw what would happen he told me at once about their intrigues and strongly urged me not to take it too hard, as by now it was apparent to all that they were acting too harshly. He said I could be confident that such violence so clearly prompted by jealousy would discredit them and benefit me, and told me not to worry about being confined in a monastery as he knew that the papal legate was only acting under pressure, and would set me quite free within a few days of his leaving Soissons. So he gave me what comfort he could, both of us shedding tears.

also in marg.; simul *C, ?E, ?S, Y*; insimul *D* [p] pugniretur *D*; puniretur *Y* [q] Quoniam *BRSDY* [r] opus *DY* [s] est *E* [t] nitebatur *TAmb* utebatur *ACEFBRSDYAmb*[1]; il s'apuioit et tenoit moult *J* [u] *om. CEFBRSDY* [v–v] episcopus presensisset *BRSDY* [w] hoc *T* [x] honoratus *D* [y] hic *E* [z–z] agere eos *T* [a] offuturam *A*; effuturam *CE*; obfuram *B before superscr. corr.* [b] nullatenus *CEBRSDY* [c] *om. D* [d] hec *A* [e] libaturum *T*

[135] Papal approval to promulgate a work of theology was not an established requirement. See Flahiff, 'Censorship of books'; Classen, *Burgundio von Pisa*, p. 61 and note.

43. [a]DE COMBVSTIONE IPSIVS LIBRI[a]

Vocatus[b] itaque statim ad[c] concilium[d] adfui,[e] et sine ullo discussionis examine meipsum compulerunt propria manu librum memoratum meum in ignem proicere; et sic combustus est.[136] Vt tamen non[f] nichil dicere uiderentur, quidam de aduersariis meis[g] id submurmurauit quod in libro scriptum deprehenderat[h] solum [i]patrem Deum[i] omnipotentem esse.[137] Quod cum legatus subintellexisset, ualde[j] admirans ei respondit hoc nec de puerulo[k] aliquo credi debere quod adeo erraret, cum communis,[l] inquid, fides[m] et teneat et profiteatur[n] tres[o] omnipotentes esse. Quo audito Terricus[p] quidam, [q]scolaris magister,[q] irridendo subintulit illud[r] Athanasii:[s] 'Et tamen non tres[t] omnipotentes, sed unus omnipotens.'[138] Quem cum episcopus suus increpare[u] cepisset et reprimere quasi reum, qui in maiestatem loqueretur, audacter[v] ille restitit et, quasi [w]Danielis uerba[w] commemorans, ait: '"[x]Sic fatui,[x] filii Israel, non[y] iudicantes neque quod uerum est cognoscentes,[z] condempnastis[a] filium[b] Israel? Reuertimini ad iudicium", et de ipso iudice[c] iudicate qui talem iudicem quasi[d] ad instructionem fidei et[e] correctionem[f] erroris[g] instituistis; qui cum[h] iudicare deberet, ore se proprio condemnauit,

43 [a–a] *rubr. TAS;* Le viij[e] chapitre, comme son livre fu ars *table in H of the (missing) contents of Dijon MS 525* [b] Vocatus *decorated initial in TB on new line; large initial ARY on new line; space for initial unfilled in D on new line* [c] in *F* [d] consilium *CD* [e] affui *ARS* [f] cum *Amb* [g] *om. BRSDY* [h] deprenderat *T;* deprehenderit *E;* deprehendit *F;* dependerat *Y* [i–i] deum patrem *YAmb* [j] *om. Y* [k] pūlo *C;* paruulo *E add. in marg. after corr. of* puerolo, *DYAmb*[1] [l] quid *CE;* communis *superscr. Ecorr.* [m] *om. DY* [n] scola *add. Y* [o] *add. E in vacant space* [p] Terricus *repeated in marg. of T by another hand;* territus *CEF;* Thierricus *D* [q–q] scholarum magister *EAmb;* magister scolaris *Y;* ung des disciplez du maistre *J;* l'un des escoliers d'Abellar *Claude Fauchet, Vie de Pierre Abellard (see the Introduction, p. c), p. 185* [r] *om. BD* [s] atthanasii *S* [t] *add. Ecorr.* [u] increniare *D* [v] audatus *D* [w–w] uerba danielis *BRSDY* [x–x] fatui *T;* sunt fatui *superscr. E after exp. of* se statui [y] neque quod *E;* recte *add. BRSDY* [z] agnoscentes *C;* cognoscentis *F* [a] condempnasti *T;* condempnatis *CE;* condempnauistis *Y* [b] filiam *Vulg.* [c] iuste *CEFD* [d] quem *Y* [e] ad *D* [f] correpcionem *AS;* correptionem *CEF;* correctionis *Y* [g] errorum *CEAmb*[1]*; om. BY* [h] eum *RDY*

---

[136] Cf. Otto of Freising, who writes that Abelard was given no opportunity to reply for fear of his abilities in debate; the bishops made him put his book into the fire with his own hand; *Gesta Friderici*, i. 49 (ed. Waitz and von Simson, p. 69).

[137] Cf. *TSum*, ii. 105–6, where Abelard writes that God the Father is omnipotent; nevertheless, he accepted that the three divine persons, who share the same essence, are together omnipotent. A problem was whether sharing the same properties meant that the divine persons are not distinct (*TSum*, iii. 38–40; cf. *TChr*, iv. 47–8, 52, 54). Later (*c.*1125), in re-presenting his arguments in *TChr*, iii. 166, 171, Abelard adds a harangue against the 'insania' of some masters in this matter (iii. 167–70). In a *Confession of faith* sent to Heloise,

43. THE BURNING OF HIS BOOK

I was then summoned and came at once before the Council. Without any questioning or discussion they compelled me to throw my book into the fire with my own hand, and thus it was burnt.[136] But so that they could appear to have something to say, one of my enemies muttered that he understood it was written in the book that only God the Father was Almighty.[137] Overhearing this, the legate replied in great surprise that one would scarcely believe a small child could make such a mistake, seeing that the faith we have in common holds and professes that there are three Almighties. Thereupon the head of a school, Thierry by name, laughed and quoted the words of Athanasius: 'And yet there are not three Almighties, but one Almighty.'[138] His bishop spoke sharply to him and rebuked him as being guilty of contempt, but he boldly stood his ground and calling to mind words of Daniel said: ' "Are you such fools, you sons of Israel, thus to condemn a son of Israel, without judging and finding out the truth? Reopen the trial" and judge the judge himself. You appointed this judge to teach the faith and to correct error; but he who should give judgement has condemned himself out of his own mouth. Today God in his mercy

perhaps *c.*1140 and based on the (ps.-)Athanasian Creed (late 4th/first half of the 5th c.), he wrote that the Son is equal to the Father in power (ed. Burnett, '*Confessio fidei ad Heloisam*—Abelard's last letter to Heloise?', p. 152; *PL* clxxviii. 376C).

[138] Ps.-Athanasius, *Symbolum 'Quicumque'*, 14 (ed. Mountain, p. 566). Cf. *Expositio Symboli Athanasii* (*PL* clxxviii. 630BC). 'Terricus quidam': according to the short biography of Abelard mentioned above in n. 5, Abelard was taught mathematics privately by one 'magister Tirricus'. The writer claims that Abelard found the subject difficult, and indeed Abelard himself admitted as much in his *Dialectica* (ed. de Rijk, p. 59 *ll.* 4–6). But the writer then stretches belief by asserting that Abelard, whom he has called an Englishman, subsequently wrote many easily found works on geometry and arithmetic (ed. Hödl, , *Die Geschichte der scholastischen Literatur*, p. 78; Mews, 'In search of a name', pp. 172–3. Probably there is confusion here with the well-known contemporary English scientist and mathematician, Adelard of Bath (1080–1152). Häring, 'Chartres and Paris revisited', pp. 279–94, clarified the life and works of one Theodoricus (Theodericus, Terricus, Therricus) Brito, a Breton who is better known as Thierry of Chartres and who wrote a commentary on Cicero's *De inventione* and on the *Ad Herennium*, a commentary and *lectiones* on Boethius' *De trinitate*, and a tract on the opening chapters of Genesis. For his writings see esp. the introduction and edn. by Häring of Thierry of Chartres, *Commentaries on Boethius*. Häring, 'Chartres and Paris revisited', p. 286, suggested that the 'Terricus quidam' of whom Abelard writes here may well be this Thierry, but was he also Abelard's tutor in mathematics? The joke found in the short biography of Abelard (see n. 5 above) relies on Tirricus' reference to a form of the cognomen—*Baiolardus*—which is found in MSS of Abelard's works which circulated in Germany and Austria; see Mews, 'In search of a name', pp. 177–9. This need not imply that 'Terricus quidam', if he was also Abelard's tutor in mathematics, was himself German and not the Breton Thierry of Chartres, for the biographer is clear that the name is *abelardus* but, following the joke, many started to say *baiolardus*.

diuina hodie[i] misericordia innocentem[j] patenter, sicut olim Susannam a falsis accusatoribus, liberante.'[139]

44. Tunc[a] archiepiscopus assurgens, uerbis prout oportebat[b] commutatis, sententiam legati confirmauit, dicens: 'Reuera, [c]domine, inquit[c] "omnipotens Pater, omnipotens Filius, omnipotens Spiritus sanctus",[140] et qui ab[d] hoc dissentit aperte deuius est nec[e] est[f] audiendus. Et modo, si placet, bonum est ut frater ille fidem suam coram omnibus exponat, ut ipsa, prout oportet,[g] uel approbetur uel improbetur atque corrigatur.' Cum autem ego[h] ad profitendam et exponendam fidem[i] meam assurgerem, ut quod sentiebam[j] uerbis propriis exprimerem,[k] aduersarii dixerunt non aliud mihi necessarium[l] esse nisi[m] ut symbolum Athanasii[n] recitarem, [o]quod quisuis[p] puer eque facere posset.[o] [141] Ac,[q] ne ex ignorantia pretenderem excusationem, quasi qui[r] uerba illa in usu non haberem, scripturam ad legendum afferri fecerunt. [s]Legi inter suspiria,[s] singultus et lacrimas, prout potui.[t] Inde, quasi reus et conuictus,[u] abbati sancti Medardi qui aderat traditus, ad claustrum eius tanquam ad carcerem trahor; [v]statimque concilium soluitur.[v]

45. Abbas autem et monachi illius monasterii, me sibi[a] remansurum [b]ulterius arbitrantes,[b] [c]summa exultatione[c] susceperunt, et cum omni diligentia tractantes consolari frustra nitebantur.[142] Deus, qui iudicas equitatem,[143] quanto tunc animi[d] felle, quanta mentis amaritudine te ipsum insanus[e] arguebam, [f]te furibundus accusabam,[f] sepius repetens illam beati[g] Anthonii[h] conquestionem: 'Ihesu[i] bone, ubi eras?'[j] [144]

[i] hominem *E* [j] et nocentem *C;* innocencie *D*

44 [a] Tum *ARD;* Tamen *Y* [b] apparebat *C* [c–c] inquit domine *Y* [d] ad *A;* ab *superscr. B* [e] non *A* [f] *om. Y* [g] est *E* [h] esse *C* [i] uitam *Y;* fidem *Y*[1] *in marg.* [j] *add. Ecorr. in marg.* [k] exponerem *F* [l] necessum *EAmb*[1] [m] nec *C* [n] atthanasii *BSD;* a(t *exp.*)thanasii *Y* [o–o] *between round brackets in F* [p] quiuis *AS;* quamuis *C;* quis uis *B;* quis *Y after exp. of* uis [q] At *RY* [r] ad *B* [s–s] Legi (*superscr.*) in ter suspriora *E* [t] Et *add. D* [u] quasi *BRSDY* [v–v] statim concilium soluitur *BRSD;* statim (que finitur *Y*[1]) concilium *Y*

45 [a] s(*exp.*)ibi *Y* [b–b] arbitrantes *CEF;* arbitrantes ulterius *BRSDY* [c–c] summa exultione *T before corr. by T*[4]*;* summa cum (*add. Y over eras. of* ?summa) exultatione *Y* [d] *om. D* [e] infamis *Amb* [f–f] te furibundus arguebam *T before corr.; om. CEF* [g] animi *add. D* [h] Antonii *F* [i] Iesu *F* [j] erat *D*

[139] Dan. 13: 48–9; see n. 126 above.

[140] Ps.-Athanasius, *Symbolum 'Quicumque'*, 13 (ed. Mountain, p. 566); also cited in *TSum*, iii. 38 and *TChr*, iv. 47.

[141] Abelard later wrote an *Exposition* of the Pseudo-Athanasian Creed printed in *PL*

clearly frees an innocent man just as he once delivered Susanna from her false accusers!'[139]

44. Then the archbishop rose to his feet and confirmed the view of the legate, changing the wording as was needed. 'Truly, my lord,' he said, 'the Father is Almighty, the Son is Almighty and the Holy Spirit is Almighty,[140] and whoever does not share this belief is clearly in error and should not be heard. And now, if it please you, it would be proper for our brother to profess his faith before us all, so that it may be duly approved or disapproved and corrected.' I then stood up to make a full profession of my faith and to explain what I thought in my own words, but my enemies declared that it was not necessary for me to do more than recite the Athanasian Creed—as any boy could do.[141] They even had the text put before me to read in case I should plead ignorance, as though I were not familiar with the words. I read it out as best I could through my tears, choked with sobs. Then I was handed over as if guilty and condemned to the abbot of St-Médard, who was present, and taken off to his cloister as if to prison. The Council then immediately dispersed.

45. The abbot and monks of St-Médard welcomed me most warmly and treated me with every consideration, thinking that I should remain with them in future. They tried hard to comfort me, but in vain.[142] O God, who judges justly,[143] with what bitterness of spirit and anguish of mind did I reproach you in my madness and accuse you in my fury, constantly repeating the lament of St Antony—'Good Jesus, where were you?'[144] All the grief and indignation, the

clxxviii. 629–32. See Häring, 'Commentaries on the Pseudo-Athanasian Creed', p. 238; *Checklist* no. 289.

[142] Godfrey 'Stag-neck' ('Gaufridus collum cervi') was abbot of St-Médard from 1121 to 1131, when he became bishop of Châlons-sur-Marne. While Abelard was at St-Médard, the prior Goswin, who had earlier attended Abelard's lectures on the Mont Sainte-Geneviève (see n. 28 above) and who was to become abbot of Anchin near Douai (1131–66), thought that Abelard was now like a wild rhinoceros. Goswin sought to mollify him by praising his deep learning, his fiery, versatile eloquence, and his many successes in disputation ('Proponebat ei, pro mulcendis eius auribus et animo deflectendo, profunditatem scientiae . . . torrentem eloquentiae ad quicquid uellet abundantem, numerositatem uictoriarum quas conflictu literario conquisisset'). He advised Abelard to become a model of integrity (*honestus*). Abelard remarked that people who talk about *honestas* often do not know what it is, to which Goswin said that Abelard would soon find out what it is from the brethren if he ever said or did anything that was not *honestum*; *Vita prima Goswini*, i. 18, in *Vita Gosvini*, ed. Gibbons; also in *Recueil des historiens*, xiv, ed. Delisle, p. 445.

[143] Cf. Ps. 95 (96): 13, Acts 17: 31, etc.

[144] Athanasius, *Vita beati Antonii interprete Evagrio* (*PL* lxxiii. 132D).

Quanto autem[k] dolore estuarem, quanta erubescentia[l] confunderer, quanta desperatione perturbarer, sentire[m] tunc potui proferre non possum.[n] Conferebam cum his que in corpore passus [o]olim fueram quanta nunc sustinerem,[o] et omnium hominum me estimabam miserrimum. Paruam illam ducebam[p] proditionem[q] in comparatione huius iniurie, et longe amplius fame quam corporis detrimentum plangebam, cum ad illam[r] ex aliqua[s] culpa deuenerim, ad hanc me tam patentem uiolentiam sincera intentio[t] amorque fidei nostre induxissent, que me ad scribendum compulerant.

46. Cum autem hoc[a] tam crudeliter et inconsiderate factum omnes ad quos fama delatum[b] est uehementer arguerent,[c] singuli qui interfuerant[d] a se culpam repellentes in alios transfundebant, adeo ut ipsi quoque emuli nostri id[e] consilio suo factum esse denegarent,[f] et legatus[g] coram omnibus inuidiam Francorum super hoc maxime detestaretur. Qui statim penitentia ductus,[h] post aliquos dies, cum ad tempus coactus satisfecisset illorum inuidie, me[i] de alieno eductum[j] monasterio ad proprium remisit, ubi fere quotquot erant olim iam, ut supra memini, infestos habebam, cum eorum uite turpitudo et impudens conuersatio me[k] suspectum penitus haberet,[l] quem[m] arguentem grauiter sustineret.[n]

47. Paucis[a] autem elapsis mensibus, occasionem eis fortuna[b] obtulit[c] qua me perdere molirentur. Fortuitu[d] namque mihi[e] quadam die legenti occurrit quedam Bede sententia [f]qua in[f] *Expositione*[g] *Actuum Apostolorum* asserit Dyonisium[h] Ariopagitam[i] Corinthiorum[j] potiusquam[k] Atheniensium[l] fuisse episcopum.[145] Quod ualde eis[m]

[k] *Ecorr. in vacant space* [l] e(*add.* Y^{1})rubescentia *Y* [m] assentire *C;* subsentire *Ecorr. in vacant space* [n] possem *D* [o] fuerem. quanta nunc fuerem. quanta sustinerem nunc *S* [p] dicebam *DY* [q] producionem *S* [r] illa *CF* [s] antiqua *?E, Amb*[1] [t] interior *Y before corr.*

46 [a] hec *RS* [b] delata *Y* [c] argueretur *C* [d] Interfuerent *S* [e] de *add. DY* [f] negarent *F* [g] Comme il fu ramené a son abbaie, et comme les moines furent esmeuz contre lui; a tel seing (*the sign is a double arrow head*). Et legatus *the table in H of the* (*missing*) *contents of Dijon MS 525* [h] est *add. Y* [i] me *Y after corr.* [j] inductum *A before corr.* [k] *om. C* [l] haberent *CEFAmb* [m] Quod *Amb*[1] [n] sustinerent *CEFAmb*

47 [a] *large initial add. Y in inner marg.* [b] fortuitu *S* [c] attulit *C* [d] fortitudo *S* [e] in *Y* [f-f] quam *BR;* quam in *S* qua *D* [g] cap. 17 *superscr. add. F* [h] Dionysium *F* [i] arriopagitam *CR;* areopagitam *EF* [j] corinphiorum *A before corr.* [k] potius quam *F* [l] atteniensium *BRSY;* archeniense *D* [m] eius *C*

blushes for shame, the agony of despair I suffered then, I cannot put into words. I compared my present plight with my physical suffering in the past, and judged myself the unhappiest of men. My former betrayal seemed small in comparison with the wrongs I now had to endure, and I wept much more for the injury done to my reputation than for the damage to my body, for that I had brought upon myself through my own fault, but this open violence had come upon me only because of the purity of my intentions and the love of our faith which had compelled me to write.

46. But as the news spread, and everyone who heard it began to condemn outright this wanton act of cruelty, the persons who had been present tried to shift the blame on to others; so much so that even my rivals denied it had been done on their advice, and the legate publicly denounced the jealousy of the French in this affair. He soon regretted his conduct and, some days later, feeling that he had satisfied their jealousy at a time when he had been under constraint, he had me brought out of St-Médard and sent back to my own monastery, where, as I recalled above, nearly all the monks who were there before were now my enemies; for their disgraceful way of life and scandalous conduct made them deeply suspicious of a man whose criticisms they could ill endure.

47. A few months later chance gave them the opportunity to work for my downfall. It happened that one day in my reading I came across a statement of Bede, in his *Commentary on the Acts of the Apostles*, which asserted that Denis the Areopagite was bishop of Corinth, not of Athens.[145] This seemed in direct contradiction to their boast that

[145] Bede, *Expositio Actuum Apostolorum et Retractatio*, xvii. 34 (ed. Laistner, pp. 73–4; *PL* xcii. 981AB). Cf. Acts 17: 34. 'One day in my reading' ('quadam die legenti'): it is likely that Abelard had now started to bring together extracts taken from Christian sources which seem to present disagreements and to require interpretation; the outcome, his *Yes and No* (*Sic et Non*), grew in stages to become a large collection arranged in 158 chapters with a prologue in which rules for enquiring into discordant statements are presented; in this he followed the example of Ivo, bishop of Chartres (d. 1115), in his *Decretum*. It is likely that the library of St-Denis possessed an important collection of manuscript books, but detailed knowledge of these is not available before the 13th c.; see Nebbiai-Dalla Guarda, *La Bibliothèque de l'abbaye de Saint-Denis*, pp. 71–5. Denis the Areopagite is mentioned in Acts 17: 34, which state that St Paul converted him to the Christian faith at Athens. Over the centuries it came to be believed (though not by Bede, d. 735) that Denis the Areopagite was the first bishop of Athens and that he brought the Christian faith to Gaul and was martyred in Paris, the place of the martyrdom being now called Montmartre and the place of his burial being the abbey that was later founded in his name. See Luscombe, 'Denis the Pseudo-Areopagite in the Middle Ages'; Jeauneau, 'Pierre Abélard à Saint-Denis'.

contrarium uidebatur, qui suum Dyonisium[n] esse illum Ariopagitam[o] iactitant,[p] [q]quem ipsum[q] Atheniensem[r] episcopum gesta eius fuisse profitentur. Quod cum reperissem,[s] quibusdam circumstancium[t] fratrum quasi iocando[u] monstraui testimonium scilicet illud[v] Bede quod nobis obiciebatur.[w] Illi uero, ualde[x] indignati, dixerunt[y] Bedam mendacissimum[z] scriptorem, et se Huldoinum[a] abbatem suum ueriorem habere testem, qui pro hoc inuestigando[b] Greciam[c] diu perlustrauit[d] et rei ueritate[e] agnita, in[f] gestis illius que[g] conscripsit,[h] hanc penitus[i] dubitationem remouit.[146] Vnde cum unus eorum me[j] importuna[k] interrogatione pulsaret quid[l] mihi super hac controuersia, Bede [m]uidelicet atque[m] Huldoini,[n] uideretur, respondi [o]Bede auctoritatem,[o] cuius scripta[p] uniuerse Latinorum frequentant[q] ecclesie,[147] grauiorem[r] mihi uideri.[148]

48. [a]DE PERSECVTIONE ABBATIS SVI ET FRATRVM IN EVM[a]

Ex[b] quo illi uehementer accensi [c]clamare ceperunt[c] nunc me patenter ostendisse quod semper monasterium [d]illud nostrum[d] infestauerim, et quod nunc maxime[e] toti regno [f]derogauerim, ei[f] uidelicet honorem illum auferens quo singulariter gloriaretur,[g] cum eorum patronum Ariopagitam[h] fuisse denegarem. Ego autem respondi nec me hoc[i] denegasse[149] nec[j] multum curandum esse utrum ipse Ariopagita[k] an aliunde[l] fuerit, dummodo[m] [n]tantam[o] apud Deum[n] [p]adeptus sit[p] coronam. [q]Illi uero ad abbatem statim concurrentes[r] quod mihi

[n] Dionysium *F* [o] ariopagitam *CR;* arreopagitam *E;* Areopagitam *F* [p] iactitatur *C* [q–q] quoniam *EF;* quem *Y after exp. of* ipsum [r] attheniensem *BRS;* archeniensem *D;* atheniensium *Y* [s] peperissem *D* [t] circonstantium *T;* circunstantium *E* [u] iocundo *D* [v] id *C* [w] obicieatur *D* [x] *om. E* [y] *?A* [z] mendacicissum *C;* mandatissimum *D* [a] holdouinum *E;* Hilduinum *F;* Huldonium *Amb; al.* Hilduinum *et recte Amb*[1] [b] inuestigendo *D* [c] graciam *C;* gretiam *E* [d] Perlustrauerit *A* [e] ueritatem *C;* ueritatis *S* [f] et *Y* [g] qui *D* [h] scripsit *ACEF* [i] ueraciter *T over eras.;* du tout *J* [j] *om. TY* [k] impertunia *B* [l] qui *D* [m–m] atque uidelicet *D* [n] Hilduini *F;* Huldonij *Amb* [o–o] Redde (*exp. Y*[1]) auctoritatem eius (eius *Y*[1]) *Y;* Bede authoritatem *F* [p] scriptura *A;* scripturam *CEF;* l'escripture *J* [q] frequantant *D;* frequentarent *F* [r] gratiorem *TACEFAmb;* grauiorem *BRSDY;* plus aggreable *J. Cf. Jeauneau, 'Pierre Abélard à Saint-Denis', p. 164n; Synan and Jeauneau, 'Some remarks'; also Letter* 11 *to Abbot Adam and the monks of St Denis, ed. Smits, p. 249, ll. 10–11 and PL clxxviii. 341A:* grauioribus . . . auctoritatibus

48 [a–a] *rubr. T in marg., S; vacant space in B;* Le ix[e] chapitre, comme il fu accusé envers son abbé *table in H of the (missing) contents of Dijon MS 525* [b] Ex *BRD on a new line; large decorated initial BR; unfilled space for initial in D* [c–c] ceperunt clamare *CEF* [d–d] nostrum *C;* nostrum illud *Y* [e] *om. D* [f–f] ei derogauerim ei *CEF* [g] *om. C* [h] Areopagitam *F* [i] *om. S* [j] me *add. E;* nec *Y*[1] [k] arriopagita *E;* Areopagita *F* [l] alius *BRSDY;* autres *J* [m] dum modo *Y* [n–n] apud deum tantam *Y* [o] tantum *S* [p–p] adepta sit *C;* sit adeptus *Y* [q–q] *om. D* [r] conterrentes *?B* currentes *S*

their Denis is the Areopagite whose history shows him to have been bishop of Athens. I showed my discovery, by way of a joke, to some of the brothers who were standing by, as evidence from Bede which was against us. They were very much annoyed and said that Bede was a complete liar and that they had a more truthful witness in their own abbot Hilduin, who had spent a long time travelling in Greece to investigate the matter; he had found out the truth and removed all shadow of doubt in the history of the saint which he had compiled himself.[146] Then one of them abruptly demanded my opinion on the discrepancy between Bede and Hilduin. I replied that the authority of Bede, to whose writings all the Latin churches have recourse,[147] carried more weight with me.[148]

48. HIS PERSECUTION BY THE ABBOT AND THE BROTHERS

In their fury at this answer they began to cry that I had now openly revealed myself as an enemy of the monastery, and had moreover disparaged the whole kingdom in seeking to destroy the honour that was its special pride by denying that their patron was the Areopagite. I said that I had not denied it,[149] nor did it much matter whether he was the Areopagite or came from somewhere else, seeing that he had won so bright a crown in the sight of God. However, they hurried straight to the abbot and told him what they accused me of. He was

[146] Hilduin, *Vita et passio S. Dionysii* ('*Post beatam et salutiferam*', *PL* cvi. 23–50). Hilduin had been abbot of St-Denis from 814 to 840. He knew and rejected Bede's opinion about the Areopagite; cf. Hilduin's *Rescriptum* ('*Exultauit cor meum*') to the Emperor Louis, 8–9 (ed. Dümmler, pp. 331–2; *PL* cvi. 17D–18D). The *Rescriptum* usually accompanied Hilduin's *Vita* in MS copies (Jeauneau, 'Pierre Abélard à Saint-Denis', pp. 164–5).

[147] 'cuius scripta . . . frequentant ecclesie': cf. *Letter* 11 to Abbot Adam and the monks of St-Denis (ed. Smits, p. 252, *ll.* 86–7; *PL* clxxviii. 343A: 'eius expositiones Latinorum maxime frequentet ecclesia'; trans. Ziolkowski, p. 142: 'the Latin church has especially frequent recourse to his commentaries').

[148] Cf. *Letter* 11, where Abelard revokes this support for Bede by turning to the 'weightier authority' ('grauior auctoritas') of Eusebius and Jerome (ed. Smits, p. 249, *ll.* 8–11, p. 252, *ll.* 74–6; *PL* clxxviii. 341A, 342D; trans. Ziolkowski, pp. 138, 142). Their testimony had been presented by Hilduin, *Rescriptum*, 8–9 (ed. Dümmler, pp. 331–2; *PL* cvi. 17D–18D), and Abelard cited it in *Letter* 11. For a similar expression ('grauissima auctoritas') cf. *TSum*, iii. 37; *TChr*, iv. 45. For a detailed demonstration of Abelard's principles for weighing or weighting authorities when they provide discrepant testimony see his prologue to *SN* (ed. Boyer and McKeon, pp. 89–111).

[149] In *Letter* 11 (ed. Smits, pp. 249–55; *PL* clxxviii. 341–4; trans. Ziolkowski, pp. 138–46) Abelard tries to meet some of the objections made by the monks of St-Denis with a suggestion that there may have been two bishops of Corinth, both called Denis, the first of whom was Denis the Areopagite who *may* be the patron of the abbey of St-Denis. (On a mistaken reference in *Letter* 11 to Aratus (a Greek poet, *c.*390–327 BC) instead of to Arator, a 6th-c. Christian Latin poet and commentator on Acts of the Apostles, see Silvestre, 'Aratus pour Arator').

imposuerant[s] nuntiauerunt;[qt] qui libenter hoc audiuit, gaudens se occasionem[u] aliquam adipisci qua me opprimeret, utpote qui quanto ceteris turpius uiuebat, magis me uerebatur. Tunc consilio suo congregato et fratribus conuocatis,[v] grauiter mihi comminatus est, et se ad regem cum festinatione missurum dixit, ut de me uindictam sumeret, tanquam regni sui gloriam et coronam[w] ei auferente.[x] [150] Et me interim[y] bene obseruari[z] precepit donec me regi traderet.[a] Ego autem ad regularem disciplinam,[151] si quid deliquissem, frustra me offerebam.

49. Tunc[a] ego[b] nequitiam eorum uehementer exhorrens, utpote qui iam[c] diu tam aduersam habuissem fortunam, penitus desperatus, quasi aduersum me uniuersus coniurasset mundus, [d]quorumdam consensu[d] fratrum mei miserantium[e] et quorumdam discipulorum nostrorum suffragio,[f] nocte latenter[g] aufugi atque ad terram comitis [h]Theobaldi proximam,[h] ubi antea [i]in cella[i] moratus fueram, abscessi.[j] [152] Ipse quippe et mihi[k] aliquantulum notus[l] erat, et oppressionibus meis quas audierat admodum[m] compaciebatur.[153] Ibi autem in castro Pruuigni[n] morari cepi,[o] in cella uidelicet quadam Trecensium[p] monachorum, quorum prior antea mihi familiaris extiterat[q] et [r]ualde me dilexerat;[r] qui[s] ualde in aduentu meo[t] gauisus, cum omni diligentia me procurabat.[u] [154]

50. Accidit autem quadam die ut ad ipsum castrum abbas noster ad predictum comitem pro quibusdam suis negotiis ueniret;[a] quo

[s] impositurì erant *FAmb*[1]   [t] nominauerunt *RY*   [u] actionem *C*   [v] conuocatis *T and Muckle; an add. by T*[1] *is too faint to read although Monfrin found* congregatis; congregatis *ACEFBRDYAmb and Monfrin;* conuocatis *preferred by Orlandi, 'Minima Abaelardiana', p. 132;* quant il ot assemblé son conseil et li frere furent assemblé *J*   [w] coronem *D*   [x] auferentem *DF*   [y] iterum *E*   [z] obseruare *TCEF;* que je fusse bien gardez *J*   [a] traderent *CE*

49 [a] Tum *AR;* Tamen *E*   [b] Comme il s'en fui de nuit, puis fist sa pais. *Tunc ego+ table in H of the (missing) contents of Dijon MS 525*   [c] tam *B before corr.*   [d–d] *T after eras. at* consensu; quorum *D;* quorumdam *Y*   [e] miserencium *Y*   [f] suffragiis *CEF*   [g] latente *E*   [h–h] christiani *Y*   [i–i] *om. D*   [j] accessi *CEFY;* abcessi *RD;* ving *J*   [k] cum *E*   [l] motus *R*   [m] ad modi *D*   [n] Pruuini *FAmb*[1]*;* priuigni *B;* pruuini *D;* p'migni *Y;* Priuigni *Amb*   [o] cepit *T before corr. by another hand*   [p] trescensum *Y but marked with a cross by Ycorr.*   [q] fuerat *S*   [r–r] ualde dilexerat *TABRSDY;* m'avoit mout amé *J*   [s] cui *C*   [t] nostro *C (after corr.?)E, F*   [u] curabat *F*

50 [a] perveniret *B*

[150] On abbot Adam's efforts to make closer links with the French crown, which included the production of the *Historia regum Francorum*, ed. Waitz, pp. 395–406, see Grosse, 'L'Abbé Adam'.

only too ready to listen and delighted to seize an opportunity to silence me, for he had the greater reason to fear me as his own life was even more scandalous than that of the rest. He summoned his council, and the chapter of the brethren, and denounced me severely, saying that he would have recourse straightaway to the king for punishment on the charge of having designs on the glory of his kingdom and on the crown.[150] Meanwhile, he put me under close surveillance until I could be handed over to the king. I offered to submit myself to the sanctions of the *Rule*[151] if I had done wrong, but in vain.

49. I was so horrified by their wickedness and in such deep despair after having borne the blows of fortune so long, feeling that the whole world had conspired against me, that with the help of a few brothers who took pity on me and the support of some of my pupils I fled secretly in the night, and went away to the neighbouring territory of Count Theobald, where once before I had stayed in a monastic cell.[152] I was slightly acquainted with the Count personally, and he had heard of my afflictions and took pity on me.[153] There I began to live in the fortified town of Provins, in a house of monks from Troyes whose prior had long been my close friend and loved me dearly. He was overjoyed by my arrival and made every provision for me.[154]

50. But one day it happened that the abbot of St-Denis came to the town to see Count Theobald on some business of his own; on hearing

[151] 'regularem disciplinam': cf. Benedict, *Rule*, c. 3, 10 and 32, 5; 54, 5; 60, 2 and 5; 62, 3 and 4; 65, 19; 70, 6.

[152] Theobald II, count of Blois and Champagne 1125–52.

[153] According to the *Carmen ad Astralabium* (ed. Rubingh-Bosscher, *vv.* 921–2) Theobald was generous to people in religious life because what he gave away were ill-gotten gains: 'Multa Theobaldus largitur religiosis / sed, si plura rapit, sunt data rapta magis.' According to a story told by Peter the Chanter in his *Verbum abbreuiatum*, written *c.*1191–2 (i, c. 44 in the long version—*textus conflatus*—ed. Boutry, , p. 295; c. 46 in the short version, *PL* ccv. 146BC), Abelard refused gifts made by Theobald for his companions unless they clearly came from his revenues ('ex redditibus meris'). On the teaching of Peter the Chanter and other Parisian masters of the late 12th c. on the subject of rapine see Bisson, *Crisis of the Twelfth Century*, pp. 445–55 and Baldwin, *Masters, Princes and Merchants*, i. 235–40. Cf. also, for Theobald, Appendix A, 5.iii.

[154] The walled town of Provins was the key to the western defences of the county of Champagne against the royal domain; cf. Hubert, 'La Frontière occidentale du comté de Champagne'; Bur, *La Formation du comté de Champagne*, Appendix 3, pp. 516–17 and Map 8 on p. 234. Between 1093 and 1122 the prior of St-Ayoul in Provins was Raoul and the priory was a dependency of the abbey of St-Pierre in Troyes (Godefroy, 'L'Histoire du prieuré de Saint-Ayoul', in *Revue Mabillon*, xxviii (1938), 30). St Ayoul came to be commemorated at the abbey of the Paraclete (3 Sept.), *Paraclete Breviary*, IIIA (ed. Waddell, p. 11); cf. *Old French Paraclete Ordinary* (ed. Waddell, p. 334).

cognito, accessi ad comitem cum priore illo, rogans eum[b] quatinus[c] [d]pro me ipse[d] intercederet ad abbatem nostrum, ut me absolueret et licentiam daret uiuendi monastice ubicunque[e] mihi[f] competens locus occurreret. Ipse autem, et qui cum eo erant [g]in consilio, rem posuerunt[g] responsuri [h]comiti super hoc[h] in ipsa die antequam recederent. Inito[i] autem consilio, uisum est eis[j] me ad aliam abbatiam uelle transire, et hoc sue[k] dedecus inmensum[l] fore. Maxime namque glorie sibi imputabant[m] quod ad eos in conuersione[n] mea diuertissem, quasi [o]ceteris omnibus[o] abbatiis contemptis, et nunc [p]maximum sibi[p] imminere[q] dicebant opprobrium si, eis abiectis, ad alios transmearem. Vnde nullatenus uel me uel comitem super hoc[r] audierunt; immo [s]mihi statim[s] comminati sunt quod,[t] nisi festinus redirem, me excommunicarent, et priori illi ad quem refugeram[u] modis omnibus interdixerunt ne me deinceps retineret, [v]nisi excommunicationis particeps esse sustineret.[v] Quo audito, tam prior ipse[w] quam ego ualde anxiati fuimus.[x]

51. Abbas autem, in[a] hac obstinatione recedens, post paucos dies defunctus est.[155] Cui cum alius successisset, conueni eum cum episcopo Meldensi, ut mihi hoc quod a predecessore[b] eius petieram[c] indulgeret.[156] Cui rei cum nec ille primo acquiesceret,[d] postea interuenientibus [e]amicis quibusdam[e] nostris regem et consilium eius super hoc compellaui;[f] et sic quod uolebam[g] impetraui. Stephanus quippe [h]regis tunc[h] dapifer, uocato in partem[i] abbate[j] et familiaribus eius, quesiuit ab eis cur me inuitum[k] retinere uellent, ex quo [l]incurrere facile scandalum possent[l] et nullam utilitatem habere, cum nullatenus uita mea et ipsorum conuenire[m] possent.[157] Sciebam autem in hoc regii[n] consilii sententiam esse ut quo minus regularis abbatia illa esset, magis regi esset subiecta atque utilis, quantum uidelicet ad lucra temporalia; unde me facile regis et suorum

[b] illum *EBRSDY* [c] quatenus *F* [d–d] pro me ipso *F;* ipse pro me *S* [e] ubique *E* [f] *om. S* [g–g] hoc (*add. Y*¹) in consilio reposuerunt *Y* [h–h] super hoc comiti *D* [i] Inuito *?E* [j] *om. E* [k] sui *A before corr.; om. CEF* [l] immensum *F* [m] imputabat *CE* [n] conuersacione *D* [o–o] preteris omnibus *CE;* prae ceteris omnibus *F;* omnibus ceteris *D* [p–p] sibi maximum sibi *ditto. D* [q] in minere *E;* innerere *?Y* [r] *add. Y*¹ [s–s] mihi statim mihi *ditto. A;* statim *YF* [t] *om. BRSDY* [u] *illegible B;* refugerem *RS;* reffugerem *D* [v–v] nisi excommunicationis particeps esse uellet *CEF;* nisi excommunicationis particeps sustineret (sustineret *exp. by Ycorr.*) *RDY* [w] ille *DY* [x] sumus *F*

51 [a] ab *CEF* [b] *om. D* [c] pecierem *S* [d] ad quiesceret *A* [e–e] quibusdam amicis *YF* [f] appellaui *CEF;* je requis *J* [g] ualebam *C* [h–h] tunc regis *F* [i] patrem *B* [j] abbatem *C* [k] inuictum *D* [l–l] incurrere scandalum possent facile

this, together with the prior I approached the count and begged him to intercede for me with the abbot and obtain his pardon and permission to live the monastic life wherever a suitable place could be found. The abbot and those with him took counsel together on the matter, so as to give the count their answer the same day, before they left. On deliberation they formed the opinion that it was my wish to transfer to another abbey and that this would be a great reproach to them, for they considered that I had brought them great glory when I entered the religious life by coming to them in preference to all other abbeys, and now it would be a serious disgrace if I cast them off and went elsewhere. Consequently they would not hear a word on the subject either from the count or from me. Moreover, they threatened me with excommunication if I did not return quickly, and they absolutely forbade the prior with whom I had taken refuge to keep me any longer, under penalty of sharing my excommunication. Both the prior and I were very much alarmed at this.

51. The abbot departed, still in the same mind, and a few days later he died.[155] When his successor was appointed, I met him with the bishop of Meaux, hoping that he would grant what I had sought from his predecessor.[156] He too was unwilling to do so at first; but through the intervention of some of my friends I appealed to the king and his council, and so got what I wanted. A certain Stephen, the king's seneschal at the time, summoned the abbot and his companions and asked why they wished to hold me against my will when this could easily involve them in scandal and do no good, as my life and theirs could never be compatible.[157] I knew that the opinion of the king's counsellors was that the less regular the abbey was, the more reason there was for it to be subject to the king and useful to him on account of its material wealth, and this made me think that I should easily win

BRD; scandalum incurrere possent facile *S;* incurrere scandalum facile possent *Y*
[m] congruere *FAmb*[1]   [n] regis *Y*

[155] Abbot Adam died on 19 Feb. 1122.

[156] Abbot Suger, consecrated 12 Mar. 1122; d. 1151. Bouchard, bishop of Meaux, 1120–34.

[157] On the powerful Garlande family and on Stephen (d. 1148), chancellor in the household of King Louis VI (1108–37), and also from 1120 seneschal, until his fall in 1127/8 (before *Letter* 1 was written), see n. 16 above; also Bournazel, *Le Gouvernement capétien*, pp. 35–40. Suger had benefited from the patronage of the Garlande family. In a letter to Suger which Bernard, abbot of Clairvaux, wrote *c.*1127, Bernard described Stephen as being both a cleric and a soldier in appearance but in reality a monster who was neither (*Letter* 78, 11, ed. Leclercq and Rochais in *S. Bernardi Opera*, vii. 208–9). For similar criticism cf. the *Chronique de Morigny*, ed. Mirot, pp. 42–3.

assensum assequi[o] credideram; sicque actum est. Sed ne[p] gloriationem suam quam de me habebat monasterium nostrum amitteret,[q] concesserunt mihi ad [r]quam uellem[s] solitudinem[r] transire dummodo nulli me abbatie subiugarem; hocque in presentia regis et suorum utrimque[t] assensum est et confirmatum.

52. Ego itaque[a] [b]ad solitudinem quandam[c] in Trecensi pago[b] mihi antea cognitam [d]me contuli,[d] ibique a quibusdam terra mihi donata, assensu episcopi terre, oratorium quoddam in nomine sancte Trinitatis ex callis[e] et culmo primum[f] construxi; ubi cum quodam clerico nostro latitans,[g] illud uere Domino[h] poteram decantare: 'Ecce elongaui fugiens et mansi in solitudine.'[158] Quod cum cognouissent[i] scolares, ceperunt undique concurrere, et relictis ciuitatibus et castellis solitudinem inhabitare, et pro amplis domibus parua tabernacula sibi construere, et pro delicatis cibis[j] herbis aggrestibus et pane[k] cibario uictitare,[l] et pro mollibus stratis culmum[m] sibi et stramen comparare, et pro[n] mensis[o] glebas erigere, ut[p] uere[q] eos priores philosophos imitari crederes, de quibus et[r] Iheronimus[s] [t]in secundo[t] *Contra Iouinianum* his commemorat uerbis: 'Per quinque[u] sensus, quasi[v] per quasdam[w] fenestras, uitiorum ad animam introitus est. Non[x] potest[y] metropolis [z]et arx mentis[z] capi, nisi [a]per portas[a] irruerit hostilis[b] exercitus. Si circensibus quispiam delectatur,[c] si athletarum certamine, si mobilitate[d] histrionum, si formis mulierum, [e]si splendore[e] gemmarum, uestium[f] et ceteris huiusmodi[g] per oculorum fenestras anime capta[h] libertas est, et impletur illud propheticum: "Mors intrauit per fenestras nostras."[159] Igitur[i] cum per has

[o] consequi *T before corr.*; ass(. . .?) T^1 *in marg.* [p] me *C* [q] admitteret *CE;* amittere *S* [r–r] quam (quem *before corr. by another hand*) uellem (*superscr. by another hand*); solitudinem *A;* quem uellem solitudinem *CDY* [s] uellam *S* [t] utr(u *exp.*)inque *A;* utriusque *CE;* utrinque *R*

52 [a] Comme il fonda premierement l'abbaie du Paraclet. *Ego itaque xx table in H of the (missing) contents of Dijon MS 525* [b–b] ad solitudinem in trecensi pago *BRSD;* in trecensi pago ad solitudinem *Y;* ung lieu solitaire (c'est a dire en ung desert). . .ou boure de Troyes *J* [c] *om. S* [d–d] *om. Y;* transiui Y^1 [e] cannis *A after corr.;* callamis *E;* callis *exp. by Fcorr.;* al. calamis *add. F in marg.;* cal(a Y^1)mis *Y;* calamis *Amb* [f] primo *ACEFRDY* [g] latitens *D* [h] david *D;* dauiticum *Y* [i] cognossissent *D* [j] sibi *CE* [k] pro *add. DY* [l] moctitare *A before superscr. corr.* [m] culmen *S* [n] *om. BRDY* [o] messis *Y* [p] et *T before corr. by another hand* [q] uero *D* [r] *om. F* [s] Ieronimus *CEBRDY;* Hieronymus *F* [t–t] in seculo *T;* in secundo *B followed by an unfilled space;* sec̄ondo *R;* scribendo *D;* in scribendo *Y;* in libro secundo *Amb* [u] v. *TA;* h. *C; om. Amb* [v] *om. C* [w] qua(s Y^1)dam *Y* [x] nec *Y* [y] autem *add. F* [z–z] et arx (et ars T^4 *in marg.*) mentis *TF;* arx (*?; superscr. by another hand*) mentis *A;* et ars(?) militibus *C;* appri(?) militibus *E;* et ars mentis *BRSDY* [a–a] portas *ACE;* eius(?) *add. F* [b] hostiles *E* [c] delectetur *F and Jerome* [d] mo *CE followed by blank space* [e–e] si

the consent of the king and his council—which I did. But so that the monastery should not lose the reputation gained from having me as a member, they allowed me to withdraw to any retreat I liked, provided that I did not come under the authority of any abbey. This was agreed and confirmed on both sides in the presence of the king and his advisers.

52. And so I took myself off to a lonely spot I had known before in the territory of Troyes, and there, on land given me by some people with the agreement of the local bishop, I built a sort of oratory in the name of the Holy Trinity with skins and thatch. Here I could stay hidden alone but for one of my clerks, and truly cry out to the Lord: 'Lo, I escaped far away and dwelt in solitude.'[158] No sooner was this known than scholars began to gather there from all parts, forsaking cities and towns to inhabit the wilderness, leaving large mansions to put up little tents for themselves, eating wild herbs and coarse bread instead of delicate food, spreading hay and straw in place of soft beds, and using banks of turf for tables. They could rightly be thought to be imitating the early philosophers, whom Jerome recalls in the second book of his *Against Jovinian* with these words: 'The five senses are like windows through which vices gain entry to the soul. The capital and citadel of the spirit cannot be taken except by a hostile army entering through the gates. If anyone takes pleasure in circuses and athletics, an actor's pantomime or women's beauty, the splendour of jewels and garments, or anything of this sort, the liberty of his soul is captured through the window of the eyes, and the word of the prophet is fulfilled: "Death has climbed in through our windows."[159] So when the marshalled

splandore *D;* et splendore *Y* [f] metallorum *add. F* [g] huius *BS* [h] capta(s *exp.*) *Y* [i] cui *?A*

[158] Ps. 54 (55): 8 (7). Abelard's benefactors at this time are unknown; for benefactors later on see Appendix A, 5.iii. From 1123 the bishop of Troyes was Hatto. His predecessor—Renaud II, of the house of Montlhéry—had died on 6 January 1122 before the death of abbot Adam. On the solitude cf. *Letter* 2, 6. The new oratory of the Trinity, later to be renamed the Paraclete, was by the river Ardusson in the parish of Quincey and about seven km south-east of Nogent-sur-Seine (on the present N. 422). William Godell, an English religious writing in France after the death of Heloise in 1164, mentions the *cenobium* in his *Chronicon*, ed. Bouquet, p. 675BC: 'Construxit denique cœnobium in territorio Trecassino, in prato quodam ubi legere solitus fuerat . . . quod Paraclitum nominavit'. Robert of Auxerre (d. 1212) follows this in his *Chronicon*, p. 235; likewise, William of Nangis, *custos chartarum* in the abbey of St-Denis (*fl.* late 13th c.), in his *Chronicle*, ed. Géraud, i. 32.

[159] Jer. 9: 21; also cited in *Rule* 34.

portas quasi quidam perturbationum cunei ad arcem[j] nostre mentis intrauerint,[k] ubi erit[l] libertas? ubi fortitudo eius? [m]ubi de Deo cogitatio?[m] Maxime cum tactus depingat[n] sibi etiam[o] preteritas uoluptates, et recordatione[p] uitiorum cogat animam[q] compati[r] et quodam modo[s] exercere quod non agit. His igitur[t] rationibus inuitati,[u] multi philosophorum reliquerunt[v] frequentias urbium[w] et ortulos suburbanos, ubi[x] ager irriguus et arborum[y] come et susurrus auium,[z] fontis speculum, riuus murmurans, et [a]multe oculorum auriumque[a] illecebre, ne per luxum[b] et habundantiam copiarum anime fortitudo mollesceret[c] [d]et eius[d] pudicitia[e] stupraretur.[f] Inutile quippe est crebro uidere per que aliquando captus [g]sis, et[g] eorum [h]te experimento[h] committere quibus difficulter[i] careas. Nam et[j] Pytagorei[k] huiuscemodi frequentiam declinantes,[l] in solitudine[m] et desertis locis habitare consueuerant.[n] Sed et[o] ipse Plato, cum [p]diues esset[p] et thorum eius Diogenes lutatis pedibus conculcaret,[160] ut posset uacare philosophie elegit Academiam uillam, ab urbe procul, non solum desertam, sed et pestilentem: ut cura[q] et assiduitate morborum libidinis impetus frangerentur,[r] discipulique sui nullam aliam sentirent uoluptatem nisi [s]earum rerum[s] quas discerent.'[t] [161] Talem et filii prophetarum, Helyseo[u] adherentes, uitam[v] referuntur duxisse, de quibus ipse quoque Ieronimus,[w] quasi[x] de monachis illius temporis, ad Rusticum monachum inter cetera ita scribit: 'Filii prophetarum, quos monachos [y]in ueteri legimus Testamento,[y] edificabant sibi casulas prope[z] fluenta Iordanis et, turbis [a]et urbibus[a] derelictis, polenta et herbis aggrestibus uictitabant.'[162] Tales discipuli nostri [b]ibi super[b] Arduzonem[c] fluuium[d] casulas suas edificantes, heremite magis quam scolares[e] uidebantur.[f]

[j] artem *D, ?S* [k] intrauerit *BRSD* [l] erat *S* [m–m] nisi de deo cogitatio *C;* nisi de domo cogitatio *E;* ubi cogitatio de deo *DY* [n] depinguat *TC;* de pingat *D* [o] et *E* [p] recordationem *TCE;* contreigne l'ame a piteusement souffrir la remembrance *J* [q] anima *T* [r] comparati *?E* [s] quodammodo *FRS* [t] ergo *E* [u] imitati *T illegible corr. by* T^1 *in marg.* [v] relinquerunt *BS* [w] uerbium *D* [x] nisi *E* [y] arbor *ED;* arboris *Y* [z] auium *E after corr.* [a–a] multorum aurium oculorum que *E;* multe oculorum animique *F;* multe oculorumque *Y* [b] luxuriam *CE* [c] illesceret *B;* melesceret *Y* [d–d] et eius *ditto. E* [e] pudicia *D* [f] constupraretur *F;* stuparet *Y* [g–g] sistet *B* [h–h] experimento te *tr. Y* [i] difficiliter *BRDY* [j] si *add. CE;* etsi *F; om. RDY* [k] pitagorei *A, E before corr. to* putagorei, *DY;* pithagorei *CS;* pythagorei *FR;* pythagorici *B* [l] decinantes *T before corr.* [m] sollicitudine *E* [n] consuerant *A;* consueuerunt *Jerome* [o] *om. CE* [p–p] esset diues *F* [q] eum *?A* [r] frangeretur *F and Jerome* [s–s] earumdem rerum *CE;* earum *RD;* earum scienciarum (scienciarum *add.* Y^1) *Y;* ces choses *J* [t] dicerent *E* [u] heliseo

forces of distraction have marched through these gates into the citadel of the mind, where will its liberty and its strength be? Where will be thought about God? Especially when sensibility pictures for itself past pleasures and, by recalling its vices, drives the soul to empathy and, as it were, to practise what it does not actually do. These are the considerations which have led many philosophers to leave crowded towns and the gardens outside them where they find water meadows and leafy trees, the twittering of birds, reflections in spring waters and murmuring brooks, to be so many snares for eye and ear. They fear that amidst all this luxury and abundance the soul's strength will sap and its purity be soiled. No good comes from looking often on what may one day seduce you, and from committing yourself to trying out what you find it difficult to do without. Indeed, the Pythagoreans used to shun this kind of contact and lived in solitude in the desert. Plato himself was a wealthy man (and his couch was trampled on by Diogenes with muddy feet),[160] yet in order to give all his time to philosophy he chose to set up his Academy some way from the city on a site which was unhealthy as well as deserted, so that ceaseless preoccupation with sickness would break the assaults of lust, and his pupils would know no pleasures but what they had from their studies.'[161] Such too was the life that the sons of the prophets, the followers of Elisha, are said to have led, of whom (amongst other things) Jerome writes to the monk Rusticus, as if they were the monks of their time, that 'the sons of the prophets, the monks we read about in the Old Testament, built themselves huts by the river Jordan, and abandoned crowds and towns to live on barley meal and wild herbs'.[162] My pupils built themselves similar huts on the banks of the Ardusson, and looked like hermits rather than scholars.

AESY; Heliseo *F* [v] et *add. E* [w] iheronimus *CEBRDY;* Hieronymus *F* [x] qui *Y* [y–y] in ueteri legibus testamento *T;* in Veteri Testamento legimus *F;* in ueteris legimus testamento *D;* legimus in ueteri testamento *Y* [z] propter *F;* propter *al.* prope *Jerome* [a–a] *om. CE;* urbium *F;* urbium *al.* et urbibus *Jerome* [b–b] ibi ad *CE;* ad *F* [c] auduzonem *T;* arduz quem *A;* ardaconem *BR;* ardulzonem *S;* ardacionem *D;* ardationem *Y;* Durtain *J* [d] fluviolum *BRSDY* [e] scolaribus *E* [f] uiderentur *B;* uidentur *R*

[160] Cf. Diogenes Laertius, *Vitae philosophorum*, vi. 26 (ed. Cobet, p. 139).

[161] Jerome, *Aduersus Iouinianum*, ii. 8–9 (*PL* xxiii. 310–12 (297B, 298A–C)); also cited in *TChr*, ii. 61–2.

[162] Jerome, *Epistola* CXXV *ad Rusticum monachum*, 7 (ed. Hilberg, lvi. 125, *ll.* 9–12; *PL* xxii. 1076). Cf. 4 Kgs. (2 Kgs.) 6: 1–2, cited at **26** and *Letter* 7, **2**.

53. Quanto autem illuc[a] maior scolarium erat confluentia, et quanto duriorem in[b] doctrina nostra[c] uitam sustinebant,[d] tanto amplius [e]mihi emuli[e] [f]estimabant gloriosum[f] et sibi ignominiosum. Qui cum cuncta que [g]poterant[h] in me[g] egissent, omnia cooperari mihi in bonum dolebant;[i] [163] atque ita iuxta illud Iheronimi:[j] 'Me procul ab urbibus, foro, litibus, turbis remotum, sic[k] quoque [l]ut[m] Quintilianus ait: "latentem[l] inuenit inuidia".'[164] Quia[n] apud semetipsos tacite conquerentes et [o]ingemiscentes dicebant:[o] '"Ecce[p] mundus totus post eum[q] abiit",[165] nichil persequendo[r] profecimus, sed magis [s]eum gloriosum[s] effecimus.[t] Extinguere nomen eius studuimus, sed magis accendimus.[u] Ecce in ciuitatibus omnia necessaria[v] [w]scolares ad manum habent[w] et, ciuiles delicias contempnentes, ad solitudinis inopiam confluunt et sponte miseri fiunt.' Tunc autem precipue ad scolarum[x] regimen intolerabilis me compulit paupertas, cum 'fodere[y] non ualerem et[z] mendicare erubescerem'.[166] Ad artem itaque[a] quam noueram recurrens,[b] pro labore manuum ad officium lingue compulsus sum. Scolares autem ultro mihi quelibet[c] [d]necessaria preparabant, tam in uictu scilicet[e] quam in[f] uestitu uel cultura agrorum seu in[g] expensis edificiorum, ut nulla me scilicet a studio cura domestica retardaret.[167] Cum autem oratorium nostrum modicam eorum portionem capere non posset, necessario[h] ipsum dilatauerunt, [ij]et de[j] lapidibus et lignis[k] construentes meliorauerunt.[il]

54. Quod cum in honore[a] sancte Trinitatis esset[b] fundatum[c] ac postea dedicatum, quia tamen ibi profugus ac iam desperatus diuine gratia consolationis aliquantulum respirassem, in memoria[d] huius[e] beneficii ipsum Paraclitum[f] nominaui.[168] Quod multi audientes non sine[g] magna admiratione[h] susceperunt, et nonnulli hoc

53 [a] illud *C* [b] a *CEF* [c] nostram *Y* [d] sustinebat *C* [e–e] mihi emuli mihi *ditto. D* [f–f] estimabant et gloriosum *E;* estimabant *R;* gloriosum estimabant *DY* [g–g] in me poterant *CEF* [h] potuerant *Amb*[I] [i] dicebant *DY* [j] Ieronimi *CEBRSDY;* Hieronymi *F* [k] ⟨S *rubr. exp.*⟩ sic *Y;* sicut *F* [l–l] *vacant space in Y;* emulorum *add. in another hand Y* [m] *om. CEFDY* [n] qui *Y after exp. of* a; Qui *Amb*[I] [o–o] ingemiscebant dicentes *BR;* ingemis[cat] dicentes *S before exp. of the superscr. addition* [cat]; in gemiscendo dicentes *D;* ingemiscendo dicentes *Y* [p] *A before superscr. corr.* [q] ipsum *BRSDY* [r] prosequendo *D* [s–s] gloriosum eum *CEF* [t] efficimus *S* [u] attendimus *ED* [v] uenalia *DY* [w–w] scolares ad manum eius habent *T;* scolares ad manum haberetur *C;* ad manum scolares habent *BRSDY* [x] scolarium *D* [y] confodere *S* [z] *om. F* [a] *om. CEF* [b] reuertens *Amb*[I] [c] quilibet *Y* [d] *from here to* profugus *in* **54** *written over eras. T* [e] *om. BRSDY* [f] *om. S* [g] *om. Y* [h] *add. E in vacant space* [i–i] *om. S;* li firent meilleur *J* [j–j] fi(fi *exp.*)de *Y* [k] linguis *DY* [l] meliorauerunt *TABRDYAmb;* incolauerunt *CEAmb*[I]*;* incoluerunt *F;* li firent meilleur *J*

53. But the greater the crowds of scholars who gathered there, and the harder the life they led under my teaching, the more my rivals thought this brought honour to me and shame to themselves. They had done all they could to harm me, and now they could not bear to see things turning out to my benefit;[163] and so, in the words of Jerome: 'Remote as I was from cities, public affairs, law courts, and crowds, "envy" (as Quintilian says) "sought me out in my retreat".'[164] They brooded silently over their wrongs, and then began to complain: '"Why, all the world has gone after him."[165] We have gained nothing by persecuting him but rather have increased his fame. We meant to extinguish the light of his name but all we have done is make it shine still brighter. See how the students have everything they need at hand in the cities, yet they scorn the comforts of civilization, flock to the barren wilderness and choose this wretched life of their own accord.' Now it was sheer pressure of poverty at the time which made me run a school, since I was 'not strong enough to dig and too proud to beg';[166] so I returned to the skill which I knew, and made use of my tongue instead of working with my hands. For their part, members of the school provided all I needed without asking, food, clothing, work on the land as well as building expenses, so that I should not be kept from my studies by domestic cares of any kind.[167] As my oratory could not hold even a modest proportion of their numbers, they were obliged to enlarge it, and improved it by building in wood and stone.

54. It had been founded and later dedicated in the name of the Holy Trinity, but because I had come there as a fugitive, and in the depths of my despair had been granted some comfort by the grace of God, I named it the Paraclete in memory of this gift.[168] Many who heard the name were astonished, and several people strongly criticized me on the

54 [a] nomine *TBRSDYAmb;* honore *ACEFAmb*[1]*;* en l'onnour *J* [b] est *E* [c] fundamentum *CE* [d] memoriam *F* [e] eius *CEF* [f] Paracletum *FAmb and Vulg.;* Paraclitum *& sic ubique Amb*[1] [g] solum *Y* [h] *superscr. Ecorr.*

[163] 'omnia cooperari mihi in bonum': cf. Rom. 8: 28.

[164] Jerome, *Hebraicae quaestiones in libro Geneseos, prologus* (ed. Lagarde, p. 1; *PL* xxiii. 984A (935B)); Ps.-Quintilian, *Declamationes*, xiii. 2.

[165] John 12: 19.

[166] Luke 16: 3.

[167] 'uictu et uestitu': cf. Deut. 10: 18.

[168] Paraclete: a Greek word meaning Advocate and traditionally translated as Comforter; cf. John 14: 16, 16: 7.

uehementer calumpniati sunt, dicentes non licere Spiritui sancto specialiter[i] magis quam[j] Deo Patri ecclesiam aliquam assignari; sed uel soli Filio uel toti simul Trinitati, secundum [k]consuetudinem antiquam.[k] [169]

55. Ad quam nimirum calumpniam hic eos error plurimum induxit, quod inter Paraclitum[a] et Spiritum Paraclitum[b] nichil[c] referre crederent, cum ipsa quoque Trinitas et quelibet[d] in Trinitate persona, sicut Deus uel adiutor[e] dicitur,[170] ita et[f] Paraclitus,[g] id est consolator, recte nuncupetur,[h] iuxta illud Apostoli: 'Benedictus Deus et pater domini nostri Ihesu Christi, pater misericordiarum, et Deus totius consolationis, qui consolatur[i] nos in omni tribulatione nostra',[171] et secundum quod Veritas ait: 'Et alium Paraclitum[j] dabit uobis.'[172] [k]Quid etiam impedit,[k] cum omnis ecclesia in nomine Patris et Filii et Spiritus sancti pariter consecretur, nec sit eorum [l]in aliquo possessio[l] diuersa[m] quod[n] domus Domini non ita Patri uel Spiritui sancto ascribatur[o] sicut[p] Filio? Quis titulum eius cuius est ipsa domus de fronte uestibuli radere presumat? Aut cum se Filius in sacrificium Patri obtulerit, et secundum hoc[q] in celebrationibus missarum specialiter ad Patrem orationes[r] dirigantur et hostie fiat immolatio, cur eius precipue [s]altare esse[s] non uideatur cui maxime supplicatio et sacrificium agitur? [t]Numquid[u] rectius eius [v]qui immolatur quam illius cui immolatur[v] altare dicendum est?[t] An melius dominice crucis aut sepulchri[w] uel beati Michaelis seu Iohannis[x] aut Petri uel alicuius[y] sancti, qui nec ibi immolatur[z] [a]nec eis immolatur[a] aut obsecrationes eis[b] fiunt, [c]altare quis[c] esse profitebitur?[d] Nimirum nec inter idolatras altaria uel templa aliquorum dicebantur, nisi quibus ipsi sacrificium atque obsequium impendere intendebant.[e]

[i] spiritualiter *S* [j] consuetudinem antiquam *add. T before exp.* [k–k] antiquam consuetudinem *T*

55 [a] paracletum *FAmb* [b] paracletum *FAmb* [c] nil *F* [d] quilibet *S;* quamlibet *D* [e] auditor *B* [f] itaque *CE;* ita quoque *F* [g] paracletus *FAmb* [h] noncupetur *T;* nuncupatur *FY* [i] consola *C* [j] paracletum *FAmb* [k–k] Quod (*after corr. at* o) etiam impedimentum est *Y* [l–l] possessio in aliquo *F* [m] diuisa *Amb*[1] [n] *om. Y* [o] scribatur *Y* [p] cum *RDY* [q] *om. F* [r] *add. Ecorr. in vacant space* [s–s] esse altare *E* [t–t] *written compactly over eras. in T; eras. also in marg.* [u] Nunquid *A;* Nonquid *R;* Non quid *D* [v–v] qui immolatur quam illius qui immolat *T after exp. at the end of* immolat; cui immolatur *CEF;* qui immolatur *B;* celui qui est sacrifies que a celui a qui l'en sacrefie *J* [w] sepulcrum *Y* [x] quam *add. BRSDY* [y] alius *add. F* [z] immolantur *TC;* immolan(n *?exp.*)tur *A;* qui ne soit pas illec sacrefiez *J* [a–a] nec eis immolan(n *exp. A*[1])tur *A;* nec ei immolatur *F;* ne leur sacrifie *J* [b] ei *F;* ei(s *add. Y*[1]) *Y* [c–c] altare quibus quis *D;* altare quid *Y* [d] confitebitur *T* [e] impendebant *B*

grounds that it was not permissible for a church to be assigned specifically to the Holy Spirit any more than to God the Father, but that it must be dedicated according to ancient custom either to the Son alone or to the whole Trinity.[169]

55. This false charge doubtless arose from their mistaken belief that there was no distinction between the Paraclete and the Holy Spirit as Paraclete. In fact, both the Trinity and each person in the Trinity may be addressed as God or Protector[170] and equally properly as Paraclete, that is Comforter, following the words of the Apostle: 'Blessed be God and Father of our Lord Jesus Christ, the all-merciful Father and the God of all consolation, who comforts us in all our troubles';[171] and as the Truth says: 'He will also give you another Paraclete.'[172] Since the whole Church is consecrated in the name of the Father and equally of the Son and of the Holy Spirit, and is in their possession indivisibly, what is to prevent a house of the Lord from being ascribed to the Father or to the Holy Spirit just as much as to the Son? Who would think of removing an owner's name from above his entrance? Or again, since the Son offered himself in sacrifice to the Father, and consequently in celebrations of the Mass it is the Father to whom prayers are specially directed and the Host is offered, why should an altar not chiefly be his to whom prayer and sacrifice are chiefly offered? Is it any better to say that an altar belongs to him who is sacrificed than to him to whom sacrifice is made? Would anyone claim that an altar is better named after the Lord's Cross or Sepulchre or St Michael, John, or Peter, or any saint, who is neither sacrificed there nor receives sacrifice, nor has prayers addressed to him? Surely even amongst idolators, altars and temples were said to belong only to those who received sacrifice and offering.

[169] Other examples of the dedication of churches to the Paraclete are found although they are rare and somewhat later, e.g. the Augustinian canonry at Ebelholt founded before 1175, diocese of Roskild, on the island of Seeland in Denmark, and Le Paraclet-des-Champs, an abbey of Cistercian nuns near Amiens founded in 1219. See Cottineau, *Répertoire*, i, col. 1017, and ii, col. 2186.

[170] 'adiutor': Ps. 17 (18): 3 (2), 18 (19): 15 (14), 27 (28): 7, etc.

[171] 2 Cor. 1: 3–4.

[172] John 14: 16. Two problems are discussed here. The first is how to show that the third person of the Trinity is the Paraclete or Comforter while upholding that all the divine persons are comforters; this was part of the problem which had come to the fore when Abelard's book on the Trinity was thrown on the fire at Soissons in 1121; cf. **43** above and *TChr*, iv. 67–8. The second is the tension between the demands of reason and fidelity to tradition, which also underlay Abelard's quarrel with Anselm of Laon when Anselm's 'usus' was confronted by Abelard's 'ingenium'; cf. **10** and **11** above; also *Rule* **71** and *Letter* **10**.

56. Sed fortasse dicat[a] aliquis, ideo Patri non esse uel ecclesias uel altaria dedicanda,[b] quod eius aliquod factum[c] non existit quod specialem[d] ei sollempnitatem tribuat.[e] Sed hec[f] profecto ratio ipsi hoc[g] Trinitati aufert[h] et Spiritui sancto non aufert, cum ipse quoque Spiritus [i]ex aduentu suo propriam[i] habeat Pentecostes[j] sollempnitatem, sicut[k] Filius [l]ex suo[l] natalis sui festiuitatem; sicut[m] enim Filius missus[n] in mundum, ita et [o]Spiritus sanctus in discipulos[o] propriam sibi uendicat sollempnitatem.

57. Cui etiam probabilius quam alicui[a] aliarum personarum templum ascribendum uidetur, si[b] diligentius apostolicam[c] attendamus auctoritatem atque ipsius Spiritus operationem. Nulli enim trium personarum[d] spirituale[e] templum specialiter ascribit[f] Apostolus, nisi Spiritui sancto; non enim ita templum Patris uel[g] templum Filii dicit, sicut[h] templum[i] Spiritus sancti, in prima ad Corinthios ita scribens: [j]'Qui adheret Domino, unus Spiritus est.'[173] Item:[j] 'An nescitis quia[k] corpora[l] uestra[m] templum sunt[n] Spiritus sancti qui in uobis[o] est, quem habetis a Deo,[p] et non [q]estis uestri?'[q] [174] Quis etiam[r] diuinorum sacramenta beneficiorum que[s] in ecclesia fiunt operationi[t] diuine gratie, que[u] Spiritus sanctus intelligitur, nesciat specialiter ascribi? Ex aqua[v] quippe et Spiritu sancto in baptismo renascimur, et tunc primo quasi speciale templum Deo constituimur.[w] In confirmatione[x] quoque septiformis Spiritus gratia traditur,[y] quibus[z] ipsum Dei templum adornatur atque dedicatur. Quid ergo mirum si ei persone cui specialiter spirituale[a] templum Apostolus tribuit,[b] nos corporale[c] assignemus?[d] Aut cuius[e] persone rectius ecclesia esse dicitur quam eius cuius operationi cuncta que in ecclesia ministrantur beneficia specialiter assignantur?[f] Non tamen hoc[g] ita conicimus[h] ut, cum

56 [a] dicet *CEF* [b] edificanda *D* [c] fcm̄ *TASDY;* factum *CERAmb;* festum *FAmb*[1]*;* ftm̄ *B* [d] speciale *C* [e] tribuatur *Y* [f] hoc *ABRS* [g] hac *E;* hic *D;* huius *Y* [h] *om. D* [i–i] propriam ex aduentu suo *Y* [j] pent⟨h *SD*⟩ecostes habeat *BRSDY* [k] sic *BRDY* [l–l] aduentu *add. Y*[1] [m] sic *B* [n] est *add. CE* [o–o] spiritus sanctus *T;* (. . . ?)iscipulis *T*[1] *in marg. where trimming has occurred;* spiritus sanctus in discipulis *A;* spiritus sanctus in discipulos *CEF;* spiritus sanctus *BRSDY;* li Saint Esperit envoyez es disciplez *J*

57 [a] aliter *E* [b] sed *D* [c] applicatam *Y* [d] est *add. B* [e] speciale *TCFAmb and Monfrin;* spāle *ABRSDY;* speciale *E with two dots add. by corr. over* c; spirituale *Amb*[1] *and Muckle;* especial *J* [f] scribit *CEF* [g] in *E before corr.* [h] sed *CEF;* comme *J* [i] *add. E in vacant space* [j–j] *om. BRDY* [k] quoniam *F* [l] corpora *E after corr.;* membra *F* [m] nostra *AD* [n] est *TA* [o] nobis *BRD* [p] domino *E* [q–q] sunt uestri *C;* est nostri *E* [r] *superscr. E by another hand* [s] qui *Y* [t] cooperationi *Y* [u] qua *FAmb* [v] a *Y; add. Y*[1]

56. But perhaps someone may say that neither churches nor altars should be dedicated to the Father because there is no act of his for which he is assigned a special solemnity. But this argument without question detracts from the Trinity itself, not from the Holy Spirit, since the Holy Spirit on account of his coming has his own solemnity of Pentecost, just as the Son by his coming has the feast of the Nativity; for just as the Son having been sent into the world merits his solemnity so also, having been sent to the disciples, does the Holy Spirit.

57. In fact, if we pay careful attention to apostolic authority and the workings of the Spirit himself, it seems more fitting that a temple should be ascribed to the Holy Spirit than to any other person of the Trinity. To none of the three persons does the Apostle specifically assign a spiritual temple other than the Holy Spirit, for he speaks neither of a temple of the Father nor of a temple of the Son but of a temple of the Holy Spirit when he writes in the First Letter to the Corinthians: 'Anyone who is joined to the Lord is one spirit with him',[173] and again: 'Do you not know that your body is the temple of the Holy Spirit who is in you since you received him from God? You are not your own property.'[174] Everyone knows too that the sacraments of the gifts of God administered in the Church are ascribed particularly to the action of divine grace, by which is meant the Holy Spirit. For by water and the Holy Spirit we are reborn in baptism, after which we first become a special temple of God. And in the sacrament of confirmation the sevenfold grace of the Holy Spirit is conferred on us whereby the temple of God itself is adorned and dedicated. Is it then surprising if we dedicate a material temple to the person to whom the Apostle has specially ascribed a spiritual one? Can a church be more fittingly said to be his than the person to whose action all the benefits administered in the Church are specifically ascribed? However, in first giving my oratory the name of the

[w] constituitur *D* [x] consummatione *TRY;* confirmacion *J* [y] tradimur *BRSDY* [z] etiam *add. A* [a] *? C;* speciale *Y* [b] as⟨s *F*⟩cribit *CEF;* atribuit *D* [c] *add. E in vacant space* [d] assignamus *R before corr.* [e] eius *E* [f] assignatur *E* [g] hec *ES* [h] cognouimus *or* cognoscimus *C;* cognouimus *E;* cogitamus *FAmb;* conuincimus *R;* agitamus *Amb*[1]

[173] 1 Cor. 6: 17.
[174] 1 Cor. 6: 19.

Paraclitum[i] primo [j]nostrum uocauerimus oratorium, uni ipsum persone nos dicasse fateamur, sed propter eam quam supra reddidimus causam, in memoria scilicet nostre consolationis,[j] quamquam si illo quoque, quo[k] creditur, modo id fecissemus, non esset[l] rationi aduersum, licet consuetudini incognitum.

58. [a]DE PERSECVTIONE QVORVMDAM QVASI NOVORVM APOSTOLORVM IN EVM[a]

[b]Hoc autem loco[b] me corpore latitante sed fama tunc maxime[c] [d]uniuersum mundum perambulante,[d] et illius poetici figmenti quod Echo[e] dicitur instar penitus retinente,[f] quod uidelicet plurimum[g] uocis habet sed nichil[h] substantie,[175] priores emuli, cum per se iam minus ualerent, quosdam aduersum me nouos apostolos, quibus mundus plurimum credebat, excitauerunt.[176] Quorum[i] alter regularium canonicorum uitam, [j]alter monachorum[j] se resuscitasse gloriabatur.[k] [177] Hii [l]predicando per mundum[l] discurrentes[178] et me impudenter quantum poterant[m] corrodentes, non modice[n] tam ecclesiasticis quibusdam quam secularibus[o] potestatibus me[p] contemptibilem ad tempus effecerunt; et [q]de mea tam fide quam uita[q] adeo sinistra disseminauerunt ut ipsos quoque amicorum nostrorum[r] precipuos a me auerterent;[s] et [t]si

[i] Paracletum *F* [j–j] nostrum uocauerimus oratorium uni ipsum (ipsius *S*) persone nos (nos persone nos *ditto. E*) dicasse (dedicasse *S*) fateamur, sed propter eam quam supra (supra *om. F*) reddidimus (reddimus *T*) causam in memoria scilicet (scilicet in memoriam *F* in memoriam scilicet *Amb*) nostre consolationis *TAEFSAmb;* nostrum uocauerimus oratorium uni ipsum nos scilicet nostre consolationis *C;* uel in memoria scilicet nostre consolationis nostrum uocauerimus (uacauerimus *D*) oratorium uni ipsius persone nos dedicasse fateamur (fatemur *Y*) sed propter eam (eam *om. D*) quam supra reddidimus causam *BRDY* [k] que *BR;* qui *DY* [l] est *EAmb*[1]

58 [a–a] *rubr. TA; this rubr. is added a little lower in S;* Le x[e] chapitre, comme ses premiers ennemis le difamoient tant, qu'il convint qu'il s'en fuist *table in H of the* (*missing*) *contents of Dijon MS 525* [b–b] *decorated initial T; bold, thick letters E; Y begins new paragraph* [c] *om. Amb* [d–d] uniuersum perambulante mundum *BRSY;* uniuersi perambulante mundi *D* [e] Equo *TBRS; om. D* [f] resonante *FAmb*[1]*;* retenant *J* [g] credebat *add. T before corr.* [h] nil *F* [i] *initial capital TE; decorated initial BRS;* (Q)uor(um) *D; BSD begin a new line and S adds the rubr.* de persecucione quorundam quasi nouorum apostolorum in eum [j–j] sanctus Bernardus *add. in marg. of T by a 14th-/15th-c. hand* [k] gloriabantur *CE* [l–l] per mundum predicando *D* [m] poterunt *D* [n] modicum *CEFAmb*[1] [o] scolaribus *E* [p] *om. TABRSDYAmb;* me *CEF* [q–q] de mea tam (tam *repeated in marg. by another hand*) fide quam uita *T;* tam de mea fide quam uita *ACEF;* de mea tam uita quam fide *D;* de mea tam uita *Y* [r] meorum *Y* [s] reuerterent *CE* [t–t] si quid *E;* qui *Amb*

[175] Ovid, *Metamorphoses*, iii. 359: 'corpus adhuc Echo, non vox erat' / 'Echo was still a body, not a voice' (trans. Melvill). The distinction between *uox* (here meaning simply a movement of sound or air) and *substantia* (substance) brings to mind the contemporary

Paraclete I had no thought of declaring its dedication to a single person. My reason was simply what I said above—it was in memory of the consolation I had found there. But even if I had done so in the way that is generally believed, it would not have been unreasonable, even though it is unknown to general custom.

58. HIS PERSECUTION BY SOME NEW QUASI-APOSTLES

Meanwhile, though my body lay hidden in this place, my fame certainly travelled all over the world. Even so, within my heart I reflected on that poetic creation Echo, so called because she has so large a voice but no substance.[175] My former rivals could do little by themselves, and therefore stirred up against me some new apostles in whom the world had great faith.[176] One of these boasted that he had reformed the life of the regular canons, the other the life of the monks.[177] They hurried here and there,[178] slandering me shamelessly in their preaching as much as they could, and for a while brought me into no little disrepute in the eyes of ecclesiastical as well as of secular authorities; and they spread such evil reports of my faith and way of life that they also turned some of my chief friends against me, while

enquiries of logicians into the nature of nouns and their content or meaning; cf. Appendix A, 1 and 2.iv.

[176] 'Priores emuli': perhaps including Alberic of Reims and Lotulf the Lombard; cf. **37** above: 'duo illi predicti emuli' and **42**: 'emuli mei'. But at **36** 'emuli mei' include others in addition to Alberic and Lotulf. Cf. also **12** and **39** above and *Letter* 2, **2**.

[177] Perhaps, indeed probably, Norbert of Xanten (*c.*1084–1134), the founder of the canonry of Prémontré and of the Praemonstratensian order of regular canons in 1121, and Bernard, abbot of Clairvaux (1090–1153), the leading force in the growth of the new Cistercian order of Benedictine monks. See Miethke, 'Abaelards Stellung zur Kirchereform', pp. 167–70; Grauwen, 'Het getuigenis van Abaelard over Norbert' and 'Nogmaals over Abelard'; and Ziolkowski, pp. 154–5. Partly following Muckle, 'Abelard's letter of consolation', pp. 212–13, and largely for the reasons (which are unsatisfactory) that *c.*1125 Bernard could not be described as unfriendly towards Abelard nor as a wandering preacher, Borst, 'Abälard und Bernhard', pp. 501–3, claimed that Abelard's two critics were Norbert and Hugo Farsitus. In *Sermon* 33 (*PL* clxxviii. 605C) Abelard accuses Norbert and 'his co-apostle Farsitus' (*coapostolum ejus Farsitum*) of boasting that they could raise the dead to life. (Arduini, 'Ruperto, san Norberto e Abelardo', pp. 86–8, has questioned whether Farsitus was the personal name of the co-apostle because *farsitus* or *farcitus* means well-fed, being the past participle of the verb *farcio, -ire* (to stuff, to get fat, to feed well) and a recognized term of severe criticism. On the other hand, a regular canon called Hugo Farsitus of Soissons delivered the panegyric at Norbert's funeral in 1134; see Borst, 'Abälard und Bernhard', pp. 502–3; Smits, pp. 125–6). For further negative remarks about regular canons see *Letter* 6, **14** and *Letter* 12. On Norbert see esp. Elm, 'Norbert von Xanten', and Felten, 'Norbert von Xanten'; also Felten, 'Zwischen Berufung und Amt'.

[178] 'Hii predicando per mundum discurrentes': cf. *Rule* 111. Abelard writes similarly in *Adtendite* in criticism of Cistercian monks who preach: 'prout officium predicationis exigebat per mundum discurrentibus'; 'Discurrunt per mundum . . . et predicacionibus quantum possunt uacantes, quod monachorum non est' (ed. Engels, p. 227, *ll.* 56–7 and *ll.* 65–7).

qui[t] adhuc pristini amoris erga me aliquid[u] retinerent, hoc[v] ipsi modis omnibus metu[w] illorum dissimularent.[179]

59. Deus ipse mihi testis est, quotiens[a] aliquem ecclesiasticarum personarum conuentum adunari[b] noueram, hoc[c] in dampnationem meam agi credebam. Stupefactus ilico[d] quasi super uenientis ictum fulguris, expectabam[e] ut quasi hereticus aut prophanus in conciliis[f] traherer aut sinagogis. Atque[g] ut [h]de pulice[h] ad leonem, de formica ad elefantem comparatio ducatur,[i] non me mitiori[j] animo persequebantur[k] emuli mei quam beatum[l] olim Athanasium heretici.[180] Sepe autem, Deus scit, in tantam lapsus sum[m] desperationem [n]ut Christianorum finibus excessis[o] ad gentes[p] transire disponerem[n] atque ibi quiete sub quacunque[q] tributi pactione[r] inter inimicos Christi christiane uiuere.[s] [181] Quos[t] tanto magis[u] [v]propitios me[v] habiturum credebam quanto me minus christianum ex imposito mihi crimine suspicarentur, et [w]ob hoc[w] [x]facilius ad sectam suam inclinari posse[x] crederent.[y]

60. [a]DE ABBATIA AD QVAM ASSVMPTUS EST, ET PERSECVTIONE[b] TAM FILIORVM, ID EST MONACHORVM, QVAM TYRANNI IN EVM[a]

Cum[c] autem tantis perturbationibus [d]incessanter affligerer,[d] atque hoc [e]extremum mihi superesset[e] consilium ut apud inimicos Christi

[u] aliqui *D* [v] hic *CE* [w] motu *D;* uictu *Y*

59 [a] quoties *F* [b] admirari *D* [c] hunc *CF;* hec *EY* [d] ab eo *CEF* [e] *om. E* [f] consiliis *CEFD* [g] aut *B* [h–h] de publice *T before self-corr.;* de pu (pu *exp.*) de (*superscr.*) pulice *A;* de (*Y*[1]) pulice *Y* [i] duditur *S* [j] minori *?E, FY* [k] prosequebantur *D* [l] *om. B* [m] *om. D* [n–n] *om. C* [o] dei *add. and del. E;* excedens *F* [p] gentiles *DY* [q] quoque *C* [r] panctione *T before corr. by exp.* [s] uiuerem *F* [t] *om. E* [u] integre *Amb* [v–v] me propitios *EF* [w–w] ab hoc *C;* ab his *E* [x–x] facilius me ad sectam suam inclinari *BRSDY* [y] credererent *A;* credent *D*

60 [a–a] *rubr. TS;* Quod electus in abbatem et qua consideracione s(e *add.*)uscepit *rubr. A;* Le xj[e] chapitre, comme il fu abbé d'une abbaie en Bretaingne *table in H of the (missing) contents of Dijon MS 525* [b] ne *add. in T with a thin nib and black ink* [c] *decorated initial T;* Dum *BRS* (*decorated initial on a new line in S*) *Y;* dum *D;* Comme *J* [d–d] affligerer incessanter *D* [e–e] mihi extremum superesset *CEF;* extremum mihi esset (esset michi *Y*) *BRDY*

---

[179] Hilary, who seems to have been a schoolmaster in Orleans, wrote a poem (*inc.* 'Lingua serui, lingua perfidie') lamenting the break-up of this school and claiming that a servant had made false allegations to Abelard of the bad behaviour of his students of logic; they were made to leave the oratory (better called a *ploratorium* than an *oratorium*) and disperse to Quincey: 'Tort a uers nos li mestre' / 'The Master was wrong to us' (*Versus et ludi*, no. 6, ed. Bulst and Bulst-Thiele, pp. 30–1; *Elegia*, ed. Häring, pp. 935–7; *PL* clxxviii. 1855–6). False allegations or not, some anxiety about the running of the school was likely to arise. Häring, 'Hilary of Orleans', pp. 1077–80, suggested that, although this poem appears in Paris BnF lat. 11331, fos. 1–17, along with other poems and three plays written by Master Hilary of

any who up till now had retained some of their old affection for me took fright and tried to conceal this as best they could.[179]

59. God is my witness that whenever I heard of a meeting of ecclesiastics being convened, I believed its purpose was to condemn me. Like one in terror of being struck by lightning, I expected to be brought before a council or assembly and charged with heresy or profanity. And if I may compare a flea with a lion, an ant with an elephant, my rivals persecuted me with no more mercy than heretics in the past persecuted St Athanasius.[180] Often, as God knows, I fell into such a state of despair that I thought of quitting the bounds of Christendom and going over to the heathen, there to live a quiet Christian life amongst the enemies of Christ at the cost of what tribute was asked.[181] I told myself that they would receive me more kindly and would regard me more highly as someone who, by reason of the allegations made against me, was not much of a Christian, and they would therefore believe that I could more easily be won over to their sect.

60. THE ABBEY WHICH HE ACQUIRED AND HIS PERSECUTION BY HIS SONS—THE MONKS—AS WELL AS BY A TYRANT

While I was continuously harassed by these anxieties and as a last resort had thought of taking refuge with Christ among Christ's

Orleans, it was written by a different Hilary who at the time was a student of Abelard. However, Häring later ('Die Gedichte', p. 921) seems to accept that Master Hilary of Orleans, who also left a letter collection which is full of material illustrating the schools at Orleans, Angers, and elsewhere, wrote the poem about Abelard's school and did not need to have been a student there to be able to do so. (There is, in any case, no reason to think that the *scolares* who joined Abelard included only students.) Part of the poem was published by Marchegay in 1876 from the cartulary of Le Ronceray, a convent near Angers where Hilary may have been a canon. Another poem written by Hilary (no. 8, *inc.* 'Fama mendax et Fama perfida', ed. Bulst and Bulst-Thiele, pp. 32–3), may be about Abelard, but the claim made by Latzte, 'Zu dem Gedicht *De papa scolastico*', that no. 14 (*De papa scolastico*, ed. Bulst and Bulst-Thiele, pp. 47–8) also concerns him is contested here (pp. 72 and 73). Robl, 'Der Dichter und Lehrer Hilarius von Orléans', pp. 38–41, finds the *papa scolasticus* to be a generalized caricature of the features of a famous but arrogant master of the time, Abelard not excluded. He also finds that the canon, the poet, and the master, all called Hilary, are one person. On the stylistic features of Hilary's poetry see Wollin, 'Ein Liebeslied des Petrus Abaelardus', pp. 149–55, with further references.

[180] St Athanasius (*c.*296–373), bishop of Alexandria, spent much of his life in exile. In his short *Letter* against Bernard (*Epistola contra Bernardum*) Abelard compares himself again to another suffering saint, the martyr Vincent of Saragossa (d. 304); on this see Ziolkowski, pp. 105–6 and also n. 126 above.

[181] Pope Gregory VII, in a letter to Abbot Hugh of Cluny (Jan. 1075), also expressed exasperation with those with whom he had to live: 'the Romans, that is, the Lombards and the Normans, as I often tell them, I accuse of being worse than the Jews and the heathen'; *Letter* 2. 49 (*Register*, ed. Caspar, p. 189).

ad Christum confugerem, occasionem quandam adeptus qua[f] insidias istas[g] paululum [h]declinare me credidi, incidi in Christianos atque monachos[i] gentibus[h] longe seuiores[j] atque peiores.[k] Erat[l] quippe in Britannia[m] minore,[n] in episcopatu Venecensi,[o] abbatia quedam sancti [p]Gildasii Ruiensis,[p] pastore defuncto desolata.[182] Ad quam[q] me [r]concors fratrum[r] electio[s] cum assensu principis[t] terre uocauit, atque hoc[u] ab abbate nostro et fratribus facile impetrauit;[183] sicque[v] me[w] Francorum inuidia ad Occidentem[x] sicut Iheronimum[y] Romanorum expulit[z] ad Orientem.[184] Numquam enim[a] huic rei, sciat[b] Deus, acquieuissem, nisi ut quocunque[c] modo has[d] quas incessanter sustinebam oppressiones, ut dixi, declinarem. Terra quippe barbara et terre lingua mihi incognita erat, et turpis atque indomabilis[e] illorum[f] monachorum[g] uita omnibus fere notissima,[h] et gens [i]terre illius[i] [j]inhumana atque incomposita.[185] Sicut ergo ille, qui[k] imminente sibi gladio perterritus[j] in[l] precipitium[m] se collidit et ut puncto[n] temporis mortem unam[o] differat aliam[p] incurrit, sic ego[q] ab uno periculo in[r] aliud scienter me contuli;[s] [t]ibique ad[t] horrisoni undas excubans[u] [v]Occeani, cum fugam[v] [w]mihi ulterius terre[w] postremitas non preberet,[186] sepe in orationibus[x] meis

[f] quam *T before corr. by another hand;* quas *D* [g] ipsas *BRSDY* [h–h] *om. C* [i] uel *add. F* [j] saniores (in al⟨io⟩ sceuiores *superscr. add. by another hand*) *A;* seuioribus *E;* seniores *S* [k] peioribus *?E* [l] *on a new line with decorated initial and with space left for a heading B; R likewise, although vacant space is filled with small decorative motifs; D also on a new line but lacking the initial* [m] britania *S* [n] et *add. C;* minori *S* [o] Vaneteñ (*line over* n *add. by Ecorr.*) *E;* uenecensis *Y before exp. of final* s; Venetensi *F* [p–p] gildasii rinensis *AE;* Gildasii Riuensis *F;* Gildardi riuensis *BR;* gildarsii riuensis *S;* Gilandi riuersis *D;* gildardi riuensis *Y;* Saint Gildace de Raines *J* [q] quem *C* [r–r] fratrum concors *CEF* [s] *add. Ecorr. in marg.* [t] principe *E;* principum *F* [u] hac *C;* hic *D* [v] sic *DY* [w] *om. CEF* [x] occidente *D* [y] ieronimum *AE;* Jeronimum *CBRD;* Hieronymum *F* [z] expulsit *D* [a] *om. CEF* [b] scit *F* [c] quoque *C* [d] hac *D* [e] indomalis *D;* indoma(bi *superscr. by another hand*)lis *Y* [f] eorum *F* [g] *om. CEF* [h] nouissima *BR* [i–i] ill(ius) te(rre) *DY* [j–j] *om. CE* [k] *om. D* [l] perter(r *add.* Y^1)itus *Y* [m] p̄t̄em *C; E leaves a short space unfilled;* punctim *F;* precipucium *BRS; illegible in D* [n] punctis *E;* praesentis *F* [o] *illegible abbrev. exp. by another hand in Y* [p] illam *Y* [q] ergo *Y before corr. by exp.* [r] ad *Y* [s] contulit *D* [t–t] ubique ad *BRD;* ubique ex *Y* [u] *om. TACEF* [v–v] occeani ubi quo (quo *after exp. of* cum) fugiam *Y* [w–w] ulterius terre michi *A* [x] omnibus *E before corr. in marg. by another hand*

---

[182] The abbey had been founded in the 6th c. by St Gildas. Of the rebuilding in the 11th c. there are remains in the choir and north transept. St Gildas was to be commemorated at the abbey of the Paraclete (29 Jan.), *The Paraclete Breviary*, IIIA, ed. Waddell, p. 3; cf. *Old French Ordinary of the Paraclete*, ed. Waddell, p. 334.

[183] 'Principis terre' / 'the local lord': Conan or Cono III (the Fat), count of Nantes from *c.*1103 and also duke of Brittany from 1112 (d. 1148), son of Duke Alan IV of Brittany (Alain Fergent; 1084–1112; d. 1119) and Ermengarde, daughter of Count Fulk IV of Anjou (Fulk Réchin). Before 1113 he married Maud, an illegitimate daughter of Henry, king of

enemies, an opportunity was offered me which, I believed, would bring me some respite from the plots against me. But in taking it I fell among Christians and monks who were far more savage and wicked than the heathen. There was in lower Brittany, in the diocese of Vannes, the abbey of St-Gildas de Rhuys, which the death of its abbot had left without a pastor.[182] I was invited there by the agreed choice of the monks, with the approval of the local lord, and permission from the abbot and brothers of my monastery was easily obtained.[183] Thus the jealousy of the French drove me west as that of the Romans drove Jerome east.[184] God knows, I should never have accepted this offer had I not hoped somehow to find some escape from the attacks which, as I have said, I had ceaselessly to endure. The country was foreign and the language there was unknown to me. The monks were beyond control and led a dissolute life which was well known to almost all, and the natives were brutal and lawless.[185] Like a man who rushes to a precipice in terror at the sword hanging over him, and at the very moment of escaping one death meets another, I consciously took myself from one danger to another, and there listening to the waves coming from the Ocean's horizon, at the far end of the earth where I could flee no further,[186] I often used to recall in my prayers the words

England from 1100 and duke of Normandy from 1106; cf. 'Henry I's illegitimate children' in *Complete Peerage*, xi, Appendix D, pp. 105–21 at 114, and K. Thompson, 'Affairs of State', p. 147. Conan's request that Abelard's abbot, Suger of St-Denis, should give permission for him to become abbot of a Breton house was one of a series of initiatives to bring monks to Brittany from France; cf. Bautier, 'Paris au temps d'Abélard', pp. 65–6; Chédeville and Tonnerre, *La Bretagne féodale*, pp. 69–72. Abelard is recorded as abbot of St-Gildas in the *Chronicon Ruyense* (printed by Morice in *Mémoires*, i, col. 151): 'Petrus Abaelardus Sancti Gildasii Ruyensis'. For Conan see also 71 below. A suggestion made once by L. Grodecki that Abbot Suger, when designing windows for his abbey church, and also in his written works, was influenced by hymns that Abelard wrote was later withdrawn; see Grodecki, 'Les Vitraux allégoriques de Saint-Denis' and 'Abélard et Suger'.

[184] Cf. *Vita S. Hieronymi 'Hieronymus noster'* (*PL* xxii. 178); *Vita S. Hieronymi 'Plerosque nimirum'* (*PL* xxii. 203–4); Jerome, *Epistola* XLV *ad Asellam* (ed. Hilberg, liv. 323–8; *PL* xxii. 480–4). Abelard's election took place around 1125/7.

[185] Twice in his *Dialectica* i. 3, v. 2 (ed. de Rijk, pp. 128 *ll.* 28–32, 583 *ll.* 12–13), which was written much earlier in his career, Abelard had already likened Bretons to brutes ('Britones' and 'bruti' or 'brutones'). For other near-contemporary references to the barbarousness of the Bretons see Dalarun and others, *Les Deux Vies de Robert d'Arbrissel*, pp. 136–7 and n. 19. As regards language, the Vannetais was still largely Breton-speaking; see Chédeville and Tonnerre, *La Bretagne féodale*, pp. 295–310.

[186] 'ibique . . . preberet': cf. *Hymn* 120 (Szövérffy 119), *De Sancto Gilda, abbate* 3: 'Hic indeficiens est tamquam hesperus / extremis imminens terrarum partibus, / vbi Britanniam cingens occeanus / immensis aridam contundit fluctibus' (*Hymn Collections from the Paraclete*, ed. Waddell, p. 163; *Hymns*, ed. Szövérffy, p. 242). 'Terre postremitas': St-Gildas de Rhuys is on the Presqu'île de Rhuys on the southern coast of Brittany about 28 km south of Vannes and by road about 115 km north of Nantes.

illud reuoluebam: 'A finibus terre ad te clamaui, dum anxiaretur cor meum.'[187]

61. Quanta enim anxietate[a] illa etiam[b] quam regendam susceperam[c] indisciplinata fratrum[d] congregatio cor meum die ac nocte cruciaret, cum tam[e] anime mee[f] quam corporis pericula pensarem, neminem iam latere arbitror. Certum quippe habebam,[g] si eos ad regularem[h] uitam quam professi fuerant compellere temptarem, me uiuere non posse[i] et, si[j] hoc[k] in quantum possem[l] non agerem, me dampnandum[m] esse. Ipsam etiam[n] abbatiam [o]tirannus quidam[o] in terra illa potentissimus[p] ita iam diu sibi subiugauerat, ex inordinatione scilicet ipsius[q] monasterii nactus occasionem[r] ut omnia loca monasterio adiacentia in usus proprios redegisset, ac grauioribus exactionibus[s] monachos ipsos quam tributarios Iudeos exagitaret.[188] Vrgebant[t] me monachi pro necessitudinibus[u] cotidianis, cum [v]nichil in[v] commune haberent quod eis ministrarem, sed unusquisque de propriis olim marsupiis [w]se et concubinas suas[w] cum filiis uel[x] filiabus sustentaret.[y] Gaudebant [z]me super hoc[z] anxiari, et ipsi quoque[a] furabantur et asportabant[b] que poterant, ut cum in administratione ista[c] deficerem, [d]compellerer aut[d] a disciplina cessare [e]aut omnino[e] recedere. Cum autem tota [f]terre illius barbaries pariter exlex[f] et indisciplinata[g] esset, [h]nulli erant[h] hominum ad quorum[i] confugere possem adiutorium, cum a moribus omnium [j]pariter dissiderem.[j] Foris me tyrannus ille et satellites[189] sui assidue opprimebant; intus mihi fratres incessanter insidiabantur, ut [k]illud Apostoli in me[k] specialiter dictum res ipsa indicaret:[l] 'Foris pugne. Intus timores.'[m] [190]

61 [a] anxitate *A* [b] in *B; om. RDY* [c] *om. Y* [d] fraterna *B* [e] causa *C* [f] *om. A* [g] habebam quod *all codd.; Orlandi, 'Minima Abaelardiana', p. 136, n. 7 suggested that* quod *is unnecessary here and may be a slip by the author. Note that in one MS, B, the scribe writes* habebam quod . . . non possem *but then continues to write* et . . . dampnandum esse [h] irregularem *C* [i] possem *B* [j] Ni *B;* nisi *?S;* Quod si *Amb* [k] *om. D* [l] et *add. DY* [m] dampnificandum *E;* damnificandum *Amb*¹ [n] et *C;* quidem *BRDY* [o–o] quidam tirannus *E* [p] potentissimus *ditto. B before corr. by exp.* [q] ipsius scilicet *BRSDY* [r] actionem *C* [s] ex accionibus *E* [t] Vigebant *D* [u] necessitatibus *BRSDY* [v–v] nil *F;* nichil *BRDY;* riens en commun *J* [w–w] et *add. BRS;* ut se concubinas suas et *D;* ut se et concubinas suas et *Y* [x] et *CEFBRSDY;* et *J* [y] sustentarent *ACEFDY* [z–z] super hoc *CE;* super hoc me *F* [a] sui *add. BRDY* [b] apportabant *BY;* aportabant *RD* [c] sua *CEF; om. D* [d–d] compellerer ut *T;* compellerent aut *EFAmb*¹*;* je fusse contraint au *J* [e–e] an omnino *BS;* an animo *R;* aut animo *D;* ou du tout *J* [f–f] terra iu(?) barbarus pariter exlex *C;* terra iuer barberies pariter exlex *F;* terra illius pariter barberies exlex *BRY;* terre illius pariter bar barbaries exlex *S;* terra illius pariter barbarate lex *D;* toute la restrangerie de cele terre fust sans loy *J* [g] in disciplina *S* [h–h] nullus erat *CEF;* nulla (*before corr.*) erant *Y* [i] cuius *F* [j–j] pariter diffiderem *S;*

of the Psalmist: 'From the ends of the earth I have called to thee when my heart was in anguish.'[187]

61. Everyone knows now, I think, how much anguish my tormented heart suffered night and day at the hands of that undisciplined community I had undertaken to rule, while I thought of the dangers to my soul as well as my body. I was certain at any rate that if I tried to bring them back to the regular life to which they were professed it would cost me my own life; yet if I did not do my utmost to achieve this, I should be damned. In addition, the abbey had long been subjected to a formidably powerful local tyrant who had taken advantage of the disorder in the monastery to appropriate all its adjoining lands for his own use, and was making heavier exactions from the monks than he would have done from Jews subject to tribute.[188] The monks beset me with demands for their daily needs, though there was no common allowance for me to distribute, but each one of them provided for himself, his concubines, and his sons and daughters from his own purse. They enjoyed upsetting me over this, and they also stole and carried off what they could, so that when I had reached the end of my resources I should be forced to abandon my attempt at enforcing discipline or leave them altogether. The entire barbarous population of the area was similarly lawless and out of control; there was no one I could turn to for help since I disapproved equally of the morals of them all. Outside the monastery that tyrant and his accomplices[189] never ceased to harry me; inside the brethren were always setting traps for me, until it seemed that the saying of the Apostle was meant for me: 'Quarrels outside, fears in our heart.'[190]

dissiderem pariter *D* [k–k] preparat (*underlined*) *add. E;* in me illud apostoli *Y*
[l] iudicaret *D* [m] timor *CE*

[187] Ps. 60 (61): 3 (2).

[188] The tyrant has not been identified. In charters of Redon in Brittany in the 9th c. the terms 'tiarnus' and 'tyrannus', meaning 'machtiern' or locally powerful men, are employed; see *Cartulaire de l'abbaye de Redon*, ed. Guillotin de Corson, nos. i, cxxviii, ccxlvii, cclxvii (pp. 1, 97–8, 198–9, 216–7); also Planiol, *Histoire des institutions de la Bretagne*, ii. 74–7. On the brutality of tyrants in territories which Abelard had known well before coming to St-Gildas, and on mentions of tyrants and their cruelty in his writings on logic, see Bisson, 'L'Expérience du pouvoir', pp. 104–6.

[189] Cf. *Sermon* 6: 'Satellites isti praedonesque Babylonici, per quos captivamur' (*PL* clxxviii. 428, cited by Bisson, 'L'Expérience du pouvoir', p. 105, n. 66. There are some similarities between *Sermon* 6, which is about the Babylonian exile and captivity, and this part of *Letter* 1.

[190] 2 Cor. 7: 5; cited again below at **71**. On the stubborn resistance to 'Gregorian' reform of churches in Brittany see Chédeville and Tonnerre, *La Bretagne féodale*, pp. 239–54. In a

62. Considerabam [a]et plangebam[a] quam inutilem[b] et miseram uitam ducerem, et quam infructuose tam mihi quam aliis uiuerem, et quantum[c] antea clericis profecissem et quod nunc,[d] eis propter monachos dimissis, [e]nec in ipsis[e] nec in monachis aliquem fructum haberem,[f] et quam [g]inefficax in[g] omnibus inceptis atque conatibus meis [h]redderer,[i] ut iam mihi de omnibus illud improperari rectissime deberet: 'Hic homo[h] cepit[j] edificare, et non potuit[k] consummare.'[191] Desperabam penitus, cum recordarer [l]que fugerem[l] et considerarem que incurrerem;[m] et priores molestias quasi iam nullas reputans, crebro [n]apud me[n] ingemiscens dicebam: 'Merito hec patior, [o]qui Paraclitum,[o] [pq]id est[p] consolatorem, deserens,[q] in desolationem certam me[r] intrusi et, minas euitare[s] cupiens, ad certa confugi pericula'.[t] Illud autem plurimum me cruciabat[u] quod,[v] oratorio nostro dimisso, de diuini [w]celebratione officii[w] ita ut opporteret prouidere non poteram, quoniam loci nimia paupertas uix unius hominis[x] neccessitudini sufficeret. Sed ipse quoque[y] uerus Paraclitus[z] [a]michi maxime[a] super hoc desolato ueram attulit consolationem, et[b] proprio prout debebat [c]prouidit oratorio.[c] [192]

63. [a]Accidit[b] namque[a] ut abbas noster,[c] sancti scilicet[d] Dyonisii,[e] predictam[f] illam Argenteoli[g] abbatiam, in qua[h] religionis habitum nostra illa iam in Christo soror potius[i] quam uxor Heloysa[j] susceperat,[193] tanquam[k] ad ius monasterii sui antiquitus pertinentem [l]quocunque[m] modo[l] acquireret, et conuentum inde[n] sanctimonialium,

62 [a–a] *om. C* [b] inutile *S* [c] et *RD;* et quam *S;* et *Y before exp.;* cum *Y*[1] [d] non *E;* non modo (modo *subscr.*) *F* [e–e] *om. E* [f] habere *E;* habebam *BRDY* [g–g] inefficax *CF;* efficax *E* [h–h] *om. CEF* [i] redderet *B* [j] cepi *F* [k] potui *F* [l–l] que fugeram *T;* quo fugeram *F* [m] incurreram *BRF* [n–n] a prime *R* [o–o] quia paraclitum *ACE;* quia paracletum *F* [p–p] *om. BRDY* [q–q] deserens id est consolatorem *S* [r] *om. CE* [s] uitare *Y* [t] Iuxta illud incidit in cillam cupiens uitare carybdim *add. D* [u] erudiebat *BR;* cruciebat *S;* erudiebat. Iuxta illud incidit in scillam cupiens uitare caribdim *add. Y* [v] et *S* [w–w] officii celebratione *Y* [x] *om. Y* [y] *om. BRDY* [z] paracletus *F* [a–a] maxime michi *Y* [b] ut *E* [c–c] oratorio prouidit *F before corr. by numbering the two words* 2, 1

63 [a–a] Accidit autem (*thick lettering*) siue namque *add. CE* [b] Comme il fist Heloyse abbeesse du Paraclit, *Accidit two triangles follow in the table in H of the* (*missing*) *contents of Dijon MS 525* [c] *om. BRDY* [d] *om. CFRDY* [e] dionisii *A;* Dionysii *F* [f] *om. F* [g] argentolii *CEF;* Argentolii *Amb*[1] [h] *om. Y* [i] post *C* [j] Heloyssa *F* [k] antequam *D;* tandem *E* [l–l] m *with superscr.* a *S* [m] quoque *CE* [n] *om. BRSDY* [o] expellet *D*

letter to Pope Honorius II, following a council held in Nantes in 1127, Hildebert, archbishop of Tours, reported decisions taken by the bishops and abbots of Brittany, with the support of the count, to put an end to inheritance of ecclesiastical offices and to ordinations of the sons of priests; see Hildebert, *Letter* ii. 30 (*PL* clxxi. 253B–254B).

62. I used to weep as I thought of the useless, wretched life I led, as profitless to myself as to others. I had once done so much for the clerks, and now that I had abandoned them for the monastery, all I did for them and for the monks was fruitless. I had proved ineffective in all my attempts and undertakings, so that now above all men I justly merited the reproach: 'Here is a man who started to build and was unable to finish.'[191] I was in deep despair when I remembered what I had fled from and considered what I had met with now. My former troubles were as nothing in retrospect, and I often used to sigh and tell myself that I deserved my present sufferings for deserting the Paraclete, the Comforter, and plunging myself into certain desolation; in my eagerness to escape from threats I had run into real dangers. What tormented me most of all was the thought that in abandoning my oratory I was unable to make proper provision for celebrating the Divine Office, since the place was so poor that it could barely provide for the needs of one man. But then the true Paraclete himself brought me true consolation in my great distress, and provided for the oratory as was fitting, for it was his own.[192]

63. It happened that my abbot of St-Denis by some means took possession of the abbey of Argenteuil where Heloise, now my sister in Christ rather than my wife, had put on the religious habit.[193] He claimed that it belonged to his monastery by ancient right, and forcibly expelled the community of nuns, of which she was prioress,[194] so that

[191] Luke 14: 30; also cited in the *Rule* 114.

[192] 'uerus Paraclitus . . . ueram consolationem': Waddell notes a similarity here with the rhymed formula, found in the *Ordinary of the Paraclete* after it became a convent of nuns, and used for acknowledging the reception of a death-notice at the abbey: 'Consolator dolentis anime / ac mestorum uere paraclite' (ed. Waddell in *The Old French Paraclete Ordinary*, ii. 107', *ll.* 5–6 and i. 298–9).

[193] 'my sister in Christ rather than my wife' / 'in Christo soror potius quam uxor': cf. *Letter* 3, 3; *Hymns*, preface to book 1: 'soror michi Heloysa, in seculo quondam cara, nunc in Christo karissima' (*Hymn Collections*, ed. Waddell, p. 5; *Peter Abelard's Hymnarius Paraclitensis*, ed. Szövérffy, p. 11; *PL* clxxviii. 1771); *Confessio fidei ad Heloissam* (ed. in Burnett, '*Confessio fidei ad Heloisam*', p. 152 (Latin), p. 154 (French); *PL* clxxviii. 375); *Sermons*, *prefatory Letter to Heloise*: 'ueneranda in Christo et amanda soror Heloissa' (*PL* clxxviii. 379–80); *Expositio in Hexameron, praefatio*: 'soror Heloysa, in seculo quondam cara, nunc in Christo carissima' (ed. Romig and Luscombe, p. 4; *PL* clxxviii. 731C).

[194] In an extract printed from a (lost) Calendar of the Paraclete by Duchesne–d'Amboise, p. 1187, Heloise is described as prioress of Argenteuil: 'Heloisa, neptis Fulberti Canonici Parisiensis, primo Petri Abaelardi coniux, deinde Monialis & Priorissa Argentolij'. *Helvide m(onacha)*, who may be Heloise but this name is not uncommon, is listed among the nuns of the convent of Notre Dame at Argenteuil in the mortuary roll of Vitalis, abbot of Savigny (d. autumn 1122), ed. Delisle, 'Documents paléographiques', pp. 388–40; id., *Rouleaux des morts*, p. 299; *Rouleau mortuaire du B. Vital*, ed. Delisle, pp. 22–4 and Plate X; Dépoin, *Une*

ubi illa comes nostra prioratum habebat, uiolenter expelleret.[o] [194] Que cum[p] diuersis locis exules dispergerentur,[q] oblatam [r]mihi a Domino[r] intellexi occasionem qua[s] nostro consulerem oratorio. [t]Illuc[u] itaque[t] reuersus, eam cum quibusdam aliis de eadem congregatione ipsi[v] adherentibus ad predictum oratorium inuitaui; eoque[w] illis adductis,[x] ipsum oratorium cum omnibus ei pertinentibus concessi et donaui;[195] ipsamque postmodum donationem[y] nostram,[z] assensu atque[a] interuentu episcopi terre, papa[b] Innocentius secundus ipsis et earum sequacibus per[c] priuilegium in[d] perpetuum corroborauit.[e] [196]

64. Quas ibi quidem primo[a] inopem[b] sustinentes uitam et ad tempus plurimum desolatas, diuine misericordie respectus, cui deuote seruiebant, in breui consolatus est,[c] et se eis[d] quoque uerum exhibuit Paraclitum[e] et circumadiacentes populos misericordes eis [f]atque propitios effecit.[f] Et plus, sciat[g] Deus, ut arbitror, uno anno in terrenis commodis[h] sunt multiplicate quam ego per centum si ibi permansissem. Quippe quo[i] feminarum sexus[j] est infirmior, tanto[k] earum inopia miserabilior facile humanos[l] [m]commouet affectus,[m] et earum uirtus[n] tam Deo quam hominibus est gratior.[o] [197] Tantam autem gratiam in oculis omnium illi sorori nostre, que ceteris preerat, [p]Dominus annuit,[p] ut [q]eam episcopi quasi filiam,[q] abbates quasi sororem, laici quasi matrem diligerent; et omnes pariter eius religionem,[r] prudentiam, et in omnibus incomparabilem patiencie mansue-

[p] Que tamen *D;* Quod cum *CE* [q] *add. E in vacant space* [r–r] a domino mihi *CEF* [s] quam *BRD* [t–t] Illud (*before corr.*) ita *A;* Illud inquam *C;* Illuc namque *FAmb;* Illic itaque *BR* [u] Illic *S* [v] ei *F* [w] eodemque *Y* [x] eductis *Y* [y] dampnationem *E* [z] *om. F* [a] et *Y* [b] propterea *E before corr.* [c] *om. BRSDY; add. Y*[1] [d] *om. D* [e] roborauit *CEF*

64 [a] *om. D* [b] opem *C;* in opere *E* [c] *om. CE* [d] ipsis *BRSDY* [e] paracletum *F* [f–f] atque propitios eis effectus *C;* atque propitios eis effecit *E;* atque propitios eos effecit *F;* eis atque propitios offecit *D* [g] sciebat *A before corr.;* ce scet *J* [h] praediis *FAmb*[1] [i] quanto *Amb*[1] [j] in ex (*superscr.* o) *B* [k] tato *S;* tantum *Y* [l] *om. RDY* [m–m] commouet effectus *CD;* permouet et (et *om. Amb*[1]) affectus *FAmb*[1] [n] *add. E in vacant space* [o] grauior *BRD* [p–p] Dominus autem *BR;* annuit *Y* [q–q] eam episcopi *CE;* eam episcopi quasi filiam (quasi filiam *superscr. by another hand*); deest quasi filiam uel quid simile *add. and exp. Fcorr. in marg.;* eam episcopus quasi filiam *BRSY;* episcopus quasi filiam *D* [r] relig *C;* religiosi *E;* religiosam *F* [s] admirarentur *F* [t] si *D*

Élégie latine d'Héloïse suivie du Nécrologe d'Argenteuil. Cf. also McLeod, *Héloise: A Biography*, 2nd edn., pp. 86–91 and frontispiece; *Checklist* no. 415. The possibility that Heloise composed a lament in elegiac couplets for the death of 'the shepherd of the flock', which is included in the roll in the entry from Argenteuil, while attractive is not conclusive (*inc.* 'Flet pastore pio grex desolatus adempto'; cf. Walther, *Initia Carminum*, no. 6613a;

they were now scattered as exiles in various places. I realized that this was an opportunity sent me by the Lord for providing for my oratory, and so I returned and invited her, along with some other nuns from the same convent who stayed with her, to come to the Paraclete; and once they had gathered there, I handed it over to them as a gift, and also everything that went with it.[195] Subsequently, with the approval of the local bishop acting as intermediary, my gift was confirmed by Pope Innocent II by charter to them and their successors in perpetuity.[196]

64. Their life there was full of hardship at first and for a while they suffered the greatest deprivation, but soon God, whom they served devoutly, in his mercy brought them comfort; he showed himself a true Paraclete to them too in making the local people sympathetic and kindly disposed towards them. Indeed, God knows, I think, that their worldly goods were multiplied more in a single year than mine would have been in a hundred had I remained there, for women, being the weaker sex, are the more pitiable in a state of need, easily rousing human sympathy, and their virtue is the more pleasing to God as well as to men.[197] And such favour in the eyes of all did God bestow on that sister of mine, who was in charge of the other nuns, that bishops loved her as a daughter, abbots as a sister, lay people as a mother; while all alike admired her piety and prudence and her unequalled gentleness and patience in every situation. The more rarely she allowed herself to be seen—so that she could devote herself in a

McCleod, *Héloise: A Biography*, 2nd edn., p. 88; *Checklist* no. 415). On the expulsion of the nuns from Argenteuil see Appendix A, 5.i.

[195] Cf. *Letter* 2, **6–7**; *Sermo* 30, *de eleemosyna pro sanctimonialibus de Paracleto*. On the arrival at the Paraclete of Heloise and some of the sisters from Argenteuil see Appendix A, 5.ii. Other sisters went to the abbey of Malnouë in Brie and continued to dispute their expulsion until as late as 1207; cf. *Gallia Christiana*, vii, cols. 507–15 at 508–9.

[196] The bishop was Hatto of Troyes (1123–45). On the endowments of the abbey see Appendix A, 5.iii.

[197] 'Quippe quo feminarum . . . gratior': for similar phrases cf. *Letter* 7, **26**, **29**, and **36**; *Hymns* 82 (Szövérffy 99), *De martyribus* 3, i; 90 (Szövérffy 126), *De sanctis mulieribus* 3, iv; 92 (Szövérffy 120), *De uirginibus* 1, ii and 93 (Szövérffy 121), *De uirginibus* 2, i; *Sermons* 1 (*PL* clxxviii. 383D) and 30 (*PL* clxxviii. 568C); *Carmen ad Astralabium*, ed. Rubingh-Bosscher, *vv.* 681–2. 'terrenis commodis': on the buildings of the Paraclete see Louis, 'Pierre Abélard et l'architecture monastique'. Waddell (*The Old French Paraclete Ordinary*, i. 313–18) reconstructs the general plan of the oratory and the cloister quadrangle from the 'Book of Burials' which survives in Paris, BnF fr. 14410, fos. 5^r–28^v, a late 13th-c. MS, and which has been published in the *Obituary of the Paraclete* (ed. A. Molinier in *Obituaires de la Province de Sens*, iv. 388–403; also ed. Lalore in *Collection des principaux obituaires et confraternités du diocèse de Troyes*, pp. 446–60). Waddell draws particular attention to similarities between Cistercian abbey plans and that of the Paraclete.

tudinem ammirabantur.[s] Que quanto rarius se[t] uideri permittebat, ut scilicet clauso[u] cubiculo sacris meditationibus atque[v] orationibus purius uaccaret, tanto ardentius eius presentiam atque spiritalis[w] colloquii[x] monita hii qui foris sunt efflagitabant.[y] [198]

65. [a]DE INFAMATIONE TVRPITVDINIS[a]

Cum[b] autem [c]omnes earum[c] uicini uehementer me culparent quod[d] earum inopie[e] minus quam possem et deberem consulerem,[f] et [g]facile id ⟨facere⟩ nostra saltem predicatione ualerem,[g] cepi sepius ad eas reuerti ut eis quoquomodo subuenirem.[199] In quo nec inuidie [h]mihi murmur[h] defuit, et quod[i] me facere sincera karitas [j]compellebat, solita derogantium prauitas[j] impudentissime accusabat, dicens [k]me adhuc quadam[k] carnalis[l] concupiscentie[m] oblectatione teneri, qua[n] pristine dilecte sustinere absentiam uix aut numquam paterer.[o] Qui frequenter illam beati[p] Ieronimi[q] querimoniam mecum uoluens qua[r] ad Asellam[s] de fictis amicis[t] scribens, ait: 'Nichil mihi[u] obicitur nisi sexus meus, et hoc[v] nunquam obiceretur[w] nisi cum[x] Ierosolimam[y] Paula[z] proficiscitur.'[a] [200] Et iterum: '[b]Antequam', inquit,[b] 'domum sancte Paule nossem, totius in me urbis studia[c] consonabant; omnium[d] pene iuditio[e] dignus summo [f]sacerdotio decernebar.'[f] [201] 'Sed scio per bonam et malam famam peruenire[g] ad regna celorum.'[h] [202] Cum hanc, inquam, [i]in tantum uirum[i] detractionis[j] iniuriam ad mentem reducerem, non modicam hinc consolationem carpebam,[k] inquiens: 'O si tantam suspitionis causam emuli mei in me reperirent, quanta

[u] claso *R* [v] et *E* [w] specialis *S* [x] colloqui (i *add.* Y^1) *Y* [y] afflagitabant *CEBRD;* affligebant *S*

65 [a–a] *rubr.* T^3*ABS; vacant space in R;* Le xij^{e} chapitre, comme il conversa en ladicte abbaie avec Heloyse *table in H of the (missing) contents of Dijon MS 525* [b] *decorated initial on new line TBRSY; initial missing D* [c–c] earum omnes *CEF* [d] et *S* [e] in opie *E* [f] consularem *A before corr.* [g–g] *Orlandi, 'Minima Abaelardiana', p. 134, pointed out that* facile id . . . ualerem *turns* ualerem *inadmissibly into a transitive verb. I have adopted his preferred conjecture and have added* facere. *The scribes may have been misled by the proximity of* facile *to* facere; *for a similar confusion*—facillime/facere—*see* **16**[l] *above. An alternative conj. made by Orlandi is* ⟨facere ad⟩ id . . . ualerem [h–h] murmur mihi *BRSDY* [i] que *C* [j–j] *F in marg.* [k–k] me quid adhuc *E* [l] carnali *DY* [m] concupiscentiae *T* (*sic, final* e *add. in a darker ink*) [n] qui *Amb* [o] parerer *B* [p] uero *add. E* [q] Hieronymi *FAmb* [r] *om. ACE* [s] assellam *ERSY* [t] amiciciis *Y* [u] aliud *add. F and Jerome* [v] hic *E* [w] obiicitur *F* [x] *om. B* [y] Iherosolimam *TY;* Hierosolymam *F;* Hierosolimam *Amb* [z] et Melania *add. F* [a] profisciscitur *TS;* profficistur *CE;* proficiscuntur *F;* profiscitur *?B after corr.;* proficitur *D* [b–b] inquit antequam *CEF* [c] studiam *D* [d] animum *E* [e] iudiciis *DY* [f–f] decernebar sacerdotio *CE* [g] perueniri *F and Jerome* [h] polorum *BRDY* [i–i] in quantum iuris *?E;* in tantum mater *D;* in tantam mater *Y before corr. by exp. to* tantam [j] detractationis Amb^1 [k] querebam *A;* habebam *?C, EF;* je . . . prenoye *J*

closed room without distraction to prayer and meditation on holy things—the more eagerly did those outside demand her presence and her spiritual conversation for their guidance.[198]

65. RUMOURS OF INDECENCY

But then all the neighbours began to complain strongly that I was doing less than I could and should to minister to their needs, as (they said) I was certainly well able to do, if only through my preaching. So I started to visit them more often to help them somehow.[199] This resulted in malicious rumours, and my detractors, with their usual perverseness, had the effrontery to accuse me of most shamefully doing what genuine charity prompted; they said that I was still in the grip of the pleasures of carnal concupiscence and could rarely or never bear the absence of the woman I had once loved. Often I repeated to myself St Jerome's lament in his letter to Asella about false friends: 'The only fault found in me is my sex, and that only when Paula comes to Jerusalem.'[200] And again: 'Before I knew the house of saintly Paula, my praises were sung throughout the city, and nearly everyone judged me worthy of the highest office of the Church.'[201] 'But I know well that it is through good and evil report that we make our way to the kingdom of heaven.'[202] When, as I say, I recalled the injustice of such a calumny against so great a man, I took no small comfort from it. If my rivals, I said, were to find such strong grounds for suspicion in my case, how I should suffer from their slander! But now that I have been freed from such suspicion by

[198] 'Que quanto rarius . . .': cf. *Rule* **40** and, for very similar comments about John the Baptist, *Sermon* 33 (*PL* clxxviii. 598A) and *Adtendite* (ed. Engels in '*Adtendite a falsis prophetis*', p. 227, *ll.* 61–4).

[199] Abelard did preach a *Sermon* (*Sermo* 30, *de elemosyna pro sanctimonialibus de Paraclito*, *PL* clxxviii. 564–9) to support efforts to relieve hardship while the convent of the Paraclete was still new ('hoc uero monasterium nouiter constructum', 568D; 'nouella . . . adhuc et tenera plantatio', 569A). He appealed to what seems to have been a largely lay congregation ('fratres', 564A, 565C, 567A–C; 'fratres hic congregati', 566C). The *Sermon*, of which another version has been edited by Granata in 'La dottrina dell'elemosina', pp. 54–9, contains a series of observations, largely based on biblical and patristic sources and on Seneca, concerning the use of possessions, in particular the obligation that falls upon the rich to give to the poor all superfluous or non-essential possessions. Cf. n. 153 above and Granata, pp. 32–59. Extracts from this *Sermon* were copied in 1154 by Guta, an Augustinian nun at Schwartzenthann in Alsace, with the assistance of Sintram, a canon at the nearby Augustinian house of Marbach; they concern the duty of care for religious women that falls upon priests. See Griffiths, 'Brides and *Dominae*'.

[200] Jerome, *Epistola* XLV *ad Asellam*, 2 (ed. Hilberg, liv. 324, *ll.* 19–21; *PL* xxii. 481). Also cited in *Letter* 7, **49**.

[201] Jerome, *Epistola* XLV *ad Asellam*, 3 (ed. Hilberg, liv. 325, *ll.* 6–8; *PL* xxii. 481).

[202] Jerome, *Epistola* XLV *ad Asellam*, 6 (ed. Hilberg, liv. 328, *ll.* 10–11; *PL* xxii. 483). Also cited in *Letter* 7, **49**.

me detractione[l] opprimerent! [m]Nunc uero mihi[m] diuina misericordia ab hac suspitione liberato, quomodo,[n] huius perpetrande turpitudinis facultate ablata,[o] suspitio remanet? Que[p] est[q] tam[r] impudens hec[s] criminatio nouissima?' Adeo namque [t]res ista[t] omnem[u] huius turpitudinis suspitionem apud omnes remouet, ut[v] quicunque mulieres [w]obseruare diligentius[w] student[x] eis[y] eunuchos adhibeant,[z] sicut de[a] Hester[b] et ceteris regis[c] Assueri puellis sacra narrat hystoria.[203] Legimus et potentem illum regine Candacis eunuchum uniuersis eius[d] gazis preesse; ad quem conuertendum[e] et baptizandum [f]Philippus apostolus[f] ab[g] angelo directus est.[204] Tales quippe [h]semper apud uerecundas et honestas[h] feminas tanto amplius dignitatis et familiaritatis [i]adepti sunt quanto[i] longius ab hac absistebant[j] suspitione. Ad quam quidem[k] penitus[l] remouendam maximum[m] illum Christianorum[n] philosophum Origenem,[o] [205] cum mulierum[p] quoque sancte[q] doctrine intenderet, sibi[r] ipsi manus intulisse[s] *Ecclesiastice Historie*[t] liber sextus[u] continet.[206]

66. Putabam[a] tamen in hoc mihi magis[b] quam illi diuinam misericordiam propitiam fuisse, ut quod[c] ille minus prouide creditur egisse atque inde non modicum crimen incurrisse, id aliena culpa in me ageret ut ad simile opus me liberum prepararet, ac[d] tanto minore pena[e] quanto[f] breuiore ac subita[g] ut, oppressus sompno[h] cum mihi manus inicerent,[i] [j]nichil pene fere sentirem.[j] [207] Sed [k]quod tunc[k] [l]fortc minus pertuli[m] ex uulnere, nunc[n] ex detractione diutius[o] plector; et plus ex detrimento[l] fame[p] quam ex[q] corporis crucior diminutione. Sicut enim[r] [s]scriptum est:[s] 'Melius est nomen bonum quam diuitie multe.'[208] Et ut beatus meminit Augustinus in sermone quodam *de uita et moribus clericorum*: 'Qui, fidens conscientie sue, negligit famam

[l] destructione *R;* destruccione *D;* destrictione *Y* [m–m] ut nunc mihi *D;* ut nunc me *Y* [n] quo *C* [o] oblata *S* [p] Qui *E* [q] etiam *Amb* [r] *om. D* [s] *after eras. in text of T;* hec *T*[4] *in marg.;* hinc *D;* hic *Y* [t–t] *add. E in vacant space* [u] *om. F* [v] et *D* [w–w] diligentius obseruare *EF* [x] studeat *D;* studerent *Y* [y] *om. DY* [z] exhibebant *Y* [a] ad *S* [b] hoster *D* [c] regibus *E* [d] *om. Y* [e] conuertandum *D* [f–f] apostolus philippus *RDY* [g] *add. Ycorr.* [h–h] apud uerecundas et honestas *CEF;* homines ad preuerecundas semper et honestas *BS;* et honestas (honestas *exp.*) ad preuerecundas semper honestas *R;* et apud uerecundas semper et honestas *D;* apud uerecundas semper et honestas *Y;* ces hommes . . . envers les femmes honteuses et honestes *J* [i–i] adempti sunt *E;* adeptis (*before exp. of* s) sunt quanto *B;* adeptis quanto *R;* adepta sunt quanto *D* [j] absistobant *A;* assistebant *CERSDY;* asistebant *B* [k] quippe *S;* quoque *Amb* [l] *om. CEF* [m] maximinum *B with an added letter* m *superscr. as if for corr.* [n] romanorum *add. B* [o] originem *FSD;* orig(e *exp.*)inem *R* [p] mulieribus *E;* mulieres *F* [q] sacre ?*S* [r] *om. Y* [s] indidisse *B;* incidisse *S* [t] historie eusebii *superscr. add. F* [u] sextus *CEF*

God's mercy, and the power to commit this sin has been taken from me, how can suspicion remain? What is the meaning of this latest monstrous accusation? This predicament so undermines all suspicion of indecency on the part of anyone that eunuchs are employed by those who wish to keep close watch on their wives, as sacred history tells us in the case of Esther and the other maidens of King Ahasuerus.[203] We also read that it was a eunuch under Queen Candace, a man of authority in charge of all her treasure, whom the apostle Philip was directed by the angel to convert and baptize.[204] Such men have always held positions of responsibility and familiarity in the homes of modest and honourable women simply because they are far removed from suspicion of this kind, and it was to rid himself of this entirely that Origen,[205] that very great philosopher for Christians, laid violent hands on himself when directing the religious education of women, as Book 6 of the *Ecclesiastical History* relates.[206]

66. However, I thought that in this God's mercy had been kinder to me than to him, for he is believed to have acted less than wisely and to have been strongly reproached as a result, whereas what happened to me to set me free for similar work was the fault of others and was so much less painful for being quick and sudden, for I was asleep when attacked and felt practically nothing.[207] Yet though perhaps I suffered less physical pain at the time, I am now more distressed for the calumny I must endure. My agony is less for the mutilation of my body than for the damage to my reputation, for it is written: 'A good name is more to be desired than great riches.'[208] In a sermon *On the Life and Morals of Clerics* St Augustine remarks: 'He who relies on his

66 [a] Patabam *T before corr. by T*[4] [b] *om. D* [c] scilicet *B* [d] Ac *T ?C;* ut *D* [e] penas *D* [f] quam *CEF* [g] subiecta *C* [h] sumpno *Y* [i] ñecerent *S;* inicerent *add. in vacant space in Y, probably by Y*[1] [j–j] nichil pene fere sentissem *T before corr.;* nichil pene fere sentirent *BS;* uel uere pene sentirem *D* [k–k] tunc quod *A;* quod nunc *F* [l–l] *om. CEF* [m] periculi *DY* [n] tunc *D* [o] diuitius *T before corr. by another hand, Amb;* diutius *Amb*[1] [p] forme *CE;* magis *add. F* [q] *om. D* [r] *om. F* [s–s] scribitur *BRSDY*

[203] Esther 2: 3.

[204] Cf. Acts 8: 26–7 and *Letter* 5, **34**.

[205] 'maximum . . . philosophum': cf. **34** above; also *Letters* 5, **22** and 7, **47** and *Sermon* 31 (*PL* clxxviii. 571B).

[206] Eusebius of Caesarea, *Historia ecclesiastica*, vi. 8 (ed. Mommsen, pp. 535–7; *PG* xx. 535BC). On Origen's self-castration cf. also *Letter* 5, **22**, *Letter* 7, **47** and **50**, and *Sermon* 31 (*PL* clxxviii. 571BC); also Fulk of Deuil, *Letter* to Abelard (*PL* clxxviii. 374AB).

[207] Cf. *Letter* 5, **22**.

[208] Prov. 22: 1.

suam crudelis est.’[209] Idem supra: ‘“Prouidemus,”’ inquit, ‘“bona,” ut ait Apostolus, “non solum coram Deo sed etiam[t] [u]coram hominibus.”[u] [210] [v]Propter nos consciencia nostra sufficit nobis;[v] [w]propter uos[w] fama nostra[x] non pollui[y] sed pollere [z]debet in uobis.[z] Due res sunt conscientia[a] et fama. Conscientia tibi, [b]fama proximo tuo.’[b] [211]

67. Quid[a] autem horum [b]inuidia ipsi Christo[b] uel eius membris, tam prophetis scilicet quam apostolis seu aliis patribus sanctis, obiceret si[c] in eorum[d] temporibus existeret, cum eos[e] uidelicet corpore integros tam familiari[f] conuersatione feminis precipue uiderent sociatos?[g] Vnde et beatus Augustinus [h]in libro[h] *de opere monachorum* ipsas etiam mulieres domino Ihesu[i] Christo atque apostolis ita[j] inseparabiles comites[k] adhesisse[l] demonstrat,[m] ut[n] cum eis etiam ad predicationem procederent. ‘[o][p]Ad hoc enim’,[p] inquit, ‘et fideles mulieres habentes terrenam substantiam[q] ibant cum eis et ministrabant eis de [r]sua substantia,[r] ut[s] nullius indigerent[t] horum que ad substantiam[u] uite huius pertinent.’[v] [212] ‘[w]Quod quisquis[w] [x]non putat[x] ab apostolis fieri ut cum eis sancte conuersationis[o] mulieres circuirent[y] quocunque[z] euuangelium predicabant, euuangelium audient,[a] et cognoscant[b] quemadmodum hoc[c] ipsius Domini exemplo[d] faciebant.’[213] ‘In euuangelio enim[e] scriptum est: “Deinceps et[f] ipse iter faciebat per ciuitates et castella, euuangelizans[g] regnum Dei, et duodecim[h] cum illo[i] et mulieres alique, que erant curate a spiritibus immundis[j] et infirmitatibus: Maria, que uocatur[k] Magdalene,[l] et Iohanna, [m]uxor Cuze[m] procuratoris Herodis, et Susanna, et [n]alie multe[n] que ministrabant eis[o] de facultatibus suis.”’[214] [215] Et[p] Leo nonus,[q] contra epistolam Parme-

[t] et *E* [u–u] omnibus hominibus *F* [v–v] Propter uos consciencia uestra sufficit uobis *CE* [w–w] propter nos *ABRD; om. Y* [x] uestra *CER* [y] polluit *F* [z–z] debet in nobis *CEDY* [a] *add. Bcorr. in marg.* [b–b] proximo tuo fama *BSDY;* proximo tuo sermo *R*

67 [a] Quod *Y* [b–b] inuidia ipsi (ipsi *superscr. in a smaller hand*) christi christo *A;* inuidia christi christo *D* [c] sed *D* [d] earum *B* [e] *om. CEF* [f] familiare *A before corr.* [g] societas *C;* societes *E* [h–h] *ditto. R* [i] Iesu *F* [j] *om. S* [k] comitis *B, ?C* [l] adherisisse *B* [m] demonstrant *A before exp.* [n] ucet *T;* ñ et *A;* et *add. other codd.* [o–o] *T over eras.; eras. also in lower marg.* [p–p] Ad heremum *B* [q] substenciam *D* [r–r] substantia sua *F and Augustine* [s] *om. S* [t] indigeret *A* [u] necessaria *F* [v] pertinerent *C, Y after corr. by* Y[1] *of* optinerent, *Amb* [w–w] Quod si quis *CE;* Quid quisquis (quisquid *D*) *BRSDY* [x–x] putat non potuisse *F and Augustine* [y] circuarent *T before illegible corr. by another hand;* cursitarent *Amb;* circumirent *al.* circuirent *Augustine* [z] quoque per *CE;* quacumque *al.* quocumque *Augustine* [a] audiat *F and Augustine;* audirent *S* [b] cognoscat *F and Augustine* [c] hic *E* [d] Christo *D* [e] *superscr. A by a smaller hand* [f] ut *D* [g] praedicans et euangelizans *F and Augustine* [h] xii[cim]. *T;* xii. *A;* etiam(?) 12 *E* [i] ille *E*

conscience to the neglect of his reputation is cruel to himself',[209] and earlier on says: '"Our aims", as the Apostle says, "are honourable not only in God's sight but also in the eyes of men".[210] For ourselves, conscience within us is sufficient. For your sake, our reputation should not be blemished but should be influential upon you. Conscience and reputation are two different things. Conscience concerns yourself, reputation your neighbour.'[211]

67. But what would my enemies in their malice have said to Christ himself and his followers, the prophets and apostles and other holy fathers, had they lived in their times when these men, pure in body, were seen to enjoy such friendly feminine company? Here also St Augustine in his book *On the Work of Monks* proves that women too were inseparable companions of our Lord Jesus Christ and the apostles, even to the extent of accompanying them when they preached: 'To this end faithful women who brought the fruits of the soil went with them and provided for them so that they should lack none of the necessities of this life.'[212] 'No one should believe that it was not the practice of the apostles, wherever they preached the Gospel, for women of holy life to go with them and hear the Gospel, knowing that they were following the example of the Lord himself.'[213] 'For in the Gospel it is written: "After this he made his way through towns and villages proclaiming the good news of the kingdom of God and with him went the Twelve and a number of women who had been set free from evil spirits and infirmities: Mary, known as the Magdalene, and Joanna, the wife of Chuza, Herod's steward, and Susanna, and many others who provided for them out of their own

[j] malignis *FAmb*[1]; malignis *al.* inmundis *Augustine* [k] uocabatur *BRSDY* [l] magdelene *C;* magdalena *B* [m–m] uxor Chuze *F;* uxor euze *R;* euze *Y before exp.by Y*[1] [n–n] multe alie *D* [o] ei *TAS;* eis *CEFBRDY*

[209] Augustine, *Sermo* 355, *De uita et moribus clericorum suorum sermo primus*, 1 (ed. Lambot, p. 124; *PL* xxxix. 1569A). Also cited in part in *TChr*, ii. 102 (p. 177, *ll.* 1539–40); *Sermon* 33 (*PL* clxxviii. 600B); *Confessio fidei 'Vniuersis'* (ed. Burnett in 'Peter Abelard, *Confessio fidei "Universis"*', p. 133, *l.* 20; *PL* clxxviii. 105–6) and *Apologia contra Bernardum*, 4 (ed. Buytaert, p. 361, *ll.* 44–5).

[210] 2 Cor. 8: 21.

[211] Augustine, *Sermo* CCCLV, *De uita et moribus clericorum suorum sermo primus*, 1 (ed. Lambot, p. 124; *PL* xxxix. 1569A).

[212] Augustine, *De opere monachorum*, iv. 5 (ed. Zycha, p. 538, *l.* 21–p. 539, *l.* 1; *PL* xl. 552); also cited in *Letter* 7, **12**.

[213] Augustine, *De opere monachorum*, v. 6 (ed. Zycha, p. 539, *ll.* 14–18; *PL* xl. 552); also cited in *Letter* 7, **12**.

niani[r] de Studii monasterio: 'Omnino',[s] inquit,[t] 'profitemur[u] non licere episcopo,[v] presbytero, diacono, subdiacono propriam uxorem causa religionis abicere[w] cura sua, ut[x] non[y] ei uictum et uestitum largiatur, sed non ut cum illa[z] carnaliter iaceat.[a] Sic et sanctos apostolos legimus[b] egisse, beato[c] Paulo dicente: "Numquid[d] non[e] habemus potestatem sororem mulierem[f] circumducendi, sicut fratres[g] Domini et Cephas?"[216] Vide insipiens quia non dixit: "Numquid non[h] habemus potestatem sororem[i] mulierem amplectendi",[j] sed: "circumducendi", scilicet[k] ut[l] mercede predicationis sustentarentur[m] ab eis, nec tamen deinceps foret inter eos carnale coniugium.'[217] Ipse certe Phariseus, [n]qui intra[n] se de Domino ait:[o] 'Hic, si esset propheta, sciret utique que et qualis esset[p] mulier que [q]tangit eum,[q] quia peccatrix est',[218] multo commodiorem, quantum ad humanum iudicium[r] spectat, turpitudinis[s] coniecturam [t]de Domino[t] concipere[u] poterat quam de nobis[v] isti,[w] aut[x] qui matrem eius iuueni[y] commendatam[z] [219] uel prophetas cum uiduis maxime hospitari atque conuersari uidebant,[220] multo[a] [b]probabiliorem inde suspitionem contrahere.[b]

68. Quid etiam[a] dixissent[b] isti[c] detractatores[d] nostri si Malchum[e] illum captiuum monachum, de quo beatus scribit Iheronimus,[f] eodem contubernio[g] cum uxore uictitantem[h] conspicerent?[i] Quanto id crimini ascriberent,[j] quod egregius [k]ille doctor[k] cum uidisset maxime commendans ait: 'Erat illic [l]senex quidam[l] nomine Malchus, eiusdem

[p] ut *BRY;* est *S;* et ut *D* [q] leonanus *CE;* leo nouus *S;* Leo Magnus *Amb*[1] [r] Parmenii *FAmb*[1]*;* contra epistolam Nicete abbatis *Ivo* (*ed. Brett and Brasington*) [s] eterno *B* [t] inquid *D* [u] profitentur *B;* confitemur *Ivo* (*ed. Brett and Brasington; PL clxi. 1154D*) [v] christo *D* [w] abire *R;* abjicere a *Ivo* (*ed. Brett and Brasington; PL clxi. 1155A*) [x] et *DY* [y] *om. Ivo* (*ed. Brett and Brasington*) [z] illa ex more *Ivo* (*ed. Brett and Brasington; PL clxi. 1155A*) [a] iaceat *A after corr.* [b] legissimus *B before corr.* [c] bono *D* [d] Numquam *C* [e] *om. A* [f] muliere *D* [g] frater *BRS and Ivo* (*ed. Brett and Brasington; PL clxi. 1156A*) [h] *om. S* [i] sororem nostram (nostram *exp.*) *R;* sororem et *D* [j] amplexandi *CEF;* amplectandi *SD* [k] *om. BRDY* [l] et *D* [m] sustentaretur *DY and Ivo* (*ed. Brett and Brasington; PL clxi. 1156A*) [n–n] quia intra *C;* qui contra *D* [o] *om. R;* dicebat *DY* [p] est *F* [q–q] tangit *RS;* eum tangit *DY* [r] iudicum *D* [s] turpitudo *D* [t–t] *ditto. B* [u] *T after T*[3] *has written* con *over eras.* [v] qui castrati sumus *add. in marg. by another hand in F* [w] Isti *B;* illi *R;* Illi *DY* [x] antiqui *B;* autem *DY* [y] iuuenis *R;* inuenit *S* [z] commandatam *D* [a] merito *E* [b–b] probabilior est ipsi suspectio est contrahere (contrahere *om. D*) *BRD;* probabiliorem uite suspeciorem contrahere *S;* probabilior est ipsi suspectionem contraherent *Y*

68 [a] *add. by another hand in E in vacant space;* enim *BRDY* [b] duxissent *C* [c] ipsi *D* [d] detractores *ARS* [e] nostrum *add. T before exp.;* malcum *S*

resources.'"[214] [215] Leo IX, too, in answer to a letter of Parmenian, of the monastery of Studios, says: 'We declare absolutely that no bishop, priest, deacon, or subdeacon may give up the care of his wife in the name of religion, so as not to provide her with food and clothing, though he may not lie with her carnally. This was the practice of the holy apostles, as we read in St Paul: "Have we no right to take a Christian woman about with me, like the Lord's brothers and Cephas?"[216] Take note, fool: he did not say "Have we no right to embrace a woman" but "to take about", meaning that they should support women from the profit made from their preaching, not that they should then have carnal intercourse with them.'[217] Certainly that Pharisee who said of the Lord to himself: 'If this man were a real prophet he would know who this woman is who touches him, and what sort of woman she is, a sinner',[218] could have supposed far more easily, as far as human judgement goes, that the Lord was guilty of evil-living than my enemies could imagine the same of me. Anyone who saw the Lord's mother entrusted to the care of a young man[219] or the prophets enjoying the hospitality and conversation of widows[220] would entertain far more probable suspicions.

68. And what would my detractors have said if they had seen Malchus, the captive monk of whom St Jerome writes, living together with his wife? In their eyes it would have been a great crime, though the splendid doctor had nothing but high praise for what he saw:

[f] Ieronimus *ACEFBRDY;* Hieronymus *F* [g] contabernio *F;* conturbernio *D* [h] uictantem *D;* uictitante *Y* [i] conspiceret *D* [j] conscriberent *TACEFDY;* al. adscriberent *add. F in marg.;* conscriberant *?B, RS. Cf. Orlandi, 'Minima Abaelardiana', p. 134* [k–k] doctor ille *DY*

[214] Luke 8: 1–3.

[215] Augustine, *De opere monachorum*, v. 6 (ed. Zycha, p. 540, *ll.* 9–17; *PL* xl. 553); also cited in *Letter* 7, **12**.

[216] 1 Cor. 9: 5; also cited in *Letter* 7, **12**. 'uictum et uestitum': cf. Deut. 10: 18.

[217] The passage cited here is taken from *Contra Nicetam monachum monasterii Studii*, xxvii (*PL* cxliii. 997D–998A), a polemic against Nicetas Stethatos, monk of Studios in Constantinople (d. *c.*1085), that may have been written by Humbert of Silva Candida (d. 1061). The extract is attributed to Pope Leo IX in the *Panormia* attributed to Ivo of Chartres, iii. 115 (ed. Brett and Brasington; *PL* clxi. 1155A–1156A); this may have been Abelard's source. *Contra epistolam Parmeniani*, the title given by Abelard but not by the author of the *Panormia*, is the title of a work by St Augustine (ed. Petschenig, pp. 17–142; *PL* xliii. 33–108). In *SN* c. 103 texts are assembled to illustrate the question whether all the apostles except John did or did not have wives.

[218] Luke 7: 39; cf. *Letter* 7, **3** and **50**.

[219] Cf. John 19: 26–7; also *Rule* **40** and *Sermon* 25 (*PL* clxxviii. 536D–537A).

[220] Cf., for Elias, 3 Kgs. (1 Kgs.) 17: 9.

loci[m] indigena, anus[n] quoque in eius contubernio,[o] studiosi[p] ambo religionis[q] et sic[r] ecclesie limen[s] terentes[t] ut[u] Zachariam et Elysabeth[v] de euangelio[w] crederes,[x] [221] nisi quod Iohannes in medio non erat.'[222] Cur denique a detractione sanctorum patrum se continent, quos frequenter legimus uel etiam[y] uidimus monasteria quoque[z] feminarum constituere atque eis[a] ministrare, exemplo quidem septem diaconorum, quos [b]pro se[b] apostoli[c] mensis et procurationi mulierum prefecerunt?[d] [223] Adeo namque [e]sexus infirmior fortioris[e] indiget auxilio,[f] ut semper uirum mulieri [g]quasi capud[g] preesse[h] Apostolus statuat;[224] [i]in cuius[i] etiam rei signo ipsam semper[j] uelatum[k] habere capud precipit.[l] [225]

69. Vnde non[a] mediocriter miror consuetudines has in monasteriis dudum inoleuisse,[b] quod quemadmodum uiris abbates, ita et[c] feminis abbatisse preponantur,[d] et eiusdem regule[e] professione[f] tam femine[g] quam uiri se astringant, in qua[h] tamen[i] pleraque continentur[j] que[k] a feminis tam prelatis quam subiectis nullatenus possunt adimpleri.[226] In plerisque etiam locis, ordine perturbato naturali,[227] ipsas abbatissas atque moniales[l] clericis quoque ipsis, quibus subest populus,[m] dominari conspicimus,[228] et tanto facilius eos[n] ad praua desideria inducere posse quanto[o] eis amplius[p] habent preesse, et iugum illud in eos grauissimum exercere; quod satiricus[q] ille considerans[r] ait:

Intolerabilius nichil est quam femina diues.[229]

70. Hoc[a] ego sepe apud me pertractando, quantum[b] mihi liceret sororibus illis prouidere et earum curam agere disposueram,[c] et quo me amplius reuererentur[d] corporali quoque presentia eis inuigilare;

[l–l] quidam senex *F* [m] *om. Y* [n] Anus *TE;* Augustinus *B;* annus *S* [o] tam *add. F;* conturbernio *D* [p] Studiosi *TA;* studiose *F and Jerome* [q] religiosi *F and Jerome* [r] se *E* [s] lumen *R* [t] therentes *A;* terentis *E;* commeuntes *D;* coeuntes *Y* [u] et *B;* et *add. RDY* [v] helysabeth *A;* helizebet *C;* helizabet *E;* Elizabeth *F;* elizabeth *RD;* elisabeth *S;* helizabeth *Y* [w] euuangelio *CERSDY;* ewangelio *B* [x] credens *C* [y] *add. in vacant space in E by another hand; om. BRSDY* [z] *om. BRSDY* [a] *om. D* [b–b] preesse *DY* [c] apostolis *D* [d] profecerunt *B;* proficerunt *R;* preficerent *S;* profitentur *DY;* firent ordeneurs *J* [e–e] sepius infirmior fortiori *C;* sexus infirmior fortiori *E* [f] consilio *DY* [g–g] *om. Y* [h] precem *S* [i–i] In cuius *TBR;* In eius *E* [j] super *BRDY* [k] uelatam *C* [l] precepit *Y*

69 [a] *om. E* [b] incleuisse *S* [c] *om. CEF* [d] preponerentur *CE* [e] *superscr. in B by another hand* [f] professioni *FDY;* professionem *BR* [g] mulieres *DY* [h] quam *B* [i] *om. RDY* [j] continent *Y* [k] *om. D* [l] atque *add. C* [m] populis *BR* [n] esses *S* [o] *om. Y* [p] *om. D* [q] sact(i *superscr.*)cus *before corr. by another hand to* satyricus *A; add. E in vacant space by another hand;* satericus *D* [r] desiderans *S*

'There was an old man named Malchus there, a native of the place, and an old woman living with him. Both of them were so eager for the faith, for ever wearing down the threshold of the church, that you would have thought them Zachariah and Elizabeth of the Gospel[221] but for the fact that John was not with them.'[222] Finally, why do they refrain from accusing the holy fathers themselves, when we often read or see how they founded monasteries for women too and ministered to them, following the example of the seven deacons who were appointed to wait at table and look after the women?[223] The weaker sex needs the help of the stronger, so much so that the Apostle lays down that the man must always be over the woman, as her head,[224] and as a sign of this he orders her always to have her head covered.[225]

69. And so I am much surprised that customs should have been long established in monasteries of putting abbesses in charge of women just as abbots are set over men, and of binding women by profession to the same *Rule* as men, for there is so much in the *Rule* which cannot be carried out by women, whether in authority or not.[226] In very many places, too, the natural order is upset,[227] to the extent that we see abbesses and nuns ruling clergy who have authority over the people,[228] all the more easily able to entice them to evil desires the more authority they have, holding over them as they do a heavy yoke. The satirist has this in mind when he says

Nothing is more intolerable than a rich woman.[229]

70. After much reflection I decided to do all I could to provide for the sisters, to manage their affairs, and, so that they would revere me

70 [a] Hec *A;* HOC *C;* Hoc *E in large, thick letters* [b] quantam *T, B* (*before corr.?*), *RS;* quam *CE* [c] disponeram *SD*

---

[221] Cf. Luke 1: 5–7. [222] Jerome, *Vita Malchi*, 2 (*PL* xxiii. 54B).

[223] Cf. Acts 6: 1–6; also *Letter* 7, **12** and *Sermon* 31 (*PL* clxxviii. 569–73).

[224] Cf. 1 Cor. 11: 3; also *Rule* **41**.

[225] Cf. 1 Cor. 11: 5. [226] Cf. *Letter* 6, **3–4**.

[227] Cf. *Letters* 4, **1** and 5, **1**; *Carmen ad Astralabium*, ed. Rubingh-Bosscher, *vv.* 1021–2: 'Si praelata uiris dominatum femina sumat, / peruerso dicas ordine cuncta geri.'

[228] On this question of male or female headship in a community of women religious see Appendix A, 6.i and ii. In his *Rule* **40–51** Abelard writes more fully about the direction that he believed men should give to women in religious life, although he also sets clear limits upon the men's responsibilities for the sisters at the Paraclete.

[229] Juvenal, *Satire* vi. 460. Cf. the imitation in *Carmen ad Astralabium*, ed. Rubingh-Bosscher, *v.* 525: 'intolerabilius nichil est quam uita superbi'. The nuns of Fontevraud included daughters of the aristocratic families of western France.

[e]et sic etiam earum magis necessitudinibus subuenire[e] ut,[f] cum me[g] nunc frequentior ac maior [h]persecutio filiorum[h] quam olim fratrum[i] afligeret, ad eas de[j] estu huius tempestatis quasi ad quendam[k] tranquillitatis[l] portum recurrerem atque ibi aliquantulum respirarem;[m] et qui in monachis nullum,[n] [o]aliquem saltem in[o] illis assequerer fructum,[230] ac tanto [p]id mihi fieret[p] magis saluberrimum quanto id[q] earum infirmitati[r] magis esset neccessarium.

71. Nunc autem [a]ita me[a] Sathanas impediuit ut ubi[b] quiescere[c] possim[d] aut etiam uiuere non inueniam, sed uagus et profugus,[231] ad instar maledicti[e] Caym,[f][232] ubique circumferar,[g] quem,[h] ut supra memini, 'foris pugne, intus timores'[233] incessanter[i] cruciant, immo tam foris quam intus[j] pugne pariter et timores; et multo[k] periculosior et crebrior persecutio filiorum aduersum me seuit[l] quam hostium. Istos[m] quippe [n]semper presentes[n] habeo,[o] et eorum insidias iugiter[p] sustineo.[q] Hostium uiolentiam[r] in corporis mei periculum uideo, si a claustro procedam;[s] in claustro autem filiorum, id est monachorum, mihi tanquam abbati, hoc est[t] patri, commissorum,[u] tam uiolenta quam dolosa incessanter sustineo machinamenta.[v] O quotiens [w]ueneno me[w] perdere temptauerunt, sicut et in beato[x] factum est Benedicto![y][234] Ac si hec ipsa[z] causa, qua ille peruersos deseruit[a] filios, ad hoc[b] ipsum [c]me patenter[c] tanti patris [d]adhortaretur exemplo, ne me, certo[d] uidelicet opponens[e] periculo, temerarius Dei[f] temptator potius quam amator, [g]immo mei[g] ipsius peremptor, inuenirer. A talibus autem cotidianis eorum[h] insidiis [i]cum mihi[i] in administratione cibi uel potus quantum[j] possem prouiderem, in ipso[k] altaris sacrificio toxicare[l] me moliti sunt, ueneno scilicet [m]calici immisso.[m] Qui etiam[n] quadam die, cum Namneti[o] ad comitem in egritudine sua

[d] reuerentur *AR* [e–e] et sic etiam magis earum necessitudinibus subuenire *CBRSDY;* et sic et (et *om. F*) earum necessitudinibus magis subuenire *EF; om. Amb* [f] et *codd., Amb;* Et *J;* ut *conj. Orlandi, 'Minima Abaelardiana', p. 134* [g] Comme il s'en retorna a son abbaie et comme ses moines le vouldrent occirre. *Et cum me there follows a sign—three circles and a loop—in the table in H of the* (*missing*) *contents of Dijon MS 525* [h–h] perfectio filiorum *BRS;* filiorum persequcio *D* [i] fratrem *D* [j] easdem *RDY* [k] quedam *C;* quandam *B* [l] transquilitatis *D;* transquillitatem *E* [m] respirare *AEF*, *C after corr. of* respirarer [n] nullam *DY* [o–o] aliquem saltem *T;* aliquando saltem in *E;* aliquam salutem in *DY;* toutesvoyes aucun en elles *J* [p–p] mihi fieret id *A*; id fieret mihi *EF* [q] magis *add. BR* [r] infirmati *T*

71 [a–a] ita *BRS;* me ita *DY* [b] ibi *C* [c] requiescere *ACEF* [d] possum *D* [e] maledictio *C* [f] Cain *F;* chayn *D;* chaym *Y* [g] circumferat *ABRS;* circumferor *DY* [h] quam *C;* qua *add. E in marg. by another hand;* Quia *DY* [i] me *add. DY* [j] timores incessanter pugne *add. T before exp.* [k] merito *E* [l] senit *D* [m] Istas *C* [n–n] presentes semper *F* [o] habere *R* [p] magis *C* [q] sustineri *R* [r] uiolē *R;* molē

more, to watch over them in person too and thus minister better to their needs. The persecution I was now suffering at the hands of the monks who were my sons was even more persistent and distressing than what I had endured previously from my brothers, so I thought I could turn to the sisters as a haven of peace away from raging storms, find repose there for a while, and at least achieve something amongst them, having failed with the monks.[230] Indeed, the more they needed me in their weakness, the more it would benefit me.

71. But now Satan has put so many obstacles in my path that I can find nowhere to rest or even to live; a wanderer and a fugitive,[231] I carry everywhere the curse of Cain,[232] forever tormented (as I said above) by 'quarrels outside, fears in our heart',[233] or rather, quarrels and forebodings without and within. The hostility of my sons here is far more dangerous and relentless than that of my enemies, for I have them always with me and face their traps continuously. I can see my enemies' violence as a danger to my person if I go outside the cloister; but it is within the cloister that I have to face the incessant assaults—as crafty as they are violent—of my sons, that is, of the monks entrusted to my care as their abbot and father. How many times have they tried to poison me—as happened to St Benedict![234] The same reason which led him to abandon his depraved sons might well have encouraged me to follow the example of so great a Father of the Church, lest in exposing myself to certain danger I should be thought a rash tempter rather than a lover of God, or even appear to be my own destroyer. And while I guarded as well as I could against their daily assaults by providing my own food and drink, they tried to destroy me during the sacrifice of the altar by putting poison in the

D; molem *Y* [s] recedam *F* [t] *om. SY* [u] commissoris *Y* [v] ex machina uitam *A before self-corr.*; machina uitam *Y before corr. by* Y^1 [w–w] me ueneno *F* [x] bono *D* [y] benedictio *C* [z] hec (*add. by another hand in marg.*) ipsa (*after self corr.*) *A*; hic ipsa *E*; hac ipsi *Y* [a] deserit *E* [b] hec *ES* [c–c] patenter me *A* [d–d] abhortaretur exemplo ne me certo *A* (exempla *add.* Y^1) adhortarentur exempla (exempla *om. Y*) ne (non *B*) me certe (certo *S*) *BRSDY* [e] apponens *E*; opponentes *Y* [f] *om. BRSDY* [g–g] in me met *B*; inmemeth *R*; meimet *DY* [h] *om. S* [i–i] mihi cum *E* [j] quam *C* [k] ipsos *D*; ipsas *?C* [l] tacitare *C*; intoxicare *EF*; in toxicare *Amb* [m–m] caldeici inuulso *B*

[230] Cf. *Letter* 2, 7.
[231] On monastic fugitives see Leclercq, 'Documents sur les "fugitifs"'.
[232] Cf. Gen. 4: 11 and 14.
[233] 2 Cor. 7: 5 and above at **61**.
[234] Cf. Gregory the Great, *Dialogi*, ii. 3. 3–4 (ed. Moricca, pp. 80–1; Vogüé, *SChr* cclx. 140–1; *PL* lxvi. 136A). Abelard's account of his troubles at St-Gildas is similar to Gregory's account of Benedict's unsuccessful attempts to reform a rebellious monastic community.

uisitandum uenissem, hospitatum me [p]ibi in domo[p] cuiusdam fratris [q]mei carnalis,[q] per ipsum qui[r] in comitatu [s]nostro erat famulum ueneno interficere[s] machinati sunt, ubi [t]me uidelicet[t] [u]minus a tali machinatione prouidere[u] crediderunt.[235] Diuina autem dispositione tunc actum est, ut dum [v]cibum mihi[v] apparatum non curarem, frater quidam[w] ex monachis quem[x] mecum adduxeram[y] hoc[z] cibo per ignorantiam usus[a] ibidem [b]mortuus occumberet,[b] et famulus ille[c] qui hoc[d] presumpserat tam conscientie[e] sue quam testimonio ipsius rei perterritus aufugeret.[f][236]

72. Ex tunc itaque [a]manifesta omnibus[a] eorum nequitia, patenter iam cepi eorum, prout poteram, insidias declinare, [b]et iam[b] a conuentu abbatie me[c] subtrahere et in cellulis cum paucis habitare.[237] Qui[d] si me transiturum aliquo[e] [f]presensissent, corruptos[f] per pecuniam latrones in uiis aut semitis ut me interficerent opponebant. Dum autem in istis laborarem periculis, forte me[g] die quadam de nostra lapsum equita-

[n] etiam *E after corr. by another hand* [o] nannetum *A;* Nannetum *F;* uanneti *D; om. Y* [p] in domo ibi *T but marked for corr. by T*[4] [q–q] mercarnalis *R* [r] *om. CE* [s–s] uestro erat famulum ueneno prouidere (prouidere *after corr.*) crediderunt diuina autem dispositione interficere *add. B* [t–t] uidelicet me *T* [u–u] minus a tali machinatione timere *A;* minus cauere a tali machinatione *CEF;* a tali machinatione minus prouidere *Y* [v–v] mihi cibum *BRSDY* [w] quidem *C* [x] quam *EB* [y] conduxeram *B* [z] huic *E* [a] uersus *E* [b–b] occumbit *BRDY;* occumberet *S* [c] *om. D* [d] *om. Y* [e] consenciente *A before corr.* [f] affugeret *C;* effugit *B;* effugeret *RDY;* effugerete *S*

72 [a–a] manifestata (manifesta in *superscr. before corr.*) in omnibus *A* [b–b] etiam *Amb* [c] mee *T, A before corr., CE;* moy a soustraire de leur couvent en m'abbaye *J* [d] cui *C* [e] aliqua *BRDY;* aliquam *S* [f–f] presessisseret corruptas *C;* presensissent corrutos *S*

[235] 'comitem' / 'the count': Conan III, on whom see n. 183 above; Nantes was Conan's main residence. Abelard witnessed, as abbot of St-Gildas ('Petrus Abaelardus S. Gildasii abbas'), a charter granted by Conan to the nuns of Notre-Dame du Ronceray at Angers on 15 Mar. 1128; see *Archives d'Anjou*, iii, no. 453, pp. 288–9 (original), no. 423, pp. 259–60 (copy); Morice, *Mémoires*, i, col. 559; Guillotel, *Recueil des actes des ducs de Bretagne*, pp. 414–16; *Checklist* no. 383. Among the witnesses was Ulger, bishop of Angers, on whom see Appendix A, 1, p. 521. 'Cuiusdam fratris mei carnalis' / 'one of my blood brothers': perhaps Porcarius, a canon of the cathedral of Nantes, who became a monk at the Cistercian abbey of Buzé, and who had a nephew, also a canon of Nantes, called Astralabius, both of them being mentioned in a charter issued by Bishop Bernard of Nantes and found in the cartulary of the abbey: 'Porcharius, Nannetensis ecclesiae canonicus, cum apud Buzeium monachus fieret . . . Astralabius, canonicus Nannetensis, nepos ejus'. See 'Charte mentionnant Astralabe, fils d'Abailard (1153–1157)', *Bulletin de la Société des Bibliophiles Breton*, iv (1880–1), 50–1; also Morice, *Mémoires*, i, col. 587. Bernard was bishop of Nantes from 1147 at the earliest; d. 1169 (Morice, *Histoire*, ii: *Cartulaire historique des évêques et abbés de Bretagne*, pp. xvii and cxxxix). Adam, abbot of Buzé from 1153 to 1157 at the latest (*Gallia Christiana*, xiv, col. 861), is one of the witnesses together with his monks ('Adam abbas de Buzeio et monachi sui'). These dates make it likely that Porcarius and Astralabius

chalice. One day also, when I had gone into Nantes to visit the count who was ill, and was staying there in the home of one of my blood brothers, they tried to poison me by the hand of one of the servants accompanying me, supposing, no doubt, that I should be less on my guard against a plot of that kind.[235] By God's intervention it happened that I did not care for any of the food prepared for me. But one of the monks I had brought from the abbey, ate it unknowingly and fell dead there; and the servant who had dared to do this fled in terror of his conscience as much as of the evidence of his crime.[236]

72. From then on their villainy was known to all, and I began to make no secret of the fact that I was avoiding their snares as best I could; I even removed myself from the abbey and lived in small cells with a few companions.[237] But whenever the monks heard that I was travelling anywhere they would bribe robbers and station them on the roads and paths to murder me. I was still struggling against all

were respectively Abelard's brother and son. Buzé (or Buzay or Buzais) is about 20 km west of Nantes in the diocese of Nantes and the commune of Rouans; the abbey was founded in 1135 by Ermengarde and her son Conan. For Abelard's other brothers see n. 6 above; for Astralabe see also **21** above. Less likely is the possibility that Astralabe became the abbot of Hauterive, some 7 km south of Fribourg in Switzerland, who is mentioned in a charter *c.*1162 included in the Cartulary of Hauterive, in *Liber Donationum Altaeripae*, ed. Tremp, no. 74, pp. 139–40 at 139: 'Astralabius abbas Alteripe'. Cf. also 'Liste des abbés de Hauterive depuis la fondation de ce couvent jusqu'à l'année 1302', *Mémorial de Fribourg. Recueil Périodique*, ii (1855), pp. 14–15, and (but this I have not seen) *Le Nécrologe de l'abbaye cistercienne d'Hauterive*, ed. B. de Vevey, unpublished typescript (Berne, 1957), fo. 80, where an Astralabe is named as fourth abbot of Hauterive.

[236] A similar incident is related in a letter, written in June 1166 to Master Raymond, chancellor of Poitiers cathedral, by John of Salisbury: John writes that friends in Paris have told him of an attempt to poison the bishop of Poitiers and that this had resulted in the death of a monastic prior who drank from the poisoned chalice; *Letters of John Salisbury*, ii (ed. Millor and Brooke, no. 166, p. 91). Likewise, Gerald of Wales (1145/6–1223) wrote that Peter Comestor (d. 1178/9) had heard of monks at Tours who, when their abbot was celebrating Mass, mixed poison with the wine in the chalice, so causing his death; *Gemma ecclesiastica*, i. 45 (ed. Brewer, *Opera*, ii. 122; trans. Hagen, pp. 93–4). The death of William Fitz Herbert, archbishop of York, in 1154 was also allegedly caused by poison put into the chalice during Mass by or through the agency of Osbert of Bayeux, the archdeacon of York—a charge, according to E. King, *King Stephen* (New Haven, 2010), p. 299, that was 'inherently unlikely but impossible to disprove'. Allegations of poisoning 'rarely deserve credence' according to Edbury and Rowe, *William of Tyre*, p. 20, writing of the alleged poisoning *c.*1183 of the historian William, archbishop of Tyre, at the bidding of his rival, Patriarch Eraclius: 'perhaps the entire story should be rejected out of hand as the invention of someone out to blacken Eraclius' memory. But it may contain a kernel of truth even if it is overlaid by a measure of fanciful distortion.'

[237] For a map of seventeen priories and churches dependent on the abbey see Tonnerre, *Naissance de la Bretagne*, p. 440.

tura manus Domini uehementer[h] collisit, colli uidelicet mei canalem[i] confringens. Et[j] multo[k] me amplius hec[l] fractura[m] afflixit[n] et debilitauit quam prior plaga.[238]

73. Quandoque[a] horum indomitam rebellionem[b] per excommunicationem cohercens,[c] quosdam[d] eorum, quos magis formidabam, ad hoc compuli ut fide sua seu sacramento publice mihi promitterent[e] se ulterius ab abbatia penitus recessuros,[f] nec me amplius in aliquo inquietaturos. Qui publice[g] et impudentissime tam fidem datam quam sacramenta facta[h] uiolantes,[i] tandem per auctoritatem romani[j] pontificis Innocentii, legato proprio ad hoc destinato, in presentia comitis et episcoporum hoc ipsum iurare compulsi sunt, et pleraque alia; nec sic [k]adhuc quieuerunt.[k] [239] Nuper autem cum,[l] illis quos predixi eiectis, ad conuentum[m] abbatie redissem[n] et reliquis fratribus, quos minus suspicabar,[o] me committerem, multo[p] hos peiores quam[q] illos reperi; quos[r] iam quidem[s] non de ueneno sed de gladio [t]in iugulum[t] meum tractantes[u] cuiusdam proceris terre conductu uix euasi. In quo [v]adhuc etiam[v] laboro periculo, et cotidie quasi ceruici mee[w] gladium imminentem suspitio, ut inter epulas[x] uix respirem,[y] sicut de illo legitur qui, cum[z] Dyonisii[a] tiranni[b] potentiam[c] atque opes conquisitas [d]maxime imputaret beatitudini,[d] filo[e] latenter apensum super se[f] gladium suspitiens,[g] que[h] terrenam potentiam felicitas[i] consequatur edoctus est.[240] Quod nunc [j]quoque ipse[j] de paupere monacho in abbatem promotus incessanter experior,[k] tanto scilicet[l] miserior quanto ditior[m] effectus, ut nostro[n] etiam exemplo eorum qui id sponte appetunt ambitio refrenetur.

[g] m *S* [h] me *add. BRDY;* m *add. S* [i] carnalem *A before corr., D;* canale *CE;* cauale *Y;* elle me froissa le chanolle de mon col *J. Cf. Orlandi, 'Minima Abaelardiana', p. 135;* canolam *is also a possible reading* [j] in *BR;* In *DY* [k] merito *E;* nullo *Y* [l] *om. D* [m] factura *T;* froisseure *J* [n] affluxit *D*

73 [a] quantoque *BRDY;* Quantaque *S* [b] repellionem *RSD* [c] coherens *T before corr.* [d] quorundam *C* [e] non *add. CEF* [f] recessisuros *C* [g] puplice *S* [h] sancta *Y* [i] uiolentes *T before corr., BRSD* [j] rationi *E* [k–k] quieuerunt adhuc *BRSDY* [l] tamen ?*C* [m] que *add. C* [n] redidissem *B;* reddidissem *R before corr., S;* rediissem *Y* [o] supplicabar *D* [p] merito *E;* multoque *Y* [q] quod *R* [r] Quos *T;* Quas *C* [s] quidam *Y* [t–t] inugulum *R* [u] pretractantes *Ycorr.;* pertractantes *Y* [v–v] etiam adhuc (adhuc *add. E by another hand*) *AEF;* etiam ad hoc *C;* adhuc et *DY* [w] mei *D* [x] epistolas *S* [y] repperirent ?*E* [z] *om. S* [a] Dionysii *F* [b] tirannum *BR* [c] potestatem *Amb*[1] [d–d] maxime (*superscr.*) imputaret beatitudini *E;* maximam (maxime *S*) imputaret beatitudinem *SDY* [e] filio *A before corr.* [f] *om. Y*

these perils when, as it so happened, the hand of the Lord struck me sharply one day and I fell from my saddle, breaking my collarbone. This fracture caused me far greater pain and weakened me more than my previous injury.[238]

73. Sometimes I tried to put a stop to their lawless insubordination by excommunication, and compelled those of them I most feared to promise me either on their honour or on oath taken before the rest that they would leave the abbey altogether and trouble me no more. But then they would openly and shamelessly violate both the word they had given and the oaths they had sworn, until in the end they were forced to renew their oaths on this and many other things in the presence of the count and the bishops, by the authority of Innocent, the Roman pontiff, through his special legate sent for this purpose. Even then they would not live in peace.[239] After those mentioned had been expelled, I recently came back to the abbey and entrusted myself to the remaining brothers from whom I thought I had less to fear. I found them even worse than the others. They did not deal with poison but with a sword held to my throat, and it was only under the protection of a certain lord of the land that I managed to escape. I am still in danger, and every day I imagine a sword hanging over my head, so that at meals I dare scarcely breathe, like the man we read about, who supposed the power and wealth of the tyrant Dionysius to constitute the greatest happiness, until he looked up and saw a sword suspended by a thread over his head and then he learned what sort of joy it is which accompanies earthly power.[240] This is my experience all the time: a poor monk raised to be an abbot, the more wretched as I have become more wealthy, in order that my example may curb the ambition of those who deliberately choose to seek the same.

[g] suspericiens *E;* aspiciens *Amb* [h] quam *CEY;* quo *BR* [i] felicitatis *C* [j-j] ipse quoque *BRSDY* [k] experior incessanter *BRSDY* [l] uidelicet *DY* [m] dilectior *B, ?R* [n] magis *E*

[238] The identification with Abelard of Gnato, the parasite who appears in a poem written by a contemporary poet, Hugh Primas of Orleans and Paris (no. 18, verses 94–117, ed. McDonough, pp. 64–5; ed. and trans. Adcock, p. 48)—an identification partly based on the supposition that a scar he bore (*cicatrix*, *v.* 111) resulted from a fall off his horse—has been scotched by McDonough, 'Miscellaneous notes to Hugh Primas', pp. 197–8.

[239] The legate was Geoffrey of Lèves, bishop of Chartres; cf. **40** above.

[240] The sword hung over the head of Damocles, a courtier of Dionysius I, the tyrant of Syracuse (*c.*430–367 BC); cf. Cicero, *Tusculanae disputationes*, v. 21 (61–2).

74. [a] Hec, dilectissime[a] frater in Christo, et ex diutina[b] conuersatione[c] familiarissime comes, de calamitatum mearum hystoria, in quibus quasi [d]a cunabulis[d] iugiter[e] laboro,[f] tue me desolationi[g] atque iniurie illate scripsisse sufficiat, ut, sicut in exordio prefatus sum epistole,[241] oppressionem tuam in comparatione mearum [h]aut nullam[h] aut modicam esse iudices, et tanto eam patientius feras quanto minorem consideras; illud semper in consolationem[i] assumens, quod[j] membris suis[k] de membris diaboli Dominus dixit:[l] 'Si me persecuti [m]sunt, et uos persequentur. Si mundus uos odit,[m] scitote quoniam[n] [o]me priorem[o] uobis[p] odio habuit. Si de mundo fuissetis,[q] mundus[r] quod suum erat diligeret.'[242] Et: 'Omnes', inquit Apostolus,[s] 'qui uolunt pie uiuere in Christo,[t] persequutionem patientur.'[u] [243] [v]Et alibi: 'An[v] [w]quero hominibus placere? Si adhuc hominibus placerem, Christi seruus non essem.'[w] [244] Et[x] Psalmista: 'Confusi sunt', inquit, 'qui hominibus placent, quoniam Deus spreuit eos.'[245] Que[y] diligenter [z]beatus attendens[z] Ieronimus,[a] cuius me[b] precipue in contumeliis[c] detractionum[d] heredem conspicio, ad Nepotianum scribens ait: '"Si adhuc", inquit[e] Apostolus, "hominibus placerem, Christi seruus non essem."[246] Desinit[f] placere hominibus, et [g]seruus factus est[g] Christi.'[247] Idem[h] ad Asellam[i] de fictis amicis:[j] 'Gratias ago[k] Deo[l] meo quod dignus sim[m] quem[n] mundus oderit';[o] [248] et ad Heliodorum[p] monachum: 'Erras,[q] frater, erras si putas[r] umquam[s] Christianum persequutionem non[t] pati. "Aduersarius noster,[u] tanquam leo rugiens, deuorare[v] querens circuit",[249] et tu[w] pacem putas? "Sedet in insidiis cum diuitibus"',[250] [251] etc.[x]

74 [a–a] Hoc dilectissime *AY;* Hec dilectissime *large letters in CE* [b] diutina *TSAmb; preferred by Muckle and by Orlandi, 'Minima Abaelardiana', p. 132;* diuina *ACEBRDY, preferred by Monfrin;* diuturna *F;* diuine *J* [c] conseruatione *BRSY* [d–d] ad cunabulum *S* [e] magis *C* [f] labore *D* [g] dessolacioni *A after corr. of* dissolacioni; desolato *C* [h–h] *om. Y* [i] solationem *Y* [j] in *add. Y* [k] sueis *T before corr. by exp.* [l] predixit *S* [m–m] sunt (*om. E*) et uos persequantur. Si mundus uos odit *CE;* sunt et enim si mundus uos (non *D*) odit *RD;* sunt et nos persequentur si mundus nos odit *S;* sunt uos persequentur. Si mundus uos odit *Y* [n] quia *F* [o–o] priorem me *Y* [p] *om. BRSDY* [q] quod *add. B* [r] sed *?add. C;* mundum *D* [s] apostoli *S* [t] Iesu *add. F* [u] paciuntur *S* [v–v] Et alibi (alibo *C*) aut *TACBRDY;* Et alibi an *EF;* qui(?) ut *S;* Et alibi Haud *Amb. Cf. Orlandi, 'Minima Abaelardiana', p. 134* [w–w] quero hominibus placere (placerem *S*) et Christi seruus (seruus Christi *Y*) non esssem *BRDY* [x] ut *C* [y] Quod *CEF* [z–z] attendens beatus *DY* [a] Jeronimus *CEBRDY;* Hieronymus *FAmb;* Iheronimus *S* [b] hominibus *add. S* [c] contumelia *DY* [d] detractantium *F* [e] inquid *ARD* [f] Desiit *F;* desiuit *al.* desinit *Jerome* [g–g] factus est seruus *D* [h] Illud *CE;* Et illud *F* [i] assellam *ARSY* [j] amicitiis *E* [k] ego *D* [l] domino *E*

74. This, dearest brother in Christ, and closest companion from our long life in religion, is the story of my misfortunes which have dogged me almost since I left my cradle. Let the fact that I have written it with your own affliction and the injury you have suffered in my mind suffice to enable you (as I said at the beginning of this letter)[241] to think of your suffering as little or nothing in comparison with mine, and to bear it with more patience when you can see it in proportion. Take comfort from what the Lord told his followers about the followers of the Devil: 'As they persecuted me, they will persecute you. If the world hates you, know that it hated me first. If you belonged to the world, the world would love its own.'[242] And the Apostle says: 'Persecution will come to all who want to live a godly life as Christians.'[243] And elsewhere: 'Do you think I am currying favour with men? If I still sought men's favour I should be no servant of Christ.'[244] And the Psalmist: 'They are destroyed who seek to please men, since God has rejected them.'[245] It was with this particularly in mind that St Jerome, whose heir I consider myself as regards slanders and false accusations, wrote in his letter to Nepotian: '"If I still sought men's favour", says the Apostle, "I should be no servant of Christ."[246] He has ceased to seek men's favour and is become the servant of Christ.'[247] He also wrote to Asella, concerning false friends: 'Thank God I have deserved the hatred of the world',[248] and to the monk Heliodorus: 'You are wrong, brother, wrong if you think that a Christian can ever be free of persecution. "Our adversary like a roaring lion prowls around, seeking someone to devour",[249] and do you think of peace? "He sits in ambush with the rich"',[250] [251] etc.

[m] sum *CEFBRSDY;* sum *al.* sim *Jerome* [n] quam *CED* [o] aderit *C* [p] eliodorum *BRSDY* [q] *om. S* [r] pautas *C* [s] numquam *ACEBRSDY* [t] *om. Y* [u] meus *?A;* scilicet dyabolus *add. CEF* [v] donare *D;* aliquem deuorare *Jerome* [w] *om. D;* cum *E* [x] *om. CF;* ut in occultis interficiat innocentem *add. F*

[241] 1 above.
[242] John, 15: 20, 18, and 19.
[243] 2 Tim. 3: 12.
[244] Gal. 1: 10. Cf. *Carmen ad Astralabium*, ed. Rubingh-Bosscher, *v.* 469: 'non se homini Paulus credit Christoque placere'.
[245] Ps. 52 (53): 6 (5).
[246] Gal. 1: 10.
[247] Jerome, *Epistola* LII *ad Nepotianum*, 13 (ed. Hilberg, liv. 436, *ll.* 6–8; *PL* xxii. 537).
[248] Jerome, *Epistola* XLV *ad Asellam*, 6 (ed. Hilberg, liv. 327, *ll.* 11–12; *PL* xxii. 482).
[249] 1 Pet. 5: 8.
[250] Ps. 10 (11): 8 (7).
[251] Jerome, *Epistola* XIV *ad Heliodorum monachum*, 4 (ed. Hilberg, liv. 49, *ll.* 6–10; *PL* xxii. 349).

75. His itaque documentis atque exemplis animati, tanto securius ista[a] toleremus[b] quanto iniuriosius accidunt. Que[c] si non ad meritum nobis, saltem ad purgationem aliquam proficere non dubitemus; et quoniam omnia diuina dispositione[d] geruntur,[e] in hoc se saltem quisque[f] fidelium in omni pressura consoletur,[g] quod[h] nichil inordinate fieri umquam[i] [j]summa Dei[j] bonitas permittit, et [k]quod quecumque[k] peruerse[l] fiunt optimo fine ipse terminat;[252] [m]unde et ei de omnibus[m] recte[n] dicitur: 'Fiat uoluntas tua.'[253] Quanta denique diligentium Deum illa est ex auctoritate apostolica consolatio qua[o] dicit: 'Scimus quoniam[p] diligentibus Deum omnia cooperantur in bonum',[254] etc.![q] Quod[r] diligenter ille sapientium[s] sapientissimus attendebat cum in Prouerbiis diceret: 'Non contristabit[t] iustum quicquid ei acciderit.'[255] Ex quo [u]manifeste [v]a iusticia[v] [w]eos recedere[w] demonstrat[x] quicunque pro aliquo[uy] sui[z] grauamine his irascuntur que erga se diuina dispensatione geri non dubitant,[a] et se proprie[b] uoluntati[c] magis quam diuine subiciunt,[d] et ei quod in uerbis sonat:[e] 'Fiat uoluntas tua' desideriis occultis repugnant,[f] diuine uoluntati[g] propriam anteponentes.[h] [256] Vale.[i]

75 [a] ita *TC;* ces choses *J* [b] tollemus *E* [c] Quod *CEF* [d] dispensatione *Amb*[1] [e] disponuntur et *BRDY;* geruntur et *S* [f] omnium *add. D* [g] consolaretur *BRD, Y before exp. of* -ar- [h] quia *D* [i] numquam *ACEBRDY* [j–j] dei summa *CEF* [k–k] quecumque (quodcumque *A before corr. by another hand*) *ACEF* [l] peruerso *F* [m–m] unde et de (de *om. D*) omnibus ei *BRSDY* [n] et *add. A* [o] quae *Amb* [p] ipsum *D* [q] *om. F* [r] Quid *A;* Que *CEF* [s] sapientum *ACEFBRSDY; om. Amb* [t] constrabit *A before corr. by another hand* [u–u] *ditto. Y* [v–v] amicicia *BR* [w–w] recedere eos *DY* [x] denotat *C; vacant space in E* [y] alio *BRS;* [z] suo *Amb* [a] dubitent *E* [b] proprio *D* [c] uocat *?C;* uocati *E* [d] subieciunt *R* [e] sonant *FDY* [f] repugnat *TCRS;* et *add. D;* sont contraire *J* [g] uocat *?C;* uocati *E* [h] anteponens *TBRS;* anteponunt *D;* anteponunt uoluntatem *add. Y;* mettent leur volenté *J* [i] *in majuscule T; om. BDY*

---

252 Cf. *Carmen ad Astralabium*, ed. Rubingh-Bosscher, *v.* 529–30: 'Summa Dei bonitas disponens omnia recte / que bona, que mala sunt ordinat ipsa bene'; also *vv.* 845–59. *Collationes* **128** (ed. and trans. Marenbon and Orlandi, pp. 140–1; *Dialogus*, ed. Thomas *ll.* 2173–4; *PL* clxxviii. 1655B): 'Cum enim nihil sine causa, Deo cuncta optime disponente, fiat . . .' / 'For since God disposes all things in the best way, and there can be nothing without a cause . . .' *Collationes* **219** (ed. and trans. Marenbon and Orlandi, pp. 216–17; *Dialogus*, ed. Thomas *ll.* 3312–14; *PL* clxxviii. 1679A): 'quecunque a quocunque fiant, quia

75. Let us take heart then from these proofs and examples, and bear our wrongs the more cheerfully the more we know they are undeserved. Let us not doubt that, if they add nothing to our merit, at least they contribute to the expiation of our sins. And since everything happens by divine disposition, each one of the faithful, when it comes to the test, must take comfort at least from the knowledge that God's supreme goodness allows nothing to be done outside his plan, and whatever is done wrongly, he himself brings it to the best conclusion.[252] Hence in all things it is right to say to him: 'Thy will be done.'[253] Finally, think what consolation comes to those who love God from the authority of the Apostle who says: 'We know that for those who love God all things work together for good.'[254] This is what the wisest of all wise men had in mind when he said in the book of Proverbs: 'Whatever happens to the righteous man it shall not sadden him.'[255] Here he clearly shows that those who are angered by some personal injury, though they well know it has been laid on them by divine dispensation, leave the path of righteousness and follow their own will rather than God's. They rebel in their secret hearts against the meaning of the words 'Thy will be done', and they set their own will above the will of God.[256] Farewell.

hec ex optima diuine prouidentie dispensatione contingunt, rationabiliter ac bene sic ea prouenire sicut eueniunt.' / 'whatever things are done by whomever, they take place rationally and well in the way in which they actually happen, because they happen as part of the design (which is the best) of divine providence.'

[253] Matt. 6: 10, 26: 42.

[254] Rom. 8: 28. Cf. *Comm. Rom.*, iii (viii. 28).

[255] Solomon in Prov. 12: 21. Cf. *Comm. Rom.*, iv (xii. 15).

[256] Cf. *Rule* 3. *Carmen ad Astralabium*, ed. Rubingh-Bosscher, *v.* 47: 'Semper diuine tua sit subiecta uoluntas' / 'Let your will always be subject to that of God'. *Collationes* **226** (ed. and trans. Marenbon and Orlandi, pp. 222–3; *Dialogus*, ed. Thomas *ll.* 3415–21; *PL* clxxviii. 1681A–1682A): 'Qui etiam sepe per errorem multa nobis minime profutura petimus, que diuina dispositione commodissime nobis a Deo denegantur . . . semper Deo dicendum est: "Fiat uoluntas tua"' / 'We also often through error seek many things which will in no way be to our benefit and which are most fittingly denied us by the plan devised by God . . .; we should always say . . . to God "Thy will be done".' *Ethica*, i. 7, 6 (ed. Ilgner, p. 8; ed. Luscombe, p. 12): 'Quis etenim nobis grates habeat, si in eo, quod pro ipso nos facere dicimus, uoluntatem nostram impleamus?' / 'Who has thanks for us if in what we say we are doing for him we fulfil our own will?'

⟨EPISTOLA II⟩

1. [a]DOMINO[b] SVO IMMO[c] PATRI, CONIVGI[d] SVO[a] IMMO[e] FRATRI; ANCILLA[f] SVA IMMO FILIA, IPSIVS VXOR IMMO SOROR; [g]ABAELARDO HELOYSA[g][1]

Missam ad amicum[h] pro consolatione epistolam, [i]dilectissime, uestram[i] ad me forte[j] quidam[k] nuper attulit.[2] Quam ex ipsa statim tituli fronte uestram esse considerans, tanto ardentius [l]eam cepi legere[l] quanto scriptorem ipsum carius[m] amplector, ut cuius rem perdidi uerbis[n] saltem tanquam eius [o]quadam imagine[o] recreer.

2. Erant, memini,[a] huius epistole [b]fere omnia[b] felle et absinthio plena,[3] que[c] scilicet nostre conuersionis[d] miserabilem historiam et tuas, unice, cruces assiduas[e] referebant. Complesti reuera in [f]epistola illa[f] quod in exordio[g] eius amico promisisti,[h] ut uidelicet in comparatione tuarum suas molestias [i]nullas uel paruas[i] reputaret.[4] Vbi quidem expositis prius[j] magistrorum[k] tuorum [l]in te[l] persecutionibus,[m] deinde in corpus tuum summe proditionis[n] iniuria, ad[o] condiscipulorum[p] quoque tuorum,[q] Alberici uidelicet Remensis et Lotulfi[r] Lumbardi,[s] execrabilem inuidiam et infestationem nimiam stilum contulisti. Quorum quidem suggestionibus[t] quid[u] de glorioso

Letter 2 *T* fos. 18ra–21rb; *A* fos. 14ra–16rb; *C* fos. 154^{r}–158^{r}; *E* fos. 14^{v}–17^{r}; *F* pp. 10–19; *B* fos. 14ra–16ra; *R* fos. 125vb–128rb; *S* fos. 19^{v}–25^{v}; *D* fos. 328^{r+v}; *Y* fos. 97vb–100ra; *Amb* pp. 41–8; *Amb*[1] *variants in the margins of Amb*; *J* pp. 58–70. *Headings are found in the following witnesses*: Heloyse sue (sue *om. BS*) ad ipsum deprecatoria *rubr. TBS;* epistola ((epistol)a *E*) heloysse ad p. *A* (*by another hand*), *C, E* (*by a later hand in marg.*)*; vacant space in R;* Comme Heloyse li escript ses doleurs ij[c] xij *table in H of the* (*missing*) *contents of Dijon MS 525;* Epistola heloysse misse abaelardo suo amico *Y*[1] *in vacant space;* EPISTOLA II. Quae est HELOISSAE ad PETRUM Deprecatoria *Amb*

1 [a–a] *large letters in E with space left for an initial* [b] *large initial in TABRSYAmb; space left for an initial in CD* [c] karissimo *S* [d] amori *B* [e] karissimo *S* [f] Ancilla *TY* [g–g] Abaelardo. heloysa *T;* abaelardo. heloysa *A;* abalardo heloissa *C;* abaelardo heloyssa *E;* Abaelardo Heloyssa *F;* Abaelardo. Heloysa *B;* Abaelardo heloysa *R;* abaelardo heloysa *S;* abelardo heloysa *D;* Abaelardo. heloissa *Y;* Abaelardo Heloissa *Amb* [h] nostre ami *J* [i–i] dilectissime *CEF;* uestram dilectissime *BRSDY; probably* dilectissime uestrum *in J's exemplar according to Dronke, Women Writers, p. 304, n. 12 and p. 113, who suggests that the sentence read as follows:* Missam ad amicum ⟨nostrum⟩ pro consolatione epistolam, dilectissime, vestrum ad me quidam nuper attulit. (*'Dearest one, your man has recently shown me your letter, which you sent to our friend for consolation.'*) [j] not translated in *J* [k] quidem *BRS,?D,Y;* uoz homs *J* [l–l] cepi legere eam *BRSDY* [m] carissimus *E before corr.* [n] *om. CEF* [o–o] imagine *BRY;* imagine quadam *S;* imaginem *D*

LETTER 2

1. TO HER LORD OR RATHER HER FATHER, HUSBAND OR RATHER BROTHER; FROM HIS HANDMAID OR RATHER HIS DAUGHTER, WIFE OR RATHER SISTER; TO ABELARD FROM HELOISE[1]

Not long ago, my dearest love, someone by chance brought me the letter of consolation you had sent to a friend.[2] Seeing at once from the opening passage that it was yours, I began to read it all the more eagerly since the writer is so dear to my heart. I hoped for renewal of strength, at least from the writer's words which would picture for me the reality I have lost.

2. But nearly every line of this letter was filled, I remember, with gall and wormwood,[3] as it told the pitiful story of our entry into monastic life and the cross of unending suffering which you, my one-and-only, continue to bear. In that letter you did indeed carry out the promise you made your friend at the beginning, that he would think his own troubles insignificant or nothing in comparison with your own.[4] First you revealed the persecutions you suffered from your teachers, then the supreme treachery of the mutilation of your person, and then you described the execrable envy and violent attacks of your fellow-students, Alberic of Reims and Lotulf of Lombardy. You did not gloss over what at their instigation was done to your glorious book of

2 [a] uerba *add. in marg.* A^2 [b–b] omnia fere *BRSDY* [c] *om. D* [d] conuersationis *CB;* conuersacionis *RSD* [e] assidue *RDY* [f–f] illa epistola *D;* epistola in (*followed by vacant space*) illa *Y* [g] oxordio *Amb* [h] permisisti *S* [i–i] paruas (penas *D*) aut (ut *Y*) nullas *BRSDY* [j] *om. D* [k] uitiorum *BRY;* (ini)micorum *?D* [l–l] uite *CY* [m] persecutionis *E* [n] perdicionis *A* [o] a *BY* [p] discipulorum *SD;* quibusdam discipulorum *Y* [q] suorum *E* [r] lotulphi *CEF;* lotulfi *B;* loculfi *R;* Loculfi *D;* loculphi *Y* [s] lombardi *BRSY;* Lombardi *DAmb* [t] subiestionibus *B;* subiectionibus *RS* [u] *om. DY*

---

[1] Cf. the similar phrasing in a letter from Heloise to Peter the Venerable: 'Quod itaque sorori immo ancillae concessistis, frater immo dominus impleatis' (*Letters of Peter the Venerable*, ed. Constable, i, no. 167, pp. 400–1; *PL* clxxxix. 428A).

[2] Cf. the heading of a letter of Peter of Blois (written probably 1208 × 1211): 'consolatoria missa cuidam amico . . .' (*The Later Letters of Peter of Blois*, ed. Revell, no. 66, p. 289).

[3] 'felle et absinthio plena': cf. Jer. 23: 15; Prov. 5: 4.

[4] Cf. *Letter* 1, **1** and **74**.

illo *Theologie* tue[v] opere, quid de teipso quasi in carcere damnato,[w] actum sit non pretermisisti. Inde ad abbatis tui fratrumque falsorum machinationem accessisti, et detractiones illas tibi grauissimas duorum illorum[x] pseudoapostolorum[5] a predictis emulis [y]in te[y] commotas, atque ad scandalum plerisque[z] subortum de nomine Paracliti[a] oratorio preter consuetudinem imposito. Denique ad intolerabiles illas et adhuc continuas [b]in te[b] persecutiones, crudelissimi scilicet illius exactoris, et pessimorum, quos filios nominas, monachorum profectus miserabilem historiam consummasti.

3. [a]Que cum[a] siccis oculis[6] neminem uel legere uel audire posse [b]estimem; tanto[b] dolores meos [c]amplius renouarunt[cd] quanto[e] diligentius singula[f] expresserunt, et eo magis auxerunt quo in te adhuc [g]pericula crescere[g] [h]retulisti, ut omnes pariter de uita tua desperare cogamur, et quotidie [i]ultimos[h] illos[i] de nece[j] tua rumores trepidantia nostra corda et palpitantia pectora expectent.[k] Per ipsum itaque, qui te sibi adhuc quoquomodo protegit, Christum obsecramus quatinus[l] ancillulas[m] ipsius et tuas crebris litteris de his, in[n] quibus adhuc fluctuas, naufragiis[o] certificare digneris, ut nos saltem, que tibi sole remansimus, doloris[p] uel gaudii participes[q] habeas.

4. Solent etenim dolenti nonnullam afferre[a] consolationem qui condolent, et quodlibet onus pluribus impositum leuius sustinetur siue defertur. Quod si paululum hec tempestas quieuerit, tanto amplius maturande sunt littere[b] quanto sunt iucundiores[c] future. De quibuscunque[d] autem nobis scribas,[e] non paruum [f]nobis remedium[f] conferes; hoc saltem uno quod te nostri memorem esse monstrabis. Quam iucunde[g] uero sint[h] [i]absentium littere amicorum,[i] ipse nos exemplo proprio Seneca docet, ad amicum Lucilium[j] quodam loco sic scribens: ‘Quod frequenter mihi scribis, gratias ago. Nam[k] quo [l]uno modo[l] potes te mihi ostendis.[m] Nunquam epistolam tuam accipio, quin[n] protinus una simus.[o] Si imagines

[v] tuo *DY* [w] deputato *RD;* de privato *Y* [x] uidelicet *add. RS;* scilicet *add. DY* [y–y] inde *BRY* [z] plerumque *BRDY* [a] paracleti *F;* Paracleti *Amb* [b–b] uite *TA;* vitae *Amb*

3 [a–a] Qui cum *D;* Quecumque *Y* [b–b] estima (*before add. by corr. above the line of* rem uel estimem) tanto *A;* estimemus tanto *CEF;* estimentendo *S* [c–c] renouarunt *ACE;* renouauerunt *F;* renouare amplius *D with a stroke over* -re*;* amplius renouari *Y* [d] renouare Y [e] quam *BS* [f] *om. E;* cuncta *F;* singulula *B* [g–g] crescere pericula *DY* [h–h] *om. C* [i–i] ultra suos *E;* ultra illos *F* [j] uoce *Y* [k] expectant *CERSDY* [l] quatenus *FAmb* [m] ancillas *RSDY* [n] *om. CEF* [o] naufragus *Amb*[1] [p] dolores *E* [q] particeps *A*

Theology or what amounted to a prison sentence passed on yourself. Then you went on to the plotting against you by your abbot and false brethren, the serious slanders from those two pseudo-apostles,[5] spread against you by the same rivals, and the scandal stirred up among many people because you had acted contrary to custom in naming your oratory after the Paraclete. And finally you went on to the incessant, intolerable persecutions which you still endure at the hands of that cruel tyrant and the evil monks you call your sons, and so brought your wretched story to an end.

3. No one, I think, could read or hear it dry-eyed;[6] it renewed more fully my sorrows as it expressed more diligently every detail, and it increased them all the more because you say your dangers are increasing still. All of us are driven to despair of your life, and every day we await in fear and trembling the final word of your death. And so in the name of Christ, who is still giving you some protection for his service, we beseech you to write as often as you think fit to us who are his handmaids and yours, with news of the perils in which you are still storm-tossed. We are all that are left you, so at least you should let us share your sorrow or your joy.

4. It is often some consolation in sorrow to feel that it is shared, and any burden laid on several is carried more lightly or removed. And if this storm has quietened down for a while, you must be all the more prompt to send us a letter which will be the more gladly received. But whatever you write about for us will bring us no small relief in the mere proof that you have us in mind. Letters from absent friends are welcome indeed, as Seneca himself shows us by his own example when he writes these words in one of his letters to his friend Lucilius: 'Thank you for writing to me often, the one way in which you can make your presence felt, for I never have a letter from you without the immediate feeling that we are together. If pictures of absent

4 [a] aufferre *D* [b] tue *add. E* [c] iocundiores *C before exp., SY;* recundiores *C after exp.* [d] quibuslibet *F* [e] scribis *Y* [f-f] remedium nobis *CEF* [g] reconde *C* [h] sunt *C before corr., Y* [i-i] littere amicorum absencium *BRSDY* [j] Lucillum *F;* bacilium *?D* [k] non *D* [l-l] *vacant space R;* modo *DY* [m] offendis *R* [n] Vt non *F and Seneca;* quim *D;* quoniam *Y before corr. by Y*[1] [o] sumus *D*

[5] Cf. 2 Cor. 11: 13 and *Letter* 1, 58.

[6] Cf. with reference to the Lord's Passion, *Sermon* 11: 'Quis siccis oculis hoc intelligat?' (*PL* clxxviii. 470A); also Jerome, *Epistola* XXXIX *ad Paulam de morte Blesillae*, 1 (ed. Hilberg, liv. 294, *ll.* 3–4; *PL* xxii. 465) and Horace, *Carmina*, i. 3, *v.* 18.

nobis amicorum[p] absentium[q] iucunde[r] sunt,[s] que memoriam renouant et desiderium absentie falso atque inani solatio leuant, quanto iucundiores sunt littere que [t]amici absentis ueras[t] notas afferunt?'[7] Deo autem gratias, quod hoc[u] saltem modo presentiam tuam nobis reddere nulla inuidia[v] prohiberis, nulla difficultate[w] prepediris,[x] nulla, obsecro,[y] negligentia retarderis.[z]

5. Scripsisti[a] ad amicum prolixe[b] consolationem epistole, et pro aduersitatibus quidem suis, sed[c] de tuis. Quas uidelicet tuas diligenter commemorans, cum eius intenderes[d] [e]consolationi, nostre plurimum addidisti[f] desolationi;[e] et dum eius mederi uulneribus cuperes, [g]noua quedam[g] nobis uulnera doloris[h] inflixisti et priora auxisti. Sana, obsecro, ipsa[i] que fecisti, qui que alii fecerunt curare[j] satagis.[k] Morem[l] quidem amico et socio gessisti,[m] et tam[n] amicitie quam societatis debitum persoluisti, [o]sed maiore[o] te debito[p] nobis astrinxisti,[q] quas non tam amicas quam amicissimas,[r] non tam socias quam filias, conuenit nominari, uel [s]si quod dulcius[s] et sanctius uocabulum potest[t] excogitari.[8] Quanto autem debito te erga eas[u] obligaueris, non argumentis, non testimoniis indiget,[v 9] ut quasi dubium comprobetur;[w] et si omnes taceant, res ipsa clamat.[10]

6. Huius quippe loci [a]tu, post Deum,[a] solus es fundator, solus huius oratorii constructor, solus huius congregationis edificator.[11] Nihil hic super alienum edificasti fundamentum.[12] Totum quod hic est, tua creatio est. Solitudo[13] hec[b] feris tantum, siue[c] latronibus uacans, nullam hominum habitationem nouerat, nullam domum habuerat.[d]

[p] nostrorum *add. BRSDY* [q] absencie *D* [r] reconde *C* [s] sint *CBRSDY* [t–t] amici absentes ueras *E;* uera amici absentis uestigia *F;* amici (amici *after corr. by Y*[1]) absentis ueras *Y* [u] ad *Y*, *exp. Y*[1] [v] *om. CEF* [w] diffinitate *E* [x] prohiberis (prohiberis *marked for exp.*) prepederis *T;* impedieris *B;* impediris *RY;* impendiris *D* [y] obsectio *E* [z] recitarderis *E*

5 [a] scripsi *E* [b] prolixum *T before corr.* [c] *om. RDY* [d] intenderis *Y;* studeres *Amb*[1] [e–e] consolacioni (consolacionem *R*) plurimum nostram addidisti desolacionem *RDY* [f] addisti *C;* adisti *E* [g–g] nouae quaedam *F;* noua que *S* [h] *om. F* [i] *om. DY;* ipse *Amb* [j] cruciare vel curare *B* [k] satagis *over eras. in T* [l] Moram *BS* [m] fecisti *BRD, Y before corr. by Y*[1] [n] *om. CE* [o–o] et maiori *Y* [p] debita *BRS* [q] abstrinxisti *C;* astruxisti *Y* [r] amicicissimas *E* [s–s] siquidem dilectius *B* [t–t] inueniri uel *add. CEF* [u] eas *F after corr., in marg. R* [v] indico *BRD;* iudico *Y* [w] probetur *F*

6 [a–a] post deum tu *D* [b] hic *E* [c] sine *S* [d] locus iste *add. ?C, ?E, F*

[7] Seneca, *Epistola* 40 *ad Lucilium*, 1.

friends give us pleasure, renewing our memories and relieving the pain of separation even if they cheat us with empty comfort, how much more welcome are letters which come to us in the very handwriting of an absent friend?'[7] Thank God that here at least is a way of restoring your presence to us which no envy can prevent, nor any obstacle hinder; do not then, I beseech you, allow any negligence to hold you back.

5. You wrote your friend a long letter of consolation, prompted no doubt by his adversities, but really telling of your own. The careful account you gave of these, when you were intent upon his consolation, added greatly to our desolation; in your desire to heal his wounds you have dealt us fresh wounds of grief as well as increasing the old. I beseech you, then, as you try to tend the wounds which others have caused, to heal those you have yourself inflicted. You have done right by a friend and comrade, paying your debt to friendship and companionship, but you bound yourself by a greater debt to us who should properly be called not friends so much as dearest friends, not companions but daughters, or any sweeter, holier name if such can be conceived.[8] How great the debt by which you have bound yourself to us needs neither proof nor witness,[9] were it in any doubt; if everyone kept silent, the facts themselves would cry out.[10]

6. For you alone, after God, are the founder of this place, you alone the builder of this oratory, you alone the creator of this community.[11] You have built nothing here upon another man's foundation.[12] Everything here is your own creation. This was a wilderness[13] open only to wild beasts and brigands, a place which had known no home

[8] 'si quod dulcius . . .': for the wide culture of friendship which shapes this passage see McEvoy, 'The theory of friendship'. Cf. also **10** below.

[9] Cf. Heloise in the preface to the *Problemata*, where, after illustrating Jerome's commendation of Marcella's study of scriptural questions, she writes: 'Non sunt haec documenta, sed monita, ut ex his quid debeas recorderis, et debitum soluere non pigriteritis' (*PL* clxxviii. 677D–678B).

[10] 'si omnes taceant . . .': cf. *Letter* 1, **6** and note.

[11] Cf. *Letter* 6, **33**. Also the *Cartulary of the Paraclete*: 'XI Kal. (maii) obiit Petrus Abelardus fundator' (ed. Lalore, p. vi, n. 1), an addition to the Calendar of the Paraclete in Chaumont, Bibliothèque municipale, MS 31, fol. 3v (a.d. XI. Kal. Maii): 'Obiit Petrus Abaelardus fundator', and the *Obituary of the Paraclete*: 'Anniuersarium magistri nostri Petri Abaelardi, loci huius fundatoris nostreque religionis institutoris' (*Obituaires de la province de Sens*, iv, ed. Molinier (21 Apr.), p. 412F). 'solus . . . solus . . . solus': cf. **9** below; also the doxology *Gloria in excelsis Deo*: 'tu solus Sanctus. Tu solus Dominus. Tu solus Altissimus . . .'.

[12] Cf. Rom 15: 20; *Letter* 6, **33**.

[13] Cf. *Letter* 1, **52**.

In ipsis cubilibus ferarum,[e] in ipsis latibulis latronum,[f] ubi[g] nec nominari Deus solet, diuinum erexisti tabernaculum, et Spiritus sancti proprium dedicasti[h] templum.[14] Nihil ad hoc edificandum ex regum uel principum opibus[i] intulisti, [j]cum plurima posses et maxima, ut quidquid fieret tibi soli[k] posset ascribi.[j] Clerici siue[l] scolares huc certatim ad disciplinam tuam confluentes omnia ministrabant necessaria; et [m]qui de[m] beneficiis uiuebant ecclesiasticis, nec oblationes facere nouerant sed suscipere, et qui manus ad suscipiendum, non ad dandum, habuerant, hic in oblationibus faciendis prodigi[n] atque importuni fiebant.[15]

7. Tua itaque, uere tua, hec est[a] proprie[b] in sancto proposito nouella plantatio,[16] cuius adhuc teneris maxime plantis[c] frequens, ut proficiant,[d] necessaria est[e] irrigatio. Satis ex ipsa feminei sexus natura debilis est hec plantatio et[f] infirma, [g]etiamsi non[g] esset noua. Vnde diligentiorem culturam exigit et frequentiorem, iuxta illud Apostoli: 'Ego plantaui, Apollo[h] rigauit,[i] Deus[j] autem incrementum dedit.'[k] [17] Plantauerat Apostolus atque fundauerat in fide per[l] predicationis sue doctrinam[m] Corinthios, quibus scribebat. Rigauerat[n] [o]postmodum eos[o] ipsius Apostoli discipulus[p] Apollo[q] sacris exhortationibus, et sic eis[r] incrementum uirtutum[s] diuina largita[t] est gratia. Vitis aliene uineam, quam non plantasti, in amaritudinem[u] tibi conuersam,[18] admonitionibus sepe cassis, et sacris frustra sermonibus excolis.[v] Quid tue[w] debeas attende, qui sic curam impendis[x] aliene.[y] Doces et ammones[z] rebelles, nec proficis. Frustra ante porcos[a] diuini eloquii[b] margaritas spargis.[19] Qui[c] obstinatis[d] tanta impendis,[e] quid obedientibus debeas considera. Qui tanta hostibus largiris,[f] quid filiabus debeas meditare. Atque ut[g] ceteras omittam, quanto erga me te obligaueris

[e] fera est *BRD*, *?Y before corr.* [f] *om. Y* [g] ut *BRD;* ubi *Y*[1] *over eras.* [h] edificasti *D* [i] operibus *BRS* [j–j] *om. CEF* [k] *om. BRDY* [l] seu *B* [m–m] quidem *B;* qui *DY* [n] *vacant space in B*

7 [a] *om. S* [b] propria *F* [c] plantas *D* [d] perficiant *S* [e] autem *S* [f] est *Amb* [g–g] etiam si (sed *EF*) *CEF;* etsi non *Amb* [h] appollo *E* [i] rogavit *D* [j] dominus *?C, BRSDY* [k] *om. C* [l] proprie *add. BRDY* [m] ad *add. Y* [n] Rogauerat *D* [o–o] eos postmodum *BRSDY* [p] discipulis *marked for corr. in A;* discipulos *E* [q] appollo *E* [r] eas *R before corr.* [s] *om. S* [t] largiata *D* [u] amaritudine *B* [v] ex talis *S* [w] unice *add. CE;* uineae *add. F* [x] et *add. S* [y] aliene[s] *R;* alienis *DY; D ends here* [z] admones *add. by E corr. in vacant space, Amb* [a] porcas *C;* deporcos *S* [b] eloqui *R* [c] quid *BRS* [d] estiuatis *R;* astinatis *S* [e] impendens *C* [f] satageris *R;* satagēs *Y* [g] *om. BR*

nor habitation of men. In the very lairs of wild beasts and lurking-places of robbers, where the name of God was never heard, you built a sanctuary to God and dedicated a shrine in the name of the Holy Spirit.[14] To build it you drew nothing from the riches of kings and princes, though their wealth was great and could have been yours for the asking: whatever was done, the credit was to be yours alone. Clerks and scholars came flocking here, eager for your teaching, and ministered to all your needs; and even those who had lived on the benefices of the Church and knew only how to receive offerings, not to make them, whose hands were held out to take but not to give, here became prodigal and relentless in the help they gave.[15]

7. And so it is yours, truly your own, this new plantation for God's purpose,[16] but it is sown with plants which are still very tender and need watering if they are to thrive. Through its feminine nature this plantation is weak and frail and would be so even if it were not new; and so it needs a more careful and regular cultivation, according to the words of the Apostle: 'I planted the seed and Apollos watered it; but God made it grow.'[17] The Apostle through the doctrine that he preached had planted and established in the faith the Corinthians, to whom he was writing. Afterwards the Apostle's own disciple, Apollos, had watered them with his holy exhortations and so God's grace bestowed on them growth in the virtues. You cultivate a vineyard of another's vines which you did not plant yourself and which has now turned to bitterness against you,[18] so that often your advice brings no result and your holy words are uttered in vain. You devote your care to another's vineyard; think what you owe to your own. You teach and admonish rebels to no purpose, and in vain you throw pearls of divine eloquence to pigs.[19] While you spend so much on the stubborn, consider what you owe to the obedient; you are so generous to your enemies but should reflect on what you owe to your daughters. Apart from everything else, consider the close tie by which you have bound yourself to me, and repay the debt you owe a whole

[14] Cf. *Letter* 1, **54**.

[15] Cf. *Letter* 1, **52**.

[16] 'nouella plantatio': cf Cassian, *Collationes*, xx. 4. 3: 'prima plantatio' (ed. Petschenig, xiii. 558; repr. with French trans. by Pichery, *SChr* lxiv. 60–1; *PL* xlix. 1153B). Also *Sermon* 30 (*PL* clxxviii. 569A): 'nouella eius adhuc et tenera plantatio uestris, ut crescat, colenda est eleemosynis'.

[17] 1 Cor. 3: 6. Cf. Jerome, *Epistola* VII *ad Chromatium, Jouinum et Eusebium*, 4 (ed. Hilberg, liv. 29, *ll.* 9–10; *PL* xxii. 340); *Epistola* CXXX *ad Demetriadem de servanda virginitate*, 2 (ed. Hilberg, lvi. 177, *ll.* 12–13; *PL* xxii. 1108 *sup*).

[18] Cf. Jer. 2: 21.

[19] Matt. 7: 6.

debito[h] pensa, ut quod[i] deuotis communiter debes[j] feminis, unice[k] tue deuotius soluas.[20]

8. Quot[a] autem et quantos tractatus in doctrina uel exhortatione seu etiam consolatione sanctarum feminarum sancti patres consummauerint,[b] et quanta eos[c] diligentia composuerint,[d] [e]tua melius excellentia[e] quam nostra[f] paruitas[g] nouit.[21] [h]Vnde non mediocri admiratione nostre tenera conuersacionis[i] initia tua iamdudum [j]obliuio mouit,[h] quod[j] nec[k] reuerentia Dei nec amore nostri nec [l]sanctorum patrum[l] exemplis admonitus fluctuantem me et iam diutino[m] merore[n] confectam, uel sermone[o] presentem uel epistola absentem, consolari tentaueris. Cui quidem tanto [p]te maiore debito[p] noueris obligatum quanto[q] te amplius nuptialis federe sacramenti constat esse astrictum; et eo [r]te magis mihi[r] obnoxium quo te semper, ut omnibus patet, immoderato[s] amore complexa sum.

9. Nosti,[a] karissime, nouerunt[b] omnes quanta in te amiserim et quam miserabili casu summa et ubique nota proditio meipsam quoque mihi tecum abstulerit, ut[c] incomparabiliter maior sit dolor ex amissionis modo quam ex damno. Quo uero maior est dolendi causa, maiora sunt consolationis adhibenda remedia, non utique ab alio sed a teipso, ut qui solus es in causa dolendi, solus sis [d]in gratia[d] consolandi. Solus quippe es[e] qui [f]me contristare, qui me laetificare seu consolari, ualeas.[g] Et solus es qui[fh] plurimum id mihi debeas, et[i] nunc[j] maxime, cum uniuersa que iusseris in tantum impleuerim[k] ut, cum te in aliquo offendere non possem, me ipsam pro iussu tuo perdere sustinerem.[22] Et[l] quod maius est dictuque mirabile, in tantam [m]uersus est [n]amor[m] insaniam[n] ut quod solum appetebat, hoc ipse sibi sine spe recuperationis auferret, cum ad tuam statim iussionem[23] tam habitum

[h] debite *EBRY* [i] quicquid *BS* [j] exhibes *F* [k] unicu *Y* (*sic*)

8 [a] Quod *T* [b] consummauerunt *T before corr. by exp., BRSY, om. Amb* [c] eas *T before corr.;* eos *T*ᴵ, *in marg.;* eas *ACES* [d] ut *add. B;* composuerunt *RY* [e–e] melius excellentia *R;* melius excellentia tua *Y* [f] mea *F* [g] unitas *Y;* simplicitas *Y*ᴵ [h–h] *om. CEF* [i] conuersionis *TCEFAmb;* conuersacionis *ABRSY;* conversacion *J; cf. Gilson, Heloise and Abelard, pp. 147–66; Héloïse et Abélard, pp. 172–91, 192–207* [j–j] abñtio nouit qui *Y* [k] si nec *F* [l–l] patrum sanctorum *Y* [m] diutiuo *Amb* [n] memore *R* [o] sermonem *B;* seruicio *S* [p–p] maiore debito te *Y* [q] quante *S* [r–r] te mihi magis *ACEFS;* magis esse *BRY* [s] immoderata *R*

9 [a] Nostri *Amb* [b] nouerint *A;* et nouerunt *Y* [c] et *TAmb* [d–d] in *CE;* et gratia *F* [e] est *E* [f–f] *om. CEF* [g] uales *Y* [h] quid *S* [i] *om. F* [j] tunc *Amb* [k] compleuerim *Y* [l] ut *CE* [m–m] uersus estimor *B;* uersus *R;* auersus(?) meus uersus est *Y* [n–n] amoris saniam *S*

community of devoted women by discharging it the more devotedly to her who is yours alone.[20]

8. In your pre-eminence you know better than we in our insignificance how many and how great are the treatises which the holy Fathers compiled for the instruction or exhortation or even the consolation of holy women, and with what great care they were composed.[21] And so I was not a little surprised by your forgetfulness during the fragile beginnings of our life in religion here, some time ago now, and troubled that neither reverence for God nor love for us nor the examples of the holy Fathers made you think of trying to comfort me, wavering and exhausted as I was by prolonged grief, either by word when I was with you or by letter when I was not. Yet you must know that you are bound to me by an obligation which is all the greater for the further close tie of the sacrament of marriage uniting us, and that you are the deeper in my debt because of the love I have always borne you, as everyone knows, a love which is beyond all bounds.

9. You know, dearest love, as everyone knows, how much I have lost in you, how at one wretched stroke of fortune that supreme act of flagrant treachery robbed me of my very self in robbing me of you; and how my sorrow for my loss is nothing compared with what I feel for the manner in which I lost you. Surely the greater the cause for grief the greater the need for the help of consolation, and this no one can bring but you; you who alone are the cause of my sorrow, be alone in granting me the grace of consolation. You alone indeed have the power to make me sad, to bring me joy or comfort. You alone owe me so much, particularly now when I have carried out all your orders to such an extent that when I was powerless to oppose you in anything, I found strength at your command to destroy myself.[22] I did more, strange to say—my love rose to such heights of madness that it robbed itself of what it most desired beyond hope of recovery, when at your command[23] I changed my clothing at once along with my

[20] Cf. 1 Cor. 7: 3: 'uxori uir debitum reddat'.

[21] Cf. *Letter* 7, **47**; 'tua melius excellentia quam nostra paruitas nouit'. Cf. *Epistola Heloissae ad Petrum Abaelardum* (Heloise's preface to the *Problemata*): 'uestra melius prudentia quam mea simplicitas nouit' (*PL* clxxviii. 677B) and Heloise, *Letter* to Peter the Venerable: 'ad paruitatem nostram magnitudo uestra descenderit' (*Letters of Peter the Venerable*, ed. Constable, i. 400).

[22] 'solus es . . . solus sis . . . solus quippe es . . . solus es': cf. above, **6**.

[23] 'iussionem' follows closely upon 'iusseris' and 'iussu'; cf. **15** below and *Letters* 1, **31** and 4, **14**.

ipsa quam animum immutarem, ut [o]te tam[o] corporis mei quam [p]animi unicum[p] possessorem ostenderem.

10. Nihil unquam,[a] Deus[b] scit, in te nisi te requisiui, te pure non tua concupiscens.[24] Non matrimonii federa, non dotes aliquas, expectaui, [c]non denique [d]meas uoluptates[d] sed tuas, sicut[c] ipse nosti, [e]adimplere studui.[e] Et si uxoris nomen sanctius ac ualidius uidetur,[f] dulcius [g]mihi semper[g] extitit amice uocabulum[25] aut, si non indigneris, concubine uel scorti, ut quo me uidelicet pro te amplius humiliarem, ampliorem apud te consequerer gratiam, [h]et sic etiam[h] excellentie tue gloriam minus lederem. Quod et tu ipse tui[i] gratia [j]oblitus penitus[j] non[k] fuisti[l] in ea, quam supra memini, ad amicum epistola [m]pro consolatione[m] directa, ubi et rationes nonnullas, quibus te a coniugio nostro [n]et infaustis thalamis[n] reuocare conabar,[o] exponere non es[p] dedignatus,[q] sed plerisque tacitis[r] quibus amorem [s]coniugio, libertatem uinculo[s] preferebam.[t] Deum testem inuoco, si me Augustus[u] uniuerso presidens mundo matrimonii[v] honore[w] dignaretur, totumque [x]mihi orbem[x] confirmaret in[y] perpetuo possidendum,[z] karius mihi et dignius uideretur tua dici meretrix quam illius imperatrix.[26]

[o–o] tam te *in T but marked for corr. by* T^4 [p–p] cum unicum *C;* animi unius *S;* animum *Amb*

10 [a] inquam *BR* [b] *add. B corr. in vacant space* [c–c] T^3 *over eras.; eras. also in marg.* [d–d] meas uoluptates aut uoluntates *TBRSYAmb;* mes deliz *J* [e–e] adimplere *R* studui adimplere *Y* [f] uideretur *AEF* [g–g] semper mihi *BSY* [h–h] sic et *E* [i] *om. E;* mei *F* [j–j] oblitus *CEF;* penitus oblitus *BRSY* [k] *om. S* [l] fuistis *CE* [m–m] consolatione *R;* consolationis *Y* [n–n] et (et *add.* T^1 *in marg.*) in faustis thalamis *TACEFAmb;* infaustisque thalamis (talamis *B*) *BR;* infaustis talamis *S;* infaustisque his talentis *Y* [o] cognabat *S* [p] est *ES* [q] dignatus *B* (*a space precedes*), *R* [r] tantis *R* [s–s] coniugio libertatem coniugio *F before corr.;* coniugio libertatem uingulo *B;* uicto libertatem uinculo *R;* inuito *Y* [t] *om. BS* [u] auxatus *B* [v] matrimonio *C;* matrimonii *add. in vacant space by another hand in E* [w] decorare *add.* Y^1 [x–x] orbem michi *Y* [y] *om. F* [z] presidendum *TS;* praesidendum *Amb*

[24] See *Letter* 5, **29** for Abelard's admission that his love for Heloise was lustful and not, as hers was for him, disinterested. The one who truly loves her is Christ himself: 'He is the true friend who desires yourself, not what is yours . . . It was he who truly loved you, not I' ('Verus est amicus qui teipsam non tua desiderat . . . Amabat te ille ueraciter, non ego. Amor meus . . . concupiscentia, non amor, dicendus est'). On true love being selfless see *Comm. Rom.* iii (vii. 13; pp. 201–2) where, after citing Augustine, *De diuersis quaestionibus octaginta tribus*, xxxv. 1: 'Quid amandum sit' (ed. Mutzenbecher, xlivA. 50; *PL* xl. 23) and *Enarrationes in Psalmos*, liii. 10 (ed. Dekkers and Fraipont, xxxix. 653–4; *PL* xxxvi. 626), Abelard writes: 'Ex his itaque beati Augustini uerbis aperte declaratur quae sit uera in aliquem ac sincera dilectio, ipsum uidelicet propter se, non propter sua diligit.' Also *TChr*,

mind, in order to prove you the unique possessor of my body and my mind alike.

10. God knows I never sought anything in you except yourself; I wanted simply you, nothing of yours.[24] I looked for no marriage bond, no wedding present; it was not my pleasures I sought to gratify, as you know, but yours. The name of wife may seem holier or more valid, but sweeter for me will always be the word friend[25] or, if you will permit me, concubine or whore. I believed that the more I humbled myself on your account, the more favour I should win from you, and also the less harm I should do to the glory of your reputation. You yourself on your own account did not altogether forget this in the letter of consolation I have spoken of which you wrote to a friend; there you thought fit to set out some of the reasons I gave in trying to dissuade you from binding us together in marriage and in an ill-starred bed. But you kept silent about many of my arguments for preferring love to marriage and freedom to a chain. God is my witness that if Augustus, emperor of the whole world, thought fit to honour me with marriage and conferred all the earth on me to possess forever, it would seem to me dearer and more honourable to be called not his empress but your mistress.[26]

ii. 50: 'non est in proximum caritas perfecta quae "non quaerit quae sua sunt," sed amici sui commoda'; *TSch*, i. 4 (after citing Cicero, *De inuentione*, ii. 55 (150b): 'Sunt enim qui alios amare dicuntur quacumque intentione bene illis esse desiderent. Qui cum id causa sui potius quam illorum agant, non tam hominem diligunt quam fortunam eius sequuntur, nec tam commoda ipsius quam sua in illo uenerantur; nec tale desiderium tam caritas, id est amor, ut dictum est, honestus, quam cupiditas, id est amor inhonestus ac turpis, est dicendum.'

[25] Cf. 5 above and Ovid, *Heroides*, vii. 169: 'Si pudet uxoris, non nupta, sed hospita dicar.' The word *amica*, here translated as friend, is used in the sense of sweetheart or lover.

[26] Cf. Ovid, *Heroides*, iv. 35–6: 'si mihi concedat Iuno fratremque virumque, / Hippolytum videor praepositura Iovi!' ('Should Juno grant me him who is at once her brother and her lord, I think I should prefer Hippolytus to Jove.' Phaedra's unrequited love for Hippolytus drove her to suicide.) Amboise thought Heloise's claim figurative and poetic (*Praefatio apologetica*, *PL* clxxviii. 97B), comparing it with Catullus in *Carmen* 70: 'Nulli se dicit mulier mea nubere malle / quam mihi, non si se Iuppiter ipse petat.' ('The woman I love says that there is no one whom she would rather marry than me, not even if Jove himself were to woo her.') The *Carmen* continues: 'sed mulier cupido quod dicit amanti / in uento et rapida scribere oportet aqua' ('but what a woman says to her ardent lover should be written in wind and running water'). For *meretrix* as a harlot cf. Ovid, *Ars amatoria*, i. 435–6; *Amores*, i. 10. 21; i. 15. 18; iii. 14. 9. For examples of erotic frankness on the part of clergy and of men and women in religious life in the 11th and 12th cc. see Dronke, *Women Writers of the Middle Ages*, pp. 84–92; Luscombe, 'The letters of Heloise and Abelard', pp. 21–2; D. Schaller, 'Erotische und sexuelle Thematik in Musterbriefsammlungen'; H. M. Schaller, 'Scherz und Ernst in erfunden Briefen'.

11. Non enim quo quisque ditior siue potentior, ideo et melior; fortune illud est, hoc uirtutis. Nec se[a] minime uenalem estimet esse que libentius ditiori quam pauperi nubit, et plus in marito[b] sua quam ipsum concupiscit.[27] Certe quamcunque ad nuptias hec concupiscentia ducit, [c]merces ei[c] potius quam gratia debetur. Certum [d]quippe est[d] eam res ipsas, non hominem, sequi,[e] et se, si posset, uelle prostituere ditiori, sicut inductio[f] illa[g] Aspasie[h] philosophe[i] apud[j] Socraticum[k] Eschinem cum Xenofonte[l] et uxore eius habita manifeste conuincit.[28] Quam quidem inductionem cum predicta philosopha[m] ad reconciliandos inuicem illos proposuisset, tali fine[n] conclusit: '[o]Quare, nisi[o] hoc[p] peregeritis, [q]ut neque uir[q] melior neque [r]femina in terris letior sit,[r] profecto semper[s] id, quod[t] optimum putabitis[u] esse, multo[v] maxime requiretis, [w]ut et[w] tu maritus sis[x] quam optime, et hec [y]quam optimo uiro nupta sit.'[y] [29] Sancta profecto[z] hec[a] et plus quam philosophica est[b] sententia[c] ipsius potius sophie [d]quam philosophie[d] dicenda.

12. Sanctus hic error, et beata fallacia in coniugatis, ut perfecta[a] dilectio illesa custodiat matrimonii federa non tam corporum continentia quam animorum pudicitia.[b] At quod[c] error ceteris, ueritas mihi manifesta contulerat cum quod[d] ille[e] uidelicet de suis estimarent maritis, hoc ego[f] de te, hoc[g] mundus uniuersus non tam crederet quam sciret ut [h]tanto uerior[h] in te meus amor existeret quanto ab errore longius absisteret.[i] Quis etenim[j] regum aut philosophorum tuam exequare[k] famam poterat? Que te regio aut ciuitas seu uilla[l] uidere non[m] estuabat? Quis te, rogo, in publicum procedentem conspicere[n] non [o]festinabat, ac[o] discedentem collo erecto, oculis directis non insectabatur?[p] [q]Que coniugata, que uirgo non concupiscebat absentem,

11 [a] illa *add. BRSY* [b] manu *S* [c–c] mihi res *E* [d–d] est quippe *BRY* [e] insequi *BR* [f] inductatio *B;* inducticio *R* [g] *om. CEF* [h] asphasie *B* [i] prophilosophe *R* [j] en l'ostel *J* [k] Socratis *R, Y*(*after corr.?*); sacratitum *S* [l] zenofonte *CY;* zenophonte *E;* te *preceded by a space in B;* zenofon te *R;* senofonte *S* [m] pholosopha *C;* philosophia *ES* [n] ipsam *add. S* [o–o] quare si *A after deletion of* ni *from* nisi*;* Quia nisi *CFY;* Qro nisi *E;* Quia ubi *Amb* [p] hec *SY* [q–q] neque uir *BR;* nec non *S* [r–r] femina in terris letior (eleccior *A after corr. by a second hand*) sit *TA;* mulier in terra lecior (laetior *FAmb*) sit *CEFAmb;* femina letior sit *BRY;* femina letior sit in terris *S;* il n'est en terre . . . nulle plus vaillant femme ne plus elisable *J;* femina lectior in terris sit *Cicero. In the marg. of A a note has been add. by Petrarch*: Require in libro M. Tullii inventione [s] *om. F* [t] quam *S* [u] putabaris *C;* putabatis *F;* putabis *Y* (*after corr.?*), *Amb* [v] merito *E;* mulco *marked for corr. Y* [w–w] et ut et *S* [x] *om. RY* [y–y] optimo (optime *R*) marito nupta *BRY* [z] profecte *B* [a] hoc *S* [b] *om. CEF* [c] suam *BS* [d] *om. BRY*

12 [a] profecta *B;* perfecto *C* [b] pudicia *S* [c] atque *BRS;* quod que *Y* [d] et

11. For a person's worth does not rest on wealth or power; these depend on fortune, but worth on his merits. And a woman should realize that if she marries a rich man more readily than a poor one, and desires her husband more for his possessions than for himself, she is offering herself for sale.[27] Certainly any woman who comes to marry through desires of this kind deserves wages, not favours, for clearly her mind is on the man's property, not himself, and she would be ready to prostitute herself to a richer man, if she could. This is evident from the argument, found in Aeschines Socraticus, of the philosopher Aspasia with Xenophon and his wife.[28] When she had presented it in an effort to reconcile them, the philosopher ended with these words: 'Unless you come to believe that there is no better man nor worthier woman on earth you will always still be looking for what you judge the best thing of all—to be the husband of the best of wives and the wife of the best of husbands.'[29] These are saintly words which are more than philosophic; indeed, they deserve the name of wisdom, not philosophy.

12. It is a holy error and a blessed delusion between man and wife that perfect love can keep the ties of marriage unbroken not so much through bodily continence as chastity of spirit. But what error permitted other women, plain truth permitted me, and what they thought of their husbands, the world in general believed, or rather knew to be true of yourself; so that my love for you was the more genuine for being further removed from error. What king or philosopher could match your fame? What region, city, or village did not long to see you? When you appeared in public, who (I ask) did not hurry to catch a glimpse of you, or crane her neck and strain her eyes to follow your departure? Every wife, every young girl desired

RY [e] ipse *CEF* [f] ergo *Y before corr.by Y*[1], *om. CEF* [g] Hec *B;* et hic *Y* [h–h] *in E* uerior *is add. by another hand in vacant space;* quanto minor *F which adds* maior *over* minor [i] obsisteret *C;* assisteret *Y* [j] uidelicet *Y* [k] excecare *CE* [l] nulla *S* [m] *om. R* [n] respicere *Y* [o–o] estimabat aut *Y* [p] insequebatur *RY* [q–q] *om. C*

[27] Cf. Augustine, *Enarrationes in Psalmos*, liii. 10 (ed. Dekkers and Fraipont, xxxix. 654; *PL* xxxvi. 626): 'Erubesceres si te uxor tua propter diuitias amaret; et forte si tibi paupertas accideret, de adulterio cogitaret', cited in *Comm. Rom.* iii (vii. 13; p. 202).

[28] Aspasia was a friend of Socrates and the mistress of Pericles from *c.*445 BC. Xenophon (*c.*428/7–*c.*354 BC) was also an associate of Socrates, and Aeschines Socraticus was a follower of Socrates in the 4th c.

[29] Cicero, *De inuentione*, i. 31, 51–2.

et non exardebat in presentem? Que regina uel prepotens femina gaudiis meis non[r] inuidebat[q] uel thalamis?

13. Duo autem, fateor, tibi specialiter inerant quibus[a] feminarum quarumlibet animos[b] statim allicere[c] poteras, dictandi[d] [30] [e]uidelicet et cantandi[e] gratia, que ceteros minime philosophos assecutos[f] esse nouimus. Quibus quidem, quasi ludo quodam laborem exercitii[g] recreans philosophici,[h] pleraque[i] amatorio[j] metro uel rithmo[k] composita reliquisti carmina, que pre nimia suauitate tam dictaminis[31] quam cantus sepius frequentata, tuum in ore omnium nomen incessanter tenebant,[32] ut [l]illitteratos etiam[l] melodie dulcedo tui non sineret[m] immemores esse. Atque hinc maxime in amorem tui femine[n] suspirabant. Et cum horum pars maxima carminum nostros decantaret amores, multis me regionibus [o]breui tempore[o] nuntiauit, et multarum in me feminarum accendit inuidiam.[p] [33] Quod enim[q] bonum animi uel corporis tuam[r] non exornabat adolescentiam? Quam,[s] tunc mihi inuidentem, nunc tantis[t] priuatae deliciis compati calamitas mea non compellat?[u] Quem uel quam, licet hostem primitus, debita compassio mihi nunc non emolliat? [v]Que plurimum nocens,[v] plurimum, ut nosti, sum innocens. Non enim rei effectus sed efficientis[w] affectus[x] in crimine est. [y]Nec que fiunt[y] sed quo animo fiunt equitas pensat.[34] Quem autem animum [z]in te[z] semper habuerim, solus qui expertus es[a] iudicare potes. Tuo examini cuncta committo, tuo per omnia cedo[b] testimonio.

14. Dic unum, si uales, cur[a] post conuersionem[b] nostram, quam tu solus facere decreuisti, in tantam tibi[c] negligentiam atque obliuionem[d] uenerim, ut[e] nec colloquio presentis recreer nec [f]absentis epistola consoler.[f] [35] Dic, inquam,[g] si uales, aut[h] ego quod sentio,[i] imo quod[j]

[r] *om. S*

13 [a] que per *BR;* per que *Y* [b] animas *C; om. F* [c] illicere *F* [d] dictando *R* [e–e] et cantandi uidelicet *Y;* uidelicet et contandi *S* [f] assecutas *C* [g] exercicii *T over eras.; eras. also in marg.;* exercicio *C; om. E;* exercitio *F;* exertu *S* [h] Philosophi *F* [i] plerasque *E* [j] amatori *T* [k] *A before superscr. corr. by* A^2 *to* rithimo*;* Rithimo *E;* rimo *B* [l–l] illi tantos et *R;* illiteratos et *S;* illius cantus et *Y;* etiam illiteratos *Amb* [m] *add. by another hand in E;* eos *add. Y* [n] sapientie *E* [o–o] breuiter *F* [p] inuidia *CE* [q] tunc *F* [r] *om. Y* [s] Que iam *S* [t] tantos *C* [u] compellatur *S* [v–v] Quamplurimum nocens *F;* Quod plurimum nocens *R;* Quam plurimum nocens *Y;* Et plurimum nocens *Amb;* Qui fu trop nuissans an plusieurs *J* [w] efficiens *A;* efficientes *Y* [x] effectus *B* [y–y] nec que fiant *CE;* neque fiunt *BR;* Neque enim (que Y^1) fiunt *Y* [z–z] *om. F* [a] omnes *S* [b] sancto *Y*

you in absence and was on fire in your presence; queens and great ladies envied me my joys and my bed.

13. You had besides, I admit, two special gifts with which you could at once win the heart of any woman—the gifts of composing[30] verse and song. We knew that other philosophers have rarely been successful in these, whereas for you they were no more than a diversion, a relief from the toil of doing philosophy. You have left many songs composed in amatory verse and rhyme. Because of the very great sweetness of their words[31] as much as of their tune, they have been repeated often and have kept your name continually on the lips of everyone.[32] The beauty of the melody ensured that even the unlettered did not forget you; more than anything this made women sigh for love of you. And as most of these songs told of our love, they soon made me widely known and roused the envy of many women against me.[33] For your manhood was adorned by every grace of mind and body, and among the women who envied me then, could there be one now who does not feel compelled by my misfortune to sympathize with my loss of such joys? Who is there who was once my enemy, whether man or woman, who is not moved now by the compassion which is my due? Wholly guilty though I am, I am, as you know, wholly innocent. It is not the deed but the state of mind of the doer which makes the crime, and justice should weigh not what is done but the spirit in which it is done.[34] What my intention towards you has always been, you alone who have known it can judge. I commit all to your scrutiny; I yield in all things to what you say.

14. Tell me one thing, if you can. Why, since our entry into religion, which was your decision alone, have I been so neglected and forgotten by you that I have neither encouragement in conversation with you when you are here nor consolation in a letter when you are not?[35] Tell me, I say, if you can—or I will tell you what I think and indeed what

14 [a] cum *Amb* [b] conuersionem *a call for corr. in T is indicated by T^4 with the sign* / / ; conuerssationem *C* [c] tui *F* [d] tui *add. F* [e] et *Y, but Y^1 adds* ut [f-f] epistolis absentis *F;* absentis consoler epistola *BRS;* absentis epistola *Y* [g] nunquam *Y* [h] at *C* [i] assentio *?C* [j] quam *B*

[30] 'dictandi': that is, composing and dictating.

[31] 'dictamen': the art of composition in words and dictation.

[32] Cf. Ovid, *Remedia* 363.

[33] Cf. *Letter* 1, **19**.

[34] Cf. *Letter* 6, **25** and *Rule* **70**.

[35] Cf. Ovid, *Heroides*, ii. 27.

omnes suspicantur, dicam. Concupiscentia te mihi potius quam amicitia sociauit, libidinis ardor potius[k] quam amor. Vbi igitur[l] quod desiderabas cessauit, quidquid propter [m]hoc exhibebas[m] pariter euanuit. Hec, dilectissime, non tam mea est[n] quam omnium coniectura, non tam specialis quam communis, non[o] tam priuata quam publica. Vtinam mihi soli sic[p] uideretur, atque aliquos[q] in excusationem[r] sui [s]amor tuus[s] inueniret,[t] per quos dolor meus paululum resideret! Vtinam occasiones[u] fingere possem, quibus te excusando mei[v] quoquomodo tegerem[w] uilitatem![x] [36]

15. Attende, obsecro, que requiro,[a] et parua hec[b] uideris[c] et tibi[d] facillima. Dum tui[e] presentia fraudor, uerborum saltem uotis,[f] quorum tibi[g] copia est, tue mihi imaginis presenta[h] dulcedinem. Frustra te in rebus dapsilem[i] expecto si in uerbis auarum sustineo. Nunc uero[j] plurimum a te me promereri[k] credideram, cum omnia[l] propter te compleuerim, nunc in[m] tuo maxime[n] perseuerans[o] obsequio. Quam quidem[p] iuuenculam[q] ad monastice conuersationis[r] asperitatem non religionis deuotio sed tua tantum pertraxit[s] iussio,[t] [37] ubi si [u]nihil a te[u] promerear, quam frustra laborem diiudica. Nulla mihi super hoc [v]merces expectanda[v] est a Deo, cuius adhuc amore nihil [w]me constat[w] egisse. Properantem te ad Deum[x] secuta sum habitu, imo precessi.[y] Quasi enim memor uxoris Loth retro conuerse,[38] prius [z]me sacris uestibus[z] et professione monastica quam te ipsum[a] Deo mancipasti. In quo, fateor, uno[b] minus [c]te de[c] me confidere uehementer dolui atque erubui. Eque[d] autem, Deus scit, ad[e] [f]Vulcania loca[f] te[g] properantem precedere[h] uel[i] sequi pro iussu tuo minime dubitarem.[39] Non enim mecum animus meus,[j] sed tecum erat. Sed et nunc maxime, si tecum non est, nusquam est. Esse uero sine te nequaquam[k] potest. Sed ut tecum bene sit age, obsecro. Bene

[k] *om. RY* [l] ergo *F* [m–m] hoc (*or* hec) al' exhibebas colebas *Y* [n] *om. BRY* [o] nec *CEF* [p] *om. RY* [q] alios *BS* aliis *RY* [r] excus(a *add. T*³)sionem *with a corr. sign. in marg. T;* excusionem *B;* excussionem *S* [s–s] amor tui *R;* amorem *Y* [t] ueniret *BRY* [u] actione *C;* occasionem *E* [v] nostri *B;* unde *R;* non *S;* meam *Y* [w] regerem *CESY* [x] utilitatem *BR;* uoluntatem *Y*

15 [a] quare require *BR* [b] hoc *SY* [c] uidebis *RY* [d] *om. C* [e] cuius *Y* [f] notis *EFSYAmb*¹ [g] uidelicet *C* [h] presencia *CR;* presentia *E* [i] daxilem *T, A before corr., CES;* dixissem *B;* docilem *R;* al- dapsilem *Y* [j] non *Y* [k] preueniri *Y* [l] iam *C* [m] duo *add. R* [n] maximo *BS* [o] compleueram *CEF;* compleam *F superscr., Amb*¹; presens *BR;* uerans *S;* pñs *Y* [p] quidam *B* [q] iuuencula *BRS* [r] conuersionis *Y;* conversion *J* [s] protraxit *Y* [t] uisio *R* [u–u] a te nihil *E* [v–v] expectanda merces *Y* [w–w] constat me *A* [x] adeo *E*

everyone suspects. It was desire, not affection, which bound you to me, the flame of lust rather than love. So when the end came to what you desired, any show of feeling you used to make went with it. This, most dearly beloved, is not so much my opinion as everyone's, not so much a particular or private view as the common or public one. If only it were mine alone and the love you professed could find someone to defend it and so comfort me in my grief for a while! If only I could think of some pretexts which would excuse you and somehow cover up the way you hold me cheap![36]

15. I beg you then to listen to what I ask—you will see that it is a small favour which you can easily grant. While I am denied your presence, give me at least through your words—of which you have enough and to spare—some sweet semblance of yourself. It is no use my hoping for generosity in deeds if you are grudging in words. Up to now I had thought I deserved much of you, seeing that I carried out everything for your sake and continue up to the present moment in complete obedience to you. It was not any sense of vocation which brought me as a young girl to accept the austerity of religious life, but your command alone,[37] and if I deserve no gratitude from you, you may judge for yourself how my labours are in vain. I can expect no reward for this from God, for it is clear that I have done nothing as yet for love of him. When you hurried towards God I followed you; indeed, I went first to take the veil. As if you were thinking how Lot's wife turned back,[38] you made me put on the religious habit and take my vows before you gave yourself to God. Your lack of trust in me over this one thing, I confess, overwhelmed me with grief and shame. At your command, God knows, I would equally have had no hesitation in going ahead of you or following you to Vulcan's pit.[39] For my mind was not with me but with you, and now, most of all, if it is not with you it is nowhere; truly, without you it cannot survive. See

[y] processi *S* [z–z] sacris uestibus me *Y* [a] ipsam *F* [b] ymo *CE;* ; immo *F before exp.;* imo *R* [c–c] de te *Y* [d] *E after del. of* Eg; Ego *F after deletions, Amb;* et que *BR;* Et que *Y* [e] a *S* [f–f] un feu *J* [g] *om. F* [h] procedere *CEBY* [i] et *A* [j] *om. RSY* [k] nunquam *BRY*

[36] Cf. Ovid, *Heroides*, iii. 41–2.

[37] 'iussio': cf. **9** above and *Letters* 1, **31** and 4, **14**. Also, *Problemata* 42, where Heloise asks Abelard 'utrum aliquis in eo quod facit a Domino sibi concessum, vel etiam iussum, peccare possit' ('whether anyone can sin in doing what the Lord allows or even commands him to do').

[38] Gen. 19: 26.

[39] An implicit allusion to Alcestis as in Euripides' play; cf. Dronke, *Women Writers of the Middle Ages*, p. 120.

autem tecum[l] fuerit si te propitium inuenerit, si gratiam referas pro gratia,[40] modica pro magnis, uerba pro rebus. Vtinam, dilecte, sua[m] de me dilectio minus confideret, ut [n]sollicitior esset![n] Sed quo[o] te amplius nunc securum reddidi, negligentiorem sustineo.

16. Memento, obsecro, que fecerim, et quanta debeas [a]attende. Dum[a] tecum carnali[b] fruerer uoluptate,[c] utrum id amore uel libidine agerem incertum pluribus habebatur.[d] Nunc[e] uero[f] finis indicat quo id inchoauerim principio.[41] Omnes[g] [h]denique mihi[h] uoluptates [i]interdixi,[j] ut tue parerem uoluntati. Nihil mihi reseruaui,[i] [42] nisi sic [k]tuam nunc[k] precipue fieri. Que uero tua[l] sit iniquitas perpende, si merenti amplius persoluis minus, imo[m] nihil penitus, presertim cum paruum sit quod exigeris,[n] et tibi facillimum. Per ipsum itaque cui te obtulisti[o] Deum te obsecro, ut [p]quo modo[p] potes tuam mihi presentiam reddas, consolationem uidelicet [q]mihi aliquam[q] rescribendo, hoc saltem pacto,[r] ut[s] sic recreata diuino alacrior uacem[t] obsequio. Cum[u] me ad turpes[v] olim[w] uoluptates expeteres,[x] crebris me epistolis[y] uisitabas,[z] frequenti carmine tuam in ore omnium Heloissam[a] ponebas. Me platee omnes, me domus singule resonabant.[b] Quanto autem rectius me nunc in Deum quam tunc in libidinem excitares? Perpende, obsecro, que debes; attende que postulo; et longam epistolam breui fine concludo. Vale, unice.

[l] *om. Y* [m] tua *S* [n–n] sollicior *Y* [o] de *add. B*

16 [a–a] Attende dum *Y* [b] *om. BRY* [c] uolutata *B* [d] haabebat *S* [e] eius *R;* Eius *Y* [f] autem *T;* uero *ACEFBRSY* [g] enim *add. BRY* [h–h] mihi denique *RY* [i–i] *om. Y* [j] preterdixi *B* [k–k] nunc tuam *BRSY* [l] tu *B before corr., R* [m] quin *B; om. S* [n] exigeris *A, which corrects the first* i *to* e *and also marks* s *for corr.;* exigerim *CE;* exegerim *YF* [o] obtuli *CE;* abstuli *F* [p–p] quoquo modo *CEF,?B, Amb* [q–q] aliquam mihi *CEF* [r] *unfilled space in B* [s] et *C* [t] nacem *B* [u] u *add. Y;* Cuius *E* [v] temporales *Amb* [w] *om. F* [x] expeteris *A;* expectares *C* [y] epulis *EY;* epistolis *Y*[1] [z] uiuificatus *Y* [a] heloyse *T before corr.;* heloysam *S* [b] resonebant *S before corr.*

that it fares well with you, I beseech, as it will if it finds you kind, if you give grace in return for grace,[40] small for great, words for deeds. If only your love had less confidence in me, my dear, so that you would be more concerned on my behalf! But as it is, the more I have made you feel secure in me, the more I have to bear with your neglect.

16. Remember, I implore you, what I have done, and think how much you owe me. While I enjoyed with you the pleasures of the flesh, many were uncertain whether I was prompted by love or lust; but now the end is proof of the beginning.[41] I have finally denied myself every pleasure in obedience to your will, kept nothing for myself[42] except to prove that now, even more, I am yours. Consider then your injustice, if when I deserve more you give me less, or rather, nothing at all, especially when it is a small thing I ask of you and one you could so easily grant. And so, in the name of God to whom you have dedicated yourself, I beg you to restore your presence to me in what way you can—by writing me some word of comfort, so that in this at least I may find increased strength and readiness to serve God. When in the past you sought me out for sinful pleasures your letters came to me thick and fast, and your many songs put your Heloise on everyone's lips, so that every street and house resounded with my name. Is it not far better now to summon me to God than it was then to satisfy our lust? I beg you, think what you owe me, give ear to my pleas, and I will finish a long letter with a brief ending: farewell, my one-and-only.

[40] Cf. John 1: 16.
[41] Cf. Ovid, *Heroides*, ii. 85: 'Exitus acta probat.'
[42] Cf. Virgil, *Aeneid*, iv. 315: 'nihil ipsa reliqui'.

⟨EPISTOLA III⟩

1. HELOYSE[a] DILECTISSIME[b] SORORI SVE IN CHRISTO ABAELARDVS[c] FRATER[d] EIVS IN IPSO

Quod post nostram a seculo [e]ad Deum conuersionem[e] nondum[f] tibi aliquid consolationis uel exhortationis scripserim, non negligentie mee sed tue, de qua semper plurimum[g] confido, prudentie imputandum est. Non enim eam his indigere credidi, cui abundanter quecunque[h] necessaria sunt diuina gratia impertiuit, ut[i] tam uerbis scilicet[j] quam exemplis errantes ualeas[k] docere, pusillanimes consolari, tepidos exhortari, sicut et facere iam dudum consueuisti cum sub abbatissa prioratum[l] obtineres. Quod[m] si nunc[n] tanta diligentia tuis prouideas filiabus, quanta tunc sororibus, satis esse credimus ut iam omnino superfluam doctrinam uel exhortationem nostram arbitremur. Sin autem humilitati tue[o] aliter uidetur, et in iis[p] etiam que ad Deum pertinent magisterio nostro[q] atque scriptis[r] indiges, super his que[s] uelis scribe mihi, ut ad ipsam[t] rescribam prout [u]Dominus mihi[u] annuerit.[1]

2. Deo autem gratias,[a] qui[b] grauissimorum et assiduorum periculorum meorum sollicitudinem [c]uestris cordibus[c] inspirans, afflictionis mee[d] participes uos fecit, ut orationum suffragio[e] uestrarum diuina miseratio me protegat, et uelociter Satanam sub pedibus nostris[f] conterat. Ad hoc autem precipue psalterium, quod [g]a me[g] sollicite requisisti, soror in seculo quondam chara, nunc in Christo charissima,[2] mittere maturaui. In quo uidelicet pro nostris [h]magnis

Letter 3 *T* fos. 21rb–23vb; *A* fos. 16rb–18rb; *C* fos. 158^{r}–160^{v}; *E* fos. 17^{r}–19^{r}; *F* pp. 19–27; *B* fos. 16ra–17vb; *R* fos. 128rb–130rb; *S* fos. 25^{v}–30^{r}; *Y* fos. 100ra–102ra; *Amb* pp. 48–54; *Amb*[1] *variants in the margins of Amb*; *J* pp. 70–9. *Headings are found in the following witnesses*: Rescriptum ipsius ad ipsam *rubr. TABS;* Epistola Abaelardi . . (?) . . Heloysse *add. by another hand Y;* Comme il rescript a Heloyse, en li confortant et que elle weille prier pour lui ij[c]xiij *table in H of the (missing) contents of Dijon MS 525;* EPISTOLA III. Quae est Rescriptum PETRI ad HELOISSAM *Amb*

1 [a] *with decorated initial ABR;* eloysse *with vacant space for initial C;* ELOYSSE *with vacant space for initial E;* Heloyssae *F;* heloyse *S;* Heloysse *with decorated initial Y;* Heloissae *Amb* [b] *ditto. S* [c] abaelardus *TAER;* Abaelardus *CFBYAmb* [d] suus *add. CE* [e–e] conuersionem ad deum *E* [f] numdum *TEB* [g] quam plurimum *BY* [h] quae *Amb* [i] nec *R* [j] *om. FAmb* [k] uales *E* [l] primatum *BRY* [m] Que *ACEFY;* que *BR* [n] uere *CEF;* non *R* [o] tui *R* [p] id *T* [q] *om. B* [r] scripto *CEF* [s] *om. Y* [t] ipsa *F* [u–u] mihi Dominus *Amb*

LETTER 3

1. TO HELOISE, HIS DEARLY BELOVED SISTER IN CHRIST, FROM ABELARD HER BROTHER IN HIM

If since our conversion from the world to God I have not yet written you any word of comfort or advice, it must not be attributed to indifference on my part but to your own good sense, in which I have always had such confidence that I did not think anything was needed; God's grace has bestowed on you all essentials to enable you to instruct the erring, comfort the weak, and encourage the faint-hearted, both by word and example, as, indeed, you have been doing since you first held the office of prioress under your abbess. So if you still watch over your daughters as carefully as you did previously over your sisters, it is sufficient to make me believe that any teaching or exhortation from me would now be wholly superfluous. If, on the other hand, in your humility you think differently, and you feel that you have need of my instruction and writings in matters pertaining to God, write to me what you want, so that I may answer as God permits me.[1]

2. Meanwhile thanks be to God who has filled all your hearts with anxiety for my desperate, unceasing perils, and made you share in my affliction; may divine mercy protect me through the support of your prayers and quickly crush Satan beneath our feet. To this end in particular, I hasten to send the Psalter you earnestly begged from me, my sister once dear in the world and now dearest in Christ,[2] so that you may offer a perpetual sacrifice of prayers to the Lord for

2 [a] ago *add. CEF* [b] deus *add. CEF; E adds* g *after* qui *before exp.* [c–c] uestris *T;* cordibus uestris *A* [d] me *C* [e] suffragiis *CEF* [f] uestris *CEFY* [g–g] adme *C* [h–h] et magnis *CEF*

---

[1] For the results of this suggestion that Abelard would be willing, on request, to provide instruction or writings to meet the spiritual needs of the Paraclete sisters see the Introduction above at pp. xxv–xxviii.

[2] 'soror . . . charissima': cf. *Expositio in Hexameron, preface* (ed. Romig and Luscombe, p. 4; *PL* clxxviii. 731C); *Hymns*, book 1, preface (*Hymn Collections from the Paraclete*, ed. Waddell, ii. 5; *Peter Abelard's Hymnarius Paraclitensis*, ed. Szövérffy, ii. 9; *PL* clxxviii. 1771–2); *Confessio fidei ad Heloissam*, 1 (ed. Burnett in '*Confessio fidei ad Heloisam*—Abelard's last letter to Heloise?', p. 152; *PL* clxxviii. 375C, 1862A). Also *Sermons*, *preface* (*I sermoni di Abelardo per le monache del Paracleto*, ed. De Santis, p. 86; *PL* clxxviii. 379–80).

et[h] multis excessibus, et quotidiana periculorum meorum instantia iuge Domino sacrificium immoles orationum.[3]

3. Quantum autem locum apud Deum et sanctos eius fidelium orationes optineant,[a] et[b] maxime mulierum pro charis suis, [c]et uxorum[c] pro uiris, multa[d] nobis occurrunt testimonia uel[e] exempla. Quod diligenter attendens[f] Apostolus, sine intermissione [g]orare nos[g] admonet.[4] Legimus Dominum Moysi dixisse: 'Dimitte me[h] ut irascatur furor meus.'[5] Et Ieremie:[i] 'Tu uero,' inquit,[j] 'noli orare[k] pro populo [l]hoc, et[l] non obsistas mihi.'[6] [m]Ex quibus uidelicet[m] uerbis manifeste[n] Dominus ipse profitetur orationes sanctorum quasi quoddam frenum ire[o] ipsius immittere, quo scilicet[p] ipsa coerceatur, ne quantum merita peccantium exigunt[q] ipsa[r] in eos seuiat, et[s] quem[t] ad uindictam iustitia quasi spontaneum ducit,[u] amicorum supplicatio flectat, et tanquam inuitum quasi ui quadam retineat.[7] Sic quippe oranti uel[v] oraturo dicitur: 'Dimitte me, et ne obsistas mihi.' Precipit[w] Dominus ne oretur pro impiis. Orat iustus, Domino prohibente, et ab ipso impetrat quod postulat, et irati[x] iudicis sententiam immutat. Sic quippe de Moyse subiunctum est: 'Et placatus [y]factus est Dominus[y] de malignitate quam dixit facere populo suo.'[8] Scriptum est alibi de uniuersis[z] operibus Dei:[a] 'Dixit, et facta sunt.'[9] Hoc autem loco et dixisse memoratur[b] quod de afflictione[c] populus meruerat, et [d]uirtute orationis[d] preuentus non implesse[e] quod dixerat.[10]

4. Attende itaque quanta[a] sit orationis uirtus, si quod iubemur oremus, quando id quod[b] orare Prophetam[c] Deus[d] prohibuit orando tamen obtinuit, et ab eo quod dixerat eum auertit.[e] Cui et alius Propheta dicit:[f] 'Et[g] cum iratus fueris,[h] [i]misericordie recordaberis.'[i] [11] Audiant id[j] [k]atque aduertant principes terreni,[k] qui occasione preposite[l] et edicte iustitie[m] sue[n] obstinati[o] magis quam iusti reperiuntur,

3 [a] obtineat *E* [b] *om. BRY* [c–c] uxoris *C;* uirorum *BR;* uxorum *Y* [d] merita *E* [e] et *Amb* [f] *om. F* [g–g] nos orare *CEF* [h] me *om. F* [i] Iheremie *T;* hieremie *A;* ieromie *C;* Hieremiae *FAmb;* Ieremie *BRY* [j] inquro *T; om. CEF* [k] horari *R* [l–l] hoc est *A;* hoc ut *Y* [m–m] ex quibus multis *C, ?E;* Et quidem multis *F;* ex quibus uidetur *Y* [n] manifesteque *Y* [o] ut *B* [p] ira *add. C, ?E, F* [q] exiguerint *C, add. in vacant space Ecorr.;* exigant *F* [r] ira *add. EF* [s] ut *T* (et *T*[1] *in marg.*), *Amb* [t] quam *B after corr., CE* [u] dicit *Y* [v] amico *add. T before exp.* [w] precepit *ACEFY* [x] etiam me *?R* [y–y] est dominus factus *BRY* [z] *add. in vacant space Ecorr.* [a] Christi *S* [b] commemoratur *CEF* [c] quam *add. Y* [d–d] orationis uirtute *BRY* [e] implere *Y*

4 [a] quante *E* [b] *om. C* [c] propheta *R* [d] dominus *ACEFBR* [e] aduertit *CE* [f] dixit *Y* [g] *om. Y* [h] *om. R* [i–i] i.r. *abbreviation in BR* [j] hic *C;* igitur *Y* [k–k] principes (princeps *C*) terreni atque aduertant *CEF*

our many great aberrations, and for the dangers which daily threaten me.[3]

3. We have indeed many examples as evidence of the high position in the eyes of God and his saints which has been won by the prayers of the faithful, especially those of women on behalf of their dear ones and of wives for their husbands. The Apostle observes this closely when he bids us pray continually.[4] We read that the Lord said to Moses: 'Let me alone, to vent my anger upon them',[5] and to Jeremiah: 'Therefore offer no prayer for these people nor stand in my path.'[6] By these words the Lord himself makes it clear that the prayers of the devout set a kind of bridle on his wrath and check it from raging against sinners as fully as they deserve, just as a man who is willingly moved by his sense of justice to take vengeance can be turned aside by the entreaties of his friends and forcibly restrained, as it were, against his will.[7] Thus when the Lord says to one who is praying or about to pray: 'Let me alone and do not stand in my path', he forbids prayers to be offered to him on behalf of the impious; yet the just man prays though the Lord forbids, obtains his requests, and alters the sentence of the angry judge. And so the passage about Moses continues: 'And the Lord repented and spared his people the evil with which he had threatened them.'[8] Elsewhere it is written about the universal works of God: 'He spoke, and it was.'[9] But in this passage it is also recorded that he had said the people deserved affliction, but he had been prevented by the power of prayer from carrying out what he had said.[10]

4. Consider then the great power of prayer, if we pray as we are bidden, seeing that the prophet won by prayer what he was forbidden to pray for, and turned God aside from his declared intention. And another prophet says to God: 'In thy wrath remember mercy.'[11] The lords of the earth should listen and take note, for they are found obstinate rather than just in the execution of the justice they have

[l] proposite *TF*   [m] iustiore *C*   [n] *om. E*   [o] abstinati *CE*; et rebelles *add. CEF*

---

[3] This 'psalterium' was probably a collection of Psalms, each followed by a collect or prayer. Cf. Van den Eynde, 'Les Écrits perdus d'Abélard', pp. 476–80.

[4] 1 Thess. 5: 17.   [5] Exod. 32: 10.   [6] Jer. 7: 16.

[7] Cf. *Sermon* 26 (*PL* clxxviii. 544B): 'Irae Domini sanctorum preces in tantum resistere legimus, ut nequaquam debitam possit exercere uindictam.'

[8] Exod. 32: 14.   [9] Ps. 32 (33): 9, 148: 5.

[10] Cf. *Sermon* 14 (*PL* clxxviii. 489BC).   [11] Hab. 3: 2.

et se remissos[p] uideri erubescunt si[q] misericordes fiant, et mendaces si edictum suum mutent[r] uel quod minus prouide[s] statuerunt non impleant, etsi uerba rebus[t] emendent.[u] Quos quidem[v] [w]recte dixerim Iephte[w] comparandos,[x] qui quod stulte uouerat stultius adimplens[y] [z]unicam interfecit.[z] [12] Qui uero[a] [b]eius membrum[b] [13] fieri cupit cum[c] Psalmista dicit: 'Misericordiam et iudicium cantabo tibi, Domine.'[14] 'Misericordia', sicut scriptum [d]est, 'iudicium exaltat,'[d] [15] attendens quod alibi Scriptura comminatur,[e] 'iudicium sine misericordia[f] in eum qui[g] misericordiam non facit.'[16] Quod diligenter ipse Psalmista considerans, ad supplicationem uxoris Nabal Carmeli iuramentum, quod ex[h] iustitia fecerat, de uiro eius scilicet et ipsius domo delenda, per misericordiam[i] cassauit.[j] [17] Orationem itaque [k]iustitie pretulit,[k] et quod uir deliquerat supplicatio uxoris deleuit.

5. In quo quidem[a] tibi,[b] soror, exemplum proponitur, et securitas datur, ut si huius oratio apud hominem tantum obtinuit, quid[c] apud Deum tua pro me audeat instruaris. Plus quippe Deus, qui pater est noster, filios diligit quam Dauid[d] feminam[e] supplicantem. Et ille[f] quidem[g] pius et misericors habebatur, sed[h] ipsa pietas et[i] misericordia Deus est. Et que tunc supplicabat mulier secularis erat et laica, nec ex sancte deuotionis[j] professione Domino copulata. [k]Quod si[k] ex te minus ad impetrandum sufficias, sanctus qui tecum est tam uirginum quam uiduarum conuentus, quod[l] per te non potes, obtinebit. Cum enim[m] discipulis Veritas dicat: 'Vbi[n] duo uel tres congregati fuerint[o] in nomine meo, ibi sum in medio eorum.'[18] Et rursum: 'Si duo ex uobis consenserint[p] de omni re quam petierint, fiet illud[q] a Patre meo',[19] [r]quis non[r] uideat quantum [s]apud Deum ualeat[s] sancte congregationis frequens oratio? [t]Si, ut[t] Apostolus asserit, 'multum ualet[u] oratio iusti[v] assidua',[20] [w]quid de[w] multitudine sancte congregationis [x]sperandum est?[x]

[p] iusti *add.* *CEF* [q] se *R* [r] mittent *R* [s] proinde *R* [t] eorum *CEF* [u] emendant *F* [v] etiam *Y* [w–w] recte dixerim recte *C;* recte dixerim Iepte *E* (Iepte *add. in vacant space by Ecorr.*)*;* Iepte dixerim inepte *SY* [x] ei *add.* *Y* [y] implens *Y* [z–z] uineam interfecit *R*; Vnicam interficit *Y* [a] non *add.* *Y*ᴵ [b–b] membrum eius *BRSY* [c] qui cum *T*; cui cum *ACEFBRSY;* tunc cum *Amb*; dont *J*; ei cum *conj. Muckle* [d–d] superexaltat iudicium *CEF* [e] commemorat *Y and Y*ᴵ [f] fiet *add.* *Y* [g] quia *C* [h] de *CEF* [i] penitenciam *Y* [j] cessauit *FY* [k–k] iustitie *R;* preferens iustitie *Y*

5 [a] quidam *Y* [b] tui *E* [c] quam *E* [d] dauit *A; illegible C;* dauid *add. in vacant space Ecorr.;* pater dauid *R;* pater quidem *Y* [e] *om.* *Y* [f] dauid *add.* *A*; ipse *Y* [g] qui *E;* quantum *R;* quamuis *Y* [h] et *CEF* [i] in *A* [j] prodeuotionis *C* [k–k] Quam *C* (*or* Quasi), *E* [l] *om.* *B* [m] *om.* *B; ditto.* *S* [n] nisi *S*; aliter ubi *superscr.* *S* [o] *om.* *A*; sunt *Y* [p] asserint *C* [q] illis *CE;* eis *BRY* [r–r] quia sis *B*; quid non *C* [s–s] ualeat apud deum *CEF;* ualeat *RY*

decreed and pronounced; they blush to appear lax if they are merciful, and untruthful if they change a pronouncement or do not carry out a decision which lacked foresight, even if they can emend their words by their actions. Such men could properly be compared with Jephthah who made a foolish vow and, in carrying it out even more foolishly, killed his only daughter.[12] But he who desires to be a member of his body[13] says with the Psalmist: 'I will sing of mercy and justice unto thee, O Lord.'[14] 'Mercy', it is written, 'exalts judgement',[15] in accordance with the threat elsewhere in the Scriptures: 'In that judgement there will be no mercy for the man who has shown no mercy.'[16] The Psalmist himself considered this carefully when, at the entreaty of the wife of Nabal the Carmelite, as an act of mercy he broke the oath he had justly sworn concerning her husband and the destruction of his house.[17] Thus he set prayer above justice, and the man's wrongdoing was wiped out by the entreaties of his wife.

5. Here you have an example, sister, and an assurance how much your prayers for me may prevail on God, if this woman's did so much for her husband, seeing that God who is our father loves his children more than David did a suppliant woman. David was indeed considered a pious and merciful man, but God is piety and mercy itself. And the woman whose entreaties David heard then was an ordinary lay person, in no way bound to God by the profession of holy devotion; whereas if you alone are not enough to win an answer to your prayer, the holy convent of widows and virgins which is with you will succeed where you cannot by yourself. For when the Truth says to the disciples: 'When two or three have met together in my name, I am there among them',[18] and again: 'If two of you agree about any request you have to make, it shall be granted by my Father',[19] we can all see how the communal prayer of a holy congregation must prevail upon God. If, as the apostle James says: 'A good man's prayer is powerful and effective',[20] what should we hope for from the large numbers of a holy congregation?

[t–t] si ut *perhaps over eras. in T;* sed ut *BRY* [u] ualeat *CEF* [v] iusta *CE*
[w–w] quam de *E;* qui de *?R;* que ex *Y* [x–x] est sperandum *BR*; est speranda *Y*

[12] Cf. Judg. 11: 29–40; also *Letter* 7, **30** and *Planctus III: Planctus uirginum Israel super filia Jephtae Galaditae* (ed. Meyer, *Gesammelte Abhandlungen*, i. 350–1; ed. von den Steinen in 'Die Planctus Abaelards – Jephthas Tochter', pp. 142–3; *PL* clxxviii. 1819–20).
[13] Cf. Eph. 5: 30. [14] Ps. 100 (101): 1. [15] Jas. 2: 13.
[16] Jas. 2: 13. [17] 1 Kgs. (1 Sam.) 25. [18] Matt. 18: 20.
[19] Matt. 18: 19. [20] Jas. 5: 16.

6. Nosti,[a] carissima soror, ex homelia beati Gregorii XXXVIII[b] quantum suffragium inuito seu contradicenti fratri oratio fratrum mature[c] attulerit.[21] De quo iam ad extremum ducto quanta periculi anxietate miserrima [d]eius anima[d] laboraret,[e] et quanta desperatione et tedio uite fratres ab oratione reuocaret, [f]quid ibi[f] diligenter scriptum sit tuam minime latet prudentiam.[g]

7. Atque utinam confidentius te et sanctarum conuentum sororum ad orationem inuitet, ut me scilicet [a]uobis ipse uiuum custodiat, per quem,[a] Paulo attestante, mortuos etiam suos de resurrectione mulieres acceperunt.[22] Si enim[b] Veteris et Euangelici Testamenti paginas[c] reuoluas,[d] inuenies maxima resuscitationis[e] miracula solis uel[f] maxime feminis exhibita fuisse, pro ipsis scilicet uel[g] de ipsis facta. Duos quippe mortuos suscitatos ad supplicationes maternas Vetus commemorat Testamentum, per Helyam[h] scilicet et ipsius discipulum Helyseum.[23] Euangelium uero trium tantum[i] mortuorum suscitationem a Domino factam[j] continet, que mulieribus exhibita maxime illud quod supra memorauimus[k] apostolicum dictum rebus suis[l] confirmant: 'Acceperunt [m]mulieres de resurrectione[m] [n]mortuos suos.[n]' [24] Filium quippe uidue ad portam ciuitatis Naym[o] suscitatum matri reddidit, eius compassione compunctus.[25] Lazarum quoque[p] amicum suum ad[q] obsecrationem sororum eius,[r] Marie uidelicet ac[s] Marthe, suscitauit.[26] Quo[t] etiam archisynagogi filie hanc ipsam gratiam ad petitionem patris impendente,[u] [27] 'mulieres de resurrectione mortuos suos acceperunt', cum hec uidelicet suscitata[v] proprium de morte receperit corpus, sicut [w]ille corpora[w] suorum.[28] Et paucis quidem[x] interuenientibus he facte sunt resuscitationes.[y] Vite uero nostre conseruationem multiplex [z]uestre deuotionis oratio[z] facile obtinebit. Quarum[a] tam abstinentia quam continentia Deo sacrata quanto[b] ipsi gratior habetur, tanto ipsum propitiorem[c] inueniet.[d] Et

6 [a] Et nosti *S* [b] 36 *C*; 38 *E*; tricesima octaua *F* [c] nature *TAmb;* mature *Amb*[1] [d–d] anima eius *BR* [e] *om. RY* [f–f] quam ibi *CE;* quid tibi *B* [g] sententiam *S*

7 [a–a] ipse uobis uiuum custodiat per quem *B;* uobis uiuum custodiat per quem *R;* uiuum custodiat uobis per quam *Y* [b] *ditto. S* [c] *om. CE;* historiam *F* [d] reuolues *F* [e] resurrectionis *CEFY* [f] *om. CE* [g] *del. A* [h] heliam *CE;* Heliam *Amb* [i] *om. BRY* [j] facta *C* [k] commemorauimus *T* (*after corr. of* memorauimus), *Amb* [l] ipsis *ACEFY;* temporis *BR* [m–m] de resurrectione mulieres *BRY* [n–n] m.s. *C;* mortuos scilicet *BY;* mor. s. *R* [o] naim *A;* nam *R;* iam *Y* [p] quippe *T* [q] ob *BRY* [r] suarum *BRY* [s] atque *BRY;* et *F* [t] Quomodo *F* [u] impedendo *F* [v] *om. S* [w–w] ille deus corpora *CE;* illae duae corpora *F* [x] quidam *R before corr.;* nunc *add. Y* [y] resurectiones *A;* resurrectiones *CEY* [z–z] oratio uestre deuotionis *CEF* [a] orationum *add. CEF* [b] quanta *B* [c] propitiatorium *F* [d] inuenit *Y*

6. You know, dearest sister, from the thirty-eighth homily of St Gregory how much support the prayers of his fellow brethren quickly brought a brother, although he was unwilling and resisted.[21] The depths of his misery, the fear of peril which tormented his unhappy soul, the utter despair and weariness of life which made him try to call his brethren from their prayers—all the details set out there cannot have escaped your understanding.

7. May this example give you and your convent of holy sisters greater confidence in prayer, so that I may be preserved alive for you all through him from whom, as Paul bears witness, women have even received back their dead raised to life.[22] For if you turn the pages of the Old and New Testaments you will find that the greatest miracles of being brought back to life were shown only, or mostly, to women, and were performed for or because of them. The Old Testament records two instances of men raised from the dead at the entreaties of their mothers, by Elijah, that is, and his disciple Elisha.[23] The Gospel, it is true, has three instances only of the dead being raised by the Lord but, as they were shown to women only, they provide factual confirmation of the Apostle's words I quoted above: 'Women received back their dead raised to life.'[24] It was to a widow at the gate of the city of Nain that the Lord restored her son, moved by compassion for her,[25] and he also raised Lazarus his own friend at the entreaty of his sisters Mary and Martha.[26] And when he granted this same favour to the daughter of the ruler of the synagogue at her father's petition,[27] again 'women received back their dead raised to life', for in being brought back to life she received her own body back from death just as those other women received the bodies of their dead.[28] Now these risings from death were performed with only a few interceding; and so the multiplied prayers of your shared devotion should easily win the preservation of my own life. The more God is pleased by the abstinence and continence which women have dedicated to him, the more willing he will be to grant their prayers. Moreover, it may well be that the majority of those raised from the

[21] Gregory the Great, *Homiliae in Evangelia* xxxviii, 16 (ed. Étaix, pp. 376–8; *PL* lxxvi. 1292B–1293C).

[22] Heb. 11: 35.

[23] Cf. 3 Kgs. (1 Kgs.) 17: 17–24; 4 Kgs. (2 Kgs.) 4: 18–37, 8: 1–6. Cf. *Letter* 7, 37 and *Sermon* 23 (*PL* clxxviii. 525D).

[24] Heb. 11: 35.

[25] Luke 7: 11–15.

[26] John 11: 34.

[27] Cf. Mark 5: 22–42; Luke 8: 40–56.

[28] 'Si enim Veteris et Euangelici Testamenti . . . corpora suorum': cf. *Letter* 7, 37.

plerique fortassis horum qui suscitati sunt nec fideles extiterunt, sicut nec[e] uidua predicta,[29] cui non roganti [f]filium Dominus[f] suscitauit,[g] fidelis extitisse[h] legitur. Nos autem inuicem non solum fidei colligat[i] integritas, uerum etiam eiusdem[j] religionis professio[k] sociat.

8. Vt autem sacrosanctum collegii uestri nunc[a] omittam conuentum, in quo plurimarum uirginum ac uiduarum deuotio Domino iugiter deseruit,[b] ad te unam ueniam, cuius apud Deum[c] sanctitatem plurimum non ambigo posse, et que potes mihi precipue debere, maxime nunc[d] in tante[e] aduersitatis laboranti discrimine. Memento [f]itaque semper[f] in orationibus tuis eius, qui specialiter est tuus,[30] et tanto confidentius in oratione uigila[g] quanto[h] id esse tibi[i] recognoscis[j] iustius, et ob hoc ipsi qui orandus est acceptabilius. [k]Exaudi, obsecro,[k] aure[l] cordis, quod sepius[m] audisti[n] aure corporis. Scriptum est in Prouerbiis: 'Mulier diligens [o]corona est[o] uiro suo.'[31] Et rursum:[p] 'Qui inuenit mulierem bonam, inuenit bonum: et hauriet iucunditatem a Domino.'[32] Et [q]iterum: 'Domus et diuitie dantur a parentibus, a Domino autem proprie uxor prudens.'[33] Et[q] in Ecclesiastico: 'Mulieris bone beatus uir.'[34] Et post pauca: 'Pars bona, mulier bona.'[r] [35] Et iuxta auctoritatem apostolicam: 'Sanctificatus est uir infidelis per mulierem fidelem.'[36]

9. Cuius quidem rei experimentum in[a] regno precipue nostro, id est Francorum, diuina specialiter exhibuit gratia, cum [b]ad orationem[b] [c]uidelicet uxoris[c] magis quam [d]ad sanctorum predicationem,[d] Clodoueo[e] rege ad fidem Christi conuerso, regnum[f] sic[g] uniuersum[h] diuinis legibus[i] mancipauerunt,[j] [37] ut exemplo maxime superiorum [k]ad orationis[k] instantiam inferiores[l] prouocarentur. Ad quam quidem [m]instantiam dominica nos uehementer inuitans[m] parabola 'ille,'[n] inquit, 'si perseuerauerit[o] pulsans,[p] dico uobis quia si non dabit ei

[e] uero *R* [f–f] dominus filium *BRY* [g] illa mulier *add. CEF* [h] esse *CEF* [i] collocat *CEF* [j] euuangelice *Y*[1] *after corr.* [k] proffectio *C;* profectio *E*

8 [a] *add. Bcorr.; om. R;* non *Y* [b] diseruit *F* [c] dominum *Y* [d] *om. Amb* [e] tanta *F* [f–f] semper itaque *BRY* [g] uigilia *T before corr., C* [h] tanto *E* [i] *om. RY* [j] recognosciscis *C;* recognoscere *Y*[1] *after corr.* [k–k] Obsecro exaudi *BRY* [l] ore *F* [m] sepe *BY; om. F* [n] audita *E;* et *add. S* [o–o] caro est *C;* corona *EF* [p] *om. E in vacant space* [q–q] *om. CEF* [r] *ditto. C*

9 [a] *om. SY* [b–b] orationem *CE;* oratione *F* [c–c] uxoris sue *BR;* uxoris sue regine clothildis *Y* [d–d] a sanctorum predicationem *CE;* sanctorum praedicatione *F* [e] clodaueo *C* [f] regni *Y* [g] se *TACEFBRY;* et se *S;* sic *Amb* [h] uniuersis *BRS;* uniuersi *Y* [i] Regibus *C* [j] mancipauerit *F* [k–k] *om. T; add. T*[1] *in marg.* [l] inferi *Ecorr.* [m–m] nos instantiam dominica uehementer inuitat *CEF;* instantiam (inferiores prouocarentur *del. B*) dominica uehementer nos inuitans *B;*

dead were not of the faith, for we do not read that the widow mentioned above,[29] whose son was raised without her asking, was a believer. But in our case we are bound together by the integrity of our faith and united in our profession of the same religious life.

8. But now, to leave aside the holy convent of your community, where so many virgins and widows are dedicated to continual service of the Lord, let me come to you alone, you whose holiness must surely have the greatest influence before God, and who must especially do all you can on my behalf, especially now when I am in the toils of such adversity. Always remember then in your prayers him who is especially yours.[30] Watch and pray the more confidently as you recognize your cause is just, and so more acceptable to him to whom you pray. Listen, I beg you, with the ear of your heart to what you have so often heard with your bodily ear. In the book of Proverbs it is written that 'a capable wife is her husband's crown',[31] and again: 'Find a wife and you find a good thing; so you will earn the favour of the Lord';[32] yet again: 'Home and wealth may come down from ancestors; but an intelligent wife is a gift from the Lord.'[33] In Ecclesiasticus too it says that 'a good wife makes a happy husband',[34] and a little later: 'A good wife means a good life.'[35] And we have it on the Apostle's authority that 'the unbelieving husband now belongs to God through his believing wife'.[36]

9. A special instance of this was granted by God's grace in our own country of France, when Clovis the king was converted to the Christian faith more by the prayers of his wife than by the preaching of holy men; his entire kingdom was then placed under divine law[37] so that humbler men should be encouraged by the example of their betters to persevere in prayer. Indeed, such perseverance is warmly recommended to us in a parable of the Lord which says: 'If the man perseveres in his knocking, though he will not provide for him out of

instantiam dominica nos inuitat uehementer *Y* [n] et *C, ?E, F* [o] seruauerit *Y;* perseuerauerit *Y*[1] [p] quis *add. S*

[29] Luke 7: 15.
[30] 'specialiter . . . tuus': cf. the inscription at the head of *Letter* 6: 'suo specialiter' / 'hers especially.'
[31] Prov. 12: 4.
[32] Prov. 18: 22.
[33] Prov. 19: 14.
[34] Ecclus. 26: 1.
[35] Ecclus. 26: 3.
[36] 1 Cor. 7: 14.
[37] Cf. Gregory of Tours, *Libri historiarum X*, ii. 29–31 (ed. Krusch and Levison, pp. 90–3).

eo[q] quod amicus illius[r] sit, [s]'propter improbitatem tamen[t] eius surgens dabit ei quotquot habet[u] necessarios',[38] etc.[sv] Ex hac profecto, ut ita dicam orationis improbitate,[w] sicut supra memini, Moyses diuine iustitie seueritatem eneruauit,[39] et sententiam immutauit.

10. Nosti, dilectissima,[a] quantum charitatis affectum[b] presentie mee conuentus olim uester[c] in oratione solitus sit[d] exhibere. Ad expletionem namque[e] quotidie singularum horarum specialem pro me[f] Domino supplicationem hanc offerre consueuit, ut responso proprio cum uersu[g] eius premissis et decantatis, preces his[h] et collectam[i] in hunc modum subiungeret:

Responsum:[j] Non me derelinquas, nec[k] discedas a me, Domine.[40]

Versus:[l] In adiutorium meum semper intende, Domine.[m 41]

Preces:[n] Saluum fac seruum tuum, Deus[o] meus, sperantem in te.[42]

Domine, exaudi orationem meam, et clamor meus [p]ad te ueniat.[p 43]

Oratio:[q] Deus qui per[r] seruulum[s] tuum ancillulas tuas in nomine tuo [t]dignatus es aggregare,[t] te quesumus, ut tam ipsi quam nobis in tua tribuas [u]perseuerantiam uoluntate.[u] Per Dominum,[v] etc.[44]

11. Nunc autem [a]absenti mihi[a] tanto amplius orationum uestrarum opus est suffragio, quanto maioris anxietate periculi constringor. Supplicando itaque postulo,[b] et postulando supplico, quatenus precipue nunc absens experiar quam uera charitas uestra erga absentem extiterit, [c]singulis uidelicet horis expletis hunc orationis proprie modum adnectens:

Responsum:[cd] Ne derelinquas me, Domine,[e] pater et dominator uite mee, ut[f] non corruam in conspectu aduersariorum meorum: ne gaudeat de me inimicus meus.[45]

[q] *om. F* [r] eius *F* [s–s] *om. R* [t] *om. Amb* [u] *om. CE* [v] *om. FAmb* [w] reprobitate *Y*

10 [a] karissima *Y* [b] effectum *Y* [c] noster *F* [d] scit *R* [e] nam *B, Ecorr.* [f] *om. Y* [g] conuersu *B* [h] has *F* [i] collectis *B;* collectum *R* [j] R *E;* Responsorium *F;* RS *add. in vacant space* Y^2 [k] ne *TA* [l] Versum *TA;* deus *?add. in vacant space by* Y^2 [m] *om. E* [n] *om. TABRY* [o] domine deus *CEF;* did *?B* d. d. *R* [p–p] etc CE [q] Oremus *CEFAmb*[1]*; add. in vacant space by* Y^2 [r] *om. TY; add. in marg. by* T^1 *and another hand* [s] seruum *CEF* [t–t] aggregare dignatus est *E* (dignatus est *add. in marg. Ecorr.*) [u–u] perseuerantium uoluntate *T;* perseuerantia uoluntatem *CEF;* perseuerare uoluntate *Amb* [v] nostrum *add. CE*

11 [a–a] mihi absenti mihi *BR;* michi absenti *Y* [b] *om. R;* postulo et *add. YAmb*

friendship, the very shamelessness of the request will make him get up and give him all he needs', etc.[38] It was certainly by what I might call this shamelessness in prayer that Moses (as I said above) softened the harshness of divine justice[39] and changed its sentence.

10. You know, beloved, the warmth of charity your convent once used to show me in their prayers at the times I could be with you. At the conclusion of each of the Hours every day they would offer this special prayer to the Lord on my behalf; after the proper response and versicle were pronounced and sung they added prayers and a collect, as follows:

RESPONSE: Forsake me not, O Lord, do not depart from me.[40]

VERSICLE: O Lord, make haste to help me.[41]

SUPPLICATIONS: Save thy servant, O my God, whose hope is in thee.[42]
Lord, hear my prayer, and let my cry for help come to thee.[43]

PRAYER: O God, who through thy servant hast been pleased to gather together thy handmaidens in thy name, we beseech thee to grant both to him and to us that we persevere in thy will. Through our Lord, etc.[44]

11. But now that I am not with you, there is all the more need for the support of your prayers, the more I am gripped by fear of greater peril. And so I ask of you in entreaty, and entreat you in asking, particularly now that I am absent from you, to show me how truly your charity extends to the absent by adding this form of special prayer at the conclusion of each hour:

RESPONSE: O Lord, Father and Ruler of my life, do not desert me, lest I fall before my adversaries and my enemy gloats over me.[45]

[c–c] *om. Y* [d] Responsorium *F ;* Preces *add. in vacant space Y*[2] [e] *om. BRY*
[f] et *Y*

[38] Luke 11: 8. Luke continues: 'And so I say to you, ask, and you will receive.'
[39] Exod. 32: 14.
[40] Ps. 37 (38): 22 (21); 'Ne derelinquas me, Domine Deus meus; Ne discesseris a me,' *Vulg.*
[41] Ps. 37 (38): 23 (22), 69 (70): 2 (1). [42] Ps. 85 (86): 2. [43] Ps. 101 (102): 2 (1).
[44] The formulation 'Deus . . . te quesumus ut . . .' is unusual. It is also found in the next *Oratio* and in the *Paraclete Breviary* in the first collect for the feast of Philip the Deacon (*Bre* iiiB, ed. Waddell, p. 258, *ll.* 4–6) and in the *Postulationes gratiarum sancti Spiritus* (*Bre* iiiC, ed. Waddell, pp. 401–2). Waddell in *The Old French Paraclete Ordinary*, i. 209–10, 377–9, sees in it a mark of Abelard's authorship. 'Per Dominum, etc.': 'Through our Lord Jesus Christ, your Son, who lives and reigns with you in the unity of the Holy Spirit, one God, for ever and ever. Amen.'
[45] Ecclus. 23: 1, 3 ('. . . et incidam in conspectu aduersariorum meorum . . .', *Vulg*).

Versus:[g] Apprehende arma et scutum,[h] et exsurge in adiutorium mihi. Ne gaudeat, etc.[i] [46]

Preces:[j] Saluum fac seruum tuum,[k] Deus meus, [lm]sperantem in te.[m] [47]

Mitte ei, Domine,[n] auxilium de sancto: et [o]de Sion tuere[p] eum.[oq] [48]

Esto ei, Domine, turris fortitudinis [r]a facie inimici.[lr] [49]

Domine, exaudi[s] orationem meam,[t] [u]et clamor meus ad te ueniat.[u] [50]

Oratio:[v] Deus qui per seruum[w] tuum[x] ancillulas tuas in nomine tuo dignatus es aggregare,[y] te quesumus, ut eum ab omni aduersitate protegas, et ancillis[z] tuis incolumem reddas. Per [a]Dominum, etc.[a]

12. Quod si me Dominus in manus[a] inimicorum tradiderit,[51] scilicet ut ipsi preualentes me interficiant, aut quocunque[b] casu uiam uniuerse carnis absens[c] uobis[d] ingrediar, cadauer, obsecro, nostrum[e] ubicunque[f] uel sepultum uel expositum iacuerit, ad cemeterium uestrum deferri faciatis, ubi filie uestre,[g] imo in Christo sorores, sepulcrum nostrum sepius uidentes, ad preces pro me Domino[h] fundendas amplius inuitentur.[52] Nullum quippe locum anime dolenti de peccatorum suorum errore desolate tutiorem ac[i] salubriorem arbitror quam eum qui uero[j] Paracleto,[k] id est consolatori, proprie consecratus est et de eius nomine[l] specialiter[m] insignitus. Nec Christiane sepulture locum rectius apud aliquos fideles[n] quam apud feminas Christo[o] deuotas consistere censeo. Que, de Domini[p] Iesu Christi sepultura[q] sollicite, eam[r] unguentis pretiosis et preuenerunt et subsecute sunt, et circa [s]eius sepulcrum[s] studiose uigilantes et sponsi mortem [t]lacrimabiliter plangentes,[t] [53] sicut scriptum est: 'Mulieres sedentes ad monumentum lamentabantur flentes Dominum.'[54] Primo ibidem de resurrectione eius angelica apparitione et allocutione[u] sunt

[g] Versum *TA; om. Y* [h] secutum *Amb* [i] *om. TABRAmb;* de me inimicus *Y* [j] *om. TABRY* [k] d(omine) *add. BR;* domine *add. Y* [l–l] etc *C* [m–m] etc *EF* [n] *om. F* [o–o] etc *EF* [p] tueatur *Y, Vulg* [q] t(e) *R;* te *Vulg* [r–r] etc *EF* [s] *om. E* [t] *om. F* [u–u] etc *CEF* [v] Oremus *CEFAmb*[1]; Oratio *add. in vacant space by Y*[2] [w] seruulum *AEFRY;* famulum *C* [x] et *add. F* [y] congregare *RY* [z] ancillulis *F* [a–a] dominum *TAB;* dominum nostrum etc *CE; om. RY*

12 [a] Manu *A;* manibus *Amb* [b] quoque *C* [c] absens *TBRDY;* (. . .)sentibus *T*[1] *in marg.;* absentibus *ACEF;* a *add. Amb* [d] nobis *B* [e] uestrum *B* [f] ubique *C* [g] nostre *CEFAmb;* vestrae *Amb*[1] [h] *om. F* [i] et *FY* [j] vere *F* [k] paraclito *T* [l] eius *add. RY* [m] proprie *CEF* [n] *om. E* [o] deo *BRY* [p] nostri *add. FBRY* [q] sepulture *CE* [r] eum *CEF* [s–s] sepulcrum eius *BRY* [t–t] plangentes lacrimabiliter *BRY* [u] locutione *BRY*

VERSICLE: Grasp shield and buckler and rise up to help me, lest my enemy gloats,[46] etc.

SUPPLICATIONS: Save thy servant, O my God, whose hope is in thee.[47]

Send him help, O Lord, from thy holy place, and watch over him from Zion.[48]

Be a tower of strength to him, O Lord, in the face of his enemy.[49]

Lord, hear my prayer, and let my cry for help come to thee.[50]

PRAYER: O God, who through thy servant hast been pleased to gather together thy handmaidens in thy name, we beseech thee to protect him in all adversity and restore him in safety to thy handmaidens. Through our Lord, etc.

12. But if the Lord shall deliver me into the hands of my enemies[51] so that they overcome and kill me, or by whatever chance I enter upon the way of all flesh while separated from you, wherever my body may lie, buried or unburied, I beg you to have it brought to your cemetery, where our daughters, or rather our sisters in Christ, may see my tomb more often and thereby be encouraged to pour out their prayers more fully to the Lord on my behalf.[52] There is no place, I think, more safe and salutary for a soul grieving for its sins and desolated by its transgressions than that which is specially consecrated to the true Paraclete, the Comforter, and which is particularly designated by his name. Nor do I believe that there is any place more fitting for Christian burial among the faithful than one amongst women dedicated to Christ. Women were concerned for the tomb of our Lord Jesus Christ; they came ahead and followed after, bringing precious ointments, keeping close watch around this tomb, weeping for the death of the Bridegroom,[53] as it is written: 'The women sitting at the tomb wept and lamented for the Lord.'[54] And there they were first reassured about his resurrection by the appearance of an angel

[46] Ps. 34 (35): 2; Ecclus. 23: 3. [47] Ps. 85 (86): 2. [48] Ps. 19 (20): 3 (2).
[49] Ps. 60: 4 (3). [50] Ps. 101 (102): 2 (1). [51] Cf. Dan. 3: 32.

[52] 'cadauer, obsecro, nostrum . . . ad cemeterium uestrum deferri faciatis ubi filie uestre . . . ad preces pro me . . . fundendas . . . inuitentur': cf. the prayer in an epitaph of Abelard (*inc.* 'Serui animam seruans'):'". . . ancillis redde cadauer"! / Hanc tibi fundo, Deus . . . precem' (ed. Dronke in *Abelard and Heloise in Medieval Testimonies*, pp. 49–50; repr. in *Intellectuals and Poets*, pp. 284–5; *Checklist* no. 450).

[53] Cf. Matt. 27: 61; Mark 15: 47–16: 1; Luke 23: 55–24: 1.

[54] The antiphon at the *Benedictus* in Lauds on Holy Saturday in the *Roman Breviary*, cited also in *Letter* 5, 4 and 28. Cf. Matt. 27: 61; Luke 23: 27, 55; John 20: 11.

consolate, et statim[v] ipsius resurrectionis gaudia, eo[w] [x]bis eis[x] apparente, percipere meruerunt et manibus contrectare.[y] [55]

13. Illud autem demum [a]super omnia postulo,[a] [b]ut que nunc[b] de corporis mei periculo nimia sollicitudine laboratis, tunc[c] precipue de salute anime sollicite, quantum[d] dilexeritis uiuum exhibeatis defuncto, orationum[e] uidelicet uestrarum speciali quodam et proprio suffragio.

Viue, uale, uiuantque tue ualeantque sorores. Viuite, sed Christo,[f] queso, mei memores.

[v] post *add.* *Y* [w] angelo *Y* [x–x] eis bis *RY* [y] contractare *AEY*

13 [a–a] postulo super omnia *Y* [b–b] usque nunc *T;* ut quecunque *BRY* [c] *om. E* [d] quam *C* [e] oratio *Y* [f] domino christo *CE;* Domino *Amb*[1]

and the words he spoke to them; later on they were found worthy both to taste the joy of his resurrection when he twice appeared to them, and also to touch him with their hands.[55]

13. Finally, I ask this of you above all else: at present you are over-anxious about the danger to my body, but then your chief concern must be for the salvation of my soul, and you must show the dead man how much you loved the living one by the special support of prayers chosen for him.

Live, fare you well, yourself and your sisters with you. Live, but I pray, in Christ be mindful of me.

[55] Cf. Matt. 28: 1–10; also *Letter* 7, 11.

⟨EPISTOLA IV⟩

1. [a]VNICO[b] SVO POST CHRISTVM VNICA SVA IN CHRISTO[a]

[c]Miror, unice meus, quod preter consuetudinem[c] epistolarum, immo contra ipsum ordinem naturalem rerum,[1] in ipsa fronte salutationis epistolaris me tibi preponere presumpsisti, feminam uidelicet uiro, uxorem marito, ancillam domino, monialem monacho et sacerdoti, diaconissam abbati.[d][2] Rectus quippe ordo est et honestus ut qui[e] ad superiores uel[f] ad pares scribunt, eorum quibus scribunt nomina suis anteponant; sin[g] autem ad inferiores, precedunt scriptionis ordine qui precedunt rerum dignitate.[3]

2. Illud etiam[a] non parua ammiratione suscepimus, quod[b] quibus consolationis remedium afferre debuisti desolationem auxisti, et quas mittigare debueras excitasti[c] lacrimas. Que enim nostrum [d]siccis oculis[d][4] audire possit quod circa finem epistole posuisti[5] dicens quod 'si [e]me Dominus[e] in manus inimicorum tradiderit,[6] [f]ut me scilicet preualentes interficiant',[f] etc.? O karissime, quo id animo cogitasti? Quo id ore dicere sustinuisti? Numquam[g] ancillulas[h] suas [i]adeo Deus[i] obliuiscatur ut eas tibi superstites[j] reseruet; numquam[k]

Letter 4 *T* fos. 23[vb]–27[rb]; *A* fos. 18[rb]–20[va]; *C* fos. 160[v]–164[v]; *E* fos. 19[r]–22[r]; *F* pp. 27–38; *B* fos. 17[vb]–20[ra]; *R* fos. 130[rb]–133[ra]; *S* fos. 30–6; *Y* fos. 102[ra]–104[rb]; *Amb* pp. 54–61; *Amb*[1] *variants in the margins of Amb*; *J* pp. 79–91. *Headings are found in the following witnesses*: Rescriptum ipsius ad ipsum (ipsam *S*) *rubr. TAS;* edita ordine 4[a] *F;* Comme Heloyse rescrip a P. Abaielart plus doloreusement que devant, et recite partie de la vie qu'il avoient tenue ij[c]xiiij *table in H of the* (*missing*) *contents of Dijon MS 525;* Rescriptio Heloysse ad Abaelardum *in vacant space Y*[2]*;* EPISTOLA IIII. Quae est Rescriptum HELOISSAE ad PETRUM *Amb*

1 [a–a] *another hand in F* [b] *vacant space for initial in CE; decorated initial in B;* Amico *decorated initial in R, Y* [c–c] amor uni et meus quod pre cum *B* [d] abbatissam *add. ?T*[1] *in marg., ACEF* [e] que *C* [f] et *A* [g] si *CEF*

2 [a] enim *Y* [b] pro *E* [c] excitare *A before corr.*, ad *add. BRY* [d–d] oculis siccis *Y* [e–e] me deus *CF;* deus *E* [f–f] *om. CEF* [g] numquid *BR* [h] ancillas *CEF* [i–i] deus (*superscr. by another hand*) adeo *Y* [j] superstites *superscr. by Ecorr* [k] Nomquam *R*

---

[1] Cf. *Letters* 1, **69** and 5, **1**.

[2] On deaconesses cf. *Letter* 7, **18–20** and *Rule* **26–7**.

[3] For the conventional sequence which Heloise upholds see Alberic of Montecassino, *Breviarium de dictamine*, x. 9 (ed. Bognini, p. 41): 'Antiqui mittentium nomina semper solebant preponere; moderni, humilitatis causa, nisi excellentissima sit persona mittentis,

LETTER 4

I. TO HER ONE-AND-ONLY AFTER CHRIST, SHE WHO IS HIS ALONE IN CHRIST

I am surprised, my only love, that contrary to custom in letter-writing and, indeed, to the natural order of things,[1] you have thought fit to put my name before yours in the greeting which heads your letter, so that we have woman before man, wife before husband, handmaid before lord, nun before monk and priest, and deaconess before abbot.[2] Surely the right and proper order is for those who write to their superiors or equals to put their names before their own, but in letters to inferiors, precedence in order of address follows precedence in rank.[3]

2. We were also greatly surprised when instead of bringing us the healing balm of comfort as you should have done, you increased our desolation and made the tears to flow which you should have dried. For which of us could remain dry-eyed[4] on hearing the words you wrote towards the end of your letter:[5] 'But if the Lord shall deliver me into the hands of my enemies[6] so that they overcome and kill me', etc.? Oh, dearest, what did you have in mind? How could you bear to say it? Never may God be so forgetful of his humble handmaids as to let them outlive you; never may he grant us a life which would be

semper ea consueverunt postponere' / 'The ancients always used to put the senders' names first; the moderns, out of humility, have become accustomed to put them last, except when the sender has surpassing eminence.' At x. 16 (Bognini, p. 42) Alberic gives examples in which the lesser person comes last: 'magistro clientulus, domino servulus'. His *Breviarium* was largely written in the mid-1180s and was hugely influential on later treatises on letter writing and especially on forms of address. See, for example, Magister Bernardus, *Rationes dictandi* (written in Romagna, and probably in Bologna, 1138–43, v, ed. (and attributed to Alberic of Monte Cassino) by Rockinger, i. 11: 'cum maior scribit minori, tunc enim mittentis nomen preponendum est, ut eius dignitas ipsa nominum positione monstretur' / 'when a greater person writes to a lesser one, the name of the sender is to be put first so that his dignity may be shown by the positioning of words'. On the attribution to Magister Bernardus of *Rationes dictandi* and on the composition of this work, see Worstbrock and others, *Repertorium*, pp. 24–8. See also Adalbertus Samaritanus, *Praecepta dictaminum* 3: 1–34 (written in Bologna, 1112–18; ed. Schmale, pp. 34–42; Worstbrock and others, *Repertorium*, pp. 1–6). On *salutatio* formulae according to these *dictatores* see also Lanham, *Salutatio Formulas*, pp. 94–100.

[4] 'siccis oculis': cf. *Letter* 2, **3**.

[5] Above, *Letter* 3, **12**.

[6] Cf. Dan. 3: 32.

[l]nobis illam uitam[l] concedat que omni genere mortis sit grauior.[7] Te nostras exequias celebrare, te nostras [m]Deo animas[m] conuenit commendare et quas Deo agregasti ad ipsum premittere,[n] ut nulla [o]amplius de ipsis[o] perturberis sollicitudine, et tanto [p]letior nos[p] subsequaris quanto securior de [q]nostra salute iam[q] fueris.

3. Parce, obsecro, domine, parce [a]huiusmodi dictis,[a] [8] quibus miseras miserrimas facias, et [b]hoc ipsum quod utcumque[b] uiuimus ne[c] nobis auferas ante mortem. 'Sufficit diei malicia sua',[9] et dies illa[d] [10] omnibus quos[e] inueniet[f] satis secum sollicitudinis afferet[g] omni amaritudine inuoluta.[11] 'Quid enim [h]neccesse est', inquit Seneca,[h] 'mala arcessere',[i] et ante mortem uitam perdere?[12]

4. Rogas, unice, ut quocumque casu nobis[a] absens hanc uitam finieris, ad cimiterium nostrum corpus tuum afferri faciamus,[b] ut orationum scilicet nostrarum[c] ex assidua tui memoria ampliorem assequaris fructum. At uero quomodo memoriam tui a[d] nobis labi posse suspicaris? Aut quod[e] orationi tempus[f] tunc erit commodum quando summa perturbatio nichil permittet[g] [h]quietum, cum nec[h] anima rationis sensum nec lingua sermonis retinebit usum,[i] cum mens insana,[j] in ipsum, ut ita dicam, Deum magis irata quam paccata,[k] non tam orationibus ipsum placabit[l] quam querimoniis irritabit? Flere tunc miseris tantum[m] uaccabit, non orare licebit, et te magis subsequi quam sepelire[n] maturandum erit,[o] ut potius et nos consepeliende[p] simus quam sepelire possimus; que cum in te nostram amiserimus uitam, uiuere, te recedente, nequaquam[q] poterimus. Atque utinam nec tunc[r] usque possimus! Mortis tue mentio mors quedam[s] nobis est; ipsa autem mortis huius ueritas quid,[t] si nos inuenerit, futura[u] est? Nunquam Deus [v]annuat ut[v] hoc tibi debitum superstites persoluamus, ut hoc tibi patrocinio subueniamus quod a te penitus expectamus, [w]in hoc utinam te[w] precessure[x] non secuture!

[l–l] illam nobis uitam *Y;* nobis vitam illam *Amb* [m–m] animas deo *RY* [n] permittere *Y before corr. by* Y^1 [o–o] de ipsis amplius *F* [p–p] nos *E;* nos laetior *F;* lectior nos *B* [q–q] nostra iam salute *F*

3 [a–a] huius dicens *B* [b–b] hoc (hoc *om. Amb*) ut (ut *add. over eras. T*) ipsum quodcumque (quod *over eras. T*) *T with eras. also in marg., Amb;* hoc ipsum quod utrumque *Y* [c] *om. EF* [d] *om. CEF* [e] quod *T* [f] inuenit *Y* [g] conferet *Y* [h–h] inquit seneca necesse est *CEF* [i] accrescere *Y*

4 [a] a nobis *CEF* [b] uideamus *E before corr.* [c] obtentu *add. Y* [d] nisi *B* [e] *om. Y* [f] temporis *C* [g] promittet *BR* [h–h] quietum (*? add. F*) Cum nec (hec *E*) *CEF* [i] usum *followed by a question mark in T* [j] sana *F* [k] placata *Y* [l] placaberat *B*; placebit *C* [m] tunc *BR*; non *Y* [n] possemus *add. B before exp.*

harder to bear than any form of death.[7] The proper course would be for you to perform our funeral rites, for you to commend our souls to God, and to send ahead of you those whom you assembled for God's service—so that you need no longer be troubled by worries for us, and follow after us the more gladly because freed from concern for our salvation.

3. Spare us, I beseech you, lord, spare us words such as these[8] which can only intensify our misery; do not deny us, before death, the one thing by which we live. 'Sufficient unto the day is the evil thereof',[9] and that day,[10] shrouded in bitterness, will bring with it distress enough to all it comes upon.[11] 'Why is it necessary', says Seneca, 'to summon evil' and to destroy life before death comes?[12]

4. You ask us, my one-and-only, if you chance to die when separated from us, to have your body brought to our cemetery so that you may reap a fuller harvest from the prayers we shall offer in constant memory of you. But how could you suppose that our memory of you could ever fade? Besides, what time will there be then which will be fitting for prayer, when extreme distress will allow us no peace, when the soul will lose its power of reason and the tongue its use of speech? Or when the frantic mind, more angry, as it were, with God than at peace with him, will provoke him with complaints, not appease him with prayers? In our misery then we shall have time only for tears and no power to pray; we shall be hurrying to follow, not to bury you, so that we may share your grave instead of laying you in it. If we lose our life in you, we shall not be able to go on living when you leave us. I would not even have us live to see that day, for if the mere mention of your death is death for us, what will the reality be if it finds us still alive? God grant we may never live on to perform this duty, to render you the service which we look for from you alone; in this may we go before, not after you!

[o] erunt *BR* [p] tunc sepeliende *Y* [q] numquam *Y* [r] nunc *Y* [s] *om. Y*
[t] quam *CE;* quae *F;* quod *BR* [u] factura *Y* [v–v] adiuuat ut *B;* adiuuat nec *R*
[w–w] ut te *C;* utinam te *E;* utinam *F* [x] precessiue *B*

[7] Cf. *Planctus VI: Dauid super Saul et Ionathan*, *vv.* 45–6 (77–8) : 'Et me post te uiuere / mori sit assidue'/ 'And to outlive you is for me / To perish constantly' (ed. Meyer, *Gesammelte Abhandlungen*, i. 324; ed. Weinrich in '"*Dolorum solatium*": Text und Musik', p. 68; *PL* clxxviii. 1822; trans. Lombardo and Thorburn in Levitan, p. 291).

[8] 'Parce . . . parce': see also 5 below.

[9] Matt. 6: 34.

[10] 'dies illa': cf. Isaiah 2: 17, 20; Zephaniah 1: 15; Matt. 24: 36, etc.

[11] Cf. Job 3: 5.

[12] Seneca, *Epistola ad Lucilium*, 24: 1.

5. Parce itaque, obsecro, nobis; parce itaque[a] unice saltem tue,[b] [13] huiusmodi scilicet supersedendo uerbis quibus tanquam gladiis mortis nostras transuerberas animas, ut quod mortem preuenit ipsa morte grauius sit. Confectus merore[c] animus quietus non est, nec Deo sincere potest uaccare mens perturbationibus occupata. Noli, obsecro, diuinum impedire[d] seruitium, cui nos maxime mancipasti. Omne ineuitabile quod cum acciderit merorem maximum secum inferet,[e] ut subito ueniat obtandum est, ne timore inutili diu ante cruciet cui nulla succurri[f] prouidentia potest. Quod et poeta bene considerans Deum deprecatur[g] dicens:

> Sit subitum quodcumque[h] paras, sit ceca futuri[i]
> Mens hominum fati; [j]liceat sperare timenti.[j] [14]

6. Quid autem, te amisso, [a]sperandum mihi[a] superest? Aut que[b] in hac peregrinatione causa remanendi, ubi nullum nisi[c] te remedium habeam, et nullum aliud in te nisi hoc ipsum quod uiuis, omnibus [d]de te mihi aliis[d] uoluptatibus interdictis,[e] cui[f] nec presentia tua concessum est frui ut quandoque mihi reddi ualeam? O,[g] si fas sit dici, crudelem mihi per omnia Deum! O inclementem[h] clementiam! O [i]infortunatam fortunam[i] que iam in me uniuersi conaminis[j] sui [k]tela in tantum[k] consumpsit ut quibus in alios seuiat iam non habeat! Plenam in me pharetram exhausit, ut[l] frustra iam alii bella [m]eius formident;[m] nec si ei[n] adhuc telum[o] aliquod superesset[p] locum in me uulneris inueniret.[15] Vnum inter tot uulnera metuit, ne morte supplicia finiam; et cum[q] interimere non cesset, interitum[r] tamen quem accelerat timet.

7. O[a] me miserarum miserrimam, infelicium infelicissimam, que quanto uniuersis[b] in te feminis prelata sublimiorem obtinui gradum, tanto hinc prostrata[c] grauiorem in te et in me [d]pariter perpessa[d] sum

5 [a] *om.* *ACEFBY* [b] ab *add.* *Y*[1] [c] dolore *before corr.* *T;* memore *C* [d] impendere *E* [e] affert *Y after corr. of* affertur [f] securi *?E* [g] precatur *Amb* [h] quodque *C* [i] futura *A* [j–j] liceat sapere timenti *marked for corr.* *Y*

6 [a–a] mihi sperandum *BRY* [b] absque *T*; ou quelle *J* [c] *om.* *E*; in *add.* *F* [d–d] mihi de te aliis *CEF;* a te aliis mihi *BRY* [e] intermissis *BRY* [f] tibi *Y* [g] ut *RY* [h] clementem *C* [i–i] infortuna fortuna *RY* [j] cognaminis *BR* [k–k] intantum tela *CEF* [l] nec *B* [m–m] formident eius *Y* [n] eius *marked for corr.* *Y* [o] te lum *T after eras.* [p] superest *C* [q] *om.* *RY* [r] inuitum *C*

7 [a] A *Y* [b] *om.* *Y* [c] prostacta *C* [d–d] perpessa pariter *E*

5. And so, I beseech you, spare us—spare her at least who is yours alone[13]—by refraining from words like these. They pierce our hearts with swords of death, so that what comes before is more painful than death itself. A heart which is exhausted with grief cannot find peace, nor can a mind preoccupied with anxieties genuinely devote itself to God. I beseech you not to hinder God's service to which you specially committed us. Whatever has to come to us bringing with it total grief we must hope will come suddenly, without torturing us far in advance with useless apprehension which no foresight can relieve. This is what the poet has in mind when he prays to God:

> May it be sudden, whatever you plan; may man's mind
> Be blind to future fate. May he who is afraid have hope.[14]

6. But if I lose you, what hope is left for me? What reason for continuing on life's pilgrimage, for which I have no support but you, and none in you save the knowledge that you are alive, now that I am forbidden all other pleasures in you and denied even the joy of your presence which from time to time could restore me to myself? O God—if it is right to say this—cruel to me in every way! O inclement clemency! O Fortune who is only misfortune, who has already wasted on me so many of the shafts she uses in her wider battle that she has none left with which to vent her anger on others. She has emptied a full quiver on me; henceforth no one else need fear her onslaughts, and even if she still had a single arrow she could find no place left on me to make a wound.[15] Her only dread is that through my many wounds death may end my sufferings; and though she does not cease to destroy me, she still dreads my dying which she hurries on.

7. Oh, of all wretched women I am the most wretched, and amongst the unhappy I am the unhappiest. The higher I was exalted when you preferred me to all other women, the greater was my suffering over

[13] 'Parce, obsecro, domine, parce . . . (see 3 above) . . . parce itaque, obsecro, nobis; parce itaque unice saltem tue': cf. Jerome, *Epistola* XXXIX *ad Paulam de morte Blesillae*, 6: 'Parce, quaeso, tibi, parce filiae iam cum Christo regnanti, parce saltim Eustochiae tuae' (ed. Hilberg, liv. 305, *ll.* 23–4; *PL* xxii. 471).

[14] Lucan, *De bello ciuili*, ii. 14–15.

[15] Cf. Ovid, *Ex Ponto*, ii. 7. 15–16: 'Sic ego Fortunae telis confixus iniquis / pectore concipio nil nisi triste meo' / 'So I, pierced by unjust shafts of Fortune, fashion in my breast none but gloomy thoughts'. Also ii. 7. 41–2: 'sic ego continuo Fortunae vulneror ictu, / uixque habet in nobis iam noua plaga locum' / 'I am so wounded by the steady blows of fate and have scarcely any space within me now for a further wound.'

casum! Quanto quippe altior[e] ascendentis gradus, tanto grauior corruentis casus.[16] Quam mihi [f]nobilium[g] potentium feminarum fortuna[f] umquam preponere potuit [h]aut equare?[h] [i]Quam denique adeo deiecit et dolore conficere potuit?[i] Quam [j]in te mihi[j] gloriam contulit! Quam [k]in te mihi[k] ruinam intulit! Quam mihi uehemens in [l]utramque partem[l] extitit, ut nec in bonis nec in[m] malis modum habuerit! Que, ut me miserrimam omnium faceret, omnibus ante beatiorem effecerat, ut, cum quanta perdidi pensarem, tanto me maiora consumerent[n] lamenta quanto me maiora oppresserant damna; et tanto maior amissorum succederet dolor quanto maior possessorum precesserat amor, et summe uoluptatis gaudia summa meroris[o] terminaret tristicia.

8. Et,[a] ut ex iniuria[b] maior indignatio surgeret, omnia in nobis equitatis iura pariter sunt peruersa. Dum enim solliciti amoris gaudiis frueremur et, ut turpiore sed expressiore[c] uocabulo utar, fornicationi uaccaremus, diuina nobis seueritas pepercit. Vt autem illicita licitis correximus,[d] et[e] honore coniugii turpitudinem fornicationis operuimus, [f]ira Domini[f] manum suam super nos uehementer[g] aggrauauit,[h] [17] et immaculatum non pertulit[i] thorum qui [j]diu ante[j] sustinuerat pollutum. Deprehensis in quouis adulterio uiris[k] hec[l] satis esset ad uindictam[m] pena quam pertulisti. Quod[n] ex adulterio promerentur[o] alii,[p] id tu ex coniugio incurristi per quod iam te omnibus satisfecisse confidebas iniuriis.[q] Quod[r] fornicatoribus suis[s] adultere[t] hoc[u] propria [v]uxor tibi[v] contulit, nec cum pristinis uaccaremus uoluptatibus sed cum[w] iam ad tempus segregati castius uiueremus, te quidem Parisius[x] scolis presidente et me ad imperium tuum Argenteoli[y] cum sanctimonialibus conuersante. Diuisis itaque sic nobis adinuicem[z] ut tu studiosius scolis, ego liberius orationi siue sacre lectionis meditationi uacarem; et[a] tanto nobis sanctius quanto castius degentibus,[b] solus in corpore luisti quod duo pariter commiseramus. Solus in pena fuisti, duo in culpa,[18] et, qui minus

[e] electior *C;* est *add. Y* [f–f] fortuna nobilium potencium fortunarum *Y* [g] et *add. F;* ac *add. Amb* [h–h] *om. Y* [i–i] *om. Y* [j–j] uite mihi *CEAmb*[1] [k–k] mihi uite *CE;* mihi in te *FBRY* [l–l] utramque parte *R;* utraque parte *Y* [m] *om. ACEY* [n] assumerent *C* [o] merore *C*

8 [a] *om. B* [b] niuria *R*; nimia gratia *Y* [c] etiam expressiore *E;* ex impressione *B* [d] correxerimus *T;* conuertisimes *J* [e] ut *CEF* [f–f] ira Dominus *F;* ita dominus *B* [g] *om. Y* [h] agregauit *B* [i] praetulit *F* [j–j] *blank space B*; diu in *Y* [k] uiuis *B* [l] hoc *TBSY* [m] *superscr. Ecorr* [n] Et quod *Y* [o] Promereatur *B* [p] *om. E* [q] miseriis *B, ?R* [r] Et quod *Y* [s] *om. F* [t] adultera *CE;* adulteria *F* [u] hec *CEY* [v–v] tibi uxor *BRY* [w] *om. BRY* [x] pater *F;* uel parter (*sic*) *add. F in marg.;* pater *?Y;*

my fall and yours as much, when I was flung down; for the higher the ascent, the heavier the fall.[16] Has Fortune ever set any great or noble woman above me or made her my equal, only to be similarly cast down and crushed with grief? What glory she gave me in you! What ruin she brought upon me in you! Violent in either extreme, she showed no moderation in good or evil. To make me the saddest of all women she first made me blessed above all, so that when I thought how much I had lost, my consuming grief would match my crushing loss, and my sorrow for what was taken from me would be the greater for the fuller joy of possession which had gone before; and so that the happiness of supreme ecstasy would end in the supreme bitterness of sorrow.

8. Moreover, to add to my indignation at the outrage, all the laws of equity in our case were overturned. For while we enjoyed the pleasures of an uneasy love and abandoned ourselves to fornication (if I may use an ugly but expressive word) we were spared God's severity. But when we amended our unlawful conduct by what was lawful, and atoned for the shame of fornication by an honourable marriage, then the Lord in his anger laid his hand heavily upon us,[17] and would not permit a chaste union though he had long tolerated one which was unchaste. The punishment you suffered would have been proper vengeance for men caught in open adultery. But what other men deserve for adultery came upon you through a marriage which you believed had made amends for all previous wrong-doing; what adulterous women have brought upon their lovers, your own wife brought on you. Nor was this at the time when we abandoned ourselves to our former delights, but when we had already parted and were living more chastely, you presiding over the school in Paris and I at your command living with the nuns at Argenteuil. Thus we were separated, to give you more time to devote yourself to your school, and me more freedom for prayer and meditation on the Scriptures, both of us leading a life which was the more holy as it was the more chaste. It was then that you alone paid the penalty in your body for what we had both equally done. You alone were punished though we were both to blame,[18] and you paid all though you had deserved less.

parisius *Y*[1] [y] argentolii *CEF* [z] Abinuicem *AFAmb*[1]; inuicem *C* [a] ut *CE*
[b] de gentibus *B*

[16] Cf. *Prouerbia* (Walther), no. 900: 'altior ascensus, grauior plerumque ruina'; *Prouerbia* (Schmidt), no. 34667g: 'altior quisque hoc ruina est, quo levatur altius'; no. 34670a1: 'altius quanto cadendum est, altius tanto strepis'; no. 34943: 'ascensum sequitur sepe ruina gravis.'

[17] Cf. Ps. 37 (38): 3 (2).

[18] Cf. *Letter* 5, 31.

debueras, totum pertulisti.[c] Quanto enim amplius te pro me humiliando satisfeceras, et me pariter et totum genus meum[d] sublimaueras, tanto te minus tam[e] apud Deum [f]quam apud[g] illos proditores[f] obnoxium pene reddideras.

9. O me miseram in tanti sceleris causa progenitam! O summam[a] in uiros summos et consuetam feminarum perniciem![19] Hinc de muliere cauenda scriptum est in Prouerbiis:[b] 'Nunc ergo, fili,[c] audi me, et attende uerbis[d] oris mei.[e] Ne abstrahatur in uiis[f] illius mens tua, neque[g] decipiaris semitis eius; multos enim[h] uulneratos deiecit, et fortissimi[i] quique[j] interfecti[k] sunt ab ea. Vie[l] inferi[m] domus eius, penetrantes[n] in[o] inferiora[p] mortis.'[20] Et in[q] Ecclesiaste: 'Lustraui uniuersa animo meo, et inueni amariorem morte mulierem, que [r]laqueus uenatorum[r] est, et sagena cor eius. Vincula enim[s] sunt manus eius. Qui placet Deo effugiet eam; qui autem peccator est capietur ab illa.'[21]

10. Prima statim mulier de paradyso uirum captiuauit,[22] et que ei a Domino creata fuerat in auxilium, in summum ei conuersa [a]est exitium.[a][23] Fortissimum[b] illum[c] Nazareum Domini[d] et angelo nuntiante conceptum[e] Dalila[f] sola superauit, et eum inimicis proditum et oculis priuatum ad hoc tandem dolor compulit ut se pariter cum ruina hostium opprimeret.[g][24] Sapientissimum omnium Salomonem[h] sola quam sibi [j]copulauerat[i] mulier[j] infatuauit, et[k] in tantam compulit insaniam ut[l] eum quem ad edificandum sibi [m]Dominus templum[m] elegerat, patre eius Dauid,[n] qui iustus fuerat, in hoc reprobato, ad ydolatriam[o] ipsa usque in[p] finem uite deiceret,[q] ipso [r]quem tam[r]

[c] (?) soluisti *in marg.* *Y*[1] [d] *om. CEF* [e] *om. BRY* [f–f] *marked for corr. Y* [g] *om. B*

9 [a] summa *CE* [b] propriis *C, ?E, ?B* [c] filii *C, E before corr.;* fili mi *F and Vulg.* (*Clementine*) [d] uerba *CEFY* [e] meis *C* [f] uerbis *Y* [g] ne *Y* [h] nisi *before corr. E; om. S* [i] fortissimis *E* [j] queque *C* [k] interfecti *after corr. E* [l] uia *E* [m] inferni *Y* [n] penetrantis *E* [o] *om. CEF* [p] interiora *Vulg.* [q] *om. Y* [r–r] uenatorum laqueus *BRY* [s] *om. S*

10 [a–a] exitum *C;* exitium *E;* est in exitium *BR* [b] fortissimus *E and Ecorr.;* Sortissimum *before corr. Y* [c] *om. Y* [d] deo *Y* [e] *after corr. E* [f] dalida *Y* [g] comprimeret *BY* [h] salamonem *C* [i] compuluerat *A* [j–j] mulier copulauerat *Y* [k] *T over eras.; eras. also in marg.* [l] T over eras.; eras. also in marg. [m–m] templum dominus *CEFBRY* [n] dauit *A;* dauid *add. in vacant space Ecorr* [o] idololatriam *FAmb* [p] ad *BRY* [q] *corrupt in F;* uel deficeret *add. in marg. F* [r–r] quam tam *C;* tam quam *E;* quoque *F*

[19] Cf. *Planctus IV: Israel super Samson*: 'O semper fortium / ruinam maximam / et in exitum / creatam feminam!' / 'Oh, ever of the mighty / supreme destruction, / for such

The more you had made amends and, humbling yourself for me, had raised me and all my family, the less, in the eyes of God and of your betrayers, had you made yourself deserving of such punishment.

9. What misery for me—born as I was to be the cause of such a crime! Again and again women utterly destroy the very greatest of men![19] Hence the warning about women in Proverbs: 'But now, my son, listen to me, attend to what I say: do not let your heart entice you into her ways, do not stray down her paths; she has wounded and laid low so many, and the strongest have all been her victims. Her house is the way to hell, and leads down to the halls of death.'[20] And in Ecclesiastes: 'I put all to the test . . . I find woman more bitter than death; she is a snare, her heart a net, her arms are chains. He who is pleasing to God eludes her, but the sinner is her captive.'[21]

10. It was the first woman in the beginning who lured man from Paradise,[22] and she who had been created by the Lord as his helpmate became the instrument of his total downfall.[23] And that mighty man of the Lord, the Nazirite whose conception was announced by an angel, Delilah alone overcame; betrayed to his enemies and robbed of his sight, he was driven at last by sorrow to destroy himself along with the fall of his enemies.[24] Only the woman he had slept with could make a fool of Solomon, the wisest of all men; she drove him to such a pitch of madness that although he was the man whom the Lord had chosen to build the temple in preference to his father David, who was a righteous man, she plunged him into idolatry until the end of his

catastrophe / was created woman!' (ed. and trans. Dronke, *Poetic Individuality in the Middle Ages*, p. 122; ed. Meyer, *Gesammelte Abhandlungen*, i. 370; *PL* clxxviii. 1821). Also cf. *Letter* 1, **23** and 5, **24**; *Carmen ad Astralabium*, ed. Rubingh-Bosscher, *vv.* 547–56; *TChr*, ii. 89.

[20] Prov. 7: 24–7; cf. *TChr*, ii. 90.

[21] Eccles. 7: 26–7; cf. *TChr*, ii. 90.

[22] Cf. Gen. 3; 6.

[23] Cf. Gen. 3: 23–4; also *Letter* 8, **33**; *TChr*, ii. 89, and *Planctus IV: Israel super Samson*, *vv.* 46, 38: 'exitium . . . auxilium' (ed. and trans. Dronke, *Poetic Individuality in the Middle Ages*, pp. 122–3 (3b, *l.* 5, 2a, *l.* 3); ed. Meyer, *Gesammelte Abhandlungen*, i. 370–1; *PL* clxxviii. 1821).

[24] Cf. Judg. 13: 2–25; 16: 4–31. The Nazirite is Samson. 'Fortissimum . . . conceptum': cf. *TChr*, ii. 89 and *Planctus IV: Israel super Samson*, *vv.* 7–9 (ed. and trans. Dronke, *Poetic Individuality in the Middle Ages*, pp. 121–3 (1b, *ll.* 1–3); ed. Meyer, *Gesammelte Abhandlungen*, i. 369; *PL* clxxviii. 1820–1). 'Compulit . . . opprimeret': cf. *TChr*, ii. 80; Augustine, *De ciuitate Dei*, i. 21 (ed. Dombart and Kalb, lxvii. 23; ed. Hoffmann, xl (1), p. 40; *PL* xli. 35). Dronke, *Poetic Individuality in the Middle Ages*, pp. 123–32, shows how untraditional was this representation of Samson as a man overcome by grief; see further Orlandi, 'On the text and interpretation of Abelard's *Planctus*', pp. 338–40.

uerbis quam scriptis predicabat atque docebat diuino cultu derelicto.[25] Iob sanctissimus in uxore nouissimam atque grauissimam sustinuit pugnam, que eum ad maledicendum Deo[s] stimulabat.[26] Et callidissimus temptator[t] hoc optime nouerat, quod[u] sepius expertus fuerat, uirorum uidelicet[v] ruinam in uxoribus esse facillimam. [w]Qui denique[w] etiam[x] usque ad nos consuetam extendens maliciam, quem[y] de[z] fornicatione sternere non potuit de coniugio temptauit; et bono male est usus qui[a] malo male uti non est permissus.[b]

11. Deo saltem super hoc gratias, quod[a] me ille ut suprapositas feminas in culpam ex consensu non traxit, quam tamen in causam[b] commisse malicie ex effectu[c] conuertit.[27] Sed et[d] si purget animum meum[e] innocentia[f] nec huius [g]reatum sceleris[g] consensus[28] incurrat, peccata tamen multa precesserunt[h] que me penitus immunem ab huius [i]reatu sceleris[i] esse non sinunt. Quod uidelicet[j] diu ante carnalium illecebrarum uoluptatibus seruiens,[k] ipsa tunc merui quod nunc plector; et precedentium in me peccatorum sequentia merito [l]facta sunt[l] pena, et[m] malis initiis peruersus imputandus est exitus.[29] Atque utinam huius precipue commissi dignam agere ualeam penitentiam, ut pene illi tue uulneris illati ex longa saltem penitentie contricione uicem quoquo modo recompensare queam;[n] et quod tu ad horam in corpore pertulisti, ego in omni[o] uita, ut iustum est, in contritione mentis suscipiam, et hoc [p]tibi saltem[p] modo, si non [q]Deo, satisfaciam.[q][30] Si[r] enim[s] uere[t] miserrimi [u]mei animi[u] profitear infirmitatem, qua penitentia Deum placare ualeam non inuenio, quem super hac semper[v] iniuria[w] summe crudelitatis arguo et, eius dispensationi contraria, magis eum ex indignatione offendo quam ex penitentie satisfactione mitigo. Quomodo etiam penitentia peccatorum dicitur, quantacumque sit corporis afflictio, si mens adhuc ipsam peccandi retinet uoluntatem et pristinis estuat desideriis? Facile quidem est quemlibet confitendo peccata seipsum accusare

[s] deum *CEF* [t] temptor *E* [u] quia *marked for corr. Y* [v] ut *marked for corr. Y* [w–w] Que *BY*; Qui *R* [x] etiam *after corr. E* [y] quam *Y* [z] in *Y*[1] (de *Y*) [a] que *C* [b] promissus *C*

11 [a] quia *?C* [b] eam ex causa *F* [c] affectu *TAmb;* en cause du fait *J* [d] etiam *BRY* [e] cum *add. CEF* [f] ignorantia *CBRY* [g–g] sceleris reatum *BRY* [h] precesserant *CEF* [i–i] sceleris reatu *BRY* [j] uiget *C* [k] inseruiens *F* [l–l] sunt facta *BRY* [m] Etiam *Amb* [n] quemdam *before corr. B* [o] *om. B* [p–p] platem *Y* [q–q] satisfaciam *?C;* satisfaciam deum *Y* [r] Sed *F* [s] *om. S* [t] nature *RY* [u–u] animi mei *BRSY* [v] *om. R* [w] iusticia *Y*

life, so that he abandoned the worship of God which he had preached and taught in word and writing.[25] Job, the holiest of men, fought his last and hardest battle against his wife, who urged him to curse God.[26] The cunning arch-tempter well knew from repeated experience that men are most easily brought to ruin through their wives, and so he directed his usual malice against us too, and tempted you through marriage when he could not destroy you through fornication. Denied the power to do evil through evil, he effected evil through good.

11. At least I can thank God for this: the tempter did not prevail on me to do wrong of my own consent, like the women I have mentioned, though in the outcome he made me the instrument of his malice.[27] But even if my conscience is clear through innocence, and no consent of mine makes me guilty of this crime,[28] too many earlier sins were committed to allow me to be wholly free from guilt. I yielded long before to the pleasures of carnal desires, and merited then what I weep for now. The sequel is a fitting punishment for my former sins, and an evil beginning must be expected to come to a bad end.[29] For this offence, above all, may I have strength to do proper penance, so that at least by long contrition I can make some amends for your pain from the wound inflicted on you; and what you suffered in the body for a time, I may suffer, as is right, throughout my life in contrition of mind, and thus make reparation to you at least, if not to God.[30] For if I truthfully admit to the weakness of my most unhappy soul, I can find no penitence whereby to appease God, whom I always accuse of the greatest cruelty in regard to this injustice. By opposing his ordinance, I offend him more by my indignation than I placate him by making amends through penitence. How can it be called repentance for sins, however great the mortification of the flesh, if the mind still retains the will to sin and is on fire with its old desires? It is easy enough for anyone to confess his sins, to accuse himself, or even

[25] Cf. 3 Kgs. (1 Kgs.) 3: 6–9 and 11: 1–8, where several women, not one, derange Solomon and bring him to idolatry. Cf. also *TSum*, i. 33, *TChr*, i. 59, and *TSch*, i. 105. But in *TChr*, ii. 89 one woman is held responsible for Solomon's idolatry. Cf. also *Letter* 5, 24; *Sermon* 2 (*PL* clxxviii. 402C); *Planctus IV: Israel super Samson* (ed. and trans. Dronke, *Poetic Individuality in the Middle Ages*, pp. 121–3; ed. Meyer, *Gesammelte Abhandlungen*, i. 369–71; *PL* clxxviii. 1821), and, for the selection of Samson, David, and Solomon, cf. Jerome, *Epistola* XXII *ad Eustochium* 12 (ed. Hilberg, liv. 159; *PL* xxii. 401).

[26] Cf. Job 2: 9–10.

[27] Cf. *Letter* 2, 13.

[28] 'nec huius reatum sceleris consensus incurrat': on 'consensus' to wrong as the constituent of sin cf. *Rule* 93.

[29] 'malis . . . . exitus': cf. Pope Leo the Great, *Epistola* XII. 1 (*PL* liv. 647A).

[30] Cf. *Carmen ad Astralabium*, ed. Rubingh-Bosscher, *vv*. 379–82.

aut etiam in[x] exteriori satisfactione corpus affligere; difficillimum uero est a desideriis maximarum uoluptatum auellere animum. Vnde et merito sanctus Iob cum premisisset:[y] 'Dimittam aduersum me eloquium meum',[31] id est, '[z]laxabo linguam et aperiam os per confessionem[z] in peccatorum meorum accusationem, statim adiunxit: 'Loquar in amaritudine anime mee'.[32] Quod beatus exponens Gregorius: 'Sunt', inquit, 'nonnulli qui apertis uocibus culpas fatentur, sed tamen[a] in confessione gemere nesciunt et lugenda gaudentes dicunt. Vnde qui culpas suas detestans loquitur, restat, [b]necesse est,[b] ut has in amaritudine anime[c] loquatur ut hec[d] ipsa amaritudo puniat quicquid[e] lingua [f]per mentis[f] iudicium accusat.'[33] [g]Sed hec[g] quidem amaritudo uere[h] penitentie quam rara[i] sit beatus diligenter attendens Ambrosius: 'Facilius', inquid, 'inueni qui innocentiam seruauerunt[j] quam qui[k] [l]penitentiam egerunt.'[l] [34]

12. In tantum uero ille quas pariter exercuimus amantium uoluptates dulces mihi[a] fuerunt ut nec displicere [b]mihi nec[b] uix a memoria labi possint. Quocumque loco me uertam, semper se[c] oculis meis cum[d] suis ingerunt desideriis, nec [e]etiam dormienti[e] suis illusionibus parcunt. Inter ipsa missarum sollempnia, ubi purior [f]esse debet[f] oratio, obscena[g] earum[h] uoluptatum phantasmata ita sibi[i] penitus miserrimam captiuant animam ut turpitudinibus illis magis quam orationi[j] uacem;[k] que[l] cum ingemiscere[m] debeam de commissis, suspiro potius de amissis.[n] Nec solum que egimus [o]sed loca pariter et tempora[p] in quibus hec egimus[o] ita tecum[q] nostro infixa[r] sunt animo, ut in ipsis[s] omnia tecum agam nec dormiens etiam ab his quiescam.[35] Nonnumquam etiam[t] ipso[u] motu corporis animi mei cogitationes deprehenduntur,[v] nec a uerbis[w] temperant improuisis.[x] [36]

[x] *om. F* [y] dixisset *F* [z–z] dilatabo linguam (linguam *om. Y*) et aperiam os per confessionem (per confessionem *om. RY*) *BRY* [a] cum *BR* [b–b] necesse esse *CE; om. F* [c] sue *add. BRY* [d] *om. S* [e] quamquam *E* [f–f] permanentis *R* [g–g] sed *B;* hec *RY* [h] uero *A; om. E* [i] reati *Y;* rara *Y*[1] [j] Seruauerint *F and Ambrose;* seruarunt *S* [k] congrue *add. F and Ambrose* [l–l] egerint poenitentiam *F;* poenitentiam egerint *Ambrose*

12 [a] *om. Y* [b–b] *add. probably by* T^3 *over eras. and eras. also in marg. T;* nec *Y* [c] in *add. CE;* prae *add. F* [d] in *add. C;* est in *E;* hoc est *F* [e–e] *add. in vacant space Ecorr* [f–f] debet esse *RY* [g] obcenam *E* [h] eorum *CE* [i] *om. C;* sunt *before corr. to* sibi *E;* meam *Y* [j] orationibus *Y* [k] nocere *?B before corr. to* rac(?)t; uacent *?S* [l] Quod *S* [m] ingemescere *E* [n] amicis *T before corr. by* T^4 *to* amisis; remissis *BRY* [o–o] *om. B* [p] imperia *E* [q] deo *BR;* adeo *Y* [r] fixa *C* [s] *om. E* [t] et *Amb* [u] *om. BR* [v] deprehendunt *E* [w] uobis *F* [x] impudicis *Y*

[31] Job 10: 1. [32] Job 10: 1.

to mortify his body in outward show of penance, but it is most difficult to tear the mind away from longing for the greatest pleasures. Quite rightly then, when the saintly Job said: 'I will speak out against myself',[31] that is: 'I will loosen my tongue and open my mouth in confession to accuse myself of my sins', he added at once: 'I will speak out in bitterness of soul.'[32] St Gregory comments on this: 'There are some who confess their faults aloud but in doing so do not know how to groan over them—they speak cheerfully of what should be lamented. And so whoever hates his faults and confesses them must still confess them in bitterness of spirit, so that this bitterness may punish him for what his tongue, at his mind's bidding, accuses him.'[33] But this bitterness of true repentance is very rare, as St Ambrose observes when he says: 'I have more easily found men who have preserved their innocence than men who have known repentance.'[34]

12. The lovers' pleasures we enjoyed together were so sweet to me that they cannot displease me and can scarcely fade from my memory. Wherever I turn they are always there before my eyes, bringing with them awakened longings and fantasies which will not even let me sleep. Even during the celebration of Mass, when our prayers should be purer, lewd visions of those pleasures take such a hold on my most unhappy soul that my thoughts are on their wantonness rather than on prayer. I, who should be grieving for the sins I have committed, am sighing rather for what I have lost. The things we did and also the places and times in which we did them are stamped on my heart along with your image, so that I live through them all again with you. Even in sleep I know no respite.[35] Sometimes my thoughts are betrayed in a movement of my body, or they break out in an unguarded word.[36]

[33] Gregory the Great, *Moralia in Job*, ix. 43 (ed. Adriaen, cxliii. 504; *PL* lxxv. 896C).

[34] Ambrose, *De paenitentia*, ii. 10. 96 (ed. Faller, p. 201, *ll.* 40–1; *PL* xvi. 542A).

[35] 'ita tecum nostro . . . quiescam': cf. Virgil, *Aeneid*, iv. 4–5: 'haerent infixi pectore uultus / uerbaque nec placidam membris dat cura quietem' / 'His look, his words had gone to her heart / And lodged there: she could get no peace from love's disquiet' (trans. C. Day Lewis).

[36] Cf. for the whole of **11** and **12** *Carmen ad Astralabium*, ed. Rubingh-Bosscher, *vv.* 377–84: 'ymmo uoluptatis dulcedo tanta sit huius / ne grauet ulla satisfactio propter eam. / est nostre super hoc Eloyse crebra querela / qua michi, qua secum dicere sepe solet: / "si, nisi peniteat me comississe priora, / saluari nequeam, spes michi nulla manet: / dulcia sunt adeo comissi gaudia nostri / ut memorata iuuent, que placuere nimis."' / 'The sweetness of that bliss remains remains so great that no sense of atoning for it has force. This is the burden of complaint of our Heloise, whereby she often says to me as to herself: "If I can not be saved without repenting of what I used to commit, there is no hope for me. The joys of what we did are still so sweet that, after delight beyond measure, even remembering brings relief"'; trans. Dronke, *Abelard and Heloise in Medieval Testimonies*, p. 15; repr. *Intellectuals and Poets*, p. 257).

13. [a]O uere[a] me miseram et[b] illa conquestione[c] ingemiscentis[d] [e]anime dignissimam:[e] 'Infelix ego homo, quis me liberabit de corpore mortis huius?'[37] Vtinam[f] et quod sequitur [g]ueraciter addere queam:[g] 'Gratia Dei per Iesum Christum Dominum nostrum'.[38] Hec te gratia, karissime, preuenit, et ab his tibi stimulis una corporis plaga medendo multas in anima[h] sanauit; [i]et in quo[i] tibi amplius aduersari Deus creditur propitior inuenitur, more quidem fidelissimi[j] medici qui non parcit dolori ut[k] consulat[l] saluti. Hos autem in me stimulos carnis, hec incentiua libidinis, ipse iuuenilis feruor etatis et iocundissimarum experientia uoluptatum[m] plurimum accendunt, et tanto amplius sua [n]me impugnatione[n] opprimunt quanto infirmior est natura quam impugnant. [o]

14. Castam me predicant qui[a] non deprehendunt[b] ypocritam; munditiam[c] carnis conferunt[d] in uirtutem, cum non sit corporis sed animi uirtus.[39] Aliquid laudis apud homines habens, nichil apud Deum mereor,[e] qui cordis et renum probator est[40] et 'in abscondito uidet'.[41] Religiosa hoc tempore[f] iudicor in quo iam parua pars religionis non est ypochrisis, ubi ille[g] maximis extollitur laudibus qui humanum non offendit iudicium. Et hoc fortassis aliquo modo laudabile et Deo acceptabile quoquo modo uidetur si quis uidelicet exterioris operis exemplo quacumque intentione non sit Ecclesie[h] scandalo,[i] nec iam per ipsum apud infideles nomen Domini blasphemetur,[42] nec apud carnales professionis sue ordo infametur. Atque hoc quoque[j] nonnullum est diuine gratie donum,[k] ex cuius uidelicet munere uenit non solum bona facere [l]sed etiam[l] a malis abstinere. Sed frustra istud precedit ubi[m] illud non succedit, sicut scriptum est: 'Declina a malo, et fac bonum';[43] et [n]frustra utrumque[n] geritur quod [o]amore Dei[o] non agitur.[p] In omni [q]autem, Deus scit, uite mee[q] statu,[r] te magis adhuc offendere quam Deum uereor,[s] tibi placere amplius quam ipsi appeto. Tua me ad religionis[t] habitum iussio, non diuina traxit dilectio.[44]

13 [a–a] quare *CEF* [b] in *C* [c] T^3 *over eras. and eras. also in marg. T;* questione *AEF* [d] ingemiscenti *F* [e–e] anime indignissimam *B*; anime anime dignissimam *R*; anime mee dignissimam *Y* [f] ut *Y* [g–g] uerasciter addere queam *T;* addere ueraciter queam *F* [h] animas *E* [i–i] Et quo *F* [j] fidelissime *C;* felicissimi *BR* [k] ubi *Y* [l] parcat *BR*; consulant *marked for corr. Y* [m] uoluntatum *A* [n–n] me oppugnatione *F;* inexpugnatione *BRY;* in expugnacione *S* [o] impugnat *F;* oppugnant *Amb*

14 [a] que *C* [b] deprehenderunt *Amb* [c] mundicitiam *F* [d] uel conuertunt (uel conuertunt *superscr. by another hand*) *add. A* [e] miror *add. Ecorr* [f] corpore *F;* corde Amb^1 [g] illa *F* [h] cum *add. in vacant space by another hand B* [i] scandalum *CEF* [j] quocumque *marked for corr. Y* [k] bonum *BRY*

13. In my utter wretchedness, that cry from a suffering soul could well be mine: 'Miserable creature that I am, who will free me from the body of this death?'[37] Would that I could truthfully go on: 'The grace of God through Jesus Christ our Lord'.[38] This grace, my dearest, came upon you unsought—a single wound of the body by freeing you from these torments has healed many wounds in your soul. Where God may seem to you an adversary, he has in fact proved himself kind: like an honest doctor who does not shrink from giving pain if it will bring about a cure. But for me, youth and passion and experience of pleasures which were so delightful intensify the torments of the flesh and the longings of desire, and the assault is the more overwhelming as the nature they attack is the weaker.

14. Men call me chaste; they do not know the hypocrite I am. They see purity of the flesh as a virtue, though virtue belongs not to the body but to the mind.[39] I can win some praise from men but deserve none before God, who searches our hearts and loins[40] and 'sees in our darkness'.[41] I am thought to be religious at a time such as this when there is little in religion which is not hypocrisy, when whoever does not offend human judgement is singled out for praise. And yet perhaps it seems in a way praiseworthy and somehow acceptable to God if a person gives no offence to the Church in outward behaviour, whatever his intention, and if the name of the Lord is not blasphemed among unfaithful people[42] because of him, and if he does not disgrace the Order of his profession amongst the worldly. And this too is a gift of God's grace and comes through his bounty—not only to do good but to abstain from evil—though the latter is vain if the former does not follow from it, as it is written: 'Turn from evil and do good.'[43] Both are vain if not done for love of God. In every situation in my life, as God knows, I still fear to offend you more than God, and try to please you more fully than him. It was your command, not love of God, which hauled me into the religious life.[44] Look at the unhappy

[l–l] *om. E* [m] nisi *?B* [n–n] *om. and vacant space B* [o–o] dei *Y;* amore *add.* *Y*[1]
[p] geritur *T before exp.* [q–q] autem uite mee deus scit *BRSY;* autem Deus scit vita mea *F* [r] in omni statu *CEF* [s] uerear *C* [t] religionem *E*

[37] Rom. 7: 24.
[38] Rom. 7: 25.
[39] Cf. Augustine, *De bono coniugali*, xxi. 25: 'Continentia quippe non corporis, sed animi uirtus est' (ed. Zycha, p. 218, *l.* 23–p. 219, *l.* 1; *PL* xl. 390). Also *Letter* 6, **23**.
[40] Cf. Ps. 7: 10 (9); Jeremiah 11: 20, 17: 10, 20: 12; Rev. 2: 23; also *Letter* 6, **25**.
[41] Matt 6: 4. Cf. Matt. 6: 6 and *Letter* 6, **25**.
[42] Cf. Rom. 3: 24.
[43] Ps. 36 (37): 27.
[44] Cf. *Letters* 1, **31**; 2, **9** and **15**.

Vide quam infelicem et omnibus miserabiliorem ducam uitam si tanta hic frustra sustineo, nichil habitura remunerationis in futuro. Diu te, sicut et[u] multos,[v] simulatio mea fefellit, ut religioni[w] deputares ypochrisim; et ideo, nostris te maxime commendans[x] orationibus, quod a te [y]expecto a me postulas.[y]

15. Noli, obsecro, de me tanta presumere, ne mihi cesses orando subuenire. Noli estimare sanam, ne medicaminis subtrahas gratiam. Noli non egentem credere, ne differas in necessitate subuenire. Noli ualitudinem[a] putare, ne prius corruam[b] quam sustentes[c] labentem. Multis [d]ficta sui[d] laus nocuit, et presidium quo indigebant abstulit. Per Ysaiam[e] Dominus[f] clamat: 'Popule meus, qui te beatificant[g] ipsi te decipiunt, et uiam gressuum[h] tuorum dissipant.'[i] [45] Et per Ezechielem: Ve qui consuitis,[j] inquit, 'puluillos[k] sub[l] omni cubitu[m] manus, et[n] ceruicalia sub capite [o]etatis uniuerse[o] ad decipiendas animas.'[46] E contra autem[p] [q]per Salomonem[q] dicitur: 'Verba sapientium[r] quasi stimuli,[s] et quasi claui in altum defixi'[47] qui uidelicet uulnera nesciunt palpare, sed pungere.[t]

16. Quiesce,[a] obsecro, a laude mea, ne turpem adulationis notam et mendacii crimen incurras, aut si quod[b] in me suspicaris bonum ipsum laudatum uanitatis aura uentilet. Nemo medicine[c] peritus interiorem morbum ex[d] exterioris habitus inspectione diiudicat. Nulla quicquid[e] [f]meriti apud Deum[f] optinent que reprobis eque[g] ut[h] electis communia sunt; [i]hec autem ea sunt[i] que exterius aguntur, que nulli sanctorum tam[j] studiose peragunt quantum ypochrite.[48] 'Prauum[k] est cor hominis, et[l] inscrutabile et[m] quis cognoscet illud?'[49] Et: 'Sunt uie hominis[n] que uidentur recte: nouissima autem illius deducunt[o] ad mortem.'[50] [p]Temerarium est in eo iudicium hominis[p] quod diuino tantum reseruatur examini. Vnde et[q] scriptum est: 'Ne[r] laudaueris

[u] *om. Amb* [v] multas *C* [w] religio *B before ?corr., R* [x] commendas *F;* commendatis *before corr. B, R;* commendant *Y after corr.* [y–y] postulo a me expectas *BRY*

15 [a] ualetudinem *FAmb*[1] [b] cocruam *R* [c] sustinentes *B* [d–d] sui ficta *BRSY* [e] Esaiam *Amb* [f] dicens *B* [g] beatam dicunt *F;* beatifficam *S;* beatum dicunt *Vulg.* [h] gressium *T* [i] *om. B;* discipant *C* [j] consuunt *F;* consuetis *BR;* consuitis *another hand—probably Y*[1]*—in Y* [k] *add. by another hand—probably Y*[1]*—in Y* [l] sibi *C* [m] concubitu *CE* [n] faciunt *add. F* [o–o] uniuerse etatis *FY;* etatis *R* [p] *om. BRSY* [q–q] persolationem *C* [r] sapientum *RYAmb* [s] stimulum *?C, ?B, R;* stimulus *Y* [t] pongere *S*

16 [a] quies *before corr. B, R*; Quiescas *Y* [b] quid *Y* [c] medicina *TBY*; medicinam *RS* [d] *om. CEF* [e] quicquam *AFBR;* quamquam *E;* quitquam *Y* [f–f] apud deum meritum *E* [g] recte *BRSY* [h] et *Y* [i–i] hec autem sunt ea

life I lead, pitiable beyond any other if in this world I must endure so much in vain, with no hope of future reward. For a long time my pretence has deceived you as it has deceived many, so that you regarded hypocrisy as devotion; and so, commending yourself most especially to our prayers, you ask of me what I expect of you.

15. I beseech you, do not feel so sure of me that you cease to help me by your own prayers. Do not suppose me healthy and so withdraw the grace of your healing. Do not believe I want for nothing and delay helping me in my hour of need. Do not think me strong, lest I collapse before you can sustain me. False praise has harmed many and taken from them the support they needed. The Lord cries out through Isaiah: 'O my people! Those who call you happy lead you astray and confuse the path you should take.'[45] And through Ezekiel he says: 'Woe to them who sew frills round wrists and who make ruffs for the heads of people of every age the better to ensnare souls.'[46] On the other hand, through Solomon it is said that 'the sayings of the wise are sharp as goads, like nails driven home'.[47] That is to say, nails which cannot touch wounds gently, but only pierce through them.

16. Cease praising me, I beseech you, lest you acquire the base stigma of being a flatterer or the charge of telling lies, or the breath of my vanity blows away any merit you saw in me to praise. No one with medical knowledge diagnoses an internal ailment by examining only outward appearance. What is common to the damned and the elect, things that are outwardly done, can win no favour in the eyes of God: none of the saints perform these as eagerly as hypocrites.[48] 'The heart of man is deceitful and inscrutable; who can fathom it?'[49] And: 'A road may seem straightforward to a man, yet may end as the way to death.'[50] It is rash for man to pass judgement on what is reserved for God's scrutiny, and so it is also written: 'Do not praise a man in his

add. R [j] causa *R* [k] Paruum *T;* mauues *J* [l] *om. BR* [m] *superscr. T; om. BR;* etiam *Amb* [n] *om. BRY* [o] deducaint *?T* [p–p] temerarium est cor hominis in eo iudicium *BR;* temerarium est cor hominis in eo iudicium facere *Y* [q] *om. BRSY* [r] *om. RY*

[45] Isaiah 3: 12.

[46] Ezek. 13: 18. The Douai translation (1609) reads: 'Woe to them that sew cushions under every elbow and make pillows for the heads of persons of every age to catch souls.'

[47] Eccles. 12: 11. [48] Cf. *Letter* 6, **20**. [49] Jer. 17: 9.

[50] Prov. 14: 12, 16: 25; cited also in *Comm. Rom.*, iv (xiv. 22), p. 306; *Sermon* 8 (*PL* clxxviii. 444B); and *Collationes* **72** (missing from *PL* clxxviii.1639B but given in the edn. of Marenbon and Orlandi, p. 90 and of *Dialogus*, ed. Thomas, *ll.* 1395–7).

hominem[s] in uita',[t 51] ne[u] tunc[v] uidelicet hominem laudes, dum[w] laudando[x] facere non laudabilem potes. Tanto autem mihi tua laus in me[y] periculosior est quanto gratior,[z] et tanto amplius ea capior[a] et delector quanto[b] amplius tibi per omnia placere studeo. Time, obsecro, semper de me potius quam confidas, ut tua semper sollicitudine adiuuer.[c] Nunc[d] uero precipue timendum est, ubi nullum incontinentie[e] mee[f] superest [g]in te[g] remedium.

17. Nolo, me ad uirtutem exhortans et ad pugnam[a] prouocans, dicas: 'Nam uirtus [b]in infirmitate perficitur'[b 52] et: 'Non [c]coronabitur nisi qui[c] legitime certauerit.'[53] Non[d] quero coronam uictorie; satis est mihi periculum uitare.[e] [f]Tutius euitatur[f] periculum quam committitur[g] bellum. Quocumque[h] me angulo celi Deus collocet satis mihi faciet; nullus ibi cuiquam inuidebit,[i] cum singulis quod habebunt suffecerit.[54] Cui quidem consilio nostro[j] ut ex auctoritate quoque robur[k] adiungam, beatum audiamus Iheronimum: 'Fateor imbecillitatem meam; nolo spe [l]uictorie pugnare[l] ne perdam aliquando[m] uictoriam. Quid necesse est certa dimittere et incerta[n] sectari?'[o 55]

[s] neminem *Y* [t] sua *add. CEFB* [u] nec *T* [v] sunt *E* [w] deum *Y;* dum *Y*[1] [x] laudendo *S* [y] *om. B* [z] graciosior *CEF* [a] encapior *B* [b] tanto *C* [c] adiuuor *BR* [d] Tunc *CEF* [e] inconcie *Y* [f] *om. CEF* [g–g] uite *CFY*

17 [a] pugnas *E* [b–b] perficitur in infirmitate *T but marked for corr. by T*[4] [c–c] coronabitur quis nisi qui *A;* corporaliter nisi qui *E;* coronabitur quis non *R;* coronabitur qui non *Y* [d] Et non *Y before corr.* [e] uictare *BR;* euitare *Amb* [f–f] tucius est uitare *BRSY* [g] committatur *C;* committere *RY* [h] Quoque *C* [i] inudebit *T* [j] meo (meo *marked for corr.*) nostro *A*; uestro *B* [k] roboratur *B* [l–l] uictorie repugnare *CE*; repugnare victoriae *F* [m] aliunde *CY;* alii *E* [n] certa *Y* [o] Vale *add. F; the lack of a valediction in MSS earlier than F may reflect an oversight in the course of copying.*

lifetime.'[51] By this is meant, do not praise a man while in doing so you can make him no longer praiseworthy. To me your praise is the more dangerous because I welcome it. The more anxious I am to please you in everything, the more I am won over and delighted by it. I beseech you, always be fearful for me rather than trusting, so that I may always find help in your solicitude. Now particularly you should fear, now when I no longer have in you an outlet for my incontinence.

17. I do not wish you to exhort me to virtue and summon me to the fight, saying: 'Power comes to its full strength in weakness'[52] and: 'He cannot win a crown unless he has kept the rules.'[53] I do not seek a crown of victory; avoiding danger is enough for me, and it is safer than engaging in war. In whatever corner of heaven God shall place me, I shall be satisfied. No one there will envy anyone else; what each one has will be enough.[54] Let the weight of authority reinforce what I say—let us hear St Jerome: 'I confess my weakness, I do not wish to fight in hope of victory, lest at some time I lose victory. What need is there to put aside those things that are certain and pursue those that are not?'[55]

[51] Cf. Ecclus. 11: 30.

[52] 2 Cor. 12: 9; also cited in *Letters* 6, **12**; 7, **26**, and *Sermons* 1 and 30 (*PL* clxxviii. 383D, 568C).

[53] 2 Tim. 2: 5; also cited in *Letter* 5, **32**; *Comm. Rom.*, iii (viii. 17), p. 218, *ll.* 286–7; *Ethica*, i. 2, 6 (ed. Ilgner, p. 2, *ll.* 39–40; Luscombe, p. 4, *ll.* 12–13); *Sermon* 26 (*PL* clxxviii. 540D).

[54] Cf. *Rule* **89**; *Carmen ad Astralabium*, ed. Rubingh-Bosscher, *vv.* 295–6; also *Problemata* 12 (*PL* clxxviii. 693B).

[55] Jerome, *Contra Vigilantium* 16 (*PL* xxiii. 352A). Cited more fully in *Letter* 12 (ed. Smits, p. 265; *PL* clxxviii. 350AB; trans. Ziolkowski, p. 169) and cf. *Collationes* **8** and **13** (ed. Marenbon and Orlandi, pp. 10 and 16; *Dialogus*, ed. Thomas, *ll.* 128–9, 202–3; *PL* clxxviii. 1615A, 1616D).

⟨EPISTOLA V⟩

1. SPONSE CHRISTI SERVVS EIVSDEM

In quatuor, memini, circa que tota[a] epistole tue nouissime[b] summa consistit offense tue commotionem expressisti.[1] Primo quidem super hoc conquerens[c] quod preter consuetudinem epistolarum, immo etiam contra ipsum naturalem [d]ordinem rerum,[d] [e]epistola nostra[e] [f]tibi directa[f] te mihi in salutatione preposuit.[g] Secundo quod,[h] cum uobis[i] consolationis potius remedium afferre debuissem, desolationem auxi; et quas [j]mitigare debueram[j] lacrymas[k] excitaui, illud [l]uidelicet ibidem[l] adiungens: 'Quod si me Dominus [m]in manus inimicorum tradiderit ut me scilicet preualentes interficiant',[2] etc.[m] Tertio uero ueterem illam et[n] assiduam querelam[3] tuam in Deum adiecisti,[o] [p]de modo[p] uidelicet [q]nostre conuersionis[q] ad Deum et crudelitate proditionis illius in me commisse. Denique accusationem tui contra nostram in te laudem opposuisti, [r]non cum supplicatione modica,[r] ne id[s] deinceps presumerem.

2. Quibus quidem singulis rescribere[a] decreui, non tam[b] pro excusatione mea quam pro doctrina[c] uel exhortatione tua,[4] ut eo [d]scilicet[d] libentius petitionibus assentas[e] nostris quo eas rationabilius factas intellexeris, et tanto me amplius exaudias in tuis quanto reprehensibilem minus inuenies in meis, tantoque amplius uerearis contemnere quanto minus uideris dignum[f] reprehensione.[g] [5]

Letter 5 *T* fos. 27[rb]–34[vb]; *A* fos. 20[vb]–26[ra]; *C* fos. 164[v]–171[r]; *E* fos. 22[r]–27[r]; *F* pp. 38–57; *B* fos. 20[ra]–24[va]; *R* fos. 133[ra]–138[va]; *S* fos. 36–49; *Y* fos. 104[va]–106[va]; *Amb* pp. 62–77; *Amb*[1] *variants given in the marg. of Amb*; *J* pp. 92–120. *Headings are found in the following witnesses*: Ipse rursus ad ipsam *TAS;* edita ordine 5a *add. in marg. F;* Rescribit *add. in vacant space Y*[2]*;* Comme P. Abaielart rescript a Heloyse, et la conforte par plusieurs enseignemens et auctoritez ij[c] xvj *table in H of the* (*missing*) *contents of Dijon MS 525;* EPISTOLA V. Quae est Rescriptum PETRI rursus ad HELOISSAM *Amb*

1 [a] *om. TAmb* [b] *om. BY* [c] consequens *T;* conquereris *YAmb* [d–d] ordinem *R;* rerum ordinem *Y* [e–e] epistolam nostram *C* [f–f] directa tibi *T but marked for corr. by T*[4] [g] preposui *BRSY* [h] *om. RY* [i] nobis *CB* [j–j] debueram mitigare *F* [k] ad lacrimas *BRSY* [l–l] uidelicet ibi *EF;* ibi uidelicet *B, R in marg., SY* [m–m] *om. F* [n] *om. CEF* [o] deiecisti *ACEFY* [p–p] Demum *Y* [q–q] nostre conuersationis *TEAmb*[1]*;* conuersionis nostrae *F* [r–r] cum modica non supplicacione *A;* non modicum cum supplicatione *CF;* non modica cum supplicatione *E* [s] *om. BR;* illud *Y*

2 [a] scribere *CEF* [b] *in T over eras.; eras. also in marg.* [c] tua *add. Y* [d–d] scilicet ut eo *E;* ut eo uidelicet *BRS* [e] assentias *ACEFYAmb* [f] *om. BR* [g] Ad primam querimoniam *rubr. T in text, A in marg.*

LETTER 5

1. TO THE BRIDE OF CHRIST FROM CHRIST'S SERVANT

The whole of your last letter is given up to a recital of your misery over the wrongs you suffer, and these, I note, are on four counts.[1] First, you complain that contrary to custom in letter-writing, or indeed against the natural order of the world, my letter to you put your name before mine in its greeting. Secondly, that when I ought to have offered you some remedy for your comfort I actually increased your sense of desolation and made the tears flow which I should have checked. This I did by writing: 'But if the Lord shall deliver me into the hands of my enemies, so that they overcome and kill me',[2] etc. Thirdly, you went on to your old continual complaint[3] against God concerning the manner of our entry into religious life and the cruelty of the act of treachery performed on me. Lastly, you set your self-accusations against my praise of you, and implored me with some urgency not to praise you again.

2. I have decided to answer you on each point in turn, not so much in self-justification as for your own enlightenment and encouragement,[4] so that you will more willingly grant my own requests when you understand that they have a basis of reason, listen to me more attentively on the subject of your own pleas as you find me less to blame in my own, and be less ready to refuse me when you see me less deserving of reproach.[5]

[1] The *Theologia 'Scholarium'* and the *Sententie* of Abelard open in a similar way: 'Tria sunt, ut arbitror, in quibus . . . summa consistit' (*TSch*, i, *ll.* 1–2; *Sententie*, i, *ll.* 1–2, ed. Luscombe, p. 5; i, ed. Buzzetti, p. 25; *PL* clxxviii. 1695).

[2] *Letter* 4, 2; cf. *Letter* 3, 12.

[3] 'ueterem . . . querelam': cf. *Comm. Rom.* ii (v. 19; *ll.* 336–7): 'ueterem humani generis quaerelam . . . de originali scilicet peccato'.

[4] 'pro doctrina uel exhortatione tua': cf. *Letters* 2, 8 and 3, 1.

[5] Ruys, '*Planctus magis quam cantici*', p. 41, has suggested that a sequence (*Parce continuis*), which various scholars (including Meyer, 'Zwei mittellateinische Lieder', pp. 157–9) have considered to be a possible composition of Abelard, was written as a poetic response to *Letter* 4. Dronke, who ed. and trans. two versions of the sequence in his *Medieval Latin and the Rise of the European Love-Lyric*, 2nd edn., ii. 341–52 (and see i, p. x; also Dronke, 'Postscript (1996)'), maintained that a first version of the poem pre-dates Abelard and that a later one, which has a new layer of stanzas, is the work of a *remanieur* who was not Abelard but knew Abelard's *Planctus.* More recently Dronke and Orlandi, 'New works by Abelard and Heloise?', pp. 141–2 have affirmed, on palaeographical grounds, that the attribution of *Parce continuis* to Abelard is not possible.

3. De ipso autem nostre salutationis, ut dicis,[6] ordine prepostero, iuxta [a]tuam quoque,[a] si diligenter attendas,[b] actum est sententiam. Id [c]enim quod[c] omnibus patet, tu ipsa indicasti ut, cum uidelicet ad superiores scribitur, eorum nomina preponantur. Te uero extunc me superiorem factam intelligas, quo[d] domina mea esse cepisti, Domini mei sponsa effecta, iuxta illud beati Iheronimi ad Eustochium [e]ita scribentis: 'Hec[f] idcirco, domina mea, Eustochium[eg]—dominam quippe debeo uocare sponsam Domini mei',[7] etc.[h]

4. Felix talium commercium nuptiarum ut homunculi miseri prius uxor, nunc in summi regis thalamis sublimeris. Nec ex huius honoris priuilegio[a] priori [b]tantum modo uiro[b] sed quibuscumque seruis[c] eiusdem regis prelata. Ne mireris igitur si tam uiuus quam mortuus me uestris precipue commendem orationibus, cum iure publico constet apud dominos plus eorum sponsas intercedendo posse quam ipsorum familias, dominas amplius quam seruos. In quarum quidem typo regina illa et summi regis sponsa diligenter describitur, cum in psalmo dicitur: 'Astitit regina a dextris tuis',[8] etc.[d] Ac si aperte dicatur: ista iuncto latere sponso familiarissime adheret et pariter incedit, ceteris omnibus quasi a longe absistentibus[e] uel subsequentibus.[9] De huius[f] excellentia prerogatiue sponsa[g] in Canticis exultans illa, ut ita dicam, quam Moyses duxit,[h][10] Ethiopissa dicit:[i] 'Nigra sum, sed formosa, filie[j] Ierusalem.[11] Ideo[k] dilexit me rex, et introduxit me[l] in cubiculum suum.'[12] Et rursum: 'Nolite[m] considerare quod[n] fusca sim[o] quia decolorauit me sol.'[13] In quibus quidem uerbis cum [p]generaliter anima[p] describatur contemplatiua que specialiter sponsa Christi dicitur, expressius[q] tamen ad uos[r] hoc pertinere ipse etiam

3 [a–a] quoque tuam *CEF* [b] attendebas *Y;* attendis *F* [c–c] prope eidem *?S* [d] quod *CE* [e–e] *om. S* [f] est *add. CE* [g] scribo *add. FAmb* [h] *om. FAmb*

4 [a] prius logio *B;* prouisio *Y* [b–b] modo tantum uiro (uirio B) *BR;* tantum meo (meo *marked for corr.*) uiro *Y* [c] seruos *E*; seruis uiris *B*; uiris *R; om. Y* [d] *om. CFAmb* [e] assistentibus *CEFBRSY;* adsistentibus *Amb*[1] [f] quibus *CE;* cuius *F;* eius *Y* [g] sponse *AY* [h] dixit *BSY* [i] dixit *EFBR;* duxit *C* [j] fidia *BY* [k] et ideo *BRS* [l] *om. CEF* [m] me *add. F and Vulg* [n] quia *BR* [o] sum *AFY;* suum *Amb* [p–p] anima generaliter *CEFY* [q] *in T over eras.; eras also in marg.;* Exprisius *B* [r] nos *EBY*

[6] Above, *Letter* 4, 1.

[7] Jerome, *Epistola* XXII *ad Eustochium*, 2 (ed. Hilberg, liv. 145 *ll.* 15–16; *PL* xxii. 395). Also cited in *Letter* 7, 23 and *Sermon* 30 (*PL* clxxviii. 568C). Cf. also *Rule* 44 ('Domini sponse' / 'dominas').

[8] Ps. 44 (45): 10 (9). Cited in *Sermon* 1 (*PL* clxxviii. 384A, 387C) and by Jerome, *Epistola* XXII *ad Eustochium*, 6 (ed. Hilberg, liv. 151, *ll.* 7–8; *PL* xxii. 397).

3. What you call[6] the unnatural order of my greeting, if you consider it carefully, was in accordance with your own view as well as mine. For it is common knowledge, as you yourself have shown, that in writing to superiors one puts their name first, and you must realize that you became my superior from the day when you began to be my lady on becoming the bride of my Lord; witness St Jerome, who writes to Eustochium: 'This is my reason for writing "my lady Eustochium". Surely I must address as "my lady" her who is the bride of my Lord',[7] etc.

4. It was a happy transfer of your married state as you were previously the wife of a poor mortal and now you are raised to the bed of the supreme king. By the privilege of this honour you are set not only over your former husband but over every servant of that king. So you should not be surprised if I commend myself in life as in death to the prayers of your community, seeing that in common law it is accepted that wives are better able than their households to intercede with their husbands, being ladies rather than servants. As an illustration of this, the Psalmist says of the queen and bride of the supreme king: 'On your right stands the queen',[8] etc., as if it were clearly stated that, being at his side, she is the nearest to her husband and steps forward with him, while all the rest stand apart or follow behind.[9] The bride in the Canticles, an Ethiopian (such as the one Moses took as a wife[10]) rejoices in her glorious privilege and says: 'I am black but lovely, daughters of Jerusalem;[11] therefore the king has loved me and brought me into his chamber.'[12] And again: 'Take no notice of my darkness, because the sun has discoloured me.'[13] Although it is the contemplative soul which is described generally in these words and called especially the bride of Christ, however, your outer habit also

[9] Cf. *Hymn* 94, *De uirginibus* 2–3: 'Haec incedit iuncto latere. / Et regina sponsi tenens dexteram . . .' (ed. Waddell, p. 132; ed. (no. 122), Szövérffy, p. 250); *Sermon* 1: 'Ac si aperte dicat . . . ut quasi regina celorum ei juncto latere assistas' (*PL* clxxviii. 387D). Cf. also the sequence *Virgines castae* (sometimes attributed to Abelard; see above, Introduction, p. xxxviii), stanza 5 (*Analecta Hymnica Medii Aevi*, liv (1915), p. 133; ed. with an English translation by Bell, *Abelard after Marriage*, p. 16 (and cf. pp. 230–2): 'Haec est a dextris / assistens regis / illa regina / iuncto latere' / 'This one is that queen serving at the right hand of the king / United beside him'. Bell, p. 73, suggests (from information given to him by Waddell) that Origen's first *Homily* on the Song of Songs is the source used here: 'Sponsa . . . iuncto ingreditur latere' (*Homiliae*, i. 5, ed. Baehrens, p. 34; French trans., Rousseau, p. 82).

[10] Cf. Num. 12: 1.

[11] S. of S. 1: 4. Cf. Jerome, *Epistola* XXII *ad Eustochium*, 1 (ed. Hilberg, liv. 145, *ll.* 2–3; *PL* xxii. 395).

[12] Cf. S. of S. 1: 3.

[13] S. of S. 1: 5.

uester[s] exterior habitus loquitur.[14] Ipse quippe cultus exterior nigrorum aut uilium indumentorum, instar lugubris habitus [t]bonarum uiduarum[t] mortuos quos dilexerant uiros plangentium, uos[u] in hoc mundo, iuxta Apostolum,[15] uere uiduas et desolatas ostendit, stipendiis Ecclesie sustentandas. De[v] quarum etiam[w] uiduarum luctu super occisum earum sponsum[x] Scriptura commemorat dicens: Mulieres sedentes ad monumentum lamentabantur flentes Dominum.[16]

5. Habet[a] autem Ethiopissa exteriorem in carne[b] nigredinem et, quantum ad exteriora pertinet, ceteris apparet[c] feminis deformior; cum [d]non sit tamen[d] [e]in interioribus[e] dispar sed in plerisque [f]etiam formosior atque candidior, sicut[g] in ossibus seu dentibus.[f] [17] Quorum uidelicet dentium[h] candor in[i] ipso[j] etiam[k] commendatur[l] sponso, cum dicitur: 'Et dentes eius lacte candidiores.'[18] Nigra itaque in exterioribus, [m]sed formosa in interioribus[m] [n]est quia, in hac uita crebris aduersitatum tribulationibus[n] corporaliter afflicta,[o] quasi in carne nigrescit exterius, iuxta illud Apostoli: 'Omnes qui [p]uolunt pie[p] uiuere in[q] Christo[r] tribulationem[s] patientur.'[t] [19] Sicut enim candido prosperum, ita [u]non incongrue[u] nigro designatur aduersum. Intus autem quasi in ossibus candet, quia in uirtutibus eius anima pollet, sicut scriptum est: 'Omnis gloria eius filie regis ab intus.'[20] Ossa quippe que interiora sunt, exteriori[v] carne circumdata, et ipsius carnis quam gerunt uel sustentant robur[w] ac fortitudo sunt,[21] bene[x] animam exprimunt[y] que carnem ipsam, cui inest, uiuificat,[z] sustentat, mouet atque regit, atque ei omnem ualitudinem ministrat. Cuius quidem est candor siue decor ipse quibus adornatur uirtutes. Nigra quoque est[a] in exterioribus quia, dum[b] in hac peregrinatione adhuc[c] exulat,[d] uilem et abiectam se [e]tenet in hac uita ut[e] in illa sublimetur, que 'est abscondita cum[f] Christo[g] in Deo',[h] [22] patriam iam adepta. Sic[i] uero eam sol uerus decolorat, quia celestis amor sponsi eam sic[j] humiliat, uel tribulationibus cruciat,[k] ne eam scilicet prosperitas extollat.

[s] uidetur *AEY;* et uester *C, ?F* [t–t] uiduarum bonarum *CEF;* beatarum uiduarum *Y* [u] nos *EB* [v] *om. S* [w] *om. EBR* [x] uirum *BR*

5 [a] haec *F* [b] habet *add. F* [c] que *C;* atque *E* [d–d] tamen non sit *Y* [e–e] mulieribus *Y* [f–f] (filie *Y before exp.*) ut in dentibus *Y* [g] seu *E* [h] *om. Y* [i] *om. E* [j] ipsa *Y* [k] *om. CEF* [l] commendat *Y* [m–m] *om. S* [n–n] *om. Y* [o] *om. Y* [p–p] pie uolunt *F* [q] *om. Y* [r] Iesu *add. F* [s] persecutionem *F and Vulg.* [t] paciuntur *ASY;* patiantur *C* [u–u] est congrue *BR* [v] exteriore *F* [w] *om. R* [x] unde *R* [y] exprimeret *B*; exprimere *S* [z] et *add. EF* [a] *om. F* [b] *om. Y* [c] hominis *Y* [d] exultat *Y but marked for corr.* [e–e] tenet ut in hac uita humilietur ut *Y* [f] *om. Y* [g] primo *C* [h] *om. E* [i] sicut *CEF* [j] *om. C* [k] crucia *S*

indicates that they have a particular application to you.[14] For that outer garb of black or coarse clothing, like the mourning worn by good widows who weep for the dead husbands they had loved, shows you to be in this world, in the words of the Apostle,[15] truly widowed and desolate and such as the Church should be charged to support. The Scriptures also record the grief of these widows for their spouse who was slain, in the words: 'The women sitting at the tomb wept and lamented for the Lord.'[16]

5. The Ethiopian woman is black in the outer part of her flesh and as regards exterior appearance looks less lovely than other women; yet she is not unlike them within, but in several respects she is whiter and lovelier, in her bones, for instance, or her teeth.[17] Indeed, whiteness of teeth is also praised in her spouse, in reference to 'his teeth whiter than milk'.[18] And so she is black without but lovely within; for she is blackened outside in the flesh because in this life she suffers bodily affliction through the repeated tribulations of adversity, according to the saying of the Apostle: 'Persecution will come to all who want to live a godly life as Christians.'[19] As prosperity is marked by white, so adversity may properly be indicated by black, and she is white within in her bones because her soul is strong in virtues, as it is written: 'All the glory of the king's daughter is within.'[20] For the bones within, surrounded by the flesh without, are the strength and support of the very flesh they wear or sustain,[21] and can properly stand for the soul which gives life and sustenance to the flesh itself in which it is, and to which it gives movement and direction and provision for all its well-being. Its whiteness or beauty is the sum of the virtues which adorn it. She is black too in outward things because while she is still an exile on life's pilgrimage, she keeps herself humble and abject in this life so that she may be exalted in the next life, which 'is hidden with Christ in God',[22] once she has reached her own country. So indeed the true sun changes her colour because the heavenly love of the bridegroom humbles her in this way, or torments her with tribulations lest

[14] The bride in the Song of Songs was often held to symbolize the contemplative and ascetic life of the cloister; cf. Herde, 'Das Hohelied'.

[15] Cf. 1 Tim. 5: 5, 16. Cf. *Letters* 6, **28** and 7, **18, 20, 22**.

[16] Cf. Matt. 27: 61; Luke 23: 27, 55; John 20: 11; also *Letter* 3, **12** and note.

[17] Marenbon, *The Philosophy of Peter Abelard*, p. 85, shows that there is no parallel here with Aristotle's *Historia animalium*, iii. 9.

[18] Gen. 49: 12.

[19] 2 Tim. 3: 12.

[20] Ps. 44: 14 (13).

[21] Cf. *Letter* 7, **10**.

[22] Col. 3: 3.

Decolorat eam sic, [l]id est,[l] dissimilem[m] eam[n] [o]a ceteris[o] facit, que terrenis inhiant et seculi querunt gloriam, ut sic ipsa uere[p] lilium conuallium[23] per humilitatem efficiatur, non[q] lilium quidem[r] montium,[s] sicut ille uidelicet fatue[t] uirgines[24] que de munditia carnis, uel abstinentia exteriore, apud se intumescentes, estu temptationum aruerunt.

6. Bene autem filias Iherusalem, id est, imperfectiores[a] alloquens fideles, qui filiarum potius quam filiorum nomine digni sunt, dicit:[b] 'Nolite [c]mirari',[25] etc.[c] Ac si apertius dicat: Quod sic[d] me humilio uel[e] tam uiriliter aduersitates[f] sustineo, non est mee uirtutis, sed eius gratie cui deseruio. Aliter solent heretici uel ypocrite, quantum ad faciem hominum spectat, spe terrene glorie sese uehementer humiliare uel [g]multa inutiliter tolerare.[g] De quorum quidem[h] huiusmodi[i] abiectione uel tribulatione quam sustinent, uehementer mirandum est, cum sint omnibus miserabiliores hominibus qui nec presentis uite bonis nec future fruuntur.[j] Hoc[k] itaque diligenter[l] sponsa considerans, dicit:[m] Nolite mirari cur id faciam. Sed de illis mirandum est qui inutiliter terrene laudis desiderio estuantes terrenis se priuant commodis tam hic quam in futuro miseri. Qualis quidem[n] fatuarum uirginum continentia est, que a[o] ianua sunt excluse.[26]

7. Bene etiam, quia nigra est, ut diximus,[27] et formosa, dilectam et introductam[a] se dicit in cubiculum regis,[b] id est, in secretum uel quietem contemplationis, et lectulum illum[c] de quo eadem alibi dicit: 'In lectulo meo per noctes quesiui quem[d] diligit anima mea.'[28] Ipsa quippe nigredinis[e] deformitas occultum potius quam manifestum, et secretum magis quam publicum, amat. Et que talis est uxor secreta potius uiri gaudia quam manifesta desiderat, et in lecto magis uult sentiri quam in mensa uideri. Et frequenter accidit[f] ut nigrarum[g] caro feminarum [h]quanto est[h] in aspectu deformior tanto sit in tactu suauior; atque ideo earum uoluptas secretis gaudiis quam publicis[i]

[l–l] igitur *BR;* scilicet *Y* [m] similes *Y* [n] *om. F* [o–o] *om. Y* [p] nec *B* [q] nec *B* [r] est *add. R* [s] in interitum *CEF* [t] fame *S*

6 [a] imperfectiones *T;* imperfectior *C;* imperfectorum *EF* [b] *om. E;* dici *BR;* dicit *Y;* ait *Y*[1] [c–c] mirari si etc. *CE;* me considerare quod fusca sim quia decolorauit me sol *FAmb* [d] si *E* [e] et *F* [f] aduersitatem *E* [g–g] iusta inutiliter collocare *C* [h] quidam *Y* [i] huius *S* [j] fruantur *E* [k] Hec *Y* [l] *om. Y* [m] dixit *E* [n] quidam *Y* [o] *om. ABR*

7 [a] introducta *Y* [b] *om. F* [c] istum *F* [d] quam *C* [e] nigretudinis *S* [f] *in T over eras.* [g] nigra *AEFY* [h–h] *om. Y* [i] *corrupted in E;* plurimis *F*

prosperity lifts her up. He changes her colour, that is, he makes her different from other women who thirst for earthly things and seek worldly glory, so that she may truly become through her humility 'a lily of the valley',[23] and not a lily of the heights like those foolish virgins[24] who pride themselves on purity of the flesh or an outward show of self-denial, and then wither in the fire of temptation.

6. And she rightly told the daughters of Jerusalem, that is, the weaker amongst the faithful who deserve to be called daughters rather than sons: 'Take no notice',[25] etc. She might say more openly: 'The fact that I humble myself in this way or bear adversity so bravely is due to no virtue of mine but to the grace of him whom I serve.' This is not the way of heretics and hypocrites who (at any rate when others are present) humiliate themselves to excess in hope of earthly glory and endure much to no purpose. The sort of abjection or tribulation they put up with is indeed surprising, and they are the most pitiable of men, enjoying the good things neither of this life nor of the life to come. It is with this in mind that the bride says: 'Do not wonder that I do so'; but we must wonder at those who vainly burn with desire for worldly praise and deny themselves advantages on earth so that they are as unhappy in their present life as they will be in the next. Such self-denial is that of the foolish virgins who found the door shut against them.[26]

7. And she did well to say that, because she is black, as we said,[27] and lovely, she is chosen and taken into the king's bedchamber, that is, to that secret, quiet place of contemplation, and into that little bed, of which she says elsewhere: 'Night after night on my little bed my soul has sought my true love.'[28] Indeed, the disfigurement of her blackness makes her love what is hidden rather than open, what is secret rather than public. And any such wife desires private, not public delights with her husband, and would rather be felt in bed than seen at table. Moreover it often happens that the flesh of black women is all the softer to touch though it is less attractive to look at, and for this reason the pleasure they give is greater and more suitable for private

[23] S. of S. 2: 1.
[24] Cf. Matt. 25: 2, 3, 8.
[25] S. of S. 1: 5, already cited in full at **4** in the form 'nolite considerare'. In John 5: 28 Christ says to his disciples 'Nolite mirari'.
[26] Cf. Matt. 25: 1–13.
[27] Above at **4**.
[28] S. of S. 3: 1, cited also in *Rule* **113**. For the 'lectulum contemplationis' or 'quietis' cf. *Rule* **12**, note 45.

gratior sit et conuenientior, et earum [j]uiri, ut[j] illis oblectentur,[k] magis[l] eas in cubiculum introducunt quam[m] ad publicum educunt.[n] Secundum quam[o] quidem methaphoram bene spiritalis sponsa, cum premisisset:[p] 'Nigra sum, sed formosa,'[29] statim adiunxit: 'Ideo dilexit me rex, et introduxit me in cubiculum suum,'[30] singula uidelicet singulis reddens. Hoc[q] est, quia formosa, dilexit; quia nigra, introduxit. Formosa, ut dixi, intus uirtutibus quas diligit sponsus; nigra exterius corporalium tribulationum [r]aduersitatibus.

8. Que quidem[a] nigredo, corporalium scilicet tribulationum,[r] facile fidelium[b] mentes ab amore terrenorum auellit[c] et[d] ad eterne uite desideria[e] suspendit et sepe a tumultuosa seculi[f] uita trahit ad secretum contemplationis, sicut[g] in Paulo[h] illo uidelicet nostre,[i] id est monachalis, uite primordio actum esse beatus[j] [k]scribit Ieronymus.[k] [31] Hec[l] quoque abiectio[m] indumentorum uilium secretum magis quam publicum[n] appetit, et maxima[o] humilitatis[p] ac[q] secretioris loci qui nostre[r] precipue conuenit professioni [s]custodia est. Maxime[s] namque ad publicum procedere preciosus prouocat cultus quem[t] a nullo appeti nisi ad inanem gloriam et seculi pompam beatus Gregorius [u]inde conuincit[u] quod nemo his in occulto se ornat, sed ubi conspici queat.[32] Hoc autem predictum sponse[v] cubiculum illud est ad quod ipse sponsus in Euangelio inuitat [w]orantem,[x] dicens:[w] 'Tu autem cum oraueris intra in cubiculum,[y] et [z]clauso ostio[z] ora patrem tuum.'[33] Ac si diceret: non in plateis uel[a] publicis locis, sicut ypocrite. Cubiculum itaque dicit secretum a tumultibus et aspectu[b] seculi locum ubi [c]quietius et purius[c] orari possit, qualia sunt scilicet [d]monasticharum solitudinum[d] secreta ubi claudere ostium iubemur, id est aditus[e] omnes obstruere,[f] ne puritas orationis casu aliquo[g] prepediatur et oculus noster[h] infelicem animam depredetur.[34]

[j–j] uiri *C;* uiris *E;* uiri *Y;* quando *Y*[1] [k] ablectentur *C* [l] cum *add. F* [m] cum *add. F* [n] introducunt *BR;* eductum *S;* educant *Y* [o] *om. Y* [p] premisit *Y* [q] Hec *Y* [r–r] *om. Y*

8 [a] est *add. BR* [b] fidelissimus *CEF* [c] euellit *EY* [d] *om. C* [e] gaudia *CEF* [f] *om. R* [g] *om. CE;* Quod *F* [h] principio *Y*[1] [i] meo *Y* [j] *om. E;* probatus *F;* quoque *add. Y* [k–k] ieronimus scribit *Y* [l] hoc *Y* [m] iniectio*: ?E,?F* [n] publicatum *C* [o] maximus *C;* maxime *BRY* [p] utilitatis *T;* humilitatis *ACEFBRSY;* vilitatis *Amb;* humilitatis *Amb*[1] [q] et *Y* [r] uestre *B* [s–s] custodienda est maxime *TAmb; om. BR;* cuius conditur (*?*) et maxime *Y but marked for corr.* [t] quam *C* [u–u] *om. BR;* inde conuincet *?S* [v] sponsi *F* [w–w] dicens orantem *Y* [x] oratam *S* [y] tuum *add. F* [z–z] hostio clause *E* [a] in *add. Y* [b] aspectum *C* [c–c] quiescius purius *B;* quiescius et purius *RS;* queitius *Y* [d–d] monachorum sollicitudinum *E* [e] auditus *Y* [f] astruere *TY;* abstruere *C* [g] aliquando *A* [h] uester *Y*

than for public gratification, and their husbands take them into a bedroom to enjoy them rather than parade them in public. Following this metaphor, when that spiritual bride said: 'I am black but lovely',[29] she rightly added at once: 'Therefore the king has loved me and brought me into his chamber.'[30] She relates each point to the other: because she was lovely he loved her, and because she was black he brought her into his chamber. She is lovely within, as we said before, with virtues which the bridegroom loves, and black outside from the adversity of bodily tribulation.

8. Such blackness of bodily tribulation easily turns the minds of the faithful away from love of earthly things and attaches them to the desire for eternal life, often leading them from the stormy life of the world to retirement for contemplation, as happened at the beginning of our own, that is, the monastic life in the case of the Paul of whom St Jerome writes.[31] The humiliation of coarse garments also looks to retirement rather than to public life, and is to be preserved as being most suitable for the life of humility and withdrawal which especially befits our profession. The greatest encouragement to public display is costly clothing, which is sought by none except for empty display and worldly ceremony, as St Gregory clearly shows in saying that no one adorns himself in private, only where he can be seen.[32]As for the chamber of the bride, it is the one to which the bridegroom himself in the Gospel invites anyone who prays, saying: 'But when you pray, go into a room by yourself, shut the door and pray to your Father.'[33] He could have added: not like the hypocrites, at street corners and in public places. So by a room he means a place that is secluded from the tumult and sight of the world, where prayer can be offered more purely and quietly, such as the seclusion of monastic solitude, a place where we are told to shut the door, that is, to close up every approach, lest something happen to hinder the purity of prayer and what we see distract the unfortunate soul.[34]

[29] S. of S. 1: 4.

[30] Cf. S. of S. 1: 3.

[31] Jerome, *Vita Pauli primi eremitae*, 5 (*PL* xxiii. 21A). Jerome's *Life* portrays St Paul of Thebes (d. *c*.340) as the first Christian hermit.

[32] Cf. Gregory the Great, *Homiliae in Euangelia*, xl. 3 (ed. Étaix, p. 399; *PL* lxxvi. 1305B) and *Rule* **101**.

[33] Matt. 6: 6.

[34] Cf. Lamentations 3: 51.

9. Cuius quidem consilii, immo precepti, diuini multos[a] huius habitus nostri contemptores adhuc[b] grauiter sustinemus qui, cum diuina celebrant officia claustris[c] uel[d] choris eorum reseratis, publicis tam feminarum quam uirorum aspectibus impudenter se ingerunt, et tunc precipue cum in[e] sollempnitatibus preciosis polluerint[f] ornamentis, sicut et [g]ipsi quibus[g] se[h] ostentant seculares homines. Quorum quidem iudicio tanto festiuitas habetur celebrior quanto in[i] exteriori ornatu est ditior et in epulis copiosior.[35]

10. De quorum quidem cecitate miserrima, et pauperum[a] Christi religioni[b] penitus contraria, tanto est silere[c] honestius quanto loqui turpius. Qui penitus iudaizantes[d] consuetudinem suam sequuntur [e]pro regula,[e][36] et irritum [f]fecerunt mandatum[f] Dei propter[g] traditiones suas,[37] non quod debeat[h] sed quod soleat attendentes. Cum, ut beatus etiam meminit Augustinus,[38] Dominus dixerit: 'Ego sum ueritas',[39] non: Ego sum consuetudo. Horum orationibus, [i]que aperto scilicet fiunt ostio,[i] qui [j]uoluerit se[j] commendet. Vos autem que in cubiculum celestis regis ab ipso introducte[k] atque in eius amplexibus quiescentes,[l] clauso semper ostio, ei tote[m] uacatis[n] quanto [o]familiarius ei[o] adheretis, iuxta illud Apostoli: 'Qui adheret Domino unus spiritus est',[40] tanto puriorem et[p] efficaciorem habere confidimus[q] orationem et ob[r] hoc uehementius [s]earum efflagitamus[s] opem. Quas etiam tanto deuotius pro me[t] faciendas esse credimus quanto maiore[u] nos inuicem[v] caritate colligati sumus.

11. Quod[a] uero mentione periculi[b] in quo laboro, uel mortis quam timeo, uos commoui, iuxta ipsam quoque tuam[c] factum[d] est exhortationem, immo etiam adiurationem. Sic enim prima,[e][41] quam ad me direxisti, quodam loco continet epistola:[f] 'Per ipsum itaque [g]qui te[g] sibi adhuc quoquo modo protegit Christum obsecramus [h]quatinus

9 [a] multas *E* [b] *ditto. Y* [c] claustratis *CE* [d] et *F* [e] *om. S* [f] polluerunt *BRS;* pollent *Y* [g–g] quibus ipsi *T before corr.* ipsis quibus *A* [h] *om. TAmb* [i] *om. Y*

10 [a] pauperrimi *?C, EF* [b] religiosi *E* [c] et *add. BRS* [d] iudaziantes *CE* [e–e] propterea *E* [f–f] *om. Y* [g] per *Amb* [h] deceat *C;* deneniat *E* [i–i] que aperte fiunt honeste *CEF;* que aperto hostio fiunt *BR;* fiunt *S* [j–j] se uoluerit *CF* [k] introducere *R* [l] quiescente *Y* [m] tante *E* [n] uocatis *Y* [o–o] ei familiarius *BRS* [p] *om. E* [q] credimus *Y* [r] ab *C* [s–s] earum affligatumus *C;* eorum effligitamus *S* [t] nobis *CEF* [u] maiorem *BRS* [v] inuitis *E*

11 [a] ad secundam *rubr. add. TA, add. Amb in marg.* [b] et periculi *add. Y* [c] uiam *B* [d] actum *F* [e] primo *S* [f] ecclesia *T before exp.* [g–g] qui etc *BR;* qui qui te *Y* [h–h] *om. C;* etc *EF*

9. Yet there are many wearing our habit who despise this divine counsel, or rather precept, and we find them hard to tolerate when they celebrate the divine offices with cloister or choir wide open and conduct themselves shamelessly in full view of both men and women, especially during the Mass when they are decked out in valuable ornaments like those of the worldly men to whom they display them. In their view a feast is best celebrated if it is rich in external adornment and lavish in food and drink.[35]

10. Better to keep silence, as it is shameful to speak of their wretched blindness that is wholly contrary to the religion of the poor of Christ. At heart they are like Jews, following their own custom instead of a rule,[36] making a mockery of God's command in their practices,[37] looking to usage, not duty; although, as St Augustine reminds us,[38] the Lord said: 'I am truth',[39] not 'I am custom'. Anyone who cares to may entrust himself to the prayers of these men, which are offered with doors open, but you who have been led by the king of heaven himself into his chamber and rest in his embrace, and with the door always shut are wholly given up to him, are more intimately joined to him, in the Apostle's words: 'But anyone who is joined to the Lord is one spirit with him.'[40] So much the more confidence, then, have I in the purity and effectiveness of your prayers, and the more urgently I demand your help. And I believe these prayers are offered more devoutly on my behalf because we are bound together in such great mutual love.

11. But if I have distressed you by mentioning the dangers which beset me or the death I fear, it was done in accordance with your own request, or rather, entreaty. For the first letter you wrote me[41] has a passage which says: 'And so in the name of Christ, who is still giving you some protection for his service, we beseech you to write as often

[35] Cf. *Carmen ad Astralabium*: 'qui celebrant epulis sacra natalicia largis, / non ea sic sanctos promeruisse sciant' (ed. Rubingh-Bosscher, *vv.* 809–10); 'those who celebrate sacred nativities with lavish banquets / know not how the saints deserved them'.

[36] Cf. *Letters* 6, **16** and *Rule* 71.

[37] Cf. Matt. 15: 6.

[38] Augustine, *De baptismo contra Donatistas*, iii. 6. 9 (citing Cyprian, *Sententiae episcoporum*, 30) and vi. 37. 71 (ed. Petschenig, p. 203, *ll.* 16–17 and p. 334, *ll.* 15–16; *PL* xliii. 143 and 220). Also cited in *Rule* 71.

[39] John 14: 6.

[40] 1 Cor. 6: 17.

[41] The first letter, that is, since the arrival at the Paraclete of *Letter* 1, which occasioned a renewal of contact between the couple.

ancillulas ipsius et tuas[i] crebris litteris de his, in quibus adhuc fluctuas, naufragiis certificare digneris ut nos saltem, que[j] tibi sole remansimus, doloris[k] uel gaudii participes[l] habeas. Solent etenim[m] dolenti nonnullam afferre consolationem qui condolent. Et quodlibet onus pluribus impositum[n] leuius sustinetur siue[o] defertur.'[h] [42] Quid igitur[p] arguis quod uos anxietatis mee participes feci, ad [q]quod me[q] adiurando compulisti? [r]Numquid in tanta uite, qua crucior, desperatione gaudere uos[s] conuenit? Nec doloris socie, sed gaudii tantum, uultis esse, nec 'flere cum flentibus', sed 'gaudere cum gaudentibus'?[r] [43] Nulla maior uerorum et falsorum differentia est amicorum quam quod illi aduersitati, isti[t] prosperitati, se sociant.

12. Quiesce, obsecro, ab his dictis, et huiusmodi[a] querimonias[b] compesce que[c] a uisceribus caritatis absistunt[d] longissime.[44] Aut[e] si adhuc in his offenderis, me tamen in tanto [f]periculi positum[f] articulo, et cotidiana[g] desperatione uite, de salute anime sollicitum conuenit esse, et[h] de[i] ipsa, dum licet, prouidere. Nec tu, si[j] me uere diligis, hanc exosam prouidentiam habebis. Quin[k] etiam, si quam[l] de diuina erga[m] me misericordia spem haberes, tanto amplius ab huius uite erumpnis liberari me cuperes [n]quanto eas conspicis[n] intolerabiliores. Certum [o]quipe tibi[o] est quod quisquis ab hac uita me liberet, a[p] maximis penis eruet. Quas postea incurram[q] incertum[r] est, sed a quantis absoluar[s] dubium[t] non est.

13. Omnis uita misera [a]iocundum exitum[a] habet, et quicumque aliorum[b] anxietatibus uere compatiuntur et condolent,[c] eas finiri desiderant, et cum dampnis etiam[d] suis, si quos anxios uident uere diligunt,[e] nec tam commoda propria quam illorum in ipsis attendunt. Sic[f] diu languentem filium mater etiam[g] morte languorem finire desiderat, quem tolerare ipsa non potest, et[h] eo potius orbari sustinet quam in miseria consortem habere.[i] Et quicumque amici presentia[j] plurimum oblectatur,[k] [l]magis tamen beatam esse uult[l] eius[m] absentiam

[i] a *add. Y* [j] qui *S* [k] dolores *BS* [l] particeps *A* [m] enim *Amb* [n] est *add. A* [o] seu *Y* [p] ergo *F* [q–q] quod *CE*; quam *F* [r–r] *om. CEF* [s] *om. B* [t] illi *RS*

12 [a] huius *S* [b] querimoniis *RY* [c] qui *Y* [d] assistunt *S* [e] *om. B* [f–f] positum periculi *F* [g] cotidiane *BR* [h] *om. CEF* [i] dum *Y* [j] siue *C* [k] Que *ACEFSY;* Ne *B;* Nequam *R* [l] *om. E;* qua *S* [m] gratia in *A* [n–n] quam a concupiscentiis *Y* [o–o] tibi quippe *Y* [p] *om. BR* [q] et *add. C* [r] iustum *Y* [s] absoluas *Y* [t] dum *C*

13 [a–a] exitum iocundum *A* [b] illorum *BR* [c] cum dolent *B* [d] et *BR* [e] diligenter *BRS* [f] si *T* [g] et *R* [h] ut *T* [i] *om. Y* [j] penitencia *Y*

as you think fit to us who are his handmaids and yours, with news of the perils in which you are still storm-tossed. We are all that are left you, so at least you should let us share your sorrow or your joy. It is always some consolation in sorrow to feel that it is shared, and any burden laid on several is carried more lightly or removed.'[42] Why then do you accuse me of making you share my anxiety when I was forced to do so at your own behest? When I am suffering in despair of my life, would it be fitting for you to be joyous? Would you want to be partners only in joy, not grief, 'to join in rejoicing' without 'weeping with those who weep'?[43] There is no wider distinction between true friends and false than the fact that the former share adversity, the latter only prosperity.

12. Say no more, I beseech you, and cease from complaints like these, which are so far removed from the true depths of love![44] Yet even if you are still offended by this, I am so critically placed in danger and daily despair of life that it is proper for me to take thought for the welfare of my soul, and to provide for it while I may. Nor will you, if you truly love me, take exception to my forethought. Indeed, had you any hope of divine mercy being shown me, you would be all the more anxious for me to be freed from the troubles of this life as you see them to be intolerable. At least you must know that whoever frees me from life will deliver me from the greatest suffering. What I may afterwards incur is uncertain, but from what I shall be set free is not in question.

13. Every unhappy life is happy in its ending, and those who feel true sympathy and pain for the anxieties of others want to see these ended, even to their own loss, if they really love those they see suffer and think more of their friends' advantage than of their own. So when a son has long been ill a mother wants his illness to end even in death, for she finds it unbearable, and can more easily face bereavement than have him share her misery. And anyone who takes special pleasure in the presence of a friend would rather have him happy in absence than

[k] oblectantur *CEY* [l–l] uult *B;* magis tamen uult beatam *R;* magis tamen beatam mult *Y* [m] *om. BRF*

[42] *Letter* 2, 3–4.
[43] Rom. 12: 15.
[44] Cf. *Letter* 4, 3 and 15–16; also Virgil, *Aeneid*, iv. 360: 'Desine meque tuis incendere teque querelis' / 'No more reproaches, then—they only torture us both' (trans. C. Day Lewis).

quam presentiam miseram, quia quibus subuenire non ualet erumpnas[n] tolerare non potest.[45]

14. Tibi uero nec nostra uel etiam misera concessum[a] est frui presentia. Nec nisi[b] tuis in me commodis aliquid[c] prouideas,[d] cur me miserrime[e] uiuere malis quam felicius[f] mori non uideo. Quod si nostras protendi miserias in[g] commoda tua desideras, hostis potius quam amica conuinceris. Quod si uideri refugis, ab his obsecro, sicut dixi, quiesce querimoniis.

15. Approbo[a] autem quod reprobas laudem quia in hoc ipso te laudabiliorem ostendis. Scriptum est enim: 'Iustus [b]in primordio[b] accusator est sui',[46] et:[c] 'Qui se humiliat, [d]se exaltat.'[d][47] Atque utinam sic[e] sit in animo tuo sicut et[f] in scripto! Quod si fuerit, uera est humilitas tua nec[g] pro nostris euanuerit[h] uerbis. Sed uide, obsecro, ne[i] hoc ipso laudem queras quo[j] laudem fugere uideris, et reprobes illud ore quod appetas corde. De quo ad Eustochium uirginem sic inter cetera beatus scribit Iheronimus: 'Naturali ducimur[k] malo.[l] Adulatoribus nostris libenter fauemus et quamquam nos respondeamus indignos et callidior[m] rubor ora suffundat,[n] attamen[o] ad laudem suam intrinsecus anima letatur.'[48] Talem et lasciue[p] calliditatem Galathee Virgilius[q] describit, que quod uolebat[r] fugiendo appetebat et, simulatione repulse,[s] amplius in se amantem incitabat: 'Et fugit ad salices',[t] inquit, 'et se cupit ante uideri.'[49] Antequam lateat [u]cupit se[u] fugientem uideri, ut ipsa fuga qua[v] reprobare consortium iuuenis uidetur amplius acquirat. Sic et laudes hominum, dum fugere uidemur, amplius erga nos excitamus et, cum[w] latere nos [x]uelle simulamus,[x] ne quis scilicet in nobis quid[y] laudet[z] agnoscat, amplius attendimus[a] in[b] laudem nostram imprudentes,[c] quia eo [d]laude uidemur[d] digniores. Et hec quidem, quia sepe accidunt,[e] dicimus,[f] non[g] quia de te talia[h] suspicemur qui de tua non hesitamus humilitate. Sed

[n] aerumnis *FAmb*

14 [a] circumcisum *?S* [b] ubi *TAmb* [c] aliud *F* [d] prouideat *EF* [e] miserrima *BR* [f] hostis potius *add. T before exp.*; felicibus *E* [g] *om. F*

15 [a] ad terciam *rubr. in marg. TA, in marg. Amb, rubr. in text S* [b–b] prior *F and Vulg.* [c] etiam F [d–d] exaltabitur *CF;* se exaltabitur *E* [e] si *C* [f] *superscr. by Ecorr.; om. R* [g] ne *TAmb* [h] euanuit *F* euanuerunt *BR;* euanuerint *Y* [i] nec *CEF* [j] quod *BRS* [k] dicimur *Y* [l] male *Y* [m] calidus *F* [n] perfundat *F* [o] ac tamen *TBR;* at tamen *A;* tamen *CEF;* actum *S* [p] laciue *BR* [q] uigilius *T* [r] nollebat *E;* nolebat *F;* ualebat *S* [s] repulsa *BR;* repulset *S* [t] salacices *B;* salacites *R;* salicices *S* [u–u] se cupit *Y* [v] que *T;* quando *?B;* quam *Y* [w] tamen *C* [x–x] somulamus uelle *Y* [y] quam *C* [z] laudes *T before exp.* [a] ascendimus *T;* accendimus *RS Amb*[1];

present and unhappy, for he finds suffering intolerable if he cannot relieve it.[45]

14. In your case, you are not even permitted to enjoy my presence, unhappy though it is, and so, when any provision you are able to make for me is to your own advantage, I cannot see why you should prefer me to live on in great misery rather than be happier in death. If you see your advantage in prolonging my miseries, you are proved an enemy rather than a friend. But if you hesitate to appear in such a guise, I beg you, as I said before, to cease your complaints.

15. However, I approve of your rejection of praise, for in this very thing you show yourself more praiseworthy. It is written: 'He who is first in accusing himself is just',[46] and: 'Whoever humbles himself will be exalted.'[47] May your written words be reflected in your heart! If they are, yours is true humility and will not vanish with anything I say. But be careful, I beg you, not to seek praise when you appear to shun it, and not to reject with your lips what you desire in your heart. St Jerome writes to the virgin Eustochium on this point, amongst others: 'We are led on by our natural evil. We give willing ear to our flatterers, and though we may answer that we are unworthy and an artful blush suffuses our cheeks, the soul inwardly delights in its own praise.'[48] Such artfulness Virgil describes in wanton Galatea, who sought what she wanted by flight, and by feigning rejection led on her lover more surely towards her: 'She flees to the willows and wishes first to be seen.'[49] Before she hides she wants to be seen fleeing, so that the very flight whereby she appears to reject the youth's company ensures that she obtains it. Similarly, when we seem to shun men's praise we are directing it towards ourselves, and when we pretend that we wish to hide lest anyone discovers what to praise in us, we are leading the unwary on to give us praise because in this way we appear to deserve it. I mention this because it is a common occurrence, not because I suspect such things of you; I have no doubts about your

attendamus *Y* [b] ut *Y* [c] imprudentes *TABRYAmb;* impudentes *?C, Amb*[1]*;* inpredictis *E;* impudentes praedictis *F* [d–d] laudemur *EF* [e] accidit *BR;* occidunt *Y* [f] dicemus *E* [g] *om. Y* [h] gloria *Y*

[45] Cf., and more fully, *Comm. Rom.*, iv (xii. 15) and *TSch*, iii. 117–20.

[46] Prov. 18: 17; also cited in *Rule* 37 and 69.

[47] Luke 18: 14.

[48] Jerome, *Epistola* XXII *ad Eustochium*, 24 (ed. Hilberg, p. 176, *l.* 16–p. 177, *l.* 2; *PL* xxii. 410).

[49] Virgil, *Eclogues*, iii. 65.

ab his etiam uerbis [i]te temperare[i] uolumus ne his, qui[j] te minus nouerint, uidearis, ut[k] ait[l] Iheronimus,[50] fugiendo[m] gloriam querere. Numquam te mea laus inflabit sed ad meliora prouocabit, et tanto studiosius que laudauero[n] amplecteris quanto mihi amplius[o] placere satagis. Non est laus nostra testimonium tibi religionis ut hinc[p] aliquid extollentie[q] sumas. Nec de[r] commendatione cuiusquam amicis credendum est,[s] sicut nec[t] inimicis de uituperatione.

16. Superest[a] tandem[b] ut ad antiquam illam, [c]ut diximus,[c] et assiduam querimoniam tuam ueniamus, qua[d] uidelicet de [e]nostre conuersionis[e] modo Deum potius accusare presumis quam glorificare, ut iustum est, uelis.[51] Hanc iamdudum amaritudinem animi tui tam[f] manifesto diuine misericordie consilio euanuisse credideram. Que, quanto tibi periculosior est,[g] corpus tuum pariter et[h] animam conterens, tanto miserabilior est et mihi molestior. Que[i] cum mihi per omnia placere, sicut profiteris, studeas, hoc saltem uno ut [j]me non[j] crucies, immo ut mihi summopere placeas hanc depone, cum qua mihi non potes placere neque mecum[k] ad beatitudinem peruenire. Sustinebis[l] [m]illuc me[m] sine te pergere, quem[n] [o]etiam ad Vulcania[o] loca[p] profiteris te sequi uelle?[52] [q]Hoc saltem uno[r] religionem appete ne a me ad Deum, ut credis, properante[s] diuidaris; et tanto libentius quanto quo ueniendum nobis est beatius[t] est,[u] ut tanto scilicet societas nostra sit gratior quanto felicior.[q] Memento que dixeris, recordare que scripseris, in hoc uidelicet nostre conuersionis modo quo mihi Deus amplius aduersari creditur, propitiorem mihi sicut manifestum est exstitisse. [v]Hoc uno[v] saltem hec eius dispositio tibi placeat quod mihi sit saluberrima, immo mihi[w] pariter et tibi,[x] si rationem uis[y] doloris admittat. Nec[z] te tanti[a] boni causam esse doleas, ad quod te a Deo maxime [b]creatam esse[b] non dubites. Nec quia id[c] tulerim plangas, nisi cum martyrum passionum[d] ipsiusque[e] dominice mortis commoda te contristabunt. Numquid si id [f]mihi iuste[f] accidisset, tolerabilius

[i–i] obtemperare *TBRS* [j] in *add. CEF* [k] *om. B* [l] *om. R* [m] fugere *Y* [n] laudem non *Y* [o] *om. BRS* [p] habere *BS* [q] excellencie *ERY;* excellentiae *F* [r] *om. A* [s] *om. CEF* [t] de *add. E; om. F*

16 [a] ad quartam *rubr add. TAS, in marg. Amb* [b] *om. Y* [c–c] *om. R* [d] quia *TAmb* [e–e] conuersionis nostre *T*; nostre conuersacionis *R* [f] *om. CEF* [g] *om. F* [h] *om. BR* [i] qui *Y* [j–j] non me *S* [k] *om. C* [l] Sustinebit *Y* [m–m] illud me *C;* me illuc *tr. R* [n] quam *C* [o–o] etiam ad uulcana *T;* ad multa me *Y;* neis en feus *J* [p] loca *om. codd., Amb, but cf. Letter* 2, **15** [q–q] *om. CEF* [r] immo *B; Y breaks off here in mid-column* [s] properantem *codd., Amb;* properante *Bergh, 'Studia critica', pp. 22–3;* c'est que de moy-qui me haste d'aler a Dieu, si comme tu crois – ne soies pas departie *J* [t] beatus *T* [u] *om. B*

humility. But I want you to refrain from speaking like this, so that you do not appear to those who do not know you so well to be seeking fame by shunning it, as Jerome says.[50] My praise will never make you proud, but will summon you to higher things, and the more eager you are to please me, the more anxious you will be to embrace what I praise. My praise is not a tribute to your piety which is intended to bolster up your pride, and we ought not in fact to believe in our friends' approval any more than in our enemies' abuse.

16. I come at last to what I have called your old continual complaint, in which you presume to blame God for the manner of our entry into religion instead of wishing to glorify him as you justly should.[51] I had thought that this bitterness of heart at what was so clear an act of divine mercy had long since disappeared. The more dangerous such bitterness is to you in wearing out body and soul alike, the more pitiful it is and distressing to me. If you are anxious to please me in everything, as you claim, and in this at least would end my torment, or even give me the greatest pleasure, you must rid yourself of it. If it persists you can neither please me nor attain bliss with me. Can you bear me to come to this without you—I whom you declare yourself ready to follow to Vulcan's pit?[52] Seek piety in this at least, lest you cut yourself off from me who am hastening, you believe, towards God; be the readier to do so because the goal we must come to will be blessed, and our companionship the more welcome for being happier. Remember what you have said, recall what you have written, namely that in the manner of our conversion, when God seems to have been more my adversary, he has clearly shown himself kinder. For this reason at least you must accept his will, that it is most salutary for me, and for you too, if your transports of grief will see reason. You should not grieve because you are the cause of so great a good, for which you must not doubt you were specially created by God. Nor should you weep because I have to bear this, except when our blessings through the martyrs in their sufferings and the Lord's death sadden you. If it had befallen me justly, would you find it easier to bear? Would it

[v–v] hec (Haec *F*) una *CEF* [w] tibi *BRS* [x] tui *E;* mihi *BRS* [y] *over eras. in T; add. T*[1] *in marg.* [z] Ne *AEF;* ne *C* [a] tam *R* [b–b] esse creatam *F* [c] ut *CEF* [d] passiones *F* [e] ipsaque *F* [f–f] iuste mihi *F*

[50] Jerome, *Epistola* XXII *ad Eustochium*, 27 (ed. Hilberg, p. 183, *l.* 7; *PL* xxii. 413).
[51] Cf. *Letters* 2, 8 and 15; 4, 14.
[52] Cf. *Letter* 2, 15.

ferres et minus te offenderet?[g] Profecto si sic fieret, eo modo contingeret quo[h] mihi esset ignominiosius, et inimicis laudabilius, cum illis laudem iustitia et[i] mihi contemptum acquireret culpa, nec iam quisquam quod actum est accusaret aut[j] compassione mei moueretur.

17. Vt tamen et hoc modo huius amaritudinem doloris leniamus,[a] tam iuste quam utiliter id[b] monstrabimus nobis[c] accidisse, et rectius in coniugatos quam in fornicantes ultum[d] Deum fuisse. Nosti,[e] post nostri[f] federationem[g] coniugii cum[h] Argenteoli[i] cum sanctimonialibus in claustro conuersareris,[j] me die quadam priuatim ad te uisitandam uenisse, et quid ibi tecum[k] mee[l] libidinis egerit[m] intemperantia in quadam etiam parte ipsius refectorii, cum quo alias uidelicet[n] diuerteremus non haberemus.[o] Nosti, inquam, id[p] impudentissime tunc actum esse[q] in tam reuerendo loco et summe Virgini consecrato[53]—[r]quod, et si[r] alia cessent flagitia, multo[s] grauiore dignum sit ultione. Quid pristinas fornicationes et[t] impudentissimas referam pollutiones que coniugium precesserunt? Quid summam denique proditionem meam, qua de te ipsa tuum, cum quo assidue in eius domo conuiuebam,[u] auuunculum tam turpiter seduxi? Quis me ab eo iuste prodi non censeat[v] quem tam impudenter ante[w] ipse prodideram? Putas ad tantorum criminum ultionem momentaneum illius[x] plage dolorem sufficere? Immo tantis malis tantum debitum esse commodum? Quam plagam [y]diuine sufficere[y] iustitie credis ad tantam contaminationem, ut diximus, sacerrimi loci sue matris? Certe, nisi uehementer erro, non tam illa saluberrima plaga in ultionem[z] horum conuersa est quam que cotidie[a] indesinenter sustineo.

18. Nosti etiam, quando te grauidam in meam transmisi[a] patriam, sacro[b] habitu indutam[c] monialem te finxisse, et tali[d] simulatione tue,[e] quam nunc[f] habes, religioni inreuerenter illusisse. Vnde etiam[g] pensa[h] quam conuenienter ad hanc te religionem diuina iustitia,

[g] offenderetur *S* [h] quod *C* [i] etc *E* [j] ut *Amb*

17 [a] leuiamus *BS* [b] illus *F* [c] *om. F* [d] uultum *C* [e] Noste *A* [f] nostram *R, Ecorr, F* [g] confederationem *EAmb* [h] *om. B;* ac *R* [i] argentolii *CE;* Argentolii *F* [j] conuersabaris *Amb* [k] *om. F* [l] tunc *B;* me *C* [m] egerunt *R, S before corr.* [n] *om. Amb* [o] haberes *B* [p] illud *F* [q] *om. B* [r–r] et quod si *R* [s] merito *E* [t] *om. BRS* [u] conuiuebant *BRS* [v] sentiat *F;* senserat *S* [w] autem *R* [x] unius *F* [y–y] diem sufficere *C;* sufficere diuine *R* [z] ultione *B* [a] et *add. F*

18 [a] transisti *S* [b] te *add. TABRSAmb* [c] inductam *T* [d] tituli *F* [e] mee *R;* me *S* [f] ninc *Ecorr.;* non *R* [g] et *F* [h] attende *Ecorr.*

distress you less? In fact if it had been so, the result would have been greater disgrace for me and more credit to my enemies, since justice would have won them approval while my guilt would have brought me into contempt. And no one would be stirred by pity for me to condemn what was done.

17. However, it may relieve the bitterness of your grief if I prove that this came upon us justly, as well as to our advantage, and that God's punishment was more properly directed against us when we were married than when we were living in sin. After our marriage, when you were living in the cloister with the nuns at Argenteuil and I came one day to visit you privately, you know what my uncontrollable desire did with you there, actually in a corner of the refectory, since we had nowhere else to go. I repeat, you know how shamelessly we behaved on that occasion in so hallowed a place, dedicated to the most holy Virgin.[53] Even if our other shameful behaviour was ended, this alone would deserve far heavier punishment. Need I recall our previous fornication and the wanton impurities which preceded our marriage, or my supreme act of betrayal, when I deceived your uncle about you so disgracefully, at a time when I was continuously living with him in his own house? Who would not judge me justly betrayed by the man whom I had first shamelessly betrayed? Do you think that the momentary pain of that wound is sufficient punishment for such crimes? Or rather, that so great an advantage was fitting for such great wickedness? What wound do you suppose would satisfy God's justice for the profanation such as I described of a place so sacred to his own Mother? Surely, unless I am much mistaken, that wound which was wholly beneficial was not intended as a punishment for this, but rather the daily unending torment I now endure.

18. You know too how, when you were pregnant and I took you to my own country, you disguised yourself in the sacred habit of a nun, a pretence which was an irreverent mockery of the religion you now profess. Consider, then, how fittingly divine justice, or rather, divine grace, brought you against your will to the religion which you did not

[53] 'The supreme Virgin' also appears in the sequence *Virgines castae* (sometimes attributed to Abelard; see above, Introduction, p. xxxviii; ed. in *Analecta Hymnica Medii Aevi*, liv (1915), p. 133; ed. Iversen, 'Pierre Abélard et la poésie liturgique', pp. 254–5; ed. and trans. Bell, *Abelard after Marriage*, pp. 16–20, at 16. Bell, p. 224, n. 10, notes two other references by Abelard to 'the supreme Virgin' in *Sermon* 26 (*PL* clxxviii. 542A, 544A).

immo gratia, traxerit nolentem,[i] cui uerita[j] non es[k] illudere, uolens ut [l]in ipso[l] luas habitu quod in ipsum deliquisti, et simulationis mendacio ipsa rei ueritas remedium prestet et falsitatem emendet.

19. Quod si [a]diuine in nobis[a] iustitie nostram uelis utilitatem[b] adiungere, non tam iustitiam quam gratiam Dei quod tunc[c] egit in nobis poteris appellare. [d]Attende itaque, attende,[d] carissima, quibus misericordie sue retibus[e] a profundo huius tam[f] periculosi maris nos Dominus piscauerit,[g] et a[h] quante[i] Caribdis[j] uoragine naufragos[k] licet inuitos extraxerit,[l] [54] ut merito uterque nostrum in illam prorumpere[m] posse[n] uideatur uocem: 'Dominus sollicitus est mei.'[55] Cogita et recogita in quantis ipsi nos periculis constitueramus[o] et a quantis nos eruerit[p] Dominus, et narra semper cum summa gratiarum actione quanta fecit Dominus anime nostre,[56] et quoslibet iniquos de bonitate Domini desperantes nostro consolare exemplo, ut aduertant omnes quid supplicantibus atque[q] petentibus fiat, cum iam[r] peccatoribus et[s] inuitis tanta prestentur[t] beneficia. Perpende altissimum in[u] nobis diuine consilium pietatis, et[v] quam misericorditer iudicium suum Dominus in correptionem uerterit,[w] et quam prudenter malis quoque ipsis[x] usus sit et impietatem pie [y]deposuerit, ut[y] unius partis corporis mei iustissima plaga[z] duabus[a] mederetur[b] animabus. Confer periculum et liberationis modum. Confer languorem et medicinam. Meritorum causas inspice et miserationis affectus ammirare.[c]

20. Nosti quantis turpitudinibus immoderata mea[a] libido corpora nostra addixerat,[b] ut nulla honestatis uel Dei reuerentia in ipsis etiam diebus dominice passionis uel[c] quantarumcumque sollempnitatum ab huius 'luti uolutabro'[d] [57] me reuocaret. Sed et te nolentem et,[e] prout poteras, reluctantem et dissuadentem, que natura infirmior eras,[f] sepius minis ac flagellis ad consensum trahebam. Tanto enim tibi[g] concupiscentie ardore copulatus eram[h] ut[i] miseras illas et obscenissimas uoluptates, quas etiam[j] nominare confundimur, tam Deo quam

[i] uolentem *CE* [j] ueritus *CE;* uetita *R* [k] est *CE* [l–l] ipsos *CE;* ipso *F*

19 [a–a] in nobis diuine (diuinae *F*) *CEF* [b] humilitatem *B* [c] rem *R;* tam *S* [d–d] Accente itaque arten de *?S* [e] renibus *B* [f] causa *C* [g] piscatus fuerit *ACEF* [h] *om. R* [i] quanto *BRS* [j] karipdis *T;* caripdis *CB;* charybdis *F* [k] naufragas *C* [l] extraxerunt *BR;* extraxerint *S* [m] perrumpere *Amb;* prorrompere *Amb*[1] [n] *om. R* [o] constituti eramus *Amb* [p] eruet *CE* [q] ac *ACE;* et *F* [r] tam *codd., Amb;* iam *Amb*[1] [s] *om. CEF* [t] prestantur *C;* parantur *Ecorr.;* praestantur *F* [u] *om. BR* [v] *om. C* [w] uerterunt *R;* uerterint *S* [x] bene *add. ACEFBR* [y–y] deposuerit ut (ut *over eras.*) *T; eras. also in marg.;* deposuerit et *E;* disposuerit ut *FB;* disposuerunt ut *R;* desposuerint *S*

hesitate to mock, so that you should willingly expiate your profanation in the same habit, and the truth of reality should remedy the lie of your pretence and correct your falsity.

19. And if you would allow consideration of our advantage to be an element in divine justice, you would be able to call what God did to us then an act not of justice, but of grace. See then, my beloved, see how with the dragnets of his mercy the Lord has fished us up from the depth of this dangerous sea, and from the abyss of such a Charybdis he has saved our shipwrecked selves,[54] although we were unwilling, so that each of us may justly break out in that cry: 'The Lord takes thought for me.'[55] Think and think again of the great perils in which we were and from which the Lord rescued us; tell always with the deepest gratitude how much the Lord has done for our soul.[56] Comfort by our example any unrighteous who despair of God's goodness, so that all may know what may be done for those who ask with prayer, when such benefits are granted sinners even against their will. Consider the magnanimous design of God's mercy for us, the compassion with which the Lord directed his judgement towards our chastisement, the wisdom whereby he made use of evil itself and mercifully set aside our impiety, so that by a wholly justified wound in a single part of my body he might heal two souls. Compare our danger and manner of deliverance. Compare the sickness and the medicine. Examine the cause, our deserts, and marvel at the effect, his pity.

20. You know the depths of shame to which my unbridled lust had consigned our bodies, until no reverence for decency or for God even during the days of Our Lord's Passion or of any number of sollemnities could keep me from 'wallowing in this mire'.[57] Even when you were unwilling, resisted to the utmost of your power, and tried to dissuade me, as yours was the weaker nature I often forced you to consent with threats and blows. So intense were the fires of lust which bound me to you that I set those wretched, obscene pleasures, which we blush even to name, above God as above

[z] plagas *C* [a] duobus *BR* [b] medetur *A* [c] admirari *F*

20 [a] nostra *E* [b] adduxerat *Acorr*, *?B* [c] *om. R* [d] uoluptatibus *S* [e] *om. BR* [f] eius *R* [g] *om. C*; tue *E* [h] enim *BR* [i] *om. BR* [j] et *E*

[54] Cf. *Collationes* 9 (ed. Marenbon and Orlandi, p. 12; *Dialogus*, ed. Thomas, *ll.* 139–42; *PL* clxxviii. 1615BC).

[55] Ps. 39 (40): 18 (17). [56] Cf. Ps. 65 (66): 16. [57] 2 Peter 2: 22.

mihi ipsi[k] [l]preponerem, nec[m] iam[n] aliter consulere posse diuina uideretur clementia, nisi has mihi[l] uoluptates[o] sine spe ulla omnino interdiceret.[p]

21. Vnde iustissime et clementissime, licet cum summa[a] tui auunculi proditione, ut in multis crescerem, parte illa[b] corporis mei[c] sum imminutus[d] in qua libidinis regnum[e] erat et tota huius concupiscentie causa consistebat, ut[f] iuste illud plecteretur membrum quod in[g] nobis commiserat totum, et expiaret paciendo quod deliquerat[h] oblectando, et ab his me spurcitiis[i] quibus me[j] totum quasi luto immerseram, tam mente quam corpore circumcideret; et tanto sacris etiam[k] altaribus idoniorem[l] efficeret quanto me nulla hinc amplius carnalium contagia[m] pollutionum reuocarent. Quam clementer etiam[n] in eo tantum me pati[o] uoluit membro cuius priuatio et anime [p]saluti consuleret[p] et corpus non deturparet nec ullam[q] officiorum ministrationem prepediret.[r] Immo ad omnia, que honeste geruntur, tanto me promptiorem[s] efficeret[t] quanto ab[u] huius[v] concupiscentie iugo maximo amplius liberaret.[58]

22. Cum itaque membris his uilissimis, que pro summe turpitudinis exercitio pudenda uocantur nec proprium sustinent nomen, [a]me diuina gratia[a] mundauit potius quam priuauit, quid aliud egit quam ad puritatem mundicie conseruandam sordida remouit[b] et uilia?[c] Hanc quidem munditie puritatem nonnullos sapientium[d] uehementissime[e] appetentes inferre[f] etiam sibi manum[g] audiuimus, ut hoc[h] a se penitus remouerent[i] concupiscentie flagitium. Pro quo etiam [j]stimulo carnis[j] auferendo et[k] Apostolus perhibetur[l] Dominum rogasse nec exauditum esse.[59] In exemplo est[m] [n]magnus ille[n] Christianorum philosophus Origenes[o] qui, ut hoc[p] in se penitus incendium extingueret, manus[q] sibi[r] inferre ueritus non est,[60] ac si illos ad litteram uere beatos intelligeret 'qui se ipsos propter regnum celorum

[k] *om. R* [l–l] *om. B* [m] *om.* R [n] tam *Amb* [o] uoluntates *C* [p] intercideret (interdiceret *add. F in marg.*) *FAmb*[1]

21 [a] spe *add. E* [b] una *F* [c] *om. Amb* [d] immunis *C;* minutus *Amb* [e] regimen *B* [f] *om. B* [g] *om. E* [h] deliqueram *CE and Fcorr* [i] purciciis *R* [j] *om. BR* [k] *om. BR* [l] idoneiorem *AB;* idonei oratio *F;* odoneiorem *R* [m] coniugia *R* [n] et *E; om. R* [o] *om. RS* [p–p] consuleret saluti *BS;* consisteret saluti *R* [q] ulla *C;* nullam *B* [r] impediret *BAmb*[1] [s] esse *add. A* [t] efficerent *TBR* [u] ad *E* [v] hoc *Amb*

22 [a–a] diuina me gracia (gratia *F*) *ACEFBRS* [b] remouet *B* [c] uitia *Amb* [d] sapientum *B;* sapientie tamen *R* [e] uehementis *T;* uehemencius *AS;* uehementius *CE* [f] et inferre *S* [g] manus *EF* [h] hec *S* [i] est *add. BR*

myself; nor would it seem that divine mercy could have taken action except by forbidding me these pleasures altogether, without future hope.

21. And so it was wholly just and merciful, although by means of the supreme treachery of your uncle, for me to be reduced in that part of my body which was the seat of lust and sole reason for those desires, so that I could increase in many ways; in order that this member should justly be punished for all its wrongdoing in us, expiate in suffering the sins committed for its amusement and cut me off from the slough of filth in which I had been wholly immersed in mind as in body. Only thus could I become more fit to approach the holy altars, now that no contagion of carnal impurity would ever again call me from them. How mercifully did he want me to suffer so much only in that member, the privation of which would also further the salvation of my soul without defiling my body nor preventing any performance of my duties! Indeed, it would make me readier to perform whatever can be honourably done by setting me wholly free from the heavy yoke of carnal desire.[58]

22. So when divine grace cleansed rather than deprived me of those vilest members which from their practice of utmost indecency are called 'the parts of shame' and have no proper name of their own, what else did it do but remove a foul imperfection in order to preserve perfect purity? Such purity, as we have heard, certain sages have desired so eagerly that they have mutilated themselves, so as to remove entirely the shame of desire. The Apostle too is recorded as having besought the Lord to rid him of this thorn in the flesh,[59] but was not heard. The great Christian philosopher Origen provides an example, for he was not afraid to mutilate himself in order to quench completely this fire within him,[60] as if he understood literally the words that those men were truly blessed 'who castrated themselves

[j–j] carnis stimulo *BRS* [k] *om. F* [l] se *add. BS*; prohibetur se *R* [m] etiam *F*
[n–n] ille magnus *Amb* [o] origines *S* [p] hic *BS* [q] *om. BR* [r] suas *C*

[58] Ivo of Chartres (d. 1115) cited in his *Decretum* (vi. 374, *PL* clxi. 523D–524A) a decree included in the *Capitula* of Martin of Braga (*c.*520–79) that allows a castrated man to undertake clerical office if he has not mutilated himself (c. 21, *PL* lxxxiv. 577D–578A). Otherwise (*Decretum*, vi. 37 and 75, *PL* clxi. 453 and 461) a eunuch cannot do so, as Abelard lamented in *Letter* 1, **30**.

[59] Cf. 2 Cor. 12: 7–9.

[60] Cf. Eusebius, *Historia ecclesiastica*, vi. 8 (ed. Mommsen, pp. 535–7; *PG* xx. 535BC). Cf. *Letter* 1, **65**, note 208.

castrauerunt',[61] et tales illud[s] ueraciter implere crederet quod[t] de membris[u] [v]scandalizantibus nos[v] precipit Dominus, ut ea scilicet a nobis abscindamus et proiciamus;[62] et quasi illam Ysaie prophetiam ad hystoriam magis quam ad misterium duceret, per quam ceteris[w] fidelibus eunuchos Dominus prefert, dicens: 'Eunuchi[x] si custodierint sabbata mea et elegerint que uolui, dabo eis in domo mea et in muris meis locum, et nomen melius a[y] filiis et filiabus. Nomen sempiternum dabo eis quod non peribit.'[63] Culpam tamen[z] non modicam Origenes[a] incurrit dum per penam corporis remedium culpe querit, zelum quippe Dei habens sed non secundum[b] scientiam;[64] homicidii[c] incurrit reatum, inferendo sibi manum. Suggestione diabolica uel errore maximo id ab ipso constat esse factum, quod miseratione Dei in me est ab alio[d] perpetratum. Culpam euito, non incurro. Mortem mereor et uitam assequor. Vocor[e] et reluctor. Insto criminibus et ad ueniam trahor inuitus. Orat Apostolus[f] nec exauditur. Precibus instat nec impetrat.[65] Vere 'Dominus sollicitus est mei'.[g] [66] Vadam igitur[h] et narrabo quanta fecit Dominus anime mee.[67]

23. Accede[a] et tu, inseparabilis comes, in una gratiarum actione, que[b] et[c] culpe particeps facta es[d] et gratie. Nam et tue Dominus non immemor salutis, immo plurimum tui[e] memor, qui etiam sancto quodam nominis presagio te precipue[f] suam[g] fore presignauit,[h] cum te uidelicet Heloysam, [i]id est diuinam,[i] ex proprio nomine suo quod est Heloym[j] insigniuit;[68] ipse, inquam, clementer disposuit in uno duobus consulere quos[k] diabolus in uno nitebatur[l] exstinguere. Paululum enim antequam hoc accideret, nos indissolubili lege sacramenti nuptialis inuicem astrinxerat, cum cuperem te mihi supra modum dilectam in perpetuum retinere, [m]immo[n] cum ipse iam tractaret ad se nos ambos hac occasione conuertere.[m] Si enim mihi

[s] id *F*   [t] *om. E*   [u] uerbis *R*   [v–v] nos scandalizantibus *F;* scandalizantibus non *BR;* scandalizantibus nobis *Amb*   [w] *over eras. in T*   [x] Heu michi *S*   [y] *om. B*   [z] sed *C*   [a] origenem *C*   [b] sententiam *add T before exp.*   [c] homicidium *B*   [d] illo *A;* ipso *CEF*   [e] vacor *C*   [f] opus *CE*   [g] mea *C*   [h] ergo *F*

23 [a] attende *CEBR*   [b] *om. CEF*   [c] etiam *S*   [d] est *E*   [e] tue *TACERS;* me *B*   [f] precipuam *CE*   [g] tuam *T*   [h] designauit *BR*   [i–i] id est dominam *F; om. Amb*   [j] heloyssam *CF*   [k] quod *EF*   [l] uidebatur *A*   [m–m] *om. CEF*   [n] *om. R*

[61] Matt. 19: 12.   [62] Cf. Matt. 18: 8, 19:12.

[63] Isaiah 56: 4–5. The difference between historical or literal and mystical or allegorical interpretation of Scripture—between *historia* and *mysterium*—was fundamental to patristic

for the Kingdom of Heaven's sake',[61] and believed them to be truthfully carrying out the bidding of the Lord about offending members, that we should cut them off and throw them away;[62] and as if he interpreted as historic fact, not as a hidden symbol, that prophecy of Isaiah in which the Lord prefers eunuchs to the rest of the faithful: 'The eunuchs who keep my sabbaths, and choose to do my will I will give a place in my own house and within my walls and a name better than sons and daughters. I will give them an everlasting name which shall not perish.'[63] Yet Origen is seriously to be blamed because he sought a remedy for blame in punishment of his body. True, he has zeal for God, but an ill-informed zeal,[64] and he can be accused of homicide for his self-mutilation. People think he did this either at the suggestion of the devil or in grave error but, in my case, through God's compassion, it was done by another's hand. I do not incur blame, I escape it. I deserve death and gain life. I am called and I resist. I persist in crime and am pardoned against my will. The Apostle prays and is not heard. He persists in prayer and is not answered.[65] Truly 'the Lord takes thought for me'.[66] I will go then and declare how much the Lord has done for my soul.[67]

23. Come too, my inseparable companion, and join me in thanksgiving, you who were made my partner both in guilt and in grace. For the Lord is not unmindful also of your own salvation, indeed, he has you much in mind, for by a kind of holy presage of his name he marked you out to be especially his when he named you Heloise, after his own name, Elohim.[68] In his mercy, I say, he intended to provide for two people in one, the two whom the devil sought to destroy in one; since a short while before this happening he had bound us together by the indissoluble bond of the marriage sacrament. I desired to keep you whom I loved beyond measure for myself for ever, but he was already planning to use this opportunity for our joint conversion

and medieval study of the Bible and Origen was largely responsible for making it so; see Smalley, *The Study of the Bible in the Middle Ages* (2nd edn., 1952), pp. 6–14.

[64] Cf. Rom. 10: 2.

[65] Cf. 2 Cor. 12: 8-9.

[66] Ps. 39 (40): 18 (17).

[67] Cf. Ps. 65 (66): 16.

[68] In his *TSch*, i. 69 Abelard writes that 'Heloim' is the plural form of the Hebrew word 'Hel', which means God: in the Hebrew scriptures at Genesis 1: 1 ('In the beginning God made heaven and earth') the word 'Heloim' appears, not 'Hel', and this, Abelard argues, is an indication of the divine Trinity of three persons. Similar passages occur in *TSum*, i. 6; *Tchr*, i. 8; *Expositio in Hexameron*, 57 (ed. Romig and Luscombe, p. 20; *PL* clxxviii. 739); *Sententie Magistri Petri Abaelardi*, 62 (ed. Luscombe, pp. 31–2; c. 9, ed. Buzzetti, pp. 48–9; *PL* clxxviii. 1705–6).

antea[o] matrimonio non esses copulata, facile in discessu meo a seculo uel suggestione parentum uel carnalium oblectatione uoluptatum seculo inhesisses.

24. Vide ergo quantum sollicitus nostri fuerit Dominus, quasi ad magnos[a] aliquos nos reseruaret usus, et quasi indignaretur aut doleret illa litteralis scientie talenta,[69] que utrique nostrum commiserat, ad sui nominis[b] honorem non dispensari, aut quasi etiam de incontinentissimo seruulo suo[c] uereretur[d] quod scriptum est:[e] 'Quia mulieres faciunt' etiam[f] 'apostatare sapientes.'[70] [g]Sicut et[g] de sapientissimo certum est Salomone.[71] Tue[h] uero prudentie talentum quantas quotidie Domino refert[i] usuras, que multas Domino iam spirituales filias peperisti, me penitus sterili[j] permanente, et in filiis perditionis[k] inaniter laborante.

25. O quam detestabile damnum! Quam lamentabile incommodum, si carnalium uoluptatum sordibus[a] uacans paucos cum dolore pareres[b] mundo, que nunc multiplicem prolem cum exsultatione parturis celo! Nec esses plus quam femina que nunc etiam uiros transcendis, et que[c] maledictionem Eue in benedictionem uertisti Marie.[72] O quam indecenter [d]manus ille[d] sacre, que nunc etiam diuina reuoluunt uolumina, cure muliebris obscenitatibus deseruirent! Ipse nos a contagiis huius[e] ceni,[f] a uolutabris[g] huius[h] luti,[73] dignatus est erigere[i] et[j] ad[k] seipsum ui[l] quadam[m] attrahere, qua[n] percussum uoluit Paulum conuertere,[74] et hoc ipso fortassis exemplo nostro alios quoque litterarum peritos ab hac deterrere[o] presumptione.[75]

26. Ne[a] te id igitur,[b] soror, obsecro, moueat, nec [c]patri paterne[c] nos corrigenti sis molesta, sed attende quod scriptum[d] est: 'Quos diligit Deus, hos corrigit;[e][76] castigat[f] autem omnem[g] filium quem recipit.'[77] [h]Et alibi: 'Qui parcit uirge, odit filium.'[h][78] Pena[i] hec momentanea est,[j]

[o] *om.* CEF

24 [a] magnas *C* [b] hominis *E* [c] *om. Amb* [d] ueretur *E* [e] *om. CE* [f] *om. R* [g–g] et sicut *C;* Et *Amb* [h] Tu *CF* [i] refferat *TBRAmb;* Refferat *C;* referas *EF* [j] steriles *C* [k] proditionis *R*

25 [a] sordibus *om. R* [b] parentes *T;* pereres *B;* perieres *R* [c] qui *E* [d–d] ille manus *tr. E* [e] quibus *C* [f] sceni *T* [g] uoluptabris *TACEFBRY;* uoluptabis *S;* voluptatibus *Amb;* uolutabris *Bergh, 'Studia critica' p. 23* [h] *om. R* [i] eruere *Amb*[1] [j] *om. B* [k] a *C* [l] in *FBRS* [m] quodam *C;* sagena *add. F* [n] quia *C;* que *S* [o] deterre *T;* disterrere *CEF*

26 [a] Nec *CR* [b] ergo *F* [c–c] deo *CEF* [d] dictum *F* [e] corripit *FAmb* [f] flagellat *FAmb*[1] *and Vulg.* [g] dominus *CE* [h–h] om. CEF [i] est *add. T before exp.; add. Amb* [j] *om. Amb*

to himself. Had you not been previously joined to me in wedlock, you might easily have clung to the world when I withdrew from it, either at the suggestion of your relatives or in enjoyment of carnal delights.

24. See then, how greatly the Lord was concerned for us, as if he were reserving us for some great ends, and was indignant or grieved because our knowledge of letters, the talents[69] which he had entrusted to us, were not being used to glorify his name; or as if he feared for his humble and incontinent servant, because it is written: 'Women make even the wise forsake their faith.'[70] Indeed, this is proved in the case of the wisest of men, Solomon.[71] How great an interest the talent of your own wisdom pays daily to the Lord in the many spiritual daughters you have borne for him, while I remain totally barren and labour in vain amongst the sons of perdition!

25. What a hateful loss and grievous misfortune if you had abandoned yourself to the defilement of carnal pleasures only to bear in suffering a few children for the world, when now you are delivered in exultation of numerous progeny for heaven! Nor would you have been more than a woman, whereas now you rise even above men, and have turned the curse of Eve into the blessing of Mary.[72] How unseemly for those holy hands which now turn the pages of sacred books to be devoted to indecent aspects of women's lives! God himself has thought fit to raise us up from the contamination of this filth[73] and the pleasures of this mire and draw us to him by force—the same force whereby he chose to strike and convert Paul[74]—and by our example perhaps to deter from our audacity others who are also trained in letters.[75]

26. I beg you then, sister, do not be aggrieved, do not vex the Father who corrects us in fatherly wise; pay heed to what is written: 'Whom the Lord loves he reproves'[76] for 'He lays the rod on every son whom he acknowledges.'[77] And elsewhere: 'A father who spares the rod hates his son.'[78] This punishment is momentary, not eternal, and for our

[69] 'talenta': cf. Matt 25: 15–30.
[70] Ecclus. 19: 2.
[71] Cf. 3 Kgs. (1 Kgs.) 11: 1–13; *Letter* 4, **6**.
[72] Cf. *Letter* 7, **27**.
[73] 'uolutabris . . . luti': cf. 2 Peter 2: 22.
[74] Cf. Acts 9: 3–18; 26: 13–18.
[75] 'et hoc ipso . . . presumptione': Levitan, p. 98, n. 48 (and cf. pp. xxv–xxvi) calls this sentence 'a moralistic tag which, interrupting the flow of argument through to the next paragraph, is most likely a later interpolation'. Rather, it consolidates the commendation of learning and wisdom in the course of **24** and **25**.
[76] Prov. 3: 12.
[77] Heb. 12: 6.
[78] Prov. 13: 24.

non eterna, purgationis, non damnationis. Audi prophetam et confortare: 'Non iudicabit Dominus bis [k]in idipsum,'[k] [79] et[l] 'non consurget duplex tribulatio'.[80] Attende summam illam et maximam Veritatis adhortationem: 'In patientia uestra possidebitis animas uestras.'[81] Vnde et Salomon: 'Melior est patiens uiro forti, et qui dominatur animo suo, expugnatore[m] urbium.'[82]

27. Non[a] te ad lacrimas aut ad compunctionem mouet[b] unigenitus Dei innocens pro te et omnibus ab impiissimis comprehensus,[c] distractus,[d] flagellatus et uelata[e] facie illusus[f] et colaphizatus, sputis[g] conspersus, spinis coronatus, et tandem in illo crucis[h] tunc tam[i] ignominioso patibulo inter latrones suspensus[j] atque illo tam[k] horrendo et exsecrabili[l] genere mortis interfectus?[83] Hunc semper, soror, uerum tuum et totius ecclesie sponsum pre oculis habe,[m] mente gere. Intuere hunc exeuntem ad crucifigendum pro te et baiulantem sibi crucem. Esto de populo et mulieribus que plangebant et lamentabantur eum, sicut [n]Lucas his uerbis narrat: 'Sequebatur autem multa[o] turba populi et mulierum que plangebant et lamentabantur eum.'[n] [84] Ad quas quidem benigne conuersus, clementer eis predixit futurum in ultionem sue mortis exitium[p] a[q] quo quidem, si saperent, cauere sibi per hoc possent.[r] 'Filie', inquit, 'Ierusalem, nolite flere super me [s]sed super uos ipsas flete et super filios uestros. Quoniam ecce uenient dies in quibus dicent: Beate steriles, et uentres qui[t] non genuerunt et ubera que non lactauerunt. Tunc incipient dicere montibus: Cadite super nos, et collibus: Operite nos. Quia si in uiridi ligno hec faciunt, in arido quid fiet?'[s] [85]

28. Patienti sponte[a] pro redemptione tua[b] compatere et super crucifixo [c]pro te compungere,[c] sepulcro eius mente semper assiste, et cum fidelibus feminis lamentare et luge. [d]De quibus etiam,[e] ut iam supra memini,[f] [86] scriptum est: Mulieres sedentes ad monumentum

[k–k] ipsum *AR* [l] etiam *C* [m] expugnator est *E*

27 [a] Num *Amb*[1] [b] monet *S* [c] et *add. R* [d] et *add. BRS* [e] data *BR* [f] illius *BRS* [g] spinis *S* [h] *om. ACEF* [i] *om. E* [j] *om. R* [k] tunc *TAmb* [l] inexecrabili *E* [m] habere *C; om. S* [n–n] Lucas narrat *CEF* [o] *om. B* [p] exitum *ACB* [q] *om. TE* [r] posse *C* [s–s] etc *CEF* [t] que *TBRS;* qui (?) *add. T*[1] *in marg.*

28 [a] sponse *A* [b] *in T marked for corr. by T*[1] [c–c] *om. R* [d–d] *om. CEF* [e] *om. R* [f] sicut *add. BR*

[79] Nahum 1: 9, Septuagint version. Cf. Jerome, *Commentarii in Prophetas minores*, *In Naum Prophetam*, i. 9: 'LXX . . . non vindicabit Dominus bis in idipsum in tribulatione'

purification, not damnation. Hear the prophet and take heart: 'The Lord will not judge twice on the same issue'[79] and 'no second tribulation shall arise'.[80] Listen too to that supreme and mighty exhortation of the Truth: 'By your endurance you will possess your souls.'[81] Solomon, too: 'Better be slow to anger than be a fighter; and master one's heart rather than storm a city.'[82]

27. Are you not moved to tears or remorse by the only begotten Son of God who, for you and for all mankind, in his innocence was seized by the hands of impious men, dragged along and scourged, blindfolded, mocked at, buffeted, spat upon, crowned with thorns, finally hanged between thieves on the Cross, at the time so shameful a gibbet, to die a horrible and accursed form of death?[83] Always, sister, have this man before your eyes as your true spouse and that of all the Church. Keep him in mind. Look at him going to be crucified for your sake, carrying his own cross. Be one of the crowd, one of the women who wept and lamented over him, as Luke tells: 'A great crowd of people followed, many women among them, who wept and lamented over him.'[84] To these he graciously turned and mercifully foretold the destruction which would come to avenge his death, against which they could provide, if they understood. 'Daughters of Jerusalem,' he said, 'do not weep for me; no, weep for yourselves and your children. For the days are surely coming when they will say: "Happy are the barren, the wombs that never bore a child, the breasts that never fed one." Then they will start saying to the mountains: "Fall on us", and to the hills: "Cover us." For if these things are done when the wood is green, what will happen when it is dry?'[85]

28. Have compassion on him who suffered willingly for your redemption, and look with remorse on him who was crucified for you. In your mind be always present at his tomb, weep and wail with the faithful women, of whom it is written, as I said:[86] 'The women

(ed. Adriaen, lxxviA, pp. 534, 535; *PL* xxv. 1238A, C, D). On the importance of this text in 12th-c. debates see Smalley, *The Becket Conflict and the Schools*, pp. 124–8.

[80] Nahum 1: 9, Vulgate version.

[81] Luke 21: 19.

[82] Prov. 16: 32; also cited in *Problemata*, 14 (*PL* clxxviii. 698D); *Ethica*, i. 2, 4 (ed. Ilgner, *ll.* 35–6 ff.; ed. Luscombe, p. 5); *Comm. Rom.*, iii (viii. 13, p. 217).

[83] Cf. *Comm. Rom.* ii (iii. 26, p. 116); *Sermons* 5 and 12 (*PL* clxxviii. 422C, 479–84); *Expositio Symboli Apostolorum* (*PL* clxxviii. 626C); *Problemata*, 29 (*PL* clxxviii. 714AB).

[84] Luke 23: 27.

[85] Luke 23: 28–31.

[86] Above at 4.

lamentabantur flentes Dominum.[d][87] Para cum illis sepulture eius unguenta, sed meliora, spiritualia quidem, non corporalia;[g] [h]hec enim requirit aromata qui non suscepit[i] illa. Super his toto deuotionis affectu compungere. Ad quam quidem compassionis compunctionem ipse etiam[j] per Ieremiam fideles adhortatur, dicens: 'O uos omnes qui transitis per uiam, attendite et uidete si est dolor similis sicut dolor meus!',[88] id est, si super aliquo patiente ita est per compassionem dolendum, cum ego scilicet solus sine culpa quod alii[k] deliquerint luam. Ipse autem est uia per quam fideles de exsilio[l] transeunt[m] ad patriam, qui etiam crucem, de qua sic clamat,[n] ad hoc nobis erexit scalam. Hic pro te occisus est unigenitus Dei; 'oblatus est quia uoluit'.[89]

29. Super hoc uno compatiendo dole, dolendo compatere. Et quod per Zachariam prophetam de animabus deuotis predictum est comple:[a] 'Plangent', inquit, 'planctum quasi super unigenitum, et dolebunt super eum ut doleri solet in morte primogeniti.'[90] Vide, soror, quantus sit planctus his qui regem diligunt super morte primogeniti eius et unigeniti. Intuere quo planctu familia, quo merore tota consumatur curia et, cum ad sponsam unigeniti mortui perueneris, intolerabiles ululatus eius non sustinebis. Hic tuus, soror, planctus; hic tuus sit ululatus, que te huic[b] sponso felici copulasti matrimonio. Emit te iste non suis sed seipso.[c] Proprio sanguine emit te et[d] redemit. Quantum ius [e]in te habeat[e] uide, et quam[f] [g]pretiosa sis[g] intuere. Hoc quidem pretium suum Apostolus attendens, et in hoc pretio quanti sit ipse, pro quo ipsum datur, perpendens, et quam[h] tante gratie uicem referat adnectens: 'Absit [i]michi', inquit,[i] 'gloriari nisi in cruce Domini nostri Iesu Christi per quem mihi mundus crucifixus est et ego mundo.'[91] Maior es celo, maior es mundo, cuius pretium ipse conditor mundi factus est. Quid in te, rogo, uiderit, qui nullius eget, ut pro te adquirenda usque ad agonias tam horrende atque ignominiose mortis certauerit?[j] Quid [k]in te,[k] inquam, querit[l] nisi teipsam? Verus est amicus qui teipsam non tua desiderat.[92] Verus

[g] carnalia *C* [h] om. CEF, ending in **29** [i] susceperit *TBRS* [j] *om. A* [k] alia *R* [l] auxilio *B* [m] transierunt *A* [n] clamabat *A*

29 [a] comple est *A* [b] uero *add. BR* [c] se *T* [d] ac *ABR* [e–e] habeat in te *A* [f] *om. BR* [g–g] preciosis *R* [h] quem *ARS* [i–i] inquit mihi *TBR* [j] certauerunt *BR* [k–k] *om. BR* [l] querunt *BR*

[87] Cf. Matt. 27: 61, Luke 23: 27, 55. [88] Lam. 1: 12. [89] Isa. 53: 7.
[90] Zach. 12: 10. [91] Gal. 6: 14. Cf. *Sermon* 9 (*PL* clxxviii. 446D).
[92] Cf. Heloise in *Letter* 2, **10** (and note): 'God knows I never sought anything in you except yourself; I wanted simply you, nothing of yours' / 'Nihil umquam, Deus scit, in te

sitting at the tomb wept and lamented for the Lord.'[87] Prepare with them the perfumes for his burial, but better perfumes, which are of the spirit, not of the body, for this is the fragrance he needs though he rejected the other. Be remorseful over this with all your powers of devotion, for he exhorts the faithful to this remorse and compassion in the words of Jeremiah: 'All you who pass by, look and see if there is any sorrow like my sorrow.'[88] That is, if there is some sufferer for whom you should sorrow in compassion when I alone, for no guilt of mine, atone for the sins of others. He himself is the way whereby the faithful pass from exile to their own country. He too has set up the Cross, from which he summons us, as a ladder for us to use. On this, for you, the only begotten Son of God was killed; 'he was made an offering because this was his will'.[89]

29. Grieve with compassion over him alone; in your grief share his suffering. Fulfil what was foretold of devout souls through the prophet Zachariah: 'They shall wail for him as over an only child, and shall grieve for him as for the death of a first-born son.'[90] See, sister, what great mourning there is amongst those who love their king over the death of his only and first-begotten son. Behold the lamentation and grief with which the whole household and court are consumed; and when you come to the bride of the only son who is dead, you will find her wailing intolerable and more than you can bear. This mourning, sister, should be yours and also the wailing, for you were joined to this bridegroom in blessed matrimony. He bought you not with his wealth, but with himself. He bought and redeemed you with his own blood. See what right he has over you, and know how precious you are. This is the price which the Apostle has in mind when he considers how little he is worth for whom the price was paid, and what return he should make for such a gift: 'God forbid that I should boast of anything but the Cross of our Lord Jesus Christ, through whom the world is crucified to me and I to the world!'[91] You are greater than heaven, greater than the world, for the Creator of the world himself became the price for you. What has he seen in you, I ask you, when he lacks nothing, to make him seek even the agonies of a fearful and inglorious death in order to purchase you? What, I say, does he seek in you save you? He is the true friend who desires yourself, not what is yours,[92] the true friend who

nisi te requisiui, te pure non tua concupiscens.' Cf. also *Comm. Rom.* iii. (vii. 13, pp. 201–4). For discussion of the definitions of love found in the writings of Augustine and of a contemporary of Heloise and Abelard, Walter of Mortagne, see Marenbon, *The Philosophy of Peter Abelard*, pp. 298–303 and Wielockx, 'La Sentence *De caritate*'.

est amicus qui pro te moriturus dicebat: 'Maiorem hac dilectionem nemo habet ut animam suam ponat quis[m] pro amicis suis.'[n] [93] [o]Amabat te ille ueraciter,[o] non ego. Amor meus, qui utrumque nostrum peccatis inuoluebat,[p] concupiscentia, non amor, dicendus est. Miseras [q]in te[q] meas uoluptates implebam, et hoc erat totum quod amabam. Pro te, inquis,[r] passus sum, et fortassis uerum est, sed magis per te, et hoc ipsum inuitus, non amore tui sed coactione mei, nec ad tuam salutem sed ad dolorem. [s]Ille uero salubriter, ille pro te[s] sponte passus est qui passione sua omnem curat languorem, omnem remouet passionem.

30. In hoc,[a] obsecro, non in me tua tota sit deuotio, tota compassio, tota compunctio. [b]Dole [c]in tam innocentem[c] tante crudelitatis perpetratam[d] iniquitatem, non iustam in me equitatis uindictam, immo gratiam, ut dictum est, in utrosque summam. Iniqua[e] enim es si equitatem non amas, et iniquissima si uoluntati, immo tante gratie, Dei scienter es[f] aduersa.[b] Plange tuum reparatorem, non corruptorem, redemptorem, non scortatorem, pro te mortuum Dominum, non uiuentem seruum, immo nunc primum de morte uere liberatum. Caue,[g] obsecro, ne quod dixit Pompeius[h] merenti[i] Cornelie tibi improperetur turpissime:

[j]Viuit post prelia Magnus![k]
Sed fortuna perit. Quod defles,[l] illud[m] amasti.[94]

31. Attende,[j] precor, id,[a] et erubesce nisi[b] admissas[c] turpitudines impudentissimas commendes.[d] Accipe itaque, soror, accipe, queso, pacienter que nobis acciderunt misericorditer. Virga hec est patris, non gladius persequutoris. Percutit pater ut corrigat, ne feriat[e] hostis ut occidat. [f]Vulnere mortem preuenit,[g] non ingerit; immittit ferrum[h] ut amputet morbum; corpus uulnerat et animam sanat;[f] [i]occidere debuerat[i] et uiuificat; immunditiam resecat ut mundum relinquat; punit semel ne puniat semper; patitur unus ex uulnere ut[j] duobus parcatur a morte. Duo in culpa,[k] unus in pena.[95] Id quoque tue[l]

[m] qui *T* [n] omission in CEF beginning in **28** *ends here* [o–o] Ipse enim te ueraciter amabat (amabit *F*) *CEF* [p] inuoluerat *CEF;* inuoluat *BR* [q–q] uite *R* [r] inquit *F* [s–s] ille uero pro te salubriter CEF

30 [a] me *E* [b–b] *om. CEF* [c–c] uitam ignoscentem *BR* [d] perpetrantem *T* [e] Insana *B* [f] est *T* [g] Quare *C* [h] ponperius *S* [i] menti *B;* mente *R* [j–j] *om. E* [k] mannus *TAAmb;* manus *CFBRS* [l] deflet *R* [m] *om. B*

31 [a] *om. CEF* [b] ubi *F* [c] amissas *CEF* [d] comendas *CEF* [e] ferit *Amb*[1] [f–f] *om. CEF* [g] peruenit *R* [h] *om. BR* [i–i] ut occidat. Occidere debuerat *F* [j] *over eras. in T* [k] culpam *Amb* [l] me *R*

said when he was about to die for you: 'There is no greater love than this, that a man should lay down his life for his friends.'[93] It was he who truly loved you, not I. My love, which brought us both to sin, should be called lust, not love. I took my fill of my wretched pleasures in you, and this was the sum total of my love. You say I suffered for you, and perhaps that is true, but it was really through you, and even this, unwillingly; not for love of you but under compulsion, and to bring you not salvation but sorrow. But he suffered truly for your salvation, on your behalf of his own free will, and by his suffering he cures all sickness and removes all suffering.

30. Not to me, I beseech you, should you direct all your devotion, all your compassion, all your remorse. Weep for the injustice of the great cruelty inflicted on him, not for the just and righteous payment demanded of me, or rather, as I said, the supreme grace granted us both. For you are unrighteous if you do not love righteousness, and most unrighteous if you consciously oppose the will, or more truly, the boundless grace of God. Mourn for your Saviour, not for a seducer; for your Redeemer, not for a fornicator; for the Lord who died for you, not for the servant who lives and, indeed, is for the first time truly freed from death. I beg you, beware lest Pompey's reproach to weeping Cornelia is applied to you, to your shame:

> The battle ended, the great one
> Lives, but his fortune died. It is this you now mourn
> And loved.[94]

31. Take this to heart, I pray, and blush for shame, unless you would commend the wanton vileness of our former ways. And so I ask you, sister, to accept patiently what mercifully befell us. This is a father's rod, not a persecutor's sword. The father strikes to correct, and to forestall the enemy who strikes to kill. By a wound he prevents death, he does not deal it; he thrusts in the steel to cut out disease. He wounds the body, and heals the soul; he makes to live what he should have destroyed, cuts out impurity to leave what is pure. He punishes once so that he need not punish forever. One suffers the wound so that two may be spared death; two were guilty, one pays the penalty.[95]

[93] John 15: 13.
[94] Lucan, *De bello ciuili*, viii. 84–5; also partly cited in *Comm. Rom.* iii (vii. 13, *l.* 567).
[95] Cf. *Letter* 4, 8.

infirmitati[m] nature diuina indulgetur[n] miseratione et quodam modo[o] iuste. Quo enim naturaliter sexu infirmior eras et fortior continentia, pene minus eras obnoxia.

32. Refero Domino, et[a] in hoc grates,[b] qui te tunc et[c] a pena liberauit et ad coronam reseruauit et, cum me una corporis mei passione semel[d] ab omni estu huius concupiscentie, in qua una[e] totus per immoderatam incontinentiam occupatus eram, refrigerauit[f] ne corruam, multas[g] adolescentie[h] tue maiores[i] animi passiones ex assidua carnis suggestione reseruauit[j] ad martirii coronam. Quod licet te audire tedeat et dici prohibeas, ueritas tamen id loquitur manifesta. Cui enim superest[k] pugna, superest et corona quia 'non coronabitur[l] nisi qui legitime certauerit'.[96] Mihi uero[m] nulla superest corona quia nulla subest[n] certaminis causa. Deest materia pugne cui ablatus est stimulus concupiscentie.[97]

33. Aliquid[a] tamen esse estimo si, cum hinc nullam percipiam coronam, nonnullam tamen euitem penam, et dolore unius momentanee pene multis fortassis indulgeatur[b] eternis. Scriptum [c]quippe est[c] de huius miserrime uite hominibus, immo iumentis: 'Computruerunt iumenta in [d]stercoribus suis.'[d] [98] Minus quoque meritum meum minui conqueror, dum tuum crescere non diffido. Vnum quippe sumus in Christo, una per legem matrimonii caro.

34. Quidquid est tuum mihi non arbitror alienum. Tuus autem[a] est Christus, quia facta es[b] sponsa eius. Et nunc, ut supra memini,[99] me habes seruum quem olim agnoscebas[c] dominum, magis tibi tamen amore nunc[d] spiritali[e] coniunctum quam timore subiectum. Vnde et de tuo nobis apud ipsum patrocinio[f] amplius confidimus, ut id optineam ex tua quod non possum ex oratione propria. Et nunc maxime cum cotidiana periculorum aut perturbationum instantia nec uiuere me nec orationi sinat[g] uacare nec illum [h]beatissimum imitari

[m] infirmitatis *ACEF* [n] indulgentur *BRS* [o] quodammodo *A*

32 [a] *om. FAmb* [b] gratias *Amb* [c] *om. T* [d] et *add. CF;* et *E* [e] unus *CEF* [f] refrigerauerit *TAB;* refrigerat *R* [g] multa *C;* Multam *EF* [h] adolescentiam *EF* [i] maioris *E* [j] reseruauat *E;* reseruant *F* [k] semper est *TAmb* [l] corporaliter *CE* [m] autem *B* [n] superest *AR; om. E*

33 [a] Aliquam *F* [b] indulgetur *F* [c–c] quippe *over eras.; eras. also in marg. TAmb;* quippe est *ACEFBRS* [d–d] stercoribus *CE;* stercore suo *F*

34 [a] sponssus *add. CEF* [b] est *TAEFB* [c] cognoscetas *E* [d] nec *C* [e] spiritu *S* [f] matrimonio *F* [g] signat *BR* [h–h] beatissimum imitari *TRSAmb;* eunuchum beatissimum ymitari *CE;* eunuchum beatissimum comitari (imitari *Fcorr*) *F*

That, too, was granted by divine mercy to your weaker nature and, in a way, with justice, for you were naturally weaker in sex and stronger in continence, and so the less deserving of punishment.

32. For this I give thanks to the Lord, who both spared you punishment then and reserved you for a crown to come, and who also, by a moment of suffering in my body, cooled once and for all the fires of that lust which had wholly absorbed me through my excessive incontinence, lest I be consumed. The many greater sufferings of the heart through the continual prompting of the flesh of your own youth he has reserved for a martyr's crown. Though you may weary of hearing this and forbid it to be said, the truth of it is clear. For anyone who must continue to strive there is also a crown, but 'unless he strives lawfully, he will not be crowned'.[96] No crown is waiting for me, however, because no cause for strife remains. There is no occasion for strife left in one from whom the thorn of desire has been plucked out.[97]

33. Yet I think it is something, even though I may receive no crown, if I can escape further punishment, and by the pain of a single momentary punishment may perhaps be let off much that would be eternal. For it is written of the men, or rather of the beasts of this wretched life: 'The beasts have rotted in their dung.'[98] Then too, I complain less that my own merit is diminished when I am confident that yours is increasing; for we are one in Christ, one flesh by the law of marriage.

34. Whatever is yours cannot, I think, fail to be mine, and Christ is yours since you have become his bride. Now, as I said before,[99] you have me as your servant whom in the past you recognized as your lord, more your own now when bound to you by spiritual love than one subjected by fear. And so I have increasing confidence that you will plead for us both before him and that, through your prayer, I may be granted what I cannot obtain through my own; especially now, when the daily pressure of dangers and disturbances threaten my life and give me no time for prayer. Nor can I imitate that blessed

[96] 2 Tim. 2: 5. Cf. *Letter* 4, **17**.

[97] Cf. *Collationes* **84**, **112** (ed. Marenbon and Orlandi, pp. 102–6, 128–30; *Dialogus*, ed. Thomas, *ll.* 1565–1602, 1992–2000; *PL* clxxviii. 1642D–1643C, 1651CD). Also *Ethica*, i. 7. 4 (ed. Ilgner, p. 7; ed. Luscombe, p. 12, *ll.* 5–10).

[98] Joel 1: 17.

[99] Above at **3–4**.

eunuchum[h] potentem[i] Candacis regine Ethiopum, 'qui erat super omnes[j] gazas eius',[k] et de tam longinquo 'uenerat adorare in Ierusalem'.[100] Ad quem reuertentem missus est ab angelo Philippus apostolus[l] ut eum conuerteret ad fidem quod iam ille meruerat per orationem uel sacre lectionis assiduitatem. A qua quidem ut nec in uia tunc uacaret, licet ditissimus et gentilis, magne[m] diuine dispensationis actum est beneficio ut [n]locus ei[n] Scripture[101] occurreret qui[o] opportunissimam conuersionis[p] eius occasionem[q] Apostolo[r] preberet. Ne[s] quid uero hanc petitionem nostram impediat uel impleri differat, orationem quoque ipsam, quam[t] pro nobis Domino supplices,[u] componere, et mittere tibi maturaui.

35. ORATIO.[a]

Deus,[b] qui ab ipso humane creationis exordio femina de costa uiri formata nuptialis copule sacramentum maximum sanxisti, quique immensis honoribus uel de[c] desponsata nascendo uel miracula[d] inchoando nuptias sublimasti, [e]meeque etiam fragilitatis incontinentie utcumque tibi placuit olim hoc remedium indulsisti, ne despicias ancillule tue preces quas pro meis ipsis carique mei[f] excessibus in conspectu maiestatis tue[g] supplex effundo. Ignosce, o benignissime, immo benignitas ipsa, ignosce tot[h] et tantis criminibus nostris, et ineffabilis misericordie tue multitudinem culparum nostrarum immensitas experiatur. Puni, obsecro, in presenti reos ut parcas in futuro. Puni [i]ad horam[i] ne punias in eternum. Accipe in seruos uirgam correctionis,[j] non gladium furoris. Afflige carnem ut conserues animas. Adsis purgator, non ultor, benignus magis quam iustus, pater misericors, non austerus Dominus.[k] Proba nos, Domine, et tempta sicut de semetipso rogat Propheta.[102] Ac si aperte diceret: Prius uires inspice ac secundum eas[l] temptationum onera moderare. Quod et beatus Paulus fidelibus tuis promittens ait: 'Potens[m] est enim Deus, qui non[n] pacietur uos tentari supra id quod potestis, sed[o] faciet cum tentatione[p] etiam prouentum ut possitis

[i] in domo *add. A;* potentis *F* [j] *om. CEF* [k] *om. S* [l] *om. R* [m] magno *ACFAmb* [n–n] ei locus *EF* [o] que *CE* [p] conuersationis *B;* conuersacionis *R* [q] actionis *C;* actionem *E* [r] dei *add. CEF* [s] nec *C;* Nec *E before corr.* [t] qua *A* [u] dicatis *add. CEFAmb*

35 [a] *om. CEFRS;* oratio m. p. abaelardi ad heloysam pro d(. . .?) *add. by another hand in B in marg.*; *add. Amb in marg.* [b] *large decorated initial TABRAmb* [c] *om. R* [d] miraculo *R* [e–e] etc. sequitur. In fine quos *CE;* Et sequitur in fine quos *F* [f] meique *B;* tamquam meis *Amb*[1] [g] sue *T* [h] *om. Amb* [i–i] adoro *BR*

eunuch, the high official of Candace, queen of Ethiopia, 'who had charge of all her wealth', and 'had come' from so far 'to worship in Jerusalem'.[100] He was on his way home when the apostle Philip was sent by the angel to convert him to the faith, as he had already deserved by his prayers and his assiduous reading of the Scriptures. Because he did not want to take time from this even on his journey, although he was a man of great wealth and a gentile, it came about through the great goodness of providence that the passage of Scripture[101] was before him which gave the apostle the perfect opportunity for his conversion. So that nothing may delay my petition nor defer its fulfilment, I hasten to compose and send to you this prayer, which you may offer to the Lord in supplication on our behalf.

35. PRAYER

God, who at the beginning of man's creation, in forming woman from a rib of man didst sanctify the most great sacrament of the marriage bond, and who didst glorify marriage with boundless honours by being born of one who was pledged to marriage and by the first of thy miracles; thou who moreover didst grant this remedy for the frailty of my incontinence, in such manner as pleased thee, despise not the prayers of thy handmaid which I pour out as a suppliant in the presence of thy majesty for my own excesses and those of my beloved. Pardon, O most gracious, who art rather graciousness itself, pardon our many great offences, and let the ineffable immensity of thy mercy test the multitude of our faults. Punish the guilty now, I beseech thee, that thou mayst spare them hereafter. Punish now, lest thou punish in eternity. Take to thy servants the rod of correction, not the sword of wrath. Afflict their flesh that thou mayst preserve their souls. Come as a redeemer, not an avenger; gracious rather than just; the merciful Father, not the stern Lord. Prove us, Lord, and test us, in the manner in which the prophet asks for himself,[102] as if he said openly: First consider my strength, and measure accordingly the burden of my testing. This is what St Paul promises to the faithful, when he says: 'God keeps faith, and he will not allow you to be tested beyond your powers, but when the test comes he will also provide a way out, so

[j] correptionis *AB* [k] deus *A* [l] *om. BR* [m] Fidelis *ACEF and Vulg.*; loiaulx *J* [n] *over eras. in T, add.* T^1 *in marg.* [o] si *add. BR* [p] tamptationi *TB*

[100] Cf. Acts 8: 27 and *Letter* 1, **65**.

[101] Cf. Acts 8: 32–3; Isa. 53: 7–8.

[102] Ps. 25 (26): 2.

sustinere.'[103] Coniunxisti nos, Domine, et diuisisti quando placuit tibi et quo modo placuit. Nunc[q] quod, Domine, misericorditer cepisti, misericordissime comple. Et quos[e] [r]semel a se diuisisti[r] [s]in mundo,[s] perempniter tibi coniungas in celo. [t]Spes nostra, pars nostra, expectatio nostra, consolatio nostra,[t] Domine, qui es benedictus [u]in secula. Amen.[u]

[v]Vale in Christo, sponsa Christi; in Christo uale et Christo uiue. Amen.[v]

[q] Hoc *Amb*[1] [r–r] semel diuisisti a se *CEF;* a se semel diuisisti *Amb* [s–s] inuicem *CEF* [t–t] *om. CEF* [u–u] *om. CEF* (*but add. in marg. Fcorr*) [v–v] *om. ACEF*

that you are able to sustain it.'[103] Thou hast joined us, Lord, and thou hast parted us, when and in what manner it pleased thee. Now, Lord, what thou hast mercifully begun, most mercifully end, and those whom thou hast parted for a time on earth, unite forever to thyself in heaven: thou who art our hope, our portion, our expectation and our consolation, O Lord, who art blessed world without end. Amen.

Farewell in Christ, bride of Christ; in Christ fare well and live in Christ.

[103] 1 Cor. 10: 13.

⟨EPISTOLA VI⟩

1. SVO[a] SPECIALITER[1] SVA SINGVLARITER

Ne me forte in aliquo de inobedientia causari queas, uerbis etiam immoderati doloris tue frenum impositum est iussionis,[b] ut[c] ab his [d]mihi saltem[d] in scribendo temperem, a quibus in sermone[e] non tam difficile quam impossibile est prouidere. [f]Nichil enim minus in nostra est potestate quam animus, eique magis obedire cogimur quam imperare possimus. Vnde et cum nos eius affectiones stimulant, nemo earum subitos impulsus ita repulerit ut non [g]in effecta[g] facile[h] prorumpant, et se[i] per uerba facilius effluant que promptiores animi passionum sunt note,[2] secundum quod scriptum est: 'Ex habundantia enim[j] cordis os loquitur.'[3] Reuocabo itaque manum a scripto in quibus linguam a uerbis temperare [k]non ualeo.[k] Vtinam sic animus dolentis parere promptus sit quemadmodum dextra scribentis!

2. Aliquod tamen dolori[a] remedium[b] uales conferre si non hunc omnino possis auferre. Vt enim insertum clauum alius expellit,[4] sic cogitatio noua priorem excludit, cum alias intentus animus priorum memoriam dimittere cogitur aut intermittere. Tanto uero amplius cogitatio quelibet animum occupat, et ab aliis deducit, quanto quod cogitatur honestius estimatur, et quo intendimus animum magis uidetur necessarium.

3. Omnes itaque[a] nos Christi ancille[b] et in Christo filie tue duo nunc a tua paternitate supplices postulamus, que nobis ad modum necessaria prouidemus. Quorum quidem alterum est ut nos instruere uelis unde sanctimonialium ordo ceperit, et que nostre sit professionis auctoritas.

Letter 6 *T* fos. 34vb–42ra; *A* fos. 26ra–31rb; *C* fos. 171^{r}–172^{v}, 184^{r}–188^{v}, 191^{r}; *E* fos. 27^{r}–32^{r}; *F* pp. 58–80; *B* fos. 24va–29vb; *R* fos. 138va–144va; *S* fos. 49^{r}–63^{r}; *Amb* pp. 78–93; *Amb*[I] *variants shown in the marg. of Amb; J* pp. 120–48. *Headings are found in the following witnesses*: Item eadem ad eundem (eumdem *T*) *rubr. TA;* EPISTOLA VI. Quae est eiusdem HELOISSAE ad eundem PETRUM *Amb. In F this salutation is written by another hand and a third has written in the marg.:* edita ordine 6a

1 [a] Domino *TAmb;* (S)uo *CE, which lack a decorated initial although E indicates that* s *should be added;* Quo *B. The lengthier salutations at the opening of Letters 2 and 4 begin (respectively):* Domino suo . . . *and:* Vnico (*or* Amico) suo . . . [b] uisionis *BRS* [c] et *E* [d–d] saltem mihi *CEF* [e] sermo *C* [f] *Beginning of omission in CEF; text resumes at* 3 [g–gh] ineffectum *B* [h] *om. BR* [i] *om. A* [j] *om. Amb* [k–k] *om. R*

LETTER 6

1. TO HIM WHO IS HERS ESPECIALLY[1] FROM HER WHO IS HIS UNIQUELY

I would not want to give you cause for finding me disobedient in anything, so I have set the bridle of your injunction on the words which issue from my unbounded grief; thus in writing at least I may moderate what it is difficult or rather impossible to forestall in speech. For nothing is less under our control than our mind which, having no power to command, we are forced to obey. And so when its impulses move us, none of us can stop their sudden promptings from easily breaking out, and even more easily overflowing into words which are the ever-ready indications of what is felt in the mind,[2] according to what is written: 'A man's words are spoken from the overflowing of the heart.'[3] I will therefore hold my hand back from writing words which I cannot restrain my tongue from speaking; would that a grieving mind would be as ready to obey as a writer's hand!

2. And yet you have it in your power to remedy my grief, even if you cannot entirely remove it. As one nail drives out another hammered in,[4] new thought expels old when the mind, intent on other things, is made to give up or interrupt its remembrance of what went before. The more fully, indeed, any thought engages the mind, distracting it from other things, the more such thought is considered worthwhile and the focus of the mind appears inevitable.

3. And so all we handmaids of Christ, who are your daughters in Christ, come as suppliants to demand of your paternal care two things which we see to be very necessary for ourselves. One is that you will teach us how the order of nuns began and what authority there is for

2 [a] *om. T;* dolori *T[1]ACEFAmb;* doloris *BRS* [b] remediis *R*

3 [a] tamen *CF* [b] ancillule *B;* ancillice *R*

[1] Cf. *Letter* 3, 8: 'specialiter . . . tuus'/'especially yours'.

[2] 'uerba . . . que animi passionum sunt note'. Cf. Boethius (citing Aristotle), *In Librum Aristotelis de interpretatione, editio prima* (*PL* lxiv. 297A): 'sunt ergo ea quae sunt in uoce earum quae sunt in anima passionum notae'.

[3] Matt. 12: 34.

[4] Cf. Jerome, *Epistola* CXXV *ad Rusticum monachum*, 14 (ed. Hilberg, lvi. 132, *l.* 15; *PL* xxii. 1080); Cicero, *Tusculanae disputationes*, iv. 35. 75.

Alterum uero est[c] ut aliquam nobis regulam instituas et scriptam dirigas que feminarum [d]sit propria[d] et ex integro nostre conuersacionis[e] statum habitumque describat,[f] quod nondum a patribus sanctis[g] actum esse conspeximus.[h] [5] Cuius quidem rei defectu et indigentia nunc agitur ut ad eiusdem regule professionem tam mares quam femine in monasteriis suscipiantur, et idem[i] institutionis monastice iugum imponitur infirmo sexui eque ut forti.

4. Vnam quippe nunc *Regulam* beati Benedicti apud Latinos femine profitentur eque ut[a] uiri. Quam sicut uiris [b]solummodo constat[b] scriptam esse, [c]ita et[c] ab ipsis tantum impleri posse tam subiectis pariter[d] quam prelatis.[6] Vt enim cetera nunc omittam *Regule* capitula, quid ad feminas quod[e] de cucullis, femoralibus et scapularibus ibi scriptum est?[7] Quid denique ad ipsas de tunicis aut de laneis ad carnem indumentis, cum earum humoris[f] superflui[g] menstrue purgationes hec omnino[h] refugiant?[i] Quid ad ipsas etiam[j] quod de abbate statuitur ut ipse lectionem dicat euuangelicam et post ipsam hymnum incipiat?[8] Quid de[k] mensa abbatis seorsum cum peregrinis et hospitibus constituenda?[9] Numquit nostre conuenit religioni ut uel numquam[l] hospitium uiris prebeat aut cum his quos[m] susceperit uiris abbatissa comedat? O quam facilis ad ruinam animarum uirorum ac mulierum in unum cohabitatio! Maxime uero in mensa ubi crapula dominatur et ebrietas et uinum in dulcedine bibitur 'in quo est luxuria'.[10]

[c] est *om. A* [d–d] propria sit *F* [e] conuersionis *TACEBRS and Muckle;* professionis *F;* conuersationis *Amb;* conuerssionis, & professionis *Amb*[1]*;* conversion *J; cf. Gilson, Heloise and Abelard, pp. 148–66; Héloïse et Abélard, pp. 172–91* [f] describas *CEFRS* [g] *om. RS* [h] aspeximus *CEF* [i] eidem *BS;* eiusdem *R*

4 [a] et *ACEF* [b–b] constat solummodo *CEF* [c–c] ita *CE;* et ita *S* [d] patet *add. AEFR* [e] *om. F* [f] humeres *E;* humores *F;* humeris R [g] superflue *E* [h] non *CE* [i] confugiant *A;* reffugamur *CE* [j] et *E* [k] est *EF* [l] unquam *ACEF* [m] quod *T*

[5] Rules had been specially written for religious women although, from what she writes here, it would appear that Heloise either considered them unsatisfactory or, more likely, did not know any. Examples of such rules written many centuries earlier in the West include the *Statuta sanctarum uirginum* or *Regula uirginum* of Caesarius, bishop of Arles from 503 to 542, and the *Regula ad uirgines* of Aurelianus, bishop of Arles from 546 to 551. Caesarius's rule may be the first specially written for a women's monastery; the rule of Aurelianus is largely modelled on this (cf. De Clercq, *La Législation religieuse francque*, i. 79–83). Others (see *Clavis Patrum Latinorum*, nos. 1860 and 1863) include the *Regula ad uirgines* written for the abbess of Jussanmoutier by Donatus, bishop of Besançon (d. 658 or 660) and the *Regula ad uirgines* written (it is thought) for the nuns of Eboriac or Faremoutiers by Waldebert, abbot of Luxeuil, *c.*629–70. Such Rules had come to be eclipsed since the Carolingian age

our profession. The other, that you will establish some Rule for us and write it down, a Rule which shall be suitable for women, and also describe fully the standing and manner of our religious way of life, which we find was never done by the holy Fathers.[5] Through lack and need of this it is the practice today for men and women alike to be received into monasteries to profess the same Rule, and the same yoke of monastic ordinance is laid on the weaker sex as on the stronger.

4. At present the one *Rule* of St Benedict is professed in the Latin Church by women equally with men, although, as it was clearly written for men alone, it can only be fully obeyed by men, whether subordinates or superiors.[6] Leaving aside for the moment the other articles of the *Rule*, how can women be concerned with what is written there about cowls, drawers or scapulars?[7] Or indeed, with tunics or woollen garments worn next to the skin, when the monthly purging of their superfluous humours should completely avoid such things? How are they affected by the ruling for the abbot, that he shall read aloud the Gospel himself and afterwards start the hymn?[8] What about the abbot's table, set apart for him with pilgrims and guests?[9] Which is more fitting for our religious life: for an abbess never to offer hospitality to men, or for her to eat with men she has allowed in? It is all too easy for the souls of men and women to be destroyed if they live together in one place, and especially at table, where gluttony and drunkenness are rife, and wine 'which leads to lechery'[10] is drunk with enjoyment.

by the *Rule* of St Benedict, although Benedict of Aniane (*c.*750–821) drew upon them in his *Concordia regularum* and they are found in the *Codex regularum* which has been attributed to him (see Vogüé, *Les Règles monastiques anciennes*, esp. pp. 40–1). For a summary of their appearances in the *Concordia regularum* and the *Codex regularum* see Bonnerue's introduction to his edn. of the *Concordia*, pp. 145–7. The diffusion of the *Concordia* was largely indirect, e.g. through the *Expositio in Regulam S. Benedicti* of Smaragdus of St Mihiel (d. 821); see Bonnerue's introduction, pp. 147–59. For discussion of feminine monasticism in the West from Caesarius to the 12th c., with valuable references, see Röckelein, 'Hiérarchie, ordre et mobilité dans le monachisme féminin', who notes (p. 216 and n. 45) that in general the *Rule* of St Benedict came to be followed in convents of women but with modifications on such matters as Heloise mentions in this *Letter*. See also Seilhac, 'L'Utilisation de la Règle de saint Benoît dans les monastères féminins' and, for the modifications of the *Rule* of St Benedict discussed in the present correspondence, Mohr, 'Der Gedankenaustausch'.

6 Cf. *Letter* 1, **69**.

7 Benedict, *Rule*, c. 55. Cf. *Problemata*, 35 (*PL* clxxviii. 717).

8 Cf. Benedict, *Rule*, c. 11.

9 Cf. Benedict, *Rule*, c. 56. Also, Abelard, *Rule* **38** and **112**.

10 Eph. 5: 18; cited also in *Rule* **82**. Cf. Jerome, *Epistola* XXII *ad Eustochium*, 8 (ed. Hilberg, liv. 154–5; *PL* xxii. 399), *Epistola* CVIII *ad Eustochium* (*Epitaphium sanctae Paulae*), 11 (ed. Hilberg, lv. 320, *ll.* 6–7; *PL*xxii. 887).

5. Quod et beatus precauens Ieronimus ad matrem et filiam scribens meminit dicens: 'Difficile inter epulas seruatur pudicitia.'[11] Ipse quoque[a] poeta luxurie turpitudinisque doctor, libro amatorie artis intitulato, quantam fornicationis occasionem conuiuia maxime prebeant studiose exequitur dicens:

Vinaque[b] cum bibulas sparsere[c] Cupidinis alas
permanet [d]et [e]capto stat[e] grauis ille loco.
Tunc[d] ueniunt risus,[f] tunc[g] pauper cornua sumit,
tunc[h] dolor et cure rugaque frontis[i] abit.
Illic[j] sepe animos iuuenum rapuere puelle,
et Venus in uinis[k] ignis in igne fuit.[l] [12]

6. Numquid et si feminas solas hospitio susceptas ad mensam admiserint, nullum ibi latet periculum? Certe in seducenda muliere nullum est eque facile ut lenocinium muliebre. Nec[a] corrupte mentis turpitudinem ita prompte cuiquam mulier committit sicut mulieri. Vnde et predictus Ieronimus maxime[b] secularium[c] accessus feminarum uitare propositi sancti feminas adhortatur.[13] Denique si uiris ab hospitalitate nostra exclusis[d] solas admittamus feminas,[e] quis non uideat [f]quanta exasperatione[f] uiros offendamus quorum beneficiis monasteria sexus infirmi egent, maxime si eis a quibus plus accipiunt minus aut omnino nihil largiri uideantur?

7. Quod si predicte *Regule* tenor a nobis impleri non potest, uereor ne illud [a]apostoli Iacobi[a] in nostram quoque dampnationem dictum sit: 'Quicunque [b]totam legem[b] obseruauerit, offendat autem in uno, factus est omnium reus.'[14] Quod est dicere: de hoc etiam[c] ipso reus statuitur qui peragit multa[d] quod non implet omnia. Et[e] transgressor legis efficitur ex uno cuius impletor non fuerit nisi omnibus consummatis eius preceptis. Quod ipse [f]statim diligenter[f] exponens Apostolus adiecit: 'Qui enim dixit: Non mechaberis, dixit et: Non occides. Quod si[g] non mechaberis, occidas autem, factus es[h] transgressor legis.'[15] Ac si aperte dicat: ideo quilibet reus fit de transgressione

5 [a] *om. BR* [b] Roma que *E* [c] spersere *ES* [d–d] *T over eras.* [e–e] incepto stat *T over eras.; eras. also in marg.;* cepto stat *ACBRSAmb;* stat cepto *E* [f] risque *C* [g] tum *Ovid* [h] tum *Ovid* [i] fontis *R* [j] Ibi *ACE* [k] inuenis *T;* in uenis *BRSAmb* [l] fuit *?C;* fuuit *F;* furit *BAmb*

6 [a] ne *T* [b] *om. E* [c] *om. BR* [d] seclusis *E* [e] *om. B* [f–f] quantas exasperationes *C*

7 [a–a] Iacobi apostoli *CEF* [b–b] legem totam *S* [c] hoc *T;* hoc etiam *ACEFBRS* [d] iusta *C* [e] ex *S* [f–f] diligenter statim *CEF* [g] *om. F* [h] est *E*

5. St Jerome warns us of this when he writes to remind a mother and daughter that 'it is hard to keep one's chastity at feasts'.[11] And the poet himself, that master of sensuality and shame, in his book called *The Art of Love*, describes in detail what an opportunity for fornication is provided by banquets especially:

> When wine has sprinkled Cupid's thirsty wings
> He stays and stands weighed down in his chosen place . . .
> Then laughter comes, then even the poor find plenty,
> Then sorrow and care and wrinkles leave the brow . . .
> That is the time when girls bewitch men's hearts,
> And Venus in the wine adds fire to fire.[12]

6. And even if they admit to their table only women to whom they have given hospitality, is there no lurking danger there? Surely nothing is so conducive to a woman's seduction as woman's flattery, nor does a woman pass on the foulness of a corrupted mind so readily to any but another woman; which is why St Jerome particularly exhorts women of a sacred calling to avoid contact with women of the world.[13] Finally, if we exclude men from our hospitality and admit women only, it is obvious that we shall offend and annoy the men whose services are needed by a convent of the weaker sex, especially if little or no return seems to be made to those from whom most is received.

7. But if we cannot observe the tenor of this *Rule*, I am afraid that the words of the apostle James may be quoted to condemn us also: 'If a man keeps the whole law but for one single point, he is guilty of breaking all of it.'[14] That is to say, although he carries out much of the law he is held guilty simply because he fails to carry out all of it, and he is turned into a lawbreaker by the one thing he did not keep unless he fulfilled all the law's precepts. The apostle is careful to explain this by adding at once: 'For the One who said "Thou shalt not commit adultery" also said: "Thou shalt not commit murder." You may not be an adulterer, but if you commit murder you are a lawbreaker all the same.'[15] Here he says openly that a man becomes guilty by breaking

[11] Jerome, *Epistola* CXVII *ad matrem et filiam in Gallia commorantes*, 6 (ed. Hilberg, lv. 429, *ll.* 16–17; *PL* xxii. 957).

[12] Ovid, *Ars amatoria*, i. 233–4, 239–40, 243–4.

[13] Cf. Jerome, *Epistola* XXII *ad Eustochium*, 16 (ed. Hilberg, liv. 163; *PL* xxii. 403) and *Letter* 7, **24**.

[14] Jas. 2: 10.

[15] Jas. 2: 11.

uniuscuiuslibet precepti, quia ipse Dominus, qui precipit unum, precipit et[i] aliud. Et quodcumque[j] legis uioletur preceptum, ipse contempnitur [k]qui legem[k] non in uno sed in omnibus pariter mandatis constituit.[16]

8. Vt autem pretercam illa *Regule* instituta que penitus obseruare non possumus, aut sine periculo non ualemus, ubi[a] umquam[b] ad colligendas messes conuentus monialium exire uel labores agrorum habere consueuit,[17] aut[c] suscipiendarum feminarum constantiam uno anno probauerit, [d]easque [e]tertio[d] perlecta[e] *Regula*, sicut in ipsa iubetur,[18] instruxerit?[f] Quid rursum stultius quam uiam ignotam[g] nec[h] adhuc demonstratam[i] aggredi?[j] Quid presumptuosius quam eligere ac profiteri uitam quam nescias,[k] aut uotum facere quod implere[l] non queas?[m]

9. Sed et cum omnium uirtutum [a]discretio sit mater,[a 19] et omnium bonorum [b]moderatrix[20] sit[b] ratio, quis[c] aut uirtutem aut bonum censeat quod ab istis dissentire uideat?[d] Ipsas[e] quippe uirtutes[f] excedentes modum atque mensuram, sicut Ieronimus asserit,[21] inter uitia reputari conuenit. Quis autem ab[g] omni ratione ac discretione seiunctum[h] non uideat si, ad imponenda onera eorum quibus imponuntur, ualitudines prius non discutiantur[i] ut nature constitutionem humana sequatur industria? Quis asinum sarcina tanta onerat[j] qua dignum[k] iudicat elephantem? Quis tanta pueris aut senibus quanta uiris iniungat? Tanta debilibus scilicet quanta fortibus, tanta infirmis quanta sanis, tanta feminis quanta maribus, infirmiori uidelicet sexui quanta et forti?[22] Quod diligenter beatus papa Gregorius attendens, *Pastoralis*[l] sui capitulo quarto et uicesimo,[m] tam [n]de ammonendis[n] quam de[o] precipiendis ita distinxit: 'Aliter igitur[p]

[i] *om.* *CEF* [j] quicumque *BR* [k–k] *om.* *BR*

8 [a] nisi *BRS* [b] numquam *E* [c] T^3 *over eras.* [d–d] eos quoque *C;* eos quoque 3° *E* [e–e] perlecta tertio *F* [f] instruxit *F* [g] ignoratam *C* [h] ne *T* [i] monstratam *F* [j] aggreditur *B* [k] nescias? *B* [l] complere *BRS* [m] nequeas *CEFBRS*

9 [a–a] sit mater discretio *BRS* [b–b] mediatrix sit *TAmb; illegible corr.* T^1; moderatrix sit *ACEFAmb*^{1}*;* sit moderatrix *BRS* [c] Quid *A;* Quis *ES* [d] uideatur *AAmb* [e] Ipsos *E* [f] uidens *E* [g] in *C* [h] se iunctum *TS* [i] discucientur *BS;* discuscientur *R* [j] *add.* Luscombe*; f(orte) deest* onerat, *uel quid simile Amb*^{1} [k] digna *C* [l] pastorali *T* [m] XXIIII *TABRS;* 24 *CE;* 4 *F;* XIIII *Amb* [n–n] ammonandis de *B before corr. of tr.* [o] ad *A* [p] ergo *F*

[16] In *Problemata*, 2 (*PL* clxxviii. 679C–680A) this teaching of James is discussed in a similar way. Cf. also *Problemata*, 14 (*PL* clxxviii. 702A). There is no good reason to think, as

any one of the law's commandments, for the Lord himself who laid down one also laid down the other, and whatever commandment of the law is violated, it shows disregard of him who laid down the law in all its commandments, not in one alone.[16]

8. However, to pass over those provisions of the *Rule* which we are unable to observe in every detail, or cannot observe without danger to ourselves: what about gathering in the harvest—has it ever been the custom for convents of nuns to go out to do this, or to tackle the work of the fields?[17] Again, are we to test the constancy of the women we receive during the space of a single year, and instruct them by three readings of the *Rule*, as it says there?[18] What could be so foolish as to set out on an unknown path, not yet defined, or so presumptuous as to choose and profess a way of life of which you know nothing, or to take a vow you are not capable of keeping?

9. And since discretion is the mother of all the virtues[19] and reason the moderator of all that is good,[20] who will judge anything virtuous or good which is seen to conflict with discretion and reason? For the virtues which exceed all bounds and measure are, as Jerome says,[21] to be counted among the vices. It is clearly contrary to reason and discretion if burdens are imposed without previous investigation into the strength of those who are to bear them, to ensure that human industry may depend on natural constitution. No one would lay on an ass a burden suitable for an elephant, or expect the same from children and old people as from men, the same, that is, from the weak as from the strong, from the sick as from the healthy, from women, the weaker sex, as from men, the stronger one.[22] St Gregory, the Pope, was careful to make this distinction as regards both admonition and precept in the twenty-fourth chapter of his *Pastoral Rule*: 'Therefore men are to be admonished in one way, women in

does Levitan, p. 109, n. 14, that *Letter* 6 has here been altered following the writing of the *Problemata*.

[17] Benedict, *Rule*, c. 48.

[18] Benedict, *Rule*, c. 58.

[19] Cf. below at **10** and *Rule* **89**. Also cf. *Ethica*, ii. 2 (ed. Ilgner, p. 85, *ll.* 2237–8; ed. Luscombe, p. 128, *l.* 8); *Collationes*, **115** (ed. Marenbon and Orlandi, p. 130; *Dialogus*, ed. Thomas *ll.* 2018–19; *PL* clxxviii. 1652A); *Sermon* 30 (*PL* clxxviii. 567D–568A). Also Benedict, *Rule*, c. 64, 19: 'testimonia discretionis matris uirtutum'.

[20] Cf. John Cassian, *Collationes*, ii. 4 (ed. Petschenig, p. 44; repr. with French trans. by Pichery, *SChr* xlii. 116–17; *PL* xlix. 528C): 'Omnium namque uirtutum generatrix, custos moderatrixque discretio est.'

[21] Jerome, *Epistola* CXXX *ad Demetriadem de seruanda uirginitate*, 11 (ed. Hilberg, lvi. i. 3, p. 191; *PL* xxii. 1116).

[22] Cf. *Rule* **97**.

ammonendi sunt uiri atque aliter femine, quia illis grauia, istis[q] uero sunt iniungenda[r] leuiora; et[s] illos[t] magna exerceant, istas uero leuia demulcendo conuertant.'[u] [23]

10. Certe et qui monachorum regulas scripserunt nec solum de feminis omnino tacuerunt, uerum etiam illa statuerunt[a] que eis nullatenus conuenire sciebant; satis commode innuerunt nequaquam eodem iugo regule tauri et[b] iuuence premendam esse ceruicem, quia quos dispares natura creauit, equari labore non conuenit. Huius autem discretionis beatus non immemor Benedictus, tanquam omnium iustorum spiritu plenus, pro qualitate hominum aut temporum cuncta sic moderatur in regula, ut omnia sicut ipsemet[c] uno concludit loco mensurate[d] fiant.[24] Primo itaque ab ipso incipiens abbate, precipit[e] eum ita subiectis presidere[f] ut 'secundum [g]unius,' inquit, 'cuiusque[g] qualitatem uel intelligentiam ita se omnibus conformet et aptet,[h] ut non solum detrimenta gregis sibi[i] commissi non paciatur, uerum[j] in augmentatione boni gregis gaudeat,[25] suamque fragilitatem semper suspectus sit, memineritque calamum quassatum non conterendum.'[26] 'Discernat [k]et tempora,[k] cogitans discretionem sancti[l] Iacob dicentis: Si greges meos plus in ambulando fecero[m] laborare, morientur cuncti una die.[27] Hec[n] ergo aliaque testimonia discretionis matris uirtutum[28] sumens, sic omnino[o] temperet ut [p]et fortes sit quod[p] cupiant et infirmi non refugiant.'[29]

11. Ad hanc quidem dispensationis moderationem indulgentia pertinet puerorum,[30] senum[31] et omnino debilium,[32] lectoris[a] [33] seu septimanariorum[34] coquine ante alios refectio, et in ipso etiam conuentu de ipsa cibi uel potus qualitate seu quantitate pro diuersitate hominum prouidentia, de quibus quidem singulis ibi diligenter scriptum est. Ipsa quoque statuta ieiunii tempora pro qualitate

[q] iste *add. C* [r] in(T^3)iungenda *T* [s] ut *Gregory* [t] alios *TBAmb;* illa *E* [u] concitant *F*

10 [a] *followed by eras. in T* [b] *om. R* [c] insemet *AE* [d] mansurate *BS* [e] precepit *C* [f] presidem *A;* presideri *BRS* [g–g] inquit uniuscuiusque *CEF;* uniuscuiusque *R* [h] petet *C* [i] si *E* [j] etiam *add. B* [k–k] et tempora *TACEFBRAmb; preferred by Orlandi, 'Considerazioni', pp. 57–8; om. S;* et temperet *Benedict, Muckle* [l] beati *BRS* [m] feceritis *CE* [n] He *T* [o] omnia *F, Benedict* [p–p] sit quod fortes *F;* et sit quod fortes *B;* et sic quod fortes *R;* et fortes si nec *S;* sit et fortes quod *Muckle, Pagani*

11 [a] lotioris *E*

another; for heavy burdens may be laid on men and great matters exercise them, but lighter burdens on women, who should be gently converted by less exacting means.'[23]

10. Certainly those who laid down rules for monks were not only completely silent about women but also prescribed regulations which they knew to be quite unsuitable for them, and this showed plainly enough that the necks of bullock and heifer should in no sense be brought under the same yoke of a common Rule, since those whom nature created unequal cannot properly be made equal in labour. St Benedict, who is imbued with the spirit of justice in everything, has this discretion in mind when he moderates everything in the *Rule* according to the quality of men or the times, so that, as he says himself at one point, all may be done in moderation.[24] And so first of all, starting with the abbot himself, he lays down that he shall preside over his subordinates in such a way that (he says) 'he will accommodate and adapt himself to them all in accordance with the disposition and intelligence of each individual. In this way he will suffer no loss in the flock entrusted to him but will even rejoice to see a good flock increase.'[25] 'He must also be conscious always of his own frailty and remember that the bruised reed must not be broken.'[26] 'He should also set periods of time, bearing in mind the good sense of holy Jacob when he said: If I drive my herds too hard on the road they will all die in a single day.[27] Acting on this, and on other examples of discretion, the mother of the virtues,[28] he must arrange everything so that there is always what the strong desire and the weak do not shrink from.'[29]

11. Such modification of regulations is the basis of the concessions granted to children,[30] and the old[31] and the weak in general,[32] of the feeding of the lector[33] or weekly servers[34] in the kitchen before the rest, and of the provision of food and drink in quality or quantity adapted to the diversity of the people in the monastery itself. All these matters are precisely set out in the *Rule*. He also relaxes the set times

[23] Gregory the Great, *Regula pastoralis*, iii. 1/2 (xxiv) (ed. Rommel, *SChr* ccclxxxii. 266; *PL* lxxvii. 51CD); also cited in *Rule* **97**.

[24] Benedict, *Rule*, c. 48, 9.

[25] Benedict, *Rule*, c. 2, 32.

[26] Benedict, *Rule*, c. 64, 13. Cf. Isa. 42: 3: 'calamum quassatum non conteret'/'the bruised reed he shall not break'.

[27] Cf. Gen. 33: 13.

[28] Cf. **9** above and note.

[29] Benedict, *Rule*, c. 64, 17–19.

[30] Cf. Benedict, *Rule*, c. 37; 39, 10.

[31] Cf. Benedict, *Rule*, c. 37.

[32] Cf. Benedict, *Rule*, c. 36; 40, 3.

[33] Cf. Benedict, *Rule*, c. 38, 10.

[34] Cf. Benedict, *Rule*, c. 35, 12.

temporis uel quantitate laboris ita relaxat prout nature[b] postulat infirmitas.[35] Quid, obsecro,[c] ubi iste qui sic ad hominum et temporum qualitatem omnia moderatur ut [d]ab[e] omnibus[d] sine murmuratione proferri[f] queant que[g] instituuntur?[36] [hi]Quid, inquam, de feminis prouideret,[h] si eis quoque pariter ut uiris regulam institueret?[i] Si enim in quibusdam regule rigorem pueris, senibus et debilibus pro ipsa nature debilitate uel infirmitate temperare cogitur, [j]quid de fragili sexu prouideret cuius maxime debilis et infirma natura cognoscitur?[j]

12. Perpende itaque[a] quam longe absistat ab omni[b] rationis discretione eiusdem regule professione tam [c]feminas quam uiros[c] obligari, eademque[d] sarcina tam debiles quam fortes onerari.[37] Satis [e]esse nostre[e] arbitror infirmitati, si nos ipsis ecclesie rectoribus et qui in sacris ordinibus constituti sunt clericis tam continentie quam abstinentie uirtus equauerit,[f] maxime cum Veritas dicat: 'Perfectus omnis erit, si sit sicut magister eius.'[38] [g]Quibus etiam pro magno [h]reputandum esset,[h] si religiosos laicos equiparare possemus.[g] Que namque in fortibus parua censemus, in debilibus ammiramur.[i] Et iuxta illud Apostoli: 'Virtus in infirmitate perficitur.'[39] [j]Ne uero[j] laicorum religio pro paruo ducatur, qualis fuit Abrahe, Dauid,[k] Iacob,[l] licet coniugatorum, Chrisostomus in epistola[m] ad Hebreos *Sermone* septimo[n] nobis occurrit dicens: 'Sunt multa in quibus poterit laborare ut bestiam illam incantet. Que sunt ista? Labores, lectiones, uigilie. Sed quid ad nos hoc[o] inquis[p] qui non sumus monachi? Hec mihi dicis? Dic Paulo cum dicit: "Vigilantes in omni" patientia et oratione,[40] cum dicit: "Carnis curam ne feceritis in concupiscentiis."[41] Non enim [q]monachis hec[q] scribebat[r] tantum, sed omnibus qui erant in ciuitatibus. Non enim secularis homo debet aliquid amplius habere [s]monacho quam[s] cum uxore concumbere tantum.[42] Hic enim habet ueniam, in aliis autem nequaquam, sed omnia [t]equaliter sicut monachi[t] agere debet.[u] Nam et beatitudines que a Christo dicuntur non monachis tantum dicte sunt, alioquin uniuersus mundus peribit et in angustum[v]

[b] uere *C* [c] obsecro? *Amb* [d–d] ab hominibus *R;* omnibus *S* [e] *om. S* [f] perferri *ACEF;* profiteri *Amb*[1] [g] *om. T*(*but add. T*[1])*BRS* [h–h] *om. B* [i–i] *om. C* [j–j] *om. ACEF*

12 [a] *om. ACEF* [b]omnibus *CE* [c–c] uiros quam feminas *F* [d] etc *add. A;* eadem *F* [e–e] nostre esse *BRS* [f] equa *S* [g–g] *om. ACEF* [h–h] reputandi *R* [i] ammiremur *BR* [j–j] ne *AEF;* nec *C* [k] dicendo *E* [l] Iob *TBRSAmb;* iacob *T*[1]*ACEFAmb*[1]*;* Jacob *J* [m] epistolam *F* [n] io *C* [o] hec *S* [p] inquit *TACEBRSAmb;* inquis *F, Chrysostom* [q–q] haec Monachis *Amb* [r] scribebit *B* [s–s] quam monachus nisi *Chrysostom* [t–t] sicut monachi equaliter *BRS* [u] debent *TACEBRS;* debet *FAmb, Chrysostom* [v] augustum *RS*

for fasting according to the season or the amount of work to be done, to meet the needs of natural infirmity.[35] What, I ask—when he adapts everything to the quality of men and seasons, so that all his regulations can be carried out by everyone without complaint[36]—what provision would he make for women if he laid down a Rule for them like that for men? For if in certain respects he is obliged to modify the strictness of the *Rule* for the young, the old and weak, according to their natural frailty or infirmity, what would he provide for the weaker sex whose frailty and infirmity is generally known?

12. Consider then how far removed it is from all reason and good sense if both women and men are bound by profession of a common Rule, and the same burden is laid on the weak as on the strong.[37] I think it should be sufficient for our infirmity if the virtue of continence and also of abstinence makes us the equals of the rulers of the Church themselves and of the clergy who are confirmed in holy orders, especially when the Truth says: 'Everyone will be fully trained if he reaches his teacher's level.'[38] It would also be thought a great thing if we could equal religious laymen, for what is judged unimportant in the strong is admired in the weak. In the words of the Apostle: 'Power is made perfect in weakness.'[39] But lest we should underestimate the religious commitment of the laity, of men like Abraham, David, and Jacob, although they had wives, Chrysostom reminds us in his seventh *Sermon* on the Letter to the Hebrews: 'There are many ways whereby a man may struggle to charm that beast. What are they? Toil, study, vigils. But what concern are they of ours, when we are not monks? Do you ask me that? Rather, ask Paul, when he says: "Be watchful in all tribulation and persevere in prayer"[40] and: "Give no more thought to satisfying your body with all its cravings."[41] For he wrote these things not only for monks but for all who were in the cities, and the layman should not have greater freedom than the monk, apart from sleeping with his wife.[42] He has permission for this, but not for other things; and in everything he must conduct himself like a monk. The Beatitudes too, which are the actual words of Christ, were not addressed to monks alone, otherwise the whole world must perish and he would have confined the things which belong to

[35] Cf. Benedict, *Rule*, c. 36, 9; 39, 1–2 and 10.
[36] Cf. Benedict, *Rule*, c. 40, 9.
[37] Cf. Benedict, *Rule*, c. 48.
[38] Luke 6: 40.
[39] 2 Cor. 12: 9; cf. *Letter* 4, **17** and note.
[40] Cf. Eph. 6: 18; Coloss. 4: 2.
[41] Cf. Rom. 13: 14: 'carnis curam ne feceritis in desideriis'.
[42] Cf. *Rule* **97** and note.

inclusit ea que uirtutis sunt. Et quomodo[w] honorabiles sunt nuptie[43] que nobis tantum[x] impediunt?'[44] Ex quibus quidem uerbis aperte colligitur quod quisquis[y] euuangelicis preceptis continentie uirtutem[z] addiderit, monasticam perfectionem implebit.

13. Atque[a] utinam ad hoc nostra[b] religio conscendere posset ut euuangelium impleret, non transcenderet nec[c] plusquam christiane appeteremus esse. Hinc profecto, ni[d] fallor, sancti decreuerunt Patres non ita nobis sicut uiris generalem aliquam regulam quasi nouam legem prefigere, nec magnitudine uotorum nostram infirmitatem onerare,[e] attendentes[f] illud Apostoli: 'Lex enim iram operatur. Vbi enim non est lex nec preuaricatio.'[45] Et iterum: 'Lex autem subintrauit ut abundaret delictum.'[46] Idem quoque maximus continentie predicator de infirmitate nostra plurimum confidens, et quasi ad secundas nuptias urgens iuniores[g] uiduas: 'Volo', inquit, 'iuniores nubere, filios procreare,[h] matresfamilias esse, nullam occasionem dare aduersario',[47] etc.[i] Quod et beatus Ieronimus saluberrimum esse considerans Eustochio de improuisis [j]feminarum uotis[j] consulit his uerbis: 'Si autem et ille que[k] uirgines sunt ob alias tamen culpas[l] non saluantur, quid fiet illis que prostituerunt membra Christi et mutauerunt templum [m]Spiritus sancti[m] in lupanar? Rectius[n] fuerat homini subisse coniugium, ambulasse per plana, quam [o]altiora intendentem[o] in profundum inferni cadere.'[48] Quarum etiam temerarie[p] professioni sanctus Augustinus consulens[q] in libro *De continentia*[r] *uiduali* ad Iulianam[s] scribit his uerbis: 'Que non cepit deliberet; que aggressa est perseueret. Nulla aduersario detur occasio; nulla Christo subtrahatur oblatio.'[49] Hinc etiam[t] canones nostre infirmitati consulentes decreuerunt diaconissas [u]ante quadringentos annos[u] ordinari non debere, et hoc cum diligenti probatione,[v] [50] cum a[w] uiginti annis liceat diaconos promoueri.

[w] quo *R*   [x] *vacant space in R;* tamtum *S*   [y] ex *add. B*   [z] *om. B*

13 [a] ad que *BS*   [b] mea *B*   [c] ne *TFBAmb*   [d] nisi *CE*   [e] honorare *C*   [f] attendens *RS*   [g] mulieres *CE*   [h] procurare *S*   [i] *om. Amb*   [j–j] uotis feminarum *BRS*   [k] uirgines *al.* que *Jerome*   [l] uirginitate corporum *add. Jerome*   [m–m] sancti spiritus *ABRS*   [n] Rectus *R*   [o–o] per altiora tendentem *AE;* altiora tendentem *CB;* ad altiora intendentem *F;* altiorem tendentem *RS;* ad altiora tendentem *Jerome and Rule* **67**   [p] temere *TAC, E after corr., FBRS;* temerarie *Amb, Muckle*   [q] consulans *S*   [r] continantia *S*   [s] Iulianum *ACEFAmb*   [t] et *F*   [u–u] ante xl annos *over eras. in T; eras. also in marg.*   [v] et *add. R*   [w] et *B*; *om. R*

[43] Cf. Heb. 13: 4.

[44] John Chrysostom, *Homiliae in Epistulam ad Hebraeos interprete Mutiano*, 7. 4 (*PG* lxiii. 289). Cf. *Rule* **97**. John Chrysostom—the 'golden-mouthed'—lived from *c.*347 to 407.

virtue within narrow limits. And how can marriage be honourable[43] when it weighs so heavily on us?'[44] From these words it can easily be inferred that anyone who adds the virtue of continence to the precepts of the Gospel will achieve monastic perfection.

13. Would that our religion could rise to this height—to carry out the Gospel, not to go beyond it, lest we attempt to be more than Christians! Surely this is the reason (if I am not mistaken) why the holy Fathers decided not to lay down a general Rule for us as for men, like a new law, nor to burden our weakness with a great number of vows; they looked to the words of the Apostle: 'Because law can bring only retribution; but where there is no law there can be no breach of law.'[45] And again: 'Law intruded to multiply law-breaking.'[46] The same great preacher of continence also shows great consideration for our weakness and appears to urge the younger widows to a second marriage, when he says: 'It is my wish, therefore, that young widows shall marry again, have children and preside over a home. Then they will give no opponent occasion for slander',[47] etc. St Jerome also believes this to be salutary advice, and tells Eustochium of the rash vows taken by women, in these words: 'But if those who are virgins are still not saved, because of other faults, what will become of those who have prostituted the members of Christ and turned the temple of the Holy Spirit into a brothel? It were better for a man to have entered matrimony and walked on the level than to strain after the heights and fall into the depths of hell.'[48] St Augustine too has women's rashness in taking vows in mind when he writes to Julian in his book *On the Continence of Widows*: 'May she who has not begun, think it over, and may she who has made a start, continue. No opportunity must be given to the enemy, no offering taken from Christ.'[49] Consequently, canon law has taken our weakness into account and laid down that deaconesses must not be ordained before the age of 40, and only then after thorough probation,[50] while deacons may be promoted from the age of 20.

[45] Rom. 4: 15. Cf. *Rule* 89. [46] Rom. 5: 20. [47] 1 Tim. 5: 14.

[48] Jerome, *Epistola* XXII *ad Eustochium*, 6 (ed. Hilberg, liv. 150, *ll.* 14–17, p. 151, *ll.* 12–14; *PL* xxii. 397–8); cited also in the *Rule* 79.

[49] Augustine, *De bono uiduitatis*, ix. 12 (ed. Zycha, p. 317, *ll.* 21–3; *PL* xl. 437).

[50] Cf. *SN* c. 122, 10, and the Council of Chalcedon (AD 451), 15, in the *Collectio Hispana* (*Colección canónica Hispana*, ed. Martínez Díez and Rodriguez, iii. 257, or *Collectio canonum* in *PL* lxxxiv. 169C); Ps.-Isidore, *Decretalium collectio*, 15, *PL* cxxx. 312; *Decretales Pseudo-Isidorianae* (the 'False Decretals') ed. Hinsch, p. 286. In *Letter* 7, 18 and in his *Rule* 27 Abelard cites 1 Tim. 5: 9 in support of a minimum age of 60 for the election of a widow to the diaconate.

14. Sunt et[a] in[b] monasteriis qui regulares dicuntur canonici,[51] beati Augustini [cd]quandam,[e] ut aiunt, regulam[d] profitentes,[52] qui se inferiores monachis nullatenus arbitrantur,[53] licet eos et[f] uesci[c] carnibus et lineis uti uideamus. Quorum quidem uirtutem [g]si nostra exequare[h] infirmitas posset, numquid pro minimo habendum esset?[54] Vt autem[g] nobis[i] de omnibus cibis tutius ac leuius[j] indulgeatur, ipsa quoque natura prouidit que maiore scilicet sobrietatis uirtute [k]sexum nostrum[k] premuniuit. Constat quippe multo parciore sumptu et alimonia minore feminas quam uiros[l] sustentari posse, nec eas tam leuiter[m] inebriari physica protestatur. Vnde[n] et Macrobius Theodosius[o] *Saturnaliorum* libro septimo[p] meminit his uerbis: 'Aristotiles mulieres', inquit, 'raro hebriantur,[q] crebro senes. Mulier humectissimo [r]est corpore.[r] Docet hoc et leuitas cutis et splendor. Docent precipue assidue purgationes superfluo exonerantes[s] corpus humore. Cum ergo epotum uinum in tam largum ceciderit humorem,[t] uim suam perdit,[u] nec facile cerebri sedem ferit fortitudine eius extincta.'[55] Item: 'Muliebre corpus crebis purgationibus deputatum pluribus consertum[v] foraminibus ut pateat in meatus et uias[w] prebeat[x] humori in egestionis exitum confluenti. Per hec foramina uapor uini[y] celeriter euanescit. Contra, senibus siccum [z]est corpus[z] quod probat asperitas et scalor cutis.'[56] Ex his itaque perpende quanto tutius ac iustius nature et infirmitati nostre cibus quislibet et potus indulgeri possit, quarum [a]crapula uidelicet corda[a] et hebrietate grauari facile non possunt, cum ab illa nos cibi parcitas, ab ista feminei corporis qualitas, ut dictum est, protegat.[b] Satis nostre [c]esse infirmitati[c] et maximum imputari debet,[d] si continenter ac sine proprietate uiuentes et, officiis occupate diuinis, ipsos[e] ecclesie duces uel religiosos laicos in uictu adequemus, uel eos denique qui [f]regulares canonici[f] dicuntur et se [g]precipue uitam[g] apostolicam sequi profitentur.[h]

14 [a] etiam *F* [b] *om. T* [c–c] regulam quandam ut eos et uesci *C* [d–d] quendam *S* [e] regulam quandam ut aiunt *AEF* [f] *om. BS* [g–g] *om. C* [h] adequare *EFAmb*[1] [i] *om. Amb* [j] lenius *Amb* [k–k] nostrum sexum *CE* [l] et *add. R* [m] et *add. T* [n] dum *A* [o] *om. R* [p] uii *TABRAmb;* 4 *CE;* iiii *S* [q] inebriantur *CEFAmb;* inebriebantur *B* [r–r] pectore est *R* [s] exhonera *E* [t] honorem *C* [u] et fit dilutive *add. F;* et fit dilutius *add. Macrobius* [v] fec *add. T*[1]*;* confectum *AE;* confertum *F;* consertum est *Macrobius according to some MSS; cf. Orlandi, 'Considerazioni', p. 57* [w] uia *C* [x] prebeas *R* [y] uinum *C* [z–z] corpus est *F, Macrobius* [a–a] uidelicet corda crapula *ACEFBRSAmb* [b] prorogat *A* [c–c] *om. CEF* [d] infirmitati *add. F* [e] Ipsos *BR* [f–f] canonici regulares *CEF* [g–g] *om. BR* [h] regulam *superscr. add. by an annotator in B*

[51] 'called Regular Canons'/'regulares dicuntur canonici': repeated at the end of 14 and cf. *Letter* 12 to a regular canon: 'clerics in your calling whom you call Regular Canons'; 'even you yourselves, newly called "Regular Canons" by yourselves, just as you are newly

14. In monasteries there are also those called Regular Canons,[51] professing, they say, a Rule of St Augustine,[52] who think themselves in no way inferior to monks,[53] although we see them eating meat and wearing linen. If our weakness could match their virtue, surely it would be considered no small thing?[54] And Nature herself has made provision for our being safely granted a mild indulgence in any kind of food, for our sex is protected by a greater power of sobriety. It is well known that women can be sustained on much less nourishment and at less cost than men, and medicine bears witness that they are not so easily intoxicated. And so Macrobius Theodosius in the seventh book of his *Saturnalia* notes: 'Aristotle says that women are rarely intoxicated, but old men often. Woman has an extremely humid body, as can be known from her smooth and glossy skin, and especially from her regular purgations which rid the body of superfluous moisture. So when wine is drunk and merged with so general a humidity, it loses its power and does not easily strike the seat of the brain when its strength is extinguished.'[55] Again: 'A woman's body which is destined for frequent purgations is pierced with several holes, so that it opens into channels and provides outlets for the moisture draining away to be dispersed. Through these holes the fumes of wine are quickly released. By contrast, in old men the body is dry, as is shown by their rough and wrinkled skin.'[56] From this it can be inferred how much more safely and properly our nature and weakness can be allowed any sort of food and drink; in fact we cannot easily fall victims to gluttony and drunkenness, seeing that our moderation in food protects us from the one and the nature of the female body as described from the other. It should be sufficient for our infirmity, and indeed, a high tribute to it, if we live continently and without possessions, wholly occupied by service of God, and in doing so equal the leaders of the Church themselves in our way of life or religious laymen or even those who are called Regular Canons and profess especially to follow the apostolic life.

arisen'/'tuae professionis clericos, quos canonicos regulares uocatis'; 'uos ipsi canonici regulares a uobis ipsis nouiter appellati, sicut et nouiter exorti'(ed. Smits, pp. 257, *ll.* 4–5; 267, *ll.* 285–7; *PL* clxxviii. 345A, 351A; trans. Ziolkowski, pp. 158, 171).

[52] Regular or Augustinian (or Austin) canons who adopted a *Rule* attributed to St Augustine of Hippo, ed. and trans. Lawless, pp. 73–118.

[53] Cf. *Letter* 12: 'You say, as people report, that our order is by far inferior to yours and that monks are very far removed from the dignity of clerics'/'Dicis, ut dicunt, longe ordine tuo nostrum inferiorem esse et plurimum monachos a dignitate clericorum abesse' (ed. Smits, p. 257, *ll.* 7–9; *PL* clxxviii. 345A; trans. Ziolkowski, p. 158).

[54] Cf. *Rule* 97.

[55] Macrobius, *Saturnalia*, vii. 6. 16–18. Also cited in *Rule* 85.

[56] Macrobius, *Saturnalia*, vii. 6. 18–19. Also cited but with some differences in *Rule* 85.

15. Magne postremo prouidentie est his qui Deo se per uotum obligant, ut minus uoueant et plus exequantur, ut aliquid semper[a] debitis gratia superaddant.[b] Hinc enim per semetipsam[c] Veritas ait: 'Cum feceritis omnia[d] que precepta sunt,[e] dicite: Serui inutiles sumus: que debuimus facere, fecimus.'[57] Ac si aperte diceret: Ideo inutiles et quasi pro nichilo[f] ac sine meritis reputandi, quia debitis tantum exsoluendis contenti,[g] nichil ex gratia superaddimus.[h] De quibus quidem gratis superaddendis ipse quoque Dominus alibi[i] parabolice loquens ait: Sed et si quid 'supererogaueris,[j] ego cum rediero reddam tibi'.[58]

16. Quod quidem hoc tempore multi monastice religionis temerarii professores si diligentius attenderent, et[a] in quam professionem iurarent[b] [c]antea prouiderent,[c] atque[d] ipsum regule tenorem studiose perscrutarentur, minus per ignorantiam offenderent[e] et per negligentiam peccarent. Nunc uero indiscrete omnes fere pariter[f] ad monasticam conuersationem[g] currentes,[h] inordinate suscepti inordinatius[i] uiuunt, et eadem facilitate qua ignotam regulam profitentur eam contempnentes, consuetudines quas uolunt pro lege statuunt.[j] [59] Prouidendum itaque nobis est ne id oneris[k] femine presumamus in quo uiros fere iam uniuersos[l] succumbere uidemus,[m] immo et deficere. Senuisse iam mundum conspicimus hominesque ipsos cum ceteris que[n] mundi sunt pristinum nature uigorem amisisse,[60] et iuxta illud Veritatis ipsam karitatem non tam multorum quam fere omnium refriguisse,[61] ut iam uidelicet pro qualitate hominum ipsas propter homines scriptas uel mutari uel temperari[o] necesse sit regulas.

17. Cuius quidem[a] discretionis ipse quoque beatus non immemor Benedictus ita se monastice districtionis[b] rigorem temperasse fatetur, ut descriptam a se *Regulam* comparatione priorum institutorum nonnisi quamdam honestatis institutionem et quandam conuersationis inchoationem reputet, dicens: 'Regulam autem hanc descripsimus,

15 [a] supra *F* [b] superaddat *EFAmb;* superaddent *BRS* [c] semetipsum *F* [d] *om. BRS* [e] uobis *add. F and Vulg.* [f] nullo *E* [g] contempti *TER* [h] superaddidimus *CEFSAmb* [i] *om. E* [j] supererogaueras *A*

16 [a] *om. CEF* [b] intrarent *F* [c–c] animaduerterent *Amb* [d] atqui *A* [e] offenderet *T* [f] *om. F* [g] conuersionem *codd., Amb*[1], *and Muckle;* conuersationem *Amb;* conversion *J; cf. Gilson, Heloise and Abelard, pp. 148–66* [h] currantes *B* [i] inordinaciusque *A* [j] statuerunt *T* (*but marked for corr. by T*[1])*BRS* [k] honoris *?A* [l] uniuersse *C;* uniuerse *E* [m] uideamus *TAmb; om. R* [n] qui *E* [o] temperare *Amb*

17 [a] quid *A* [b] discretionis *BRAmb*

15. Finally, it is a great sign of forethought in those who bind themselves by vow to God if they perform more than they vow, so that they add something by grace to what they owe. For the Truth says in his own words: 'When you have done all you have been told to do, say: We are merely servants; we have only done our duty.'[57] Or, in plain words: We are useless and good for nothing, and deserve no credit, just because we were content only to pay what we owed and added nothing extra as a gift. The Lord himself, speaking in a parable, says of what should be freely added: But if you 'give more in addition, I will repay you on my return'.[58]

16. If indeed many of those who rashly profess monastic observance today would pay more careful attention to this, would consider beforehand what it is that they profess in their vows, and study closely the actual tenor of their Rule, they would offend less through ignorance, and sin less through negligence. As things are, they all hurry almost equally indiscriminately into monastic life; being received without proper regulation they live with even less, and with the same readiness that they profess a Rule they do not know, despising it they set up as law customs they prefer.[59] We must therefore be careful not to impose on a woman a burden under which we see nearly all men stagger and even fall. We see that the world has now grown old, and that with all other living creatures men too have lost their former natural vigour:[60] and, in the words of the Truth, amongst many or indeed almost all men love itself has grown cold.[61] And so it would seem necessary today to change or to modify those Rules which were written for men in accordance with men's present nature.

17. St Benedict himself was also well aware of this need to discriminate, and admits that he has so tempered the rigour of monastic strictness that he regards the *Rule* he has set out, in comparison with earlier institutes, as no more than a basis for virtuous living and the beginning of a monastic life. He says: 'We have written down this Rule in order

[57] Luke 17: 10. Cf. *Rule* **89**; *Problemata*, 25 (*PL* clxxviii. 711CD).

[58] Luke 10: 35.

[59] Cf. *Letter* 5, **10** and *Rule* **71**.

[60] The ageing of the world was a familiar *topos*. Cf. e.g. Otto of Freising, *Chronica*, v, prologue: 'we behold the world . . . already failing and, so to speak, drawing the last breath of extremest old age' / 'mundum . . . iam deficientem et tanquam ultimi senii extremum spiritum trahentem cernimus' (trans. Mierow, p. 323; ed. Hofmeister, pp. 227–8). Cf. also Augustine, *Sermon* 81, 8 (*PL* xxxviii. 504–5).

[61] 'karitatem non tam multorum quam fere omnium refriguisse': cf. Matt. 24: 12: 'quoniam abundauit iniquitas, refrigescet charitas multorum' and *Rule* **97**: 'iam refrigescente pristine caritatis feruore'.

ut hanc obseruantes aliquatenus uel honestatem morum aut[c] initium conuersationis nos demonstremus habere. Ceterum ad perfectionem conuersationis qui festinat,[d] sunt doctrine sanctorum patrum, quarum obseruatio perducat[e] hominem ad celsitudinem perfectionis.'[62] Item: 'Quisquis ergo ad celestem patriam festinas,[f] hanc minimam inchoationis regulam, adiuuante Christo, perfice, et tunc demum ad maiora doctrine uirtutumque culmina, Deo protegente, peruenies.'[63] Qui, ut ipse ait,[64] [g]dum quando[g] legamus olim sanctos patres uno die psalterium explere solere, ita psalmodiam tepidis temperauit ut in ipsa per hebdomadam distributione psalmorum minore ipsorum numero monachi quam [h]clerici contenti sint.[h]

18. Quid etiam tam religioni quietique monastice contrarium est quam quod luxurie fomentum maxime[a] prestat et[b] tumultus excitat, atque[c] ipsam Dei in nobis ymaginem, qua[d] prestamus ceteris, id est, rationem delet? Hoc autem uinum est quod supra omnia uictui pertinentia plurimum Scriptura dampnosum asserit et caueri[e] ammonet. De quo et maximus ille sapientum in Prouerbiis meminit dicens: 'Luxuriosa res uinum et tumultuosa ebrietas. Quicumque his[f] delectatur non erit sapiens.'[65] [g]'Cui ue?[g] Cuius[h] patri ue?[i] Cui[j] rixe? Cui fouee? Cui sine causa uulnera? Cui suffusio[k] oculorum? Nonne his qui morantur in uino et student calicibus[l] epotandis?[m] Ne intuearis uinum quando flauescit cum splenduerit in uitro color eius. Ingreditur blande, sed in nouissimo mordebit ut coluber, et sicut[n] regulus uenena diffundet.[o] Oculi tui uidebunt extraneas,[p] et cor tuum loquetur peruersa. Et eris sicut dormiens[q] in medio mari,[r] [s]et quasi[s] sopitus gubernator amisso clauo. Et dices:[t] Verberauerunt me, sed non dolui; traxerunt[u] me, et ego[v] non sensi. Quando[w] euigilabo, et[x] rursus uina reperiam.'[y] [66] Item: 'Noli regibus, [z]O Lamuel,[a] noli regibus[z] dare uinum, quia nullum secretum est ubi [b]regnat ebrietas,[b]

[c] *T over eras.; eras. also in marg.* [d] festinant *F;* festinati *S* [e] perducit *F* [f] festinans *R* [g–g] cum *FAmb* [h–h] contempti ((cont)enti *T*[1] *in a now trimmed marg.*) clerici sunt *T;* clerici sunt contenti *AB;* clerici contenti *CE;* clerici contenti essent *FAmb*[1]*;* clerici sint contenti *RS;* Clerici contenti sint *Amb*

18 [a] *om. R* [b] *T over eras.; eras. also in marg.* [c] itaque *CEF* [d] quam *T*[1]*AC;* qua *T*[3] [e] causam *F* [f] Quique hoc *C* [g–g] Que *C* [h] *om. C* [i] uel *R* [j] cuius *BRS* [k] suffusitio *T;* suffossio *F* [l] in calicibus *C;* in calicibus *E after correction of* in talibus [m] eptitandis *T;* epudendis *BR;* epudandis *S* [n] quasi *F* [o] *om. B* [p] extranen *BR* [q] dormies *E* [r] maris *CEF* [s–s] *om. B* [t] dicens *F* [u] extraxerunt *R* [v] *om. CEF* [w] Cum *E* [x] Et *B* [y] etc *add. EF* [z–z] *om. F* [a] samuel *CE* [b–b] ebrietas (hebrietas *R*) regnat *BRS*

that by practising it we may show that we have attained some degree of virtue and the rudiments of monastic observance. But for anyone who would hasten towards perfection of the monastic life, there are the teachings of the holy Fathers, observance of which may lead a man to the summit of perfection.'[62] And again: 'Whoever you are, then, who hasten to the heavenly kingdom, observe, with Christ's help, this minimum Rule as a beginning, and then you will come finally to the higher peaks of doctrine and virtue, under the protection of God.'[63] He also specifically says[64] that, whereas we read that the holy Fathers of old used to complete the psalter in a single day, he has modified psalmody for the lukewarm so as to spread the psalms over a week; the monks may then be content with a smaller number of them, as the clergy are.

18. Moreover, what is so contrary to the religious life and peace of the monastery as the thing which most encourages sensuality and starts up disturbances, which destroys our reason, the very image of God in us, whereby we are raised above the rest of creation? That thing is wine, which the Scriptures declare to be the most harmful of any form of nourishment, warning us to beware of it. The wisest of wise men refers to it in Proverbs in these words: 'Wine is reckless and strong drink quarrelsome; no one who delights in it grows wise.'[65] 'Who will know woe, as his father will, and quarrels, brawls, bruises without cause and bloodshot eyes? Those who linger late over their wine, and look for ready-mixed wine. Do not look at the wine when it glows and sparkles in the glass. It goes down smoothly, but in the end it will bite like a snake and spread venom like a serpent. Then your eyes will see strange sights, and your mind utter distorted words; you will be like a man sleeping in mid-ocean, like a drowsy helmsman who has lost his rudder, and you will say: They struck me and it did not hurt, dragged me off and I felt nothing. When I wake up I shall turn to wine again.'[66] And again: 'Do not give wine to kings, O Lemuel, never to kings, for there is no privy council where drinking prevails.

[62] Benedict, *Rule*, c. 73, 1–2.

[63] Benedict, *Rule*, c. 73, 8–9.

[64] Cf. Benedict, *Rule*, c. 18, 22–5 and **31** below.

[65] Prov. 20: 1; cited also in *Rule* **82**.

[66] Prov. 23: 29–35; cited also in *Rule* **82**. Levitan (p. 116, n. 39; and cf. p. 108, n. 9, p. 117, n. 44) writes that the passage cited here, like some others cited in this letter, 'seems to be imported' from the *Rule*. He makes a similar claim in reverse, for a passage cited from Jerome in *Rule* 83, that it is 'likely to have been imported as an interpolation' from *Letter* 6 (= 5 according to Levitan, p. 219, n. 153). However, the reproduction of texts cited in *Letter* 6 is to be expected in the course of the two replies given to *Letter* 6 in the letter collection.

ne forte bibant[c] et obliuiscantur iudiciorum et mutent[d] causam filiorum pauperis.'[67] Et in Ecclesiastico scriptum est: 'Vinum et mulieres apostatare[e] faciunt sapientes, et arguunt sensatos.'[68] Ipse quoque Ieronimus ad Nepotianum scribens de uita clericorum, et quasi grauiter indignans quod sacerdotes legis ab omni quod inebriare[f] potest[g] abstinentes nostros in hac abstinentia superent,[h] 'nequaquam',[i] inquit, 'uinum redoleas ne audias illud philosophi: hoc non est osculum porrigere sed[j] propinare.[69] Vinolentos[k] sacerdotes et Apostolus dampnat et lex uetus prohibet: "qui altario[l] deseruiunt"[70] uinum et siceram[m] non bibant.[71] Sicera[n] Hebreo[o] sermone omnis potio nuncupatur que inebriare[p] potest, siue illa que[q] fermento conficitur, siue pomorum succo, aut faui decoquuntur[r] in [s]dulcem et barbaram[s] potionem,[t] aut palmarum fructus exprimuntur in liquorem, coctisque frugibus aqua pinguior colatur.[u] Quicquid[v] inebriat et statum mentis[w] euertit, fuge similiter ut uinum.'[72]

19. Ecce quod regum[a] deliciis interdicitur, sacerdotibus penitus denegatur, et cibis[b] omnibus periculosius esse constat. Ipse tamen tam spiritualis uir[c] beatus Benedictus dispensatione quadam presentis etatis indulgere monachis cogitur. 'Licet', inquit, 'legamus uinum monachorum omnino non esse,[73] sed quia nostris temporibus id[d] monachis persuaderi non potest',[74] etc. Legerat, ni fallor, quod in *Vitis Patrum* scriptum est his uerbis: 'Narrauerunt quidam [e]abbati Pastori[e] [f]de quodam monacho[f] quia[g] non bibebat[h] uinum, et dixit eis[i] quia [j]uinum monachorum omnino[j] non est.'[75] Item post aliqua: 'Facta est aliquando celebratio missarum in monte abbatis Antonii et inuentum est ibi cenidium[k] uini. Et tollens[l] unus de senibus paruum uas,[m] calicem portauit [n]ad abbatem[n] Sisoi et dedit ei. Et

[c] bibent *B* [d] mittant *TR;* mutant *BS* [e] apostare *F* [f] inebriari *T;* in ebrietate *E, B before corr. by another hand, R before corr.* [g] potum *exp. B, R* [h] superant *ACEF* [i] Nunquam *F, Jerome* [j] uinum *add. FAmb, Jerome* [k] uinolentes *TR;* uinolantes *BS* [l] altari *CEF, Jerome* [m] sinceram *TCE* [n] sincera *CEF but F adds in marg.:* F(orte) Sicera [o] hebreorum *C* [p] inebrietate *C;* in ebrietate *E* [q] ex *add. F* [r] decoquitur *TCERAmb;* dequoquitur *ABS;* decoquuntur *F, Jerome* [s–s] dulce et herbarum *TBRS;* dulcedine et herbarum *ACE;* dulcem et barbaram *F, Jerome;* dulcedinem et herbarum *Amb* [t] pociones *A* [u] coloratur *F, Jerome* [v] Quid quid *E* [w] mentus *F*

19 [a] *T before corr. by exp.; eras. also in marg.* [b] cibus *CBR* [c] *over eras. in T; eras. also in marg.* [d] his *T;* hoc *Amb* [e–e] Abbati pastori *Amb* [f–f] monacho de quodam *T but marked for corr. by* T^4 [g] qui *A, Vitae;* quod *F* [h] bibat *S* [i] *om. R* [j–j] uinum monachorum *ACE;* omnino potus monachorum *F* [k] uasculum *F;* modicum *Jerome* [l] extollens *Amb* [m] id est *add. F* [n–n] Abbati *F*

If they drink they may forget what they have decreed and neglect the pleas of the poor for their sons.'[67] In Ecclesiasticus too it is written: 'Wine and women rob the wise of their wits and are a hard test for good sense.'[68] Jerome himself also, when writing to Nepotian about the life of the clergy, and apparently highly indignant because the priests of the Law abstain from anything which could intoxicate them and surpass our own priests in such abstinence, says: 'Never smell of wine, lest you hear said of you the well known word of the philosopher: This is not offering a kiss but proffering a cup.[69] The Apostle equally condemns priests who are given to drink, and the Old Law forbids it: "Those who serve the altar"[70] shall not drink wine or strong drink.[71] By strong drink in Hebrew is understood any drink which can intoxicate, whether produced by fermentation or from apple juice, or from honeycombs which have been distilled into a sweet, rough drink, or when the fruits of date palms are pressed into liquid, or water is enriched with boiled grain. Whatever intoxicates and upsets the balance of the mind, shun it like wine.'[72]

19. See how what is forbidden kings to enjoy is wholly denied to priests, and is known to be more dangerous than any food. And yet so spiritual a man as St Benedict himself is compelled to allow it to monks as a sort of concession to the times in which he lived. 'Although', he says, 'we read that wine is no drink for monks,[73] yet because nowadays monks cannot be persuaded of this',[74] etc. He had read, if I am not mistaken, these passages in the *Lives of the Fathers*: 'Certain people told Abbot Pastor that a particular monk drank no wine, to which he replied that wine was not for monks.'[75] And further on: 'There was once a celebration of the Mass on the Mount of Abbot Antony, and a jar of wine was found there. One of the elders took a small vessel, carried a cupful to Abbot Sisoi and gave it to him. He

[67] Prov. 31: 4–5; cited also in *Rule* 82.

[68] Ecclus. 19: 2; cited also in *Rule* 82. 'Quid etiam tam religioni quietique monasticae . . . arguunt sensatos': cf. *Rule* 82.

[69] Cf. *Rule* 83 and n. 326.

[70] 1 Cor. 9: 13: 'Nescitis quoniam qui in sacrario operantur, quae de sacrario sunt, edunt; et qui altari deseruiunt, cum altari participant?'

[71] Cf. Lev. 10: 9; Deut. 29: 6; 1 Tim. 3: 3; Tit. 1: 7. Also Luke 1: 15: 'erit enim (*sc.* Ioannes) magnus coram Domino: et uinum et siceram non bibet.'

[72] Jerome, *Epistola* LII *ad Nepotianum*, 11 (ed. Hilberg, liv. 434, *ll.* 2–11; *PL* xxii. 536–7). 'Ipse quoque Hieronymus . . . fuge similiter ut uinum': cf. *Rule* 83 and notes 326–9.

[73] Cf. *Vitae patrum, Verba seniorum*, v. 4. 31 (*PL* lxxiii. 868D).

[74] Benedict, *Rule*, c. 40, 6; also cited in *Rule* 84. The passage continues: 'let us at least agree to drink sparingly'.

[75] *Vitae patrum, Verba seniorum*, v. 4. 31 (*PL* lxxiii. 868D); also cited in *Rule* 84.

bibit[o] semel,[p] et secundo et accepit et bibit. Obtulit ei et tertio, sed non accepit dicens: Quiesce, frater,[q] an[r] nescis quia [s]est Sathanas?'[s] [76] Et iterum de abbate Sisoi:[t] 'Dicit:[u] ergo Abraham discipulus[v] eius: Si occurritur in Sabbato et Dominica ad ecclesiam, et biberit[w] tres calices, [x]ne multo est?[x] Et dixit senex: Si non esset Sathanas, non esset multum.'[77]

20. Vbi umquam,[a] queso, carnes a Deo damnate sunt uel monachis interdicte? Vide, obsecro, et attende qua neccessitate *Regulam* temperet in eo etiam[b] quod periculosius est monachis, et quod eorum non esse nouerit, quia uidelicet huius abstinentia temporibus suis monachis iam persuaderi non poterat. Vtinam eadem dispensatione et in hoc tempore ageretur ut uidelicet in his que media[c] boni et mali atque indifferentia dicuntur,[d] [78] tale temperamentum fieret[e] ut quod iam persuaderi non ualet, professio[f] non exigeret, mediisque omnibus sine scandalo concessis, sola[g] interdici peccata sufficeret, et sic quoque in cibis sicut in uestimentis dispensaretur, ut quod uilius comparari[h] posset ministraretur, et[i] per omnia neccessitati, non superfluitati, consuleretur.[j] [79] Non enim magnopere sunt curanda que nos regno Dei non preparant,[k] uel que nos minime Deo commendant. Hec uero sunt omnia que exterius geruntur, et eque reprobis ut electis,[l] eque ypocritis[m] ut religiosis communia sunt.[80] Nichil quippe inter Iudeos et Christianos ita separat sicut exteriorum operum et interiorum discretio,[81] presertim cum inter filios Dei et[n] diaboli sola caritas discernat[o] quam plentitudinem[p] legis et finem precepti Apostolus uocat.[82] Vnde et ipse hanc operum gloriam prorsus extenuans ut fidei preferat [q]iustitiam Iudeum[q] alloquens dicit:[r] 'Vbi est ergo[s] gloriatio tua? Exclusa est. Per quam legem? Factorum? Non, sed per legem fidei. Arbitramur enim[t] hominem

[o] *om. F* [p] senis *S* [q] super *S* [r] Aut *TA;* autem *C* [s–s] Satanas est *F* [t] sildi *S* [u] dixit *CE;* Dixit *F* [v] discipulis *?A, BAmb* [w] frater *add. F* [x–x] multum ne isti *F;* ne multum est *Amb, Vitae*

20 [a] numquam *RS* [b] et *E* [c] sunt *add. F* [d] dicunt *E* [e] fiet *T*(fieret *T*¹)*BRS* [f] perfectio *F* [g] solum *CEF* [h] compari *A* [i] *om. EF* [j] consuletur *R;* consularetur *S* [k] preparent *E* [l] deiectis *Amb* [m] reprobis ypocritis *S* [n] filios *add. F* [o] decernat *A* [p] quem *S* [q–q] iusticiam in deum *BRS;* institiam, Iudaeam *Amb* [r] dixit *CE* [s] *om. TFAmb* [t] eum *Amb*

[76] *Vitae patrum, Verba seniorum*, v. 4. 36 (*PL* lxxiii. 869CD); also cited in *Rule* **84**.

[77] *Vitae patrum, Verba seniorum*, v. 4. 37 (*PL* lxxiii. 869D); also cited in *Rule* **84**.

[78] Cf. below **26** and note; also *Rule* **97**.

[79] Cf. *Rule* **77** and **93**.

[80] Cf. *Letters* 4, **16** and 6, **25–6** and *Rule* **92**; *Comm. Rom.* i (ii. 6, p. 78, *ll.* 65–8); iv (xiv. 17, p. 304); *Collationes* **116**, **205** (ed. Marenbon and Orlandi, pp. 130–1, 206; *Dialogus*, ed.

drank once, and a second time he took it and drank, but when it was offered a third time he refused, saying: Peace, brother, do you not know it is Satan?'[76] It is also said of Abbot Sisoi: 'His disciple Abraham then asked: If this happens on the Sabbath and the Lord's Day in church, and he drinks three cups, is that too much? If it were not Satan, the old man replied, it would not be much.'[77]

20. On the question of meat: where, I ask you, has this ever been condemned by God or forbidden to monks? Look, pray, and mark how of necessity St Benedict modifies the *Rule* on this point too (though it is more dangerous for monks and he knew it was not for them), because in his day it was impossible to persuade monks to abstain from meat. I would like to see the same dispensation granted in our own times, with a similar modification regarding matters which fall between good and evil and are called indifferent,[78] so that vows would not compel what cannot now be gained by persuasion. If concession were made without scandal on neutral points, it would be enough to forbid only what is sinful. Thus thc same dispensations could be made for food as for clothing, so that provision could be made of what can be purchased more cheaply, and, in everything, necessity not superfluity could be our consideration.[79] For things which do not prepare us for the Kingdom of God or commend us least to God call for no special attention. These are all outward works which are common to the damned and elect alike, as much to hypocrites as to the truly religious.[80] For nothing so divides Jew from Christian as the distinction between outward and inner works,[81] especially since between the children of God and those of the devil love alone distinguishes: what the Apostle calls the sum of the law and the object of what is commanded.[82] And so he also disparages pride in works in order to set above it the righteousness of faith, and thus addresses Jewry: 'What room then is left for human pride? It is excluded. And on what principle? Of works? No, but through the principle of faith. For our

Thomas, *ll.* 2025–30, 3158–65; *PL* clxxviii. 1652B, 1676AB); *Ethica*, i. 1. 6; i. 2. 8; i. 17. 1; i. 29. 5–30, 1 (ed. Ilgner, p. 1, *ll.* 14–16, p. 3, *ll.* 52–4, p. 18, *ll.* 461–3, p. 30, *ll.* 774–84; ed. Luscombe, p. 2, *ll.* 13–16, p. 4, *ll.* 24–5, pp. 27, *l.* 35–28, *l.* 2, pp. 44, *l.* 26–46, *l.* 1); *Carmen ad Astralabium*, ed. Rubingh-Bosscher, *v.* 302; *SN*, *versio prima*, c. 141, no. 7a (ed. Boyer and McKeon, p. 609): 'ABAIELARDUS: . . . Exteriora . . . opera aeque reprobris sicut sanctis communia sunt'; *SN* c. 142 ('Quod opera factorum non iustificent hominem et contra'); *Sententie*, **275** (ed. Luscombe, p. 14; c. 34, ed. Buzzetti, p. 154, *ll.* 33–5; *PL* clxxviii. 1755A).

[81] Cf. *Comm. Rom.*, i (i. 17, p. 65, *ll.* 642–5); *Problemata*, 1 (*PL* clxxviii. 679B) and 24 (*PL* clxxviii. 710AB).

[82] Cf. Rom. 13: 10; 1 Tim. 1: 5.

iustificari per fidem sine operibus legis.'[83] Item: 'Si enim [u]Abraham ex operibus[v] iustificatus est, habet gloriam, sed non apud Deum. Quid enim dicit[w] Scriptura? Credidit Abraham Deo,[u] et reputatum est ei ad iustitiam.'[84] Et rursum:[x] 'Ei', inquit, 'qui non operatur, credenti[y] autem in eum[z] qui iustificat impium, deputatur fides eius ad iustitiam secundum propositum gratie Dei.'[85]

21. Idem etiam omnium ciborum esum Christianis indulgens, et ab his ea[a] que iustificant distinguens: 'Non est', inquit, 'regnum Dei esca et potus, sed iustitia et pax et gaudium in Spiritu sancto.'[86] 'Omnia quidem munda sunt, sed malum est homini qui per offendiculum manducat.[b] Bonum est non manducare[c] carnem et non bibere uinum, neque in quo frater tuus [d]offendatur aut scandalizetur[d] aut infirmetur.'[87] Non enim hoc loco ulla[e] cibi[f] comestio interdicitur, sed comestionis offensio qua uidelicet quidam[g] ex conuersis Iudeis scandalizabantur, cum uiderent[h] ea quoque comedi que lex interdixerat. Quod[i] quidem scandalum apostolus etiam Petrus cupiens euitare, grauiter ab ipso est obiurgatus et salubriter correptus,[j] sicut ipsemet Paulus ad Galathas scribens commemorat.[88] Qui rursus Chorinthiis scribens: 'Esca autem nos non commendat[k] Deo.'[89] Et rursum: 'Omne[l] quod in macello uenit manducate';[90] 'Domini est[m] terra et plenitudo eius.'[91] Et ad Colossenses:[n] 'Nemo ergo uos iudicet in cibo aut[o] in potu.'[92] Et post aliqua: 'Si mortui[p] estis cum Christo ab elementis huius mundi, quid[q] adhuc tanquam uiuentes in mundo decernitis? Ne[r] tetigeritis neque gustaueritis neque contrectaueritis:[s] que sunt omnia in interitu [t]ipso usu[t] secundum preceptum[u] et doctrinas hominum.'[93] Elementa huius mundi uocat prima legis[v] rudimenta secundum carnales obseruantias, in quarum uidelicet doctrina, quasi in addiscendis[w] litteralibus elementis, primo se

[u–u] habraham deo *C* [v] legis *add. CER* [w] dixit *E* [x] et *add. EF* [y] credendi *E* [z] Deum *Amb*

21 [a] *om. BRS* [b] mandeat *E* [c] mendicare *R* [d–d] offendatur aut (*over eras.; eras. also in marg.*) scandalizetur *T;* scandalizatur aut offendatur *CE;* scandalizetur aut offendatur *F* [e] illa *CEF* [f] sibi *B* [g] quidem *CEBRS* [h] uiderint *E* [i] Que *S* [j] correctus *TCAmb* [k] condempnat *BR* [l] Omni *B* [m] in *C;* et *E before corr. by exp.* [n] calossenses *C;* colocenses *RS* [o] et *F* [p] mortuis *C* [q] quidquid *CEF* [r] nec *B* [s] contractaueritis *C* [t–t] ipsa uissu *C;* ipso uissu *EF;* ipso uisu *R* [u] precepta *CEF and Vulg.* [v] mundi *add. T* [w] adiscendo *E*

[83] Rom. 3: 27–8.

[84] Rom. 4: 2–3; also cited in *Rule* **91**; *Collationes*, **21** (ed. Marenbon and Orlandi, p. 26;

argument is that a man is justified by faith without observances of the law.'[83] And again: 'For if Abraham was justified by works, then he has a ground for pride, but not before God: for what does Scripture say? Abraham put his faith in the Lord and that faith was counted to him as righteousness.'[84] Once more: 'But if without any work he simply puts his faith in him who makes a just man of the sinner, then his faith is indeed counted as righteousness according to God's gracious plan.'[85]

21. The Apostle also allows Christians to eat all kinds of food and distinguishes from it those things which count as righteous. 'The Kingdom of God', he says, 'is not eating and drinking, but justice and peace and joy in the Holy Spirit.'[86] 'All things indeed are pure in themselves, but anything is bad for the man who gives offence by his eating. It is a good thing not to eat meat and not to drink wine, nor to do anything which may offend or scandalize or weaken your brother.'[87] In this passage there is no eating of food forbidden, only the giving of offence by eating, because certain converted Jews were scandalized when they saw things being eaten which the Law had forbidden. The apostle Peter was also trying to avoid giving such offence when he was seriously rebuked and wholesomely corrected, as Paul himself recounts in his letter to the Galatians.[88] Paul also writes to the Corinthians: 'Certainly food does not commend us to God.'[89] And again: 'You may eat anything sold in the meat market';[90] 'the earth is the Lord's and all that is in it'.[91] And to the Colossians: 'Allow no one therefore to take you to task about what you eat or drink',[92] and later on: 'If you died with Christ and passed beyond the elements of this world, why do you behave as though still living the life of the world? Do not touch this, do not taste that, do not handle the other: these are all things which perish as we use them, all based on the precepts and teachings of men.'[93] The elements of the world are what he calls the first rudiments of the law dealing with carnal observances, in the practice of which, as in learning the rudiments of

Dialogus, ed. Thomas, *l.* 372; *PL* clxxviii. 1620B); *Sermon* 3 (*PL* clxxviii. 398C). Cf. *Comm. Rom.*, ii (iv. 2–3, pp. 122–3).

[85] Rom. 4: 5. Cf. *Comm. Rom.*, ii (iv. 5, pp. 123–4).

[86] Rom. 14: 17. Cf. *Comm. Rom.*, iv (xiv. 17, p. 304).

[87] Rom. 14: 20–1. Cf. *Comm. Rom.*, iv (xiv. 20–1, p. 305).

[88] Cf. Gal. 2: 11–14.

[89] 1 Cor. 8: 8.

[90] 1 Cor. 10: 25.

[91] 1 Cor. 10, 26; cf. Ps. 23 (24): 1.

[92] Coloss. 2: 16.

[93] Coloss. 2: 20–2.

mundus, id est, carnalis adhuc populus exercebat.[94] Ab his quidem elementis, id est, carnalibus obseruantiis tam[x] Christus[y] quam sui mortui sunt, cum nichil his debeant, iam[z] non in hoc mundo uiuentes, hoc est, inter carnales figuris intendentes et decernentes,[a] id est, distinguentes quosdam cibos uel quaslibet res ab aliis, atque ita dicentes:[b] 'Ne[c] tetigeritis' hec uel illa, etc.[d][95] Que scilicet tacta uel gustata[e] uel[f] contrectata,[g] inquit Apostolus,[96] sunt in interitu anime ipso suo usu[h] quo uidelicet ipsis ad aliquam etiam utimur utilitatem[i] 'secundum', inquam, 'preceptum et doctrinas hominum',[97] id est, carnalium et legem carnaliter intelligentium potius quam Christi uel suorum.

22. Hic enim cum ad predicandum ipsos[a] destinaret apostolos, ubi magis ipsi[b] ab omnibus scandalis prouidendum erat, omnium tamen ciborum esum[c] [d]ita eis[d] indulsit, ut apud quoscumque suscipiantur hospitio,[e] ita sicut illi uictitent,[f] 'edentes' scilicet 'et bibentes que apud illos sunt'.[98] Ab hac[g] profecto Dominica suaque disciplina illos recessuros ipse iam Paulus per Spiritum prouidebat. De quibus ad Thymotheum scribit dicens: 'Spiritus autem manifeste dicit, quia in nouissimis temporibus discedent[h] quidam[i] a fide, attendentes spiritibus erroris et doctrinis demoniorum in[j] ypochrisi loquentium mendatium prohibentium nubere, abstinere a cibis quos Deus creauit ad percipiendum cum gratiarum actione fidelibus, et his qui cognouerunt ueritatem, quia omnis creatura Dei [k]bona est[k] et nichil reiciendum[l] quod cum gratiarum actione percipitur. Sanctificatur enim per uerbum Dei [m]et[n] orationem. Hec[o] proponens fratribus, bonus eris minister Christi Ihesu, enutritus[p] uerbis fidei[m] et bone doctrine quam assecutus es.'[99]

23. Quis denique Iohannem eiusque discipulos abstinentia nimia[a] se macerantes[b] ipsi[c] Christo eiusque discipulis in religione non preferat, si corporalem[d] oculum ad exterioris abstinentie intendat exhibitionem? De quo etiam ipsi discipuli Iohannis aduersus Christum et suos

[x] tamquam *B* [y] Christi *Amb* [z] Iam *BR* [a] discernentes *R;* decernantes *S* [b] dicens *R* [c] nec *CEF* [d] *om. Amb* [e] gusta *S* [f] et *A* [g] conuersa *E* [h] iussu *CEF* [i] humilitatem *T before exp. of* h *and* m; humilitatem *Amb;* vilitatem, *& in al*(*io*) *Cod*(*ice*) vtilitatem *Amb*[1]; proufit *J*

22 [a] eos *E* [b] ipsis *A* [c] *om. B* [d–d] eis ita *Amb* [e] hospites *F* [f] uictaretur *C;* euitassent *Ecorr.;* uiuerent *F;* lactitent *R* [g] hoc *ACFB* [h] discedant *F* [i] quibus *C;* quidem *RS* [j] et *F* [k–k] *om. TR;* bona *ACEBSAmb* [l] reiciandum *S* [m–m] *om. C* [n] per *add. F* [o] hoc *E* [p] et nutritus *AEF;* et enutritus *Amb*

letters, the world, that is, a people still carnal, was engaged.[94] But those who are Christ's own are dead as regards these rudiments or carnal observances, for they owe them nothing, as they no longer live in this world among carnal people who pay heed to forms and distinguish or discriminate between certain foods and similar things, and so say: 'Do not touch' this or that,[95] etc. For such things when touched or tasted or handled, says the Apostle,[96] are destructive to the soul in the act of using them for some purpose 'in accordance with the precepts and teachings of men',[97] that is, of carnal beings who interpret the law in a worldly sense and not in the way of Christ or of his own.

22. When Christ sent his apostles out to preach, at a time when it was even more necessary to avoid any scandal, he allowed them to eat any kind of food, so that wherever they might be shown hospitality they could live like their hosts, 'eating and drinking what was in the house'.[98] Paul certainly foresaw through the Holy Spirit that they would fall away from this, the Lord's teaching and his own, and wrote on the subject to Timothy: 'The Spirit says expressly that in after-times some will desert from the faith and give their minds to subversive doctrines inspired by devils who speak lies in hypocrisy. They forbid marriage and demand abstinence from certain foods, though God created them to be enjoyed with thanksgiving by believers who have inward knowledge of the truth. For everything that God created is good, and nothing is to be rejected when it is taken with thanksgiving, since it is hallowed by God's own word and by prayer. By offering such advice as this to the brotherhood you will prove a good servant of Jesus Christ, bred in the precepts of our faith and of the sound instruction which you have followed.'[99]

23. But if anyone turns his bodily eye to the display of outward abstinence, he would then prefer John and John's disciples, wasting away through excessive fasting, to Christ and his disciples: and indeed, John's disciples who were apparently still following Jewish

23 [a] *om. R* [b] maturantes *E* [c] pro *add. R* [d] *om. R*

[94] Cf. *Letter* 10 (ed. Smits, p. 241, *ll.* 72–5; *PL* clxxviii. 337B; trans. Ziolkowski, p. 88); *Sermon* 5 (*PL* clxxviii. 417D); *Expositio in Hexameron*, 9 (ed. Romig and Luscombe, p. 6; *PL* clxxviii. 731D–732D); *Problemata*, 14 (*PL* clxxviii. 699D).

[95] Cf. Coloss. 2: 21.

[96] Cf. Coloss. 2: 21–2.

[97] Coloss. 2: 22.

[98] Luke 10: 7.

[99] 1 Tim. 4: 1–6.

murmurantes, tanquam adhuc in exterioribus iudaizantes, ipsum interrogauerunt Dominum[e] dicentes: 'Quare nos et[f] Pharisei ieiunamus[g] frequenter, discipuli autem tui non ieiunant?'[100] Quod diligenter [h]beatus attendens[h] Augustinus, et quid inter uirtutem et uirtutis[i] exhibitionem referat distinguens,[j] [k]ita que[k] fiunt exterius pensat ut[l] nichil meritis[m] superaddant[n] opera. [o]Ait quippe[o] sic in libro *de bono coniugali*: 'Continentia non corporis sed animi[p] uirtus est.[101] Virtutes autem animi aliquando in corpore[q] manifestantur, aliquando in habitu latent,[r] sicut martyrum[s] uirtus apparuit[t] in tolerando passiones.'[102] Item: 'Iam enim erat in Iob patientia quam nouerat Dominus,[u] et cui testimonium perhibebat, sed hominibus innotuit[v] temptationis examine.'[103] Item: 'Verum ut[w] apertius intelligatur quomodo sit uirtus in habitu etiamsi[x] non sit in opere, loquor de exemplo de quo nullus dubitat Catholicorum.[y] [z]Dominus Iesus,[z] quod in ueritate carnis esurierit et[a] sitierit[b] et[c] manducauerit et biberit, nullus ambigit eorum qui ex eius euuangelio fideles sunt. Num[d] igitur non[e] erat in illo continentie uirtus a cibo et potu, quanta erat in Iohanne Baptista? "Venit enim Iohannes non[f] manducans neque[g] bibens et dixerunt: Demonium habet. Venit filius hominis manducans et bibens et dixerunt: Ecce homo uorax[h] [i]et potator uini,[i] amicus publicanorum et peccatorum." '[104] [105] [j]Item: 'Deinde[j] ibi subiecit cum de Iohanne ac de se illa dixisset:[k] "Iustificata est[l] sapientia a filiis suis",[106] [m]qui uirtutem continentie uident[m] in habitu animi semper esse debere, in opere autem pro rerum ac temporum oportunitate manifestari, sicut uirtus patientie[n] sanctorum [o]martirum.[p] Quo circa sicut[o] non est impar meritum [q]patientie in Petro qui passus est, et in Iohanne qui passus non est, sic non est impar meritum[q] continentie in Iohanne qui nullas expertus est nuptias, et in Abraham qui filios generauit. Et

[e] *om. CEF* [f] a *R* [g] ieiunauimus *S* [h–h] attendens beatus *T* [i] uirtutes *C* [j] attendens *Amb* [k–k] itaque que *TBRS;* itaque *E* [l] *add. in T by* T^3 *; eras. in marg.; om. A* [m] meriti *AEF* [n] superhabundant *C;* superadent *S* [o–o] ait. Quippe *F* [p] anime *TACEBRS; cf. Letter* 4, 14 *and Carmen ad Astralabium, ed. Rubingh-Bosscher, v. 197;* l'ame *J* [q] opere *Augustine* [r] *om. Amb* [s] martyrii *F, Augustine* [t] emicuit apparuitque *F, Augustine* [u] Deus *F, Augustine* [v] notuit *C* [w] apparens *add. R* [x] et si *E* [y] Christianorum *add. F* [z–z] Dominus enim noster Iesus Christus *F;* Dominus enim Iesus *Augustine* [a] ac *F* [b] sacierit *R* [c] *om. F, Augustine* [d] nec *CE;* Non *BRS* [e] *om. CE* [f] neque *F* [g] & *Amb* [h] uerax *ERS* [i–i] et uinarius *F;* uinaria *al.* potator uini *Augustine* [j–j] Item quod Dominus *F;* Item Dominus *Augustine* [k] est mathei.xi. *add. in marg. B* [l] inquit *add. F* [m–m] qui uidet (uident *Augustine*) continentiae uirtutem *F, Augustine* [n] sapiencie *E* [o–o] *om. E;* martyrum in opere apparuit, retrorsum(*?*) uero aequo sanctorum in habitu fuit. Quocirca (sicut *om. F*) *F* [p] in opera apparuit *add. Augustine* [q–q] *marked for corr.* T^1*; om. ACEF and J*

custom in outward matters grumbled against Christ and his disciples, and even questioned the Lord himself: 'Why is it that John's disciples and the disciples of the Pharisees are fasting but yours are not?'[100] In examining this passage and determining the difference between virtue and exhibition of virtue, St Augustine concludes that as regards outward matters, works add nothing to merit. In his book *On the Good of Marriage* he says: 'Continence is a virtue not of the body but of the mind.[101] But the virtues of the mind are displayed sometimes in works, sometimes in natural habit, as when the virtue of martyrs has been seen in their endurance of suffering.'[102] Also: 'Patience was already in Job; the Lord knew this and gave proof of knowing it, but he made it known to men through the ordeal of Job's testing.'[103] And again: 'So that it may truly be better understood how virtue may be in natural habit though not in works, I will quote an example of which no Catholic is in doubt. That the Lord Jesus, in the truth of the flesh, was hungry and thirsty and ate and drank, no one can fail to know who is faithful to his Gospel. Yet surely the virtue of continence was as great in him as in John the Baptist? "For John came neither eating nor drinking and men said he was possessed. The Son of man came eating and drinking and they said: Look at him, a glutton and a drinker, a friend of tax gatherers and sinners!"'[104] [105] Again: 'Then, after having said those things of John and himself, he added: "And yet God's wisdom is proved right by its own children",[106] for they see that the virtue of continence ought always to exist in natural habit but is shown in practice only in appropriate times and seasons, as was the virtue of endurance in the holy martyrs. And so just as the merit of endurance is not greater in the case of Peter who suffered martyrdom than in John who did not, so John who never married wins no greater merit for continence than Abraham who fathered children, for the

[100] Matt. 9: 14.

[101] 'Continentia . . . est': cf. *Letter* 4, **14** and *Carmen ad Astralabium*, ed. Rubingh-Bosscher, *v.* 197.

[102] Augustine, *De bono coniugali*, xxi. 25 (ed. Zycha, p. 218, *l.* 23–p. 219, *l.* 3; *PL* xl. 390). Also cited in *SN* c. 130, 6 and (in part) c. 143, 16. On the reading 'in corpore' in both *SN* and here—it makes good sense in the context although Augustine wrote 'in opere' and *Muckle* followed him—see Dronke, *Women Writers of the Middle Ages*, pp. 140–3.

[103] Augustine, *De bono coniugali*, xxi. 25 (ed. Zycha, p. 219, *ll.* 6–8; *PL* xl. 390). Also cited in *SN* c. 130, 7. Cf. Job 1–2.

[104] Matt. 11: 18–19; cited also in *Rule* **92**.

[105] Augustine, *De bono coniugali*, xxi. 26 (ed. Zycha, p. 220, *ll.* 9–19; *PL* xl. 390–1). Also cited in *SN* c. 130, 8. Cf. *Sententie* **274** (ed. Luscombe, p. 142, *ll.* 3247–54; c. 34, ed. Buzzetti, p. 153, *ll.* 10–17; *PL* clxxviii.1754D).

[106] Matt. 11: 19.

illius enim celibatus et illius conubium pro distributione temporum Christo militauerunt. Sed continentiam[r] Iohannes et[s] in opere, Abraham uero in[t] solo habitu habebat. Illo itaque tempore cum et lex, dies patriarcharum subsequens, maledictum dixit[u] qui non excitaret semen in[v] Israel; et qui[w] poterat non promebat, sed tamen habebat.[107] Ex quo autem "uenit plenitudo temporis"[108] ut diceretur: "Qui potest capere, capiat";[109] qui habet, operatur; qui[x] operari noluerit, non se habere mentiatur.'[110]

24. Ex his liquide uerbis colligitur solas apud Deum merita uirtutes obtinere, et quicumque[a] uirtutibus pares sunt, quantumcumque distent[b] operibus, equaliter ab ipso[c] promereri.[d] Vnde quicumque [e]uere sunt[e] Christiani sic toti[f] circa interiorem hominem sunt occupati, ut eum[g] scilicet uirtutibus ornent ac uitiis mundent, ut[h] de exteriori nullam uel minimam assumant curam. Vnde et ipsos legimus apostolos ita rusticane et uelut inhoneste in ipso etiam Domini comitatu se habuisse, ut, uelut omnis reuerentie atque[i] honestatis obliti, cum[j] per sata transirent spicas uellere, fricare[k] et comedere[111] more puerorum non erubescerent, nec de ipsa etiam manuum ablutione, cum cibos essent[l] accepturi, sollicitos esse.[112] Qui cum a non nullis quasi de immunditia arguerentur, eos Dominus excusans, 'non lotis', inquit, 'manibus manducare, non coinquinat hominem'.[113] Vbi et statim [m]generaliter adiecit ex nullis exterioribus animam inquinari, sed ex his tantum[m] que de corde prodeunt, que sunt, inquit, cogitationes,[n] adulteria, homicidia, etc.[114] Nisi enim prius praua[o] uoluntate animus corrumpatur,[115] peccatum esse non poterit, quicquid exterius agatur in corpore. Vnde et bene ipsa quoque adulteria siue homicidia ex corde procedere dicit,[p] que et sine tactu[q] corporum perpetrantur iuxta illud: 'Qui uiderit mulierem ad [r]concupiscendum eam,[r] iam mechatus est eam[s] in corde suo',[116] et:[t]

[r] continentie *E* [s] *om. ACEF* [t] *om. CEF* [u] dicit *?A;* duxit *CF* [v] *om. BRS* [w] non *add. codd., Amb;* ne *add. J; cf. SN c. 130, 9; Problemata 42* (*PL clxxviii. 723C*) [x] quia *C*

24 [a] quibus *C* [b] distant *A before corr., BRS* [c] a Christo *A;* in Christo *CEF* [d] dicuntur *add. EF* [e–e] sunt uere *T* [f] *om. F* [g] enim hominem *C;* eum hominem *EF* [h] unde *B* [i] et *F* [j] *om. B* [k] fabricare *TAmb* [l] scilicet apostoli *add. C;* scilicet apostoli essent *E;* licet Apostoli essent *F* [m–m] *om. C* [n] malae *add. F and Vulg.* [o] parua *T but corr. to* praua *in marg. by a later hand* [p] dixit *C* [q] contactu *Amb*[1] [r–r] concupiscendam *FAmb* [s] *om. CEAmb* [t] Et *FAmb*

[107] Cf. *Letter* 7, 43 and n. 277.
[108] Gal. 4: 4.
[109] Matt. 19: 12.

celibacy of the one and the marriage of the other both fought for Christ in accordance with the difference of their times. Yet John was continent in practice as well, Abraham only as a habit. At the time after the days of the Patriarchs, when the Law declared a man to be accursed if he did not perpetuate his race in Israel, a man who could have continence did not reveal himself, but even so, he had it.[107] Afterwards "the term was completed"[108] when it could be said: "Let the man accept it who can",[109] and if he can, put it into practice; but if he does not wish to do so, he must not claim it untruthfully.'[110]

24. From these words it is clear that virtues alone win merit before God, and that those who are equal in virtue, however different in works, deserve equally of him. Consequently, those who are true Christians are wholly occupied with the inner man, so that they may adorn him with virtues and purify him of vices, but they have little or no concern for the outer man. We read that the apostles themselves were so simple and almost rough in their manner, even when in the company of the Lord, that they were apparently forgetful of respect and propriety, and when walking through the cornfields were not ashamed to pick the ears of corn and strip and eat them[111] like children. Nor were they careful about washing their hands before taking food;[112] but when they were rebuked by some for what was thought an unclean habit, the Lord made excuses for them, saying that 'to eat without first washing his hands does not defile a man'.[113] He then added the general ruling that the soul is not defiled by any outward thing but only by what proceeds from the heart—thoughts, adulteries, murders, and so on.[114] For unless the mind be first corrupted by an evil will,[115] whatever is done outwardly in the body cannot be a sin. He also rightly says that even adultery or murder proceed from the heart and can be perpetrated without bodily contact, as in the words: 'If a man looks upon a woman with a lustful eye he has already committed adultery with her in his heart',[116] and:

[110] Augustine, *De bono coniugali*, xxi. 26 and xxii. 27 (ed. Zycha, p. 221, *ll.* 10–15; p. 221, *l.* 16–p. 222, *l.* 5; *PL* xl. 390–1, 391–2). Also cited in *SN* c. 130, 9 and (in part) in *Problemata*, 42 (*PL* clxxviii. 723BC).

[111] Cf. Matt. 12: 1.

[112] Cf. Matt. 15: 2; also *Rule* **92**.

[113] Matt. 15: 20.

[114] Cf. Matt.15: 18–19. Cf. *Rule* **93**; *Problemata*, 24 (*PL* clxxviii. 709D–711A).

[115] Cf. *Rule* **81**.

[116] Matt. 5: 28. Also cited in *Ethica*, i. 15. 5 (ed. Ilgner, p. 16, *ll.* 411–14; ed. Luscombe, p. 24, *ll.* 21–3).

'Omnis qui odit fratrem suum homicida est.'[117] Et tactis uel lesis corporibus minime peraguntur, quando uidelicet per uiolentiam opprimitur aliqua uel per iustitiam coactus iudex interficit[u] reum.[118] Omnis quippe homicida, sicut scriptum est, non habet partem in regno [v]Christi et[v] Dei.[119]

25. Non itaque magnopere que fiunt sed quo animo fiant pensandum est,[120] si illi placere studemus qui cordis et renum probator est[121] et 'in abscondito uidet',[122] 'qui iudicabit occulta[a] hominum', Paulus inquit, 'secundum Euangelium meum',[123] hoc est, secundum mee predicationis doctrinam. Vnde et modica uidue oblatio que fuit duo[b] minuta, id est, quadrans,[c][124] omnium diuitum oblationibus copiosis prelata est ab illo cui dicitur: 'Bonorum meorum non eges',[125] cui magis oblatio ex offerente quam offerens placet ex oblatione, sicut scriptum est: 'Respexit Dominus ad Abel et ad munera eius',[126] ut uidelicet prius[d] deuotionem offerentis[e] inspiceret, et sic[f] ex ipso[g] donum oblatum[h] gratum haberet. Que quidem[i] animi deuotio[j] tanto maior in Deo habetur quanto in [k]exterioribus minus est animus occupatus, et tanto humilius ei deseruimus, ac magis debere[l] cogitamus, quanto de[k] exterioribus que fiant minus confidimus. Vnde et Apostolus post communem ciborum indulgentiam de qua, ut supra meminimus,[127] Thimoteo scribit, de exercitio quoque corporalis laboris adiunxit dicens: 'Exerce autem teipsum ad pietatem. Nam corporalis exercitatio [m]ad modicum[m] utilis est. Pietas autem[n] ad omnia utilis est, promissionem habens uite que nunc est et future',[128] quoniam[o] pia mentis[p] in Deum deuotio et hic ab ipso meretur

[u] interficere *Amb* [v–v] *om. Amb*

25 [a] facta *CEF* [b] de *S* [c] deo *add. CEF* [d] ad *add. B* [e] offerens *T before corr. in marg. by T*⁴ [f] se *E* [g] ipsa *Amb*¹ [h] ablatum *E* [i] est *add. BRS* [j] et *add. F* [k–k] *om. Amb.* [l] deseruire *add. CEF* [m–m] ad modum *TAmb;* ad modicum *T*¹*ACEFBRS and Vulgate* [n] aut *E* [o] Quam *F* [p] existens *add. C, Ecorr.;* domus *add. F*

---

117 1 John 3: 15.

118 Cf. *Ethica*, i. 15. 1–2 (ed. Ilgner, pp. 15–16, *ll.* 398–404; ed. Luscombe, p. 24, *ll.* 9–14).

119 Cf. 1 John 3: 15.

120 Cf. Augustine, *De sermone Domini in monte*, ii. 13. 46 (ed. Mutzenbecher, p. 137, *ll.* 1004–5; *PL* xxxiv. 1289): 'Non ergo quid quisque faciat, sed quo animo faciat considerandum est'; also *Enarrationes in Psalmos*, xxxi. 2. 4 (ed. Dekkers and Fraipont, xxxviii. 227; *PL* xxxvi. 259). Cf. *Letter* 2, 13 and *Rule* 70; *Tchr.*, v. 41, *ll.* 583–5; *Comm. Rom.*, i (i. 17, ed. Buytaert, p. 65, *ll.* 640–5) and iv (xiv. 23, ed. Buytaert, p. 306, *ll.* 324–5); *Ethica*, i. 17. 3; i. 25. 3 (ed. Ilgner, p. 18, *ll.* 471–2, p. 26, *ll.* 685–6; ed. Luscombe, p. 28, *ll.* 9–10, p. 40, *ll.* 9–

'Everyone who hates his brother is a murderer.'[117] Such acts are not necessarily committed by contact with or injury to the body, as when, for instance, a woman is violently assaulted or a judge compelled in justice to kill a man.[118] For no murderer, it is written, has a place in the Kingdom of Christ and of God.[119]

25. And so it is not so much what things are done as the mind in which they are done that we must consider,[120] if we wish to please him who tests the heart and the loins[121] and 'sees in hidden places',[122] 'who will judge the secrets of men', says Paul, 'in accordance with my gospel',[123] that is, according to the doctrine of his preaching. Consequently, the modest offering of the widow, which was two tiny coins worth a farthing,[124] was preferred to the lavish offerings of all the rich by him to whom it is said: 'You have no need of my goods',[125] and who takes pleasure in the offering because of the giver rather than in the giver because of his offering, as it is written: 'The Lord received Abel and his gift with favour',[126] that is, he looked first at the devotion of the giver and was pleased with the gift offered because of him. Such devotion of the heart is valued more highly by God the less it is concerned with outward things, and we serve him with greater humility and think more of our duty to him the less we put our trust in outward things. The Apostle too, after writing to Timothy on the subject of a general indulgence about food, as I said above,[127] went on to speak of training the body: 'Keep yourself in training for the practice of religion. The training of the body brings limited benefit, but the benefits of religion are without limit, since it holds promise not only for this life but for the life to come.'[128] For the pious devotion of the mind to God wins from him both what is

10); *Collationes* **211** (ed. Marenbon and Orlandi, p. 211; *Dialogus*, ed. Thomas, *ll.* 3225–6; *PL* clxxviii. 1677C); *Adtendite* (ed. Engels in '*Adtendite a falsis prophetis*', p. 226 *ll.* 20–1); *Sermon* 14 (*PL* clxxviii. 492A); *SN*, prologue (ed. Boyer and McKeon, p. 99).

121 Cf. Ps. 7: 10 (9); Jer. 11: 20, 17: 10, 20: 12; Rev. 2: 23; also *Letter* 4, **14**; *Ethica*, i. 25. 3 (ed. Ilgner, p. 26, *l.* 688; ed. Luscombe, p. 40, *l.* 17); *Comm. Rom.*, i. (ii. 6, ed. Buytaert, p. 78, *l.* 62), and *Sermon* 14 (*PL* clxxviii. 492A).

122 Matt. 6: 4 and 6; cited also in *Letter* 4, **14**; *Ethica*, i. 25. 3 (ed. Ilgner, p. 26, *ll.* 688–9; ed. Luscombe, p. 40, *l.* 12), and *Adtendite* (ed. Engels in '*Adtendite a falsis prophetis*', p. 226, *l.* 20). Cf. also *Comm. Rom.*, i (ii. 6, ed. Buytaert, p. 78, *l.* 62), and *Sermon* 14 (*PL* clxxviii. 492A).

123 Rom. 2: 16.

124 Cf. Mark 12: 42–4.

125 Ps. 15 (16): 2.

126 Gen. 4: 4.

127 See **22** above.

128 1 Tim. 4: 7–8.

necessaria et in futuro perpetua. Quibus quidem documentis quid aliud docemur quam Christiane sapere et cum Iacob de domesticis animalibus[q] refectionem patri prouidere, non cum Esau de siluestribus curam sumere,[129] et in exterioribus iudaizare?[130] Hinc et illud est Psalmiste: 'In me sunt, Deus, uota tua, que[r] reddam, laudationes tibi.'[131] Ad hoc quoque [s]illud adiunge[s] poeticum: 'Ne te quesiueris extra.'[132]

26. Multa sunt et innumerabilia tam secularium quam ecclesiasticorum doctorum testimonia quibus ea que fiunt[a] exterius, et[b] indifferentia uocantur, non magnopere curanda esse docemur.[133] Alioquin legis opera et seruitutis[c] eius, sicut ait Petrus,[134] importabile iugum euangelice libertati esset preferendum, et suaui iugo[135] Christi et [d]eius honeri[d] leui. Ad quod quidem suaue iugum et honus leue[e] per semet ipsum Christus nos inuitans: 'Venite', inquit, 'qui laboratis et honerati [f]estis',[136] etc.[f] Vnde et predictus Apostolus quosdam iam ad Christum conuersos, sed adhuc opera legis retineri[g] censentes[h] uehementer obiurgans, sicut in Actibus Apostolorum scriptum est, ait: 'Viri fratres, quid temptatis Deum[i] imponere iugum super ceruicem discipulorum, quod neque patres nostri neque nos portare potuimus, sed per gratiam [j]Domini Ihesu[j] credimus saluari quemadmodum et illi?'[137]

27. Et tu ipse, obsecro, non solum Christi, uerum etiam huius imitator Apostoli, discretione, sicut et nomine, sic operum precepta moderare ut[a] infirme conuenit nature, [b]et ut[b] diuine laudis plurimum uacare[c] possimus[d] officiis. Quam[e] quidem hostiam, exterioribus omnibus sacrificiis reprobatis,[f] Dominus commendans ait: 'Si esuriero,[g] non dicam tibi; meus est enim orbis terre et plenitudo eius.[h] Numquid manducabo carnes taurorum? Aut sanguinem hyrcorum potabo? Immola Deo sacrificium laudis, et redde Altissimo uota tua,

[q] animabus *B* [r] quas *Amb*[1] [s–s] adiunge illud *BRS*

26 [a] sunt *BRAmb* [b] ex *TEBRSAmb*[1] [c] seruituti *E* [d–d] oneri eius *F* [e] *om. R* [f–f] estis, et ego reficiam uos *F;* estis *Amb* [g] retinere *Amb* [h] cessantes *BR;* censcantes *S* [i] Deum *exp. E* [j–j] domini nostri ihesu christi *BF*

27 [a] et *T* [b–b] ut et *F* [c] uocare *RS* [d] possumus *E* [e] Qandam *A;* Quadam *C* [f] reprobatus *R* [g] esurireo *Amb* [h] *om. R*

[129] Cf. Gen. 27. [130] Cf. **19** above.
[131] Ps. 55 (56): 12. [132] Persius, *Satires*, i. 7.
[133] Cf. **20** above and *Rule* **97**. Also *Collationes*, **116**, **205** (ed. Marenbon and Orlandi, pp. 130–1, 206; *Dialogus*, ed. Thomas *ll.* 2026, 3162–3; *PL* clxxviii. 1652B, 1676A); *Comm.*

necessary in this life and things eternal in the life to come. By these examples are we not surely taught to think as Christians, and like Jacob to provide for our Father a meal from domestic animals and not go after wild game with Esau,[129] and act the Jew in outward things?[130] Hence the verse of the Psalmist: 'Within me, God, are your vows which I shall give back as praises.'[131] To this add the words of the poet: 'Do not look outside yourself.'[132]

26. There are many, indeed innumerable, testimonies from the learned, both secular and ecclesiastic, to teach us that we should care little for what is performed outwardly and called indifferent.[133] Otherwise the works of the Law and the insupportable yoke of its bondage, as Peter calls it,[134] would be preferable to the freedom of the Gospel and the easy yoke and light burden of Christ.[135] Christ himself invites us to this easy yoke and light burden in the words: 'Come to me, all you who labour and are burdened',[136] etc. The apostle Peter also sharply rebuked certain people who were already converted to Christ but believed they should still keep to the works of the Law, as it is recorded in the Acts of the Apostles: 'My brothers, why do you provoke God by laying on the shoulders of these converts a yoke which neither we nor our fathers were able to bear? No, we believe that it is by the grace of the Lord Jesus that we are saved, and so are they.'[137]

27. Do you then also, I beg you, who seek to imitate not only Christ but also this apostle, in discrimination as in name, modify your instructions for works to suit our weak nature, so that we can be free to devote ourselves to the offices of praising God. This is the offering which the Lord commends, rejecting all outward sacrifices, when he says: 'If I am hungry I will not tell you, for the world and all that is in it are mine. Shall I eat the flesh of your bulls or drink the blood of he-goats? Offer to God the sacrifice of thanksgiving and pay your vows to

Rom., i (ii. 6, ed. Buytaert, p. 78 *l.* 65); *Ethica*, i. 30. 1 (ed. Ilgner, p. 30 *ll.* 779–80; ed. Luscombe, p. 44 *ll.* 30–1), and Seneca, *Epist. ad Lucilium*, 118; Jerome, *Epistola* CXII *ad Augustinum*, 16 (ed. Hilberg, lv. 386; *PL* xxii. 926).

134 Cf. Acts 15: 10.

135 Cf. Matt. 11: 30.

136 Matt. 11: 28. Also cited in *Rule* **90**; *Sermon* 3 (*PL* clxxviii. 404B). Cf. *Ethica*, i. 48. 4 (ed. Ilgner, p. 47; ed. Luscombe, p. 72), and *Sermon* 5 (*PL* clxxviii. 422C). The passage continues: 'and I will give you relief'.

137 Acts 15: 7, 10–11. Also cited in *Rule* **90** and *Comm. Rom.*, ii (iv. 15, ed. Buytaert, p. 145). Cf. *Sermon* 3 (*PL* clxxviii. 404C).

et inuoca me[i] in die tribulationis; [j]et eruam te, et honorificabis me.'[j] [138]

28. Nec[a] id quidem ita loquimur ut laborem operum corporalium respuamus cum necessitas postulauerit, sed ne ista magna putemus que corpori seruiunt, et officii diuini celebrationem prepediunt,[b] presertim cum ex auctoritate apostolica id precipue deuotis indultum sit feminis ut aliene procurationis sustententur officiis magis quam de opere proprii laboris. Vnde ad Timotheum Paulus: 'Si quis fidelis habet uiduas, subministret illis, et non grauetur ecclesia ut his, que uere uidue sunt, sufficiat.'[139] Veras[c] quippe uiduas dicit quascumque Christo deuotas,[d] quibus non solum maritus mortuus est, uerum etiam[e] mundus crucifixus est[f] et ipse mundo.[140] Quas recte de stipendiis[g] Ecclesie tamquam de propriis sponsi sui redditibus sustentari conuenit.[141] Vnde et Dominus ipse matri sue procuratorem apostolum potius quam uirum eius preuidit,[h] [142] et apostoli septem diaconos, id est, Ecclesie ministros qui deuotis ministrarent feminis instituerunt.[143]

29. Scimus quidem et Apostolum Thessalonicensibus scribentem quosdam otiose uel curiose uiuentes adeo constrinxisse ut preciperet: 'Quoniam siquis non uult operari, non manducet',[144] et beatum Benedictum maxime pro otiositate uitanda opera manuum iniunxisse.[145] Sed numquid Maria otiose sedebat ut uerba Christi audiret, Martha tam ei quam Domino laborante, et de quiete sororis tamquam inuida murmurante[a] quasi que 'sola pondus diei et estus'[146] portauerit?[147] Vnde et hodie frequenter murmurare eos cernimus, qui in exterioribus laborant, cum his, qui diuinis [b]occupati sunt[b] officiis, terrena ministrant. Et sepe de his, que tyranni rapiunt, minus conqueruntur [c]quam que[c] desidiosis, ut aiunt, istis et otiosis exoluere coguntur. Quos tamen non solum uerba Christi audire, uerum etiam in his assidue legendis et decantandis occupatos considerant esse. Nec[d] attendunt non esse magnum, ut ait Apostolus,[148] si eis communicent[e]

[i] *om. B* [j–j] etc *CEF*

28 [a] Ne *ABRS* [b] impediunt *Amb*¹ [c] Vere *CEF;* uerax *S* [d] a *add. BR;* et *add. S* [e] ita *E before exp.; add. Ecorr.;* et *Amb* [f] *om. B* [g] dispendiis *TAmb;* spiendis *?C* [h] prouidit *Amb*¹

29 [a] murmurantem *E* [b–b] miste *add. and exp. T;* occupate sunt. sunt *ditto. BR* [c–c] quam que de hiis que *CE;* quam de his que *F* [d] Nec *Amb* [e] communirent *T before corr. by T*¹

the Most High. Call upon me in time of trouble and I will come to your rescue, and you shall honour me.'[138]

28. We do not speak like this with the intention of rejecting physical labour when necessity demands it, but so as not to attach importance to things which serve bodily needs and obstruct the celebration of the divine office, particularly when on apostolic authority the special concession was granted to devout women of being supported by services provided by others rather than by their own labour. Thus Paul writes to Timothy: 'If any among the faithful has widows in the family, he must support them himself: the Church must be relieved of the burden, so that it may be free to support those who are widows in the full sense.'[139] By widows in the full sense he means all women devoted to Christ, for whom not only are their husbands dead but the world is crucified and they too to the world.[140] It is right and proper that they should be supported from the funds of the Church as if from the personal resources of their husbands.[141] Hence the Lord provided his mother with an apostle to care for her instead of her own husband,[142] and the apostles appointed seven deacons, or ministers of the Church, to minister to devout women.[143]

29. We know of course that when writing to the Thessalonians the Apostle sharply rebuked certain idle busybodies with the instruction: 'A man who will not work shall not eat',[144] and that St Benedict instituted manual labour for the express purpose of preventing idleness.[145] But was not Mary sitting idle in order to listen to the words of Christ, while Martha was working for her as much as for the Lord and grumbling rather enviously about her sister's repose, as if she had to bear 'the burden and heat of the day'[146] alone?[147] Similarly today we see those who work on external things often complaining as they serve the earthly needs of those who are occupied with divine offices. Indeed, people often protest less about what tyrants seize from them than about what they are compelled to pay to those whom they call lazy and idle, although they observe them not only listening to Christ's words but also busily occupied in reading and chanting them. They do not see that it is no great matter, as the Apostle says,[148]

[138] Ps. 49 (50): 12–15.
[139] 1 Tim. 5: 16.
[140] Cf. Gal. 6: 14.
[141] Cf. *Letters* 5, 4; 7, 18 and 22.
[142] Cf. John 19: 26–7.
[143] Cf. Acts 6: 5; also *Letter* 7, 12.
[144] 2 Thess. 3: 10.
[145] Benedict, *Rule*, c. 48, 1.
[146] Matt. 20: 12.
[147] Cf. Luke 10: 39–42; also *Rule* 127.
[148] 1 Cor. 9: 11.

corporalia a quibus expectant spiritalia, nec indignum esse ut qui terrenis intendunt his, qui spiritalibus[f] occupantur, deseruiant. Hinc etenim ex ipsa quoque legis sanctione ministris ecclesie hec salubris otii libertas concessa est[g] ut tribus Leui nichil hereditatis terrene[h] perciperet quo expeditius Domino deseruiret, sed de labore aliorum decimas et oblationes susciperet.[149]

30. De abstinentia quoque ieiuniorum quam magis uitiorum quam ciborum Christiani appetunt, si quid Ecclesie[a] institutioni[b] superaddi decreueris,[c] deliberandum est,[d] et quod nobis expedit instituendum.[150]

31. Maxime uero de officiis ecclesiasticis et de ordinatione psalmorum prouidendum est ut in hoc saltem, si placet, nostram exoneres[a] infirmitatem ne, cum psalterium per ebdomadam[b] expleamus, eosdem necesse sit psalmos repeti.[c] Quam etiam[d] beatus Benedictus, [e]cum eam[e] pro uisu suo distribuisset, in aliorum quoque[f] optione[g] sua[h] id reliquit admonitio ut [i]si, cui[i] melius uideretur, aliter ipsos ordinaret,[j] [151] attendens[k] uidelicet quod per temporum successionem ecclesie decor creuerit, et que prius rude susceperat fundamentum, postmodum edificii nacta est ornamentum.

32. Illud autem pre omnibus [a]diffinire te[a] uolumus quid[b] de euangelica lectione in uigiliis[c] nocturnis nobis agendum sit.[152] Periculosum quippe nobis[d] uidetur eo tempore ad nos sacerdotes aut [e]diaconos admitti, per quos hec lectio recitetur, quas precipue ab[e] omni hominum accessu atque aspectu segregatas esse conuenit, tum[f] ut sincerius [g]Deo uacare[g] possimus, [h]tum etiam[h] ut a temptatione[i] tutiores simus.

33. Tibi nunc, domine, dum uiuis incumbit[a] instituere[b] de nobis quid in perpetuum tenendum[c] sit nobis. Tu quippe post Deum huius loci fundator, tu per Deum nostre congregationis es plantator,[153] tu cum

[f] spiritibus *BRS* [g] *om. ACFBSAmb* [h] *om. R*

30 [a] ecclesiastice *BRS* [b] constitutioni *F* [c] superaddecreueras *B* [d] *om. F*

31 [a] exoneris *S* [b] *ditto. R* [c] repleti *T before corr. by exp.* [d] et *before corr. by Ecorr* [e–e] *vacant space in B* [f] quorum *EF* [g] actione *TCEFAmb* [h] *om. BRS* [i–i] sic in *BR;* sic cui *S* [j] ipsos *add. B* [k] Attendens *Amb*

32 [a–a] te diffinire *CEF* [b] quod *F* [c] euuangeliis *T before corr. by exp.* [d] *om. Amb* [e–e] *om. C* [f] cum *R* [g–g] uacare deo *BRS* [h–h] tamen eciam *R* [i] attempcione *ES*

33 [a] incombit *TS; om. BR* [b] instruere *R* [c] tenandum *S*

if they have to make material provision for those to whom they look for things of the spirit, nor is it unbecoming for men occupied with earthly matters to serve those who are devoted to the spiritual. That is why the ministers of the Church were also granted by the sanction of the Law this salutary concession of freedom through leisure, whereby the tribe of Levi should have no patrimony in the land, the better to serve the Lord, but should receive tithes and offerings from the labour of others.[149]

30. As regards fasts, which Christians hold to be abstinence from vices rather than from food, you must consider whether anything should be added to what the Church has instituted, and order what is suitable for us.[150]

31. But it is chiefly in connection with the offices of the Church and ordering of the psalms that provision is needed, so that here at least, if you think fit, you may allow some concession to our weakness, and when we recite the psalter in full within a week it shall not be necessary to repeat the same psalms. When St Benedict divided up the week according to his view, he left instructions that others could order the psalms differently, if it seemed better to do so,[151] for he expected that with the passage of time the ceremonies of the Church would become more elaborate, and that from a rough foundation would arise a splendid edifice.

32. Above all, we want you to decide what we ought to do about reading the Gospel in the Night Office.[152] It seems to us hazardous if priests and deacons, who should perform the reading, are allowed among us at such hours, when we should be especially segregated from the approach and sight of men in order to devote ourselves more sincerely to God and to be safer from temptation.

33. It is for you then, my lord, while you live, to establish for us what we should adhere to for all time, for after God you are the founder of this place, through God you are the planter of our community,[153]

[149] Cf. Num. 18: 20–1.

[150] Cf. *Rule* **100**.

[151] Benedict, *Rule*, c. 18, 22; cf. **17** above. In his *Rule* Abelard gave no reply to this request by Heloise for guidance on the Offices and the ordering of the Psalms; see *Rule* **52–3**, **64–7**, and **74–6**. Evidence of Abelard's contributions to the Offices is discussed in the Introduction on pp. xxxvii–xxxviii above.

[152] According to Benedict, *Rule*, c. 11, in the vigils for Sunday twelve lessons should be read, four of them from the New Testament.

[153] Cf. 1 Cor. 3: 6.

Deo nostre [d]sis religionis[d] institutor.[154] Preceptorem alium post te fortassis habiture sumus, et qui[e] super alienum aliquid[f] edificet fundamentum,[155] ideoque,[g] ueremur,[h] de nobis minus futurus sollicitus uel a nobis minus audiendus, et[i] qui denique, si eque uelit, non eque possit. Loquere tu nobis, et audiemus.[156] Vale.[j]

[d–d] religionis sis *CEFBRS* [e] quid *T* [f] aliud *FAmb*[1] [g] Ideoque *EFAmb* [h] ne *add. A* [i] Et *FB* [j] valete *R*

with God you should be the instructor of our religious life.[154] After you we may perhaps have another to guide us, one who will build something upon another's foundation,[155] and so, we fear, he may be less likely to feel concern for us, or be less readily heard by us; or indeed, he may be no less willing, but less able. Speak to us, and we shall hear.[156] Farewell.

[154] Cf. *Letter* 2, **6** and note.
[155] Cf. Rom. 15: 20; *Letter* 2, **6**.
[156] 'Loquere tu nobis, et audiemus': Exod. 20: 19.

⟨EPISTOLA VII⟩

ITEM PETRI AD EAMDEM

1. Caritati[a] tue, karissima soror, de ordine[b] tue professionis tam tibi quam spiritalibus filiabus tuis sciscitanti,[c] [d]unde scilicet[d] monialium ceperit religio,[e] paucis, si potero, [g]succincteque rescribam.[f 1]

2. Monachorum siquidem siue monialium ordo a Domino nostro Ihesu Christo religionis sue formam plenissime sumpsit,[2] quamuis et ante ipsius incarnationem nonnulla[a] huius propositi tam in uiris quam in feminis precesserit inchoatio. Vnde et Ieronimus ad Rusticum[b] scribens: 'Filios', inquit, 'prophetarum quos monachos [c]legimus in Veteri Testamento',[c 3] etc. Annam quoque uiduam templo et diuino cultui[d] assiduam Euangelista commemorat, que pariter cum [e]Symeone Dominum[e] in templo suscipere et prophetia repleri meruerit.[f 4] Finis itaque Christus,[g] iusticie et omnium bonorum consummatio, in plenitudine temporis ueniens[5] ut inchoata[h] perficeret bona uel[i] exhiberet incognita, sicut utrumque sexum uocare uenerat atque redimere,[6] ita utrumque sexum [j]in uero monachatu[j] sue congregationis dignatus est adunare, ut inde tam [k]uiris quam[k] feminis[l] huius professionis daretur auctoritas, et omnibus perfectio uite proponeretur [m]quam imitarentur.[m] Ibi quippe cum apostolis ceterisque discipulis, cum matre ipsius, sanctarum legimus[n 7] conuentum mulierum que

Letter 7 *T* fos. 42rb–59ra; *A* fos. 31va–42ra; *C* fos. 191^{r}–195^{v}, 183^{r+v}, 189^{r+v}, 173^{r}–176^{v}; *E* fos. 32^{r}–40^{r}; *F* pp. 80–119; *B* fos. 29vb–40vb; *R* fos. 144va–157ra; *S* fos. 63^{r}–74^{v}; *H* fos. 11ra–12rb; *Amb*, pp. 94–129; *Amb*^{1} *variants given in the marg. of Amb; J* pp. 148–213. *Headings are found in the following witnesses*: *rubr. T;* Rescriptum ad ipsam de auctoritate (actoritate *A*) uel dignitate ordinis sanctimonialium *rubr. AS;* Heloyssae sorori charissimae Abaelardus in Christo (edita ordine 7^{a} *add. by another hand*) *F;* Comme P. Abaielart rescript a Heloyse, dont l'ordre des nonnains print son commencement, et de quele auctorité il est et quele rigle eles doivent tenir ij^{c} xxij *table in H of the* (*missing*) *contents of Dijon MS 525;* Ci rescript Pierre Abaielart a Heloys de l'auctorité ou la digneté de l'ordre des saintes nonnains *J;* EPISTOLA VII. Quae est rursum PETRI ad HELOISSAM, De origine Sanctimonialium *Amb*

1 [a] *decorated initial TBRS;* Karitati *decorated initial A; unfilled space for initial CE;* Charitati *FAmb* [b] *T* (*marked for corr.*),*ACEBRSAmb;* origine *?T*^{1}, *F, Muckle;* nessance *J* [c] siscitanti *E;* suscitanti *Amb* [d–d] scilicet unde *CEF* [e] origo *F* [f–f] succincte describam *B*

2 [a] non ullam *S* [b] Eustochium *codd., Amb* [c–c] in ueteri testamento legimus *F* [d] semper *add. CEF* [e–e] symone deum *S* [f] meruit *ACEF* [g] Christo *TACE* [h] incoacta *S* [i] et *BR* [j–j] in uero mona(chatu) *add. over eras. by T*^{3}; *eras. also in*

LETTER 7

FROM PETER TO HELOISE

1. My dearest sister, out of love you and your spiritual daughters have sought to know about the order which you profess and about the origins of the religious life of nuns. I will give, if I can, a short and succinct reply.[1]

2. The order of both monks and nuns certainly owes the form of their religion very largely to our Lord Jesus Christ,[2] though even before his incarnation there had been several previous indications of this intention amongst both women and men. So Jerome in a letter to Rusticus writes of 'the sons of the prophets who, we read, were called monks in the Old Testament',[3] etc. The Evangelist also mentions Anna, the widow who was regularly in attendance at the Temple and present at divine worship, and who equally with Simeon was found worthy to receive the Lord in the Temple and be granted the gift of prophecy.[4] Therefore, when Christ, the apogee of justice and consummation of all blessings, came in the fullness of time[5] to perfect blessings unfinished or reveal those unknown, just as he had come to summon and redeem both sexes,[6] so he thought fit to unite them both in the true monastic life of his own congregation, so that thereafter both men and women should be given authority for their profession and all have set before them a perfect way of life to imitate. In the same gospel we read[7] of a community of holy women, including

marg.; Viuere monachatu *R* [k–k] *om. BR* [l] monachis feminis *T before exp.* [m–m] postquam imitaretur *C;* potius quam imitaretur *EF* [n] sanctarum *add. F*

---

[1] For comparable salutations see *Letter* 8, the prefaces to the first book of the *Paraclete Hymnary* and to the collection of *Sermons*, and the letter of dedication which prefaces the *Expositio* of the *Hexameron*. At the end of this *Letter* (**51**) its subject is summarized again: 'de auctoritate . . . ordinis uestri, et insuper de commendatione proprie dignitatis' / 'concerning the authority for your order, and also in commendation of its special position'.

[2] Cf. *Institutiones nostre*, i, p. 9: 'Institutiones nostre sumunt exordium a doctrina Christi'/'our observance is based on the teaching of Christ' (ed. Waddell, p. 9; *PL* clxxviii. 313C, where 'Instructiones' is printed in place of 'Institutiones').

[3] Jerome, *Epistola* CXXV *ad Rusticum monachum*, 7 (ed. Hilberg, lvi. 125, *ll.* 9–10; *PL* xxii. 1076); 4 Kgs. (2 Kgs.) 6: 1. Cf. *Letter* 1, **26** and note 88.

[4] Cf. Luke 2: 25–38; also **17** below.

[5] Cf. Gal. 4: 4 and *Sermon* 5 (*PL* clxxviii. 418BC).

[6] Cf. *Hymn* 88 (Szövérffy 124), *De sanctis mulieribus*, 1, I.

[7] Cf. Luke 8: 1–3; Acts 1: 14, 2: 44–5.

scilicet seculo abrenuntiantes omnemque proprietatem abdicantes[o] ut solum possiderent Christum, sicut scriptum est: 'Dominus pars hereditatis mee',[8] deuote illud compleuerunt quo omnes, secundum regulam a Domino traditam, conuersi a[p] seculo ad huius uite communitatem initiantur.[q] 'Nisi quis renuntiauerit omnibus que possidet, non potest meus [r]esse discipulus.'[r] [9]

3. Quam deuote autem Christum he beatissime mulieres ac uere moniales sequute fuerint, quantamque gratiam et honorem deuotioni earum tam[a] ipse Christus quam postmodum apostoli exhibuerint, sacre diligenter historie continent. Legimus in euuangelio[b] murmurantem Phariseum, qui hospitio Dominum susceperat, ab ipso esse correctum,[c] et peccatricis mulieris obsequium hospitio eius longe[d] esse prelatum.[10] Legimus[11] et, Lazaro iam resuscitato cum ceteris discumbente, Martham sororem eius solam mensis ministrare, et Mariam copiosi[e] libram unguenti pedibus dominicis infundere, propriisque capillis ipsos[f] extergere,[g] huiusque copiosi[h] unguenti odore domum ipsam impletam[i] fuisse, ac de precio ipsius, quia tam inaniter consumi uideretur, Iudam in concupiscentiam ductum et discipulos indignatos esse.[12] Satagente itaque Martha de cibis, Maria disponit[j] de unguentis, et quem illa reficit interius, hec lassatum fouet[k] exterius. Nec nisi feminas Domino ministrasse Scriptura commemorat euuangelica, que proprias etiam facultates in cotidianam eius alimoniam dicarant,[l] et ei precipue huius uite necessaria procurabant.[m] [13] Ipse discipulis in mensa,[14] ipse in ablutione pedum humillimum se ministrum exhibebat.[15] A nullo uero[n] discipulorum uel etiam uirorum hoc eum suscepisse nouimus obsequium,[16] sed solas, ut diximus, feminas in his uel ceteris humanitatis obsequiis ministerium impendisse. Et[o] sicut in illo Marthe, ita in isto nouimus

[o] abhortantes *R* [p] *om. Amb* [q] quietem inuitantur *F* [r–r] discipulus esse *BRS*

3 [a] causa *E* [b] euuangeliis *B;* euangelium *R* [c] correptum *FS, Muckle* [d] *om. CEF* [e] pretiosi *F; cf. John 12: 3* [f] pedes *superscr. add. E* [g] tergere *BR* [h] pretiosi *F; cf. John 12: 3* [i] repletam *BR* [j] disposuit *Amb* [k] refouet *Amb* [l] dicarent *RS* [m] ministrabant *CEF* [n] *om. R* [o] ut *CEF*

[8] Ps. 15 (16): 5. [9] Luke 14: 33.

[10] Luke 7: 36–47. Cf. **6** and **50** below and *Letter* 1, **67**; *Hymn* 97 (Szövérffy 129), *De sancta Maria Magdalena*, 2, III; *Sermon* 11 (*PL* clxxviii. 462C–463C).

[11] John 12: 1–6. Cf. Matt. 26: 6–9; Mark 14: 3–5; also *Sermon* 11 (*PL* clxxviii. 455AB, 462C–463C). Philip the Chancellor (chancellor of Notre Dame, Paris, d. 1236) remarked in

Christ's own mother, who along with the apostles and the other disciples renounced the world and gave up all property in order to possess Christ alone, as it is written: 'The Lord is the share of my inheritance.'[8] They devoutly fulfilled the duty whereby, according to the rule first laid down by the Lord, all renounce the world to be admitted to the community of this life: 'Unless a man takes leave of his possessions he cannot be a disciple of mine.'[9]

3. The devotion with which these women of great holiness, who were true nuns, followed Christ, and the favour and honour Christ himself and subsequently the apostles showed to their devotion are carefully recorded in the sacred Scriptures. We read in the gospel that when the Pharisee, who had hospitably received the Lord, started to complain he was rebuked by him, and the service of the woman who was a sinner was greatly preferred to his hospitality.[10] We read too[11] how, when Lazarus had been raised from the dead and was sitting with the rest, his sister Martha served the tables alone, while Mary poured a pound of costly ointment over the Lord' s feet and wiped them with her hair, until the whole house was filled with the ointment's fragrance. At this apparently useless expenditure of the money it cost, Judas was filled with greedy desire and the disciples were indignant.[12] So, while Martha busied herself with the meal and Mary poured out her ointments, the former restored the inner man and the latter refreshed the outer in his weariness. Nor does the Gospel record that the Lord was served by any save women, who even assigned their own possessions to his daily maintenance and provided him especially with the necessities of this life.[13] He himself performed the humblest services for his disciples at table[14] and in washing their feet,[15] but we know that he accepted such attention from none of them, nor indeed from any man.[16] Only women, as we said, did service in these and all other kindly attentions. And just as we know of Martha's service at table, so we know of Mary's service, in

a sermon that Abelard, also in a sermon, commended the humility shown in anointing feet, contrasting this with adulation shown in anointing the head: 'Hii sunt personarum acceptiores, maioribus (maroribus *in the edition*) adulantes, quos magister Petrus Abalardus confundit in sermone suo dum capam suam purpuream exspolians adorauit'; ed. in N. Bériou, 'La Madeleine dans les Sermons parisiens du XIIIe siècle', in *Mélanges de l'École française de Rome. Moyen Âge*, 104 (1992), p. 317. Professor Robert E. Lerner kindly showed this passage to me. In *Sermon* 11 Abelard does not make this comment.

[12] Cf. **6** below.

[13] Cf. Luke 8: 3; also **10** below and *Letter* 1, **67**.

[14] Cf. Luke 22: 27.

[15] Cf. John 13: 5.

[16] Cf. *Sermon* 11 (*PL* clxxviii. 455CD).

obsequium Marie, que quidem in hoc exhibendo tanto fuit deuotior quanto [p]ante fuerat[p] criminosior. Dominus, aqua[q] in peluim missa,[r] illius ablutionis peregit officium,[17] hoc uero ipsa ei lacrimis intime conpunctionis, non [s]exteriori aqua,[s] exhibuit.[18] Ablutos discipulorum pedes linteo Dominus extersit,[19] hec pro linteo capillis[t] usa est.[20] Fomenta unguentorum insuper addidit, que nequaquam Dominum adhibuisse[u] legimus.

4. Quis etiam ignoret mulierem in tantum de ipsius gratia presumpsisse, ut capud quoque eius superfuso delibuerit ungento?[a] [21] Quod quidem [b]ungentum non de alabastro extractum, sed fracto alabastro memoratur effusum,[22] ut nimie deuotionis uehemens exprimeretur desiderium[b] que[c] ad nullum[d] ulterius usum illud reseruandum censebat, quo in tanto usa sit obsequio. In quo etiam ipsum iam unctionis defectum[e] factis[f] ipsis exhibet quem antea Daniel futurum predixerat, postquam uidelicet inungeretur[g] sanctus sanctorum.[23] Ecce enim sanctum sanctorum mulier inungit, et eum pariter hunc esse quem credit,[h] et quem uerbis Propheta presignauerat, factis ipsa proclamat. Que est ista, queso, Domini benignitas, aut que mulierum dignitas, ut tam caput quam pedes suos ipse nonnisi feminis preberet[i] inungendos? Que est ista, obsecro, infirmioris sexus prerogatiua ut summum Christum, omnibus sancti Spiritus ungentis ab ipsa eius conceptione delibutum,[24] mulier quoque inungeret et, quasi corporalibus sacramentis eum in regem et sacerdotem consecrans, Christum, id est, unctum corporaliter ipsum efficeret?[j] [25]

5. [a]Scimus primum a patriarcha Iacob in typum Domini[b] lapidem unctum fuisse,[26] et postmodum regum siue sacerdotum unctiones, seu quelibet unctionum sacramenta nonnisi uiris celebrare permissum est, licet baptizare nonnumquam mulieres presumant. Lapidem olim patriarcha,[c] templum nunc et altare pontifex[d] oleo sanctificat. Viri itaque sacramenta figuris inprimunt. Mulier uero in ipsam[e] operata

[p–p] fuerat ante *BRS* [q] aquam *TC* [r] ipsa *T* [s–s] exteriorem aquam *F* [t] capitis *add. R* [u] exibuisse *CE;* exhibuisse *F*

4 [a] unguentorum *B* [b–b] *T*[3] *over eras.; eras. also in marg.* [c] quod *CE* [d] multum *Amb* [e] defecit *S;* effectum *Muckle* [f] *om. R* [g] vngeretur *Amb* [h] credidit *CEF* [i] prebent *R* [j] efficeretur *S*

5 [a] *beginning of lacuna in CEF that ends in* **6** [b] deum *S* [c] pontifex *add. B* [d] *om. B* [e] ipsa *S*

[17] Cf. John 13: 5.
[18] Cf. Luke 7: 38.
[19] Cf. John 13: 5.
[20] Cf. Luke 7: 38; John 12: 3.

performing which she showed greater devotion having been the more sinful before. The Lord performed his duty of washing feet with water poured into a basin,[17] but she did the same for him, not with water from an external source but with the tears of deepest remorse.[18] When he had washed the disciples' feet the Lord dried them with a towel,[19] but instead of a towel she used her hair.[20] She then went on to apply ointments, but nowhere do we read that the Lord made use of them.

4. It is, moreover, generally known that the woman was so confident of his favour that she anointed his head too with ointment poured over it.[21] This was not taken from a bottle, but is said to have been poured out when the bottle was broken,[22] so that she could give expression to her passionate longing for a supreme act of devotion, judging that what had been used for so great a service should not be kept for any further use. The effect of this anointing was to reveal in actual deeds who it was—the Holy of Holies—whose anointing Daniel had earlier predicted.[23] See how a woman anoints the Holy of Holies, and by her deed proclaims him to be both the one in whom she believed and him whom the prophet had foretold in words. Tell me, what is this kind favour of the Lord or the high status of women which made him offer his head as well as his feet for anointing to none but women? What, pray, is that privilege of the weaker sex whereby a mere woman should anoint the supreme Christ who was already steeped in all the unguents of the Holy Spirit from the hour of his conception,[24] and as if consecrating him king and priest with bodily sacraments should make him in the body the Christ, that is, the Anointed?[25]

5. We know that a stone was first anointed as a symbol of the Lord by the patriarch Jacob,[26] and that the later anointings of kings or priests were permitted only to men to perform, though women might sometimes presume to baptize. As the patriarch in the past sanctified a stone by pouring oil on it, so the bishop today sanctifies church and altar. Thus men perform the sacraments on symbols, but a woman

[21] Cf. Matt. 26: 7; Mark 14: 3. In *SN* c. 105 ('Quod eadem Maria tam caput Domini quam pedes unxerit et contra') Abelard collects the texts in the Gospels which suggest that either one Mary or two anointed the head and the feet of Jesus.

[22] Cf. Mark 14: 3.

[23] Cf. Dan. 9: 24–6.

[24] Cf. Isa. 11: 2–3; also Amos 6: 6 ('optimo unguento delibuti').

[25] Cf. *Sermon* 11 (*PL* clxxviii. 455C); *Hymn* 91 (Szövérffy 127), *De sanctis mulieribus* 4, II; *SN* c. 74, 'Quod Christus corporaliter quoque unctus fuisse legatur et contra.'

[26] Gen. 28: 18. Cf. *Sermon* 28 *de dedicatione ecclesiae* (*PL* clxxviii. 551B–555A).

est ueritate, sicut et ipsa protestatur Veritas, dicens:[f] 'Opus bonum operata est in me.'[27] Christus ipse a muliere, Christiani a uiris inunguntur—capud ipsum, scilicet, a[g] femina, membra a uiris. Bene autem effudisse unguentum non stillasse super capud eius mulier memoratur,[28] secundum quod de ipso sponsa in Canticis precinit, dicens: 'Ungentum effusum[h] nomen tuum.'[29] Huius quoque ungenti copiam per illud quod a[i] capite usque ad horam uestimenti defluit[j] Psalmista[k] mistice prefigurat[l] dicens: 'Sicut ungentum in capite, quod descendit in barbam, barbam Aaron, quod[m] descendit in oram uestimenti eius.'[30]

6. Trinam Dauid unctionem,[a] sicut et Ieronimus in Psalmo sexto et uicesimo meminit,[31] accepisse legimus, trinam et Christum siue Christianos. Pedes quippe Domini siue capud muliebre susceperunt ungentum. Mortuum uero ipsum Ioseph ab Arimathia et Nichodemus, sicut refert Iohannes,[32] cum aromatibus sepelierunt. Christiani quoque trina sanctificantur unctione, quarum una fit in baptismo, altera in confirmatione, tercia uero infirmorum est. Perpende itaque[b] mulieris dignitatem, a qua[c] uiuens Christus bis inunctus, tam in[d] pedibus scilicet quam in capite,[33] regis et sacerdotis suscepit sacramenta. Myrre uero et aloes ungentum, quod ad conseruanda corpora mortuorum adhibetur,[34] ipsius Dominici corporis incorruptionem futuram presignabat, quam etiam quilibet electi in resurrectione sunt adepturi.[ef] [g]Priora autem mulieris[g] ungenta singularem eius tam regni quam sacerdotii demonstrant dignitatem, unctio quidem[h] capitis superiorem, pedum uero[i] inferiorem. Ecce regis[j] etiam[k] sacramentum [l]a muliere suscipit,[m] qui tamen oblatum a uiris sibi regnum suscipere respuit, et ipsis eum in regem rapere uolentibus aufugit.[35] Celestis non terreni regis mulier sacramentum peragit;[l] eius, inquam, qui de semetipso postmodum ait: 'Regnum meum non est de hoc mundo.'[36] Gloriantur episcopi cum, aplaudentibus populis, terrenos inungunt reges, cum mortales consecrant

[f] dominus *S* [g] e *BR* [h] est *add. BR* [i] in *S* [j] defuit *T;* defluxit *Amb;* defluit *Amb*[1] [k] psalmis *T but* T^4 *adds* u *over the letter* i *and* T^1 *adds* t; psamis *?R;* psalmus *S* [l] prefigurauit *A* [m] Quod *TAR*

6 [a] illo cum dicitur *R* [b] *om. B* [c] aqua *T* [d] *om. A* [e] *end of lacuna in CEF beginning in* 5 [f] adepti *Amb;* adepturi *Amb*[1] [g–g] hec ergo huius mulieris *CEF;* Priora autem mulieres *Amb* [h] quidam *S* [i] *om. F* [j] rex; *?C, EFAmb*[1] [k] *om. C* [l–l] *ditto. R* [m] suscepit *BR*

---

[27] Matt. 26: 10; Mark 14: 6.
[28] Matt. 26: 7; Mark 14: 3.
[29] S. of S. 1: 2.
[30] Ps. 132 (133): 2; cf. Exod. 30: 30.

did this for the very truth, as the Truth itself bears witness, saying: 'It is a good work she has done for me.'[27] Christ himself was anointed by a woman as Christians are by men; that is to say, the head itself by a woman, the members by men. And that the woman is said to have done well in pouring out the ointment and not trickling it over his head[28] accords with what the Bride says of him in Canticles: 'Your name is ointment poured out.'[29] The full flow of this oil is also prefigured in a mystical way by the Psalmist when he speaks of 'fragrant oil poured upon the head and running down to the beard, down Aaron's beard to the collar of his robes'.[30]

6. We read that David received a threefold anointing, as Jerome notes in his *Commentary* on the twenty-sixth Psalm,[31] and threefold too is that of Christ and Christians. The feet and head of the Lord received oil from a woman, but his dead body was buried with spices by Joseph of Arimathaea and Nicodemus, as John relates.[32] Christians too receive a threefold sacrament of anointing, one at baptism, a second at confirmation, a third on their sick bed. Think then of the woman's privileged position, for it was by her that Christ was twice anointed in his lifetime, on both feet and head,[33] and received the sacraments of king and priest. The ointment of myrrh and aloes, which is used to preserve the bodies of the dead,[34] signified that the body of the Lord would be free from corruption, and this will be granted also to the chosen at the resurrection. But the earlier ointments of the woman indicate the dignity of his kingship and priesthood, the anointing of the head showing the higher, of the feet the lower status. See then how he accepted the sacrament of kingship from a woman, though he refused to accept the kingdom offered him by men and fled from those who wished to take him by force and make him king.[35] The woman performed the sacrament of a heavenly, not an earthly, king for him who later said of himself: 'My kingdom is not of this world.'[36] Bishops feel pride when they anoint earthly kings before an applauding populace, when clad in magnificent vestments embroidered with

[31] Jerome, *Commentarioli in Psalmos*, xxvi. 1 (ed. Morin, p. 201). Cf. Ps.- Jerome, *Breuiarium in Psalmos*, *PL* xxvi. 948. For the three anointings of David see 1 Kgs. (1 Sam.) 16: 13, 2 Kgs. (2 Sam.) 2: 4, and 5: 3.

[32] John 19: 38–40.

[33] Cf. Luke 7: 38.

[34] Cf. Ambrose, *Expositio euangelii secundum Lucam*, ii. 44 (ed. Adriaen, p. 51; ed. Schenkl, p. 66; *PL* xv. 1569).

[35] Cf. John 6: 15.

[36] John 18: 36.

sacerdotes, splendidis et inauratis uestibus adornati. Et sepe[n] his benedicunt quibus Dominus maledicit.[o] Humilis mulier, non mutato habitu, non preparato cultu, ipsis quoque indignantibus apostolis, hec[p] in Christo sacramenta peragit, non prelationis officio, sed deuotionis[q] merito. O magnam fidei constantiam! O inestimabilem caritatis[r] ardorem,[s] que 'omnia credit, omnia sperat, omnia sustinet'![37] [t]Murmurat Phariseus dum[u] a peccatrice [v]pedes dominici[v] inunguntur.[38] Indignantur patenter[w] apostoli quod de capite quoque mulier presumpserit.[39] Perseuerat ubique[x] mulieris fides immota, de benignitate Domini[y] confisa, nec ei in utroque dominice commendationis desunt suffragia. Cuius quidem ungenta quam accepta, quam grata Dominus habuerit, ipsemet[z] profitetur cum sibi hec reseruari postulans indignanti Iude dixerit:[a] 'Sine illam ut in die sepulture mee seruet illud.'[40] Ac si diceret: Ne repellas hoc eius obsequium a uiuo, ne deuotionis eius exhibitionem in hac quoque re auferas defuncto.

7. Certum quippe est sepulture quoque dominice sanctas mulieres aromata parasse, quod tunc ista utique minus satageret, si nunc repulsa uerecundiam[a] sustinuisset.[b] [c]Qui etiam quasi [d]de[c] tanta mulieris presumptione discipulis indignantibus [e]et, ut Marcus meminit,[41] in eam frementibus,[e] cum eos mitissimis[d] fregisset responsis, in tantum hoc extulit beneficium ut ipsum Euuangelio inserendum[f] esse censeret, et cum ipso pariter ubique predicandum esse prediceret, in memoriam, scilicet, et laudem mulieris que id fecerit, in quo[g] non mediocris arguebatur presumptionis.[42] Quod nequaquam de aliis quarumcumque personarum obsequiis auctoritate dominica[h] sic commendatum[i] esse legimus[j] atque sancitum. Qui etiam[k] [l]uidue pauperis[l] elemosinam omnibus [m]templi preferens[m] oblationibus, quam accepta sit ei feminarum deuotio diligenter ostendit.[43]

[n] *om. BR* [o] maledixit *F* [p] *om. CEF;* hoc *S* [q] delationis *CEAmb;* dilectionis *F;* dilationis *F in marg.;* dilectionis. Par(acletensi) *Cod(ice)* deuotionis *Amb*[1] [r] caritatem *E;* charitatem *F* [s] *om. CEF* [t] beginning of lacuna in CEF to 7 [u] *om. BR* [v–v] dominici pedes *AR* [w] pariter *S* [x] vtique *Amb*[1] [y] *om. R* [z] *om. B* [a] direxit *T;* dix(it?) *T*[1]*;* dixit *Amb*

7 [a] uerecundia *S* [b] *end of lacuna in CEF beginning in* 6 [c–c] de qua quidem *CEF* [d–d] de (qua quidem *add.*) . . . mitissimis *ditto. C* [e–e] *om. CEF* [f] miserendum *T before corr. to* inserendum *by a later hand in marg.;* miserandum *S* [g] *om. R* [h] domini *R* [i] commandatum *S* [j] benignius *B* [k] Qui d(?) *C;* Quiderima *E* [l–l] pauperis uidue *BRS* [m–m] preferens templi *CEF*

gold they consecrate mortal priests; and often they give their blessing to those whom Lord curses. The humble woman, with no change of garment and no prepared ritual, and in the face also of the indignation of the apostles, performed these sacraments on Christ not by virtue of priestly office but as a service of devotion. Such great constancy of faith, such inestimable fervour of love, 'which in all things is ready to trust, to hope and to endure'![37] The Pharisee complained when the Lord's feet were anointed by a sinner.[38] The apostles did not hide their indignation that a woman should presume to do the same to his head as well.[39] But in each situation her faith remained unmoved, trusting in the Lord's kind favour, and on both occasions the Lord's approval did not fail to support her. How acceptable and pleasing to the Lord were her ointments he himself declared when he required them to be reserved for himself, and answered Judas, who spoke out in indignation: 'Leave her alone. Let her keep it for the day of my burial.'[40] It was as if he were saying: Do not stop her serving the living man lest you take away the display of her devotion to the dead as well.

7. It is, of course, quite true that holy women prepared spices for the Lord's burial, which that woman would have been less eager to do had she now been pushed aside and put to shame. And when the disciples were indignant that the woman should have presumed too much and, as Mark relates,[41] spoke angrily against her, he first checked them with soft answers and then so highly extolled her service that he thought it should be inserted in the Gospel and preached wherever the Gospel was preached, as a memorial and a tribute to the woman who had done what had incurred the charge of no mean presumption.[42] Nowhere do we read of the services of any other persons whatsoever receiving such authority and sanction from the Lord. When, moreover, he preferred the poor widow's alms to all the offerings of the Temple, his concern was to show how acceptable he found the devotion of women.[43]

[37] 1 Cor. 13: 7. Cf. **10** below.
[38] Cf. Luke 7: 39. Cf. **3** above, **50** below and *Letter* 1, **67**.
[39] Cf. Matt. 26: 8; Mark 14: 4, and **3** above.
[40] John 12: 7.
[41] Mark 14: 4.
[42] Cf. Mark 14: 9 and the antiphon in the *Breviary of the Paraclete* on Tuesday in Holy Week (*Bre* IIIA, ed. Waddell, p. 127).
[43] Cf. Mark 12: 41–4; Luke 21: 1–4.

8. [a]Ausus quidem est Petrus se ipsum et coapostolos suos pro Christo omnia reliquisse profiteri,[44] et Zaccheus, desideratum Domini aduentum suscipiens, dimidium bonorum suorum pauperibus[b] largitur, et in quadruplum, si quid defraudauit, restituit.[45] Et multi alii maiores in Christo seu pro Christo fecerunt expensas et longe preciosiora in obsequium obtulerunt diuinum[c] uel pro Christo reliquerunt, nec [d]ita tamen[d] dominice[e] commendationis[f] laudem adepti sunt sicut[g] femine.

9. Quarum quidem deuotio quanta semper erga eum extiterit, ipse quoque dominice uite exitus patenter insinuat. He quippe, ipso apostolorum principe negante et dilecto Domini fugiente[a] uel ceteris dispersis apostolis,[46] intrepide perstiterunt, nec eas a Christo, uel in passione uel in morte, formido aliqua uel desperatio separare potuit, ut[b] eis specialiter[c] illud[d] Apostoli congruere uideatur: 'Quis nos separabit a caritate Dei? tribulatio? an angustia?' etc.[e][47] Vnde Matheus, cum de se pariter et ceteris retulisset: 'Tunc discipuli omnes, relicto eo, fugerunt',[48] perseuerantiam postmodum supposuit mulierum, que ipsi etiam crucifixo quantum permittebatur adsistebant. 'Erant', inquit, 'ibi mulieres multe a longe que sequute fuerant Ihesum a Galilea, ministrantes ei',[49] etc.[f] Quas denique ipsius quoque sepulchro immobiliter adherentes, idem diligenter euuangelista describit, dicens: 'Erant autem Maria Magdalene et altera Maria sedentes contra sepulchrum.'[50] De quibus etiam mulieribus Marchus commemorans ait: 'Erant autem et mulieres de longe aspicientes, inter quas erat Maria[g] Magdalene, et Maria Iacobi minoris et Ioseph mater, et Salome. Et[h] cum esset in Galilea sequebantur[i] eum et[j] ministrabant ei, et alie multe que simul cum eo ascenderant Iherosolimam.'[51] Stetisse autem iuxta crucem et crucifixo se etiam astitisse Iohannes, qui prius aufugerat,[k] narrat, sed perseuerantiam premittit mulierum quasi earum[l] exemplo animatus esset ac reuocatus. 'Stabant',[m] inquit, 'iuxta crucem Ihesu mater eius et soror matris eius, Maria Cleophe, et Maria Magdalene. Cum uidisset ergo[n] Ihesus matrem et discipulum stantem',[52] etc.

8 [a] *beginning of long lacuna in CEF which ends in 11 below* [b] domini *add. BR* [c] dimidium *BR* [d–d] *add. over eras. T*[3]*; eras. also in marg.* [e] domini *A* [f] commandacionis *S* [g] *om. A*

9 [a] fugiante *S* [b] Vt *Amb* [c] spiritualiter *R* [d] *om. B* [e] *om. Amb* [f] *om. Amb* [g] maria *AB; om. TRSAmb* [h] Que *BRS* [i] subsequebantur *A* [j] ut *B* [k] aufregerat *R;* aufegerat *S* [l] eorum *R* [m] autem *add. ABRS* [n] igitur *R*

8. Peter was indeed so bold as to boast that he and his fellow apostles had left everything for Christ.[44] And when Zacchaeus received the Lord on his longed-for visit he bestowed half his possessions on the poor and, if he had gained anything by fraud, he repaid it four times over.[45] Many others too went to greater expense on Christ or for Christ or offered far greater riches in his service or relinquished them for Christ, yet they did not win praise and commendation from the Lord as the women did.

9. How great the devotion of the women had always been to him was clearly shown in his death. For when the leader of the apostles denied him and the apostle whom the Lord loved fled and the rest scattered,[46] the women stood firm and fearless, nor could any dread or desperation separate them from Christ either in his suffering or at his death; so that to them especially the words of the Apostle seem to apply: 'Who shall separate us from the love of Christ? Can affliction or hardship?'[47] etc. Thus when Matthew had related of himself and the others: 'Then all the disciples forsook him and fled',[48] he went on to speak of the constancy of the women who supported the Lord at his crucifixion as far as they were permitted to do. 'A number of women', he says, 'were also present watching from a distance; they had followed Jesus from Galilee and waited on him',[49] etc. The same evangelist describes how they also remained without moving by his sepulchre: 'Mary Magdalene was there and the other Mary, sitting opposite the grave.'[50] Mark also mentions these women: 'A number of women were also present, watching from a distance. Among them were Mary of Magdala, Mary the mother of James the younger and of Joseph, and Salome, who had all followed him and waited on him when he was in Galilee, and there were several others who had come up to Jerusalem with him.'[51] John, who had previously fled, tells how he stood by the cross and stayed with the crucified Christ, but he first speaks of the constancy of the women, as if he had been stirred and called back by their example: 'Near the cross of Jesus stood his mother and his mother's sister, Mary of Clopas and Mary of Magdala. So, when Jesus saw his mother and the disciple standing by',[52] etc.

[44] Cf. Matt. 19: 27; Mark 10: 28; Luke 18: 28. [45] Cf. Luke 19: 2–8.
[46] Cf. Matt. 26: 56, 69–75; Mark 14: 50, 66–72; Luke 22: 54–62; John 18: 15–17, 25–7.
[47] Rom. 8: 35. [48] Matt. 26: 56. [49] Matt. 27: 55.
[50] Matt. 27: 61; cf. the antiphon in the *Breviary of the Paraclete* for Vespers on Holy Friday and None on Holy Saturday (*Bre* IIIA, ed. Waddell, pp. 135, 138).
[51] Mark 15: 40–1.
[52] John 19: 25–6; cf. *Sermon* 11 (*PL* clxxviii. 478AB). On Mary of Clopas see Bauckham, *Gospel Women*, pp. 203–23.

10. Hanc autem sanctarum constantiam mulierum et discipulorum defectum longe ante beatus Iob in persona Domini prophetauit, dicens: 'Pelli mee, consumptibus[a] carnibus,[b] adhesit os meum, et derelicta sunt[c] tantummodo labia circa dentes meos.'[53] In osse quippe, quod carnem et pellem sustentat et gestat, fortitudo est corporis.[54] In corpore igitur Christi, quod est Ecclesia, os ipsius dicitur[d] Christiane fidei stabile fundamentum siue feruor ille caritatis de quo canitur: 'Aque multe non poterunt extinguere caritatem',[55] etc.[e] De quo et Apostolus: 'Omnia', inquit, 'suffert, omnia credit, omnia sperat, omnia sustinet.'[56] Caro autem in corpore pars interior[f] est et pellis exterior. Apostoli ergo interiori [g]anime cibo[g] predicando intendentes et mulieres corporis necessaria procurantes carni comparantur et pelli. Cum itaque carnes consumerentur, os Christi adhesit pelli, quia, scandalizatis in passione Domini apostolis, et de morte ipsius desperatis, sanctarum deuotio feminarum perstitit immobilis, et ab osse Christi minime recessit, quia fidei uel[h] spei uel caritatis constantiam in tantum retinuit, ut nec a mortuo mente disiungerentur aut corpore. Sunt et uiri naturaliter tam mente quam corpore [i]feminis fortiores.[i] Vnde et merito per carnem, que uicinior est ossi, uirilis natura, per pellem muliebris infirmitas designatur. Ipsi[j] quoque apostoli, quorum est reprehendendo lapsus aliorum mordere, dentes Domini dicuntur.[57] Quibus tantummodo labia, id est, uerba potius quam facta, remanserunt,[k] cum iam desperati de Christo magis loquerentur quam pro Christo quid operarentur. Tales profecto illi erant[l] discipuli quibus in castellum Emaus euntibus et loquentibus adinuicem de his omnibus que acciderant ipse[m] apparuit, et eorum desperationem correxit.[58] Quid denique Petrus uel ceteri discipulorum preter uerba tunc habuerunt cum ad dominicam uentum esset passionem, et ipse Dominus futurum eis de passione sua scandalum predixisset? 'Et si omnes', inquit Petrus, 'scandalizati fuerint in te, ego numquam [n]scandalizabor.'[59] Et iterum:[n] 'Etiam si oportuerit me mori tecum, non te negabo. Similiter et omnes discipuli dixerunt.'[60] Dixerunt, inquam, potius quam fecerunt. Ille[o]

10 [a] consumptis *BRS* [b] *om. S* [c] *om. B* [d] dixit *TAmb* [e] *om. Amb* [f] exterior *S* [g–g] cybo anime *A* [h] *om. ABRS* [i–i] fortiores feminis *B* [j] Illi *R* [k] remanserunt *TR;* remanserant *S* [l] apostoli *add. but exp. T* [m] ipsi *Amb* [n–n] scandalizabo etc *B;* scandalizabor etc. Et iterum *S* [o] enim *add. Amb*

[53] Job 19: 20. Abelard's commentary on this verse is largely based on Gregory the Great, *Moralia in Iob*, xliv. 57–8 (ed. Adriaen, cxliiiA, pp. 732–3; *PL* clxxv. 1068–9).

[54] Cf. *Letter* 5, 5.

10. This constancy of the holy women and the defection of the disciples had long before been prophesied by the blessed Job in the person of the Lord who said: 'My bone sticks to my skin as my flesh rots and my lips are wasted around my teeth.'[53] For the strength of the body rests in the bone which sustains and supports flesh and skin.[54] Thus in Christ's body, which is the Church, the firm foundation of Christian faith is said to be his bone, as is that fire of love celebrated in verse: 'Many waters cannot quench love',[55] etc. The Apostle also says of love that 'in all things it is ready to accept, to trust, to hope and to endure'.[56] The flesh is the inner part of the body, the skin the outer, and so the apostles whose concern is to preach with the inner food of the soul and the women who provide necessities for the body are compared with flesh and skin. Thus, when the flesh of Christ was consumed, bone adhered to skin, for the apostles lost faith during the Lord's suffering and lost hope at his death, but the devotion of the holy women stood firm and did not shrink at all from the bone of Christ, because it retained such constancy in faith, hope, and love that the women would not be parted from the dead Christ either in mind or in body. Men are naturally stronger than women in mind and body, and so man's nature is properly indicated by the flesh which is nearer the bone, and woman's weakness by the skin. The apostles themselves whose duty is to bite by rebuking the failings of others are called Christ's teeth.[57] They were left only with lips, that is, with words rather than deeds, when in their despair they spoke of Christ instead of acting on his behalf. Such indeed were the disciples who, on their way to the village of Emmaus, were talking among themselves of all that had happened, when the Lord himself appeared and rebuked them for losing hope.[58] And what had Peter or the rest of the disciples to show except words, when the hour of the Lord's suffering had come, and the Lord himself had foretold that they would lose faith on account of his suffering? 'Though all lose faith in you', said Peter, 'I will never lose faith.'[59] And again: 'Even if I must die with you, I will never disown you. And all the disciples said the same.'[60] Those were just words, I say, not deeds. The foremost and

[55] S. of S. 8: 7. Also cited in *Sermon* 18 (*PL* clxxviii. 503B); cf. *Hymn* 93 (Szövérffy 121), *De uirginibus* 2, III.

[56] 1 Cor. 13: 7. Cf. **6** above and *Sermon* 18 (*PL* clxxviii. 503AB).

[57] Cf. Mic. 3: 5.

[58] Luke 24: 13–35. Cf. Pope Gregory the Great, *Moralia in Iob*, xiv. 50, 58 (ed. Adriaen, cxliiiA. 733; *PL* lxxv. 1069).

[59] Matt. 26: 33.

[60] Matt. 26: 35; cf. Mark 14: 31.

primus et maximus apostolorum qui tantam in uerbis habuerat constanciam ut [p]Domino diceret:[p] 'Tecum paratus sum et in carcerem et in mortem ire',[61] cui[q] tunc et Dominus ecclesiam suam specialiter[r] committens, dixerat: 'Et tu aliquando conuersus confirma fratres tuos',[62] ad unam ancille uocem ipsum negare non ueretur, nec[s] semel id agit sed tercio ipsum adhuc uiuentem denegat.[63] Et a uiuo pariter omnes discipuli uno temporis puncto fugiendo[t] deuolant,[64] a quo nec in morte uel mente uel corpore femine sunt disiuncte. Quarum beata illa peccatrix, mortuum etiam querens et Dominum suum confitens, ait: 'Tulerunt Dominum de monumento.'[65] Et iterum: 'Si tu sustulisti eum, dicito mihi ubi posuisti eum[u] et ego eum tollam.'[66] Fugiunt arietes, immo et pastores Dominici gregis; remanent oues intrepide.[67] Arguit nos[v] Dominus tanquam infirmam carnem, quod in articulo etiam[w] passionis sue nec una hora cum eo potuerunt uigilare.[68] Insomnem ad sepulchrum illius noctem in lacrimis femine ducentes, resurgentis gloriam prime[x] uidere meruerunt. Cui fideliter in mortem quantum dilexerint[y] uiuum, non tam uerbis quam rebus exhibuerunt. Et de ipsa etiam, quam[z] circa eius passionem et mortem habuerunt sollicitudinem, resurgentis uita prime sunt letificate.[69] Cum enim, secundum Iohannem,[70] Ioseph ab Arymathia et Nichodemus corpus Domini ligantes linteis cum aromatibus sepelirent, refert Marchus de earum[a] studio quod Maria Magdalene et Maria Ioseph[b] aspiciebant ubi poneretur.[71] De his quoque Lucas commemorat, dicens: 'Sequute autem mulieres que cum Ihesu uenerant de Galilea; uiderunt monumentum et quemadmodum positum erat corpus eius, et reuertentes parauerunt aromata', non[c] satis uidelicet habentes aromata Nichodemi nisi et adderent sua. 'Et sabbato quidem siluerunt secundum mandatum'.[72] Iuxta Marchum uero, cum transisset sabbatum, summo mane in ipso die resurrectionis uenerunt ad monumentum Maria Magdalene et Maria [d]Iacobi et Salome.[d] [73]

[p–p] doceret *R* [q] Cui *Amb* [r] uel spiritualiter *add.* *T*[1] [s] Nec *Amb*
[t] fugiando *S* [u] *om.* *Amb* [v] hos *?T, BSAmb* [w] *om.* *A* [x] primo *BR*
[y] dilexerunt *A* [z] *f(orte)* quia *Amb*[1] [a] eorum *BR* [b] ihesu mater *?B*
[c] Nec *Amb* [d–d] salome et *B;* et salome *R;* iacobi et salomee *S*

[61] Luke 22: 33. [62] Luke 22: 32.
[63] Cf. Matt. 26: 69–75; Mark 14: 66–72; Luke 22: 55–62; John 18: 17, 25–7.
[64] Cf. Matt. 26: 56; Mark 14: 50.
[65] John 20: 2. [66] John 20: 15.
[67] Cf. *Hymn* 113 (Szövérffy 51) for Compline on Good Friday, II.

the greatest of the apostles, who had shown such constancy in words that he said to the Lord: 'I am ready to go with you to prison and to death',[61] he to whom the Lord said, when specifically entrusting his Church to him: 'And when you have come to yourself, you must lend strength to your brothers',[62] did not hesitate to disown him at a single word from a serving-maid.[63] Nor did he do so just once, but three times he disowned the Lord while he still lived, while the disciples, one and all, at the same moment deserted the living Christ and fled.[64] But the women were not parted from him either in mind or in body even in death. Amongst them that holy sinner sought out his dead body and confessed her Lord saying: 'They have taken the Lord out of the tomb',[65] and again: 'If you have taken him, tell me where you have put him, and I will take him away.'[66] The rams, or rather the shepherds, of the Lord's flock ran off, but the ewes remained unafraid.[67] The Lord rebuked the former as weak flesh because at the very moment of his suffering, they could not stay awake even for an hour.[68] But the women passed a sleepless night weeping at his tomb, and were judged worthy to be the first to see the glory of the risen Lord. By their faithfulness at his death they showed in actions not words how much they loved him in life, and because of their solicitude to his suffering and death, they were the first to be gladdened by his resurrection to life.[69] For when, according to John,[70] Joseph of Arimathaea and Nicodemus buried the Lord's body, and wrapped it with spices in strips of linen cloth, Mark says of the devotion of the women that they watched to see where he was laid.[71] Luke also relates of them that 'the women who had come with Jesus from Galilee followed; they took note of the tomb and how his body was laid. Then they returned home and prepared spices'—evidently they thought the spices brought by Nicodemus were insufficient unless they added their own—'and on the Sabbath day they rested, as they were commanded to do'.[72] But, according to Mark, when the Sabbath was ended, very early in the morning, on the very day of the resurrection, Mary Magdalene, Mary the mother of James, and Salome came to the tomb.[73]

[68] Cf. Matt. 26: 40.

[69] Cf. *Hymn* 91 (Szövérffy 127), *De sanctis mulieribus* 4, III.

[70] Cf. John 19: 38–9.

[71] Cf. Mark 15: 47.

[72] Cf. Luke 23: 55–6. Cf. the antiphon in the *Breviary of the Paraclete* at the office of Lauds on Holy Saturday (*Bre* IIIA, ed. Waddell, p. 137).

[73] Cf. Mark 16: 1–2.

11. Nunc, quoniam deuotionem earum ostendimus, honorem quem meruerunt[a] prosequamur. Primo angelica uisione sunt consolate de resurrectione Domini iam completa, demum[b] ipsum Dominum prime uiderunt et tenuerunt.[74] Prior quidem Maria Magdalene, que ceteris feruentior erat, postea ipsa simul et alie, de quibus scriptum est quod post angelicam uisionem exierunt de monumento currentes nuntiare discipulis resurrectionem Domini. 'Et ecce Ihesus occurrit illis, dicens: "Auete." Ille autem accesserunt et tenuerunt pedes eius et adorauerunt eum. Tunc ait illis[c] Ihesus: "Ite, nunciate fratribus meis ut eant in Galileam; ibi me uidebunt."'[75] De quo et Lucas prosequtus ait: 'Erat Maria[d] Magdalene, et Iohanna et Maria Iacobi et cetere que cum eis erant, que dicebant ad apostolos hec.'[76] Quas etiam ab angelo primum fuisse missas ad apostolos nuntiare [e]hec non[e] reticet Marchus ubi[f] angelo mulieribus loquente scriptum est: 'Surrexit, non est hic. Sed ite, dicite[g] discipulis eius et Petro quia precedet uos in Galileam.'[77] Ipse etiam Dominus primo Marie Magdalene apparens ait illi: 'Vade ad[h] fratres meos et dic eis: Ascendo ad Patrem meum',[78] etc.[i] Ex quibus colligimus has sanctas mulieres quasi apostolas super apostolos esse constitutas,[79] cum[j] ipse ad eos, uel a Domino uel ab angelis misse, summum illud resurrectionis gaudium nuntiauerunt quod expectabatur ab omnibus, ut per eas apostoli primum addiscerent quod toti mundo postmodum predicarent. Quas etiam post resurrectionem, Domino occurrente,[k] salutari ab ipso Euangelista supra memorauit ut, tam occursu suo quam salutatione, quantam erga eas sollicitudinem et gratiam haberet ostenderet. Non enim aliis

11 [a] meruerint *Amb* [b] Deinde *RS* [c] *om. Amb* [d] *om. Amb* [e–e] *om. R* [f] nec *B* [g] discite *T* [h] et *A* [i] *om. Amb* [j] Cum *Amb* [k] occurrante *T*

[74] Cf. Matt. 28 : 1–8 ; also Mark 16: 5–9; Luke 24: 4–10 and 23; John 20: 11–14 and *Letter* 3, **12**. On the differences between the Gospel accounts of the resurrection cf. *Problemata* 5 (*PL* clxxviii. 683B–685C) and *SN* c. 86: 'Quod dominus resurgens primo apparuerit Mariae Magdalenae et non.'

[75] Matt. 28: 8–10. Cf. the antiphon in the *Breviary of the Paraclete* at the office of Vespers on Holy Saturday (*Bre* IIIA, ed. Waddell, p. 140).

[76] Luke 24: 10. On the women and the resurrection see Bauckham, *Gospel Women*, pp. 257–310.

[77] Mark 16: 6–7.

[78] John 20: 17.

[79] Cf. **32** below and *Sermon* 13: 'Apostolorum apostola' (*PL* clxxviii. 485AB). Abelard may have known Jerome, *Commentarii in Prophetas minores: In Sophoniam, prologus*: 'Dominum resurgentem primum aparuisse mulieribus, et apostolorum illas fuisse apostolas' (ed. Adriaen, lxxviA, p. 655; *PL* xxv. 1338B). However, use of the title of apostle or apostle of the apostles to declare the paschal role of the Magdalene is well attested before and during the 12th c. and Saxer, *Le Culte de Marie Madeleine*, pp. 340–50 gives examples taken

11. Now that we have shown their devotion let us go on to the honour they have merited. First of all, they were comforted by a vision of an angel concerning the resurrection of the Lord, which had already been accomplished.[74] Then they were the first to see and touch the Lord himself, and first among them was Mary Magdalene, who loved him more ardently than the rest; but later on, she and the others (it is written), after the vision of the angel, 'came out of the tomb and ran to tell the disciples' that the Lord was risen. And there, coming to meet them, was Jesus. '"Greetings"', he said, 'and they came up to him and clasped his feet, falling prostrate before him. Then Jesus said to them: "Go and tell my brothers that they must go to Galilee. They will see me there."'[75] In his account Luke also says: 'The women were Mary Magdalene, Joanna, and Mary the mother of James, and they, with the other women who were with them, told this to the apostles.'[76] Mark too indicates that the women were sent first by the angel to give the news to the apostles when he writes that the angel said to them: 'He is risen; he is not here. But go and tell his disciples and Peter that he is going on before you into Galilee.'[77] And the Lord himself, on his first appearance to Mary Magdalene, said to her: 'Go to my brothers and tell them that I am ascending to my Father',[78] etc. From this we infer that these holy women were, so to speak, female apostles, set over the apostles,[79] since they were sent either by the Lord or by angels to announce the great joy of the resurrection, which all were awaiting; so that the apostles might first learn through them what they would later preach themselves to the whole world. Moreover, the Evangelist quoted above relates that after the resurrection, when the Lord came to meet the women, he greeted them, so that both by his meeting and his greeting them he could show how much concern and gratitude he felt for them. For we do not read of his

from writings of Odo of Cluny, Honorius of Autun, and Peter of Celle as well as Abelard. See too Bernard of Clairvaux, *Sermo in Cantica* 75, 8: 'apostolae Apostolorum' (ed. Leclercq, Talbot, and Rochais in *S. Bernardi Opera*, ii. 251, *l.* 28). S. Haskins, *Mary Magdalen*, p. 220 and Pl. 43, draws attention to a painting in the Psalter of Jutte Tersina of Liechtenfels, *c.*1200, which bears the inscription 'Sancta Maria Magdalena apostolorum apostola'. For an early example from the 3rd c. see the *Commentary* on the Song of Songs usually attributed to St Hippolytus, where Mary Magdalene and also Martha are said to be apostles for the apostles through being sent to them by the risen Christ (*Hippolyts Kommentar zum Hohenlied*, p. 67). Sanctuaries dedicated to St Mary Magdalene are well attested in the ecclesiastical province of Sens and include one of the dependencies of the abbey of the Paraclete, the priory of Trainel (near Nogent-sur-Seine in Aube; see Map 1 in the Introduction at p. xxxvi), which was founded by the early 1140s (Saxer, *Le Culte de Marie Madeleine*, p. 117; *Cartulaire de l'abbaye du Paraclet*, ed. Lalore, pp. 65–6; McLeod, *Héloïse*, pp. 216–18).

proprium salutationis uerbum, quod est 'Auete', eum legimus protulisse, imo[l] [m]et a[m] salutatione antea discipulos inhibuisse, cum eis diceret: 'Et neminem per uiam salutaueritis',[80] quasi hoc[n] priuilegium nunc usque deuotis feminis reseruaret quod per semet ipsum eis exhiberet immortalitatis gloria iam potitus. Actus quoque Apostolorum, cum referant statim post ascensionem Domini apostolos[o] a monte Oliueti Iherusalem redisse, et illius sacrosancti[p] conuentus religionem diligenter describant, non est deuotionis sanctarum mulierum perseuerantia pretermissa, cum dicitur: 'Hi [q]omnes erant,[q] perseuerantes unanimiter in orationibus cum mulieribus et Maria matre Ihesu.'[r] [81]

12. [a]Vt autem de Hebreis pretermittamus feminis que,[a] primo conuerse ad fidem, uiuente adhuc Domino in carne et predicante, formam huius religionis inchoauerunt, de uiduis quoque Grecorum que ab apostolis postea suscepte sunt consideremus,[b] quanta scilicet diligentia, quanta cura ab apostolis et ipse tractate sint[c] cum ad ministrandum eis gloriosisimus signifer christiane militie Stephanus prothomartyr, cum quibusdam aliis spiritalibus uiris, ab ipsis apostolis fuerit constitutus. Vnde in eisdem Actibus[d] Apostolorum scriptum est: 'Crescente numero discipulorum factum[e] est murmur Grecorum aduersus Hebreos quod despicerentur in[f] ministerio cotidiano uidue eorum. Conuocantes autem duodecim apostoli multitudinem discipulorum dixerunt: Non est equum [g]derelinquere nos[g] uerbum Dei, et ministrare mensis. Considerate ergo, fratres, uiros ex [h]omnibus uobis[h] boni testimonii septem, plenos Spiritu sancto et sapientia, quos constituamus super hoc opus. Nos uero orationi et ministerio uerbi instantes erimus. Et placuit sermo coram[i] multitudine. Et elegerunt Stephanum plenum [j]fide et[j] Spiritu sancto, et Philippum et Prochorum et Nicanorem[k] et Timotheum[l] et [m]Parmenam et[m] Nicholaum[n] Antiochenum. Hos statuerunt ante conspectum apostolorum, et orantes imposuerunt eis manus.'[82] Vnde et continentia Stephani

[l] uno *T;* uiro *B* [m–m] et (a *superscr.*) *T;* ista *Amb* [n] ad *B* [o] *om. B* [p] sacrosancte *R* [q–q] erant omnes *Amb* [r] *end of long lacuna in CEF that begins in* 8 *above*

12 [a–a] multas autem (autem *later add. in E*)*;* hebreas pretermittendo feminas que (in *C*) *CEF* [b] considerantes *S* [c] sunt *CEF* [d] acceptibus *S* [e] factus *TAERS;* Factus *B* [f] *om. S* [g–g] nos derelinquere *F* [h–h] nobis omnibus *B;* uobis *F and Vulg.* [i] omni *add. F and Vulg.* [j–j] *om. BR* [k] nicanorum *S* [l] Timonem *F* [m–m] Parmanam et *TCEFB;* parmenam et *add. by another hand in marg. A, R Amb* [n] aduenam *add. F and Vulg.*

having greeted others with that special word of greeting, that is *Avete*; but rather that he had previously forbidden the disciples to give greeting when he said to them: 'Greet no one on the road',[80] as if from then on he reserved for devout women that privilege which he revealed to them in his own person, after he had already gained the glory of immortality. Again, when the Acts of the Apostles relate that immediately after the Lord's ascension the apostles returned from the Mount of Olives to Jerusalem, and describe the religious worship of that holy community, mention is made of the sustained devotion of the holy women, in the words: 'All there were constantly at prayer together, and with them a group of women, including Mary the mother of Jesus.'[81]

12. Next, passing over Jewish women who were early converts to the Faith when the Lord was still living in the flesh and preaching, and who then inaugurated the form of their religious profession, let us consider the widows of the Greeks, for they were subsequently received by the apostles, and were also treated with the greatest care and solicitude at the time when the apostles appointed that glorious standard-bearer of the Christian army, Stephen the first martyr, and several other men filled with the Spirit, to wait on them. For it is written in the Acts of the Apostles: 'When the disciples were increasing in number, the Greeks made a complaint against the Jews that in the daily distribution their widows were being overlooked. So the Twelve called all the disciples together and said: "It would not be right for us to neglect the word of God in order to wait at table. Therefore, brothers, you must look from among yourselves for seven men of good reputation, men filled with the Holy Spirit and wisdom, for us to appoint to this duty, while we shall devote ourselves to prayer and to the ministry of the Word." Their proposal was acceptable to all, and they elected Stephen, a man filled with faith and the Holy Spirit, together with Philip, Prochorus, Nicanor, Timothy, Parmenas, and Nicholas of Antioch. These they presented to the apostles, who prayed and laid hands on them.'[82] Thus the

[80] Luke 10: 4.

[81] Acts 1: 14.

[82] Acts 6: 1–6. Cf. *Letter* 6, **28** and *Sermons* 31and 32 (*I sermoni di Abelardo per le monache del Paracleto*, ed. De Santis, pp. 219–33; *PL* clxxviii. 569–82). Both sermons are addressed to the sisters of the Paraclete and are on St Stephen, one of the seven deacons whose feast was specially celebrated there; cf. *The Old French Paraclete Ordinary*, ed. Waddell, p. 334. Cf. Waddell, 'Peter Abelard as creator of liturgical texts', p. 273 ff. and id., 'St. Bernard and the Cistercian Office', p. 82.

admodum commendatur, quod ministerio atque obsequio sanctarum feminarum fuerit deputatus.[o] [83] Cuius[p] quidem obsequii[q] ministratio, quam excellens sit et tam Deo quam ipsis apostolis accepta, ipsi tam propria oratione quam manuum impositione protestati sunt, quasi hos, quos in hoc constituebant, adiurantes ut fideliter agerent,[r] et[s] tam benedictione sua quam oratione[t] eos adiuuantes ut possent. Quam etiam[u] Paulus administrationem ad apostolatus sui plenitudinem ipse[v] sibi uendicans, 'numquid non habemus', inquit, 'potestatem sororem mulierem circumducendi[w] sicut et ceteri apostoli?'[84] Ac si aperte diceret: Numquid etiam[x] sanctarum mulierum conuentus nos habere ac nobiscum in predicatione [y]ducere permissum est, sicut ceteris apostolis, ut ipse uidelicet eis[z] in[a] predicatione de [b]sua substantia[b] necessaria ministrarent? Vnde Augustinus in libro *de opere monachorum*: 'Ad hoc', inquit, 'et fideles mulieres habentes terrenam substantiam[c] [d]ibant cum eis[dy] et ministrabant eis de [e]sua substantia,[e] ut nullius indigerent horum que ad substantiam[f] huius uite pertinent.'[85] Item: 'Quod quisquis [g]non putat[g] ab apostolis fieri, ut cum eis sancte conuersationis mulieres circuirent,[h] quocumque[i] euangelium predicabant, euangelium audiat[j] et cognoscat[k] quemadmodum hoc ipsius Domini exemplo faciebant.'[86] 'In euangelio enim scriptum est: "Deinceps et ipse iter faciebat per ciuitates et castella euangelizans[l] regnum[m] Dei, et duodecim cum illo et mulieres alique que erant curate a spiritibus immundis[n] et infirmitatibus, Maria que uocatur Magdalene,[o] et Ioanna uxor Cuze[p] procuratoris[q] Herodis, et Susanna, et alie multe, que ministrabant ei[r] de [s]facultatibus suis."'[s] [87] [88] Vt hinc quoque pateat Dominum etiam[t] in[u] predicatione sua proficiscentem ministratione mulierum corporaliter sustentari, et eas ipsi pariter cum apostolis quasi inseparabiles comites adherere.

13. Demum[a] uero, huius professionis religione in feminis pariter ut in uiris multiplicata in ipso statim ecclesie nascentis exordio, eque sicut

[o] depositus *C* [p] cuiusdam *B* [q] *om. F* [r] agerent *?T;* facerent *R;* fagerent *S* [s] *om. CEF* [t] sua *add. BR* [u] ut *add.* T^1*ACE;* et *add. F* [v] *om. E* [w] conducendi *S* [x] *om. EAmb* [y–y] *over eras. in T* [z] ei *F* [a] *om. R* [b–b] substantia sua *CEF* [c] sustenciam *S* [d–d] stant cum *R* [e–e] substantia sua *EF, Augustine* [f] necessaria *F, Augustine;* sustanciam *S* [g–g] putat non potuisse *F, Augustine* [h] circumirent *Amb;* circumirent *al.* circuirent *Augustine* [i] quoque *CS;* quacumque *al.* quocumque *Augustine* [j] audiant *TACEBRS;* audiat *F, Augustine* [k] cognoscant *TACEBRS*; cognoscat F, Augustine [l] praedicans et euangelizans *F, Augustine* [m] uerbum *BRS* [n] malignis *F and Vulg.;* malignis *al.* immundis *Augustine* [o] madelene *C* [p] cute *BR;* Chuze *F* [q] regis *add. BS* [r] eis *C;* eis *al.* ei *Augustine* [s–s] suis facultatibus *CE;* facultatibus *F* [t] *om. BR* [u] *om. R*

continence of Stephen was highly commended and he was assigned to the ministry and service of holy women.[83] How excellent was his performance of this service, as acceptable to God as to the apostles, they bore witness both by their prayer and laying on of hands, as if they were adjuring those whom they appointed to act faithfully, and helping them as much as they could both by blessing and by prayer. St Paul also claimed this ministry for himself as the supreme fulfilment of his apostolate, when he said: 'Have we not the right to take a Christian woman about with us, like the other apostles?'[84] In plain words: Is it not permitted to us to have groups of holy women accompanying us in our preaching, as it was to the other apostles, so that while they preached the women could provide for their needs from their own resources? Hence Augustine in his book *On the Work of Monks* says: 'To this end, faithful women who had worldly goods went with them and made provision for them so that they should lack none of the necessities of this life.'[85] And: 'If any one does not believe that it was the practice of the apostles to take with them women of holy life wherever they preached the Gospel, he has only to hear the Gospel to know that they did this following the example of the Lord himself.'[86] 'For there it is written: "After this he went journeying from town to town and village to village, proclaiming the good news of God. With him were the Twelve and a number of women who had been set free from evil spirits and infirmities: Mary, known as the Magdalene, Joanna, the wife of Chuza, Herod's steward, and Susanna, and many others. These women provided for them out of their own resources."'[87] [88] It is therefore evident that the Lord also had his bodily needs supplied by the service of women when he set out on his preaching, and that they, along with the apostles, remained with him as his inseparable companions.

13. Then as the observance of this profession spread among women as among men, women, like men, had their own accommodation in

13 [a] Deinde *CFBRSAmb*[1]

[83] Cf. Acts 6: 1–5.

[84] 1 Cor. 9: 5; cf. *Letter* 1, **67**.

[85] Augustine, *De opere monachorum*, iv. 5 (ed. Zycha, p. 538, *l.* 21–p. 539, *l.* 1; *PL* xl. 552). Also cited in *Letter* 1, **67**.

[86] Augustine, *De opere monachorum*, v. 6 (ed. Zycha, p. 539, *ll.* 14–18; *PL* xl. 552). Also cited in *Letter* 1, **67**.

[87] Luke 8: 1–3.

[88] Augustine, *De opere monachorum*, v. 6 (ed. Zycha, p. 540, *ll.* 9–17; *PL* xl. 553). Also cited in *Letter* 1, **67**.

uiri ita et femine propriorum per se monasteriorum habitacula possederunt. Vnde[b] et[c] *Ecclesiastica Hystoria* laudem Phylonis[d] [e]dissertissimi Iudei,[e] quam non solum dixit, uerum etiam magnifice scripsit, de[f] Alexandrina sub Marco ecclesia, ita inter cetera libro secundo, capitulo [g]septimo decimo,[g] commemorat:[h] [89] 'In multis est', inquit, 'orbis terre[i] partibus hoc genus hominum.'[90] Et post aliqua: 'Est autem in singulis locis consecrata orationi[j] domus que appellatur semneion[k] uel monasterium.'[l] [91] Item infra: 'Itaque non solum subtilium[m] intelligunt hymnos ueterum, sed[n] ipsi faciunt nouos[o] in Deum, omnibus eos et metris et sonis [p]honesta satis[p] et[q] suaui[r] compage modulantes.'[92] Item, plerisque de abstinentia eorum[s] premissis et diuini[t] cultus officiis, adiecit: 'Cum uiris autem quos dicimus sunt et femine in quibus [u]plures iam[u] grandeue sunt uirgines integritatem et[v] castitatem corporis non necessitate aliqua sed deuotione seruantes, dum[w] sapientie studiis semet gestiunt non solum anima sed et[x] corpore consecrare,[y] indignum ducentes libidini mancipare uas ad capiendam sapientiam preparatum et edere mortalem partum[z] eas a quibus diuini uerbi concubitus sacrosanctus et immortalis expetitur, ex quo posteritas relinquatur, nequaquam corruptele mortalitatis obnoxia.'[93] Item ibidem de Phylone: 'Etiam de conuentibus eorum scribit ut seorsum quidem uiri seorsum etiam [a]in eisdem locis[a] femine congregentur, [b]ut et[b] uigilias sicut apud nos fieri moris[c] est, peragant.'[94]

14. Hinc illud [a]est in laude[a] Christiane phylosophye, hoc est monastice prerogatiue,[95] quod et[b] *Tripartita*[c] commemorat[d] *Hystoria*, non minus[e] a feminis quam a[f] uiris arrepte. Ait quippe sic libro primo, capitulo undecimo: 'Huius elegantissime phylosophye princeps [g]fuit quidem,[g] sicuti[h] quidam dicunt, Helyas propheta et

[b] de(. . .) T^1 [c] in *CF* [d] philo(. . .) T^1 [e–e] iudei dissertissimi *B* [f] De *T* [g–g] ia *?C, E;* 16 *F;* xvi *BRAmb* [h] *om. BRS* [i] *om. BR* [j] orationis *S* [k] sennior *TAS;* semnor *CER;* ϛεμνύον *F;* semñor *B;* Seniuor *Amb* [l] μοναϛύριον *F* [m] subtilissimum *C;* subtilium *Hymn. Praef.* 2, 2, *but Silvestre, 'A propos d'une édition récente', p. 97, draws attention to Eusebius-Rufinus, ed. Mommsen, p. 149: subtilius* [n] etiam *F* [o] *om. S* [p–p] honestatis *B* [q] *om. CE* [r] sua in *BS* [s] *om. Amb* [t] omni *S* [u–u] iam plures *CEF* [v] ac *Amb* [w] de *?C;* De *F* [x] etiam *?T^1, E Amb; om. R* [y] consecrate *TBR;* consecrare *?T^1* [z] pratum *S* [a–a] in (*add. in marg.*) eisdem eciam locis *A;* in eisdem locis etiam *CE;* in eisdem locis et *F* [b–b] et ut *ACFBRAmb* [c] mos *Amb*

14 [a–a] in laude est *R* (*but an insertion was intended before* in) [b] *om. FAmb* [c] Tripertita *AS* [d] commemorat *inserted into E;* narrat *inserted into F* [e] nunquam *C* [f] *om. Amb* [g–g] quidem *CE;* quidem fuit *F and Cassiodorus-Epiphanius* [h] sicut *F*

their own monasteries from the very beginning of the infant Church. And so the *Ecclesiastical History* in book 2, chapter 17, relates amongst other matters that Philo, a highly learned Jew, paid tribute both in spoken and in eloquent written words to the Church of Alexandria under Mark,[89] saying: 'Such people are to be found in many parts of the world',[90] and a little later: 'In each of these places there is a building consecrated to prayer which is called a sanctuary or monastery.'[91] Again: 'Thus they not only understand the exquisite hymns of earlier writers but also compose new hymns to God, setting them to all sorts of metres and melodies in true and pleasing harmony.'[92] Again, leaving out several passages on their abstinence and the offices of living worship, it says: 'With the men of whom we have spoken there are also women, several of whom are virgins of advanced age. They have preserved their integrity and bodily chastity not from any necessity but through their dedication, in their eagerness to devote themselves to the study of wisdom not only in spirit but in body; for they think it unworthy for the vessel which is prepared for the receipt of wisdom to be given up to lust, and for those from whom is required a sacred and immortal cohabitation with the divine word which may leave a posterity in no way subject to mortal corruption, to give birth to mortal offspring.'[93] And in the same passage it says of Philo: 'In writing of their communities he also describes the segregation of men and women who live in the same place, so that they may keep vigils as is the custom with us.'[94]

14. Hence the words in praise of Christian philosophy, that is, of the monastic privilege,[95] embraced as eagerly by women as by men, which are recorded in the *Tripartite History*, book 1, chapter 11: 'The founder of this greatly refined philosophy was (as some say) Elijah the

[89] 'Vnde et . . . commemorat'; cf. , *Hymn Collections from the Paraclete*, preface to bk. 2 (ed. Waddell, p. 47 *l.* 22–p. 48 *l.* 3; *Peter Abelard's Hymnarius Paraclitensis*, ed. Szövérffy, p. 80; *PL* clxxviii. 1787–8). Philo, a Hellenistic Jewish writer and exegete (*c.*30 BC–AD 45), lived in Alexandria and became an important influence in the Jewish community there.

[90] Eusebius, *Historia ecclesiastica*, ii. 17 (ed. Mommsen, p. 145, *l.* 15; *PG* xx. 178B).

[91] Ibid., p. 147, *ll.* 1–2; *PG* xx. 178C.

[92] Ibid., p. 149, *ll.* 3–5; *PG* xx. 179B. Also cited in *Hymn Collections from the Paraclete*, preface to bk. 2 (ed. Waddell, p. 48 *ll.* 5–8; *Peter Abelard's Hymnarius Paraclitensis*, ed. Szövérffy, p. 80; *PL* clxxviii. 1787–8).

[93] Eusebius, *Historia ecclesiastica*, ii. 17 (ed. Mommsen, p. 151, *ll.* 5–12; *PG* xx. 182BC).

[94] Ibid., p. 153 *ll.* 2–4; *PG* xx. 183A.

[95] 'Christiane phylosophye': cf. *Sermon* 33 (*PL* clxxviii. 585B).

[i]Baptista Iohannes.[i] Phylo autem Phytagoricus[j] suis temporibus refert undique egregios Hebreorum in quodam predio circa [k]stagnum Marian[k] in colle positum[l] phylosophatos.[96] Habitaculum uero eorum et cibos et conuersationem talem introducit qualem et nos nunc apud Egyptiorum monachos esse conspicimus. Scribit[m] eos ante solis occasum non gustare cibum, uino semper et sanguinem habentibus abstinere, cibum eis[n] esse[o] panis et salis et ysopi[97] et[p] potum aque. Mulieres[q] eis cohabitare, seniores[r] uirgines propter amorem philosophye spontanea uoluntate nuptiis abstinentes.'[98] Hinc et illud est Ieronimi in libro *de illustribus uiris*, capitulo septimo,[s] de laude Marci et ecclesie sic scribentis: 'Primus[t] Alexandrie Christum annuntians constituit ecclesiam [u]tante doctrine et uite continentie,[u] ut[v] omnes sectatores Christi ad exemplum sui cogeret.[99] Denique Phylo, disertissimus Iudeorum, uidens Alexandrie primam ecclesiam adhuc iudaizantem, quasi[w] in laudem [x]gentis sue[x] librum super[y] eorum conuersione[z] scripsit,[100] et quomodo Lucas narrat Ierosolime credentes omnia habuisse communia,[101] sic[a] ille quod Alexandrie sub Marco doctore fieri cernebat, memorie[b] tradidit.'[102] Item capitulo undecimo: 'Phylo Iudeus, natione Alexandrinus, de genere sacerdotum idcirco a nobis inter scriptores ecclesiasticos ponitur, quia librum de prima[c] Marci euangeliste apud Alexandriam scribens ecclesia in nostrorum laude uersatus est, non solum eos ibi, sed in multis quoque prouinciis esse commemorans,[d] et habitacula eorum dicens monasteria. Ex quo apparet[e] talem primum Christo credentium fuisse ecclesiam quales nunc monachi esse nituntur,[f] et cupiunt[g] ut nichil[h] cuiusquam proprium sit, nullus inter eos diues, nullus pauper,

[i–i] Iohannes baptista *B* [j] Phytagorius *T;* (Phytagori)cus *T*[1]*;* phytagoricus *A;* pittagoricus *C;* pithagoricus *E;* Pytagoricus *F;* phytagorius *B;* pitagorius *R;* phitagorius *S;* Pythagoricus *Amb;* Phytagorius *al.* Phytagoricus *Cassiodorus-Epiphanius* [k–k] stagnum marian *T*(*after corr.*), *A;* stagnum mariam *T*(*before corr.*), *CEFBRS;* stagnum Maria *Amb;* un estanc que l'en appelle Maria *J;* lacum . . . Mariae *Eusebius* (*trans. Rufinus*) [l] posito *F* [m] enim *add. A* [n] ait *?C, EF* [o] erat *E but inserted in a smaller hand* [p] *om. F* [q] et ait *add. CEF* [r] semet *E* [s] VIII. *Amb, Jerome* [t] Primum *Jerome* [u–u] tanta doctrina et uitae continentia *F, Jerome* [v] et *T;* ut *T*[1] [w] *om. Amb* [x–x] sue gentis *E* [y] supra *F* [z] conuersionem *E;* conuersatione *Jerome* [a] et *add. FAmb, Jerome* [b] memorieque *Jerome* [c] penitentia *inserted by a smaller hand in E* [d] memorans *inserted by a smaller hand in E, F, Jerome* [e] *exp. E;* uidetur *superscr. E* [f] imitantur *TACEBRS and a reading in a MS of Jerome;* nituntur *F, Jerome* [g] capiunt *TAB;* esse *add. CE;* cupiunt *FRS, Jerome* [h] nil *F*

[96] In his *De uita contemplatiua*, cited by Eusebius in his *Historia ecclesiastica*, Philo provided an idealized description of this Jewish community of pious philosophers who lived

prophet and then John the Baptist. Philo the Pythagorean also relates that in his day eminent Jews used to congregate from all parts in a farmhouse on a hill near Lake Mareotis, and there study philosophy.[96] He speaks of their dwelling-places and food and way of life as being such as we see today amongst the monks of Egypt, and says that they tasted no food before sunset and always abstained from wine and anything containing blood, with bread and salt and hyssop[97] for food and water for drink. Women lived with them, virgins who were no longer young and abstained from marriage of their own free will because of their love of philosophy.'[98] And so Jerome, in chapter 8 of his book *On Illustrious Men*, writes as follows in praise of Mark and his church: 'He was the first to proclaim Christ in Alexandria and to found a church, and was of such great learning and continence of life that he compelled all followers of Christ to follow his example.[99] Then when Philo, the most learned of the Jews, saw that the first church of Alexandria was observing Jewish rites, he wrote a book on the conversion of his people, as if in their praise,[100] and just as Luke tells how all the faithful in Jerusalem had all things in common,[101] so he put on record the events he witnessed in Alexandria under the direction of Mark.'[102] Again, in chapter 11: 'Philo the Jew, a native of Alexandria and one of a family of priests, is included by us amongst ecclesiastical writers because in his book about the first church of Mark the Evangelist in Alexandria, he writes in praise of our fellow Christians. He records their presence both in Alexandria and in many other provinces, and refers to their dwelling-places as monasteries. From this it appears that at its start the church consisted of believers in Christ whose example is followed by monks today: they desire that nothing should be anyone's personal property, that no one among them should be rich or poor, that their possessions should be

near Lake Mareotis (Bahra Mariyut), south-west of Alexandria, Marea (El 'Amirīya) being a town at the south-western end of the lake. Eusebius regarded them as Christians. On these devotees, the Therapeutae, see esp. the introduction by Daumas to the French trans. by Miquel of Philo's work.

[97] Hyssop: an aromatic herb.

[98] Cassiodorus–Epiphanius, *Historia ecclesiastica tripartita*, i. 11 (ed. Jacob and Hanslik, p. 35, *ll.* 49–55, 62–3, 64 to p. 36, *l.* 1; *PL* lxix. 897CD). Cf. Eusebius, *Historia ecclesiastica*, ii. 17 (ed. Mommsen, pp. 147–55, esp. 153; *PG* xx. 178BC).

[99] The tradition, attested by Eusebius, that St Mark the Evangelist founded the church of Alexandria is unreliable; see Pearson, 'Earliest Christianity in Egypt', pp. 137–45; and id., 'Christianity in Egypt', pp. 995–6.

[100] Philo, *De uita contemplatiua*.

[101] Cf. Acts 2: 44, 4: 32.

[102] Jerome, *De uiris illustribus*, viii (ed. Bernoulli, p. 12; ed. Herding, p. 14; *PL* xxiii. 621B–623A).

patrimonia[i] egentibus diuidantur, orationi uacetur, et psalmis, doctrine quoque et continentie, quales et Lucas refert primum Iherosolime fuisse credentes.'[103]

15. Quod si ueteres reuoluamus[a] hystorias, reperiemus in ipsis feminas, in his que ad Deum pertinent uel ad quamcumque religionis singularitatem, a uiris non fuisse disiunctas. Quas etiam pariter ut uiros diuina cantica non solum cecinisse, uerum etiam composuisse sacre tradunt hystorie. Primum quippe canticum de liberatione Israelitici populi non solum uiri sed etiam mulieres Domino decantauerunt,[104] hinc statim[b] diuinorum officiorum[c] in ecclesia celebrandorum auctoritatem ipse adepte. Sic quippe scriptum est: 'Sumpsit ergo Maria prophetes,[d] soror Aaron, tympanum in manu sua; egresseque[e] sunt omnes mulieres post eam cum tympanis et choris quibus precinebat, dicens: Cantemus Domino, [f]gloriose enim magnificatus est',[105] etc.[f] Nec ibi quidem Moyses commemoratur[g] propheta, nec[h] precinisse[i] dicitur sicut[j] Maria, nec tympanum aut[k] chorum [l]uiri habuisse[l] referuntur sicut mulieres. Cum itaque Maria precinens prophetes[m] commemoratur, uidetur ipsa non tam dictando uel recitando quam prophetando[n] canticum istud[o] protulisse.[106] Que etiam cum ceteris precinere describitur,[p] quam[q] ordinate siue concorditer psallerent demonstratur. Quod autem non solum uoce uerum etiam tympanis et choris cecinerunt,[r] non solum [s]earum maximam[s] deuotionem insinuat, uerum etiam mystice specialis[t] cantici in congregationibus monasticis formam diligenter exprimit. Ad quod et Psalmista nos exhortatur,[u] dicens: 'Laudate eum in tympano et choro',[107] hoc est in[v] mortificatione carnis[108] et[w] concordia illa caritatis de qua scriptum est quia 'multitudinis credentium erat cor unum et anima una'.[x] [109] Nec uacat etiam a misterio quod egresse[y] ad cantandum referuntur,[110] in quo anime contemplatiue[z] iubili figurantur.[a] Que dum ad celestia se suspendit [b]quasi terrene habitationis[b]

[i] *add. CEF*

15 [a] resoluamus *F* [b] statis *T* [c] *om. C* [d] *inserted by another hand in E;* Prophetissa *F* [e] egresse *B* [f–f] gloriose etc *CE;* gloriose enim magnificatus est *FAmb* [g] commoratur *F* [h] *om. T but add. T*[1] [i] precuisse *S;* precinuisse *F* [j] sed *F* [k] nec *A before corr. in marg.* [l–l] habuisse uiri *CEFBRS* [m] *inserted by another hand in E;* Prophetissa *F* [n] prophectizando *C* [o] illud *CEF* [p] dicitur *CEF* [q] cum *CE* [r] cecinerent *CE;* cecinerint *Amb* [s–s] maximam earum *F* [t] Spiritalis *AAmb;* spiritualis *CF* [u] hortatur *ER;* horatur *B* [v] *om. B* [w] *om. C* [x] in Domino *add. F* [y] egisse *Amb* [z] contemplatiui *EF* [a] fugiuntur *A* [b–b] *om. CEF*

distributed among the needy, and they should give their time to prayer and the psalms and also to learning and continence, as Luke recounts the believers in Jerusalem did in the early days.'[103]

15. Moreover, if we turn the pages of the Old Testament we shall find that in those matters which concern God or some special point of religion, the women there are not segregated from men; indeed, they are said not only to have sung but also to have composed religious songs as much as men did. Women as well as men sang to the Lord the first song on the liberation of the people of Israel,[104] and from this they won for themselves authority to celebrate the divine offices in the Church. For thus it is written: 'And Miriam the prophetess, Aaron's sister, took up her tambourine, and all the women went out after her, dancing to tambourines. And Miriam led them in singing the refrain: Let us sing to the Lord for he is exalted in triumph',[105] etc. There is no mention here of the prophet Moses nor is he said to have led the singing as Miriam did; neither is there anything about men dancing like the women to tambourines. Thus, when Miriam is called a prophetess as she led the singing, this seems to be not so much because of her speaking or chanting as for being prophetical in her song;[106] and when she is also described as leading the others in song, it shows how they sang in due order and harmony. The fact that they sang not unaccompanied but with tambourines and dancing not only suggests the depth of their devotion but also carefully shows in a mystical way that a special kind of chanting is found in monastic communities. The Psalmist also exhorts us to follow this example, in the words: 'Praise him with drums and dancing';[107] that is, with mortification of the flesh[108] and harmony in love about which it is written that 'the body of believers was united in heart and soul'.[109] There is symbolic meaning too in the fact that the women are said to have gone out to sing,[110] for this represents the joyful singing of the contemplative soul when it clings to heavenly things and leaves behind, as it were, the secure defences

[103] Jerome, *De uiris illustribus*, xi (ed. Bernoulli, p. 14; ed. Herding, p. 16; *PL* xxiii. 625B–627A).

[104] Cf. Exod. 15: 1–21.

[105] Exod. 15: 20–1.

[106] Cf. *Sermon* 13 *on Easter Day* (*PL* clxxviii. 484B–485A); *Hymn* 43 (Szövérffy 59), *De resurrectione Domini* I.

[107] Ps. 150: 4. Also cited in *Sermon* 13 (*PL* clxxviii. 484D).

[108] Cf. *Sermon* 13 (*PL* clxxviii. 484D).

[109] Acts 4: 32.

[110] Cf. Exod. 15: 20.

castra[c] [111] deserit, et de ipsa contemplationis sue intima dulcedine hymnum spiritalem summa exultatione Domino persoluit. Habemus [d]ibi quoque[d] Debbore[e] et Anne nec non Iudith uidue cantica, sicut[f] et in Euangelio Marie[g] matris Domini.[112] Que uidelicet Anna,[h] Samuelem paruulum suum offerens tabernaculo Domini,[113] auctoritatem suscipiendorum infantium[i] monasteriis dedit. Vnde Ysidorus fratribus in cenobio Honoriacensi[j] [114] constitutis, capitulo quinto: 'Quicumque', inquit, 'a parentibus propriis in monasterio fuerit[k] delegatus, nouerit se ibi[l] perpetuo mansurum.[m] Nam Anna Samuelem puerum[n] Deo obtulit, qui[o] et in ministerio templi, quo a matre fuerat[p] functus,[q] permansit, et ubi constitutus est deseruiuit.'[115] Constat etiam filias Aaron pariter cum fratribus suis ad sanctuarium et hereditariam sortem Leui adeo pertinere, ut hinc quoque eis Dominus alimoniam[r] instituerit, sicut scriptum est in libro Numeri, ipso ad[s] Aaron sic dicente: 'Omnes primitias sanctuarii quas offerunt filii[t] Israel Domino, tibi dedi et filiis ac[u] filiabus tuis iure perpetuo.'[116] Vnde nec a[v] clericorum ordine mulierum religio disiuncta uidetur. Quas etiam ipsis nomine coniunctas esse [w]constat, cum[w] uidelicet tam diaconissas quam diaconos appellemus,[x] ac si in utrisque[y] tribum Leui et[z] quasi Leuitas agnoscamus. Habemus etiam in eodem libro uotum illud maximum, et consecrationem Nazareorum Domini eque feminis sicut et uiris esse institutum,[a] ipso ad Moysen Domino sic dicente: 'Loquere ad filios Israel, et dices ad eos: Vir siue mulier cum fecerint uotum ut sanctificentur, et se uoluerint Domino consecrare, uino et omni quod inebriare potest abstinebunt. Acetum ex uino et ex qualibet alia potione[b] et quicquid de uua[c] exprimitur non bibent. Vuas

[c] castrum *Amb* [d–d] ibique *C* [e] delbore *C;* Delborae *FAmb;* Deborae *Amb*¹ [f] *om. F* [g] *om. F* [h] *om. B* [i] infantum *T* [j] Honorianensi *TAEBRSAmb;* honoriacensi *C;* Honoriacensi *FAmb*¹*;* Honoire *J* [k] fuit *TAmb* [l] sibi *BRS and Smaragdus* [m] semansurum *C;* remanssurum *E;* remansurum *F;* permansurum *Benedict of Aniane;* mansurum *Benedict of Aniane, MS T* [n] *om. BR* [o] Qui *TA, Amb;* Quid *C;* quique *Benedict of Aniane, Smaragdus* [p] *om. T but* (fue)rat *add. T*¹ *in trimmed marg.* [q] deputatus *Gratian* [r] elemozinam *C* [s] *om. BRS* [t] filiis *S* [u] ad et *R;* ac et *S* [v] *om. S* [w–w] constitutum *T* [x] appellamus *CEF* [y] utris *A* [z] etiam *F* [a] constitutum *F* [b] posicione *R* [c] una *S*

---

[111] 'terrene habitationis castra'; cf. *Sermon* 10: 'uoluptates carnis quasi quaedam castra', 'castra . . . id est uoluptates carnis' (*PL* clxxviii. 450A and B).

[112] Cf. Judg. 5: 2–31; 1 Kgs. (1 Sam.) 2: 1–10; Judith 16: 2–21; Luke 1: 46–55. Also *Problemata* 33 (*PL* clxxviii. 715C–716B).

[113] Cf. 1 Kgs. (1 Sam.) 1: 24–8.

[114] An unidentified monastery according to Cottineau, *Répertoire*, i, col. 1429, who cited Mabillon, *Annales*, i. 331: 'Isidorus, scripta monastica Regula quam sanctis fratribus in

of an earthly habitation[111] and, on the innermost delight of its contemplation and with the greatest exultation, performs for the Lord a hymn of the spirit. In the Old Testament too we find the songs of Deborah and Hannah as well as that of the widow Judith, just as we read in the Gospel of the song of Mary, the mother of the Lord.[112] Indeed, it was Hannah who set a precedent for the reception of small children into monasteries by presenting her little son Samuel to the Temple of the Lord.[113] And so in chapter 5 Isidore says to the brethren placed in the monastery of Honorian:[114] 'Whoever has been placed by his own parents in a monastery should know that he is to remain there for ever. For Hannah gave her son Samuel to God, and he remained in the ministry of the Temple where he had been appointed by his mother, and served where he was placed.'[115] It is also clear that the daughters of Aaron were attached to the sanctuary and to the hereditary priesthood of Levi on equal terms with their brothers, for the Lord provided alimony for them too, as is recorded in the Book of Numbers when he says to Aaron: 'All the first fruits of sanctuary which the children of Israel set aside for the Lord I have given to you, and to your sons and daughters as a due in perpetuity.'[116] Thus it appears that the religious life of women was not a separate one from the order of clergy, and indeed, the women were linked with the men by name, since we speak of deaconesses as well as deacons, as if we recognize in them a kind of female Levite along with the tribe of Levi. In the same Book we find the solemn vow and consecration of the Nazirites of the Lord, which was laid down for women as well as for men in the words of the Lord to Moses: 'Speak to the sons of Israel and say to them: All those, men or women, who have made a vow of dedication and have decided to consecrate themselves to the Lord, shall abstain from wine and strong drink. They shall not drink vinegar made from wine or any other drink, nor any juice pressed from grapes,

coenobio Honoriacensi constitutis nuncupavit. Quodnam hoc monasterium cui haec regula praescripta est, incertum.'

[115] This passage, missing from c. 4 of the *Regula monachorum* of Isidore of Seville (d. 636) as found in *PL* lxxxiii. 872, appears in c. 4 of the same work as presented in the collection of *Rules* or *Codex regularum* attributed to Benedict of Aniane (Hérault; d. 821) (*PL* ciii. 558D–559A). It was also cited by Benedict of Aniane in his *Concordia regularum*, c. 66, iii (ed. Bonnerue, clxviiiA, p. 593; *PL* ciii. 1308B) and by Smaragdus, abbot of St-Mihiel (Meuse; d. after 825) in his *Expositio in Regulam S. Benedicti*, c. 59 (written soon after 816; ed. Spannagel and Engelbert, p. 300, *ll.* 4–8; *PL* cii. 905AB; trans. Barry, p. 481); likewise by Gratian, *Concordia discordantium canonum*, Causa 20, Q. 1, c. 4.

[116] Num. 18: 19; cf. Num. 18: 11. At Num. 18: 8 the first fruits seem to be assigned to Aaron and his sons.

recentes[d] siccasque[e] non comedent [f]cunctis diebus quibus ex uoto Domino consecrantur. Quicquid ex uinea est ab[g] uua passa usque ad acinum non comedent[f] omni tempore separationis sue.'[117]

16. Huius quidem religionis illas fuisse arbitror excubantes ad ostium tabernaculi, de quarum speculis Moyses uas composuit in quo lauarentur Aaron et filii eius, sicut scriptum est: posuit[a] Moyses labrum[b] eneum, in quo lauarentur Aaron et filii eius, quod 'fecit de speculis mulierum que excubabant[c] ad ostium tabernaculi'.[118] Diligenter magne deuotionis earum feruor describitur, que clauso etiam tabernaculo foribus eius adherentes sanctarum uigiliarum excubias celebrabant, noctem etiam ipsam in orationibus ducentes, et ab[d] obsequio diuino uiris quiescentibus non uacantes. Quod uero clausum eis tabernaculum memoratur, uita penitentium congrue designatur, qui ut se durius penitentie lamentis afficiant a ceteris segregantur. Que profecto uita specialiter monastice professionis esse perhibetur, cuius uidelicet ordo nichil aliud[e] esse dicitur quam quedam parcioris[f] penitentie forma.[119] Tabernaculum uero ad cuius ostium excubabant, illud est[g] mystice intelligendum, de quo ad Hebreos Apostolus scribit: 'Habemus altare de quo [h]non habent edere[h] hi qui tabernaculo deseruiunt',[120] id est, quo participare digni non sunt, qui corpori suo, in quo hic quasi in castris ministrant, uoluptuosum impendunt obsequium.[121] Ostium uero[i] tabernaculi finis est uite presentis, quando hinc[j] anima exit[k] de corpore et futuram ingreditur uitam. Ad hoc ostium excubant qui de exitu huius uite et introitu future solliciti sunt, et sic penitendo[l] disponunt[m] hunc exitum ut illum mereantur introitum. De hoc quidem cotidiano introitu [n]et exitu[n] sancte ecclesie illa est oratio Psalmiste: 'Dominus custodiat introitum tuum et exitum tuum.'[122] Tunc enim simul introitum[o] et[p] exitum nostrum custodit cum nos hinc exeuntes et iam per penitentiam purgatos, illuc[q] statim introducit.[r] Bene autem prius introitum quam exitum nominauit, non tam uidelicet ordinem quam dignitatem

[d] rescentes *C* [e] siccas et *S* [f-f] *om. BR* [g] ex *CEF*

16 [a] *TA with a large initial, CR;* possuit *E;* Posuit *FB also with a large but less ostentatious initial;* Apposuit *Amb* [b] barum (*exp.*) labrum *T;* librum *S* [c] excubant *TABRS;* excu *E* [d] omni *add. B* [e] *om. B* [f] pressioris *CEF* [g] etiam *add. R* [h-h] edere non habent potestatem *add. F* [i] *om. R* [j] hic *CEF* [k] *om. C* [l] penitudo *T* [m] deponunt *BR* [n-n] *om. CEF* [o] tuum *add. A* [p] *om. BRS* [q] illud *C* [r] introduxit *C*

[117] Num. 6: 2–5. For Nazirites cf. also *Letter* 1, **26** and *Rule* **82**.

nor eat fresh grapes or dried, during the whole period of their vow of consecration to the Lord. They shall eat nothing that comes from the vine, neither the juice of the grapes nor the lees, for all the days of their vow.'[117]

16. Of this persuasion, I believe, were those women who kept watch at the door of the tabernacle—the women whose mirrors Moses used to make the basin for Aaron and his sons to wash in, as it is written: Moses set up the bronze basin for Aaron and his sons to wash in, making it 'out of the mirrors of the women who kept watch at the doors of the Tent of the Presence'.[118] The warmth of their great devotion is clearly indicated: they stayed by the doors of the tabernacle when it was closed, and kept the watches of the holy vigils, spending even the night in prayer, and not relaxing in their divine service while the men rested. The fact that the tabernacle was closed to them properly signifies the life of penitents who are segregated from other people so that they may suffer more severely in their penitential laments. Such a life is ascribed particularly to the monastic profession, for monastic order is said to be nothing other than a milder form of penance.[119] The tabernacle at the door of which they kept watch is also to be understood in a mystical way as that of which the Apostle writes to the Hebrews: 'We have an altar, at which those who serve the sacred tent have no right to eat',[120] that is, those are unworthy to participate who give pleasure to their own bodies in which, as in a camp, they give service in this life.[121] The door of the tabernacle is the end of this present life, when the soul leaves the body and enters into the life to come. At this door watch is kept by those who are solicitous about departure from this life and entry into the life to come, and by their penitence so arrange their departure from here that they may merit entry there. On the subject of this daily coming and going in the holy Church the Psalmist prays: 'May the Lord guard your coming and your going',[122] for he guards both our coming and our going at the moment when we leave our life here and, being purged by penitence, are led by him immediately into the life to come. And the Psalmist rightly named our coming before he named our going, with worthiness rather than sequence in mind, for leaving

[118] Cf. Exod. 30: 18–19; 38: 8. Abelard's comment on these verses is partly based on Gregory the Great, *Homiliae in Euangelia*, xvii. 10 (ed. Étaix, pp. 124–5; *PL* lxxvi. 1143–4).

[119] Cf. *Problemata* 14 (*PL* clxxviii. 700A).

[120] Heb. 13: 10.

[121] Cf. *Sermons* 10 and 33 (*PL* clxxviii. 449C–450B, 583D).

[122] Ps. 120 (121): 8.

attendens,[s] cum hic exitus uite mortalis[t] in dolore sit, ille uero introitus eterne summa sit exultatio. Specula uero earum opera sunt exteriora ex quibus anime turpitudo uel decor diiudicatur, sicut ex speculo corporali qualitas humane faciei. Ex istis earum speculis uas componitur in quo se abluant Aaron et filii eius, quando sanctarum feminarum opera et tanta infirmi sexus in Deo constantia pontificum et presbyterorum negligentiam uehementer increpant, et ad compunctionis lacrimas precipue mouent. Et si,[u] [v]prout oportet, ipsi earum sollicitudinem gerant, hec ipsarum opera peccatis illorum[w] ueniam[v] per quam abluantur preparant. Ex his profecto speculis uas sibi compunctionis beatus parabat[x] Gregorius cum, sanctarum uirtutem feminarum et infirmi sexus in martyrio[y] uictoriam admirans et ingemiscens, querebat quid barbati[z] dicturi sint[a] uiri, cum tanta pro Christo delicate puelle sustineant et[b] tanto agone sexus fragilis triumphet, ut frequentius ipsum gemina[c] uirginitatis[d] et martyrii corona pollere nouerimus.[e] [123]

17. Ad has quidem, ut dictum est,[124] ad ostium tabernaculi excubantes, et que iam quasi Nazaree Domini suam ei uiduitatem consecrauerant,[a] beatam illam Annam pertinere non ambigo, que singularem Domini Nazareum Dominum[b] Ihesum Christum in templo [c]cum sancto Symeone pariter[c] meruit[d] suscipere, et, ut plusquam propheta[e] fieret, ipsum eadem hora qua Symeon per Spiritum agnoscere et presentem demonstrare ac[f] publice predicare.[125] [g]Cuius quidem laudem Euangelista diligentius prosequutus ait: 'Et erat Anna prophetissa, filia Phanuel, de tribu Aser. Hec processerat [h]in diebus multis,[h] et uixerat cum uiro suo annis septem a uirginitate sua. Et hec uidua erat usque ad annos octoginta quatuor, que non discedebat de templo, ieiuniis et obsecrationibus[i] seruiens nocte [j]ac die.[j] Et hec,[k] ipsa hora superueniens, confitebatur[l] Domino et loquebatur omnibus qui expectabant redemptionem[m] Ierusalem.'[n] [126] Nota singula que dicuntur et perpende quam studiosus[o] in huius uidue laude fuerit Euangelista et quantis

[s] accedens *C* [t] mortalitatis *ABR* [u] non *BR;* sicut *S* [v–v] *om. C* [w] eorum *BR* [x] preparat *BR;* preparabat *S* [y] Martyrie *R* [z] barbari *Amb* [a] sunt *AFAmb* [b] in *C* [c] geminam *C* [d] *over eras. in T; eras. also in marg.* [e] nouimus *R*

17 [a] consecrabant *F* [b] nostrum *add. B* [c–c] pariter cum sancto Symeone *BR* [d] meruerint *E* [e] Prophetissa *F* [f] et *F* [g] lacuna in CEF to end of section [h–h] uidelicet multis *A where another hand adds above this* in diebus*;* uidelicet multis in diebus *BR* [i] orationibus *?T*[1], *A* [j–j] om. R [k] hac *Amb* [l] confiteatur *B* [m] *om. A* [n] Israel *Amb*[1], *Vulg.* (*Clementine*) [o] studiosius *T*

mortal life is painful but our entry into eternal life is a supreme joy. The mirrors of the women are the outward works whereby the foulness or the brightness of the soul can be judged, just as the quality of the human face can be seen in a material mirror. From their mirrors the basin is made for Aaron and his sons to wash in; the works of holy women and the deep devotion of the weaker sex to God are a stern rebuke to the negligence of prelates and priests, and move them to tears of remorse as nothing else can. Then, if they pay heed to these women, as they should, the women's work prepares forgiveness for their sins whereby they shall be washed away. From these mirrors St Gregory prepared a basin of remorse for himself, when he sighed in admiration for the virtue of holy women and the victory of the weaker sex in martyrdom and asked: 'What are bearded men to say when delicate girls endure so much for Christ, and their frail sex triumphs in such great agony that we know it is more often they who win the double crown of virginity and martyrdom?'[123]

17. These women, as I have said,[124] kept watch at the door of the tabernacle and had already, like the Nazirites of the Lord, dedicated their widowhood to him. I have no doubt that blessed Anna should be counted among them, for she was found equally worthy with holy Simeon to receive in the temple that special Nazirite of the Lord, the Lord Jesus Christ, and, moreover, so that she might become more than a prophet, recognized him through the Holy Spirit, revealed him, and publicly proclaimed him at the same time as did Simeon.[125] Indeed, the Evangelist is explicit when writing in praise of her: 'There was also a prophetess, Anna the daughter of Phanuel, of the tribe of Asher. She was well advanced in years, and had lived seven years with her husband after marriage, and then as a widow until the age of 84. She never left the temple but worshipped day and night with fasting and prayer. She came up at that very moment and began to confess to the Lord and speak to all who were looking for the liberation of Jerusalem.'[126] Note every detail and mark how anxious the Evangelist was to praise this widow and extol her excellence in

[123] Cf. Gregory the Great, *Homiliae in Euangelia*, xi. 3 (ed. Étaix, p. 75; *PL* lxxvi. 1116A). Cf. *Hymn* 93 (Szövérffy 121), *De uirginibus* 2, IV. For the 'double crown' cf. also **41** below.

[124] At **16** above.

[125] Cf. Luke 2: 25–38 and **2** above. 'Nazareum': cf. Matt. 2: 23.

[126] Luke 2: 36–8. Cf. **2** above.

preconiis excellentiam eius extulerit. Cuius quidem prophetie[p] gratiam quam habere solita erat et parentem eius et tribum et, post septem annos quos cum uiro sustinuerat, longeuum sancte uiduitatis tempus quo se Domino mancipauerat et assiduitatem eius in templo et ieiuniorum et orationum instantiam et[q] confessionem laudis[r] [s]quas grates[s] Domino referebat et publicam eius predicationem de promisso et nato Saluatore diligenter expressit. Et Symeonem[t] quidem iam superius Euangelista de iusticia, non de prophetia, commendauerat, nec in eo tante continentie uel abstinentie uirtutem nec diuini sollicitudinem obsequii fuisse memorauit[127] nec de eius ad alios[u] predicatione quicquam adiecit.

18. Huius quoque professionis[a] atque propositi ille sunt uere uidue de quibus ad Thymotheum scribens [b]Apostolus ait:[b] 'Viduas honora, que uere uidue sunt.'[128] [c]Item: 'Que autem uere[d] uidua est, et desolata, speret in Deum, et instet obsecrationibus et orationibus nocte ac die. Et hoc precipe[e] ut irreprehensibiles sint',[129] etc.[c] Et iterum: 'Si quis fidelis habet uiduas, subministret illis, et non grauetur ecclesia, ut his que uere[f] uidue sunt sufficiat.'[130] Veras[g] quippe uiduas dicit[h] que uiduitatem suam secundis nuptiis non dehonestauerunt,[i] uel que deuotione magis quam necessitate sic perseuerantes Domino se dicarunt. Desolatas[j] dicit que sic omnibus abrenuntiant ut nullum terreni [k]solatii subsidium[k] retineant, uel qui earum curam agant[l] [m]non habent.[m] Quas quidem et[n] honorandas esse precipit, et de stipendiis ecclesie censet[o] sustentari, tanquam de propriis redditibus sponsi earum Christi. Ex quibus etiam quales [p]ad diaconatus ministerium sint[p] eligende diligenter describit, dicens: 'Vidua eligatur non minus sexaginta annorum que fuerit unius uiri uxor,[q] in operibus bonis testimonium habens, si filios educauit, si hospitio suscepit, si sanctorum pedes lauit, si tribulationem pacientibus subministrauit, si omne [r]bonum opus[r] consecuta est. Adolescentiores autem uiduas

[p] prophetice *T before corr. by exp.*; prophetissae *Amb* [q] *om. TAmb* [r] *S breaks off here due to loss of leaves* [s–s] qua gratis *A* [t] simeon *A;* symeon *R* [u] de *add. BR*

18 [a] perfectionis *FAmb*[1] [b–b] ait Apostolus *E* [c–c] *om. C* [d] *om. A* [e] Precipue *BRAmb* [f] uere' *F;* uerae *Amb* [g] uere *E;* Vere' *F* [h] dici *A* [i] honestauerunt *BR* [j] Dosolatas *T* [k–k] subsidium solatii *CEF* [l] gerant *F* [m–m] *add. in marg. by another hand in E* [n] ut *BR* [o] cesset *R* [p–p] sint ad dyaconatus (diaconatus *F*) ministerium *CEF* [q] *om. R* [r–r] opus bonum; *CEBR*

terms of the warmest appreciation. He took pains to describe the gift of prophecy she usually enjoyed, her father and tribe, the seven years she lived with her husband, and then the long period of her holy widowhood, during which she had devoted herself to the Lord, her constant attendance in the Temple and her unremitting fasting and prayer, her confession of praise to the Lord and the thanks she gave him, and her public preaching of the birth of the promised Saviour. On the other hand, the Evangelist previously praised Simeon for his upright character, not for any prophetic gift, and made no mention of his having so great a virtue of continence or abstinence, nor such concern for divine worship;[127] nor did he add anything about his preaching to others.

18. The same profession and way of life is also followed by those who are true widows, of whom the Apostle wrote to Timothy: 'Honour widows who are widows in the true sense.'[128] Also: 'But a woman who is truly widowed and left desolate will set her hopes on God and devote herself day and night to supplication and prayer. Remind them of this too so that they may be blameless',[129] etc. And again: 'If any Christian believer has widows in his family he should support them and not let them be a burden on the congregation, so that it may support those who are widows in the true sense.'[130] By true widows he means women who have not dishonoured their widowhood by a second marriage, or who from devotion rather than necessity have steadfastly dedicated themselves to the Lord. By desolate he means widows who renounce everything, so that they retain no earthly comfort for their support or have no one to care for them; he gives instructions that they are to be honoured and says that they should be supported from church funds as if from personal gifts from Christ their spouse. He also describes in detail what sort of widows should be chosen to wait on the deacons: 'A widow should not be chosen under 60 years of age. She must have been the wife of only one husband, and show proof of good works, whether she has brought up children, given hospitality, washed the feet of God's people, helped those who are in distress, and been active in all kinds of good work.

[127] Cf. Luke 2: 25.

[128] 1 Tim. 5: 3. On widows cf. **20** and **22** below and *Letters* 5, **4** and 6, **28** and *Rule* **27**. Cf. also a nearly contemporary work of uncertain authorship, *Speculum virginum*, vii, *ll.* 461–73 (ed. Seyfarth, p. 206).

[129] 1 Tim. 5: 5 and 7.

[130] 1 Tim. 5: 16.

deuita.'[s] [131] Quod quidem beatus exponens Ieronimus: 'Deuita', inquit,[t] 'in[u] ministerio diaconatus preponere[v] ne malum pro bono detur exemplum.'[132] Si uidelicet iuniores ad hoc eligantur, que ad temptationem[w] proniores et natura leuiores, nec per experientiam longeue etatis prouide,[x] malum exemplum his prebeant quibus maxime bonum dare debuerant. Quod quidem malum[y] exemplum in iunioribus uiduis, quia iam[z] Apostolus certis[a] didicerat experimentis, aperte profitetur, et consilium insuper aduersum hoc prebet. Cum enim premisisset: 'Adolescentiores autem uiduas deuita',[b] [133] [c]causam huius rei[c] et consilii sui medicamentum statim apposuit, dicens: 'Cum enim luxuriate fuerint in Christo, nubere uolunt,[d] habentes dampnationem quia primam fidem irritam fecerunt. [e]Simul autem et otiose discunt circumire[f] domos, non solum otiose sed et uerbose et curiose loquentes que non oportet.[e] Volo ergo iuniores nubere, filios procreare, matresfamilias esse, nullam occasionem[g] dare aduersario maledicti gratia. Iam enim quedam conuerse sunt retro[h] Sathanan.'[134]

19. Hanc quoque Apostoli prouidentiam de diaconissis scilicet eligendis beatus Gregorius sequutus, Maximo,[a] Siracusano episcopo, scribit his uerbis: 'Iuuenculas abbatissas[b] uehementissime prohibemus. Nullum igitur episcopum[c] fraternitas tua nisi sexagenariam[d] uirginem cuius uita[e] hoc[f] atque mores exegerint[g] uelare[h] permittat.'[i] [135] Abbatissas quippe quas nunc dicimus antiquitus diaconissas uocabant, quasi ministeriales potius quam matres.[136] Diaconus quippe

[s] de uita *TA* [t] aliis *add. Muckle* [u] aliis *Souter and PL, Supplementum* [v] *om. Amb* [w] temptationes *R* [x] et *add. T* [y] *om. Amb* [z] *om. R* [a] cunctis *R* [b] de uita *TA* [c–c] Huius rei causam *CEF;* causa huius rei *R* [d] nolunt *B* [e–e] *om. CEF* [f] circuire *BR* [g] occasitatem *B;* occiositatem *R* [h] retro post *add. F*

19 [a] Maximiano *F, Gregory* [b] fieri *add. F, Gregory* [c] *om. F* [d] sexariam *BR* [e] uitam *TABRAmb;* etas *F* [f] *om. Amb.* [g] exigerint *BR* [h] uelari *F* [i] permittent *?B*

[131] 1 Tim. 5: 9–11. Also cited in *Rule* **27**. In *Letter* 6, **13** Heloise refers to legislative canons which have decreed that the minimum age for a woman to become a deaconess should be 40 years. If she was born *c.*1095 (cf. Robl, '*Hersindis mater*', p. 54 (§7 and n.)), Heloise was herself about 40 when she was named abbess of the oratory of the Holy Trinity by Pope Innocent II in a privilege dated 17 June 1135 (*Checklist* no. 417). On deaconesses see Appendix A, 6. iii.

[132] Not Jerome but Pelagius, *Expositiones xiii epistularum Pauli: Expositio in 1 Timotheum* (ed. Souter, p. 495; *PL, Supplementum*, 1, pp. 1354–5). Pelagius' *Commentary* on the Epistles of St Paul was revised by Cassiodorus and his pupils in the mid-6th c. Cf. John the

But avoid choosing younger widows.'[131] St Jerome explains this as follows: 'Avoid preferring them to others for waiting on the deacons lest you find yourselves with a bad example instead of a good one.'[132] For if younger widows are chosen for this who are more prone to temptation and naturally more frivolous, lacking the foresight which comes from experience in a long life, they may set a bad example to those to whom especially they ought to have set a good one. Jerome openly ascribes this bad example to younger widows because the Apostle had learned this from actual experience and offered advice against it; for after he had said: 'But avoid choosing younger widows',[133] he added the reason for this warning and gave advice to remedy the situation, saying: 'For when their passions draw them away from Christ, they want to marry, and then they are condemned for breaking their first promise. At the same time they learn to be idle and go from house to house, and not only idle but gossips and busybodies, speaking of things best left unspoken. It is my wish therefore that younger widows should remarry, have children, preside over a home, and give no opponent occasion for slander. For there have already been some who have taken the wrong turning and gone to the devil.'[134]

19. St Gregory also follows the Apostle's wise ruling on the choosing of deaconesses, when he writes as follows to Maximus, bishop of Syracuse: 'We absolutely forbid the choice of young women as abbesses. Therefore, see that your fraternity allows no bishop to give the veil except to a virgin of 60 years whose life and morals have proved her claim.'[135] Those whom we now call abbesses were called deaconesses in former times, as if in recognition of their service rather than of their being mothers to those in their care;[136] for deacon means

Deacon, *In Epistolam* 1 *ad Timotheum*, v. 11 (*PL* xxx. 883D). Cited also in Jerome's name in *Sermon* 31 (*PL* clxxviii. 572C) and less fully in *Comm. Rom.*, iv (xvi. 2, p. 327).

[133] 1 Tim. 5: 11. [134] 1 Tim. 5: 11–15.

[135] Gregory the Great, *Registrum epistularum*, IV, 11 (ed. Norberg, cxl. 229; ed. Ewald and Hartmann, i. 245; *PL* lxxvi. 681B).

[136] Cf. *Comm. Rom.*, iv (xvi. 2, p. 327): 'Quas itaque antiquitus diaconissas, id est ministras, nunc abbatissas, id est matres, uocamus', and *Rule* **26**. Heloise calls herself deaconess (and also, according to some MSS, abbess) in her salutation in *Letter* 4, **1**. In *Comm. Cantab.* (ed. Landgraf, part 3, pp. 574–5), preference is given to speaking of deaconesses as ministers, not as abbesses. They lead a group of women but minister to the poor: 'mulieres huiusmodi (*sc.* diaconisse), que aliis in ministratione pauperum presunt, hodie abatisse vocantur, que convenientiori vocabulo iuxta dominicam sententiam, que est: Qui maior est vestrum . . . fiat minister vester (cf. Matt. 23: 11), ministre appellantur.' See further on deaconesses Appendix A, 6. iii.

minister interpretatur, et diaconissas[j] [k]ab administratione potius[k] quam [l]a prelatione[l] nuncupandas[m] esse censebant, secundum quod ipse Dominus tam exemplis quam uerbis instituit dicens: 'Qui maior est uestrum [n]erit minister uester.'[n] [137] Et iterum: 'Numquit[o] [p]maior est,[p] qui recumbit an qui ministrat? [q]Ego autem in medio uestrum sum, sicut qui ministrat.'[q] [138] Et alibi: 'Sicut filius hominis non uenit ministrari sed ministrare.'[139] Vnde Ieronimus hoc ipsum nomen abbatis, quo [r]iam gloriari multos[r] nouerat, ex ipsa Domini auctoritate non mediocriter ausus est arguere.[s] Qui uidelicet eum locum exponens, quo scriptum[t] est in epistola ad Galatas: 'Clamantem, abba pater',[140] [u]'abba', inquit, 'hebraicum est,[v] [w]hoc ipsum[w] significans[x] quod pater. Cum[y] autem abba pater[u] hebreo syroque sermone dicatur, et Dominus[z] in Euangelio precipit[a] nullum patrem uocandum esse[b] nisi Deum,[141] nescio qua licentia in monasteriis uel uocemus[c] hoc nomine alios uel uocari nos acquiescamus. Et certe ipse precepit[d] hoc qui dixerat non esse iurandum.[142] Si non iuramus nec patrem[e] quempiam nominemus. Si de patre interpretabimur[f] aliter, et de iurando [g]aliter sentire[g] cogemur.'[143]

20. Ex his profecto diaconissis Pheben illam fuisse constat quam Apostolus [a]Romanis diligenter[a] commendans et pro[b] ea exorans ait: 'Commendo autem uobis Pheben sororem nostram, que est in ministerio ecclesie que est[c] Cenchris,[144] ut eam suscipiatis in Domino [d]digne sanctis[d] et assistatis ei in quocunque negotio uestri[e] indiguerit. [f]Etenim ipsa[f] quoque astitit multis et mihi ipsi.'[145] Quem quidem locum tam Cassiodorus quam Claudius exponentes ipsam illius ecclesie diaconissam fuisse profitentur. [g]Cassiodorus: 'Significat', inquit, 'diaconissam fuisse matris ecclesie, quod in partibus[h] Grecorum hodie [i]usque quasi militie[i] causa peragitur. Quibus et baptizandi usus in ecclesia non negatur.'[146] Claudius: 'Hic locus',

[j] diaconissa *F* [k–k] potius administrationem *CEF* [l–l] ad prelationem *CE;* praelationem *F;* amplatione *BR* [m] non cupiendas *B* [n–n] erit enim *B;* maior erit u. *R* [o] Nunquid *AAmb;* Nam quia *F* [p–p] est maior *Amb* [q–q] *om. C* [r–r] iam gloriari multas *E;* iam multos gloriori iam *BR* [s] augere *R* [t] quod scriptum *TCE;* qui scriptus *FAmb*[1] [u–u] *om. A* [v] *om. B;* eum *R* [w–w]idipsum *F, Jerome* [x] signans *CE* [y] siue *B* [z] noster *add. F* [a] praecipiat *F, Jerome* [b] *om. F* [c] uocamus *E* [d] precipit *AEFBR* [e] quidem *add. F, Jerome* [f] interpretamur *C* [g–g] sentire aliter *BR*

20 [a–a] diligenter romanis *CEFBR* [b] post *BR* [c] in *add. Amb* [d–d] digne satis *A; om. CE* [e] uestro *TBRAmb* [f–f] ut u. Ipsa enim *C* [g–g] *om. CEF but marked for corr. in E* [h] pactibus *Amb* [i–i] T^3 *over eras.;* quod que si militie *BR*

minister, and it was thought that they should be called deaconesses after their ministry instead of their office, in accordance with what the Lord himself had laid down, both by example and by word: 'The greatest among you must be your servant.'[137] Again: 'Which is the greater, the one who sits at table or the one who serves? Yet here am I among you like a servant.'[138] And elsewhere: 'Just as the Son of Man came not to be served but to serve.'[139] Jerome accordingly argued boldly in no uncertain terms against the very name of abbot, knowing that many boasted of it and had the Lord's authority to do so; for in expounding the passage in the Letter to the Galatians which says: 'Crying, "Abba! Father!"'[140] he says: 'Abba is a Hebrew word which means the same as Father. But since Abba means Father in the Hebrew and Syrian tongue, and the Lord in the Gospel says that no one is to be called father except God,[141] I do not know with what licence we either call others by that name in monasteries, or allow ourselves to be so called. This was clearly what the Lord instructed when he forbade swearing:[142] if we do not swear neither may we name any man father. If we give another meaning to the word father we shall also have to think differently about swearing.'[143]

20. There can be no doubt that one of these deaconesses was the Phoebe whom the Apostle expressly commends to the Romans with this plea on her behalf: 'I commend to you our sister Phoebe, who serves the church at Cenchreae.[144] Give her, in the fellowship of Christ, a welcome worthy of God's people, and stand by her in any business in which she needs your help, for she has herself been a good friend to many, including myself.'[145] Both Cassiodorus and Claudius in their exposition of this passage state that she was a deaconess of that church. Cassiodorus says that 'it means that she was a deaconess of a Mother Church, a practice which continues in some of the Greek communities up to the present day, as a sort of military training. Such women were permitted to administer baptism in the Church.'[146]

[137] Matt. 23: 11. [138] Luke 22: 27. [139] Matt. 20: 28.
[140] Gal. 4: 6. [141] Cf. Matt. 23: 8. [142] Cf. Matt. 5: 34.
[143] Jerome, *Commentarii . . . in epistolam ad Galatas*, ii. 4 (*PL* xxvi. 374AB (400AB)).
[144] Cenchreae: one of the ports of Corinth.
[145] Rom. 16: 1–2. See also on deaconesses Appendix A. 6. iii.
[146] Not found in the *Expositio S. Pauli epistolae ad Romanos* (*PL* lxviii. 415–506), a work of the school of Cassiodorus (d. *c.*580), once attributed to Primasius of Hadrumetum in north Africa (also 6th c.). Also cited, and attributed to Cassiodorus, in *Comm. Rom.*, iv (xvi. 2, p. 327) and in *Sermon* 31 (*PL* clxxviii. 572B). The *Expositio*, based on one by Pelagius, was anonymous to Cassiodorus and his circle, who purged it of Pelagian errors; it was later used by Claudius of Turin; see Souter, *The Earliest Latin Commentaries*, p. 210.

inquit, 'apostolica auctoritate docet etiam feminas in ministerio ecclesie constitui. In quo officio positam Pheben apud ecclesiam que est Cenchris Apostolus magna cum laude et commendatione[j] prosequitur.'[gk] [147] Quales etiam ipse ad Tymotheum scribens, inter ipsos colligens diaconos,[l] [m]simili morum[m] instructione uitam earum instituit.[148] Ibi quippe ecclesiasticorum ministeriorum[n] ordinans gradus, cum ab episcopo ad diaconos[o] descendisset, 'diacones',[p] inquit, 'similiter pudicos, non bilingues,[q] non multo[r] uino deditos, non turpe luchrum sectantes, habentes mysterium[s] fidei in conscientia pura. [t]Et hi[t] autem probentur primum, et sic ministrent, nullum crimen [u]habentes. Mulieres similiter pudicas esse,[v] non detrahentes, sobrias, fideles in omnibus. [w]Diacones sint unius uxoris uiri, qui filiis suis bene presint[x] et suis domibus. Qui enim bene ministrauerint gradum bonum sibi acquirent, et multam fiduciam in fide que est in Christo Ihesu.'[149] Quod itaque ibi de diaconibus dixit: 'non bilingues', hoc[y] de diaconissis dicit: 'non detrahentes'. Quod ibi: 'non multo uino deditos', hic dicit: 'sobrias'. Cetera uero que ibi sequuntur hic breuiter comprehendit[z] dicens:[a] 'fideles in omnibus'.[150] Qui etiam sicut episcopos siue diaconos esse prohibet digamos,[b] ita etiam[c] diaconissas unius uiri uxores instituit[d] esse, ut iam supra meminimus.[151] 'Vidua', inquit, 'eligatur non minus sexaginta annorum, que fuerit unius uiri uxor, in operibus bonis testimonium habens, si filios educauit, si hospitio recepit, si sanctorum pedes lauit, si tribulationem pacientibus[e] subministrauit, si omne opus bonum subsequuta[f] est. Adolescentiores autem uiduas deuita.'[wg] [152] [h]In qua quidem[hu] diaconissarum [i]descriptione[j] uel[k] instructione[l] quam diligentior fuerit Apostolus quam in premissis tam episcoporum quam diaconorum

[j] Mendacione *R* [k] prosequatur *BR* [l] diacones *B;* dyacones *R* [m–m] simili in eorum *EF;* semil morum *B; R leaves a space sufficient for about 10 characters* [n] ministrorum *FAmb*[1] [o] diacones *C;* dyacones *E* [p] diaconos *A; om. B* [q] bilinguentes *C, E before corr. by exp.* [r] *E before corr. by exp.* [s] ministerium *B* [t–t] Et: Hi *Amb* [u–u] habentes etc ubi *CE* [v] *om. F* [w–w] *om. F* [x] possint *BR* [y] hic *B* [z] *T*[3] *over eras.; eras. also in marg.* [a] *om. Amb* [b] bigamos *Amb*[1] [c] et *Amb* [d] constituit *BR* [e] parentibus *RAmb* [f] sub(*T*[3] *over eras.*)sequuta *T; eras. also in marg.* [g] etc. *add. TABR* [h–h] Vbi non tantam *F* [i–i] u[m] tam dyaconorum quam episcoporum potest apostolica (apostolus *E*) ubi etiam caute *CE;* uirum tam diaconorum quam episcoporum ponit Apostolus. Vbi et caute *F* [j] descriptionem *EF* [k] siue *CE* [l] instructionem *F*

---

[147] According to Buytaert, this passage, which is also cited in *Comm. Rom.*, iv (xvi. 2, ed. Buytaert, p. 327), comes from the unpublished Commentary on Romans by Claudius, bishop of Turin (9th c.) which is found in Paris, BnF lat. 2392, fo. 64[ra]. Also cited and attributed to Claudius in *Sermon* 31 (*PL* clxxviii. 572BC).

Claudius says: 'This passage informs us on apostolic authority that women were appointed to service in the Church. Phoebe, who held office in the church at Cenchreae, was warmly praised and commended by the Apostle.'[147] In writing to Timothy the Apostle also grouped such women with deacons, with similar moral guidance to regulate their lives.[148] For in presenting the grades of ecclesiastical ministry, when he had come down from the bishop to deacons, he said: 'Deacons likewise must be men of high principle, not indulging in double talk, given neither to excessive drinking nor to money-grubbing. They must combine a pure conscience with a firm hold on the deep truths of our faith. They too must first be subject to scrutiny, and if they are found blameless, they may serve. Their wives equally must be women of high principle, who will not talk scandal, sober and trustworthy in every way. A deacon must be faithful to one wife, good at managing his children and his household. For those who have served well will earn a high standing for themselves, and great assurance in their work for the faith in Christ Jesus.'[149] So what he said there about deacons, that they must not indulge in double talk, he now says of deaconesses, that they must not talk scandal. 'Not given to excessive drinking' is followed by 'sober' but all the subsequent points are briefly summed up in the words 'trustworthy in every way'.[150] Similarly, just as he forbids a bishop and a deacon to be twice married, he lays down that a deaconess should be the wife of only one husband, as we have already said:[151] 'A widow should not be chosen under 60 years of age. She must have been the wife of only one husband, and show proof of good works, whether she has brought up children, given hospitality, washed the feet of God's people, helped those who are in distress, and been active in all kinds of good work. But avoid choosing younger widows.'[152] It can easily be determined how much more punctilious the Apostle was in this description or guidance of deaconesses than in his regulations

[148] Cf. *Sermon* 31: 'Idem quoque apostolus, cum supra in eadem Epistola post episcopos etiam diaconorum vitam ordinaret, institutionem quoque diaconarum illis conjunxit' (*PL* clxxviii. 572C).

[149] 1 Tim. 3: 8–13. Also cited in *Sermon* 31 (*PL* clxxviii. 572CD). Cf. Jerome, *Epistola* XIV *ad Heliodorum*, who cites verses 8–10 (ed. Hilberg, liv. 56; *PL* xxii. 352).

[150] Cf. *Comm. Cantab.* (ed. Landgraf, part 3, p. 574).

[151] 18 above and cf. *Sermon* 31: 'quemadmodum . . . diaconos quoque, sicut episcopos, unius uxoris viros approbat, ita . . . diaconissarum ordinem instituens, eas etiam unius viri uxores maxime commendat' (*PL* clxxviii. 572D).

[152] 1 Tim. 5: 9–11. Also cited at 18 above and in *Rule* 27 and (less fully) in *Sermon* 31 (*PL* clxxviii. 572D).

institutionibus facile est assignare. Quippe quod ait: 'in operibus bonis[m] testimonium habens' uel 'si hospitio recepit', nequaquam in diaconibus memorauit. Quod[n] uero adiecit: 'si sanctorum pedes lauit, si tribulationem', etc., tam in episcopis quam in diaconis tacitum est. Et episcopos quidem et diaconos[o] dicit: 'nullum crimen habentes'.[153] Istas uero non solum irreprehensibiles esse precipit,[p] uerum etiam 'omne opus bonum' subsequutas dicit.[154]

21. Caute etiam[i] de maturitate [a]etatis earum[a] prouidit, ut in omnibus auctoritatem habeant, dicens: 'non minus sexaginta annorum', et non solum uite earum, uerum[b] etiam etati longeue in multis probate reuerentia deferatur. Vnde et Dominus, licet Iohannem plurimum diligeret,[155] Petrum tamen seniorem tam ipsi quam ceteris prefecit.[156] [c]Minus quippe omnes indignantur seniorem sibi quam iuniorem preponi, et libentius[c] seniori paremus quem[d] non solum uita priorem uerum etiam[e] natura et ordo temporis fecit. Hinc et[f] Ieronimus [g]in primo[g] *contra Iouinianum*, cum de prelatione Petri meminerit:[h] 'Vnus', inquit, 'eligitur ut, capite constituto, scismatis tollatur occasio. Sed cur non Iohannes electus est?[i] Etati delatum est, quia Petrus senior erat, ne[j] adhuc adolescens et[k] pene puer progresse etatis hominibus preferretur, et magister bonus (qui occasionem iurgii debuerat auferre discipulis) in adolescentem quem dilexerat causam prebere uideretur inuidie.'[157] Hoc[l] abbas ille diligenter considerabat qui, sicut in *Vitis Patrum* scriptum est, iuniori fratri qui primus ad conuersionem uenerat primatum abstulit, et maiori[m] eum[n] tradidit hoc[o] uno tantum quia hic illum[p] etate precedebat.[158] [q]Verebatur quippe ne ipse etiam frater carnalis indigne ferret iuniorem sibi preponi. [r]Meminerat ipsos quoque[r] apostolos de duobus ipsorum indignatos esse cum apud Christum, matre interueniente, prerogatiuam quandam affectasse uiderentur,[159] maxime cum unus horum esset duorum qui ceteris iunior erat apostolis, ipse[s] uidelicet Iohannes de quo modo diximus.

[m] *add. BR* [n] Que *A* [o] diacones *A* [p] precepit *A*

21 [a–a] earum etatis *CEF* [b] sed *F* [c–c] *om. C* [d] quam *AE* [e] et *C;* et *add. Amb* [f] *om. F* [g–g] *om. BR* [h] *Ecorr.;* meminit *F* [i] *F adds in marg.* viros? virgo?; virgo *Jerome* [j] nec *CF* [k] ac *F* [l] Haec *F* [m] maiora *B* [n] abstulit *add. A* [o] hic *BR* [p] illam *E* [q] *lacuna in CEF which ends in 23 below* [r–r] Meminatur quoque ipsos *BR* [s] Ipse *Amb*

[153] 1 Tim. 3: 10. [154] 1 Tim. 5:10.

for bishops and deacons. For what he says about showing proof of good works and giving hospitality is not applied to deacons; and when he goes on to speak of washing the feet of God's people and helping those in distress, there is no mention of either bishops or deacons. To be sure, he says of both bishops and deacons that they must be found blameless,[153] but he rules that the women must not only be blameless but 'active in all kinds of good work'.[154]

21. He also made careful provision for the deaconesses to be of mature age, saying that they 'should not be under 60 years of age'. This was to establish their authority over the others, and to ensure that reverence be paid not only to their way of life but also to their advanced age, tested in many ways. This is why the Lord, though he loved John so much,[155] set Peter, the older man, over him and the rest,[156] for all men are less resentful when an older rather than a younger man is given authority over them, and we are more willing to obey an older man who owes his precedence to nature and age as well as to his way of life. So also Jerome in the first book of his *Against Jovinian*, says with reference to the prelacy of Peter: 'One was chosen to remove all chance of schism once a head was appointed. But why was John not chosen ? Regard was paid to age, because Peter was the older man, so that one who was still a youth, almost a boy, should not be given precedence over men of advanced age, and the good master (who had an obligation to remove all occasion for quarrelling from his disciples) should not appear to provide a cause for jealous feeling against the young man he had loved.'[157] This was the consideration which prompted the abbot in the *Lives of the Fathers* to remove the office of prior from a younger brother, who had come first to conversion, and transfer it to an older one, for the sole reason that the latter was senior in age.[158] He must have feared that even a brother in the flesh would take it amiss if a younger man were given authority over him. He remembered that the apostles themselves were indignant when two of their number appeared to have sought some special favour from Christ at their mother's intervention,[159] especially as one of them was the youngest of the apostles, John in fact, of whom we spoke above.

[155] Cf. John 13: 23, 19: 26, 20: 2, 21: 7 and 20.
[156] Cf. Matt. 16: 16–19.
[157] Jerome, *Aduersus Iouinianum*, i. 26 (*PL* xxiii. 247AB).
[158] Cf. *Vitae Patrum*, *Verba seniorum*, v. 10. 113 (*PL* lxxiii. 932D).
[159] Cf. Matt. 20: 20–4; Mark 10: 35–41. The two apostles are James and John, sons of Zebedee.

22. Nec solum in diaconissis instituendis apostolica plurimum inuigilauerit[a] cura, uerum generaliter erga sancte professionis uiduas quam studiosius[b] extiterit liquet, ut omnem amputet [c]temptationis occasionem.[c] Cum enim premisisset: 'Viduas honora que uere uidue sunt'[160] statim adiecit: 'Si qua autem uidua filios aut nepotes habet, discat[d] primum domum suam regere et mutuam uicem reddere parentibus.'[161] Et post aliqua: 'Si quis', inquit, 'suorum[e] et maxime domesticorum curam non habet, fidem negauit, et est infideli deterior.'[162] In quibus quidem uerbis simul et debite prouidet humanitati et proposite religioni ne uidelicet sub[f] obtentu religionis paruuli deserantur inopes, et carnalis compassio erga[g] indigentes sanctum uidue perturbet propositum, et retro respicere cogat, et nonnumquam etiam usque ad sacrilegia trahat, et aliquid suis porrigat quod de communi defraudet. Vnde necessarium prebet[h] consilium ut, que domesticorum cura sunt implicite, antequam ad ueram uiduitatem transeuntes diuinis se penitus obsequiis mancipent, hanc uicem suis parentibus reddant ut, sicut eorum cura fuerunt educate, ipse quoque posteris suis eadem lege prouideant. Qui etiam uiduarum religionem exaggerans, eas instare precipit obsecrationibus et orationibus nocte et die. De quarum etiam necessitudinibus admodum solicitus, 'siquis fidelis', inquit, 'habet uiduas subministret illis et non grauetur ecclesia ut his que uere uidue sunt sufficiat.'[163] Ac si aperte dicat: Si qua est uidua que tales habeat domesticos qui ei necessaria de facultatibus suis ualeant ministrare, ipsi super hoc ei prouideant ut ceteris sustentandis publici sumptus ecclesie possint sufficere. Que quidem sententia patenter ostendit, siqui erga huiusmodi uiduas suas obstinati sunt, eos ad hoc debitum ex apostolica auctoritate constringendos esse. Qui non solum earum necessitudini, uerum etiam prouidens honori, 'uiduas', inquit, 'honora que uere uidue sunt'.[164]

23. [a]Tales illas[b] fuisse credimus quarum alteram ipse matrem,[c] alteram Iohannes euuangelista dominam, ex sancte professionis reuerentia uocat.[d] 'Salutate',[e] inquit Paulus ad Romanos scribens,

22 [a] inuigilauit *Amb* [b] *A* (*but marked for corr.*),*BRAmb* [c–c] occasionis temptationem *BR* [d] dicat *R* [e] sanctorum *A* [f] quod *B* [g] *om. BR* [h] patet *Amb*

23 [a] *CEF resume with* huius sancti propositi illas uiduas *CEF* [b] *om. A* [c] Paulus matrem *CF;* Paulus *E* [d] uocant *CF* [e] Saluator *BR*

---

[160] 1 Tim. 5: 3; cf. **21** above.
[161] 1 Tim. 5: 4.
[162] 1 Tim. 5: 8.
[163] 1 Tim. 5: 16; cf. **18** above.

22. Nor was it only in the appointment of deaconesses that the Apostle showed particular care and concern, for it is clear how attentive he was to widows of holy profession in general, in order to cut off every opportunity of temptation. For when he had said: 'Honour widows who are widows in the true sense',[160] he went on at once to add: 'But if a widow has children or grandchildren she must first learn to manage her household and repay the debt she owes to her parents.'[161] And a little later: 'If anyone does not look after his own relatives, especially if they are living in his house, he has denied the faith and is worse than an unbeliever.'[162] In these words he provided for the claims of humanity as well as of religious profession to ensure that, under the pretext of religion, young children shall not be left destitute and that human compassion for the needy shall not interrupt the holy profession of the widow and force her to look back, and sometimes even lead her to sacrilege, if she makes provision for her family by defrauding the community. Hence the necessary advice that before women who are involved in domestic responsibilities may pass to true widowhood, and devote themselves wholly to the service of God, they must discharge their debt to their parents and, as they themselves were brought up in their parents' care, by the same rule, they must make provision for their own offspring. The Apostle also extends the religious duties of widows, bidding them be active day and night in supplication and prayer, and he is also much concerned with their personal needs. 'If any Christian believer', he says, 'has widows in his family he should support them and not let them be a burden on the congregation, so that it may support those who are widows in the true sense.'[163] He could have said openly that if any widow has people in her family able to supply her with necessities from their own resources, they should provide for her in this respect, so that the public funds of the Church can be sufficient to support the others. This injunction clearly shows that people who stubbornly neglect their obligations towards widows of this kind must be compelled to do their duty on the authority of the Apostle, who looked not only to their needs but also to the tribute due to them when he said: 'Honour widows who are widows in the true sense.'[164]

23. Such we believe were those women of whom the Apostle calls one his mother and John the Evangelist calls another his lady, out of reverence for their holy profession. In writing to the Romans Paul

'Rufum electum in Domino et matrem eius et meam.'[165] Iohannes uero[f] in secunda quam scribit epistola, 'senior', inquit, 'electe[g] domine et natis eius',[166] etc. A qua etiam se diligi postulans inferius adiunxit: 'Et nunc rogo te domina ut diligamus alterutrum.'[167] [h]Cuius quoque[h] fretus auctoritate beatus[i] Ieronimus, ad uestre professionis uirginem Eustochium[j] scribens, eam appellare dominam[k] non erubuit,[l] immo [m]cur etiam[m] debuerit statim apposuit, dicens: 'Hec[n] idcirco, domina mea[o] Eustochium,[p] dominam quippe debeo uocare[q] sponsam Domini mei',[168] etc.[r]

24. Qui etiam postmodum in eadem epistola[a] huius sancti propositi prerogatiuam omni terrene felicitatis glorie superponens[b] ait: 'Nolo [c]habeas consortia matronarum,[c] nolo ad nobilium[d] accedas domos,[e] nolo[f] frequenter uideas[g] quod contempnens uirgo esse uoluisti. Si ad imperatoris uxorem concurrerit[h] ambitio salutantium, cur tu facis iniuriam uiro tuo? Ad hominis[i] coniugem[j] sponsa Dei quid properas? Disce in hac parte[k] superbiam sanctam; [l]scito te[l] [m]esse illis[m] meliorem.'[169] Qui etiam ad uirginem Deo dicatam[n] scribens de consecratis[o] Deo uirginibus, quantam in celo beatitudinem et in terra possideant dignitatem, [p]ita exorsus ait: 'Quantam in celestibus beatitudinem uirginitas sancta possideat,[p] preter[q] Scripturarum testimonia ecclesie[r] etiam consuetudine edocemur, qua[s] addiscimus[t] peculiare illis[u] subsistere meritum, quarum[v] specialis[w] est consecratio. Nam cum unaqueque[x] turba credentium paria [y]gratie dona[y] percipiat,[z] et hisdem omnes sacramentorum benedictionibus glorientur, iste [a]proprium aliquid[a] pre ceteris habent, dum de illo sancto et immaculato ecclesie grege, quasi sanctiores purioresque hostie[b] pro uoluntatis sue meritis a [c]Spiritu sancto[c] eliguntur,[d] et per summum sacerdotem Dei offeruntur altario.'[170] Item:[e] 'Possidet ergo uirginitas

[f] *om. R* [g] dilecte *BR* [h–h] Cuius cumque *B;* Cuiusque *R* [i] *om. BR* [j] Euthochium *E* [k] animam *E* [l] eribuit *B* [m–m] etiam cur *CEF* [n] Hoc *Amb* [o] mi *F* [p] Euthocium *E;* scribo *add. F* [q] debes *add. F* [r] *long lacuna begins here in A due to loss of folios and ends in 33 below*

24 [a] ecclesia *F* [b] supponens *E* [c–c] habeas consortium matronarum *FAmb*[1]*;* consortia matronarum habeas *BR* [d] nobilissimarum *C* [e] domos accedas *F* [f] te *add. F, Jerome* [g] uiduas *E;* uidere *Jerome* [h] concurret *E;* concurrit *FBR, Jerome* [i] ominis *BR* [j] coniugis *BR* [k] partem *R* [l–l] Scitote *R* [m–m] illis esse *F, Jerome* [n] dedicatam *B* [o] consecratione *C* [p–p] *om. C* [q] post *F, Jerome* [r] ecclesiam *BR* [s] que *B;* quia *F;* qua *superscr. F* [t] discimus *F* [u] illi *F, Jerome* [v] cuius *F, Jerome* [w] spiritalis *TACE;* specialis *FBR, Jerome* [x] Uniuersa *F, Jerome* [y–y] dona gratiae *F* [z] percipiant *TABR;* percipient *CE;* percipi *F;* percipiat *Jerome* [a–a] aliquid proprium *F* [b] hostium *F* [c–c] sancto Spiritu *F;* & *add. Amb* [d] eligantur *E* [e] *om. F*

greets 'Rufus, a chosen servant of the Lord, and his mother, whom I call mother too.'[165] And John says in his second Letter: 'From the Elder: Greetings to the lady, the chosen one, and to her children',[166] etc. He also asks her to love him, for later on he says: 'And now I have a request for you, dear lady: let us love one another.'[167] St Jerome also acted on John's authority when, in writing to Eustochium, a virgin of your own profession, he was not ashamed to call her his lady, and indeed immediately gave the reason why he should do so: 'I write my lady Eustochium because I must call my lady her who is the bride of my Lord.'[168]

24. Later on in the same letter, when he sets the privilege of this sacred calling above every boast of earthly happiness, he says: 'I do not wish you to consort with married women and visit the houses of the nobility, nor to see frequently what you set aside when you decided to be a virgin. The ambition of courtiers may make them gather round the wife of the Emperor, but why should you insult your own husband? You are the bride of God; why hurry to the wife of a man? Develop a holy pride in this matter, and know that you are better then they.'[169] And in writing to a dedicated virgin about virgins consecrated to God, telling her how they will enjoy great happiness in heaven and high honour on earth, he says: 'We are also taught how holy virginity shall enjoy great happiness in heavenly things by the practice of the Church, quite apart from the testimony of the Scriptures, for from this we learn that there is a special merit in those women who are spiritually consecrated. Although one and all in the throng of the faithful receive similar gifts of grace, and all alike rejoice in the same sacramental blessings, those women have something which belongs to them rather than the others when they are chosen by the Holy Spirit from that holy and spotless flock of the Church, for the merits of their intention, as holier and purer offerings, and are presented at God's altar by his high priest.'[170] And again:

[164] 1 Tim. 5: 3. Also cited at **18** above.

[165] Rom. 16: 13.

[166] 2 John 1: 1.

[167] 2 John 5.

[168] Jerome, *Epistola* XXII *ad Eustochium*, 2 (ed. Hilberg, liv. 145, *ll.* 15–16; *PL* xxii. 395). Also cited in *Letter* 5, 3 and *Sermon* 30 (*PL* clxxviii. 568C).

[169] Jerome, *Epistola* XXII *ad Eustochium*, 16 (ed. Hilberg, liv. 163, *ll.* 10–12, 13–17; *PL* xxii. 403). Cf. *Letter* 6, **6**.

[170] Not Jerome; probably Pelagius, *Epistula ad Claudiam de uirginitate* (ed. Halm, p. 225; *PL* xxx. 163AB); written *c*.404–6.

et[f] quod alii non habent dum[g] et peculiarem obtinet gratiam[h] et proprio, ut ita dixerim, consecrationis priuilegio gaudet.'[171]

25. Virginum quippe consecrationem, nisi periculo mortis urgente, celebrari alio tempore non licet quam in Epyphania et albis Paschalibus et in apostolorum natalitiis,[a] nec nisi a summo sacerdote, id est episcopo, tam ipsas quam ipsarum sacris capitibus imponenda uelamina sanctificari.[172] Monachis autem, quamuis eiusdem sint professionis uel ordinis et dignioris sexus, etiam si sint uirgines, qualibet die benedictionem et[b] ab[c] abbate suscipere tam ipsis quam propriis eorum indumentis, id est cucullis, permissum est. Presbyteros quoque et ceteros inferioris gradus clericos semper in ieiuniis quatuor temporum, et episcopos omni die dominico constat ordinari posse.[173] Virginum autem consecratio quanto[d] preciosior tanto rarior, precipuarum exsultationem sollempnitatum sibi uendicauit. De quarum scilicet[e] uirtute mirabili uniuersa amplius congaudet ecclesia, sicut et Psalmista predixerat his uerbis: 'Adducentur regi uirgines post eam.'[174] Et rursum: 'Afferentur in leticia et exultatione, adducentur in templum regis.'[175] Quarum[f] etiam consecrationem Matheus apostolus[g] simul et euuangelista composuisse uel dictasse refertur, sicut in eius *Passione* legitur, ubi et ipse pro earum consecratione uel uirginalis propositi defensione martyr occubuisse[h] memoratur.[176] Nullam uero benedictionem uel clericorum uel monachorum apostoli nobis scriptam reliquerunt.[i]

26. Quarum quoque religio sola ex nomine sanctitatis est insignita, cum ipse a sanctimonia, id est[a] sanctitate, sanctimoniales sint[b] dicte. Quippe quo infirmior est [c]feminarum[c] sexus, gratior[d] [e]est Deo[e] atque perfectior earum uirtus,[177] iuxta ipsius quoque Domini[f] testimonium

[f] quod alii habent et *F, Jerome* [g] ueram *E;* et communem *add. F, Jerome* [h] *om. R*

25 [a] nataliis *R* [b] *om. E* [c] *om. R* [d] tanto *E* [e] *om. Amb* [f] Quam *Amb;* Quarum *Amb*[1] [g] *om. R* [h] obulisse *C;* occubuisse *Ecorr* [i] relinquerunt *TCE*

26 [a] a *add. BR* [b] sunt *Amb* [c–c] sexus feminarum *E* [d] gaudior *BR;* eo gratior *add. F* [e–e] deo est *CEFR* [f] *om. CEF*

[171] Not Jerome; probably Pelagius, *Epistula ad Claudiam de uirginitate* (ed. Halm, p. 225; *PL* xxx. 163BC).

[172] Cf. Pope Gelasius I, *Epistola* IX *ad Episcopos Lucanae*, 12 (*PL* lix. 52BC). Cited by Ivo of Chartres, *Decretum*, vii, c. 36 (*PL* clxi. 553D). 'Albis Paschalibus': white robes were worn in the week following Easter.

'Therefore virginity possesses what others do not have, since it gains special grace and rejoices in what I may call its particular privilege of consecration.'[171]

25. For the consecration of virgins, unless they are in imminent danger of death, may not be celebrated at any time except at Epiphany and in Easter week and on the birthdays of the apostles. Nor are they or the veils to be laid on their sacred heads to be blessed by anyone but the high priest, that is, by the bishop.[172] Monks, on the other hand, although they are of the same profession or order and of a worthier sex, even if they are virgins, are permitted to receive the blessing, both for themselves and for their garments, that is, their cowl, on any day and from an abbot. Priests also and other lower grades of clergy can always be ordained on Ember Days and the bishops on any Sunday, as is generally known.[173] But the consecration of virgins, being more precious and so rarer, has claimed for itself the joyous celebration of the principal festivals, and the whole Church widely rejoices in their marvellous virtue, as the Psalmist had foretold in these words: 'Virgins shall follow her into the presence of the king.'[174] And again: 'In joy and exultation they shall be brought; they shall be taken into the temple of the king.'[175] The apostle and evangelist Matthew is also said. to have written or dictated on the subject of their consecration, as we read in his *Passion*, where he is also said to have died a martyr himself in the cause of their consecration or in defence of their virginal calling.[176] But no written form of blessing for clergy or monks has been left to us by the apostles.

26. The religious order of women is also the only one to be distinguished by the name of sanctity, since nuns are called *sanctimoniales* from *sanctimonia*, which means sanctity. And just as the female sex is weaker so the virtue of women is more pleasing to God and more perfect,[177] according to the testimony of the Lord himself;

[173] Cf. Pope Gelasius I, *Epistola* IX. 11 (*PL* lix. 52B), and for bishops cf. Leo I, *Epistola* VI. 6 (*PL* liv. 620A). The minor orders were generally held to be those of acolyte, exorcist, reader, and doorkeeper, while the major orders were bishop, priest, deacon, and subdeacon, but there was no uniformity of reckoning. Four groups of three Ember Days in the year (the 'quattuor tempora') were set aside for fasting and for ordinations. Cf. also **41** below.

[174] Ps. 44: 15 (14).

[175] Ps. 44: 16 (15).

[176] Cf. *Acta S. Matthaei* II. 19 (*Acta Sanctorum*, Sept. VI, p. 224).

[177] Cf. **29** and **36** below; also *Letter* 1, **64** and note.

quo infirmitatem Apostoli ad certaminis coronam exhortans ait: 'Sufficit tibi gratia mea: nam uirtus in infirmitate perficitur.'[178] Qui[g] etiam de corporis sui, quod est ecclesia, membris per eundem loquens apostolum,[h] ac si precipue tam [i]infirmorum membrorum honorem commendaret, in eadem subiunxit epistola, hoc est [j]ad Corinthios[j] prima: 'Sed multo magis que uidentur membra corporis[i] infirmiora[k] esse necessariora[l] sunt: et[m] que putamus ignobiliora [n]membra esse corporis[n] his [o]habundantiorem honorem[o] [p]circumdamus. Et que inhonesta [q]nostra sunt,[q] habundantiorem[p] honestatem[r] habent. Honesta autem[s] nostra[t] nullius egent. Sed Deus temperauit corpus ei cui deerat,[u] habundantiorem[v] tribuendo[w] honorem ut[x] non sit scisma in corpore, sed in idipsum[y] pro inuicem sollicita sint membra.'[179] Quis autem [z]adeo integre[z] per diuine gratie dispensationem hec[a] in aliquo dixerit[b] adimpleri, sicut in ipsa muliebris[c] sexus infirmitate, quem[d] tam culpa quam natura contemptibilem fecerat?[180] Circumspice singulos in hoc sexu gradus, non solum uirgines ac[e] uiduas seu coniugatas, uerum etiam ipsas scortorum abhominationes, et in eis Christi gratiam uidebis ampliorem ut, iuxta dominicam et apostolicam sententiam, sint 'nouissimi primi, et primi nouissimi',[181] et[f] 'ubi habundauit delictum superabundet[g] et gratia'.[182]

27. Cuius quidem diuine gratie beneficia uel honorem feminis exhibita, [a]si ab ipso[a] [b]mundi repetamus[c] exordio,[b] reperiemus statim mulieris creationem quadam precellere[d] dignitate, cum ipsa scilicet[e] in paradyso, uir extra creatus sit, ut hinc precipue mulieres admoneantur[f] attendere quam sit earum naturalis patria paradysus, et quo amplius eas celibem paradysi uitam sequi conueniat.[183] [g]Vnde Ambrosius in libro *de Paradyso*: 'Et apprehendit', inquit, 'Deus hominem quem fecit et posuit eum in paradyso.[184] Vides quoniam

[g] Lapsus memoriae *add. Amb in marg.* [h] apostolus *E* [i–i] *ditto. C* [j–j] eorum *E* [k] infirmioris *TE;* infirmiora *add. by a later hand in marg. T* [l] necessaria *CEBR* [m] Et *TAmb* [n–n] esse membra corporis *E* [o–o] habundantiorem honorem (honorem *exp.*) honestatem (*exp.*) honorem *T;* habundantiorem *E;* honorem habundantiorem *F, Vulg* [p–p] *om. CE* [q–q] sunt nomina *F;* sunt nostra *Vulg* [r] *om. C* [s] enim *BR* [t] necessario *F* [u] dederat *Amb* [v] habundatiorem *T* [w] retribuendo *T before corr. by exp.* [x] id *BR* [y] ipsum *BR* [z–z] integre adeo *CEF* [a] hoc *CEF* [b] duxerit *F* [c] muliebri *BR* [d] quam *CEF* [e] aut *CEFBR* [f] ut T^1E [g] semper habundet *T*

27 [a–a] *om. BR* [b–b] exordio mundi repetamus *T but marked for corr. by* T^4*;* mundi repetamus exordio *T after corr.* [c] reperamus *E* [d] preexcellere *CE* [e] quoque $CEFAmb^1$ [f] moneantur *F* [g–g] *om. CEF*

for when he was urging on the weakness of the Apostle towards the crown of strife, he said: 'My grace is all you need for power comes to its full strength in weakness.'[178] And in speaking through the same Apostle of the members of his body which make up the Church, as if he wished to commend especially the honour of the members who are so weak, he went on to say in the same letter, the first to the Corinthians: 'Those members of the body which appear to be the weaker ones are much more indispensable, and those parts of the body which we regard as less honourable are treated with fuller honour. To our unseemly parts is given a fuller seemliness, whereas our seemly parts need nothing. But God has balanced the parts of the body by giving fuller honour to the part which lacked it, so that there may be no sense of division in the body but all its parts have the same concern for each other.'[179] But who would say that there has been so complete a fulfilment through the dispensation of divine grace in anything as in the very weakness of women's sex, which sin as well as nature had made to be despised?[180] Look at all the grades within this sex, not only virgins and widows and married women but also prostitutes with their abominable practices, and you will find the grace of Christ to be fuller in the latter, so that, in accordance with the words of the Lord and of the Apostle, 'the last shall be first and the first last',[181] and 'where sin abounded, grace will be even greater'.[182]

27. Indeed, if we consider the benefits of this divine grace or the honour conferred on women from the very beginning of the world, we shall soon find that the creation of woman was marked by a special distinction since she was created in paradise but man was created outside it. Women are therefore especially advised to consider how paradise is their natural home, and how much more appropriate it is for them to lead the celibate life of paradise.[183] Hence Ambrose in his book *On Paradise* says: 'God took the man he had made and set him in paradise.[184] You see how he already existed when he was taken. He

[178] 2 Cor. 12: 9; partly cited in *Letter* 6, **12**; cf. *Letter* 4, **17** and note 52.

[179] 1 Cor. 12: 22–5. From 1 Cor. but not from the 'same epistle'.

[180] Cf. *Expositio in Hexameron* **255–8**, **264–6** (ed. Romig and Luscombe, pp. 59–61; *PL* clxxviii. 760C–751A, 761CD;); *Hymn* 27 (Szövérffy 27).

[181] Matt. 20: 16.

[182] Cf. Rom. 5: 20. Also *Hymns* 88 (Szövérffy 124), *De sanctis mulieribus* 1, I–II and 91 (Szövérffy 127), *De sanctis mulieribus* 4, III.

[183] Cf. *Sermon* 26 (*PL* clxxviii. 542CD); *Hymn* 89 (Szövérffy 125), *De sanctis mulieribus* 2, II; *SN* c. 52, 'Quod Adam extra paradisum sit conditus et contra'.

[184] Cf. Gen. 2: 15.

qui erat apprehenditur. In paradyso eum collocauit. Aduerte quia extra paradysum uir factus est et mulier intra paradysum. In inferiori[h] loco uir melior inuenitur et illa que in meliore loco facta est inferior reperitur.'[g] [185] Prius[i] quoque Dominus Euam, totius originem mali, restaurauit in Maria quam Adam in Christo reparauit.[186] Et sicut a muliere [j]culpa, sic a muliere[j] cepit gratia[k] [187] et uirginitatis refloruit prerogatiua. Ac prius in Anna et Maria, uiduis et uirginibus, sancte professionis forma est[l] exhibita quam in Iohanne uel apostolis monastice religionis exempla uiris proposita.

28. Quod si post Euam Debbore,[a] Iudith, Hester uirtutem intueamur, profecto non mediocrem robori uirilis sexus inferemus erubescentiam.[188] Debbora[b] quippe, dominici iudex [c]populi, uiris[c] deficientibus dimicauit et, deuictis hostibus populoque Domini[d] liberato, potenter triumphauit.[189] Iudith inermis cum abra sua terribilem exercitum est aggressa[e] et, unius[f] Holofernis proprio ipsius[g] gladio capud amputans, sola uniuersos strauit hostes, et desperatum populum suum liberauit.[190] Hester, Spiritu latenter suggerente,[191] contra ipsum etiam legis decretum gentili copulata regi, impiissimi Aman consilium et crudele[h] regis preuenit edictum, [i]constitutam regieque[i] deliberationis sententiam, quasi uno temporis momento,[j] in contrarium conuertit.[192] Magne ascribitur uirtuti, quod Dauid[k] in funda et lapide Goliam aggressus est et deuicit:[193] Iudith uidua ad hostilem procedit exercitum sine funda et lapide,[l] sine omni adminiculo armature dimicatura.[194] Hester solo uerbo populum suum[m] liberat et conuersa [n]in hostes[n] sententia[o] corruerunt ipsi in laqueum quem tetenderant.[p] [195] Cuius quidem insignis facti memoria singulis annis apud Iudeos sollempnem meruit [q]habere leticiam.[q] [196] Quod nequaquam aliqua uirorum facta quantumcumque splendida obtinuerunt.[r]

[h] inferiore *B, Jerome* [i] Primus *C* [j–j] *om. CEF* [k] ita *add. F* [l] *om. Amb*

28 [a] Delborae *Amb* [b] Delbora *Amb;* Debora *Amb*[1] [c–c] a plurimis *CE;* exeantur plurimia *F;* apostoli auris *R* [d] Dei *F* [e] egressa *C* [f] ipsius *CEF* [g] *om. CEF* [h] *in T the last two letters* (le) *are add. over eras. by T*[3]*; eras. also in marg.* [i–i] constitutam regie *C;* regie *E;* constitutamque regie *FAmb;* constitutam regie et *BR* [j] *om. BR* [k] dauid *Ecorr* [l] et *add. CEF* [m] *om. CEF* [n–n] ad hostium *CEF* [o] sententiam *CEFB;* sentenciam *R* [p] tenderant *E;* tentenderant *B* [q–q] letitiam habere *B* [r] obtinuerint *R*

---

[185] Ambrose, *De Paradiso*, iv. 24 (ed. Schenkl, p. 280, *ll.* 7–9, 11–12, 13–14, 16–18; *PL* xiv. 283D–284A). Cf. *Expositio in Hexameron* **393** (ed. Romig and Luscombe, pp. 88–9; *PL* clxxviii. 776BC).

[186] Cf. *Letter* 5, **25**.

was placed in paradise. See that man was made outside paradise and woman within. Man, the better person, is found in the lesser place; and woman, the lesser person, was made in the better place.'[185] The Lord also restored Eve, the source of all evil, in Mary before he renewed Adam in Christ.[186] Just as fault began in woman, so did grace,[187] and the privilege of virginity flowered again. Moreover, the form of their sacred calling was shown to widows and virgins in the persons of Anna and Mary before men were given examples of the monastic way of life in John or the apostles.

28. If after Eve we consider the virtue of Deborah, Judith, and Esther, we shall make the male sex, for all its vigour, blush deeply for shame.[188] Deborah was one of the judges of the Lord's people; when men were weak she gave battle, and when the enemy was defeated and the Lord's people set free, she was mighty in triumph.[189] Judith made her way to a terrifying army, unarmed and alone with her maidservant, and cut off the head of Holofernes with his own sword. She destroyed all her enemies single-handed and set free her people who had lost hope.[190] Esther, at the secret prompting of the Spirit,[191] became the wife of a heathen King in defiance of the Law's decree. She forestalled the plan of impious Haman and the king's cruel edict and reversed in a trice the sentence passed after royal deliberation.[192] David's courage is said to be outstanding when he attacked and overthrew Goliath with sling and stone; but the widow Judith set out against a hostile army with neither sling nor stone,[193] to do battle unsupported by any weapon.[194] Esther by her word alone set free her people, and when the sentence was reversed against her enemies, they fell into the trap of their own setting.[195] The memory of this famous deed has earned among the Jews the tribute of an annual festival of rejoicing,[196] something which no deeds of men, however glorious, have ever won.

[187] Cf. *Hymn* 88 (Szövérffy 124), *De sanctis mulieribus* 1, I.

[188] For Deborah and Judith cf. *Hymn* 89 (Szövérffy 125), *De sanctis mulieribus* 2, III. These and other examples of womanly strength are found in a nearly contemporary work of uncertain authorship, *Speculum virginum*, iv, *ll.* 551–665 (ed. Seyfarth, pp. 105–7). Cf. also Peter the Venerable's *Letter* (115) to Heloise, ed. Constable, i. 305–6.

[189] Cf. Judg. 4 and 5.

[190] Cf. Judith 10–13; also *Rule* 82.

[191] 'Spiritu latenter suggerente': cf. *Sermon* 4 (*PL* clxxviii. 412B).

[192] Cf. Esther 8.

[193] 1 Kgs. (1 Sam.) 17: 50.

[194] Cf. Judith 10.

[195] Cf. Esther 8; also *Hymn* 90 (Szövérffy 126), *De sanctis mulieribus* 3, III.

[196] The Jewish Feast of Purim or Lots; cf. Esther 9: 20–31.

29. Quis incomparabilem matris septem filiorum constanciam non miretur, quos una cum matre apprehensos, sicut Machabeorum hystoria narrat, rex impiissimus Antiochus ad carnes porcinas contra legem edendas, nisus est frustra compellere?[197] Que materne[a] immemor nature et humane affectionis ignara, nec nisi Deum[b] pre oculis habens quot sacris exhortationibus suis ad coronam filios premisit tot[c] ipsa[d] martyriis[e] triumphauit, proprio ad extremum martyrio[f] consumata.[198] Si totam ueteris testamenti seriem[g] reuoluamus, quid[h] huius mulieris constancie[i] comparare poterimus? Ille ad extremum uehemens temptator beati Iob, imbecillitatem humane nature contra mortem considerans, 'pellem', inquit, 'pro pelle et [j]uniuersa dabit homo[j] pro anima sua'.[199] In tantum enim omnes angustiam[k] mortis naturaliter horremus, ut sepe ad defensionem unius membri alterum opponamus,[l] et pro uita hac conseruanda nulla uereamur incommoda. Hec uero non solum sua[m] sed propriam et filiorum animas perdere sustinuit ne unam legis incurreret[n] offensam. Que est ista, obsecro,[o] ad quam compellebatur transgressio? Numquid abrenuntiare Deo uel thurificare[p] ydolis cogebatur? Nichil, inquam,[q] aliud[r] [s]ab eis[s] exigebatur nisi ut carnibus uescerentur[t] [200] quas lex eis interdicebat. O fratres et commonachi,[201] qui tam impudenter cotidie contra regule institutionem ac uestram[u] professionem ad carnes inhiatis, quid[v] ad huius [w]mulieris constantiam[w] dicturi estis? Numquid tam inuerecundi estis, ut cum hec[x] auditis erubescentia[y] non confundamini? Sciatis, fratres, quod de regina austri Dominus incredulis exprobrat[z] dicens:[a] 'Regina austri surget in iudicio cum generatione ista, et condempnabit eam',[202] multo amplius uobis de huius mulieris constantia improperandum esse,[b] que et longe[c] maiora fecerit et uos[d] uestre professionis[e] [f]uoto religioni[f] artius[g] astricti estis. Cuius quidem tanto agone uirtus examinata,[h] hoc

29 [a] mater suae *Amb* [b] Dominum *Amb, Muckle* [c] quot *BR* [d] ipsos *CE* [e] martyrii *BR* [f] martirii *Ecorr. in marg.* [g] *om. BR* [h] cui *F* [i] constantiam *CEF* [j–j] universa quae habet homo dabit *F* [k] angustias *Amb* [l] apponamus *C* [m] suam *CEF* [n] incurrerent *F;* occurreret *BR* [o] *om. F* [p] transficare *C* [q] inquit *BR* [r] *om. FAmb* [s–s] *om. BR* [t] uesceretur *T*¹*BR* [u] nostram *Amb* [v] Quid *B* [w–w] instantiam mulieris *B;* instanciam mulieris *R* [x] hoc *CE* [y] erubescentiam *CEAmb* [z] exprobat *R* [a] *om. R* [b] est *CEF* [c] lege *F* [d] nos *R* [e] *om. CEF* [f–f] religionis voto *CEF;* uoto religionis *R* [g] arctius *EFAmb* [h] uel refecisse *add. C*

[197] Cf. 2 Macc. 7.

[198] Cf. *Hymn* 82 (Szövérffy 99), *De martyribus* 3, II.

[199] Job 2: 4. Cf. Gregory the Great, *Moralia in Iob*, iii. 4. 5 (ed. Adriaen, cxliii. 117; *PL* lxxv. 601).

29. Who does not marvel at the incomparable steadfastness of the mother of seven sons, as recounted in the history of the Maccabees? They were arrested along with their mother, and King Antiochus, most evil of men, then tried in vain to force them to eat pigs' flesh, forbidden by the Law.[197] Regardless of her maternal feelings and heedless of human affection, with her eyes fixed on God alone, the mother triumphed in as many martyrdoms as the mother of sons she sent ahead of her to the Crown with holy exhortations, and was the last to die by her own martyrdom.[198] We can go through the whole course of the Old Testament but what can we find to compare with the steadfast determination of this woman? The tempter of holy Job, who was unremitting in his pressure to the end, was thinking of the frailty of human nature in the face of death when he said: 'Skin for skin! A man will give up all he has to save his own life.'[199] For we all naturally dread the pain of death so keenly that in defence of one part of the body we will offer another, and are prepared to face any hardship in order to preserve the life we have. But this woman endured the loss of all she had, of her own and her sons' lives, rather than commit a single offence against the Law. And what, pray, was this transgression to which she was being driven? Was she being forced to renounce God and burn incense to idols? No, nothing was demanded of her and her sons except that they should eat flesh[200] forbidden them by the Law. O brothers and fellow monks,[201] who hanker after meat so shamelessly every day, in defiance of the practice of the *Rule* and your own profession, what have you to say about the steadfastness of this woman? Are you too impudent to blush for shame on hearing this? Know, brothers, that what the Lord said about the Queen of the South as a reproof to those lacking faith—'The Queen of the South will appear at the Judgement when this generation is on trial and condemn it'[202]—would be far better applied as a reproach to yourselves with regard to this woman's constancy, for she achieved far greater things, while you are more strictly bound to religious life by the vow of your profession. Her courage was tested in

[200] Cf. 2 Macc. 7: 1.

[201] Abelard turns aside to deliver a general reproach to monks (and perhaps lay brothers too) who crave meat, including his fellow monks in his abbey of St-Gildas. This form of address ('fratres et commonachi') is also found in *Sermon* 33 on St John the Baptist (*PL* clxxviii. 582B); *Letter* 11 to Abbot Adam and the monks of St-Denis (ed. Smits, p. 249; *PL* clxxviii. 341A; trans. Ziolkowski, p. 138); *Soliloquium* (ed. Burnett in 'Peter Abelard "Soliloquium"', p. 888; *PL* clxxviii. 1878A).

[202] Matt. 12: 42; cf. *Letter* 9 to the sisters of the Paraclete (ed. Smits, p. 233; *PL* clxxviii. 333B; trans. Ziolkowski, p. 28).

in ecclesia priuilegium obtinere meruit ut[i] eius martyrium solempnes lectiones atque missam habeat,[203] quod[j] nulli antiquorum sanctorum concessum est, quicunque scilicet aduentum Domini moriendo preuenerunt, quamuis in ipsa Machabeorum[k] hystoria Eleazarus ille uenerabilis senex, unus[l] de primoribus Scribarum eadem causa martyrio iam coronatus fuisse referatur.[204] [m]Sed quia, ut diximus,[205] quo naturaliter femineus sexus est infirmior, eo [n]uirtus eius Deo est[n] acceptabilior et honore dignior,[206] nequaquam martyrium illud in festiuitate memoriam meruit cui femina non interfuit, quasi pro magno non habeatur si fortior sexus fortiter[o] paciatur. Vnde et in laude predicte femine amplius Scriptura prorumpens, ait: 'Supra modum autem mater mirabilis et bonorum memoria digna, que pereuntes septem filios sub unius diei tempore conspiciens[p] bono animo ferebat propter spem quam in Deo[q] habebat. Singulos illorum[r] hortabatur fortiter, repleta sapientia et feminee cogitationi masculinum animum inserens.'[m] [207]

30. Quis in laudem uirginum unicam[a] illam[b] Iepte filiam assumi non censeat que, ne uoti licet inprouidi reus pater haberetur et diuine gratie beneficium promissa fraudaretur hostia, uictorem patrem in iugulum proprium animauit?[c] [208] Quid hec,[d] [e]queso, in agone martyrum[e] factura esset, si forte ab infidelibus negando Deum apostatare cogeretur?[209] Numquid interrogata de Christo cum illo iam apostolorum principe diceret: 'Non[f] noui illum?'[210] Dimissa per duos menses a patre libera, his completis[g] redit[h] ad patrem occidenda. Sponte morti[i] se ingerit et eam magis prouocat quam ueretur. Stultum patris plectitur uotum et paternum redimit mendacium,[j] amatrix maxima ueritatis. Quantum [k]hunc in se[k] lapsum abhorreret[l] quem[m] [n]in patre[n] non sustinet! Quantus hic est uirginis feruor tam in

[i] et *BR* [j] quot *BR* [k] monachorum *CE* [l] usus *CE* [m–m] *om. CEF* [n–n] uirtus est (eius T^1) deo est *T;* uirtus eius est deo *B,* virtus est Deo *Amb* [o] fortiori *Amb* [p] concipiens *BR* [q] domino *BR;* Domino *Amb* [r] eorum *BR*

30 [a] vineam *Amb* [b] *om. R* [c] animaduertit *F* [d] hic *E;* hoc *BR* [e–e] in agone martirum queso *CE;* in agone martyrum quaeso *F* [f] *om. E* [g] expletis *CEF* [h] rediit *CEF* [i] morte *R* [j] mandatum *Amb* [k–k] nunc in se *E;* habuisse *BR* [l] abhorret *R* [m] quam C [n–n] ipse *B*

---

[203] Cf. *Hymn* 89 (Szövérffy 125), *De sanctis mulieribus* 2, III.

[204] Cf. 2 Macc. 6: 18–31.

[205] At **26** above and cf. **36** below.

[206] Cf. *Letter* 1, **64** and the references cited there.

[207] 2 Macc. 7: 20–1.

agony so intense that she was found worthy to be granted the privilege in the Church of solemn readings and a Mass,[203] a concession given to none whatever of the holy men of old who met their death before the coming of the Lord, even though in the same history of the Maccabees the old and revered Eleazar, one of the leaders of the Scribes, is recorded as having received a martyr's crown for the same reason.[204] But, as we have said,[205] since the virtue of the female sex is naturally weaker, and her virtue more acceptable to God and worthier of honour,[206] a martyrdom in which no woman had a part has never won recognition in the feasts of the Church, as if it were of no great importance if the manly sex should suffer manfully. And so in fuller praise of the woman mentioned above Scripture bursts into the words: 'But the mother was especially admirable and worthy of honourable remembrance, for she watched her seven sons all die in the space of a single day, but bore it bravely because of her hopes in the Lord. She encouraged each one of them without flinching; she was filled with wisdom and reinforced her woman's thoughts with a manly spirit.'[207]

30. Who would not think that Jephthah's only daughter should be added to the list of virgins we praise? She gave her father the strength to take her own life in his hour of victory, lest he be held to account for his vow, rash though it was, and lest the gift he received by divine grace be cheated of its promised victim.[208] What, I wonder, would she have done in a contest for martyrs, were pagans to have compelled her to renounce her faith by denying God?[209] Would she, if questioned about Christ, have said with him who was already leader of the apostles: 'I do not know the man'?[210] Sent away by her father for two months of freedom, she then returned to her father to be killed. She went to meet death of her own accord and challenged it more than dreaded it. Her father's foolish vow was punished while she saved him from a broken promise by her great love of truth. How she would have abhorred such a lapse in herself when she could not bear it in her father! How great the love of this virgin, as much for her father in the

[208] Cf. Judg. 11: 30–40. Jephthah's vow was that, if he was victorious against the Ammonites, he would offer as a holocaust to Yahweh the first person he met on returning to his house. Cf. also *Letter* 3, 5; *Planctus III*: *Planctus uirginum Israel super filia Jephtae Galaditae* (ed. Meyer, i. 347–52; ed. von den Steinen, pp. 142–3; *PL* clxxviii. 1819–20); *Hymns* 89 and 90 (Szövérffy 125 and 126), *De sanctis mulieribus* 2, IV and 3, I. On *Planctus III* cf. Alexiou and Dronke, 'The Lament of Jephta's daughter'.

[209] Cf. *TChr*, ii. 77.

[210] Luke 22: 57.

carnalem quam in celestem[o] patrem! Que simul morte[p] sua et hunc[q] a mendacio liberare et illi[r] promissum decreuit conseruare. Vnde merito tanta hec[s] puellaris animi fortitudo prerogatiua quadam id meruit obtinere ut per annos singulos filie Israel in unum conuenientes quasi quibusdam sollempnibus hymnis festiuas uirginis agant exequias, et[t] de passione uirginis compuncte piis[u] planctibus compatiantur.[211]

31. Vt autem cetera omnia pretermittamus, quid tam necessarium[a] nostre redemptioni[b] et totius mundi [c]saluti fuerit[c] quam sexus femineus qui nobis ipsum peperit saluatorem? Cuius quidem honoris singularitatem mulier illa que prima irrumpere ausa est ad beatum Hylarionem illi admiranti[d] opponebat[e] dicens: 'Quid auertis[f] oculos? Quid[g] rogantem fugis? Noli me[h] mulierem aspicere sed miseram. Hic sexus genuit saluatorem.'[i] [212] Que gloria huic [j]poterit comparari[j] quam in Domini matre adeptus est sexus iste? Posset utique, si uellet, redemptor noster de uiro [k]corpus assumere,[k] sicut primam feminam de corpore uiri uoluit formare.[213] Sed hanc sue humilitatis singularem gratiam ad infirmioris sexus transtulit honorem.[214] Posset et alia parte muliebris[l] corporis digniore nasci quam ceteri homines, eadem qua concipiuntur uilissima portione nascentes.[215] Sed ad incomparabilem infirmioris corporis honorem longe amplius ortu suo consecrauit eius genitale, quam uiri fecerat ex circumcisione.

32. Atque ut[a] hunc singularem uirginum nunc omittam[b] honorem, libet ad ceteras quoque[c] feminas, sicut proposuimus, stilum conuertere. Attende itaque quantam[d] statim gratiam aduentus Christi[e] Helysabeth coniugate, quantam[f] exhibuit Anne uidue.[216] [g]Virum Helysabeth Zachariam, magnum Domini sacerdotem, incredulitatis[h] diffidentia [i]mutum adhuc tenebat[i] dum in aduentu et salutatione Marie ipsa mox Helysabeth, Spiritu sancto repleta, et exultantem in utero suo paruulum sensit et prophetiam [j]iam de ipso[j] completo

[o] *Ecorr* [p] mater *R* [q] illum *F* [r] huic *F* [s] *om. F* [t] Et *B* [u] ei *add. BR*

31 [a] ueterum *?B* [b] redemptionis *CEFR* [c–c] fuit saluti *CEF* [d] admirant *C* [e] apponebat *E* [f] aduertis *BR* [g] quam *C* [h] *om. F, Jerome* [i] saluator *CEF* [j–j] comparari poterit *F* [k–k] corpus corpus assumere *ditto. F;* corpus posset assumere *B;* corpus post assumere *R* [l] mulieris *Amb*

32 [a] in *T* [b] demittam *E* [c] *om. Amb* [d] quemdam *C* [e] *om. B* [f] quanta *CE* [g–g] *om. CEF* [h] incrudelitatis *T* [i–i] multum tenebat adhuc *BR* [j–j] de ipso iam *R*

flesh as for her father in heaven! She determined by her death both to save one from falsehood and to keep for the other what had been promised. And so this girl's great strength of mind was rightly held to have a special claim to be granted the privilege that every year the daughters of Israel assemble to hold a kind of funeral service with solemn hymns for her, and to share in sympathy the virgin's sufferings with pious laments.[211]

31. Passing over all other examples, has anything been as necessary for our redemption and for the salvation of the whole world as the female sex which gave birth to our Saviour himself for our sake? The woman who was the first to challenge an astonished St Hilarion about the unique nature of this honour asked him: 'Why do you avert your eyes? Why shun my plea? Do not look on me as a woman but a woman to be pitied. This sex of mine gave birth to the Saviour.'[212] What glory could be compared with what that sex won in the person of the Mother of God? Our Redeemer, had he wished, could have taken his body from a man, just as he chose to create the first woman from a man's body.[213] But he transferred this special favour of his humility to honour the weaker sex.[214] He could have been born from another and worthier part of a woman's body, unlike other men who are born from the vilest part where they are conceived.[215] But instead, to the incomparable honour of the weaker body, he hallowed its genitals far more by his birth than he had done those of a man through circumcision.

32. And now, to say no more for the present about the singular honour granted to virgins, I would like to turn my pen to other women, as I proposed to do. So consider the great favour bestowed by the coming of Christ on Elizabeth, a married woman, and Anna, a widow.[216] Zachariah, Elizabeth's husband and a high priest of the Lord, still remained dumb for the lack of trust shown by his unbelief, while at the arrival and greeting of Mary, Elizabeth, filled with the Holy Spirit, immediately felt the baby leap for joy in her womb. She was the first to proclaim Mary's conceiving, which had already

[211] Cf. Judg. 11: 39–40; also *Planctus III: Planctus uirginum Israel super filia Jephtae Galadite*, i, *vv.* 9–14 (ed. Meyer, i. 347; ed. von den Steinen, p. 142; *PL* clxxviii. 1819); *Hymn* 90 (Szövérffy 126), *De sanctis mulieribus* 3, II.

[212] Jerome, *Life of St Hilarion*, 13 (*PL* xxiii. 33C).

[213] Cf. *Sermons* 1 and 26 (*PL* clxxviii. 379A–380A, 542A); also Augustine, *Sermon* 51, 2 (*PL* xxxviii. 334–5).

[214] Cf. *Sermon* 5 (*PL* clxxviii. 419C).

[215] Cf. Augustine, *De Genesi ad litteram*, ix. 16 (ed. Zycha, p. 290; *PL* xxxiv. 405).

[216] Cf. *Hymn* 91 (Szövérffy 127), *De sanctis mulieribus* 4, I.

Marie conceptu prima proferens plusquam propheta extitit.[217] Presentem quippe ilico uirginis conceptum nunciauit, et ipsam Domini matrem ad magnificandum super hoc ipso Dominum concitauit.[g] Excellentius autem[k] prophetie donum in Helysabeth uidetur completum[l] conceptum statim[m] Dei Filium agnoscere quam in Iohanne ipsum iamdudum natum ostendere. Sicut igitur[n] Mariam Magdalenam apostolorum dicimus apostolam,[218] sic nec[o] istam prophetarum dicere dubitemus prophetam[p] [q]siue ipsam[r] beatam uiduam Annam, de qua supra latius actum est.[q] [219]

33. Quod si hanc prophetie gratiam usque ad gentiles etiam extendamus, Sibilla uates in medium procedat, et que ei de Christo reuelata[a] sunt proferat. Cum qua[b] si uniuersos conferamus prophetas, ipsum[c] etiam Ysaiam, que, ut Ieronimus asserit, non tam propheta quam euuangelista dicendus est,[220] uidebimus in hac quoque[d] gratia feminam uiris longe prestare. De qua Augustinus contra quinque[e] hereses testimonium [f]proferens ait:[f] 'Audiamus [g]quid etiam[g] Sibilla uates eorum de eodem dicat: "Alium", inquit, "dedit Dominus[h] [i]hominibus fidelibus[i] colendum." [j]Item:[k] "Ipse[l] tuum cognosce Dominum[m] Dei Filium esse."[j] Alio loco Filium Dei symbolum[n] appellat, id est [o]consiliarium uel consilium.[o] Et Propheta dicit: "Vocabunt[p] nomen eius[q] admirabilis,[r] consiliarius."''[221] [222] De qua rursus idem pater[s] Augustinus[t] in octauo decimo *de ciuitate Dei*: 'Eo', inquit, 'tempore nonnulli Sibillam Eritream[u] uaticinatam[v] ferunt', quam 'quidam magis credunt'[w] esse Cumanam. 'Et sunt' eius[x] '[y]uiginti septem[y] uersus' qui, 'sicut eos quidam Latinis[z] uersibus est interpretatus, hoc continent:

> "Iudicii signum: tellus[a] sudore madescet.
> E celo rex adueniet per secla futurus,
> Scilicet [b]in carne[b] presens, ut iudicet orbem"',[223] etc.[c]

[k] enim *CEFB* [l] *om. CEFBR* [m] statum *E* [n] ergo *F* [o] et *BR* [p] Prophetissam *F* [q] *om. CEF* [r] uel ipsam *add. BR*

33 [a] translate *Ecorr* [b] que *CE* [c] ipsam *R* [d] parte de *CE;* parte Dei *F* [e] *om. Amb* [f–f] ait proferens *C;* ait profferens *E* [g–g] *om. BR;* etiam quid *CE* [h] Deus *Quodvultdeus* [i–i] omnibus fidelibus *BR;* filiis hominum *F* [j–j] esse *om. F* [k] *long lacuna in A, beginning in 23 above due to loss of folios, ends here* [l] ipsum *Amb*[1] [m] Deum *Quodvultdeus* [n] symbolon *TC;* symbolum *AE;* simbolum *R*; *συνβολιον F* [o–o] consilium uel consiliarium *F;* consiliarum *Amb* [p] Vocabitur *F* [q] *om. R* [r] mirabilis *Amb* [s] pariter *F* [t] *add. R* [u] erecteam *T* (*before corr.*); ericteam *T*(*after corr.*), *AR;* eriteam *CE;* Erythream *F* er(*space for one character*)tream *B;* Erictream *Amb* [v] uacinatam *C* [w] credebant *CEF* [x] eiusdem *CE* [y–y] xx et vij *TA* [z] et stantibus *add. Augustinus* [a] stellus *T* (*but marked with a cross by T*[1]); telus *C* [b–b] ut carnem *Augustine* [c] *om. FAmb*

happened, and she revealed herself as more than a prophet,[217] for there and then she announced the conceiving of the virgin before her and prompted the mother of the Lord to magnify him for just this. The gift of prophecy seems to have been more perfectly realized in Elizabeth, who immediately recognized the Son of God once he was conceived, than in John, who revealed him some time after his birth. So just as we call Mary Magdalene the apostle of the apostles,[218] we should have no hesitation in calling Elizabeth the prophet of the prophets or Anna, the holy widow about whom we wrote more fully earlier.[219]

33. If we also extend this gracious gift of prophecy to the pagans, let the soothsaying Sibyl come forward and tell what was revealed to her concerning Christ. Compare with her all the prophets, even including Isaiah who—Jerome says—should be called evangelist rather than prophet,[220] and we shall see again that in this grace a woman far outstrips men. When presenting the evidence against five heresies Augustine says of her: 'Let us hear what the Sibyl, their soothsayer, also says on this. "The Lord", she says, "gave to faithful men another man to worship."' Again: "You should know that your Lord is the Son of God." Elsewhere she names the Son of God a symbol which is counsellor or counsel. The Prophet also says: "His name shall be called Wonderful, Counsellor."'[221] [222] The same father Augustine also says in the eighteenth book of *The City of God*: 'It was at that time, according to some accounts, that the Erythraean Sibyl made her predictions, though some prefer to believe that it was the Sibyl of Cumae. There are twenty-seven verses which in the Latin verse translation which someone made contain the following lines:

> In token of the judgement day the earth shall drip sweat.
> Eternally to reign a king shall come from heaven
> And judge the world, present in the flesh,[223] etc.

[217] Cf. Luke 1: 5–55. [218] Cf. 11 above. [219] Cf. 17 above.

[220] Jerome, *Commentarii in Esaiam, Prologus* (ed. Adriaen, p. 1; *PL* xxiv. 18); *Praefatio in Librum Isaiae* (*PL* xxviii. 771B); *Epistola* LIII *ad Paulinum*, 8 (ed. Hilberg, liv, p. 460, *ll.* 13–14; *PL* xxii. 547). Also Augustine, *De ciuitate Dei*, xviii. 29 (ed. Dombart and Kalb, xlviii. 619; ed. Hoffmann, ii. 306; *PL* xli. 585). [221] Cf. Isa. 9: 6.

[222] Not Augustine but Quoduultdeus, *Aduersus quinque haereses*, 3 (ed. Braun, p. 266; *PL* xlii. 1103).

[223] Augustine, *De ciuitate Dei*, xviii. 23 (ed. Dombart and Kalb, xlviii. 613 and 614; ed. Hoffmann, ii. 297, 299; *PL* xli. 579–80). The oracles of the Sybils, female seers, were a part of ancient Greek and Roman religion, one Sybil being associated with Erythrae in Asia Minor opposite the island of Khíos (Chios), another, near Naples, with Cumae, which had historic links with Sicily. A list of ten Sibyls, made by Varro, is found in Lactantius,

Quorum[d] quidem uersuum prime littere in greco coniuncte id sonant: 'Iesus Christus, [e]filius Dei[e] saluator.'[224] 'Infert[f] etiam Lactentius[g] quedam de Christo uaticinia Sibille. "In manus", inquit, "infidelium postea ueniet; dabunt[h] Deo alapas manibus incestis, et impurato[i] ore expuent[j] uenenatos sputos;[k] dabit[l] uero[m] ad uerbera[n] suppliciter[o] [p]sanctum dorsum.[p] Et colaphos accipiens tacebit, ne quis agnoscat quod uerbum uel unde[q] uenit,[r] ut[s] inferis loquatur, et spinea corona coronetur.[t] Ad cibum autem fel et ad sitim acetum dederunt;[u] [v]inhospitalitatem[w] hanc monstrabunt mensam. Ipsa enim insipiens [x]gens tuum Deum[x] non intellexisti, ludentem[y] mortalium mentibus, sed spinis coronasti, fel[z] miscuisti. Templi uelum scindetur, et in medio die nox erit tribus horis; [a]et morietur tribus diebus[a] somno suscepto; et tunc ab inferis regressus ad lucem[b] ueniet primus resurrectionis principio ostensus."'[vc] [225] [226]

34. Hoc[a] profecto Sibille uaticinium, ni[b] fallor, maximus ille poetarum nostrorum Virgilius audierat atque attenderat, cum in quarta *Egloga*[c] futurum in proximo sub Augusto Cesare, tempore consulatus Pollionis, mirabilem cuiusdam pueri[d] de celo ad terras mittendi, qui etiam peccata mundi tolleret et quasi[e] seculum nouum in mundo mirabiliter ordinaret, precineret[f] ortum, ammonitus, ut ipsemet ait, Cumei[g] carminis uaticinio, hoc est, Sibille que Cumea[h] dicitur. Ait quippe sic, quasi adhortans[i] quoslibet ad congratulandum sibi et concinendum seu scribendum de hoc tanto puero nascituro, in comparatione cuius omnes alias[j] materias quasi infimas[k] et uiles reputat, dicens:

> Sicilides[l] Muse paulo maiora canamus.
> Non omnes arbusta iuuant[m] humilesque mirice.[n]

[d] Maiori *B* [e–e] Dei filius *Augustine* [f] Inserit *Augustine* [g] lacentius *TE;* lactencius *ABR;* operi suo *add. F* [h] Dabunt *Amb* [i] in purato *T;* inpurato *A;* impure *Amb*[1] [j] expuerint *A* [k] sputus *F* [l] Dabunt *R* [m] deus *CEF* [n] uerba *R* [o] simpliciter *F* [p–p] dorsum sanctum *B;* dorsum *R* [q] unum *BR* [r] uenerit *BR* [s] uel *CEF; om. Amb* [t] coronabitur *?T, ?E, FAmb;* corroborabitur *C* [u] diferetur *?C;* defferent *E* [v–v] etc. multa *CE;* et caetera multa *F* [w] In hospitalitatem *Amb;* inhospitalitatis *Augustine, Muckle* [x–x] *ditto. R* [y] laudentem *T;* laudandum *Amb* [z] et horridum fel *Augustine* [a–a] *om. B* [b] ad inuicem *R* [c] ostenso *Augustine*

34 [a] hec *CE* [b] nisi *CEF* [c] eglogla *T* (*but marked with a cross by T*[1]); egloga *ACEBR;* Ecloga *FAmb* [d] pueri *Ecorr* [e] qui *F* [f] precineret *R* [g] cum ei *B* [h] cumena *TBR;* cumea *ACEF;* Cumana *Amb;* Cumaea *Amb*[1] [i] adhuc exhortans *F* [j] aliquas *B but* alias *in marg.* [k] infirmas *CEAmb*[1] [l] Sicilides *TAE;* cicilides *C;* Sicelides *FRAmb;* sicendes *B* [m] mumiant *C* [n] morte *C*

The initial letters of these verses in Greek when joined together read: 'Jesus Christ, son of God, the Saviour'.[224] 'Lactantius also includes some of the Sibyl's prophecies about Christ. "Afterwards", he says, "he will fall into the hands of unbelievers. They will deal God blows with their polluted hands and spit poisoned spittle from their unclean mouths, but he will humbly offer his holy back to their lashes. And he will be silent as he receives these blows so that no one may know that he comes as the Word or whence he comes, so that he may speak to those down in Hell and be crowned with a crown of thorns. They have given him gall for his food and vinegar for his thirst; this is the table of inhospitality they will display. For you foolish people did not recognize your God, when he mocked the minds of mortals, but you crowned him with thorns and mixed gall for him. The veil of the Temple shall be rent and in the middle of the day there will be night for three hours. And he will die, falling asleep for three days, and then return from Hell into light to be the first to be revealed at the beginning of the resurrection." '[225] [226]

34. Surely, unless I am mistaken, Virgil, the greatest of our poets, had heard and noted this prophecy of the Sibyl when in his fourth *Eclogue* he foretold the marvellous birth soon to take place during the reign of Augustus Caesar in Pollio's consulship: the birth of a child to be sent down from heaven to earth to take away the sins of the world and miraculously to establish, as it were, a new age in the world. It was suggested to him, as he himself says, by the prophecy of the Cumaean song, that is, by the song of the Sibyl who is called Cumaean. He speaks as follows, as if exhorting all men to give thanks amongst themselves and to sing or write of this mighty child about to be born, in comparison with whom he judges all other subjects base and cheap:

> Sicilian Muses, let us sing a little of nobler themes!
> Hedgerow and humble tamarisk do not please all.

Divinae institutiones, i. 6 (ed. Brandt, pp. 20–2; *PL* vi. 140–4). Jewish and Christian authors from at least the 2nd c. AD found compatibilities between the oracles and the teachings of the Old and New Testament.

[224] Augustine, *De ciuitate Dei*, xviii. 23 (ed. Dombart and Kalb, xlviii. 613; ed. Hoffmann, ii. 297; *PL* xli. 579).The Greek word for fish *'ΙΧΘΥΣ*—in Christian art and literature a symbol of Christ—contains the initial letters of the phrase *'Ιησους Χριστος Θεου Υίος Σωτηρ*, Jesus Christ, Son of God, Saviour.

[225] Cf. Lactantius, *Diuinae Institutiones*, iv. 18–19 (ed. Brandt, pp. 349–64; *PL* vi. 502–13); written *c.*304–13.

[226] Augustine, *De ciuitate Dei*, xviii. 23 (ed. Dombart and Kalb, xlviii. 614–15; ed. Hoffmann, ii. 299–300; *PL* xli. 580–1). The lines from 'De qua Augustinus contra quinque hereses . . .' to here are also found in *TSum*, i. 60–1, *TChr*, i. 126–7, and *TSch*, i. 189–90.

Vltima Cumei uenit iam carminis etas,
Magnus ab integro seclorum nascitur ordo.
Iam redit[o] et uirgo, redeunt Saturnia regna,
Iam noua progenies celo[p] demittitur[q] alto,[227] etc.[228]

Inspice singula Sibille dicta et quam integre et aperte Christiane fidei de Christo summam[r] complectatur. Que nec diuinitatem nec humanitatem nec utrumque ipsius[s] aduentum nec utrumque iudicium prophetando uel[t] scribendo pretermisit; primum quidem iudicium [u]quo iniuste[v] [w]iudicatus est in passione, et[x] secundum[u] quo iuste[w] iudicaturus est mundum in maiestate.[229] Que, nec descensum eius ad inferos nec resurrectionis gloriam pretermittens, non[y] solum prophetas uerum etiam ipsos supergressa uidetur euuangelistas, qui de hoc eius descensu minime scripserunt.

35. Quis[a] non etiam illud tam familiare prolixumque[b] colloquium miretur quo ipse solus solam illam gentilem et Samaritanam mulierem [c]tam diligenter[c] dignatus est instruere, de quo et ipsi uehementer obstupuerunt apostoli?[230] [de]A qua[e] etiam infideli et de uirorum suorum multitudine reprehensa potum ipse[f] uoluit postulare, quem nichil ulterius alimenti ab aliquo nouimus[g] requisisse. Superueniunt apostoli et emptos ei cibos offerunt, dicentes: 'Rabbi,[h] manduca',[231] nec oblatos[i] suscipi uidemus, sed hoc quasi in excusationem [j]ipsum pretendisse: 'Ego cibum habeo manducare quem uos nescitis.'[232] Potum ipse a muliere postulat, a quo se illa excusans beneficio, 'quomodo', inquit, 'tu, Iudeus cum sis, bibere a me poscis[k] que sum mulier Samaritana? Non enim coutuntur Iudei Samaritanis.'[233] Et iterum: 'Neque in quo haurias habes, et puteus altus est.'[234] Potum itaque a muliere infideli et id negante desiderat, qui oblatos ab apostolis cibos non curat.

[o] reddit *E* [p] a celo *add. C;* e celo *add. E* [q] mittitur *C;* dimittitur *R* [r] summa *CEF* [s] eius *F* [t] ibi *BR* [u–u] *om. E* [v] iuste *C* [w–w] *om. C* [x] humilitate *add. F* [y] nec *CEF*

35 [a] Quid *F before corr., BR* [b] promissumque *B* [c–c] *om. E* [d] *lacuna CEF, ending in 36* [e–e] Aqua *T* [f] etiam *add. B* [g] nouissimus *R* [h] rabi *TAR* [i] ablatos *R* [j] *lacuna BR, ending in 39* [k] possis *T*

[227] Virgil, *Eclogue* iv. 1–6. For the Sybil of Cumae and Virgil's visit there see Virgil, *Aeneid*, vi. 42–155.

[228] The lines from 'Hoc profecto Sibille uaticinium . . .' to here are also found in *TChr*, i. 128 and *TSch*, i. 191. Cf. Augustine, *De ciuitate Dei*, x. 27 (ed. Dombart and Kalb, xlvii. 302; ed. Hoffmann, ii. 493; *PL* xli. 305). In *SN* c. 25, 7–8 Abelard quotes Jerome, who

The final age of Cumaean song is come,
The mighty sequence of ages born anew.
The Virgin now returns, and Saturn's reign,
Now a new race descends from heaven on high,[227] etc.[228]

Look at everything the Sibyl says and see how completely and clearly she covers the sum of Christian faith about Christ. In her prophesying or writing she omits neither his divinity nor his humanity nor his first and second coming nor either of his two judgements, that is, the first judgement whereby he was unjustly judged at the time of his passion and the second whereby he will justly judge the world in majesty.[229] She passes over neither his descent into hell nor the glory of his resurrection, and so she can be seen to surpass not only the prophets but the evangelists themselves, who wrote very little about this descent.

35. Everyone too will marvel at the long and intimate conversation Christ had with the woman who was pagan and a Samaritan and on her own, when he thought fit to give her careful advice: a conversation which very much astonished the apostles.[230] He chose to ask for a drink of water from an unbeliever, a woman he had rebuked for having many husbands, though we know of no other request by him to anyone for sustenance. The apostles came on the scene and offered him the food they had bought, saying: 'Rabbi, eat',[231] but we do not read that he accepted what they offered but that he replied as if excusing himself: 'I have food to eat of which you do not know.'[232] He asked for a drink from the woman but she excused herself from giving it to him, saying: 'How can you, a Jew, ask for a drink from me, a Samaritan woman? For Jews do not associate with Samaritans.'[233] And again: 'You have nothing to draw water with, and the well is deep.'[234] So he wanted water from a woman and an unbeliever and who refused, but ignored the food proffered by the apostles.

opposed the view that the pagans knew about the Trinity and the Incarnation ('incongrua testimonia', *Epistola* LIII *ad Paulinum* 4 and 7, ed. Hilberg, liv. 449, 453; *PL* xxii. 543, 544–5). See McGinn, '*Teste David cum Sibylla*', on the Sibylline tradition in the Middle Ages; also Dronke, 'Hermes and the Sybils', pp. 229–31, on differences between Abelard and Augustine over the Sibyl.

229 The lines from 'Que nec diuinitatem . . .' to here are also found in *TSum*, i. 60, *TChr*, i. 126, and *TSch*, i. 189.

230 Cf. John 4: 5–42.

231 John 4: 31.

232 John 4: 32.

233 John 4: 9.

234 John 4: 11.

36. Que est ista, queso, gratia quam exhibet infirmo sexui ut uidelicet a muliere hac postulet aquam qui omnibus tribuit uitam? Que, inquam, nisi ut patenter insinuet tanto sibi mulierum uirtutem esse gratiorem quanto earum natura[a] esse constat infirmiorem,[235] et se[b] tanto amplius earum salutem desiderando sitiret quanto mirabiliorem earum uirtutem constat esse. Vnde et cum a femina potum postulat, huic precipue siti sue per salutem feminarum satisfieri uelle se insinuat. Quem potum etiam cibum uocans, 'Ego', inquit, 'cibum habeo manducare quem uos nescitis.'[236] Quem postmodum exponens cibum adiungit: 'Meus cibus est ut faciam uoluntatem patris mei';[237] hanc uidelicet quasi singularem sui patris uoluntatem esse innuens ubi de salute agitur infirmioris sexus.[c] Legimus et familiare colloquium cum Nichodemo illo Iudeorum principe Dominum habuisse, quo illum quoque ad se [d]occulte uenientem[d] de salute sua ipse instruxerit,[e] sed illius colloquii non tantum tunc[f] fructum esse consequutum.[238] [g]Hanc quippe Samaritanam et spiritu prophetie repletam esse tunc constat, quo uidelicet Christum et ad Iudeos iam uenisse et ad gentes uenturum esse professa est, cum dixerit: 'Scio quia Messyas uenit, qui dicitur Christus; cum ergo[h] uenerit ille nobis annuntiabit omnia.'[239] Et[i] multos ex ciuitate illa propter uerbum mulieris ad Christum cucurrisse, et in eum credidisse, et ipsum duobus diebus apud se retinuisse,[240] qui tamen alibi discipulis ait: 'In uiam gentium ne abieritis, et in ciuitates[j] Samaritanorum ne intraueritis.'[241] Refert alibi idem Iohannes quosdam ex gentilibus qui ascenderant Ierosolimam ut adorarent in die festo, per Phylippum et Andream Christo nuntiasse quod eum uellent uidere.[242] Nec[k] tamen eos esse admissos commemorat nec illis postulantibus tantam Christi copiam esse concessam quantam huic Samaritane nequaquam id petenti, a[l] qua eius in gentibus predicatio cepisse uidetur. Quam[m] non solum conuerterit[n] sed per eam, ut dictum est, multos acquisiuit.[243] Illuminati statim per stellam Magi et ad Christum conuersi, nullos[o] exhortatione sua uel doctrina ad eum traxisse referuntur,[p] sed

36 [a] naturam *AAmb* [b] sic *A* [c] *end of lacuna CEF, beginning in 35* [d–d] uehementer *C;* uenientem *EF* [e] instruxit *CEF* [f] hunc *TAmb*[1]*;* tunc *T*[1]*AAmb; om. CEF* [g–g] *om. CEF* [h] igitur *A* [i] et *Amb* [j] ciuitate *Amb* [k] Non *Amb* [l] A *Amb* [m] quam *Amb* [n] conuertit *Amb* [o] multos *Amb* [p] feruntur *A*

[235] Cf. **26** and **29** above.
[236] John 4: 32.
[237] John 4: 34.
[238] John 3: 1–12.
[239] John 4: 25. Blamires, in *The Case for Women*, pp. 195–6 and in '*Caput a femina*', pp. 62–3, contrasts Abelard's enthusiasm for the Samaritan woman with Augustine, *In*

36. What then is that favour which he shows the weaker sex, he who has given life to all, in asking for water from this woman? I repeat, what is it if it is not his intention to make clear that the weaker a woman's nature is, the more pleasing to him is her virtue,[235] and that his thirst and his desire for their salvation is all the greater the more remarkable their virtue is seen to be? And so when he asks for a drink from the woman, more than anything else he makes it known that his thirst will be quenched through the salvation of women. He also calls this drink food, saying: 'I have food to eat of which you do not know.'[236] Later, to explain this food, he adds: 'My food is to do the will of my father',[237] implying that there is something special about the will of his father where the salvation of the weaker sex is concerned. We read also how the Lord held an intimate conversation with Nicodemus, one of the leading Jews, who came to him in secret and also received instruction on his salvation, though that conversation was not so fruitful in its results.[238] For we know that the Samaritan woman was at that moment filled with the spirit of prophecy and that she professed that Christ had already come to the Jews and would come to the pagans, saying: 'I know that the Messiah is coming. He is called Christ. When he comes, he will tell us everything.'[239] It is known too that because of what this woman said, many people from the town hurried to Christ and believed in him, and kept him with them for two days,[240] although elsewhere he tells the disciples: 'Do not take the road to pagan places nor enter any Samaritan town.'[241] John also relates elsewhere how some of the pagans who had come up to Jerusalem to worship at the festival told Christ through Philip and Andrew that they wished to see him,[242] but he says nothing about their being admitted, nor that he responded as generously to their request as he did to the Samaritan woman, who asked for nothing. It was with her that this preaching to pagans seems to have begun, for he not only converted her but, as I have said, through her many others.[243] At the sight of the star the Magi immediately saw the light and were converted to Christ, but they are not recorded as having brought any others to him through

Johannis Evangelium, xv. 10–30 (ed. Willems, pp. 154–63; *PL* xxxv. 1513–21). Like John Chrysostom Abelard is more favourable to the Samaritan woman than to Nicodemus; see, for example, Chrysostom, *In Joannem Homilia* 32: 'mulier . . . multo sapientior Nicodemo; nec modo sapientior, sed et fortior' (*PG* lix. 184).

[240] Cf. John 4: 39–40.

[241] Matt. 10: 5.

[242] Cf. John 12: 20–2.

[243] Cf. John 4: 41.

[244] Cf. Matt. 2: 1–12.

soli accessisse.[gq] [244] Ex quo etiam[r] liquet quantam a Christo gratiam in gentibus mulier sit adepta que, precurrens et ciuitati nuntians eius aduentum et que audierat predicans, tam[s] propere[t] ipsa multos de populo suo[u] est lucrata.

37. Quod si ueteris testamenti uel euuangelice scripture paginas reuoluamus, summa illa de resuscitatis mortuis beneficia diuinam gratiam feminis precipue uidebimus impendisse, nec nisi ipsis uel de ipsis hec miracula facta fuisse. Primo quippe[a] per Helyam et Helyseum ad intercessionem matrum filios ipsarum resuscitatos [b]et eis redditos[b] esse legimus.[245] Et Dominus ipse,[c] uidue cuiusdam filium suum[d] [246] et archisinagogi filiam[247] et rogatu sororum Lazarum[248] resuscitans, hoc immensi miraculi beneficium maxime feminis impendit.[249] Vnde illud est Apostoli ad Hebreos scribentis: 'Acceperunt mulieres [e]de resurrectione mortuos suos.'[e] [250] [fg]Nam[h] et puella suscitata[i] mortuum recepit corpus et cetere femine in consolationem sui quos plangebant mortuos receperunt suscitatos.[g] [251] Ex quo etiam liquet quantam semper feminis exhibuerit gratiam quas tam sua quam suorum resuscitatione primo letificans, nouissime quoque ipse propria resurrectione[fj] eas plurimum extulit quibus, [k]ut dictum est,[k] [252] primum apparuit.

38. [a]Quod etiam hic sexus in populo persequente, quodam[b] erga Dominum naturali compassionis affectu, uisus est promereri. Vt enim Lucas meminit, cum eum uiri ad crucifigendum ducerent, femine ipsorum sequebantur plangentes ipsum atque lamentantes. Quibus ipse conuersus, et quasi pietatis huius uicem in ipso statim passionis articulo misericorditer eis referens, futurum ut cauere queant predicit[c] exitium:[d] 'Filie', inquit, 'Ierusalem, nolite flere super me, sed super uos ipsas flete, et super filios uestros. Quia ecce uenient dies in quibus dicent: Beate steriles, et uentres que[e] non genuerunt',[253] etc.[f] Ad cuius etiam liberationem iniquissimi iudicis[254] uxorem antea

[q] accessione *A* [r] *om. EF* [s] tamen *F* [t] prope *A* [u] *om. CEF*

37 [a] quidem *F* [b–b] *om. Amb* [c] ipsi *E* [d] *om. F* [e–e] mortuos suos de resurrectione *CE* [f–f] *om. C* [g–g] *om. EF* [h] *illegible add. by T¹ in marg.* [i] resuscitata *A* [j] insurrectione *E* [k–k] *om. CEF*

38 [a] *lacuna CEF, ending in 39* [b] *a cross is placed in the marg. of T facing this sentence* [c] predixit *A* [d] exitum *TACEFAmb;* exi(. . .?)*T¹;* exitium *Amb¹*; le destruisement *J* [e] qui *Amb* [f] *om. Amb*

[245] Cf. 3 Kgs. (1 Kgs.) 17: 17–24; 4 Kgs. (2 Kgs.) 4: 18–37, 8: 1–6. Also *Letter* 3, 8 and *Sermon* 33 (*PL* clxxviii. 525D).

exhortation or teaching; they alone came to him.[244] From this it is surely clear what a great favour a woman brought to pagans from Christ, when she ran ahead and told her town of his arrival, and proclaimed what she had heard so that in so short a time she won over many of her people.

37. If we turn the pages of the Old Testament or of the Gospels we shall see that divine grace mainly bestowed upon women was the supreme blessing of raising the dead to life, and that these miracles were not performed except with regard to them or for them. We read that first of all through Elijah and Elisha sons were raised to life at their mothers' intercession and restored to them.[245] And the Lord himself, in bringing back to life the son of a widowed mother,[246] and the daughter of the leader of the synagogue,[247] and also Lazarus at his sisters' plea,[248] bestowed the blessing of this greatest of miracles on women above all.[249] Hence the words of the Apostle in writing to the Hebrews: 'Women received back their dead raised to life.'[250] For the girl who was restored took back her own dead body, and the other women for their consolation received back restored to life those whom they had mourned as dead.[251] This clearly shows how greatly Christ always favoured women first in bringing them joy in restoring themselves and their children to life, and finally too at his own resurrection when, as has been said,[252] he so greatly honoured the women to whom he appeared first.

38. Among the people who followed him, the female sex is seen to have won favour through their natural feeling of compassion for the Lord, for, as Luke records, when the men led him away to be crucified, their women followed, mourning and weeping for him. He turned to them and, as if, out of pity, in the very hour of his suffering, he wished to make a return for their devotion, he foretold the end to come so that they could guard against it. 'Daughters of Jerusalem', he said, 'do not weep over me, but weep for yourselves and your children. For the days will surely come when people will say: Happy are the barren and the wombs which never bore a child',[253] etc. Matthew also relates that the wife of his most unjust judge[254] had

[246] Cf. Luke 7: 12–16.
[247] Cf. Mark 5: 22–43; Luke 8: 41–56.
[248] Cf. John 11: 1–44.
[249] Cf. John 11: 44.
[250] Cf. Heb. 11: 35.
[251] 'Quod si ueteris testamenti . . . suscitatos': cf. *Letter* 3, 7.
[252] At 11 above.
[253] Luke 23: 28–9.
[254] Pontius Pilate.

fideliter laborasse Matheus commemorat, dicens: 'Sedente autem illo pro tribunali, misit ad illum uxor eius dicens: Nichil tibi et iusto illi; multa enim passa sum hodie per uisum propter eum.'[255] Quo etiam predicante, solam feminam de tota turba in tantam eius laudem legimus extulisse uocem, ut beatum exclamaret uterum qui eum portauerit, et ubera que suxerit.[g 256] A quo et statim piam confessionis sue, licet uerissime, correctionem meruit audire, ipso confestim ei respondente: 'Quin imo beati qui audiunt uerbum Dei et custodiunt illud.'[257]

39. Solus Iohannes inter apostolos Christi hoc priuilegium amoris obtinuit ut dilectus Domini uocaretur.[258] De Martha autem et[a] Maria ipse scribit Iohannes quia 'diligebat Ihesus Martham et sororem eius Mariam et Lazarum'.[259] Ipse idem Apostolus, qui ex[b] priuilegio, ut dictum est, amoris se unum a Domino dilectum esse[c] commemorat, hoc ipso priuilegio quod nulli aliorum ascripsit apostolorum feminas insigniuit. In quo etiam honore, [d]cum etiam[d] fratrem earum ipsis aggregaret, eas tamen illi preposuit quas in amore precellere credidit.[e]

40. Libet denique ut [a]ad fideles seu[b] Christianas[a] redeamus[c] feminas et[d] diuine respectum[e] misericordie in ipsa etiam publicorum abiectione scortorum et stupendo predicare et predicando stupere. Quid enim[f] abiectius quam Maria Magdalene uel Maria Egyptiaca[g] secundum uite statum pristine? Quas uero postmodum uel[h] honore uel merito diuina amplius gratia sublimauit? Illam quidem quasi in apostolico[i] permanentem[j] cenobio, ut iam supra commemorauimus,[260] hanc[k] uero, ut scriptum est,[261] supra humanam uirtutem anachoretarum agone dimicantem,[l] ut in utrorumque[m] monachorum proposito[262] sanctarum uirtus feminarum premineat,[n] et illud quod incredulis [o]ait Dominus:[o] 'Meretrices precedent uos[p] in regnum Dei',[263] ipsis etiam[q] fidelibus uiris improperandum[r] uideatur,[s] et secundum sexuum [t]seu uite differentiam fiant 'nouissimi primi et primi nouissimi'.[264]

[g] sugserit *T;* sugserrit *A after corr. of* suggedit

39 [a] ex *T* [b] ex *T, perhaps after corr. by* T^4 [c] esse *T* [d–d] et *T;* cum et *A;* etsi *Amb* [e] *lacuna BR, beginning in 35, ends here; lacuna CEF, beginning in 38, ends here*

40 [a–a] Christianas seu fideles *F* [b] ad *add. E* [c] uideamus *BR* [d] *om. TBRAmb* [e] indicium *CF;* renosum *?E;* respectu *RAmb* [f] etiam *T;* est *Amb* [g] egyptiace *BR* [h] in *B* [i] apostolica *E* [j] praeeminentem *F* [k] hac *Amb* [l] dimicante *TBAmb* [m] utraque *BR* [n] peniteat *?B,?R* [o–o] ait Domine *B;* Dominus ait *Amb* [p] nos *B* [q] et *Amb* [r] esse *add. CEF* [s] uideantur *BR* [t] T^2 *takes over here from T*

previously worked faithfully for the Lord's release: 'While he was sitting in court his wife sent him this message: Have nothing to do with that innocent man, for I have been troubled all day by a dream about him.'[255] Again, while he was preaching, only a woman out of the whole crowd raised her voice in praise of him, crying out that happy was the womb which bore him and the breasts he sucked.[256] She was immediately privileged to hear a devout correction of her confession of faith, genuine though it was, when he replied immediately: 'No, happy are those who hear the word of the Lord and keep it.'[257]

39. John alone among Christ's apostles was granted love's privilege of being called the beloved of the Lord,[258] though John himself writes of Martha and Mary: 'Now Jesus loved Martha and her sister Mary and Lazarus.'[259] So the same Apostle who records, as has been said, that he alone enjoyed the privilege of being loved by the Lord, distinguished these women by the very privilege he ascribed to no other apostle, and, although in referring to this honour he added their brother's name to theirs, he placed the sisters' names first, believing that they came first in the Lord's love.

40. Finally, to return to faithful or Christian women, we may proclaim with wonder the consideration shown by divine mercy even to the degradation of common prostitutes. Could anything be more sordid than the early life of Mary Magdalene or Mary the Egyptian? Yet divine grace later raised them high, to do them honour or for their merit. The former remained permanently in, as it were, the community of the apostles, as we recalled above,[260] and of the latter it is recorded[261] that she struggled with superhuman courage against what anchorites suffer, so that holy women should give a lead in both kinds of monastic life[262] and so that the Lord's saying to incredulous hearers: 'Harlots shall enter the kingdom of God before you',[263] be seen to apply also to faithful men: the last of either sex or of either way of life 'shall be first and the first last'.[264]

[255] Matt. 27: 19.
[256] Cf. Luke 11: 27.
[257] Cf. Luke 11: 28.
[258] Cf. John 13: 23, 19: 26, 20: 2, 21: 7 and 20.
[259] John 11: 5.
[260] At 11 above.
[261] Cf. *Vitae Patrum*, i. *Vita sanctae Mariae Aegyptiacae* (*PL* lxxiii. 671–90).
[262] 'utrorumque monachorum proposito': that is, the cenobitic or conventual and the eremitic or solitary way of monastic life.
[263] Matt. 21: 31.
[264] Matt. 20: 16.

41. Quis denique ignoret feminas exhortationem Christi et consilium Apostoli tanto[a] castimonie zelo esse complexas ut pro conseruanda[b] carnis pariter ac mentis integritate[c] [d]Deo se per[d] martyrium[e] offerrent[f] holocaustum,[265] et gemina triumphantes corona[266] agnum sponsum uirginum quocumque[g] ierit sequi studerent?[h] [267] Quam quidem uirtutis perfectionem, raram in uiris,[i] crebram[j] in feminis esse cognouimus.[k] [268] Quarum etiam nonnullas tantum in hac carnis prerogatiua zelum habuisse legimus ut non sibi manum inferre dubitarent ne quam Deo uouerant incorruptionem amitterent[l] et ad sponsum[m] [n]uirginum non[n] uirgines peruenirent.[o] [269] Qui etiam sanctarum [p]deuotionem uirginum[p] in tantum sibi gratam esse monstrauit ut gentilis[q] populi multitudinem ad beate Agathe suffragium concurrentem, uelo eius contra estuantis Ethne terribilem ignem opposito,[r] tam a[s] corporis quam anime liberaret[t] incendio.[270] Nullam nouimus monachi[u] cucullam beneficii tanti gratiam esse adeptam. Legimus quidem ad tactum pallii Helye Iordanem esse diuisum, et ipsi pariter et Helyseo uiam per terram prebuisse,[271] uelo autem uirginis immensam [v]adhuc infidelis[v] [w]populi multitudinem tam[x] mente saluari quam corpore, et sic eis conuersis[w] ad celestia uiam patuisse. Illud quoque non modicum sanctarum dignitatem commendat feminarum quod in suis ipse[y] uerbis consecrantur, dicentes: 'Anulo[z] suo[a] subarrauit me',[272] etc;[b] 'Ipsi sum desponsata',[273] [c]etc.[d] Hec quippe uerba sunt beate Agnetis in quibus uirgines suam professionem[c] facientes Christo desponsantur.

42. [a]Si quis[b] etiam uestre[c] religionis formam ac dignitatem apud gentiles cognoscere curet, atque nonnulla inde quoque exempla ad

41 [a] quanto *C* [b] seruanda *R* [c] integritatem *CE* [d–d] deo se *E;* deo deo in *F* [e] maritum *?E;* martyrii *F* [f] offenderent *BR* [g] quoque *C* [h] studeant *CEF* [i] ueris *R* [j] crebam *R* [k] cognoscimus *EF* [l] admitterent *CE* [m] sponsam *BR* [n–n] uirginem *TACEBRAmb;* uirginum non *F* [o] peruenerunt *BR* [p–p] uirginum deuotionem *CEF* [q] gentiles *E* [r] apposito *A* [s] *om. B* [t] liberauerit *Amb* [u] monachis *BR* [v–v] infidelis *ACE;* infidelibus *F;* infidelis adhuc *BR* [w–w] *om. CEF* [x] quam *BR* [y] in se *BR* [z] A nullo *F;* a ullo *R;* Annullo *Amb* [a] fidei suae *Vita S. Agnetis* [b] *om. Amb* [c–c] *om. C* [d] *om. Amb*

42 [a–a] *om. CEF* [b] Siquis *TB* [c] nostre *BR*

[265] 'pro conseruanda carnis pariter ac mentis integritate Deo se per martyrium offerrent holocaustum'. Cf. **50** below: 'ut . . . integritatem . . . carnis conseruarent', *Sermon* 1 *on the Annunciation to Mary*: 'integritate corporis pariter et mentis conservata' (*PL* clxxviii. 385B) and *Hymn* 92, III, *on Virgins*: 'integra tam spiritu quam corpore, / holocaustum uerum fit ex uirgine' (ed. Waddell, p. 130; Szövérffy (120, III), p. 245). Bell, *Peter Abelard after Marriage*, pp. 239–45 and p. 17, also draws attention to a phrase in stanza 6 of the sequence *Virgines*

41. In short, everyone knows that women embraced the guidance of Christ and the counsel of the Apostle with such great zeal for chastity that in order to preserve integrity of body and mind alike they gave themselves in martyrdom as a burnt offering to God[265] and, triumphant with a double crown,[266] sought to follow the lamb, the virgins' spouse, wherever he would go.[267] Such perfection of courage we know to be rare in men but not uncommon in women,[268] some of whom are said to have had so great a zeal for this special quality of the flesh that they did not hesitate to lay hands on themselves, lest they should lose the purity they had dedicated to God, and not come as virgins to the virgins' spouse.[269] God has also shown that the devotion of holy virgins is so pleasing to him that when a great crowd of pagans hastily gathered to seek the intercession of St Agatha and spread out her veil against the fearful flames of seething Etna, he saved them from burning in both body and soul.[270] We know of no monk's cowl receiving the grace of such a benefit, although we read that at the touch of Elijah's cloak the Jordan was divided so that he and also Elisha could cross over on dry ground.[271] But by the veil of a virgin a huge number of people, still unbelievers, was saved both in mind and body and, so converted, the way to heaven opened before them. Holy women have a further high tribute paid to them in that they are consecrated using their own words, saying: 'With this ring he has espoused me',[272] etc.; 'I am betrothed to him',[273] etc. These are the words of St Agnes whereby the virgins making their profession are betrothed to Christ.

42. If anyone seeks to know what was the form and status among unbelievers of your religious way of life, and to draw from there

castae sometimes ascribed to Abelard (see above, Introduction, p. xxxviii): 'Holocaustum Domino / Offerent ex integro / uirgines carne / integrae mente.'

[266] 'gemina . . . corona': cf. also **16** above and *Hymn* 68 (Szövérffy 89), *De ss. Petro et Paulo* 1, II.

[267] Cf. Rev. 14: 4 and **50** below.

[268] Cf. *Hymn* 92 (Szövérffy 120), *De uirginibus* 1, II.

[269] Cf. **50** below.

[270] Cf. *Acta Sanctae Agathae*, 15 (*Acta Sanctorum*, Feb., I, p. 624).

[271] Cf. 4 Kgs. 2: 8; also *Sermon* 16 (*PL* clxxviii. 500A).

[272] *Vita Sanctae Agnetis*, 1, 3 (*Acta Sanctorum*, Jan., II, p. 715). Cf. the Roman Pontifical of the 12th c. in *Le Pontifical romain au moyen âge*, ed. Andrieu, i. 163: 'Annulo suo subarrhavit me dominus meus Iesus Christus et tamquam sponsam decoravit me corona.' On the consecration ceremony for female religious see Metz, *La Femme et l'enfant dans le droit canonique médiéval*, essay VII: 'La couronne et l'anneau dans la consécration des vierges' (first published in the *Revue des sciences religieuses*, xxviii (1954), pp. 113–32).

[273] *Breuiarium Romanum*, *Pars hiemalis*, p. 682 (the antiphon before the seventh lesson on the feast of St Agnes, 21 Jan.): 'Ipsi sum desponsata, cui Angeli seruiunt, cuius pulchritudinem sol et luna mirantur'. Cf. the 12th-c. Roman Pontifical in *Le Pontifical romain au moyen âge*, ed. Andrieu, i. 161.

exhortationem uestram inducere, facile deprehendet[d] in ipsis etiam nonnullam huius propositi institutionem precessisse, excepto quod ad fidei pertinet tenorem; et multa in illis, sicut et in Iudeis, precessisse que ex utrisque congregata ecclesia retinuit sed in melius commutauit. Quis enim[e] nesciat uniuersos clericorum ordines, ab hostiario usque ad episcopum, ipsumque tonsure[f] usum ecclesiastice qua clerici fiunt, et ieiunia quattuor temporum,[274] et azimorum sacrificium, nec non ipsa sacerdotalium indumentorum ornamenta, et nonnulla dedicationis uel alia sacramenta, a synagoga ecclesiam[g] assumpsisse?[275] Quis etiam ignoret ipsam,[h] utilissima dispensatione, non solum secularium dignitatum gradus in regibus ceterisque principibus, et nonnulla legum[i] decreta uel philosophice discipline documenta in conuersis gentibus retinuisse, uerum etiam quosdam ecclesiasticarum dignitatum gradus uel continentie formam et corporalis mundicie religionem ab eis accepisse? Constat quippe nunc episcopos uel archiepiscopos presidere ubi tunc flamines uel archiflamines habebantur, et que tunc templa demonibus sunt instituta, postea Domino fuisse consecrata et sanctorum memoriis insignita.[a]

43. Scimus et in gentibus[a] precipue prerogatiuam uirginitatis enituisse,[276] cum maledictum legis[b] ad nuptias Iudeos coherceret,[277] et[c] in tantum gentibus [d]hanc uirtutem[d] seu mundiciam[e] carnis acceptam[f] extitisse ut in templis earum[g] magni[h] feminarum conuentus [i]celibi se uite dicarent.[j] Vnde Ieronymus *in epistola*[k] *ad Galathas*, libro[l] tertio: 'Quid nos', inquit, 'oportet facere in quorum condempnationem habet et Iuno[m] uniuiras et Vesta uniuirgines[n] et alia ydola continentes?'[278] Vniuiras autem et uniuirgines[o] dicit quasi monachas[p] que uiros[q] nouerant et monachas[r] uirgines. Monos enim, unde[s] monachus, id est, solitarius dicitur, unum sonat.[279] Qui etiam

[d] deprehendit *B* [e] *om. Amb* [f] censure *R* [g] *om. BR* [h] ipsum *Amb* [i] *om. BR*

43 [a] gentilibus *R* [b] Regis *C* [c] Et *ABR* [d–d] *om. E* [e] mundicia *B* [f] accepta *BR* [g] eorum *F* [h] *vacant space in C, om. EF* (*F provides a comma*) [i] *H starts here* [j] dedicarent *B* [k] epistolam *FAmb* [l] in libro *B* [m] muro *C;* juno *?Ecorr;* uino *B* [n] uniuirgines *TACBRHAmb;* uirgines *Ecorr, F* [o] uniuirgines *TAC, Ecorr, Amb;* uirgines *FBR* [p] monachis *T;* vniuiras *add. Amb* [q] uniuiras *superscr. add. by T² or by another hand in T* [r] uniuirgines *superscr. add. by T² or by another hand in T, add. Amb* [s] unum *B;* unum inde *add. H*

---

[274] Cf. note 173.

[275] Cf. *Sermon* 3 (*PL* clxxviii, 406D–7B); Isidore of Seville, *De ecclesiasticis officiis*, ii. 4–15 (ed. Lawson, pp. 55–73; *PL* lxxxiii. 779–94).

[276] Cf. *TChr*, ii. 94.

examples to encourage you, she will easily find among them too some sort of earlier organization for those of your calling, except in such matters as belong to the tenor of the faith. Many things existed among them, as among the Jews, which the Church has drawn together from both sources and retained, though changed for the better. For it is well known that all the ranks of the clergy, from doorkeeper to bishop, even the use of the ecclesiastical tonsure signifying a cleric, the fasts of the Ember Days,[274] the sacrifice of unleavened bread, as well as the ornaments of priestly vestments and the sacraments of dedication and so forth, were taken over by the Church from the synagogue.[275] It is also well known that the Church has retained, by a most useful dispensation, not only the degrees of secular rank enjoyed by kings and other princes, as well as some legal enactments and examples of philosophical teaching in use amongst converted pagans, but has also taken from them certain grades of ecclesiastical offices, and even the state of continence and the observance of bodily purity. There can be no doubt that bishops and archbishops now hold authority where there were formerly flamens and archflamens, and temples set up for demons then were subsequently consecrated to the Lord and dedicated in the memory of saints.

43. We know too that, although the curse of the Law forced the Jews into marriage,[276] the privilege of virginity was held in particular honour by pagans,[277] and this virtue or purity of the flesh was so highly regarded by them that in their temples large communities of women devoted themselves to the celibate life. Hence Jerome writing *on the Letter to the Galatians* asks in his third book: 'What should we do? Juno has her women who were married once only, Vesta her virgins, and other idols their continent servants, so we stand condemned.'[278] He says that the women married once only and the virgins were like female monks who have known men and monastic virgins. For *monos*, from which 'monk', that is, 'a solitary', is derived, means 'one'.[279] He also cites many examples of chastity or continence

[277] Cf. the passage from Augustine, *De bono coniugali*, xxii. 27 cited in *Letter* 6, **23**, and note 110); also *Collationes* **59** (ed. Marenbon and Orlandi, p. 72 and note 166; *Dialogus*, ed. Thomas, *ll.* 1113–14; *PL* clxxviii. 1633C); *Sermons* 1 and 26 (*PL* clxxviii. 382C, 384C, 539D); *Problemata* 42 (*PL* clxxviii. 723A–724A), and *Ethica*, i. 12. 3 (ed. Ilgner, pp. 12–13; ed. Luscombe, p. 20, *ll.* 6–8).

[278] Jerome, *Commentarii . . . in Epistolam ad Galatas*, iii. 6. 10 (*PL* xxvi. 433BC (462B)). Also cited in *TChr*, ii. 109.

[279] Cf. *Rule* **14**; *Letter* 12 (ed. Smits, pp. 259–61; *PL* clxxviii. 346B–347C; trans. Ziolkowski, pp. 161–3); *Sermon* 33 (*PL* clxxviii. 588D); *Problemata* 14 (*PL* clxxviii. 698C).

libro primo *contra*[t] *Iouinianum*, multis[u] de castitate uel continentia gentilium feminarum inductis exemplis, 'scio',[v] inquit, 'in cathalogo feminarum[w] me plura dixisse, ut que[x] Christiane pudicicie despiciunt fidem, discant saltem ab ethnicis castitatem'.[280] Qui, in eodem, supra illam quoque continentie uirtutem adeo commendauit ut[y] [z]hanc precipue mundiciam[z] carnis in omni gente Dominus approbasse[a] uideatur, et nonnullis eam[b] infidelibus quoque uel collatione meritorum uel exhibitione miraculorum extulisse.[281] 'Quid referam', inquit, 'sibillam[c] Erythream[d] atque Cumanam[e] et octo[f] reliquas?[g] Nam Varro decem fuisse autumat, quarum insigne uirginitas[h] est et uirginitatis premium diuinatio.'[282] Item: 'Claudia uirgo uestalis, cum in suspicionem[i] uenisset stupri, fertur cingulo[j] duxisse ratem[k] quam [l]hominum milia[l] trahere nequiuerant.'[283] [m]Et Sydonius Claremontensis[m] episcopus in propenticon[n] ad libellum suum ita loquitur:[o]

> [p]Qualis nec Tanaquil fuit nec illa,
> quam tu, Trecipitine,[q] procreasti,
> qualis nec Phrigie dicata[r] Veste
> que[s] contra satis Albulam tumentem
> duxit uirgineo ratem capillo.[p] [284]

Augustinus *de ciuitate Dei*, libro secundo et uicesimo: 'Iam si ad eorum miracula ueniamus que facta [t]a diis suis[t] [u]martyribus opponunt[u] nostris,[v] nonne etiam[w] ipsa pro nobis facere et nobis reperientur omnino proficere? Nam inter magna miracula deorum[x] suorum profecto magnum illud est quod Varro commemorat uestalem uirginem, cum periclitaretur falsa suspicione de stupro, cribrum[y] implesse[z] aqua de Tyberi, et ad suos[a] iudices nulla eius parte stillante portasse.[285] Quis aque [b]pondus tenuit tot cauernis patentibus?[c] Itane

[t] *om. A* [u] mulieris *H* [v] Sentio *F and Jerome* [w] multo *add. F* [x] qui *E* [y] In *C* in *E* [z–z] hac precipue munditia *CE* [a] approbare *CEF* [b] in *add. ABRH;* etiam in *Amb* [c] Sibillas *F, Jerome* [d] erietheam *T;* erietheam *A;* eritheam *CEBH;* Erithream *F* [e] cumaneam *C* [f] viii *TA;* vi *C;* vii *BRH* [g] Reliquias? *R* [h] uirginitas *A;* uirginita *H followed by a space sufficient for three characters* [i] suspicione *BRH* [j] tam *add. H* [k] nauem *F, Jerome* [l–l] multa millia hominum *add. F, Jerome* [m–m] ut hoc etiam sidonius (sydonius *E*) clarmontensis (claremontensis *E*) *CE;* Hoc etiam Sidonius Claromontensis *F;* Et si dominus claromontensis *H* [n] prapemptico *F;* propenticum *BRH;* propemtico *Amb* [o] Reffert *CE;* refert *F* [p–p] *om. CEF* [q] precipitine *BRH;* Tricipitine *Amb, Sidonius* [r] est *add. BH* [s] circa *TAmb* [t–t] ad hiis suis *E* [u–u] opponunt martyribus *F* [v] *om. E* [w] *om. H* [x] *corrupt in CE* [y] cribum *C* [z] de *add. CE* [a] eos *E* [b–b] pondus super cribum tenuit? Quia tot cauernis patentibus nihil inde in terram cadere permisit? Itane Deus omnipotens qui ipsa creauit elementa *F, Augustine* [c] patientibus *Amb*

amongst pagan women in the first book of his *Against Jovinian* and he then adds: 'I know that I have spoken at some length in my catalogue of women, in the hope that those who think little of faith in Christian modesty shall at least learn chastity from the heathen.'[280] Earlier on in the same book he praised the virtue of continence so warmly that he makes it appear that the Lord had especially approved that purity of the flesh among all peoples and he even extolled it in some of the pagans, either by comparing their merits or by setting out the miracles they had performed.[281] 'What shall I say', he asks, 'of the Erythraean and Cumean Sibyl and the eight others? For Varro declares that they were ten in number, distinguished by their virgin state, for which the gift of prophecy was their reward.'[282] Again: 'The Vestal virgin Claudia, under suspicion of unchastity, is said to have used her girdle to pull along a boat which thousands of men had been unable to move.'[283] Sidonius, bishop of Clermont, also says in the Preface to his book:

> Such as was neither Tanaquil, nor she
> Whom you, Trecipitinus, fathered once,
> Nor she, to Phrygian Vesta dedicated,
> Who with her virgin hair did draw a boat
> Against the swollen tide of Albula.[284]

Augustine writes in book 22 of his *City of God*: 'And now if we turn to the miracles performed by their gods which they set against those of our martyrs, we shall surely find that they support our arguments and fully benefit us. Indeed, among the great miracles of their gods is one recorded by Varro of the Vestal virgin, who was falsely suspected of unchastity and in danger of her life. She is said to have filled a sieve with water from the Tiber and brought it to her judges without spilling a drop.[285] Who held the weight of the water when there were

[280] Jerome, *Aduersus Iouinianum*, i. 47 (*PL* xxiii. 276B (288–9)). On the Jovinianist controversy see *Letter* 1, **24**, n. 81.

[281] Cf. *TChr*, ii. 106 and 108.

[282] Jerome, *Aduersus Iouinianum*, i. 41 (*PL* xxiii. 270 (283)). Also cited in *TChr*, ii. 104.

[283] Jerome, *Aduersus Iouinianum*, i. 41 (*PL* xxiii. 271 (283)). Also cited in *TChr*, ii. 106. Cf. Ovid, *Fasti*, iv. 305–72.

[284] Sidonius Apollinaris, *Carmina*, xxiv, *Propempticon ad libellum*, *vv.* 39–43 (ed. Loyen, pp. 165–6; ed. Lütjohann, pp. 262–3; ed. and trans. Anderson, pp. 320–3; *PL* lviii. 746B); also cited in *TChr*, ii. 106. For Tanaquil and for Trecipitinus, father of Lucretia, cf. Livy, *Ab urbe condita*, i. 34 and 59.

[285] This miracle is not recorded in the collection made by R. Agahd of the traces of Varro's *Antiquities* found in the *De ciuitate Dei* (*Varronis Antiquitatum Rerum Divinarum Libri* . . .). Cf. Valerius Maximus, *Facta et dicta memorabilia*, viii. 1. 5.

Deus omnipotens terreno[b] corpori[d] graue pondus auferre non poterit, ut in eodem elemento habitet uiuificatum corpus in quo uoluerit uiuificans spiritus?'[286]

44. Nec mirum si hiis uel aliis Deus miraculis infidelium quoque castitatem extulerit, uel officio demonum extolli permiserit, ut tanto amplius nunc fideles ad ipsam animarentur quanto hanc in[a] infidelibus quoque amplius exaltari cognouerint.[b] Scimus et Cayphe prelationi,[c] non persone, prophetie[d] gratiam [e]esse collatam,[e] [287] et pseudo quoque apostolos miraculis nonnumquam[f] choruscasse, et hec non personis eorum set officio[g] esse concessa.[288] Quid igitur[h] mirum si Dominus non personis infidelium feminarum sed uirtuti continentie ipsarum[i] hoc[j] concesserit,[k] ad innocentiam [l]uirginis saltem[l] liberandam et false accusationis improbitatem conterendam? Constat quippe amorem continentie bonum esse etiam[m] in infidelibus, sicut[n] et coniugalis pactionis obseruantiam donum Dei apud omnes esse; ideoque[o] mirabile[p] non[q] uideri, si sua dona, non errorem infidelitatis, per signa que infidelibus fiunt, non fidelibus,[r] Deus honoret, maxime quando per hec,[s] ut dictum est,[289] et[t] innocentia liberatur et peruersorum hominum malicia reprimitur, et ad hoc[u] quod ita[v] magnificatur bonum homines amplius cohortantur,[w] per[x] quod tanto minus ab infidelibus quoque peccatur quanto amplius a uoluptatibus carnis receditur. Quod nunc etiam, cum plerisque aliis, aduersus predictum incontinentem hereticum beatus[y] non inconuenienter induxit [z]Ieronimus, [a]ut que[b] non miratur in Christianis, erubescat in ethnicis.[c] [290] Quis etiam dona Dei [d]esse[za] deneget, potestatem[d] etiam infidelium principum,[e] etsi peruerse ipsa[f] utantur, uel amorem iusticie uel mansuetudinem quam habent [g]lege instructi[g] naturali uel cetera que decent principes? Quis bona esse[h] contradicat

[d] corpore *E;* corporum *R;* corporis *H*

44 [a] *om. E* [b] cognoverunt *E* [c] prelatione *CEBRH* [d] *om. TAmb* [e–e] collatam esse *H* [f] nonnusquam *TAmb* [g] officiis *F* [h] ergo *F* [i] earum *CEFH* [j] *om. FBRH* [k] concessit *CEF* [l–l] etiam virginis *F;* uirginitatis saltem *H* [m] et *CAmb* [n] sic *H* [o] Ideoque *TBRH* [p] est *add. CE* [q] debet *add. F* [r] *A adds a colon, Amb adds a comma* [s] hoc *CEF* [t] *om. Amb* [u] huc *H* [v] ad tam *H* [w] cohortentur *H* [x] et *C* [y] beatum *E* [z–z] *om. CE* [a–a] *om. F* [b] quod *H* [c] erumpnis *B;* empnicis *R* [d–d] deneget esse potestate *H* [e] principium *R* [f] ipsi *E* [g–g] lege instructa *E;* legem instructi *F* [h] *superscr. by another hand over* e *in A; om. CEF*

[286] Augustine, *De ciuitate Dei*, xxii. 11 (ed. Dombart and Kalb, xlviii. 830; ed. Hoffmann, ii. 617; *PL* xli. 774); also cited in *TChr*, ii. 106-a (Montecassino MS 174).
[287] Cf. John 11: 51.

so many gaping holes? Has not almighty God the power to do away with the heavy weight of an earthly body in order to enable the revived body to live in the same element as that which the revived spirit has chosen?'[286]

44. Nor is it surprising if God has extolled the chastity even of a pagan in these and other miracles, nor if he has allowed it to be extolled by the agency of demons, in order that believers now may be more inspired to practise chastity the more they know it was exalted amongst pagans. We know too that the gift of prophecy was conferred not on the person but on the priesthood of Caiaphas;[287] and that at times false apostles also leaped to fame through the miracles they performed, and that these were allowed them not in their persons but because of the office they held.[288] What wonder then if the Lord granted this concession to pagan women, not to their persons but to their virtue of continence, so that at least a virgin's innocence could be freed from suspicion and the wickedness of a false accusation be destroyed. It is generally accepted that love of continence is a good thing even amongst pagans, just as the observance of the marriage bond is a gift of God to all. So it should seem no marvel if God honours his own gifts, not the error of unbelief, through signs shown to unbelievers, not only to believers, especially when through these, as has been said,[289] innocence wins freedom and the spite of wicked men is curbed; and when people are further encouraged towards this good thing because it is esteemed in this way and reduces sin, even amongst pagans, the more they withdraw from the pleasures of the flesh. St Jerome accordingly introduced this quite suitably, amongst several other points, into his attack on the incontinent heretic named above, so that what one might blush to find in pagans one should not be surprised to find in Christians.[290] Again, who would deny to be gifts of God the power of rulers, even when they are unbelievers and may make wrong use of it, or any love of justice or clemency they may have under the guidance of natural law, or anything else proper to princes? Who would gainsay these things are good just because they

[288] Cf. Matt. 24: 24; Augustine, *De diuersis quaestionibus LXXXIII*, lxxix. 3 (ed. Mutzenbecher, p. 228; *PL* xl. 92). Cf. *TSum*, i. 33–4, *TChr*, i. 59–60, *TSch*, i. 105–6.

[289] At **43** above.

[290] The heretic is Jovinian. Cf. *Letter* 1, **24**, and **43** above.

[291] Augustine, *De ciuitate Dei*, xii. 6 (ed. Dombart and Kalb, xlviii. 360; ed. Hoffmann, i. 574; *PL* xli. 353); *Contra Iulianum opus imperfectum*, i. 66 and 114 (ed. Zelzer, p. 64 and p. 132; *PL* xlv. 1085 and 1124).

quia malis sunt permixta,[i] presertim cum, ut beatus astruit Augustinus et manifesta ratio testatur, mala esse [j]nequeant nisi in[j] natura bona?[291] Quis [k]non illud[k] approbet[l] quod poetica perhibet sententia: 'Oderunt peccare boni uirtutis amore'?[m] [292] Quis Vespasiani[n] nondum[o] imperatoris miraculum quod Suetonius[p] refert, de ceco uidelicet[q] et claudo per eum curatis, non magis approbet quam neget, ut eius uirtutem amplius emulari uelint principes;[293] aut quod de anima Traiani beatus egisse Gregorius refertur?[r] [294] [s]Nouerunt homines in coeno[t] margaritam[u] legere[295] et a paleis grana discernere. Et dona sua infidelitati adiuncta Deus ignorare non potest, nec quicquam horum que fecit[v] odire. Que, quo amplius signis choruscant, tanto amplius sua esse demonstrat, nec hominum prauitate sua inquinari posse, et qualis sit fidelibus sperandus[w] qui talem se exhibet infidelibus.[s] Quantam[x] autem apud infideles dignitatem deuota illa templis pudicicia sit adepta uindicta uiolationis indicat. Quam scilicet uindicatam[y] Iuuenalis commemorans in quarta *Satira* contra Crispinum sic de ipso ait:

Cum quo nuper uittata[z] iacebat,
Sanguine adhuc uiuo terram subitura sacerdos.[296]

Vnde et Augustinus *de ciuitate Dei* libro tertio: 'Nam et ipsi', inquit, 'Romani antiqui in stupro detectas[a] Veste[b] sacerdotes[c] uiuas[d] defodiebant; adulteras[e] autem feminas, quamuis aliqua dampnatione, nulla tamen morte plectebant: usque adeo grauius que[f] putabant abdita[g] diuina quam humana cubilia uindicabant.'[297]

45. Apud nos autem Christianorum cura principum tanto amplius uestre[a] prouidit castimonie quanto eam sanctiorem esse non dubitatur. Vnde Iustinianus[b] Augustus: 'Si quis', inquit, 'non dicam rapere sed attemptare[c] tantum[d] [e]causa iungendi matrimonium[e] sacras

[i] Permissa *H* [j–j] nequeunt ubi *H* [k–k] illud non *CEF* [l] approbat *A before corr., RH* [m] oderunt peccare mali formidine pene *add. H* [n] uaspasiani *BR* [o] nundum *B;* mundi *R* [p] suedonius *A;* sutonius *B* [q] *om. E* [r] Reffert *CE* [s–s] *om. CEF* [t] sceno *T;* ceno *H;* caeno *classical Latin* [u] marguaritam *R* [v] fecerit *Amb* [w] spectandus *TAmb* [x] *C, which resumes here, adds in marg. two dots* [y] uindictionem *E* [z] uitata *ACBR;* uitatta *H;* vitiate *Amb* [a] deiectas *A;* deiectos *H* [b] Vestales *F* [c] sacerdotis *E* [d] etiam *add. F;* uiuos *H* [e] ad adulteras *E* [f] *om. F* [g] adyta *F, Augustine;* audita *RH*

45 [a] nostre *FH;* nostrae *Amb;* vestrae *Amb*[1] [b] manus *add. C* [c] attentare *FRAmb* [d] tamen *H* [e–e] matrimonium iungendi causa *B*

---

[292] Horace, *Epistolae*, i. 16. 52. Also cited in *Ethica*, i. 48. 9 (ed. Ilgner, p. 48 ; ed. Luscombe, p. 72 *ll.* 33–4) and *TChr*, ii. 27.

are mixed with evil, especially since, as St Augustine adds and reason clearly affirms, there cannot be evils except in a nature which is good?[291] Who does not agree with the poet's maxim: 'From love of virtue the good hate to err',[292] and approve rather than deny the miracle performed by Vespasian before he became emperor as related by Suetonius, that of the blind man and the lame man he healed, so that rulers may more eagerly desire to emulate his virtue?[293] And approve too what St Gregory is reported to have done for the soul of Trajan?[294] Men know how to pick a pearl out of the mire[295] and to distinguish grain from chaff, and God cannot fail to know the gifts he has bestowed on unbelief, nor can he hate any of the things he has made. The more brightly these shine out by signs, the more fully he shows that they are his, and what is his cannot be corrupted by the depravity of men; and when he reveals himself in this light to unbelievers, he shows too what believers should hope him to do for them. The high standing acquired by chastity among pagans dedicated to the service of their temples is shown by the punishment for its violation, the penalty which Juvenal recalls in his fourth *Satire* against Crispinus:

> with whom a robed Vestal recently lay,
> Who now must be entombed, her heart still beating.[296]

So too Augustine in the third book of his *City of God* says: 'For in antiquity, when vestal priestesses were caught in acts of fornication the Romans used to bury them alive. On the other hand, adulterous women they did condemn to some punishment but not to death in any form, so much more severe was their penalty for desecration of their supposed divine sanctuaries than of the human marriage bed.'[297]

45. With us, Christian princes are all the more concerned to safeguard your chastity, the more sacred it is universally held to be. Accordingly, the emperor Justinian declared that 'if anyone has dared, I will not say to rape, but only to solicit the sacred virgins with a view to

[293] Suetonius, *de uita Caesarum*, viii. 7; cf. *TChr*, ii. 111.

[294] Pope Gregory the Great through his tears was said to have freed the deceased Emperor Trajan from the torments of hell. Cf. John the Deacon, *Life* of Pope Gregory the Great, ii. 44 (*PL* lxxv. 104D–106A), cited by Abelard, *SN* c. 106, 26 and (less fully) *TChr*, ii. 112.

[295] Cf. Matt. 13: 44–6.

[296] Juvenal, *Satire* iv. 9–10.

[297] Augustine, *De ciuitate Dei*, iii. 5 (ed. Dombart and Kalb, xlvii. 68; ed. Hoffmann, i. 114; *PL* xli. 82).

uirgines ausus fuerit, capitali pena[f] feriatur.'[298] Ecclesiastice quoque sanctio discipline, que penitentie remedia non mortis supplicia querit, quam seuera sententia lapsus uestros[g] preueniat non est dubium. Vnde illud est Innocentii pape Victricio episcopo Rothomagensi capitulo tertio decimo: 'Que[h] Christo spiritualiter nubunt et a sacerdote uelantur, si postea uel publice nupserint uel occulte corrupte fuerint, non eas admittendas esse ad agendam penitentiam nisi is[i] cui[j] se coniunxerant[k] de hac uita discesserit.'[l] [299]

46. Hee[a] uero que necdum[b] sacro uelamine tecte,[c] tamen[d] in proposito uirginali semper se [e]simulauerunt permanere[e] licet uelate non fuerint,[f] hiis agenda aliquanto[g] tempore [h]penitentia[i] est,[h] quia sponsio earum a Domino[j] tenebatur. Si enim[k] inter homines solet[l] bone fidei contractus nulla ratione dissolui, quanto magis ista pollicitatio quam cum Deo[m] pepigerunt solui sine uindicta non poterit? Nam si apostolus Paulus que a proposito uiduitatis discesserant[n] dixit[o] eas habere condempnationem 'quia primam fidem irritam fecerunt',[300] quanto magis[p] uirgines que prioris propositionis fidem minime seruauerunt? Hinc et Pelagius ille notabilis ad filiam Mauritii: 'Criminosior est', inquit, 'Christi adultera quam mariti. Vnde pulchre Romana ecclesia tam seueram nuper de huiusmodi[q] statuit sententiam ut [r]uix uel[r] penitentia dignas iudicaret[s] que sanctificatum Deo corpus libidinosa coinquinatione uiolassent.'[301]

47. [a]Quod si[a] perscrutari uelimus quantam curam, quantam diligentiam et[b] caritatem sancti doctores, ipsius[c] Domini et apostolorum exemplis incitati, deuotis semper exhibuerint feminis, reperiemus eos summo[d] dilectionis zelo deuotionem[e] earum amplexos fuisse et fouisse[f] [g]et[h] multiplici doctrine uel exhortationis studio earum religionem iugiter[g] instruxisse atque[i] auxisse.[302] Atque, ut ceteros

[f] pene *C* [g] nostros *AEFH; om. C* [h] Quod *AR* [i] his *CE;* hi *F* [j] qui qui *ditto. F* [k] coniunxerat *C;* adiunxerint *BH;* adiunxerat *R* [l] decesserit *AH;* discesserint *F;* descesserit *R*

46 [a] Haec *Amb* [b] nec *BRH* [c] recte *A;* sunt tectae *F;* rectae *Amb* [d] cum *BR* [e–e] simulauerint permanere *CAmb;* permanere simulauerunt *F* [f] fuerunt *A* [g] aliquando *BR;* aliquo *H* [h–h] est penitencia *EH* [i] agenda *BR* [j] deo *H* [k] Sin *H;* Si vero *Amb* [l] sit *Ecorr* [m] Domino *F* [n] Recesserant *CEF* [o] dicit *CEF* [p] pocius *ACEBRH;* potius *F* [q] huius *BR* [r–r] uix uel *TABRH, Jerome;* uix illas *CEF* [s] indicare *BRH*

47 [a–a] si autem *CEF* [b] quantam *add. C* [c] ipsi *A* [d] sume *C;* summe *EH;* summae *F* [e] d(. . .?) *T*¹*;* dilectionem *B* [f] fauisse *H* [g–g] *om. C* [h] ac *F* [i] *om. C*

matrimony, he shall be punished with death'.[298] It is also well known that the sanction of ecclesiastical teaching, which seeks the remedies of penitence, not the penalty of death, provides against your lapses with the severest of sentences. Hence these words of Pope Innocent to Victricius, bishop of Rouen, chapter 13: 'If women who are spiritually wedded to Christ and are veiled by the priest publicly marry or are secretly seduced, they are not to be permitted to do penance unless the man they have associated with has departed this life.'[299]

46. Yet those who have not yet received the sacred veil but have always given the appearance of intending to remain in the virginal state, though unveiled, must do penance for a certain time, because their bridal vow was accepted by the Lord. For if among men a contract made in good faith may not be broken for any reason, far less could the pact they have made with God go unpunished if broken. And if the apostle Paul said that those who abandoned their status of widow should stand condemned 'for having broken their original promise',[300] far more should virgins be condemned when they have not kept at all the promise of their former intention. The remarkable Pelagius therefore wrote to the daughter of Mauritius: 'An adulteress against Christ is more culpable than one against her husband. And so the Roman Church acted well in recently passing judgement on cases of this kind with such severity that it condemned women who had violated a body dedicated to God by lustful pollution as scarcely worthy even of penance.'[301]

47. And if we want to examine the extent of the care, concern, and charity which the holy doctors of the Church, inspired by the examples of the Lord himself and of the apostles, have always shown to devout women, we shall find that they have cultivated and cherished women's devotion with the utmost warmth of affection, and have continually instructed and increased their religion with a variety of doctrinal or exhortatory works.[302] And, to say nothing of

[298] *Codex Iustinianus*, i. 3. 5 (*Corpus Iuris Ciuilis*, ed. Krueger and others, ii. 19).

[299] Pope Innocent I (d. 417), *Epistola* ii. 13 (*PL* xx. 478B–479A. Cf. JL I, p. 44; *PL* lvi. 525B–526A). Cited by Ivo of Chartres, *Decretum*, vii, c. 17 (*PL* clxi. 549A).

[300] 1 Tim. 5: 12.

[301] Pelagius (probably), *Epistula ad Claudiam de uirginitate* (ed. Halm, p. 250. Cf. Pope Innocent I, *Epistola* ii. 13 (*PL* xx. 478B–479A). The passage cited appears among the works of Sulpicius Severus (first sentence only, *PL* xx. 241C), of pseudo-Jerome (*Epistola* xiii, *PL* xxx. 175C (181A)), and of Benedict of Aniane (second sentence only, in the *Codex regularum* attributed to him, *PL* ciii. 684BC). For Pelagius' views about the ascetic life and the Jovinianist controversy see Hunter, *Marriage, Celibacy, and Heresy in Ancient Christianity*, pp. 259–68.

[302] Cf. *Letter* 2, 8.

omittam, precipui doctores ecclesie producantur in medium, Origines,[j] scilicet,[k] Ambrosius atque Ieronimus. Quorum quidem primus ille, uidelicet maximus Christianorum phylosophus,[l] religionem feminarum tanto [m]amplexus est zelo[m] ut sibi [n]manus ipse[n] inferret, sicut[o] *Ecclesiastica* refert[p] *Historia*, ne ulla[q] eum suspicio a doctrina uel exhortatione mulierum abduceret.[r] [303]

48. Quis etiam ignoret quantam[a] ecclesie diuinorum messem librorum rogatu Paule et Eustochii beatus reliquerit Ieronimus?[304] Quibus inter cetera sermonem etiam de assumptione matris Domini iuxta earum petitionem scribens, idipsum profitetur dicens: 'Set quia negare [b]non queo[b] quicquid iniungitis, nimia[c] uestra deuinctus[d] dilectione experiar quod[e] hortamini.'[305] Scimus autem nonnullos maximorum doctorum tam ordinis quam uite dignitate sublimium nonnumquam ad eum de longinquo scribentes parua ab eo requisisse scripta nec impetrasse. Vnde et illud est beati Augustini in secundo[f] *Retractationum* libro: 'Scripsi et[g] duos libros ad [h]presbyterum Ieronimum[h] sedentem in Bethleem, unum de origine anime,[i] alium de sententia [j]apostoli Iacobi,[j] ubi ait: "Quicumque totam legem seruauerit, offendat autem in uno, factus est omnium reus",[306] de utroque consulens eum. Sed in illo[k] priore questionem quam proposui[l] ipse non solui, in posteriore autem quid michi de illa soluenda[m] uideretur non[n] tacui. Sed utrum hoc approbaret etiam[o] illum[p] consului. Respondit[q] autem laudans eandem consultationem[r] meam, sibi tamen ad respondendum ocium[s] non esse respondit. Ego uero quousque esset in corpore hos libros[t] edere nolui, ne forte responderet[u] aliquando, et[v] cum ipsa responsione eius pocius ederentur. Illo autem defuncto edidi.'[307]

49. Ecce uirum tantum tanto tempore pauca[a] et parua rescripta a predicto uiro expectasse nec accepisse. Quem[b] quidem ad peticionem[c] predictarum feminarum in tot et tantis uoluminibus uel transferendis

[j] origenes *AE;* Origenes *F* [k] ac *add. CE* [l] scilicet Origenes *add. H* [m–m] amplius est zelo amplexus *H* [n–n] ipse manus *F* [o] Et sicut *BR;* ut sicut *H* [p] narrat *H* [q] ullam *R* [r] aduerteret *H*

48 [a] quantum *B* [b–b] nequeo *F, Ps.-Jerome* [c] anima *CE* [d] deuictus *F, Ps.-Jerome;* ductus *H* [e] quae *F, Ps.-Jerome* [f] iii *BRH* [g] etiam *F, Augustine* [h–h] Hieronymum presbyterum *F* [i] hominis *add. F, Augustine* [j–j] Iacobi apostoli *F* [k] *om. Amb* [l] posui *H* [m] soluanda *H* [n] ipse non *F;* ipse non *al.* non *Augustine* [o] et *Amb* [p] ipsum *CE* [q] Rescripsit *FAmb*[1], *Augustine* [r] consulacionem *RH* [s] occiosum *H* [t] in corpore *add. CE* [u] renderet *A;* reprehenderet *H* [v] aut *CEF*

49 [a] *om. EF* [b] Quam *R* [c] predicationem *CE*

the rest, let me cite the leading doctors of the Church, Origen, Ambrose, and Jerome. The first of these, indeed the greatest Christian philosopher, favoured the religion of women so warmly that he laid hands on himself, as the *Ecclesiastical History* relates, lest any suspicion might draw him away from the teaching or exhortation of women.[303]

48. Everyone knows too that St Jerome harvested a great number of holy books which he left to the Church at the request of Paula and Eustochium;[304] and he admits that very thing when writing, amongst other things, a sermon on the Assumption of the Mother of the Lord at their petition: 'But because I cannot refuse anything you ask of me', he says, 'being bound by your great love, I shall attempt what you urge me to do.'[305] Yet we know that several of the greatest scholars, men of the highest standing both in rank and in their manner of life, who wrote to him on several occasions and from far away, begging him for some small piece of writing, did not obtain it. Hence the words of St Augustine in the second book of his *Retractations*: 'I also wrote two books for Jerome the priest when he was living in Bethlehem, one on the origin of the soul, the other on the saying of the apostle James: "If a man keeps the whole law except for one point where he fails, he is guilty of breaking it all."[306] I consulted him on each book. In the former I failed to solve the question I set myself, and in the latter I did not conceal what seemed to me to be the solution, but I asked him whether he approved of it. He replied, praising me for consulting him, but said he had not the leisure to answer. I was therefore unwilling to publish these books as long as he was alive in case he might perhaps reply someday, and they could be better published with his reply. But now that he is dead I have published them.'[307]

49. See how so great a man waited for so long for a few short lines from the one we named above, but received nothing. Yet we know that Jerome toiled over the copying or composition of so many

[303] Eusebius of Caesarea, *Historia ecclesiastica*, vi. 8 (ed. Mommsen, pp. 535–7; *PG* xx. 535BC). Cf. **50** below; also *Letter* 1, **65** and note 208.

[304] Cf. *Rule* **128**; also *Letter* 9 (ed. Smits, p. 219; *PL* clxxviii. 325AB; trans. Ziolkowski, p. 10).

[305] Paschasius Radbertus (as Ps.-Jerome), *Epistula beati Hieronymi ad Paulam et Eustochium de assumptione sanctae Mariae Virginis*, 1 (ed. Ripberger, p. 109; *PL* xxx. 122C).

[306] Jas. 2: 10.

[307] Augustine, *Retractationum libri*, ii. 45 (71) (ed. Mutzenbecher, pp. 126–7; ed. Knoll, p. 184, *ll.* 4–16; *PL* xxxii. 649).

uel dictandis sudasse[d] cognouimus, longe eis maiorem quam episcopo reuerentiam in hoc[e] exhibens. Quarum fortassis tanto amplius[f] uirtutem amplectitur studio, nec contristare[g] sustinet, quanto earum naturam fragiliorem considerat. Vnde et nonnumquam zelus caritatis eius erga huiusmodi[h] feminas tantus esse deprehenditur, ut in earum laudibus aliquatenus ueritatis tramitem excedere uideatur, quasi in seipso illud expertus quod alicubi commemorans:[i] 'Caritas', inquit,[j] 'mensuram non habet.'[308] Qui in ipso statim exordio *Vite* sancte Paule,[k] quasi[l] attentum sibi lectorem preparare desiderans, ait: 'Si cuncta [m]mei corporis[m] membra uerterentur[n] in linguas, et omnes artus humana uoce resonarent, nihil dignum sancte ac uenerabilis Paule uirtutibus dicerem.'[309] Descripsit et[o] nonnullas sanctorum Patrum uenerabiles uitas, atque miraculis choruscas, in quibus longe mirabiliora sunt que referuntur.[310] Nullum tamen eorum tanta[p] [q]laude uerborum[q] extulisse uidetur quanta hanc uiduam commendauit. Qui[r] etiam ad Demetriadem[s] uirginem scribens, tanta eius laude[t] [u]frontem ipsius[u] insigniuit epistole ut [v]non in[v] modicam labi uideatur adulationem. 'Inter omnes', inquit, 'materias quas ab infancia[w] usque ad hanc etatem uel mea uel notariorum scripsi manu, nichil presenti opere difficilius. Scripturus[x] enim ad Demetriadem,[y] uirginem Christi, que et nobilitate et diuiciis prima est in [z]urbe Romana,[z] si[a] cuncta [b]uirtutibus eius[b] congrua dixero, adhulari putabor.'[311] Dulcissimum quippe uiro sancto fuerat quacumque[c] arte uerborum fragilem naturam ad ardua uirtutis[d] studia promouere. Vt autem opera nobis quam uerba in hoc[e] certiora prebeant argumenta, tanta huiusmodo feminas excoluit caritate ut immensa eius sanctitas neuum[f] sibi proprie imprimeret fame. Quod et ipse quidem ad Asellam de fictis amicis atque sibi detrahentibus scribens, inter cetera commemorat dicens: 'Et licet me sceleratum [g]quidam putent et[g] omnibus flagiciis [h]obrutum, tu tamen[h] bene facis quod ex tua mente etiam malos bonos putas. Periculosum quippe est de seruo alterius iudicare,[312] et non facilis uenia praua dixisse de rectis.

[d] laudasse *CE* [e] hac *C* [f] ampliori *F* [g] constristari *F;* conscrutare *R* [h] huius *R* [i] commemoratus *BRH* [j] inquid *A;* autem *C;* ait *F* [k] Paulam *F* [l] que *H* [m–m] corporis mei *FAmb* [n] uirerentur *C* [o] eciam *H* [p] tante *E* [q–q] uerborum *BR;* uerborum laude *H* [r] Que *E* [s] demetrianem *RH* [t] laudem *C* [u–u] ipsius frontem *BRH* [v–v] in non *A* [w] adolescentia *F, Jerome* [x] scripture *C* [y] democriadem *H* [z–z] orbe Romano *F, Jerome* [a] Si *RH* [b–b] eius uirtutibus *Amb* [c] quoque *C* [d] uirtutum *F* [e] hac *E* [f] *om. A;* nouum *B;* uouum *R;* nom *H* [g–g] *indecipherable in C;* quidam et *E;* quidem et *F;* quid *H* [h–h] obrutum, et puo (*sic*) peccatis meis etiam haec parua sint tamen tu *F*

lengthy volumes at the request of the women we mentioned, showing them far more respect in this than he showed a bishop. Perhaps he cherished their virtue with more concern, and could bear less to sadden them the frailer he believed their nature to be. And sometimes the warmth of his love for women of this kind appears to be so great that he seems to go somewhat beyond the bounds of truth in their praise, as if he felt in himself what he mentions elsewhere: 'Love has no limit.'[308] At the very beginning of his *Life* of St Paula, as though wishing to prepare the attentive reader, he says: 'If all the members of my body were turned into tongues and all my limbs resounded with a human voice, I could not speak well enough of the virtues of the holy and venerable Paula.'[309] He has described the venerable lives of several of the holy Fathers, lives radiant with miracles where the events recorded are far more wonderful,[310] yet he seems to have lavished on none of them as many words of praise as he employs to commend this widow. Again, in writing to the virgin Demetrias, he began his letter with such remarkable praise of her that he seems to give way to excessive adulation. 'Of all the subjects', he says, 'on which I have written from my childhood to now, either in my own hand or in that of scribes, none has been more difficult than the present work. For when I start to write to Demetrias, the virgin of Christ, who in her noble birth and her wealth ranks highest in the city of Rome, if I say everything which befits her virtues, I shall be thought to flatter her.'[311] So much pleasure had it given this holy man to help forward a frail nature to the strenuous pursuit of virtue by whatever art of words. And because actions furnish us with more cogent arguments than words in a matter like this, he displayed such warmth of affection when cultivating women of this kind that, notwithstanding his immense sanctity, he blotted his own reputation. This he records himself when writing to Asella about his detractors and false friends. Amongst other things he says: 'Although some men think me atrocious, smothered by every sort of vice, you yourself do well to think that even evil men may be good. It is dangerous to judge another's slave,[312] and pardon is not easy for slander of the righteous.

[308] Jerome, *Epistola* XLIV *Paulae et Eustochii ad Marcellam*, 1 (ed. Hilberg, liv. 329, *l.* 3; *PL* xxii. 483).

[309] Jerome, *Epistola* CVIII *ad Eustochium uirginem* (*Epitaphium sanctae Paulae*), 1 (ed. Hilberg, lv. 306, *ll.* 3–5; *PL* xxii. 878).

[310] The *Vitae* are of Paul, Malchus, and Hilarion.

[311] Jerome, *Epistola* CXXX *ad Demetriadem de seruanda uirginitate*, 1 (ed. Hilberg, lvi. 175, *l.* 15– p. 176, *l.* 2; *PL* xxii. 1107).

[312] Cf. Rom. 14: 4.

Osculabantur [i]quidam michi manus,[i] et ore uipereo detrahebant.[j] Dolebant labiis,[k] corde gaudebant. Dicant quid umquam[l] in me aliter senserint[m] [n]quam quod[n] Christianum decebat.[o] Nichil michi[p] obicitur nisi sexus meus. Et hoc numquam obiceretur[q] nisi cum Ierosolimam[r] Paula[s] proficiscitur.'[313] Item: 'Antequam domum sancte Paule noscerem,[t] tocius in me urbis studia consonabant. Omnium pene iudicio dignus summo sacerdocio decernebar.[u] Sed postquam eam pro [v]suo merito sanctitatis[v] uenerari, colere, suscipere[w] cepi, omnes me illico deseruere uirtutes.'[314] Et post[x] aliqua: 'Saluta', inquit, 'Paulam et Eustochium, uelint nolint,[y] in Christo meas.'[315]

50. Legimus [a]et Dominum ipsum tantam beate meretrici familiaritatem exhibuisse,[a] ut qui eum inuitauerat Phariseus, ob[b] hoc iam penitus [c]de ipso[c] diffideret, apud se dicens: 'Hic si esset propheta, sciret utique que et qualis est[d] que tangit eum',[e] [316] etc.[f] Quid ergo mirum si pro lucro talium animarum ipsa Christi membra eius incitata[g] exemplo proprie[h] fame [i]detrimentum non effugiunt?[j] Quod quidem Origenes,[k] ut dictum est,[317] cum cuperet euitare, grauius sibi corporis[i] detrimentum inferre sustinuit. Nec solum in doctrina uel exhortatione feminarum mira sanctorum Patrum caritas innotuit, uerum etiam in earum consolatione ita uehemens nonnumquam extitit ut ad[l] earum dolorem leniendum[m] nonnulla fidei aduersa promittere mira [n]eorum compassio[n] uideatur. Qualis quidem[o] [p]illa est[p] beati Ambrosii consolatio quam[q] super[r] morte Valentiniani imperatoris sororibus eius scribere ausus est, et eius qui cathechuminus sit defunctus[s] salutem[t] astruere, quod longe a catholica fide atque[u] euangelica[v] ueritate uidetur dissidere.[w] [318] Non enim ignorabant quam accepta[x] Deo semper extiterit uirtus infirmioris sexus. Vnde, et cum innumeras uideamus uirgines matrem Domini in huius

[i–i] mihi manus quidam *CEF* [j] *add. F* [k] *add. CEF* [l] unquam *AE;* inquam *BRH* [m] assenserunt *C;* senserunt *Amb* [n–n] quam quam *R;* quemquam *H;* quam *Jerome* [o] decebant *A;* dicebat *H* [p] aliud *add. F, Jerome* [q] abiiceretur *C;* obiicitur *F;* obiceret *H;* obicitur *al.* obiceretur *Jerome* [r] ierosolima *R* [s] parua *R* [t] nocerem *B;* nossem *F, Jerome* [u] discernebar *BR* [v–v] sui mariti sanctitatem *C;* sui mariti sanctitate *E* [w] suspicere *FAmb*[1]*;* suspicere *al.* suscipere *Jerome* [x] dicit *add. E* [y] mundes *add. F*

50 [a–a] *om. BRH* [b] ab *H* [c–c] *om. H* [d] mulier *add. F* [e] illum *F* [f] *om. CEFAmb* [g] incitatiua *A;* incitantes *CEF;* incitati *BRH* [h] proprio *E* [i–i] *om. H* [j] refugiunt *BR* [k] origines *R* [l] *om. E* [m] leuiendum *R;* leuiandum *H* [n–n] eorum compassione *CE;* earum compassione *F;* compassio eorum *BR* [o] siquidem *CEF* [p–p] est illa *F* [q] qua *BRH* [r] supra *F* [s] diffinitus *C* [t] salute *BRH* [u] et *F* [v] euuangelica *ABR* [w] defficere *CE;* deficere *F;* diffidere *RH* [x] accepto *CE*

Certain men used to kiss my hands and then disparage me with a viper's tongue. They grieved with their lips and rejoiced in their hearts. Let them say what they have perceived in me which was not becoming to a Christian. The only fault found in me is my sex, and fault would never be found with this except when Paula comes to Jerusalem.'[313] Again: 'Before I knew the house of the saintly Paula, my praises were sung throughout the city, and nearly everyone judged me worthy of the highest offices of the Church. But after I began to revere and venerate and support her, as she deserved for her holiness, all my virtues suddenly left me.'[314] And a little further on he says: 'Greet Paula and Eustochium, who, whether they are willing or no, are mine in Christ.'[315]

50. We read too that the Lord himself showed such friendly affection for the saintly whore that the Pharisee who had invited him began inwardly to lose faith in him because of this, and said to himself: 'If this man were a prophet he would know who and what this woman is who is touching him',[316] etc. What wonder then if in order to gain such souls the members of Christ themselves are fired by his example and do not escape damage to their own reputations? It was when he sought to avoid this that Origen, as was said above,[317] took upon himself to inflict a greater damage on his own body. Nor has the wonderful affection of the holy Fathers shown itself only in the teaching or exhortation of women; for their comfort it has sometimes shown itself so ardent that to console women in grief their compassion seems to promise certain miracles which are contrary to the faith. An example of this is the consolation offered by St Ambrose on the death of the emperor Valentinian, in a letter written to his sisters, when he ventured to promise him salvation because he died a catechumen; this can be seen to differ widely from the Catholic faith and the truth of the Gospel.[318] The Fathers were indeed well aware how acceptable to God the virtue of the weaker sex has always been. Consequently, even though we see countless virgins following

[313] Jerome, *Epistola* CXXX *ad Asellam*, 1 and 2 (ed. Hilberg, liv. 323, *l.* 13–p. 324, *l.* 3, p. 324, *ll.* 8–9, 16–17, 19–21; *PL* xxii. 480–1). 'Nichil mihi obicitur . . . proficiscitur': also cited in *Letter* 1, **65**.

[314] Jerome, *Epistola* XLV *ad Asellam*, 3 (ed. Hilberg, liv. 325, *ll.* 6–8, 18–20; *PL* xxii. 481). 'Antequam domum . . . decernebar': also cited in *Letter* 1, **65**.

[315] Jerome, *Epistola* XLV *ad Asellam*, 7 (ed. Hilberg, liv. 328, *ll.* 12–13; *PL* xxii. 484).

[316] Luke 7: 39; also cited in *Letter* 1, **67**. Cf. also **3** and **6** above.

[317] At **47** above.

[318] Cf. Ambrose, *De obitu Valentiniani consolatio*, 51–6 (ed. Faller, pp. 354–6; *PL* xvi. 1435A–1437A). Cited in *SN* c. 106, 22–5; also *TChr*, ii. 113–14.

excellentie proposito sequi, paucos agnoscimus uiros huius uirtutis gratiam adeptos [y]ex qua quocumque[y] ierit[z] ipsum sequi agnum ualerent.[319] Cuius quidem zelo uirtutis, cum nonnulle sibi manum inferrent[a] ut quam Deo uouerant integritatem etiam carnis conseruarent, non solum hoc [b]in eis[b] non est reprehensum, sed apud plerosque hec ipsarum martyria titulos ecclesiarum meruerunt.[c] [320] Desponsate quoque uirgines, si antequam uiris suis carnaliter misceantur monasterium decreuerint[d] eligere et, [e]homine reprobato,[e] sponsum sibi Deum efficere,[f] liberam in hoc habent facultatem, quam nequaquam uiris legimus indultam. Quarum etiam plereque tanto [g]ad castimoniam[g] zelo sunt accense ut non solum contra legis decretum[321] pro custodienda castitate uirilem presumerent habitum, uerum etiam inter monachos tantis preminerent[h] uirtutibus ut abbates fieri mererentur. Sicut de beata legimus Eugenia, que sancto etiam Heleno[i] episcopo conscio, immo[j] iubente, uirilem habitum sumpsit, et ab eo baptizata[k] monachorum collegio est sociata.[322]

51. Hec ad [a]nouissimarum peticionum[a] tuarum primam, soror in Christo carissima, me satis rescripsisse arbitror, de auctoritate uidelicet ordinis uestri,[b] et insuper de commendatione proprie dignitatis, ut tanto studiosius uestre[c] professionis propositum amplectamini, quanto eius excellentiam amplius[d] noueritis. Nunc ut secundam quoque, Domino annuente,[e] perficiam, uestris id meritis et orationibus obtineam.[f] Vale.[g]

[y–y] quocumque *R;* ut quecumque *H* [z] Regit *C* [a] refferrent *B* [b–b] sanctis *H* [c] meruerint *H* [d] decreuerunt *B;* decreuerit *F* [e–e] habere Repropato (*sic*) *C* [f] *illegible add. here* T^1*;* afficere *F* [g–g] castimonie *BRH* [h] presumerent *A* [i] hebeno *C* [j] etiam *add. CEF* [k] bapti . . . am *corrupt T*

51 [a–a] peticionum nouissimarum *AC;* petitionem novissimarum *EFAmb* [b] nostri *CEFBR* [c] nostre *R* [d] eius *add. E* [e] annuante *H* [f] obtineant *B;* optineant *R* [g] VALE *T with decorated capitals, Amb;* Vale *A* (*which proceeds without interruption to Letter 8*), *CE* (*which leave the rest of the line blank*), *F* (*which leaves the rest of this and the following page blank and begins Letter 1 on the next page 121*)*;* Valete *BR* (*which leave the rest of the line blank*), *H* (*which adds without interruption:* Epistola magistri petri abaielardi concludendo pariter de supradictis).

the Mother of God in pursuit of this excellence, we know of few men who have been granted the grace of this virtue to enable them to follow the Lamb wherever he goes.[319] Indeed, in their zeal for virtue, many women have laid hands on themselves so that they might preserve the integrity of the flesh which they had vowed to God; yet not only is this no reproach to them, but their martyrdom has won them dedications of churches in many places.[320] Betrothed virgins too if, before they have had carnal intercourse with their husbands, they have decided to choose monastic life, to reject men, and to make God their bridegroom, have freedom of action in this such as we never read was granted to men. A great many of these virgins have been fired with such zeal for purity that not only have they assumed male attire in defiance of the Law,[321] in order to preserve their chastity, but they have also been so outstanding amongst monks for their great virtues that they have deserved to become abbots. This we read in the case of St Eugenia, who put on male clothing with the full knowledge of her bishop, St Helenus, or rather did so at his command, and was then baptized by him and admitted to a community of monks.[322]

51. Dearest sister in Christ, I think I have written enough in answer to the first of your latest requests, concerning the authority for your order, and also in commendation of its special position, so that you may more warmly embrace the calling of your profession through better understanding of its excellence. Now let me have the support of your merits and your prayers so that, God willing, I may also complete the second. Farewell.

[319] Cf. Rev. 14: 4; also **41** above and *Sermon* 1 (*PL* clxxviii. 381D and 383D).

[320] Cf. Augustine, *De ciuitate Dei*, i. 26 (ed. Dombart and Kalb, xlvii. 26–7; ed. Hoffmann, i. 46; *PL* xli. 39), on self-inflicted violence as a way of preserving chastity; cited in *SN* c. 155, 11. Cf. also Jerome, *Commentarii . . . in Ionam*, i. 12 (ed. Adriaen, pp. 390–1; *PL* xxv. 1129): 'in persecutionibus non licet proprie perire manu, absque eo ubi castitas periclitatur, sed percutienti colla submittere'. And cf. **41** above.

[321] Cf. Deut. 22: 5.

[322] Cf. *Vitae Patrum*, i. *Vita sanctae Eugeniae*, i. (*PL* lxxiii. 605–20).

⟨EPISTOLA VIII⟩

1. Peticionis[a] tue parte iam aliqua prout potuimus absoluta, superest Domino annuente[b] de illa que restat parte tam tuis quam spiritalium tuarum filiarum desideriis complendis operam dare.[1]

2. Restat quippe, iuxta predicte uestre postulationis ordinem,[2] aliquam uobis[a] institutionem[b] quasi quandam propositi uestri[c] regulam a nobis scribi et uobis tradi, ut certius ex scripto quam ex consuetudine habeatis quid[d] uos sequi conueniat. Nos itaque partim consuetudinibus bonis, partim scripturarum testimoniis uel rationum nitentes[e] fulcimentis, hec omnia in unum conferre decreuimus ut spiritale Dei templum[3] quod estis uos hiis[f] decorare[g] quasi quibusdam egregiis exornare picturis ualeamus, et[h] ex pluribus imperfectis, quoad[i] possumus,[j] unum[k] opusculum consummare.

3. In quo quidem opere Zeusim pictorem[4] imitantes,[a] ita facere instituimus in templo spiritali sicut ille disposuit faciendum[b] in corporali. [c]Hunc enim, ut in *Rethorica* sua Tullius meminit,[c] Crothoniate[d] asciuerunt ad quoddam templum quod religiosissime[e] colebant excellentissimis picturis decorandum.[5] Quod ut diligentius faceret quinque sibi uirgines pulcherrimas de populo illo[f] elegit quas[g] sibi pingenti assistentes,[h] intuens earum pulcritudinem, pingendo imitaretur. Quod duabus de causis factum esse credibile est: tum uidelicet quia,[i] ut predictus[j] meminit doctor,[k] maximam periciam[l] [m]in depingendis mulieribus pictor ille adeptus fuerat; tum etiam[m] quia naturaliter puellaris forma elegantior et delicatior uirili compositione[n] censetur. Plures autem uirgines ab eo eligi supra memoratus philosophus ait, quia[o] nequaquam credidit in una se reperire [p]posse puella

Letter 8 *T* fo. 59[rb–vb]; *A* fo. 42[r+v]; *C* fos. 176[v]–177[v]; *E* fo. 40[r+v]; *B* fos. 40[vb]–41[rb]; *R* fo. 157[ra+va]; *H* fo.12[r+v]; *Amb* pp. 130–1; *Amb*[1] *variants given in the marg. of Amb. Headings are found in the following witnesses*: Epistola magistri petri abaielardi concludendo pariter de supradictis *rubr. H;* EPISTOLA VIII. Quae est eiusdem Petri ad Heloissam, Institutio, seu Regula Sanctimonalium *Amb*

1 [a] *large initial in TABRHAmb; initial lacking in CE* [b] annuante *HAmb*

2 [a] nobis *BR* [b] Institutionem *CAmb* [c] nostri *BRH* [d] quod *B* [e] inittentes *?E;* intendendes *B;* intentes *R;* utentes *H* [f] habens *Amb* [g] et *add. H* [h] ut *H* [i] quod *Amb.* [j] poterimus *H;* possimus *Amb* [k] nostrum *H*

3 [a] imitentes *BR;* de zeusi in rosa capitulo nature sub tali signo lxxxi *add. in marg. H* [b] facere *E* [c–c] *underlined in H* [d] crothoniante *E* [e] religiosisse *RH*

LETTER 8

1. Some part of your request has already been answered, as far as I was able, and it remains, God willing, for me to turn my attention to the rest of it by fulfilling the wishes of your spiritual daughters and yourself.[1]

2. For I still have to meet the second part of your demand[2] by putting in writing for you some instruction to be a kind of Rule for your calling and to deliver this to you, so that the written word may give you more certainty than custom about what you should follow. Relying, therefore, partly on good practices and partly on the testimony of the Scriptures with the support of reason, I have decided to put all these together, in order to adorn the spiritual temple of God[3] which you are by embellishing it with certain choice pictures, and from several imperfect elements to create as far as I can a single, complete work.

3. In this I intend to imitate the painter Zeuxis,[4] and work on the spiritual temple as he planned his achievement on a material one. For, as Tully records in his *Rhetoric*, the people of Croton appointed him to decorate with the best possible pictures a certain temple for which they had the highest veneration.[5] So that he might do so more surely he chose from the people the five most beautiful maidens and looked at them as they sat by him while he worked, so that he could copy their beauty in his painting. This was probably done for two reasons: first, as the philosopher I quoted above remarks, Zeuxis had developed his greatest skill in portraying women; secondly, because maidenly beauty is naturally considered more refined and delicate than the male figure. Moreover, Tully says that he chose several girls because he did not believe he could find all the limbs of a single one equally lovely, since so

[f] *add. in marg. Ecorr.*; suo *H* [g] quathenus *Ecorr* [h] assistens *A* [i] *om. H*
[j] inpredictus *A* [k] propter *add. H* [l] *om. C* [m–m] *om. BRH*
[n] compassione *CE;* compactione *Amb*[1] [o] quia quod *TAB;* pro *C;* quod *ERH*
[p–p] puella posse omnia membra *CE*

[1] For comparable salutations see *Letter* 7, 1 and note.
[2] Cf. *Letter* 6, 3.[3] Cf. 1 Cor. 3: 16; 2 Cor. 6: 16.
[4] Zeuxis, the painter, of Heraclea in Lucania; *floruit* in the late 5th c. BC.
[5] Cicero, *De inuentione rhetorica*, ii. 1. Near Croton (today Crotone) in the 'toe' of Italy was the celebrated temple of Juno or Hera Lacinia.

membra omnia[p] equaliter formosa,[q] nullique umquam a natura tantam pulcritudinis gratiam[r] esse collatam ut equalem in omnibus membris pulcritudinem haberet, ut nichil ex omni parte perfectum in compositione[s] corporum ipsa expoliret, tamquam uni sic omnia commoda conferret ut non haberet quid[t] ceteris largiretur.

4. Sic et nos ad depingendam anime pulcritudinem et sponse Christi describendam perfectionem, in qua[a] uos[b] tamquam speculo[c] quodam[d] unius[e] spiritalis uirginis semper pre oculis habite decorem uestrum uel turpitudinem deprehendatis, [f]proposuimus ex multis sanctorum patrum documentis uel consuetudinibus monasteriorum optimis[f] uestram instruere conuersationem, singula queque prout memorie occurrerint delibando,[g] et quasi in unum fasciculum congregando que uestri[h] propositi sanctitati[i] congruere uidebo, nec solum que de monachabus[j] uerum etiam que de monachis instituta sunt.[k] Quippe sicut nomine et continentie professione nobis estis coniuncte, ita etiam[l] fere omnia nostra uobis competunt instituta.

5. Ex hiis ergo, ut diximus, plurima quasi quosdam flores decerpendo quibus uestre lilia castitatis adornemus, multo maiore studio describere debemus uirginem Christi quam predictus Zeusis depingere simulachrum ydoli. Et ille quidem quinque uirgines quarum speciem imitaretur sufficere credidit. Nos uero[a] pluribus patrum documentis exuberantem copiam habentes, auxilio freti diuino, perfectius [b]uobis opusculum[b] relinquere non desperamus quo ad sortem uel descriptionem illarum quinque prudentium uirginum pertingere[c] ualeatis quas[d] in depingenda uirgine Christi Dominus nobis in Euangelio proponit.[6] Quod ut possimus sicut uolumus uestris orationibus impetremus. [e]Valete in Christo sponse[f] Christi.[e]

[q] forma *C* [r] nouimus *add. H* [s] computatione *C;* compunctione *?E* [t] quod *CEAmb*

4 [a] quam *B* [b] nos *CE* [c] speculum *H* [d] *om. BRH* [e] unus *B* [f–f] *om. E* [g] deliberando *CH* [h] nostri *?B* [i] sanctitate *A* [j] monachalibus *H* [k] *om. Amb.* [l] et *Amb*

5 [a] de *add. CE* [b–b] opusculum uobis *CE;* nobis opusculum *R* [c] pertinare *H* [d] qua *E* [e–e] *om. CE; TCE—but not ABRH—continue after a short space and on a new*

much grace and beauty had never been conferred by nature on any one so as to give her equal beauty in every feature; for nature in creating bodies produces nothing which is perfect in every detail, as though she would have nothing left to bestow on the rest if she conferred all her advantages on one.

4. I too, then, in wishing to depict the beauty of the soul and describe the perfection of the bride of Christ, in which you may discover your own beauty or blemish as in the mirror of one spiritual virgin always held before your eyes, propose to instruct your religious life through the many documents of the holy Fathers and the best customs of monasteries, gathering each blossom as it comes to mind and collecting in a single bunch what I shall see will accord with the sanctity of your calling; and choosing what was instituted not only for nuns but also for monks. For as in name and profession of continence you are one with us, so nearly all our usages are suitable for you.

5. Gathering from these then, as I have said, many things as if they were flowers with which to adorn the lilies of your chastity, I must describe the virgin of Christ with far greater care than that which Zeuxis applied to painting the likeness of an idol. Indeed, he believed that five maidens were sufficient for him to copy their beauty; but I have abundant riches in the records of the Fathers and, trusting in God's aid, do not despair of leaving you a more finished work, whereby you may be able to attain to the lot or description of those five wise virgins whom the Lord sets before us in the Gospel in depicting the virgin of Christ.[6] May I be granted the power to achieve this through your prayers. Greetings to you in Christ, Brides of Christ.

line with Tripertitum instructionis uestre . . . (*the Institutio or Rule*). *The copyist in B adds a rubr:* Anno domini millesimo centesimo lx^{o}iiii. Heloysa obiit paracliti abbatissa. Anno domini millesimo centesimo xl^{o}ii. obiit petrus abahelardi perypateticus. *H adds a rubr. colophon*: Expliciunt epistole petri abaielardi et heloyse. primitus eius amice postmodum uxoris. scripte parisius per me mathiam rivalli in domo episcopi ambianensis. Anno domini millesimo. ccc^{o}. lx^{o}. primo. mense decembris. [f] sponsa *B*

[6] Cf. Matt. 25: 1–13.

THE RULE

⟨INSTITUTIO⟩

1. Tripertitum[a] instructionis nostre[b] [1] tractatum fieri decreuimus in describenda atque munienda[c] religione uestra et diuini obsequii[d] celebratione disponenda[e] in quibus religionis monastice summam arbitror consistere, ut uidelicet continenter et sine proprietate uiuatur,[f] silentio maxime studeatur.[2] Quod quidem iuxta dominicam euangelice regule disciplinam[3] lumbos precingere,[4] omnibus renunciare,[5] ociosum uerbum cauere.[g] [6]

2. Continentia uero castitatis illa est quam suadens Apostolus ait: que innupta est et uirgo 'cogitat que domini sunt, ut sit sancta corpore et spiritu'.[7] [a]Corpore, inquit, toto, non uno membro, ut ad nullam scilicet lasciuiam in factis uel in dictis eius aliquod membrum declinet. Spiritu uero tunc sancta est quando eius mentem nec consensus inquinat[8] nec superbia inflat, sicut illarum quinque fatuarum uirginum que, dum ad uendentes oleum recurrerent, extra ianuam remanserunt. Quibus iam clausa ianua, frustra pulsantibus et

Institutio *T* fos. 59vb–88vb; *C* fos. 177^{v}–182^{v}, 190^{r+v}, 196^{r}–207^{v}; *E* fos. 40^{v}–53^{v}; *Amb* pp. 131–97; *Amb*[I] variants in the marg. of *Amb*

1 [a] Large decorated initial *T;* vacant space for an initial followed by large letters *CE* [b] uestre *CE;* vestrae *Amb* [c] in *add. C;* commendenda uel innuenda in *add. E* [d] in *add. CE* [e] *in T a space follows adequate for c.10 characters* [f] ac *add. Amb.* [g] *in T a space follows; in E a double stroke // is add. as if to indicate a break in the text*

2 [a–a] *om. CE*

[1] In *Letter* 6, 3 Heloise asked Abelard to institute and put into writing a Rule which was suited to women: *ut aliquam nobis regulam instituas et scriptam dirigas que feminarum sit propria*. In *Letter* 8, 2 Abelard calls his contribution an Institute, which, he writes, is like a Rule: *aliquam uobis institutionem quasi quandam propositi uestri regulam a nobis scribi.* Its instruction (1) is provided in a spirit of guidance. Waddell (*The Paraclete Statutes*, pp. 31–5) maintains that it was written to replace rather than to complement the *Rule* of St Benedict at the Paraclete. In general, religious houses in this period followed a traditional Rule, usually that of St Benedict or of St Augustine, but might supplement it with an *institutio* or customs or statutes to complete and to give precision to their observances; this has been demonstrated with reference to 12th-c. papal bulls by J. Dubois, 'Les Ordres religieux au XIIe siècle'. On some of the differences (which are by no means static or unequivocal) between Rules, written *consuetudines* or customs, statutes and institutes, see Melville, 'Regeln – *Consuetudines* – Texte – Statuten', who draws attention (p. 22, n. 77) to the distinction made (shortly after Abelard wrote his *Institutio*) by Pope Innocent II between the *Rule* of St Augustine, which was adopted by the order of Praemonstratensian canons (and generally also by other bodies of regular canons), and the *Institutio* proper to the

THE RULE

1. I have decided that in describing and fortifying your religion and arranging the celebration of divine service, the treatise for your instruction shall be divided into three parts,[1] in which I believe the sum of monastic faith to rest: that is, a life of continence and one without personal possessions and, above all, the observance of silence.[2] This is, in accordance with the Lord's teaching in the commandments of the Gospel,[3] to be ready with belts fastened,[4] to forsake everything,[5] and to avoid idle talk.[6]

2. Continence is indeed the practice of chastity which the Apostle enjoins when he says: 'The unmarried woman cares for the Lord's business and her aim is to be dedicated to him in body as in spirit.'[7] In body, he says, as a whole, and not in one member, so that none of her members may fall into lasciviousness in deed or word. She is dedicated in spirit when her mind is neither defiled by compliance nor puffed up with pride,[8] like the minds of those five foolish virgins who ran back to the oil-sellers and then were left outside the door. They beat vainly upon the door which was already shut and cried:

Praemonstratensians themselves: 'Ordinem quoque, et propositum vestrum canonice vivendi secundum Beati Augustini regulam, et institutionem Praemonstratensis Ecclesiae, nullus audeat immutare, vel super vos ordinem alterius professionis inducere'; *Privilegium* of Pope Innocent II for Floreffe abbey, near Namur, dated 21 Dec. 1138 (*PL* clxxix. 381–2, at 381D; JL 7924). In seeking to accommodate Heloise's request, Abelard's *Institutio* seems designed to provide an innovative adaptation for the Paraclete sisters of their *Rule* which was that of St Benedict (mentioned at **21** and **67** below). Studies of Abelard's *Institutio* include Leclercq, '*Ad ipsam sophiam Christum*' (in both French and German); Lutterbach, '"Ein Herz und eine Seele"'; Mohr, 'Der Gedankenaustausch'; and Porter, 'The convent of the Paraclete'. The *Institutio* does not appear to have been adopted at the Paraclete (Waddell, *The Paraclete Statutes*, p. 332); *Institutiones nostre* (on which see the Introduction, pp. xxxiv–xxxvii) appear to provide regulations to suit the needs of the Paraclete order.

[2] Cf. the opening of *TSch*, i. 1 and *Sententie* 1 (ed. Luscombe, p. 5; ed. Buzzetti p. 25; *PL* clxxviii. 1695A): 'Tria sunt, ut arbitror, in quibus humane salutis summa consistit.'

[3] Cf. *Institutiones nostre*, i (in *The Paraclete Statutes*, ed. Waddell, p. 9 (commentary on pp. 67–77); *PL* clxxviii. 313C).

[4] Cf. Luke 12: 35.

[5] Cf. Luke 14: 33.

[6] Cf. Matt. 12: 36.

[7] 1 Cor. 7: 34.

[8] On consent to concupiscence cf. **93** below; also *Sermon* 1 (on the Annunciation and the chastity of Joseph, *PL* clxxviii. 381C–382C), and *Problemata* 14 (on concupiscence, *PL* clxxviii. 697C).

clamantibus:[b] 'Domine, domine, aperi nobis', terribiliter sponsus ipse respondet: 'Amen, dico uobis, nescio uos.'[a] [9]

3. Tunc autem relictis omnibus nudum Christum nudi sequimur,[10] sicut sancti fecerunt apostoli, cum propter eum non solum terrenas possessiones aut carnalis propinquitatis affectiones, uerum etiam proprias postponimus uoluntates, ut non nostro uiuamus arbitrio sed prelati nostri regamur imperio, et ei qui nobis loco Christi presidet tamquam Christo penitus pro Christo subiciamur.[a] Talibus enim ipsemet dicit: 'Qui uos audit, me audit, et qui uos spernit, ipse[b] me spernit.'[11] Qui si etiam, quod absit, male uiuat cum bene precipiat, non est tamen ex uitio hominis [c]sententia[d] contempnenda Dei.[c] [12] De quolibet ipsemet precipit dicens: 'Que dixerint uobis, seruate et facite; secundum uero opera eorum nolite facere.'[13] Hanc autem ad Deum spiritalem a seculo conuersionem ipsemet diligenter describit dicens: 'Nisi quis renunciauerit omnibus que possidet, non potest meus esse discipulus.'[14] Et iterum: 'Si quis uenit ad me et non odit patrem suum[e] aut matrem et uxorem et filios [f]et fratres[f] et sorores, adhuc autem et animam suam, non potest meus esse discipulus.'[15] Hoc autem est[g] odire[h] patrem [i]uel matrem[i] etc. affectiones carnalium propinquitatum nolle [j]sequi, sicut[k] et odire animam suam est uoluntatem propriam sequi nolle.[j] Quod alibi quoque precipit dicens: 'Si quis uult post me uenire, abneget semetipsum et tollat crucem suam et sequatur me.'[16] Sic enim propinquantes [l]post eum[m] uenimus,[l] hoc est, eum maxime imitando sequimur qui[n] ait: 'Non ueni facere uoluntatem [o]meam, sed[o] eius qui misit me',[17] ac si dicere cuncta per obedientiam agere.[18]

4. [a]Quid est enim abnegare[a] semetipsum nisi carnales affectiones propriamque uoluntatem postponere et alieno, non suo, regendum arbitrio se committere? Et sic profecto crucem suam non ab alio[b]

[b] clamentibus *Amb*

3 [a] subiciatur *CE* [b] ipse *om. E* [c–c] contemnenda *E* [d] *om. E* [e] *om. CE* [f–f] *om. E* [g] *om. CE* [h] *as in Late Latin* (*Classical Latin:* odisse) [i–i] *om. CE* [j–j] *om. C by homoeoteleuton* [k] sicuti *E* [l–l] uenimus post eum *E* [m] *om. C* [n] sicut *E* [o–o] *om. T;* meam(?) uolu(ntatem) s(ed) *add.* T^1 *in the marg., which has been trimmed;* uo(luntatem) *add. E*

4 [a–a] Quid enim abneget *Amb* [b] illo *C*

[9] Matt. 25: 11.

[10] 'nudum Christum nudi sequimur': cf. Jerome, *Epistola* CXXV *ad Rusticum monachum*, 20 (ed. Hilberg, lvi. 142; *PL* xxii. 1085).

'Lord, Lord, open to us', but the bridegroom himself gave a terrible reply: 'Truly I know you not.'[9]

3. Then, too, in forsaking everything we follow naked a naked Christ,[10] as the holy apostles did, when for his sake we put behind us not only our earthly possessions and affection for our kindred in the flesh, but also our own wishes, so that we may not live by our own will but be ruled by the command of our superior, and may wholly submit ourselves for Christ to him who presides over us in the place of Christ, as if to Christ. For Christ himself says: 'Whoever listens to you, listens to me; whoever rejects you, rejects me.'[11] Even if he lives an evil life (which God forbid), so long as his precepts are good, God's utterance must not be rejected because of the vice of the man.[12] God himself enjoins this, saying: 'What they tell you, observe and do; but do not follow their practices.'[13] This spiritual conversion from the world to God he also describes accurately himself, saying: 'Unless a man part with all his possessions he cannot be a disciple of mine';[14] and again: 'If anyone comes to me and does not hate his father and mother, wife and children, brothers and sisters, even his own life, he cannot be a disciple of mine.'[15] Now, to hate father or mother etc. is to refuse to yield to affection for kindred in the flesh, just as to hate one's own life is to renounce one's own will. This too he enjoins elsewhere, saying: 'If anyone wishes to be a follower of mine, he must leave self behind, take up his cross, and come with me.'[16] For in thus drawing near to him we are his followers, that is, by closely imitating him we follow him who says: 'I have come not to do my own will but the will of him who sent me.'[17] It is as if he said: let everything be done under obedience.[18]

4. For what is renouncing self if not for a man to put behind him carnal affections and his own will and commit himself to being ruled by another's judgement and not his own? And so he does not receive

[11] Luke 10: 16.

[12] 'ex uitio hominis sententia condemnenda Dei': cf. Cicero, *De inuentione*, i. 94; also D'Anna, 'Abelardo et Cicerone', p. 336.

[13] Matt. 23: 3.

[14] Luke 14: 33; also cited in *Letter* 7, 1.

[15] Luke 14: 26.

[16] Luke 9: 23.

[17] John 6: 38.

[18] 'Et iterum: Si quis . . . agere': cf. *Letter* 1,75; *Ethica*, i. 7. 6–8, 3–5 (ed. Ilgner, pp. 7–8; ed. Luscombe, p. 12, *ll.* 14–31); *Problemata* 28 (*PL* clxxviii. 712D); *Sermon* 10 (*PL* clxxviii. 450CD).

suscipit sed ipsemet tollit per quem,[c] scilicet, ei mundus crucifixus est[d] et ipse mundo,[19] cum spontaneo proprie professionis uoto mundana sibi et terrena desideria interdicit, quod est uoluntatem propriam non sequi. Quid enim carnales aliud appetunt nisi implere quod uolunt? Et que est terrena delectatio[e] nisi proprie uoluntatis impletio, eciam quando id quod uolumus labore maximo siue periculo agimus? Aut quid est aliud[f] crucem ferre, id est cruciatum aliquem sustinere, nisi contra uoluntatem nostram aliquid fieri quantumcumque illud uideatur facile nobis esse uel utile? Hinc alius Ihesus longe inferior in Ecclesiastico ammonet, dicens: 'Post concupiscentias [g]tuas non eas, et a uoluntate tua auertere. Si prestes anime tue concupiscentias[g] eius, faciet te in gaudium inimicis tuis.'[20]

5. Cum uero ita tam rebus nostris quam nobis ipsis penitus renunciamus, tunc uere omni proprietate abiecta uitam illam apostolicam inimus, que omnia in commune reducit, sicut scriptum est: 'Multitudinis credentium erat cor unum et anima una. Nec quisquam eorum que possidebat aliquid suum esse dicebat, sed erant illis omnia communia. Diuidebatur autem singulis prout cuique opus erat.'[21] Non enim equaliter omnes egebant, et ideo non equaliter omnibus distribuebatur, sed [a]singulis prout[a] opus erat. Cor unum[b] fide, quia corde creditur; anima una, quia eadem ex caritate uoluntas ad inuicem, cum hoc unusquisque alii quod sibi uellet; nec sua magis quam aliorum commoda quereret uel ad communem utilitatem ab omnibus omnia referrentur, nemine[c] que sua sunt, sed que Ihesu Christi, querente seu affectante.[22] Alioquin nequaquam sine proprietate uiueretur, que magis in ambitione quam in possessione consistit.

6. Ociosum uerbum seu superfluum idem est quod multiloquium. Vnde Augustinus *Retractationum* libro primo: 'Absit', inquit, 'ut multiloquium deputem, quando necessaria dicuntur, [a]quantalibet sermonum multitudine ac prolixitate dicantur.'[a] [23] Hinc autem per

[c] *vacant space in E;* quam *Amb* [d] sit *T* [e] dilectio *CE* [f] quam *add. E* [g–g] *om. C by homoeoteleuton*

5 [a–a] prout singulis *CE* [b] in *add. CE* [c] affectante *add. C;* affectante ea *add. E*
6 [a–a] *om. CE*

[19] Cf. Gal. 6: 14.
[20] Jesus, son of Sirach, in Ecclus. 18: 30–1. Cf. Benedict, *Rule*, c. 7, 19.
[21] Acts 4: 32, 35. Cf. *Institutiones nostre*, i (*The Paraclete Statutes*, ed. Waddell, p. 9 (commentary on pp. 67–77); *PL* clxxviii. 313C); and Augustine, *Epistola* ccxi. 5 (ed. Goldbacher, lvii. 359–60; *PL* xxxiii. 960).

his cross from another but takes it up himself, so that through it the world may be crucified to him and he to the world,[19] when by the voluntary offering of his own profession he denies himself worldly and earthly desires: which is a renunciation of his own will. For what else do the carnal seek, except to carry out their will, and what is earthly pleasure if not the fulfilment of our will, even when we attain our desires only with the greatest risk or effort? What is bearing a cross, that is, enduring some form of suffering, if not doing something against our will, however easy or profitable it seems to us? The other Jesus, who was by far the lesser, warns us of this in Ecclesiasticus when he says: 'Do not let your passions be your guide, but restrain your desires. If you indulge yourself with all that passion fancies, it will make you the butt of your enemies.'[20]

5. It is only when we wholly renounce both our possessions and ourselves that all that we own is cast away and we truly enter into the apostolic life, which reduces everything to a common store; as it is written: 'The whole body of believers was united in heart and soul. Not one of them claimed any of his possessions as his own, but everything was held in common. It was distributed to each according to his need.'[21] For they were not equally in want, and so it was not distributed in equal shares to all, but in accordance with each man's need. They were united in heart through faith, because it is through the heart that we believe; and united in soul because there was one mutual will through love, since each one wished the same for his neighbour as for himself and did not seek his own advantage rather than another's, or because everything was brought together by all for the common good, and no one sought or pursued what was his but what was of Jesus Christ.[22] Otherwise they could never have lived without property, which consists in ambition rather than possession.

6. An idle or superfluous word and too much talk are the same thing. Hence St Augustine says in the first book of his *Retractations*: 'Far be it from me to hold that there is too much talk when necessary words are spoken, however long-winded and prolix they may be.'[23] And in

[22] 'corde creditur': cf. Rom. 10: 10; 'nec sua . . . quereret': cf. 1 Cor. 10: 24; 'que sua sunt . . . querente': cf. Phil. 2: 21. Cf. also *TChr*, ii. 49.

[23] Augustine, *Retractationes*, Prologue 2 (ed. Mutzenbecher, p. 5; ed. Knoll, p. 8, *ll*. 7–9; *PL* xxxii. 583–4). For discussion of **6–11** (silence) and **12–21** (solitude) see J. A. Smith, 'The virtue of stillness: Abelard and monastic silence'.

Salomonem dicitur: 'In multiloquio non deerit peccatum. Qui autem moderatur labia sua prudentissimus est.'[24] Multum ergo cauendum est in quo peccatum non deest, et tanto studiosius huic morbo prouidendum est quanto periculosius[b] et difficilius euitatur. Quod beatus prouidens Benedictus: 'Omni tempore', inquit, 'silentium[c] debent studere[d] monachi.'[25] Plus quippe esse[e] constat silentio studere quam silentium habere. Est enim studium uehemens applicatio animi ad aliquid gerendum. Multa uero negligenter agimus uel inuiti sed nulla studiose nisi uolentes uel intenti.

7. Quantum uero difficile sit uel utile linguam refrenare apostolus Jacobus diligenter attendens ait: 'In multis enim offendimus omnes. Si quis in uerbo non offendit, hic perfectus est uir.'[26] [a]Idem ita:[a] 'Omnis natura bestiarum et uolucrum et serpentium et ceterorum domantur, et domita sunt a natura humana.'[27] Qui simul considerans quanta sit in lingua malorum materia et omnium bonorum consumptio, supra sic et infra loquitur: 'Lingua quidem modicum membrum, quantus ignis, quam magnam siluam incendit; uniuersitas iniquitatis, inquietum malum plenum ueneno mortifero.'[28] Quid autem ueneno periculosius uel cauendum amplius? Sicut[b] ergo uenenum uitam extinguit, sic loquacitas religionem penitus euertit. Vnde idem superius: 'Si quis putat se', inquit, 'religiosum esse, non refrenans linguam suam sed seducens cor suum, huius uana est religio.'[29] Hinc et in Prouerbiis scriptum est: 'Sicut urbs patens et absque murorum ambitu, ita uir qui non potest in loquendo cohibere spiritum suum.'[30] Hoc[c] ille senex diligenter considerabat, qui de loquacibus fratribus ei in uia sociatis, Antonio dicente: 'Bonos fratres inuenisti tecum, abba?' respondit: 'Boni sunt siquidem,[d] sed habitatio eorum non habet ianuam. Quicumque uult intrat in stabulo[e] et soluit asinum.'[31] Quasi enim ad[f] presepe Domini anima nostra ligatur, sacre se meditationis in eo quadam[g] ruminatione reficiens, a quo quidem presepi[h] soluitur, atque huc et illuc toto mundo per cogitationes discurrit, nisi eam clausura taciturnitatis retineat. [i]Verba quippe intellectum anime inmittunt ut ei quod intelligit intendat et per

[b] est *add. CE* [c] silentio *T*¹*Amb* [d] custodire *CE* [e] ipse *CE*

7 [a–a] Item infra *E* [b] Sic *E* [c] hic *E* [d] quidem *CE* [e] stabulum *Amb, Vitae patrum* [f] a *CE* [g] se *add. E* [h] anima *add. E* [i–i] *om. CE*

[24] Prov. 10: 19.
[25] Benedict, *Rule*, c. 42, 1. Cf. *Problemata* 14 (*PL* clxxviii. 698C).
[26] Jas. 3: 2.
[27] Jas. 3: 7.

the person of Solomon it is also said that 'where men talk too much sin is not far away; the man who holds his tongue is wise'.[24] We must therefore guard against what is sinful and take all the greater precautions against this evil, the more dangerous and difficult it is to avoid. St Benedict provides for this when he says: 'At all times monks ought to practise silence.'[25] Evidently to practise or study silence means more than to keep silence, for study is the intense concentration of the mind on doing something. We do many things carelessly or unwillingly, but nothing studiously unless we are willing and apply ourselves.

7. Just how difficult it is to bridle the tongue, but how beneficial, the apostle James carefully considers when he says: 'All of us often go wrong: the man who never says a wrong thing is perfect.'[26] Again, he says: 'Beasts and birds of every kind, creatures that crawl on the ground and all others are tamed and have been tamed by mankind.'[27] Between these two statements, when he considers how much matter for evil there is in the tongue and destruction of all that is good, he says: 'The tongue is a small member of the body, but how great a fire! How vast a forest it can set alight! It is a world of wickedness, an intractable evil, charged with deadly venom.'[28] What is more dangerous than venom or more to be shunned? As venom destroys life, so idle talk means the complete destruction of religion. And so James says earlier on: 'A man may think he is religious, but if he has no control over his tongue he is deceiving himself, and his religion is futile.'[29] Hence it is said in Proverbs: 'Like a city that is breached and left unwalled is a man who cannot control his temper in speech.'[30] This is what the old man had in mind when he made the following reply to Antony who had asked about the talkative brethren accompanying him on his way: 'Have you found good brethren to be with you, Father'? 'No doubt they are good but their dwelling has no door. Anyone who likes can go into the stable and untie the ass.'[31] It is as though our soul were tethered to the manger of the Lord, refreshing itself there by ruminating on sacred thoughts, but once untied from the manger it runs here and there all over the world in its thought, unless the bar of silence keeps it in. Words do indeed impart understanding to the soul, so that it may direct itself towards what

[28] Jas. 3: 5–6, 8. Cf. *Carmen ad Astralabium*, ed Rubingh-Bosscher, *v.* 237.

[29] Jas. 1: 26.

[30] Prov. 25: 28.

[31] *Vitae patrum*, *Verba seniorum*, v. 4. 1 (*PL* lxxiii. 864D). St Antony of Egypt (251?–356), hermit.

cogitationem hereat.[32] Cogitatione uero Deo loquimur sicut uerbis hominibus. Dumque huc uerbis hominum intendimus necesse est ut inde ducamur, nec Deo simul et hominibus intendere ualemus.[i]

8. Nec solum ociosa, uerum etiam que utilitatis [a]aliquid habere[a] uidentur uitanda sunt uerba, eo quod facile a necessariis ad ociosa, ab ociosis ad noxia ueniatur.[33] [b]Lingua quippe, ut Iacobus ait, 'inquietum malum';[34] quo ceteris minor est aut subtilior membris tanto mobilior, et ceteris motu lassescentibus ipsa cum non mouetur fatigatur, et quies ipsa ei fit onerosa. Que quanto in uobis[c] subtilior, et ex mollicie corporis uestri[d] flexibilior, tanto mobilior et etiam[e] in uerba pronior existit et omnis malicie seminarium patet. Quod in uobis precipue uicium Apostolus notans, omnino feminis in ecclesia loqui interdicit, nec de hiis etiam que ad Deum pertinent nisi domi uiros interrogare permittit. Et in hiis etiam discendis uel quibuscumque[f] faciendis silentio eas precipue subicit Tymotheo super hiis ita scribens: 'Mulier in silentio discat cum omni subjectione. Docere autem mulieri non permitto neque dominari in uirum, sed esse in silentio.'[35]

9. Quod si laicis et coniugatis[a] feminis ita de silentio prouiderit, quid uobis est faciendum? Qui rursus eidem cur hoc preceperit innuens, uerbosas eas et loquentes cum non oportet arguit.[b] Huic igitur tante pesti remedium aliquod prouidentes, hiis saltem penitus locis uel temporibus linguam continua taciturnitate domemus, in oratorio[c] scilicet, in claustro, dormitorio,[d] refectorio, et in omni commestione et coquina, et post Completorium deinceps, hoc maxime ab[e] omnibus obseruetur. Signis uero hiis locis uel temporibus, si necessarium est, pro uerbis utamur. De quibus [f]etiam signis[f] docendis seu[g] addiscendis diligens habeatur cura [h]per que, etiamsi uerbis quoque opus est, ad colloquium inuitetur loco congruo et ad hoc instituto.[36] Et expletis breuiter uerbis illis necessariis, redeatur ad priora, uel quod oportunum est fiat.[h] Nec tepide corrigatur uerborum aut signorum excessus, sed uerborum precipue in quibus maius imminet periculum.

8 [a–a] habere aliquid *E* [b] *beginning of lacuna in CE, ending in* 9 [c] nobis *Amb* [d] nostri *Amb* [e] *om. Amb* [f] quecumque *T*

9 [a] et *add. T* [b] *end of lacuna in CE beginning in* 8 [c] oratione *Amb* [d] et *add. E* [e] de *E* [f–f] *om. CE* [g] uel *CE* [h–h] *om. CE*

---

[32] Cf. *Sermons* 14 and 9 (*PL* clxxviii. 490AB, 446A).

[33] 'ab ociosis ad noxia ueniatur': cf. Gregory the Great, *Dialogi*, iii. 15. 16 (ed. Vogüé, cclx. 324; *PL* lxxvii. 253B).

it understands and adhere to this by thinking;[32] and by thinking we speak to God as we do in words to men. While we tend towards the words of men it is necessary for us to be led from there, for we cannot tend towards God and man at the same time.

8. Not only idle words but also those which seem to have some purpose should be avoided, because it is easy to pass from the necessary to the idle, and from the idle to the harmful.[33] The tongue, as James says, is 'an intractable evil',[34] and being smaller and more sensitive than all the other parts of the body it is the more mobile, so that whereas the others are wearied by movement, it does not tire when moving and finds inactivity a burden. The more sensitive it is in you, and the more flexible from your softness of body, the more mobile and given to words it is, and can be seen to be the seedbed of all evil. The Apostle marks this vice especially in you when he absolutely forbids women to speak in church, and even on matters which concern God he permits them only to question their husbands at home. In learning such things, or whatever things are to be done, he particularly subjects them to silence, writing thus to Timothy on the point: 'A woman must be a learner, listening quietly and with due submission. I do not permit a woman to be a teacher, nor must woman domineer over man; she should be quiet.'[35]

9. If he has made these provisions for silence in the case of lay and married women, what ought you to do? Again, in showing Timothy why he has ordered this, he explains that women are gossips and speak when they should not. So, to provide a remedy for so great a plague, let us subdue the tongue by perpetual silence, at least in these places or times: at prayer, in the cloister, the dormitory, the refectory, and during all eating and cooking, and let this be specially observed by all from Compline onwards. If necessary in these places or times let us use signs instead of words. Careful attention must be paid to teaching and learning these signs, and if words are also needed for this, the speaker must be asked to speak in a suitable place chosen for the purpose.[36] Once the necessary words are briefly said, she should return to her former duties or the next suitable task. Any excess of words or signs must be firmly corrected, words especially, in which lies the greater danger.

[34] Jas. 3: 8.

[35] 1 Tim. 2: 11–12.

[36] On monastic sign language see Constable, *The Reformation of the Twelfth Century*, p. 198, with further references; some examples are given by Coulton, *Five Centuries of Religion*, i, Appendix 9, pp. 473–6.

10. Cui profecto multo magnoque periculo et beatus Gregorius succurrere uehementer cupiens, septimo[a] *Moralium* libro sic nos instruit: 'Dum ociosa', inquit, '[b]uerba cauere[b] negligimus,[c] ad noxia peruenimus. Hinc seminantur stimuli, oriuntur rixe, accenduntur faces odiorum, pax tota extinguitur cordium. Vnde bene per Salomonem dicitur: "Qui dimittit aquam, capud est iurgiorum."[37] Aquam quippe dimittere est linguam in fluxum eloquii relaxare. Quo contra et in bonam partem asserit dicens: "Aqua profunda[d] ex ore uiri."[38] Qui ergo dimittit aquam capud est iurgiorum quia, qui linguam non refrenat, concordiam dissipat. Vnde[e] scriptum est: "Qui imponit stulto silentium, iras mitigat." '[39] [40]

11. Ex quo nos manifeste ammonet[a] in hoc precipue uicio corrigendo districtissimam adhibere[b] censuram ne eius uindicta ullatenus[c] differatur, et per hoc [d]maxime religio periclitetur. Hinc quippe detractiones, lites, conuicia et[d] nonnumquam conspirationes et coniurationes germinantes totum religionis edificium non[e] tam labefactant quam euertunt. Quod quidem uicium cum amputatum fuerit, non omnino fortasse praue cogitationes extinguuntur, sed ab alienis cessabunt corruptelis. Hoc unum uicium fugere quasi religioni sufficere arbitraretur[f] abbas Macharius ammonebat, sicut scriptum est hiis uerbis: 'Abbas Macharius, maior in Scyti, dicebat fratribus: "Post Missas ecclesias[g] fugite, fratres." Et dixit ei unus fratrum: "Pater, ubi habemus fugere amplius a solitudine ista?" Et ponebat digitum suum in ore suo dicens: "Istud[h] est quod fugiendum dico." Et sic intrabat in cellam suam et claudens ostium sedebat solus.'[41] Hec uero silentii uirtus que, ut ait Iacobus, perfectum hominem reddit,[42] et de quo[i] Ysaias predixit: 'Cultus iusticie silentium',[43] tanto a sanctis patribus feruore est arrepta quod, sicut scriptum est, abbas Agatho[j] per triennium lapidem in ore suo mittebat donec taciturnitatem disceret.[44]

10 [a] VIII° *T;* 6° *C* [b–b] cauere uerba *CE* [c] negligemus *E* [d] uerba *add. Gregory* [e] *A space follows in T adequate for 10 characters;* Vnde e diuerso *Gregory*

11 [a] *om. E* [b] debere *add. CE* [c] nullattenus *C;* nullatenus *E* [d–d] *om. C* [e] ut *CE* [f] arbitrabatur *CE;* arbitratus *Amb*[1] [g] ecclesiae *Vitae patrum* [h] Illud *CE* [i] qua *Amb* [j] agathon *C*

[37] Prov. 17: 14. [38] Prov. 18: 4.
[39] Prov. 26: 10.

10. St Gregory was most anxious to forestall this frequent and serious danger when he instructs us in the seventh book of his *Morals*: 'When we are careless about guarding against idle words, we come on to harmful ones. By these provocation is sown, quarrels arise, the torches of hatred are set alight, and the whole peace of the heart is destroyed. And so it is well said through Solomon: "Letting out water starts quarrels."[37] To let out water is to let loose the tongue in a flood of eloquence. On the other hand he says approvingly: "Man's utterance is like water which runs deep."[38] So he who lets out water is a source of quarrels because he does not bridle his tongue and breaks up concord. Thus it is written: "He who makes a fool keep silence softens anger."'[39] [40]

11. This is a clear warning that we should employ the strictest censure to correct this vice above all, lest its punishment be deferred and religion thereby greatly endangered. From this spring slander, litigation, and abuse, and often conspiracies and plots which do not so much undermine the whole structure of religion as overthrow it. Once this vice has been cut out, evil thoughts may not perhaps be wholly extinguished but they will cease to corrupt others. Abbot Macarius told his brethren to shun this one vice as though he thought that was sufficient for their religion, as it is written in these words: 'Abbot Macarius, the elder in Scetis, said to his brethren: "After Mass, brothers, flee from the churches." One of them said to him: "Father, where can we flee further than this wilderness?" He put his finger on his lips and answered: "That is what I say you are to flee." So saying he went into his cell, shut the door and sat down alone.'[41] This virtue of silence which, as James says, makes a man perfect,[42] and of which Isaiah prophesied that 'the harvest of righteousness is quietness',[43] was seized on so eagerly by the holy Fathers that, it is written, abbot Agatho carried a stone in his mouth for three years until he should learn to keep silence.[44]

[40] Gregory the Great, *Moralia in Iob*, vii. 37. 57 (ed. Adriaen, cxliii. 378; *PL* lxxv. 800).

[41] *Vitae patrum*, *Verba seniorum*, v. 4. 27 (*PL* lxxiii. 868C). St Macarius 'the Great' of Egypt (*c.*300–*c.*390), who founded one of the chief centres of Egyptian monasticism in Scetis (Wadi-el-Natrun, about 100 km north-west of Cairo) where more than fifty monasteries were established in the 4th c.

[42] Cf. Jas. 3: 2.

[43] Isa. 32: 17.

[44] Cf. *Vitae patrum*, *Verba seniorum*, v. 4. 7 (*PL* lxxiii. 865B).

12. Quamuis[a] locus non saluet, multas tamen prebet opportunitates ad religionem facilius obseruandam[b] et tucius muniendam;[c] et multa religionis auxilia uel impedimenta ex eo consistunt. Vnde et filii prophetarum quos, ut ait Ieronymus, monachos legimus in Veteri Testamento, ad solitudinis secretum se transtulerunt, preter fluenta Iordanis casulas suas constituentes.[45] Iohannes quoque et discipuli eius quos etiam propositi nostri principes habemus, et deinceps Paulus, Antonius, Macharius, et qui precipue in nostro floruerunt proposito, tumultum seculi et plenum temptationibus mundum fugientes, ad quietem solitudinis lectulum sue contemplationis contulerunt, ut uidelicet Deo possent sincerius uacare.[46] Ipse quoque Dominus, [d]ad quem nullus temptationis motus accessum habebat, suo nos erudiens exemplo, cum aliqua uellet agere precipua[e] secreta petebat, et populares declinabat tumultus. Hinc ipse Dominus nobis quadraginta dierum abstinentia heremum consecrauit,[47] turbas in heremo refecit,[48] et ad orationis puritatem, non solum a turbis, uerum etiam ab apostolis secedebat.[49] Ipsos quoque apostolos etiam[f] in monte seorsum instruxit atque constituit,[50] et transfigurationis sue gloria solitudinem insigniuit,[51] et exhibitione resurrectionis sue discipulos communiter in monte letificauit,[52] et de monte in celum ascendit,[53] et cetera[d] quecumque[g] magnalia in solitudinibus uel secretis operatus est locis. Qui etiam Moysi uel antiquis patribus in solitudinibus apparens, et per solitudinem ad terram promissionis populum transducens,[54] [h]ibique populo diu detento[h] legem tradens,[i] [55] manna pluens,[56] aquam de petra educens,[57] crebris apparitionibus ipsum consolans,[58] et mirabilia operans,[59] patenter docuit quantum[j] eius singularitas solitudinem pro nobis amet, cui purius in ea uacare possumus.

12 [a] *TCEAmb begin a new section here. TC leave one line blank; TE decorate the initial; C leaves a space for the initial to await the painter; EAmb open with majuscule letters:* QUAMVIS LOCUS *E,* QUAMVIS *Amb* [b] conseruandam *CE* [c] commendendam *E* [d–d] *om. CE* [e] precipue *Amb* [f] et *Amb* [g] q*om. E* [h–h] et *C;* in *E* [i] ibi *add. CE* [j] quantam *E*

[45] Jerome, *Epistola* CXXV *ad Rusticum monachum*, 7 (ed. Hilberg, lvi. 125, *ll.* 9–10; *PL* xxii. 1076). Cf. **14** below and *Letter* 1, **26** and note.

[46] Cf. Jerome, *Epistola* LVIII *ad Paulinum presbyterum*, 5 (ed. Hilberg, liv. 534; *PL* xxii. 583), cited at **14** below. For John the Baptist as 'princeps' of the monastic life cf. below at **112**, *Letter* 7, **14** and *Letter* 12 (ed. Smits, pp. 260–1; *PL* clxxviii. 347AC; trans. Ziolkowski, pp. 162–3); *Sermon* 33 (*PL* clxxviii. 585C, 586A, 587B, 596C). For John and the origins of 'propositi nostri' cf. *Adtendite* (ed. Engels in '*Adtendite a falsis prophetis*', p. 227, *l.* 47).

St Paul of Thebes (d. *c.*345), the 'first hermit'; St Antony of Egypt (251?–356), hermit; St Macarius—see n. 41 above. Cf. *Letters* 1, **26**, **52** and 7, **2**. 'lectulum sue contemplationis' ('the narrow bed of contemplation'): cf. S. of S. 3: 1 and below at **14**, **17**, **112**, **113**; also

12. Although a place cannot bring salvation, it still provides many opportunities for easier observance and safeguarding of religion, and many aids or impediments to religion depend on the place. And so the sons of the prophets, whom, as Jerome says, we read of as monks in the Old Testament, removed themselves to the secret places of the wilderness and set up huts by the waters of the Jordan.[45] John also and his disciples, whom we regard as the first of our calling, and after them Paul, Antony, Macarius, and all those who have been pre-eminent among us, fled from the tumult of their times and the world full of temptations, and carried the bed of their contemplation to the peace of the wilderness, so that they could devote themselves to God more sincerely.[46] The Lord himself also, whom no stirrings of temptation could ever have touched, teaches us by his example, for he sought hidden places particularly and avoided the clamour of the crowd whenever he had something special to do. Thus he consecrated the desert for us by his forty days of fasting,[47] refreshed the crowds in the desert,[48] and for purity of prayer withdrew not only from the crowds of people but even from the apostles.[49] The apostles too he set apart on a mountain to receive instruction and appointment;[50] he honoured the wilderness by the glory of his transfiguration[51] and gladdened the apostles assembled on a mountain by the revelation of his resurrection;[52] he ascended into heaven from a mountain,[53] and all his miracles were performed either in lonely or in hidden places. He also appeared to Moses or the patriarchs of old in the wilderness, and through the wilderness he led his people to the promised land;[54] there too he delivered the Law to the people long held captive,[55] rained manna,[56] brought out water from a rock[57] and comforted them with frequent apparitions[58] and the miracles he worked.[59] In this he plainly taught them how much his aloneness finds pleasure in our being in a lonely place where we can more purely devote ourselves to him.

Letter 5, 7 and *Letter* 12 (ed. Smits, p. 263; *PL* clxxviii. 348BD; trans. Ziolkowski, pp. 166–7) and *Sermon* 28 (*PL* clxxviii. 552CD); and on the use by other writers of this metaphor cf. Constable, 'Metaphors for religious life', pp. 234–5.

47 Cf. Matt. 4: 1–2; Mark 1: 13; Luke 4: 1–2.

48 Cf. Matt. 14: 13–21; Mark 6: 30–44; Luke 9: 10–17; John 6: 1–13.

49 Cf. Matt. 14: 22–3; Mark 6: 45–6; John 6: 15.

50 Cf. Matt. 5: 1–7: 29; Mark 3: 13–19; Luke 6: 12–16.

51 Cf. Matt. 17: 1–8; Mark 9: 1–7; Luke 9: 28–36.

52 Cf. Matt. 28: 16.

53 Cf. Mark 16: 19; Luke 24: 50–1; Acts 1: 9.

54 Cf. Exod. 15: 22.

55 Cf. Exod. 19–20.

56 Cf. Exod. 16: 1–5.

57 Cf. Exod. 17: 1–6; Num. 20: 1–11.

58 Cf. Exod. 19: 16, 34: 5, 40: 32–6; Num. 9: 15.

59 Cf. Exod. 15: 22–5, 17: 8–13; Num. 11: 16–34, 21: 4–11.

13. Qui etiam libertatem mystice onagri solitudinem amantis diligenter describens, et uehementer approbans, ad beatum Iob loquitur dicens: 'Quis dimisit onagrum liberum, et uincula eius quis soluit? [a]Cui dedi[a] in solitudine domum et tabernacula eius in terra salsuginis. Contempnit multitudinem ciuitatis;[b] clamorem exactoris non audit. [c]Circumspicit montes pascue sue, et uirentia queque perquirit.'[c] [60] Ac si aperte dicat: Quis hoc fecit nisi ego? Onager quippe, quem siluestrem asinum uocamus, monachus est qui secularium rerum[d] uinculis absolutus ad tranquillam uite solitarie libertatem se contulit, et seculum fugiens in seculo non remansit.[61] Hinc in terra salsuginis habitat, cum membra eius per abstinentiam sicca sunt et arida.[62] Clamorem exactoris non audit sed uocem, quia uentri non superflua sed necessaria impendit. Quis enim tam importunus exactor et cotidianus exactor[e] quam uenter? Hic clamorem, [f]id est[f] immoderatam postulationem, habet in superfluis et delicatis cibis in quo minime est audiendus.[63] Montes pascue sunt illi uite uel doctrine sublimium[g] patrum quas[h] legendo et[i] meditando reficimur. Virentia queque dicit uniuersa uite celestis et immarcessibilis scripta.[64]

14. Ad quod nos precipue beatus Ieronymus exhortans sic Helyodoro scribit monacho: 'Interpretare uocabulum monachi, hoc est nomen tuum. Quid facis in turba qui solus es?'[65] Idem et nostram a clericorum uita distinguens, ad Paulinum[a] presbyterum scribit hiis uerbis: 'Si officium uis exercere presbyteri, si episcopatus te uel opus uel onus[b] forte delectat,[c] uiue in urbibus et castellis, et aliorum salutem fac lucrum anime tue. Si[d] cupis esse, quod diceris, monachus, id est solus, quid facis in urbibus que utique non sunt solorum habitacula sed multorum? Habet unumquodque propositum principes suos. Et ut ad nostra[e] ueniamus, episcopi et presbyteri habeant ad exemplum apostolos et apostolicos uiros, quorum honorem possidentes habere nitantur et meritum. Nos autem habeamus

13 [a–a] cui dedit *C before corr.;* Cui dedit *Amb* [b] civis *Amb* [c–c] *om. E* [d] uirorum *CE;* virorum *& in aliq.* vitiorum *Amb*[1] [e] *om. CE* [f–f] et *C* [g] sublimissimorum *C* [h] quibus *CE* [i] uel *CE*

14 [a] Paulum *TCEAmb;* Paulinum *Sermon 33 (PL clxxviii. 585B), Letter 12 to a regular canon (Smits p. 260 l. 83; PL clxxviii. 346C), Jerome* [b] honor *Letter 12 (Smits p. 260 l. 88; PL clxxviii. 346D);* honos *al.* onus, honor *Jerome* [c] delectant *E* [d] Sin autem *Letter 12 (Smits p. 260 l. 90; PL clxxviii. 346D), Jerome* [e] nostram *TCEAmb;* nostra *Sermon 33 (PL clxxviii. 585B), Letter 12 (Smits p. 260 l. 93; PL clxxviii. 346D), Jerome;* nostram uitam *Muckle*

[60] Job 39: 5–8. Also cited in *Sermon* 33 on St John the Baptist (*PL* clxxviii. 582B).
[61] Cf. *Sermon* 33 (*PL* clxxviii. 582C).

13. He also takes pains to describe in a mystical way the freedom of the wild ass which loves the wilderness, and warmly approves of it, saying to holy Job: 'Who has set the wild ass free and let it range at will? I have made its home in the wilderness and its lair in the salting. It disdains the noise of the city and is deaf to the driver's shouting; it roams the hills as its pasture and searches for anything green.'[60] It is as though he says openly: Who has done this, if not I? Now the wild ass, which we call the ass of the woodland, is the monk, who is freed from the chains of worldly things and has taken himself off to the peace and freedom of the solitary life; he has fled from the world and not remained in it.[61] And so he lives in the salting land and his members through abstinence are parched and dry.[62] He is deaf to the driver's shouting but hears his voice, because he provides for his stomach not what is superfluous but what is needed; for who is so demanding and unremitting a driver as the stomach? It shouts when it makes its immoderate demands for superfluous foods and delicacies, and this is when it should least be heard.[63] The hills for his pasture are the lives and teachings of the sublime Fathers, by reading and meditating on which we are refreshed. By 'anything green' is meant the entire Scriptures on the heavenly and unfading life.[64]

14. In specially exhorting us on this St Jerome writes as follows to the monk Heliodorus: 'Consider the meaning of the word "monk", your name. What are you doing in a crowd, when you are a solitary?'[65] And in drawing the distinction between our life and that of the clergy, he also writes to the priest Paulinus: 'If you want to perform the duties of a priest, if the work—or burden—of the episcopate happens to please you, then live in cities and towns and make the salvation of others a profit to your soul. If you desire to be, as you say, a monk, that is, a solitary, what are you doing in cities, the homes not of solitaries but of crowds? Every calling has its leaders and, to come to our own way of life, bishops and priests should take as their example the apostles and apostolic men, whose positions they occupy and to whose merit they should try to attain. For us, the leaders of our

[62] Cf. *Sermon* 33 (*PL* clxxviii. 583D–4A).
[63] Cf. *Sermon* 33 (*PL* clxxviii. 584BC).
[64] Cf. *Sermon* 33 (*PL* clxxviii. 584C–585A).
[65] Jerome, *Epistola* XIV *ad Heliodorum monachum*, 6 (ed. Hilberg. liv. 52, *ll.* 5–6; *PL* xxii. 350). Also cited in *Letter* 12 (ed. Smits p. 259, *ll.* 69–70; *PL* clxxviii. 346B; Ziolkowski, p. 161), *Sermon* 33 (*PL* clxxviii. 589A and 596D) and (in part) *Problemata* 14 (*PL* clxxviii. 698C). Cf. **20** below and *Letter* 7, **43**.

propositi nostri principes Paulos, Antonios,[f] Hilariones, Macharios:[g] et, ut ad scripturarum auctoritatem[h] redeam, noster princeps Helyas, Helyseus,[i] [j]nostri duces et filii prophetarum,[j] qui habitabant in agris et[k] solitudine,[l] et faciebant sibi tabernacula prope[m] fluenta Iordanis.[66] De hiis sunt et illi filii Rechab qui uinum et siceram non bibebant, qui morabantur in tentoriis, qui Dei [n]per Ieremiam uoce[n] laudantur, quod[o] non deficiat de stirpe eorum uir stans coram Domino.'[67] [68] Et nos ergo, ut coram Domino stare et eius obsequio parati magis ualeamus assistere,[p] tabernacula nobis erigamus in solitudine, ne[q] lectulum nostre quietis[69] frequentia hominum concuciat, quietem turbet, ingerat temptationes, mentem a sancto euellat proposito.

15. Ad quam quidem liberam uitae tranquillitatem,[a] beatum Arsenium Domino dirigente, omnibus immo[b] manifestum datum est exemplum. Vnde et scriptum est: 'Abbas Arsenius, cum adhuc esset in palatio, orauit ad Dominum dicens: "Domine, dirige me ad salutem." Et uenit ei uox dicens: "Arseni, fuge homines et sanaberis."[c] Idem ipse ac discedens ad monachalem uitam, rursum orauit, eumdem sermonem dicens: "Domine, dirige me ad salutem." Audiuitque uocem dicentem sibi: "Arseni, fuge, tace, quiesce; he enim sunt radices non peccandi." [70] Ille igitur hac[d] una diuini precepti regula instructus, non solum homines fugit, sed eos etiam a se fugauit. Ad quem archiepiscopo suo cum quodam iudice quadam die uenientibus, et edificationis sermonem [e]ab eo requirentibus, ait: '"Et si dixero uobis, custodietis?" Illi[e] autem promiserunt se custodire. Et dixit eis: "Vbicumque audieritis Arsenium, approximare nolite." Alia iterum uice archiepiscopus eum uisitans, misit primo uidere si aperiret. Et mandauit ei dicens: "Si uenis, aperio tibi, sed si tibi aperuero, omnibus aperio, et tunc iam ultra hic non sedeo." Hec audiens archiepiscopus dixit: "Si eum persecuturus uado, numquam uadam ad hominem sanctum." '[71] Cuius etiam sanctitatem

[f] Antonios, Julianos *Jerome* [g] Macharium *TCE;* Macharios *Amb, Jerome* [h] materiam *TCEAmb;* auctoritatem *Sermon 33* (*PL clxxviii. 585B*), *Letter 12* (*Smits p. 260 l. 97; PL clxxviii. 346D*), *Jerome* [i] helyseus *T;* h(. . .) T^1; noster Helisaeus *Amb, Jerome* [j–j] duces prophetarum *T;* duces et filii prophetarum *CE;* nostri duces filii prophetarum *Sermon 33* (*PL clxxviii. 585C*) *and Letter 12* (*Smits p. 260 l. 98; PL clxxviii. 347A*), *Jerome* [k] in *add. E* [l] solitudinibus *Jerome* [m] preter *TAmb;* prope *CE, Sermon 33* (*PL clxxviii. 585C*), *Letter 12* (*Smits p. 260 l. 100; PL clxxviii. 347A*); propter *al.* prope *Jerome* [n–n] uoce per Ieremiam *CE;* per Hieremiam voce *Amb, Jerome* [o] et promittitur eis quod *Jerome* [p] absistere *E;* adsistere *Amb* [q] in *CE*

15 [a] ad *add. CE* [b] in uno *CEAmb* [c] saluaberis *CE* [d] hec *TCE;* Hae *Amb* [e–e] *om. CE*

calling should be the Pauls, Antonies, Hilarions, and Macariuses, and, to return to the Scriptures, let our leaders be Elijah and Elisha, the chief of the prophets, who lived in fields and in the wilderness and made themselves huts by the river Jordan.[66] Amongst these too are the sons of Rechab who drank neither wine nor cider, who lived in tents and are praised by the voice of God through Jeremiah saying that they shall not lack a descendant to stand before the Lord.'[67] [68] Let us therefore set up huts for ourselves in the wilderness, so that we may be better able to stand before the Lord and, being prepared, take part in serving him, and so that the society of men will not jolt the bed of our repose,[69] disturb our rest, breed temptations, and distract our minds from our holy calling.

15. When the Lord directed holy Arsenius to this freedom and peace in life, we were all given a clear example in this one man. Thus it is written: 'When abbot Arsenius was still in the palace he prayed to the Lord, saying: "Lord, guide me to salvation." And a voice came to him, saying: "Arsenius, flee from men and you will be saved." He retired to the monastic life and prayed again, in the same words: "Lord, guide me to salvation." He heard a voice say to him: "Arsenius, flee, be silent, be at peace, for these are the roots of not sinning."'[70] And so, acting on this one rule of the divine command, he not only fled from men but even drove them from him. One day his archbishop came to him, along with a certain judge, and asked him for a sermon of edification. '"If I give you one," said Arsenius, "will you follow it?" They promised that they would. Then he said to them: "Wherever you hear of Arsenius, do not go there." On another occasion the archbishop was visiting him and sent first to see if he would open his door. He sent back word: "If you come, I will open to you, but if I open to you I am opening to all, and then I can stay here no longer." Hearing this, the archbishop said: "If my coming will harass him, I will never go to this holy man."'[71] To a certain Roman

[66] Cf. 4 Kgs. (2 Kgs.) 6: 1.
[67] Cf. Jer. 35: 6–19.
[68] Jerome, *Epistola* LVIII *ad Paulinum presbyterum*, 5 (ed. Hilberg, liv. 533, *ll.* 15–21, p. 534, *ll.* 3–14; *PL* xxii. 582–3), cited more fully in *Letter* 12 (ed. Smits, p. 260; *PL* clxxviii. 346D–347A; trans. Ziolkowski, p. 162) and less fully in *Sermon* 33 (*PL* clxxviii. 585BC). Cf. **12** above and *Letter* 1, **26** and **52**.
[69] 'lectulum nostre quietis': cf. **12** above and n. 45.
[70] *Vitae patrum*, *Verba seniorum*, v. 2. 3 (*PL* lxxiii. 858AB).
[71] *Vitae patrum*, *Verba seniorum*, v. 2. 4 (*PL* lxxiii. 858BC).

cuidam Romane matrone uisitanti dixit: '"Quomodo presumpsisti tantam nauigationem assumere? Nescis quia mulier es, et non debes exire quoquam? Aut[f] ut uadas Romam, et dicas aliis mulieribus quia uidi Arsenium, et faciant[g] mare uiam mulierum uenientium ad me?" Illa autem dixit: "Si uoluerit me Deus[h] reuerti Romam, non permitto aliquem[i] uenire huc; sed ora pro me et memor esto mei semper." Ille autem respondens dixit ei: "Oro Deum ut deleat memoriam tui de corde meo." Que audiens hec egressa est turbata.'[72] Hic quoque, sicut scriptum est, a Marcho abbate requisitus cur fugeret homines, respondit: 'Scit Deus quia diligo homines, sed cum Deo pariter et hominibus esse non possum.'[73]

16. In tantum uero sancti patres conuersationem hominum atque noticiam abhorrebant ut non nulli eorum, ut illos a se penitus remouerent, insanos se fingerent et, quod dictu mirabile est, hereticos [a]etiam se[a] profiterentur. Quod, [b]si quis uoluerit,[b] legat in *Vitis Patrum* de abbate Symone qualiter se preparauit iudici prouincie ad se uenienti, qui se uidelicet sacco cooperiens et tollens in manu sua panem et caseum, sedit in ingressu celle sue et cepit manducare.[74] Legat et de illo anachoreta qui, cum [c]quosdam sensisset obuiam sibi[c] cum lampadibus occurrere, expolians se uestimenta sua, misit in flumen et stans nudus cepit ea lauare. Ille autem qui ministrabat ei hec[d] uidens erubuit, et rogauit homines dicens: '"Reuertimini, quia senex noster sensum perdidit." Et ueniens ad eum dixit ei: "Quid hoc[e] fecisti, abba? Omnes enim qui te uiderunt dixerunt quia demonium habet senex." Ille autem respondit: "Et ego hoc uolebam audire."'[75] Legat insuper[f] de abbate Moyse qui, ut a se penitus iudicem prouincie remoueret, 'surrexit ut fugeret in palude. Et occurrit ei ille iudex cum suis et interrogauit eum, dicens: "Dic nobis, senex, ubi est cella abbatis Moysi?" Et dicit[g] eis: "Quid uultis eum inquirere? Homo fatuus est et hereticus"',[76] etc.[h] Quid etiam de abbate Pastore qui nec se a iudice prouincie uideri permisit ut [i]sorori sue supplicanti[i] filium de carcere liberaret?[77] Ecce potentes seculi cum magna ueneratione et deuotione sanctorum presentiam postulant, et

[f] An *Vitae patrum* [g] facias *Vitae patrum* [h] Dominus *Amb* [i] aliquam *Vitae patrum*

16 [a–a] se etiam *C* [b–b] si (*exp.*) qui si uoluerit *T;* quis si non nouerit *CE* [c–c] sensisset quasdam (quosdam *E*) sibi obuiam *CE* [d] *om. CE* [e] hic *Amb* [f] e *add. T before exp.;* et *add. Amb* [g] dixit *Amb* [h] *om. CAmb* [i–i] sorori sue supplicantes *T;* sororis sue supplicantis *Amb*

matron who came to visit his holiness, Arsenius said: "Why have you presumed to undertake such a voyage? You must know you are a woman and should not travel at all. Or do you intend to return to Rome and tell other women that you have seen Arsenius, so that they will make the sea a highway for women coming to see me?" She replied: "If the Lord wishes me to return to Rome, I shall not allow anyone to come here. Only pray for me, and remember me always." But he answered: "I pray God to wipe out the memory of you from my heart." Hearing this she went away dismayed.'[72] It is also recorded that, when Arsenius was asked by abbot Mark why he fled from men, he replied: 'God knows that I love men, but I cannot be equally with men and with God.'[73]

16. The holy Fathers did indeed so shun the conversation and attention of men that many of them feigned madness, in order to drive men from them, and, remarkable to relate, even professed to be heretics. Anyone who likes may read in the *Lives of the Fathers* about abbot Simon, and how he prepared himself for a visit from the judge of the province; he covered himself with a sack and, holding bread and cheese in his hand, sat at the door of his cell and started eating.[74] He may read too of the hermit who, when he saw people coming towards him with lanterns, pulled off his clothes, threw them into the river, and standing there naked began to wash them. His servant blushed for shame at the sight and asked the men to go away, saying: '"Our old man has lost his senses." Then he went to him, and said: "Why did you do this, father? All who saw you said the old man is possessed." He replied: "That is what I wanted to hear."'[75] Let him read also of abbot Moses who, in order to keep a judge of the province well away from him, 'got up and fled into a marsh. The judge and his followers came along and enquired: "Tell us, old man, where is the cell of abbot Moses"? He replied: "Why do you want to look for him? The man is crazy and a heretic,"'[76] etc. And what of abbot Pastor, who even refused to be seen by the judge of the province in order to free from prison the son of his own sister, in answer to her plea?[77] You see then how the presence of the saints is sought by the powerful

[72] *Vitae patrum*, *Verba seniorum*, v. 2. 7 (*PL* lxxiii. 859AB)
[73] *Vitae patrum*, *Verba seniorum*, v. 17. 5 (*PL* lxxiii. 973D)
[74] *Vitae patrum*, *Verba seniorum*, v. 8. 18 (*PL* lxxiii. 908D).
[75] *Vitae patrum*, vii. 12. 7 (*PL* lxxiii. 1035C).
[76] *Vitae patrum*, *Verba seniorum*, v. 8. 10 (*PL* lxxiii. 907B).
[77] Cf. *Vitae patrum*, *Verba seniorum*, v. 8. 13 (*PL* lxxiii. 907D–908A).

illi etiam cum summo sui dedecore eos [j]a se penitus[j] repellere student!

17. Vt autem sexus etiam uestri in hac re uirtutem cognoscatis, quis digne predicare sufficiat uirginem illam[a] [b]que beatissimi quoque Martini uisitationem respuit ut uacaret contemplationi?[b] Vnde ad Oceanum[c] monachum Ieronymus scribens: 'In beati', inquit, 'Martini *Vita* legimus commemorasse Sulpicium quod transiens sanctus Martinus uirginem quandam moribus et castitate precelsam[d] cupiens salutare. Illa noluit, sed exenium[e] misit,[f] et per fenestram respiciens ait sancto uiro: "Ibi, pater, ora, quia numquam [g]sum a uiro uisitata."[g] Quo audito gratias egit Deo sanctus Martinus quod talibus imbuta moribus castam custodierit uoluntatem. Benedixit eam et abiit, leticia plenus.'[78] Hec reuera de[h] contemplationis sue lectulo surgere dedignata uel uerita, pulsanti ad ostium amico parata erat dicere: 'Laui pedes meos, quomodo inquinabo illos?'[79]

18. O quante sibi imputarent iniurie episcopi uel prelati huius temporis si hanc ab Arsenio uel ab hac uirgine repulsam pertulissent! Erubescant ad ista, si qui nunc in solitudine morantur, monachi cum episcoporum frequentia gaudent, cum eis proprias[a] in quibus suscipiantur fabricant domos, cum seculi potentes quos turba comitatur, uel ad quos confluit, non solum non fugiunt sed adsciscunt[b] et, occasione hospitum domos multiplicantes, quam quesierunt solitudinem redigunt in ciuitatem. Hac profecto antiqui et callidi temptatoris[c] machinatione omnia fere huius temporis monasteria, cum prius in solitudine constituta fuissent ut homines fugerentur,[d] postea feruore religionis refrigescente[80] homines asciuerunt;[e] et seruos atque ancillas congregantes uillas maximas in locis monasticis construxerunt, et sic ad seculum redierunt, immo ad se traxerunt seculum. Qui se miseriis maximis implicantes, et maxime seruituti tam ecclesiasticarum quam terrenarum potestatum[f] alligantes, dum ociose appeterent uiuere et de alieno uictitare labore, ipsum quoque monachi, hoc est solitarii,

[j–j] penitus a se *Amb*

17 [a] *om. E* [b–b] *om. CE* [c] occeanum *T* [d] preexcelsam C [e] xenium *Amb*, *Jerome* [f] misit ei *Jerome* [g–g] a viro sum visitata *Amb* [h] *om. CE*

18 [a] propria *C* [b] *T*[1] *adds a cross here in marg.* [c] hostis *CE* [d] fugent *E* [e] adsciverunt *Amb* [f] potestatem *TCE*

[78] Ps.-Jerome, *Epistola* XLII *ad Oceanum de uita clericorum*, 10 (*PL* xxx. 291CD). Not in the *Vita Martini* written by Sulpicius Severus *c.*394 but in his *Dialogus*, i (ii. 12), written

in the world with great veneration and devotion, while their aim is to keep people at a distance, even at the loss of their own dignity!

17. Now, so that you may know the virtue of your own sex in this matter, could anyone adequately tell of that virgin who refused a visit even from St Martin, so that she could devote herself to contemplation? Jerome writes of this to the monk Oceanus: 'In the *Life of St Martin*, we read that Sulpicius relates how St Martin when travelling wished to call on a certain virgin who was outstanding for her morals and chastity. She refused, but sent him a gift, and looking from her window said to the holy man: "Offer prayer where you are, father, for I have never been visited by a man." Hearing this St Martin thanked God that a woman of such morals had kept her desire for chastity. He blessed her and departed, filled with joy.'[78] This woman in fact disdained or feared to rise from the bed of her contemplation, and was prepared to say to a friend knocking at her door: 'I have washed my feet, how shall I defile them?'[79]

18. O what an insult to themselves would the bishops or priests of our day consider it if they received such a rebuff from Arsenius or this virgin! If any monks still remain in solitude, let them blush for such things since they delight in the society of bishops, build them special houses for their entertainment, do not shun worldly potentates whom a crowd accompanies or gathers round but rather invite them and, by multiplying their buildings on the pretext of hospitality, change the solitary place they sought into a city. Indeed, by the craft and cunning of the old tempter, nearly all the monasteries of today which were formerly founded in solitude so that men could be avoided, now that religious fervour has subsided,[80] have invited men to them, have assembled manservants and maidservants, and built great villages on monastic sites; and thus they have returned to the world, or rather have brought the world to them. By involving themselves in such great inconvenience and binding themselves in total slavery both to ecclesiastical and secular powers, while they seek to live at ease and enjoy the fruits of another's labour, they have lost the very name of

*c.*403, where Sulpicius' friend Postumianus from Aquitaine illustrates Martin's ideals in a series of stories (ed. Halm, pp. 194–5; *PL* xx. 209C–210B).

[79] Cf. **12** above and n. 45.

[80] 'postea feruore religionis refrigescente': cf. *Sermon* 33: 'Iam quippe refrigescente, imo extincto religionis feruore' (*PL* clxxviii. 587C).

nomen[81] pariter amiserunt et uitam. Qui etiam sepe tantis urgentur incommodis ut, dum suos et res eorum tutari laborant, proprias[g] amittant, et frequenti incendio uicinarum domorum ipsa quoque monasteria cremantur.[82] Nec sic tamen ambitio refrenatur.

19. Hi[a] quoque districtionem monasterii qualemcumque non ferentes, ac per uillas, castella, ciuitates se se dispergentes, binique[b] uel terni aut eciam singuli sine aliqua obseruatione regule uictitantes, tanto secularibus deteriores sunt hominibus quanto a[c] professione sua amplius apostatantur. Qui habitationum quoque suarum sicut[d] sua abutentes obedientias loca sua nominant, ubi nulla regula tenetur, ubi nulli rei nisi uentri et carni obeditur, ubi cum propinquis uel familiaribus suis manentes, tanto liberius agunt[e] quod uolunt quanto minus a conscientiis suis uerentur.[83] In quibus profecto [f]impudentissimis apostatis[f] excessus illos criminales esse dubium non est qui in ceteris ueniales sunt hominibus. Qualium omnino uitam non solum non[g] attingere sed nec audire sustineatis.[h]

20. Vestre uero infirmitati tanto magis est solitudo necessaria quanto carnalium temptationum bellis [a]minus hic[a] infestamur et minus ad corporalia per sensus euagamur.[b] Vnde et beatus Antonius: 'Qui sedet', inquit, 'in solitudine et quiescit, a tribus bellis eripitur, id est auditus, locutionis et uisus; et contra unum [c]habebit tantummodo[c] pugnam, id est cordis.'[84] Has quidem uel ceteras heremi comoditates insignis ecclesie doctor Ieronymus diligenter attendens, et ad eas Helyodorum monachum uehementer adhortans, exclamat dicens: 'O heremus familiarius[d] Deo gaudens![e] Quid agis, frater, in seculo, qui maior es mundo?'[85]

[g] suas *CE*

19 [a] Hic *T* [b] bini *C* [c] *om. CE* [d] in *add. C;* et *add. EAmb* [e] agere *TCE* [f–f] impudentissimus in apostatis *TCE* [g] *om. CEAmb* [h] substineatis *Amb*

20 [a–a] hic minus *CE* [b] euadamus *CE* [c–c] tantummodo habebit *Amb* [d] familiari *Amb, Jerome* [e] congaudens *C*

[81] 'monachi, hoc est solitarii, nomen': cf. **14** above.

[82] An example of such a fire hazard, and of steps taken to remove it, has been shown to me by Dr J. Kerr. It is found in the *Eulogy* for Euphemia, abbess of Wherwell in Hampshire (d. 1257), printed in trans. in Spear, *Leadership in Medieval English Nunneries*, Appendix D, pp. 217–18: 'The court of the abbey manor, owing to the useless mass of squalid buildings, and the propinquity of the kitchen to the granary and old hall, was in much danger of fire.

monk, that is, of solitary,[81] as well as their monastic life. They also often fall a victim to other misfortunes: while struggling to protect the persons and possessions of their followers they lose their own, and in the frequent fires which break out in adjoining buildings the monasteries are burned down as well.[82] Yet not even this checks their ambition.

19. There are those too who will not submit to monastic restriction of any kind, but are scattered in twos and threes amongst the villages, towns, and cities, or even live alone, without observance of a rule, and are thereby worse than men of the world the more they fall away from their profession. They also make misuse of the places where their people dwell as much they do their own, calling these obediences, though no rule is kept there and no obedience shown except to the belly and the flesh, and there they live with relatives and friends, behaving as freely as they wish, as they have so little to fear from their own consciences.[83] There can be no doubt that in shameless apostates such as these, excesses are criminal which in other men are venial. You should not permit yourselves to take example from such lives nor even to hear of them.

20. Solitude is indeed all the more necessary for your woman's frailty, inasmuch as for our part we are less attacked by the conflicts of carnal temptations and less likely to stray towards bodily things through the senses. Hence St Antony says: 'Whoever sits in solitude and is at peace is rescued from three wars, that is, wars of hearing, speech, and sight; he shall have only one thing to fight against, the heart.'[84] These and all the other advantages of the desert the famous Doctor of the Church Jerome has particularly in mind in giving urgent counsel to the monk Heliodorus: 'O desert rejoicing in the presence of God! What are you doing in the world, brother, when you are greater than the world?'[85]

The mother Euphemia . . . demolished the whole of these buildings . . . and erected a new hall of suitable size and height. She also built a new mill, some distance from the hall.'

[83] For similar criticism of monks living away from their abbeys in properties which were sometimes called obediences cf. *Sermon* 33 (*PL* clxxviii. 589AC); also Luscombe, 'Pierre Abélard et le monachisme', pp. 275–6.

[84] *Vitae patrum*, *Verba seniorum*, v. 2. 3 (*PL* lxxiii. 858A). Cf. Exod. 12: 10–12; 15: 24; 16: 2–12; 17: 1–7. St Antony of Egypt (251?–356) is traditionally seen as the 'founder' of the anchorite or eremitical variety of monasticism.

[85] Jerome, *Epistola* XIV *ad Heliodorum monachum*, 10 (ed. Hilberg, liv. 59, *ll.* 15–16; *PL* xxii. 354); cf. **14** above.

21. Nunc uero quia ubi construi monasteria conuenit disseruimus, qualis et ipsa loci positio esse debeat ostendamus. Ipsi autem monasterii loco constituendo, sicut quoque beatus consuluit[a] Benedictus, ita, si fieri potest, prouidendum est ut intra monasterii septa contineantur illa maxime que monasteriis sunt necessaria, id est ortus, aqua, molendinum, pistrinum cum furno, et loca quibus cotidiana [b]exerceant sorores[b] opera, ne foras uagandi detur occasio.[86]

22. Sicut[a] in castris seculi, ita et in castris Domini, id est congregationibus monasticis, constituendi sunt qui presint ceteris. Ibi quippe[b] [c]imponitur unus,[c] ad cuius nutum omnia gerantur, preest omnibus. Qui etiam pro multitudine exercitus uel diuersitate officiorum sua non nullis imperciens onera, quosdam sub se adhibet magistratus qui diuersis hominum cateruis aut officiis prouideant. Sic et in monasteriis fieri necesse est [d]ut ibi una omnibus[d] presit matrona, ad cuius considerationem atque arbitrium omnes relique omnia operentur, [e]nec ulla ei in aliquo presumat obsistere uel etiam ad aliquod eius preceptum murmurare.[e] Nulla quippe hominum congregatio[f] uel quantulacumque domus unius familia consistere potest incolumis nisi unitas in ea conseruetur, ut uidelicet totum eius regnum[g] in unius persone magisterio[h] consistat.[87] [i]Vnde et archa, typum ecclesie gerens cum multos tam in longo quam in lato cubitos haberet, in uno consummata est.[88] Et in Prouerbiis scriptum est:[i] 'Propter peccata terre multi principes eius.'[89] Vnde etiam Alexandro mortuo, multiplicatis regibus, mala quoque multiplicata sunt. Et Roma pluribus communicata rectoribus concordiam tenere non potuit. Vnde Lucanus in primo sic meminit:

Tu causa malorum
Facta tribus [j]dominis communis,[j] Roma, nec umquam
In turbam missi feralia federa regni.[90]

Et post pauca:

Dum terra fretum terramque leuabit
Aer et longi[k] uoluent Titana[l] labores

21 [a] consulit *C after corr. of* consuluit, *E* [b–b] exerceant sorores *CEAmb*

22 [a] *TCEAmb open a new section, T by starting a new line with a paragraph marker, C by emphasizing the initial, EAmb by using majuscule letters* [b] *T*[1] *makes an illegible add. in the marg.* [c–c] imponitur (a unu *add. and exp.*) unus *T;* ponitur unus *CE;* imperator unus *Amb* [d–d] sic ut in omnibus una *CE* [e–e] *om. CE* [f] congratulatio uel congregatio *E* [g] regimen *E* [h] ministerio *Amb*[1] [i–i] Vnde in proverbiis *CE* [j–j] Dominus *Amb* [k] longe *T* [l] tytana *T*

21. Now that we have discussed where monasteries should be set up, let us show what the layout of the site should be. In planning the site of the actual monastery, and in accordance with the *Rule* of St Benedict, provision should be made, if possible, for those things which are particularly necessary for monasteries to be contained within its precincts, that is, a garden, water, a mill, a bakehouse with oven, and places where the sisters may carry out their daily tasks without any need for straying outside.[86]

22. As in the army camps of the world, so in the camps of the Lord, that is, in monastic communities, people must be appointed to be in authority over the rest. In an army there is one commander over all, at whose bidding everything is carried out, but because of the size of his army and the complexity of his duties he shares his burdens with several others, and appoints subordinate officers to be responsible for various duties or companies of men. Similarly in convents it is also necessary for one matron to preside over all; the others must do everything in accordance with her decision and judgement, and no one must presume to oppose her in anything or even to grumble at any of her instructions. No community of people nor even a small household in a single house can continue as a whole unless unity is preserved in it, and complete control rests on the authority of a single person.[87] And so the Ark, as a model for the Church, was many cubits long and wide but rose to a single point.[88] It is written in Proverbs: 'For its sins a land has many rulers.'[89] Hence on the death of Alexander, when kings were multiplied, evils were multiplied too. Rome could not maintain concord when authority was shared amongst many rulers. Lucan reminds us in his first book:

> You, Rome, have been the cause of your own ills,
> Shared in three masters' hands; the pacts spell death
> Of power that never should devolve on many.[90]

A little later he says:

> So long as earth supports the sea and is itself
> Poised in the air, the sun rolls on its course,

[86] Benedict, *Rule*, c. 66, 6.

[87] Cf. Jerome, *Epistola* CXXV *ad Rusticum monachum*, 15 (ed. Hilberg. lvi. 133; *PL* xxii. 1080) cited below at **24**. Also D'Anna, 'Abelardo e Cicerone', p. 363 ff.

[88] Cf. Gen. 6: 14–15.

[89] Prov. 28: 2.

[90] Lucan, *De bello ciuili*, i. 84–6.

[m]Noxque diem celo totidem per signa sequetur,[n]
Nulla fides regni sociis, omnisque potestas
Impaciens consortis erit.[91]

23. Tales[a] profecto[b] illi erant discipuli sancti Frontonii abbatis quos ipse, in ciuitate in qua natus est, cum usque ad septuaginta congregasset et magnam ibidem gratiam tam apud Deum quam apud homines adeptus esset; relicto tamen[c] monasterio ciuitatis cum mobilibus rebus nudos secum ad heremum traxit. Qui postmodum more Israelitici populi aduersus Moysen conquerentis quod eos etiam de Egipto, relictis ollis carnium et habundantia terre, in solitudinem eduxisset, murmurantes incassum dicebant: 'Numquid sola in heremo castitas que in urbibus non est? Cur itaque non in ciuitatem reuertimur de qua ad tempus exiuimus? An in heremum solum Deus exaudiet orantes? Quis cibo angelorum uiuat? Quem peccorum et ferarum delectat fieri socium? Quanta nos habet necessitas hic morari? Cur itaque non regressi in locum in quo nati sumus benedicimus Dominum?'[92]

24. Hinc et Iacobus admonet apostolus: 'Nolite', inquit, 'plures magistri fieri, fratres mei, scientes quoniam maius iudicium sumitis.'[a] [93] Hinc quoque Ieronymus ad Rusticum monachum de institutione uite scribens: 'Nulla', inquit, 'ars absque magistro discitur. Etiam [b]multa animalia[b] et ferarum greges ductores secuntur suos. In apibus unam precedentem[c] relique subsecuntur. Grues unum[d] secuntur ordine literato. Imperator unus, iudex unus[e] prouincie. Roma, ut condita est, duos fratres simul habere reges non potuit [f]et parricidio dedicatur. In Rebecce utero Esau et Iacob bella gesserunt.[94] Singuli ecclesiarum episcopi, singuli archipresbyteri, singuli archidiaconi, et omnis ordo ecclesiasticus suis rectoribus nititur. In naue unus gubernator. In domo unus dominus. In quamuis grandi exercitu unius signum spectatur.[fg] Per hec omnia ad illud tendit oratio ut doceam te, non tuo arbitrio dimittendum, sed uiuere debere in monasterio sub unius disciplina patris consortioque multorum.'[h] [95]

[m] beginning of lacuna in CE, ending in 24 [n] sequatur *T*

23 [a] *in marg. of T some rubr. letters have been erased* [b] profecto e *add. and exp. T;* et *add. Amb* [c] *om. Amb*

24 [a] *end of lacuna in CE, beginning in 22* [b–b] animalia multa *CE;* muta animalia *Amb, Jerome* [c] et *add.* E [d] unam *Jerome* [e] unius *TCE* [f–f] et parricidio etc *CE* [g] expectatur *Jerome* [h] ut ab alio *add. T;* multorum ut ab alio discas humilitatem *Jerome*

Night follows day through the zodiac's signs,
No trust binds fellow rulers and every power
Rejects a partner.[91]

23. Such, surely, were those disciples of the abbot St Frontonius, whom he had assembled to the number of seventy in the city where he was born. He had won great favour there in the eyes of God and men, but then he left the monastery in the city, and with their movable goods took them naked with him into the desert. After a while, like the Israelites complaining against Moses because he had led them out of Egypt into the wilderness, abandoning their fleshpots and their wealth in the land, they started grumbling foolishly. 'Is chastity only to be found in the desert and not in town'? they asked. 'Why can't we go back to the city we have left? Will God hear our prayers only in the desert? Who can live by the bread of angels? Who wants to have livestock and wild beasts for company? Why do we have to stay here? Why can't we return and bless the Lord in the place where we were born?'[92]

24. Hence the apostle James gives warning: 'My brothers, not many of you should try to teach others; be sure that if you do, you will be judged with greater severity.'[93] Similarly, Jerome in writing to the monk Rusticus on the conduct of his life says: 'No skill is learned without a teacher. Even dumb animals and herds of wild beasts follow their leaders; amongst bees, one goes first and the rest follow, and cranes follow one of their number in regular order. There is one emperor, one judge of a province. When Rome was founded there could not be two brothers as kings at the same time, and this was settled by fratricide. Esau and Jacob fought in Rebecca's womb.[94] The churches each have one bishop, one dean, and one archdeacon, and every order in the Church depends on its rulers. In a ship there is one helmsman, in a house one master; in an army, however large, men look to the standard of one man. By all these examples my discourse aims at teaching you that you must not be left to your own will, but must live in a monastery under the discipline of one father and in fellowship with many.'[95]

[91] Ibid., 89–93.

[92] Cf. *Vitae patrum*, i: *Vita Frontonii*, 2 (*PL* lxxiii. 439BC). Frontonius or Fronto, a 2nd-c. abbot at Nitria, near modern el-Barnudj, about 40 miles south-east of Alexandria and close to Lake Mareotis.

[93] Jas. 3: 1.

[94] Gen. 25: 22.

[95] Jerome, *Epistola* CXXV *ad Rusticum monachum*, 15 (ed. Hilberg, liv. 133; *PL* xxii. 1080).

25. Vt[a] igitur in omnibus concordia seruari possit unam omnibus preesse conuenit cui per omnia omnes[b] obediant. Sub hac etiam, quasi magistratus quosdam, nonnullas alias personas prout ipsa decreuerit constitui oportet. Que quibus officiis ipsa preceperit et quantum uoluerit presint, ut sint[c] uidelicet iste quasi duces uel consules in exercitu dominico. Relique autem omnes tamquam milites uel pedites, istarum cura eis preuidente, aduersus malignum eiusque satellites libere pugnent.

26. Septem uero personas ex uobis ad omnem monasterii administrationem necessarias esse credimus atque sufficere, portariam scilicet, cellerariam,[a] uestiariam, infirmariam, cantricem,[b] sacristam et ad extremum diaconissam, quam nunc abbatissam nominant.[96] In hiis itaque castris et diuina quadam milicia—sicut scriptum est: 'Milicia est uita hominis super terram',[97] [c]et alibi: 'Terribilis ut castrorum acies ordinata'[c] [98]—uicem imperatoris cui[d] per omnia obeditur ab omnibus obtinet diaconissa. Sex uero alie sub ea, quas dicimus officiales, ducum siue consulum loca possident. Omnes uero relique moniales,[e] quas [f]uocamus claustrales,[f] militum more diuinum peragunt expedite seruicium. Conuerse autem, que etiam seculo renunciantes obsequio monialium se dicarunt habitu quodam religioso, non tamen monastico, quasi pedites inferiorem optinent gradum.[99]

27. Nunc uero superest, Domino inspirante, huius milicie gradus singulos ordinare, ut aduersus impugnationes demonum [a]uere sit quod dicitur:[a] 'castrorum acies ordinata'. Ab ipso itaque,[b] ut dictum est, capite, quod diaconissam dicimus, huius institutionis ducentes[c] exordium de ipsa primitus disponamus, per quam [d]sunt omnia disponenda.[d] Huius uero sanctitatem, [e]sicut in precedenti meminimus epistola,[e] beatus Paulus apostolus[f] Thymotheo scribens, quam eminentem et probatam oporteat esse diligenter describit dicens: 'Vidua eligatur non minus sexaginta annorum, [g]que fuerit unius uiri uxor, in operibus bonis testimonium habens, si filios educauit, si hospicio recepit, si sanctorum pedes lauit, si tribulationem pacientibus subministrauit, si omne opus bonum subsecuta est. Adolescentiores[h]

25 [a] *preceded by a paragraph marker in T* [b] *om. E* [c] *om. CE*

26 [a] cellariam *C* [b] cantatricem *CE;* cartaticem *sed male Amb*[1] [c–c] *om. CE* [d] cuius *E before corr. in marg.* [e] *om. CE* [f–f] claustrales uocamus *CE*

27 [a–a] uera sit *CE* [b] inquam *TAmb;* ita(que) *T*[1] *in marg., which has been trimmed* [c] ducentem *E* [d–d] omnia disponenda sunt *CE* [e–e] *om. CE* [f] *om. CE* [g–g] etc. *CE* [h] Adolescentes *Amb*

25. So that concord may therefore be maintained in all things, it is proper for one sister to be over all, and for all to obey her in everything. Some other sisters should also be appointed as officials to serve under her as she herself decides. They shall take charge of the duties she has ordered and as far as she wishes, as though they were dukes or counts serving in the army of their Lord, while all the rest are the soldiers or infantry who are under the direction of the others and shall fight freely against the evil one and his accomplices.

26. Seven persons out of your number are, I think, all that are needed for the entire administration of the convent: portress, cellaress, wardrober, infirmarian, chantress, sacristan, and lastly the deaconess, who is now called the abbess.[96] And so in this camp, and in this kind of service in the army of the Lord—as it is written that 'Man's life on earth is like service',[97] and elsewhere: 'Awesome as a regimented army'[98]—the deaconess has the place of the commander who is obeyed by all in everything. The six under her, the officials as we call them, hold the positions of dukes or counts; while all the other nuns, whom we call the claustral sisters, perform their service for God promptly, like knights. And the lay sisters, who have also renounced the world and dedicated themselves to serving the nuns, wear a kind of religious, though not a monastic, habit and, like foot-soldiers, hold a lower rank.[99]

27. Now, under the Lord's inspiration, it remains to marshal the several ranks of this army so it may truly be what is called 'a regimented army' to meet the assaults of demons. And so, starting at the head of this institution, with the deaconess as we call her, let us first dispose of her through whom all must be disposed. First of all, her sanctity: as I said in my preceding letter, St Paul in writing to Timothy describes in detail how outstanding and proved this must be: 'A widow should be chosen who is not under sixty years of age. She must have been faithful in marriage to one man, and must produce evidence of good deeds performed, showing whether she has had the care of children, or given hospitality, or washed the feet of God's people, or supported those in distress—in short, whether she has taken every opportunity of doing

[96] 'diaconissam', 'abbatissam': cf. *Letter* 7, **19**. In *Institutiones nostre*, 6 (*The Paraclete Statutes*, ed. Waddell, p. 10; *PL* clxxviii. 314D) an additional office is mentioned, that of prioress.

[97] Job 7: 1.

[98] S. of S. 6: 9.

[99] On the lay sisters see Appendix A, 6. iv.

autem uiduas deuita',[100] etc.[i] Idem supra de diaconissis, cum etiam diaconorum institueret uitam, 'Mulieres', inquit, 'similiter pudicas, non detrahentes, sobrias, fideles in omnibus'.[101] Que quidem omnia quid intelligentie uel rationis habeant, quantum estimamus, epistola precedente nostra satis disseruimus, maxime cur eam Apostolus unius uiri et prouecte uelit esse etatis.[g] [102]

28. Vnde non mediocriter miramur quomodo perniciosa hec in ecclesia consuetudo inoleuit, ut que uirgines sunt pocius quam que uiros cognouerunt ad hoc eligantur, et frequenter iuniores senioribus preficiantur, cum tamen Ecclesiastes dicat: 'Ve tibi terra cuius rex puer est',[103] et cum illud beati Iob omnes pariter approbemus: 'In antiquis est sapientia, et in multo tempore prudentia.'[104] Hinc et in Prouerbiis scriptum est: 'Corona dignitatis senectus que in uiis iusticie reperietur.'[105] Et in Ecclesiastico: 'Quam speciosum caniciei iudicium et a presbyteris cognoscere consilium! Quam speciosa ueterani sapientia et gloriosus intellectus et consilium! Corona senum multa pericia et gloria illorum timor Dei.'[106] Item: 'Loquere maior natu; decet enim te.'[107] 'Adolescens, loquere in tua causa uix [a]enim necesse fuit.[a] Si bis[b] interrogatus fueris, habeat capud responsum tuum. In multis esto quasi inscius,[c] et audi tacens simul et querens, [d]et loqui[d] in medio magnatorum[e] non presumas, et ubi sunt senes, non multum[f] loquaris.'[108] Vnde et presbyteri qui in ecclesia populo presunt seniores interpretantur, ut ipso quoque nomine quales esse debeant doceatur. Et qui sanctorum[g] *Vitas* scripserunt, quos nunc abbates dicimus, senes appellabant.[109]

29. Modis itaque omnibus prouidendum est ut in electione uel consecratione diaconisse consilium precedat Apostoli, ut uidelicet talis eligatur que ceteris uita et doctrina preesse debeat, et etate quoque morum maturitatem polliceatur, et que obediendo meruerit imperare, et operando magis quam audiendo *Regulam* didicerit, et

[i] *om. Amb*

28 [a–a] *add. TCE;* cum necesse fuerit *add. Amb; cf. Ecclus., prologus:* ipsos loquentes necesse est esse peritos [b] hiis *CE* [c] insciens *C* [d–d] *add. TCE Amb* [e] magnatum *Amb*[I] [f] multa *E* [g] patrum *add. CE*

[100] 1 Tim. 5: 9–11. Also cited in *Letter* 7, **18** and **20**; cf. notes 131 and 152 there.

[101] 1 Tim. 3: 11; also cited in *Letter* 7, **20**; cf. n. 149 there.

[102] Cf. *Letter* 7, **18–20**.

[103] Eccles. 10: 16.

[104] Job 12: 12. Gold, *The Lady and the Virgin*, pp. 96–8, contrasts the approval shown at the Benedictine house of Le Ronceray at Angers for the election as abbess in about 1122 of Mabilia, a nun since childhood, and the choice by Robert of Arbrissel in 1115 of Petronilla

good. Avoid younger widows',[100] etc. And earlier on, when he was laying down rules for the life of deacons, he says about deaconesses: 'Their wives, equally, must be high-principled, not given to talking scandal, sober and trustworthy in every way.'[101] I have said enough in my last letter to show how highly I value the meaning and reasoning behind all these words, especially the reason why the Apostle wishes her to be the wife of one husband alone and to be advanced in age.[102]

28. And so I am much surprised that the pernicious practice has arisen in the Church of appointing virgins to this office rather than women who have known men, and often of putting younger over older women. Yet Ecclesiastes says: 'Woe betide the land where a boy is king',[103] and we all approve the saying of holy Job: 'There is wisdom in age and long life brings understanding.'[104] It is also written in Proverbs: 'Grey hair is a crown of glory if it shall be won by a virtuous life',[105] and in Ecclesiasticus: 'How beautiful is the judgement of grey hairs and counsel taken from the old! How beautiful the wisdom of the aged, how glorious their understanding and counsel! Long experience is the old man's crown and his pride is the fear of the Lord.'[106] Again: 'Speak, if you are old, for it is your privilege.'[107] 'If you are young, speak in your own case, but not much. If you are asked twice, let your reply be brief. For the most part be like a man who does not know and can listen in silence while making enquiries. Do not be familiar among the great, nor talk much before your elders.'[108] So the priests who have authority over the people in the Church are understood to be elders, so that their very name may teach what they ought to be. And the men who wrote the *Lives of the Saints* gave the name of elder to those whom we now call abbots.[109]

29. Thus in every way care must be taken when electing or consecrating a deaconess to follow the advice of the Apostle, and to elect one who must be above all the rest in her life and learning, and of an age to promise maturity in conduct; by her obedience she should be worthy of giving orders, and through practising the *Rule* rather

of Chemillé as abbess of his foundation at Fontevraud on the ground that her experience as a formerly married woman made her more suitable than an inexperienced virgin (*Cartulaire de l'abbaye du Ronceray*, ed. Marchegay, p. 19; Andrew of Fontevraud, *Vita altera Roberti de Arbrissello*, 5, in *PL* clxii. 1060).

[105] Prov. 16: 31.

[106] Ecclus. 25: 6–8.

[107] Ecclus. 32: 4.

[108] Ecclus. 32: 10–13.

[109] Books iii, v, vi, and vii of the *Vitae patrum* contain the *Verba seniorum* (*Sayings of the Elders*).

firmius nouerit.[110] Que si litterata non fuerit, sciat se non ad philosophicas scolas uel disputationes dialeticas sed ad doctrinam uite et operum[a] exhibitione[b] accomodari, sicut de Domino scriptum est: 'Qui cepit facere et docere',[111] prius uidelicet facere, postmodum[c] docere, quia melior atque perfectior est doctrina operis quam sermonis, facti quam uerbi.[112] Quod diligenter attendamus ut scriptum est: 'Dixit abbas Ypitius: "Ille est uere sapiens[d] qui facto suo alios docet, non qui uerbis." '[113] Nec parum consolationis et confidentie super hoc affert. [e]Attendatur et[e] illa quoque beati Antonii ratio qua uerbosos confutauit philosophos, eius uidelicet tamquam ydiote et illitterati[f] hominis magisterium irridentes: 'Respondete',[g] inquit, 'mihi quid prius est, sensus an littere? Et quid cuius exordium est, sensus ex litteris an littere oriuntur ex sensu? Illis asserentibus quia sensus esset auctor[h] atque inuentor litterarum ait: Igitur cui sensus incolumis[i] est, hic litteras non requirit.'[114] Audiat quoque illud Apostoli et confortetur in Domino: 'Nonne stultam fecit Deus sapientiam huius mundi?'[115] Et iterum: 'Que stulta sunt mundi elegit Deus [j]ut confundat sapientes; et infirma elegit Deus ut confundat fortia. Et ignobilia mundi et contemptibilia elegit Deus ut[j] ea que non sunt tamquam ea que sunt destrueret,[k] ut non glorietur omnis caro in conspectu eius.'[116] Non enim, sicut ipse postmodum dicit,[l] in sermone est[m] regnum Dei, sed in uirtute. Quod si de aliquibus melius cognoscendis ad Scripturam recurrendum[n] esse censuerit, a litteratis hoc requirere et addiscere non erubescat,[o] nec in hiis litteraturarum[p] documenta contempnat, sed [q]diligenter suscipiat,[q] cum ipse quoque apostolorum princeps coapostoli sui Pauli publicam correctionem[r] diligenter exceperit.[117] [s]Vt enim beatus quoque meminit Benedictus: 'Sepe minori[t] reuelat Dominus quod melius est.'[s] [118]

29 [a] operis *E* [b] exhibitionem *Amb* [c] postea *CE* [d] passiens *CE* [e–e] et attendatur *C;* et attendat *E* [f] illyteratus *C* [g] Et respondete *Amb* [h] actor *C* author *Amb* [i] incolumus *C* [j–j] *om. CE by homoeoteleuton* [k] destruat *Amb* [l] non *add. CE* [m] *om. CE* [n] reuertendum *Amb* [o] erubescant *CE* [p] literarum *Amb* [q–q] deuote (*exp.*) diligenter suscipiat *T;* deuote et diligenter suscipiat *Amb* [r] correptionem *Amb*[1] [s–s] *om. CE* [t] iuniori *Benedict*

[110] Cf. 1 Tim. 5; also **27** above and *Letters* 6, **13** and 7, **18**.

[111] Acts 1: 1; also cited with a similar comment in *TChr*, ii. 45.

than hearing it she should have learned it and know it well.[110] If she is not lettered let her know that she should accustom herself not to philosophic studies nor dialectical disputations but to teaching of life and the performance of works. As it is written of the Lord: he 'set out to do and teach',[111] that is, he taught afterwards what he did first, for teaching through works rather than speech,[112] the deed before the word, is better and more thorough. Let us pay careful heed to what abbot Ipitius is recorded to have said: 'He is truly wise who teaches others by his action, not by words.'[113] He gives us no little comfort and encouragement thereby. We should listen too to the argument of St Antony which confounded the wordy philosophers who laughed at his authority as being that of a foolish and illiterate man: 'Tell me', he said, 'which comes first, understanding or letters? Which is the beginning of the other—does understanding come from letters or letters from understanding?' When they declared that understanding was the author and inventor of letters, he said: 'So if a man's understanding is sound, he has no need of letters.'[114] She should hear too the words of the Apostle, and be strengthened in the Lord: 'Has not God made the wisdom of this world look foolish?'[115] And again: 'To shame the wise, God has chosen what the world counts as folly. God has chosen the base and contemptible things of the world so as to bring to nothing what is now in being so that no human flesh may boast in his presence.'[116] For the kingdom of God, as he says later, is not a matter of talk but of power. But if to gain better understanding of some things the deaconess thinks she should have recourse to the Scriptures, she should not be ashamed to ask and learn from the lettered, nor despise the evidence of their education in these matters, but accept it devoutly and thoughtfully, just as the leader of the apostles himself thoughtfully accepted public correction from his fellow apostle Paul.[117] For, as St Benedict also remarks: 'The Lord often reveals what is better to the lesser man.'[118]

[112] 'perfectior est doctrina . . . facti quam uerbi': cf. 30 below and *Letter* 1, 1.

[113] *Vitae patrum, Verba seniorum*, v. 10. 75 (*PL* lxxiii. 925). Not Ipitius, but Iperchio.

[114] Athanasius, *Vita beati Antonii abbatis interprete Euagrio*, 45, in *Vitae patrum*, i (*PL* lxxiii. 158BC). Also cited in part or alluded to in *Collationes* 73 (ed. Marenbon and Orlandi, p. 92; *Dialogus*, ed. Thomas, *ll.* 1411–12; *PL* clxxviii. 1639C).

[115] 1 Cor. 1: 20.

[116] 1 Cor. 1: 27–9.

[117] Cf. Gal. 2: 11; also *SN, prologue* (ed. Boyer and McKeon. p. 97, *ll.* 203–8).

[118] Cf. Benedict, *Rule*, c. 3, 3. Cf. *Sermon* 26 (*PL* clxxviii. 543D).

30. Vt autem amplius dominicam sequamur prouidentiam, quam Apostolus [a]quoque supra[a] memorauit,[119] numquam de nobilibus aut potentibus seculi nisi maxima incumbente necessitate et certissima ratione fiat hec electio. Tales namque, de genere suo facile confidentes aut gloriantes, aut presumptuose aut superbe fiunt; et tunc, maxime quando indigene[b] sunt, earum prelatio perniciosa fit monasterio. [c]Verendum quippe est ne uicinia suorum eam presumptiorem reddat, et frequentia ipsorum grauet aut inquietet monasterium, atque ipsa per suos religionis perferat detrimentum, aut aliis ueniat in contemptum iuxta illud Veritatis: 'Non est propheta sine honore nisi in patria sua.'[120] Quod beatus quoque prouidens Ieronymus ad Helyodorum scribens, cum pleraque annumerasset que monachis officiunt in sua morantibus patria, 'ex hac', inquit, 'supputatione illa summa nascitur monachum in patria sua perfectum esse non posse. Perfectum esse autem nolle delinquere est.'[c] [121] Quantum uero est animarum dampnum si minor in religione fuerit que religionis preest magisterio? Singulis quippe subiectis singulas uirtutes exhibere sufficit. In hac autem omnium[d] exempla debent eminere uirtutum, ut omnia que aliis preceperit propriis preueniat exemplis, ne[e] ipsa que precipit moribus oppugnet,[f] et quod uerbis edificat factis ipsa destruat, et de ore suo uerbum correctionis auferatur, cum ipsa in aliis erubescat corrigere que constat eam committere.[122]

31. [a]Quod quidem Psalmista ne ei eueniat Dominum precatur dicens: 'Et ne auferas de ore meo [b]uerbum ueritatis[b] usquequaque.'[123] Attendebat quippe illam grauissimam Domini increpationem, de qua et ipse alibi meminit dicens: 'Peccatori autem dixit Deus: Quare tu enarras iustitias meas et assumis testamentum meum per os tuum? Tu uero odisti disciplinam et proiecisti sermones meos retrorsum.'[ca] [124] [d]Quod studiose precauens[d] Apostolus: 'Castigo', inquit,[e] 'corpus meum et in seruitutem redigo, ne forte cum aliis predicauerim ipse reprobus efficiar.'[125] Cuius quippe uita despicitur

30 [a–a] supra quoque *CE* [b] indigne *E* [c–c] *om. CE* [d] omnia *CE* [e] nec *C* [f] oppugnatur *CE*

31 [a–a] *om. CE* [b–b] veritatem *Amb* [c] retro *Amb* [d–d] Vnde dicebat apostolus *CE* [e] *om. CE*

---

[119] Cf. 1 Cor. 1: 27–8, cited above in **29**. The previous verse, 1 Cor. 1: 26, not cited in **29**, also underlies this passage: 'Videte enim uocationem uestram fratres, quia non multi sapientes secundum carnem, non multi potentes, non multi nobiles.'

30. So that we may better follow the Lord's injunction which the Apostle recorded above,[119] we should never let this election be made from the nobility or the powerful in the world except under pressure of great necessity and for sound reason. Such women, from their easy confidence in their breeding, become boastful or presumptuous or proud, and, especially when they are native to the district, their authority becomes damaging to the convent. Precautions must be taken against her becoming presumptuous because of the proximity of her kindred, and the convent's being burdened or disturbed by their numbers, so that religion suffers harm through her people and she comes under contempt from others. In accordance with the Truth: 'A prophet is not without honour, save in his own country.'[120] St Jerome also made provision for this when he wrote to Heliodorus and enumerated several things which stand in the way of monks who stay in their own country. 'The conclusion of these considerations', he says, 'is that a monk cannot be perfect in his own country; and not to wish to be perfect is a sin.'[121] But what damage to souls will there be if she who is the authority over religion is lacking in religion herself? For it is sufficient for her subordinates if each of them displays a single virtue. But in her examples of all the virtues should shine out, so that she can be a living example of all she enjoins on the others, and not contradict her precepts by her morals, nor destroy by her own deeds what she builds in words; in order that the word of correction may not fall away from her lips when she is ashamed to correct in others the errors she is known to commit herself.[122]

31. The Psalmist prays to the Lord lest this happens to him: 'Rob not my mouth of the power to tell the truth',[123] he says, for he was expecting that stern rebuke of the Lord to which he refers elsewhere: 'God's word to the wicked man is this: What right have you to recite my laws and make so free with the words of my covenant, you who hate correction and turn your back when I am speaking?'[124] The Apostle too was careful to provide against this: 'I punish my own body', he says, 'and make it know its master, for fear that after preaching to others I should find myself rejected.'[125] For anyone

[120] Matt. 13: 57.
[121] Jerome, *Epistola* XIV *ad Heliodorum monachum*, 7 (ed. Hilberg, liv.. 54, *ll.* 16–18; *PL* xxii. 352).
[122] 'exemplis', 'uerbis', 'factis': cf. **29** above and *Letter* 1, 1.
[123] Ps. 118 (119): 43.
[124] Ps. 49 (50): 16–17.
[125] 1 Cor. 9: 27.

restat ut et predicatio uel doctrina contempnatur. Et cum curare quis alium debeat, si in eadem laborauerit infirmitate recte ipsi ab egroto improperatur: 'Medice, [f]cura teipsum.'[f] [126]

32. Attendat sollicite quisquis[a] ecclesie preesse uidetur quantam ruinam casus eius prebeat cum ipse ad precipicium secum pariter subiectos trahat. 'Qui soluerit', inquit Veritas, 'unum de mandatis istis minimis, et docuerit sic homines, minimus uocabitur in regno celorum.'[127] Soluit quippe mandatum qui contra agendo infringit ipsum, et exemplo suo corrumpens alios 'in cathedra pestilentie'[128] doctor residet.[b] Quod si quislibet hoc agens minimus habendus est in regno celorum, hoc est in ecclesia presenti, quanti habendus est pessimus prelatus a cuius negligentia non sue tantum sed omnium subiectarum animarum sanguinem Dominus requirit?[129] Vnde bene Sapientia talibus comminatur: 'Data est a Domino potestas uobis et uirtus ab altissimo qui interrogabit opera uestra et cogitationes scrutabitur. Quoniam cum essetis ministri regni illius, non recte iudicastis neque custodistis legem iusticie. [c]Horrende etiam[c] cito apparebit uobis, quoniam iudicium durissimum in[d] hiis qui presunt, fiet. Exiguo enim conceditur misericordia. Potentes autem potenter tormenta pacientur,[e] [f]et fortioribus fortior instat cruciatio.'[f] [130]

33. Sufficit quippe unicuique subiectarum animarum a proprio sibi prouidere delicto. Prelatis autem etiam[a] in peccatis alienis mors imminet. Cum enim augentur dona, rationes etiam[b] crescunt donorum, et cui plus committitur plus ab eo exigitur.[131] Cui quidem periculo tanto maxime prouidere in Prouerbiis ammonemur cum dicitur: 'Fili, si spoponderis pro amico tuo, defixisti[c] apud extraneum manum tuam. Illaqueatus es uerbis oris tui et captus propriis sermonibus. Fac ergo quod dico, fili mi, et temetipsum[d] libera, quia incidisti [e]in manum proximi tui. Discurre, festina, suscita amicum tuum, ne dederis sompnum oculis tuis,[e] nec dormitent palpebre tue.'[132] Tunc enim pro amico sponsionem facimus cum

[f-f] curat teipsum *C;* curate ipsum *E*

32 [a] quis *C* [b] presidet *CE* [c-c] horrendo et *E* [d] *om. CE* [e] passienter *CE* [f-f] *om. CE*

33 [a] et *Amb* [b] *om. CE* [c] indefixisti *CE* [d] te ipsum *CE* [e-e] etc usque *CE*

---

[126] Luke 4: 23.
[127] Matt. 5: 19.
[128] Ps. 1: 1.
[129] 'sanguinem Dominus requirit': cf. Ps. 9: 13 (12).

whose life is despised must see his preaching or teaching condemned as well, and a man who should heal another but suffers from the same infirmity is rightly reproached by the sick man: 'Physician, heal yourself.'[126]

32. Whoever is seen to have authority in the Church must think carefully what ruin his own fall will bring about when he takes his subjects along with him to the precipice. 'If any man', says the Truth, 'breaks even the lowest of the Lord's commandments and teaches others to do the same, he will be the least in the kingdom of Heaven.'[127] He breaks a commandment who infringes it by acting against it and, if he corrupts others by his own example, he sits as a teacher in 'the chair of pestilence'.[128] But if anyone acting thus is to be called the least in the kingdom of Heaven, that is in the Church here on earth, what are we to call a superior who is utterly vile and because of whose negligence the Lord demands the lifeblood not only of his own soul but of all the souls subject to him?[129] And so the Book of Wisdom rightly curses such men: 'It is the Lord who gave you your authority, and your power comes from the Most High. He will put your actions to the test and scrutinize your intentions. Though you are viceroys of his kingly power, you have not been upright judges; you do not stand up for the law of justice. Swiftly and terribly will he descend on you, for judgement falls relentlessly on those in high places. The small man may find pardon, but the powerful will be powerfully tormented, and a cruel trial awaits the mighty.'[130]

33. It is sufficient for each of the subject souls to provide for itself against its own misdeed, but death hangs over those who also have responsibility for the sins of others for, when gifts are increased, the reasons for gifts are also multiplied, and more is expected of him to whom more is committed.[131] We are warned in Proverbs to guard against so great a danger, when it says: 'My son, if you pledge yourself to a friend and stand surety for a stranger, if you are caught by your promise, trapped by some words you have said, do what I now tell you and save yourself, my son, when you fall into another man's power. Run, hurry, rouse your friend, let not your eyes sleep nor your eyelids slumber.'[132] For we pledge ourselves to a friend

[130] Wisdom 6: 4–9. [131] Cf. Luke 12: 48.
[132] Prov. 6: 1–4.

aliquem caritas nostra in nostre congregationis conuersationem[f] suscipit. Cui nostre prouidencie curam promittimus sicut et ille nobis obedientiam suam. Et sic quoque manum nostram apud eum defigimus cum sollicitudinem nostre operationis erga eum spondendo constituimus. Tum et in manum eius incidimus, quia nisi nobis ab ipso prouiderimus ipsum anime nostre interfectorem senciemus. Contra quod periculum adhibetur consilium cum subditur: 'discurre, festina', etc.

34. Nunc igitur huc, nunc illuc deambulans, more prouidi et impigri ducis, castra sua sollicite giret uel scrutetur, ne per alicuius negligentiam ei qui 'tamquam leo circuit, querens quem deuoret'[133] aditus pateat. Omnia mala domus sue prior agnoscat, ut ab ipsa prius possint corrigi quam a ceteris agnosci et in exemplum trahi. [a]Caueat illud quod stultis uel negligentibus beatus improperat Ieronymus: 'Solemus mala nostre domus scire nouissimi ac liberorum ac coniugum uicia, uicinis canentibus, ignorare.'[a] [134] Attendat que hic[b] presidet[c] quia tam corporum quam animarum custodiam suscepit. [d]De custodia uero corporum ammonetur cum dicitur in Ecclesiastico: 'Filie tibi sunt? Serua corpus illarum et non ostendas faciem tuam hylarem ad illas.'[135] Et iterum: 'Filia patris abscondita est uigilia, et sollicitudo eius aufert sompnum ne quando polluatur.'[136] Polluimus uero corpora nostra non solum fornicando sed quodlibet indecens in ipsis operando, tam lingua quam alio membro seu quolibet membro sensibus corporis ad uanitatem aliquam abutendo. Sicut scriptum est: 'Mors intrat per fenestras nostras',[137] hoc est, peccatum ad animam per quinque sensuum instrumenta.[d]

35. Que uero mors grauior aut custodia periculosior quam animarum? 'Nolite', inquit Veritas, 'timere eos qui occidunt corpus, anime uero non habent quid faciant.'[138] Si quis hoc audit consilium, quis non magis mortem corporis quam anime timet? Quis non magis gladium quam mendacium cauet? Et[a] tamen scriptum est: 'Os quod mentitur occidit animam.'[139] Quid tam facile interfici quam anima potest? Que sagitta cicius fabricari[b] quam peccatum ualet?[c] Quis sibi a cogitatione

[f] conuersionem *C*

34 [a–a] *om. CE* [b] sic *Amb* [c] possidet *C* [d–d] *om. CE*

35 [a] *add. CE* [b] fabricata *E* [c] ualebit *C*

[133] 1 Pet. 5: 8.

[134] Jerome, *Epistola* CXLVII ad Sabinianum, 10 (ed. Hilberg, lvi. 327; *PL* xxii. 1203); cited also in *Letter* 1, **20**.

when our charity admits someone into the life of our community; we promise him the care of our supervision, as he promises his obedience to us. So too we stand surety for him by joining hands when we confirm our willingness to work on his behalf; and we fall into his power because unless we make provision for ourselves against him, we shall find that he is the slayer of our soul. It is against this danger that the advice is given: 'Run, hurry', etc.

34. And so now here, now there, like a watchful and tireless captain, let our deaconess go carefully round her camp and watch lest through any negligence a way is opened to him who 'like a lion prowls around looking for someone to devour'.[133] She must be the first to know all the evils of her house, so that she may correct them before they are known to the rest and taken as a precedent. Let her beware too of the charge St Jerome lays against the foolish or negligent: 'We are always the last to learn what has gone wrong in our own home, and we do not know of the faults of our wives and children even though they are the talk of the neighbourhood.'[134] She who thus presides must remember that she has taken on the care of bodies as well as of souls, and concerning the former there is advice for her in the words of Ecclesiasticus: 'Have you daughters? See that they are chaste, and do not be too lenient with them.'[135] Again: 'A daughter is a secret anxiety to her father, and the worry of her takes away his sleep for fear she may be defiled.'[136] But we defile our bodies not only by fornication but by doing anything improper with them, as much by the tongue as by any other member, or by abusing the bodily senses in any member for some idle whim. So it is written: 'Death comes in through our windows',[137] that is, sin enters the soul by means of the five senses.

35. What death is more grievous or care more perilous than that of souls? 'Do not fear those who kill the body but cannot kill the soul',[138] says the Truth. But if anyone hears this, does he not still fear the death of the body rather than of the soul? Who would not avoid a sword rather than a lie? And yet it is written: 'A lying tongue is death to the soul.'[139] What can be destroyed so easily as the soul? What arrow can be fashioned so speedily as a lie? Who can safeguard

[135] Ecclus. 7: 26. [136] Ecclus. 42: 9–10.
[137] Jer. 9: 21. Also cited in *Letter* 1, 37 and *Problemata* 28 (*PL* clxxviii. 712D).
[138] Matt. 10: 28 and Luke 12: 4.
[139] Wisd. 1: 11.

saltem prouidere potest? Quis propriis peccatis prouidere sufficit nedum alienis? Quis carnalis pastor spiritales oues a lupis spiritalibus, inuisibiles ab inuisibilibus, custodire sufficiat? Quis raptorem non timeat qui infestare non cessat, quem nullo possumus excludere uallo, nullo interficere uel ledere gladio? Quem incessanter insidiantem, et maxime religiosos persequentem, iuxta illud Abacuc: Esce illius electe,[140] Petrus apostolus cauendum adhortatur dicens: 'Aduersarius uester diabolus tamquam leo [d]rugiens circuit, querens quem deuoret.'[d] [141] Cuius quanta sit presumptio in deuoratione nostra ipse Dominus beato Iob dicit: 'Absorbebit fluuium et non mirabitur; et habet fiduciam quod influat Jordanis in os eius.'[142]

36. Quid enim[a] aggredi non presumat qui ipsum quoque Dominum aggressus est temptare, qui [b]de paradiso primos statim[b] parentes captiuauit, et de apostolico cetu ipsum etiam quem Dominus elegerat apostolum rapuit? Quis ab eo locus tutus? Que claustra [c]illi non sunt[c] peruia? Quis ab eius insidiis prouidere? Quis eius fortitudini ualet resistere? Ipse est qui, uno impulsu concuciens quatuor angulos domus sancti uiri Iob, filios et filias innocentes oppressit et extinxit.[143] Quid sexus infirmior aduersus eum[d] poterit? Cui seductio eius tantum timenda est quantum femine? Hanc quippe ipse primum seduxit, et per ipsam uirum eius pariter et totam posteritatem captiuauit.[144] [e]Cupiditas maioris boni possessione minoris mulierem priuauit.[e] Hac[f] quoque arte[g] nunc facile mulierem seducet, cum preesse magis quam prodesse cupierit, rerum ambitione uel honoris ad hoc[h] impulsa. Quod autem horum precesserit sequentia probabunt. Si enim[i] delicatius uixerit prelata quam subiecta, uel si supra necessitatem aliquid sibi peculiare uendicauerit, non dubium est hoc eam concupisse. Si preciosiora postmodum quam antea quesierit ornamenta, profecto uana tumet[j] gloria. Qualis prius extiterit postmodum apparebit. Quod prius exhibebat,[k] utrum uirtus fuerit an simulatio indicabit prelatio.

[d–d] *om. C;* etc *E*

36 [a] *om. E* [b–b] de paradiso (statim paradiso *add. and exp. T*) primos statim *TCE;* de paradiso statim primos *Amb* [c–c] non sunt illi *C;* non sunt illis *E* [d] ipsum *Amb* [e–e] *om. CE* [f] Hanc *CE* [g] autem *C;* ante *E* [h] huc *CE* [i] vero *Amb* [j] timet *C;* Contra eos qui ambiunt prelationes *add. in marg. TAmb* [k] exhibebit *T*

himself, if only against a thought? Who is able to watch out for his own sins, let alone those of others? What shepherd in the flesh has the power to protect spiritual sheep from spiritual wolves, both alike invisible? Who would not fear the robber who never ceases to lie in wait, whom no wall can shut out, no sword can kill or wound? He is forever plotting and persecuting, with the religious as his chosen victims, for, in the words of Habakkuk, they 'enjoy rich fare',[140] and it is against him that the apostle Peter urges us to be on our guard, saying: 'Your enemy the devil, like a roaring lion, prowls around looking for someone to devour.'[141] How confident he is of devouring us the Lord himself says to holy Job: 'The flooded river he drinks unconcerned: he is confident he can draw up Jordan into his mouth.'[142]

36. For what would he not be bold enough to try who tried to test the Lord himself? It was he who took our first parents straight from Paradise to captivity, and even snatched an apostle whom the Lord had chosen from the apostles' company. What place is safe from him, what doors are not unbarred to him? Who can take action against his plots or stand up to his strength? It was he who struck with a single stroke the four corners of the house of holy Job, and crushed and killed his innocent sons and daughters.[143] What then can the weaker sex do against him? Who but women have his seductive ways so much to fear? It was a woman he first seduced, and through her husband too, and so made captive all their descendants.[144] His desire for a greater good robbed her of her possession of a lesser good, and by the same wiles he can still easily seduce a woman when her desire is for authority, not for service, and when she is brought to this through ambition for wealth or status. Which of the two mattered more to her, the sequel will show. For if she lives more luxuriously when in authority than she did as a subordinate, or claims any special privilege for herself beyond what is necessary, there can be no doubt that she coveted this. If she seeks more costly ornaments after than before, it is certain that she is swollen with vainglory. What she was before will afterwards appear, and her office will reveal whether what she displayed before was true virtue or pretence.

[140] Cf. Hab. 1: 16.
[141] 1 Pet. 5: 8.
[142] Job 40: 18.
[143] Cf. Job 1: 19.
[144] Cf. Gen. 3 and *Letter* 4, **10**.

37. Trahatur ad prelationem magis quam ueniat, dicente Domino: 'Omnes quotquot uenerunt,[a] fures sunt et latrones.'[145] '"Venerunt" ', inquit Ieronymus, 'non qui missi sunt.'[146] Sumatur pocius ad honorem quam sibi sumat honorem. Nemo enim, inquit Apostolus, 'sibi sumit honorem, sed qui uocatur a Deo, tamquam Aaron'.[147] Vocata lugeat tamquam ad mortem deducta; repulsa gaudeat tamquam a[b] morte liberata. Erubescimus ad uerba que dicimus ceteris meliores. Cum autem in electione nostra rebus ipsis hoc exhibetur, impudenter[c] sine pudore sumus. Quis enim nesciat meliores ceteris[d] preferendos? Vnde libro *Moralium*[e] quarto et uicesimo: 'Non [f]autem debet[f] hominum ducatum suscipere qui nescit homines [g]bene ammonendo increpare, ne qui ad hoc eligitur,[g] ut aliorum culpas corrigat, quod[h] resecare[i] debuit ipse committat.'[148] In qua tamen electione, si forte hanc impudentiam [j]aliquo leui uerbo repulsamus,[j] per aures oblatam recusamus dignitatem. Hanc profecto in nos[k] accusationem proferimus quo iustiores et digniores uideamur. O quot in electione sua flere uidimus corpore et ridere corde! Accusare se tamquam indignos, et per hoc gratiam sibi et fauorem humanum magis uenari, attendentes quod scriptum est: 'Iustus prior accusator est sui!'[149] Quos[l] postea, cum accusari contingeret et se eis occasio cedendi[m] offerret, importunissime et impudentissime suam sibi[n] prelationem deffendere nituntur quam se inuitos suscepisse fictis lacrimis et ueris accusationibus sui monstrauerant. [o]Quot in ecclesiis uidimus canonicos episcopis suis reluctantes cum ab eis ad sacros ordines cogerentur, et se indignos tantis ministeriis profitentes, nec omnino uelle adquiescere, quos cum forte clerus ad episcopatum postmodum eligeret nullam aut leuem perpessus est repulsam? Et qui heri, sicut aiebant, anime sue periculum uitantes diaconatum refugiebant, iam quasi una nocte iustificati de altiore gradu precipicium non uerentur.[o] [150] De qualibus quidem in ipsis scriptum est Prouer-

37 [a] veniunt *Amb* [b] *om. CE* [c] siue *add. C* [d] ceteros *T* [e] maiorum *C* [f–f] debet autem *TAmb* [g–g] bene ammonendo (admonendo *Amb*) increpare. Qui (et *C*) ad hoc eligitur (eligatur *CE*) *TCEAmb;* bene uiuendo praeire ne qui ad hoc eligitur *Gregory* [h] et *C* [i] resecari *codd., Amb;* resecare *Gregory* [j–j] aliquando (*?E*) leui uerborum repulsa tamen *TCEAmb;* aliquo leui uerbo repulsamus *my conj.* [k] uos *C* [l] Quid *C;* Quod *E* [m] *om. CE* [n] *om. CE* [o–o] *om. CE*

[145] John 10: 8.

[146] Jerome, *Dialogi aduersus Pelagianos*, ii. 17 (ed. Moreschini, p. 77; *PL* xxiii. 554).

[147] Heb. 5: 4.

[148] Gregory the Great, *Moralia in Iob*, xxiv. 25. 54 (ed. Adriaen, cxliiiB. 1228; *PL* lxxvi. 318).

37. She should be brought to office, not come to it herself, in accordance with the Lord's words: 'Those who have come of themselves are all thieves and robbers'[145]—'who have come', Jerome notes, not 'who were sent'.[146] She should be raised to the honour, not take it on herself, for 'nobody', the Apostle says, 'takes the honour on himself; he is called by God, as Aaron was'.[147] If called, she should mourn as though led to her death; if rejected, rejoice as though delivered from death. When we are said to be better than the rest we blush to hear the words, but when this is proved by the fact of our election, we shamelessly lose all shame. For who does not know that the better are preferable to the rest? So in the twenty-fourth book of *Morals* it is said: 'No one should undertake the leadership of men if he does not know how to rebuke men by admonishing them properly. Nor should the one chosen to correct the faults of others commit himself what he ought to have rooted out.'[148] But if in the election we try with some light word to reject this immodesty, and audibly decline the position offered, we immediately incur the charge of trying to appear more righteous and worthy than we are. How many have we seen at their election with tears in their eyes and laughter in their hearts, accusing themselves of unworthiness and thereby courting more approval and human support for themselves! They had in mind the words: 'The just man is the first to accuse himself',[149] but afterwards when they were blamed and given a chance to retire they were completely shameless and persistent in their efforts to defend the position which they had declared themselves unwilling to accept, with feigned tears and well-founded accusations of themselves. In how many churches have we seen canons resisting their bishops when compelled by them to take holy orders, professing themselves unworthy of such offices and quite unwilling to comply! Yet should the clergy subsequently elect them to the episcopate they are given only a frivolous refusal or none at all. And those who yesterday were avoiding the diaconate to escape endangering their souls, so they said, apparently find justification overnight, and have no fears of downfall from a higher office.[150] In the same book of Proverbs it

[149] Prov. 18: 17, also cited at **69** below.

[150] Julia Barrow, in a study of cathedral chapters in France, England, and Germany ('Grades of ordination and clerical careers, *c.* 900–*c.* 1200'), provides evidence of reluctance on the part of cathedral canons in the 12th c. to progress from the subdiaconate to higher clerical grades, and especially of reluctance to become priests, since priests were tied to the daily service of an altar and to full-time residence, and demand for priests to celebrate private masses was intensifying. But she suggests (p. 51) that 'it is likely that there was usually no serious shortage of candidates for the diaconate in cathedral chapters', although the diaconate did incur a higher level of responsibility.

biis: 'Homo stultus plaudet manibus cum spoponderit pro amico.'[151] Tunc enim miser gaudet unde pocius [p]lugendum ei[p] esset, cum ad regimen aliorum ueniens in cura subiectorum propria professione ligatur, a quibus magis amari quam timeri debet.

38. Cui profecto pestilentie quantum possumus prouidentes omnino interdicimus ne delicatius aut mollius uiuat prelata quam subiecta, ne priuatos habeat secessus ad comedendum uel dormiendum, sed cum sibi commisso grege cuncta peragat, et tanto eis amplius prouideat quanto eis[a] amplius presens assistit.[b] Scimus quidem beatum Benedictum de peregrinis et hospitibus maxime sollicitum mensam abbatis [c]cum illis seorsum[c] constituisse.[152] Quod licet tunc pie sit constitutum, postea tamen utilissima monasteriorum dispensatione ita est immutatum ut abbas a conuentu non recedat, et fidelem dispensatorem peregrinis prouideat. Facilis quippe est inter epulas lapsus,[153] et tunc discipline magis est inuigilandum. Multi etiam occasione hospitum sibi magis quam hospitibus propicii fiunt,[d] et hinc maxima suspitione leduntur absentes et murmurant.[154] [e]Et tanto prelati minor est auctoritas quanto eius uita suis est magis incognita. Tunc quoque tolerabilior omnibus quelibet habetur inopia, cum ab omnibus eque participatur, maxime uero a prelatis. Sicut in Catone quoque didicimus. Hic quippe, ut scriptum est, 'populo secum siciente' oblatum sibi aque paululum respuit et effudit 'suffecitque omnibus unda'.[fe] [155] Cum igitur prelatis maxime sobrietas sit necessaria, tanto eis parcius est uiuendum quanto per eos ceteris[g] prouidendum. Qui etiam ne donum Dei, hoc est prelationem sibi concessam, in superbiam conuertant, et maxime subiectis per hoc insultent, audiant quod scriptum est: 'Noli esse sicut leo in domo tua, euertens domesticos tuos et opprimens subiectos [h]tibi.'[156] [i]'Odibilis coram Deo [j]est et hominibus[j] superbia.'[157] '[k]Inicium superbie hominis apostatare a

[p–p] ei lugendum *CEAmb*

38 [a] eos *C* [b] assistat *CE;* assistet *Amb* [c–c] seorsum cum illis seorsum *ditto. TCE* [d] sunt *Amb* [e–e] *om. CE* [f] unde Lucanus ait *T; om. Amb* [g] est *add. CE* [h] beginning of lacuna in E, ending in 39*; E writes* etc. *here* [i] beginning of lacuna in C, ending in 39 [j–j] et hominibus est *Amb* [k–k] *om. Amb by homoeoteleuton*

[151] Prov. 17: 18.

[152] Benedict, *Rule*, c. 56. Cf. **112** below, *Letter* 6, **4** and *Adtendite* (ed. Engels, '*Adtendite a falsis prophetis*', p. 228, *ll.* 83–5).

[153] Cf. Jerome, *Letter* CXVII *ad matrem et filiam in Gallia commorantes*, 6 (ed. Hilberg, lv. 429, *ll.* 16–17; *PL* xxii. 957; cited in *Letter* 6, **5**: 'Difficile inter epulas seruatur pudicitia.'

is written of such people: 'A foolish man applauds when he stands as surety for a friend';[151] for the poor wretch rejoices though he should rather mourn when he assumed authority over others, and binds himself by his own declaration to caring for his subordinates, by whom he ought to be loved rather than feared.

38. To provide against this evil as far as we can we absolutely forbid the superior to live in greater luxury and comfort than her subordinates. She must not have private apartments for eating or sleeping, but should do everything along with the flock entrusted to her, and be better able to make provision for them the more she is present in their midst. We know of course that St Benedict was greatly concerned about pilgrims and guests and set a table apart for the abbot to be with them.[152] Though this was a pious provision at the time, it was afterwards amended by a dispensation which is highly beneficial to monasteries, whereby the abbot does not leave the monks but provides a faithful steward for the pilgrims; for it is easy for discipline to be relaxed at table,[153] and that is the time when it should be more strictly observed. There are many too who use hospitality as an opportunity to think of themselves rather than of their guests, so that those who are not present are troubled by the gravest suspicions and make complaints.[154] The authority of a superior is weakened the less his way of life is known to his people; moreover, any shortage there may be can be more easily accepted by all when it is shared by all, and especially by superiors. This we have learned from the example of Cato, who, it is written, 'when the people with him were thirsty', rejected and poured away the few drops of water offered him 'so that all were satisfied'.[155] Since therefore sobriety is so necessary for those in authority, they must live sparingly, and the more so as provision for the others rests with them. And lest they turn the gift of God, that is, the authority conferred on them, into pride, and so show themselves insolent to their subjects, let them hear what is written: 'Do not play the lion in your house, upsetting your household and oppressing your servants.'[156] 'Pride is hateful to God and man.'[157] 'The beginning of pride in man is renunciation of God,

[154] Cf. **101** below; *Adtendite* (ed. Engels, '*Adtendite a falsis prophetis*', p. 228, *ll.* 83–7) and *TChr*, ii. 57.

[155] Cf. Lucan, *De bello ciuili*, ix. 498–510. Cf. *Carmen ad Astralabium*, ed. Rubingh-Bosscher *vv.* 63–4 and, more generally, *TChr*, ii. 56–9.

[156] Ecclus. 4: 35.

[157] Ecclus. 10: 7

Deo, quoniam ab eo qui fecit illum recessit cor eius, quoniam inicium [l]omnis peccati est[l] superbia.'[k] [158] 'Sedes ducum superborum destruxit Dominus, et sedere fecit mites pro eis.'[159] 'Rectorem te posuerunt? Noli extolli. Esto in illis quasi unus ex ipsis.'[160] Et apostolus Tymotheum erga subiectos instruens, 'seniorem', inquit, 'ne increpaueris, sed obsecra ut patrem, iuniores ut fratres, anus ut matres, iuuenculas ut sorores'.[161] 'Non uos me', inquit Dominus, 'elegistis, sed ego elegi uos',[162] etc.[m]

39. Vniuersi alii prelati a subiectis eliguntur et ab eis creantur et constituuntur, quia non ad dominium[a] sed ad ministerium assumuntur.[b] Hic[c] autem solus uere est Dominus et subiectos sibi ad seruiendum habet eligere. Nec tamen se dominum sed ministrum exhibuit, et suos iam ad dignitatis arcem aspirantes proprio confutat exemplo dicens: 'Reges gentium dominantur eorum, et qui potestatem habent super eos, benefici uocantur. Vos autem non sic',[163] etc.[d] Reges igitur gentium imitatur quisquis in subiectis dominium appetit magis quam ministerium, et timeri magis quam amari satagit, et, de prelationis sue magisterio intumescens, 'amat primos recubitus in cenis et primas cathedras in synagogis et salutationes in foro et uocari ab hominibus Rabbi'.[164] Cuius quidem uocationis honorem ut nec nominibus gloriemur, et in omnibus humilitati prouideatur, 'uos autem', inquit Dominus, 'nolite uocari Rabbi. Et patrem nolite uocare[e] uobis[f] super terram.'[165] Et postremo uniuersam prohibens gloriationem, 'qui se', inquit, 'exaltauerit, humiliabitur'.[g] [166]

40. Prouidendum quoque est ne per absentiam pastorum grex periclitetur, et ne prelatis extrauagantibus intus disciplina torpeat. Statuimus itaque ut diaconissa magis spiritalibus quam corporalibus intendens nulla exteriore cura monasterium deserat, [a]set circa subiectas tanto sit magis sollicita quanto magis assidua, et tanto sit hominibus quoque presentia eius uenerabilior quanto rarior,[167] sicut[a] scriptum est: 'Aduocatus a potentiore, discede. Ex hoc enim magis te aduocabit.'[168] [b]Si qua uero legatione monasterium egeat, monachi uel

[l–l] peccati est omnis *codd.* [m] *om. Amb*

39 [a] Dominum *Amb* [b] adsumuntur *Amb* [c] Contra prelatos austeros *add. in marg. TAmb* [d] *om. Amb* [e] uocari *T* [f] *om. Amb* [g] *end of lacuna in CE, beginning in* 38

40 [a–a] *om. CE* [b] *beginning of lacuna in CE, ending in* 50; *CE write* etc. *here*

since the heart withdraws from God who made him, just as pride in any form is the beginning of sin.'[158] 'The Lord has overturned the seats of proud princes and enthroned the gentle in their place.'[159] 'Have they chosen you to preside? Do not put on airs; behave to them as one of themselves.'[160] And the Apostle in giving instructions to Timothy about his subordinates says: 'Never be harsh to an elder; appeal to him as though he were your father. Treat the younger men as brothers, the older women as mothers and the young as your sisters.'[161] 'You did not choose me', says the Lord, 'I chose you',[162] etc.

39. All other prelates are elected by their subjects and are created and set up by them, because they are chosen not to lord over men but to minister to them. God alone is truly Lord and has the power to choose his subjects for his service. Yet he did not show himself as a lord but as a servant, and when his disciples were already aspiring to high seats of power he rebuked them by his own example, saying: 'You know that in the world rulers lord it over their subjects, and those in authority are called benefactors; but it shall not be so with you',[163] etc. Whoever imitates such kings seeks lordship over his subjects rather than service to them and works to be feared, not loved, and being swollen with pride in his authority 'likes to have places of honour at feasts and the chief seats in the synagogue, to be greeted respectfully in the market place and to be addressed as Rabbi'. As for the honour of this title, we should not take pride in names but look to humility in everything. 'But you', says the Lord, 'must not be called Rabbi[164] and do not call any man on earth father.'[165] And afterwards he forbade self-glorification altogether, saying: 'Whoever exalts himself shall be humbled.'[166]

40. We must also make sure that the flock is not imperilled by the absence of its shepherds, and discipline slacken within when authority strays from its duties. And so we rule that the deaconess, whose care is for spiritual rather than material matters, must not leave her convent for any external concern, but be the more solicitous for her subordinates the more active she is. Thus her appearances in public will be more highly valued for their rarity,[167] as it is written: 'If a great man invites you, keep away, and he will be the more pressing in his invitation.'[168] But if the convent needs emissaries, the monks or their

[158] Ecclus. 10: 14–15.
[159] Ecclus. 10: 17.
[160] Ecclus. 32: 1.
[161] 1 Tim. 5: 1.
[162] John 15: 16.
[163] Luke 22: 25.
[164] Matt. 23: 6–7.
[165] Matt. 23: 8–9.
[166] Matt. 23: 12.
[167] 'tanto . . . quanto rarior': cf. *Letter* 1, **64**.
[168] Ecclus. 13: 12.

eorum conuersi ea fungantur. Semper enim uiros mulierum necessitudinibus oportet prouidere, et, quo earum maior religio, amplius uacant Deo et maiori uirorum egent patrocinio. Vnde et matris Domini curam agere Joseph ab angelo ammonetur quam tamen cognoscere non permittitur.[169] Et ipse Dominus moriens, quasi alterum filium matri sue prouidit, qui eius temporalem ageret curam.[170] Apostoli quoque quantam deuotis curam impenderent feminis dubium non est, ut iam satis alibi meminimus, quarum[c] etiam obsequiis diaconos septem instituerunt.[171] Quam quidem nos auctoritatem sequentes, ipsa etiam rei necessitate hoc exigente, decreuimus monachos et eorum conuersos, more apostolorum et diaconorum in hiis que ad exteriorem pertinent curam, monasteriis feminarum prouidere. Quibus maxime propter missas necessarii sunt monachi, propter opera uero conuersi.[172]

41. Oportet itaque, sicut Alexandrie sub Marcho euangelista legimus esse factum in ipso ecclesie nascentis exordio, ut monasteriis feminarum monasteria non desint uirorum,[173] et per eiusdem religionis uiros omnia extrinsecus feminis administrentur. Et tunc profecto monasteria feminarum firmius propositi sui religionem obseruare credimus si spiritalium uirorum prouidentia gubernentur, et idem tam ouium quam arietum pastor constituatur, ut qui uidelicet uiris ipse quoque presit feminis, et semper iuxta [a]institutionem apostolicam:[a] capud mulieris sit uir sicut uiri Christus et Christi Deus.[174] Vnde et monasterium beate Scolastice, in possessione fratrum monasterii situm, fratris quoque prouidentia regebatur, et crebra ipsius uel fratrum uisitatione instruebatur et consolabatur.[175]

42. De cuius quoque regiminis prouidentia beati Basilii *Regula*, quodam loco nos instruens, ita continet: 'Interrogatio: Si oportet

[c] quorum *T;* quarum *Amb*

41 [a–a] Apostolicam institutionem *Amb*

---

[169] Cf. Matt. 1: 20.

[170] Cf. John 19: 26; also *Letter* 1, **67**.

[171] Cf. Acts 6: 1–5; also *Letter* 7, **12**.

[172] On the monks and lay brothers at the Paraclete see Appendix A, 6. i and iv. According to *Institutiones nostre*, 8, no veiled sisters (that is, virgins who have received episcopal consecration) may ever leave their convent to undertake any business or to visit the home of any lay person. For matters concerning their order nuns and lay sisters who are trustworthy on account of their age as well as their example should be sent between the houses. No mention is made in *Institutiones nostre* of monks or lay brothers undertaking external tasks on the nuns' behalf: 'Quod non egredimur. Statutum tenemus quod nulla uelata causa cuiuscumque necessitatis egrediatur ad forensia negocia uel ingrediatur domum

lay brothers should supply them, for it is always men's duty to provide for women's needs, and the greater the religious devotion of the nuns, the more they give themselves up to God and have need of men's protection. And so Joseph was bidden by the angel to care for the mother of the Lord, though he was not allowed to sleep with her.[169] The Lord himself at his death chose for his mother a second son who should take care of her in material things.[170] There is no doubt either, as I have said sufficiently elsewhere, that the apostles paid great attention to devout women and appointed the seven deacons for their service.[171] We too, then, acting on this authority and in accordance with the demands of the situation, have decided that monks and lay brothers, like the apostles and deacons, shall provide for the external needs of convents of women. The monks are necessary especially to celebrate Mass, the lay brothers for other tasks.[172]

41. It is therefore essential, as we read was the practice in Alexandria under Mark the Evangelist in the early days of the infant Church, that monasteries of men should be near at hand for convents of women,[173] and that all external affairs should be conducted for the women through men of the same religious life. And indeed we believe that convents then maintain the religion of their calling more firmly, if they are ruled by the guidance of spiritual men, and the same shepherd is set over the ewes as well as the rams: that is, that women shall come under the same authority as men, and always in accordance with the ruling of the Apostle: woman's head is man as man's head is Christ and Christ's is God.[174] And so the convent of St Scholastica, which was situated on land belonging to the brethren of a monastery, was also under the supervision of one of the brothers, and was given both direction and comfort through frequent visits by him or the other brothers.[175]

42. A passage in the *Rule* of St Basil also instructs us on this kind of supervision: 'Question: Shall the presiding brother, apart from the

cuiuslibet secularis. Ad familiaria uero negocia et ad custodiam rerum nostrarum mittimus in domos nostras probatas tam etate quam uita et moniales et conuersas.' (*The Paraclete Statutes*, ed. Waddell, p. 11 (with commentary on pp. 109–17); *PL* clxxviii. 315A).

[173] Eusebius, *Historia ecclesiastica*, ii. 16. 1–2; 17. 19–24 (ed. Mommsen, pp. 141, 151–3; *SChr* xxxi. 71, 76–7; *PG* xx. 174AB, 178B–183B). Cf. Philo, *The Contemplative Life*, 32–3, 68–9, 83–9 (trans. Coulson, pp. 131–2, 155, 165–9); also *Letter* 7, 13–14.

[174] Cf. 1 Cor. 11: 3, and also Appendix A, 6. i.

[175] According to Gregory the Great, *Dialogi*, ii. 33 (ed. Vogüé, pp. 230–4; *PL* lxvi. 194AB), Benedict and some of his monks met his sister, Scholastica, once a year when she came to a house outside the gate of his monastery to talk about spiritual matters and to pray together.

eum qui preest, extra eam que sororibus preest, loqui aliquid quod ad edificationem pertineat uirginibus? Responsio: Et quomodo seruabitur illud preceptum Apostoli dicentis: "Omnia" uestra "honeste et secundum ordinem fiant?" '[176] [177] Item sequenti capitulo: 'Interrogatio: Si conuenit eum qui preest cum ea que sororibus preest frequenter loqui, et maxime si aliqui de fratribus per hoc leduntur? Responsio: Apostolo dicente: "Vt quid enim libertas iudicatur ab aliena conscientia?"'[178] Bonum est imitari eum dicentem: "Quia non sum usus[a] potestate mea,[b] ne offendiculum aliquod ponerem[c] euangelio Christi."[179] Et quantum fieri potest, et rarius uidende sunt et breuius est sermocinatio finienda.'[180] Hinc et illud est Hyspalensis concilii: 'Consensu communi decreuimus ut monasteria uirginum in prouincia Betica monachorum ministratione ac presidio gubernentur. Tunc enim salubria Christo dicatis uirginibus prouidemus quando eis spiritales patres eligimus, quorum non solum gubernaculis tueri, sed etiam doctrinis edificari possint. Hac tamen circa monachos cautela seruata ut, remoti ab earum peculiaritate, nec usque ad uestibulum habeant accedendi permissum familiare; sed[d] neque abbatem uel eum qui preficitur extra eam que preest loqui uirginibus Christi aliquid quod ad institutionem morum pertinet licebit. Nec cum sola que preest frequenter eum colloqui oportet, set sub testimonio duarum aut trium sororum. Ita ut rara sit accessio, breuis locutio. Absit enim ut[e] monachos, quod etiam dictu nephas est, Christi uirginibus familiares esse uelimus[f] sed, iuxta quod iussa regularia uel canonum ammonent, longe discretos atque seiunctos. Eorum tantum gubernaculis[g] easdem deputamus constituentes ut unus monachorum probatissimus eligatur cuius cure sit predia earum rusticana uel urbana intendere, fabricas struere, uel si quid aliud ad necessitatem monasterii prouidere, ut Christi famule pro anime sue tantum utilitate sollicite solis diuinis cultibus uiuant, operibus suis inseruiant. Sane is qui ab abbate suo proponitur[h] iudicio sui episcopi comprobetur. Vestes autem ille isdem cenobiis faciant a quibus tuitionem expectant.

42 [a] visus *Amb* [b] uti *add. TAmb* [c] *om. T; demus Vulg.;* darem *Rufinus* [d] et *Amb* [e] ne *add. Amb* [f] velim *Amb* [g] gabernaculis *T* [h] praeponitur *Amb*

[176] 1 Cor. 14: 40.

[177] Basil of Caesarea, *Regula a Rufino latine versa, Interrogatio* 197 (ed. Zelzer, pp. 215–16), included in the *Codex regularum* attributed to Benedict of Aniane (*PL* ciii. 551C). The *Rule* of St Basil (*c.*330–79) was translated into Latin by Rufinus *c.*396.

nun who presides over the sisters, say anything to edify the virgins? Answer: How else shall the precept of the Apostle be observed, which says: "Let all be done decently and in order"?'[176 177] And in the following chapter: 'Question: Is it seemly for him who presides to converse frequently with her who presides over the sisters, especially if some of the brethren are offended by this? Answer: Although the Apostle asks: "Is my freedom to be called in question by another man's conscience"?[178] It is good to follow him when he says: "But I have availed myself of no such right, lest I should offer any hindrance to the gospel of Christ."[179] As far as possible the sisters should be seldom seen and conversation kept brief.'[180] On this there is also the decision of the Council of Seville: 'By common consent we have decreed that the monasteries of virgins in the province of Baetica shall be ruled through the ministration and authority of monks. For we can best provide what is salutary for virgins dedicated to Christ by choosing for them spiritual fathers whose guidance can give them protection and whose teaching provide edification. But proper precautions must be taken so that the monks do not intrude on the privacy of the nuns, nor have general permission even to approach the entrance. Neither the abbot nor anyone in authority over them apart from their superior shall be permitted to say anything to the virgins of Christ concerning regulations for their moral life; nor should he speak often with the superior alone, but in the presence of two or three sisters. Access should be rare and speech brief. God forbid the unmentionable—that we should wish the monks to be familiar with the virgins of Christ; they must be kept separate and far apart, as the statutes of the rule and the canons lay down. We commit the nuns to their charge in the sense that one man, the best proved of the monks, shall be chosen to take over the management of their lands in the country or town, and also the erection of buildings, or provision of whatever else is needed by the convent, so that the handmaids of Christ may be concerned only with the welfare of their souls, may live only for divine worship and performance of their own works. Of course, the one proposed by his abbot must have the approval of his bishop. The sisters for their part should make clothing for the monasteries to which they look for guidance, since they will receive

[178] 1 Cor. 10: 29.

[179] Cf. 1 Cor. 9: 12.

[180] Basil of Caesarea, *Regula a Rufino latine versa, Interrogatio* 198 (ed. Zelzer, p. 216), included in the *Codex regularum* attributed to Benedict of Aniane (*PL* ciii. 551CD).

Ab hiisdem denuo, ut predictum est, laborum fructus et procurationis suffragium recepture.'[181]

43. Hanc nos itaque prouidentiam sequentes monasteria feminarum monasteriis uirorum ita semper esse subiecta uolumus ut sororum curam fratres agant,[182] et unus utriusque[a] tamquam pater presideat ad cuius prouidentiam utraque spectent monasteria, et utrorumque in Domino quasi 'unum sit ouile et unus pastor'.[183] Que quidem spiritalis fraternitatis societas tanto gratior tam Deo quam hominibus fuerit quanto ipsa perfectior omni sexui ad conuersionem uenienti sufficere possit, ut uidelicet monachi uiros, moniales feminas suscipiant, et omni anime de salute sua cogitanti possit ipsa consulere. Et quicumque cum uxore[b] uel matre aut sorore uel filia seu aliqua cuius curam gerit conuerti uoluerit, plenum ibi solacium reperire possit. Et tanto maioris caritatis affectu[c] sibi utraque monasteria sint connexa, et pro se inuicem sollicita, quanto que ibi sunt persone propinquitate aliqua uel affinitate amplius sunt coniuncte.[184]

44. Prepositum autem monachorum, quem abbatem nominant, sic etiam monialibus preesse uolumus ut eas, que Domini sponse sunt cuius ipse seruus est, proprias recognoscat dominas, nec eis preesse sed prodesse gaudeat. Et sit tamquam dispensator in domo regia qui non imperio dominam premit, set prouidentiam erga eam gerit ut ei de necessariis statim obediat, et in noxiis eam non audiat, et sic exterius cuncta minstret ut thalami secreta numquam nisi iussus introeat. Ad hunc igitur modum seruum Christi sponsis Christi prouidere uolumus, et[a] earum pro Christo fideliter curam gerere, et de omnibus que oportet cum diaconissa tractare, nec ea inconsulta quicquam de ancillis Christi uel de hiis que ad eas pertinent eum statuere, nec ipsum cuiquam earum nisi per eam quicquam precipere uel loqui presumere. Quociens uero eum diaconissa uocauerit ne tardet uenire, et que ipsa ei consuluerit de hiis quibus ipsa uel ei subiecte opus habent non moretur exequi quantum ualet. Vocatus

43 [a] vtrisque *Amb* [b] *om. Amb* [c] affectui *Amb*

44 [a] ut *T*

[181] *Concilium Hispalense*, AD 619, canon 11 (Mansi, *Concilia*, x. 560). Province of Baetica: in southern Spain, now Andalucía and part of Granada.

[182] 'ut sororum curam fratres agant': in letters of grace issued by Pope Adrian IV on 13 Feb. 1156, Heloise, abbess, and the sisters of the Paraclete were given licence to bury deceased brethren ('fratres') at the monastery (*Checklist* no. 422; *Cartulaire de l'abbaye du*

in return, as I said, the fruits of the monks' labour and support of their protection.'[181]

43. In accordance with this provision, then, we want convents of women always to be subject to monasteries of men, so that the brothers may take care of the sisters[182] and one man preside over both like a father whose authority each community shall recognize, and thus for both in the Lord 'there will be one flock and one shepherd'.[183] Such a society of spiritual brotherhood should be the more pleasing to God as it is to man, the more perfectly it is able to meet the needs of either sex coming for conversion, the monks taking in the men and the nuns the women, so that it can provide for every soul seeking its own salvation. And whoever wishes to be converted along with a mother, sister, daughter, or any other woman for whom he is responsible will be able to find complete consolation there, and the two monasteries should be joined by a greater affection of charity and a concern for each other the more closely their members are united by some kinship or affinity.[184]

44. The one placed in charge of the monks, whom they call the abbot, we want to preside over the nuns too in such a way that he regards those who are the brides of the Lord whose servant he is as his own ladies, and so be glad to serve them rather than rule them. He should be like a steward in a king's palace who does not oppress the queen by his powers but treats her wisely, so that he obeys her at once in necessary matters but pays no heed to what might be harmful, and performs all his services outside the bedchamber without ever penetrating its privacy unbidden. In this way, then, we want the servant of Christ to provide for the brides of Christ, to take charge of them faithfully for Christ, and to discuss everything necessary with the deaconess, so that he makes no decisions about the handmaids of Christ and their concerns without consulting her and issues no instructions or presumes to speak to any of them except through her. But whenever the deaconess summons him he should be prompt to come, and not delay carrying out as far as he is able whatever she advises him about the needs of herself or her subordinates. When

Paraclet, ed. Lalore, no. 8, pp. 16–17; also ed. Tribout de Morembert, 'Quatre bulles', p. 104).

[183] John 10: 16.

[184] On the presence of relatives of Heloise in the community of the Paraclete see *Letter* 1, 2, n. 6.

autem a diaconissa numquam nisi in manifesto et sub testimonio probatarum personarum ei loquatur, nec ei proximus adiungatur, nec prolixo sermone eam detineat.[185]

45. Omnia uero que ad uictum aut uestitum pertinent,[a] et si que etiam pecunie fuerint, aput ancillas Christi congregabuntur uel reseruabuntur, et inde fratribus necessaria tradentur de hiis que sororibus supererunt. Omnia itaque fratres exteriora procurabunt, et sorores ea tantum que intus a mulieribus agi conuenit, componendo scilicet uestes etiam fratrum uel abluendo, panem etiam conficiendo et ad coquendum tradendo et coctum suscipiendo. Ad ipsas etiam cura lactis et eorum que inde fiunt pertinebit, et gallinarum uel anserum nutritura, et quecumque conuenientius mulieres agere quam uiri possunt.

46. Ipse uero prepositus, quando constitutus fuerit, in presentia episcopi et sororum iurabit quod eis fidelis in Domino dispensator erit, et earum corpora a carnali contagio sollicite obseruabit. In quo si forte, quod absit, episcopus eum negligentem deprehenderit, statim eum tamquam periurii reum deponat.

47. Omnes quoque fratres in professionibus suis hoc se sororibus sacramento astringent[a] quod nullatenus eas grauari consencient et earum carnali mundicie pro posse suo prouidebunt. Nullus igitur uirorum nisi licentia prepositi ad sorores accessum habebit, nec aliquid eis missum nisi a preposito transmissum suscipietur.

48. Nulla umquam sororum septa monasterii egredietur, sed omnia exterius, sicut dictum est, fratres procurabunt, et in fortibus fortes sudabunt operibus.[186]

49. Nullus umquam fratrum septa hec ingredietur nisi obtenta[a] prepositi et diaconisse licentia, cum aliqua hoc necessaria uel honesta exegerit causa. Si quis forte contra hoc presumpserit, absque dilatione de monasterio proiiciatur.

45 [a] pertinet *Amb*

47 [a] adstringent *Amb*

49 [a] licentia *T;* obtenta *Amb*

[185] Dalarun, in 'Nouveaux Aperçus', pp. 57–65, presents a case for seeing in Abelard's endeavour here to strike a balance between the responsibilities of the abbot and of the deaconess of the Paraclete an indication that he knew the earliest statutes of the abbey of Fontevraud and that in this letter he was at times responding to them.

summoned by the deaconess he should speak to her openly, in the presence of approved persons, and not approach too near nor detain her with prolonged talk.[185]

45. Anything to do with food or clothing, and money too, if there is any, shall be collected amongst the handmaids of Christ, or set aside so that what is surplus to the sisters' requirements can be made over to the brothers. And so the brothers shall attend to all external affairs, and the sisters confine themselves to what can suitably be done indoors by women, such as making clothes for themselves and the brothers, doing the washing, kneading bread and putting it to bake, and handling it when baked. They shall also take charge of the milk and its products, and of feeding hens or geese, and whatever women can do more conveniently than men.

46. On his appointment the one placed in charge of the monks shall himself swear in the presence of the bishop and the sisters that he will be to them a faithful steward in the Lord, and will carefully keep their bodies from carnal contamination. If by chance, which God forbid, the bishop finds him negligent in this, he must depose him at once as guilty of perjury.

47. All the brothers too, in making their profession, shall bind themselves by oath to the sisters not to consent to harass them in any way, and to guarantee their bodily purity as far as they can. None of the men, therefore, except with the permission of their head, shall have access to the sisters, nor receive anything sent by them unless it comes from him.

48. None of the sisters shall ever leave the precincts of the convent, but everything outside, as was said above, shall be the brothers' concern, for men should sweat over men's work.[186]

49. None of the brothers shall ever enter these precincts, unless he has obtained leave from the one placed in charge and the deaconess for some necessary or worthy reason. If anyone ventures to do so, he shall be expelled from the monastery immediately.

[186] In *Institutiones nostre*, 6 and 8 provision is made for nuns and lay sisters, but not nuns who are also consecrated virgins, to go outside the convent on community business (*The Paraclete Statutes*, ed. Waddell, pp. 10, 11 (commentary on pp. 102, 109–17); *PL* clxxviii. 314D, 315A). Cf. n. 172 above.

50. Ne tamen uiri fortiores feminis in aliquo eas grauare presumant, statuimus eos quoque nichil presumere contra uoluntatem diaconisse, sed omnia ipsos etiam ad nutum eius peragere, et omnes pariter tam uiros quam feminas ei professionem facere, et obedientiam promittere, ut tanto pax firmior habeatur et melius seruetur concordia quanto fortioribus minus licebit, et tanto minus fortes debilibus obedire grauentur quanto earum uiolentiam minus uereantur. Et quanto amplius hic humiliauerit se apud Deum amplius exaltari certum sit.[a] [187]

51. Hec in presenti de diaconissa dicta sufficiant. Nunc ad officiales stylum inclinemus.

52. [a]Sacrista,[b] que et thesauraria, toti oratorio prouidebit, et omnes que ad ipsum pertinent claues et que ipsi necessaria sunt ipsa seruabit, et si que fuerint oblationes ipsa suscipiet; et de hiis que in oratorio [c]sunt necessaria[c] faciendis uel reficiendis et de toto eius ornatu curam aget. Ipsius quoque prouidere est de hostiis, de uasis et[d] libris altaris, et toto eius ornatu, de reliquiis, de incenso, de luminaribus, de horologio,[e] de signis pulsandis. Hostias uero, si fieri potest, uirgines conficiant, et frumentum purgent unde fiant, et altaris pallas abluant. Reliquias autem uel uasa altaris numquam ei uel alicui monialium contingere licebit, nec etiam pallas nisi cum eis tradite ad lauandum fuerint.[188] Sed ad hoc uel[f] monachi uel eorum conuersi uocabuntur et expectabuntur. Et si necesse fuerit, aliqui sub ea ad hoc officium instituantur, qui hec contingere cum opus fuerit digni sint, et archis ab ea reseratis hec inde ipsi sumant uel ibi reponant. Hec quidem que sanctuario presidet uite mundicia preeminere debet, et[g] que si fieri potest mente cum corpore sit integra, et eius tam abstinentia quam continentia sit probata. Hanc precipue de compoto lune instructam esse oportet ut secundum temporum rationem oratorio prouideat.[189]

53. Cantrix toti choro prouidebit et diuina disponet officia, et de doctrina cantandi uel legendi magisterium habebit, et de eis que ad scribendum pertinent uel dictandum. Armarium quoque librorum

50 [a] *end of lacuna in CE, beginning in* 40

52 [a] beginning of lacuna in CE, ending in 67 [a] Sacrifica *Amb* [c–c] necessaria sunt *Amb* [d] de *add. Amb* [e] horlogio *Amb* [f] *om. Amb* [g] *om. Amb*

[187] Cf. Matt. 23: 12.

50. But so that the men, being stronger than the women, shall not make too heavy demands on them, we make it a rule that they shall impose nothing against the will of the deaconess, but do everything at her bidding and, all alike, men and women, shall make profession to her and promise obedience; for peace will be more soundly based and harmony better preserved the less freedom is allowed to the stronger, while the men will be less burdened by obedience to the weaker women the less they have to fear violence from them. The more a man has humbled himself before God, the higher he will certainly be exalted.[187]

51. Let this be enough for the moment about the deaconess. Now let us turn our pen to the officers under her.

52. The Sacristan, who is also the Treasurer, shall provide for the whole oratory; and she herself must keep all the keys that belong to it and everything necessary to it. If there are any offerings she shall receive them, and she shall have charge of making or remaking whatever is needed in the oratory and caring for all its furnishings. It is her duty too to see to the hosts, the vessels, the books for the altar and all its fittings, the relics, incense, lights, clock, and striking of the bells. If possible the nuns should prepare the hosts themselves and purify the flour they are made from, and wash the altar-cloths. But neither the sacristan nor any of the sisters shall ever be allowed to touch the relics or the altar-vessels, nor even the altar-cloths except when these are given them to be washed.[188] They must summon the monks or the lay monks for this and await their coming. If necessary, some of them may be appointed to serve under the sacristan for this duty, who shall be thought fit to touch these things when the need arises, and take them out or replace them when she has unlocked the chests. The sister in charge of the sanctuary must be outstanding in purity of life, whole in mind as in body, if possible, and her abstinence and continence must be proved. She must be particularly well taught to calculate the phases of the moon, so that she can provide for the oratory according to the order of the seasons.[189]

53. The Chantress shall be responsible for the whole choir, and shall arrange the divine offices and direct the teaching of singing and reading, and of everything to do with writing or composition. She

[188] Cf. Burchard of Worms, *Decretum*, viii. 84 (*PL* cxl. 808B).

[189] One very widely circulated source of guidance for computing the course of the moon and the Paschal cycle was Bede's *De temporum ratione* (ed. Jones; trans. Wallis).

custodiet, et ipsos inde tradet atque suscipiet, et de ipsis scribendis uel aptandis curam suscipiet uel sollicita erit. Ipsa ordinabit quomodo sedeatur in choro et sedes dabit, et a quibus legendum sit uel cantandum prouidebit, et inscriptionem componet sabbatis recitandam in capitulo, ubi omnes ebdomadarie describantur.[a] [190] Propter que maxime litteratam eam esse conuenit, et precipue musicam non ignorare. Ipsa etiam post diaconissam toti discipline prouidebit et, si forte illa rebus alienis fuerit occupata, uices illius in hoc exequetur.[b] [191]

54. Infirmaria ministrabit infirmis, et eas obseruabit tam a culpa quam ab indigentia. Quicquid infirmitas postulauerit tam de cibis quam de balneis uel quibuscumque aliis est eis indulgendum. Notum [a]quippe est[a] prouerbium in talibus: 'Infirmis non est lex posita.'[192] Carnes eis nullatenus denegentur nisi sexta feria uel precipuis uigiliis aut ieiuniis quatuor temporum seu quadragesime. A peccato autem tanto amplius coherceantur quanto amplius de exitu suo cogitandum incumbit. Maxime uero tunc silentio studendum est in quo exceditur plurimum et orationi instandum sicut scriptum est: 'Fili, in tua infirmitate ne despicias teipsum, sed ora Deum et ipse curabit te. Auertere a delicto et dirige manus, et ab omni delicto munda cor tuum.'[193] Oportet quoque infirmis prouidam semper assistere custodiam que cum opus fuerit statim subueniat[194] et domum omnibus instructam esse que infirmitati illi sunt necessaria. De medicamentis quoque, si necesse est, pro facultate loci prouidendum erit. Quod facilius fieri poterit si que infirmis preest non fuerit expers medicine. Ad quam etiam de hiis que sanguinem minuunt cura pertinebit. Oportet autem aliquam flebotomie[b] peritam esse, ne uirum propter hoc ad mulieres ingredi necesse sit. Prouidendum [c]etiam est[c] de officiis horarum et communione, ne desint infirmis ut saltem dominico die communicetur, confessione semper et satisfactione quam potuerint preeuntibus. De

53 [a] scribentur (*exp.*) describantur *T;* describentur *Amb* [b] infirmaria *add. T*

54 [a–a] est quippe *Amb* [b] fleobotomie *T;* flebotomiae *Amb* [c–c] est etiam *Amb*

[190] In his *Rule*, especially in c. 11, 35 and 63, Benedict had outlined his idea of 'ordo' in the monastery, which included arrangements for sitting in choir and for the tasks of each week.

[191] The last sentence of the section on the chantress ends in *T* (*CE* here lack text) with the word *infirmaria*, is followed by a space on the line, and then by a paragraph marker and an initial capital to start a new section on a new line, *Infirmaria ministrabit infirmis. . .* It seems more likely that the first *infirmaria*, not found in *Amb*, is a mistake and that the correct reading should show that the chantress (*ipsa*) is responsible after the deaconess for

shall also take charge of the book-cupboard, shall hand books out from it and receive them back, undertake the task of copying or binding them, or see that this is done. She shall decide how the sisters are to sit in choir and assign the seats, arrange who are to read or sing, and shall draw up the list, to be recited on Saturdays in Chapter, in which all the duties of the week are set out.[190] Hence it is most important for her to be lettered, and especially to have some knowledge of music. She shall also be responsible for all instruction after the deaconess and, if she is otherwise engaged, shall take her place.[191]

54. The Infirmarian shall take care of the sick, and shall protect them from sin as well as from want. Whatever their sickness requires, baths, food or anything else, is to be allowed them; for there is a well-known saying: 'No law has been laid down for the sick.'[192] Meat is not to be denied them on any account, except on the sixth day of the week or on the chief vigils or the fasts of the Ember Days or of Lent. But they should all the more be restrained from sin the more it is incumbent on them to think of their departure. That is the time when they should most observe silence, as they are very near their end, and concentrate on prayer, as it is written: 'My son, if you have an illness, do not neglect it but pray to the Lord, and he will heal you. Renounce your sin, amend your ways, and cleanse your heart from all sin.'[193] There must also be a watchful nurse always with the sick to answer their call at once when needed,[194] and the infirmary must be equipped with everything necessary for their illness. Medicaments too must be provided, according to the resources of the convent, and this can more easily be done if the sister in charge of the sick has some knowledge of medicine. Those who have a period of bleeding shall also be in her care. And there should be someone with experience of blood-letting, or it would be necessary for a man to come in amongst the women for this purpose. Provision must also be made for the sick not to miss the offices of the Hours and communion; on the Lord's Day at least they should communicate, as far as possible always after confession and penance.

all instruction, and if the deaconess (*illa*) is otherwise engaged should take her place. The infirmarian, busy with the sick in the infirmary, seems less likely to be called upon for this. *Institutiones nostre* shed no light on the uncertainty; they provide for a prioress in addition to an abbess and a chantress.

[192] Not found but cf. *Carmen ad Astralabium*, ed. Rubingh-Bosscher, *v.* 597: 'Infirmis legem positam non esse fatemur' and 1 Tim. 1: 9: 'lex iusto non est posita, sed iniustis' (I owe this reference to Carolinne White).

[193] Ecclus. 38: 9–10.

[194] Cf. Benedict, *Rule*, c. 36, 7.

unctione quoque infirmorum beati Iacobi apostoli sententia sollicite custodiatur,[195] ad quam quidem faciendam, tunc maxime cum de uita egrotantis desperatur, inducantur ex monachis duo seniores sacerdotes cum diacono qui sanctificatum oleum secum afferant et, conuentu sororum assistente, interposito tamen pariete, ipsi hoc celebrent sacramentum. Similiter, cum opus fuerit, de communione agatur. Oportet itaque domum infirmarum sic aptari ut ad hec facienda monachi facilem habeant accessum et recessum, nec conuentum uidentes nec ab eo uisi.

55. Singulis autem diebus semel ad minus diaconissa cum celleraria infirmam tamquam Christum uisitent ut de necessitatibus eius sollicite prouideant, tam in corporalibus quam spiritualibus, et illud a Domino audire mereantur: 'Infirmus eram et uisitastis[a] me.'[196]

56. Quod si egrotans ad exitum propinquauerit, et in extasi agonie uenerit, statim aliqua ei assistens ad conuentum properet cum tabula et eam pulsans exitum sororis nunciet, totusque conuentus quacumque[a] hora sit diei uel noctis ad morientem festinet, nisi ecclesiasticis prepediatur[b] officiis. Quod si acciderit, quod nichil est operi Dei preponendum,[197] satis est diaconissam cum aliquibus quas elegerit accelerare et conuentum postmodum sequi. Quecumque uero ad hunc tabule pulsum[c] occurrerint statim letaniam inchoent quousque sanctorum et sanctarum inuocatio compleatur, et tunc uel[d] psalmi uel cetera que ad exequias pertinent subsequantur. Quam salubre uero sit ad infirmos ire siue mortuos, Ecclesiastes diligentur attendens ait: 'Melius est ire ad domum luctus quam ad domum conuiuii. In illa enim finis cunctorum amonetur hominum, et uiuens cogitat quid futurus[e] sit.'[198] Item: 'Cor sapientium ubi tristicia est [f]et cor stultorum ubi leticia.'[f][199]

57. Defuncte[a] uero corpusculum a sororibus statim abluatur et aliqua uili sed munda interula et caligis indutum feretro imponatur, uelo capite obuoluto. Que quidem indumenta firmiter corpori consuantur siue ligentur nec ulterius moueantur. Ipsum corpus a sororibus in

55 [a] visitasti *Amb*

56 [a] quaecumque *Amb* [b] impediatur *Amb*[1] [c] cursum *T* [d] *om. Amb* [e] futurum *Vulg.* [f-f] *om. Amb*

57 [a] *T opens a new section here*

[195] Cf. Jas. 5: 14

For the anointing of the sick, the precept of St James the apostle is to be carefully observed,[195] and in order to do this, especially when the sick woman's life is despaired of, two of the older priests with a deacon must be brought in from the monks, bringing with them the holy oil; then they must administer the sacrament in the presence of the whole convent, though divided off by a screen. Communion shall be celebrated when needed in the same way. It is therefore essential for the infirmary to be so arranged that the monks can easily come and go to administer these sacraments without seeing the sisters or being seen by them.

55. Once at least every day the deaconess and the Cellaress should visit the sick woman as if she were Christ, so that they may carefully provide for her bodily as well as her spiritual needs, and show themselves worthy to hear the words of the Lord: 'I was sick and you visited me.'[196]

56. But if the sick woman is near her end and has reached her death-agony, someone who is with her must at once go quickly through the convent beating on a wooden board to give warning of the sister's departure. The whole convent, whatever the hour of day or night, must then hurry to the dying, unless prevented by the offices of the Church. Should this happen, as nothing must come before the work of God,[197] it is enough if the deaconess and a few others she has chosen shall hasten there and the convent follow later. Those who gather at the beating of the board should begin the Litany at once, until the invocation of the saints, male and female, is completed, and then either psalms should follow or other prayers of death. How salutary it is to go to the sick or the dead Ecclesiastes points out with care, when he says: 'Better to go to the house of mourning than to the house of feasting; for there a warning is given of the lot of every man, and the living should take this to heart.'[198] Likewise: 'The wise man's heart is where there is grief, and the fool's heart where there is joy.'[199]

57. The body of the dead woman must then be washed at once by the sisters, clad in some cheap but clean garment and stockings, and laid on a bier, her head covered by the veil. These coverings must be firmly stitched or bound to the body and not afterwards removed. The body

[196] Matt. 25: 36; also Benedict, *Rule*, c. 36, 1–2.
[197] Cf. Benedict, *Rule*, c. 43, 3.
[198] Eccles. 7: 3.
[199] Eccles. 7: 5.

ecclesia delatum monachi cum oportuerit sepulture tradant, et sorores interim in oratorio psalmodie uel orationibus intente uacabunt. Diaconisse uero sepultura id tantum pre ceteris habeat honoris ut cilicio solo totum eius corpus inuoluatur et in eo quasi in sacco tota consuatur.

58. Vestiaria[a] totum quod ad curam indumentorum spectat prouidebit tam in calciamentis scilicet quam in ceteris omnibus. Ipsa tonderi oues faciet, coria calciamentorum suscipiet. Linum seu lanam excolet et colliget et totam curam telarum habebit. Filum et acum et forfices omnibus ministrabit. Totam dormitorii curam habebit et stratis omnibus prouidebit. De mantilibus quoque mensarum et manutergiis et uniuersis pannis curam aget incidendis, suendis, abluendis. Ad hanc maxime illud pertinet: 'Quesiuit lanam et linum et operata est consilio manuum suarum. Manum suam misit ad colum et digiti sui apprehenderunt fusum. Non timebit domui sue a frigoribus niuis. Omnes enim domestici eius uestiti duplicibus et ridebit in die nouissimo. Considerauit semitas domus sue et panem ociosa non comedit. Surrexerunt filii eius et beatissimam predicauerunt eam.'[200] Hec suorum operum habebit instrumenta et prouidebit de suis operibus que quibus debeat iniungere sororibus. Ipsa enim nouiciarum curam aget donec in congregationem suscipiantur.

59. Celleraria curam habebit de hiis omnibus que pertinent ad uictum, de cellario, refectorio, coquina, molendino, pistrino cum furno, de hortis etiam et uiridariis et agrorum tota cultura, de apibus quoque, armentis et pecoribus cunctis, seu auibus necessariis. Ab ipsa requiretur quicquid de cibis necessarium erit. Hanc maxime non esse auaram conuenit sed promptam et uoluntariam ad omnia necessaria tribuenda. 'Hilarem enim datorem diligit Deus.'[201] Quam omnino prohibemus ne de administrationis sue dispensatione sibi magis quam aliis sit propicia nec priuata sibi paret fercula nec sibi reseruet quod[a] aliis defraudet. 'Optimus', inquit Ieronimus, 'est dispensator qui sibi nichil reseruat.'[202] Iudas, sue dispensationis abutens officio, cum loculos haberet de cetu periit apostolico.[203] Ananias quoque et Saphira uxor eius sua[b] retinendo sententiam mortis exceperunt.[204]

58 [a] Vestiararia *T*

59 [a] quae *Amb* [b] *om. Amb*

[200] Prov. 31: 13, 19, 21, 25, 27–8. [201] 2 Cor. 9: 7.

[202] Jerome, *Epistola* LII *ad Nepotianum*, 16 (ed. Hilberg, liv. 440, *ll.* 5–6; *PL* xxii. 539).

shall be carried into the church by the sisters for the monks to give it proper burial, and the sisters meanwhile shall devote themselves to psalm-singing and prayer in the oratory. The burial of a deaconess shall have only one feature to distinguish it from that of others: her entire body shall be wrapped only in a cloth of hair and sewn up in this as in a sack.

58. The Wardrober shall be in charge of everything to do with clothing, and this includes shoes. She shall have the sheep shorn and receive the hides for shoes, spin and card flax or wool, take entire charge of weaving, and supply everyone with needle, thread, and scissors. She shall also be personally responsible for the dormitory and provide bedding for all, and also for tablecloths, towels, and cloths of every kind, and shall see to cutting and sewing and also washing them. To her especially the words apply: 'She seeks wool and flax and works by the skill of her hands. She sets her hand to the distaff and her fingers grasp the spindle. She will have no fear for her household when it snows, for all her servants are wrapped in two cloaks and she can laugh at tomorrow. She keeps her eye on the ways of her household and does not eat the bread of idleness. Her sons rise up and call her blessed.'[200] She shall keep the tools necessary for her work, and shall arrange what part of it to assign to which of the sisters. She shall have charge of the novices until they are admitted into the community.

59. The Cellaress shall be responsible for everything connected with food, for the cellar, refectory, kitchen, mill, bakehouse and its oven, and also the gardens, orchards, and the entire cultivation of the fields. She shall also take charge of bees, herds, and all livestock, and all the poultry that is needed. She shall be expected to provide all the essentials to do with food, and it is most important that she should not be grudging but ready and willing to provide everything required. 'For God loves a cheerful giver.'[201] We absolutely forbid her to favour herself above the others in dispensing her stores; she must neither prepare private dishes for herself nor keep anything for herself by defrauding the others of it. 'The best steward', says Jerome, 'is one who keeps nothing for himself.'[202] Judas abused his office of steward when he had charge of the common purse and left the company of the apostles.[203] Ananias too and Sapphira his wife were condemned to death for keeping money back.[204]

[203] Cf. John 13: 29–30.
[204] Cf. Acts 5: 1–11; also **109** below and Benedict, *Rule*, c. 57, 5–6.

60. Ad portariam siue hostiariam, quod idem est, pertinet de suscipiendis hospitibus uel quibuslibet aduenientibus et de hiis nunciandis uel adducendis ubi oporteat et de cura hospitalitatis. Hanc etate et mente discretam esse conuenit ut sciat accipere responsum et reddere et que uel qualiter suscipiendi sint an non sint diiudicare.[205] Ex qua maxime tamquam ex uestibulo Domini religionem monasterii decorari oportet cum ab ipsa eius noticia incipiat. Sit igitur blanda[a] uerbis, mitis alloquio, ut in hiis quoque quos excluserit conuenienti reddita ratione caritatem studeat edificare. Hinc enim scriptum est: 'Responsio mollis frangit iram; sermo durus suscitat furorem.'[206] Et alibi: 'Verbum dulce multiplicat amicos et mitigat inimicos.'[207] Ipsa quoque sepius pauperes uidens meliusque cognoscens, si qua eis de cibis aut uestimentis distribuenda sunt, distribuet. Tam ipsa uero quam cetere officiales, si suffragio uel solatio aliquarum eguerint, dentur eis a diaconissa uicarie.[208] Quas precipue de conuersis assumi conuenit ne aliqua umquam monialium diuinis desit officiis siue capitulo uel refectorio.[209]

61. Domunculam iuxta portam habeat in qua ipsa uel eius uicaria presto sit semper aduenientibus,[210] ubi etiam ociose non maneant, et tanto amplius silentio studeant quanto earum loquacitas hiis quoque qui extra sunt facilius potest innotescere. Ipsius profecto est non solum homines quos oportet arcere, uerum etiam rumores penitus excludere, ne ad conuentum temere deferantur; et ab ipsa est exigendum quidquid[a] in hoc quoque fuerit excessum. Si quid uero audierit quod scitu opus sit, ad diaconissam secreto referet ut ipsa super hoc si placet deliberet. Mox autem, ut ad portam pulsatum uel inclamatum fuerit, que[b] presto est querat a superuenientibus qui sint aut quid uelint portamque si opportuerit statim aperiat ut aduenientes suscipiat. Solas quippe feminas intus hospitari licebit. Viri autem ad monachos dirigentur. Nullus itaque aliqua de causa intus admittetur nisi consulta prius et iubente diaconissa. Feminis autem statim patebit introitus. Susceptas uero feminas seu uiros quacumque occasione introeuntes portaria in cellula sua pausare faciet donec a diaconissa uel sororibus, si necessarium est uel oportunum, eis

60 [a] blandis *Amb*

61 [a] quicquid *Amb* [b] qui *T*

---

[205] Cf. Benedict, *Rule*, c. 66, 1.

[206] Prov. 15: 1. Cf. *Carmen ad Astralabium*, ed. Rubingh-Bosscher *vv.* 695–6.

60. The Portress or Doorkeeper (which means the same) has the duty of receiving guests and all comers, announcing them or bringing them to the proper place, and dispensing hospitality. She should be discreet in years and mind, so that she will know how to receive and give an answer, and to decide who and who not to admit, and in what way.[205] She especially, as if she were the vestibule of the Lord, should be an ornament for the religious life of the convent, since knowledge of it starts with her. She should therefore be gentle of speech and mild in manner, and should try by giving a suitable reason to establish a friendly relationship even with those she has to turn away. For it is written: 'A soft answer turns away anger, but a sharp word makes tempers hot.'[206] And elsewhere: 'A pleasant word wins many friends and soothes enemies.'[207] She also, as she sees the poor more regularly and knows them better, should share out what food and clothing there is for distribution; but if she or any of the officials need support or comfort, the deaconess should appoint deputies for them,[208] taking these generally from the lay sisters, lest some of the nuns are absent from the divine offices or from Chapter or the refectory.[209]

61. The Portress should have a lodge by the gate, where she or her deputy can always be ready for visitors;[210] they must not sit idle and, as their talk may easily be heard outside, they should be careful to observe silence. Indeed, her duty is not only to deny entrance to people who must be kept out but also to exclude entirely any rumours, so that they are not carelessly allowed into the convent, and she must be called to account for any failure in this matter. But if she hears what ought to be known, she should report it privately to the deaconess so that she may think it over if she wishes. As soon as there is any knocking or clamour at the gate the Portress must ask the newcomers who they are and what they want and, if necessary, open the gate at once to admit them. Only women shall be entertained inside; men must be directed to the monks. Thus no man may be admitted for any reason, unless the deaconess has been previously consulted and has issued instructions, but entrance shall be granted to women at once. The women when admitted, or the men allowed to enter on some occasion, must be made to wait by the Portress in her cell, until the deaconess or the sisters, if it is necessary or fitting, shall

[207] Ecclus. 6: 5. [208] Cf. Benedict, *Rule*, c. 66, 5.
[209] On the lay sisters and lay brothers see Appendix A, 6. iv.
[210] Cf. Benedict, *Rule*, c. 66, 2.

occurratur. Pauperibus uero que ablutione pedum indigent hanc quoque hospitalitatis gratiam ipsa diaconissa seu sorores diligenter exhibeant.[211] Nam et apostolis[c] ex hoc Dominus[d] precipue humanitatis obsequio dictus est diaconus, sicut in *Vitis* quoque *Patrum* quidam ipsorum meminit dicens: 'Propter te homo Saluator factus diaconus, precingens se lintheo, lauit pedes discipulorum precipiens eis fratrum pedes lauare.'[212] Hinc Apostolus de diaconissa meminit dicens: 'Si hospicio recepit, si sanctorum pedes lauit.'[213] Et ipse Dominus: 'Hospes', inquit, 'eram et collegistis me.'[214]

62. Officiales omnes preter cantricem de hiis instituantur que litteris non intendunt si ad hoc tales reperiri possint ydonee ut litteris uacare liberius queant.

63. Oratorii ornamenta necessaria sint, non superflua, munda magis quam preciosa. Nichil igitur in eo de auro uel de argento compositum sit preter unum calicem argenteum uel plures etiam si necesse sit. Nulla de serico sint ornamenta preter stolas aut phanones. Nulla in eo sint ymaginum sculptilia. Crux ibi lignea tantum erigatur ad altare in qua si forte ymaginem Saluatoris placeat depingi non est prohibendum. Nullas uero alias ymagines altaria cognoscant. Campanis duabus monasterium sit contentum. Vas aque benedicte ad introitum oratorii extra collocetur ut ea sanctificentur mane ingressure uel post Completorium egresse.[a]

64. Nulle monialium horis desint canonicis sed statim, ut pulsatum fuerit signum, omnibus aliis postpositis ad diuinum properetur officium, modesto tamen incessu.[215] Introeuntes autem secreto oratorium dicant que poterunt: 'Introibo in domum tuam, adorabo ad templum sanctum tuum',[216] etc. Nullus in choro liber teneatur nisi officio presenti necessarius. Psalmi aperte et distincte ad intelligendum

[c] apostolus *TAmb* [d] *om. Amb*

63 [a] *in T there follows a space adequate for 7 characters*

[211] A story was told in the 13th c. by Étienne de Bourbon, a Dominican friar, of how Abelard ('magister Petrus Abalar') had been shabbily treated when visiting an abbey poorly clad and on foot but received with honour on a later occasion when he arrived in splendour with a mounted escort. On being invited to address the monks in their chapter he rebuked them, asking how they would have received Christ. See *Anecdotes historiques, légendes et apologues tirés du recueil inédit d'Étienne de Bourbon, dominicain du XIIIe siècle*, ed. Lecoy de la Marche (Société de l'histoire de France; Paris, 1877), no. 508, p. 439; summary in French in Lecoy de la Marche, *L'Esprit de nos aïeux, anecdotes et bons mots tirés des manuscrits du XIIIe siècle* (Paris 1888), pp. 56–7. For a scriptural parallel cf. Jas. 2: 1–9. Professor Robert E. Lerner has kindly drawn to my attention another story told in a 13th-c. sermon about

come to them. In the case of poor women whose feet need to be washed, the deaconess herself or the sisters shall duly perform this charitable act of hospitality.[211] For the Lord too was called deacon by the apostles chiefly for this service to humanity, as someone has recorded in the *Lives of the Fathers*, saying: 'For you, O men, the Saviour became a deacon, girding himself with a towel and washing the disciples' feet, and telling them to wash their brothers' feet.'[212] And so the Apostle says of the deaconess: 'If she has given hospitality and washed the feet of God's people.'[213] And the Lord himself says: 'I was a stranger, and you took me in.'[214]

62. All the officials, except the Chantress, should be chosen from the sisters who do not study letters if there are others better fitted to make use of greater freedom for their studies.

63. The ornaments for the oratory should be necessary, not superfluous, and clean rather than costly. There should be nothing made of gold or silver in it apart from one silver chalice, or more than one if needed. There must be no furnishings of silk, apart from the stoles or maniples, and no carved images. Nothing but a wooden cross shall be set up on the altar there, though if the sisters like to paint the statue of the Saviour, that is not forbidden. But the altars must have no other statues. The convent must be content with a pair of bells. A vessel of holy water should be set outside the entrance to the oratory, for the sisters to bless themselves with when they go in in the morning and come out after Compline.

64. None of the nuns may be absent from the canonical hours, but as soon as the bell is rung, everything must be put down and each sister go quickly, with modest gait, to the divine office.[215] As they come separately into the oratory, let all who can, say: 'Through thy great love I shall come into thy house, and bow low towards thy holy temple',[216] etc. No book is to be kept in the choir except the one needed for the office at the time. The psalms should be said clearly and

people who do not, as Christ had done, wash the feet of the poor but pour ointment only on the heads of the rich: 'Hii sunt personarum acceptores, maioribus (*ed.* marioribus) adulantes, quos magister Petrus Abalardus confundit in sermone suo dum capam suam purpuream exspolians adorauit'; ed. N. Bériou, 'La Madeleine dans les sermons parisiens du XIIIe siècle', *Mélanges de l'École française de Rome. Moyen Âge*, 104 (1992), p. 317.

[212] *Vitae patrum, Verba seniorum*, vi. 4. 8 (*PL* lxxiii. 1016).

[213] 1 Tim. 5: 10; cf. *Letter* 7, **20**.

[214] Matt. 25: 35.

[215] Cf. Benedict, *Rule*, c. 43, 1–2.

[216] Ps. 5: 8 (7).

dicantur, et tam moderata sit psalmodia uel cantus ut que uocem habent infirmam sustinere ualeant. Nichil in ecclesia legatur aut cantetur nisi de autentica sumptum scriptura, maxime autem de nouo uel ueteri testamento.[217] Que utraque sic per lectiones distribuantur ut ex integro per annum in ecclesia legantur. Expositiones uero ipsorum uel sermones doctorum seu quelibet scripture aliquid edificationis habentes ad mensam uel in capitulo recitentur, et ubicumque opus sit omnium lectio concedatur.[218] Nulla autem legere uel cantare presumat nisi quod prius preuiderit. Si qua forte di hiis aliquid in oratorio uiciose protulerit, ibidem supplicando coram omnibus satisfaciat secreto dicens: 'Ignosce, Domine, etiam hac uice negligentie mee.'[219]

65. Media[a] autem nocte, secundum institutionem propheticam, ad Vigilias nocturnas surgendum est propter quod adeo tempestiue cubandum est ut has uigilias ferre natura ualeat infirma,[220] et omnia que ad diem pertinent cum luce fieri possint, sicut et beatus Benedictus instituit.[221] Post Vigilias autem ad dormitorium redeatur antequam hora matutinarum Laudum pulsetur. Et si quid noctis adhuc superest, infirme sompnus non negetur nature. Maxime namque sompnus lassatam recreat naturam[222] et pacientem operis reddit et sobriam conseruat et alacrem. Si que tamen psalterii uel aliquarum lectionum meditatione indigent, ut beatus quoque meminit Benedictus, uacare ita debent ut quiescentes non inquietent.[223] Ideo namque meditationi hoc loco potius quam lectioni dixit ne lectio aliquorum quietem impediret aliorum. Qui etiam cum ait: 'A fratribus qui indigent',[224] profecto nec ad hanc meditationem compulit. Nonnumquam tamen si doctrina etiam cantus opus est, de hoc similiter prouidendum est hiis quibus necesse est.

65 [a] *T opens a new section here, on a new line and inset from the margin*

[217] Cf. Benedict, *Rule*, c. 9, 8.

[218] A very full guide, known as the *Ordinary of the Paraclete*, to the choice and arrangement of liturgical material at the Paraclete, including hymns and the cycle of readings in the church, the refectory, and the cloister, as well as a guide to processions and accompanying chants, and indications too of books in the abbey in which such materials will be found, survives in a late 13th-c. MS in Paris, BnF fr. 14410. This is a translation into Old French of an earlier Latin manuscript. The late 15th- or early 16th-c. MS Chaumont, Bibliothèque municipale 31—the *Breviary of the Paraclete*—supplements this material with texts for the day and night Offices; these show that little alteration was made over the intervening centuries. Most of the material shows Cistercian influence, but some is also taken from contributions made by Abelard, which include, besides hymns and sermons, many shorter pieces. On all this Chrysogonus Waddell is an outstanding guide; see

distinctly so as to be understood, and any chanting or singing must be pitched so that anyone with a weak voice can sustain the note. Nothing may be said or sung in church which is not taken from an authoritative source, and chiefly from the Old or New Testament.[217] These are to be divided amongst the lessons so that both are read in their entirety in the course of the year. But expositions of the Scriptures or sermons of the Doctors of the Church or any other writings of an edifying nature shall be read aloud in the refectory or in Chapter; the reading of all these is permitted where the need is felt.[218] No one must presume to read or sing without previous preparation, and if anyone happens to mispronounce something in the oratory, she must make amends on the spot by prayer in the presence of all, saying softly to herself: 'Yet again, Lord, forgive my carelessness.'[219]

65. All must rise at midnight for the nocturnal Vigils as the prophet enjoins, and so they must retire to bed early, so that their weak nature can sustain these Vigils[220] and all the tasks for the day can be done in daylight, as St Benedict also laid down.[221] After the Vigils they should return to the dormitory until the hour is struck for morning Lauds. If any of the night still remains, sleep should not be denied their weakness, for sleep more than anything refreshes weary nature,[222] makes it able to endure toil, and keeps it equable and alert. However, if any feel a need to meditate on the Psalter or some of the readings, as St Benedict also says, they should devote themselves to this but without disturbing those who are asleep,[223] for Benedict refers here to meditation rather than reading, lest the reading of some disturb the sleep of others. And when he spoke of 'the brothers who feel a need',[224] he was certainly not compelling anyone to meditate in this way. But if there is sometimes also a need for instruction in chanting, this will also have to be met for those for whom it is necessary.

Waddell, *The Old French Paraclete Ordinary and the Paraclete Breviary*, ed. Waddell (2 vols.) and *The Paraclete Breviary* (*Bre* IIIA–C), ed. Waddell, and the Introduction above at pp. xxxvii–xxxviii; also for sermons for the Paraclete see *I sermoni di Abelardo per le monache del Paracleto*, ed. De Santis, pp. 29–32. On the possibility that the *Ordinary* indicates that the Paraclete book collection included a copy of the exposition of Ezekiel which Abelard began to write at Laon (*Letter* 1, 11) see *The Old French Paraclete Ordinary*, ed. Waddell, i, *Introduction*, pp. 167–9.

[219] Cf. Benedict, *Rule*, c. 45.

[220] Cf. Ps. 118 (119): 62; Benedict, *Rule*, c. 16, 4; 8.

[221] Cf. Benedict, *Rule* c. 41, 8–9.

[222] Cf. *Collationes* 16 (ed. Marenbon and Orlandi, p. 20; *Dialogus*, ed. Thomas, *ll.* 275–6; *PL* clxxviii. 1618B).

[223] Cf. Benedict, *Rule*, c. 8, 3.

[224] Benedict, *Rule*, c. 8, 3.

66. Hora uero matutina die statim illucescente peragatur et exorto lucifero, si prouideri potest, ipsa pulsetur.[225] Qua completa reuertatur ad dormitorium. Quod si estas fuerit, quia tunc breue est tempus nocturnum et longum matutinum, aliquantulum ante Primam dormire non prohibemus donec sonitu facto excitantur.[a] De qua etiam quiete post matutinales uidelicet Laudes beatus Gregorius secundo *Dialogorum* capitulo, cum de uenerabili uiro Libertino loqueretur, meminit[b] dicens: 'Die uero erat altera pro utilitate monasterii causa constituta. Expletis igitur ymnis matutinalibus, Libertinus ad lectum abbatis uenit, orationem sibi humiliter petiit', etc.[c] [226] Hec igitur quies matutinalis a pascha usque ad equinoctium autumpnale, ex quo [d]uidelicet nox[d] incipit diem excedere, non denegetur.

67. Egresse autem de dormitorio manus[a] abluant et acceptis libris in claustro sedeant legentes uel cantantes donec Prima pulsetur. Post Primam uero in capitulum eatur et omnibus ibi residentibus lectio *Martyrologii* legatur, luna ante pronunciata. Vbi postmodum uel aliquo sermonis edificio fiat uel aliquid de *Regula* legatur et exponatur.[b] Deinde si que corrigenda sunt uel disponenda, prosequi hec[c] oportet.

68. Sciendum[a] uero[b] est nec monasterium nec domum aliquam inordinatam dici debere si qua ibi inordinate fiant, sed si[c] cum facta fuerunt non sollicite corrigantur. Quis enim locus a peccato penitus expers? Quod diligenter [d]beatus attendens Augustinus,[d] cum clerum[e] suum instrueret, ita[f] quodam loco meminit:[g] 'Quantumlibet[h] enim uigilet[i] disciplina domus mee, homo sum et inter homines uiuo nec mihi arrogare audeo ut domus mea melior sit quam arca Noe, ubi[j] tamen [k]inter octo[k] homines unus inuentus est reprobus,[227] aut[l] quam domus Abrahe, ubi dictum est: "Eiice[m] ancillam et filium eius";[228] [n]aut[o] domus Ysaac[p]—"Iacob dilexi, Esau odio habui"[n] [229]—aut[q] domus Iacob, ubi lectum patris filius incestauit;[230] aut[r] domus Dauid cuius filius[s] cum sorore concubuit,[231] alter contra[t] patris tam

66 [a] excitentur *Amb* [b] nemini *T* [c] *om. Amb* [d–d] *om. Amb*

67 [a] *om. Amb* [b] *end of lacuna in CE, beginning in* 51. *Before resuming the text CE here make a comment:* quibus uero officialibus supra nominatis ordinatis querendum in fine *C;* quibus scilicet officialibus supranominatis ordinatis concludit in fine *E* [c] *om. Amb*

68 [a] *TCEAmb open a new section on a new line* [b] hoc *add. CE* [c] non *CE* [d–d] beatus Augustinus attendens *C;* attendens beatus augustinus *E* [e] clericum *Ecorr* [f] in *CEAmb* [g] dicens *add. Amb* [h] Quantum *E before corr. in marg.* [i] inuigilet *CE* [j] *om. E* [k–k] tamen inter sex(*?*) *add. E in marg.* [l] melior sit *add. Amb, Jerome* [m] Eice *T; an unclear add. is made by* T^1 *in marg.*; eiice *Ecorr*; Eijce *Amb* [n–n] *om. CE* [o] melior quam *add. Amb, Augustine* [p] cuius de duobus

66. The morning Hour should be celebrated as soon as day dawns, and, if it can be arranged, the bell should be rung at sunrise.[225] When it is ended the sisters should return to the dormitory, and, if it is summer, and the night is short and the morning long, we are willing for them to sleep a little before Prime, until they are woken by the bell. Such sleep after morning Lauds is mentioned by St Gregory in the second chapter of his *Dialogues* when speaking of the venerable Libertinus: 'But on the second day there was a case to be heard for the benefit of the monastery. And so, after morning hymns had been sung, Libertinus came to the abbot's bedside and humbly sought a prayer for himself',[226] etc. This morning sleep shall accordingly be permitted from Easter until the autumn equinox, after which the night begins to exceed the day.

67. On coming out of the dormitory they must wash their hands and then take books and sit in the cloister reading or chanting until Prime is rung. After Prime they should go to Chapter, and when all are seated there, a lesson from the *Martyrology* should be read, after the day of the month is announced. After this there should either be some edifying sermon or something from the *Rule* should be read out and expounded. Then if there are matters to correct or arrange they should go on to these.

68. But it must be understood that neither a monastery nor any home should be called irregular if irregularities occur there, but only if they are not afterwards carefully corrected. For is any place wholly faultless? St Augustine took due note of this in a certain passage when he was instructing his clergy: 'However strict the discipline in my house, I am a man and I live among men. I would not venture to claim that my house is better than Noah's Ark, where one amongst eight persons was found to be a reprobate;[227] or better than the house of Abraham, where it was said: "Drive out this slave-girl and her son";[228] or better than the house of Isaac and the twins of whom the Lord said: "I love Jacob, I hate Esau";[229] or better than the house of Jacob, where a son defiled his father's bed;[230] or better than the house of David, where one son slept with his sister[231] and another rebelled

geminis dictum est *add. Augustine* [q] melior quam *add. Amb, Augustine* [r] melior quam *add. Amb, Augustine* [s] unus *add. Amb* [t] quam *C*

[225] Cf. Benedict, *Rule*, c. 8, 4.
[226] Gregory the Great, *Dialogi*, i. 2. 9 (ed. Moricca, p. 24; Vogüé, p. 32; *PL* lxxvii. 161C).
[227] Cf. Gen. 7: 13; 9: 20–7. [228] Gen. 21: 10. [229] Mal. 1: 2–3.
[230] Cf. Gen. 35: 22; 49: 4. [231] Cf. 2 Kgs. (2 Sam.) 13: 14.

sanctam[u] mansuetudinem rebellauit;[232] aut[v] cohabitatio apostoli Pauli qui, si inter omnes bonos habitaret, non diceret: "Foris pugne, intus timores",[233] [w]nec loqueretur: "Nemo est homo qui germane de uobis sollicitus sit. Omnes que sua sunt querunt",[w] [234] etc.;[x] aut[y] cohabitatio ipsius Christi, in qua undecim boni perfidum et furem Iudam tolerauerunt;[235] aut[z] postremo quam celum unde angeli ceciderunt.'[236] [237] Qui etiam nos ad disciplinam monasterii plurimum exhortans annexuit dicens: 'Fateor coram Deo ex quo Deo[a] seruire cepi quomodo difficile sum expertus meliores quam qui in monasteriis [b]profecerunt. Ita non sum expertus peiores quam qui in monasteriis ceciderunt. Ita ut hinc arbitror in Apocalypsi scriptum: "Iustus iustior fiat et sordidus sordescat adhuc." '[b] [238] [239]

69. Tanta igitur correctionis [a]districtio sit[a] ut quecumque in altera uiderit quod corrigendum sit et celauerit grauiori subiaceat discipline quam illa que hoc commisit. Nulla igitur uel suum uel alterius delictum accusare differat. Quecumque uero se accusans alias preuenerit, sicut scriptum est: 'Iustus prior [b]est accusator[b] sui',[240] mitiorem meretur disciplinam si eius cessauerit [c]negligentia. Nulla uero [d]aliam excusare[d] presumat nisi forte diaconissa[c] ab aliis ignotam rei ueritatem interroget. Nulla umquam aliam [e]cedere pro quacumque culpa presumat[e] nisi cui iniunctum fuerit a[f] diaconissa.[241] Scriptum est autem de disciplina correctionis: 'Disciplinam Domini, fili mi, ne abicias; ne deficias cum ab eo corriperis.[g] Quem enim diligit Dominus[h] corripit, et quasi pater in filio complacet sibi.'[i] [242] Item: 'Qui parcit uirge, odit filium; qui autem diligit illum,[j] instanter erudit.'[243] 'Pestilente flagellato stultus sapientior erit.'[244] 'Mulctato pestilente sapientior erit paruulus.'[245] '[k]Flagellum equo et chamus asino et uirga dorso imprudentium.'[246] 'Qui corripit hominem gratiam[l] postea inueniet apud eum magis quam ille qui per lingue

[u] *om. C* [v] melior quam *add. Amb, Augustine* [w–w] *om. CE* [x] om. *Amb* [y] melior quam *add. Amb, Augustine* [z] melior *add. Amb, Augustine* [a] ipso *C;* ipsi *E* [b–b] etc. *CE*

69 [a–a] sit districtio *CE* [b–b] accusator est *CE* [c–c] *om. C* [d–d] excusare aliam *E* [e–e] cedere presumat post quamcumque culpam *CE* [f] ad *C* [g] corripieris *E* [h] deus *E* [i] *om. C* [j] *om. CE* [k–k] *om. CE* [l] *om. Amb*

---

[232] Cf. 2 Kgs. (2 Sam.) 15.
[233] 2 Cor. 7: 5.
[234] Phil. 2: 20–1.
[235] Cf. John 13: 29.
[236] Cf. Luke 10: 18; Rev. 12: 7–9.
[237] Augustine, *Epistola* lxxviii. 8 (ed. Goldbacher, xxxiv. 343, *l.* 13–p. 344, *l.* 13; *PL* xxxiii. 271–2).
[238] Cf. Rev. 22: 11.

against the holy mildness of his father;[232] or better than the company of the apostle Paul who, had he lived among good men, would not have said: "Quarrels all round us, forebodings within",[233] nor would he have said: "There is no one here who takes a genuine interest in your concerns; they are all bent on their own ends",[234] etc.; nor better than the company of Christ himself, in which eleven good men had to put up with the traitor and thief Judas;[235] nor better, lastly, than heaven from where the angels fell.'[236] [237] Augustine also, in pressing us to seek the discipline of the monastery, added: 'I confess before God, from the day on which I began to serve God, I have had difficulty in finding better men than those who have made progress in monasteries, but equally I have found none worse than those in monasteries who have fallen. Hence, I think, it is written in the Apocalypse: "Let the good man persevere in his goodness and the filthy man stay in his filth."'[238] [239]

69. Correction must therefore be rigorous, to the extent that any sister who has seen but concealed something to be corrected in another shall be subjected to a harsher discipline than the offender. So no one should put off denouncing her own or another's wrongdoing. Whoever anticipates the others in accusing herself deserves a milder punishment if her negligence has ceased, as it is written: 'The just man is the first to accuse himself.'[240] But no one shall presume to make excuses for another unless the deaconess happens to question her about the truth of a matter which is unknown to the rest. No one shall ever presume to strike another for any fault unless she has been ordered to do so by the deaconess.[241] It is written of the discipline of correction: 'My son, do not spurn the Lord's correction nor be cast down at his reproof; for those whom he loves the Lord reproves, as a father punishes a favourite son.'[242] Again: 'A father who spares the rod hates his son, but one who loves him keeps him in order.'[243] 'Strike a scornful man and a fool will be wiser.'[244] 'Punish a scornful man and the simple will be wiser.'[245] 'A whip for the horse, a halter for the ass, and a rod for the back of fools.'[246] 'Who takes a man to task will in the end win more thanks than the man with a flattering

[239] Augustine, *Epistola* lxxviii. 9 (ed. Goldbacher, xxxiv. 344, *l.* 14–p. 345, *l.* 3; *PL* xxxiii. 272).
[240] Prov. 18: 17; also cited at **37** above and in *Letter* 5, **15**.
[241] Cf. Benedict, *Rule*, c. 70, 2.
[242] Prov. 3: 11–12.
[243] Prov. 13: 24.
[244] Prov. 19: 25.
[245] Prov. 21: 11.
[246] Prov. 26: 3.

blandimenta decipit.'[k] [247] 'Omnis autem disciplina in presenti quidem[m] uidetur non esse gaudii, sed meroris. Postea autem fructum paccatissimum exercitatis per eam reddet iusticie.'[248] 'Confusio patris est in filio indisciplinato; [n]filia autem fatua in deminoratione erit.'[249] 'Qui diligit filium, assiduat illi flagella ut letetur in nouissimo. Qui docet filium, laudabitur in illo et in medio domesticorum in illo gloriabitur.'[o] [250] 'Equus indomitus euadet durus et filius remissus euadet preceps. Lacta filium tuum et pauentem te faciet. Lude cum eo et contristabit te.'[n] [251]

70. In discussione uero consilii cuilibet [a]suam proferre[a] sententiam licebit sed quicquid omnibus uideatur diaconisse[b] decretum immobile teneatur in cuius arbitrio cuncta consistunt, etiamsi, quod absit, ipsa[c] fallatur et, quod deterius est, ipsa constituat.[252] Vnde et illud est beati Augustini libro *Confessionum*: 'Multum peccat qui inobediens est suis prelatis in aliquo, si uel meliora eligat quam ea que sibi iubentur.'[253] Multo quippe melius est nobis bene facere[d] quam bonum facere, nec tam quod fiat quam[e] quomodo uel quo[f] animo fiat pensandum est.[254] Bene uero fit quicquid per obedientiam fit, etiamsi[g] quod fit bonum esse minime uideatur. Per omnia itaque prelatis est obediendum, quantacumque sint dampna rerum, si nullum apparet anime periculum. Prouideat prelatus ut bene precipiat quia subiectis bene obedire sufficit, nec suam, sicut professi sunt, sed prelatorum sequi uoluntatem.[255]

71. Omnino[a] enim prohibemus ut numquam consuetudo rationi preponatur nec umquam aliquid deffendatur quia sit consuetudo, sed quia ratio; nec quia sit usitatum, sed quia bonum; et tanto libentius excipiatur quanto melius apparebit. Alioquin iudaizantes[b] legis antiquitatem Euangelio[c] preferamus.[256] Ad quod beatus Augustinus de concilio[d] Cypriani pleraque[e] asserens testimonia quodam loco ait: '"Qui contempta ueritate presumit consuetudinem sequi, aut circa fratres inuidus est et malignus quibus ueritas reuelatur,[f] aut circa Deum[g] ingratus est cuius inspiratione ecclesia eius

[m] quid *Amb* [n–n] etc. *CE* [o] gloriatur *Amb*

70 [a–a] proferre suam *E* [b] diaconissa *T; T*[1] *puts a cross in marg.;* diaconissa tamquam *add. C;* dyaconisse tanquam *add. E* [c] *om. CE* [d] benefacere *E* [e] quod *add. TAmb* [f] *om. Amb* [g] etiam *E*

71 [a] Omnibus *Amb*[1] [b] iudaziantes *CE* [c] eo modo *CE* [d] consilio *CEAmb* [e] pluraque *CE* [f] regulatur *C* [g] *om. CE*

[247] Prov. 28: 23. [248] Heb. 12: 11. [249] Ecclus. 22: 3.
[250] Ecclus. 30: 1–2. Cf. *Carmen ad Astralabium*, ed. Rubingh-Bosscher *v.* 263.

tongue.'[247] 'Discipline is never pleasant; at the time it seems painful, but later, for those trained by it, it yields a harvest of peace and goodness.'[248] 'There is shame in being the father of a spoilt son, and the birth of a foolish daughter will bring loss.'[249] 'A man who loves his son will whip him often so that he may have joy in him in the end.'[250] 'An unbroken horse turns out stubborn, and an unchecked son turns out headstrong. Pamper your son and he will shock you; play with him and he will grieve you.'[251]

70. In a discussion on what counsel to take, it shall be open to anyone to offer her opinion, but whatever everyone else thinks, the decision of the deaconess must not be swayed, for everything depends on her will, even if (which God forbid) she may be mistaken and decide on a worse course.[252] For as St Augustine says in his *Confessions*: 'He who disobeys his superiors in anything sins greatly, even if he chooses what is better than what is commanded him.'[253] It is indeed far better for us to do well than to do good, and we must think less of what should be done and more of the manner and spirit in which to do it.[254] A thing is well done which is done obediently, even if what is done seems the least good thing. And so superiors must be obeyed in everything, whatever the material harm, if there is no apparent danger to the soul. The superior must take care that he orders well since it is sufficient for his subjects to obey well and not to follow their own will but, as they professed, that of their superiors.[255]

71. Now we absolutely forbid that custom should ever be set above reason; a practice must never be defended on grounds of custom but only of reason, not because it is usual but because it is good, and it should be more readily accepted the better it is shown to be. Otherwise like the Jews we should set the antiquity of the Law before the Gospel.[256] On this point St Augustine several times gives proof from the counsel of Cyprian, and says in one passage: 'Whoever despises truth and presumes to follow custom is either ill-disposed and hostile towards his fellow-men, to whom truth is revealed, or he is ungrateful

[251] Ecclus. 30: 8–9.

[252] Cf. Benedict, *Rule*, c. 3, 1–5.

[253] Not found but cf. *Confessions*, i. 10. 16 (ed. Verheijen, p. 9): 'Non enim meliora eligens inoboediens eram.'

[254] Cf. *Letters* 2, **13** and 6, **25**.

[255] Cf. Benedict, *Rule*, c. 3, 6.

[256] Cf. *Letters* 5, **10** and 6, **16**; *Carmen ad Astralabium*, ed. Rubingh-Bosscher *v.* 247; *Letter* 10 (ed. Smits, pp. 243–5; *PL* clxxviii. 338B–339B; trans. Ziolkowski, pp. 90–3).

instruitur." '[257] Item: '"In Euangelio Dominus: 'Ego sum', inquit, 'Veritas.'[258] Non dixit: Ego sum consuetudo. Itaque, ueritate manifestata,[h] cedat consuetudo ueritati."'[259] Item: '"[i]Reuelatione facta ueritatis, cedat error ueritati, quia et Petrus, qui prius circumcidebat,[j] cessit Paulo predicanti ueritatem."'[260] Item[i] libro quarto *de Baptismo*: '"Frustra quidem, qui ratione uincuntur, consuetudinem nobis obiiciunt, quasi consuetudo maior sit ueritate aut non sit in spiritualibus sequendum quod in melius fuit a Spiritu sancto reuelatum." Hoc plane uerum est quia ratio et ueritas consuetudini preponenda est.'[261] Gregorius septimus Wimundo[k] episcopo: 'Et certe, ut beati Cypriani utamur sententia, quelibet consuetudo, quantumuis uetusta, quantumuis uulgata, ueritati est omnino postponenda,[l] et usus qui ueritati est contrarius abolendus.'[262]

72. Quanto etiam[a] amore ueritas quoque uerborum amplectenda sit[b] ammonemur in Ecclesiastico cum dicitur: 'Pro anima tua non confundaris dicere uerum.'[263] Item: 'Non contradicas uerbo ueritatis ullo[c] modo.'[264] Et iterum: 'Ante omnia opera uerbum uerax precedat te et ante omnem actum consilium stabile.'[265] Nichil etiam in auctoritatem ducatur[d] quia geritur a multis, sed quia probatur a sapientibus et bonis. 'Stultorum', inquit Salomon, 'infinitus est numerus.'[266] [e]Et iuxta Veritatis assertionem: 'Multi uocati, pauci uero electi.'[267] Rara sunt queque preciosa, et que habundant numero minuuntur precio.[e] [268] Nemo enim in consilio maiorem hominum partem [f]set meliorem, sequatur.[f] [269] Nec etas hominis sed sapientia

[h] manifesta *CE* [i–i] *om. CE* [j] ccumcidebat *T; T*[1] *puts a cross in marg. here* [k] aduersario *add. CE;* Willimundo *Amb*[1] [l] preponenda *TAmb*

72 [a] autem *CE* [b] *om. Amb.* [c] nullo *CE* [d] ducamur *E* [e–e] *om. CE* [f–f] *om. E*

---

[257] Augustine, *De baptismo contra Donatistas*, iii. 5. 8 (ed. Petschenig, p. 203, *ll.* 10–14; *PL* xliii. 143), citing Cyprian, *Sententiae episcoporum*, 28.

[258] John 14: 6.

[259] Augustine, *De baptismo contra Donatistas*, iii. 6. 9 (ed. Petschenig, p. 203; *PL* xliii. 143), citing Cyprian, *Sententiae episcoporum*, 30; also cited in part in *Letter* 5, **10**.

[260] Augustine, *De baptismo contra Donatistas*, iii. 7. 10 (ed. Petschenig, p. 203, *ll.* 22–4; *PL* xliii. 143), citing Cyprian, *Sententiae episcoporum*, 56.

[261] Augustine, *De baptismo contra Donatistas*, iv. 5. 7 (ed. Petschenig, p. 228, *ll.* 1–6; *PL* xliii. 157), citing Cyprian, *Epistola* lxxiii. 13. Also cited in *Letter* 10 (ed. Smits, pp. 243–4; *PL* clxxviii. 338C; trans. Ziolkowski, pp. 90–1); cf. Ivo of Chartres, *Decretum*, iv. 235 (*PL* clxi. 315AB).

[262] Cf. Ivo of Chartres, *Decretum*, iv. 213 (written *c.*1094; *PL* clxi. 311BC); also *Panormia* (commonly attributed to Ivo), ii. 166 (written *c.*1095; *PL* clxi. 1121A and JL 5277). Ivo gives as the source of the quotation a letter from Pope Gregory VII (1073–85) to Wimundus

to God on whose inspiration his Church is founded.'[257] Again: 'In the Gospel the Lord says "I am Truth."[258] He did not say: I am custom. And so as truth was made manifest, custom must yield to truth.'[259] Again: 'Since the truth was revealed, error must yield to truth, just as Peter, who was previously circumcised, yielded to Paul who preached truth.'[260] Similarly, in the fourth book *On Baptism* he writes: 'In vain do those who are vanquished by reason plead custom against us, as though custom were greater than truth or as if in spiritual matters we should not follow what was revealed for the better by the Holy Spirit. This is clearly true because reason and truth must be set before custom.'[261] Gregory the Seventh writes to Bishop Wimund: 'And certainly, in the words of St Cyprian, any custom, however long established and widespread, must stand second to truth, and practice which is contrary to truth must be abolished.'[262]

72. And we are told how lovingly we should adhere to the truth in speech by Ecclesiasticus when he says: 'Do not be ashamed to speak the truth for your soul's sake',[263] and: 'Do not contradict the truth in any way',[264] and again: 'A true word should come before every enterprise, and steady counsel before every deed.'[265] Nothing must be taken as a precedent because it is done by many but because it is approved by the wise and good. As Solomon says: 'The number of fools cannot be counted',[266] and as the Truth declares: 'Many are called but few are chosen.'[267] Valuable things are rare, and multiplication of numbers diminishes value.[268] In taking counsel no one should follow the larger number of men but the better men;[269] it is not a man's years which should be considered but his wisdom, and

(Guitmund), bishop of Aversa. Also ed. and trans. Cowdrey in *The 'Epistolae Vagantes' of Pope Gregory VII*, Appendix A, no. 67, p. 151. See Ladner, 'Two Gregorian letters', pp. 225–35, and, more briefly, Ladner, *The Idea of Reform*, p. 138, on the sources of this principle in Tertullian, Cyprian, and Augustine, and on its actuality for the 'Gregorian' and papal reform movement in the 11th c.; also Leisching, 'Consuetudo und ratio', and Gouron, ' "Non dixit: Ego sum consuetudo" '.The first, but not the second, of two sentences which constitute the fragment as it is found in Ivo appears in *Letter* 10 (ed. Smits, p. 244; *PL* clxxviii. 338C; trans. Ziolkowski, p. 91): 'Gregory VII wrote to Wimund, bishop of Aversa: "If perhaps you adduced custom, what the Lord says should be pointed out: 'I am,' he said, 'the truth'; he did not say, 'I am custom." ' ('Gregorius VII Wimundo auersano episcopo: "Si consuetudinem fortassis opponas, aduertendum fuerit quod Dominus dicit: 'Ego sum', inquit, 'ueritas'; non ait: 'ego sum consuetudo" '). Cf. John 14: 6.

[263] Ecclus. 4: 24.
[264] Ecclus. 4: 30.
[265] Ecclus. 37: 20.
[266] Eccles. 1: 15. To be cited again in **109** below.
[267] Matt. 20: 16, 22: 14. To be cited again in **109** below.
[268] Cf. *Proverbia* (Walther), nos. 19123b, 30430.
[269] Cf. *Carmen ad Astralabium*, ed. Rubingh-Bosscher, *v.* 253.

consideretur, nec amicicia sed ueritas attendatur.[270] Vnde et poetica est illa sententia: 'Fas est et ab hoste doceri.'[271]

73. Quociens autem opus[a] est consilio[b] non differatur et, si de rebus precipuis est deliberandum, conuocetur conuentus.[272] In minoribus autem rebus discuciendis sufficiet diaconissa paucis ad se de maioribus personis conuocatis.[273] Scriptum quoque est de consilio: 'Vbi non est gubernator populus corruit. [c]Salus autem ubi multa consilia.'[274] 'Via stulti recta in oculis eius. Qui autem sapiens est[d] audit consilia.'[c][275] 'Fili, sine consilio [e]nihil facias et post factum non penitebis.'[e][276] Si forte sine consilio aliquid prosperum habet euentum, non excusat [f]hominis presumptionem fortune beneficium.[f] [g]Sin autem post consilium nonnumquam errant, potestas que consilium quesiuit, rea non tenetur[h] presumptionis. Nec tam culpandus est qui credidit quam quibus ipse errando acquieuit.[g]

74. Egresse uero capitulum hiis quibus oportet operibus intendant, legendo scilicet uel cantando siue manibus operando usque ad Terciam. [a]Post Terciam autem Missa dicatur ad quam quidem celebrandam unus ex monachis sacerdos ebdomadarius instituatur. Quem profecto,[b] si copia tanta sit, cum diacono et subdiacono uenire oportet, qui ei quod necessarium est administrent uel quod suum est et ipsi operentur. Quorum accessus uel recessus ita fiant ut sororum conuentui nullatenus pateant. Si uero plures necessarii fuerint,[c] de hiis prouidendum erit et ita semper si fieri potest ut monachi propter Missas monialium numquam conuentui suo in officiis desint diuinis.

75. Si uero communicandum a sororibus fuerit, senior eligatur sacerdos qui post Missam eas communicet, egressis inde prius diacono et subdiacono propter tollendam temptationis occasionem. Ter uero ad minus in anno totus communicet conuentus, id est Pascha, Penthecoste et Natale Domini, sicut a patribus est institutum de secularibus etiam hominibus.[277] Hiis autem communionibus ita se preparent ut tercio die ante ad confessionem et congruam satisfactionem omnes accedant et terno se panis et aque ieiunio et oratione

73 [a] *om. CE* [b] consilium *CE* [c–c] etc. *CE* [d] *om. Amb* [e–e] etc. *CE* [f–f] *om. E* [g–g] *om. CE* [h] teneatur *Amb*

74 [a] *beginning of lacuna in CE, ending in* 76 [b] praesto *Amb*[1] [c] et *add. Amb*

[270] Cf. *Proverbia* (Walther), no. 62: 'Amicus Plato, sed magis amica ueritas.'

[271] Ovid, *Metamorphoses*, iv. 428. Also cited in *TChr* (*CT*), iii. 8c and *TSch*, ii. 33.

regard should be paid not to friendship but to truth.[270] Hence also the words of the poet: 'Even from a foe it is right to learn.'[271]

73. But whenever there is need for counsel it must not be postponed and, if important matters are to be debated, the whole convent should be assembled.[272] For discussing minor affairs it will be enough for the deaconess to meet a few of the senior nuns.[273] It is also written concerning counsel that 'the people fares ill that has no guidance, but safety reigns where counsel abounds'.[274] 'The fool is right in his own eyes, but the wise man listens to counsel.'[275] 'Do nothing, my son, except with counsel, and afterwards you will have no regrets.'[276] If something done without taking counsel happens to have a successful outcome, fortune's kindness does not excuse the doer's presumption. But if after taking counsel men sometimes err, the authority which sought counsel is not held guilty of presumption, and the man who believed his advisers is not so much to be blamed as those with whom he agreed in their error.

74. On coming out from Chapter the sisters should apply themselves to suitable tasks, reading or chanting or handiwork until Terce. After Terce Mass shall be said, and to celebrate this one of the monks shall be appointed the priest of the week. If numbers are large he must come with a deacon and subdeacon to assist him as necessary or to perform duties on their own. Their coming and going must be so arranged that they are unseen by the sisters. If more were needed, arrangements shall be made for them, and permanently so if possible, so that the monks never miss divine offices in their own monastery because of the Masses for the nuns.

75. If the sisters are to take communion, one of the older priests must be chosen to administer it to them after Mass and after the deacon and subdeacon have first withdrawn, to remove any risk of temptation. Three times at least in the year the whole convent must communicate, at Easter, Pentecost, and the Nativity of the Lord, as was ordained by the Fathers for the laity also.[277] For these communions they must prepare themselves in the following way: three days before they should all make their confession and do suitable penance, and by three days of

[272] Cf. Benedict, *Rule*, c. 3, 1. [273] Cf. Benedict, *Rule*, c. 3, 12.
[274] Prov. 11: 14. [275] Prov. 12: 15. [276] Ecclus. 32: 24.
[277] Cf. Ivo of Chartres, *Decretum*, ii. 27 (*PL* clxi. 167A); Gratian, *Decretum*, D. 2, c.16 *de consecratione*.

frequenti purificent cum omni humilitate et tremore, illam Apostoli terribilem apud se retractantes sententiam: 'Itaque', inquit, 'quicumque manducauerit panem uel biberit calicem Domini indigne, reus erit corporis et sanguinis Domini. Probet autem seipsum homo, et sic de pane illo edat et[a] calice bibat. Qui enim manducat et bibit indigne, iudicium sibi manducat et bibit, non diiudicans corpus Domini. Ideo inter uos multi infirmi et imbecilles, et dormiunt multi. Quod si nosmetipsos diiudicaremus, non utique iudicaremur.'[b] [278]

76. Post Missam quoque ad opera redeant usque ad Sextam, et nullo tempore ociose uiuant sed unaqueque id quod potest et quod oportet operetur. Post Sextam autem prandendum est nisi ieiunium fuerit; tunc enim Nona est expectanda et in quadragesima etiam Vespera.[279] Nullo[a] uero tempore conuentus careat lectione, quam cum diaconissa terminare uoluerit, dicat: 'Sufficit.' Et statim ad grates Domino referendas ab omnibus surgatur. Estiuo tempore post prandium usque ad Nonam quiescendum est in dormitorio, et post Nonam ad opera redeundum usque ad Vesperas. Post Vesperas autem uel statim cenandum est uel potandum. Et inde[b] secundum temporis considerationem[c] ad collationem eundum.[280] Sabbato autem ante collationem mundicie fiant in ablutione uidelicet pedum et manuum, in quo quidem obsequio diaconissa famuletur cum ebdomadariis que coquine deseruierunt.[281] Post collationem uero ad Completorium statim est ueniendum; inde dormitum est eundum.[d]

77. De uictu[a] autem et uestitu apostolica teneatur sententia qua dicitur: 'Habentes autem alimenta et quibus tegamur, hiis contenti[b] simus.'[282] Vt uidelicet necessaria sufficiant, non superflua querantur; et quod uilius poterit comparari uel facilius haberi et sine scandalo sumi, id[c] concedatur.[283] Solum quippe scandalum proprie conscientie uel alterius in cibis Apostolus uitat, sciens quia non est cibus in uitio sed appetitus.[284] 'Qui manducat', inquit, 'non manducantem non spernat;[d] qui non manducat, manducantem non iudicet. [e]Tu

75 [a] de *add. Amb* [b] dijudicaremur *Amb*

76 [a] *illegible addition by* T^1 *in marg.* [b] etiam *add. Amb* [c] consuetudinem *Amb* [d] *in T there follows a space adequate for 8 characters; end of lacuna in CE, beginning in* 74

77 [a] *A new section opens here in T,C (which writes* De uictu *in bold letters), E (which writes* De uictu autem *in large, thick letters on a new line) and Amb* [b] contempti *CE* [c] re *Amb* [d] et *add. CE* [e–e] *om. E*

---

[278] 1 Cor. 11: 27–31. [279] Cf. Benedict, *Rule*, c. 41, 1–7.

[280] St Benedict in his *Rule*, c. 42, established a daily reading or collation from the

fasting on bread and water and repeated prayer, purify themselves humbly and fearfully, taking to themselves those terrible words of the Apostle: 'It follows that anyone who eats the bread or drinks from the cup of the Lord unworthily will be guilty of desecrating the body and blood of the Lord. A man must test himself before eating his share of the bread and drinking from the cup. For he who eats and drinks unworthily eats and drinks judgement on himself if he does not discern the body of the Lord. That is why many of you are feeble and sick and a number have died. But if we judged ourselves we should not be judged at all.'[278]

76. After Mass they should return again to their work until Sext and not waste any time in idleness; everyone must do what she can and what is right for her. After Sext they should have lunch, unless it is a fast-day, when they must wait until None, and in Lent even until Vespers.[279] But at no time must the convent be without reading, which the deaconess may end when she wishes by saying: Enough. And then they should all rise at once to render thanks to God. In summer they should rest in their dormitory after lunch until None, and after None return to work until Vespers. Immediately after Vespers they should eat and drink, and then, in the time left available, they should go to the collation;[280] but on Saturday, before the collation, they should be made clean by washing of feet and hands. The deaconess should also participate in this rite along with the sisters on duty for the week in the kitchen.[281] After the collation they are to come at once to Compline, and then retire to sleep.

77. As regards food and clothing, the opinion of the Apostle must be followed in which he says: 'As long as we have food and something to wear let us rest content.'[282] That is, necessities should be sufficient and superfluous things not sought. They should be allowed whatever can be bought cheaply or easily obtained and taken without giving offence,[283] for the Apostle avoids only what foods will offend his own or his brother's conscience, knowing that it is not the food which is at fault but the appetite for it.[284] 'The man who eats', he says, 'must not hold in contempt the man who does not, and he who does not eat must not pass

Conferences of John Cassian (*c.*360–after 430). The *Conferences* record conversations with leading figures in eastern monasticism.

[281] Cf. Benedict, *Rule*, *c.* 35, 7–9.

[282] 1 Tim. 6: 8.

[283] Cf. **95** below, *Letter* 6, **20**, and Benedict, *Rule*, c. 55, 7.

[284] Cf. **81**, **93**, and **96** below.

quis es qui iudicas alienum seruum?[e] Qui manducat, Domino manducat; gratias enim agit Deo. Et qui non manducat, Domino non manducat; et gratias agit Deo. Non [f]ergo amplius[f] inuicem iudicemus, sed hoc iudicate magis, ne ponatis offendiculum fratri uel scandalum. Scio et confido in Domino Iesu, quia nichil commune per ipsum, nisi qui existimat quid commune esse. Non est regnum Dei esca et potus, sed iusticia et pax et gaudium in Spiritu sancto. Omnia quidem munda sunt, sed malum est homini qui per offendiculum manducat. Bonum est non manducare carnem et non bibere uinum, neque in quo frater tuus offendatur aut scandalizetur.'[285] Qui etiam post scandalum fratris de proprio scandalo ipsius, qui contra[g] conscientiam suam comedit,[h] adiungit[i] dicens: 'Beatus qui non iudicat semetipsum in eo quod probat. Qui autem discernit, si manducauerit, dampnatus est, quia non ex fide. Omne autem quod non est ex fide, peccatum est.'[286]

78. In omni quippe quod agimus contra conscientiam nostram, et[a] contra hoc quod credimus, peccamus. Et in eo quod probamus, hoc est per legem quam approbamus atque recipimus, iudicamus nosmetipsos atque dampnamus si illos uidelicet comedimus cibos quos discernimus, hoc est secundum[b] legem excludimus et separamus tamquam immundos. Tantum enim est testimonium conscientie nostre ut hec nos apud Deum maxime accuset uel excuset. Vnde et Iohannes in prima sua meminit epistola: 'Karissimi, si cor nostrum non reprehenderit nos,[c] fiduciam habemus ad Deum. Et[d] quicquid petierimus, accipiemus[e] ab eo, quoniam mandata eius custodimus, et ea que sunt placita coram eo[f] facimus.'[287] Bene itaque et Paulus superius ait nichil esse commune per Christum, nisi ei qui commune quid esse putat,[288] hoc est immundum et interdictum [g]si sibi[g] credit. Communes quippe cibos dicimus qui secundum legem mundi[h] uocantur, quod eos scilicet lex a suis excludens quasi hiis qui extra legem sunt exponat[i] et publicet. Vnde et communes femine immunde sunt et communia queque uel publicata uilia sunt uel minus cara.[289] Nullum itaque cibum per Christum asserit esse communem, id est immundum, quia lex Christi nullum interdicit nisi, ut dictum est, propter scandalum remouendum uel proprie scilicet conscientie uel

[f–f] amplius ergo *C;* amplius E [g] autem *E* [h] comendit *C;* comendit *E*
[i] *om. CE*

78 [a] *om. C* [b] per *Amb* [c] uos uel nos *CE* [d] ut *CE* [e] accipiamus *CE*
[f] Deo *CE* [g–g] (=sibi) sibi *T;* sibi *CE* [h] immundi *CE* [i] apponat *C*

judgement on one who does. Who are you to pass judgement on someone else's servant? He who eats has the Lord in mind when he eats, since he gives thanks to God; and he who abstains has the Lord in mind no less, since he too gives thanks to God. Let us therefore cease judging one another, but rather make this judgement: that no obstacle or stumbling-block be placed in the way of a brother. I know on the authority of the Lord Jesus that nothing is unclean in itself, only if a man considers a particular thing unclean. The kingdom of God is not eating and drinking but justice, peace, and joy in the Holy Spirit. For everything is pure but bad for a man who by his eating causes another to fall. It is good not to eat meat and not to drink wine and not to do anything which causes your brother's downfall.'[285] And after the offence to his brother he goes on to speak of the offence to himself of a man who eats against his own conscience: 'Happy is the man who does not bring judgement upon himself by what he approves. But a man who has doubts is guilty if he eats, because his action does not arise from his conviction, and anything which is not from conviction is sin.'[286]

78. For in all that we do against our conscience and against our beliefs we are sinning; and in what we test by the law which we approve and accept, we judge and condemn ourselves if we eat those foods which we discriminate against or exclude by the law and set apart as unclean. So great is the testimony of our conscience that this more than anything accuses or excuses us before God. And so John writes in his First Letter: 'Dear friends, if our conscience does not condemn us, then we can approach God with confidence, and obtain from him whatever we ask, because we keep his commandments and do what he approves.'[287] It was, therefore, well said by Paul in the passage above that nothing is unclean in the eyes of Christ, but only for the man who considers a thing unclean,[288] that is, if he thinks it impure and forbidden to him. Indeed, we call certain foods unclean which according to the Law are clean, because the Law in forbidding them to its own people may still offer them publicly to those outside the Law. Hence common women are unclean, and common things which are offered publicly are cheap or less dear.[289] And so the Apostle asserts that no food is common or unclean in the eyes of Christ because the law of Christ forbids nothing except, as is said, to remove offence to one's own conscience or

[285] Rom. 14: 3–4, 6, 13–14, 17, 20–1.
[286] Rom. 14: 22–3.
[287] 1 John 3: 21–2.
[288] Cf. Rom. 14: 14.
[289] Cf. 73 above.

aliene. De qua et alibi dicit: 'Quapropter, si esca scandalizat[j] fratrem meum, non manducabo carnem[k] in eternum, ne fratrem meum scandalizem.'[290] 'Non sum liber? Non sum Apostolus?'[291] etc.[l] Ac si diceret: numquid non habeo illam libertatem quam Dominus apostolis dedit de quibuslibet scilicet edendis uel de stipendiis aliorum sumendis? Sic quippe cum apostolos mitteret quodam loco ait: 'Edentes et bibentes que apud illos sunt',[292] nullum uidelicet[m] cibum a ceteris distinguens. Quod diligenter Apostolus attendens et omnia ciborum genera, etiamsi sint infidelium cibi, et ydolatita[n] Christianis esse licita studiose prosequitur, solum, ut diximus, in cibis scandalum uitans. 'Omnia', inquit, 'licent, sed non omnia [o]expediunt. Omnia mihi licent, sed non omnia[o] edificant. Nemo quod suum est querat,[p] sed quod alterius. Omne quod in macello uenit manducate, nihil interrogantes propter conscientiam. "Domini est terra et plenitudo eius."[293] Si quis uocat uos infidelium ad cenam et uultis ire, omne quod uobis apponitur manducate, nihil interrogantes propter conscientiam. Si quis autem dixerit: hoc immolatum est ydolis, nolite manducare propter illum qui indicauit[q] et[r] propter conscientiam. Conscientiam autem[s] dico non tuam, sed alterius. Sine offensione estote Iudeis et gentibus et ecclesie Dei.'[294]

79. Ex quibus uidelicet Apostoli uerbis manifeste colligitur nullum nobis[a] interdici quo sine offensa proprie conscientie uel aliene uesci possimus. Sine offensa uero proprie conscientie tunc agimus si propositum uite quo saluari possumus nos seruare[b] confidimus, sine offensa autem aliene si eo modo uiuere credimur quo saluemur. Eo quidem modo uiuemus si omnibus necessariis nature indultis peccata uitemus,[c] nec de nostra uirtute presumentes illi uite iugo [d]per professionem[d] nos obligemus quo pregrauati succumbamus;[e] et tanto sit grauior casus quanto fuerat professionis altior gradus. Quem quidem casum et stulte professionis uotum Ecclesiastes preueniens ait: 'Si quid uouisti Deo ne moreris reddere. Displicet enim ei infidelis et stulta promissio. Sed quodcumque uoueris redde. Melius est non uouere quam post uotum promissa non reddere.'[295] Cui quoque periculo [f]apostolicum occurrens[f] consilium, 'uolo',

[j] scandalizet *E* [k] *om. E* [l] *om. Amb* [m] scilicet *E* [n] idolotyta *Amb* [o–o] *om. CE by homoeoteleuton* [p] quaerit *Amb*[1] [q] iudicauit *TAmb;* iudicat *CE;* indicauit *Vulg.* [r] *om. CE* [s] *om. Amb*

79 [a] cibum *add. CE* [b] saluare *CE* [c] uitamus *CE* [d–d] professione *Amb* [e] subcumbamus *CE* [f–f] occurrens Apostolicum *Amb*

another's. On this he says elsewhere: 'And therefore if food be the downfall of my brother, I will never eat meat any more, for I will not be the cause of my brother's downfall.'[290] 'Am I not a free man? Am I not an apostle'?[291] etc.—as if he were to say: Have I not the freedom which the Lord gave to the apostles, to eat whatever I like or to take alms from others? For when the Lord sent out the apostles, he said in a certain passage: 'Eating and drinking what they have',[292] and thus he made no distinction between kinds of food. Noting this, the Apostle is careful to say that any kind of food, even if it is the food of unbelievers and consecrated to idols, is permitted to Christians and only the giving of offence in food is to be avoided: 'There are no forbidden things, but not everything does good. Nothing is forbidden me, but not everything helps to build the community. Nobody should look to his own interests, but those of the other man. You may eat anything sold in the meat market without raising questions of conscience; for "the earth is the Lord's and everything in it".[293] If an unbeliever invites you to a meal and you care to go, eat whatever is put before you without raising questions of conscience. But if someone says to you: This food has been offered in sacrifice to idols, then, out of consideration for him who told you and for conscience's sake, do not eat it—not your conscience, I mean, but the other man's. Give no offence to Jews or Greeks or to the Church of God.'[294]

79. From these words of the Apostle it is plain that nothing is forbidden us which we can eat without offence to our own or another's conscience. We eat without offence to our own conscience if we are sure that we are keeping to that course of life whereby we can be saved, and without offence to another's if we are believed to be living in a manner leading to salvation. We shall indeed live in this manner if we permit everything necessary to our nature while avoiding sin, and if we are not overconfident of our strength so as to bind ourselves by profession to a rule of life too heavy for us, under which we may fall: and the higher the degree of our profession, the heavier the fall would be. Such a fall, and such a foolish vow of profession, Ecclesiastes forestalls when he says: 'When you make a vow to God do not be slow to pay it, for he has no use for unbelievers and foolish promises. Pay whatever you owe. Better not vow at all than vow and fail to pay.'[295] On this hazard too the Apostle advises, saying: 'It is my wish that younger

[290] 1 Cor. 8: 13.
[291] 1 Cor. 9: 1.
[292] Luke 10: 7.
[293] Ps. 23 (24): 1.
[294] 1 Cor. 10: 22–9, 32.
[295] Eccles. 5: 3–4. Cf. *Carmen ad Astralabium*, ed. Rubingh-Bosscher *v.* 357: 'ne uoueas maiora deo quam soluere possis / set tua sint factis uota minora tuis.'

inquit, 'iuniores nubere, filios procreare, [g]matresfamilias esse, nullam occasionem dare aduersario maledicti gratia. Iam enim quedam conuerse sunt retro Sathanam.'[g] [296] Etatis[h] infirme naturam considerans, remedium uite laxioris opponit periculo melioris. Consulit residere in imo ne precipicium detur ex alto. Quod[i] et beatus secutus Ieronimus Eustochium uirginem instruens[j] ait: 'Si autem et ille que uirgines sunt ob alias tamen culpas non saluantur, quid fiet illis que prostituerunt membra Christi et mutauerunt templum Spiritus sancti in lupanar? Rectius fuerat homini subisse coniugium, ambulasse per plana, quam ad altiora tendentem in profundum inferni cadere.'[297]

80. Quod si eciam uniuersa reuoluamus Apostoli dicta, numquam[a] eum reperiemus secunda matrimonia nisi feminis indulsisse, sed uiros maxime ad continentiam exhortans ait: 'Circumcisus aliquis uocatus est? Non adducat prepucium.'[298] Et iterum: 'Solutus es ab uxore? Noli querere uxorem.'[299] Cum Moyses tamen, uiris magis quam feminis indulgens, uni uiro plures simul feminas, non uni femine plures uiros, concedat; et districtius adulteria[b] feminarum quam uirorum puniat.[300] 'Mulier', inquit Apostolus, 'si mortuus fuerit uir eius, liberata est a lege uiri ut non sit adultera si fuerit cum alio uiro.'[301] Et alibi: 'Dico autem non nuptis et uiduis: Bonum est illis si sic permaneant, sicut et ego. Quod si non se continent, nubant. Melius est enim nubere quam uri.'[302] Et iterum: 'Mulier,[c] si dormierit uir eius, liberata est; cui uult nubat, tantum in Domino. Beatior autem erit si sic permanserit, secundum consilium meum.'[303] Nam secunda tantum matrimonia infirmo sexui concedit, [d]uerum etiam ea nullo concludere audet numero, sed cum dormierint earum uiri nubere aliis permittit.[d] Nullum matrimoniis earum prefigit numerum,[e] dummodo fornicationis euadant reatum.[f] Sepius magis nubant[g] quam semel fornicentur; [h]ne se[i] uni prostituant,[j] multis carnalis commercii debitum soluant. Que tamen debiti solutio non est penitus

[g–g] etc. *CE* [h] enim *add. E* [i] Quem *T, ?E, Amb;* Quod T^1C [j] instituens *Amb*

80 [a] nusquam *E* [b] adultera *Amb* [c] *om. E* [d–d] *om. CE* [e] matrimonium *C* [f] nec *add. CE* [g] *om. CE* [h–h] *om. CE but E marks this for corr.* [i] si *Amb* [j] prostituantur *Amb*

[296] 1 Tim. 5: 14–15; also cited in *Letter* 6, 13.

[297] Jerome, *Epistola* XXII *ad Eustochium*, 6 (ed. Hilberg, liv. 150, *ll.* 14–17, p. 151, *ll.* 12–14; *PL* xxii. 397–8); also cited in *Letter* 6, 13.

widows shall remarry, have children, preside over a home, and give no opponent occasion for slander. For there have already been some who have taken the wrong turning and gone to the devil.'[296] Out of consideration for the nature of youth's frailty, he sets the remedy of a freer way of life against the risk of attempting a better one, and advises us to stay in a lowly position lest we fall from a high one. Following him St Jerome also instructs the virgin Eustochium: 'But if those who are virgins may not be saved on account of other faults, what shall become of those who have prostituted the members of Christ and turned the temple of the Holy Spirit into a brothel? It would have been better for mankind to undergo matrimony, to tread level ground, than to aim at the heights and fall into the depths of hell.'[297]

80. And if we search through all the words of the Apostle we shall never find that he allowed a second marriage except to women. To men he preaches continence saying: 'If anyone was circumcised before he was called, he should not disguise it.'[298] And again: 'If you are free of a wife, do not seek one.'[299] Moses, on the other hand, was more indulgent to men than to women, and allowed one man several wives at the same time, but not one woman several husbands; and he punished the adulteries of women more severely than those of men.[300] 'A woman', says the Apostle, 'if her husband dies is free from the law of her husband, so that she does not commit adultery if she consorts with another man.'[301] And elsewhere: 'To the unmarried and to widows I say this: It is a good thing if they stay as I am myself, but if they cannot control themselves, they should marry. Better be married than burn with desire.'[302] Again: 'A wife, if her husband is dead, is free to marry whom she will, as long as it is in the Lord. But she will be happier if she stays in accordance with my advice.'[303] Not only does he allow a second marriage to the weaker sex but he does not venture to set a limit to the number, simply permitting them to take other husbands when theirs are dead. He fixes no limit to their marriages, provided that they are not guilty of fornication. They should marry often rather than fornicate once, and pay the debts of the flesh to many rather than be prostituted

[298] 1 Cor. 7: 18.

[299] 1 Cor. 7: 27.

[300] Cf. Gen. 16 for Abraham's wives. I do not know of Mosaic evidence of harsher punishment for adulteresses than for adulterers unless this be thought to be implied in Matt. 19: 9 or John 8: 4–5. Cf. Lev. 20: 10; Num. 5; Deut. 22: 22–30, and *Problemata* 42 (*PL* clxxviii. 723D–724A).

[301] Rom. 7: 3.

[302] 1 Cor. 7: 8–9.

[303] 1 Cor. 7: 39–40.

immunis a peccato,[304] sed indulgentur minora ut maiora uitentur peccata.[h]

81. Quid igitur mirum si id in quo nullum est omnino [a]conceditur ne[a] peccatum incurrant,[b] hoc est alimenta quelibet necessaria, non superflua? Non est enim, ut dictum est,[305] [c]cibus in uicio[c] sed appetitus, cum uidelicet libet quod non licet et concupiscitur quod interdictum est et nonnumquam impudenter sumitur unde maximum scandalum generatur.

82. Quid uero inter uniuersa hominum alimenta tam periculosum est uel dampnosum et religioni nostre uel [a]sancte quieti[a] contrarium quantum uinum?[306] Quod maximus ille sapientum diligenter attendens ab[b] hoc maxime nos dehortatur dicens: 'Luxuriosa res uinum, et tumultuosa ebrietas. Quicumque hiis delectatur non erit sapiens.'[307] [c]'Cui ue? Cuius patri ue?[c] Cui rixe? Cui fouee? Cui sine causa uulnera? Cui suffosio oculorum? Nonne hiis qui morantur in uino et student calicibus epotandis? Ne[d] intuearis uinum quando flauescit, cum splenduerit in uitro color eius. Ingreditur blande, sed in nouissimo mordebit ut coluber, et sicut regulus uenena diffundet. Oculi tui uidebunt extraneas, et cor tuum [e]loquetur peruersa.[e] Et eris sicut dormiens in medio mari[f] [g]et quasi sopitus gubernator, amisso clauo. Et dices: Verberauerunt me et non dolui, traxerunt me et ego non sensi. Quando euigilabo [h]et rursus[h] uina reperiam?'[g] [308] Item: 'Noli regibus, O Lamuel,[i] noli regibus dare uinum, quia nullum secretum est ubi regnat ebrietas, [j]ne forte bibant et obliuiscantur iudiciorum et mutent[k] causam filiorum pauperis.'[j] [309] Et in Ecclesiastico scriptum est: 'Operarius ebriosus non locupletabitur, [l]et qui spernit modica, paulatim decidet.[l] Vinum et mulieres apostatare faciunt sapientes et arguunt sensatos.'[310] Ysaias quoque uniuersos preteriens cibos solum in causam captiuitatis populi commemorat uinum. 'Ve', inquit, 'qui consurgitis mane ad ebrietatem sectandam et

81 [a–a] concedatur nec *CE* [b] incurrent *E* [c–c] in uitio cibus *E*

82 [a–a] quieti sancte *E* [b] ad *TCE* [c–c] *om. CE* [d] non *CE* [e–e] peruersa loquetur *CE* [f] maris *CE* [g–g] etc. *CE* [h–h] rursus et *Amb* [i] Samuel *CE* [j–j] etc. *CE* [k] mittant *TAmb* [l–l] *om. CE*

[304] Cf. **97** below; also *SN* c. 130; *Problemata* 42 (*PL* clxxviii. 723A–730B); *Ethica*, i. 11–13 (ed. Ilgner, pp. 11–15; ed. Luscombe, pp. 17–23). Also *Sententie* **231–3** (ed. Luscombe, pp. 122–4; ed. Buzzetti, pp. 135–6; *PL* clxxviii. 1745B–176A).

[305] Cf. **77** above; also **93** and **96** below. Cf. *Problemata* 42 (*PL* clxxviii. 723–30, esp. 725B, 727AB—also cited in *SN* c. 130, 12—and 729B), where Abelard collects passages from St

to one: such payment is not wholly free from sin,[304] but lesser sins are permitted so that greater may be avoided.

81. No wonder, then, that what has no sin at all is allowed them lest they commit sin; that is, foods which are necessary and not superfluous. For, as we said,[305] the food is not to blame but the appetite, when pleasure is taken in what is not permitted, and forbidden things are desired and sometimes shamelessly snatched, which causes very serious offence.

82. But what amongst all the foods of men is so dangerous, injurious. and contrary to our religion or to holy quiet as wine?[306] The wisest of men well understood this when he particularly warns us against it, saying: 'Wine is reckless, and strong drink quarrelsome. No one who delights in these will be wise.'[307] 'Who knows misery? Whose father knows misery? Who has quarrels, falls into holes, has unexplained bruises and bloodshot eyes? Those who linger late over wine, and devote themselves to emptying cups. Do not look on wine when it glows and sparkles in the glass. It goes down smoothly, but in the end it will bite like a snake and spread venom like a serpent. Then your eyes will see strange sights, and your heart will utter distorted words; you will be like a man sleeping in mid-ocean, like a drowsy helmsman who has lost his rudder, and you will say: They struck me and it did not hurt, dragged me off and I felt nothing. When I wake up I shall turn to wine again.'[308] Again: 'Do not give wine to kings, O Lemuel, never to kings! There are no secrets where drinking prevails. If they drink they may forget what they have decreed and neglect the pleas of the sons of the poor.'[309] And in Ecclesiasticus it is written: 'A drunken workman will never grow rich; carelessness in small things leads little by little to ruin. Wine and women rob the wise of their wits and find faults in men of good sense.'[310] Isaiah, too, passes over all foods and mentions only wine as a reason for the captivity of his people. 'Shame on you', he says, 'who rise in the morning to go in pursuit of liquor

Augustine to compare good and bad aspects of marriage with the appetite for food and drink. Cf. Augustine, *De bono coniugali*, ix and xvi. 18 (ed. Zycha, pp. 210–11; *PL* xl. 380 and 385). The morality of both the pleasures of sexual intercourse and of food is also considered in *Ethics*, i. 11–13 (ed. Ilgner, pp. 11–15; ed. Luscombe, pp. 17–23).

[306] Cf. on wine *Letter* 6, **18**.

[307] Prov. 20: 1; also cited in *Letter* 6, **18**.

[308] Prov. 23: 29–35; also cited in *Letter* 6, **18** and cf. **86** below.

[309] Prov. 31: 4–5; also cited in *Letter* 6, **18** and cf. **86** below.

[310] Ecclus. 19: 1–2; also cited in part in *Letter* 6, **18**.

potandum usque ad uesperam, ut uino estuetis. Cythara et lyra et tympanum et tybia [m]et uinum[m] in conuiuiis uestris, et opus Domini non respicitis. Propterea captiuus ductus est populus meus, quia non habuit scientiam.'[311] 'Ve qui potentes estis ad bibendum uinum et uiri fortes ad miscendam ebrietatem.'[312] Qui etiam de populo usque ad sacerdotes et prophetas querimoniam extendens ait: '[n]Verum hii quoque pre uino nescierunt et pre ebrietate errauerunt.[n] Sacerdos et propheta nescierunt pre ebrietate; absorti sunt a uino, [o]errauerunt in ebrietate, nescierunt uidentem, ignorauerunt iudicium. Omnes enim mense replete sunt uomitu sordiumque, ita ut non esset ultra locus. Quem docebit scientiam et quem intelligere faciet auditum?'[o] [313] Dominus[p] per Ioel dicit: 'Expergiscimini,[q] ebrii, et flete qui bibitis uinum in dulcedine.'[314] Non enim uti prohibet uino[r] in necessitate, sicut Apostolus inde Tymotheo consulit, 'propter stomachi frequentes infirmitates':[315] [s]non tantum infirmitates set frequentes.[s] Noe primus uineam plantauit, nesciens [t]adhuc fortassis[t] ebrietatis malum, et inebriatus femora denudauit, quia uino coniuncta est luxurie turpitudo. Qui etiam superirrisus a filio maledictionem in eum intorsit et seruitutis [u]illum sententia[u] obligauit que antea nequaquam facta esse cognouimus.[316] Loth uirum sanctum ad incestum nullatenus trahi nisi per ebrietatem filie ipsius prouiderunt.[317] Et beata uidua superbum Olofernem nonnisi hac arte illudi posse et prosterni credidit.[318] Angelos antiquis patribus apparentes et ab eis hospicio susceptos carnibus non uino usos esse legimus;[319] et maximo illi et primo principi nostro Helye in solitudinem latenti corui mane et uespere panis et carnium alimoniam, non uini, ministrabant.[320] Populus etiam Israeliticus,[v] delicatissimis in heremo cibis maxime coturnicum educatus,[w] [321] nec uino usus fuisse nec ipsum appetisse legitur.[322] [x]Et refectiones ille panum et piscium quibus in solitudine populus sustentabatur uinum nequaquam habuisse referuntur.[x] Solummodo nuptie que indulgentiam habent incontinentie

[m–m] *om. E* [n–n] *om. CE* [o–o] etc. *CE* [p] etiam *add. CE* [q] expergimiscimini *TAmb* [r] uinum *T* [s–s] *om. CE* [t–t] fortassis adhuc *CE* [u–u] sententia illum *Amb* [v] israelicticus *E* [w] aduocatus *C* [x–x] *om. CE*

[311] Isa. 5: 11–12, 13. [312] Isa. 5: 22.
[313] Isa. 28: 7–9. [314] Joel 1: 5.
[315] 1 Tim. 5: 23; cited also at **86** below. Cf. Jerome, *Epistola* XXII *ad Eustochium*, 8 (ed. Hilberg, liv. 154–5; *PL* xxii. 399); *Epistola* LII *ad Nepotianum presbyterum*, 11 (ed. Hilberg, liv. 434; *PL* xxii. 537).
[316] Cf. Gen. 9: 20–7; also Jerome, *Epistola* XXII *ad Eustochium*, 8 (ed. Hilberg, liv. 155; *PL* xxii. 399).

and drinking until evening, when you are heated with wine. At your feasts you have harp and lute, timbrel and pipe and wine, but no regard for the work of the Lord. My people are led into exile for want of perception.'[311] 'Shame upon you, mighty drinkers, champions at mixing drinks.'[312] Then he extends his lament from the people to priests and prophets, saying: 'These too are fuddled with wine and bemused with drinking. Priest and prophet are stupid with drinking; they are sodden with wine, bemused with liquor; they do not recognize the one who sees and have forgotten about judgement. Every table is covered with vomit and filth and no place was left. To whom shall the Lord teach knowledge? Whom shall he compel to listen and understand?'[313] Through Joel the Lord says: 'Wake up, you drunkards, and weep for the sweet wine you drink.'[314] Not that he forbids wine when necessary, for the Apostle recommends it to Timothy 'for the frequent ailments of your stomach'[315]—not ailments only, but frequent ones. Noah was the first to plant a vineyard, still not knowing perhaps of the evil of intoxication, and, when drunk, exposed his bare thighs, because with wine comes the shame of lechery. When mocked by his son he put a curse on him and bound him by a sentence of servitude which we know had never been done before.[316] Lot was a holy man, and so his daughters saw that he could never be led into incest except through drunkenness.[317] And the holy widow believed that Holofernes in his pride could never be tricked and brought low except by this device.[318] The angels who visited the patriarchs of old and were hospitably received by them took food, we are told, but not wine.[319] Elijah too, the greatest and first of our leaders, when he had retired to the wilderness was brought the nourishment of bread and meats by the ravens morning and evening, but not wine.[320] The children of Israel also, we read, were fed in the desert mainly on the delicate flesh of quails,[321] but neither received nor desired wine.[322] And those repasts of loaves and fishes wherewith the people were sustained in the wilderness are nowhere said to have included wine. Only a wedding, at which one may indulge, was granted the miracle of wine 'and the dissipation that goes

[317] Cf. Gen. 19: 30–8; also Jerome, *Epistola* XXII *ad Eustochium*, 8 (ed. Hilberg, liv. 155–6; *PL* xxii. 399).

[318] 'beata uidua': Judith. Cf. Judith 12: 12 – 13: 13; also *Letter* 7, 28 and *Hymn* 89 (Szövérffy 125), *De sanctis mulieribus* 2, III.

[319] Cf. Gen. 18: 1–8.

[320] Cf. 3 Kgs. (1 Kgs.) 17: 6; also Jerome, *Epistola* XXII *ad Eustochium*, 9 (ed. Hilberg, liv. 156; *PL* xxii. 400).

[321] Cf. Exod. 16: 13.

[322] Cf. Exod. 16–17.

uini 'in quo est luxuria'[323] miraculum habuerunt.[324] Solitudo uero que propria est monachorum habitatio, carnium magis quam uini beneficium nouit. Summa etiam [y]illa in lege[y] Nazareorum religio, qua[z] se Domino consecrant, uinum et quod inebriare potest solummodo uitabant.[325] Que namque uirtus, quod[a] bonum in ebriis manet?

83. Vnde non solum uinum, uerum etiam omne quod inebriare potest, antiquis quoque sacerdotibus legimus interdici. De quo et[a] Ieronimus ad Nepocianum de uita clericorum scribens, et grauiter indignans quod sacerdotes legis ab omni quod inebriare potest abstinentes nostros in hac abstinentia superent, 'nequaquam', inquit, 'uinum redoleas ne audias illud philosophi: hoc non est osculum porrigere sed propinare.[326] [b]Vinolentos sacerdotes et Apostolus dampnat et lex uetus prohibet: "qui altario deseruiunt"[327] uinum et siceram non bibent.[c] [328] Sicera Hebreo sermone[d] omnis pocio nuncupatur que inebriare potest, siue illa que fermento conficitur siue pomorum succo, aut faui decoquuntur in dulcem[e] et barbaram[f] potionem, aut palmarum fructus exprimuntur in liquorem, coctisque frugibus aqua pinguior colatur.[g] Quicquid inebriat et statum mentis euertit, fuge similiter ut uinum.'[b] [329] Ex *Regula* sancti Pachomii: 'Vinum et liquamen absque loco egrotantium nullus attingat.'[330]

84. Quis etiam uestrum[a] non audierit[b] uinum monachorum penitus non esse[331] et in tantum [c]olim a monachis abhorreri ut [d]ab ipso uehementer dehortantes[d] ipsum Sathanam appellarent? Vnde[e] in *Vitis Patrum* [f]scriptum legimus: 'Narrauerunt quidam abbati Pastori de quodam monacho quia[g] non bibebat uinum, et dixit eis quia uinum monachorum omnino non est.'[332] Item post aliqua: 'acta est aliquando celebratio missarum in monte abbatis Antonii, et inuentum est ibi cenidium[h] uini. Et tollens unus de senibus paruum uas,[i] calicem

[y–y] in lege illa *CE* [z] quo *TCE* [a] namque *add. CE*

83 [a] *om. Amb* [b–b] etc. *CE* [c] bibant *Jerome* [d] *Amb add. in marg.*: Haec iam antea scripsit iijsdem omnino verbis. *Cf. Letter 6, 18* [e] dulce *TAmb* [f] herbarum *TAmb* [g] coloratur *Jerome*

84 [a] nostrum *EAmb*[1] [b] audiet *E* [c–c] olim horreri etc. ante Recitatum(*?*) est *C* [d–d] *om. E* [e] ut *E* [f–f] habetur (*or* legetur) et ante recitatum est *E* [g] qui *Vitae* [h] enidium *add. in vacant space in T by T*[5]; modicum *Vitae* [i] *om. Vitae*

[323] Eph. 5: 18. Cited also in *Letter* 6, 4.
[324] Cf. John 2: 1–10.
[325] Cf. Num. 6: 3; also, for the Nazirites, cf. *Letters* 1, 26 and 7, 15.

with it'.[323] [324] But the wilderness, the proper habitation of monks, knew the benefit of meats rather than wine. Again, the cardinal point in the law of the Nazirites, whereby they dedicated themselves to God, forbade only wine and strong drink.[325] For what strength or goodness remains in the drunken?

83. Thus not only wine, but anything which can intoxicate, we read, was also forbidden to the priests of old. And so Jerome, in writing to Nepotian about the life of the clergy, and highly indignant because the priests of the Law abstain from all strong drink and so surpass our clergy in abstinence, says: 'Never smell of wine, lest you hear said of you the well known word of the philosopher: This is not offering a kiss but proffering a cup.[326] The Apostle condemns priests who are given to drink and the Old Law equally forbids it: "Those who serve the altar"[327] shall not drink wine or strong drink.[328] By strong drink in Hebrew is understood any drink which can intoxicate, whether produced by fermentation or from apple juice, or from honeycombs which have been distilled into a sweet, rough drink, or when the fruits of date palms are pressed into liquid, or water is enriched with boiled grain. Whatever intoxicates and upsets the balance of the mind, shun it like wine.'[329] According to the *Rule* of St Pachomius: 'No one shall have access to wine and liquor except in the sickroom.'[330]

84. Which of you has not heard that wine in any form is not for monks,[331] and was so greatly abhorred by the monks of old that in their stern warnings against it they called it Satan? And so we read in the *Lives of the Fathers*: 'Certain people told abbot Pastor that a particular monk drank no wine, to which he replied that wine was not for monks.'[332] And further on: 'Once there was a celebration of Mass on Abbot Antony's Hill, and a jar of wine was found there. One of the elders took a small vessel, carried a cupful to abbot Sisoi and gave it to

[326] Not found, but G. Duurama has kindly drawn my attention to Novatian, *De cibis iudaicis*, vi. 7: 'quorum (*sc.* ebriorum) quisquis salutat, non osculum dat, sed propinat' (*CCSL* iv. 101; *PL* iii. 962BC).

[327] Cf. 1 Cor. 9: 13: 'Nescitis quoniam qui in sacrario operantur, quae de sacrario sunt, edunt; et qui altari deseruiunt, cum altari participant ?'

[328] Cf. Lev. 10: 9; Deut. 29: 6; 1 Tim. 3: 3; Tit. 1: 7. Also Luke 1: 15 ('erit enim (*sc.* Ioannes) magnus coram Domino: et uinum et siceram non bibet').

[329] Jerome, *Epistola* LII *ad Nepotianum presbyterum*, 11 (ed. Hilberg, liv. 434, *ll.* 2–11; *PL* xxii. 536–7). 'De quo et Ieronimus . . . fuge similiter ut uinum': also in *Letter* 6, 18.

[330] Pachomius, *Praecepta*, c. 45 (*PL* xxiii. 69C; *Pachomiana Latina*, p. 24).

[331] Cf. Benedict, *Rule*, c. 40, 6; also *Letter* 6, 19.

[332] *Vitae patrum*, *Verba seniorum*, v. 4. 31 (*PL* lxxiii. 868D); also cited in *Letter* 6, 19.

portauit ad abbatem Sysoi et dedit ei. Et bibit semel, et secundo et[j] accepit et bibit. Obtulit[k] ei etiam tertio, sed non accepit dicens: Quiesce, frater, an nescis quia est Sathanas?'[333] Et iterum de abbate Sysoi: 'Dicit ergo Abraham discipulus eius: Si occurritur in Sabbato et Dominica ad ecclesiam et biberit tres calices, ne multo[l] est? Et dixit senex: Si non esset Sathanas, non esset multum.'[cf 334] Hinc et beatus non immemor Benedictus, cum dispensatione quadam monachis uinum indulgeret, ait: 'Licet legamus uinum monachorum omnino non esse,[335] sed quia nostris temporibus id [m]monachis persuaderi[m] non potest',[n 336] etc.[o]

85. Quid enim mirum, si monachis penitus non sit indulgendum, quod feminis quoque, quarum in se [a]est natura[a] debilior et tamen contra [b]uinum fortior, ipsum[b] omnino beatus interdicit[c] Ieronimus? Hic[d] enim Eustochium uirginem Christi de conseruanda instruens uirginitate uehementer adhortatur dicens: 'Si quid itaque in me potest esse consilii, si experto creditur, hoc primum moneo et obtestor ut sponsa Christi uinum fugiat pro ueneno. [e]Hec aduersus adolescentiam prima sunt arma demonum. Non sic auaricia quatit, inflat superbia, delectat ambitio. Facile aliis caremus uiciis. Hic hostis intus inclusus est. Quocumque pergamus nobiscum portamus inimicum. Vinum et adolescentia duplex incendium uoluptatis. Quid oleum flamme adicimus? Quid ardenti corpusculo fomenta ignium ministramus?'[e 337] Constat tamen ex eorum documentis qui de phisica scripserunt multo minus feminis quam uiris uirtutem uini preualere posse. Cuius quidem rei rationem inducens Machrobius Theodosius septimo[f] Saturnaliorum libro sic ait: 'Aristotiles [g]mulieres, inquit,[g] raro inebriantur, crebro senes. Mulier humectissimo est corpore. Docet hoc et lenitas[h] cutis et splendor. Docent precipue assidue purgationes superfluo exhonerantes corpus humore. Cum ergo[i] epotum uinum in tam largum ceciderit humorem uim suam perdit, nec facile cerebri sedem ferit fortitudine eius exstincta.'[338] Item: 'Muliebre corpus crebris purgationibus depuratum pluribus consertum foraminibus ut pateat in meatus et uias prebeat humori [j]in

[j] *om. Vitae* [k] Attulit *Vitae* [l] multum *Vitae* [m–m] persuaderi monachis *CE;* monachis penitus persuaderi *Amb* [n] potuit *E* [o] etc.: *add. Luscombe*

85 [a–a] natura est *CE* [b–b] ipsum fortior uinum *CE* [c] interdicat *CE* [d] hinc *CE* [e–e] etc *CE* [f] iiii *T;* 4 *CEAmb* [g–g] inquit mulieres *CE* [h] leuitas *?C, Amb* [i] igitur *CE* [j–j] *om. CE*

[333] *Vitae patrum, Verba seniorum*, v. 4. 36 (*PL* lxxiii. 869CD); also cited in *Letter* 6, 19.

him. He drank once, and he took it a second time and drank, but when it was offered a third time he refused, saying: Peace, brother, do you not know this is Satan?'[333] It is also said of abbot Sisoi: 'His disciple Abraham then asked: If this happens on the Sabbath and the Lord's Day in church, and he drinks three cups, is that too much? If it were not Satan, the old man replied, it would not be much.'[334] St Benedict had this in mind when he allowed wine to monks by special dispensation, saying: 'Although we read that wine is never for monks,[335] but because in our times it is impossible to persuade monks of this',[336] etc.

85. It is not surprising, then, that if wine is strictly denied to monks, St Jerome absolutely forbids it to women, whose nature is weaker in itself, though stronger as regards wine. He uses strong words when instructing Eustochium, the Bride of Christ, how to preserve her virginity: 'And so, if there is any counsel in me, if my experience is to be trusted, this is my first warning and testimony. The Bride of Christ must avoid wine like poison. It is the first weapon of demons against youth. Greed does not make her waver nor pride bolster her up nor ambition seduce her in the same way. We can easily forgo the other vices, but this is a foe shut up within us. Wherever we go we carry the enemy with us. Wine and youth are the twin fires of lust. Why throw oil on the flame? Why add the fuel of fire to the burning body?'[337] And yet it is well known from the evidence of those who have written about medicine that wine has much less power over women than men. Macrobius Theodosius, in the seventh book of his *Saturnalia*, gives a reason for this: 'Aristotle says that women are rarely intoxicated, but old men often. Woman has an extremely humid body, as can be known from her smooth and glossy skin, and especially from her regular menstruations, which rid the body of a superfluous humour. So when wine is drunk and descends into such a plentiful humour, it loses its power and when its strength has gone it does not readily strike the seat of the brain.'[338] Again: 'A woman's body which is cleansed by frequent purgations is formed with several apertures and opens into channels and provides outlets for fluid

[334] *Vitae patrum, Verba seniorum*, v. 4. 37 (*PL* lxxiii. 869D); also cited in *Letter* 6, **19**.
[335] Cf. *Vitae patrum, Verba seniorum*, v. 4. 31 (*PL* lxxiii. 868D); also *Letter* 6, **19**.
[336] Benedict, *Rule*, c. 40, 6; also cited in *Letter* 6, **19**.
[337] Jerome, *Epistola* XXII *ad Eustochium*, 8 (ed. Hilberg, liv. 154, *ll.* 11–20; *PL* xxii. 399).
[338] Macrobius, *Saturnalia*, vii. 6. 16–17; also cited in *Letter* 6, **14**.

egestionis exitum confluenti.[j] Per hec foramina uapor uini celeriter euanescit.'[339]

86. Qua igitur ratione id monachis indulgetur quod infirmiori sexui denegatur? Quanta est insania id eis concedere quibus amplius potest nocere et aliis negare? Quid denique stultius id quod religioni magis est contrarium et a Deo plurimum facit apostatare religionem non abhorrere? Quid impudentius quam id quod regibus[340] quoque et sacerdotibus legis[341] interdicitur Christiane perfectionis abstinentiam non uitare, immo in hoc maxime delectari? Quis namque ignoret quantum in hoc tempore clericorum precipue uel monachorum studium circa cellaria uersetur ut ea scilicet diuersis generibus uini repleant, herbis illud,[a] melle et speciebus condiant ut tanto facilius se inebrient[b] quanto delectabilius potent,[c] et tanto se magis ad libidinem incitent quanto amplius uino estuent?[d] Quis hic non tam error quam furor ut qui se maxime per professionem continentie obligant, minus [e]se ad conseruandum uotum[e] preparent, immo ut minime custodiri possit efficiant? Quorum profecto si claustris retinentur corpora, corda libidine plena sunt et in fornicationem inardescit animus. Scribens ad Tymotheum Apostolus 'noli', inquit, 'adhuc aquam bibere, sed uino modico utere propter stomachum tuum et frequentes [f]infirmitates tuas.'[f][342] Cui propter infirmitatem [g]uinum conceditur[g] modicum. Constat utique[h] quia sanus sumeret nullum. Si uitam profitemur apostolicam, et precipue formam uouemus penitentie et fugere seculum proponimus, cur eo maxime delectamur quod proposito nostro maxime aduersari uidemus et uniuersis est alimentis delectabilius?[i] Diligens penitentie descriptor beatus Ambrosius nihil in uictu penitentium preter uinum accusat dicens: 'An quis putat illam penitentiam ubi adquirende ambitio dignitatis, ubi uini effusio, ubi ipsius copule coniugalis usus? [j]Renunciandum seculo est. Facilius inueni qui innocentiam seruauerint quam qui congrue [k]egerint penitentiam.'[kj][343] Idem[l] in libro *de fuga seculi* 'bene', inquit, 'fugis si oculus tuus fugiat calices et fialas ne fiat libidus[m] dum moratur in uino.'[344] Solum de omnibus alimentis in fuga seculi

86 [a] et *add. CE* [b] inebriant *CE* [c] potant *CE* [d] estuant *CE* [e–e] ad conservandum votum se *Amb* [f–f] tuas infirmitates *CE* [g–g] conceditur vinum *Amb* [h] quippe *CE* [i] detestabilius *CE* [j–j] *om. CE* [k–k] poenitentiam egerint *Amb* [l] Item *CE* [m] libidinosus *Amb*

[339] Macrobius, *Saturnalia*, vii. 6. 18; also cited in *Letter* 6, 14.
[340] Cf. Prov. 31: 4–5, cited at 82 above and in *Letter* 6, 18.

flowing out to be dispersed. Through these channels the vapour of wine quickly disappears.'[339]

86. On what grounds, then, should monks be allowed what is denied to the weaker sex? What madness is it to permit it to those it can harm more while denying it to others? What could be more foolish than that religion should not abhor what is so contrary to religion and takes us furthest away from God? What could be more shameless than that the abstinence of Christian perfection should not shun or, rather, should especially delight in what is forbidden to kings[340] and priests of the Law?[341] For who does not know that today the attention of clerics in particular, and of monks, revolves round cellars, to see how they can fill them with different varieties of wine, how to flavour it with herbs, honey, and spices, so that they may get drunk more easily because they drink more pleasurably, and the more they are warmed by wine, the more they rouse themselves to lust? What error, or rather, what folly is this, when those who bind themselves most stringently by their profession of continence make less preparation for keeping their vow, and even do what makes it least likely to be kept? Though their bodies are confined to the cloister their hearts are filled with lust and minds on fire for fornication. In writing to Timothy the Apostle says: 'Stop drinking nothing but water; take a little wine for your digestion, for your frequent ailments.'[342] Timothy is allowed a little wine for his ailments because it is clear that when in good health he would take none. If we profess the apostolic life and especially vow to follow the way of repentance, if we preach withdrawal from the world, why do we particularly delight in what we see to be wholly contrary to our purpose and more delectable than any food? St Ambrose in his detailed description of repentance condemns nothing in the diet of the penitent except wine. 'Does anyone think', he asks, 'that repentance exists where there is still ambition for high position, pouring out of wine and conjugal enjoyment of sexual union? Renunciation of the world can more easily be found among those who have kept their innocence than among those who have done fitting penance.'[343] Again, in his book *On Renouncing the World* he says: 'You renounce it well if your eye renounces cups and flagons lest it becomes lustful in lingering over wine.'[344] Wine is the only form of

[341] Cf. Lev. 10: 9.

[342] 1 Tim. 5: 23; also cited at **82** above.

[343] Ambrose, *De paenitentia*, ii. 10. 96 (ed. Faller, p. 201, *ll.* 41–4, 40–1; *PL* xvi. 541–2).

[344] Ambrose, *De fuga saeculi*, ix. 56 (ed. Schenkl, p. 206, *ll.* 9–10; *PL* xiv. 594D).

uinum commemorat, et hoc uinum, si fugiamus, bene nos seculum fugere asserit, quasi omnes seculi uoluptates ex hoc uno[n] pendeant; [o]nec etiam dicit si gula fugiat eius gustum, uerum etiam oculus uisum, ne libidine et uoluptate ipsius capiatur quod frequenter intuetur. Vnde et illud est Salomonis quod supra meminimus: 'Ne intueamur uinum quando flauescit, cum splenduerit in uitro color eius.'[o] [345] [p]Sed quid et hic,[p] queso, dicemus qui, ut tam gustu eius quam uisu oblectemur[q] cum illud melle, herbis uel speciebus diuersis condierimus, fialis etiam ipsum propinari uolumus?

87. Beatus Benedictus, uini coactus indulgentiam faciens, 'saltem uel hoc', inquit, 'consenciamus non usque ad sacietatem bibamus, set parcius, quia "uinum apostatare [a]facit etiam[a] sapientes."'[346] [347] O utinam usque ad sacietatem bibere sufficeret ne maioris rei transgressionis ad superfluitatem efferremur! Beatus etiam Augustinus, monasteria ordinans clericorum et eis *Regulam* scribens, Sabbato tantum et Dominica [b]uinum eis indulget dicens: 'Sabbato et Dominica,[b] sicut consuetudo[c] est, qui uolunt uinum accipiant',[348] tum uidelicet pro reuerentia dominice diei et ipsius uigilie que est Sabbatum, tum etiam quia tunc dispersi per cellulas fratres congregabuntur. Sicut etiam[d] in *Vitis Patrum* beatus commemorat Ieronimus scribens de loco quem Cellia nominauit hiis uerbis: 'Singuli per cellulas manent. Die tamen Sabbati et Dominica in unum ad ecclesiam coeunt et ibi semetipsos inuicem tamquam e[e] celo redditos uident.'[349] Vnde[f] profecto conueniens erat hec indulgentia ut insimul[g] conuenientes aliqua recreatione congauderent, non tam dicentes quam sencientes: 'Ecce quam bonum [h]et quam iocundum habitare fratres in unum.'[h] [350]

88. Ecce,[a] si a carnibus[b] abstineamus, magnum quid nobis imputatur quantacumque superfluitate ceteris uescamur, si multis expensis diuersa piscium fercula comparemus, si piperis et specierum sapores misceamus, si, cum inebriati mero fuerimus, calices herbatorum et phialas[c] pigmentorum superaddamus! Totum id excusat uilium abstinentia carnium dummodo eas publice non uoremus, quasi

[n] uino *CEAmb*[1] [o–o] *om. CE* [p–p] etc. Quid ad *T* [q] delectamur (*exp.*) oblectemur *T*

87 [a–a] etiam facit *CE* [b–b] *om. CAmb* [c] constitutum *Augustine* [d] et *Amb* [e] *om. CAmb* [f] Vbi *CE* [g] simul *CE* [h–h] etc. *CE*

88 [a] Contra illos (qui a) carnibus absti(nent) et ceteris superflu(e) uescuntur et pota(nt) *add. in marg. TAmb; in T the letters between brackets have been lost through trimming* [b] carnalibus *CE* [c] fialas *EAmb*

nutriment he mentions in this book, and he says that we renounce the world well if we renounce wine, as if all the pleasures of the world depend on this alone: nor does he say 'if the palate renounces the taste of it' but 'if the eye renounces the sight', lest it be captivated by lust and delight in what it often sees. Hence the words of Solomon which we quoted above: 'Do not look on wine when it glows and sparkles in the glass.'[345] But what, pray, are we to say when we have flavoured it with honey, herbs, or different spices so as to enjoy its taste as well as the sight of it, and then want to drink it by flagons?

87. St Benedict was compelled to grant indulgence for wine, saying: 'Let us agree at least on this, that we should drink temperately, not to satiety, for "wine robs even the wise of their wits".'[346] [347] If only our drinking could stop at satiety and not be carried on to the greater sin of excess! St Augustine, too, in setting up monasteries for clerics and writing a *Rule* for them, says: 'Those who wish may have wine on Saturdays and Sundays, as agreed upon.'[348] This was out of reverence for the Lord's Day and its vigil, the Sabbath, and also because at that time the brothers scattered amongst the cells were gathered together. Likewise in the *Lives of the Fathers* also St Jerome says, when writing of the place he named the Cells: 'They stay each in his own cell, but on the Sabbath and the Lord's Day they go together to Church, and there they see each other as if returned from heaven.'[349] This indulgence was therefore surely suitable at a time when they met together and could enjoy some relaxation, and feel as well as say: 'How good it is and how pleasant for brothers to live together!'[350]

88. But if we abstain from meat, what a reproach it is to us if we eat everything else to excess, if we procure varied dishes of fish at vast expense, mingle the flavours of pepper and spices, and, when we are drunk on neat wine, go on to cups of herb-flavoured liquor and flagons of spiced drink! Abstinence from plain meat excuses all this provided that we do not guzzle in public—as if quality rather than

[345] Prov. 23: 31, cited above at **82**.

[346] Ecclus. 19: 2

[347] Benedict, *Rule*, c. 40, 6–7.

[348] *Ordo monasterii* or *Disciplina monasterii*, 7; also known as the *Regula secunda*, part of the *Rule* ascribed to Augustine of Hippo, *c.*397, and usually held to be addressed to men (ed. Verheijen, p. 150; ed. and trans. Lawless, pp. 76–7; *PL* xxxii. 1459).

[349] Not Jerome but Rufinus (*c.*345–411), trans., *Historia monachorum*, 22 (*PL* xxi. 444C–445A).

[350] Ps. 132 (133): 1.

ciborum qualitas magis quam superfluitas in culpa sit, cum solam Dominus crapulam et ebrietatem nobis interdicat,[351] hoc est, cibi pariter et uini superfluitatem [d]pocius quam qualitatem.[d] Quod et diligenter beatus attendens Augustinus, nichilque[3] in alimentis preter uinum ueritus nec ullam[f] ciborum qualitatem distinguens, [g]hoc in abstinentia satis[g] esse credidit quod breuiter[h] expressit: 'Carnem', inquit, 'uestram domate ieiuniis et abstinentia [i]esce uel potus quantum ualitudo permittit.'[i] [352] Legerat, nisi fallor, illud beati Athanasii in *Exhortatione ad monachos*: 'Ieiuniorum quoque non sit uolentibus[j] certa mensura, sed in quantum possibilitas ualet nisi[k] laborantis extensa que, preter dominicam diem, semper sint solempnia si[l] uotiua sint.'[353] Ac si diceret: si ex uoto suscipiuntur, deuote compleantur omni tempore nisi in dominicis diebus. Nulla hic ieiunia[m] prefiguntur sed quantum [n]permittit ualitudo.[n] Dicitur enim:[o] 'Solam nature facultatem inspicit et ipsam sibi modum prefigere permittit, sciens quoniam in nullis delinquitur si modus in omnibus teneatur.'[354] Vt uidelicet nec remissius quam oportet[p] uoluptatibus resoluamur, sicut de populo medulla tritici et meracissimo uino educato[q] scriptum est: 'Incrassatus est dilatatus[r] et recalcitrauit.'[355] Nec supra modum abstinentia macerati uel omnino uicti succumbamus uel murmurantes mercedem amittamus[s] uel de singularitate gloriemur. Quod Ecclesiastes preueniens ait: 'Iustus perit in sua iusticia. Noli esse iustus multum neque plus sapias quam necesse est, ne [t]obstupescas',[356] hoc est, ne tua[t] quasi admirans singularitate intumescas.

89. Huic uero diligentie sic omnium uirtutum mater discretio[357] presit ut que quibus imponat onera[a] sollicite uideat, unicuique scilicet secundum propriam uirtutem et naturam sequens pocius quam trahens, nequaquam usum saturitatis[b] set abusum auferat superfluitatis, et sic extirpentur[c] uicia ne ledatur[d] natura. Satis est infirmis si peccata uitent, etsi non ad[e] perfectionis cumulum conscendant. Sufficit quoque paradisi angulo residere si martyribus non possis considere.[f] [358] Tutum est uouere modica ut maiora debitis superaddat

[d–d] *om.* C [e] nichil *C;* nihil *E* [f] illam *CE* [g–g] hec in abstinentia *E* [h] *om. E, where a space is left* [i–i] *om. C* [j] nolentibus *CE* [k] nisu *T;* uisu *C* [l] non *Amb* [m] ieiuniorum tempora *CE* [n–n] ualitudo permittit *CE* [o] *om. CE* [p] uenientes *add. CE* [q] inducato *CE* [r] dilectus *C;* dillectus *E* [s] admittamus *CE* [t–t] obstupescas de tua *TAmb;* obstupescas (stupescas *C*) hoc est ne tua *CE*

89 [a] homines *CE* [b] satietatis *CAmb;* saturitatis *Amb*[1] [c] extirpantur *CE* [d] delectatur *CE* [e] *om. CE* [f] contendere *C;* consedere *E*

superfluity of food were to blame, although the Lord forbids us only dissipation and drunkenness,[351] that is, superfluity in food and drink alike, not quality. St Augustine takes note of this: he has no fears for any form of nourishment save wine, and makes no distinction of quality in foods when he says briefly what he believes to be sufficient abstinence: 'Subdue your flesh by fasting and by abstinence from food and drink as far as your health permits.'[352] If I am not mistaken, he had read that in St Athanasius' *Exhortation to monks*: 'Let there be no fixed measure of fasts for the willing, but let these last as long as possible, without being prolonged by effort, and except on the Lord's Day, if vowed they should be solemnly observed.'[353] In other words: If they are undertaken by vow they should be devoutly carried out, except on the Lord's Day. No fasts are fixed in advance but are to last as far as health permits, for it is said: 'He regards solely the capacity of nature and lets it set its own limit, knowing that there is failure in nothing if moderation is kept in everything.'[354] And so we should not be relaxed in our pleasures more than is right, like the people nourished on wheat germ and the finest wine, of whom it is written: 'He grew fat, he grew bloated and unruly';[355] nor should we succumb, famished and wholly defeated by excessive fasting, and lose our reward by complaining, or glory in our singularity. Ecclesiastes foresees this and says: 'The righteous man perishes in his righteousness. Do not be over-righteous nor wiser than is necessary, lest you are bewildered',[356] that is to say, do not be carried away by pride in your own singularity .

89. Let discretion, the mother of all the virtues,[357] preside over zeal and look carefully to see on whom she may lay which burdens, that is, on each according to his capacity, following nature rather than putting pressure on it, and removing not the habit of sufficiency but the abuse of superfluity, so that vices are rooted out but nature is unharmed. It is enough for the weak if they avoid sin, although they may not rise to the peak of perfection, and sufficient also to rest in a corner of Paradise if you cannot take your seat with the martyrs.[358] It

[351] Cf. Luke 21, 34; also **92** and **93** below and Benedict, *Rule*, c. 39, 7–9.
[352] Augustine, *Epistola* ccxl. 8 (ed. Goldbacher, lvii. 361, *ll.* 15–16; *PL* xxxiii. 960).
[353] Ps.-Athanasius, *De obseruationibus monachorum* cited in an appendix to the *Codex regularum* attributed to Benedict of Aniane (*PL* ciii. 667B).
[354] Not found. [355] Deut. 32: 15. [356] Eccles. 7: 16–17.
[357] 'omnium uirtutum mater discretio': cf. *Letter* 6, **9** and note.
[358] Cf. *Letter* 4, **17** and *Carmen ad Astralabium*, ed. Rubingh-Bosscher *vv.* 295–6.

gratia. Hinc enim scriptum est: 'Cum feceritis omnia que precepta sunt, dicite: Serui inutiles sumus; que debuimus[g] facere, fecimus.'[359] 'Lex', inquit Apostolus, 'iram operatur. Vbi enim non est lex, nec preuaricatio.'[360] Et iterum: 'Sine [h]lege enim[h] peccatum mortuum erat. Ego autem uiuebam sine lege aliquando. Sed cum uenisset mandatum, peccatum reuixit. Ego autem mortuus sum, et inuentum est mihi mandatum quod erat ad uitam, hoc est, ad mortem. Nam peccatum occasione accepta per mandatum seduxit me, et per illud me occidit ut fiat supra modum peccans peccatum per mandatum.'[361] Augustinus ad Simplicianum: 'Ex prohibitione, aucto desiderio, dulcius factum est, et ideo fefellit.'[362] Idem in libro *questionum octaginta trium*: 'Suasio delectationis ad peccatum uehementior est cum adest prohibitio.'[363] [i]Hinc et illud est poeticum:[i] 'Nitimur in uetitum semper cupimusque negata.'[364] Attendat hoc[j] cum tremore[k] quisquis se iugo alicuius regule quasi noue legis professioni uult alligare.[365] Eligat quod possit, timeat quod non possit.[366] Nemo legis efficitur reus nisi qui [l]eam fuerit ante[l] professus. Antequam profitearis, delibera. Cum professus fueris, obserua. Ante est uoluntarium quod postea fit necessarium. 'In domo Patris mei', dicit Veritas, 'mansiones multe sunt.'[367] Sic et[m] plurime sunt quibus illuc perueniatur uie. Non dampnantur coniuges, sed facilius[n] saluantur continentes. Non ad hoc ut saluemur[o] sanctorum patrum superaddite sunt[p] regule, sed ut facilius saluemur et purius Deo uacare possimus. 'Et si', inquit Apostolus, 'nupserit uirgo, non peccabit; tribulationem tamen carnis[q] habebunt huiusmodi.[r] Ego autem uobis parco.'[368] Item:[s] 'Mulier que innupta est et uirgo cogitat que Domini sunt [t]ut sit sancta corpore et spiritu. Que autem nupta est cogitat que sunt mundi, quomodo placeat uiro.[t] Porro hoc ad utilitatem uestram dico,[u] non ut laqueum uobis iniciam,[v] sed ad[w] id quod honestum est et quod

[g] debemus *C* [h–h] enim lege *CE* [i–i] Hinc . . . poeticum *om. Amb* [j] hic *E; om. Amb* [k] haec *add. Amb* [l–l] ante eam fuerit *CE* [m] etiam *Amb* [n] *om. E* [o] saluaremur *Amb* [p] sunt additae *Amb* [q] *om. CE* [r] huius *CE* [s] et *add. TCE* [t–t] etc. *CE* [u] *T*[1] *adds a cross in marg. here* [v] inijciam *Amb* [w] *om. C*

[359] Luke 17: 10; also cited in *Letter* 6, 15.

[360] Rom. 4: 15; also cited in *Letter* 6, 13 and in *Comm. Rom.*, ii (iv. 15, ed. Buytaert, p. 145).

[361] Rom. 7: 8–11, 13; also cited in *Comm. Rom.*, iii (vii. 8, ed. Buytaert, pp. 198–9).

[362] Augustine, *De diuersis quaestionibus ad Simplicianum*, i. 1. 5 (ed. Mutzenbecher, p. 11; *PL* xl. 104).

[363] Augustine, *De diuersis quaestionibus octaginta tribus*, lxvi. 5 (ed. Mutzenbecher, p. 156; *PL* xl. 63).

is safe to vow in moderation so that grace may add more to what we owe; for of this it is written: 'When you have done all you have been told to do, say: We are merely servants; we have only done our duty.'[359] 'The Law', says the Apostle, 'can bring only retribution: only where there is no law can there be no breach of law.'[360] And again: 'Where there is no law, sin is dead. Once when there was no law, I was alive, but when the commandment came, sin sprang to life and I died. The commandment was meant to lead me to life, but in my case it led to death, because sin took advantage of the commandment to seduce me, and through the commandment killed me. And so, through the commandment, sin became more powerful than ever.'[361] Augustine writes to Simplician: 'By being prohibited desire has increased, it has become sweeter and so deceived me.'[362] Similarly, in the book of *Eighty-Three Questions*: 'The persuasiveness of pleasure towards sin is more urgent when there is prohibition.'[363] Hence the poet says: 'We always seek what is forbidden and desire what is denied.'[364] Let him pay heed to this with reverence, who wishes to bind himself under the yoke of any rule, as though by obedience to a new law.[365] Let him choose what he can, fear what he cannot.[366] No one is held liable under a law unless he has accepted its authority. Think carefully before you accept it, but once you have done so, keep it. What was voluntary before afterwards becomes compulsory. 'There are many dwelling places', says the Truth, 'in my Father's house.'[367] So too there are many ways whereby we may come to them. The married are not damned, but the continent are more easily saved. The rulings of the holy Fathers were not added on so that we can be saved, but so that we can be saved more easily and be enabled to devote ourselves more purely to God. 'If a virgin marries', says the Apostle, 'she does no wrong. But such people will have trouble in the flesh, and my aim is to spare you.'[368] Again: 'The unmarried and virgin woman cares for the Lord's business; her aim is to be holy both in body and spirit. But the married woman cares for worldly things and her aim is to please her husband. In saying this I have no desire to keep you on a tight rein; I am thinking simply of your own good, of what is seemly, and of your freedom to wait upon

[364] Ovid, *Amores*, iii. 4. 17; cited also in *Collationes* **26** (ed. Marenbon and Orlandi, p. 36; *Dialogus*, ed. Thomas *l.* 529; missing from *PL* clxxviii. 1622C); *TChr*, ii. 21 and *Comm. Rom.*, iii (vii. 9, ed. Buytaert, p. 198, *l.* 381).

[365] Cf. *Letter* 6, **13** and **15**.

[366] Cf. **79** above and note.

[367] John 14: 2.

[368] 1 Cor. 7: 28.

facultatem prebeat sine impedimento Deum obseruandi.'[x] [369] Tunc uero facillime id agitur cum a seculo corpore quoque recedentes claustris nos monasteriorum recludimus, ne nos seculares inquietent tumultus.

90. Nec solum qui legem suscipit, sed qui legem imponit prouideat ne multiplicatis preceptis transgressiones multiplicet.[370] Verbum Dei ueniens, uerbum abbreuiatum fecit super terram. Multa Moyses locutus est et tamen, ut ait Apostolus: 'Nichil ad perfectum adduxit lex.'[371] Multa profecto et in tantum grauia ut apostolus Petrus eius precepta neminem potuisse portare profiteatur, dicens: 'Viri fratres, quid temptatis Deum imponere iugum super ceruicem discipulorum, quod neque[a] patres nostri neque nos portare potuimus? Sed per gratiam Domini Ihesu credimus saluari, quemadmodum et illi.'[372] Paucis Christus de edificatione morum et sanctitate uite apostolos instruxit et perfectionem docuit. Austera remouens et grauia, suauia precepit et leuia quibus omnem consummauit religionem. 'Venite', inquit, 'ad me omnes qui [b][c]laboratis et onerati estis, et ego reficiam uos.[c] Tollite iugum meum super uos [d]et discite a me, quia mitis sum et humilis corde, et inuenietis requiem animabus uestris.[d] Iugum enim meum suaue [e]est et onus meum leue.'[e][b] [373]

91. Sic enim sepe in operibus bonis sicut in negociis agitur[a] seculi. Multi quippe in negocio plus laborant et minus lucrantur. Et multi exterius amplius affliguntur et minus interius apud Deum proficiunt qui cordis pocius quam operis inspector est. Qui etiam quo in exterioribus amplius occupantur minus ad interiora uacare possunt; et quanto apud homines qui de exterioribus iudicant amplius innotescunt, maiorem gloriam apud eos assecuntur et facilius per elationem seducuntur. Cui Apostolus occurrens errori opera uehementer extenuat et fidei iustificationem amplificans ait: 'Si enim Abraham ex operibus iustificatus est, habet gloriam, sed non aput Deum.[b] Quid enim dicit Scriptura? Credidit Abraham Deo et reputatum est ei ad iusticiam.'[374] [c]Et iterum: 'Quid ergo dicemus?[d]

[x] obsecrandi *Vulg.*

90 [a] nec *Amb* [b–b] etc. *C* [c–c] etc. *E* [d–d] etc. *E* [e–e] etc. *E*

91 [a] agat *CE* [b] Dominum *Amb* [c] beginning of lacuna in CE, ending in 92 [d] dicimus *Amb*

[369] 1 Cor. 7: 34–5.
[370] Cf. Rom. 9: 28; also *Comm. Rom.*, iv (ix. 28, ed. Buytaert, pp. 245–6).
[371] Heb. 7: 19; also cited in *SN* c. 140, 3; *Collationes* **65**, ed. Marenbon and Orlandi,

the Lord without distraction.'[369] The time for this to be most easily done is when we withdraw from the world in body too, and shut ourselves in the cloisters of monasteries lest we are disturbed by the tumult of the world.

90. Not only he who receives but he who imposes a law should take care not to multiply transgressions by multiplying restrictions.[370] The Word of God came down to earth and curtailed the word on earth. Moses said many things, and yet, in the words of the Apostle, 'The Law brought nothing to perfection.'[371] He did indeed say many things, which were so burdensome that the apostle Peter declares that no one can endure his precepts: 'Men and brothers, why do you provoke God, laying on the shoulders of these disciples a yoke which neither we nor our fathers were able to bear? No, we believe that it is by the grace of the Lord Jesus that we are saved, and so are they.'[372] Christ chose only a few words to give the apostles moral instruction and teach the holiness of life and the way of perfection. He set aside what was austere and burdensome and taught sweetness and light, which for him was the sum of religion. 'Come to me', he said, 'all you who labour and are overburdened, and I will give you rest. Shoulder my yoke, and learn from me, for I am gentle and humble in heart, and you will find rest for your souls. For my yoke is pleasant to bear and my load is light.'[373]

91. We often treat our good works as we do the business of the world, for many in their business labour more and gain less, and many outwardly afflict themselves more but inwardly make less progress in the sight of God, who looks at the heart rather than works. The more they are taken up with outward things, the less they can devote themselves to inner ones; and the more they shine out amongst men, who judge by externals, the greater the fame they seek among them, and the more easily they are led astray by pride. The Apostle deals with this error when he firmly belittles works and extols justification by faith, saying: 'For if Abraham was justified by works, then he has a ground for pride, but not before God. For what does Scripture say? Abraham put his faith in the Lord and that faith was counted as righteousness.'[374] And again: 'Then what are we to say? That Gentiles,

p. 82; *Dialogus*, ed. Thomas, *l.* 1242; *PL* clxxviii.1635D; *Sermon* 5 (*PL* clxxviii. 417D); *Problemata* 7 and 14 (*PL* clxxviii. 689CD and 699D).

[372] Acts 15: 7, 10–11; also cited in *Letter* 6, **26** and *Comm. Rom.*, ii (iv. 15, ed. Buytaert, p. 145).

[373] Matt. 11: 28–30; cf. *Letter* 6, **26** and n. 136.

[374] Rom. 4: 2–3; cf. *Letter* 6, **20** and n. 84.

Quod gentes que non sectabantur iusticiam, apprehenderunt iusticiam; iusticiam autem que ex fide est. Israel uero, sectando legem iusticie, in legem iusticie non peruenit. Quare? Quia non ex fide, sed quasi ex operibus.'[375] Illi quod catini est uel parapsidis[e] de foris mundantes, de interiori mundicia minus prouident et, carni magis quam anime uigilantes, carnales pocius sunt quam spirituales.

92. Nos uero Christum in interiori[a] homine per fidem habitare cupientes, pro modico ducimus exteriora que tam reprobis quam electis sunt communia,[376] attendentes quod scriptum est: 'In me sunt, Deus, uota tua, que reddam, laudationes tibi.'[b] [377] [c]Vnde et exteriorem illam legis abstinentiam[c] non sequimur quam nihil iusticie certum est conferre.[378] Nec quicquam nobis in cibis Dominus interdicit nisi crapulam et ebrietatem,[379] id est superfluitatem. Qui etiam quod nobis indulsit in seipso exhibere non erubuit, licet hinc multi scandalizati non mediocriter improperarent. Vnde et per semet ipsum loquens: 'Venit Iohannes', inquit, 'non manducans et non bibens et [d]dixerunt: [e]Demonium habet.[d] Venit Filius hominis manducans et bibens[e] [f]et dixerunt:[f] Ecce homo uorax et potator uini',[380] etc.[g] Qui etiam, suos excusans quod non sicut discipuli Iohannis ieiunarent, nec eciam manducantes corporalem illam mundiciam abluendarum manuum magnopere curarent,[381] 'non possunt', inquit, 'lugere filii sponsi quamdiu cum illis [h]est sponsus',[382] etc.[h] Et alibi: 'Non quod intrat in os coinquinat hominem, [i]sed quod procedit ex ore. Que autem procedunt de ore, de corde exeunt, et ea coinquinant hominem.[i] Non lotis autem manibus manducare, non coinquinat hominem.'[i] [383]

93. Nullus itaque cibus inquinat[a] animam sed appetitus cibi uetiti.[384] Sicut enim corpus nonnisi corporalibus inquinatur sordibus, sic nec anima nisi spiritalibus.[385] Nec timendum est quicquid agatur in corpore si animus ad consensum non trahitur; nec confidendum de

[e] paropsidis *Amb*

92 [a] exteriori *Amb* [b] *end of lacuna in CE, beginning in* 91 [c–c] Illam ergo exteriorem legis abstinentiam ciborum *CE* [d–d] dixerunt. ecce homo demonium habet *C* [e–e] *Ecorr in marg.* [f–f] *om. E* [g] *om. Amb* [h–h] sponsus est *Amb* [i–i] etc *CE*

93 [a] coinquinat *C*

---

[375] Rom. 9: 30–2. Also cited in part in *Problemata* 1 (*PL* clxxviii. 679B).
[376] Cf. *Letters* 4, **16**, and 6, **20**, n. 80. [377] Ps. 55 (56): 12.
[378] Cf. *Problemata* 15 (*PL* clxxviii. 703B).

who were not seeking righteousness, found it, a righteousness, however, that comes from faith; whereas Israel sought a law of righteousness but never achieved it. Why was this? Because their efforts were not based on faith, but (as they supposed) on works.'[375] They clean the outside of the pot or dish but pay less attention to cleanliness inside, they watch over the flesh more than the soul, and so are fleshly rather than spiritual.

92. But we who desire Christ to dwell in the inner man by faith, think little of outward things which are common to the sinner and the chosen.[376] We heed the words: 'I am bound by vows to thee, O God, and will redeem them with praise of thee.'[377] So we do not practise that outward abstinence prescribed by the Law, which certainly confers no righteousness.[378] Nor does the Lord forbid us anything in the way of food except dissipation and drunkenness,[379] that is, excess; and he was not ashamed to display in himself what he has allowed to us, although many of those present took offence and sharply rebuked him. With his own lips he says: 'John came neither eating nor drinking, and they said: He is possessed. The Son of Man came eating and drinking, and they said: Look at him! a glutton and a drinker',[380] etc. He also excused his own disciples because they did not fast like the disciples of John, nor when they were about to eat did they bother much about bodily cleanness and hand-washing.[381] 'The children of the bridegroom', he said, 'cannot be expected to mourn when the bridegroom is with them',[382] etc. And elsewhere: 'A man is not defiled by what goes into his mouth but by what comes out of it. What comes out of the mouth has its origins in the heart, and that is what defiles a man; but to eat without first washing his hands, that cannot defile him.'[383]

93. Therefore no food defiles the soul, only the appetite for forbidden food.[384] For as the body is not defiled except by bodily filth, so the soul can only be defiled by spiritual filth.[385] We need not fear anything done in the body if the mind is not prevailed on to consent. Nor should we put our trust in bodily cleanliness if the mind is

[379] Cf. Luke 21: 34; also **88** above.
[380] Matt. 11: 18–19; cf. *Letter* 6, **23**.
[381] Cf. Matt. 15: 2; also *Letter* 6, **24**.
[382] Matt. 9: 15 .
[383] Matt. 15: 11, 18, 20. Cf. *Letter* 6, **23**; *Problemata* 24 (*PL* clxxviii. 709D–711A) and *Ethica*, i. 14. 2 (ed. Ilgner, p. 15; ed. Luscombe, pp. 22–5).
[384] Cf. **77** and **81** above; also **96** below.
[385] Cf. *Ethica*, i. 14. 1–2 (ed. Ilgner, p. 15; ed. Luscombe, p. 22 *l.* 26–p. 24 *l.* 2).

mundicia carnis si mens uoluntate[b] corrumpitur.[386] In corde igitur tota mors anime consistit et uita. Vnde et Salomon in Prouerbiis: 'Omni custodia serua cor tuum, quoniam ex ipso uita procedit.'[387] [c]Et, iuxta predictam Veritatis assertionem, ex corde procedunt que coinquinant hominem[388] quoniam bonis uel malis desideriis anima dampnatur uel saluatur.[c] Set quoniam anime et carnis in unam coniunctarum personam maxima est unio, summopere prouidendum est ne carnis delectatio ad consensum animam trahat et, dum nimis indulgetur carni, ipsa lasciuiens reluctetur spiritui, et quam oportet subici incipiat dominari.[389] Hoc autem cauere poterimus si necessariis omnibus concessis superfluitatem, ut sepius dictum est, penitus amputemus et infirmo sexui nullum ciborum usum sed omnium denegemus abusum.[d] Omnia concedantur sumi sed nulla immoderate consumi. 'Omnis', inquit Apostolus, 'creatura Dei bona[e] et nihil reiciendum quod cum gratiarum actione percipitur. [f]Sanctificatur enim per uerbum Dei et orationem. Hoc proponens fratribus bonus eris minister Christi Iesu, enutritus uerbis fidei et bone doctrine quam assecutus es.'[f] [390] Et nos igitur cum Tymotheo hanc Apostoli insecuti doctrinam, et iuxta dominicam sententiam nihil in cibis nisi crapulam et ebrietatem uitantes,[391] sic omnia temperemus ut ex omnibus infirmam naturam sustentemus, non uicia nutriamus. Et [g]quo queque[g] amplius sua superfluitate possunt nocere temperamenti magis accipiant. Maius quippe est ac laudabilius temperate comedere quam omnino abstinere. [h]Vnde et beatus Augustinus in libro *de bono coniugali*, cum de corporalibus ageret sustentamentis, 'nequaquam', inquit, 'eis bene utitur, nisi qui et uti non potest. Multi quidem facilius se abstinent ut non utantur quam temperant ut bene utantur. Nemo tamen potest eis sapienter uti, nisi potest et continenter non uti.'[392] Ex hoc habitu et Paulus dicebat: 'Scio et habundare et penuriam pati.'[393] Penuriam quippe pati quorumcumque hominum est, sed scire penuriam pati magnorum est. Sic et habundare

[b] uoluptate non *CE* [c–c] *om. CE* [d] *T adds a cross in marg. here* [e] est *add. CE* [f–f] etc. *CE* [g–g] quoque *CE* [h–h] *om. CE*

[386] 'consensum', 'uoluntate': in his *Ethica*, i. 3. 1–4, 3; i. 7. 1–10, 9, Abelard refined his concept of sin in such a way that sin should properly be defined not as an evil will or desire but as consent to evil (ed. Ilgner, pp. 3–4, 7–11; ed. Luscombe, pp. 4 *l.* 29–6 *l.* 24, 10 *l.* 28–16 *l.* 32). Cf. *Problemata* 13 and 24 (*PL* clxxviii. 696A, 710CD). But on occasions (as here and at **96** below) he was more flexible. Cf. for example *Carmen ad Astralabium*, ed. Rubingh-Bosscher *vv.* 741–2, *Comm. Rom.*, ii (v. 19, ed. Buytaert, p. 164 *ll.* 354–78) and *Sententie* **267–9**, **274** (ed. Luscombe, *ll.* 3173–3202, *ll.* 3241–2; c. 33, 34, ed. Buzzetti, p. 150 *l.* 30–151

corrupted by the will.[386] Thus the whole life and death of the soul depends on the heart, as Solomon says in Proverbs: 'Guard your heart more than any treasure, for it is the source of all life.' [387]And according to the words of the Truth we have quoted, what defiles a man comes from the heart,[388] since the soul is lost or saved by evil or good desires. But since soul and flesh are closely conjoined in one person, special care must be taken lest the pleasure enjoyed by the flesh leads the soul to comply, and when the flesh is overindulged it grows wanton, resists the spirit and begins to dominate where it should be subject.[389] However, we can guard against this if we allow all necessities but, as we have often said, cut off completely any excess, and so deny the weaker sex not the use of foods but abuse of all of them. Let everything be permitted to be taken but nothing consumed beyond moderation. 'For everything', says the Apostle, 'that God created is good, and nothing is to be rejected when it is taken with thanksgiving, since it is hallowed by God's own word and prayer. By offering such advice as this to the brethren you will prove a good minister of Jesus Christ, bred in the precepts of our faith and of the sound instruction which you have followed.'[390] Let us therefore, with Timothy, follow the teaching of the Apostle, and in accordance with the words of the Lord shun nothing in food except dissipation and drunkenness;[391] let us moderate everything so that we sustain weak nature in every way but do not nurture vices. Whatever can do harm by excess must be the more strictly moderated, for it is better and more praiseworthy to eat in moderation than to abstain altogether. Thus St Augustine, in his book *On the Good of Marriage*, when he deals with bodily sustenance, says that 'a man makes no good use of these things unless he can also abstain from them. Many find it easier to abstain and not use at all than to be moderate and use well. But no one can use wisely unless he can also restrain himself from using.'[392] St Paul also said of this habit: 'I know both what it is to have plenty and what it is to suffer need.'[393] To suffer need is the lot of all men, but to know how to suffer need is granted only to great men. So too, any man can begin to have plenty,

l. 56, p. 153 *ll.* 4–5; *PL* clxxviii. 1753BD, 1754C). On one occasion, in *Letter* 4, 11, Heloise writes of consent which brings guilt.

[387] Prov. 4: 23.

[388] Cf. Matt. 15: 18.

[389] Cf. *Problemata* 14 and 28; also *Sermon* 10 (*PL* clxxviii. 697C, 712D, 449CD).

[390] 1 Tim. 4: 4–6.

[391] Cf. Luke 21: 34; also 88 and 92 above.

[392] Augustine, *De bono coniugali*, xxi. 25 (ed. Zycha, p. 219, *l.* 25–p. 220, *l.* 3; *PL* xl. 390).

[393] Phil. 4: 12.

quisquam [i]hominum incipere[i] potest, scire autem habundare nonnisi eorum est quos habundantia non corrumpit.[h]

94. De uino itaque quia, [a]sicut dictum est, 'luxuriosa res est et tumultuosa',[394] ideoque[a] tam continentie quam silentio maxime contrarium, aut omnino femine abstineant propter Deum,[395] sicut uxores gentilium ab hoc inhibentur metu adulteriorum, aut ita ipsum aqua temperent ut et siti pariter et sanitati consulat et uires nocendi non habeat. [b]Hoc autem fieri credimus si huius mixture quarta pars ad minus aque fuerit.[b] [396] Difficilimum uero est ut ad positum[c] nobis potum sic obseruemus ut non usque ad sacietatem inde bibamus, sicut de uino beatus precipit Benedictus.[397] Ideoque tucius arbitramur ut nec sacietatem interdicamus nec[d] inde[e] periculum incurramus. Non enim sacietas, ut sepe iam diximus,[398] set superfluitas in crimine est. Vt uero pro medicamento herbata uina conficiantur aut etiam [f]purum uinum[f] sumatur non prohibendum est. Quibus tamen conuentus numquam utatur sed separatim ab infirmis hec degustentur.

95. [a]Triticee quoque medulle similaginem omnino prohibemus, sed semper, cum habuerint triticum, tercia pars ad minus grossioris annone misceatur. Nec calidis umquam oblectentur panibus, sed qui ad minus uno die ante cocti fuerint.[a] [399] Ceterorum uero alimentorum prouidentiam sic habeat diaconissa ut, [b]sicut iam prefati sumus,[b] [400] quod uilius poterit comparari uel facilius haberi, infirmi sexus nature subueniat. [c]Quid enim stultius quam, cum sufficiant nostra, emamus aliena? Et cum sint domi necessaria, queramus extra superflua? Et cum sint ad manum que sufficiunt,[d] laboremus ad illa que superfluunt?[c] De qua quidem necessaria discretionis moderatione non tam humano quam angelico seu etiam dominico instructi documento, nouerimus ad huius uite necessitudinem transigendam non tam qualitatem ciborum exquirere quam hiis que presto sunt contentos esse. Vnde et Abraham carnibus apparatis

[i–i] *om. T but add. in marg. by T*[5]

94 [a–a] *om. CE* [b–b] *om. CE* [c] adpositum *Amb* [d] ne *Amb* [e] vitae *Amb*[1] [f–f] uinum purum *CEAmb*

95 [a–a] *om. CE* [b–b] *om. CE* [c–c] *om. CE* [d] sufficiant *Amb*

[394] Prov. 20: 1; cf. **82** above and *Letter* 6, 18.

[395] Cf. *Problemata* 31 (*PL* clxxviii. 715AB).

[396] Cf. *Institutiones nostre*, 5 (*The Paraclete Statutes*, ed. Waddell, p. 10 (commentary on p. 97); *PL* clxxviii. 314C).

[397] Benedict, *Rule*, c. 40, 6; cf. **87** above.

but to know how to have plenty is granted only to those whom plenty does not corrupt.

94. As regards wine then, because, as has been said, 'it is a sensual and a turbulent thing',[394] and so very much opposed both to continence and to silence, women should either abstain altogether, for God's sake,[395] just as the wives of the Gentiles are forbidden it through fear of adultery, or they should mix it with enough water to make it satisfy their thirst and benefit their health while not being strong enough to hurt them. This we believe can be done if at least a quarter of the mixture is water.[396] It is indeed very difficult when drink is set before us to make sure that, as St Benedict instructed, we do not go on drinking to sufficiency.[397] And so we think it safer not to forbid sufficiency and run the risk of a rule being broken, for it is not this, as we have often said, which is culpable, but superfluity.[398] The preparation for medicinal purposes of wine mixed with herbs or even the drinking of neat wine is not to be forbidden, so long as the convent in general never takes these and they are drunk by the sick separately.

95. Fine wheat flour we absolutely forbid; whenever the sisters use flour, a third part at least of coarser grain must be mixed with it. And they must never enjoy bread hot from the oven, but eat only what has been baked at least one day before.[399] As for other foods, as we have already said,[400] the deaconess must see that what can be cheaply bought or easily obtained shall meet the needs of their weaker nature. For what could be more foolish than to buy extras when our own resources are sufficient? And to look outside for superfluous things when we have in the house all we need? And to exert ourselves for the sake of more when we have enough at hand? We are taught this necessary moderation and discretion not so much by human as by angelic example, or even by that of the Lord himself, and should therefore know that for meeting the needs of this life we should not seek particular kinds of food but rest content with what we have; for the angels fed on meat set before them

[398] Cf. **88**, **89**, and **92** above. A similar view on drinking wine is expressed in a near contemporary work of uncertain authorship, *Speculum virginum*, v, *ll.* 661–703 (ed. Seyfarth, pp. 136–7).

[399] White flour, while not the sole preserve of the wealthy, was a delicacy. These restrictions on the preparation of bread do not occur in *Institutiones nostre* 5 (*The Paraclete Statutes*, ed. Waddell, p. 10 (commentary on pp. 94–5); *PL* clxxviii. 314C).

[400] 77 above.

angeli uescuntur,[401] et inuentis in solitudine piscibus ieiunam multitudinem dominus Ihesus refecit.[402] Ex quo uidelicet manifeste docemur indifferenter tam carnium quam piscium esum non esse respuendum, et eum precipue sumendum qui et offensa peccati careat et, sponte se offerens, faciliorem habeat apparatum et minorem exigat expensam.

96. Vnde et Seneca, maximus ille paupertatis et continentie sectator et summus inter uniuersos philosophos morum edificator,[403] 'propositum', inquit, 'nostrum est secundum naturam uiuere. Hoc contra naturam est torquere corpus suum et faciles [a]odisse mundicias et squalorem appetere et cibis non tantum uilibus uti, sed tetris[b] et horridis. Quemadmodum desiderare delicatas res luxurie est, ita[c] usitatas et non magno parabiles fugere dementie. Frugalitatem exigit philosophia,[d] non penam. Potest tamen esse non incomposita frugalitas;[a] hic mihi modus placet.'[404] Vnde et Gregorius *Moralium* libro trigesimo, cum in[e] ipsis hominum moribus non tam ciborum quam animorum qualitatem [f]attendendam esse doceret[f] ac gule temptationes distingueret, 'aliquando', inquit, 'cibos lautiores querit, aliquando quelibet sumenda preparari accuratius appetit.'[g] [405] [h]Nonnumquam uero et abiectius est quod desiderat et tamen ipso estu immensi desiderii deterius[i] peccat. Ex Egipto populus eductus in heremo occubuit quia despecto manna cibos carnium peciit quos lautiores putauit.[406] Et primogenitorum gloriam Esau amisit quia magno estu desiderii uilem cibum, id est, lenticulam concupiuit quam dum uendendis etiam primogenitis pretulit, quo in illam appetitu anelaret indicauit.[407] Neque enim cibus sed appetitus in uicio est.[h] [408] Vnde et[j] lauciores cibos plerumque sine culpa sumimus et abiectiores non sine reatu conscientie degustamus. [k]Hic quippe quem diximus, Esau, primatum per lenticulam[k] perdidit, et Helyas in heremo uirtutem corporis carnes edendo seruauit.[l] [409] [m]Vnde et antiquus hostis, quia non cibum sed cibi concupiscentiam esse causam dampnationis intelligit, et primum sibi hominem non carne sed pomo subdidit,[410] et secundum

96 [a–a] etc usque *CE* [b] certis *TAmb* [c] & *add. Amb* [d] Philosophiae *Amb* [e] *om. Amb* [f–f] esse attendendam daret *CE* [g] Contra uehementes appetitores etiam uilium ciborum. *add. in marg. T* [h–h] etc *CE* [i] *om. Amb* [j] *om. CE* [k–k] esau enim primatum per lenticulam *C;* esau enim (primogenitam per lenticulam *add. Ecorr*) *E* [l] seruabit *?E, Amb* [m–m] *om. CE*

[401] Cf. Gen. 18: 8. [402] Cf. Mark 8: 7–8; John 6: 9–11.

[403] Cf. *Sermon* 24 (*PL* clxxviii. 535D); *Comm. Rom.*, i (i. 1, ed. Buytaert, p. 50); *TSch*, i. 198 (ed. Buytaert and Mews, p. 403).

by Abraham,[401] and the Lord Jesus refreshed a hungry multitude with fishes found in the wilderness.[402] From this we are surely to learn that we are to eat meat or fish without distinguishing between them, and to take especially what is without offence of sin and is freely available, and consequently easier to prepare and less costly.

96. And so Seneca, the greatest devotee of poverty and continence, and of all philosophers the supreme teacher of morals,[403] says: 'Our motto, as we all know, is to live according to nature. It is against nature for a man to torment his body, to hate simple cleanliness and seek out dirt, to eat food which is not only cheap but disgusting and revolting. Just as a craving for delicacies is a token of extravagance, avoidance of what is familiar and cheaply prepared is madness. Philosophy calls for simple living, not a penance, and a simple way of life need not be a rough one. This is the standard I approve.'[404] Gregory too, in the thirtieth book of his *Morals*, when teaching that in forming men's character we should pay attention to the quality of their minds, not of their foods, and distinguishing between the temptations of the palate, says: 'At one moment it seeks more delicate food, at another it desires its chosen dishes to be more carefully prepared.'[405] Yet sometimes what it craves is quite humble, but it sins more by the very heat of its immense desire. The people led out of Egypt met death in the wilderness because they despised manna and wanted meat, which they thought a finer food.[406] And Esau lost the birthright of the firstborn because he craved with burning desire for lentils, a cheap food, and proved with what an appetite he longed for it by preferring it to the birthright he sold.[407] Not the food but the appetite is at fault.[408] And so we can often be blameless when we take finer foods but eat humbler fare with guilt on our conscience. The Esau we spoke of lost his rights as the firstborn for the sake of lentils, while Elijah in the desert maintained his bodily strength by eating meat.[409] Thus our old enemy, knowing that it is not food but lust for food which is the cause of damnation, brought the first man into his power not with meat but with an apple,[410] and he tempted the second

404 Seneca, *Ad Lucilium*, i. 5. 4 ff.
405 Gregory the Great, *Moralia in Iob*, xxx. 18. 60 (ed. Adriaen, cxliiiB. 1531; *PL* lxxvi. 556).
406 Cf. Num. 11: 4–34.
407 Cf. Gen. 25: 29–34.
408 Cf. **77**, **81**, and **93** above.
409 Cf. 3 Kgs. (1 Kgs.) 17: 6.
410 Cf. Gen. 3.

non carne sed pane temptauit.[411] Hinc est quod plerumque Adam culpa committitur etiam cum abiecta et uilia sumuntur. Ea itaque sumenda sunt que nature necessitas querit et non que edendi libido suggerit. Minori uero desiderio concupiscimus que minus preciosa esse uidemus et que magis habundant et uilius emuntur, sicut est communium cibus carnium qui et infirmam multo ualidius quam pisces confortat, et minores expensas et faciliorem habet apparatum.[m]

97. Vsus autem[a] carnium ac[b] uini, sicut et nuptie, intermedia boni et mali, hoc est, indifferentia[412] computantur, licet copule nuptialis usus omnino peccato non careat,[413] et uinum omnibus alimentis periculosius existat. Quod profecto si temperate sumptum religioni [c]non interdicitur, quid aliorum timemus alimentorum dummodo in eis modus non[c] excedatur? Si beatus ipsum Benedictus quod monachorum non esse profitetur, quadam tamen dispensatione monachis huius temporis, iam refrigescente pristine caritatis feruore,[414] concedere cogitur,[415] quid cetera [d]indulgere feminis non[d] debeamus, que adhuc eis nulla professio interdicit? Si pontificibus ipsis et ecclesie sancte rectoribus, si denique monasteriis clericorum sine offensa carnibus etiam uesci licet, quia nulla scilicet [e]professione ab eis religantur,[e] [416] quis has culpet[f] feminis indulgeri, maxime si in ceteris maiorem tolerent districtionem? 'Sufficit' quippe 'discipulo ut sit sicut magister eius',[417] et magna uidetur crudelitas[g] si quod monasteriis clericorum indulgetur monasteriis feminarum prohibeatur. Nec paruum etiam estimandum est si femine, cum cetera monasterii districtione, in hac una carnium indulgentia religione fidelium laicorum inferiores non sint, presertim cum, teste Crisostomo, nihil liceat[h] secularibus quod non licet[i] monachis, excepto concumbere tantum cum uxore.[418] Beatus quoque Ieronimus clericorum religionem non inferiorem quam monachorum iudicans ait: 'Quasi quicquid in monachos dicitur non redundet in clericos qui [j]patres sunt[j] monachorum!'[419] Quis etiam ignoret omnino discretioni contrarium esse si tanta debilibus quanta fortibus imponantur onera, si tanta feminis quanta uiris iniungatur abstinentia?[420] De quo etiam, si quis

97 [a] ergo *CE* [b] et *CE* [c–c] *om. E* [d–d] indulgere (non *add.* T^1) feminis *T;* non indulgere feminis *Amb* [e–e] ab eis professione relegantur *CE* [f] culpe *CE* [g] credulitas *CAmb* [h] licet *Amb* [i] liceat *Amb* [j–j] sunt patres *Amb*

[411] Cf. Matt. 4: 3.
[412] 'intermedia . . . indifferentia': cf. *Letter* 6, **20** and **26** and n. 133.
[413] Cf. **80** above.

not with meat but with bread.[411] Consequently the fault of Adam is often committed when plain and ordinary food is taken. So what should be eaten are what nature's needs require, not those suggested by a passion to eat. But we crave with less desire for what we see is not so costly, but is more plentiful and cheaper to buy, for example, the ordinary kind of meat which is much more strengthening than fish for a weak nature, and is less expensive and easier to prepare.

97. The use of meat and wine, like marriage, is considered to lie between good and evil, that is, it is indifferent,[412] although copulation in marriage is not wholly free from sin,[413] and wine brings more hazards than any other food. Then if a moderate consumption of wine is not forbidden to religion, what have we to fear from other foods, so long as moderation is maintained? If St Benedict declares that wine is not for monks and yet is obliged, at a time when the fervour of early Christian charity was cooling off,[414] to allow it by special dispensation to the monks of his time,[415] why should we not allow women other things which up to now no vow has forbidden them? If even bishops and rectors of the Holy Church, if indeed monasteries of clerks are even allowed to eat meat without offence, because they are not bound by any profession of abstinence,[416] who can find fault if women are allowed this too, especially if in other respects they submit to a much stricter discipline? 'It is sufficient for a pupil to be like his master',[417] and it seems over-severe if what is allowed to monasteries of clerks is denied to convents of women. Nor should it be considered of little importance if women, subject to the other restrictions of the monastic life, are not inferior to the faithful laity in this one indulgence of meat, especially since, as Chrysostom bears witness: 'Nothing is allowed to laymen that is not allowed to monks except being in bed with a wife.'[418] St Jerome too, judging the religion of clerks to be not inferior to that of monks, says: 'As though whatever is said for monks does not redound on clerks, who are the fathers of monks!'[419] And who does not know that it is against all good sense if the same burdens are imposed on the weak as on the strong, if as much abstinence is enjoined on women as on men?[420] If

[414] 'refrigescente . . . feruore': cf. Matt. 24: 12 and *Letter* 6, **16**.

[415] Benedict, *Rule*, c. 40, 6. Cf. *Letter* 6, **20** and **17**.

[416] Cf. *Letter* 6, **14**.

[417] Matt. 10: 25.

[418] Cf. John Chrysostom, *Homiliae in Epistulam ad Hebraeos interprete Mutiano, Homilia* 7, *cap.* 4 (*PG* lxiii. 289); also *Letter* 6, **12**.

[419] Jerome, *Epistola* LIV *ad Furiam*, 5 (ed. Hilberg, liv. 471, *ll.* 6–8; *PL* xxii. 552).

[420] Cf. *Letter* 6, **9**.

supra ipsum nature documentum auctoritatem efflagitet, beatum quoque super hoc Gregorium consulat. Hic quippe magnus ecclesie tam rector quam doctor, de hoc quoque ceteros ecclesie doctores diligenter instruens, libri *Pastoralis* capitulo[k] uigesimo quarto[l] ita meminit: 'Aliter igitur ammonendi sunt uiri atque aliter femine, quia illis grauia, istis uero sunt iniungenda leuiora; [m]ut[n] illos magna exerceant, istas uero leuia demulcendo conuertant.'[421] Que enim parua sunt in fortibus magna reputantur in debilibus.[m] Quamuis[o] hec quoque uilium licentia carnium minus habeat oblectamenti quam ipse piscium uel auium carnes, quas minime tamen [p]nobis beatus[p] interdicit Benedictus.[422] De quibus etiam Apostolus, cum diuersas species[q] carnis distingueret, 'non omnis', inquit, 'caro eadem caro, sed alia hominum, alia peccorum, [r]alia uolucrum, alia autem[s] piscium.'[423] Et pecorum quidem et auium carnes in sacrificio Domini lex ponit, pisces uero nequaquam, ut[r] nemo piscium esum[t] mundiorem Deo quam carnium credat. Qui etiam tanto est onerosior paupertati uel carior quanto piscium minor est copia quam carnium et minus infirmam corroborat naturam, ut in altero magis grauet, in altero magis subueniat.

98. Nos itaque fortune pariter et nature hominum consulentes, nihil in alimentis, ut diximus, nisi superfluitatem interdicimus, [a]ipsumque ita[a] carnium siue ceterorum esum temperamus ut omnibus concessis maior sit abstinentia monialium quam quibusdam interdictis modo sit monachorum. Igitur ipsum quoque carnium esum ita temperari uolumus ut non amplius quam semel [b]in die sumant, nec diuersa inde[b] fercula eidem persone parentur [c]nec seorsum aliqua superaddantur pulmenta[c] nec ullatenus ei uesci liceat plusquam ter in ebdomada, prima uidelicet feria, tercia et quinta feria, quantecumque etiam festiuitates intercurrant.[424] Quo namque solempnitas maior est, maioris abstinentie deuotione est celebranda. Ad quod nos egregius doctor Gregorius Nazianzenus,[d] uehementer exhortans [e]libro tertio[e] *de Luminibus* uel *Secundis Epiphaniis*, ait: 'Diem festum celebremus,

[k] capitulum *T* [l] 24 *CE* [m–m] etc. *CE* [n] et *T* [o] Contra illos qui (absti)nent uel abst(inen)dum predican(t a) carnibus et non (aliis) cibis; *add. in marg. of TAmb* (*but partly lost in T through trimming*) [p–p] beatus nobis *CE* [q] absque *C;* s *E followed by a space* [r–r] etc. usque *CE* [s] *om. Amb* [t] *om. T*

98 [a–a] Ipsum itaque *Amb* [b–b] inde sumant in die (in die *superscr. Ecorr.*) nec diuersa inde *CE* [c–c] *om. CE by homoeoteleuton* [d] nazanzenus *T* [e–e] in libro *CE*

anyone demands authority for this beyond the evidence of nature, let him consult St Gregory on this point too. For this great Rector and Doctor of the Church gives considered instruction to other Doctors of the Church on this matter in the twenty-fourth chapter of his *Pastoral*: 'And so men should be admonished in one way, women in another, for heavy burdens may be laid on men but lighter ones on women, and great matters may exercise men but small ones may divert women soothingly.'[421] Small things for strong people are found to be large ones in the weak. And although this freedom to eat cheap meat is a source of less pleasure than eating the flesh of fishes or birds, St Benedict does not forbid us these.[422] The Apostle also, when he distinguishes between different kinds of flesh, says: 'Not all flesh is the same; there is flesh of men, flesh of animals, flesh of birds, and flesh of fish.'[423] Now the law of the Lord assigns the flesh of animals and of birds to sacrifice, but not that of fish, so no one may suppose that eating fish is purer in the eyes of God than eating meat. Fish is also more of a hardship to the poor, being dearer since it is in shorter supply than meat, and less strengthening for a weak nature, so that on the one hand it is more of a burden and, on the other, gives less help.

98. We therefore, considering both the resources and nature of mankind, forbid nothing in the matter of food except excess, as we have said, and we regulate the eating of meat as of everything else in such a way that the nuns can show greater abstinence with everything allowed them than is the case now with monks to whom some things are not allowed. And so we wish to make it a rule for the eating of meat that the sisters do not take it more than once a day, that different dishes must not be prepared for the same person nor any separate courses added, nor may meat ever be eaten more than three times a week, on the first, third and fifth days, whatever feast-days intervene.[424] For the more solemn the feast, the more dedicated should be the abstinence which celebrates it. This is warmly recommended to us by the famous doctor Gregory of Nazianzus in the third book *On Lights* or *The Second Epiphany*, where he says: 'Let us celebrate a

[421] Gregory the Great, *Regula pastoralis*, iii. 1/2 (xxiv) (ed. Rommel, ccclxxxii. 266; *PL* lxxvii. 51CD); also cited in *Letter* 6, 9.

[422] Cf. Benedict, *Rule*, c. 39, 11.

[423] 1 Cor. 15: 39.

[424] Meat is forbidden in *Institutiones nostre* 5 (*The Paraclete Statutes*, ed. Waddell, p. 10 (commentary on pp. 95–6); *PL* clxxviii. 314C).

non uentri indulgentes, sed spiritu exultantes.'[425] Idem libro [f]quarto *de Pentecoste*[f] *et Spiritu sancto*: 'Et[g] hic est noster festus dies', ait, 'in anime thesauros perhenne aliquid et perpetuum recondamus, non ea que pertranseunt et dissoluuntur. [h]Sufficit corpori malitia sua; non indiget copiosiore materia, nec insolens bestia abundantioribus cibis ut insolentior fiat et uiolentius urgeat.'[426] Idcirco autem spiritaliter magis est agenda solempnitas[h] quam et beatus Ieronimus eius discipulus secutus in epistola sua de acceptis muneribus ita quodam loco meminit: 'Vnde nobis sollicicius prouidendum ut solempnem diem[i] non tam ciborum habundantia quam spiritus exultatione celebremus, quia ualde absurdum est nimia saturitate honorare uelle martyrem quem sciamus Deo placuisse ieiuniis.'[427] Augustinus de penitentie medicina: 'Attende tot martyrum milia. Cur enim natalicia eorum conuiuiis turpibus celebrare delectat [j]et eorum uitam sequi honestis moribus non delectat?'[428]

99. [a]Quociens uero carnes deerunt duo eis fercula qualiumcumque pulmentorum concedimus nec superaddi pisces prohibemus.[429] Nulli uero preciosi sapores cibis apponantur in conuentu, sed hiis contente sint que in terra quam inhabitant nascuntur. Fructibus uero nonnisi in cena uescantur. Pro medicamento autem quibus opus fuerit uel herbas uel radices seu fructus aliquos[b] uel alia huiusmodi[c] numquam prohibemus mensis apponi. Si qua forte peregrina monialis hospicio recepta mensis intererit, ferculo ei aliquo superaddito caritatis senciat humanitatem, de quo quidem si quid distribuere uoluerit, licebit. Hec autem uel si plures fuerint in maiore mensa residebunt et eis diaconissa ministrabit, postea cum aliis que mensis ministrant comestura.[ad] Si qua uero sororum parciori cibo carnem domare uoluerit, nullatenus hoc ipsa nisi per obedientiam presumat, et nullatenus hoc ei denegetur, si hoc non leuitate[e] sed uirtute uideatur

[f–f] iiii[o] de pentechosten *T;* iiii. de Penthecoste *Amb;* Contra illos qui diebus festiuis se ingurgitant *add. T in marg.* [g] *om. CE* [h–h] etc *CE* [i] ut *add. CE* [j] beginning of lacuna in E, ending in 99

99 [a–a] *om. C* [b] aliquot *Amb* [c] huius *T* [d] end of lacuna in E, beginning in 98 [e] lenitate *Amb*

[425] Rufinus, *Oratio* III. *De luminibus de secundis epiphaniis*, 20, in *Orationum Gregorii Nazianzeni nouem interpretatio* (ed. Engelbrecht, p. 136). Cf. Gregory of Nazianzus, *Oratio* XXXIX *in sancta Lumina*, 20 (*PG* xxxvi. 358D—in the Latin trans. by the Maurists).

[426] Rufinus, *Oratio* IV. *De pentecoste et de spiritu sancto*, 1, in *Orationum Gregorii Nazianzeni nouem interpretatio* (ed. Engelbrecht, p. 142). Cf. Gregory of Nazianzus, *Oratio* XLI *in Pentecosten*, 1 (*PG* xxxvi. 430B—in the Latin trans. by the Maurists).

feast-day not by indulging the belly but exulting in the spirit.'[425] And in the fourth book *On Pentecost and the Holy Spirit* he says: 'This is our feast-day; let us store away in the soul's treasure-house something perennial and everlasting, not things which perish and melt away. Sufficient for the body is its own evil; it needs no richer matter, nor does the insolent beast need more lavish food to make it more insolent and violent in its demands.'[426] And so a feast-day should rather be kept spiritually, as St Jerome, Gregory's disciple, says in his letter about accepting gifts, where there is this passage: 'Thus we must take special care to celebrate the solemnity with exultation of spirit rather than abundance of food, for it is palpably absurd to honour by overindulgence a martyr whom we know to have pleased God by his fasting.'[427] Augustine says of the medicine of penitence: 'Consider all the thousands of martyrs. Why do we take pleasure in celebrating their birthdays with disgraceful banquets and not in following the example of their lives in honest ways?'[428]

99. Whenever the convent has a meatless day, the nuns are to be allowed two courses with a selection of portions to which we do not forbid adding fish.[429] But no costly condiments may be used in the food in the convent, and the sisters must content themselves with the produce of the land where they live. Fruit, however, they should eat only for supper. But as medicine for those who need it, we never forbid herbs or root vegetables, or any fruits or other similar things to appear on the table. If there happens to be any pilgrim nun staying as a guest and present at a meal, she should be shown the courtesy of charity by being offered an extra dish and, if she wishes to share this, she may. She and any other guests should sit at the high table and be served by the deaconess, who will then eat later with those who wait at table. If any of the sisters wishes to mortify the flesh by a stricter diet, on no account may she do so except by way of obedience, but on no account shall this be refused her if her reason for wanting it seems sound and not frivolous, and her strength is sufficient to bear it. But no one must ever be permitted to be missing from the convent for this

[427] Jerome, *Epistola* XXXI *ad Eustochium de munusculis*, 3 (ed. Hilberg, liv. 251, *ll.* 12–16; *PL* xxii. 446).

[428] Augustine, *Sermo* 351 *de utilitate paenitentiae*, 4 (*PL* xxxix. 1548). Cf. *Carmen ad Astralabium*, ed. Rubingh-Bosscher *vv.* 809–10.

[429] Cf. Benedict, *Rule*, c. 39, 1–3; *Institutiones nostre* 5 (*The Paraclete Statutes*, ed. Waddell, p. 10 (commentary on pp. 96–8); PL clxxviii. 314C).

appetere quod eius firmitudo ualeat tolerare. [f]Nulli tamen umquam permittatur ut per hoc [g]desit conuentui,[g] nec ut aliquam diem sine cibo transigat. Sagiminis condimento sexta feria numquam utantur, sed quadragesimali cibo contente, sponso suo ea die passo, quadam compaciantur abstinentia. Illud uero non solum prohibendum sed uehementer est abhorrendum quod in plerisque monasteriis agi solet, quod uidelicet parte aliqua panis que superest esui, et pauperibus est reseruanda, manus et cultellos mundare et extergere solent, et ut mappis parcant mensarum panem polluunt pauperum, immo eius qui se attendens in pauperibus ait: 'Quod uni ex minimis meis fecistis, mihi fecistis.'[f][430]

100. De abstinentia ieiuniorum generalis institutio ecclesie illis[a] sufficiat, nec supra fidelium laicorum religionem in hoc eas[b] grauare presumimus nec uirtuti uirorum earum[c] infirmitatem in hoc preferre audemus. [d]Ab equinoctio uero autumpnali usque ad Pascha propter dierum breuitatem unam in die comestionem sufficere credimus.[e] Quod quia non pro abstinentia religionis, sed pro breuitate dicimus temporis, nulla hic ciborum genera distinguimus.[d][f]

101. Preciose[a] uestes quas omnino Scriptura damnat summopere fugiantur. De quibus nos precipue Dominus dehortans et dampnati diuitis superbiam de hiis accusat et Iohannis humilitatem econtrario commendat.[431] Quod beatus diligenter attendens Gregorius *Omelia Euangeliorum* sexta: 'Quid est', inquit, 'dicere: "Qui mollibus uestiuntur in domibus regum sunt",[432] nisi aperta sententia demonstrare quia[b] non celesti sed terreno regno militant qui pro Deo perpeti aspera fugiunt sed, solis exterioribus dediti, presentis uite molliciem delectationemque querunt?'[433] Idem *Omelia* quadragesima: 'Sunt nunnulli qui cultum subtilium preciosarumque uestium non putant esse peccatum. Quod uidelicet si culpa non esset, nequaquam sermo Dei tam uigilanter exprimeret quod diues, qui torquebatur apud[c] inferos, bisso et purpura indutus fuisset.[434] Nemo quippe uestimenta precipua nisi ad inanem gloriam querit, uidelicet ut honorabilior ceteris esse uideatur. Nam quia[d] pro sola inani[e] gloria uestimentum

[f–f] *om. CE* [g–g] *T;* conventu *Amb, who notes in marg.:* locus corruptus

100 [a] uobis *CE* [b] uos *CE* [c] uestram *CE* [d–d] *om.* CE [e] credamus *Amb* [f] distinguemus *Amb*

101 [a] *TEAmb open a new section here* [b] quod *TEAmb;* quia T^1C [c] ad *Amb* [d] *om. Amb* [e] uana *CE*

reason, nor spend a whole day without food. They must never use lard for flavouring on the sixth day of the week, but be content with Lenten food, and by their abstinence share the suffering of their bridegroom on that day. But one practice, common in many monasteries, is not only to be forbidden but strictly abhorred, that is, the habit of cleaning and wiping the hands and knives on some of the bread which is left uneaten and kept for the poor, so that in wishing to spare the tablecloths they pollute the bread of the poor, or indeed, the bread of him who treats himself as one of the poor when he says: 'Anything you did for the least of my brothers, you did for me.'[430]

100. As regards abstinence at fasts, the general ruling of the Church should be sufficient for them. We are not prepared to burden them in this beyond the observance of the faithful laity nor to go as far as to set their weakness above the strength of men. But from the autumn equinox until Easter, because the days are short, we think one meal a day is enough. But because the reason for this is seasonal shortness, not monastic abstinence, we make no distinction between kinds of food.

101. Costly clothes, which Scripture utterly condemns, must be absolutely banned. The Lord warns us especially against them, and condemns the pride in them of the rich man who was damned, while by contrast he commends the humility of John.[431] St Gregory draws attention to this in his sixth *Homily on the Gospels*: 'What does it mean to say: "Those who wear fine clothes are to be found in the homes of kings",[432] unless to state in plain words that those who refuse to endure hardships for God's sake fight not for a heavenly but an earthly kingdom, and by devoting themselves only to outward show, seek the softness and pleasure of this present life?'[433] And in his fortieth *Homily* he says: 'There are some who do not think that the fashion of fine and costly clothes is a sin. But surely if it were not blameworthy, the Word of God would never say so explicitly that the rich man who was tormented in hell had been clothed in linen and purple.[434] For no one seeks special garments except for vainglory, in order to appear more honourable than others. That costly clothing is

[430] Matt. 25: 40.
[431] Cf. Matt. 11: 8–11; Luke 7: 25–8, 16: 19; also *Institutiones nostre* 3 (*The Paraclete Statutes*, ed. Waddell, pp. 9–10 (commentary on pp. 85–9); *PL* clxxviii. 313D–314C).
[432] Matt. 11: 8; Luke 7: 25.
[433] Gregory the Great, *Homiliae in Euangelia*, vi. 3 (ed. Étaix, p. 41; *PL* lxxvi. 1097).
[434] Cf. Luke 16: 19.

preciosius queritur, res ipsa testatur quod[f] nemo uult ibi[g] pretiosis uestibus indui, ubi ab aliis non possit uideri.'[435] A quo et prima Petri Epistola seculares et coniugatas feminas [h]dehortans ait: 'Similiter et mulieres subdite sint uiris suis ut et, si qui non credunt uerbo, per mulierum conuersationem sine uerbo lucrifiant, considerantes in timore castam conuersationem uestram.[h] Quarum [i]sit non[i] extrinsecus capillatura [j]aut circumdatio auri aut indumenti uestimentorum[k] cultus, sed qui absconditus corde est homo, incorruptibilitate quieti et modesti spiritus, quod est in conspectu Domini locuplex.'[j] [436] Bene autem feminas pocius quam uiros ab hac uanitate censuit dehortandas quarum infirmus animus id amplius appetit quo per eas et in eis amplius incitari[l] luxuria possit. Si autem seculares hinc inhibende sunt femine, quid Christo deuotas conuenit prouidere, quarum hoc ipsum illis est cultus quod sunt inculte?[m] Quecumque igitur hunc appetit cultum uel non renuit oblatum castitatis perdit [n]testimonium. Et quecumque talis est non se religioni preparare sed fornicationi credatur,[n] nec tam monialis quam meretrix censeatur. Cui et ipse cultus est tamquam[o] lenonis preconium qui incestum[p] prodit animum, sicut scriptum est: 'Amictus corporis et risus dentium et ingressus hominis enunciant[q] de illo.'[437]

102. [a]Legimus Dominum in Ioanne, ut iam supra meminimus,[438] uilitatem seu asperitatem uestium pocius quam esce commendasse atque laudasse. 'Quid existis',[b] inquit, 'in desertum uidere? Hominem mollibus uestitum?'[439] etc.[c] Habet enim nonnumquam usus preciosorum ciborum utilem aliquam dispensationem, sed uestium nullam.[a] Que uidelicet uestes quanto sunt preciosiores tanto carius custodiuntur, et [d]minus usitate[d] minus proficiunt, et ementem amplius grauant, et pre subtilitate sui facilius possunt corrumpi et minus corpori prebent fomenti. Nulli uero panni magis quam nigri lugubrem penitentie habitum decent,[440] [e]nec adeo sponsis Christi pelles alique conueniunt sicut agnine, ut ipso quoque habitu agnum sponsum uirginum indute uideantur uel induere moneantur.[441]

[f] quia *CE* [g] *om. CE* [h–h] dicens *CE* [i–i] non sit *CE* [j–j] etc. *CE* [k] vestimentorius *Amb* [l] imitari *Amb* [m] stultius *CE* [n–n] *om. CE* [o] tam *CE* [p] incestuosum *CE* [q] enunciant *unclear in C;* eueniant *E*

102 [a–a] *om. CE* [b] exiistis *Amb* [c] *om. Amb* [d–d] *om. Amb* [e] beginning of lacuna in CE, ending in 104

sought for vainglory alone is proved by the fact that no one cares to wear costly clothes where others cannot see him.'[435] The First Letter of Peter warns lay and married women against the same thing: 'In the same way wives should be obedient to their husbands, so that if there are any who do not believe the word they may be won over without a word by observing your chaste and reverent behaviour. Your beauty should reside, not in outward adornment—the braiding of the hair, or the wearing of gold, or the putting on of dress—but hidden in your heart, in the incorruptibility of a quiet and modest spirit which is precious in the sight of God.'[436] And he rightly thought that women rather than men should be warned against this vanity, for their weak minds desire more strongly what enables luxuriance to find fuller expression in them and through them. But if lay women are to be forbidden these things, what care must be taken by women dedicated to Christ? Their fashion is not to have fashion; so whoever wants fashion, or does not decline it if offered, loses the proof of her chastity. Any such person would be thought to be preparing herself not for religion but for fornication, and judged to be not a nun but a whore. Moreover, fashion itself is the badge of the bawd and betrays an unclean mind, as it is written: 'A man's clothes and the way he laughs and the way he walks tell you what he is.'[437]

102. We read, as we said above,[438] that the Lord praised and commended the cheapness and roughness of John's clothing rather than of his food. 'What did you go out to see in the wilderness?' he asked. 'A man clad in fine clothes?'[439] For there are times when the serving of costly food can usefully be conceded, but none for the wearing of costly clothing. Indeed, the more costly clothes are, the more carefully they are kept and the less they are used; and the less useful they are, the greater the burden they are to their purchaser; and being so fine they are damaged more easily and give less warmth to the body. Black clothes are most fitting of all for the mournful garb of penitence,[440] and lambs' wool the most suitable for the brides of Christ, so that even in their habits they can be seen to wear, or be told to wear, the wool of the Lamb, the bridegroom of virgins.[441]

[435] Gregory the Great, *Homiliae in Euangelia*, xl. 3 (ed. Étaix, p. 399; *PL* lxxvi. 1305).
[436] 1 Pet. 3: 1–4.
[437] Ecclus. 19: 27.
[438] Cf. above in **101**.
[439] Matt. 11: 7–8.
[440] Cf. *Letter* 5, 4.
[441] For similar advice to wear clothes made of lambs' wool, found in a poem addressed to a sister and friend, see Appendix A, 7.

103. Vela uero earum non de serico, sed de tincto aliquo lineo panno fiant. Duo autem uelorum genera esse uolumus ut alia sint scilicet uirginum iam ab episcopo[a] consecratarum, alia uero minime.[442] Que uero predictarum[b] sunt uirginum crucis sibi signum habeant impressum quo scilicet ipse integritate quoque corporis ad Christum maxime pertinere monstrentur; et sicut in consecratione distant[c] a ceteris, ita et hoc habitus signo distinguantur, quo et quique fidelium territi magis abhorreant in concupiscentiam earum exardescere. Hoc autem signum uirginalis mundicie in summitate capitis candidis expressum filis uirgo gestabit, et hoc nullatenus antequam ab episcopo consecretur gestare presumat. Nulla autem alia uela hoc signo insignita sint.

104. Interulas mundas ad carnem habeant in quibus etiam cincte semper dormiant. Culcitrarum quoque molliciem uel linteaminum usum infirme ipsarum non negamus nature. Singule uero dormiant et comedant. Nulla penitus indignari presumat si uestes uel quecumque alia sibi ab aliquibus transmissa alii que amplius indiget concedantur sorori.[443] Sed tunc maxime gaudeat cum in sororis necessitate fructum habuerit eleemosyne, uel se respexerit non solum sibi sed aliis uiuere. Alioquin ad sancte societatis fraternitatem non pertinet, nec proprietatis sacrilegio caret.[a]

105. Sufficere autem ad corpus contegendum credimus interulam,[a] pelliceam togam et, cum multum exasperauerit frigus, insuper mantellum, [b]quo uidelicet mantello pro opertorio quoque uti iacentes poterunt.[444] Oportebit autem,[b] pro[c] infestatione uermium uel grauamine sordium abluendarum, hec omnia[d] esse duplicia [e]indumenta, sicut ad litteram in laude fortis et prouide mulieris Salomon ait: 'Non timebit domui sue a frigoribus niuis; omnes enim domestici eius uestiti duplicibus.'[e] [445] Quorum ita sit moderata longitudo ut ultra oram[f] sotularium non procedant, ne puluerem moueant. [g]Manice uero extensionem brachiorum et manuum non excedant.[g] Crura uero

103 [a] ipso *Amb* [b] pudictarum *Amb* [c] distare *Amb*

104 [a] *end of lacuna in CE, beginning in* 102

105 [a] interualla *C; vacant space in E* [b–b] *om. CE; T*[1] *here adds a cross* [c] uero *add. CE* [d] *om. CE* [e–e] purus *?C;* prout *E* [f] horam *TC* [g–g] *om. CE*

[442] Reference is made to episcopal blessing and consecration in a solemn privilege granted to the Oratory of the Holy Trinity (the Paraclete) by Pope Innocent II and dated 17 June 1135 (*Cartulaire de l'abbaye du Paraclet*, ed. Lalore no. 2, p. 3; *Checklist* 417). Cf. *The Paraclete Statutes*, ed. Waddell, pp. 111–12.

103. Their veils should not be made of silk but of dyed linen cloth, and we wish there to be two sorts of veil, one for the virgins already consecrated by the bishop, the other for those not consecrated.[442] The veils of the former should have the sign of the Cross marked on them, so that their wearers shall be shown by this to belong particularly to Christ in the integrity of their virginity; and, as they are set apart from the others by their consecration, they should also be distinguished by this marking on their habit which shall act as a deterrent to any of the faithful against becoming inflamed with desire for them. This sign of virginal purity the nun shall wear on the top of her head, marked in white thread, and she should not presume to wear it before she is consecrated by the bishop. No other veils may bear this mark.

104. They should wear clean undergarments next to the skin, and always sleep in them, girded; nor do we deny their weak nature the softness of feather mattresses and the use of linen sheets. But each one must sleep and eat alone. No one should venture to be indignant if the clothing or anything else passed on to her by someone else is made over to another sister who has a greater need.[443] But she should look on it as an occasion for rejoicing when she enjoys the benefit of having given something as an act of charity, or sees herself as living for others and not only for herself. Otherwise she does not belong to the sisterhood of a holy society, and is not free of the sacrilege of having possessions.

105. It should be sufficient, we think, for them to wear an undergarment, a tunic of felt and, when the cold is very severe, a cloak as well.[444] This they can also use as a coverlet when lying in bed. To prevent infestation by vermin and to allow accumulation of dirt to be washed away, there should be a second set of all these garments, exactly as Solomon says in praise of the capable and provident housewife: 'She will not fear for her household when snow comes, for all her servants are double-wrapped.'[445] These clothes must not be made so long as to go below the ankles and stir up dust, and the sleeves must not extend beyond the length of the arms and hands. Their legs

[443] The sisters of Fontevraud under their earliest statutes were not allowed to borrow or lend each other's clothes (Dalarun and others, *Les Deux Vies de Robert d'Arbrissel*, p. 390, no. 12: 'Ut non mutuentur ad invicem vestes suae').

[444] Peter the Venerable defended the use of furs at Cluny, against criticism from Bernard of Clairvaux, in *Letters* 28 and 111 (ed. Constable, i. 62–4, 282, with notes in ii. 116–17).

[445] Prov. 31: 21. Cf. Benedict, *Rule*, c. 55, 10.

et pedes calige, [h]pedules et[h] sotulares muniant.[446] [i]Nec umquam occasione religionis nude pedes incedant. In lectis culcitra una, puluinar auriculare, lodex et linteolum sufficiant. Caput uero muniant uitta candida et uelum desuper nigrum et pro tonsura capillorum pilleum agninum, cum opus fuerit, supponatur.[i] [447]

106. Nec[a] in uictu tantum aut uestitu superfluitas euitetur, uerum etiam in edificiis aut quibuslibet possessionibus.[b] In edificiis quidem hoc manifeste dinoscitur[c] si ea maiora uel pulcriora quam necesse sit componantur, uel si nos ipsa sculpturis uel picturis ornantes non habitacula pauperum edificemus, sed palatia regum erigamus. '"Filius hominis"', inquit Ieronimus, '"non habet ubi capud reclinet",[448] et tu amplas porticus et ingentia tectorum[d] spacia metiris?'[449] Cum preciosis uel pulchris delectamur equitaturis, non solum superfluitas sed elationis uanitas innotescit. Cum autem animalium greges uel terrenas multiplicamus possessiones, tunc se ad exteriora dilatat ambicio, et quanto plura possidemus in terra tanto amplius de ipsis cogitare cogimur et a[e] contemplatione celestium deuocamur.[f] Et licet corpore claustris recludamur, hec tamen que foris sunt et diligit animus sequi cogitur et se pariter huc et[g] illuc cum illis diffundit, et quo plura possidentur que amitti possunt maiori nos[h] metu cruciant, et quo preciosiora[i] sunt amplius diliguntur et ambitione sui miserum magis illaqueant animum.

107. Vnde omnino prouidendum est ut domui nostre sumptibusque nostris certum prefigamus modum, nec supra necessaria uel appetamus aliqua uel recipiamus oblata uel retineamus suscepta. Quicquid enim necessitati superest in rapina possidemus, et tot pauperum mortis rei sumus quot inde sustentare potuimus.[450] Singulis igitur annis, cum collecta fuerint uictualia, prouidendum est quantum sufficiat per annum et, si qua superfuerint, pauperibus non[a] tam danda sunt quam reddenda.

[h–h] et pedules *C;* et pedules et *E* [i–i] *om. CE*

106 [a] *TEAmb mark the opening of a new section here* [b] ac *add. C;* et *add. E* [c] disnoscitur *C;* dissoluitur *E* [d] rectorum *T* [e] *om. E* [f] reuocamur *E* [g] *om. C* [h] *om. CE* [i] preciosiosiora *T*

107 [a] *om. CE*

---

[446] Cf. Benedict, *Rule*, c. 55, 1. The difference between 'pedules' and 'sotulares' (*subtalares* in classical Latin) is that the former cover the ankle or lower leg and the latter do not. Gaiters might be a better translation of 'pedules' than socks but the word is now little used.

and feet should be protected by shoes, socks, and slippers,[446] and they are never to go barefoot on account of religion. On their beds a single mattress, bolster, pillow, blanket, and sheet should suffice. They should wear a white band on their heads with the black veil over it, and because of their close-cropped hair a cap of lambs' wool may be worn if needed.[447]

106. Excess must be avoided not only in diet and clothing but also in buildings or any possessions. In buildings excess is plain to see when they are made larger or finer than necessary, or if we adorn them with sculpture or paintings so as to set up palaces fit for kings instead of dwelling-places for the poor. '"The Son of Man", says Jerome, "has nowhere to lay his head",[448] but you are measuring out magnificent colonnades and spacious halls?'[449] When we take pleasure in costly or beautiful horses the emptiness of pride is displayed as well as excess; and when we multiply herds of animals or earthly possessions, our ambition extends to outward things. And the more possessions we have on earth, the more we are obliged to think of these and are called away from contemplation of heavenly things. And although we may be enclosed in cloisters in the body, the mind still loves things outside, has an urge to pursue them, and at the same time dissipates itself in all directions with them. The more we possess which can be lost, the greater the fear which torments us, and the more costly these are, the more they are loved and ensnare the wretched mind with ambition to have them.

107. And so every care must be taken to set a firm limit to our household and our expenditure, and beyond what is necessary not to desire anything, receive any offering, or keep what we have accepted. Whatever is over and above our needs we possess by robbery, and are guilty of the deaths of all the poor whom we could have helped from the surplus.[450] Every year then, when the produce has been gathered in, sufficient provision must be made for the year, and anything left over must not so much be given as given back to the poor.

[447] Cf. *Institutiones nostre* 4 (*The Paraclete Statutes*, ed. Waddell, p. 10 (commentary on pp. 89–93); *PL* clxxviii. 314C), where provision is made for mattresses, bolsters, and linen sheets, if such are available.

[448] Matt. 8: 20.

[449] Jerome, *Epistola* XIV *ad Heliodorum monachum*, 6 (ed. Hilberg, liv. 52, *ll.* 3–4; *PL* xxii. 350).

[450] Cf. *Carmen ad Astralabium*, ed. Rubingh-Bosscher *vv.* 415–16; *Sermon* 30 *de eleemosyna pro sanctimonialibus de Paraclito* (*PL* clxxviii. 564D, 566BC)

108. Sunt qui prouidentiae modum ignorantes, cum redditus paucos habeant, multam[a] habere familiam gaudent. De cuius quidem procuratione dum grauantur, impudenter hanc querentes mendicant uel que non habent uiolenter ab illis extorquent. Tales etiam iam nonnullos monasteriorum patres conspicimus qui de multitudine conuentus gloriantes, non tam bonos filios quam multos habere student; et magni uidentur in oculis suis si inter multos maiores habeantur. Quos quidem ut ad suum trahant dominium, cum aspera [b]eis deberent[b] predicare, leuia[c] promittunt, et nulla examinatione antea probatos quos indiscrete suscipiunt, facile apostatantes perdunt. Talibus, ut uideo, [d]improperabat Veritas[d] dicens: 'Ve uobis qui circuitis mare et aridam ut faciatis unum proselitum; quem cum feceritis, facitis illum filium gehenne duplo quam uos.'[451] Qui profecto minus de multitudine gloriarentur si salutem animarum magis quam numerum quererent, et de suis uiribus in ratione sui regiminis reddenda minus presumerent.

109. Paucos Dominus elegit apostolos, et de ipsa electione sua unus in tantum apostatauit ut pro ipso Dominus diceret: 'Numquid[a] ego duodecim uos elegi? Et unus ex uobis diabolus est.'[452] Sicut autem de apostolis Iudas, sic et de septem diaconibus Nicholaus periit.[453] Et cum paucos [b]adhuc apostoli[b] congregassent, Ananias et Saphira uxor eius mortis excipere sententiam meruerunt.[454] Quippe et ab ipso antea Domino cum multi abissent discipulorum retrorsum pauci cum ipso remanserunt.[455] Arta quippe uia est que ducit ad uitam et pauci ingrediuntur per eam. Sicut econtrario lata est et spaciosa que ducit ad mortem, et multi sunt qui se ultro ingerant,[456] quia sicut ipse Dominus [c]testatur alibi:[c] 'Multi uocati, pauci uero electi.'[457] [d]Et iuxta Salomonem: 'Stultorum infinitus est numerus.'[d] [458] Timeat itaque quisquis de[e] multitudine gaudet subiectorum, ne in eis, iuxta dominicam assertionem, pauci reperiantur electi, et ipse immoderate gregem suum multiplicans, minus ad custodiam eius sufficiat ut ei

108 [a] multum *McLaughlin, Pagani* [b–b] deberent eis *CEAmb* [c] lenia *Amb;* Contra illos qui circum(ueni)unt alios ut (intre)nt religionem (qu)i in multitudine gloriantur et (per) mundum discurrunt *add. in marg. T* (*before trimming of letters in marg.*), *Amb; McLaughlin* (*p. 282, n. 67*) *misplaces this heading earlier in the text* [d–d] ueritas improperabat *CE*

109 [a] Nonne *Amb*[1] [b–b] apostoli adhuc *CE* [c–c] alibi testatur *CE* [d–d] *om. CE* [e] *om. CE*

[451] Matt. 23: 15.

[452] John 6: 71.

108. There are some who lack foresight and, though their resources are small, like to have a large household but, when harassed by the responsibility to provide for it, they go begging without shame, or extort forcibly from others what they do not have themselves. We see several abbots of monasteries who are like this. They boast of the numbers in their community and care more about having many sons than about having good ones; and they stand high in their own eyes if they are regarded as greater for being among many. To draw these numbers under their rule they make smooth promises when they should preach harsh words, and through broken vows they easily lose those taken in indiscriminately and approved without any test. As I see it, the Truth rebuked such men saying: 'Alas for you, for you travel over sea and land to win one convert; but when you have won him, you make him twice as fit for hell as yourselves.'[451] They would surely boast less of their numbers if they sought to save souls rather than count them, and presumed less on their strength when giving an account of their rule.

109. The Lord chose only a few apostles, and one of those he chose fell so far away that the Lord said of him: 'Have I not chosen you twelve? Yet one of you is a devil.'[452] And as Judas was lost to the apostles, so was Nicholas to the seven deacons;[453] then when the apostles had gathered together no more than a few, Ananias and Sapphira his wife earned sentence of death.[454] Indeed, many of his disciples had previously fallen away from the Lord himself, and few stayed with him.[455] The road which leads to life is narrow, and few set foot on it, but by contrast the road that leads to death is wide, with plenty of room, and many choose to go that way.[456] For as the Lord testifies elsewhere: 'Many are called but few are chosen',[457] and according to Solomon: 'The number of fools cannot be counted.'[458] And so whoever rejoices in the large numbers of those beneath him should fear lest, in the words of the Lord, few may be found to be chosen, and he who unduly increases the size of his flock may be less capable of watching over them, so that the words of the Prophet may

[453] One of the seven elected deacons (cf. Acts 6: 5), Nicholas was thought by some of the Church Fathers to have established a heretical sect called Nicholaite (cf. Rev. 2: 6 and 15).
[454] Cf. Acts 5: 1–11; cf. **59** above.
[455] Cf. Matt. 26: 31, 56; Mark 14: 27, 50; John 16: 32, 18: 6.
[456] Cf. Matt. 7: 13–14.
[457] Matt. 20: 16, 22: 14. Also cited in **72** above..
[458] Eccles. 1: 15. Also cited in **72** above.

recte a spiritalibus illud propheticum dici possit: 'Multiplicasti gentem, non magnificasti leticiam,'[459] Tales utique scilicet de multitudine gloriantes, dum tam pro suis quam suorum necessitatibus sepius exire atque ad seculum redire et mendicando discurrere coguntur, curis se corporalibus magis quam spiritalibus implicant et infamiam sibi magis quam gloriam acquirunt. [f]Quod quidem in feminis tanto magis est erubescendum quanto eas per mundum discurrere[460] uidetur minus tutum.[f]

110. Quisquis igitur quiete uel honeste cupit uiuere et officiis uacare diuinis et tam Deo quam seculo carus haberi, timeat aggregare quos non possit procurare, nec in expensis suis de alienis confidat marsupiis, nec elemosinis petendis sed dandis inuigilet. Apostolus ille magnus Euangelii predicator, et habens potestatem de Euangelio sumptus accipere, laborat manibus ne quos grauare uideatur et gloriam suam euacuet.[461] Nos ergo, quorum non est predicare sed peccata plangere,[462] qua temeritate uel impudentia mendicantes querimus? Vnde hos, quos inconsiderate congregamus, sustentare possumus?[a] Qui etiam sepe in tantam prorumpimus insaniam ut, cum predicare nesciamus, predicatores conducamus et, pseudoapostolos nobiscum circumducendo, cruces et philacteria reliquiarum gestemus, ut tam hec quam uerbum Dei seu etiam figmenta diaboli simplicibus et ydiotis uendamus Christianis, et eis promittamus quecumque ad extorquendos nummos proficere credimus.[463] Ex qua quidem impudenti cupiditate que sua sunt, non que Ihesu Christi, querente,[464] quantum iam ordo noster, et ipsa diuini predicatio uerbi uiluerit,[b] neminem iam latere arbitror.

111. Hinc et ipsi abbates uel qui maiores in monasteriis uidentur, potentibus seculi et mundanis curiis sese importune ingerentes, iam magis curiales[a] esse quam cenobite didicerunt,[b] [465] et fauorem hominum quacumque arte uenantes, crebrius cum hominibus fabulari quam cum Deo loqui consueuerunt. Illud sepe frustra legentes atque negligentes uel audientes sed non exaudientes quod beatus Antonius

[f-f] *om. CE*

110 [a] possimus *T* [b] uoluerit *CE*

111 [a] carnales (*exp.*) curiales *T;* carnales *Amb* [b] didiscerunt *CE*

---

[459] Isaiah 9: 3.
[460] 'per mundum discurrere': cf. *Letter* 1, 58 and n. 179.
[461] Cf. 1 Thess. 2: 9; 1 Cor. 9: 15 and *Sermon* 33 (*PL* clxxviii. 592).

rightly be applied to him: 'You have made their numbers greater; you have not increased their joy.'[459] Such men as boast of numbers, and are often obliged to meet their own needs and those of their people by going out and returning to the world to run round begging, entangle themselves in bodily rather than spiritual cares, and incur disgrace instead of winning glory. This is surely all the more shameful for women who seem less safe when out in the world.[460]

110. So whoever desires to live quietly and virtuously, to devote himself to the divine offices and be held as dear to God as to the world, should hesitate to gather together those for whom he cannot provide. He should not rely on other men's purses to meet his costs, and he should supervise the giving, not the seeking, of alms. The Apostle and great preacher of the Gospel had authority from the Gospel to accept gifts for his expenses, but he worked with his hands so as not to appear a burden to anyone nor detract from his glory.[461] How bold and shameless then are we, whose business is not preaching but lamenting our sins,[462] if we go begging? How can we support those we have thoughtlessly brought together? Not knowing how to preach ourselves, we also often break out into such madness that we hire preachers and take false apostles around with us, carrying crosses and reliquaries to sell these as much as the Word of God, or other such figments of the devil, to guileless and foolish Christians, and we promise them whatever we believe will enable us to extort money.[463] How far our Order and the very preaching of the divine Word is debased by such shameless cupidity, which seeks what is its own and not of Jesus Christ,[464] is known, I think, to all.

111. Consequently abbots themselves or those who appear to have authority in monasteries take themselves off to pester the secular powers and the courts of the world, having already learned to be courtiers rather than monks.[465] They woo men's favour by any device. They have grown accustomed to gossip with men more frequently than they speak with God. They often read St Antony's warning but to no

[462] 'Nos . . . plangere': cf. Jerome, *Contra Vigilantium*, 15 (*PL* xxiii. 351B); also *Sermon* 33 (*PL* clxxviii. 603A); *Adtendite* (ed. Engels, '*Adtendite a falsis prophetis*', p. 226 *l.* 46 and p. 227 *ll.* 55–7).

[463] Cf. *Sermon* 33 (*PL* clxxviii. 592D–593A).

[464] Cf. Phil. 2: 21.

[465] Cf. *Sermon* 33 (*PL* clxxviii. 588D–589A). Around 1116/19, Guibert, abbot of Nogent (dioc. of Laon), made a powerful attack on relic-mongers in *De sanctis et eorum pigneribus*, ed. Huygens.

ammonet, dicens: 'Sicut pisces, si tardauerint in sicco, moriuntur, ita et monachi tardantes extra cellulam, aut cum uiris secularibus immorantes, [c]a quietis proposito resoluuntur.[c] Oportet ergo sicut piscem in mari, ita et nos ad cellam recurrere, ne forte foris tardantes obliuiscamur interioris custodie.'[466]

112. Quod ipse quoque monastice scriptor *Regule*, scilicet beatus Benedictus, diligenter attendens, quasi in monasteriis assiduos uelit esse abbates et super custodiam sui gregis sollicite stare tam exemplo quam scripto patenter edocuit. Hic enim, cum[a] a fratribus ad sacratissimam sororem suam uisitandam profectus, cum ipsa eum pro edificatione saltem nocte una uellet retinere, aperte professus est manere extra cellam nullatenus se posse. Nec ait quidem: non possumus, sed: non possum, quia hoc per eum fratres, non ipse posset, nisi hoc ei[b] Domino, sicut postmodum actum est, reuelante.[467] Vnde et, cum *Regulam* scriberet, nusquam de abbatis sed solummodo fratrum egressu meminerit.[468] De cuius etiam assiduitate ita caute prouidit ut in uigiliis dominicorum et[c] festorum dierum euangelicam lectionem, et que illi adiuncta sunt, nonnisi ab abbate precipiat dici.[469] Qui etiam instituens ut mensa abbatis cum peregrinis et hospitibus sit semper et, quociens minus sunt hospites [d]cum eo,[d] quos uoluerit de fratribus uocare, seniore uno tantum aut duobus dimissis cum fratribus,[470] patenter insinuat numquam in tempore mense abbatem monasterio debere deesse, et ut delicatis principum ferculis iam assuetus cibarium[e] panem monasterii subiectis derelinquat.[471] De qualibus[f] quidem Veritas: 'Alligant', inquit, 'onera grauia et importabilia et imponunt in humeros hominum; digito autem suo nolunt ea mouere.'[472] Et alibi de falsis predicatoribus: 'Attendite a falsis prophetis qui ueniunt ad uos',[473] etc. [g]Veniunt, inquit, per se, non a Deo missi uel exspectantes ut pro eis mandetur.[g] Iohannes Baptista, princeps noster[474] cui pontificatus hereditate cedebat, semel ab urbe recessit ad heremum, pontificatum[h] scilicet pro monachatu, ciuitates

[c–c] *om. CE*

112 [a] *om. CE* [b] & a *add. Amb* [c] uel *CE* [d–d] cum *TCE; add. Amb* [e] cibarium *TCE;* (. . .)arium *add. T*[1] [f] quibus *CE* [g–g] *om. CE* [h] relinquens *add. CE*

[466] *Vitae patrum*, *Verba seniorum*, v. ii. 1 (*PL* lxxiii. 858A).

[467] 'Manere extra cellam nullatenus possum' ('I cannot possibly stay away from my cell'), in Gregory the Great, *Dialogi*, ii. 33 (ed. Moricca, p. 126; Vogüé, pp. 230–4, at p. 230; *PL* lxvi. 194A–196B at 194A). Benedict's sister, Scholastica, wanted him to spend the night in

purpose, ignoring it or hearing it without heeding it: 'As fish die if they linger on land, so too do monks if they linger outside the cell or stay among men of the world, free from their vow of quiet. So, like fishes in the sea, we should hurry back to the cell, lest by lingering outside we forget to care for what is within.'[466]

112. The author of the monastic *Rule*, St Benedict himself, also paid serious attention to this. He wished abbots to be active inside their monasteries and to keep careful watch over their flock, and he openly taught this by example as well as in his text. For when he had left his brothers to go to visit his most holy sister, and she wished him to stay for at least a night, he said plainly that it was impossible for him to stay away from his cell. In fact, he did not say 'we cannot' but 'I cannot', for the brothers might do so with his permission, but he could not without a revelation from the Lord, which later came.[467] And so when he came to write the *Rule*, he made no mention of the abbot's but only of the brothers' going out of the monastery,[468] and he made careful provision for the abbot's continual presence by laying down that on the vigils of Sundays and feast-days, the Gospel and what follows it should be read by the abbot alone.[469] And when he rules that the abbot's table shall always be shared with pilgrims and guests, and that whenever there are few guests he shall invite to it any of the brothers he likes, leaving only one or two senior brothers with the rest,[470] he evidently implies that at mealtimes the abbot should never be absent from the monastery nor, like one accustomed to the delicate dishes of princes, leave the ordinary bread of the monastery to subordinates.[471] Of such men the Truth says: 'They make up packs too heavy to carry and pile them on men's shoulders, but will not raise a finger to lift the load themselves.'[472] And elsewhere, of false preachers: 'Beware of false prophets who come to you',[473] etc. They come of themselves, says the Truth, not sent by God nor waiting to be summoned. John the Baptist, our leader,[474] to whom priesthood came by inheritance, withdrew from the city to the wilderness just

spiritual conversation with her on the joys of the heavenly life. He refused but her prayer was granted when a violent thunderstorm prevented him from returning to his monastery.

[468] Benedict, *Rule*, c. 29; 51, 1; 67. [469] Cf. Benedict, *Rule*, c. 11, 9–10.

[470] Cf. Benedict, *Rule*, c. 56; also *Letter* 6, 4 and above at 38.

[471] Cf. 38 above and n. 149.

[472] Matt. 23: 4. Also cited in part in *Adtendite* (ed. Engels, '*Adtendite a falsis prophetis*', p. 228 *ll.* 85–6).

[473] Matt. 7: 15.

[474] 'Iohannes Baptista, princeps noster': cf. **12** above and n. 45.

pro solitudine deserens; et ad eum populus exibat, non[i] ipse ad populum introibat.[j] [475] Qui cum tantus esset ut Christus[k] crederetur, et multa[l] in ciuitatibus corrigere posset,[476] in illo iam erat lectulo[477] unde pulsanti dilecto respondere paratus erat: 'Exspoliaui me tunica mea, [m]quomodo induar illa? Laui pedes meos, quomodo inquinabo illos?'[478]

113. Quisquis itaque quietis monastice secretum desiderat, lectulum magis quam lectum se habere gaudeat.[479] De lecto quippe, ut Veritas ait, 'unus assumetur et alter relinquetur'.[480] Lectulum uero sponse esse legimus, id est anime contemplatiue Christo arcius copulate et summo ei desiderio adherentis.[481] Quem quicumque intrauerit neminem esse relictum legimus. De quo et ipsamet loquitur: 'In lectulo meo pernoctans quesiui quem diligit anima mea.'[482] A quo etiam lectulo ipsa surgere dedignans uel formidans pulsanti dilecto quod supra meminimus respondet.[483] Non enim sordes nisi extra lectum suum esse credit quibus inquinari pedes metuit.[484] Egressa est Dina ut alienigenas uideret et corrupta est.[485] Et sicut Malcho illi captiuo monacho ab abbate suo predictum est et ipse postmodum est expertus, ouis que de ouili egreditur cito lupi morsibus patet.[a] [486] Ne igitur multitudinem congregemus pro qua egrediendi occasionem queramus,[b] immo et egredi compellamur, et cum detrimento nostri lucra[c] faciamus aliorum, ad modum uidelicet plumbi quod ut argentum seruetur in fornace consumitur. Verendum pocius est ne et plumbum pariter et argentum fornax uehemens consumat temptationum. [d]Veritas, inquiunt, ait: 'Et eum qui uenit ad me, non eiciam foras.'[487] Nec nos eici susceptos uolumus, sed de suscipiendis prouideri[e] ne, cum eos intus susceperimus, nos ipsos extra pro eis

[i] nec *Amb* [j] intrabat *CE* [k] esse *add.* CE [l] nulla *Amb* [m] beginning of lacuna in CE, ending in 113

113 [a] *end of lacuna in CE, beginning in* 112 (*C has* etc.) [b] sumamus *CE* [c] lucrum *Amb* [d] beginning of lacuna in CE, ending in 114 [e] providere *Amb*

---

[475] Cf. *Letter* 12 (ed. Smits, p. 262, *ll.* 148–55; *PL* clxxviii. 348AB; trans. Ziolkowski, p. 165); *Sermon* 33 (*PL* clxxviii. 597C–598B); *Adtendite* (ed. Engels, '*Adtendite a falsis prophetis*', p. 227, *ll.* 47–64).

[476] 'Iohannes Baptista . . . posset': cf. *Sermon* 33 (*PL* clxxviii. 597C–598A); *Adtendite* (ed. Engels, '*Adtendite a falsis prophetis*', p. 227); *Letter* 12 (ed. Smits, p. 261 *l.* 132 – 262 *l.* 155; *PL* clxxviii. 347C–348B; trans. Ziolkowski, pp. 164–5).

[477] 'lectulo': S. of S. 3: 1 and cf. **12** above and n. 45.

[478] S. of S. 5: 3; partly cited also at **17** above.

[479] Cf. *Sermon* 31 (*PL* clxxviii. 569D–570A).

once, leaving his priestly life for a monastic one and cities for solitude. People went out to him, he did not go in to the people.[475] When he was so great that he was believed to be Christ and could correct many things in the cities,[476] he was already in that bed[477] from which he was ready to answer to the knocking of the Beloved: 'I have taken off my tunic, am I to put it on again? I have washed my feet, am I to dirty them again?'[478]

113. Whoever therefore wishes to learn the secret of monastic quiet must be glad to have a narrow bed and not a wide one.[479] From the wider bed, as the Truth says, 'one will be taken, and the other left'.[480] But we read that the narrow bed belongs to the bride, that is to the contemplative soul which is more closely joined to Christ, and clings to him with the strongest desire.[481] None, we read, have been left who lay on this, and the bride herself says of it: 'By night on my narrow bed I sought him whom my soul loves.'[482] She also refuses or fears to rise from this narrow bed, but answers to the knocking of the Beloved in the way we have recalled.[483] For she believes that outside her bed is the dirt she fears will soil her feet.[484] Dinah went out to see alien women and was defiled.[485] And as was foretold to Malchus, that captive monk, by his abbot, and he afterwards found out for himself, the sheep which leaves the sheepfold is soon exposed to the bite of the wolf.[486] So let us not assemble a crowd for whom we look for an excuse, or even a compelling reason, for going out to raise money for others with detriment to ourselves, like lead melted in the furnace so that silver may be saved. We must rather beware lest lead and silver alike are consumed in the burning furnace of temptation. The Truth, men argue, says: 'The man who comes to me I will never turn away.'[487] Nor do we want to turn away those who have been admitted, but to be careful about admitting them, lest when we have taken them in we have

[480] Luke 17: 34.
[481] 'Lectulum': S. of S. 3:1 and cf. **12** above and n. 45.
[482] S. of S. 3: 1; cited also in *Letter* 5, 7.
[483] Cf. **112** above and *Letter* 12 (ed. Smits, p. 263; *PL* clxxviii. 348BD; trans. Ziolkowski, p. 166).
[484] Cf. Lam. 1: 9 ('sordes eius in pedibus eius'); also *Letter* 12 (ed. Smits, p. 262 *l.* 163 – p. 263 *l.* 167, p. 263 *l.* 194 – p. 264 *l.* 203; *PL* clxxviii. 348BC, 349AB; trans. Ziolkowski, pp.166–7) and *Sermons* 28 and 33 (*PL* clxxviii. 552C, 595C–596A)
[485] Cf. Gen. 34: 1; also *Planctus I: Dinae filiae Iacob*, *vv.* 8–13 (ed. Meyer, *Gesammelte Abhandlungen*, i. 366; ed. Dronke, *Poetic Individuality*, p. 146; *PL* clxxviii. 1817) and Jerome, *Epistola* XXII *ad Eustochium*, 25 (ed. Hilberg, liv.179; *PL* xxii. 411).
[486] Cf. Jerome, *Vita Malchi* 3 (*PL* xxiii. 55B).
[487] John 6: 37.

eiciamus. Nam et ipsum Dominum non susceptum eiecisse legimus, sed offerentem se respuisse. Cui quidem dicenti: 'Magister, sequar te quocumque ieris.'[488] [f]Ipse enim repellens eum[f] respondit: 'Vulpes foueas habent',[489] etc.

114. Qui etiam de sumptibus nos ante prouidere, cum aliquid facere meditamur cui sint ipsi necessarii, diligenter ammonet, dicens: 'Quis nostrum[a] uolens turrim edificare, nonne prius sedens computat sumptus qui necessarii sunt, si habet ad perficiendum, ne posteaquam posuerit fundamentum, et non potuerit perficere, omnes qui uiderint incipiant illudere ei dicentes: Quia hic homo cepit edificare et non potuit consummare?'[b] [490] Magnum[c] est si[d] unum quis saluare sufficiat, et periculosum est [e]multis eum[e] prouidere qui uix ad custodiam sui[f] sufficit uigilare. Nemo uero studiosus est in custodiendo nisi qui pauidus fuerit in suscipiendo. Et nemo sic perseuerat in incepto[g] sicut qui tardus est et prouidus ad incipiendum. [h]In quo quidem tanto maior feminarum sit prouidentia, quanto earum infirmitas magna minus tolerat onera et quiete plurimum est fouenda.[h]

115. Speculum[a] anime Scripturam sacram constat esse in quam quilibet legendo uiuens, intelligendo proficiens, morum suorum pulcritudinem cognoscit uel deformitatem deprehendit, ut illam uidelicet augere, hanc studeat remouere. Hoc nobis speculum beatus commemorans Gregorius in secundo *Moralium* ait: 'Scriptura sacra mentis oculis quasi quoddam speculum opponitur ut interna nostra facies [b]in ipsa uideatur. Ibi[c] etenim feda,[d] ibi pulcra nostra cognoscimus.[e] Ibi sentimus quantum proficimus, ibi a profectu quam longe distamus.'[491] Qui autem Scripturam conspicit quam non intelligit quasi cecus ante [f]oculos speculum[f] tenet in quo qualis sit cognoscere non ualet,[492] nec doctrinam querit in Scriptura ad quam ipsa est tantummodo facta; et tamquam asinus applicetur ad lyram,[493]

[f–f] *om. Amb*

114 [a] vestrum *Amb* [b] *end of lacuna in CE, beginning in* 113 [c] enim *add. CE* [d] uel se *add. codd., Amb* [e–e] eum multis *CE* [f] *om. CE* [g] coepto *Amb* [h–h] *om. CE*

115 [a] *TEAmb indicate the beginning of a new section* [b–b] etc. *CE* [c] Vbi *CE* [d] cognoscimus *add. Amb* [e] conspicimus (*exp.*) cognoscimus *T;* conspicimus *Amb* [f–f] oculos *TAmb;* oculos speculum *add.* Cousin, McLaughlin

[488] Matt. 8: 19.

[489] Matt. 8: 20: 'Foxes have their holes, the birds their roosts, but the Son of Man has nowhere to lay his head.'

[490] Luke 14: 28–30. Cf. *Letter* 1, **62**.

[491] Gregory the Great, *Moralia in Iob*, ii. 1. 1 (ed. Adriaen, cxliii. 59; *PL* lxxv. 553).

to go away ourselves on their account. For the Lord himself, we read, did not turn away anyone once admitted, but rejected some who offered themselves. To a man who said: 'Master, I will follow you wherever you go',[488] he replied: 'The foxes have holes',[489] etc.

114. He also carefully warns us to consider first the necessary cost when we are thinking of doing something. 'Would any of you', he says, 'think of building a tower without first sitting down and calculating the necessary cost, to see whether he can afford to finish it? Otherwise, if he has laid the foundation and then is unable to finish, all onlookers will laugh at him. Here is a man, they will say, who started to build and could not finish.'[490] It is a great thing if someone is able to save one man, and dangerous for one who is scarcely able to look after himself to take care of many. No custodian is diligent who has not been cautious in granting admission, and no one perseveres in an undertaking like the man who takes time and who gives forethought before making a start. In this indeed women show greater foresight, because their weakness is less able to bear heavy burdens and most in need of quiet support.

115. It is clear that sacred Scripture is a mirror of the soul, in which anyone who lives by reading and advances by understanding perceives the beauty of his own ways or discovers their ugliness, so that he may work to increase the one and remove the other. Reminding us of this mirror, St Gregory says in the second book of his *Morals*: 'Sacred Scripture is set before the mind's eye as if it were a mirror in which our inward face may be seen reflected. For there we see our beauty or recognize our hideousness, there we perceive how far we are advancing and how far we are from advancing.'[491] But whoever looks at Scripture without understanding is like a blind man holding a mirror to his eyes, unable to see what sort of man he is,[492] nor does he look for the teaching of Scripture for which alone it was composed. Like an ass before a lyre,[493] he sits idly before Scripture, and has, as it

[492] In her preface to the Scriptural *Problemata* that the Paraclete sisters asked Abelard to solve for them, Heloise refers to this and other advice by Abelard that they should see the Scriptures as a mirror of the soul which shows the soul's beauty or deformity; anyone who reads the Scriptures without understanding is blind: 'Quibus saepius in tantum Scripturae sacrae doctrinam commendasti, ut eam animae speculum dicens, quo decor eius vel deformitas cognoscatur, nullam Christi sponsam hoc carere speculo permittebas . . . Addebas insuper, ad exhortationem nostram, ipsam Scripturae lectionem non intellectam esse quasi speculum oculis non videntis appositum' (*PL* clxxviii. 678B).

[493] Cf. **122** below.

sic ociosus sedet ad Scripturam, et quasi panem appositum habet quo ieiunus non reficitur, dum uerbum Dei nec se per intelligentiam penetrante, nec alio ei docendo frangente, inutiliter cibum habet qui ei nullatenus prodest.[b]

116. Vnde et Apostolus generaliter ad Scripturarum studium nos adhortans,[a] 'quecumque', inquit, 'scripta sunt, ad nostram [b]doctrinam scripta sunt ut per patientiam et consolationem Scripturarum spem habeamus.'[b] [494] Et alibi: 'Implemini Spiritu sancto, loquentes uobismetipsis in psalmis et ymnis et canticis spiritalibus.'[495] Sibi quippe uel secum loquitur qui quod profert intelligit uel de intelligentia uerborum suorum fructum facit. Idem ad Tymotheum: 'Dum uenio', inquit, 'attende lectioni, [c]exhortationi, doctrine.'[c] [496] Et iterum: 'Tu uero permane in hiis que didicisti et credita[d] sunt tibi, sciens a quo didiceris, et quia ab infantia sacras litteras nosti que te possunt instruere ad salutem, per fidem que est in Christo Iesu. Omnis scriptura diuinitus inspirata utilis est [e]ad docendum, ad arguendum, ad corripiendum, ad erudiendum in iusticia, ut perfectus sit[f] homo Dei ad omne opus bonum instructus.'[e] [497] Qui etiam ad intelligentiam Scripture Corinthios ammonens, ut que uidelicet aliis[g] de Scriptura locuntur exponere ualeant, 'sectamini', inquit, 'caritatem, emulamini spiritualia, magis autem[h] ut prophetetis.[i] Qui enim loquitur lingua, non hominibus loquitur sed Deo. Qui autem prophetat, ecclesiam edificat. [j]Et ideo qui loquitur lingua, oret ut interpretetur. Orabo spiritu, orabo et mente; psallam spiritu, psallam et mente. Ceterum si benedixeris spiritu, quis suplet[k] locum ydiote? Quomodo dicet Amen super tuam benedictionem, quoniam quid dicas nescit? Nam tu quidem bene gratias agis, sed alter non edificatur. Gratias ago Deo quoniam omnium uestrum lingua loquor. Sed in ecclesia uolo quinque uerba sensu meo loqui ut[l] et alios instruam quam decem millia uerborum.[m] Fratres, nolite effici pueri[n] sensibus, sed malicia paruuli estote,[j] sensibus autem perfecti.'[498]

116 [a] exhortans *CE* [b–b] etc. *CE* [c–c] etc. *CE* [d] traddita *CE* [e–e] etc. *CE* [f] est *Amb.* [g] alii *TAmb* [h] autem spiritus *add. TAmb;* enim *CE;* autem *Vulg.* [i] proffitiatis *E;* proficiatis *Amb*[1] [j–j] etc. usque bene ita *CE* [k] implebit *Amb* [l] *om. Amb* [m] uerborum in lingua *Vulg.* [n] parvi *Amb*

[494] Rom. 15: 4.

[495] Ephes. 5: 18–19. Also cited in *Sermon* 14 (*PL* clxxviii. 490A).

[496] 1 Tim. 4: 13.

[497] 2 Tim. 3: 14–17.

were, bread set before him on which he does not break his fast. When he can neither penetrate the word of God through understanding nor have it broken open for him by another's teaching, he has no use for food which brings him no good.

116. Hence the Apostle, in a general exhortation to us to study the Scriptures, says: 'Everything that was written was written for our instruction, so that through patience and the comfort that the Scriptures bring, we may have hope.'[494] And elsewhere: 'Be filled with the Holy Spirit; speak to yourselves in psalms, hymns, and spiritual songs.'[495] For a man who speaks to himself or with himself understands what he is saying or from understanding makes his words fruitful. To Timothy he says: 'Until I arrive, devote yourself to reading, exhortation, and teaching.'[496] And again: 'But for your part, stand by the truths you have learned and are assured of. Remember from whom you learned them; remember that from early childhood you have been familiar with the sacred writings that have the power to lead you to salvation through faith in Christ Jesus. Every divinely inspired scripture is useful for teaching the truth and refuting error, for correction and instruction in righteousness, so that the man who belongs to God may be perfected and equipped for good work of every kind.'[497] And when he is exhorting the Corinthians to understand Scripture so that they can explain to others what they say of Scripture, he says: 'Make love your aim and spiritual gifts your aspiration and, above all, the gift of prophecy. For anyone who speaks with his tongue speaks to God, not to other people, but he who prophesies builds up the Church. And so he who speaks with his tongue should pray for understanding. I shall pray in spirit, I shall pray in my mind as well; I shall sing hymns in spirit, I shall sing hymns in my mind as well. Otherwise, if you only bless God in spirit, who will replace the plain man? How will he be able to say Amen to your blessing, for he has no idea what you are saying? True enough, you give thanks, but the other receives no benefit. I thank God that I speak in the language of you all, but in church I would rather speak five words that instruct others than ten thousand. Brothers, do not be childish in your thoughts; be as little children as far as wickedness is concerned but grown up in your thinking.'[498]

[498] 1 Cor. 14: 1–2, 4, 13, 15–20; also cited in *TSch*, ii. 52, 54; 1 Cor. 14: 16–20, also cited in part in *Sermon* 14 (*PL* clxxviii. 490A); 1 Cor. 14: 16, also cited in *Expositio symboli apostolorum* (*PL* clxxviii. 621A).

117. Loqui lingua dicitur qui ore tantum uerba format, non intelligentia exponendo ministrat. Prophetat uero siue interpretatur qui more[a] prophetarum, qui uidentes dicuntur, id est intelligentes, ea que dicit intelligit, ut ipsa exponere possit. [b]Orat ille spiritu siue psallit qui solo prolationis flatu uerba format, non mentis intelligentiam accomodat. Cum uero spiritus noster orat, id est nostre prolationis flatus solummodo uerba format, nec quod ore profertur corde concipitur, mens nostra sine fructu est quem in oratione uidelicet habere debet, ut ipsa scilicet ex intelligentia uerborum in Deum compungatur atque accendatur.[b] [499] [c]Vnde hanc[c] in uerbis perfectionem nos ammonet habere, ut non more puerorum[d] uerba tantum sciamus proferre, uerum etiam intelligentie sensum in hiis habere, atque aliter nos orare uel psallere infructuose protestatur. Quem et beatus sequens Benedictus: 'Sic stemus', inquit, 'ad psallendum ut mens nostra concordet uoci nostre.'[500] Hoc et[e] Psalmista precipiens ait: 'Psallite sapienter',[501] ut uidelicet uerborum prolationi sapor et condimentum intelligentie non desit, et cum ipso ueraciter [f]dicere Domino[f] ualeamus: 'Quam dulcia faucibus meis [g]eloquia tua',[g] [502] etc.[h] Et alibi: 'Non in tibiis', inquit,[i] 'uiri[j] beneplacitum erit ei.'[503] Tibia quippe sonitum emittit ad delectationem uoluptatis, non ad intelligentiam mentis. Vnde bene in tybiis cantare nec in hoc Deo placere dicuntur qui melodia sui cantus sic oblectantur ut nulla hinc edificentur intelligentia. Qua etiam ratione, inquit Apostolus,[504] cum benedictiones in ecclesia fiunt, respondebitur Amen, si quod oratur in illa benedictione non intelligitur? Vtrum uidelicet bonum sit quod oratio postulat aut non? Sic enim sepe multos ydiotas et litterarum sensum ignorantes uidemus in ecclesia per errorem plura[k] sibi nociua quam utilia precari, ueluti cum dicitur: 'ut sic transeamus per bona temporalia ut non amittamus eterna'. Facile ipsa [l]consimilis uocis affinitas[l] nonnullos sic decipit, ut uel sic dicant: ut nos amittamus eterna, uel ita proferant: ut non admittamus

117 [a] *om. CE* [b–b] *om. CE* [c–c] quam *CE* [d] plurimorum *Amb* [e] *om. CE* [f–f] domino dicere *CEAmb* [g–g] *om. CE* [h] *om. Amb* [i] *om. Amb* [j] *om. CE* [k] nonnulla *TAmb* [l–l] uocis confinitas consimilis *CE*

[499] In his writings on logic, when discussing the relation between words and the concepts they may signify, Abelard never uses the expression 'flatus vocis' (a mere puff of the voice—cf. Appendix A, 1). But here and henceforth he contrasts 'prolationis flatus' (a mere puff of speech) with words which are spoken with understanding when the Scriptures are read and prayers are offered. He often returns to this favourite theme. Cf. *Letter* 1, **24**, **27**; *Letter* 9 to the sisters of the Paraclete (ed. Smits, pp. 219–37; *PL* clxxviii. 325–36; trans. Ziolkowski, pp. 10–33); *Carmen ad Astralabium*, ed. Rubingh-Bosscher *v.* 15; *Hymn* 2; *Comm. Rom.*, iv

117. A man who forms words with his mouth only is said to speak with his tongue; he does not provide understanding through explanation. But one who prophesies or interprets in the manner of the prophets, who are called seers, that is, understanders, understands the things he says and so can explain them. The former prays or sings in spirit but forms his words only by breathing and pronouncing them, without making available understanding from his mind. When our spirit prays, that is, when we form words only by breathing and pronouncing them so that what the mouth speaks is not taken into the heart, our mind does not benefit by prayer as it should, so as to be moved and fired towards God by an understanding of the words.[499] And so the Apostle urges us to seek this ideal with words, so that we may not, like children, only know how to say them, but may also have a sense of the meaning in them; or else, he argues, our praying and hymn-singing does no good. Following him, St Benedict says: 'Let us stand to sing the psalms so that mind and voice may be in harmony.'[500] The Psalmist too tells us to 'sing hymns with understanding',[501] so that the words we speak do not lack the savour and seasoning of meaning, and with him we can truthfully say to the Lord: 'How sweet are thy words in my mouth', and elsewhere:[502] 'He will take no pleasure in a man's flute',[503] for the flute gives out sounds for the gratification of pleasure, not for understanding in the mind. And so men are said to sing well to the flute but not to please God in doing so, because they delight in the melody of their singing but, without understanding, they gain no benefit. And how, asks the Apostle,[504] can people answer Amen after blessings in church if no one understands what is prayed for during the blessing, whether the object of the prayer is good or not? For we often see in church many ordinary and illiterate people pray by mistake for things which will bring them more harm than benefit. For example, when saying: 'May we so pass through the good things of this world that we lose not sight of those that are eternal', some people are easily confused by the similarity in sound so that either they say that we lose sight of things eternal (*nos amittamus*) or that we admit not things eternal (*non*

(xii. 14, ed. Buytaert, p. 280); *Expositio symboli apostolorum* (*PL* clxxviii. 620B–621A); *Sermon* 14, *expositio dominicae orationis* (*I sermoni di Abelardo per le monache del Paracleto*, ed. De Santis, pp. 207–10; *PL* clxxviii. 489C–490C); *TSch*, *prefatio* (ed. Buytaert and Mews, pp. 313–16) and ii. 52–61.

[500] Benedict, *Rule*, c. 19, 7.

[501] Ps. 46 (47): 8 (7); also cited by Benedict, *Rule*, c. 19, 4.

[502] Ps. 118 (119): 103.

[503] Ps. 146 (147): 10.

[504] Cf. 1 Cor. 14: 16.

eterna. Cui etiam periculo Apostolus prouidens ait: 'Ceterum si benedixeris spiritu', id est prolationis tantum flatu uerba[m] benedictionis formaueris, non sensu mentem audientis instruxeris, 'quis suplet locum ydiote?'[505] id est, quis de assistentibus, quorum est respondere, id aget respondendo quod ydiota non ualet, immo nec debet? 'Quomodo dicet Amen?'[506] etc.,[n] cum uidelicet nesciat utrum in maledictionem [o]pocius quam benedictionem[o] inducas? Denique que[p] Scripture non habent intelligentiam, quomodo sermonis edificationem sibi ministrabunt, aut etiam *Regulam* exponere uel intelligere, aut uiciose prolata corrigere ualebunt?

118. Vnde non mediocriter miramur que inimici suggestio in monasteriis hoc egit ut nulla ibi de intelligendis Scripturis sint studia, sed de cantu tantum uel de [a]uerbis solummodo[a] formandis, non intelligendis, habeatur disciplina, quasi ouium balatus plus utilitatis habeat quam pastus.[507] Cibus quippe est anime et spiritalis refectio ipsi diuina intelligentia Scripture. Vnde et Ezechielem prophetam ad predicandum Dominus destinans eum prius uolumine cibat quod statim in eius ore factum est mel dulce.[508] De quo etiam cibo scriptum est in Ieremia: 'Paruuli pecierunt panem et non erat qui frangeret eis.'[509] Panem quippe paruulis frangit qui littere sensum simplicioribus aperit. Hii uero paruuli panem frangi postulant, cum de intelligentia Scripture animam saginari desiderant, sicut alibi Dominus testatur: 'Emittam famem in terram,[b] non famem[c] panis neque sitim aque, set audiendi uerbum Domini.'[510]

119. Hinc autem econtrario antiquus hostis famem et sitim audiendi uerba hominum et rumores seculi claustris monasteriorum immisit, ut uaniloquio uacantes diuina tanto amplius fastidiamus eloquia quanto magis sine dulcedine uel condimento intelligencie nobis fiunt insipida. Vnde et Psalmista, ut supra meminimus: 'Quam dulcia [a]faucibus meis eloquia tua! Super mel ori meo.'[a] [511] Que

[m] *om. C* [n] *om. Amb* [o–o] *om. CE* [p] qui *Amb*

118 [a–a] notis tantummodo *CE* [b] terra *Amb* [c] *om. CE*

119 [a–a] etc. *CE*

[505] 1 Cor. 14: 16. [506] 1 Cor. 14: 16.

[507] Abelard does not name monasteries. According to H. Röckelein ('Die Heilige Schrift in Frauenhand', pp. 169, 174), the Praemonstratensian and other reformed orders discouraged biblical study by religious women; on the other hand, this was well promoted in Benedictine convents in Germany, Hildegard of Bingen (1098–1179) being not an exception but an example of a long tradition of sustained biblical study by religious women.

admittamus). To guard against this hazard the Apostle says: 'If, moreover, you bless in spirit', that is, if you form the words of the blessing only by breathing their sound and do not convey their meaning to the mind of the listener, 'who will replace the plain man?',[505] that is, who among the congregation whose duty it is to respond, will give a response which a plain man cannot or should not give? 'How will he say Amen?',[506] etc., when he has no idea whether you are invoking a curse rather than a blessing? Finally, if the sisters have no understanding of Scripture, how will they be able to instruct each other by word, or even to explain or understand the *Rule*, or correct false citations from it?

118. So we very much wonder what prompting by the Devil brought about the present situation in monasteries whereby there are no studies there on how to understand the Scriptures, but only training in singing or just in pronunciation without understanding the words, as if the bleating of sheep were more useful than their feeding.[507] For the food of the soul and its spiritual refreshment is the God-given understanding of Scripture, and so, when the Lord destined the prophet Ezekiel for preaching, he first fed him on a scroll which immediately became in his mouth sweet as honey.[508] Of such food Jeremiah also writes: 'Young children begged for bread but there was no one to break it for them.'[509] He breaks bread for young children who reveals the meaning of letters to the very simple, and these children ask for bread to be broken when they long for their souls to be fed with an understanding of Scripture, as the Lord bears witness elsewhere: 'I will send famine on the land, not hunger for bread nor thirst for water, but for hearing the word of the Lord.'[510]

119. On the other hand, the old enemy has implanted in monastic cloisters a hunger and thirst for hearing men's words and worldly gossip, so that by giving ourselves up to empty talk we may tire of the word of God, and the more so if we find it tasteless because it lacks the sweetness and savour of meaning. Hence the Psalmist, as we recalled above: 'How sweet are thy words on my palate, sweeter than honey in my mouth',[511] and he at once went on to say what this

In *Letter* 9, following again the example of St Jerome, Abelard encourages the Paraclete sisters to study the three languages of Scripture, Hebrew, Greek, and Latin.

508 Cf. Ezek. 3: 3.

509 Lam. 4: 4.

510 Amos 8: 11.

511 Ps. 118 (119): 103; partly cited also in **107** above.

quidem dulcedo in quo consisteret statim annexuit dicens: 'A mandatis tuis intellexi',[512] id est, a mandatis tuis pocius quam humanis intelligentiam accepi, illis uidelicet eruditus atque instructus. Cuius quidem intelligentie que sit utilitas non pretermisit, subiungens: 'Propterea odiui omnem uiam iniquitatis.'[513] Multe quippe iniquitatis uie ita per se sunt aperte ut facile omnibus in odium uel contemptum ueniant, sed omnem iniquitatis uiam nonnisi per eloquia diuina cognoscimus,[b] ut omnes euitare possimus. Hinc et illud est: 'In corde meo abscondi eloquia tua, ut non peccem [c]tibi.'[514] [d]In corde pocius recondita sunt quam in ore sonantia, cum eorum intelligentiam meditatio nostra retinet.[cd] Quorum quidem intelligencie quanto minus studemus, minus has iniquitatis uias cognoscimus atque uitamus, et minus a peccato nobis prouidere ualemus.

120. Que quidem negligencia tanto amplius in monachis qui ad perfectionem aspirant est arguenda quanto hec eis facilior esset doctrina qui et sacris habundant libris et quietis ocio perfruuntur. Quos quidem de multitudine scriptorum gloriantes, set ab eorum lectione uacantes, senex ille in *Vitis Patrum* egregie arguit, dicens: 'Prophete conscripserunt[a] libros; patres autem nostri[b] uenerunt post eos et operati sunt in eis plurima. Et iterum[c] successores illorum commendauerunt illos memorie. Venit autem generatio hec[d] que nunc est et [e]scripsit ea[e] in cartis atque membranis et reposuit in fenestris ociosa.'[515] Hinc et abbas Palladius ad discendum pariter et docendum nos uehementer adhortans ait: 'Oportet animam secundum Christi uoluntatem conuersantem aut discere fideliter que nescit aut docere manifeste que nouit. Si autem utrumque cum possit non uult, insanie morbo laborat. Initium enim recedendi a Deo fastidium doctrine est, et cum non appetit illud quod semper anima esurit, quomodo diligit Deum?'[516] Hinc et beatus Athanasius[f] in *Exhortatione monachorum* in tantum discendi uel legendi studium commendat, ut per hoc etiam orationes intermitti suadeat: 'Pergam', inquit, 'per tramitem uite[g] nostre. Primum abstinentie cura, ieiunii patiencia, orandi assiduitas, et legendi uel, si quis adhuc litterarum expers sit, audiendi sit

[b] cognoscamus *Amb*   [c–c] etc. *C*   [d–d] *om. E*

120 [a] scripserunt *Amb*   [b] uestri *TC;* nostri *EAmb, Vitae*   [c] Etenim *Amb*   [d] *om. Amb*   [e–e] scripsit et *TC;* scripsit ea *E, Vitae;* scripsit *Amb*   [f] Anastasius *TAmb;* anathasius *C;* anathanasius *E*   [g] uite *T;* uie *CE;* viae *Amb;* vitae *Amb*[1]

[512] Ps. 118 (119): 104.   [513] Ps. 118 (119): 104.   [514] Ps. 118 (119): 11.
[515] *Vitae patrum, Verba seniorum,* v. 10. 114 (*PL* lxxiii. 933A).

sweetness should be: 'From thy precepts I have had understanding',[512] that is, I gained understanding from thy precepts rather than men's, and was taught and instructed by them. Nor did he overlook what is to be gained from such understanding, adding: 'Therefore have I hated every path of wrongdoing.'[513] Many paths of wrongdoing are, of course, so plainly seen for what they are that they easily come to be hated and despised by all, but only through the word of God can we know every one of them so as to avoid them all. Hence it is also written: 'I have treasured thy words in my heart, so that I may not sin against thee.'[514] They have been treasured in the heart rather than uttered in the mouth when our meditation retains understanding of them. But the less we care about understanding, the less we recognize and shun these paths of wrongdoing, and the less we can guard ourselves against sin.

120. Such negligence is all the more reprehensible in monks, who aspire to perfection, as they have more opportunities for learning and have an abundance of sacred books and they enjoy peace and quiet: by them this teaching should be taken in more easily. Monks who boast about the numbers of written works they have but find no time to read them are admirably rebuked by that elder in the *Lives of the Fathers*, who says: 'The prophets wrote books, and your forebears came after and did much work on them. Then their successors committed them to memory. But now comes the present generation, which has copied them on paper and parchment and put them back to stand idle in alcoves.'[515] So too, abbot Palladius, in firmly urging us to learn as well as to teach, says: 'It behoves the soul which lives in accordance with the will of Christ either to learn faithfully what it knows not or to teach openly what it knows. But if it is unwilling, though able, to do either, it suffers from the disease of madness. For boredom with learning is the beginning of a withdrawal from God, and how can a man love God when he does not seek that for which the soul always hungers?'[516] St Athanasius too, in his *Exhortation to Monks*, recommends the practice of learning or reading so highly that he even allows prayers to be interrupted for this. 'Let me trace the course of our life', he says. 'First must come care for abstinence, endurance of fasting, perseverance in prayer, and the desire to read or, if there be any who are still illiterate,

[516] *Vitae patrum*, *Verba seniorum*, v. 10. 67 (*PL* lxxiii. 924A). Cf. Palladius of Helenopolis, *Historia Lausiaca* (*c.*420; *PL* lxxiv. 251): 'cum initium defectionis sit doctrinae satietas ac disciplinae fastidium'. I am grateful to Carolinne White for help with this reference.

desiderium cupiditate discendi. Hec enim prima sunt quasi lactantium cunabulorum in Dei agnitione crepundia.'[517] Et post aliqua cum premisisset: 'Orationibus uero ita instandum est ut[h] uix eas aliquod tempus interpolet', postea subiecit: 'Has, si fieri potest, sola legendi intercapedo disrumpat.'[518] Neque enim alias Petrus apostolus ammoneret: 'Parati semper estote ad rationem reddendam ad omnes poscentes uos de uerbo fidei uestre et spei.'[519] Et Apostolus: 'Non cessamus pro uobis orantes ut impleamini agnitione eius in omni sapientia et intellectu spiritali.'[520] Et rursum: 'Verbum Christi habitet in uobis habundanter in omni sapientia.'[521] Nam in Veteri Testamento similem hominibus curam sacre preceptionis inculcauit eloquium. Sic enim Dauid ait: 'Beatus uir qui non abiit in consilio impiorum', etc.,[i] 'sed in lege Domini uoluntas eius',[522] etc.[j] Et ad Ihesum Naue [k]Deus loquitur:[k] [l]'Non recedet liber iste de manibus tuis, et meditaberis in eo die ac nocte.'[l] [523]

121. [a]Hiis quoque[b] negotiis malarum cogitationum lubrica frequenter se ingerunt et, quamuis ipsa sedulitas animum ad Deum prestet intentum, efficit tamen in se mordax seculi cura sollicitum. Quod si hoc frequenter importune patitur religioso labori deditus, numquam profecto illis carebit ociosus.[a] Et beatus papa Gregorius libro *Moralium* undeuicesimo: 'Que tempora', inquit, 'iam nunc inchoasse ingemiscimus, cum multos intra ecclesiam positos cernimus qui[c] nolunt operari quod intelligunt, aut hoc ipsum quoque sacrum eloquium intelligere ac nosse contempnunt. A ueritate enim auertentes auditum ad fabulas conuertuntur, dum "omnes que sua sunt querunt, [d]non que Ihesu Christi".[524] Scripta Dei ubique [e]reperta opponuntur[e] oculis, sed[f] hec cognoscere homines dedignantur. Pene nullus scire querit[g] quod credidit.'[525]

[h] quod *TAmb;* ut *CE, Ps.-Athanasius* [i] & in via peccatorum non stetit, & in cathedra pestilentiae non sedit *add. Amb* [j] *om. Amb* [k–k] *om. CE* [l–l] Non recedat volumen legis huius de ore tuo sed meditaberis in eo diebus ac noctibus *Vulg.*

121 [a–a] *om. CE* [b] se *add. T* [c] quia *TCEAmb;* qui *Gregory* [d] beginning of lacuna in CE, ending in 122 [e–e] reperta cognoscuntur (*exp. T*) opponuntur *TAmb;* reperta oppununtur *Gregory* [f] si *T;* sed *CE, Gregory, McLaughlin;* Si *Amb* [g] quaerat *Amb*

[517] Ps.-Athanasius, *De obseruationibus monachorum,* included in an appendix to the *Codex regularum* attributed to Benedict of Aniane (d. 821; *PL* ciii. 665A–666A).

to listen in eagerness to learn. For these are the first cradle-songs, as it were, of suckling infants, in knowledge of God.'[517] And a little later, after saying: 'Your prayers should be so assiduous that scarcely any interval should come between them', he then adds: 'If possible, they should be interrupted only by intervals for reading.'[518] Nor would the apostle Peter give different advice: 'Always be ready to give an answer to all who ask you to account for your faith and hope.'[519] And the Apostle: 'We have not ceased to pray for you, that you may be filled with knowledge of God in all wisdom and spiritual understanding.'[520] And again, 'Let the word of Christ dwell in you abundantly, in all wisdom.'[521] In the Old Testament, too, the word of God implanted in men a similar care for sacred teaching. Thus David says: 'Happy is the man who does not take the wicked for his guide', etc., 'but his will is set on the law of the Lord.'[522] And to Joshua God says: 'This book of the law must not leave your hands and you must ponder over it day and night.'[523]

121. Moreover, on top of these difficulties the dangers of bad thoughts often insinuate themselves, and, although assiduous attention may keep the mind intent on God, the gnawing worries of the world make it restless. If one who devotes himself to the task of religious life experiences this frequently and troublesomely, an idle person is surely never free of it. St Gregory the Pope, in the nineteenth book of his *Morals*, says: 'We are saddened that the time has now come when we see many holding office in the Church who are unwilling to perform what they understand or treat as unimportant a knowledge and understanding of the very words of God. Closing their ears to truth they turn to fables, while "they pursue their own ends, not the cause of Jesus Christ".[524] God's Scriptures, everywhere to be found, are put before their eyes, but they refuse to study them. Scarcely anyone seeks to know what he believes.'[525]

[518] Ibid., 667CD).

[519] 1 Pet. 3: 15; also cited in *Letter* 13 (ed. Smits, p. 274; *PL* clxxviii. 355A; trans. Ziolkowski, p. 183).

[520] Coloss. 1: 9.

[521] Coloss. 3: 16.

[522] Ps. 1: 1–2.

[523] Josh. 1: 8.

[524] Phil. 2: 21.

[525] Gregory, *Moralia in Iob*, xix. 30. 56 (ed. Adriaen, cxliiiA. 1002; *PL* lxxvi. 136A).

122. Ad quod etiam plurimum ipsos et professionis sue *Regula* et sanctorum patrum adhortantur exempla.[a] Nichil quippe[b] de doctrina uel studio cantus ammonet Benedictus, cum ipse plurimum de lectione precipiat, et ipsa[c] legendi tempora sicut et laborandi diligenter assignet,[526] et in tantum [d]de ipsa quoque[d] dictandi seu scribendi doctrina prouideat, ut inter necessaria que ab abbate monachi sperare debeant tabulas etiam et grafium non pretermittat.[527] Qui cum inter cetera iubeat quod in capite quadragesime 'omnes' monachi 'singulos accipiant codices de[e] bibliotheca quos per ordinem ex integro legant',[528] quid hoc magis ridiculosum quam lectioni uacare et intelligentie operam non dare? [f]Notum quippe est illud sapientis prouerbium: 'Legere et non intelligere, negligere est.'[529] Tali quippe lectori merito illud philosophi[g] [h]anonos lyras[h] improperandum est,[f][530] quasi enim asinus est ad lyram lector librum tenens, id ad quod liber est factus agere non ualens.[531] Multo etiam salubrius [i]tales lectores alias[i] intenderent ubi aliquid utilitatis inesset quam ociose uel scripture litteras inspicerent uel folia uersarent. In quibus profecto lectoribus illud Ysaie compleri manifeste uidemus: 'Et erit', inquit, 'uobis uisio omnium sicut uerba libri signati, quem cum dederint scienti litteras dicent: Lege istum. Et respondebit: Non possum, signatus est enim. Et dabitur liber nescienti litteras diceturque ei: Lege. Et respondebit: Nescio litteras. Et dixit Dominus: Eo quod appropinquat [j]populus iste[j] ore suo et labiis suis glorificat me; cor autem eius longe est a me [k]et timuerunt me mandato hominum et doctrinis. Ideo ecce ego addam ut admirationem faciam populo huic miraculo grandi et stupendo. Peribit enim sapientia a sapientibus eius, et intellectus prudentium eius abscondetur.'[532] Scire quippe litteras in claustris dicuntur quicumque illas proferre didicerunt. Qui profecto quantum ad intelligentiam spectat se nescire legere[l] profitentes, librum qui traditur habent signatum eque ut illi quos illitteratos ibidem dicunt. Quos quidem Dominus arguens dicit eos ore et labiis pocius quam corde sibi

122 [a] *end of lacuna in CE, beginning in* 121 (*C writes* etc.) [b] enim *CE* [c] etiam *add. CE* [d–d] quoque de ipsa *CE* [e] ex *Amb* [f–f] *om. CE* [g] philosophye *T;* Phil. *Amb* [h–h] Anonas *T;* Ano liras T^1*;* ἀλλ ὄγος λυρας *Amb* [i–i] lectores tales aliis *CE* [j–j] iste populus *E* [k–k] *om. CE* [l] legem *Amb*

[526] Benedict, *Rule*, c. 47, 1.

[527] Benedict, *Rule* c. 55, 19.

[528] Benedict, *Rule*, c. 48, 15; also 16.

[529] Cato, *Distichs*, prologue (ed. Boas, p. 4; ed. Nève, p. 22; ed. Chase, p. 12); *Prouerbia* (Walther), 13639a. Also cited in *TSch*, ii. 57.

[530] Cf. Boethius, *De consolatione philosophiae*, i, *prosa* iv (ed. Bieler, xciv. 6; trans. Watts, p. 40: 'Do you understand this . . . or are you like the proverbial donkey deaf to the lyre?').

122. And yet both the *Rule* they profess and the example of the holy Fathers urge them to do so. Benedict in fact says nothing about teaching or studying chant, though he gives much instruction about reading, and carefully assigns times for this as for manual work.[526] In his provision for teaching composition or writing, among the essentials for which the monks must look to the abbot, he includes tablets and pens.[527] And when among other things he orders that 'at the beginning of Lent all the monks shall receive a book each from the library, which they shall read all the way through in full',[528] what could be more absurd than for them to give time to reading if they do not take pains to understand? There is a well-known saying of a wise man: 'To read and not to understand is not to read';[529] and to such a reader the philosopher's reproach about the ass and the lyre is rightly applicable,[530] for a reader who holds a book but cannot handle what it was made for is like an ass with a lyre.[531] Readers such as this would more profitably concentrate on what might be of some use to them, instead of idly looking at written letters and turning pages, for in them we see the words of Isaiah clearly fulfilled: 'Every vision will become for you like the words of a sealed book. Give such a book to one who can read and say: Read this, and he will answer: I cannot, for it is sealed. Give it to one who cannot read and say: Read, and he will answer: I cannot read. The Lord has said: Because these people approach me with their mouths and honour me with their lips while their hearts are far from me and their fear of me is but a precept of men, learned by rote, therefore yet again I must strike awe into these people with some great and resounding miracle. For the wisdom of their wise men shall vanish and the discernment of the discerning shall be lost.'[532] In the cloister those who have learned to pronounce letters are said to know them, but those who admit that, as far as understanding is concerned, they cannot read, have given to them a book which is just as much sealed as it is for those whom they say are illiterate. The Lord rebukes them, saying that they approach him with their mouths and lips rather than with their hearts, because they

Also Martianus Capella, *De nuptiis Philologiae et Mercurii*, viii. 807 (ed. Willis, p. 305: ὄνος λύρας); Phaedrus, *Aesop's Fables* (ed. Postgate, Perotti's Appendix, 12; ed. and trans. Perry, pp. 390–1). These sources are cited, with further references, by Jeauneau in *Rethinking the School of Chartres*, p. 13, notes and fig. 2, a photograph of the statue on the south side of the *Clocher Vieux* of Chartres cathedral of an ass who tries to play the lyre (cf. Jeauneau, *L'Âge d'or des écoles de Chartres*, pp. 11–12). Also cited in Greek (ονω λύρα) by Jerome, *Epistola* LXI *ad Vigilantium*, 4 (ed. Hilberg, liv. 581, *l.* 7; *PL* xxii. 605).

[531] Cf. **115** above.

[532] Isa. 29: 11–14.

appropinquare, quia que proferre utcumque ualent intelligere minime possunt. Qui dum diuinorum eloquiorum scientia careant, magis consuetudinem hominum quam utilitatem Scripture obediendo secuntur. Propter hoc Dominus eos quoque, qui sapientiores[m] inter eos uidentur et doctores resident, excecandos esse comminatur.[k]

123. Maximus[a] ecclesie doctor et monastice professionis honor Ieronimus[b] nos ad amorem litterarum adhortans[c] ait: 'Ama scientiam litterarum[d] et carnis uicia non amabis.'[533] Quantum laborem et expensas in doctrina earum consumpserit eius quoque testimonio didicimus.[e] Qui inter cetera que ipsemet de proprio scribit studio, ut nos etiam uidelicet suo instruat exemplo, ad Pammachium[f] et Oceanum quodam loco sic meminit: 'Dum essem iuuenis miro discendi feruebam amore nec iuxta quorumdam presumptionem ipse me docui. Apollinarem audiui frequenter Antiochie et colui cum me in Scripturis sanctis erudiret.[534] [g]Iam canis spargebatur capud[g] et[h] magistrum pocius quam discipulum decebat. Perrexi tamen Alexandriam; audiui Didimum; in multis ei gracias ago.[535] Quod nesciui didici.[i] Putabant me homines finem fecisse discendi. Rursus Ierosolime et Bethleem, [j]quo[k] labore, quo precio, Baraninam[l] Hebreum nocturnum habui preceptorem! Timebat enim Iudeos et mihi alterum sese exhibebat Nichodemum.'[j] [536] Memori profecto [m]mente hic[m] recondiderat quod in Ecclesiastico legerat: 'Fili, a iuuentute tua excipe doctrinam et usque ad canos inuenies sapientiam.'[537] [n]In quo ipse non solum Scripture uerbis, uerum etiam sanctorum patrum instructus exemplis, inter ceteras excellentis illius monasterii[o] laudes hoc de singulari exercicio eius in Scripturis diuinis adiecit: 'Scripturarum uero diuinarum meditationem et intellectum atque scientie diuine numquam tanta uidimus exercicia, ut singulos pene eorum oratores credas in diuinam esse sapientiam.'[n] [538]

[m] sapientes *Amb*

123 [a] etiam *add. CE* [b] qui *add. TAmb* [c] exhortans *CE* [d] Scripturarum *Letter 9, Heloise in the preface to the Problemata, Jerome* [e] didiscimus *CE* [f] pamnachium *T* [g–g] *om. CE* [h] ipse *add. CE* [i] didisci *CE* [j–j] etc. *CE* [k] qua *T* [l] Baranniam *Amb* [m–m] hic mente *CE* [n–n] *om. CE* [o] deuitā̄s *add. T;* monasterii divitissimas *conj. McLaughlin*

---

[533] Jerome, *Epistola* CXXV *ad Rusticum monachum*, 11 (ed. Hilberg, lvi. 130, *ll.* 3–4; *PL* xxii. 1078). Also cited in *Letter* 9 (ed. Smits, p. 219; *PL* clxxviii. 325B; trans. Ziolkowski, p. 11) and in Heloise's letter-preface to the *Problemata* (*PL* clxxviii. 678C).

[534] Apollinaris or Apollinarius of Laodicea, *c.*310–*c.*390.

are able to pronounce words after a fashion but are quite unable to understand them. Lacking knowledge of the Word of God, they are led by human custom, not the benefit of Scripture. Therefore the Lord threatens that even those among them who appear learned and sit as doctors among them shall be blinded.

123. Jerome, the greatest doctor of the Church and glory of the monastic profession, in urging us to love of letters says: 'Love knowledge of letters and you will not love the vices of the flesh.'[533] We have learned from his own testimony how much labour and expense it cost him to learn them. Amongst other things which he writes about his own studies for the purpose of instructing us by his example, he recalls in a passage addressed to Pammachius and Oceanus: 'When I was a young man I was on fire with a marvellous love of learning. I did not teach myself, as some men are rash enough to do. I frequently heard Apollinaris at Antioch and was devoted to him when he taught me the Holy Scriptures.[534] My hair was already flecked with grey and I should have been a teacher rather than a pupil, yet I went on to Alexandria and heard Didymus, to whom I am grateful for much,[535] learning from him what I did not know. Men thought I had come to an end of learning, but I returned to Jerusalem and Bethlehem, and there I had Baraninas the Jew as my teacher—with what labour and expense! He taught at night, for he feared the Jews, and to me he was a second Nicodemus.'[536] Surely Jerome had stored away in his memory what he had read in Ecclesiasticus: 'My son, seek learning while you are young, and when your hair is white you will still find wisdom.'[537] Thus educated, not only in the words of Scripture but also through the example of the holy Fathers, he added to the wealth of tributes paid to his excellent monastery one on its exceptional training in the Holy Scriptures: 'Never have we seen such a degree of training in meditating on and understanding the Holy Scriptures; you might suppose nearly every one of them to be the public orator for sacred wisdom.'[538]

[535] Didymus the Blind, *c.*313–98.

[536] Jerome, *Epistola* LXXXIV *ad Pammachium et Oceanum*, 3 (ed. Hilberg, lv. 122, *l.* 9; *PL* xxii. 745); also cited in *Letter* 9 (ed. Smits, pp. 230–1; *PL* clxxviii. 331CD; trans. Ziolkowski, pp. 24–5). For Nicodemus who came to Jesus by night cf. John 3: 1–21 and *Letter* 7, **36**.

[537] Ecclus. 6: 18.

[538] Not Jerome but Rufinus, trans., *Historia monachorum*, 21 in *Vitae patrum*, ii (*PL* xxi. 444B). In 386 Jerome settled in a monastery at Bethlehem.

124. Sanctus etiam Beda, sicut in *Hystoria* refert *Anglorum*, a puero in monasterium susceptus: 'Cunctum', inquit, 'ex eo tempus uite in eiusdem monasterii habitatione peragens, omnem meditans[a] Scripturis operam dedi atque, inter obseruantiam discipline regularis et cotidianam cantandi in ecclesia curam, semper aut discere aut scribere dulce habui.'[539] Nunc uero qui[b] in monasteriis erudiuntur adeo stulti perseuerant ut, litterarum sono contenti,[c] nullam de intelligentia curam[d] assumant, nec cor instruere sed linguam student. [e]Quos patenter illud Salomonis arguit prouerbium: 'Cor sapientis querit doctrinam et os stultorum pascetur imperitia',[540] cum uidelicet uerbis que non intelligit oblectatur.[e] Qui profecto tanto minus Deum amare et in eum accendi possunt quanto amplius ab [f]intelligentia eius[f] et a sensu Scripture de ipso nos erudientis absistunt.

125. Hoc autem [a]duabus maxime[a] de causis[b] in monasteriis accidisse credimus, uel per laicorum scilicet conuersorum seu etiam ipsorum prepositorum inuidiam, uel propter uaniloquium ociositatis cui hodie plurimum claustra monastica uacare uidemus.[541] Isti profecto nos[c] terrenis magis quam spiritalibus secum[d] intendere cupientes, illi sunt qui tamquam Allophili[e] fodientem puteos Ysaac persecuntur, et eos replendo congerie terre aquam ei satagunt prohibere.[542] Quod beatus exponens Gregorius libro *Moralium* sexto decimo ait: 'Sepe cum eloquiis sacris intendimus malignorum spirituum insidias grauius toleramus, quia menti nostre terrenarum cogitationum puluerem aspergunt[f] [g]ut intentionis nostre oculos a luce intime uisionis obscurent.'[543] Quod nimium Psalmista pertulerat cum dicebat: 'Declinate a me, maligni, et scrutabor mandata Dei mei',[544] uidelicet patenter insinuans quia mandata Dei perscrutari non poterat cum malignorum spirituum insidias in mente tolerabat. Quod etiam in Ysaac opere Allophilorum prauitate cognoscimus designari qui puteos quos Ysaac foderat terre congerie replebant. Nos enim nimirum puteos fodimus cum in Scripture sacre abditis sensibus alta penetramus. Quos tamen occulte replent Allophili quando nobis ad alta

124 [a] meditandis *Bede* [b] *om. CE* [c] correpto *C;* contempto *E* [d] scripturam *C* [e–e] *om. CE* [f–f] eius intelligentia *Amb*

125 [a–a] maxime duabus *CE* [b] *add. CE* [c] *om. CE* [d] *om. CE* [e] Allofili *Amb* [f] spargunt *Amb*[1] [g–g] etc. bene ita *?C, E*

[539] Bede, *Historia ecclesiastica gentis Anglorum*, v. 24 (ed. Colgrave and Mynors, p. 566; ed. Plummer, i. 357; *PL* cxcv. 288C). The text of Bede reads: 'aut discere aut docere aut scribere': 'to learn or to teach or to write'.

124. The Holy Bede too, who had been received into a monastery as a boy, says in his *History of the English People*: 'From then on I spent all my life living in the same monastery, applying myself entirely to the study of the Scriptures; and amid the observance of the discipline of the *Rule* and the daily task of singing in the church, it has always been my delight to learn and write.'[539] But those who are educated in monasteries today are so persistent in their stupidity that, being content with the sound of letters, they pay no attention to understanding them, and care only to instruct the tongue, not the heart. They are openly rebuked in a proverb of Solomon: 'The heart of a discerning man seeks knowledge, but the mouth of fools feeds on folly',[540] that is, when a man finds pleasure in words he does not understand. Such men are the less able to love God and be warmed towards him, the further they keep themselves from understanding him and appreciating the Scripture that teaches us about him.

125. Moreover, we believe this situation has arisen in monasteries for two main reasons: because of dislike on the part of the lay brothers, or even of those placed in charge of them, and through idle chatter for which we see monastic cloisters provide much leisure time today.[541] Men like this try to engage us and themselves in earthly rather than spiritual matters. They are like the Philistines who harassed Isaac when he was digging wells by filling them with heaps of earth to try to keep water from him.[542] St Gregory explains this in the sixteenth book of his *Morals*: 'Often when we try to concentrate on the word of God we are more seriously troubled by the designs of evil spirits who scatter the dust of earthly thoughts in our minds, so that they may conceal the eyes of our concentration from the light of inward vision.'[543] This the Psalmist had suffered excessively when he said: 'Go away, you evil-doers, and I will keep the commandments of my God.'[544] He clearly meant that he could not keep the commandments of God when his mind was standing up to the assaults of evil spirits. This we also recognize in the wickedness of the Philistines in respect of Isaac's work, as they heaped earth into the wells he had dug. For we are surely digging wells when we penetrate deeply into the hidden meanings of Holy Scripture. As we reach into the depths Philistines

540 Prov. 15: 14.

541 On the *conversi* or lay brothers see Appendix A, 6. iv.

542 Cf. Gen. 26: 15.

543 Gregory the Great, *Moralia in Iob*, xvi. 18. 23 (ed. Adriaen, cxliiiA 812; *PL* lxxv. 1131).

544 Ps. 118 (119): 115.

tendentibus immundi spiritus terrenas cogitationes ingerunt et quasi inuentam diuine scientie aquam tollunt. Sed quia nemo hos hostes sua uirtute superat per Eliphat[h] dicitur: 'Eritque omnipotens contra hostes tuos et argentum coaceruabitur tibi.'[545] Ac si diceretur: dum malignos spiritus Dominus sua a te uirtute repulerit, diuini in te eloquii talentum lucidius crescit.[g]

126. Legerat iste, nisi fallor, magni Christianorum philosophi Origenis *Omelias* in Genesi et de eius hauserat puteis quod nunc de hiis loquitur puteis. Ille quippe spiritualium puteorum fossor studiosus non solum ad eorum potum sed etiam effossionem nos uehementer adhortans, expositionis predicte *Omelia* undecima[a] [546] ita loquitur: 'Temptemus facere etiam illud quod Sapientia commonet, dicens: "Bibe aquam[b] [c]de tuis fontibus et de tuis puteis et sit tibi fons tuus proprius."[c] [547] Tempta ergo et tu, o auditor, habere proprium puteum et proprium fontem ut et tu, cum apprehenderis librum Scripturarum, incipias etiam ex proprio sensu proferre aliquem intellectum et, secundum[d] ea que in ecclesia didicisti, tempta et tu bibere de fonte ingenii tui. [e]Est intra te natura aque uiue, sunt uene perhennes et irrigua fluenta rationabilis sensus, si modo non sint terra et rudibus completa. Sed satage fodere terram tuam et purgare sordes, id est ingenium,[f] amouere desidiam et torporem cordis excutere. Audi enim quod dicit Scriptura: "[g]Punge oculum et profer lacrimam; punge cor et profer sensum."[g] [548] Purga etiam et tu ingenium tuum ut aliquando etiam "de tuis fontibus" bibas et de[h] tuis puteis haurias "aquam uiuam".[549] Si enim suscepisti in te uerbum Dei, si accepisti ab Ihesu "aquam uiuam" et fideliter accepisti, fiet in te "fons aque salientis in uitam eternam".[e] [550] [551] Idem *Omelia* sequente de puteis Ysaac [i]supra memoratis:[i] 'Quos', inquit, 'Philistini terra[j] repleuerant, illi sine dubio qui intelligenciam spiritalem claudunt ut neque ipsi bibant, neque alios bibere permittant. [k]Audi Dominum dicentem: "Ve uobis, Scribe et Pharisei, quoniam tulistis clauem scientie, neque[l]

[h] Eliphat *TAmb;* Eliphaz *Vulg.*

126 [a] XI *TCE;* XII *Amb* [b] aquas *Origen* [c–c] de cisterna tua, et fluenta putei tui; deriuentur fontes tui foras *Vulg.* [d] de *CE* [e–e] etc. bene ita *CE* [f] ingenii tui *Origen* [g–g] pungens oculum deducens lacrimas, et qui pungit cor proferet sensum *Vulg.* [h] *om. T* [i–i] *om. CE* [j] *om. CE* [k–k] etc. *CE* [l] non *Amb*

[545] Job 22: 25.
[546] Not the eleventh but the twelfth *Homily*.
[547] Cf. Prov. 5: 15–16 in the Vulgate version.

furtively fill them up, letting loose the earthy thoughts of an evil spirit and, as it were, taking away from us the water we found of sacred learning. But no one can overcome these enemies by his own power, as we are told through Eliphaz: 'The Almighty shall be your defence against your enemies, and he will be your silver heaped up.'[545] That is, when the Lord has driven evil spirits away from you by his power, the silver talent of the divine Word will shine more brightly in you.

126. St Gregory, if I am not mistaken, had read the *Homilies* on Genesis of the great Christian philosopher Origen, and had drawn from Origen's wells what he now says about these wells. For that zealous digger of spiritual wells strongly urges us not only to drink from them but also to dig our own. He says in the eleventh *Homily* of his exposition:[546] 'Let us try also to do what Wisdom bids us, saying: "Drink water from your own springs and your own wells. Let your spring be yours alone."[547] So try also, my listener, to have your own well and your own spring, so that, when you take up a book of the Scriptures, you also may start to show some understanding of it from your own perception; and try too, in the light of what you have learned in church, to drink from the spring of your own ability. You have within you a source of living water, open channels and flowing streams of rational perception, as long as they are not clogged with earth and rubbish. Try to dig your ground and clear the filth from your mind; remove idleness and inertia from your heart. Hear what Scripture says: "Hurt the eye and tears will flow; hurt the heart and you will make it sensitive."[548] So clean your mind and then someday you too may drink "from your springs" and draw "living water"[549] from your wells. For if you have taken the word of God into yourself, if you have received "living water" from Jesus and received it with faith, it shall become in you "a spring of water gushing out into everlasting life".'[550] [551] In the next *Homily* Origen says of the wells of Isaac we spoke of: 'Those which the Philistines had filled with earth are surely men who close their spiritual understanding, so that they neither drink themselves nor allow others to drink. Hear the word of the Lord: "Alas for you, Scribes and Pharisees! You have taken away the key of knowledge; you did not go in yourselves, and did not

[548] Cf. Ecclus. 22: 24 in the Vulgate version.
[549] Gen. 26: 19.
[550] John 4: 14.
[551] Origen, *In Genesim homiliae interprete Rufino*, xii. 5 (ed. Baehrens, p. 112; ed. Doutreleau, pp. 306–9; *PG* xii. 229BD).
[552] Cf. Luke 11: 52 in the Vulgate version; also Matt. 23: 13.

ipsi introistis, [m]neque uolentes permisistis'',[m] [552] [553] etc.[n] 'Nos uero numquam cessemus puteos aque uiue fodiendo et nunc quidem uetera, nunc etiam noua discuciendo efficiamur similes illi euangelico scribe de quo Dominus dixit: "Qui profert de thesauro suo noua et uetera."'[554] [555] Item: 'Redeamus ad Ysaac et fodiamus cum ipso puteos aque uiue. Etiamsi obsistunt Philistini, etiamsi rixantur, nos tamen perseueremus cum ipso puteos fodiendo ut et nobis dicatur: "Bibe aquam [o]de tuis uasis et de tuis puteis";[o] [556] et in tantum fodiamus ut superhabundent aque putei "in plateis"[557] nostris, ut non solum nobis sufficiat scientia Scripturarum, sed et alios doceamus et instruamus ut [p]bibant homines, bibant[p] et pecora, quia et Propheta dicit: "Homines et iumenta saluos facies, Domine."'[558] [559] Et post aliqua: 'Qui Philistinus est', inquit, 'et terrena sapit,[560] nescit in omni terra inuenire aquam, inuenire rationabilem sensum. Quid tibi prodest habere eruditionem et nescire ea uti, habere sermonem et nescire loqui? Istud opus[q] proprie puerorum est Ysaac qui in omni terra fodiunt puteos aque uiue.'[k] [561]

127. Vos [a]autem non sic sed[a] uaniloquio penitus supersedentes quecumque discendi gratiam assecute sunt, de hiis que ad Deum pertinent erudiri studeant, sicut de beato scriptum est uiro: 'Sed in lege Domini uoluntas eius et in lege eius meditabitur die ac nocte.'[562] [b]Cuius quidem assidui studii in lege Domini que sequatur utilitas statim adiungitur: 'Et erit tamquam lignum quod plantatum est secus decursus aquarum',[563] etc.[c] Quasi enim lignum aridum est et infructuosum quod fluentis diuinorum eloquiorum non irrigatur, de quibus scriptum est: 'Flumina de uentre eius fluent aque uiue.'[564] Hec illa sunt fluenta de quibus in laude sponsi canit sponsa in Canticis eum describens: 'Oculi eius sicut columbe super riuulos aquarum que lacte sunt lote et resident iuxta fluenta plenissima.'[565] Et uos igitur lacte lote, id est candore castimonie nitentes, iuxta hec fluenta quasi columbe residete; et[d] hinc

[m–m] et eos qui introibant prohibuistis *Vulg.* [n] *om. Amb* [o–o] de cisterna tua et fluenta putei tui *Vulg.* [p–p] bibant. Homines bibant *Amb* [q] *om. Amb*

127 [a–a] ergo *CE* [b–b] *om. CE* [c] *om. Amb* [d] ut *Amb*

[553] Origen, *In Genesim homiliae interprete Rufino*, xiii. 2 (ed. Baehrens, p. 114, *l.* 25 – p. 115 *l.* 1; ed. Doutreleau, p. 314; *PG* xii. 231AB).

[554] Matt. 13: 52.

[555] Origen, *In Genesim homiliae interprete Rufino*, xiii. 3 (ed. Baehrens, p. 116 *ll.* 25–8; ed. Doutreleau, p. 320; *PG* xii. 232C).

[556] Cf. Prov. 5: 15 in the Vulgate version.

[557] Prov. 5: 16.

permit those who wished to enter",'[552] [553] etc. 'But let us never cease from digging wells of living water; and by discussing new things as well as old, let us make ourselves like the Scribe in the Gospel, of whom the Lord said: "He could produce from his store things both old and new."'[554] [555] Again: 'Let us return to Isaac and dig with him wells of living water. Even if the Philistines obstruct us, even if they use violence, let us carry on digging wells, so that to us too it may be said: "Drink water from your cisterns and your wells."[556] And let us dig until the waters from our wells overflow "on our streets",[557] so that our knowledge of the Scriptures is not only sufficient for ourselves but sufficient for us also to teach others and show them how to drink. Let our flocks drink too, as the Prophet also says: "Man and beast you will save, O Lord."'[558] [559] Later on Origen says: 'He who is a Philistine, and has a taste for earthly things,[560] does not know where in the earth to find water, where to find a rational perception. What do you gain by having learning and not knowing how to use it, having speech but being unable to talk? To do that is the task of Isaac's boys who dig wells for living water in every land.'[561]

127. You must not be like this but refrain altogether from idle talk, while those of you who have been given the grace of learning must strive for instruction in the things that are of God, as is written of the happy man: 'The law of the Lord is his delight, the law his meditation day and night.'[562] What profit follows his diligent study of the law of the Lord is added at once: 'And he will be like a tree planted by a watercourse',[563] etc., Something that is not watered by the streams of the words of God is like a dry and fruitless tree. Of these streams it is written: 'Rivers of living water shall flow out from within him',[564] and these are the streams of which the bride sings in the Song of Songs in praise of the bridegroom, describing him thus: 'His eyes are like doves beside brooks of water, bathed by the milky water as they sit by the flooding streams.'[565] You too, then, are bathed by the milky water, that is, you are aided by the whiteness of chastity, and must sit like

558 Cf. Ps. 35: 7 in the Vulgate version.

559 Origen, *In Genesim homiliae interprete Rufino*, xiii. 4 (ed. Baehrens, p. 121 *ll*. 4–13; ed. Doutreleau, pp. 330–2; *PG* xii. 235D–236A).

560 Cf. Phil. 3: 19.

561 Origen, *In Genesim homiliae interprete Rufino*, xiii. 3 (ed. Baehrens, p. 117 *ll*. 5–10; ed. Doutreleau, p. 320; *PG* xii. 232D–233A). The final reference to wells being dug in every land seems to be based on Gen. 26: 17–33.

562 Ps. 1: 2.

563 Ps. 1: 3.

564 John 7: 38.

565 S. of S. 5: 12.

sapientie haustus sumentes, non solum discere, sed et docere et aliis tamquam oculi uiam possitis ostendere, et sponsum ipsum non solum conspicere, sed et aliis ualeatis describere. De cuius quidem singulari sponsa que ipsum aure cordis concipere meruit scriptum esse nouimus: 'Maria autem conseruabat omnia uerba hec, conferens in corde suo.'[566] Hec igitur summi Verbi genitrix, uerba eius in corde pocius habens quam in ore, ipsa etiam diligenter conferebat, quia studiose singula discuciebat et inuicem sibi ea conferebat, quam congrue scilicet inter se conuenirent omnia. Nouerat iuxta mysterium legis omne animal immundum dici, nisi quod ruminat et ungulam findit. Nulla quippe est anima munda nisi que, meditando quantum capere potest, diuina ruminat precepta et in hiis exsequendis[e] discretionem habeat, ut non solum bona, sed et bene, hoc est recta, faciat intentione.[567] Diuisio quippe ungule pedis discretio est animi de qua scriptum est: [f]'Si recte offeras, recte autem non diuidas, peccasti.'[f][b] [568]

128. 'Si quis diligit me', inquit Veritas, 'sermonem meum seruabit.'[569] Quis autem uerba uel precepta Domini sui seruare obediendo poterit, nisi hec prius intellexerit? Nemo studiosus erit in exequendo, nisi qui attentus fuerit in audiendo. [a]Sicut et de beata illa legitur muliere que, ceteris omnibus postpositis, sedens secus pedes Domini audiebat uerbum illius, illis uidelicet auribus intelligentie quas ipsemet requirit, dicens: 'Qui habet aures audiendi, audiat.'[a] [570] Que[b] si in tante feruorem deuotionis accendi non ualetis, imitamini saltem et[c] amore et studio sanctarum litterarum beatas illas sancti Ieronimi discipulas, Paulam et Eustochium, quarum precipue rogatu tot uoluminibus ecclesiam predictus doctor illustrauit.[d] [571]

[e] exequendis *Amb* [f–f] Nonne si bene egeris, recipies: si autem male, statim in foribus peccatum aderit? *Vulg.*

128 [a–a] *om. CE* [b] Quod *TAmb;* Que *CE* [c] etiam *CE* [d] *CE add*: Expliciunt epistole uenerabilis petri abaelardi et eius regula pro monialibus paracliti qui contemporaneus fuit (*henceforth E only*) beato bernardo qui ergo floruerunt anno ab incarnatione domini millesimo centesimo uel circiter unde bernardus etatis lxiii annorum obdormiuit in domino anno m° c° liii° anno a constitutione domus cisterciensi lvi° fuit enim constituta anno domini m° nonagesimo vii° qua bernardus 22 annorum intrauit. *In E this colophon is inserted by a contemporary hand, possibly Ecorr.*

---

[566] Luke 2: 19; cf. *Letter* 6, **29**.

[567] Cf. *Ethica*, i. 36 (ed. Ilgner, pp. 35–6; ed. Luscombe, pp. 54–5), where Abelard pursues the theme that merit in the sight of God does not follow from doing good things, but from also doing them well, that is, with a good or a right intention. But those who believe that they are acting well (*bene agere*) whenever they think that their intention is good or right (*bonam uel rectam intentionem*) can be mistaken. Using the example of those who persecuted Christian martyrs, and who thought that they were serving God, he writes that a

doves by these streams, so that by drawing from them draughts of wisdom you may be able not only to learn but also teach, and be like eyes showing others the way, not only seeing the bridegroom but able to describe him to others. Of his special bride, whose merit it was to conceive him by the ear of her heart, we know it is written: 'But Mary treasured all these words and pondered them in her heart.'[566] Thus, having his words in her heart rather than on her lips, the Mother of the supreme Word pondered them carefully, considering each one attentively, comparing them with each other, seeing how closely they all fitted together. She knew that according to the mystery of the Law every animal is called unclean unless it chews the cud and divides the hoof. And so no soul is clean unless by meditating to the best of its ability it chews the cud of God's teachings and shows understanding in fulfilling them, so that it not only does good things but does them well, that is, with the right intention.[567] For division of the hoof is the mind's ability to distinguish, about which it is written: 'If you offer rightly but do not divide rightly, you have sinned.'[568]

128. 'If anyone loves me', says the Truth, 'he will keep my word.'[569] But who can obediently keep to the words or the precepts of the Lord unless he has first understood them? No one will be careful in obeying unless he has been attentive in listening, like that blessed woman of whom we read that, putting everything else aside, she sat at the Lord's feet listening to his word, listening with ears of understanding as he himself asks, saying: 'If you have ears to hear, then hear.'[570] Yet if they cannot to be kindled to such fervour of devotion, you can at least in your love and study of sacred writings model yourselves on those blessed disciples of St Jerome, Paula and Eustochium, for it was mainly at their request that this doctor with so many volumes lit up the Church.[571]

good intention is not one that seems good but one that is good or right. Cf. also *TSch*, iii. 116; *Comm. Rom.*, i (iii. 12, ed. Buytaert, p. 105, *ll.* 304–8); *Comm. Cantab.* (ed. Landgraf, pt. 1, pp. 179–80).

[568] Gen. 4: 7 (Septuagint). Cf. *Sermon* 14 (*I sermoni di Abelardo per le monache del Paracleto*, ed. De Santis, pp. 215–16; *PL* clxxviii. 494AB); *Expositio orationis dominicae* (ed. Burnett in 'The *Expositio orationis dominicae*', p. 71, *ll.* 137–51).

[569] John 14: 23.

[570] Matt. 11: 15.

[571] *Letter* 7, 48. In her preface to the Scriptural *Problemata* which Heloise later asked Abelard to solve, she drew attention to the example Jerome had set, and which Abelard had invoked, for the study by religious ladies of questions concerning sacred texts: 'Beatus Hieronymus sanctae Marcellae studium, quo tota fervebat circa quaestiones sacrarum litterarum maxime commendans ac vehementer approbans, quantis eam super hoc praeconiis laudum extulerit, vestra melius prudentia quam mea simplicitas novit' (*PL* clxxviii. 677B).

APPENDIX A

FURTHER NOTES

1. Abelard's early education in dialectic (*Letter* 1, 2)

Dialectic was taught widely in eleventh-century schools as at that of the abbey of Bec by Lanfranc and Anselm or of the cathedral of Tours by Berengar. From the late tenth century textbooks of dialectic included Porphyry's *Isagoge*, Aristotle's *Categories* and *Interpretation*, Boethius' commentaries on these and his works on syllogisms, topics, and division. Peripatetics were students of Aristotle, and Abelard became known as 'the peripatetic from Le Pallet' ('Peripateticus Palatinus') or perhaps (cf. *Letter* 1, 4 and 51) 'the peripatetic in the royal palace' or 'court'. Hence the titles given to him in MS copies of commentaries attributed to him, the *Editiones super de interpretatione*, *de diuisionibus* and *Isagoge*: 'Petri Abaelardi iunioris palatini summi peripatetici . . .'[1] and in one MS of his *Theologia 'Summi boni'*: 'Petri abaelardi palatini perhipatetici telogia',[2] as well as by his pupil John of Salisbury[3] and in the *Metamorphosis Golye episcopi*, a poem written around the time of Abelard's death in 1142.[4]

Abelard studied at Loches and Tours (Indre-et-Loire) under Roscelin in the 1090s, and apparently for some time, according to a letter from Roscelin to Abelard: 'in the church of Tours and Loches, where you sat at my feet for such a long time, the least among your master's pupils'.[5] Abelard names Roscelin as his teacher in his *Dialectica*, where he rejects one of his opinions about parts and a whole as absurd.[6] According to a short biography of Abelard (for which see *Letter* 1, 2, n. 5), Abelard was at one time a pupil of master Roscius (Roscelin) but, as he did not pay much attention to his lectures, Roscelin made him attend for a whole year.[7] Not dissimilarly Otto

[1] *Scritti di logica*, ed. Dal Pra, introd., p. xv. The attribution of these works to Abelard is not supported in current scholarship; see Martin, 'A Note'; Cameron, 'Abelard's Early Glosses'.

[2] *TSum*, ed. Buytaert and Mews, introd., p. 64.

[3] *Metalogicon*, i. 5. 13 etc. and *Policraticus*, ii. 22, ed. Webb, p. 129 *l.* 13; ed. Keats-Rohan, p. 134, *l.* 241.

[4] Ed. Huygens, stanza 54. On this see Dronke, *Abelard and Heloise in Medieval Testimonies*, pp. 16–18; repr. in *Intellectuals and Poets*, pp. 260–2, and Clark, 'Love and learning in the "Metamorphosis Golye Episcopi"'.

[5] 'Turonensis ecclesia uel Locensis, ubi ad pedes meos magistri tui discipulorum minimus tam diu resedisti'; ed. Reiners, p. 65; *PL* clxxviii. 360C (*Letter* 15).

[6] 'magistri nostri Roscellini tam insana sententia', *Dialectica*, ed. de Rijk, p. 554 *l.* 37–p. 555 *l.* 1.

[7] 'auditor aliquando magistri Roscii. Cepit eum cum exfestucatione quadam sensuum illius audire. Attamen imperauit sibi ut per annum lectionibus ipsius interesset', ed. Hödl, *Die Geschichte der scholastischen Literatur*, p. 78; Mews, 'In search of a name', p. 172.

of Freising (*c.*1115–58), who studied in Paris and who wrote in the *Gesta Friderici*, i. 49 (ed. Waitz and von Simson, p. 69) that Roscelin was Abelard's first teacher, also comments that in his arrogance and excessive self-confidence Abelard could scarcely bring himself to listen to his masters. Roscelin, in his letter to Abelard, was clearly upset that Abelard had turned against him and had shown ingratitude for the teaching given him while he was growing out of boyhood into youth.[8]

Little is known of Roscelin's teaching. Jolivet has collected the available testimonies.[9] Iwakuma suggested, controversially, that the Munich MS, Bayerische Staatsbibliothek Clm 14779, may contain Roscelin's commentaries on Porphyry (fos. 31^{r}–36^{v}) and *Interpretation* (fos. 44^{r}–66^{r}), and also on Boethius' *De hypotheticis syllogismis* and *De differentiis topicis* (fols. 67^{v}–86^{v} and 87^{r}–105^{v}).[10] Teachers of logic considered the language-aspects (*in voce*) of universal substances such as those of genera (e.g. animal) and species (e.g. horse); another approach was to consider what these are in reality (*in re*). Anselm of Bec and Canterbury commented in his *Epistola de incarnatione uerbi* that Roscelin thought that universals were nothing more than a puff of the voice ('flatus uocis').[11] Otto of Freising in *Gesta Friderici*, i. 49 wrote that Roscelin first established an *in voce* position: 'primus nostris temporibus in logica sententiam vocum instituit'.[12] John of Salisbury, who also studied in Paris, wrote in 1159 that Roscelin's opinions on *voces* had almost completely vanished along with their author.[13] Iwakuma suggested that logicians known as *vocales* first become apparent in the generation before Roscelin, *c.* 1080.[14] Most of the known texts of logic from this period are still unpublished, but for their characteristics and a survey see Marenbon, 'Logic at the turn of the twelfth century'. It seems unlikely that the text entitled *Sententia de universalibus secundum magistrum R.* was written in Roscelin's school.[15]

Roscelin's excursions into the doctrine of the divine Trinity and the Incarnation are not unconnected to his work in logic and underwent investigation, perhaps in 1092, at a church council brought together by

[8] 'beneficiorum, quae tibi tot et tanta a puero usque ad iuvenem sub magistri nomine et actu exhibui, oblitus in verba malitiae meam adversus innocentiam adeo prorupisses, ut fraternam pacem linguae gladio vulnerares', ed. Reiners, p. 63; *PL* clxxviii. 357C–358C (*Letter* 15).

[9] Jolivet, 'Trois variations médiévales', pp. 114–28.

[10] Iwakuma, '"Vocales" or Early Nominalists', pp. 57–62. The first two of these are *P7* and *H5* in the lists presented in *Glosses and Commentaries on Aristotelian Logical Texts*, ed. Burnett. *P7* is ed. by Iwakuma in '"Vocales" or early nominalists', pp. 74–100.

[11] Anselm, *Opera*, ed. Schmitt, i. 285 (a draft version written at Bec before 1093), and ii. 9 (the complete work finished at Canterbury after 1093).

[12] Ed. Waitz and von Simson, p. 69.

[13] *Metalogicon*, ii. 17, ed. Hall, p. 81 *ll.* 18–20.

[14] In '"Vocales" or early Nominalists' and '"Vocales" revisited'.

[15] First published by B. Hauréau in *Notices et extraits*, 5 (1892), pp. 325–8, later by Picavet, *Roscelin*, pp. 139–41, and more recently by Dijs, 'Two anonymous 12th century tracts', pp. 113–17. On the origin of the text see see Dijs, pp. 88–91.

Rainald, archbishop of Reims; they were also heavily criticized by Anselm of Bec in his *Epistola de incarnatione uerbi.*[16] In later years Abelard also attacked Roscelin's views concerning the divine Trinity; see the notes at *Letter* 1, **35**, **37**, and **39**; also at **34**.

Abelard perhaps also studied at Angers under 'magister noster V.', who may be either Master Ulger or Master Vasletus.[17] Mentions of 'our master' in the *Dialectica* also encompass William of Champeaux, Abelard's teacher when later he arrived in Paris.

2. William of Champeaux (*Letter* 1, **3–9**)

2.i (*Letter* 1, **3**)

Once a pupil of Anselm of Laon and of a certain Manegold—both highly influential teachers even if Manegold is not the better-known Manegold of Lautenbach (d. *c.*1103)[18]—William of Champeaux (*c.*1070 or earlier–1122) taught at Laon and then at Paris from 1103 and perhaps from *c.*1095; in 1106 he became archdeacon of Paris.[19]

2.ii (*Letter* 1, **6**)

In a letter received by his provost between 26 October 1111 and March 1112,[20] a German student from Bamberg wrote of William that as archdeacon he was almost the closest person to the king; he was still teaching, however, and he was a heavenly teacher, but he had given away all his possessions and since Easter (i.e. 1111) he had been living in a very poor church. Like the late master Manegold he did not charge fees and he taught both secular and sacred subjects: 'Parisius sum modo, in scolis magistri Gwillelmi, summi uiri omnium huius temporis, quos ego nouerim in omni genere doctrinae. Cuius uocem cum audimus, non hominem sed quasi angelum de caelo loqui putamus; nam et dulcedo uerborum eius et profunditas sententiarum quasi humanum modum transcendit. Qui cum esset archidiaconus fereque apud regem primus, omnibus quae possidebat dimissis, in praeterito pascha ad quandam pauperrimam ecclesiolam, soli Deo seruiturus, se contulit; ibique

[16] *Opera*, ed. Schmitt, i. 281–90, incomplete draft; ii. 3–41, final version. Cf. Southern, *Saint Anselm: A Portrait*, pp. 174–81; Mews, 'St Anselm and Roscelin', 'Nominalism and theology before Abelard', 'St Anselm, Roscelin and the See of Beauvais', and 'The Trinitarian docrine of Roscelin' (with an indication here of two short theological treatises by Roscelin found in the Munich MS Staatsbibliothek, Clm 4600); also Sharpe, 'Anselm as author', pp. 35–45.

[17] Cf. Abelard, *Dialectica*, ed. de Rijk, introd., pp. xix–xx (Ulger); Beonio-Brocchieri Fumagalli, *The Logic of Peter Abelard*, pp. 38–9 (Vasletus).

[18] See Caiazzo, 'Manegold'.

[19] See Michaud, *Guillaume de Champeaux* (now dated); J. Châtillon, 'De Guillaume de Champeaux à Thomas Gallus', pp. 139–46; Godet, 'Guillaume de Champeaux'; Miramon, 'Quatre notes biographiques'.

[20] For the date see Miramon, 'Quatre notes biographiques', p. 75, n. 132.

postea omnibus undique ad eum uenientibus gratis et causa Dei solummodo, more magistri Manegaldi beatae memoriae, deuotum ac benignum se praebuit. Iamque tantum studium regit tam in diuinis quam in humanis scientiis, quantum nec uidi nec meo tempore usquam terrarum esse audiui.' The letter was included in the letter collection completed by 1125 by Ulrich, a member of the cathedral chapter at Bamberg.[21]

Miramon has shown that, although William gave up some of his ecclesiastical revenues in 1108, he continued after his conversion to be active both as archdeacon and teacher, and he witnessed an act as archdeacon on 23 March 1112.[22] That these changes had some connection with a reversal of alliances that had taken place at the beginning of the reign of Louis VI, probably in 1108, and that had brought the Garlandes back into power, has been argued by Bautier.[23] But, as the student indicates and Abelard states twice, on becoming a regular canon William did not leave Paris (neither the *urbs* or town nor the *civitas* or city) at this time. The details of his moves are not clear: the monastery to which he took himself may have been Saint-Denis-de-la-Châtre (or de-la-Chartre) on the Île de la Cité on the corner of the rue de la Cité and the quai de la Corse,[24] or it may have been, and at some stage it was, the old chapel of St-Victor located on a Merovingian site on the left bank of the river Seine outside the gates of the city (now around the Rue and Place Jussieu, Paris, 5e), where a new abbey of regular canons was or was being established. William certainly entered—indeed, he founded—this new abbey. As for William being ambitious for promotion in the church, a contrary view to that of Abelard is found in *De vita vere apostolica*, v. 17, a work of uncertain authorship, perhaps that of Honorius Augustodunensis or Rupert of Deutz, written in the late 1120s: 'Nam nostra etiam memoria beatus Willelmus Catalaunensis episcopus, cum esset perfectus regularis canonicus, omniumque judicio probatus, terque licet subterfugisset, tandem invitus episcopus efficitur.'[25]

Hildebert of Lavardin, bishop of Le Mans, wrote to William to encourage him to overcome his religious scruples and continue teaching.[26] Both Hildebert and the student from Bamberg commended William's teaching for its moral and personal goodness.

2.iii (*Letter* 1, 6)

Rhetoric, along with grammar and dialectic, was a part of logic in the broad sense of the term and for several centuries there had been interplay at a

[21] *Codex Udalrici*, *Letter* 160, ed. P. Jaffé in *Monumenta Bambergensia* (Bibliotheca Rerum Germanicarum, v; Berlin, 1869), p. 286.

[22] 'Quatre notes biographiques'.

[23] 'Paris au temps d'Abélard', pp. 62–3.

[24] A suggestion made by Miramon, 'Quatre notes biographiques', p. 56 and supported by Grondeux, 'Guillaume de Champeaux', pp. 11–12.

[25] *PL* clxx. 659.

[26] *Letter* i. 1, *PL* clxxi. 141–3 at 141A; cf. von Moos, *Hildebert von Lavardin*, pp. 103–7, 136–7.

theoretical level in studies of these three linguistic arts. Two works on rhetoric, a commentary on Cicero's *De inuentione* (*inc.* 'In primis') and a commentary on *Rhetorica ad Herennium* (*inc.* 'Etsi cum Tullius'), anonymous in all but one manuscript, have been claimed for William of Champeaux.[27] They include criticism of Master Roscelin, who 'distorted dialectic' ('deprauauit dialecticam') and they show familiarity with student life in Laon and with the teaching of Masters Manegold and Anselm of Laon. The grammatical teaching of William of Champeaux and of other masters from about 1080 is reported directly and indirectly in an evolving series of *Glosulae super Priscianum*.[28] Abelard intended to write or lecture on rhetoric and, although the *Rethorica* he mentions twice in his Glosses on book 4 of Boethius' *Topics* or *De differentiis topicis*[29] has not been found, these Glosses (written *c.*1117–21) are concerned with Boethius' exposition of rhetorical topics as found in Cicero's *De inuentione*.[30] Likewise, Abelard mentions a work of his own on grammar ('nostra . . . Grammatica', *Tchr*, iv. 155) which has also not been found, but his writings on logic are infiltrated by many grammatical discussions and mentions of William's teaching of grammar.[31] Iwakuma identifies commentaries on the *Isagoge*, *Categories*, and *Interpretation* which seem to be connected with, if not written by, William.[32] Other sources of knowledge of his teaching are the *Introductiones dialectice secundum Wilgelmum* and the similar *Introductiones dialectice artis secundum G. Paganellum*[33] and the *Quaestiones Victorinae*.[34]

William was also a theologian some of whose *Sententie* have been traced.[35]

[27] By Fredborg in 'Commentaries' (see too Ward and Fredborg, 'Rhetoric').

[28] On which see Grondeux and Rosier-Catach, 'Les *Glosulae super Priscianum* et leur tradition', in *Arts du langage et théologie*, pp. 107–79.

[29] Ed. Dal Pra, pp. 263 *l.* 25 and 267 *l.* 16.

[30] Ed. Dal Pra, pp. 256–68; new edn., Fredborg, 'Abelard on rhetoric', pp. 61–80; cf. Ward, *Ciceronian Rhetoric*, pp. 108–11.

[31] See Rosier-Catach, 'Abélard et les grammairiens', and Pinzani, *The Logical Grammar of Abelard*. For references to William's teaching on Boethius' *De differentiis topicis* see Green-Pedersen, 'William of Champeaux on Boethius' *Topics*'; also Libera, 'Guillaume de Champeaux'.

[32] 'Pierre Abélard et Guillaume de Champeaux', pp. 101–22, and '*Pseudo-Rabanus super Porphyrium*'. These are *P3*, *P14*, *C8*, *C14*, *H9*, *H11* in *Glosses and Commentaries*, ed. Burnett.

[33] Ed. Iwakuma in '*Introductiones dialecticae*'; and see Iwakuma, 'William of Champeaux and the *Introductiones*' and 'William of Champeaux on Aristotle's Categories'.

[34] Ed. de Rijk, *Logica modernorum*, ii. 2, pp. 731–69; see too ii. 1, pp. 130–46, 524). On William's writings and teachings see also Guilfoy, 'William of Champeaux' and Mews, '*Logica* in the service of philosophy'. On the continuing need for caution in attributing writings and teachings to William see Jacobi, 'William of Champeaux'.

[35] Ed. Lottin, *Psychologie et morale*, v. 189–227); see also Bertola, 'Le critiche di Abelardo ad Anselmo di Laon ed a Guglielmo di Champeaux', and Jolivet, 'Données sur Guillaume de Champeaux', who underlines William's influence and importance for the development of both the arts of the trivium and of theology.

2.iv (*Letter* 1, **6**)

The first theory of universals that Abelard ascribes to William in *Letter* 1, **6** is 'realist': a universal noun which is predicable of many (e.g. the species 'man' as in 'Socrates is a man', 'Plato is a man') signifies the same thing (*res*) in all its individuals, the differences between them being accidental (height, colour, etc.). The second, revised theory held that the universal is not an essence but is what is not different between e.g. Socrates and Plato (the 'indifference theory'). Both theories are set in a broader light than here by Abelard in his *Logica 'Nostrorum petitioni sociorum'* (or *Glossulae*), written in the early 1120s, where he first reviews three definitions of the universal to be found in the ancient authorities, (1) as *res* or a thing, (2) as *intellectus* or a concept, (3) as *sermo* or a word which is meaningful in a particular way. His further exploration of the first and second definitions makes reference to two views similar to those ascribed to William in *Letter* 1, **6**. The third view finds more favour: the universal is a word, not in the sense of a physical utterance or verbal sound or *uox* (cf. the view ascribed to Roscelin above on p. 528), but of a word which signifies, i.e. *sermo*.[36] John of Salisbury associates Abelard with this *sermo* theory which, he writes, has gained and still retains (in 1159) many followers.[37] According to Iwakuma, Abelard's claim that William changed his view on the status of universal entities may be reflected in a commentary on Porphyry, perhaps written by him and after Abelard's attack, in which the 'indifference theory' is found.[38] References to William and criticisms of his views on predication, appellation, and signification are found in other surviving writings by Abelard on dialectic, including his Glosses on Boethius' *On Topical Differences* or *Super Topica Glossae*: 'praeceptor noster Willelmus',[39] and his *Dialectica*: 'magister noster W.'.[40] On Abelard as a nominalist (not a vocalist) and on criticisms made of nominalists by Alberic of Paris during Abelard's later years ('nominalis sectae acerrimus impugnator', according to John of Salisbury,[41] see Marenbon, 'Vocalism, nominalism' and *Philosophy of Peter Abelard*, pp. 52–3.

[36] Ed. Geyer in *Peter Abaelards philosophische Schriften*, ii: (1) pp. 512–13; (2) pp. 513–14; (3) pp. 514–15, with further exploration at pp. 515–22 and 522–4.

[37] *Metalogicon*, ii. 17, ed. Hall, p. 81, *ll.* 20–4.

[38] See Iwakuma, 'Pierre Abélard et Guillaume de Champeaux', pp. 118–20, who prints passages found in Paris, BnF lat. 17813, fos. 8vb–10vb (*P14* in *Glosses and Commentaries*, ed. Burnett).

[39] Ed. Dal Pra, p. 271 *ll.* 38–9.

[40] Ed. de Rijk, e.g. on pp. 112–13 and p. 541 *l.* 32. On these pages see Jolivet, 'Données sur Guillaume de Champeaux', pp. 239–41, 246, and 'Trois variations médiévales', p. 141 ff. Cf. also *Dialectica*, ed. de Rijk, pp. 67 *l.* 5, 82 *l.* 7, 135 *ll.* 28–9, 195 *l.* 12, 200 *l.* 7, 201 *l.* 2, 271 *l.* 38, and 541 *l.* 32, and de Rijk, *Logica modernorum*, ii, 1, pp. 182–6, 203–6; Iwakuma, 'The realism of Anselm' and 'Pierre Abélard et Guillaume de Champeaux'.

[41] *Metalogicon*, ii. 10, ed. Hall, p. 71, *ll.* 11–12.

2.v (*Letter* 1, 8)

A further two moves by William are narrated here: (1) from the city (*civitas*) to a vill remote from the town (*urbs*) with his fellow canons and with his school; (2) back to the *urbs* with his brethren in his former monastery, where he resumes teaching. (1) seems to be a brief move to Notre-Dame de Puiseaux (diocese of Sens; about 163 km south of Paris), where King Louis VI endowed a regular canonry before 18 April in 1112.[42] (2) is a brief return to St-Victor. In 1113, between May 21 and August 2 at Châlons, and probably on the occasion of William's consecration as bishop of Châlons, King Louis VI endowed the regular canons and the church of St-Victor near the city of Paris ('ecclesia Beati Victoris que iuxta Parisiorum civitatem sita est') with almost all the same properties and privileges previously bestowed on Puiseaux.[43] Puiseaux now became a priory of St-Victor. On the position of the new abbey in the wider history of communities of regular (Augustinian) canons in northern France at this time (e.g. Arrouaise, *c.*1106, Prémontré, 1120) see J. Führer, 'L'abbaye de Saint-Victor'. Cf. also Robert of Torigny, *De immutatione ordinis monachorum*: 'Eodem tempore (i.e. following the foundation of the Cistercian order) magister Willermus de Campellis, qui fuerat archidiaconus Parisiensis, vir admodum litteratus et religiosus, habitum canonici regularis assumens, cum aliquibus discipulis suis, extra urbem Parisius, in loco ubi erat quaedam capella sancti Victoris martyris, coepit monasterium aedificare clericorum.' This is part of a passage in *De immutatione ordinis monachorum* which was inserted into Robert's *Cronica*, *anno* 1112.[44]

3. Anselm of Laon (*Letter* 1, 10–12)

3.i (*Letter* 1, 10)

Anselm had taught the arts and theology at the cathedral school of Laon since the 1090s at the latest; he was also chancellor from 1095, dean from no later than 1111, and archdeacon from 1114. His brother Ralph taught with him and continued to do so after Anselm's death in 1117 until his own death in or after 1133; he was archdeacon and chancellor from 1118. Although caught up in the violence in Laon in 1107 when the bishop, Gaudri, was among those murdered, Anselm unquestionably enjoyed great respect and authority during and beyond his lifetime. His chief fame rested on his teaching of theology. This took the form of glossing the Bible and discussing

[42] *Recueil des actes de Louis VI*, ed. Dufour, i. 131–6, no. 64. Cf. J. Führer, *König Ludwig VI. und die Kanonikerreform*, pp. 221–4; Schoebel, *Archiv und Besitz der Abtei St. Viktor*, pp. 88–97.

[43] *Recueil*, i. 173–80, no. 80.

[44] Ed. Delisle in *Chronique de Robert de Torigni*, ii. 160; ed. Bethmann, p. 484; *PL* ccii. 1313A. See too Ehlers, *Hugo von St Viktor*, p. 5 ff. and Anhang 1, pp. 178–80; Willesme, 'Saint-Victor au temps d'Abélard'; Miramon, 'Quatre notes biographiques'; and Mews, 'William of Champeaux, the Foundation of St Victor'.

sentences or teachings which were found in or might be formed from passages in authoritative texts. A later teacher of theology in Paris, Peter the Chanter (d. 1197), wrote that Anselm began, but was unable to complete, a new and systematic *Gloss*, later to be commonly called the *Glossa ordinaria*, of the entire Old and New Testament. This was built up during the twelfth century and the task involved the selection and arrangement on a large scale of glosses and of passages taken from patristic and other sources, offering authoritative literal, allegorical, and moral interpretations of the Bible. The extent of Anselm's personal contributions remains uncertain but the completed *Gloss* was very widely used for centuries.[45] Sentences attributed (or not attributed) to Anselm as well as to other more or less contemporary teachers, including William of Champeaux, are reported, along with sentences taken from patristic sources, in some fifty *florilegia* or collections which continued to be written by students or others over several decades.[46] On Abelard's stay at Laon see Châtillon, 'Abélard et les écoles', pp. 146–60; Clanchy and Smith, 'Abelard's Description of the School of Laon'.

3.ii (*Letter* 1, 11)

Otto of Freising, in *Gesta Friderici*, i. 49, writes that Abelard found Anselm's teaching, like that of William of Champeaux, vacuous and that he did not listen to him for long.[47] Abelard's 'arrogance of intellect and joy of combat'—illustrated by his rejection of his masters—are among the features which led Haskins to write of him, in his classic work, *The Renaissance of the Twelfth Century*, that 'the personality might turn up in any subsequent epoch'.[48] But much earlier the learned and caustic Rather of Verona (890–974) observed of the schools he found that 'he learned little from his teachers, much more from himself'.[49] Of this, and of the dissociation and alienation of intellectuals from the schools during the tenth century, Leonardi has written: 'This was not an unusual attitude to take; rather, it was symptomatic of many intellectuals of the time, from Liutprand of Cremona (920–72) to Gerbert of Aurillac (940–1003).'[50]

[45] For this see Smalley, *The Study of the Bible in the Middle Ages*, pp. 46–82 (for Peter the Chanter see p. 50); Southern, *Scholastic Humanism*, ii. 25–35; Giraud, *Per verba magistri*, pp. 84–101, 496; and L. Smith, *Glossa Ordinaria*. A facsimile reprint of the *editio princeps* (Adolph Rusch of Strasburg, 1480–1) is *Biblia latina cum glossa ordinaria*, ed. Froehlich and Gibson.

[46] On this see especially Lottin, *Psychologie et morale*, v; Flint, 'The "School of Laon": A reconsideration'; Colish, 'Another look at the School of Laon'; Southern, *Scholastic Humanism*, ii. 36–48, and Giraud, *Per verba magistri*, pp. 185–436. Editions of sentences from Laon are problematic; some have been published by Lottin, *Psychologie et morale*, v.

[47] Ed. Waitz and von Simson, p. 69.

[48] *Renaissance of the Twelfth Century*, pp. 258–9.

[49] *Phrenesis*, ii. 70–1, ed. Reid, p. 200.

[50] 'Intellectual Life', p. 188; I have added the dates. See also Jaeger, *The Envy of Angels*, pp. 217–19 on 'teacher insulting' in the tenth and early eleventh centuries.

In 1116–17 Anselm of Laon, together with bishop William of Champeaux and their disciples, was to be challenged again by Rupert of Deutz, then a monk of St Lawrence near Liège, on account of his views on evil and the will of God. Rupert went to Laon and to Châlons-sur-Marne to confront Anselm and William, although Anselm died immediately after Rupert arrived in Laon.[51]

4. The castration (*Letter* 1, **29**)

Bautier thought that Fulbert's name disappeared from the lists of canons of Notre-Dame between 1117 and 1122 and that this suggested that the mutilation of Abelard occurred at the earliest in 1117 and also that Fulbert for some time withdrew or was suspended from his duties in the chapter.[52] Of all the documents found in the *Histoire générale de Paris. Cartulaire général de Paris*, i, and which date from Fulbert's first appearance as subdeacon of Notre Dame in 1107 (nos. 143 and 145; either he or another Fulbert appears as a canon in no. 130, 1102) to *c.*1124 (no. 201, *c.*1124; no. 203, 1124), only nos. 174 and 175 (both dated 1117) contain the names of two, not three, subdeacons and they do not include Fulbert. Three subdeacons but not Fulbert are named in no. 179 (1118). However, Fulbert is named as subdeacon in no. 182, dated 1 April 1119. Robl suggested that Fulbert enjoyed immunity and that his occasional non-appearance in some documents (e.g. no. 149, 1108) may be due to other reasons.[53]

In a letter to Abelard Fulk, prior of Deuil, a Benedictine priory about 13 km north of Paris and about 5 km away from the abbey of St-Denis, after paying tribute to Abelard's earlier successes as an inspiring, albeit a highly lecherous, teacher,[54] offers consolation of sorts: the castration was (as Abelard himself admitted) a just act of providence; it also brought him into the monastic life. Fulk knew what had happened and was writing shortly after the event.[55] He does not name Heloise or Fulbert but he does mention the punishment by blinding and castration of some of the perpetrators of the crime and may obliquely refer to confiscation of Fulbert's possessions while seeking to commend the bishop and the canons for doing as much as they could ('quantum potuerunt', 'quantum licuit') to ensure that justice was done: 'quidam illorum, qui tibi nocuerunt, oculorum privatione et genitalium abscissione mutilati sunt. Ille autem qui per se factum abnegat, iam ab omni possessione sua bonorum suorum comportatione exturbatus est. Noli ergo canonicos vel episcopum tui sanguinis effusores vel perditores vocare, qui propter te et propter se, quantum potuerunt, iustitiae intenderunt' (*PL*

[51] See Rupert, *De uoluntate Dei* (*PL* clxx. 437–54), *De omnipotentia Dei* (*PL* clxx. 453–78), and *Super quaedam capitula regulae divi Benedicti*, 1 (*PL* clxx. 482C–483B); also Van Engen, *Rupert of Deutz*, pp. 181–220.

[52] Bautier, 'Paris au temps d'Abélard', p. 56, n. 1.

[53] '*Hersindis mater*', pp. 64–5.

[54] See *Letter* 1, **15**, n. 59.

[55] 'paulo'; *Epistola ad Abaelardum*, *PL* clxxviii. 371C, *l.* 11.

clxxviii. 375B); 'Plangit ergo hoc tuum vulnus et damnum venerabilis episcopi benignitas, qui, quantum licuit, vacare justitiae studuit' (*PL* clxxviii. 374B). Deuil lay beneath the fortress of Montmorency, which was in the possession of the Bouchard branch of the Montmorency family to which Heloise and her uncle may have been related;[56] Fulk may have been moved to write this letter in order to protect Fulbert, his relatives, and his affinity who are mentioned here in *Letter* 1, **29**: 'auunculus et consanguinei seu affines eius'. In a part of Fulk's letter published by Duchesne–d'Amboise in 1616 and by Cousin,[57] but suppressed in *PL* clxxviii. 375A in order to avoid scandal, Fulk reports that Abelard was thinking of launching an expensive appeal in Rome; this may have been before or shortly after July 1118 because Pope Gelasius II (who died at Cluny on 2 February 1119) was forced to leave Rome after 22 July. His successor Callixtus II arrived in Rome in June 1120.

In a short poem, perhaps written shortly after the crime and beginning with the words 'Ornavere due te quondam, Gallia, gemme', sympathy is expressed for 'Mathias, the consul and Peter the philosopher . . . both jewels (of Gaul)'—for Mathias who was castrated following adultery, for Peter who 'fell by a supreme betrayal . . . destroyed by a like fall. This was the public downfall of the highest men . . . Only the wife of Peter is free of guilt: there was no consent on her part, to make her culpable.' ('Phil(os)ophus summa prodicione ruit . . . clade ruit simili . . . Sola tamen Petri coniux est criminis expers, Consensus nullus quam facit esse ream.'[58] Mathias may be Count Matthew II of Nantes (d. *c.*1103), son of Duke Hoël I of Brittany (1066–84) and younger brother of Duke Alan IV of Brittany (1084–1112). The vassals of Mathias included one Daniel of Le Pallet, Abelard's birthplace—'Danihel de Palatio', whose name appears together with that of Mathias, count of Nantes, in a deed of gift made to the abbey of Marmoutiers.[59] The poet compares Abelard's fall to those of Adam, Samson, and Solomon, as does Heloise in *Letter* 4, **10**. A suggestion made by Dickey,[60] that the mention, made in the gloss *In primis* on *De inuentione*, of a man who lost his testicles as a punishment for sleeping with a nun is a reference to Abelard seems unlikely since Heloise was not a nun at the time of the castration and the commentary seems to have been written before this occurred.[61] For other examples of

[56] *Letter* 1, **16**, n. 61.

[57] Cousin, i. 706, *l.* 5 up—p. 707, *l.* 14. Also by Van den Eynde, 'Détails biographiques sur Pierre Abélard,' p. 219 from BnF MSS lat. 2545 and 13057; see *Checklist* no. 386.

[58] Ed. Dronke in *Abelard and Heloise in Medieval Testimonies*, pp. 45–6, trans. p. 19; repr. in *Intellectuals and Poets*, p. 281, trans. p. 263; also in *Abaelardiana*, ii. 279.

[59] Printed in Morice, *Mémoires*, i, col. 474. See Dronke, *Abelard and Heloise in Medieval Testimonies*, pp. 20, 46; repr. in *Intellectuals and Poets*, pp. 264, 281; Benton in *Abaelardiana*, i. 275 and n. 7; Dronke in *Abaelardiana*, ii. 279; Everard, *Brittany and the Angevins*, pp. 28–9.

[60] In 'Some Commentaries', p. 15.

[61] Fredborg, 'Commentaries', pp. 4–5; Ward, *Ciceronian Rhetoric*, p. 217 and note. The commentary has been briefly mentioned on p. 523 above.

castration as a punishment for sexual and other offences see Constable. 'Aelred of Rievaulx and the Nun of Watton', pp. 215–16 and nn. 31 and 32, and Constable, 'Nun of Watton'.

5. The expulsion of the nuns from Argenteuil and the foundation of the abbey of the Paraclete (*Letter* 1, 63–4)

5.i. The expulsion (*Letter* 1, 63)

The agreement of King Louis VI and his son Philip to the request of Suger to restore Argenteuil to the abbey of St-Denis was given, on the advice of Matthew of Albano, the papal legate, on 14 April 1129, at Reims.[62] The nuns were replaced by monks. Suger claimed that the monastery belonged to St-Denis and had been alienated in unfortunate circumstances for a limited period in the time of Charlemagne, but that previous attempts to recover it had failed. Suger also claimed that the conduct of the nuns had become deplorable.[63] A number of female convents was suppressed around this time. Bautier described the expulsion from Argenteuil as scandalous, being supported also by documents forged at St-Denis.[64] Grant noted that it was supported by respected bishops and consolidated the abbey's properties along the north bank of the Seine, and further that a question may be raised over the reputation of the nunnery in the light of what Abelard admitted having done once with Heloise in the refectory there (*Letter* 5, 17).[65] Waldman provides a full examination of the sources and draws attention to Suger's reputation for improving the quality of religious life,[66] but his arguments and those of others such as Grant[67] that documents were forged to provide support for Suger's claims have been questioned.[68]

5.ii. The nuns' arrival at the Paraclete (*Letter* 1, 63)

The coming of Heloise and other nuns to the Paraclete at Abelard's behest was recorded by William Godell, writing in France after the death of Heloise in 1164: 'magister Petrus Abaelardus . . . Construxit denique cœnobium in territorio Trecassino, in prato quodam ubi legere solitus fuerat, in quo Sanctimoniales plurimas epistolari [*episcopali* in *Robert of Auxerre*] auctoritate congregavit, quod Paraclitum nominavit. Quibus Sanctimonialibus quondam

[62] See J. Dufour, *Recueil des actes de Louis VI*, ii, no. 281, pp. 100–6.

[63] Suger, *Vita Lodovici Grossi regis* (ed. Lecoy de la Marche, pp. 114–15; ed. Waquet, pp. 216–18; trans. Cusimano and Moorhead, pp. 126–7, and *De administratione sua* and *Testamentum* (ed. Lecoy de la Marche, pp. 160–1, 338; cf. also pp. 368, 369, 441–2). See also Pouget, 'La légende carolingienne à Saint-Denis', p. 58.

[64] 'Paris au temps d'Abélard', pp. 71–5.

[65] *Abbot Suger*, pp. 192–3.

[66] 'Abbot Suger and the Nuns of Argenteuil', 246–9.

[67] *Abbot Suger*, pp. 190–2.

[68] See Groten, 'Die Urkunde'; Clausen, 'Suger, faussaire de chartes', p. 114; Morelle, 'Suger et les archives', pp. 117–39; Führer, *König Ludwig VI*, pp. 222–5 at p. 222.

uxorem suam religiosam fœminam, et litteris tam hebraicis quàm latinis adprimè eruditam, nomine Heluisam præfecit Abbatissam.'[69] Robert of Auxerre (d. 1212) incorporates this into his *Chronicon*,[70] as does William of Nangis (late thirteenth century), in whose chronicle a reviser adds a mention of the eviction of the nuns from Argenteuil, [addition between brackets]: 'coenobium . . . quod Paraclitum nominavit. In quo sanctimoniales plurimas congregavit, et quamdam religiosam feminam, quondam uxorem suam, litteris latinis et hebraicis eruditam [quae monacha apud Argentolium effecta fuerat, sed inde, cum aliis pluribus, per industriam Sugerii abbatis sancti Dionysii in Francia, postmodum ejecta,] eis abbatissam praefecit.'[71]

5.iii. The endowments of the Paraclete (*Letter* 1, 63–4)

A first 'priuilegium' of Pope Innocent II, given at Auxerre, confirming for Heloise, prioress, and the sisters of the Oratory of the Holy Trinity the possessions of their house, is dated 28 November 1131.[72] This date provides a *terminus post quem* for the writing of *Letter* 1. Further papal confirmations were obtained in the lifetime of Heloise (now always named abbess)[73] from Innocent II (17 June 1135 at Pisa, JL 7715; 30 December, probably in 1142, JL 8176), Lucius II (15 March 1144, JL 8522), Eugenius III (1 November 1147, JL 9155), Anastasius IV (26 January 1154, JL 9822), Adrian IV (13 February 1156, JL 10144;[74] 1 December 1157, JL 10314; 24 November 1156×1158, JL 10344), and Alexander III (6 April 1163, JL 10846). Cf. *Checklist*, nos. 417–25: in nos. 417 (1135) and 419 (1144) the Oratory is named as the Oratory of the Holy Trinity; in nos. 418, 422, and 424 (probably 1142, 1156 and 1156×1158) of the Paraclete; in nos. 420, 421, 423, and 425 (1147, 1154, 1157, and 1163) of the Holy Spirit. Bernard of Clairvaux in *Letter* 278 (written in 1150) writes of the 'abbess of the Paraclete'.[75] Cf. the late thirteenth-century 'Book of Burials' at the Paraclete, Paris, BnF fr. 14410, fo. 13^{v}:[76] *Heleuis premiere abbeesse*; also the obituary of Noëfort near Meaux, one of the houses that were to be dependent on the Paraclete: *Heloysa, prima abbatissa huius religionis*.[77] Other benefactors include Count Theobald of Troyes, who in 1133 and 1146 confirmed grants made to the nuns by one Galo and his wife Adelaudis and by Milo, lord of

[69] *Chronicon*, ed. Bouquet, *Recueil*, xiii. 675.

[70] *MGH* Scriptores, xxvi, p. 235.

[71] *Chronique*, ed. Géraud, i. 32–3.

[72] Cf. JL 7513; *Checklist* no. 416.

[73] See Benton, 'Fraud, Fiction and Borrowing', p. 488, n. 48.

[74] Reproduced with French trans. by Parisse, *Les Nonnes au Moyen Âge*, p. 71.

[75] Ed. Leclercq and Rochais in *S. Bernardi Opera*, vii. 190.

[76] Published in the *Obituary of the Paraclete*, ed. Molinier in *Obituaires de la province de Sens*, 4 (16 May), p. 394C; ed. Lalore, no. 86, p. 452; also no. 303, p. 466.

[77] *Obituary of the Paraclete*, ed. Molinier, *Obituaires de la province de Sens*, 4 (28 Apr.), p. 205A.

Nogent, King Louis VI who exempted the nuns in 1135 from payment of royal customs, and Archbishop Henry of Sens, who granted tithes in 1136.[78]

6. The governance of the Paraclete

6.i. A male superior? (*Letter* 1, **69**, *Rule* **40–51**)

In *Letter* 1, **69** and in the *Rule* **41**, **43–4** Abelard proposed that the Paraclete be governed by a man since monasteries of women should be subject to monasteries of men. In *Letter* 1, **70** he writes that the nuns need him and that he wished to minister to them. In writing in favour of there being a male head of a female community, examples from Prémontré and the Cluniac order will also have passed through his mind. At Prémontré before 1143, under Norbert's successor Hugh of Fosses, the sisters, who were physically separated from the canons but occupied the same site, were subject to a prioress who was herself subject to the abbot in important matters.[79] At the Cluniac nunnery of Marcigny-sur-Loire (dioc. Autun), which had been founded *c.*1055 by abbot Hugh and his brother to house their mother, there was alongside the women's house a priory for monks, who were responsible for the temporal administration of the nunnery and for meeting some of the spiritual needs of the nuns. The abbot of Cluny was also abbot of Marcigny, the two institutions—although 73 km apart—being a single community; there was a prioress but the abbess was Our Lady.[80] Marcigny proved to be a model for other Cluniac and also non-Cluniac nunneries.[81] On the rule of female religious by men cf. Gratian, *Concordia discordantium canonum* C. 18 q. 2 c. 24: 'Puellarum monasteria monachorum presidio et ministratione regantur.' Cf. also the early thirteenth-century biography of St Gilbert of Sempringham, the founder in England in the mid-twelfth-century of a double order for nuns and canons: 'as is laid down in the decrees of the fathers it is essential that communities of maidens be controlled through the support and administration of monks and clerks' / 'sicuti patrum decreta diffiniunt, necesse est ut monasteria puellarum, presidio et administratione monachorum vel clericorum regantur'.[82]

However, Paraclete charters, some of which mention that Heloise was prioress or abbess, make no mention of a male superior, although there were

[78] For these see *Checklist* nos. 426, 432, 427, 428 and *Cartulaire de l'abbaye du Paraclet*, ed. Lalore, pp. 62–3, 70–1, 64, 64–5; for other grants made in the lifetime of Heloïse see *Checklist*, nos. 429–31, 433–41, and *Cartulaire*, ed. Lalore, pp. 65–6, 66–8, 69–70, 73–4, 71–3, 74–5, 75–6, 76–7, 77–8, 78–9, 79–81, 69. For references in documents written in the Paraclete to Abelard as the founder see *Letter* 2, n. 11.

[79] See Van Waefelghem, 'Les Premiers Statuts', pp. 63–6; Fontette, *Les Religieuses*, pp. 14–18.

[80] See Hunt, *Cluny under St. Hugh*, pp. 186–94; Wollasch, 'A Cluniac Necrology', pp. 162–6.

[81] Cf. Röckelein, 'Frauen im Umkreis der Benediktinischen Reformen', pp. 286–91, 324.

[82] *The Book of St Gilbert*, ed. R. Foreville and G. Keir (OMT, 1987), pp. 46–7.

clerics attached to the abbey[83] and monks too.[84] The *Institutiones nostre* likewise do not mention a male superior but refer to an abbess, a prioress, and nuns as well as lay brothers and lay sisters (*conuerse*, *conuersi*, *sorores laice*).[85]

Jenal, gives a clear account of the relationship between the male and female members of the abbey envisaged in the *Rule*,[86] while Felten skilfully separates 'theory' (found in the *Rule* and in *Letter* 1) and 'practice' (found in other sources, which show the Paraclete gaining freedom from outside interference and from want as well as gaining six daughter houses by 1163).[87]

6.ii. A female superior? (*Letter* 1, **69**)

Links between nunneries and the men, both religious and lay, who were attached to them took many different forms, including rule of men by women.[88] Among the monasteries that Abelard will have had in mind when writing *Letter* 1, **69**, and where a woman ruled as abbess, were the Benedictine abbeys of Saint-Sulpice-la-Forêt and Fontevraud. Saint-Sulpice-la-Forêt was in Brittany, about 17 km by road north-east of Rennes. This was a linked house of men and women founded on ducal land around 1112 by Raoul de La Fustaye (d. 1129). It grew rapidly.[89] Raoul seems also to have been a companion of Robert of Arbrissel (d. 1116), a Breton who founded for men and women the abbey of Fontevraud south of the river Loire between Saumur and Chinon (dioc. Poitiers). From 1115, when Petronilla of Chemillé became abbess of Fontevraud, the male members of the abbey and of its rapidly growing number of dependent houses in different parts of France were subject to the direction of the nuns and the abbess.[90]

Before 1121 in a letter to the bishop of Paris Abelard had defended Robert, whom he called 'that excellent herald of Christ' ('egregium illum preconem Christi'),[91] from attack by Roscelin of Compiègne. In a letter to Abelard Roscelin objected to Robert's reception of women into religious life against the

[83] *The Paraclete Statutes*, ed. Waddell, pp. 100–1.

[84] *Cartulaire de l'abbaye du Paraclet*, ed. Lalore, no. 56 (dated 1155), p. 75: 'monachi ecclesie Paracliti'.

[85] See 6, 7, 11A–E, *The Paraclete Statutes*, ed. Waddell, pp. 10–15 (commentary on pp. 99–109, 127–96); *PL* clxxviii. 314D–317A.

[86] Jenal, '*Caput autem mulieris vir*'.

[87] Felten, 'Verbandsbildung von Frauenklöstern'.

[88] See Parisse, 'Doppelkloster' and, for England, S. Thompson, *Women Religious*, esp. pp. 54–79; Knowles and Hadcock, *Medieval Religious Houses: England and Wales*. 2nd edn., p. 200, and Golding, *Gilbert of Sempringham and the Gilbertine Order*.

[89] See Guillotel, 'Les Premiers Temps' and Everard, 'The Abbey of Saint-Sulpice-la-Forêt,' pp. 108–11.

[90] On Robert of Arbrissel, his historians and their sources, and on Petronilla and the statutes of Fontevraud, see Dalarun and others, *Les Deux vies*; Dalarun, *L'Impossible Sainteté*; Bienvenu, *L'Étonnant Fondateur*; and Kerr, *Religious Life for Women*, pp. 1–10, 15–63.

[91] Ed. Smits, p. 280, *l.* 27; *PL* clxxviii. 357B, *ll.* 8–9; trans. Ziolkowski, p. 195. For evidence of a lost 'letter' written by Roscelin against Robert, see Dolbeau,'Deux catalogues inédits de bibliothèques médiévales,' p. 342.

wishes of their husbands.[92] A similar accusation was made against Robert by Marbod, archdeacon of Angers and from 1096 till 1123 bishop of Rennes.[93]

6.iii. Deaconesses (*Letter* 7, **18–20**, *Rule* **24–51**)

Abelard's discussion of deaconesses in the New Testament and in the early church leads into discussion in *Letter* 7 and in the *Rule* of what should be the functions of the deaconess at the Paraclete, and encompasses their election or consecration (*Letter* 7, **18**; *Rule* **29**, **37**), their ministry (*Letter* 7, **19–20**; *Rule* **24–51**), and the stricter requirements imposed upon them in comparison with their male counterparts, the deacons (*Letter* 7, **20**). At the Paraclete, according to Abelard, a deaconess (or deaconess-abbess, *Rule* **26**) should be responsible for the spiritual life of the sisters within the convent while a community of monks, led by a provost or abbot, should look after the material and external interests of the convent (*Rule* **26–51**). The abbot is the spiritual father and steward (*dispensator*) of the nuns (*Rule* **43–4**, **46**) and the monks provide priests to say Mass (*Rule* **74–5**). In a review of some contemporary errors (*Tchr*, iv. 80) Abelard distanced himself from the view of one of two masters, who were blood-brothers and conceited, that a woman could consecrate the bread and wine in the sacrament of the altar. On deaconesses and abbesses in the early medieval Western church, and on rites for their consecration or ordination, see Macy, *The Hidden History of Women's Ordination*, pp. 64–88, 95 and notes 44–5, Appendix 1 and 2. Other studies include Gryson, *Le Ministère des femmes dans l'Église ancienne* and Martimort, *Les Diaconesses: Étude historique*.

In *Comm. Rom.*, iv (xvi. 1, p. 326) Abelard writes that Paul commends Phoebe, his sister not in the flesh but in the faith, to the Romans in his prayers, and that she is believed to have brought to Corinth his Letter to the Romans. Abelard writes also that she is said to have been a rich noblewoman who from her own resources and those of others ministered to the needs of the believers in Cenchreae, following the example of the holy women who assisted the Lord and the apostles. Abelard adds (p. 327) a passage taken from Origen's *Comm. in Epistolam ad Romanos*, x. 17 (*PG* xiv. 1278AB) in which Origen writes that Paul teaches with apostolic authority that women were appointed to hold office in the church as female ministers, as Phoebe was in Cenchreae.[94] There follow (p. 327) three more passages. Two of these,

[92] Roscelin, *Letter* to Abelard, 3–4, ed. Reiners, pp. 65–7; *PL* clxxviii. 360D–362A (*Letter* 15); *Letter* 14, ed. Smits, p. 280; *PL* clxxviii. 357B; trans. Ziolkowski, p. 195. On Roscelin's accusation see Dalarun and others, *Les Deux vies*, pp. 501, 622–30; also Luscombe, 'From Paris to the Paraclete', pp. 256–8.

[93] *Epist.* 25 in Dalarun and others, *Les Deux vies*, p. 548, and see Mews, 'Robert d'Arbrissel, Roscelin et Abélard', pp. 38–42, and 'Negotiating the boundaries of gender in religious life', pp. 113–25.

[94] 'Origenes: "Apostolica auctoritate docet etiam feminas in ministerio ecclesiae constitui. In quo officio positam Phoeben apud ecclesiam 'quae est Cenchris' magna cum laude

attributed to Jerome, are taken from commentaries by John the Deacon (*fl.* after 554) on Paul;[95] here female deacons, appointed to the diaconate, are said to administer baptism and to undertake the ministry of the Word in eastern parts, a model being Priscilla, the wife of Aquila (cf. Acts 18: 2). The third passage, attributed to Epiphanius (St Epiphanius, *c.*315–403, bishop of Salamis), is found among the letters of Jerome; here Epiphanius writes that he has never ordained deaconesses and has not caused divisions in the church ('Numquam ego ordinaui diaconissas et ad alias misi prouincias neque feci quidquam ut ecclesiam scinderem').[96] In *Sermon* 31, addressed to the sisters of the Paraclete (*dilectissimae sorores*, *PL* clxxviii. 572A), on the feast of the nativity of St Stephen and the other deacons, Abelard introduces Paul's commendation of Phoebe to the Romans by remarking of the women who served the Lord and the apostles that the holy doctors called them *diaconae* or deaconesses and on many occasions wrote that Paul attached to the order of the diaconate, which began with men, female deacons who were equal to the male deacons.[97] The commentary on 1 Timothy in *Comm. Cantab.*,[98] after briefly summarizing the history of the *ordo mulierum*, that is, of deaconesses and their ministry, in both the Old and the New Testament, presents Phoebe as the head of a group of sacred widows and also as a minister to travellers and the poor. A deaconess is both in charge of other women and a minister. Deaconesses do not read the Gospel during Mass, though they can do so in the morning office (*matutinis*), nor can they lay on hands as deacons do, but they give blessings of their own and their position is very similar to that of deacons; this is why Paul treats of both together in his epistle: 'apostolus, quia diacones et diaconisse tam affine habent officium, vicissime de illis instruit'.[99]

et commendatione prosequitur, quia in necessitatibus apostolicisque laboribus adstiterit. Locus hic duo docet, et haberi feminas ministras in ecclesia et tales debere assumi in ministerium, quae adstiterint multis et per bona officia usque ad apostolicam laudem meruerint peruenire."'

95 *In Epistolam ad Romanos*, 16; *PL* xxx. 743C and *In Epistolam 1 ad Timotheum*, v. 11; *PL* xxx. 926C; the latter passage is also cited in *Sermon* 31, *PL* clxxviii. 572C.

96 *Epistola* LI, 2, ed. Hilberg, liv. 398; *PL* xxii. 519. Abelard shows no knowledge of the complaints made by Epiphanius against women becoming bishops and priests in defiance of St Paul, 1 Cor. 14: 34 (*Panarion*, i. 3. 49: *adversus Quintillianos*, *PG* xli. 879–82).

97 'Perpendite et quanto vos honore divina gratia sublimaverit, qui vos primum suas et postmodum apostolorum habuit diaconas, cum tam illis quam istis cunctis viduis de suis facultatibus constet ministrasse. Unde et ipsas tam diaconas quam diaconissas appellare doctores sancti consuevere. De quarum etiam mensis ordo diaconatus in praedictis viris incoeptus, ad dominicam altaris mensam postmodum est translatus; ut qui diaconarum fuerant diaconi, nunc levitae efficiantur Christi. Quibus pariter et feminas in hoc diaconatus ordine ab Apostolo conjunctas esse, doctores sancti multis profitentur in locis'; *PL* clxxviii. 572AB).

98 Ed. Landgraf, pt. 3, pp. 574–5.

99 Ibid., p. 575.

6.iv. Lay sisters and lay brothers (*Rule* **26**, **40**, **124**)

The position of *converse* and their male equivalents, the *conversi*, in monastic communities in the twelfth century varied from one house to another. According to Abelard, the *converse* serving the nuns at the Paraclete, and wearing a different habit, were not nuns but they were part of the community. Traditionally, *converse* or *conversi* participated in the divine office with the nuns or monks, but a newer type of lay converts, both sisters and brothers, also appeared in the late eleventh and twelfth centuries who, while being part of the religious community, usually lived and prayed apart from the professed nuns or monks. These lay *converse* or *conversi* were typically servants, if not also of humble birth, and practised a simpler form of religious life; this was to become a feature of the Cistercian order and elsewhere. They are mentioned in *Institutiones nostre*, 7 as labourers.[100] In *Institutiones nostre*, 10 the Paraclete ruled that a woman who joins the community as a lay sister should never afterwards become a nun.[101] This statute is modelled on statute 22 of the Cistercian order, which forbade a lay brother to become a monk. On this statute and on its ambiguity—whether the statute applied to entrants who were or were not already *converse* is not clear—see Waddell, *The Paraclete Statutes*, pp. 123–5 and Appendix 2, p. liv. On *conversi* (in the military as well as in the religious orders) and *converse*, see Constable, *The Reformation of the Twelfth Century*, pp. 74–81, 99–100; also Constable, *Medieval Monasticism*, nos. 768–75; Leclercq, 'Comment vivaient les frères convers'; and Peter the Venerable, *Letters*, ed. Constable, ii. 175.

7. Clothing (*Rule* **102**)

Within a small collection of poems (two of which clearly concern Abelard and Heloise) found in the Orleans MS Bibliothèque municipale 284, pp. 183–4, there is one which offers advice, similar to that given here in the *Institutio*, to spurn costly clothes and to wear clothes made of lambs' wool. It is addressed to a sister and friend (*soror*, *amica*) who is wedded to Christ, the Lamb of God. The text is this:

Nec catus in nitida seruari pelle ualebit,
  nec mulier, cultus si p(r)eciosus erit.
Sepe, soror, rogo te preciosas spernere uestes,
  quas, cui nupsisti, non amat, immo uetat.
Verus hic est agnus: agninas appete uestes,
  ut (s)ponsum uestis exprimat ipsa suum!
Indutam Christum te monstret uestis, amica!
  Agnus hic est: agni pellibus indue te!

[100] *The Paraclete Statutes*, ed. Waddell, p. 11 (commentary on pp. 104–9); *PL* clxxviii. 314D–315A).

[101] *The Paraclete Statutes*, ed. Waddell, p. 11; *PL* clxxviii. 315B.

Ar(c)ha Dei uirgo est, celesti dedita sponso,
textus minus caris [est] pellibus arca fuit:
scilicet his, que protegerent, non que decorarent,
que pacientes sint pulueris et pluuie.[102]

Wollin noticed the evident similarity of the advice about clothing found in the poem and in Abelard's *Institutio* and thought that Abelard was the author of the poem.[103] On a number of occasions also in his corrrespondence Abelard addresses Heloise as *soror* and *amica*. Dronke did not think that these verses were addressed specifically to Heloise.[104] *Ll.* 1–2 of the poem are similar to *vv.* 665–6 of the *Carmen ad Astralabium* (ed. Rubingh-Bosscher): 'nec catus poterit seruari pelle nitente, / nec mulier cultus si preciosus erit'.

[102] Ed. Wollin, 'Neue Textzeugen', pp. 221–2. Previously ed. Dronke, 'Orleans, Bibl. mun. 284', pp. 280–1, where he reads 'Arha' in *l.* 9 and 'texta' in *l.* 10.

[103] 'Neue Textzeugen', pp. 220–6.

[104] '*Abelard and Heloise in Medieval Testimonies*, p. 48; repr. in *Intellectuals and Poets*, p. 283.

APPENDIX B

WRITINGS OF PETER ABELARD AND HELOISE

Collected Editions

Duchesne, André, and Amboise, François d':

Du *PETRI ABAELARDI SANCTI GILDASII IN BRITANNIA ABBATIS ET HELOISAE CONJVGIS EJVS . . . OPERA, NVNC PRIMVM EX MMS CODD. ERVTA & IN LVCEM EDITA STUDIO AC DILIGENTIA ANDREAE QVERCETANI TVRONENSIS . . . PARISIIS . . . M.DCXVI . . .*

Amb *PETRI ABAELARDI FILOSOFI ET THEOLOGI, ABBATIS RVYENSIS, ET HELOISAE CONIVGIS EIVS PRIMAE PARACLETENSIS ABBATISSAE OPERA NVNC PRIMVM EDITA EX MMS. CODD. V. ILLVST. FRANCISCI AMBOESII . . . PARISIIS . . . M.DCXVI . . .*

Cousin: *Petrus Abaelardus. Opera hactenus seorsim edita nunc primum in unum collegit . . . V. Cousin adjuvantibus C. Jourdain et E. Despois* (2 vols.; Paris, 1849, 1859; repr. Hildesheim, 1970).

PL clxxviii (Paris, 1855).

Editions of the Letter Collection

Duchesne–d'Amboise, pp. 3–197.

Petri Abaelardi abbatis Ruyensis et Heloissae abbatissae Paracletensis epistolae a prioris editionis erroribus purgatae et cum cod. MS. collatae cura Ricardi Rawlinson . . . (London, 1718; repr. with a new title page, Oxford, 1728).

Cousin, i. 1–37, 72–213.

PL clxxviii. 113–314.

For the editions of Muckle and McLaughlin, see below.

Pagani: *Epistolario di Abelardo ed Eloisa* a cura di Ileana Pagani con considerazioni sulla trasmissione del testo di Giovanni Orlandi (Classici Latini; Turin, 2004). Pagani reproduces with a few corrections the editions of the letter collection made by Muckle and McLaughlin, *Letter* 9 (Smits), the prefaces to the *Hymns* (Waddell), the *Sermons* (*PL* clxxviii), the *Expositio in Hexameron* (*PL* clxxviii), the *Problemata* (*PL* clxxviii), the *Confession of Faith* to Heloise (Burnett), and the letters exchanged between Peter the Venerable and Heloise (Constable). All texts are translated into Italian and are supported by valuable notes and indexes.

Lettres d'Abélard et Héloïse. Texte établi et annoté par E. Hicks and T. Moreau. Préface par M. Zink. Introduction de J.-Y. Tilliette (Livre de Poche 'Lettres gothiques', no. 4572; Paris, 2007). Includes *Letters* 1–8 and the *Rule*, with a critical apparatus, brief notes, and a new French translation. For the principles on which this edition of the Latin text is based reference should be made to pp. xliv–liv of the work of Hicks which is cited below under *The Old French Translation*.

Letter 1 (Historia calamitatum)

Recueil des historiens des Gaules et de la France, xiv (1806; repr. 1877), pp. 278–94 from Duchesne and from Paris, BnF lat. 2923 (not complete).

Muckle, J. T., ed., 'Abelard's letter of consolation to a friend (*Historia Calamitatum*)', *Mediaeval Studies*, xii (1950), 163–213.

Monfrin: *Abélard, Historia calamitatum. Texte critique avec une Introduction*, ed. J. Monfrin (Bibliothèque des textes philosophiques; Paris, 1959; 4ème tirage, 1978). Monfrin also includes an edition from **T**, **T**^{1}, **A**, and **J** of *Letters* 2, 4, and the end of 5.

Letters 2–5

Muckle, J. T., ed., 'The personal letters between Abelard and Heloise: Introduction, authenticity and text', *Mediaeval Studies*, xv (1953), 47–94.

Letters 6–7

Muckle, J. T., ed., 'The letter of Heloise on religious life and Abaelard's first reply', *Mediaeval Studies*, xvii (1955), 240–81.

Letter 8 with the Rule or Institutio

McLaughlin, T. P., ed., 'Abelard's Rule for religious women', *Mediaeval Studies*, xviii (1956), 241–92.

The Old French Translation

Génin, F., 'Première Lettre d'Abailard, traduction inédite de Jean de Meun', *Bulletin du Comité historique des monuments écrits de l'histoire de France, Histoire-Sciences-Lettres*, ii (Paris, 1850), 175–91, 265–92.

Jean de Meun. Traduction de la première épître de Pierre Abélard (Historia calamitatum), ed. C. Charrier (Paris, 1934).

Schultz, E., '"La Vie et les Epistres Pierres Abaelart et Heloys sa fame": A Translation by Jean de Meun and an Old French Translation of Three Related Texts: A Critical Edition of MS 920 (Bibliothèque Nationale)' (Ph.D. diss., University of Washington, 1969).

Le lettere di Abelardo ed Eloisa nella traduzione di Jean de Meun, i: *Testo*; ii: *Introduzione – Apparato – Note – Indice sellettivo delle forme – Indice dei nomi propri*, ed. F. Beggiato (2 vols.; Modena, 1977).

Hicks: *La Vie et les epistres Pierres Abaelart et Heloys sa fame. Traduction du XIIIe siècle attribuée à Jean de Meun. Avec une nouvelle édition des textes* *latins d'après le ms. Troyes Bibl. mun. 802*, i: *Introduction, textes*, ed. E. Hicks (Nouvelle Bibliothèque du Moyen Âge, xvi; Paris, 1991). Hicks placed the Latin text and the old French translation of *Letters* 1–7 on facing pages and illustrated the relationship between the Latin text and the translation in a detailed apparatus. For the Latin text (see pp. xliv–liv) he made use of the editions of Monfrin and Muckle and also collated the Troyes MS 802. Hicks died in 2004; no further volume has appeared.

Other Translations of the Letter Collection

Dutch

De minnebrieven van Abelard en Heloïse. Inleidung en historische verklarung door M. Gelaude. Nederlandse vertaling door V. Heylen (Antwerp, 1980). *Letters* 1–5 and the opening of *Letter* 6.

English

The Letters of Abelard and Heloise now First Translated from the Latin by C. K. Scott Moncrieff (London, 1925). *Letters* 1–8 (with the *Rule*).

The Letters of Abelard and Heloise, translated with an Introduction by Betty Radice (Penguin Classics; Harmondsworth, 1974). *Letters* 1–6, summary of 7, 8 (with the *Rule*).

Abelard and Heloise: The Story of His Misfortunes and the Personal Letters, translated with an Introduction and Notes by Betty Radice; Wood-engravings by Raymond Hawthorn (The Folio Society; London, 1977). *Letters* 1–5 with part of 6.

Radice: *The Letters of Abelard and Heloise*, translated with an Introduction and Notes by Betty Radice, revised by M. T. Clanchy (Penguin Classics; London, 2003). *Letters* 1–6, summary of 7, 8 (with the *Rule*).

Levitan: *Abelard and Heloise: The Letters and Other Writings*, translated with introduction and notes by W. Levitan (Indianapolis, IN, 2007). *Letters* 1–8 (with the *Rule*).

McLaughlin with Wheeler: *The Letters of Heloise and Abelard: A Translation of their Collected Correspondence and Related Writings*, translated and edited by M. M. McLaughlin with B. Wheeler (The New Middle Ages; New York, 2009). *Letters* 1–8 (with the *Rule*).

The Story of Abelard's Adversities. A Translation with Notes of the 'Historia calamitatum', trans. J. T. Muckle, with a preface by E. Gilson (Toronto, 1954). 2nd rev. edn. in the series Medieval Sources in Translation, iv (Toronto, 1964).

Letter 7 trans. V. Morton in *Guidance for Women in Twelfth-Century Convents*, with an interpretive essay by J. Wogan-Browne (Library of Medieval Women; Woodbridge, 2003), pp. 50–95. *Letters* 1–8 (with the *Rule*).

French

Lettres d'Abailard et d'Héloïse traduites sur les manuscrits de la Bibliothèque royale par E. Oddoul, précédées d'un essai historique par M. et Mme. Guizot. Édition illustrée par J. Gigoux (2 vols., Paris, 1839; repr., with some changes, 1980 (Plan-de-la-Tour, Var)).

Abailard et Héloïse: Essai historique par M. et Mme. Guizot, suivi des lettres d'Abailard et Héloïse traduites sur les manuscrits de la Bibliothèque royale par E. Oddoul (new edn.; Paris, 1853).

Abélard et Héloïse, Correspondance, trans. P. Zumthor (Collection 10/18, Série 'Bibliothèque du moyen âge'; Paris, 1979). *Letters* 1–5.

Pierre Abélard: Lamentations. Histoire de mes malheurs. Correspondance avec Héloïse, trans. P. Zumthor (Actes sud, Collection Babel, lii; Paris, 1992). *Letters* 1–5.

Héloïse et Abélard: Lettres et vies. Introduction, traduction, notes, bibliographie et chronologie, ed. Y. Ferroul (Paris, 1996).

Abélard et Héloïse, Correspondance, trans. O. Gréard, Preface by E. Gilson (Folio classique; Paris, 2000). First published in 1859, revised by E. Bouyé.

E. Hicks and T. Moreau. See above, p. 537.

Héloïse et Abélard, Correspondance. Édition bilingue, ed. and trans. R. Oberson (Paris, 2008). Includes the Latin text printed by Duchesne–d'Amboise.

German

Abaelard: Die Leidensgeschichte und der Briefwechsel mit Heloïsa, ed. E. Brost (Sammlung Weltliteratur, Mittellateinische Literatur; 4th edn.; Heidelberg, 1979).

Abaelards 'Historia calamitatum'. Text – Übersetzung – literaturwissenschaftliche Modellanalysen, ed. D. N. Hasse (De Gruyter Texte; Berlin, 2002), pp. 3–101 (with the Latin text, based on the editions listed above of Muckle, Monfrin, and Hicks, on facing pages).

Italian

Pagani. See above., p. 537.

Other Letters

Apologia

Apologia contra Bernardum, ed. E. M. Buytaert (Petri Abaelardi Opera Theologica, i; *CCCM* xi; 1969), pp. 357–68.

Ruf, P., and Grabmann, M., eds., 'Ein neuaufgefundenes Bruchstück der Apologia Abaelards', *Sitzungsberichte der Bayerischen Akademie der Wissenschaften. Philo.- hist. Abteilung*, 5 (1930).

Eng. trans. Ziolkowski, pp. 116–29.

Confessio fidei ad Heloissam (Confession of faith to Heloise)

Cousin, i. 680–1.
PL clxxviii. 375–8.
Burnett, C. S. F., ed., '"*Confessio fidei ad Heloisam*"—Abelard's last letter to Heloise? A discussion and critical edition of the Latin and medieval French versions', *Mittellateinisches Jahrbuch*, xxi (1986), 147–55, edn. at pp. 152–5.
Ed. with Italian trans. Pagani, pp. 748–51.
Old French trans. (see above), ed. Beggiato, i. 237–9; Hicks, pp. 149–50.
English trans. Radice, pp. 211–12; Levitan, pp. 260–1; McLaughlin with Wheeler, pp. 209–10.

Confessio fidei 'Vniuersis' (Confession of faith 'Vniuersis')

Cousin, ii. 719–23.
PL clxxviii. 105–8.
Burnett, C. S. F., ed., 'Peter Abelard, *Confessio fidei "Universis"*: A critical edition of Abelard's reply to accusations of heresy', *Mediaeval Studies*, xlviii (1986), 111–38; edn. at pp. 132–8.
Old French trans. (see above), ed. Beggiato, i. 241–6; Hicks, pp. 151–5.

Letters 9–14

Cousin, i. 225–36, 618–24, 681–99; ii. 150–1.
PL clxxviii. 325–58.
Smits: *Peter Abelard. Letters IX–XIV*, ed. E. R. Smits (Groningen, 1983).
English trans. Ziolkowski; also McLaughlin with Wheeler, pp. 195–207, 271–91.

Letter 9

Eng. trans. Morton in V. Morton, *Guidance for Women in Twelfth-Century Convents* with an interpretive essay by J. Wogan-Browne (Library of Medieval Women; Woodbridge, 2003), pp. 121–38; also McLaughlin with Wheeler, pp. 195–207.
Ed. with Italian trans. in Pagani, pp. 666–97.

Letter 10

Eng. trans. McLaughlin with Wheeler, pp. 271–8.
Partial edn. in C. Waddell, *The Twelfth Century Cistercian Hymnal before c. 1147* (2 vols.; Cistercian Liturgy Series, i–ii; Gethsemani Abbey, Trappist, Ky., 1984), ii. 5–8 (commentary, i. 64–70).
Italian trans. in E. Arborio, E., '*Dacci oggi il nostro pane*': *Sermo 14 e Lettera 10* (Testi dei padri della chiesa, xlix; Magnano, 2001), pp. 25–35.

Epistola ad Petrum Venerabilem (Heloise, Letter to Peter the Venerable)

Cousin, ii. 715.

Epistola Heloisae abbatissae ad dominum abbatem, ed. G. Constable, in *The Letters of Peter the Venerable*, i (Cambridge, Mass., 1967), *Letter* 167, pp. 400–1.

English trans. Radice, p. 285; Levitan, pp. 272–3; McLaughlin with Wheeler, p. 299.

Epistola contra Bernardum (Letter against Bernard, abbot of Clairvaux)

Epistola contra Bernhardum abbatem, ed. J. Leclercq in 'Études sur S. Bernard et le texte de ses écrits', *Analecta Sacri Ordinis Cisterciensis*, ix (1953), 104–5.

Klibansky, R., ed., 'Peter Abailard and Bernard of Clairvaux: A letter by Abailard', *Mediaeval and Renaissance Studies*, v (1961), 1–27, at pp. 6–7.

Eng. trans. Ziolkowski, pp. 108–10.

Expositio in Hexameron, letter-preface addressed to Heloise

Cousin, i. 626–7.

PL clxxviii. 731–2.

Petri Abaelardi Expositio in Hexaemeron, Prefatio, ed. M. Romig and D. Luscombe (Petri Abaelardi Opera Theologica, v; *CCCM* xv; 2004), pp. 3–5.

Hymns, letter-prefaces addressed to Heloise. See *Hymns* below

Problemata, letter-preface addressed by Heloise to Abelard (Epistola Heloissae ad Petrum Abaelardum)

Cousin, i. 237–8.

PL clxxviii. 677–8.

Eng. trans. Levitan, pp. 257–9; McLaughlin with Wheeler, pp. 213–14.

Edn. with Italian trans. Pagani, pp. 740–3.

Sermons, letter-preface addressed to Heloise

Cousin, i. 350.

PL clxxviii. 379–80.

I sermoni di Abelardo per le monache del Paracleto, ed. De Santis, p. 86.

Eng. trans. Ziolkowski, pp. 70–2.

Ed. with Italian trans. Pagani, pp. 722–5.

Other Writings

Adtendite. See Sermons, '*Adtendite a falsis prophetis*'

Apologia. See above under *Other Letters*

Capitula haeresum XIV

Anonymi Capitula haeresum Petri Abaelardi, ed. E. M. Buytaert (Petri Abaelardi Opera Theologica, ii; *CCCM* xii; 1969), pp. 473–80.

Carmen ad Astralabium

Cousin, i. 340–3; ii. 344–9.
PL clxxviii. 1759–66.
Peter Abelard, Carmen ad Astralabium: A Critical Edition, ed. J. M. A. Rubingh-Bosscher (Groningen, 1987).
English trans. of selected passages by S. Lombardo and B. Thorburn in Levitan, pp. 294–301.
See also C. Wollin, 'Neue Textzeugen des *Carmen ad Astralabium* des Petrus Abaelardus', *Sacris Erudiri*, xlvi (2007), 187–240.

Collationes (or Dialogus inter Philosophum, Iudaeum et Christianum)

Cousin, ii. 643–715.
PL clxxviii. 1609–82.
Peter Abelard, Collationes, ed. and trans. J. Marenbon and G. Orlandi (OMT; Oxford, 2001).
Petrus Abaelardus, Dialogus inter Philosophum, Iudaeum et Christianum, ed. R. Thomas (Stuttgart-Bad Cannstatt, 1970).

Comm. Cantab.

Commentarius Cantabrigiensis in Epistolas Pauli e Schola Petri Abaelardi, ed. A. M. Landgraf (Notre Dame University Publications in Mediaeval Studies, ii, 4 parts; Notre Dame, Ind., 1937–45).

Comm. Rom.

Cousin, ii. 152–356.
PL clxxviii. 783–978.
Commentaria in epistolam Pauli ad Romanos, ed. E. M. Buytaert (Petri Abaelardi Opera Theologica, i; *CCCM* xi; 1969), pp. 39–340.
An *Abbreviation* of this work is ed. A. M. Landgraf, 'Petri Abaelardi Expositionis in Epistolam S. Pauli ad Romanos Abbreviatio', *Bohoslavia*, xxxi (1936), 7–45.
Eng. trans. of Prologue and an extract in A. Minnis and others, *Medieval Literary Theory*, pp. 100–5.

Confessio fidei ad Heloissam (*Confession of faith to Heloise*). See above under *Other Letters*

Confessio fidei 'Vniuersis' (*Confession of faith 'Vniuersis'*). See above under *Other Letters*

De intellectibus

Ed. in *La psicologia di Abelardo e il Tractatus de intellectibus*, ed. L. Urbani Ulivi (Rome, 1976), pp. 101–27.

Ed. with a French translation, *Abélard: Des intellections*. Texte établi, traduit, introduit et commenté par P. Morin (Sic et Non; Paris, 1994).

Dialectica

Partial edn. Cousin in *Ouvrages inédits d'Abélard* (Paris, 1836), pp. 171–503.

Petrus Abaelardus. Dialectica, ed. L. M. de Rijk (Wijsgerige Teksten en Studies, i; Assen, 1956; 2nd edn., Assen, 1970).

Dialogus inter Philosophum, Iudaeum et Christianum. See *Collationes*

Editio super Porphyrium, Glossae in Categorias, Editio super Aristotelem de Interpretatione, Editio super Boethium de divisionibus

Partial edn. of literal glosses on Porphyry and the *Categories* and of the beginning of glosses on *De interpretatione* in *Ouvrages inédits d'Abélard*, ed. V. Cousin (Paris, 1836), pp. 551–93, 597–601.

Full edn. by M. Dal Pra in *Pietro Abelardo, Scritti filosofici* (Nuova biblioteca filosofica, ser. II, vol. iii; Rome, 1954), pp. 3–203; 2nd edn., Dal Pra, *Pietro Abelardo, Scritti di logica* (Pubblicazioni della Facoltà di lettere e filosofia dell'Università di Milano, xxxiv; Sezione a cura dell'Istituto di storia della filosofia, iii; Florence, 1969), pp. 3–203.

These glosses are also known as the *Introductiones parvulorum*. Abelard's authorship now seems very unlikely; see Martin, 'A note' and Cameron, 'Abelard's early glosses'. His *Introductiones parvulorum* (mentioned in his *Dialectica*, ed. de Rijk, pp. 329, 353, 482) have not been traced.

Epithalamica

Waddell, C., ed. with melody and trans., '"Epithalamica": An Easter sequence by Peter Abelard', *Musical Quarterly*, lxxii (1986), 239–71, at pp. 248–52.

Dronke, P., ed., 'Amour sacré et amour profane au moyen âge latin: Témoignages lyriques et dramatiques', in P. Dronke, *Sources of Inspiration: Studies in Literary Transformations, 400–1500* (Storia e Letteratura, cxcvi; Rome, 1997), pp. 375–95, at 394–5.

Bell, T. J., ed. and trans., *Peter Abelard after Marriage: The Spiritual Direction of Heloise and her Nuns through Liturgical Song* (Cistercian Studies Series, ccxi; Kalamazoo, Mich., 2007), pp. 21–3.

See also Colette, 'Un ensemble de *planctus* attribués à Abélard'.

Epitome theologiae christianae. See *Sententie*

Ethica or Scito te ipsum

Cousin, ii. 593–642.

PL clxxviii. 633–78.

Ed. with an English trans. in D. E. Luscombe, *Peter Abelard's Ethics* (OMT; Oxford, 1971).

Ed. D. E. Luscombe, with an Italian trans. by M. Dal Pra, *Pietro Abelardo, Conosci te stesso o Etica* (Classici della filosofia, xi; Florence, 1976).

Ed. R. M. Ilgner in *Petri Abaelardi Opera Theologica*, iv (*CCCM* cxc; 2001).

Ed. with a German trans. by R. M. Ilgner in *Petrus Abaelardus. Scito te ipsum. Erkenne dich selbst* (Fontes Christiani, xliv; Turnhout, 2011).

Expositio in Hexameron

Expositio in Hexameron edita a Mary Romig auxilium praestante David Luscombe and *Abbreuiatio Petri Abaelardi Expositionis in Hexameron edita a Charles Burnett auxilium praestante David Luscombe* (Petri Abaelardi Opera Theologica, v; *CCCM* xv; 2004).

The *Expositio* (without the *Abbreuiatio*) is also in Cousin, i. 625–79 and *PL* clxxviii. 731–84.

Parts of the *Expositio* which are not included in *PL* clxxviii. 731–84 were ed. E. M. Buytaert in 'Abelard's *Expositio in Hexaemeron*', *Antonianum*, xliii (1968), 163–94.

Ed. of the preface with Italian trans. by Pagani, pp. 730–3.

English trans. of the preface by Ziolkowski, pp. 60–3.

Expositio orationis dominicae

Burnett, C. S. F., ed., 'The *Expositio orationis dominicae "Multorum legimus orationes"*: Abelard's Exposition on the Lord's Prayer?', *Revue bénédictine*, xcv (1985), 66–72.

See *Checklist*, pp. 184–5 and no. 287.

Expositio symboli apostolorum

Cousin, i. 603–15.

PL clxxviii. 617–30.

Expositio symboli Athanasii

Cousin, i. 615–17.

PL clxxviii. 629–32.

Glossae super Peri hermeneias

Petrus Abaelardus. Glossae super Peri hermeneias, ed. K. Jacobi and C. Strub (*CCCM* ccvi; 2010). And see *Logica 'Ingredientibus'* below.

Glossae super Porphyrium secundum vocales

Part ed. B. Geyer in *Peter Abaelards philosophische Schriften*, iii: *Aus den anonymen Glossen des Cod. Ambr. M 64 sup.* (*BGPTMA*, xxi (4); Münster, 1933; 1973²), pp. 581–8.

Complete but unreliable edn. by C. Ottaviano in *Testi medioevali inediti* (Fontes Ambrosiani, iii; Florence, 1933), *Glossae super librum Porphyrii secundum vocales*, pp. 106–207.

Glossae super Topica

Super Topica Glossae, ed. M. Dal Pra in *Pietro Abelardo: Scritti filosofici* (Nuova biblioteca filosofica, ser. II, vol. iii; Rome, 1954), pp. 205–330; 2nd edn., *Pietro Abelardo: Scritti di logica* (Pubblicazioni della Facoltà di lettere e filosofia dell'Università di Milano, xxxiv; Sezione a cura dell'Istituto di storia della filosofia, iii; Florence, 1969), pp. 205–330.

Hebet sidus. See *Bibliography: Primary Sources*

Hymns (Paraclete Hymnary)

Cousin, i. 295–328.

PL clxxviii. 1765–1816.

Petri Abaelardi Peripatetici Palatini Hymnarius Paraclitensis sive Hymnorum Libelli Tres ad fidem codicum Bruxellensis et Calmontani, ed. G. M. Dreves (Paris, 1891; repr. Bologna, 1970).

Peter Abelard's Hymnarius Paraclitensis: An Annotated Edition with Introduction, i: *Introduction to Peter Abelard's Hymns*; ii: *The Hymnarius Paraclitensis. Text and Notes*, ed. J. Szövérffy (Albany, NY, 1975).

Hymn Collections from the Paraclete, i: *Introduction and Commentary*; ii: *Edition*, ed. C. Waddell (Cistercian Liturgy Series, viii–ix; Gethsemani Abbey, Trappist, Ky., 1989, 1987). Waddell shows the sometimes variant numbering of the hymns found in the edn. of Szövérffy.

Eng. trans. Sister Jane Patricia in *The Hymns of Abelard in English Verse* (Lanham, Md., 1986).

Ed. of the prefaces to the three books of *Hymns* with Italian trans. by Pagani, pp. 704–17.

Eng. trans. of the prefaces in C. J. Mews, 'Liturgy and identity at the Paraclete: Heloise, Abelard and the evolution of Cistercian reform', in Stewart and Wulfstan, *Poetic and Musical Legacy*, pp. 30–3 and Ziolkowski, pp. 40–51.

Institutio or *Rule*. See *Editions of the Letter Collection* above

Introductio ad theologiam. See *TSch*

Introductiones parvulorum. See above, *Editio super Porphyrium*

Logica 'Ingredientibus'

Peter Abaelards philosophische Schriften, i: *Die Logica 'Ingredientibus'*, ed. B. Geyer (*BGPTMA* xxi (1–3); 1919–27).

Part of the third part of the *Logica 'Ingredientibus'—Super Periermenias* XII–XIV—has been ed. L. Minio-Paluello in *Twelfth-Century Logic: Texts and Studies*, ii: *Abaelardiana inedita* (Rome, 1958), pp. 3–108. For an edn. by Jacobi and Strub of the whole of this commentary see *Glossae super Peri hermeneias* above.

For the glosses on Boethius, *De differentiis topicis*, which are associated by some with the *Logica 'Ingredientibus'*, see *Glossae super Topica* above.

English trans. of passages in this work treating of universals in P. Spade, *Five Texts on the Medieval Problem of Universals: Porphyry, Boethius, Abelard, Duns Scotus, Ockham* (Indianapolis, 1994), pp. 26–56.

Logica 'Nostrorum petitioni sociorum'

Peter Abaelards philosophische Schriften, ii: *Die Logica 'Nostrorum petitioni sociorum'. Die Glossen zu Porphyrius. Mit einer Auswahl aus anonymen Glossen, Untersuchungen und einem Sachindex*, ed. B. Geyer (*BGPTMA*, xxi (4); 1933, 1973^{2}), pp. 505–80.

Lux orientalis

A poem in praise of the Virgin Mary attributed to Abelard and ed. Wollin, 'Zwei geistliche Gedichte des Petrus Abaelardus', pp. 296–303. *Checklist* no. 359.

Parce continuis. See *Bibliography: Primary Sources*

Planctus

Cousin, i. 333–9.

PL clxxviii. 1817–24.

Pietro Abelardo, I 'Planctus'. Introduzione, testo critico, trascrizioni musicali, ed. G. Vecchi (Istituto di filologia romanza della Università di Roma: Collezione di testi e manuali, xxxv; Modena, 1951).

Planctus I: Dinae filiae Jacob, II: Jacob super filios suos, IV: Israel super Samson, V: David super Abner, VI: David super Saul et Jonathan, ed. W. Meyer, *Gesammelte Abhandlungen zur Mittellateinischen Rhythmik*, i (Berlin, 1905), pp. 355–74.

Planctus I: Dinae filiae Jacob, IV: Israel super Samson, VI: David super Saul et Jonathan, ed. P. Dronke in *Poetic Individuality in the Middle Ages: New Departures in Poetry, 1000–1150* (2nd edn.; Westfield Publications in

Medieval Studies, i; Westfield College: University of London, 1986), pp. 146, 121–3 (with trans.), 203–9 (with melody transcribed by I. Bent).

Planctus III: *Virginum Israel super filia Jephtae Galaditae*, ed. W. Meyer and W. Brambach in W. Meyer, *Gesammelte Abhandlungen zur Mittellateinischen Rhythmik*, i (Berlin, 1905), pp. 340–6.

Ed. von den Steinen, 'Die Planctus Abaelards – Jephthas Tochter', *Mittellateinisches Jahrbuch*, iv (1967), 122–44.

Planctus V. Text and French translation in A. Wouters, 'Un larme pour Abner: une lamentation de l'Ancien Testament remaniée par Pierre Abélard', in Jolivet and Habrias, ed., *Pierre Abélard. Colloque international de Nantes*, pp. 295–306.

Planctus VI: *David super Saul et Jonathan*, ed. L. Weinrich, '"*Dolorum solatium*": Text und Musik von Abaelards Planctus David', *Mittellateinisches Jahrbuch*, v (1968), 59–78. Transcription with melody by Ian Bent in P. Dronke, *Poetic Individuality in the Middle Ages: New Departures in Poetry, 1000–1150* (2nd edn.; Westfield Publications in Medieval Studies, i; Westfield College: University of London, 1986), pp. 203–8. See also Colette, 'Un ensemble de *planctus* attribués à Abélard'.

English trans. of *Planctus* III and VI by S. Lombardo and B. Thorburn in Levitan, pp. 284–92.

French trans. in *Pierre Abélard: Lamentations. Histoire de mes malheurs. Correspondance avec Héloise*, ed. P. Zumthor (Actes sud, Collection Babel, lii; Arles, 1992).

German trans. in *Peter Abaelard als Dichter. Mit einer erstmaligen Übersetzung seiner Klagelieder ins Deutsche*, trans. U. Niggli (Tübingen, 2007).

Italian edn. and trans. M. Sannelli, *Pietro Abelardo: Planctus* (Littera, iii; Trento, 2002).

Problemata

Cousin, i. 237–95.

PL clxxviii. 677–730.

Eng. trans. E. M. McNamer, *The Education of Heloise: Methods, Content and Purpose of Learning in the Twelfth Century* (Medieval Studies, viii; Lewiston, NY, 1991), pp. 111– 83.

Also McLaughlin with Wheeler, pp. 213–67.

Rule or *Institutio*. See *Editions of the Letter Collection* above

Scito teipsum. See *Ethica*

Sententie

Excerpts in Cousin, ii. 567–92.

PL clxxviii. 1695–1758.

Sententie Magistri Petri Abaelardi, ed. D. Luscombe with the assistance of

J. Barrow, C. Burnett, K. Keats-Rohan, and C. J. Mews, and *Liber Sententiarum Magistri Petri*, ed. C. J. Mews with the assistance of D. Luscombe (Petri Abaelardi Opera Theologica, vi; *CCCM* xiv; 2006).

Sententie magistri Petri Abelardi (Sententie Hermanni), ed. S. Buzzetti (Pubblicazioni della Facoltà di lettere e filosofia dell'Università di Milano, ci; Sezione a cura del'Istituto di Storia della Filosofia, xxxi; Florence, 1983).

Sententiae Florianenses

Sententiae Florianenses, ed. H. Ostlender (Florilegium Patristicum, xix; Bonn 1929).

Sententie secundum M. Petrum

Ed. L. Minio-Paluello in *Twelfth-Century Logic: Texts and Studies*, ii: *Abaelardiana inedita* (Rome, 1958), pp. 109–21.

Sermons

Sermons 1–34, *PL* clxxviii. 379–610.

Sermons 2, 4, 14, 26 (= 25 in *PL* clxxviii), 32, and 34, ed. P. De Santis in *I sermoni di Abelardo per le monache del Paracleto* (Mediaevalia Lovaniensia, Series 1/Studia, xxxi; Leuven, 2002).

Sermon 30, ed. A. Granata, 'La dottrina dell'elemosina nel sermone "Pro Sanctimonialibus de Paraclito" di Abelardo', *Aevum*, xlvii (1973), 32–59, at pp. 54–9.

German trans. in E. Brost, *Abaelard: Die Leidengeschichte und der Briefwechsel mit Heloisa* (Sammlung Weltliteratur; Mittellateinische Literatur; 4th edn.; Heidelberg, 1979), pp. 388–99.

Sermon 'Adtendite a falsis prophetis', ed. L. J. Engels, '*Adtendite a falsis prophetis* (Ms. Colmar 128, ff. 152v/153v): Un texte de Pierre Abélard contre les Cisterciens retrouvé? in *Corona Gratiarum: Miscellanea patristica, historica et liturgica Eligio Dekkers O.S.B. XII lustra complenti oblata* (2 vols.; Bruges, 1975), ii. 195–228.

Eng. trans. in C. Waddell, '*Adtendite a falsis prophetis*: Abelard's earliest known anti-Cistercian diatribe', *Cistercian Studies Quarterly: An International Review of the Monastic and Contemplative Spiritual Tradition*, xxxix (2004), 371–98.

SN: Sic et non

Excerpts in *Ouvrages inédits d'Abélard*, ed. V. Cousin (Paris, 1836), pp. 1–163.

PL clxxviii. 1329–1610.

Peter Abailard, Sic et Non: A Critical Edition, ed. B. B. Boyer and R. McKeon (Chicago, 1976–7).

Eng. trans. of Prologue in A. Minnis and others, *Medieval Literary Theory*, pp. 87–100.

Soliloquium

Cousin, ii. 727–9.
PL clxxviii. 1876–80.
Ed. and trans. C. Burnett, 'Peter Abelard "*Soliloquium*": A critical edition', *Studi medievali*, 3ª ser., xxv (2) (1984), 857–94.

Super Topica Glossae. See *Glossae super Topica* above

TChr: Theologia Christiana

Cousin, ii. 357–566, 804–9.
PL clxxviii. 1123–1330.
Theologia Christiana, ed. E. M. Buytaert (Petri Abaelardi Opera Theologica, ii; *CCCM* xii; 1969), pp. 69–372.

TSch: Theologia 'Scholarium'

Cousin, ii. 1–149.
PL clxxviii. 979–1114.
Theologia 'Summi boni', Theologia 'Scholarium', ed. E. M. Buytaert and C. J. Mews (Petri Abaelardi Opera Theologica, iii; *CCCM* xiii; 1987), pp. 309–549.
Short versions (*tsch*) ed. Buytaert (Petri Abaelardi Opera Theologica, ii; *CCCM* xii; 1969), pp. 399–451 (introd., pp. 373–98).

TSum: Theologia 'Summi boni'

Abaelards 1121 zu Soissons verurtheilter Tractatus de unitate et trinitate divina, ed. R. Stölzle (Freiburg im Breisgau, 1891).
Peter Abaelards Theologia 'Summi boni', ed. H. Ostlender (*BGPTMA* xxxv (2–3); 1939).
Theologia 'Summi boni', Theologia 'Scholarium', ed. E. M. Buytaert and C. J. Mews (Petri Abaelardi Opera Theologica, iii; *CCCM* xiii; 1987), pp. 83–201.
French trans. in *Abélard, Du bien suprême (Theologia Summi boni)*. Introduction, traduction et notes, ed. and trans. J. Jolivet (Cahiers d'études médiévales, iv; Montreal, 1978).
French trans. in *Abélard, De l'unité et de la trinité divines (Theologia Summi boni)*. Introduction, traduction et notes, ed. and trans. J. Jolivet (Sic et non; Paris, 2001). Takes into account the edition of the Latin text by Buytaert and Mews.
Ed. with German trans. in *Peter Abaelard, Theologia Summi boni. Tractatus de unitate et trinitate divina. Abhandlung über die göttliche Einheit und*

Dreieinigkeit . . . Lateinisch-Deutsch, ed. and trans. U. Niggli (Meiner: Philosophische Bibliothek, cccxcv; Hamburg, 1989; repr. Hamburg, 1991). Introduction, Latin text from the edition by Ostlender with some corrections—with reference also to the edition by Buytaert and Mews—and with German translation on facing pages, and notes.

Tractatus de intellectibus. See *De intellectibus*

Tractatus de unitate et trinitate diuina. See *TSum*

Versus de sancta Maria virgine, inc. *Lux orientalis*

Ed. C. Wollin, 'Zwei geistliches Gedichte des Petrus Abaelardus', pp. 302–3

Versus in laudem crucis, inc. *Quam venerabilis*

Ed. C. Wollin, 'Zwei geistliches Gedichte des Petrus Abaelardus', p. 310

APPENDIX C

DOCUMENTS RELATING TO THE EARLY HISTORY OF THE ORATORY OF THE PARACLETE

'Book of *Burials*'. See *Obituary of the Paraclete*

Breviary of the Paraclete

Bre iiiA: *The Paraclete Breviary, Chaumont, Bibliothèque Municipale Manuscript 31*, iiiA: *Edition, Kalendar and Temporal Cycle*, ed. C. Waddell (Cistercian Liturgy Series, v; Gethsemani Abbey, Trappist, Ky., 1983).

Bre iiiB: *The Paraclete Breviary, Chaumont, Bibliothèque Municipale, Manuscript 31*, iiiB: *Edition, The Sanctoral Cycle*, ed. C. Waddell (Cistercian Liturgy Series, vi; Gethsemani Abbey, Trappist, Ky., 1983).

Bre iiiC: *The Paraclete Breviary, Chaumont, Bibliothèque Municipale, Manuscript 31*, iiiC: *Edition, Common of Saints, Varia, Indices*, ed. C. Waddell (Cistercian Liturgy Series, vii; Gethsemani Abbey, Trappist, Ky., 1983).

Cartulary of the Paraclete

Cartulaire de l'abbaye du Paraclet, ed. C. Lalore (Collection des principaux Cartulaires du diocèse de Troyes, ii; Paris, 1878).

Charters and Bulls for the Paraclete

See *Cartulary of the Paraclete* (above); also *Checklist*, nos. 416–41, and H. Tribout de Morembert, 'Quatre bulles pour l'abbaye du Paraclet (1156–1208) conservées aux Archives municipales de Metz', *Annuaire de la Société d'Histoire et d'Archéologie de la Lorraine*, lxix (1969), pp. 103–6.

Diurnal of the Paraclete. See *Breviary of the Paraclete*

Hymnary of the Paraclete (Hymnarius Paraclitensis)

Petri Abaelardi Peripatetici Palatini Hymnarius Paraclitensis sive Hymnorum Libelli Tres ad fidem codicum Bruxellensis et Calmontani, ed. G. M. Dreves (Paris, 1891; repr. Bologna, 1970).

Institutio or *Rule*. See *Editions of the Letter Collection* in Appendix A

Institutes. See *Institutiones nostre*

Institutiones nostre

The Paraclete Statutes, Institutiones nostrae. Troyes, Bibliothèque Municipale

Ms 802, ff. 89r–90v. Introduction, Edition, Commentary, ed. C. Waddell (Cistercian Liturgy Series, xx; Gethsemani Abbey, Trappist, Ky., 1987).

Cousin, i. 213–24.

PL clxxviii. 313–26.

English trans. by C. J. Mews, 'Heloise, the Paraclete liturgy and Mary Magdalen', in Stewart and Wulstan, *Poetic and Musical Legacy*, pp. 109–12; also by McLaughlin with Wheeler, pp. 313–15.

Obituary of the Paraclete

Obituaires de la Province de Sens, iv: *Diocèses de Meaux et de Troyes*, ed. A. Molinier (*Recueil des historiens de la France*, ed. A. Boutillier du Retail and P. Piétresson de Saint-Aubin; Paris, 1923), pp. 388–403 ('Book of Burials'), pp. 404–30 (*Obituary*)

Collection des principaux obituaires et confraternités du diocèse de Troyes, ed. C. Lalore (Collection de documents inédits relatifs à la ville de Troyes et à la Champagne méridionale publiés par la Société académique de l'Aube, ii; Troyes, 1882), pp. 12, 446–60 ('Book of Burials'/'Livre des sépultures'), pp. 460–73 (extracts from an 18th-century copy, now Troyes, Médiathèque, MS 2540, of the *Obituary*/'Necrologium Paracliti').

Ordinary or Ordinal of the Paraclete

The Old French Paraclete Ordinary, Paris, Bibliothèque nationale, Ms. français 14410, and the Paraclete Breviary, Chaumont, Bibliothèque Municipale Ms 31, i: *Introduction and Commentary* by C. Waddell; ii: *The Old French Paraclete Ordinary, Paris, Bibliothèque nationale Ms. français 14410. Dual Transcription. Edition*, ed. C. Waddell (Cistercian Liturgy Series, iii and iv; Gethsemani Abbey, Trappist, Ky., 1985 and 1983).

Problemata. See *Problemata* in Appendix A.

Rule. See *Institutio* above

Sermons for the Paraclete. See *Sermons* in Appendix A

CONCORDANCE

The following is a concordance between (*a*) the sections of the present edition; (*b*) the column numbers with letters of the edition in *PL* clxxviii (reprinted from Duchesne–d'Amboise); (*c*) the line numbers of the edition made by Monfrin of *Letters* 1, 2, and 4; (*d*) the page numbers of the editions of Muckle and McLaughlin; (*e*) the sections of the edition of Pagani. For full details of these editions see Appendix B, pp. 537–8.

(*a*)	(*b*)	(*c*)	(*d*)	(*e*)
Letter 1				
1	113A	1	175	1
2	113A	8	175	2
3	115B	31	176	3
4	116A	45	176	4
5	117A	58	177	4
6	118A	70	177	5
7	119C	101	178	5
8	120A	117	179	5–6
9	122A	155	179	7
10	123A	164	180	8
11	124A	180	180	9
12	125B	222	181	10
13	126A	241	181	11
14	126A	252	181	11
15	126C	272	182	11
16	126D	280	182	12
17	127B	300	183	13
18	128A	332	183	14
19	128B	347	184	14
20	128C	363	184	14
21	129A	377	184	15
22	129C	400	185	16
23	129C	410	185	16
24	130A	425	185	17–18
25	131A	467	186	18
26	131B	483	187	19
27	132D	551	189	19
28	133A	559	189	20
29	133B	573	189	20
30	135A	592	190	21
31	136A	623	190	21
32	136B	642	191	22
33	136C	654	191	23
34	137A	663	191	23
35	140A	690	192	24
36	142A	702	192	24
37	146A	721	193	25
38	147A	736	193	26
39	147B	751	193	27
40	148A	782	194	28
41	149A	823	195	29
42	149B	838	195	30
43	150A	868	195	31
44	150C	891	196	31
45	151A	910	196	32
46	153A	928	197	32
47	153A	941	198	33
48	155A	962	198	34
49	155B	982	198	35
50	156A	996	198	36
51	156C	1017	199	36
52	159A	1038	199	37
53	161C	1094	200	38
54	162A	1120	201	39
55	162B	1130	201	39
56	162D	1158	201	39
57	162D	1167	202	40
58	163C	1196	202	41
59	164A	1213	203	42
60	164C	1229	203	43
61	166A	1255	204	44
62	167A	1283	204	45
63	168A	1304	205	46
64	170A	1321	205	47
65	173A	1341	206	48
66	177A	1381	207	49
67	177B	1400	207	50
68	178B	1445	208	51
69	178C	1464	208	51
70	178D	1477	209	52
71	179A	1489	209	53

(a)	(b)	(c)	(d)	(e)
72	179D	1523	210	54
73	180A	1534	210	54
74	180B	1560	210	55
75	181A	1589	211	56

Letter 2

(a)	(b)	(c)	(d)	(e)
1	181B	4	68	1
2	181B	9	68	1–2
3	182B	32	68	3–4
4	182C	43	68	4
5	183A	62	69	5–6
6	183C	76	69	6
7	183D	92	70	7
8	184B	114	70	8
9	184C	127	70	9
10	184D	143	70	10
11	185A	162	71	11
12	185C	178	71	11–12
13	185D	194	71	12–13
14	186B	217	72	14
15	186C	231	72	15
16	187A	257	73	15–16

Letter 3

(a)	(b)	(c)	(d)	(e)
1	187A		73	1
2	187D		73	2–3
3	188A		74	4
4	189A		74	5
5	189B		74	6
6	189D		75	7
7	189D		75	8
8	190C		75	9
9	190D		76	10
10	191A		76	11
11	191C		76	12
12	192A		76	13
13	192C		77	14

Letter 4

(a)	(b)	(c)	(d)	(e)
1	191D	2	77	1
2	193A	11	77	2
3	193B	26	77	2
4	193C	33	78	3
5	193D	54	78	3
6	194A	67	78	4
7	194B	81	78	4
8	194D	97	79	5
9	195B	122	79	5
10	195C	133	79	6–7
11	195D	153	80	7–8
12	196D	193	80	9
13	197A	208	81	9–10
14	197B	221	81	10–11
15	197D	247	81	11
16	198A	261	82	11–12
17	198C	282	82	13

Letter 5

(a)	(b)	(c)	(d)	(e)
1	199A		82	1
2	199B		83	1
3	199B		83	2
4	199C		83	2
5	200C		84	3
6	201B		84	3
7	201D		84	4
8	202A		85	5
9	202C		85	6
10	202D		85	7
11	203B		86	8
12	203C		86	9
13	203D		86	9
14	204A		86	9
15	204A		87	10
16	204D		87	11
17	205C		88	12
18	206A		88	13
19	206A		88	14
20	206C		89	15
21	206D		89	15
22	207A		89	16
23	207D		90	17
24	208A		90	18
25	208B		90	18
26	208C		91	18
27	208D		91	19
28	209B		91	20
29	209C		91	21
30	210B		92	22
31	210C		92	23
32	210D		93	24
33	211A		93	25
34	211B		93	25
35	212A		93	26

Letter 6

(a)	(b)	(c)	(d)	(e)
1	213A		241	1
2	213B		241	2
3	213B		242	3
4	213C		242	4
5	214A		242	5
6	214B		242	6
7	214C		243	7

(*a*)	(*b*)	(*c*)	(*d*)	(*e*)
8	214D		243	8
9	215A		243	9
10	215C		243	10
11	215D		244	11
12	216B		244	12
13	216D		245	13
14	217B		245	14–15
15	218A		246	15
16	218B		246	15–16
17	218C		246	16
18	219A		247	17
19	219D		248	18
20	220B		248	19
21	220D		248	20
22	221C		249	21
23	222A		249	22
24	222D		250	23
25	223C		251	24
26	224A		251	25
27	224B		252	26
28	224C		252	27
29	225A		252	28
30	225B		252	29
31	226A		252	30
32	226A		253	31
33	226B		253	32

Letter 7

(*a*)	(*b*)	(*c*)	(*d*)	(*e*)
1	225D		253	1
2	225D		253	1
3	227A		254	1–2
4	227D		254	2
5	228A		254	3
6	228C		255	4
7	229B		255	5
8	229C		256	6
9	229D		256	7–8
10	230B		256	8
11	231D		258	9–10
12	232C		258	11–12
13	233D		259	13–14
14	234C		260	14
15	235A		261	15–16
16	236B		262	17
17	237B		263	18
18	238A		263	19–20
19	238D		264	21
20	239B		264	22
21	240B		265	22–4
22	240D		266	25–6
23	241C		266	26
24	241D		267	26
25	242B		267	26–7
26	242D		268	28
27	243B		268	29–30
28	243D		269	31
29	244A		269	31–3
30	245A		270	34
31	245C		270	35
32	245D		271	36
33	246B		271	37
34	247A		272	37
35	247C		272	38
36	247D		273	39
37	248D		273	40
38	249A		274	40
39	249C		274	41
40	249D		274	42
41	250A		275	42
42	250C		275	43
43	251A		276	43
44	251D		277	44
45	253A		278	45–6
46	253B		278	46
47	253C		278	47
48	253D		279	48
49	254B		279	49
50	255B		280	49
51	256C		281	50

Letter 8

(*a*)	(*b*)	(*c*)	(*d*)	(*e*)
1	255D		242	1
2	257A		242	1
3	257A		242	1
4	257C		243	2
5	257D		243	2

Institutio

(*a*)	(*b*)	(*c*)	(*d*)	(*e*)
1	258A		243	3
2	258B		243	4
3	258C		243	5
4	259A		244	6
5	259B		244	7
6	259D		244	8
7	260A		245	9
8	260C		245	10
9	261A		246	10–12
10	261B		246	12
11	261C		246	12
12	262A		246	13
13	262C		247	14
14	263A		247	15

(a)	(b)	(c)	(d)	(e)
15	263C		248	16
16	264B		249	17
17	264D		249	18
18	265A		249	19
19	265C		250	20
20	265D		250	21
21	266A		250	22
22	266B		250	23
23	266D		251	24
24	267A		251	24
25	267C		252	25
26	267C		252	25
27	268A		252	26–7
28	268B		252	27
29	268D		253	28
30	269C		253	29–30
31	270A		254	30
32	270B		254	31
33	270D		254	31
34	271B		255	32
35	271C		255	33
36	272A		255	33
37	272C		256	34
38	273B		257	35
39	274A		257	36
40	274B		257	37
41	274D		258	38
42	275A		258	39
43	276A		259	40
44	276B		259	41
45	276D		259	42
46	276D		260	43
47	277A		260	43
48	277A		260	43
49	277B		260	43
50	277B		260	43
51	277B		260	43
52	277C		260	44
53	277D		260	45
54	278A		261	46
55	278D		261	47
56	278D		261	47
57	279B		261	47
58	279C		262	48
59	279D		262	49
60	280A		262	50
61	280C		262	51
62	281A		263	51
63	281B		263	52
64	281B		263	53
65	281D		263	54
66	282A		264	55
67	282B		264	56
68	282C		264	57
69	283A		265	58
70	283D		265	59
71	284A		265	60
72	284C		266	61
73	284D		266	61
74	285A		267	62
75	285B		267	63
76	285D		267	64
77	286A		267	65
78	286C		268	66
79	287C		269	66–7
80	288A		269	67
81	288C		269	67
82	288D		270	68–71
83	290A		271	71
84	290D		271	71
85	290D		272	72
86	291B		272	73
87	292B		273	74
88	292D		273	75–6
89	293B		274	77
90	294B		275	78
91	294D		275	79
92	295A		276	80
93	295C		276	81–2
94	296C		277	83
95	296D		277	84
96	297B		277	85–6
97	298A		278	87–8
98	299A		279	89–90
99	299C		280	91
100	300B		280	92
101	300B		280	93
102	301A		281	93–4
103	301C		281	94
104	301D		282	95
105	301D		282	95
106	302B		282	96
107	302C		282	97
108	302D		282	98
109	303A		283	99–100
110	303C		283	100
111	304A		283	100
112	304B		284	101
113	305A		284	102–3
114	305C		285	104
115	306A		285	105
116	306B		285	106

(a)	(b)	(c)	(d)	(e)	(a)	(b)	(c)	(d)	(e)
117	306D		286	107	123	310C		289	113
118	307D		287	108	124	311A		290	113–14
119	308A		287	109	125	311C		290	114–15
120	308C		287	110	126	312A		290	115
121	309C		288	111	127	313A		291	116
122	309D		288	112	128	314A		292	117

BIBLIOGRAPHY

The primary sources listed in Appendix B, Writings of Peter Abelard and Heloise, and in Appendix C, Documents relating to the Early History of the Oratory of the Paraclete, have been integrated here under the title or author's name. Editions which have appeared in articles in journals may be found under Secondary Works.

PRIMARY SOURCES

Abelard, Peter, *Apologia contra Bernardum*, ed. E. M. Buytaert (Petri Abaelardi Opera Theologica, i; *CCCM* xi; 1969), pp. 357–68.

—— *Carmen ad Astralabium: A Critical Edition*, ed. J. M. A. Rubingh-Bosscher (Groningen, 1987).

—— *Collationes*, ed. and trans. J. Marenbon and G. Orlandi (OMT; Oxford, 2001).

—— *Comm. Cantab.—Commentarius Cantabrigiensis in Epistolas Pauli e Schola Petri Abaelardi*, ed. A. M. Landgraf (Notre Dame University Publications in Mediaeval Studies, ii, 4 parts; Notre Dame, Ind., 1937–45).

—— *Comm. Rom.—Commentaria in epistolam Pauli ad Romanos*, ed. E. M. Buytaert (Petri Abaelardi Opera Theologica, i; *CCCM* xi; 1969), pp. 39–340.

—— *Dialectica*. First Complete Edition of the Parisian Manuscript with an Introduction, ed. L. M. de Rijk (2nd rev. edn.; Wijsgerige Teksten en Studies, i; Assen, 1970).

—— *Dialogus inter Philosophum, Iudaeum et Christianum*, ed. R. Thomas (Stuttgart-Bad Cannstatt, 1970).

—— *Ethica*, ed. R. M. Ilgner (Petri Abaelardi Opera Theologica, iv; *CCCM* cxc; 2001).

—— *Ethica*, ed. with an English trans. in D. E. Luscombe, *Peter Abelard's Ethics* (OMT; Oxford, 1971).

—— *Expositio in Hexameron*, ed. M. Romig and D. Luscombe (Petri Abaelardi Opera Theologica, v; *CCCM* xv; 2004), pp. 3–5.

—— *Glossae super Peri hermeneias*, ed. K. Jacobi and C. Strub (*CCCM* ccvi; 2010).

—— *Historia Calamitatum*: *The Story of Abelard's Adversities: A Translation with Notes of the Historia calamitatum*, trans. J. T. Muckle, with a preface by E. Gilson (Toronto, 1954). 2nd revised edn. in the series Mediaeval Sources in Translation, iv (Toronto, 1964).

—— *Hymn Collections from the Paraclete*, i: *Introduction and Commentary*; ii:

Edition, ed. C. Waddell (Cistercian Liturgy Series, viii–ix; Gethsemani Abbey, Trappist, Ky., 1989, 1987).

—— *The Hymns of Abelard in English Verse*, trans. Sister Jane Patricia (Lanham, Md., 1986).

—— *Institutiones nostrae*, in *The Paraclete Statutes, Institutiones nostrae. Troyes, Bibliothèque Municipale Ms 802, ff. 89r–90v. Introduction, Edition, Commentary*, ed. C. Waddell (Cistercian Liturgy Series, xx; Gethsemani Abbey, Trappist, Ky., 1987).

—— *Letters IX–XIV*, ed. E. R. Smits (Groningen, 1983).

—— *Logica 'Nostrorum petitioni sociorum'*, in *Peter Abaelards philosophische Schriften*, ii: *Die Logica 'Nostrorum petitioni sociorum'. Die Glossen zu Porphyrius. Mit einer Auswahl aus anonymen Glossen, Untersuchungen und einem Sachindex*, ed. B. Geyer (*BGPTMA*, xxi (4); 1933, 1973²), pp. 505–80.

—— *Opera*, ed. V. Cousin with C. Jourdain and E. Despois (2 vols.; Paris, 1849, 1859; repr. Hildesheim, 1970).

—— *Peter Abelard's Hymnarius Paraclitensis: An Annotated Edition with Introduction*, i: *Introduction to Peter Abelard's Hymns*; ii: *The Hymnarius Paraclitensis. Text and Notes*, ed. J. Szövérffy (Albany, NY, 1975).

—— *Petri Abaelardi abbatis Ruyensis et Heloissae abbatissae Paracletensis epistolae a prioris editionis erroribus purgatae et cum cod. MS. collatae*, ed. Richard Rawlinson (London, 1718; repr. with a new title page, Oxford, 1728).

—— *Petri Abaelardi filosofi et theologi, abbatis Ruyensis, et Heloisae coniugis eius primae paracletensis abbatissae Opera*, ed. François d'Amboise (Paris, 1616).

—— *Petri Abaelardi Peripatetici Palatini Hymnarius Paraclitensis sive Hymnorum Libelli Tres ad fidem codicum Bruxellensis et Calmontani*, ed. G. M. Dreves (Paris, 1891; repr. Bologna, 1970).

—— *Petri Abaelardi Sancti Gildasii in Britannia abbatis et Heloisae conjugis ejus . . . Opera*, ed. André Duchesne (Paris, 1616).

—— *Planctus III*: *Virginum Israel super filia Jephtae Galaditae*, ed. W. Meyer and W. Brambach in W. Meyer, *Gesammelte Abhandlungen zur Mittellateinischen Rythmik*, i (Berlin, 1905), pp. 340–6.

—— *Planctus VI*: *David super Saul et Jonathan*, ed. L. Weinrich, '"*Dolorum solatium*": Text und Musik von Abaelards Planctus David', *Mittellateinisches Jahrbuch*, v (1968), 59–78. Transcription with melody by Ian Bent in P. Dronke, *Poetic Individuality in the Middle Ages: New Departures in Poetry, 1000–1150* (2nd edn.; Westfield Publications in Medieval Studies, i; Westfield College: University of London, 1986), pp. 203–8.

—— *I sermoni di Abelardo per le monache del Paracleto*, ed. P. De Santis (Mediaevalia Lovaniensia, Series I/Studia, xxxi; Leuven, 2002).

—— *Scritti filosofici*, ed. M. Dal Pra (Nuova biblioteca filosofica, ser. II, vol. iii; Rome, 1954), pp. 3–203; 2nd edn., *Pietro Abelardo, Scritti di logica* (Pubblicazioni della Facoltà di lettere e filosofia dell'Università di Milano, xxxiv; Sezione a cura dell'Istituto di storia della filosofia, iii; Florence, 1969), pp. 3–203.

—— *Sententie Magistri Petri Abaelardi*, ed. D. Luscombe with the assistance of J. Barrow, C. Burnett, K. Keats-Rohan, and C. J. Mews, and *Liber Sententiarum Magistri Petri*, ed. C. J. Mews with the assistance of D. Luscombe (Petri Abaelardi Opera Theologica, vi; *CCCM* xiv; 2006).

—— *Sententie magistri Petri Abelardi (Sententie Hermanni)*, ed. S. Buzzetti (Pubblicazioni della Facoltà di lettere e filosofia dell'Università di Milano, ci; Sezione a cura del'Istituto di Storia della Filosofia, xxxi; Florence, 1983).

—— *SN—Sic et Non: A Critical Edition*, ed. B. B. Boyer and R. McKeon (Chicago, 1976–7).

—— *Soliloquium*, ed. C. Burnett, in 'Peter Abelard "*Soliloquium*": A critical edition', *Studi medievali*, 3[a] ser., xxv (2) (1984), 857–94.

—— *TChr—Theologia Christiana*, ed. E. M. Buytaert (Petri Abaelardi Opera Theologica, ii; *CCCM* xii; 1969), pp. 69–372.

—— *TSch—Theologia 'Summi boni', Theologia 'Scholarium'*, ed. E. M. Buytaert and C. J. Mews (Petri Abaelardi Opera Theologica, iii; *CCCM* xiii; 1987), pp. 309–549.

—— *TSum—Theologia 'Summi boni', Theologia 'Scholarium'*, ed. E. M. Buytaert and C. J. Mews (Petri Abaelardi Opera Theologica, iii; *CCCM* xiii; 1987), pp. 83–201.

—— and Heloise, *Abelard and Heloise: The Letters and Other Writings*, trans. with introduction and notes by W. Levitan (Indianapolis, IN, 2007).

—— —— *Abélard et Héloïse, Correspondance*, trans. O. Gréard, Preface by E. Gilson (Folio classique; Paris, 2000). First published in 1859, revised by E. Bouyé.

—— —— *Epistolario di Abelardo ed Elisa*, ed. Ileana Pagani with comments on the transmission of the text by Giovanni Orlandi (Classici Latini; Turin, 2004).

—— —— *Le lettere di Abelardo ed Eloisa nella traduzione di Jean de Meun*, i: *Testo*; ii: *Introduzione – Apparato – Note – Indice sellettivo delle forme – Indice dei nomi propri*, ed. F. Beggiato (2 vols.; Modena, 1977).

—— —— *The Letters of Abelard and Heloise*, trans. with an Introduction by Betty Radice (Penguin Classics; Harmondsworth, 1974).

—— —— *The Letters of Abelard and Heloise*, trans. with an Introduction and Notes by Betty Radice, rev. M. T. Clanchy (Penguin Classics; London, 2003).

—— —— *The Letters of Heloise and Abelard: A Translation of their Collected Correspondence and Related Writings*, trans. and ed. M. M. McLaughlin with B. Wheeler (The New Middle Ages; New York, 2009).

Abelard, Peter, and Heloise, *Lettres d'Abélard et Héloïse*, ed. and annotated E. Hicks and T. Moreau; Préface by M. Zink; Introduction by J.-Y. Tilliette (Livre de Poche 'Lettres gothiques', no. 4572; Paris, 2007).

—— —— *La Vie et les epistres Pierres Abaelart et Heloys sa fame. Traduction du XIIIe siècle attribuée à Jean de Meun. Avec une nouvelle édition des textes latins d'après le ms. Troyes Bibl. mun. 802*, i: *Introduction, textes*, ed. E. Hicks (Nouvelle Bibliothèque du Moyen Âge, xvi; Paris, 1991).

Acta Conciliorum Oecumenicorum, ed. E. Schwartz (4 vols.; Berlin, 1914–40).

Acta Sanctorum, collecta . . . a Sociis Bollandianis (3rd edn.; Paris, 1863–).

Adalbertus Samaritanus, *Praecepta dictaminum*, ed. F.-J. Schmale (*MGH*, Quellen zur Geistesgeschichte des Mittelalters, iii; Weimar, 1961).

Aelred of Rievaulx, *De spirituali amicitia*, ed. A. Hoste (*CCCM* i; 1971).

Alberic of Monte Cassino, *Breviarium de dictamine*, ed. (in part) L. Rockinger in *Briefsteller und Formelbücher des eilften bis vierzehnten Jahrhunderts* (2 vols.; Quellen und Erörterungen zur bayerischen und deutschen Geschichte, ix (1–2); Munich, 1863–4), i. 29–46.

——*Breviarium de dictamine*, ed. F. Bognini (Edizione Nazionale dei Testi Mediolatini, xxi, Serie 1, xii; Florence, 2008).

—— *Dictaminum radii*, ed. D. M. Inguanez and H. M. Willard in *Alberici Casinensis Flores rhetorici* (Miscellanea Cassinese, xiv; Montecassino, 1938).

Amboise, François d', *Oeuvres complètes*, i *(1568–1584)*, ed. D. Ughetti (Naples, 1973).

Ambrose, *De fuga saeculi*, ed. C. Schenkl (*CSEL* xxxii (2); 1897); *PL* xiv. 569–96. (*PL* references to Ambrose (other than to *PL Supplementum*) are to the first edition.)

—— *De obitu Valentiniani consolatio*, ed. O. Faller (*CSEL* lxxiii; 1955); *PL* xvi. 1357–84.

—— *De paenitentia*, ed. O. Faller (*CSEL* lxxiii; 1955); *PL* xvi. 465–524.

—— *De paradiso*, ed. C. Schenkl (*CSEL* xxxii (1); 1896); *PL* xiv. 275–314.

—— *Expositio evangelii secundum Lucam*, ed. M. Adriaen (*CCSL* xiv; 1957); ed. C. Schenkl (*CSEL* xxxii (4); 1902); *PL* xv. 1527–1850; *PL Supplementum*, i. 569–75.

Analecta Hymnica Medii Aevi, ed. C. Blume and G. M. Dreves (55 vols.; Leipzig, 1886–1922; repr. Frankfurt am Main, 1961).

Andreas Cappellanus, *De amore libri tres*, ed. E. Trojel (Copenhagen, 1892).

Andrew of Fontevraud, *Vita altera Roberti de Arbrissello*, *PL* clxii. 1057–78.

Anselm of Bec and Canterbury, *The Major Works*, ed. B. Davies and G. R. Evans (Oxford World Classics; Oxford, 1998).

—— *Opera omnia*, ed. F. S. Schmitt (6 vols., Edinburgh, 1946–61).

Anselm of Havelberg, *Vita Adalberti II Moguntini*, in *Monumenta Moguntina*, ed. P. Jaffé (Bibliotheca Rerum Germanicarum, iii; Berlin, 1866), pp. 568–603.

Archives d'Anjou: Recueil de documents et mémoires inédits sur cette province publié sous les auspices du Conseil général de Maine-et-Loire, iii, ed. P. Marchegay (Angers, 1854).

Athanasius, *Vita beati Antonii interprete Evagrio*, *PL* lxxiii. 125–69.

Augustine of Hippo, *Confessiones*, ed. L. Verheijen (*CCSL* xxvii; 1981).

—— *Contra epistolam Parmeniani*, ed. M. Petschenig (*CSEL* li; 1908).

—— *Contra Faustum Manichaeum*, ed. I. Zycha (*CSEL* xxv; 1891).

—— *Contra Iulianum imperfectum opus*, ed. M. Zelzer (*CSEL* lxxxv (1); 1974).

—— *De baptismo contra Donatistas*, ed. M. Petschenig (*CSEL* li; 1908).

—— *De bono coniugali*, ed. I. Zycha (*CSEL* xli; 1900).

—— *De bono viduitatis*, ed. I. Zycha (*CSEL* xli; 1900).

—— *De civitate Dei*, ed. B. Dombart and A. Kalb (*CCSL* xlvii–xlviii; 1955); ed. E. Hoffmann (*CSEL* xl (1–2); 1899–1900).

—— *De diversis quaestionibus ad Simplicianum*, ed. A. Mutzenbecher (*CCSL* xliv; 1970).

—— *De diversis quaestionibus octaginta tribus*, ed. A. Mutzenbecher (*CCSL* xlivA; 1975).

—— *De doctrina christiana*, ed. J. Martin (*CCSL* xxxii; 1962).

—— *De Genesi ad litteram*, ed. I. Zycha (*CSEL* xxviii (1); 1894).

—— *De opere monachorum*, ed. I. Zycha (*CSEL* xli; 1900).

—— *De sermone Domini in monte*, ed. A. Mutzenbecher (*CCSL* xxxv; 1967).

—— *De Trinitate*, ed. W. J. Mountain and F. Glorie (*CCSL* l–lA; 1968).

—— *Enarrationes in Psalmos*, ed. E. Dekkers and J. Fraipont (*CCSL* xxxviii–xl; 1956); *Enarrationes in Psalmos* 1–32, ed. C. Weidmann (*CSEL* xciii (1A); 2003).

—— *Epistulae*, ed. A. Goldbacher (*CSEL* xxxiv, xliv, lvii, lviii; 1895–1923).

—— *In Iohannis evangelium tractatus CXXIV*, ed. R. Willems (*CCSL* xxxvi; 1954).

—— *Ordo monasterii*, ed. L. Verheijen, *La Règle de Saint Augustin* (2 vols.; Études Augustiniennes; Paris, 1967), i, pp. 148–52.

—— *Regularis informatio*, ed. L. Verheijen, *La Règle de Saint Augustin* (2 vols.; Études Augustiniennes; Paris, 1967), i, pp. 417–37.

—— *Retractationum libri*, ed. A. Mutzenbecher (*CCSL* lvii; 1984); ed. P. Knoll (*CSEL* xxxvi; 1902); *PL* xxxii. 583–656.

—— *Rule*, ed. L. Verheijen in *La Règle de saint Augustin* (2 vols.; Études augustiniennes; Paris, 1967), i; ed. with English trans. G. Lawless in *Augustine of Hippo and his Monastic Rule* (Oxford, 1987).

—— *Sermones*, *PL* xxxviii–xxxix.

—— *Sermones*, I–L, ed. C. Lambot (*CCSL* xli; 1961).

—— *Sermo CCCLV, De moribus clericorum sermo primus*, ed. C. Lambot in *Sancti Aurelii Augustini, Sermones selecti duodeviginti* (Stromata Patristica et Mediaevalia, i; Utrecht, 1950), pp. 123–31.

Aurelianus of Arles, *Regula ad uirgines* (*PL* lxviii. 399–406).

Aut me cecatum furor excusabit amoris, ed. P. Dronke in *Abaelardiana* (*see* Bibliography: Secondary Works), ii. 280.

Basil of Caesarea, *Regula a Rufino Latine versa*, ed. K. Zelzer (*CSEL* lxxxvi; 1986); *PL* ciii. 485–554.

Bede, *De temporum ratione*, ed. C. W. Jones in *Bedae opera didascalica* (*CCSL* cxxiiiB; 1977), pp. 263–460; trans. with introduction, notes, and commentary, F. Wallis, *Bede: The Reckoning of Time* (Translated Texts for Historians, 29; Liverpool; repr. with corrections 2004).

—— *Expositio Actuum Apostolorum et Retractatio*, ed. M. L. W. Laistner (*CCSL* cxxi; 1983), pp. 1–99; *PL* xcii. 937–96.

—— *Historia ecclesiastica gentis Anglorum*, ed. B. Colgrave and R. A. B. Mynors, *Bede's Ecclesiastical History of the English People* (OMT; Oxford, 1969); ed. C. Plummer, *Baedae Historia Ecclesiastica gentis Anglorum: Venerabilis Baedae opera historica* (2 vols.; Oxford, 1896); *PL* xcv. 21–290.

Benedict of Aniane, *Codex regularum* (attributed to Benedict), *PL* ciii. 393–700.

—— *Concordia regularum*, ed. P. Bonnerue in *Benedicti Anianensis Concordia Regularum* (*CCCM* clxviii (Preface, Concordances, Indexes) and clxviiiA (Text); 1999); *PL* ciii. 701–1380.

Benedict of Nursia, *Rule*, ed. with concordance J. Neufville; French trans. and notes, A. de Vogüé, *La Règle de Saint Benoît* (2 vols.; *SChr* clxxxi–clxxxii; Paris, 1972).

Berengar, *Apologia* and *Letters*, ed. R. M. Thomson in 'The satirical works of Berengar of Poitiers: An edition with introduction', *Mediaeval Studies*, xlii (1980), 89–138; *PL* clxxviii. 1857–76.

—— *Epistola contra Cartusienses*, ed. J. Leclercq, 'Autour de la correspondance de S. Bernard' in '*Sapientiae Doctrina*', in *Mélanges . . . Dom Hildebrand Bascour* (Leuven, 1980), pp. 192–8.

Bernard of Clairvaux, *Opera*, ed. J. Leclercq with C. Talbot and H. M. Rochais in *Sancti Bernardi Opera* (8 vols.; Rome, 1957–77).

—— *Opere di San Bernardo*, ed. F. Gastaldelli with Italian trans. and notes (vols. i, ii, iv, v (1–2), vi (1–2); Milan, 1984, 1990, 2000, 2006–8, 1986–7).

Bernardus. See Magister Bernardus.

Bible. See *Biblia Latina* and Vulgate.

Biblia Latina cum glossa ordinaria, ed. K. Froehlich and M. Gibson (4 vols., Turnhout, 1992).

Boethius, *Commentarii in librum Aristotelis* περι ἑρμηνειας, ed. C. Meiser (2 parts; Teubner; Leipzig, 1877–8).

—— *De consolatione philosophiae*, ed. L. Bieler (*CCSL* xciv; 1957); trans. V. E. Watts, *Boethius, The Consolation of Philosophy* (Penguin Classics; Harmondsworth, 1969).

—— *De syllogismo categorico*, *PL* lxiv, pp. 793–832.

—— *Porphirii Isagoge translatio*, ed. L. Minio-Paluello (Aristoteles Latinus, i, vi–vii; Bruges, 1966).

Bonfons, P., *Les Fastes: Antiquitez et choses plus remarquables de Paris* (Paris, 1605).

Breviarium Romanum (Mechelen, 1919).

Burchard of Worms, *Opera*, *PL* cxl.

Caesarius of Arles, *Oeuvres monastiques*, i: *Oeuvres pour les moniales*, ed. and trans. A. de Vogüé and J. Courreau (*SChr* cccxlv; 1988), pp. 170–273.

—— *The Rule of Nuns of St Caesarius of Arles*, trans. M. C. McCarthy (The Catholic University of America Studies in Mediaeval History; Washington, DC, 1960); partial English trans. by E. Amt in E. Amt (ed.), *Women's Lives in Medieval Europe: A Sourcebook* (London, 1993), pp. 221–31.

—— *Statuta sanctarum uirginum* or *Regula uirginum*, ed. G. Morin (Sancti Caesarii episcopi Arelatensis Opera omnia nunc primum in unum collecta; 2 vols.; Maredsous, 1937–42), ii. 101–29; *PL* lxvii. 1105–16 and *PL Supplementum*, v. 402-3.

Camuzat, N., *Promptuarium sacrarum antiquitatum Tricassinae dioecesis* (Troyes, 1610).

Carmina Burana, ed. A. Hilka and O. Schumann (2 vols. in 4 parts; Heidelberg, 1930–70).

Cartulaire de l'abbaye de Redon en Bretagne, ed. A. Guillotin de Corson (Collection de documents inédits sur l'histoire de France. Première série, Histoire politique; Paris, 1863).

Cartulaire de l'abbaye du Paraclet, ed. C. Lalore (Collection des principaux Cartulaires du diocèse de Troyes, ii; Paris, 1878).

Cartulaire de l'abbaye du Ronceray d'Angers (1028–1184), ed. P. Marchegay (Paris, 1900).

Cassian, *Conferences* (*Conlationes*), ed. M. Petschenig in *Editio altera supplementis aucta curante* G. Kreuz (*CSEL* xiii; 2004); repr. (with modifications) of Petschenig with French trans. and an introd. by E. Pichery in *SChr* xlii, liv, lxiv (1955–9).

Cassiodorus, *Expositio psalmorum*, ed. M. Adriaen (*CCSL* xcvii–xcviii; 1958).

Cassiodorus–Epiphanius, *Historia ecclesiastica tripartita*, ed. W. Jacob and R. Hanslik (*CSEL* lxxi; 1952); *PL* lxix. 879–1214.

Cato, *Catonis Disticha*, ed. J. Nève (Liège 1926); repr. of the edn. by E. Baehrens in *Poetae latini minores* (Leipzig, 1881), iii.

—— *Distichs*, ed. M. Boas in *Disticha Catonis* (Amsterdam, 1952).

—— *The Distichs of Cato*, ed. W. J. Chase (University of Wisconsin Studies in the Social Sciences and History, vii; Madison, 1922).

Catullus, *Carmina*: *C. Valerii Catulli Carmina*, ed. R. A. B. Mynors (Scriptorum classicorum bibliotheca Oxoniensis; Oxford, 1958).

Chrétien de Troyes, *Chansons courtoises*, ed. M. C. Zai (Bern, 1974).

—— *Le Chevalier au lion (Yvain)*, ed. M. Roques (Paris, 1982).

La Chronique de Morigny, 1095–1152, ed. L. Mirot (2nd edn.; Collection des textes pour servir à l'étude et à l'enseignement de l'histoire, xli; Paris, 1912).

Cicero, *De inventione*, in *M. Tulli Ciceronis Scripta . . .* , fasc. 2: *Rhetorici libri duo qui vocantur de inventione*, ed. E. Stroebel (Teubner; Stuttgart, 1977).

—— *Opera omnia . . . consilio et auctoritate Collegii Ciceronianis Studiis provehendis*, ed. H. Drexler (S. Casciani Val di Pesa, 1964).

—— *Tusculanae disputationes*, in *M. Tulli Ciceronis Scripta . . .* fasc. 43, ed. T. Schiche (Teubner; Leipzig, 1915).

Clavis Patrum Latinorum, ed. E. Dekkers and Ae Gaar (3rd edn.; *CCSL*; 1995).

Collectio canonum (ascribed to Isidore of Seville), *PL* lxxxiv. 23–848.

Collectio Hispana, in *La Colección canónica Hispana*, ed. G. Martínez and F. Rodriguez (Monumenta Hispaniae Sacra, Serie Canónica i–iv; Madrid, 1966–84), iii (1982).

Collection des principaux obituaires et confraternités du diocèse de Troyes, ed. C. Lalore (Collection de documents inédits relatifs à la ville de Troyes et à la Champagne méridionale publiés par la Société académique de l'Aube, ii; Troyes, 1882).

Corpus iuris civilis, ed. P. Krueger and others (3 vols.; Dublin, 1872–95) and later editions; repr. Frankfurt am Main, 1967–8).

Declamationes pseudo-Quintilianeae. See Ps.-Quintilian.

De profundis. A *planctus* attributed to Abelard in a MS from Nevers. See Colette, 'Un ensemble de *planctus* attribués à Abélard'.

Diogenes Laertius, *Vitae philosophorum*, in *Diogenis Laertii de clarorum philosophorum vitis, dogmatibus et apophthegmatibus libri decem*, ed. C. G. Cobet. Greek and Latin (Paris, 1850).

Donatus of Besançon, *Regula ad uirgines*, *PL* lxxxvii. 273–98; English trans. by J. A. McNamara and J. Halborg, *The Ordeal of Community and the Rule of Donatus of Besançon* (Toronto, n.d.).

Epiphanius of Salamis, *Panarion* or *Adversus octaginta haereses*, *PG* xli. 173–1200; xlii. 9–832.

Epistolae duorum amantium: Briefe Abaelards und Heloises?, ed. E. Könsgen (Mittellateinische Studien und Texte, 8; Leiden, 1974); text reproduced by C. J. Mews, *The Lost Love Letters of Heloïse and Abelard: Perceptions of Dialogue in Twelfth-Century France*, with English trans. by N. Chiavaroli and C. J. Mews (New York, 1999).

—— French trans. by E. Wolff, *La Lettre d'amour au moyen âge: Boncompagno da Signa, La Roue de Venus; Baudri de Bourgeuil, Poésies; Manuscrit de Tegernsee, Lettres d'amours; Manuscrit de Troyes, Lettres de deux amants (Héloïse et Abélard?)* (Paris, 1996).

—— French trans. by S. Piron, *Lettres des deux amants, attribuées à Héloïse et Abélard* (Paris, 2005); includes Könsgen's Latin text.

—— Italian trans. by G. Ballanti, *Un epistolario d'amore del XII secolo (Abelardo e Eloisa?)* (Rome, 1988).

Eudes Rigaud, *Regestrum visitationum archiepiscopi rothomagensis*, in *Journal des visites pastorales d'Eude Rigaud, archévêque de Rouen, MCCXLVIII–MCCLXIX*, ed. T. Bonnin (Rouen, 1852).

—— *The Register of Eudes of Rouen*, trans. S. M. Brown; ed. J. F. O'Sullivan (Records of Civilization, Sources and Studies, lxxii; New York, 1964).

Eusebius of Caesarea, *Historia ecclesiastica*, in *Eusebius Werke*, ii: *Die Kirchengeschichte*, ed. E. Schwartz; *Die lateinische Übersetzung des Rufinus*, ed. T. Mommsen (Die Griechischen Christlichen Schriftsteller der ersten drei Jahrhunderte; 2 vols.; Leipzig, 1903–8); French trans. of the Greek text by G. Bardy, *SChr* xxxi, xli, lv, lxxiii (1952–60); *PG* xx. 9–906, trans. H. Valesius (Paris, 1659).

Expositio in orationem dominicam 'Inter omnia quae fragilitas', *PL* clxxviii. 611–18. Sometimes attributed to Abelard; cf. *Checklist*, pp. 184–5 and no. 348.

Fulk of Deuil, *Epistola ad Abaelardum*, *PL* clxxviii. 371–6. A passage omitted from this edition was published by Van den Eynde, 'Détails biographiques sur Pierre Abélard', p. 219; English trans. by W. L. North online: <http://www.fordham.edu/halsall/source/fulk-abelard.html>; French trans. by Y. Ferroul, *Héloïse et Abélard: Lettres et vies* (Paris, 1996), pp. 197–205.

Gallia Christiana in provincias ecclesiasticas distributa . . . (16 vols.; Paris, 1716–1865).

Gallia Christiana novissima, i–vii (Montbéliard, 1899–1920).

Gelasius I, Pope, *Epistolae et Decreta*, *PL* lix. 13–190.

Gerald of Wales, *Gemma ecclesiastica*, ed. J. S. Brewer in *Giraldi Cambrensis Opera* (8 vols.; Rolls Series; London, 1861–91), ii (1862); trans. J. J. Hagen, *Gerald of Wales, the Jewel of the Church: A Translation of* Gemma ecclesiastica *by Giraldus Cambrensis* (Davis Medieval Texts and Studies, ii; Leiden, 1979).

—— *Itinerarium Kambriae*, ed. J. F. Dimock in *Giraldi Cambrensis Opera*, vi. 3–152; trans. L. Thorpe, *The Journey through Wales and the Description of Wales* (Penguin Classics; Harmondsworth, 1978).

Gerhoh of Reichersberg, *Opera*, *PL* cxciii–cxciv.

Gilbert Crispin, *Vita Herluini*, ed. A. S. Abulafia and G. R. Evans in *The Works of Gilbert Crispin* (Auctores Britannici Medii Aevi, viii; London, 1986), pp. 183–212.

Girard, Bernard de, *L'Histoire de France* (Paris, 1576; rev. edn. 1585).

Glosses and Commentaries on Aristotelian Logical Texts: The Syriac, Arabic and Medieval Latin Traditions, ed. C. S. F. Burnett (Warburg Institute Surveys and Texts, xxiii; London, 1993).

Glosulae super Priscianum: glosses on Priscian, which survive in a number of copies of the *Institutiones grammaticae*. Cf. Grondeux and Rosier-Catach, '*Glosulae super Priscianum*'.

Grandrue, Claude de, Catalogue of the manuscripts of the abbey of St-Victor. See G. Ouy and V. Gerz von Büren, *Le Catalogue de la bibliothèque de l'abbaye de Saint-Victor* under Secondary Sources.

Gratian of Bologna, *Concordia discordantium canonum*, ed. E. Friedberg in *Corpus iuris canonici*, i: *Decretum magistri Gratiani* (Leipzig, 1879).

Gregory the Great, Pope, *Dialogorum libri IV*, ed. U. Moricca (Fonti per la storia d'Italia, lvii; Rome, 1924); ed. A. de Vogüé (*SChr* ccli, cclx, cclxv; 1978–80); *PL* lxxvii. 127–432.

—— *Homiliae in Evangelia*, ed. R. Étaix (*CCSL* cxli; 1999); *PL* lxxvi. 1075–312.

—— *Homiliae in Hiezechielem*, ed. M. Adriaen (*CCSL* cxlii; 1971).

—— *Moralia in Iob*, ed. M. Adriaen (*CCSL* cxliii–cxliiiB; 1979–85).

—— *Registrum epistularum*, ed. D. Norberg (*CCSL* cxl–cxlA; 1982); ed. P. Ewald and L. M. Hartmann (*MGH*, Epistolae i–ii; 1887–91, 1892–9; repr. 1992); *PL* lxxvii. 431–1352.

—— *Regula pastoralis*, ed. F. Rommel in *Grégoire le Grand, Règle pastorale*, with introd., notes and index by B. Judic and French trans. by C. Morel (*SChr* ccclxxxi–ccclxxxii (1992); *PL* lxxvii. 13–128.

Gregory VII, Pope, *The 'Epistolae Vagantes' of Pope Gregory VII*, ed. and trans. H. E. J. Cowdrey (OMT; Oxford, 1972).

—— *Register*, ed. E. Caspar in *Das Register Gregors VII.* (*MGH*, Epistolae selectae ii, 2 parts; 1920, 1923).

Gregory of Nazianzus, *Orationes*. See Rufinus.

Gregory of Tours, *Libri historiarum X*, ed. B. Krusch and W. Levison (*MGH*, Scriptores rerum Merovingicarum, i (1); Hannover, 1951).

Guibert of Nogent, *Ad commentarios in Genesim. Proemium*, *PL* clvi. 19–22.

—— *De sanctis et eorum pigneribus*, ed. R. B. C. Huygens (*CCCM* cxxviii, 1993), pp. 79–175; *PL* clvi. 607–80.

—— *De vita sua*, ed. with French trans. E.-R. Labande, *Guibert de Nogent: Autobiographie* (Les Classiques de l'Histoire de France au Moyen Âge, xxxiv; Paris, 1981); Eng. trans. by C. C. Swinton Bland, revised by J. F. Benton in *Self and Society in Medieval France: The Memoirs of Abbot Guibert of Nogent (1064?–c.1125)*, ed. J. F. Benton with an introduction and notes (New York, 1970; repr. Toronto, 1984, etc.).

Guillaume de Lorris. See *Roman de la Rose*.

Hebet sidus, no. 169 in *Carmina burana*; ed. and trans. P. Dronke in *Medieval Latin and the Rise of the European Love-Lyric* (2nd edn.; Oxford, 1968), i. 313–14; English trans. by S. Lombardo and B. Thorburn in Levitan, pp. 279–80. (A song sometimes attributed to Abelard; see Dronke and Orlandi, 'New works by Abelard and Heloise?', pp. 140–1 with further references).

Hermann of Tournai, *Liber de restauratione monasterii Sancti Martini Tornacensis*, ed. G. Waitz (*MGH*, Scriptores, xiv; Hannover, 1883).

Hilary of Orleans, *Elegia*: ed. N. M. Häring in 'Die Gedichte und Mysterienspiele des Hilarius von Orleans', *Studi medievali*, 3[a] ser., xvii (1976), 915–68, at 935–7; ed. Bulst (see below), pp. 30–1; *PL* clxxviii. 1855; *Hilarii versus et ludi*, ed. J. J. Champollion-Figeac (Paris, 1838), pp. 14–16; repr. F. J. E. Raby, *The Oxford Book of Medieval Latin Verse* (2nd edn.; Oxford, 1959), pp. 243–5; partly ed. P. Marchegay, 'Charte en vers de l'an 1121 composé par Hilaire, disciple d'Abailard et chanoine du Ronceray d'Angers', *Bibliothèque de l'École des Chartes*, xxxvii (1876), 245–52.

—— *Versus et ludi*: *Hilarii versus et ludi*, ed. J. B. Fuller (New York, 1928); *Hilarii Aurelianensis Versus et Ludi. Epistulae. Ludus Danielis Belovacensis*, ed. W. Bulst and M. L. Bulst-Thiele; *Anhang*: M. Bielitz, *Die Egerton Handschrift. Bemerkungen zur Musik des Daniel-Spiels von Beauvais* (Mittellateinische Studien und Texte, ed. P. G. Schmidt, xvi; Leiden, 1989).

Hildebert of Lavardin, *Letters*, *PL* clxxi. 141–312.

Hilduin, *Rescriptum* to the Emperor Louis, '*Exultavit cor meum*', ed. E. Dümmler (*MGH*, Epistolae, v, Epistolae Karolini Aevi, iii; 1898–9), no. 20, pp. 327–35; *PL* cvi. 13–22.

—— *Vita et passio S. Dionysii, 'Post beatam et salutiferam'*, *PL* cvi. 23–50.

Hippolytus, *Commentary* on the Song of Songs, German trans. G. Nathanael Bonwetsch in *Hippolyts Kommentar zum Hohenlied* (Texte und Untersuchungen, NF viii (2); Leipzig, 1902).

Histoire générale de Paris: Cartulaire général de Paris ou Recueil de documents . . ., ed. R. de Lasteyrie, i (Paris, 1887).

Historia regum Francorum monasterii sancti Dionysii, ed. G. Waitz (*MGH*, Scriptores, ix; Hannover, 1851).

Horace, *Opera*, ed. E. C. Wickham, new edn. by H. W. Garrod (Scriptorum classicorum Bibliotheca Oxoniensis; Oxford, n.d.).

Huc usque, me miseram, no. 126 in *Carmina burana*. (A song which has sometimes been attributed to Heloise. See Dronke and Orlandi, 'New works by Abelard and Heloise?', pp. 143–4, with further references).

Hugh Métel, *Epistolae*, ed. L. Hugo in *Sacrae antiquitatis monumenta historica, dogmatica, diplomatica* (2 vols.; Saint-Die, 1731), ii. 312–412; *Letters* to Heloise, ed. and trans. C. J. Mews, 'Hugh Metel, Heloise, and Peter Abelard: The Letters of an Augustinian Canon and the Challenge of Innovation in Twelfth-Century Lorraine', *Viator*, xxxii (2001), 59–91, at pp. 89–91.

Hugh Primas, *Poems*: *The Oxford Poems of Hugh Primas and the Arundel Lyrics edited from Bodleian Library MS. Rawlinson G. 109 and British Library MS. Arundel 384* by C. J. McDonough (Toronto Medieval Latin

Texts; Toronto, 1984); trans. and ed. F. Adcock, *Hugh Primas and the Archpoet* (Cambridge Medieval Classics, ii; Cambridge, 1994).

Hugo of Bologna, *Rationes dictandi prosaice*, ed. L. Rockinger in *Briefsteller und Formelbücher des eilften bis vierzehnten Jahrhunderts* (2 vols.; Quellen und Erörterungen zur Bayerischen und Deutschen Geschichte, ix (1–2); Munich, 1863–4), i. 47–96.

Hymn Collections from the Paraclete, i: *Introduction and Commentary*; ii: *Edition*, ed. C. Waddell (Cistercian Liturgy Series, viii–ix; Gethsemani Abbey, Trappist, Ky., 1989, 1987). Includes the numbering of the hymns found in *Peter Abelard's Hymnarius Paraclitensis*, ed. Szövérffy.

Innocent I, Pope, *Epistolae*, *PL* xx. 463–609.

Isidore of Seville, *De ecclesiasticis officiis*, ed. C. M. Lawson (*CCSL* cxiii; 1989); *PL* lxxxiii. 737–826.

—— *Etymologiarum sive originum libri*, ed. W. M. Lindsay (Oxford, 1911).

—— *Regula monachorum*, ed. with Spanish trans. J. Campos Ruíz and I. Roca Meliá in *Santos Padres Españoles*, ii: *San Leandro, San Isidoro, San Fructuoso: Reglas monásticas de la España uisigoda. Los tres libros de la 'Sentencias'* (Biblioteca de Autores Cristianos: Santos Padres Españoles, ii; Madrid, 1971), pp. 77–125; *PL* lxxxiii. 867–94; also included within the *Codex regularum* attributed to Benedict of Aniane (d. 821), *PL* ciii. 554–72.

Isidore Mercator. See Ps.-Isidore.

Italia pontificia sive Repertorium privilegiorum et litterarum a Romanis pontificibus ante annum MCLXXXXVIII . . ., ed. P. F. Kehr, i: *Roma* (Berlin, 1906).

Ivo of Chartres, *Letters*, ed. J. Leclercq in *Yves de Chartres: Correspondance I (1090–1098)* (Les Classiques de l'Histoire de France au Moyen Âge; Paris, 1949).

—— *Opera*, *PL* clxi–clxii.

—— *Panormia* (attributed to Ivo), ed. M. Brett and B. Brasington, online and dated 06/10/2009: <http://project.knowledgeforge.net/ivo/panormia.html>.

James of Vitry, *Exempla*, in *Die Exempla des Jacob von Vitry: Ein Beitrag zur Geschichte der Erzählungs-Literatur des Mittelalters*, ed. G. Frenken (Quellen und Untersuchungen zur lateinischen Philologie des Mittelalters, v (1); Munich, 1914).

Jean de Meun, *Traduction de la première épître de Pierre Abélard (Historia calamitatum)*, ed. C. Charrier (Paris, 1934).

—— *See also Roman de la Rose*.

Jehan le Fèvre, *Le Livre de Leesce*, ed. A.-G. Van Hamel in *Les Lamentations de Matheolus et le Livre de Leesce de Jehan le Fèvre, de Resson. (Poèmes français du XIVe siècle)* (2 vols.; Bibliothèque de l'École des Hautes Études. Sciences philologiques et historiques, xcv–xcvi; Paris, 1892, 1905).

Jerome, *Aduersus Iouinianum*, *PL* xxiii. 211–338. (*PL* references to works of Jerome, other than references to *PL Supplementum*, are to the first edition.)

—— *Apologia*, ed. P. Lardet (*CCSL* lxxix; 1982).

—— *Breuiarium in Psalmos*, *PL* xxvi. 821–1270.

—— *Commentarii in Danielem*, ed. F. Glorie (*CCSL* lxxvA; 1964); *PL* xxv. 491–584.

—— *Commentarii in Esaiam*, ed. M. Adriaen (*CCSL* lxxiii (1); 1963); *PL* xxiv. 17–678.

—— *Commentarii in Ezechielem*, ed. F. Glorie (*CCSL* lxxv; 1964); *PL* xxv. 15–490.

—— *Commentarii in Prophetas minores*, ed. M. Adriaen (*CCSL* lxxvi–lxxviA; 1969–70); *PL* xxv. 815–1578.

—— *Commentarioli in Psalmos*, ed. G. Morin (*CCSL* lxxii; 1959), pp. 163–245; *PL Supplementum*, ii. 29–75.

—— *Commentarius in Ionam*, ed. M. Adriaen (*CCSL* lxxvi; 1969); *PL* xxv. 1117–52.

—— *Commentum in Joelem*, ed. M. Adriaen (*CCSL* lxxvi; 1969); *PL* xxv. 947–88.

—— *Commentarii in iv epistulas Paulinas (ad Galatas, ad Ephesios, ad Titum, ad Philomenon)*, *PL* xxvi. 307–618.

—— *Contra Vigilantium*, *PL* xxiii. 339–52.

—— *De perpetua virginitate Beatae Mariae adversus Helvidium*, *PL* xxiii. 183–206.

—— *De viris illustribus*, ed. C. A. Bernoulli in *Hieronymus und Gennadius de viris inlustribus* (Sammlung ausgewählte kirchen- und dogmengeschichtlicher Quellenschriften, xi; Freiburg im Breisgau, 1895); ed. G. Herding in *Hieronymi de viris inlustribus liber. Accedit Gennadii Catalogus virorum inlustrium* (Teubner; Leipzig, 1879); *PL* xxiii. 601–720.

—— *Dialogi adversus Pelagianos*, ed. C. Moreschini (*CCSL* lxxx; 1990); *PL* xxiii. 495–590.

—— *Epistolae*, ed. J. Hilberg in *Epistularum Pars* I: *Epistulae* I–LXX, *Epistularum Pars* II: *Epistulae* LXXI–CXX, *Epistularum Pars* III: *Epistulae* CXXI–CLIV, *Indices* (M. Kemptner). *Editio altera supplementis aucta* (*CSEL* liv, lv, lvi; 1996); *PL* xxii. 325–1224; *PL Supplementum*, ii. 19–26.

—— *Hebraicae quaestiones in libro Geneseos*, ed. P. de Lagarde (*CCSL* lxxii; 1959), pp. 1–56; *PL* xxiii. 935–1010.

—— *Liber interpretationis Hebraicorum nominum*, ed. P. de Lagarde (*CCSL* lxxii; 1959), pp. 57–161; *PL* xxiii. 771–858.

—— *Praefatio in librum Isaiae*, *PL* xxviii. 771–4.

—— *Vita Hilarionis*, ed. A. Bastiaensen in *Vite dei Santi*, iv (Scrittori greci e latini, Fondazione Valla; Rome, 1975), pp. 72–141; *PL* xxiii. 29–54.

—— *Vita Malchi*, ed. C. C. Mierow in *Classical Essays Presented to J. A. Kleist* (St Louis, 1946), pp. 31–60; *PL* xxiii. 55–62.

Jerome, *Vita Pauli primi eremitae*, *PL* xxiii. 17–28.

John Chrysostom, *Homiliae in Epistulam ad Hebraeos interprete Mutiano*, *PG* lxiii. 1–236.

—— *In Joannem Homiliae*, *PG* lix. 23–482.

John the Deacon, *Commentarii in Epistulas S. Pauli*, *PL* xxx. 645–902.

—— *Life of Pope Gregory the Great (S. Gregorii papae vita)*, *PL* lxxv. 41–242.

John of Salisbury, *The Letters of John of Salisbury*, i: *The Early Letters (1153–1161)*, ed. W. J. Millor and H. E. Butler, rev. C. N. L. Brooke; ii: *The Later Letters (1163–1180)*, ed. W. J. Millor and C. N. L. Brooke (OMT; Oxford, 1986 and 1979).

—— *Metalogicon*, ed. J. B. Hall with K. S. B. Keats-Rohan (*CCCM* xcviii; 1991).

—— *Policraticus*, ed. C. C. J. Webb (Oxford, 1909); books 1–4, ed. K. S. B. Keats-Rohan, *Ioannis Saresberiensis Policraticus I–IV* (*CCCM* cxviii; 1993).

Josephus, Flavius, *Opera*, ed. G. Dindorfius in *Flavii Josephi Opera. Graeca et Latina* (2 vols.; Paris, 1845–7); *The Works of Josephus. Complete and Unabridged. New Updated Edition*; trans. W. Whiston (Peabody, Mass., 1987); *Josephus in Nine Volumes*, trans. H. St. J. Thackeray and others (Loeb Classical Library; Cambridge, Mass., 1926–65).

Juvenal, *Satires*, ed. A. Weidner (Teubner; Leipzig, 1889).

Lactantius, *Divinae Institutiones*, ed. S. Brandt (*CSEL* xix (1); 1890).

Leo I, Pope, *Epistulae*, *PL* liv. 593–1218.

Liber Donationum Altaeripae: Cartulaire de l'abbaye cistercienne d'Hauterive (XIIe–XIIIe siècles), ed. E. Tremp, trans. I Bissegger-Garin (Mémoires et documents publiés par la Société d'histoire de la Suisse romande, 3ème série, xv; Lausanne, 1984).

Livy, *Ab urbe condita*, ed. R. S. Conway and C. F. Walters in *Titi Livi ab urbe condita* (3 vols.; Scriptorum classicorum bibliotheca Oxoniensis; Oxford, 1919–28).

Lucan, *De bello ciuili*, ed. D. R. Shackleton Bailey (Teubner; Stuttgart, 1988); trans. J. D. Duff (Loeb Classical Library; Cambridge, Mass., 1928); book 1, ed. with a commentary, P. Roche, *Lucan: De Bello Ciuili, Book 1* (Oxford, 2009).

Mabillon, J. *Annales ordinis sancti Benedicti*, (Paris, 1703–7).

Macrobius, *Saturnalia*, ed. J. Willis in *Ambrosii Theodosii Macrobii Saturnalia* (Teubner; Leipzig, 1963).

Magister Bernardus, *Rationes dictandi*, ed. (and attributed to Alberic of Monte Cassino) L. Rockinger in *Briefsteller und Formelbücher des eilften bis vierzehnten Jahrhunderts* (2 vols.; Quellen und Erörterungen zur bayerischen und deutschen Geschichte, ix (1–2); Munich, 1863–4), i. 1–28;

trans. (and considered to be anonymous) by J. J. Murphy in *Three Medieval Rhetorical Arts* (Berkeley, 1971), pp. 1–25.

Mansi, *Concilia*: *Sacrorum Conciliorum nova et amplissima collectio*, ed. G. D. Mansi and others (55 vols.; Florence, Venice, Paris, Arnhem, and Leipzig, 1759–1962).

Marbod, *Carmina*, *PL* clxxi. 1647–86, 1717–36.

Martianus Capella, *De nuptiis Philologiae et Mercurii*, ed. J. Willis (Teubner; Leipzig, 1983).

Masson, P., *Annalium libri quattuor* (Paris, 1577; repr. 1578).

Matheolus. *See* Jehan le Fèvre.

Metamorphosis Golye episcopi, ed. R. B. C. Huygens in 'Mitteilungen aus Handschriften III: Die Metamorphose des Golias', *Studi medievali*, 3[a] ser., iii (1962), 764–72, and again in *Serta mediaevalia: Textus varii saeculorum X–XIII in unum collecti* (*CCCM* clxxi–clxxiA; 2000), ii. 801–15 (with a note on more recent literature).

Novatian, *De cibis iudaicis*, ed. G. F. Diercks (*CCSL* iv (1972), pp. 79-101; *PL* iii. 953-64).

Obituaires de la Province de Sens, iv: *Diocèses de Meaux et de Troyes*, ed. A. Molinier (Recueil des historiens de la France, ed. A. Boutillier du Retail and P. Piétresson de Saint-Aubin; Paris, 1923).

The Old French Paraclete Ordinary, Paris, Bibliothèque nationale, Ms. français 14410, and the Paraclete Breviary, Chaumont, Bibliothèque Municipale Ms 31, i: *Introduction and Commentary* by C. Waddell; ii: *The Old French Paraclete Ordinary, Paris, Bibliothèque nationale Ms. français 14410. Dual Transcription. Edition*, ed. C. Waddell (Cistercian Liturgy Series, iii and iv; Gethsemani Abbey, Trappist, Ky., 1985 and 1983).

Omnia sol temperat, no. 136 in *Carmina burana*. (A song which has sometimes been attributed to Abelard or Heloise. See Dronke and Orlandi, 'New works by Abelard and Heloise?', p. 143, with further references.)

Orderic Vitalis, *The Ecclesiastical History of Orderic Vitalis*, ed. and trans. M. Chibnall (OMT; 6 vols.; Oxford, 1968–80).

Origen, *Commentaria in Epistolam S. Pauli ad Romanos*, *PG* xiv. 833–1292.

—— *Homiliae in Canticum Canticorum interprete Rufino*, ed. W. A. Baehrens (*Origenes Werke*, viii; Die griechischen christlichen Schriftsteller der ersten drei Jahrhunderte, xxxiii; Leipzig, 1925), pp. 26–60; French trans. with introduction and notes, O. Rousseau, *Origène, Homélies sur le Cantique des Cantiques* (2nd edn.; *SChr* xxxviibis; Paris, 1966); *Commentarium in Canticum Canticorum interprete Rufino*, ed. W. A. Baehrens in *Origenes Werke*, viii. 61–241.

—— *Homilien zum Hexateuch in Rufins Übersetzung*, i: *Die Homilien zu Genesis, Exodus und Leviticus* (*Origenes Werke*, vi; Die griechischen christlichen Schriftsteller der ersten drei Jahrhunderte, xxix; Leipzig, 1920).

Origen, *In Genesim homiliae interprete Rufino*, ed. W. A. Baehrens in *Origenes Werke*, vi (Die griechischen christlichen Schriftsteller der ersten drei Jahrhunderte, xxix; Leipzig, 1920); ed. L. Doutreleau in *Origène, Homélies sur la Genèse* (*SChr* viibis; Paris, 1976).

Ornavere due te quondam, Gallia, gemme . . . , ed. P. Dronke in *Abelard and Heloise in Medieval Testimonies*, pp. 45–6, trans. p. 19 (repr. in *Intellectuals and Poets*, p. 281, trans. p. 263); also in *Abaelardiana* (*see* Bibliography, Secondary Works), ii. 279.

Otloh of St. Emmeram, *Vita Wolfkangi*, ed. G. Waitz (*MGH*, Scriptores, iv; Hannover, 1925), pp. 521–42.

Otto of Freising, *Chronica*, ed. A. Hofmeister in *Ottonis episcopi Frisingensis Chronica sive Historia de duabus civitatibus* (*MGH*, Scriptores rerum Germanicarum in usum scholarum, xlv; Hannover, 1912; repr. 1984); trans., with an introduction and notes, C. C. Mierow, *The Two Cities: A Chronicle of Universal History to the Year 1146 A.D. by Otto, Bishop of Freising*, with a foreword and updated bibliography by K. F. Morrison (Records of Western Civilization; New York, 2002).

—— *Gesta Friderici*, ed. G. Waitz and B. von Simson in *Ottonis et Rahewini Gesta Friderici I. Imperatoris* (*MGH*, Scriptores rerum Germanicarum in usum scholarum, xlvi; Hannover, 1912; repr. 1997).

Ovid, *Amores*, ed. and trans. G. Showerman in *Ovid in Six Volumes*, i: *Heroides and Amores* (2nd edn. rev. by G. P. Goold; Loeb Classical Library; Cambridge, Mass., 1977).

—— *Ars amatoria*, ed. E. J. Kenny (Scriptorum classicorum bibliotheca Oxoniensis; Oxford, 1961).

—— *Ex Ponto*, ed. and trans. A. L. Wheeler in *Ovid in Six Volumes*, vi: *Tristia. Ex Ponto* (2nd edn. rev. by G. P. Goold; Loeb Classical Library; Cambridge, Mass., 1988).

—— *Fasti*, ed. E. H. Alton, D. E. W. Wormell, and E. Courtney in *P. Ovidi Nasonis Fastorum libri sex* (Teubner; Leipzig, 1988).

—— *Heroides*, ed. H. Dörrie (Texte und Kommentare, vi; Berlin, 1971); trans. H. Isbell in *Ovid, Heroides* (Penguin Classics; London, 1990).

—— *Metamorphoses*, ed. W. S. Anderson (4th edn.; Teubner; Leipzig, 1988); trans. A. D. Melvill, with an introdution and notes by E. J. Kenney (Oxford, 1986).

—— *Remedia amoris*, ed. E. J. Kenny (Scriptorum classicorum bibliotheca Oxoniensis; Oxford, 1961).

Pachomius, *Praecepta*, ed. A. Boon in *Pachomiana Latina: Règle et Épîtres de S. Pachome* (Bibliothèque de la Revue d'histoire ecclésiastique, vii (Louvain, 1932); *PL* xxiii. 65–86.

Papsturkunden in Frankreich, NF iv: *Picardie*, ed. J. Ramackers (Abhandlungen der Akademie der Wissenschaften in Göttingen, Philologisch-historische Klasse, Dritte Folge, xxvii; Göttingen, 1942).

Papsturkunden in Frankreich, NF vii: *Nördliche Ile de France und Vermandois*, ed. D. Lohrmann (Abhandlungen der Akademie der Wissenschaften in Göttingen, Philologisch-historische Klasse, Dritte Folge, xcv; Göttingen, 1976).

The Paraclete Breviary, Chaumont, Bibliothèque Municipale Manuscript 31, iiiA: *Edition, Kalendar and Temporal Cycle*; iiiB: *Edition, The Sanctoral Cycle*; iiiC: *Edition, Common of Saints, Varia, Indices*, ed. C. Waddell (Cistercian Liturgy Series, v–vii; Gethsemani Abbey, Trappist, Ky., 1983).

The Paraclete Statutes, Institutiones nostrae. Troyes, Bibliothèque Municipale Ms 802, ff. 89r–90v. Introduction, Edition, Commentary, ed. C. Waddell (Cistercian Liturgy Series, xx; Gethsemani Abbey, Trappist, Ky., 1987).

Parce continuis, ed. W. Meyer in 'Zwei mittellateinische Lieder in Florenz', in *Studi letterari e linguistici dedicati a Pio Rajna* (Milan, 1911), pp. 157–9; ed. and trans. P. Dronke in *Medieval Latin and the Rise of the European Love-Lyric* (2nd edn.; Oxford, 1968), ii. 341–52; see also i, p. x; *Checklist*, no. 361. A love song which has sometimes been claimed for Abelard; the claim is disputed by Dronke here and in 'Postscript (1996)' and in Dronke and Orlandi, 'New works by Peter Abelard?', pp. 141–2.

Parisius Petrus est velata matre profectus, ed. P. Dronke in *Abelard and Heloise in Medieval Testimonies*, p. 45, trans. p. 19 (repr. in *Intellectuals and Poets*, p. 280, trans. p. 263); also in *Abaelardiana* (*see* Bibliography, Secondary Works), ii. 278–9.

Paschasius Radbertus, *Epistula beati Hieronymi ad Paulam et Eustochium de assumptione sanctae Mariae Virginis*, ed. A. Ripberger (*CCCM* lviC; 1985), pp. 97–172; *PL* xxx. 122–42.

Pelagius, *Epistola ad Claudiam de virginitate*, ed. C. Halm in *Sulpicii Severi Opera* (*CSEL* i; 1866), pp. 225–50.

—— *Expositiones xiii epistularum Pauli*, ed. A. Souter in *Pelagius' Expositions of Thirteen Epistles of St Paul. II* (Texts and Studies: Contributions to Biblical and Patristic Literature, ed. J. Armitage Robinson; Cambridge, 1926); *PL Supplementum*, i. 1110–1374.

Peter of Blois, *The Later Letters of Peter of Blois*, ed. E. Revell (Auctores Britannici Medii Aevi, xiii; Oxford, 1993).

Peter of Celle, *The Letters of Peter of Celle*, ed. and trans. J. Haseldine (OMT; Oxford, 2001); *PL* ccii. 405–636.

Peter the Chanter, *Verbum abbreviatum*, ed. M. Boutry in *Petri Cantoris Parisiensis Verbum adbreviatum. Textus conflatus* (*CCCM* cxcvi; 2004); *PL* ccv. 21–554 (short version and *textus alter*).

Peter the Venerable, *The Letters of Peter the Venerable*, ed. G. Constable (2 vols.; Cambridge, Mass., 1967).

—— *Letter* 15 to Heloise in an old French trans., ed. M. Zink in 'Traduction française attribuée à Jean de Meun de la lettre de Pierre le Vénérable à

Héloïse', in Jolivet and Louis, eds., *Pierre Abélard–Pierre le Vénérable*, pp. 29–37; Latin text and old French trans. ed. Hicks, pp. 156–61; edn. with Italian trans. of *Letters* 115 (Peter to Heloise), 167 (Heloise to Peter) and 168 (Peter to Heloise), in *Epistolario di Abelardo ed Elisa*, ed. Pagani, pp. 756–75; English trans. by Radice, pp. 217–27, by Levitan, pp. 265–75, and by McLaughlin with Wheeler, pp. 293–302.

Phaedrus, *Fabulae Aesopiae cum Nicolai Perotti Prologo et decem novis fabulis*, ed. J. P. Postgate (Scriptorum classicorum bibliotheca Oxoniensis; Oxford, n.d. but *c.*1920); *Aesop's Fables*, ed. and trans. B. E. Perry in *Babrius and Phaedrus* (Loeb Classical Library; Cambridge, Mass., 1965).

Philip of Harvengt, *Opera*, *PL* cciii.

Philo of Alexandria, *On the Contemplative Life* (*De uita contemplatiua*), ed. and trans. F. H. Coulson in *Philo in Ten Volumes* (Loeb Classical Library; Cambridge, Mass., 1941), ix. 112–69; introduction and notes F. Daumas, French trans. P. Miquel, in *Les Oeuvres de Philon d'Alexandrie*, ed. P. Arnaldez and others, xxix (Paris, 1963).

Le Pontifical romain au moyen âge, ed. M. Andrieu (3 vols.; Vatican City, 1938–41).

Porphyry, *Isagoge*, trans. Boethius, ed. L. Minio-Paluello with the aid of B. G. Dod (Aristoteles Latinus, i (6–7); Bruges, 1966).

Primo quasdam eligo, ed. H. Brinkmann, in *Geschichte der lateinischen Liebesdichtung im Mittelalter* (Halle/Saale, 1925; repr. Tübingen, 1979), pp. 33–4; ed. with English trans. Dronke, *Medieval Latin and the Rise of the Religious Love Lyric*, ii. 366–7; ed. Wollin, 'Ein Liebeslied des Petrus Abaelardus', p. 131.

Priscian, *Institutiones grammaticae*, ed. M. Hertz (2 vols.) in H. Keil, *Grammatici latini*, ii–iii; Leipzig, 1855–9).

Proverbia (Walther): *Proverbia sententiaeque latinitatis medii aevi. Lateinische Sprichwörter und Sentenzen des Mittelalters*, ed. H. Walther (5 vols.; Carmina Medii Aevi Posterioris Latina, ii (1–5); Göttingen, 1963–7).

Proverbia (Schmidt): *Proverbia sententiaeque latinitatis medii ac recentioris aevi. Nova series. Lateinische Sprichwörter und Sentenzen des Mittelalters und der frühen Neuzeit*, ed. P.-G. Schmidt (3 vols.; Carmina Medii Aevi Posterioris Latina, ii (7–9); Göttingen, 1982–6).

Ps.-Athanasius, *Symbolum 'Quicumque'*, ed. W. J. Mountain with the assistance of F. Glorie (*CCSL* lA; 1968), Appendix C, pp. 566–7.

Ps.-Augustine, *Principia dialecticae*, *PL* xxxii. 1409–20.

Ps.- Jerome, *Epistula* XLII *ad Oceanum de vita clericorum*, *PL* xxx. 297–301.

Ps.-Isidore, *Collectio canonum*, in *Collectio Hispana Decretales* ed. P. Hinsch, *Decretales Pseudo-Isidorianae et Capitula Angelramni* (Leipzig, 1863); *PL* cxxx. 7–1174.

Ps.-Quintilian, *Declamationes XIX maiores Quintiliano falso ascriptae*, ed. L. Håkanson (Teubner; Stuttgart, 1982).

Quodvultdeus, *Sermo* 10, *Adversus quinque haereses*, ed. R. Braun (*CCSL* lx; 1976), pp. 259–301; *PL* xlii. 1101–16.

Rabanus Maurus, *Expositio in Ezekielem*, *PL* cx. 493–1084.

Rabutin, Roger de, *Les Lettres de Messire Roger de Rabutin, Comte de Bussy* (3 parts; 4 vols.; Paris, 1687; new edn. (Paris, 1720).

Ralph Tortaire, *Carmina*, ed. M. B. Ogle and D. M. Schullian (Papers and Monographs of the American Academy in Rome, viii; Rome, 1933).

Rather of Verona, *Phrenesis*, ed. P. L. D. Reid, in *Ratherii Veronensis Opera, Fragmenta, Glosae* (*CCCM* xlviA; 1984), pp. 197–218; Eng. trans., P. L. D. Reid, *The Complete Works of Rather of Verona* (Binghampton, NY, 1991), pp. 244–62.

Recueil des actes de Louis VI roi de France (1108–1137), ed. J. Dufour (4 vols.; Paris, 1992–4).

Recueil des historiens des Gaules et de la France. Rerum Gallicarum et Francicarum Scriptores, ed. M. Bouquet and others (24 vols.; Paris, 1840–1904; new edn. of vols. 1–19, ed. L. Delisle; Paris, 1869–80).

Répertoire des documents nécrologiques français, i, ed. J.-L. Lemaître (Recueil des historiens de la France; *Obituaires*, vii; Paris, 1980).

Richard of Poitiers, *Chronicon*, ed. G. Waitz (*MGH*, Scriptores, xxvi; Hannover, 1882), pp. 74–82.

Robert of Arbrissel: A Medieval Religious Life. Documents translated and annotated by B. L. Venarde (Medieval Texts in Translation; Washington, DC, 2003).

Robert of Auxerre, *Chronicon* (*MGH*, Scriptores, xxvi; 1882), pp. 219–76.

Robert of Torigny, *Cronica*, ed. L. C. Bethmann (*MGH*, Scriptores, vi; 1844; repr. 1980), pp. 475–535.

—— *De immutatione ordinis monachorum. De abbatibus et abbatiis Normannorum et aedificatoribus earum*, ed. L. Delisle in *Chronique de Robert de Torigni, abbé du Mont Saint-Michel* (2 vols.; Rouen, 1872–3), ii. 181–206; *PL* ccii. 1309–20.

Roman Breviary: *Breviarium Romanum* (Mechelen, 1919).

Le Roman de la Rose par Guillaume de Lorris et Jean de Meun, ed. E. Langlois (5 vols.; Société des anciens textes français; Paris, 1914–24); *Guillaume de Lorris et Jean de Meun, Le Roman de la Rose*, ed. F. Lecoy (3 vols.; Les Classiques français du moyen âge; Paris, 1965–70).

Roscelin, *Letter* to Abelard: *Epistola ad Abaelardum*, ed. J. Reiners in *Der Nominalismus in der Frühscholastik: Ein Beitrag zur Geschichte der Universalienfrage im Mittelalter* (*BGPMA* viii (5); 1910), pp. 62–80; *PL* clxxviii. 357–72.

Rouleau mortuaire du B. Vital, abbé de Savigny. Édition phototypique, ed. L. Delisle (Paris, 1909).

Rufinus, *Orationum Gregorii Nazianzeni novem interpretatio*, ed. A. Engelbrecht (*CSEL* xlvi (1); 1910). See also Basil of Caesarea.

Rufinus (trans.), *Historia monachorum*, *PL* xxi. 387–462.

Rule of St Augustine. See Augustine, *Rule*.

Rule of St Benedict. See Benedict of Nursia, *Rule*.

Rupert of Deutz, *Opera*, *PL* clxvii–clxx.

—— *Super quaedam capitula regulae divi Benedicti abbatis*, *PL* clxx. 477–538.

Sanderus, A., *Bibliotheca Belgica Manuscripta* (2 vols.; Lille, 1641).

Seneca, *Epistolae ad Lucilium*, ed. L. D. Reynolds in *L. Annaei Senecae ad Lucilium Epistulae morales* (2 vols.; Scriptorum classicorum bibliotheca Oxoniensis; Oxford, 1965).

Sententia de universalibus secundum magistrum R., ed. B. Hauréau in *Notices et Extraits de quelques manuscrits latins de la Bibliothèque Nationale*, v (Paris, 1892), 325–8; ed. F. Picavet in *Roscelin: Philosophe et théologien* (Paris, 1911), pp. 139–41; ed. J. Dijs in 'Two anonymous 12th-century tracts on universals', *Vivarium*, xxviii (1990), 113–17.

Sententiae Anselmi, ed. F. Bliemetzrieder in *Anselms von Laon systematische Sentenzen* (*BGPTMA* xviii (2–3); 1919), pp. 47–153.

Servi animam servans, ancillis redde cadaver!, ed. P. Dronke in *Abelard and Heloise in Medieval Testimonies*, p. 49; repr. in *Intellectuals and Poets*, pp. 284–5.

Sidonius Apollinaris, *Carmina xxiv*, ed. A. Loyen in *Sidoine Apollinaire, Poèmes* (Collection Budé; Paris, 1960); ed. C. Lütjohann (*MGH*, Auctores antiquissimi, viii; 1887), pp. 173–264; ed. W. B. Anderson (Loeb Classical Library; London, 1936–66); *PL* lviii. 639–48.

Smaragdus, *Expositio in Regulam s. Benedicti*, ed. A. Spannagel and P. Engelbert (Corpus consuetudinum monasticarum, viii; Siegburg,1974); *PL* cii. 691–932; trans. D. Barry in *Smaragdus of Saint-Mihiel: Commentary on the Rule of St Benedict* (Cistercian Studies Series, ccxii; Kalamazoo, Mich., 2008).

Speculum virginum, ed. J. Seyfarth (*CCCM* v; 1990).

Suetonius, *De uita caesarum*, ed. M. Ihm (Teubner: Leipzig, 1908).

Suger, *De administratione sua (Liber de rebus in administratione sua gestis)* and *Testamentum*, in *Oeuvres complètes de Suger*, ed. A. Lecoy de la Marche (Société de l'histoire de France; Paris, 1867), pp. 151–209, 333–41.

—— *Vita Lodovici Grossi regis*, in *Oeuvres complètes de Suger*, ed. Lecoy de la Marche, pp. 5–149; ed. H. Waquet, *Suger, Vie de Louis VI le Gros* (Les Classiques de l'histoire de France au Moyen Âge, xi; Paris, 1929; 2nd edn., 1964); English trans. by R. C. Cusimano and J. Moorhead in *The Deeds of Louis the Fat* (Washington, DC, 1992).

Sulpicius Severus, *Opera*, ed. C. Halm (*CSEL* i; 1866); *PL* xx. 79–248.

Symbolum 'Quicumque'. See Ps.-Athanasius.

Terence, *Comoediae*, ed. R. Kauer and W. M. Lindsay (Scriptorum classicorum bibliotheca Oxoniensis; Oxford, 1926).

Thierry of Chartres, *Commentaries on Boethius*, ed. N. M. Häring in

Commentaries on Boethius by Thierry of Chartres and his School (Pontifical Institute of Mediaeval Studies, Studies and Texts, xx; Toronto, 1971).

—— *In Ciceronis De inventione*, ed. P. Thomas (Paris, 1884).

Thomas of Morigny, *Disputatio catholicorum patrum contra dogmata Petri Abailardi*, ed. N. M. Häring in 'Thomas of Morigny, *Disputatio*'. For this see *Bibliography: Secondary Works.*

Tres ex condicto dixere: ruamus in unum, ed. P. Dronke, in *Abaelardiana* (*see* Bibliography, Secondary Works), ii. 279.

Valerius Maximus, *Factorum et dictorum memorabilium libri novem*, ed. C. Kempf (Teubner; Leipzig, 1888).

Varro, *Antiquitates*, ed. R. Agahd in *M. Terentii Varronis Antiquitatum Rerum Divinarum libri I, XIV, XV, XVI* (Teubner; Leipzig, 1898).

Villon, François, *Le Testament Villon*, ed. J. Rychner and A. Henry, i: Text; ii: Commentary (2 vols.; Textes littéraires français; Geneva, 1974).

Virgil, *The Aeneid*, trans. C. Day Lewis, with an Introduction and Notes by J. Griffin (Oxford World's Classics; Oxford, 1998).

Virgines castae, ed. in *Analecta Hymnica Medii Aevi*, liv (1915), p. 133; ed. Iversen, 'Pierre Abélard et la poésie liturgique', pp. 254–5; ed. and trans. Bell, *Abelard after Marriage*, pp. 16–20.

Vita Gosvini, ed. R. Gibbons in *Beati Gosvini vita celeberrimi Aquicinctensis monasterii abbatis septimi, a duobus diversis coenobii monachis separatim exarata; e veteribus ms. nunc primum edita* (Douai, 1620); extracts in *Recueil des historiens des Gaules et de la France*, xiv, ed. M.-J.-J. Brial; 2nd edn. by L. Delisle (Paris, 1877), pp. 442–8.

Vita S. Agnetis, in *Acta Sanctorum* (for which see above), Jan., ii. 715–18.

Vita S. Hieronymi, '*Hieronymus noster*', *PL* xxii. 175–84.

Vita S. Hieronymi, '*Plerosque nimirum*', *PL* xxii. 201–14.

Vita Hugonis abbatis Marchianensis, ed. E. Martène and U. Durand in *Thesaurus novus anecdotorum*, iii (Paris, 1717), cols. 1709–36.

Vitae Patrum, *PL* lxxiii.

Vulgate: *Biblia sacra iuxta Vulgatam Versionem*, adiuvantibus B. Fischer, I. Gribomont, H. D. F. Sparks, W. Thiele recensuit et brevi apparatu instruxit R. Weber (2 vols.; Stuttgart, 1969).

—— *Biblia Sacra iuxta Vulgatam Clementinam nova editio*, ed. A. Colunga and L. Turrado (6th edn.; Biblioteca de autores cristianos; Madrid, 1982).

Walter Map, *Dissuasio Valerii ad Ruffinum philosophum ne uxorem ducat*, in Map's *De nugis curialium* (*Courtiers' Trifles*), distinction iv, chapters 3, 4 and the beginning of 5, ed. and trans. M. R. James, rev. C. N. L. Brooke and R. A. B. Mynors (OMT; Oxford, 1983; rev. edn., 1994), pp. 289–313.

Walter of Mortagne, *Epistola ad Abaelardum*, ed. H. Ostlender (Florilegium patristicum, xix; Bonn, 1929), pp. 34–40.

William of Champeaux, *Sententiae*, ed. O. Lottin in *Psychologie et morale aux XIIe et XIIIe* siècles, v; Gembloux, 1959), pp. 189–227.

William of Champeaux. For works of grammar, rhetoric, and dialectic which have been claimed for William or show association with him see Appendix A, 2. iii.

William Godell, *Chronicon*, ed. M. Bouquet in *Recueil des historiens des Gaules et de la France*, xiii; Paris, 1786), pp. 671–7.

William of Nangis, *Chronicle*, ed. H. Géraud in *Chronique latine de Guillaume de Nangis de 1113 à 1300 avec les continuations de cette chronique de 1300 à 1368* (2 vols.; Paris, 1843).

SECONDARY WORKS

Abaelardiana, i: J. F. Benton, 'Poems from Orleans, Bibl. Mun. MS 284, p. 183–184'; ii: P. Dronke, 'Orleans, Bibl. mun. 284: An edition of the poems and fragments on p. 183–184'; iii: E. Pellegrin, 'Orleans, Bibl. mun. 284. Description'; iv: J. F. Benton, 'Appendix. *Mundus deciduus*, possibly by Alan of Lille', in *AHDLMA* xlix (1982; published in 1983), 273–95.

Alexiou, M., and Dronke, P., 'The lament of Jephta's daughter: Themes, traditions, originality', *Studi medievali*, 3ª ser., xii (1971), 819–63. Repr. in Dronke, *Intellectuals and Poets*, pp. 345–88.

Allegro, G., *La teologia di Pietro Abelardo fra letture e pregiudizi* (Scrinium, ix; Palermo,1990). Reviews earlier scholarship concerning Abelard's theology.

Alverny, M.–T. d', 'Comment les théologiens et les philosophes voient la femme', *Cahiers de civilisation médiévale*, xx (1977), 105–29.

Arduini, M. L., 'Ruperto, san Norberto e Abelardo: Per l'edizione delle "Opera minora Ruperti abbatis Tuitensis" ', in A. Ambrosioni and M. Ferrari, eds., *Medioevo e latinità: Studi in memoria di E. Franceschini* (Milan, 1993), pp. 51–92.

Asni, R., 'Abélard et Héloïse sur l'écran et la scène de 1900 à nos jours', in Jolivet and Habrias, eds., *Pierre Abélard. Colloque international de Nantes*, pp. 185–203.

Baldwin, J. W., 'A campaign to reduce clerical celibacy at the turn of the twelfth and thirteenth centuries', in *Études d'histoire du droit canonique dédiées à Gabriel Le Bras* (Paris, 1965), ii. 1041–53.

—— *Masters, Princes and Merchants: The Social Views of Peter the Chanter and his Circle* (2 vols.; Princeton, 1970).

Barrow, Julia, 'Grades of ordination and clerical careers, *c.* 900–*c.* 1200', *Anglo-Norman Studies*, xxx; *Proceedings of the Battle Conference* 2007, ed. C. P. Lewis (Woodbridge, 2008), pp. 41–61.

Bauckham, R., *Gospel Women: Studies of the Named Women in the Gospels* (London, 2002).

Baumgartner, E., 'De Lucrèce à Héloïse, remarques sur deux "exemples" du "Roman de la Rose" de Jean de Meun, *Romania*, xcv (1974), 433–42.

Bautier, R.-H., 'Les Origines et les premiers développements de l'abbaye de

Saint-Victor de Paris', in J. Longère, ed., *L'Abbaye parisienne de Saint-Victor au moyen âge* (Bibliotheca Victorina, i; Paris, 1991), pp. 23–52.

—— 'Paris au temps d'Abélard', in Jolivet, ed., *Abélard en son temps*, pp. 21–77.

Bayle, P., *Dictionnaire historique et critique* (2nd edn., 3 vols.; Amsterdam, 1702).

Bell, T. J., *Peter Abelard after Marriage: The Spiritual Direction of Heloise and her Nuns through Liturgical Song* (Cistercian Studies Series, ccxi; Kalamazoo, Mich., 2007).

Benton, J. F., 'Appendix. *Mundus deciduus*, possibly by Alan of Lille'. See *Abaelardiana*, iv.

—— 'The correspondence of Abelard and Heloise', in *Fälschungen im Mittelalter*, v: *Fingierte Briefe. Frömmigkeit und Fälschung. Realienfälschungen* , pp. 95–120. Repr. in Benton, *Culture, Power and Personality*, pp. 487–512.

—— *Culture, Power and Personality in Medieval France*, ed. T. N. Bisson (London, 1991).

—— 'Fraud, fiction and borrowing in the correspondence of Abelard and Heloise', in Jolivet and Louis, eds., *Pierre Abélard–Pierre le Vénérable*, pp. 469–511. Repr. in Benton, *Culture, Power and Personality*, pp. 417–53.

—— 'The Paraclete and the Council of Rouen of 1231', *Bulletin of Medieval Canon Law*, NS iv (1974), 33–8. Repr. in Benton, *Culture, Power and Personality*, pp. 411–16.

—— 'Philology's search for Abelard in the *Metamorphosis Goliae*', *Speculum*, l (1975), 199–217. Repr. in Benton, *Culture, Power and Personality*, pp. 455–73.

—— 'Poems from Orleans, Bibl. Mun. MS 284, p. 183–184'. See *Abaelardiana*, i.

—— 'A reconsideration of the authenticity of the correspondence of Abelard and Heloise', in Thomas and others, eds., *Petrus Abaelardus (1079–1142)*, pp. 41–52. Repr. in Benton, *Culture, Power and Personality*, pp. 475–86.

—— and Prosperetti Ercoli, F.,'The style of the *Historia calamitatum*: A preliminary test of the authenticity of the correspondence attributed to Abelard and Heloise', *Viator*, vi (1975), 58–86.

Beonio-Brocchieri, M. T., *Introduzione a Abelardo* (Bari, 1974).

—— *The Logic of Peter Abelard* (Dordrecht, 1969).

Beonio-Brocchieri Fumagalli, M. T., *Eloisa e Abelardo* (Milan, 1984)

—— *Heloise und Abaelard* (Munich, 1986).

Bergh, B., 'Studia critica in Historiam calamitatum inque epistolas Abaelardi et Heloisae', *Eranos*, xcvii (1999), 20–3.

Berlioz, J., *Identifier sources et citations* (L'Atelier du médiéviste, i; Turnhout, 1994).

Bernards, M., '*Nudus nudum Christum sequi*', *Wissenschaft und Weisheit*, xiv (1951), 148–151.

Bertola, E., 'Le critiche di Abelardo ad Anselmo di Laon ed a Guglielmo di Champeaux', *Rivista di filosofia neo-scolastica*, lii (1960), 495–522.

Beyer, H., 'Abälard-Heloise-Briefwechsel und der Conte du Gral in ihrer Zeit', *Zeitschrift für Kirchengeschichte*, c (1989), 3–32.

Bibolet, F., '*Bibliotheca Pithoena*: Les manuscrits des Pithou. Une histoire de fraternité et d'amitié', in Nebbiai-Dalla Guarda and Genest, eds., *Du copiste au collectionneur: Mélanges . . . André Vernet*, pp. 497–521.

Bibolet, F., Les Pithou et l'amour des livres', in Fragonard and Leroy, eds., *Les Pithou*, pp. 295–304.

Bienvenu, J.-M., *L'Étonnant Fondateur de Fontevraud: Robert d'Arbrissel* (Nouvelles éditions latines; Paris, 1981).

Billanovich, G., and Ouy, G., 'La Première Correspondence échangée entre Jean de Montreuil et Coluccio Salutati', *Italia medioevali e umanistica*, vii (1964), 337–74.

Birge Vitz, E., 'Type et individu dans l'"autobiographie" médiévale: Étude d'*Historia Calamitatum*', *Poétique*, xxiv (1975), 426–45.

Bisson, T. N., *The Crisis of the Twelfth Century: Power, Lordship, and the Origins of European Government* (Princeton, 2009).

—— 'L'Expérience du pouvoir chez Pierre Abélard (c. 1100–1142)', in Jolivet and Habrias, eds., *Pierre Abélard. Colloque international de Nantes*, pp. 91–108.

Blamires, A., '*Caput a femina, membra a viris*: Gender polemic in Abelard's letter "On the Authority and Dignity of the Nun's Profession" ', in D. Townsend and A. Taylor, eds., *The Tongue of the Fathers: Gender and Ideology in Twelfth-Century Latin* (Philadelphia, 1998), pp. 55–79.

—— *The Case for Women in Medieval Culture* (Oxford, 1997).

—— 'No outlet for incontinence: Heloise and the question of consolation', in Wheeler, ed., *Listening to Heloise*, pp. 287–301.

—— Pratt, K., and Marx, C. W., eds., *Woman Defamed and Woman Defended: An Anthology of Medieval Texts* (Oxford, 1992).

Bliemetzrieder, F., 'Robert von Melun und die Schule Anselms von Laon', *Zeitschrift fur Kirchengeschichte*, liii (1934), 117–70.

Boiadjiev, T., 'Die Marginalisierung als *principium individuationis* des mittelalterlichen Menschen am Beispiel Abaelards', in J. A. Aertsen and A. Speer, eds., *Individuum und Individualität im Mittelalter* (Miscellanea Mediaevalia, xxiv; Berlin, 1996), pp. 111–23.

Bondéelle-Souchier, A., 'Claude-Robert Jardel, de Braine, collectionneur de manuscrits (1712–1788)', in Nebbiai-Dalla Guarda and Genest, eds., *Du copiste au collectionneur, Mélanges . . . André Vernet*, pp. 615–51.

Borst, A., 'Abälard und Bernhard', *Historische Zeitschrift*, clxxxvi (1958), 497–526.

Bourgain, P., 'Héloïse', in Jolivet, ed., *Abélard en son temps*, pp. 211–37.

—— with M.-C. Hubert, *Le Latin médiéval* (L'Atelier du Médiéviste, x; Turnhout, 2005).

Bournazel, E., *Le Gouvernement capétien au XIIe siècle. 1108–1180. Structures sociales et mutations institutionelles* (Limoges,1975).

Boussard, J., *Nouvelle Histoire de Paris: De la fin du siège de 885–886 à la mort de Philippe Auguste* (Paris, 1976).

Bozzolo, C., 'L'Humaniste Gontier Col et la traduction française des lettres d'Abélard et Héloïse', *Romania*, xcv (1974), 199–215.

Brinkmann, H., 'Astrolabius', *Münchener Museum für Philologie des Mittelalters und der Renaissance*, v (1932), 168–201.

Brook, L. C., 'Bussy-Rabutin and the Abelard–Heloise correspondence', in R. Ellis and R. Tixier, eds., *The Medieval Translator*, v: *Proceedings of the Intenational Conference of Conques (26–29 July 1993)* (Turnhout, 1996), pp. 284–301.

—— 'Christine de Pisan, Heloise, and Abelard's holy women', *Zeitschrift für romanischen Philologie*, cix (1993), 556–63.

Brooke, C. N. L., 'Gregorian reform in action: Clerical marriage in England, 1050–1200', *Cambridge Historical Journal*, xii (1) (1956), 1–21; appendix, xii (2), pp. 187–8. Repr. in S. Thrupp, ed., *Change in Medieval Society* (New York, 1964), pp. 49–71.

—— *The Medieval Idea of Marriage* (Oxford, 1989). Italian trans., *Il matrimonio nel Medioevo* (Bologna, 1991).

Brown, P. R., and Peiffer II, J. C., 'Heloise, dialectic, and the Heroides', in Wheeler, ed., *Listening to Heloise*, pp. 143–60.

Brundage, J. A., 'Concubinage and marriage in medieval canon law', *Journal of Medieval History*, i (1975), 1–17.

Bruni, F., '"Historia calamitatum", "Secretum", "Corbaccio": Tre posizioni su luxuria (amor) e superbia (gloria)', in G. Tournoy, ed., *Boccaccio in Europe* (Louvain, 1977), pp. 23–52.

Bulst, W., 'Liebesbriefgedichte Marbods', in *Liber Floridus: Festschrift Paul Lehmann* (St. Ottilien, 1950), pp. 287–301.

Bur, M., *La Formation du comté de Champagne v. 950–v. 1150* (Publications de l'Université de Nancy, ii; Nancy, 1977).

Burnett, C. S. F., '*Confessio fidei ad Heloisam*—Abelard's last letter to Heloise? A discussion and critical edition of the Latin and medieval French versions', *Mittellateinisches Jahrbuch*, xxi (1986), 147–55.

—— 'The *Expositio orationis dominicae "Multorum legimus orationes"*: Abelard's exposition on the Lord's Prayer?', *Revue bénédictine*, xcv (1985), 66–72.

—— 'Notes on the tradition of the text of the *Hymnarius Paraclitensis* of Peter Abelard', *Scriptorium*, xxxviii (1984), 295–302.

—— 'Peter Abelard, *Confessio fidei "Universis"*: A critical edition of

Abelard's reply to accusations of heresy', *Mediaeval Studies*, xlviii (1986), 111–38.

—— ed., *Glosses and Commentaries on Aristotelian Logical Texts: the Syriac, Arabic and Medieval Latin Traditions* (Warburg Institute Surveys and Texts, 23; London, 1993).

—— 'Peter Abelard "Soliloquium": A critical edition', *Studi medievali*, 3[a] ser., xxv (2) (1984), 857–94.

Buytaert, E. M., 'Abelard's Expositio in Hexaemeron', *Antonianum*, xliii (1968), 163–94.

—— ed., *Peter Abelard: Proceedings of the International Conference. Louvain, May 10–12, 1971* (Mediaevalia Lovaniensia Series I, Studia, ii; Louvain and The Hague, 1974).

Caiazzo, I., 'Manegold, *Modernorum Magister Magistrorum*', in Rosier-Catach, ed., *Arts du langage et théologie*, pp. 317–49.

Calabrese, M., 'Ovid and the female voice in the *De Amore* and the letters of Abelard and Heloise', *Modern Philology*, xcv (1997), 1–26.

Camargo, M., *Ars dictaminis, ars dictandi* (Typologie des sources du moyen âge occidental, lx; Turnhout, 1991).

Cameron, M., 'Abelard's early glosses: Some questions', in Rosier-Catach, ed., *Arts du langage et théologie*, pp. 647–62.

—— 'The development of early twelfth-century logic: A reconsideration', ibid., pp. 677–94.

Carnandet, J.-B., *Notice sur le bréviaire d'Abailard conservé à la bibliothèque de Chaumont (Haute-Marne)* (Paris, 1851).

Charrier, C., *Héloïse dans l'histoire et dans la légende* (Paris, 1933).

—— *Jean de Meun: Traduction de la première épître de Pierre Abélard (Historia calamitatum)* (Paris, 1934).

Châtillon, F., 'Notes abélardiennes. I. Sur le caractère d'Abélard: '*animo levis*'. II. *Vehementer*, mot typiquement abélardien. III. Inconduite d'Abélard avant la rencontre d'Héloïse', *Revue du moyen âge latin*, xx (1964), 276–334.

—— 'Notes abélardiennes (suite). IV.'Abélard mutilé cite l'*Eunuque* de Térence', *Revue du moyen âge latin*, xxi (1965), 98–103.

—— and D'Angomont, Th., 'Notes abélardiennes (suite)', *Revue du moyen âge latin*, xxxv (1979), 43–51, 141–5.

Châtillon, J., 'Abélard et les écoles', in Jolivet, ed., *Abélard en son temps*, pp. 133–60.

—— 'De Guillaume de Champeaux à Thomas Gallus: Chronique d'histoire littéraire et doctrinale de l'école de Saint-Victor', *Revue du moyen âge latin*, viii (1952), 139–62, 247–72.

Chédeville, A. and Tonnerre, N.-Y., *La Bretagne féodale, XIe–XIIIe siècle* (Rennes, 1987).

Cipollone, M., 'In margine ai *Problemata Heloissae*', *Aevum*, lxiv (1990), 227–44.

Clanchy, M. T., *Abelard: A Medieval Life* (Oxford, 1997).

—— 'The Letters of Abelard and Heloise in today's scholarship', in Radice, pp. lviii–lxxxiv.

—— and Smith, L., 'Abelard's description of the school of Laon: What might it tell us about early scholastic teaching?', *Nottingham Medieval Studies*, liv (2010), 1–34.

Clark, J. R., 'Love and learning in the "Metamorphosis Golye Episcopi" ', *Mittellateinisches Jahrbuch*, xxi (1986), 156–71.

Classen, P., *Burgundio von Pisa. Richter – Gesandter – Übersetzer* (Sitzungsberichte der Heidelberger Akademie der Wissenschaften, Philosophisch-historische Klasse, Jahrgang 1974, 4. Abhandlung; Heidelberg, 1974).

—— *Gerhoch von Reichersberg* (Wiesbaden, 1960).

Clausen, J. P., 'Suger, faussaire de chartes', in Grosse, ed., *Suger en question*, pp. 109–16.

Colette, M.-N., 'Un ensemble de *planctus* attribués à Abélard dans un prosaire nivernais (Manuscrit Paris, BNF, nal 3126)', in Jolivet and Habrias, eds., *Pierre Abélard. Colloque international de Nantes*, pp. 277–94.

Colish, M., 'Another look at the School of Laon', *AHDLMA* lxi (1986), 7–22.

Complete Peerage: The Complete Peerage of England, Scotland, Ireland . . . by G. E. C. (i.e. G. E. Cokayne). New edn. by V. Gibbs (13 vols.; London, 1910–59).

Constable, G., 'Aelred of Rievaulx and the nun of Watton: An episode in the early history of the Gilbertine Order', in D. Baker, ed., *Medieval Women* (Studies in Church History, Subsidia, i; Oxford, 1978), pp. 205–26.

—— 'The authorship of the *Epistolae duorum amantium*: A reconsideration', in Olson and Kerby-Fulton, eds., *Voices in Dialogue*, pp. 167–78. (A shortened version of Constable, 'Sur l'attribution des *Epistolae duorum amantium*'.)

—— 'The concern for sincerity and understanding in liturgical prayer, especially in the twelfth century', in I. Vaslef and H. Buschhausen, eds., *Classica et Mediaevalia: Studies in Honor of Joseph Szövérffy* (Medieval Classics: Texts and Studies, xx; Washington, DC, 1986), pp. 17–30.

—— *Letters and Letter-Collections* (Typologie des sources du moyen âge occidental, xvii; Turnhout, 1976).

——'Medieval Latin metaphors', *Viator*, xxxviii (2007), 1–20.

—— *Medieval Monasticism: A Select Bibliography* (Toronto Medieval Bibliographies, vi; Toronto, 1976).

—— 'Nun of Watton', *Oxford Dictionary of National Biography*, xli (Oxford, 2004), p. 274.

—— *The Reformation of the Twelfth Century* (Cambridge, 1996).

Constable, G., 'Suger's Monastic Administration', in Gerson, ed., *Abbot Suger and St Denis*, pp. 17–32.

—— 'Sur l'attribution des *Epistolae duorum amantium*', *Académie des Inscriptions et Belles-Lettres. Comptes rendus des séances de l'année 2001, novembre-décembre*, pp. 1679–93.

Cook, B. M., 'The shadow on the sun: The name of Abelard's son', in Stewart and Wulstan, eds., *Poetic and Musical Legacy*, pp. 152–5.

Cottineau, L. H., *Répertoire topo-bibliographique des Abbayes et Prieurés* (3 vols.; Macon, 1939; repr. Turnhout, 1995).

Coulton, G. G., *Five Centuries of Religion* (4 vols.; Cambridge, 1923–50).

Courtenay, W. J., *Parisian Scholars in the Early Fourteenth Century: A Social Portrait* (Cambridge Studies in Medieval Life and Thought, 4th ser., no. xli; Cambridge, 1999).

Crosby, S. McK., *The Royal Abbey of Saint-Denis from its Beginnings to the Death of Suger, 475–1151*, ed. and completed by P. Z. Blum (Yale Publications in the History of Art, xxxvii; New Haven, 1987).

Cupiccia, M., 'Progressi nello studio del cursus: I metodi statistici e il caso di Eloisa e Abelardo', *Filologia mediolatina*, v (1998), 37–48.

Dalarun, J., *L'Impossible Sainteté: La vie retrouvée de Robert d'Arbrissel (v. 1045–1116), fondateur de Fontevraud* (Histoire; Paris, 1985).

—— 'Nouveaux Aperçus sur Abélard, Héloïse et le Paraclet', *Francia*, xxxii (2005), 19–66.

—— *Robert d'Arbrissel, fondateur de Fontevraud* (Paris, 1986).

—— *Robert of Arbrissel: Sex, Sin, and Salvation in the Middle Ages*, trans. B. L. Venarde (Washington, DC, 2006).

—— ed., *Robert d'Arbrissel et la vie religieuse dans l'Ouest de la France. Actes du Colloque de Fontevraud, 13–16 décembre 2001* (Disciplina monastica, i; Turnhout, 2004).

—— and Giordanengro, G., Le Huërou, A., Longère, J., Poirel, D., and Venarde, B. L., *Les Deux Vies de Robert d'Arbrissel fondateur de Fontevraud: Légendes, écrits et témoignages. The Two Lives of Robert of Arbrissel Founder of Fontevraud: Legends, Writings and Testimonies* (Disciplina monastica, iv; Turnhout, 2006).

D'Anna, G., 'Abelardo e Cicerone', *Studi medievali*, 3ª ser., x (1969), 333–419.

De Clercq, C., *La Législation religieuse francque de Clovis à Charlemagne (507–814)*, i (Louvain, 1936).

Delhaye, P., 'Le Dossier anti-matrimonial de l'*Adversus Jovinianum* et son influence sur quelques écrits latins du XIIᵉ siècle', *Mediaeval Studies*, xiii (1951), 65–86.

—— 'L'Organisation scolaire au XIIᵉ siècle', *Traditio*, v (1947), 211–68.

Delisle, L., *Le Cabinet des manuscrits de la Bibliothèque impériale* (2 vols.; Paris, 1868).

—— 'Des documents paléographiques concernant l'usage de prier pour les morts', *Bibliothèque de l'École des Chartes*, 2e sér., iii (1846), 361–411.

—— *Rouleaux des morts du IXe au XVe siècle* (Paris, 1866).

Dépoin, J., *Une Élégie latine d'Héloïse suivie du nécrologe d'Argenteuil et autres documents inédits . . . .2e édition accompagnée d'un facsimilé* (Pontoise, 1897).

Dereine, C., 'Conon de Preneste', *Dictionnaire d'histoire et de géographie ecclésiastiques*, xiii (1956), pp. 461–71.

De Robertis, D., 'Il senso della propria storia ritrovato attraverso i classici nella *Historia calamitatum* di Abelardo', *Maia*, xvi (1964), 6–54.

De Santis, P., 'Abelardo interprete del Cantico dei Cantici per il Paracleto?', *Pascua Mediaevalia: Studies voor Prof. Dr. J. M. de Smet* (Mediaevalia Lovanensia, Series I/Studia x; Leuven, 1983), pp. 284–94.

—— 'Osservazioni sulla lettera dedicatoria del sermonario di Abelardo', *Aevum*, lv (1981), 262–71.

Deutsch, S. M., 'Abälards Verurteilung zu Sens 1141: Nach den Quellen kritisch dargestellt', in *Symbolae Joachimicae: Festschrift des Königlichen Joachimsthalschen Gymnasiums* (2 vols.; Berlin, 1880), i. 1–54.

Dickey, M.,'Some commentaries on the *De inventione* and *Ad Herennium* of the eleventh and early twelfth centuries', *Mediaeval and Renaissance Studies*, vi (1968), 1–41.

Dictionnaire de théologie catholique, ed. A. Vacant and others (15 vols.; Paris 1899–1950).

Dictionnaire d'histoire et de géographie ecclésiastiques, ed. A. Baudrillart and others (Paris, 1912–).

Dictionnaire du Moyen Âge, ed. C. Gauvard, A. de Libera, and M. Zink (Paris, 2002).

Dijs, J., 'Two anonymous 12th-century tracts on universals', *Vivarium*, xxviii (1990), 85–117.

Dolbeau, F., 'Deux catalogues inédits de bibliothèques médiévales', in A. Bihrer and E. Stein, eds., *Nova de Veteribus: Mittel- und neulateinische Studien für Paul Gerhard Schmidt* (Munich, 2004), pp. 326–55.

Dronke, P., *Abelard and Heloise in Medieval Testimonies* (Glasgow, 1976). Repr. in Dronke, *Intellectuals and Poets*, pp. 247–94.

—— 'Amour sacré et amour profane au moyen âge latin: Témoignages lyriques et dramatiques', in Dronke, *Sources of Inspiration*, pp. 375–93.

—— 'Francesca and Heloise', *Comparative Literature*, xxvii (1975), 113–35.

—— 'Heloise, Abelard, and some recent discussions', in Dronke, *Intellectuals and Poets*, pp. 323–42.

—— 'Heloise and Marianne: Some reconsiderations', *Romanische Forschungen*, lxxii (1960), 223–56.

—— 'Heloise's *Problemata* and letters: Some questions of form and content', in Thomas and others, eds., *Petrus Abaelardus (1079–1142)*, pp. 53–73. Repr. in Dronke, *Intellectuals and Poets*, pp. 295–322.

Dronke, P., 'Hermes and the Sibyls: Continuations and creations', in Dronke, *Intellectuals and Poets*, pp. 219–44.

—— *Intellectuals and Poets in Medieval Europe* (Storia e Letteratura, clxxxiii; Rome, 1992).

—— *Medieval Latin and the Rise of the European Love-Lyric*. i: *Problems and Interpretations*; ii: *Medieval Latin Love-Poetry. Texts Newly Edited from the Manuscripts and for the Most Part Previously Unpublished* (2nd edn.; Oxford, 1968).

—— 'Orleans, Bibl. mun. 284: An edition of the poems and fragments on p. 183–184'. See *Abaelardiana*, ii.

—— *Poetic Individuality in the Middle Ages* (Oxford, 1970). For the 2nd edn. of this work see next.

—— *Poetic Individuality in the Middle Ages: New Departures in Poetry, 1000–1150* (2nd edn.; Westfield Publications in Medieval Studies, i; Westfield College: University of London, 1986).

—— 'Postscript (1996)' to Dronke, 'The return of Eurydice', in Dronke, *Sources of Inspiration*, pp. 281–92.

—— review of Wheeler, ed., *Listening to Heloise*, in *International Journal of the Classical Tradition*, viii (2001–2), 134–9.

—— review of Szövérffy, *Peter Abelard's Hymnarius Paraclitensis*, in *Mittellateinisches Jahrbuch*, xiii (1978), 307–11.

—— *Sources of Inspiration: Studies in Literary Transformations, 400–1500* (Storia e Letteratura, cxcvi; Rome, 1997).

—— *Women Writers of the Middle Ages* (Cambridge, 1984). Italian trans., *Donne e cultura nel Medioevo* (Milan, 1986).

—— ed., *A History of Twelfth-Century Western Philosophy* (Cambridge, 1988).

—— and Orlandi, G., 'New works by Abelard and Heloise?', *Filologia mediolatina*, xii (2005), 123–77.

Dubois, J., 'Les Ordres religieux au XIIe siècle selon la Curie romaine', *Revue bénédictine*, lxxviii (1968), 283–309.

Du Pouget, M., 'La Légende carolingienne à Saint-Denis: La donation de Charlemagne au retour de Roncevaux', in *Actes du Colloque de Saint-Jean-Pied-de-Port (12 Août 1978). La Bataille de Roncevaux* (Bulletin de la Société des Sciences, Lettres et Arts de Bayonne, cxxxv (1979), pp. 53–63.

East, W. G., 'Abelard's allusive style', *Mittellateinisches Jahrbuch*, xxxiv (1999), 41–9.

—— 'Abelard's anagram', *Notes and Queries*, ccxl (Sept. 1995), 269.

Edbury, P. W., and Rowe, J. G., *William of Tyre: Historian of the Latin East* (Cambridge Studies in Medieval Life and Thought, 4th ser., viii; Cambridge, 1988).

Ehlers, J., *Hugo von St. Viktor: Studien zum Geschichtsdenken und zur*

Geschichtsbescreibung des 12. Jahrhunderts (Frankfurter Historische Abhandlungen, vii; Wiesbaden, 1973).

Elm, K., 'Norbert von Xanten: Bedeuting—Persönlichkeit—Nachleben', in id., ed., *Norbert von Xanten*, pp. 267–318.

—— ed., *Norbert von Xanten: Adeliger – Ordenstifter – Kirchenfürst* (Cologne, 1984).

—— and Parisse, M., eds., *Doppelklöster und andere Formen der Symbiose männlicher und weiblicher Religiosen im Mittelalter* (Berlin, 1992).

Engels, L. J., 'Abélard écrivain', in Buytaert, ed., *Peter Abelard*, pp. 12–37.

—— '*Adtendite a falsis prophetis* (Ms. Colmar 128, ff. 152V/153V): Un texte de Pierre Abélard contre les Cisterciens retrouvé?', in *Corona Gratiarum: Miscellanea patristica, historica et liturgica Eligio Dekkers O.S.B. oblata* (Instrumenta Patristica, xi; Bruges, 1975), ii. 195–228.

—— and Kingma, J., '*Hos ego versiculos*: De editio princeps van werken van Abaelard', in *Bibliotheek, Wetenschap en Cultuur. Opstellen aangeboden aan mr. W. R. H. Koops bij zijn afscheid als bibliothecaris der Rijksuniversiteit te Groningen* (Groningen, 1990), pp. 238–61.

Enright, A., 'Peace and the politics of education: François Pithou and the *Collège de Troyes*', in Fragonard and Leroy, eds., *Les Pithou*, pp. 89–103.

Esneval, A. d', 'La Division de la Vulgate latine en chapitres dans l'édition parisienne du XIIIe siècle', *Revue des sciences philosophiques et théologiques*, lxii (1978), 559–68.

Everard, J. A., 'The abbey of Saint-Sulpice-la-Forêt and royal patronage in England', *Nottingham Medieval Studies*, xlvii (2003), 106–47.

—— *Brittany and the Angevins: Province and Empire, 1158–1203* (Cambridge, 2000).

Evergates, T., 'Aristocratic women in the county of Champagne', in id., ed., *Aristocratic Women in Medieval France* (Philadelphia, 1999), pp. 74–110.

—— 'Nobles and Knights in Twelfth-Century France', in T. N. Bisson, ed., *Cultures of Power: Lordship, Status and Process in Twelfth-Century Europe* (Philadelphia, 1995), pp. 11–35.

Fälschungen im Mittelalter. Internationaler Kongress der Monumenta Germaniae Historica, München, 16.–19. September 1986 (6 vols.; *MGH*, Schriften, xxxiii (1–6); Hannover, 1988–90).

Felten, F. J., 'Norbert von Xanten: Von Wanderprediger zum Kirchenfürsten', in Elm, ed., *Norbert von Xanten*, pp. 69–157.

—— 'Verbandsbildung von Frauenklöstern: Le Paraclet, Prémy, Fontevraud mit einem Ausblick auf Cluny, Sempringham und Tart', in H. Keller and F. Neiske, eds., *Vom Kloster zum Klosterverband: Das Werkzeug der Schriftlichkeit* (Münsterische Mittelalter-Schriften, lxxiv; Munich, 1997), pp. 277–341.

—— 'Zwischen Berufung und Amt: Norbert von Xanten und seinesgleichen im ersten Viertel des 12. Jahrhunderts', in G. Andenna, M. Breitenstein, and G. Melville, eds., *Charisma und religiöse Gemeinschaften im Mittelalter. Akten des 3. Internationalen Kongresses des 'Italienisch-deutschen Zentrums für Vergleichende Ordensgeschichte'* (Vita Regularis, xxvi; Münster, 2005), pp. 103–49.

Ferrante, J. M., *To the Glory of her Sex: Women's Roles in the Composition of Medieval Texts* (Bloomington, Ind., 1997).

Ferroul, Y., 'Abelard's blissful castration', in J. J. Cohen and B. Wheeler, eds., *Becoming Male in the Middle Ages* (New York, 1997), pp. 129–49.

—— 'Bienheureuse castration: Sexualité et vie intellectuelle à l'époque d'Abélard', *Bien diere et bien aprandre*, iv (1986), 1–28.

—— *Héloise et Abélard, Lettres et vies: Introduction, traduction, notes, bibliographie et chronologie* (Paris, 1996).

Flahiff, G. B., 'The censorship of books in the twelfth century', *Mediaeval Studies*, iv (1942), 1–22.

Flint, V. I. J., 'The "School of Laon": A reconsideration', *Recherches de théologie ancienne et médiévale*, xliii (1976), 89–110. Repr. in Flint, *Ideas in the Medieval West: Texts and Contexts* (London, 1988).

Folz, R., 'Otton de Freising, témoin de quelques controverses intellectuelles de son temps', *Bulletin de la Société historique et archéologique de Langres*, xiii (1958), 70–89.

Fontette, M. de, 'Recherches sur les origines des moniales chartreuses', in *Études d'histoire du droit canonique dédiées à Gabriel Le Bras* (Paris, 1965), pp. 1143–51.

—— *Les Religieuses à l'âge classique du droit canon: Recherches sur les structures juridiques des branches féminines des ordres* (Bibliothèque de la Société d'Histoire ecclésiastique de la France; Paris, 1967).

Fortia d'Urban, A. J. F. le Marquis de, *Histoire et ouvrages de Hugues Métel ou Mémoires pour servir à l'histoire ecclésiastique du douzième siècle* (Paris, 1839), pp. 29–51.

Fraioli, D., 'The importance of satire in Jerome's *Adversus Jovinianum* as an argument against the authenticity of the *Historia calamitatum*', in *Fälschungen im Mittelalter*, v: *Fingierte Briefe. Frömmigkeit und Fälschung. Realienfälschungen*, pp. 167–200.

Fragonard, M.-M., and Leroy, P.-E., eds., *Les Pithou: Les lettres et la paix du royaume. Actes du Colloque de Troyes des 13–15 avril 1998* (Colloques, congrès et conférences sur la Renaissance. Collection dirigé par Claude Blum, xxxviii; Paris 2003).

Franceschini, E., review of Monfrin in *Aevum*, xxxv (1961), 395–6.

Frank, D. K., 'Abelard as imitator of Christ', *Viator*, i (1970), 107–13.

Fredborg, K. M., 'Abelard on rhetoric', in Mews, Nederman, and Thomson, eds., *Rhetoric and Renewal*, pp. 55–80.

—— 'The commentaries on Cicero's *De inventione* and *Rhetorica ad Here-*

nnium by William of Champeaux', *Cahiers de l'Institut du Moyen Âge grec et latin*, xvii (Copenhagen, 1976), 1–39.

—— 'Speculative grammar', in Dronke, ed., *History of Twelfth-Century Western Philosophy*, pp. 177–95.

—— 'Tractatus Glosarum Prisciani in MS Vat. Lat. 1486', *Cahiers de l'Institut du Moyen Âge grec et latin*, xxi (Copenhagen, 1977), 21–44.

Fromm, H., 'Gottfried von Strassburg und Abaelard', in *Beiträge zur Geschichte der deutschen Sprache und Literatur*, xcv, *Sonderheft: Festschrift für Ingeborg Schröbler* (Tübingen, 1973), pp. 196–216.

Führer, J., 'L'Abbaye de Saint-Victor dans la réforme canoniale', in Poirel, ed., *L'École de Saint-Victor*, pp. 57–77.

—— *König Ludwig VI. und die Kanonikerreform* (Europäische Hochschulschriften, iii, 1049; Frankfurt a. M., 2008).

Gams, P. B., *Series episcoporum ecclesiae catholicae* (Regensburg, 1873–86; repr. Graz, 1957).

Gaudemet, J., *Le Mariage en Occident* (Paris, 1987). Italian trans. as *Il matrimonio in Occidente* (Turin, 1989).

Génin, F., 'Première Lettre d'Abailard, traduction inédite de Jean de Meun', *Bulletin du Comité historique des monuments écrits de l'histoire de France, Histoire-Sciences-Lettres*, ii (Paris, 1850), 175–91, 265–92.

Georgianna, L.,' "In any corner of heaven": Heloise's critique of monasticism', *Mediaeval Studies*, xlix (1987), 221–53. Repr. with some changes in Wheeler, ed., *Listening to Heloise*, pp. 187–216.

Gerson, P. L., ed., *Abbot Suger and St Denis: A Symposium* (New York, 1986).

Gilson, E., *Heloise and Abelard*, trans. L. K. Shook (Chicago, 1953).

—— *Héloïse et Abélard* (Paris, 1948; 3rd and expanded edn., 1964).

Giraud, C., 'L'École de Laon entre arts du langage et théologie', in Rosier-Catach, ed., *Arts du langage et théologie*, pp. 351–71.

—— *'Per verba magistri': Anselme de Laon et son école au XIIe siècle* (Bibliothèque d'histoire culturelle, viii; Turnhout, 2010).

—— 'Le Recueil de sentences de l'école de Laon *Principium et causa*: Un cas de pluri-attribution', in *Parva pro magnis munera: Études de littérature tardo-antique et médiévale offertes à François Dolbeau par ses élèves*, ed. M. Goullet (Turnhout, 2009), pp. 245–69.

Godefroy, J., 'L'Histoire du prieuré de Saint-Ayoul de Provins et le récit des miracles du saint', *Revue Mabillon*, xxvii (1937), 94–107; xxviii (1938), 29–48, 84–98, 112–25.

Godet, P., 'Guillaume de Champeaux', *Dictionnaire de théologie catholique*, vi (1976).

Godman, P., *The Silent Masters: Latin Literature and its Censors in the High Middle Ages* (Princeton, 2000).

Gold, P. S., *The Lady and the Virgin: Image, Attitude, and Experience in Twelfth-Century France* (Women in Culture and Society; Chicago, 1985).

Golding, B., 'Authority and discipline at the Paraclete, Fontevraud, and Sempringham', in G. Melville and A. Müller, eds., *Mittelalterliche Orden und Klöster im Vergleich: Methodische Ansätze und Perspektiven* (Vita regularis, xxxiv; Berlin, 2007), pp. 87–111.

—— *Gilbert of Sempringham and the Gilbertine Order c.1130–c.1300* (Oxford, 1995).

Gouron, A., '"Non dixit: Ego sum consuetudo" ', *Zeitschrift der Savigny-Stiftung für Rechtsgeschichte. Kanonistische Abteilung*, cv (1988), 133–40.

Grabmann, M., *Die Geschichte der scholastischen Methode* (2 vols.; Freiburg im Breisgau, 1911; repr. Darmstadt, 1957).

Granata, A., 'La dottrina dell'elemosina nel sermone *Pro sanctimonialibus de Paraclito* di Abelardo', *Aevum*, xlvii (1973), 32–59.

Grant, L., *Abbot Suger of St-Denis: Church and State in Early Twelfth-Century France* (The Medieval World; London, 1998).

—— 'Arnulf's Mentor: Geoffrey of Lèves, Bishop of Chartres', in *Writing Medieval Biography, 750–1250: Essays in Honour of Professor Frank Barlow*, ed. D. Bates, J. Crick, and S. Hamilton (Woodbridge, 2006), pp. 173–84.

—— 'Geoffrey of Lèves, bishop of Chartres, "Famous wheeler and dealer in secular business" ', in Grosse, ed., *Suger en question*, pp. 45–56.

Grauwen, W. M., 'Gaufried, bisschop van Chartres (1116–1149), vriend van Norbert en van de "Wanderprediger" ', *Analecta Praemonstratensia*, lviii (1982), 161–209.

—— 'Het getuigenis van Abaelard over Norbert van Gennep', *Analecta Praemonstratensia*, lxiii (1987), 5–25.

—— 'Nogmaals over Abelard, Bernard en Norbert', *Analecta Praemonstratensia*, lxv (1989), 162–5.

—— *Norbert, Erzbischof von Magdeburg (1126–1134)*, trans. L. Horstkötter (2nd edn.; Duisburg, 1986).

Green-Pedersen, N. J., 'William of Champeaux on Boethius' *Topics* according to Orleans Bibl. mun. 266', *Cahiers de l'Institut du Moyen Âge grec et latin*, xiii (Copenhagen, 1974), 13–30.

Griffiths, F. J., 'Brides and *Dominae*: Abelard's *Cura monialium* at the Augustinian monastery of Marbach', *Viator*, xxxiv (2003), 57–88.

—— 'The Cross and the *Cura monialium*: Robert of Arbrissel, John the Evangelist, and the pastoral care of women in the age of reform', *Speculum*, lxxxiii (2008), 303–30.

—— 'Men's duty to provide for women's needs: Abelard, Heloise, and their negotiation of the *Cura monialium*', *Journal of Medieval History*, xxx (2004), 1–24.

Grodecki, L., 'Abélard et Suger', in Jolivet and Louis, eds., *Pierre Abélard–*

Pierre le Vénérable, pp. 279–84. Repr., id., *Le Moyen Âge retrouvé: De l'an mil à l'an 1200* (2 vols.; Paris, 1986), i. 217–22.
—— 'Les Vitraux allégoriques de Saint-Denis', *Art de France*, i (1961), 19–46.
Grondeux, A., 'Guillaume de Champeaux, Joscelin de Soissons, Abélard et Gosvin d'Anchin: Étude d'un milieu intellectuel', in Rosier-Catach, ed., *Arts du langage et théologie*, pp. 3–43.
—— 'Sainteté et grammaire: Figures d'une mésentente. Gosvin d'Anchin, Bernard d'Anchin et les "Notae Dunelmenses"', in M. Goullet, ed., *Parva pro magnis munera: Études de littérature tardo-antique et médiévale offertes à François Dolbeau par ses élèves* (Instrumenta patristica et mediaevalia, li; Turnhout, 2009), pp. 883–918.
—— and Rosier-Catach, I., 'Les *Glosulae super Priscianum* et leur tradition', in Rosier-Catach, ed., *Arts du langage et théologie*, pp. 107–79.
Grosse, R., 'L'Abbé Adam, prédécesseur de Suger', in Grosse, ed., *Suger en question*, pp. 31–43.
—— *Saint-Denis zwischen Adel und König: Die Zeit vor Suger (1053–1122)* (Beihefte der Francia, lvii; Stuttgart, 2002).
—— ed., *Suger en question: Regards croisés sur Saint-Denis* (Pariser Historische Studien, lxviii; Munich, 2004).
Groten, M., 'Die Urkunde Karls des Grossen für St.-Denis von 813 (D. 286), eine Fälschung Abt Sugers?', *Historisches Jahrbuch*, cviii (1988), 1–36.
Gryson, R., *Le Ministère des femmes dans l'Église ancienne* (Recherches et Synthèses, Section d'histoire, iv; Gembloux, 1972).
Guillotel, H., 'Les Premiers Temps de l'abbaye de Saint-Sulpice la Forêt', *Bulletin de la Société d'Histoire et d'Archéologie de Bretagne* (1971–4), 60–2.
—— *Recueil des actes des ducs de Bretagne, 944–1148* (Paris, Faculté de droit, thèse, 1971).
Halphen, L., *Paris sous les premiers Capétiens (987–1223)* (Paris, 1909).
Häring, N. M., 'Abelard yesterday and today', in Jolivet and Louis, eds., *Pierre Abélard–Pierre le Vénérable*, pp. 341–403.
—— 'Chartres and Paris revisited', in J. R. O'Donnell, ed., *Essays in Honour of Anton Charles Pegis* (Toronto, 1974), pp. 258–303.
—— 'Commentaries on the Pseudo-Athanasian Creed', *Mediaeval Studies*, xxxiv (1972), 208–52.
—— 'Die Gedichte und Mysterienspiele des Hilarius von Orléans', *Studi medievali*, 3ª ser., xvii (1976), 915–68.
—— 'Hilary of Orleans and his letter collection', *Studi medievali*, 3ª ser., xiv (1973), 1069–1122.
—— 'Thomas of Morigny, *Disputatio catholicorum patrum contra dogmata Petri Abailardi*', *Studi medievali*, 3ª ser., xxii (1981), 299–376.
—— 'Die vierzehn *Capitula Heresum Petri Abaelardi*', *Cîteaux*, xxxi (1980), 32–52.

Häring, N. M., 'The writings against Gilbert of Poitiers by Geoffrey of Auxerre', *Analecta Cisterciensia*, xxii (1966), 21–8.

Haseldine, J. P., ed., *Friendship in Medieval Europe* (Stroud, 1999).

Haskins, C. H., *The Renaissance of the Twelfth Century* (Cambridge, Mass., 1927).

Haskins, S., *Mary Magdalen: Myth and Metaphor* (New York, 1993).

Herde, R., 'Das Hohelied in der lateinischen Literatur des Mittelalters bis zum 12. Jahrhundert', *Studi medievali*, 3[a] ser., viii (1967), 957–1073. Also published separately (Spoleto, 1968).

Hicks, E., ed. *Le Débat sur le Roman de la Rose* (Bibliothèque du XVe siècle, liii; Paris, 1977).

Histoire littéraire de la France par des religieux bénédictins de la congrégation de S. Maur (Paris, 1733–).

Hödl, L., *Die Geschichte der scholastischen Literatur und der Theologie der Schlüsselgewalt*, i (*BGPTMA* xxxviii (4); Münster i. W., 1960).

Howlett, D. R., 'Arithmetic rhythms in Latin letters', *Archivum Latinitatis Medii Aevi* (Bulletin du Cange), lvi (1998), 195–225.

—— 'Some criteria for editing Abelard', *Archivum Latinitatis Medii Aevi* (Bulletin du Cange), li (1993), 195–202.

Hubert, J., 'La Frontière occidentale du comté de Champagne du XIe au XIIIe siècle', in *Recueil de travaux offerts à M. Cl. Brunel* (Mémoires et documents publiés par la Société de l'École des Chartes, xii; 2 vols.; Paris, 1955), ii. 14–30.

Huchet, J.- C., 'La Voix d'Héloïse', *Romance Notes*, xxv (1985), 271–87.

Huglo, M., 'Abélard, poète et musicien', *Cahiers de civilisation médiévale*, xxii (1979), 349–61.

—— 'Un Nouveau Prosaire nivernais', *Ephemerides liturgicae*, lxxi (1957), 3–30.

Hunt, N., *Cluny under St Hugh, 1049–1109* (London, 1967).

—— ed., *Cluniac Monasticism in the Central Middle Ages* (Readings in European History; London, 1971).

Hunt, R. W., 'Studies on Priscian in the eleventh and twelfth centuries', *Mediaeval and Renaissance Studies*, i (1943), 194–231; ii (1950), 1–56.

Hunter, D. G., *Marriage, Celibacy, and Heresy in Ancient Christianity: The Jovinianist Controversy* (Oxford Early Christian Studies; Oxford, 2007).

Huot, S., *The* Romance of the Rose *and its Medieval Readers: Interpretation, Reception, Manuscript Transmission* (Cambridge Studies in Medieval Literature, xvi; Cambridge, 1993).

Irvine, M., 'Abelard and (re)writing the male body: Castration, identity, and remasculinization', in J. J. Cohen and B. Wheeler, eds., *Becoming Male in the Middle Ages* (New York, 1997), pp. 87–106.

—— 'Heloise and the gendering of the literate subject', in R. Copeland, ed., *Criticism and Dissent in the Middle Ages* (Cambridge, 1996), pp. 87–114.

Iversen, G., 'Continuité et renouvellement à Nevers: Réflexions sur le répertoire du "prosaire-tropaire Nivernais" Paris BN na 3126', in W. Arlt and G. Björkvall, eds., *Recherches nouvelles sur les tropes liturgiques* (Stockholm, 1993), pp. 271–308.

—— 'Pierre Abélard et la poésie liturgique', in Jolivet and Habrias, eds., *Pierre Abélard. Colloque international de Nantes*, pp. 233–60.

Iwakuma, Y., 'The *Introductiones dialecticae secundum Wilgelmum* and *secundum G. Paganellum*', *Cahiers de l'Institut du Moyen Âge grec et latin*, lxiii (Copenhagen, 1993), 45–114.

—— 'Pierre Abélard et Guillaume de Champeaux dans les premières années du XIIe siècle: Une étude préliminaire', in J. Biard, ed., *Langage, Sciences, Philosophie au XIIe siècle* (Sic et Non; Paris, 1999), pp. 93–123.

—— '*Pseudo-Rabanus super Porphyrium*', *AHDLMA*, lxxv (2008), 43–196.

—— 'The realism of Anselm and his contemporaries', in Luscombe and Evans, eds., *Anselm, Aosta, Bec and Canterbury*, pp. 120–35.

—— '"Vocales" or early nominalists', *Traditio*, xlvii (1992), 37–111.

—— '"*Vocales*" revisited', in C. Burnett, ed., *The Word in Medieval Logic, Theology and Psychology* (Turnhout, 2009), pp. 81–171.

—— 'William of Champeaux and the *Introductiones*', in H. A. G. Braakhuis and C. H. Kneepkens, eds., *Aristotle's Peri Hermeneias in the Latin Middle Ages: Essays on the Commentary Tradition* (Artistarium Supplementa, x; Groningen, 2003), pp. 1–30.

—— 'William of Champeaux on Aristotle's *Categories*', in J. Biard and I. Rosier-Catach, eds., *La Tradition médiévale des Catégories (XIIe–XVe siècles)* (Philosophes médiévaux, xlv; Louvain, 2003), pp. 313–28.

Jacobi, K., 'William of Champeaux: Remarks on the tradition in the manuscripts', in Rosier-Catach, ed., *Arts du langage et théologie*, pp. 261–71.

Jaeger, C. S., *Ennobling Love: In Search of a Lost Sensibility* (Philadelphia, 1999).

—— *The Envy of Angels: Cathedral Schools and Social Ideals in Medieval Europe 950–1200* (Philadelphia, 1994).

—— '*Epistolae duorum amantium* and the ascription to Heloise and Abelard', in Olson and Kerby-Fulton, eds., *Voices in Dialogue*, pp. 125–66.

—— 'Peter Abelard's silence at the Council of Sens (1140)', *Res publica litterarum*, iii (1980), 31–54.

—— 'The Prologue to the *Historia calamitatum* and the "authenticity question"', *Euphorion*, lxxiv (1980), 1–15. Cf. Silvestre (below), review of Jaeger.

—— 'A reply to Giles Constable', in Olson and Kerby-Fulton, eds., *Voices in Dialogue*, pp. 179–86.

Jansen, K. L., *The Making of the Magdalen: Preaching and Popular Devotion in the Later Middle Ages* (Princeton, 2000).

Janson, T., *Prose Rhythm in Medieval Latin from the 9th to the 13th Century* (Acta Universitatis Stockholmiensis: Studia Latina Stockholmiensia, xx; Stockholm, 1975).

—— 'Schools of cursus in the twelfth century and the letters of Heloise and Abelard', in C. Leonardi and E. Menestò, eds., *Retorica e poetica tra i secoli XII e XIV. Atti del secondo Convegno internazionale di studi dell'Associazione per il Medioevo e l'Umanesimo latini (AMUL) in onore e memoria di Ezio Franceschini, Trento e Rovereto 3–5 ottobre 1985* (Quaderni del 'Centro per il Collegamento degli Studi Medievali e Umanistici nell'Università di Perugia', xviii; Perugia, 1988), pp. 169–200.

Jeauneau, E., *L'Âge d'or des écoles de Chartres* (Chartres, 1995).

—— 'Pierre Abélard à Saint-Denis', in Jolivet, ed., *Abélard en son temps*, pp. 161–73. Repr. in Jeauneau, *Tendenda vela: Excursions littéraires et digressions philosophiques à travers le Moyen Âge* (Instrumenta patristica et mediaevalia; Research on the Inheritance of Early and Medieval Christianity, xlvii; Turnhout 2007), pp. 167–91.

—— *Rethinking the School of Chartres*, trans. from the French by C. P. Desmarais (Rethinking the Middle Ages, iii; University of Toronto Press, 2009).

Jenal, G.,'*Caput autem mulieris vir* (I Kor II, 3): Praxis und Begründung des Doppelklosters im Briefkorpus Abaelard-Heloisa', *Archiv für Kulturgeschichte*, lxxvi (1994), 285–304.

Jeudy, C., 'La Correspondance d'Abélard et Héloïse: À propos d'un manuscrit nouveau', in *Autour de George Sand: Mélanges offerts à Georges Lubin* (Centre d'Étude des Correspondances des XIXe et XXe siècles, U.P.R. 422 du C.N.R.S. Faculté des Lettres et Sciences Sociales, Université de Brest (1992), pp. 133–43.

—— 'Un Nouveau Manuscrit de la *Correspondance* d'Abélard et Héloïse', *Latomus*, l (1991), 872–81.

Johnson, P., *Equal in Monastic Profession: Religious Women in Medieval France* (Chicago, 1991).

Jolivet, J., 'Abélard entre chien et loup', *Cahiers de civilisation médiévale*, xx (1977), 307–22.

—— *Abelardo: Dialettica e mistero* (Milan, 1996).

—— 'Doctrines et figures de philosophes chez Abélard', in Thomas and others, eds., *Petrus Abaelardus (1079–1142)*, pp. 103–20.

—— 'Données sur Guillaume de Champeaux, dialecticien et théologien', in J. Longère, ed., *L'Abbaye parisiennne de Saint-Victor au Moyen Âge: Communications présentées au XIIIe Colloque d'humanisme médiéval de Paris (1986–1988)* (Bibliotheca Victorina, i; Turnhout, 1991), pp. 235–51.

—— 'Sur quelques critiques de la théologie d'Abélard', *AHDLMA*, xxx (1963), 7–51. Repr. in id., *Aspects de la pensée médiévale: Abélard. Doctrines du langage* (Paris, 1987), pp. 7–51.

—— 'Trois variations médiévales sur l'universel et l'individu: Roscelin, Abélard, Gilbert de la Porrée', *Revue de métaphysique et de morale*, xcvii (1992), 111–55.

—— ed., *Abélard en son temps. Actes du Colloque international organisé à l'occasion du 9e centenaire de la naissance de Pierre Abélard (14–19 mai 1979)* (Paris, 1981).

—— and Habrias, H., eds., *Pierre Abélard. Colloque international de Nantes* (Collection 'Histoire'; Rennes, 2003).

—— and Louis, R., eds., *Pierre Abélard–Pierre le Vénérable: Les courants philosophiques, littéraires et artistiques en Occident au milieu du XIIe siècle. Abbaye de Cluny, 2 au 9 juillet 1972* (Colloques internationaux du CNRS, dxlvi; Paris, 1975).

Kauffman, L. S., 'The irremediable: Heloise to Abelard', in ead., *Discourses of Desire: Gender, Genre, and Epistolary Fictions* (Ithaca, NY, 1986), pp. 63–89.

Kearney, E., 'Peter Abelard as biblical commentator: A study in the *Expositio in Hexaemeron*', in Thomas and others, eds., *Petrus Abaelardus (1079–1142)*, pp. 199–209.

—— '*Scientia* and *sapientia*: Reading sacred Scriptures at the Paraclete', in E. R. Elder, ed., *From Cloister to Classroom* (Kalamazoo, Mich., 1986), pp. 111–29.

Kelso, Jr., C., 'Women in power: Fontevrault and the Paraclete compared', *Comitatus: A Journal of Medieval and Renaissance Studies*, xxii (1991), 55–69.

Kerr, B. M., *Religious Life for Women c. 1100–c.1350: Fontevraud in England* (Oxford Historical Monographs; Oxford, 1999).

Klibansky, R., 'Peter Abailard and Bernard of Clairvaux: A letter by Abailard', *Medieval and Renaissance Studies*, v (1961), 1–27.

Kluge, E.-H., 'Roscelin and the medieval problem of universals', *Journal of the History of Philosophy*, xiv (1976), 405–14.

Kindermann, U., 'Abaelards Liebesbriefe', *Euphorion*, lxx (1976), 287–95.

Kneepkens, C. H., 'There is more in a biblical quotation than meets the eye: On Peter the Venerable's letter of consolation to Heloise', in *Media latinitas: A Collection of Essays to Mark the Occasion of the Retirement of L. J. Engels* (Steenbrugge, 1996), pp. 89–100.

Knowles, D., *The Evolution of Medieval Thought* (London 1962); 2nd edn. rev. D. E. Luscombe and C. N. L. Brooke (Harlow, 1988).

—— and Hadcock, R. N., *Medieval Religious Houses: England and Wales* (2nd edn.; Harlow, 1971, reissued 1994).

Könsgen, E., ' "Der Nordstern scheint auf den Pol": Baudolinos Liebesbrief an Beatrix, die Kaiserin – oder "Ex epistolis duorum amantium" ', in A. Bihrer and E. Stein, eds., *Nova de veteribus: Mittel- und neulateinische Studien für Paul Gerhard Schmidt* (Munich, 2004), pp. 1113–21.

Kolb, H., review of von Moos, *Mittelalterforschung und Ideologiekritik*, in *Euphorion*, lxviii (1974), 286–95.

Kouamé, T., *Le Collège de Dormans-Beauvais à la fin du Moyen Âge: Stratégies politiques et parcours individuels à l'Université de Paris (1370–1458)* (Education and Society in the Middle Ages and Renaissance, 22; Leiden, 2005).

Ladner, G. B., *The Idea of Reform: Its Impact on Christian Thought and Action in the Age of the Fathers* (Cambridge, Mass., 1959).

—— 'Two Gregorian letters: On the sources and nature of Gregory VII's reform ideology', *Studi Gregoriani*, v (1956), 221–42.

I laici nella 'Societas Christiana' dei secoli XI e XII. Atti della terza Settimana internazionale di studio, Mendola, 21–27 agosto 1965 (Pubblicazioni dell'Università cattolica del Sacro Cuore, Contributi 3 S.: Varia 5; Miscellanea del Centro di studi medioevali, v; Milan, 1968).

Lanham, C. D., *Salutatio Formulas in Latin Letters to 1200: Syntax, Style, and Theory* (Münchener Beiträge zur Mediävistik und Renaissance-Forschung, xxii; Munich, 1975).

Latzke, Th., 'Abälard, Hilarius und das Gedicht 22 der Ripollsammlung', *Mittellateinisches Jahrbuch*, viii (1973), 70–89.

—— 'Zu dem Gedicht *De papa scolastico* des Abaelardschülers Hilarius', *Mittellateinisches Jahrbuch*, xiii (1978), 86–99.

Laurie, H. C. R.,'Cligès and the legend of Abelard and Heloise', *Zeitschrift für romanische Philologie*, cvii (1991), 325–42.

—— 'Heloise and her achievement', in ead., *The Making of Romance: Three Studies* (Geneva, 1991), ch. 3, pp. 95–119.

—— 'The *Letters* of Abelard and Heloise: A source for Chrétien de Troyes?', *Studi medievali*, 3ª ser., xxvii (1986), 123–46.

Leclercq, J., '*Ad ipsam sophiam Christi*: Das monastische Zeugnis Abaelards', in *Sapienter ordinare: Festgabe für Erich Kleineidam* (Leipzig, 1969), pp. 179–98. (The next entry is a French version of this study.)

—— '*Ad ipsam sophiam Christum*: Le témoignage monastique d'Abélard', *Revue d'ascétique et de mystique*, xlvi (1970), 161–82.

—— 'L'Amitié dans les lettres au Moyen Âge: Autour d'un manuscrit de la bibliothèque de Pétrarque', *Revue du Moyen Age latin*, i (1945), 391–410.

—— 'Autour de la correspondance de S. Bernard', in '*Sapientiae Doctrina*': *Mélanges de théologie et de littérature offerts à Dom Hildebrand Bascour* (Leuven, 1980), pp. 185–98.

—— 'Comment vivaient les frères convers', *Analecta Cisterciensia*, xxi (1965), 239–58. Also in *I Laici nella 'Societas Christiana'*, pp. 152–82.

—— 'Documents sur les "fugitifs" ', *Analecta Monastica: Textes et études sur la vie des moines au moyen âge*, 7th ser., by R. Grégoire and others (Studia Anselmiana, liv; Rome, 1965), pp. 87–145.

—— *Études sur le vocabulaire monastique du moyen âge* (Studia Anselmiana, xlviii; Rome, 1961).
—— 'Études sur S. Bernard et le texte de ses écrits', *Analecta Sacri Ordinis Cisterciensis*, ix (1–2) (1953).
—— 'Les Formes successives de la lettre-traité de saint Bernard contre Abélard', *Revue bénédictine*, lxxviii (1968), 87–105.
—— 'Modern psychology and the interpretation of medieval texts', *Speculum*, xlviii (1973), 476–90.
—— 'Notes abélardiennes', *Bulletin de la Société SIEPM*, viii–ix (1966–7), 59–62.
—— *Otia monastica: Études sur le vocabulaire de la contemplation au moyen âge* (Studia Anselmiana, li; Rome, 1963).
Lefèvre, G., *Les Variations de Guillaume de Champeaux et la question des universaux: Étude suivie de documents originaux* (Travaux et Mémoires de l'Université de Lille, VI, xx; Lille, 1898).
Leisching, P., 'Consuetudo und ratio im Dekret und der Panormia des Bischofs Ivo von Chartres', *Zeitschrift der Savigny-Stiftung für Rechtsgeschichte*, cv, *Kanonistische Abteilung*, lxxiv (1988), 535–41.
Lemarignier, J.-F., *Le Gouvernement royal aux premiers temps Capétiens (987–1108)* (Paris, 1965).
Le Noble, A., 'Deux préfaces inédites d'Abailard', *Annales de philosophie chrétienne*, 3e sér., ix (1844), 18–21.
—— 'Lettre inédite d'Abailard à Héloïse', *Bibliothèque de l'École des Chartes*, iii (1841–2), 172–82.
Leonardi, C., 'Intellectual Life', in *The New Cambridge Medieval History*, iii: *c. 900–c. 1024*, ed. T. Reuter (Cambridge, 1999), pp. 186–211.
Lesne, E., *Les Écoles de la fin du VIIe siècle à la fin du XIIe* (Histoire de la propriété ecclésiastique en France, v; Lille, 1940).
Le Vot, G., 'Que savons-nous sur la musique des *Planctus* d'Abélard?' in Zumthor, *Pierre Abélard: Lamentations* (see *Bibliography: Writings of Abelard and Heloise – Other Translations of the Letter Collection – French*), pp. 107–22.
Lexikon des Mittelalters, ed. L. Lutz and others (10 vols.; Munich, 1977–98).
Libera, A. de, *L'Art des généralités* (Paris, 1999).
—— 'Guillaume de Champeaux', in *Dictionnaire du Moyen Âge*, ed. Gauvard, de Libera, and Zink, pp. 634–5.
Light, L., 'Versions et révisions du texte biblique', in P. Riché and G. Lobrichon, eds., *Le Moyen Âge et la Bible* (Paris, 1984), pp. 75–93.
Linscheid-Burdich, S., *Suger von Saint-Denis: Untersuchungen zu seiner Schriften 'Ordinatio' – 'De consecratione' – 'De administratione'* (Beiträge zur Altertumskunde, cc; Munich, 2004).
Little, E. F., 'Relations between St. Bernard and Abelard before 1138', *Cistercian Studies*, xxviii (1977), 155–68.

Lobrichon, G., *Héloïse: L'amour et le savoir* (Paris, 2005).

Lottin, O., *Psychologie et morale aux XIIe et XIIIe siècles*, v: *Problèmes d'histoire littéraire. L'école d'Anselme de Laon et de Guillaume de Champeaux* (Gembloux, 1959).

Louis, R., 'Pierre Abélard et l'architecture monastique: L'abbaye du Paraclet, au diocèse de Troyes', in *L'Architecture monastique: Actes et travaux de la recherche franco-allemande des historiens d'art, 1951* (Numéro spécial du Bulletin des relations artistiques France-Allemagne (Mayence), mai, 1951, 8 pp.).

Luscombe, D. E., 'Denis the Pseudo-Areopagite in the Middle Ages from Hilduin to Lorenzo Valla', in *Fälschungen im Mittelalter*, i: *Kongressdaten und Festvorträge. Literatur und Fälschung*, pp. 133–52.

—— 'Excerpts from the letter collection of Heloise and Abelard in Notre Dame (Indiana) ms 30', in *Pascua Mediaevalia: Studies voor Prof Dr. J. M. De Smet* (Mediaevalia Lovaniensia, Series 1/Studia, x; Leuven, 1983), pp. 529–44.

—— 'From Paris to the Paraclete: The correspondence of Abelard and Heloise', The Raleigh Lecture in History, *Proceedings of the British Academy*, lxxiv (1988), 247–83.

——'The letters of Heloise and Abelard since "Cluny 1972" ', in Thomas and others, eds., *Petrus Abaelardus (1079–1142)*, pp. 19–39.

—— *Peter Abelard* (Historical Association; London, 1979).

—— 'Peter Abelard and the poets', in Marenbon, ed., *Poetry and Philosophy*, pp. 155–71.

—— 'Pierre Abélard et l'abbaye du Paraclet', in Jolivet and Habrias, eds., *Pierre Abélard. Colloque international de Nantes*, pp. 215–29.

—— 'Pierre Abélard et le monachisme', in Jolivet and Louis, eds., *Pierre Abèlard–Pierre le Vénérable*, pp. 271–8.

—— *The School of Peter Abelard: The Influence of Abelard's Thought in the Early Scholastic Period* (Cambridge Studies in Medieval Life and Thought, 2nd Series, xiv; Cambridge, 1969, repr. 1970).

—— 'St Anselm and Abelard: A restatement', in *Saint Anselm—A Thinker for Yesterday and Today. Anselm's Thought Viewed by Our Contemporaries*, in C. Viola and F. Van Fleteren, eds., *Proceedings of the International Anselm Conference. Centre National de Recherche Scientifique Paris* (Texts and Studies in Religion, xc; Lewiston, NY, 2002), pp. 445–60.

—— and Evans, G. R., eds., *Anselm: Aosta, Bec and Canterbury. Papers in Commemoration of the Nine-Hundredth Anniversary of Anselm's Enthronement as Archbishop, 25 September 1093* (Sheffield, 1996).

Lutterbach, H., '"Ein Herz und eine Seele . . .": Peter Abaelards Lebensregel für Klosterfrauen', *Studien und Mitteilungen zur Geschichte des Benediktinerordens und seiner Zweige*, cx (1999), 99–123.

Mabillon, J., *Annales ordinis sancti Benedicti*, i–iv (Paris, 1703–7).

McDonough, C. J., 'Miscellaneous notes to Hugh Primas and Arundel 1', *Mittellateinisches Jahrbuch*, xiv (1979), 187–99.

McEvoy, J., 'The theory of friendship in the Latin Middle Ages: Hermeneutics, contextualisation and the transmission of ancient texts and ideas from *c.* AD 350 to *c.* 1500', in Haseldine, ed., *Friendship in Medieval Europe*, pp. 3–44.

McGinn, B., '*Teste David cum Sibylla*: The significance of the Sibylline tradition in the Middle Ages', in J. Kirshner and S. F. Wemple, eds., *Women of the Medieval World: Essays in Honor of John H. Mundy* (Oxford, 1985), pp. 7–35.

McLaughlin, M. M., 'Abelard as autobiographer: The motives and meaning of his "Story of Calamities" ', *Speculum*, xlii (1967), 463–88.

—— 'Heloise the abbess: The expansion of the Paraclete', in Wheeler, ed., *Listening to Heloise*, pp. 1–17.

—— 'Peter Abelard and the dignity of women: Twelfth-century "feminism" in theory and practice', in Jolivet and Louis, eds., *Pierre Abélard–Pierre le Vénérable*, pp. 287–334.

McLaughlin, T. P., 'Abelard's Rule for religious women', *Mediaeval Studies*, xviii (1956), 241–92.

McLeod, E., *Héloïse: A Biography* (London 1938; 2nd edn., London, 1971, with an additional, brief preface but the same pagination); Italian trans., *Eloisa* (Milan, 1951).

McNamer, E. M., *The Education of Heloise: Methods, Content and Purpose of Learning in the Twelfth Century* (Medieval Studies, viii; Lewiston, NY, 1991).

Macy, G., *The Hidden History of Women's Ordination: Female Clergy in the Medieval West* (Oxford, 2008).

Mann, J., *Feminizing Chaucer* (Chaucer Studies; Cambridge, 2002).

Marenbon, J., 'Authenticity revisited', in Wheeler, ed., *Listening to Heloise*, pp. 19–33.

—— 'Logic at the turn of the twelfth century: A synthesis', in Rosier-Catach, ed., *Arts du langage et théologie*, pp. 181–217.

—— 'Lost love letters? A controversy in retrospect', *International Journal of the Classical Tradition*, xv (2008), 267–80.

—— 'Medieval Latin glosses and commentaries on Aristotelian logical texts, before *c.* 1150 AD', in Burnett, ed., *Glosses and Commentaries*, pp. 77–127.

—— *The Philosophy of Peter Abelard* (Cambridge, 1997).

—— 'The rediscovery of Peter Abelard's philosophy', *Journal of the History of Philosophy*, xliv (2006), 331–51.

—— 'Vocalism, nominalism and the commentaries on the Categories from the earlier twelfth century', *Vivarium*, xxx (1992), 51–61.

—— ed., *Poetry and Philosophy in the Middle Ages: A Festschrift for Peter Dronke* (Mittellateinische Studien und Texte, xxix; Leiden, 2001).

Martène, E., and Durand, U., *Voyage littéraire de deux religieux bénédictins de la congrégation de S. Maur* (3 parts in 2 vols.; Paris, 1717–24).

Martimort, A. G., *Les Diaconesses: Étude historique* (Bibliotheca Ephemerides Liturgicae, Subsidia, xxiv; Rome, 1982). English trans. (San Francisco, 1986).

Martin, C. J., 'A note on the attribution of the *Literal Glosses* in Paris, BnF, lat. 13368 to Peter Abaelard', in Rosier-Catach, ed., *Arts du langage et théologie*, pp. 605–46.

Melville, G., 'Regeln – *Consuetudines* – Texte – Statuten: Positionen für eine Typologie des normativen Schrifttums religiöser Gemeinschaften im Mittelalter', in *Regulae – Consuetudines – Statuta: Studi sulle fonti normative degli ordini religiosi nei secoli centrali del Medioevo*, ed. C. Andenna and G. Melville (Vita regularis, xxv; Münster, 2005), pp. 5–38.

Metz, R., *La Femme et l'enfant dans le droit canonique médiéval* (Variorum Reprints, CS222; London, 1985).

Mews, C. J., *Abelard and Heloise* (Great Medieval Thinkers; Oxford, 2005).

—— *Abelard and his Legacy* (Variorum Collected Studies Series, CS704; Aldershot, 2001).

—— 'Aspects of the evolution of Peter Abelard's thought on signification and predication', in J. Jolivet and A. de Libera, eds., *Gilbert de Poitiers et ses contemporains* (History of Logic, v; Naples, 1987), pp. 15–41. Repr. with the same pagination in Mews, *Abelard and his Legacy*.

—— 'La Bibliothèque du Paraclet du XIIIe siècle à la Révolution', *Studia monastica*, xxvii (1985), 31–60 (with an *Appendice* by Mews and C. S. F. Burnett: 'Les Épitaphes d'Abélard et d'Héloïse au Paraclet et au prieuré de Saint-Marcel à Chalon-sur-Saône', pp. 61–7). Repr. with the same pagination in Mews, *Reason and Belief*.

—— 'Cicero and the boundaries of friendship in the twelfth century', *Viator*, xxxviii (2007), 369–84.

—— 'The Council of Sens 1141, Abelard, Bernard and the fear of social upheaval', *Speculum*, lxxvii (2002), 342–82.

—— 'The development of the *Theologia* of Peter Abelard', in Thomas and others, eds., *Petrus Abaelardus (1079–1142)*, pp. 183–98. Repr. with the same pagination in Mews, *Abelard and his Legacy*.

—— 'Heloise', in A. Minnis and R. Voaden, eds., *Medieval Holy Women in the Christian Tradition, c. 1100–c. 1500* (Turnhout, 2010), pp. 267–89.

—— 'Heloise, the Paraclete liturgy and Mary Magdalen', in Stewart and Wulstan, eds., *Poetic and Musical Legacy*, pp. 100–12.

—— 'Hugh Métel, Heloise, and Peter Abelard: The letters of an Augustinian canon and the challenge of innovation in twelfth-century Lorraine', *Viator*, xxxii (2001), 59–91.

—— 'In search of a name and its significance: A twelfth-century anecdote about Thierry and Peter Abaelard', *Traditio*, xliv (1988), 171–200. Repr. with the same pagination in Mews, *Reason and Belief.*

—— 'Interpreting Abelard and Heloise in the fourteenth and early fifteenth centuries: The criticisms of Christine de Pisan and Jean Gerson', in P. J. J. M. Bakker and others, eds., *Chemins de la pensée médiévale: Études offertes à Zénon Kaluza* (Textes et Études du Moyen Âge, xx; Turnhout, 2002), pp. 709–24.

—— 'Un Lecteur de Jérome au XIIe siècle: Pierre Abélard', in Y.-M. Duval, ed., *Jérome entre l'Occident et l'Orient: XVIe centenaire du départ de saint Jérome de Rome et de son installation à Bethléem. Actes du Colloque de Chantilly (septembre 1986)* (Paris, 1988), pp. 431–44. Repr. with the same pagination in Mews, *Abelard and his Legacy.*

—— 'Les Lettres d'amour perdues d'Héloïse et la théologie de Pierre Abélard', in Jolivet and Habrias, eds., *Pierre Abélard. Colloque international de Nantes*, pp. 137–59.

—— 'The lists of heresies imputed to Peter Abelard', *Revue bénédictine*, xcv (1985), 73–110. Repr. with the same pagination in Mews, *Abelard and his Legacy.*

—— 'Liturgy and identity at the Paraclete: Heloise, Abelard and the evolution of Cistercian reform', in Stewart and Wulstan, eds., *Poetic and Musical Legacy*, pp. 19–33.

—— '*Logica* in the service of philosophy: William of Champeaux and his influence', in R. Berndt, ed., *Schrift, Schreiber, Schenker: Studien zur Abtei Sankt Viktor in Paris und den Viktorinen* (Corpus Victorinum, Instrumenta, i; Berlin, 2005), pp. 77–117.

—— *The Lost Love Letters of Heloise and Abelard: Perceptions of Dialogue in Twelfth-Century France.* With a translation by N. Chiavaroli and C. J. Mews (New York, 1999).

—— 'A neglected gloss on the "Isagoge" by Peter Abelard', *Freiburger Zeitschrift für Philosophie und Theologie*, xxxi (1984), 35–55. Repr. with the same pagination in Mews, *Abelard and his Legacy.*

—— 'Negotiating the boundaries of gender in religious life: Robert of Arbrissel and Hersende, Abelard and Heloise', *Viator*, xxxvii (2006), 113–48.

—— 'Nominalism and theology before Abaelard: New light on Roscelin of Compiègne', *Vivarium*, xxx (1992), 4–33. Repr.with the same pagination in Mews, *Reason and Belief.*

—— 'On dating the works of Peter Abelard', *AHDLMA* lii, Année 1985 (1986), 73–134. Repr. with the same pagination in Mews, *Abelard and his Legacy.*

—— 'On some recent publications relating to Peter Abelard', *Archa Verbi*, i (2004), 119–27.

—— *Peter Abelard* (Authors of the Middle Ages, v; Aldershot, 1995).

Mews, C. J., 'Peter Abelard's *Theologia Christiana* and *Theologia 'Scholarium'* re-examined', *Recherches de théologie ancienne et médiévale*, lii (1985), 109–58. Repr. with the same pagination in Mews, *Abelard and his Legacy*.

—— 'Philosophical themes in the *Epistolae duorum amantium*: The first letters of Heloise and Abelard', in Wheeler, ed., *Listening to Heloise*, pp. 35–52.

—— *Reason and Belief in the Age of Roscelin and Abelard* (Variorum Collected Studies Series, dccxxx (London, 2002).

—— 'Robert d'Arbrissel, Roscelin et Abélard', *Revue Mabillon*, NS vii (= lxxxi) (2009), 33–54.

—— 'St Anselm and Roscelin: Some new texts and their implications 1: The *De Incarnatione verbi* and the *Disputatio inter Christianum et Gentilem*', *AHDLMA* lviii, Année 1991, pp. 55–97; 'St. Anselm and Roscelin: Some new texts and their implications 2: A vocalist essay on the Trinity and intellectual debate *c.* 1080–1120', *AHDLMA* lxv, Année 1998, pp. 39–90. Repr. with the same pagination in Mews, *Abelard and his Legacy*.

—— 'St Anselm, Roscelin and the See of Beauvais', in Luscombe and Evans, eds., *Anselm: Aosta, Bec and Canterbury*, pp. 106–19. Repr. with the same pagination in Mews, *Reason and Belief*.

—— 'The *Sententie* of Peter Abelard', *Recherches de théologie ancienne et médiévale*, liii (1986), 130–83. Repr.with the same pagination in Mews, *Abelard and his Legacy*.

—— 'Thèmes philosophiques dans les *Epistolae duorum amantium*: Les premières lettres d'Héloïse et Abélard', in J. Biard, ed., *Langages, sciences, philosophies au XIIe siècle* (Sic et Non; Paris, 1999), pp. 23–38.

—— 'The Trinitarian doctrine of Roscelin of Compiègne and its influence: Twelfth-century nominalism and theology reconsidered', in A. de Libera and others, eds., *Langages et philosophie: Hommage à Jean Jolivet* (Études de philosophie médiévale, lxxiv (Paris, 1997), pp. 347–64. Repr. with the same pagination in Mews, *Reason and Belief*.

—— *La Voix d'Héloïse: Un dialogue de deux amants*, trans. E. Champs with F.-X. Putallaz and S. Piron (Vestigia, xxxi; Fribourg, 2005).

—— 'William of Champeaux, Abelard and Hugh of Saint-Victor: Platonism, theology and Scripture in early-twelfth century France', in R. Berndt, ed., *Bibel und Exegese in der Abtei Saint-Victor zu Paris: Form und Funktion eines Grundtextes im europäischen Rahmen* (Corpus Victorinum, Instrumenta, iii; Münster, 2009), pp. 131–63.

—— 'William of Champeaux, the foundation of Saint-Victor (Easter, 1111), and the evolution of Abelard's early career', in Rosier-Catach, ed., *Arts du langage et théologie* (2011), pp. 83–104.

—— and Burnett, C. S. F., 'Les Épitaphes d'Abélard et d'Héloise au Paraclet et au prieuré de Saint-Marcel à Chalon-sur-Saône'. Appendix to Mews, 'La Bibliothèque du Paraclet', pp. 61–7.

—— and Jolivet, J., 'Peter Abelard and his influence', in G. Fløistad, ed., *La Philosophie contemporaine: Chroniques nouvelles* VI. *Philosophie et science au Moyen Age* (Dordrecht, 1990), i. 105–40.

—— Nederman, C. J., and Thomson, R. M., eds., *Rhetoric and Renewal in the Latin West 1100–1540: Essays in Honour of John O. Ward* (Disputatio, ii; Turnhout, 2003).

Meyer, W., *Gesammelte Abhandlungen zur Mittellateinischen Rhythmik*, i (Berlin, 1905).

—— 'Zwei mittellateinische Lieder in Florenz', *Studi letterari e linguistici dedicati a Pio Rajna* (Milan, 1911), pp. 149–66.

Michaud, E., *Guillaume de Champeaux et les écoles de Paris au XIIe siècle d'après des documents inédits* (2nd edn.; Paris, 1867).

Miethke, J., 'Abaelards Stellung zur Kirchenreform: Eine biographische Studie', *Francia*, i (1972), 158–92.

—— 'Theologenprozesse in der ersten Phase ihrer institutionellen Ausbildung: Die Verfahren gegen Peter Abaelard und Gilbert von Poitiers', *Viator*, vi (1975), 87–116.

Minnis, A., Scott, A. B., and Wallace, D., *Medieval Literary Theory and Criticism, c.1100–c.1375: The Commentary Tradition* (Oxford, 1991—rev. edn.)

Miramon, C. de, 'Quatre notes biographiques sur Guillaume de Champeaux', in Rosier-Catach, ed., *Arts du langage et théologie*, pp. 45–82.

Misch, G., *Geschichte der Autobiographie*, iii: *Das Mittelalter* 2: *Das Hochmittelalter im Anfang* (Framkfurt a. M., 1959).

Mohr, R., 'Der Gedankenaustausch zwischen Heloisa und Abaelard über eine Modifizierung der *Regula Benedicti* für Frauen', *Regulae Benedicti Studia*, v (1976–7), 307–33.

Montfaucon, B. de, *Bibliotheca Bibliothecarum Manuscriptorum nova* (2 vols.; Paris, 1739).

Monfrin, J., 'Le Problème de l'authenticité de la correspondance d'Abélard et d'Héloïse', in Jolivet and Louis, eds., *Pierre Abélard–Pierre le Vénérable*, pp. 409–24.

Moore, G., *Héloïse and Abélard* (2 vols.; London, 1921; repr. in 1 vol., London, 1926).

Moos, P. von, 'Abaelard, Heloise und ihr Paraklet: Ein Kloster nach Mass. Zugleich eine Streitschrift gegen die ewige Wiederkehr hermeneutischer Naivität', in G. Melville and M. Schürer, eds., *Das Eigene und das Ganze: Zum Individuellen im mittelalterlichen Religiosentum* (Vita regularis, xvi; Münster, 2002), pp. 563–620. Repr. in Moos, *Abaelard und Heloise*, pp. 233–301, with an additional excursus (2005) on pp. 282–92 concerning the *Epistulae duorum amantium*.

—— *Abaelard und Heloise: Gesammelte Studien zum Mittelalter*, i, ed.

G. Melville (Geschichte: Forschung und Wissenschaft, xiv; Münster, 2005).

—— 'Die Bekehrung Heloises', *Mittellateinisches Jahrbuch*, xi (1976), 95–125. Repr. in Moos, *Abaelard und Heloise*, pp. 9–47.

—— *Consolatio: Studien zur mittellateinischen Trostliteratur über den Tod und zum Problem der christlichen Trauer* (4 vols.; Munich, 1971–2).

—— contribution to discussion of Payen, 'La Pensée d'Abélard', in Jolivet and Louis, eds., *Pierre Abélard–Pierre le Vénérable*, p. 521.

—— 'Cornelia und Heloise', *Latomus*, xxxiv (1975), 1024–59. Repr. in Moos, *Abaelard und Heloise*, pp. 129–62.

—— 'Die *Epistolae duorum amantium* und die säkulare Religion der Liebe: Methodenkritische Vorüberlegungen zu einem einmaligen Werk mittellateinischer Briefliteratur', *Studi medievali*, 3ª ser., xliv (1) (2003), 1–115.

—— 'Heloise und Abaelard', in K. Corino, ed., *Gefälscht! Betrug in Politik, Literatur, Wissenschaft, Kunst und Musik* (Nordlingen, 1988), pp. 150–61. Repr. with additional comments in Moos, *Abaelard und Heloise*, pp. 199–213.

—— 'Heloise and Abaelard: Eine Liebesgeschichte vom 13. zum 20. Jahrhundert', in *Mittelalter und Moderne: Entdeckung und Rekonstruktion der mittelalterlichen Welt. Kongressakten des 6. Symposium des Mediävistenverbandes in Bayreuth 1995* (Sigmaringen, 1997), pp. 77–99. Repr. in Moos, *Abaelard und Heloise*, pp. 215–31.

—— *Hildebert von Lavardin 1056–1133: Humanitas an der Schwelle des höfischen Zeitalters* (Pariser Historische Studien, iii; Stuttgart, 1965).

—— 'Literary aesthetics in the Latin Middle Ages: The rhetorical theology of Abelard', in Mews, Nederman, and Thomson, eds., *Rhetoric and Renewal in the Latin West*, pp. 81–98. English version of Moos, 'Eine theologisch-rhetorische Antwort des 12. Jahrhunderts'.

—— 'Lucan und Abaelard', in G. Gambier, ed., *Hommages à André Boutémy* (Collection Latomus; Brussels, 1976), pp. 413–43. Repr. in Moos, *Abaelard und Heloise*, pp. 99–128.

—— *Mittelalterforschung und Ideologiekritik: Der Gelehrtenstreit um Heloise* (Kritische Information, xv; Munich, 1974).

—— '*Palatini quaestio quasi peregrini*: Ein gestriger Streitpunkt aus der Abaelard-Heloise-Kontroverse nochmals überprüft', *Mittellateinisches Jahrbuch*, ix (1974), 124–58. Repr. in Moos, *Abaelard und Heloise*, pp. 49–97 with a new title: 'Der Briefdialog zwischen Abaelard und Heloise: ein Existentielles *Sic et Non*.'

—— 'Petrus Abaelardus, *Epistulae*', in *Kindlers neues Literatur Lexikon*, xiii (Munich, 1991), pp. 198–201.

—— '*Post Festum* – Was kommt nach der Authentizitätsdebatte über die Briefe Abaelards und Heloises?', in Thomas and others, eds., *Petrus*

Abaelardus (1079–1142), pp. 75–100. Repr. in Moos, *Abaelard und Heloise*, pp. 163–97.

—— 'Le Silence d'Héloïse et les idéologies modernes', in Jolivet and Louis, eds., *Pierre Abélard–Pierre le Vénérable*, pp. 425–68.

—— 'Eine theologisch-rhetorische Antwort des 12. Jahrhunderts', in *Literarische Interessenbildung im Mittelalter (DFG-Tagung, Maurach 1991)* (Stuttgart, 1993), pp. 431–51. Repr. in Moos, *Abaelard und Heloise*, pp. 303–25 with a new title: 'Was galt im lateinischen Mittelalter als das Literarische an der Literatur? Eine theologisch-rhetorische Antwort Abaelards'. For an English version see von Moos, 'Literary Aesthetics in the Latin Middle Ages'.

Morelle, L., 'Suger et les archives', in Grosse, ed., *Suger en question*, pp. 117–39.

Morice, Dom Hyacinthe, *Mémoires pour servir de preuves à l'histoire ecclésiastique et civile de Bretagne* (3 vols.; Paris, 1742–6).

Morice, P.-H. (Dom Hyacinthe Morice), *Histoire ecclésiastique et civile de Bretagne* (2 vols.; Paris, 1750–6).

Muckle, J. T., 'Abelard's letter of consolation to a friend (*Historia Calamitatum*)', *Mediaeval Studies*, xii (1950), 163–213.

—— 'The letter of Heloise on the religious life and Abaelard's first reply', *Mediaeval Studies*, xvii (1955), 240–81.

—— 'The personal letters between Abaelard and Heloise', *Mediaeval Studies*, xv (1953), 47–94.

Murard, J., 'Les Pithou et l'école', in Fragonard and Leroy, eds., *Les Pithou*, pp. 65–88.

Murphy, J. J., *Medieval Rhetoric: A Select Bibliography* (Toronto Medieval Bibliographies, iii; Toronto, 1971).

—— *Rhetoric in the Middle Ages: A History of Rhetorical Theory from Augustine to the Renaissance* (Berkeley, 1974).

Nebbiai-Dalla Guarda, D., *La Bibliothèque de l'abbaye de Saint-Denis en France du IX*[e] *au XVIII*[e] *siècle* (Paris, 1985).

—— and Genest, J.-F., eds., *Du copiste au collectionneur: Mélanges d'histoire des textes et des bibliothèques en l'honneur d'André Vernet* (Bibliologia: Elementa ad librorum studia pertinentia, xviii; Turnhout, 1998).

Newman, B., 'Authority, authenticity and the repression of Heloise', *Journal of Medieval and Renaissance Studies*, xxii (1992), 121–57. Reprinted in Newman, *From Virile Woman to Woman Christ*, ch. 2, pp. 46–75.

—— *From Virile Woman to Woman Christ: Studies in Medieval Religion and Literature* (Middle Ages Series; Philadelphia, 1995).

Niggli, U., 'Berengar von Poitiers: Verteidigung Abaelards gegen Bernhard von Clairvaux', in Niggli, ed., *Peter Abaelard*, pp. 317–54.

—— 'Heloisa und Abaelard oder Heloisas Sehnsucht nach Freundschaft', in

E. Donnert, ed., *Europa in der Frühen Neuzeit: Festschrift für Günter Mühlpfordt*, vii (Vienna, 2008), pp. 1–53.

—— 'Zum Briefwechsel mit Heloisa: Erotische Konfession und klösterliche Instruktion', in Niggli, ed., *Peter Abaelard*, pp. 91–113.

—— ed., *Peter Abaelard: Leben – Werk – Wirkung* (Freiburg i. B., 2003).

Nolhac, P. de, *Pétrarque et l'humanisme* (2 vols., 2nd edn.; Paris, 1907; repr. 1965).

Nouvet, C., 'La Castration d'Abélard: Impasse et substitution', *Poétique*, lxxxiii (1990), 259–80.

Nye, A., 'Philosophy: A woman's thought or a man's discipline? The letters of Abelard and Heloise', *Hypatia*, vii (1992), 1–22.

Ohly, F., *Hohelied-Studien: Grundzüge einer Geschichte der Hoheliedauslegung des Abendlandes bis um 1200* (Schriften der Wissenschaftlichen Gesellschaft an der Johann Wolfgang Goethe-Universität, Frankfurt am Main, Geisteswissenschaftliche Reihe, i; Wiesbaden, 1958).

Olson, L., and K. Kerby-Fulton, K., eds., *Voices in Dialogue: Reading Women in the Middle Ages* (Notre Dame, Ind., 2005).

Orlandi, G., 'Classical Latin satire and medieval elegiac comedy', in P. Godman and O. Murray, eds., *Latin Poetry and the Classical Tradition: Essays in Medieval and Renaissance Literature* (Oxford, 1990), pp. 97–114.

—— 'Considerazioni sulla trasmissione del testo', in Pagani, pp. 55–66.

—— 'Metrica e statistica linguistica come strumenti nel metodo attributivo', *Filologia mediolatina*, vi–vii (1999–2000), 9–32.

—— 'Metrical and rhythmical clausulae in medieval Latin prose: Some aspects and problems', *Proceedings of the British Academy*, cxxix (2005), 395–412; consolidated bibliography, pp. 413–41.

—— '*Minima Abaelardiana*: Note sul testo del *Historia calamitatum*', *Res publica litterarum*, iii (1980), 131–38. Repr. in Orlandi, *Scritti di filologia mediolatina*, ed. P. Chiesa, A. M. Fagnoni, R. E. Guglielmetti, and G. P. Maggioni (Millenio Medievale, lxxvii; Strumenti e studi, NS xix; Florence 2008), pp. 731–40. Cf. Silvestre, review of Orlandi (1984).

—— 'On the text and interpretation of Abelard's *Planctus*', in Marenbon, ed., *Poetry and Philosophy*, pp. 327–42.

—— See also Dronke, P., and Orlandi, G., 'New works by Peter Abelard and Heloise?', *Filologia mediolatina*, xii (2005), 123–77.

Ott, L., *Untersuchungen zur theologischen Briefliteratur der Frühscholastik* (*BGPTMA* xxxiv; Münster i. W., 1937).

Ouy, G., *Les Manuscrits de l'abbaye de Saint-Victor: Catalogue établi sur la base du répertoire de Claude de Grandrue (1514)* (2 vols.; Bibliotheca Victorina, x; Turnhout, 1999).

—— 'Simon de Plumetot (1371–1443) et sa bibliothèque', in P. Cockshaw, M.-C. Garand, and P. Jodogne, eds., *Miscellanea Codicologica F. Masai dicata MCMLXXIX*, ii (Les Publications de Scriptorium, viii; Ghent, 1979), pp. 353–81.

—— and Gerz von Büren, V., *Le Catalogue de la bibliothèque de l'abbaye de Saint-Victor de Paris de Claude de Grandrue 1514* (Paris, 1983).

Pagani, I., 'Il Cantico dei Cantici nella produzione paraclitense di Abelardo', in R. E. Guglielmetti, ed., *Il Cantico dei Cantici nel Medioevo. Atti del Convegno Internazionale dell'Università degli Studi di Milano e della Società Internazionale per lo Studio del Medioevo Latino (S. I. S. M. E. L.), Gargnano sul Garda, 22–24 maggio 2006* (Florence 2008), pp. 425–49.

—— 'L'Epistolario di Abelardo ed Eloisa: Un gioco di specchi?', *Filologia mediolatina*, xi (2004), 123–42.

—— 'Epistolario o dialogo spirituale? Postille ad un'interpretazione della corrispondenza di Abelardo ed Eloisa', *Studi medievali*, 3^{a} ser., xxvii (1986), 241–318.

—— 'Il problema dell'attribuzione dell'Epistolario di Abelardo ed Eloisa: Status quaestionis', *Filologia mediolatina*, vi–vii (1999–2000), 79–88.

Parisse, M., 'Doppelkloster', in *Lexikon des Mittelalters*, iii. 1257–9.

—— *Les Nonnes au Moyen Âge* (Le Puy, 1983).

Payen, J.-C., 'La Pensée d'Abélard et les textes romans du xiie siècle', in Jolivet and Louis, eds., *Pierre Abélard–Pierre le Vénérable*, pp. 513–21.

Pearson, B. A., 'Christianity in Egypt', in *Anchor Bible Dictionary*, ed. D. N. Freedman (6 vols.; New York, 1992), i. 954–60.

—— 'Earliest Christianity in Egypt: Some observations', in id. and J. E. Goehring, eds., *The Roots of Egyptian Christianity* (Minneapolis, 1990), pp. 132–59.

Pellegrin, E., 'Orleans, Bibl. mun. 284. Description'. See *Abaelardiana*, iii.

Penco, G., 'S. Giovanni Battista nel ricordo del monachesimo medievale', *Studia monastica*, iii (1961), 7–32.

Pernoud, R., *Héloïse et Abélard* (Paris, 1970). Eng. trans. by P. Wiles, *Heloise and Abelard* (London, 1973).

Picavet, F., *Roscelin: Philosophe et théologien d'après la légende et d'après l'histoire. Sa place dans l'histoire générale et comparée des philosophies médiévales* (Paris, 1911).

Pinzani, R., *The Logical Grammar of Abelard* (New Synthese Historical Library, Texts and Studies in the History of Philosophy, li; Dordrecht, 2003). English trans. of *La grammatica logica di Abelardo* (Quaderni di *Philo<:>Logica*, i; Parma, 1995).

Piron, S., *Lettres des deux amants, attribuées à Héloïse et Abélard* (Paris, 2005).

Planiol, M., *Histoire des institutions de la Bretagne* (4 vols.; Mainz, 1981–2).

Podlech, A., *Abaelard und Heloisa oder die Theologie der Liebe* (Munich, 1990).

Poirel, D., ed., *L'École de Saint-Victor de Paris: Influence et rayonnement du*

Moyen Âge à l'époque moderne (Bibliotheca Victorina, xxii; Turnhout, 2010).

Polheim, K., *Die lateinische Reimprosa* (Berlin, 1925; 2nd edn. unchanged, Berlin, 1963).

Poole, R. L., *Illustrations of the History of Medieval Thought and Learning* (2nd edn.; London, 1920).

Porter, J. M. B., 'The convent of the Paraclete: Heloise, Abelard and the Benedictine tradition', *Studia monastica*, xli (1999), 151–69.

Pranger, M. B., 'Elective affinities: Love, hatred, playfulness and the self in Bernard and Abelard', in S. E. Gersh and B. Roest, eds., *Medieval and Renaissance Humanism: Rhetoric, Representation and Reform* (Leiden, 2003), pp. 55–72.

Quinto, R., *Doctor Nominatissimus: Stefano Langton (+1228) e la tradizione delle sue opera* (*BGPTMA*, NF xxxix (Münster i. W., 1994).

Raby, F. J. E., *A History of Christian-Latin Poetry from the Beginnings to the Close of the Middle Ages* (2nd edn.; Oxford, 1953).

Raison, L., and Niderst, R., 'Le Movement érémitique dans l'Ouest de la France à la fin du XIe siècle et au début du XIIe', *Annales de Bretagne*, lv (1948), 1–46.

Resnick, I. M., 'Odo of Tournai and the problem of universals', *Journal of the History of Philosophy*, xxxv (1997), 355–74.

Rijk, L. M. de, *Logica modernorum: A Contribution to the History of Early Terminist Logic*, i: *On the Twelfth-Century Theories of Fallacy* (Assen, 1962); ii. 1 and 2: *The Origin and Early Development of the Theory of Supposition* (Assen, 1967).

Robertson, Jr., D. W., *Abelard and Heloise* (New York, 1972).

Robl, W., 'Der Dichter und Lehrer Hilarius von Orléans', online (2003) at <http://www.abaelard.de/abaelard>

—— 'Goswin von Anchin, ein Widersacher Peter Abaelards', in Niggli, ed., *Peter Abaelard*, pp. 267–91.

—— *Heloisas Herkunft: Hersindis Mater* (Munich, 2001).

—— '*Hersindis Mater*: Neues zur Familiengeschichte Heloisas mit Ausblicken auf die Familie Peter Abaelards', in Niggli, ed., *Peter Abaelard*, pp. 25–89.

—— 'Petrus Venerabilis: Briefe zur Rettung Abaelards?', in Niggli, ed., *Peter Abaelard*, pp. 293–315.

Röckelein, H., 'Frauen im Umkreis der Benediktinischen Reformen des 10. bis 12. Jahrhunderts: Gorze, Cluny, Hirsau, St. Blasien und Siegburg', in G. Melville and A. Müller, eds., *Female "vita religiosa" between Late Antiquity and the High Middle Ages: Structures, Developments, and Spatial Contexts* (Vita Regularis, xlvii; Berlin, 2011), pp. 275–327.

—— 'Die Heilige Schrift in Frauenhand', in P. Carmassi, ed., *Präsenz und Verwendung der Heiligen Schrift im christlichen Frühmittelalter: Exegetische*

Literatur und liturgische Texte (Wolfenbütteler Mittelalter Studien, xx; Wiesbaden, 2008), pp. 139–209.

—— 'Hiérarchie, ordre et mobilité dans le monachisme féminin', in F. Bougard, D. Iogna- Prat, and R. Le Jan, eds., *Hiérarchie et stratification dans l'occident médiéval (400–1100)* (Collection haut Moyen Âge, ed. R. Le Jan, vi; Turnhout, 2008), pp. 205–20.

Rosier-Catach, I., 'Abélard et les grammairiens: Sur la définition du verbe et la notion d'inhérence', in P. Lardet, ed., *La Tradition vive: Mélanges d'histoire des textes en l'honneur de Louis Holtz* (Bibliologia, xx; Turnhout, 2003), pp. 143–59.

—— 'Abélard et les grammairiens: Sur le verbe substantif et la prédication', *Vivarium*, xli (2003), 176–248.

—— 'Grammar', in *The Cambridge History of Medieval Philosophy*, ed. R. Pasnau with C. Van Dyke (2 vols.; Cambridge, 2010), i. 196–216.

—— ed., *Arts du langage et théologie aux confins des XIe et XIIe siècles: Textes, maîtres, débats* (Studia Artistarium; Études sur la Faculté des arts dans les Universités médiévales, xxvi; Turnhout, 2011).

Roudaut, F., 'Note sur Étienne Pasquier et Pierre Pithou' in Fragonard and Leroy, eds., *Les Pithou*, pp. 305–12.

Rouse, M. A., and Rouse, R. H., *Authentic Witnesses: Approaches to Medieval Texts and Manuscripts* (Notre Dame, Ind., 1991).

Rouse, R. H., and Rouse, M. A., *Illiterati et uxorati: Manuscripts and their Makers. Commercial Book Producers in Paris, 1200–1500* (2 vols.; London, 2000).

Ruhe, E., *'De amasio ad amasiam': Zur Gattungsgeschichte des mittelalterlichen Liebesbriefes* (Beiträge zur romanischen Philologie des Mittelalters, x; Munich, 1975).

Russell, J. B., *Dissent and Reform in the Early Middle Ages* (Publications of the Center for Medieval and Renaissance Studies, i; Berkeley, 1965).

Ruys, J. Feros, '"La douceur d'une vie paternelle": La représentation de la famille dans les oeuvres poétiques d'Abélard', in Jolivet and Habrias, eds., *Pierre Abélard. Colloque international de Nantes*, pp. 205–13.

—— '*Eloquencie vultum depingere*: Eloquence and *Dictamen* in the love letters of Heloise and Abelard', in Mews, Nederman, and Thomson, eds., *Rhetoric and Renewal*, pp. 99–112.

—— 'Hearing medieval voices: Heloise and *Carmina Burana* 126', in Stewart and Wulstan, eds., *Poetical and Musical Legacy*, pp. 91–9.

—— '*Planctus magis quam cantici*: The generic significance of Abelard's *Planctus*', *Plainsong and Medieval Music*, xi (2002), 37–44.

—— '*Quae maternae immemor naturae*: The rhetorical struggle over the meaning of motherhood in the writings of Heloise and Abelard', in Wheeler, ed., *Listening to Heloise*, pp. 323–39.

Ruys, J. Feros, 'Role-playing in the letters of Heloise and Abelard', *Parergon*, xi (1993), 53–78.

—— '*Ut sexu sic animo*': The resolution of sex and gender in the *Planctus* of Abelard', *Medium Aevum*, lxxv (2006), 1–23.

Saxer, V., *Le Culte de Marie Madeleine en Occident: Des origines à la fin du Moyen Âge* (Cahiers d'archéologie et d'histoire, iii; Auxerre, 1959).

Schaller, D., 'Erotische und sexuelle Thematik in Musterbriefsammlungen des 12. Jahrhunderts', in *Fälschungen in Mittelalter*, v: *Fingierte Briefe. Frömmigkeit und Fälschung. Realienfälschungen*, pp. 63–77.

—— 'Probleme der Überlieferung und Verfasserschaft lateinischer Liebesbriefe des hohen Mittelalters', *Mittellateinisches Jahrbuch*, iii (1966), 25–36.

Schaller, H. M., 'Scherz und Ernst in erfunden Briefen des Mittelalters', in *Fälschungen im Mittelalter*, v: *Fingierte Briefe. Frömmigkeit und Fälschung. Realienfälschungen*, pp. 86–93.

Schieffer, T., *Die päpstlichen Legaten in Frankreich vom Vertrage von Meersen (870) bis zum Schisma von 1130* (Historische Studien, cclxiii; Berlin, 1935).

Schmid, K., 'Bemerkungen zur Personen- und Memorialforschung nach dem Zeugnis von Abaelard und Heloise', in D. Geuenich and O. G. Oexle, eds., *Memoria in der Gesellschaft des Mittelalters* (Veröffentlichungen des Max-Planck-Instituts für Geschichte, cxi; Göttingen, 1994), pp. 74–127.

Schmidt, P.-G., *Proverbia*: see *Proverbia* (Schmidt) in *Bibliography: Primary Sources*.

Schoebel, M., *Archiv und Besitz der Abtei St. Viktor in Paris* (Pariser historische Studien, xxxi; Bonn, 1991).

Schreckenberg, H., *Die Flavius-Josephus-Tradition in Antike und Mittelalter* (Arbeiten zur Literatur und Geschichte des hellenistischen Judentums; Leiden, 1972).

Seilhac, L. de, 'L'Utilisation de la Règle de saint Benoît dans les monastères féminins', in *Atti del 7° Congresso internazionale di studi sull'alto Medioevo: Norcia, Subiaco, Cassino, Montecassino, 29 Settembre – 5 Ottobre 1980: San Benedetto nel suo tempo* (2 vols.; Spoleto, 1982), ii. 527–49.

Sharpe, R., 'Anselm as author: Publishing in the late eleventh century', *Journal of Medieval Latin*, xix (2009), 1–87.

Silvestre, H., 'A propos d'une édition récente de l'*Hymnarius Paraclitensis* d'Abélard', *Scriptorium*, xxxii (1978), 91–100.

—— 'Aratus pour Arator: Un singulier lapsus d'Abélard', *Studi medievali*, 3ª ser., xxvii (1986), 221–4.

—— 'Héloïse', in *Dictionnaire d'histoire et de géographie ecclésiastiques*, xxiii (1990), cols. 946–58.

—— 'Héloïse et le témoignage du *Carmen ad Astralabium*', *Revue d'histoire ecclésiastique*, lxxxiii (1988), 635–60.

—— 'L'Idylle d'Abélard et Héloïse: La part du roman', *Académie Royale de Belgique, Bulletin de la Classe des Lettres et des Sciences Morales et Politiques*, 5e ser., lxxi (1985), 157–200.

—— 'Die Liebesgeschichte zwischen Abaelard und Heloise: Der Anteil des Romans', in *Fälschungen im Mittelalter*, v: *Fingierte Briefe. Frömmigkeit und Fälschung. Realienfälschungen*, pp. 121–65.

—— 'Pourquoi Roscelin n'est-il pas mentionné dans l'*Historia calamitatum*?', *Recherches de théologie ancienne et médiévale*, xlviii (1981), 218–24.

—— 'Réflexions sur la thèse de J. F. Benton relative au dossier "Abélard et Héloïse" ', *Recherches de théologie ancienne et médiévale*, xliv (1977), 211–16.

—— review of Jaeger, 'The Prologue to the "*Historia Calamitatum*" ', in *Bulletin de théologie ancienne et médiévale*, xiii (1981), 78–89.

—— review of Orlandi, '*Minima Abaelardiana*', in *Bulletin de théologie ancienne et médiévale*, xiii (1981), 625–6.

—— review of *Abaelardiana*, ii: Dronke, 'Orleans, Bibl. Mun. 284', in *Bulletin de théologie ancienne et médiévale*, xiii (1981), 804–6.

—— 'Sage ou subtile Héloïse', *Revue du moyen âge latin*, xlv (1989), 17–20.

Simon, G., 'Untersuchungen zur Topik der Widmungsbriefe mittelalterlicher Geschichtsschreiber bis zum Ende des 12. Jahrhunderts', I. *Archiv für Diplomatik*, iv (1958), 52–119; II. *Archiv für Diplomatik*, v (1959), 73–153.

Smalley, B., *The Becket Conflict and the Schools: A Study of Intellectuals in Politics* (Oxford 1973).

—— 'Les Commentaires bibliques de l'époque romane: Glose ordinaire et gloses périmées', *Cahiers de civilisation médiévale*, iv (1961), 15–22.

—— 'Jean de Hesdin, O. Hosp. S. Ioh.', *Recherches de théologie ancienne et médiévale*, xxviii (1961), 283–330. Repr. in Smalley, *Studies in Medieval Thought and Learning*, pp. 345–92.

—— *Studies in Medieval Thought and Learning from Abelard to Wyclif* (London, 1981).

—— *The Study of the Bible in the Middle Ages* (2nd edn.; Oxford, 1952; 3rd edn. with a new Preface, Oxford, 1982).

Smith, A. C., 'The *Problemata* of Heloise', in L. J. Churchill and others, eds., *Women Writing Latin*, ii: *Medieval Women Writing Latin* (New York, 2002), pp. 173–96.

Smith, J. A., 'The virtue of stillness: Abelard and monastic silence', *American Benedictine Review*, lix (2008), 291–303.

Smith, L., *The Glossa Ordinaria: The Making of a Medieval Bible Commentary* (Leiden, 2009).

Souter, A., *The Earliest Latin Commentaries on the Epistles of St Paul* (Oxford, 1927).

Southern, R. W., *Saint Anselm: A Portrait in a Landscape* (Cambridge, 1990).

—— *Scholastic Humanism and the Unification of Europe*, i: *Foundations* (Oxford, 1995); ii: *The Heroic Age* (Oxford, 2001).

Spear, V., *Leadership in Medieval English Nunneries* (Woodbridge, 2005).

Steinen, W. von den, 'Die Planctus Abaelards – Jephthas Tochter', *Mittellateinisches Jahrbuch*, iv (1967), 122–44.

—— 'Les Sujets d'inspiration chez les poètes latins du XIIe siècle. II: Abélard et le subjectivisme', *Cahiers de civilisation médiévale*, ix (1966), 363–73.

Stella, F., '*Epistolae duorum amantium*: Nuovi paralleli testuali per gli inserti poetici', *Journal of Medieval Latin*, xviii (2009), 374–97.

—— 'Il Cantico dei Cantici negli epistolari d'amore del XII secolo', in R. E. Guglielmetti, ed., *Il Cantico dei Cantici nel Medioevo. Atti del Convegno Internazionale dell'Università degli Studi di Milano e della Società Internazionale per lo Studio del Medioevo Latino (S. I. S. M. E. L.), Gargnano sul Garda, 22–24 maggio 2006* (Florence 2008), pp. 451–74.

Stewart, M., and Wulstan, D., eds., *The Poetic and Musical Legacy of Heloise and Abelard: An Anthology of Essays by Various Authors* (Wissenschaftliche Abhandlungen/Musicological Studies, lxxviii; Ottawa, 2003).

Strecker, K., 'Dies irae', *Zeitschrift für deutsches Altertum*, li (1909), 227–55.

Sullivan, T., *Parisian Licentiates in Theology: A Biographical Register*, i: *The Religious Orders*; ii: *The Secular Clergy* (Education and Society in the Middle Ages and Renaissance, xviii, xxxvii; Leiden, 2004, 2011).

Sweeney, E., *Logic, Theology and Poetry in Boethius, Abelard and Alan of Lille* (New York, 2006).

Synan, E. A., and Jeauneau, E., 'Some remarks on the Muckle translation of Abelard's Adversities', *Mediaeval Studies*, lvii (1995), 337–43.

Szövérffy, J., 'False use of "unfitting" hymns: Some ideas shared by Peter the Venerable, Peter Abelard and Heloise', *Revue bénédictine*, lxxxix (1979), 187–99. Repr. in *Peter Abelard's Hymnarius Paraclitensis*, ed. Szövérffy, pp. 537–49.

—— '*Peccatrix quondam femina*: A survey of the Mary Magdalen hymns', *Traditio*, xix (1963), 79–146.

—— *Psallat Chorus Caelestium: Religious Lyrics of the Middle Ages, Hymnological Studies and Collected Essays* (Medieval Classics: Texts and Studies (Berliner Reihe), xv; Berlin, 1983).

Taylor, A., 'A second Ajax: Peter Abelard and the violence of dialectic', in D. Townsend and A. Taylor, eds., *The Tongue of the Fathers: Gender and Ideology in Twelfth-Century Latin* (Philadelphia, 1998), pp. 14–34.

Thomas, R., 'Anselms *fides quaerens intellectum* im *Proslogion* und Abaelards *rationibus fides astruenda et defendenda* im *Dialogus inter philosophum, iudaeum et christianum*. Eine Vergleichserörterung', *Analecta Anselmiana*, v (1976), 297–310.

—— and others, eds., *Petrus Abaelardus (1079–1142): Person, Werk und Wirkung* (Trierer theologische Studien, xxxviii; Trier, 1980).

Thompson, K., 'Affairs of State: The illegitimate children of Henry I', *Journal of Medieval History*, xxix (2003), 129–51.

Thompson, S., *Women Religious: The Founding of English Nunneries after the Norman Conquest* (Oxford, 1991).

Thomson, R. M., 'The satirical works of Berengar of Poitiers: An edition with introduction', *Mediaeval Studies*, xlii (1980), 98–138.

Tilliette, J.-Y., 'Le Sens et la composition du florilège de Zurich (Zentralbibliothek, ms. C 58): Hypothèses et propositions', in P. Stotz and M. C. Ferrari, eds., *Non recedet memoria eius: Beiträge zur Lateinischen Philologie des Mittelalters im Gedenken an Jakob Werner (1861–1944)* (Lateinische Sprache und Literatur des Mittelalters, xxviii; Bern, 1995), pp. 147–67.

Tombeur, P., '*De polygraphia*', in A. Maierú, ed., *Grafia e interpunzione del latino nel medioevo* (Lessico intellettuale Europeo, xli; Rome, 1987), pp. 69–101.

Tonnerre, N.-Y., 'Le Comté nantais à la fin du XIe siècle', in Jolivet, ed., *Abélard en son temps*, pp. 11–20.

—— *Naissance de la Bretagne: Géographie historique et structures sociales de la Bretagne méridionale (Nantais et Vannetais) de la fin du VIIIe siècle à la fin du XIIe siècle* (Angers, 1994).

'Très sage Héloïse'. Catalogue d'exposition. Hors série de la revue *La Vie en Champagne* (Troyes, June 2001).

Tribout de Morembert, H., 'Quatre bulles pour l'abbaye du Paraclet (1156–1208) conservés aux Archives municipales de Metz', *Annuaire de la Société d'Histoire et d'Archéologie de la Lorraine*, lxix (1969), 103–6.

Troncarelli, F.,'"*Immoderatus amor*", Abelardo, Eloisa e Andrea Capellano', *Quaderni medievali*, xxxiv (1992), 6–58.

Tweedale, M., *Abailard on Universals* (Amsterdam, 1976).

Ughetti, D., *François d'Amboise, 1550–1619* (Biblioteca di cultura, lv; Rome, 1974).

Van de Kieft, C., 'Deux diplômes faux de Charlemagne pour Saint-Denis du XIIe siècle', *Le Moyen Âge*, lxix (1963), 223–45.

Van den Eynde, D., 'Chronologie des écrits d'Abélard à Héloïse', *Antonianum*, xxxvii (1962), 337–49.

—— 'Détails biographiques sur Pierre Abélard', *Antonianum*, xxxviii (1963), 217–23.

—— 'Du nouveau sur deux maîtres lombards contemporains du Maître des Sentences', *Pier Lombardo*, i (1953), 6–8.

—— 'En marge des écrits d'Abélard: Les "Excerpta ex regulis Paracletensis monasterii"', *Analecta Praemonstratensia*, xxxviii (1962), 70–84.

—— 'Les Écrits perdus d'Abélard', *Antonianum*, xxxvii (1962), 467–80.

Van den Eynde, D., 'Le Recueil des sermons de Pierre Abélard', *Antonianum*, xxxvii (1962), 17–54.

Van Engen, J. H., *Rupert of Deutz* (Publications of the UCLA Centre for Medieval and Renaissance Studies, xviii; Berkeley, 1983).

Van Hoecke, W., and Welkenhuysen, A., eds., *Love and Marriage in the Twelfth Century* (Mediaevalia Lovaniensia, Series I: Studia, viii; Leuven, 1981).

Vanni Rovighi, S., 'Un dibattito sull'autenticità dell'epistolario di Abelardo ed Eloisa', *Aevum*, l (1976), 357–9.

Van Waefelghem, R., 'Les Premiers Statuts de l'ordre de Prémontré', *Analecta Ordinis Praemonstratensis*, ix (1913), 63–6.

Venarde, B. L., '*Praesidentes negotiis*: Abbesses as managers in twelfth-century France', in S. K. Cohn, Jr. and S. A. Epstein, eds., *Portraits of Medieval and Renaissance Living: Essays in Memory of David Herlihy* (Ann Arbor, 1996), pp. 189–205.

—— *Women's Monasticism and Medieval Society: Nunneries in France and England, 890–1215* (Ithaca, NY, 1997).

Vergani, F., '"*Sententiam vocum seu nominum non caute theologiae admiscuit*": Ottone di Frisinga di fronte ad Abelardo', *Aevum*, lxiii (1989), 193–224.

Verger, J., 'Abélard et les mileux sociaux de son temps', in Jolivet, ed., *Abélard en son temps*, pp. 107–31.

—— *L'amour castré: L'histoire d'Héloïse et Abélard* (Collection Savoir: Lettres; Paris, 1996).

—— *Culture, enseignement et société en Occident aux XIIe et XIIIe siècles* (Rennes, 1999).

Vernet, A., 'Études médiévales', *Études augustiniennes* (Paris, 1981), pp. 500–29.

—— 'La Tradition manuscrite et la diffusion des ouvrages d'Abélard', in Jolivet and Louis, eds., *Pierre Abélard–Pierre le Vénérable*, pp. 405–8.

Vidmanova, A., review of *Peter Abelard's Hymnarius Paraclitensis*, ed. Szövérffy, in *Cahiers de civilisation médiévale*, xxi (1978), 310–12.

Vieillard-Troïekouroff, M., 'L'Église Sainte-Geneviève de Paris au début du XIIe siècle', in Jolivet, ed., *Abélard en son temps*, pp. 83–94.

Vitz, E. B., 'Type et individu dans l'"autobiographie" médiévale', *Poétique*, xxiv (1975), 426–45.

Vogüé, A. de, 'Échos de Philon dans la vie de saint Sulpice de Bourges et dans la Règle d'Abélard pour le Paraclet', *Analecta Bollandiana*, ciii (1985), 359–65.

—— *Les Règles monastiques anciennes (400–700)* (Typologie des sources du moyen âge occidental, xlvi (Turnhout, 1985).

Voltmer, E., 'Abaelard und Heloise oder die Macht von Gemeinschaft und Erinnerung: Gedanken über neue Wege aus einer alten Kontroverse', in F. Burgard, C. Cluse, and A. Haverkamp, eds., *Liber amicorum necnon et amicarum für Alfred Heit: Beiträge zur mittelalterlichen Geschichte und geschichtlichen Landeskunde* (Trierer historische Forschungen, xxviii; Trier, 1996), pp. 327–37.

Vot. See Le Vot.

Waddell, C., '*Adtendite a falsis prophetis*: Abelard's earliest known anti-Cistercian diatribe', *Cistercian Studies Quarterly: An International Review of the Monastic and Contemplative Spiritual Tradition*, xxxix (2004), 371–98.

—— 'Cistercian influence on the Abbey of the Paraclete? Plotting data from the Paraclete book of burials, customary and necrology', in T. N. Kinder, ed., *Perspectives for an Architecture of Solitude: Essays on Cistercian Art and Architecture in Honor of Peter Fergusson* (Medieval Church Studies, xi; Studia et Documenta, xiii; Turnhout, 2004), pp. 329–40.

—— '"Epithalamica": An Easter sequence by Peter Abelard', *Musical Quarterly*, lxxii (1986), 239–71.

—— 'Heloise and the abbey of the Paraclete', in M. Williams, ed., *The Making of Christian Communities in Late Antiquity and the Middle Ages* (London, 2005), pp. 103–16.

—— 'Peter Abelard as creator of liturgical texts', in Thomas and others, eds., *Petrus Abaelardus (1079–1142)*, pp. 267–86.

—— 'Peter Abelard's *Letter 10* and Cistercian liturgical reform', in J. R. Sommerfeldt, ed., *Studies in Medieval Cistercian History*, ii (Cistercian Studies Series, xxiv; Kalamazoo, Mich., 1976), pp. 75–85.

—— 'St Bernard and the Cistercian Office at the Abbey of the Paraclete', in E. R. Elder and J. R. Sommerfeldt, eds., *The Chimera of his Age: Studies on Bernard of Clairvaux* (Studies in Medieval Cistercian History, v; Kalamazoo, Mich., 1980), pp. 76–121.

Waldmann, T. G., 'Abbot Suger and the Nuns of Argenteuil', *Traditio*, xli (1985), 239–72; French trans. by J. Dufour, 'L'Abbé Suger et les nonnes d'Argenteuil', *Le vieil Argenteuil: Bulletin de la Société Historique et Archéologique d'Argenteuil & du Parisis*, xxix (1986–7), 5–26.

Walther, H., *Initia Carminum ac Versuum Medii Aevi Posterioris Latinorum* (Göttingen, 1959).

—— *Proverbia*: see *Proverbia* (Walther) in Bibliography: Primary Sources.

Ward, J. O., *Ciceronian Rhetoric in Treatise, Scholion and Commentary* (Typologie des sources du moyen âge occidental, lviii; Turnhout, 1995).

—— and Chiavaroli, N., 'The young Heloise and Latin rhetoric: Some preliminary comments on the "lost" love letters and their significance', in Wheeler, ed., *Listening to Heloise*, pp. 53–119.

—— and Fredborg, K. M., 'Rhetoric in the time of William of Champeaux', in Rosier-Catach, ed., *Arts du langage et théologie*, pp. 219–23.

Weinrich, L., '"*Dolorum solatium*": Text und Musik von Abaelards Planctus David', *Mittellateinisches Jahrbuch*, v (1968), 59–78.

—— 'Peter Abelard as musician I', 'Peter Abelard as musician II', *Musical Quarterly*, lv (1969), 295–312, 464–86.

Wheeler, B., 'Origenary fantasies: Abelard's castration and confession', in J. J. Cohen and B. Wheeler, eds., *Becoming Male in the Middle Ages* (The New Middle Ages, iv; New York, 1997), pp. 107–28.

—— ed., *Listening to Heloise: The Voice of a Twelfth-Century Woman* (The New Middle Ages; New York and Basingstoke, 2000).

Wielockx, R. 'La Sentence *De caritate* et la discussion scolastique sur l'amour', *Ephemerides theologicae Lovanienses*, lviii (1982), 50–86, 334–56; lix (1988), 26–45.

Willesme, J.-P., 'Saint-Victor au temps d'Abélard', in Jolivet, ed., *Abélard en son temps*, pp. 95–105.

Williams, J. R., 'The cathedral school of Reims in the time of Master Alberic, 1118–1136', *Traditio*, xx (1964), 93–114.

Wilson, K., and McLeod, G., 'Textual Strategies in the Abelard/Heloise Correspondence', in Wheeler, ed., *Listening to Heloise*, pp. 121–42.

Wilson, K. M., and Makowski, E. M., *Wykked Wyves and the Woes of Marriage: Misogamous Literature from Juvenal to Chaucer* (SUNY Series in Medieval Studies; Albany, NY, 1990).

Wischerman, E. M., *Marcigny-sur-Loire* (Münstersche Mittelalter-Schriften, xlii; Munich, 1986).

Wollasch, J., 'A Cluniac necrology from the time of Abbot Hugh', in Hunt, ed., *Cluniac Monasticism*, pp. 143–90.

Wollin, C., 'Ein Liebeslied des Petrus Abaelardus in Bloomington (Indiana)', *Revue bénédictine*, cxix (2009), 121–63.

—— 'Neue Textzeugen des *Carmen ad Astralabium* des Petrus Abaelardus', *Sacris erudiri*, xlvi (2007), 187–240.

—— 'Zwei geistliche Gedichte des Petrus Abaelardus', *Sacris erudiri*, xlvii (2008), 291–319.

Worstbrock, F. J., 'Ein Lucanzitat bei Abaelard und Gotfrid', *Beiträge zur Geschichte der deutschen Sprache und Literatur*, xcviii (Tübingen, 1976), 351–6.

—— Klaes, M., and Lütten, J., *Repertorium der artes dictandi des Mittelalters*, i: *Von den Anfängen bis um 1200* (Münstersche Mittelalter-Schriften, lxvi; Munich, 1992).

Wulstan, D., '*Novi modulaminis melos*: The music of Heloise and Abelard', *Plainsong and Medieval Music*, xi (2002), 1–23.

Zerbi, P., 'Abelardo ed Eloisa: Il problema di un amore e di una corrispondenza', in Van Hoecke and Welkenhuysen, eds., *Love and Marriage in the Twelfth Century*, pp. 130–61.

—— 'In Cluniaco vestra sibi perpetuam mansionem elegit: Petri Venerabilis *Epistola 98*', in Zerbi, *Tra Milano e Cluny: Momenti di vita e cultura ecclesiastica nel secolo XII* (Italia sacra: Studi e documenti di storia ecclesiastica, xxviii; Rome 1978), pp. 373–95. A repr. with minor corrections of Zerbi, 'Remarques sur l'*Epistola 98* de Pierre le Vénérable'.

—— 'La Condannna di Soissons (1121)', in Zerbi, *'Philosophi' e 'Logici'*, pp. 39–55.

—— *'Ecclesia in hoc mundo posita': Studi di storia e di storiografia medioevale raccolti in occasione del 70° genetliaco del autore*, ed. M. P. Alberzoni (Biblioteca erudita, vi; Milan, 1993).

—— '*Panem nostrum supersubstantialem*: Abelardo polemista ed esegeta nell'ep. X', in *Contributi dell'Istituto di storia medievale*, ii: *Raccolta di studi in memoria di Sergio Mochi Onory* (Milan, 1972), pp. 624–38. Repr. in Zerbi, *'Ecclesia in hoc mundo posita'*, pp. 491–509.

—— *'Philosophi' e 'Logici': Un ventennio di incontri e scontri: Soissons, Sens, Cluny (1121–1141)* (Rome, 2002).

—— 'Un recente dibattito sul'autenticità della *Historia Calamitatum* e della corrispondenza fra Abelardo ed Eloisa: Note critiche e metodologiche', in *Studi di letteratura e di storia in memoria di Antonio Di Pietro* (Pubblicazioni della Università Cattolica del Sacro Cuore: Scienze filologiche e letteratura, viii; Milan, 1977), pp. 3–43.

—— 'Remarques sur l'*Epistola 98* de Pierre le Vénérable', in Jolivet and Louis, eds., *Pierre Abélard–Pierre le Vénérable*, pp. 215–34.

—— 'San Bernardo di Chiaravalle e il concilio di Sens', in *Studi su S. Bernardo di Chiaravalle nell'ottavo centenario della canonizzazione. Convegno internazionale – Certoza di Firenze, novembre 1974* (Rome, 1975), pp. 49–73.

Ziolkowski, J., 'Lost and not yet found: Heloïse, Abelard and the *Epistolae duorum amantium*', *Journal of Medieval Latin*, xiv (2004), 171–202.

WEBSITES

www.abaelard.de/abaelard/000001buch.htm
www.abaelard.de/abaelard/040103pallet.htm
www.abaelard.de/abaelard/091000buehne.htm

INDEX OF PARALLELS WITH OTHER WRITINGS OF ABELARD AND HELOISE

INDEX OF QUOTATIONS AND ALLUSIONS TO THE BIBLE

OLD TESTAMENT

NEW TESTAMENT

INDEX OF OTHER QUOTATIONS AND ALLUSIONS

(I) THE ABBEY OF THE PARACLETE

(II) OTHER WORKS

INDEX OF MANUSCRIPTS

GENERAL INDEX